T0213695

Lecture Notes in Computer Science   10302

Commenced Publication in 1973
Founding and Former Series Editors:
Gerhard Goos, Juris Hartmanis, and Jan van Leeuwen

Editorial Board

More information about this series at http://www.springer.com/series/7412

François Lauze · Yiqiu Dong
Anders Bjorholm Dahl (Eds.)

Scale Space and Variational Methods in Computer Vision

6th International Conference, SSVM 2017
Kolding, Denmark, June 4–8, 2017
Proceedings

Springer

Editors
François Lauze 🆔
University of Copenhagen
Copenhagen
Denmark

Anders Bjorholm Dahl
Technical University of Denmark
Kongens Lyngby
Denmark

Yiqiu Dong
Technical University of Denmark
Kongens Lyngby
Denmark

ISSN 0302-9743   ISSN 1611-3349 (electronic)
Lecture Notes in Computer Science
ISBN 978-3-319-58770-7   ISBN 978-3-319-58771-4 (eBook)
DOI 10.1007/978-3-319-58771-4

Library of Congress Control Number: 2017940251

LNCS Sublibrary: SL6 – Image Processing, Computer Vision, Pattern Recognition, and Graphics

Printed on acid-free paper

This Springer imprint is published by Springer Nature
The registered company is Springer International Publishing AG
The registered company address is: Gewerbestrasse 11, 6330 Cham, Switzerland

Preface

The 6th International Conference on Scale Space and Variational Methods in Computer Vision (SSVM 2017, http://ssvm2017.compute.dtu.dk/) was held in the beautiful Danish fjord city of Kolding, eastern Jutland, Denmark. Following the previous meetings, we kept the style of gathering people in a slightly remote and scenic place in order to encourage fruitful discussions during the day and in the evening. This conference, born in 2007 in Ischia, Italy, has become a major event in the communities with common research interests in scale space, variational, geometric, and level set methods and their numerous applications in computer vision and more generally in imaging science. SSVM 2017 was announced in January 2016 and it attracted the attention of an important international scientific audience of authors coming from more than 16 countries. We received 77 double-blind submissions. The papers underwent a peer-review process similar to that of high-level journals in the field: each paper was reviewed by at least three members of the Program Committee as well as by other referees. The reviews and the papers were then considered by the conference chairs. We acknowledge P. Weiss, J. Lellmann, M. Nikolova, and Y. Quéau for their significant review work on manuscripts submitted to the conference. Finally, 55 manuscripts were selected for SSVM 2017. Among them, 24 articles were selected for oral presentation and 31 for poster presentation. All these 12-page-long original articles are contained in this book. A best student paper award was given during the conference. Following the tradition of the previous SSVM conferences, we invited outstanding scientists to give keynote presentations. This year, we were happy to welcome the following invited keynote lectures:

- Christine de Mol (Université Libre de Belgique, Bruxelles, Belgium): "NonNegative Matrix Factorization and Blind Imaging with Positivity"
- Maurizio Falcone (Università di Roma La Sapienza, Roma, Italy): "Recent Developments in the Shape-from-Shading Problem";
- Marco Loog (Delft University of Technology, Delft, The Netherlands): "Scale, Saliency, and Supervised Learning";
- Per Christian Hansen (Technical University of Denmark, Lyngby, Denmark): "ART Performance".

We would like to thank the authors for their contributions and the members of the Program Committee and the additional reviewers for their time and valuable comments during the review process. We are grateful to the organizers of the previous editions of this conference for precious tips on how to organize the event: Fiorella Sgallari (SSVM 2007), Xue-Cheng Tai (SSVM 2009), Yana Katz (SSVM 2011), Arjan Kuijper (SSVM 2013), Jean-François Aujol (SSVM 2015) gave us the most fresh information, as well as Joachim Weickert. Further, we would like to thank Lene Winther Hagelsjær (CAP Partner) and Christen Artagnan Sørensen (University of Copenhagen) for their enthusiastic help in the financial management. Finally, we are lucky to acknowledge the generous support of the Carsberg Foundation, the Center for Stochastic Geometry and Advanced Bioimaging (CSGB), the Otto Mønsted Fund, the Department of Computer Science, University of Copenhagen, IH Food AS, and Zebicon AS. The manuscripts of all past SSVM editions were published by Springer in the *Lecture Notes in Computer Science* series as well: LNCS 4485 (Ischia, Italy 2007), LNCS 5567 (Voss, Norway 2009), LNCS 6667 (Ein Gedi, Israel 2011), LNCS 7893 (Leibnitz, Austria 2013), and LNCS 9087 (Lège-Cap Ferret, France 2015). It is interesting to observe the evolution of the topics covered by this conference. They naturally reflect the progress of mathematical and application-driven ideas in the field as well as the advent of powerful computers. This is expressed by the interest in more realistic mathematical models, the use of novel mathematical tools for modeling and for scientific computing, the advance in the processing of huge data volumes (e.g., in video and in 3D, especially magnetic resonance and tomographic imaging). These new trends are well represented in this book.

April 2017   François Lauze
                                                                          Yiqiu Dong
                                                                  Anders Bjorholm Dahl

Organization

Organizing Committee

François Lauze	DIKU, University of Copenhagen, Denmark
Yiqiu Dong	DTU Compute, DTU, Denmark
Anders Bjorholm Dahl	DTU Compute, DTU, Denmark

Program Committee

Luis Alvarez	Universidad de Las Palmas de Gran Canaria, Spain
Jean-François Aujol	University of Bordeaux, France
Coloma Ballester	Unversitat Pompeu Fabra, Spain
Michael Breuß	BTU Cottbus-Senftenberg, Germany
Freddy Bruckstein	Technion, Israel
Andres Bruhn	University of Stuttgart, Germany
Antonin Chambolle	CMAP, École Polytechnique, France
Raymond Chan	Chinese University of Hong Kong, Hong Kong, SAR China
Daniel Cremers	TU München, Germany
Agnès Desolneux	CMLA, ENS Cachan, France
Remco Duits	Eindhoven University, The Netherlands
Jalal Fadili	ENSICAEN, France
Michael Felsberg	Linköping University, Sweden
Luc Florack	Eindhoven University of Technology, The Netherlands
Yann Gousseau	Telecom ParisTech, France
Atsushi Imiya	Chiba University, Japan
Arjan Kuijper	Fraunhofer IGD, Germany
Tony Lindeberg	KTH Royal Institute of Technology, Sweden
Dirk Lorenz	University of Braunschweig, Germany
Simon Masnou	Université Lyon I, France
Serena Morigi	University of Bologna, Italy
Mila Nikolova	CNRS ENS Cachan, France
Nicolas Papadakis	University of Bordeaux, France
Thomas Pock	TU Graz, Austria
Martin Rumpf	University of Bonn, Germany
Otmar Scherzer	University of Vienna, Austria
Christoph Schnörr	University of Heidelberg, Germany
Carola-Bibiane Schönlieb	University of Cambridge, UK
Fiorella Sgallari	University of Bologna, Italy
Gabriele Steidl	University of Kaiserslautern, Germany
Xue-Cheng Tai	University of Bergen, Norway

Bart ter Haar Romeny   Eindhoven University of Technology, The Netherlands
Joachim Weickert   Saarland University, Germany
Martin Welk   UMIT Hall/Tyrol, Austria

Scientific and Reviewing Committee

Martin S. Andersen   DTU Compute, DTU, Denmark
Marcelo Bertalmio   Universitat Pompeu Fabra, Spain
Laure Blanc-Feraud   CNRS Sophia Antipolis, France
Kristian Bredies   University of Graz, Austria
Aurélie Bugeau   Labri, Université de Bordeaux, France
Martin Burger   Westfälische Wilhelms-Universität Münster, Germany
Thomas Corpetti   CNRS, Rennes, France
Vedrana Dahl   DTU Compute, DTU, Denmark
Anders Bjorholm Dahl   DTU Compute, DTU, Denmark
Sune Darkner   DIKU, University of Copenhagen, Denmark
Yiqiu Dong   DTU Compute, DTU, Denmark
Jean-Denis Durou   IRIT, France
Vincent Duval   Inria Paris, France
Virginia Estellers   TU München, Germany
Weihong Guo   Case Western Reserve University, USA
Moncef Hidane   INSA Val de Loire, France
SungHa Kang   Georgia Tech, USA
Charles Kervrann   Inria Rennes, France
Ron Kimmel   Technion, Israel
Stefan Kunis   University of Osnabrück, Germany
Said Ladjal   LTCI, Telecom Paristech, France
François Lauze   DIKU, University of Copenhagen, Denmark
Carole Le Guyader   INSA Rouen, France
Antonio Leitao   Federal University of Santa Catarina, Brazil
Jan Lellmann   University of Lübeck, Germany
Marco Loog   Delft University of Technology, The Netherlands
Lionel Moisan   Université Paris Descartes, France
Rasmus Paulsen   DTU Compute, DTU, Denmark
Esben Plenge   DIKU, University of Copenhagen, Denmark
Yvain Quéau   TU München, Germany
Julien Rabin   ENSICAEN, France
Tammy Riklin Raviv   Ben-Gurion University, Israel
Chen Sagiv   SagivTech Ltd, Israel
Nir Sochen   Tel Aviv University, Israel
Stefan Sommer   DIKU, University of Copenhagen, Denmark
Jon Sporring   DIKU, University of Copenhagen, Denmark
Kim Steenstrup Pedersen   DIKU, University of Copenhagen, Denmark
Vinh-Thong Ta   Labri, Université de Bordeaux, France
Pierre Weiss   CNRS Toulouse, France

Tieyong Zeng   Hong Kong Baptist University, Hong Kong,
                                    SAR China
Xiaoqun Zhang   Shanghai Jiao Tong University, China

Additional Reviewers

Kireeti Bodduna   Saarland University, Germany
Noémie Debroux   INSA Rouen, France
Sabine Müller   Saarland University, Germany
Thomas Vogt   University of Lübeck, Germany
Tao Wu   TU München, Germany

Keynote Speakers

Christine De Mol   Université Libre de Bruxelles, Belgium
Maurizio Falcone   La Sapienza, Università di Roma, Italy
Per Christian Hansen   DTU Compute, DTU, Denmark
Marco Loog   Delft University of Technology, The Netherlands

Financial Committee

Lene Winther Hagelskjær   CAP Partners
Christen Artangan Sørensen   DIKU, University of Copenhagen, Denmark

Webmaster

Rasmus Dalgas Kongskov   DTU Compute, DTU, Denmark

Sponsoring Institutions

The Center for Stochastic Geometry and Advanced Bioimaging (CSGB)
The Carlsberg Foundation
The Otto Mønsted Foundation
The Department of Computer Science, University of Copenhagen (DIKU)
IH Food AS
Zebicon AS

Contents

Tomographic Reconstruction

Optical Flow, Motion Estimation and Registration

3D Vision

Scale Space and PDE Methods

Spatio-Temporal Scale Selection in Video Data

Tony Lindeberg[✉]

Computational Brain Science Lab,
Department of Computational Science and Technology,
School of Computer Science and Communication,
KTH Royal Institute of Technology, Stockholm, Sweden
tony@kth.se

Abstract. We present a theory and a method for simultaneous detection of local spatial and temporal scales in video data. The underlying idea is that if we process video data by spatio-temporal receptive fields at multiple spatial and temporal scales, we would like to generate hypotheses about the spatial extent and the temporal duration of the underlying spatio-temporal image structures that gave rise to the feature responses. For two types of spatio-temporal scale-space representations, (i) a non-causal Gaussian spatio-temporal scale space for offline analysis of pre-recorded video sequences and (ii) a time-causal and time-recursive spatio-temporal scale space for online analysis of real-time video streams, we express sufficient conditions for spatio-temporal feature detectors in terms of spatio-temporal receptive fields to deliver scale covariant and scale invariant feature responses. A theoretical analysis is given of the scale selection properties of six types of spatio-temporal interest point detectors, showing that five of them allow for provable scale covariance and scale invariance. Then, we describe a time-causal and time-recursive algorithm for detecting sparse spatio-temporal interest points from video streams and show that it leads to intuitively reasonable results.

1 Introduction

A basic paradigm for video analysis consists of performing the first layers of visual processing based on successive layers of spatio-temporal receptive fields (Hubel and Wiesel [1]; DeAngelis et al. [2]; Zelnik-Manor and Irani [3]; Laptev and Lindeberg [4]; Simonyan and Zisserman [5]).

A general problem when applying the notion of receptive fields in practice, however, is that the types of responses that are obtained in a specific situation can be strongly dependent on the scale levels at which they are computed. Figure 1 show illustrations of this problem by showing snapshots of spatio-temporal receptive field responses over multiple spatial and temporal scales for a video sequence and different types of spatio-temporal features computed from it. Note how qualitatively different types of responses are obtained at different

The support from the Swedish Research Council (Contract 2014-4083) and Stiftelsen Olle Engkvist Byggmästare (Contract 2015/465) is gratefully acknowledged.

© Springer International Publishing AG 2017
F. Lauze et al. (Eds.): SSVM 2017, LNCS 10302, pp. 3–15, 2017.
DOI: 10.1007/978-3-319-58771-4_1

Spatio-temporal scale-space representation L

Second-order temporal derivative L_{tt}

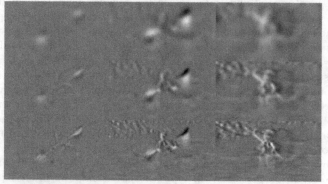

The spatial Laplacian of the second-order temporal derivative $\nabla^2_{(x,y)} L_{tt}$

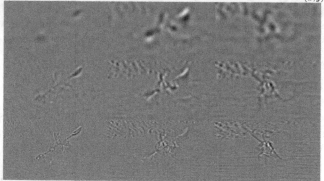

Fig. 1. Time-causal spatio-temporal scale-space representation $L(x, y, t; \; s, \tau)$ with its second-order temporal derivative $L_{tt}(x, y, t; \; s, \tau)$ and the spatial Laplacian of the second-order temporal derivative $\nabla^2_{(x,y)} L_{tt}$ computed from a video sequence in the UCF-101 dataset (Kayaking_g01_c01.avi) at 3×3 combinations of the spatial scales (bottom row) $\sigma_{s,1} = 2$ pixels, (middle row) $\sigma_{s,2} = 4.6$ pixels and (top row) $\sigma_{s,1} = 10.6$ pixels and the temporal scales (left column) $\sigma_{\tau,1} = 40$ ms, (middle column) $\sigma_{\tau,2} = 160$ ms and (right column) $\sigma_{\tau,2} = 640$ ms using a logarithmic distribution of the temporal scale levels with distribution parameter $c = 2$. (Image size: 320×172 pixels of original 320×240 pixels. Frame 90 of 226 frames at 25 frames per second.)

spatio-temporal scales. At some spatio-temporal scales, we get strong responses due to the movements of the paddle or the motion of the paddler in the kayak. At other spatio-temporal scales, we get relatively larger responses because of the movements of the here unstabilized camera. A computer vision system intended to process the visual input from general spatio-temporal scenes does therefore need to decide what responses within the family of spatio-temporal receptive fields over different spatial and temporal scales it should base its analysis on as well as about how the information from different subsets of spatio-temporal scales should be combined.

For purely spatial data, the problem of performing spatial scale selection is nowadays rather well understood. Given the spatial Gaussian scale-space concept (Koenderink [6]; Lindeberg [7,8]; Florack [9]; ter Haar Romeny [10]), a general methodology for performing spatial scale selection has been developed based on local extrema over spatial scales of scale-normalized differential entities (Lindeberg [11]). This general methodology has in turn been successfully applied to develop robust methods for image-based matching and recognition that are able to handle large variations of the size of the objects in the image domain.

Much less research has, however, been performed on developing methods for choosing locally appropriate temporal scales for spatio-temporal analysis of video data. While some methods for temporal scale selection have been developed (Lindeberg [12]; Laptev and Lindeberg [13]; Willems *et al.* [14]), these methods suffer from either theoretical or practical limitations. The subject of this article is to present an extended theory for spatio-temporal scale selection in video data.

2   Spatio-Temporal Receptive Field Model

For processing video data at multiple spatial and temporal scales, we follow the approach with idealized models of spatio-temporal receptive fields of the form

$$T(x_1, x_2, t; \; s, \tau; \; v, \Sigma) = g(x_1 - v_1 t, x_2 - v_2 t; \; s, \Sigma) \, h(t; \; \tau) \qquad (1)$$

as previously derived, proposed and studied in Lindeberg [8,15,16], where we specifically here choose as temporal smoothing kernel over time either (i) the non-causal Gaussian kernel

$$h(t; \; \tau) = g(t; \; \tau) = \frac{1}{\sqrt{2\pi\tau}} e^{-t^2/2\tau} \qquad (2)$$

or (ii) the time-causal limit kernel (Lindeberg [16, Eq. (38)])

$$h(t; \; \tau) = \Psi(t; \; \tau, c) \qquad (3)$$

defined via its Fourier transform of the form

$$\hat{\Psi}(\omega; \; \tau, c) = \prod_{k=1}^{\infty} \frac{1}{1 + i \, c^{-k} \sqrt{c^2 - 1} \sqrt{\tau} \, \omega}. \qquad (4)$$

For simplicity, we consider space-time separable receptive fields with image velocity $v = (v_1, v_2) = (0, 0)$ and set the spatial covariance matrix to $\Sigma = I$.

3   Spatial-Temporal Scale Covariance and Scale Invariance

In the corresponding spatio-temporal scale-space representation

$$L(x_1, x_2, t;\ s, \tau) = (T(\cdot, \cdot, \cdot;\ s, \tau) * f(\cdot, \cdot, \cdot)) (x_1, x_2, t;\ s, \tau) \tag{5}$$

we define scale-normalized partial derivates (Lindeberg [16, Eq. (108)]

$$L_{x_1^{m_1} x_2^{m_2} t^n, norm} = s^{(m_1+m_2)\gamma_s/2} \tau^{n\gamma_\tau/2} L_{x_1^{m_1} x_2^{m_2} t^n} \tag{6}$$

and consider homogeneous spatio-temporal differential invariants of the form

$$\mathcal{D}L = \sum_{i=1}^{I} \prod_{j=1}^{J} c_i\, L_{x^{\alpha_{ij}} t^{\beta_{ij}}}, = \sum_{i=1}^{I} \prod_{j=1}^{J} c_i\, L_{x_1^{\alpha_{1ij}} x_2^{\alpha_{2ij}} t^{\beta_{ij}}}, \tag{7}$$

where the sum of the orders of spatial and temporal differentiation in a certain term $\sum_{j=1}^{J} |\alpha_{ij}| = \sum_{j=1}^{J} \alpha_{1ij} + \alpha_{2ij} = M$ and $\sum_{j=1}^{J} \beta_{ij} = N$ does not depend on the index i of that term. Consider next an independent scaling transformation of the spatial and the temporal domains of a video sequence

$$f'(x_1', x_2', t') = f(x_1, x_2, t) \quad \text{for} \quad (x_1', x_2', t') = (S_s\, x_1, S_s\, x_2, S_\tau\, t) \tag{8}$$

where S_s and S_τ denote the spatial and temporal scaling factors, respectively. Then, a homogeneous spatio-temporal derivative expression of the form (7) with the spatio-temporal derivatives $L_{x_1^{m_1} x_2^{m_2} t^n}$ replaced by scale-normalized spatio-temporal derivatives $L_{x_1^{m_1} x_2^{m_2} t^n, norm}$ according to (6) transforms according to

$$D'_{norm} L' = S_s^{M(\gamma_s-1)} S_\tau^{N(\gamma_\tau-1)} D_{norm} L. \tag{9}$$

This result follows from a combination and generalization of Eq. (25) in (Lindeberg [11]) with Eqs. (10) and (104) in (Lindeberg [17]).

With the temporal smoothing performed by the scale-invariant limit kernel according to (3), the temporal scaling transformation property does, however, only hold for temporal scaling transformations that correspond to exact mappings between the discrete temporal scale levels in the time-causal temporal scale-space representation and thus to temporal scaling factors $S_\tau = c^i$ that are integer powers of the distribution parameter c of the time-causal limit kernel.

Specifically, the scale covariance property (9) implies that if we can detect a spatio-temporal level $(\hat{s}, \hat{\tau})$ such that the scale-normalized expression $D'_{norm} L'$ assumes a local extremum at a point $(\hat{x}, \hat{y}, \hat{t};\ \hat{s}, \hat{\tau})$ in spatio-temporal scale space, then this local extremum is preserved under independent scaling transformations of the spatial and temporal domains and is transformed in a scale-covariant way

$$(\hat{x}, \hat{y}, \hat{t};\ \hat{s}, \hat{\tau}) \mapsto (S_s\, \hat{x}, S_s\, \hat{y}, S_\tau\, \hat{t};\ S_s^2\, \hat{s}, S_\tau^2\, \hat{\tau}). \tag{10}$$

The properties (9) and (10) constitute a theoretical foundation for scale-covariant and scale-invariant spatio-temporal feature detection.

4   Scale Selection in Non-Causal Gaussian Spatio-Temporal Scale Space

In this section, we will perform a closed-form theoretical analysis of the spatial and temporal scale selection properties that are obtained by detecting simultaneous local extrema over both spatial and temporal scales of different scale-normalized spatio-temporal differential expressions. We will specifically analyze how the spatial and temporal scale estimates $\hat{s}$ and $\hat{\tau}$ are related to the spatial extent s_0 and the temporal duration τ_0 of the underlying spatio-temporal image structures.

4.1   Differential Entities for Spatio-Temporal Interest Point Detection

Inspired by the way neurons in the lateral geniculate nucleus (LGN) respond to visual input (DeAngelis et al. [2]), which for many LGN cells can be modelled by idealized operations of the form (Lindeberg [15, Eq. (108)])

$$h_{LGN}(x, y, t;\ s, \tau) = \pm(\partial_{xx} + \partial_{yy})\, g(x, y;\ s)\, \partial_{t^n}\, h(t;\ \tau), \tag{11}$$

we consider the scale-normalized Laplacian of the first- and second-order temporal derivatives

$$\nabla^2_{(x,y),norm} L_{t,norm} = s^{\gamma_s} \tau^{\gamma_\tau/2} (L_{xxt} + L_{yyt}), \tag{12}$$

$$\nabla^2_{(x,y),norm} L_{tt,norm} = s^{\gamma_s} \tau^{\gamma_\tau} (L_{xxtt} + L_{yytt}). \tag{13}$$

Inspired by the way the determinant of the spatial Hessian matrix constitutes a better spatial interest point detector than the spatial Laplacian operator (Lindeberg [18]), we consider extensions of the spatial Laplacian of the first- and second-order temporal derivatives into the determinant of the spatial Hessian of the first- and second-order temporal derivatives

$$\det \mathcal{H}_{(x,y),norm} L_{t,norm}\ = s^{2\gamma_s} \tau^{\gamma_\tau} (L_{xxt} L_{yyt} - L^2_{xyt}), \tag{14}$$

$$\det \mathcal{H}_{(x,y),norm} L_{tt,norm} = s^{2\gamma_s} \tau^{2\gamma_\tau} (L_{xxtt} L_{yytt} - L^2_{xytt}). \tag{15}$$

Over three-dimensional joint space-time, we can also define the determinant of the spatio-temporal Hessian

$$\det \mathcal{H}_{(x,y,t),norm} L = s^{2\gamma_s} \tau^{\gamma_\tau} (L_{xx}L_{yy}L_{tt} + 2L_{xy}L_{xt}L_{yt} \\ -L_{xx}L^2_{yt} - L_{yy}L^2_{xt} - L_{tt}L^2_{xy}) \tag{16}$$

and make an attempt to define a spatio-temporal Laplacian of the form

$$\nabla^2_{(x,y,t),norm} L = s^{\gamma_s}(L_{xx} + L_{yy}) + \varkappa^2 \tau^{\gamma_\tau} L_{tt}, \tag{17}$$

where we have introduced a parameter $\varkappa^2$ to make explicit the arbitrary scaling factor between temporal vs. spatial derivatives that influences any attempt to add derivative expressions of different dimensionality.

4.2 Scale Calibration for a Gaussian Blink

Consider a spatio-temporal model signal defined as a Gaussian blink with spatial extent s_0 and temporal duration τ_0

$$f(x,y,t) = g(x,y;\ s_0)\,g(t;\ \tau_0) = \frac{1}{(2\pi)^{3/2}s_0\sqrt{\tau_0}}\,e^{-(x^2+y^2)/2s_0}\,e^{-t^2/2\tau_0}, \quad (18)$$

for which the spatio-temporal scale-space representation is of the form

$$L(x,y,t;\ s,\tau) = g(x,y;\ s_0+s)\,g(t;\ \tau_0+\tau). \quad (19)$$

To calibrate the scale selection properties of the spatio-temporal interest point detectors $\nabla^2_{(x,y),norm}L_{tt,norm}$, $\det\mathcal{H}_{(x,y),norm}L_{tt,norm}$ and $\det\mathcal{H}_{(x,y,t),norm}L$, we require that at the origin $(x,y,t)=(0,0,0)$ the scale-normalized spatio-temporal differential expression should assume its strongest extremum over spatial and temporal scales at spatio-temporal scale level

$$\hat{s} = s_0, \qquad \hat{\tau} = q^2\tau_0. \quad (20)$$

Here, we have introduced a parameter $q < 1$ to enforce temporal scale calibration to a finer temporal scale than τ_0, to enable shorter temporal delays and thus faster responses for feature detection performed based on a time-causal spatio-temporal scale-space representation. By calculating the scale-normalized feature response at the origin for each one of the feature detectors, differentiating with respect to the spatial and temporal scale parameters and solving for the zero-crossings over spatial and temporal scales, we find that the spatial scale-normalization powers γ_s and γ_τ in the scale-normalized spatio-temporal derivatives (6) should be set to $\gamma_s = 1$ for all three operators and to

$$\gamma_{\tau,\nabla^2_{(x,y)}L_{tt}} = \gamma_{\tau,\det\mathcal{H}_{(x,y)}L_{tt}} = \frac{3q^2}{2(q^2+1)}, \quad (21)$$

$$\gamma_{\tau,\det\mathcal{H}_{(x,y,t)}} = \frac{5q^2}{2(q^2+1)}. \quad (22)$$

4.3 Scale Calibration for a Gaussian Onset Blob

Consider next a spatio-temporal pattern defined as a Gaussian onset blob with spatial extent s_0 and temporal duration τ_0

$$f(x,y,t) = g(x,y;\ s_0)\int_{u=0}^{t} g(u;\ \tau_0)\,du$$

$$= \frac{1}{(2\pi)^{3/2}s_0\sqrt{\tau_0}}\,e^{-(x^2+y^2)/2s_0}\int_{u=0}^{t} e^{-u^2/2\tau_0}\,du, \quad (23)$$

for which the spatio-temporal scale-space representation is of the form

$$L(x,y,t;\ s,\tau) = g(x,y;\ s_0+s)\int_{u=0}^{t} g(u;\ \tau_0+\tau)\,du. \quad (24)$$

To calibrate the scale selection properties of the spatio-temporal interest point detectors $\nabla^2_{(x,y),norm}L_{t,norm}$ and $\det \mathcal{H}_{(x,y),norm}L_{t,norm}$, we require that at the origin $(x, y, t) = (0, 0, 0)$ the scale-normalized spatio-temporal differential entity should assume its strongest extremum at spatio-temporal scale level

$$\hat{s} = s_0, \qquad \hat{\tau} = q^2 \tau_0. \tag{25}$$

By again calculating the scale-normalized response at the origin and differentiating with respect to the spatial and temporal scale parameters, we find that the spatial scale-normalization powers γ_s and γ_τ in the scale-normalized spatio-temporal derivatives (6) should for both operators be set to $\gamma_s = 1$ and

$$\gamma_\tau = \frac{q^2}{q^2 + 1}. \tag{26}$$

4.4   Lack of Scale Covariance for the Spatio-Temporal Laplacian

For the attempt to define a scale-normalized spatio-temporal Laplacian operator

$$\nabla^2_{(x,y,t),norm}L = s^{\gamma_s}(L_{xx} + L_{yy}) + \varkappa^2 \tau^{\gamma_\tau} L_{tt}, \tag{27}$$

the equations that determine the spatial and temporal scale estimates are unfortunately hard to solve in closed form for general values of the scale normalization powers γ_s and γ_τ. For the specific case of $\gamma_s = 1$ and $\gamma_\tau = 1$, we can, however, note that the resulting scale estimates

$$\hat{s} = s_0 \left(\frac{5}{2 + \varkappa^2} - 1 \right) \quad \text{and} \quad \hat{\tau} = 2\tau_0 \left(2 - \frac{5}{2 + \varkappa^2} \right) \tag{28}$$

will be explicitly dependent on the relative scaling factor $\varkappa^2$ between the derivatives with respect to the temporal $vs.$ the spatial dimensions. This situation is in clear contrast to the other spatio-temporal differential entities treated above, for which a multiplication of the temporal derivative by a factor $\varkappa$ does not affect the spatial or temporal scale estimates. This property does in turn imply that the spatio-temporal scale estimates will not be covariant under independent relative rescalings of the spatial and temporal dimensions. These theoretical arguments explain why the scale estimates from the spatial and temporal selection mechanisms in [13] were later empirically found to not be sufficiently robust.

5   Spatio-Temporal Interest Points Detected as Spatio-Temporal Scale-Space Extrema over Space-Time

In this section, we shall use the above scale-normalized differential entities for detecting spatio-temporal interest points. The overall idea of the most basic form of such an algorithm is to simultaneously detect both spatio-temporal points $(\hat{x}, \hat{y}, \hat{t})$ and spatio-temporal scales $(\hat{s}, \hat{\tau})$ at which the scale-normalized differential entity $(\mathcal{D}_{norm}L)(x, y, t; s, \tau)$ simultaneously assumes local extrema with respect to both space-time (x, y, t) and spatio-temporal scales (s, τ).

5.1 Time-Causal and Time-Recursive Algorithm for Spatio-Temporal Scale-Space Extrema Detection

By approximating the spatial smoothing operation by convolution with the discrete analogue of the Gaussian kernel over the spatial domain [7], which obeys a semi-group property over spatial scales, and approximating the time-causal limit kernel by a cascade of first-order recursive filters [16, Eq. (56)]), we can state an algorithm for computing the time-causal and time-recursive spatio-temporal scale-space representation and detecting spatio-temporal scale-space extrema of scale-normalized differential invariants from it as follows:

1. Determine a set of temporal scale levels τ_k and spatial scale levels s_l at which the algorithm is to operate by computing spatio-temporal scale-space representations at these spatio-temporal scales.
2. Compute time constants $\mu_k = (\sqrt{1 + 4r^2(\tau_k - \tau_{k-1})} - 1)/2$ according to (Lindeberg [16, Eqs. (58) and (55)]) for approximating the time-causal limit kernel by a cascade of recursive filters, where r denotes the frame rate and the temporal scale levels τ_k are given in units of $[\text{seconds}]^2$.
3. For each temporal scale level, initiate a temporal buffer for temporal scale-space smoothing at this temporal scale $B(x,y,k) = f(x,y,0)$.
4. For each spatial and temporal scale level initiate a small number of temporal buffers for the nearest past frames. (This number should be equal to the maximum order of temporal differentiation.)
5. Loop forwards over time t (in units of time steps):
   (a) Loop over the temporal scale levels k in ascending order:
       i. Perform temporal smoothing according to (with $B(x,y,0) = f(x,y,t)$)

$$B(x,y,k) := B(x,y,k) + \frac{1}{1+\mu_k}(B(x,y,k-1) - B(x,y,k)). \quad (29)$$

       ii. Initiate spatio-temporal scale-space representation at current temporal scale $L(x,y,t;\ s_1,\tau_k) = T(x,y;\ s_1) * B(x,y,k)$.
       iii. Loop over the spatial scale levels s_l in ascending order:
            A. Compute spatio-temporal representations at coarser spatial scales using the semi-group property over spatial scales

$$L(\cdot,\cdot,t;\ s_l,\tau_k) = T(\cdot,\cdot;\ s_l - s_{l-1}) * L(\cdot,\cdot,t;\ s_{l-1},\tau_k). \quad (30)$$

   (b) For all temporal and spatial scales, compute temporal derivatives using backward differences over the short temporal buffers of past frames.
   (c) For all temporal and spatial scales, compute the scale-normalized differential entity $(\mathcal{D}_{norm}L)(x,y,t;\ s_l,\tau_k)$ at that spatio-temporal scale.
   (d) For all points and spatio-temporal scales $(x,y;\ s_l,\tau_k)$ for which the magnitude of the post-normalized differential entity is above a pre-defined threshold $|(\mathcal{D}_{postnorm}L)(x,y,t;\ s_l,\tau_k)| \geq \theta$, determine if the point is either a positive maximum or a negative minimum in comparison to its

nearest neighbours over space (x, y), time t, spatial scales s_l and temporal scales τ_k. Because the detection of local extrema over time requires a future reference in the temporal direction, this comparison is not done at the must recent frame but at the nearest past frame.

i. For each detected scale-space extremum, compute more accurate estimates of its spatio-temporal position $(\hat{x}, \hat{y}, \hat{t})$ and spatio-temporal scale $(\hat{s}, \hat{\tau})$ using parabolic interpolation along each dimension [17, Eq. (115)]. Do also compensate the magnitude estimates by a magnitude correction factor computed for each dimension.

When detecting local extrema with respect to the spatial, temporal and scale dimensions, we order the comparisons with respect to the nearest neighbours in each dimension and stop performing the comparisons at any point in spatio-temporal scale-space as soon as it can be stated that a spatio-temporal point $(x, y, t; s, \tau)$ is neither a local maximum or a local minimum.

5.2 Experimental Results

Figure 2 shows the result of detecting spatio-temporal interest points in this way from the same video sequence as used for the illustrations in Fig. 1. For this experiment, we used 21 spatial scale levels between $\sigma_s = 2$ and 21 pixels and 7 temporal scale levels between $\sigma_\tau = 40$ ms and 2.56 s with distribution parameter $c = 2$ for the time-causal limit kernel. To obtain comparable numbers of features from the different feature detectors, we adapted the thresholds on the scale-normalized differential invariants $\nabla^2_{(x,y),norm} L_{t,norm}$, $\nabla^2_{(x,y),norm} L_{tt,norm}$, $\det \mathcal{H}_{(x,y),norm} L_{t,norm}$, $\det \mathcal{H}_{(x,y),norm} L_{tt,norm}$, $\det \mathcal{H}_{(x,y,t),norm} L$ and $\nabla^2_{(x,y,t),norm} L$ such that the average number of features from each feature detector was 50 features per frame.

As can be seen from the results, all of these feature detectors respond to regions in the video sequence where there are strong variations in image intensity over space and time. There are, however, also some qualitative differences between the results from the different spatio-temporal interest point detectors. The LGN-inspired feature detectors $\nabla^2_{(x,y),norm} L_{t,norm}$ and $\nabla^2_{(x,y),norm} L_{tt,norm}$ respond both to the motion patterns of the paddler and to the spatio-temporal texture corresponding to the waves on the water surface that lead to temporal flickering effects and so do the operators $\det \mathcal{H}_{(x,y),norm} L_{t,norm}$ and $\det \mathcal{H}_{(x,y),norm} L_{tt,norm}$. The more corner-detector-inspired feature detector $\det \mathcal{H}_{(x,y,t),norm} L$ responds more to image features where there are simultaneously rapid variations over all the spatial and temporal dimensions.

5.3 Covariance and Invariance Properties

From the theoretical scale selection properties of the spatial scale-normalized derivative operators according to the spatial scale selection theory in (Lindeberg [11]) in combination with the temporal scale selection properties of the temporal scale selection theory in (Lindeberg [17]) with the scale covariance

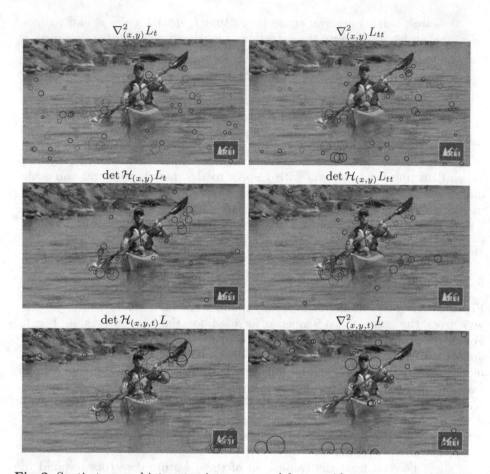

Fig. 2. Spatio-temporal interest points computed from a video sequence in the UCF-101 dataset (Kayaking_g01_c01.avi, cropped) for different scale-normalized spatio-temporal entities and using the presented time-causal and time-recursive spatio-temporal scale-space extrema detection algorithm with the temporal scale-space smoothing performed by a time-discrete approximation of the time-causal limit kernel for $c = 2$ based on recursive filters coupled in cascade and temporal scale calibration based on $q = 1$: (top left) The spatial Laplacian of the first-order temporal derivative $\nabla^2_{(x,y)} L_t$. (top right) The spatial Laplacian of the second-order temporal derivative $\nabla^2_{(x,y)} L_{tt}$. (middle row left) The determinant of the spatial Hessian of the first-order temporal derivative $\det \mathcal{H}_{(x,y)} L_t$. (middle row right) The determinant of the spatial Hessian of the second-order temporal derivative $\det \mathcal{H}_{(x,y)} L_{tt}$. (bottom row left) The determinant of the spatio-temporal Hessian $\det \mathcal{H}_{(x,y,t)} L$. (bottom row right) The spatio-temporal Laplacian $\nabla^2_{(x,y,t)} L$. Each figure shows a snapshot at frame 90 with a threshold on the magnitude of the scale-normalized differential expression determined such that the average number of features is 50 features per frame. The radius of each circle reflects the spatial scale of the spatio-temporal scale-space extremum. (Image size: 320×172 pixels of original 320×240 pixels. Frame 90 of 226 frames at 25 frames per second.)

of the underlying spatio-temporal derivative expressions $\nabla^2_{(x,y),norm}L_{t,norm}$, $\nabla^2_{(x,y),norm}L_{tt,norm}$, $\det \mathcal{H}_{(x,y),norm}L_{t,norm}$, $\det \mathcal{H}_{(x,y),norm}L_{tt,norm}$ and $\det \mathcal{H}_{(x,y,t),norm}L$ described in (Lindeberg [16]), it follows that these spatio-temporal interest point detectors are truly scale covariant under independent scaling transformations of the spatial and the temporal domains if the temporal smoothing is performed by either a non-causal Gaussian $g(t; \tau)$ over the temporal domain or the time-causal limit kernel $\Psi(t; \tau, c)$. From the general proof in Sect. 3, it follows that the detected spatio-temporal interest points transform in a scale-covariant way under independent scaling transformations of the spatial and the temporal domains.

6   Summary and Discussion

We have presented a theory and a method for performing simultaneous detection of local spatial and temporal scale estimates in video data. The theory comprises both (i) feature detection performed within a non-causal spatio-temporal scale-space representation computed for offline analysis of pre-recorded video data and (ii) feature detection performed from real-time image streams where the future cannot be accessed and memory requirements call for time-recursive algorithms based on only compact buffers of what has occurred in the past.

As a theoretical foundation for spatio-temporal scale selection, we have stated general results regarding covariance and invariance properties of spatio-temporal features defined from video data with independent scaling transformations of the spatial and the temporal domains. For five spatio-temporal differential invariants: (i)–(ii) the spatial Laplacian of the first- and second-order temporal derivatives, (iii)–(iv) the determinant of the spatial Hessian of the first- and second-order temporal derivatives and (v) the determinant of the spatio-temporal Hessian matrix, we have analysed the theoretical scale selection properties of these feature detectors and shown how scale calibration of these feature detectors can be performed to make the spatio-temporal scale estimates reflect the spatial extent and the temporal duration of the underlying spatio-temporal features that gave rise to the feature responses.

For an attempt to define a spatio-temporal Laplacian, we have on the other hand shown that this differential expression is not scale covariant under independent rescalings of the spatial and temporal domains, which explains a previously noted poor robustness of the scale selection step in the spatio-temporal interest point detector based on the spatio-temporal Harris operator [13].

To allow for different trade-offs between the temporal response properties of time-causal spatio-temporal feature detection (shorter temporal delays) in relation to signal detection theory, which would call for detection of image structures at the same spatial and temporal scales as they occur, we have specifically introduced a parameter q to regulate the temporal scale calibration to finer temporal scales $\hat{\tau} = q^2 \tau_0$ as opposed to the more common choice $\hat{s} = s_0$ over the spatial domain. According to a theoretical analysis of scale selection properties in non-causal spatio-temporal scale space, the results predict that this parameter should reduce the temporal delay by a factor of q: $\Delta t \mapsto q\,\Delta t$. An experimental quantification of the scale selection properties in time-causal spatio-temporal scale space in a longer version of this paper confirm that a substantial decrease in temporal delay is obtained. The specific choice of the parameter q should be optimized with respect to the task that the spatio-temporal selection and the spatio-temporal features are to be used for and given specific requirements of the application domain.

We have also presented an explicit algorithm for detecting spatio-temporal interest points in a time-causal and time-recursive context, in which the future cannot be accessed and memory requirements call for only compact buffers to store partial records of what has occurred in the past and presented experimental results of applying this algorithm to real-world video data for the different types of spatio-temporal interest point detectors that we have studied theoretically.

References

1. Hubel, D.H., Wiesel, T.N.: Brain and Visual Perception: The Story of a 25-Year Collaboration. Oxford University Press, Oxford (2005)
2. DeAngelis, G.C., Ohzawa, I., Freeman, R.D.: Receptive field dynamics in the central visual pathways. Trends Neurosci. **18**, 451–457 (1995)
3. Zelnik-Manor, L., Irani, M.: Event-based analysis of video. In: Proceedings of the Computer Vision and Pattern Recognition (CVPR 2001), pp. II:123–II:130 (2001)
4. Laptev, I., Lindeberg, T.: Local descriptors for spatio-temporal recognition. In: MacLean, W.J. (ed.) SCVMA 2004. LNCS, vol. 3667, pp. 91–103. Springer, Heidelberg (2006). doi:10.1007/11676959_8
5. Simonyan, K., Zisserman, A.: Two-stream convolutional networks for action recognition in videos. In: Advances in Neural Information Processing Systems, pp. 568–576 (2014)
6. Koenderink, J.J.: The structure of images. Biol. Cyb. **50**, 363–370 (1984)
7. Lindeberg, T.: Scale-Space Theory in Computer Vision. Springer, Heidelberg (1993)
8. Lindeberg, T.: Generalized Gaussian scale-space axiomatics comprising linear scale-space, affine scale-space and spatio-temporal scale-space. J. Math. Imaging Vis. **40**, 36–81 (2011)
9. Florack, L.M.J.: Image Structure. Springer, Heidelberg (1997)
10. ter Haar Romeny, B.: Front-End Vision and Multi-Scale Image Analysis. Springer, Heidelberg (2003)
11. Lindeberg, T.: Feature detection with automatic scale selection. Int. J. Comp. Vis. **30**, 77–116 (1998)
12. Lindeberg, T.: On automatic selection of temporal scales in time-casual scale-space. In: Sommer, G., Koenderink, J.J. (eds.) AFPAC 1997. LNCS, vol. 1315, pp. 94–113. Springer, Heidelberg (1997)
13. Laptev, I., Lindeberg, T.: Space-time interest points. In: ICCV, pp. 432–439 (2003)
14. Willems, G., Tuytelaars, T., Gool, L.: An efficient dense and scale-invariant spatio-temporal interest point detector. In: Forsyth, D., Torr, P., Zisserman, A. (eds.) ECCV 2008. LNCS, vol. 5303, pp. 650–663. Springer, Heidelberg (2008). doi:10.1007/978-3-540-88688-4_48

15. Lindeberg, T.: A computational theory of visual receptive fields. Biol. Cybern. **107**, 589–635 (2013)
16. Lindeberg, T.: Time-causal and time-recursive spatio-temporal receptive fields. J. Math. Imaging Vis. **55**, 50–88 (2016)
17. Lindeberg, T.: Temporal scale selection in time-causal scale space. J. Math. Imaging Vis. **58**, 57–101 (2017). doi:10.1007/s10851-016-0691-3
18. Lindeberg, T.: Image matching using generalized scale-space interest points. J. Math. Imaging Vis. **52**, 3–36 (2015)

Dynamic Texture Recognition Using Time-Causal Spatio-Temporal Scale-Space Filters

Ylva Jansson[(✉)] and Tony Lindeberg

Computational Brain Science Lab,
Department of Computational Science and Technology,
School of Computer Science and Communication,
KTH Royal Institute of Technology, Stockholm, Sweden
{yjansson,tony}@kth.se

Abstract. This work presents an evaluation of using time-causal scale-space filters as primitives for video analysis. For this purpose, we present a new family of video descriptors based on regional statistics of spatio-temporal scale-space filter responses and evaluate this approach on the problem of dynamic texture recognition. Our approach generalises a previously used method, based on joint histograms of receptive field responses, from the spatial to the spatio-temporal domain. We evaluate one member in this family, constituting a joint binary histogram, on two widely used dynamic texture databases. The experimental evaluation shows competitive performance compared to previous methods for dynamic texture recognition, especially on the more complex Dyn-Tex database. These results support the descriptive power of time-causal spatio-temporal scale-space filters as primitives for video analysis.

1   Introduction

The ability to derive properties of the surrounding world from time-dependent visual input is a key functionality of a computer vision system, and necessary for any artificial or biological agent that is to use visual input for interpreting a dynamic environment. For this purpose, there has been intensive research into areas such as action recognition, dynamic texture and scene understanding, automatic surveillance, video-indexing and retrieval, etc.

For biological vision, local image measurements in terms of receptive fields constitute the first processing layers [1]. In computer vision, spatial receptive fields based on the Gaussian scale-space concept have been demonstrated to be a powerful front-end for solving a large range of visual tasks. The theoretical properties of scale-space filters enable the design of methods invariant or robust to natural image transformations [2–4]. Also, such axiomatically derived first processing layers, which can be shared among different tasks, free resources both

The support from the Swedish Research Council (Contract 2014-4083) and Stiftelsen Olle Engkvist Byggmästare (Contract 2015/465) is gratefully acknowledged.

F. Lauze et al. (Eds.): SSVM 2017, LNCS 10302, pp. 16–28, 2017.
DOI: 10.1007/978-3-319-58771-4_2

for learning higher level features from data and during on-line processing. This could prove especially useful for high-dimensional video data.

For a real-time visual system or to model biological vision, such a visual front-end cannot utilise information from the future. For time-critical applications (such as self-driving cars) where also a small difference in response time matters, the ad-hoc solution of using a time-delayed truncated Gaussian temporal kernel would imply unnecessarily long temporal delays. Recently, a new framework for *time-causal spatio-temporal scale-space filters*, or equivalently *spatio-temporal receptive fields*, was introduced by Lindeberg [2]. These idealised receptive fields show a strong connection to biology in the sense that they very well model receptive field shapes of neurons in the LGN and V1 [2,4]. The purpose of this study is a first evaluation of using these time-causal spatio-temporal receptive fields as visual primitives for video analysis.

As a first application, we have chosen the problem of dynamic texture recognition. A dynamic texture or spatio-temporal texture can be naively defined as "texture + motion" or more formally as a spatio-temporal pattern that exhibits certain stationarity properties and self-similarity over both space and time [5]. Examples of dynamic textures are windblown vegetation, fire, waves, a flock of flying birds or a flag flapping in the wind. Recognising different types of dynamic textures is important for visual tasks such as automatic surveillance (e.g. detecting forest fires), video indexing and retrieval (e.g. return all images set on the sea) and to enable artificial agents to understand and interact with the world.

In this paper, we start by presenting a new family of video descriptors in the form of joint histograms of spatio-temporal receptive field responses, thereby generalising a previous method by Linde and Lindeberg [6] from the spatial to the spatio-temporal domain. We then evaluate one member of this family constituting a joint binary histogram on two widely used dynamic texture databases. It will be shown that our preliminary descriptor shows highly competitive performance compared to previous methods for dynamic texture recognition, thus supporting the applicability of these time-causal spatio-temporal receptive fields as primitives for video analysis.

2   Related Work

Some of the first methods for dynamic texture recognition were based on *optic flow*, see e.g. Nelson and Polana [7]. Another early approach for both synthesis and recognition was to model dynamic textures as *linear dynamical systems* (LDS), see e.g. work by Soatto et al. [8]. To enable recognition less dependent on global spatial appearance, the LDS approach has been extended to bags of dynamical systems (BoS) as by Ravichandran et al. [9] and Wang et al. [10], where the latter approach also combines local LDS descriptors with soft coding and an extreme learning machine (ELM) classifier. Previous approaches utilising *spatio-temporal filtering* are e.g. the oriented energy representations by Wildes and Bergen [11] and Derpanis and Wildes [12], where the latter represents *pure dynamics* of spatio-temporal textures by capturing space-time orientation by means of 3D Gaussian derivative filters. Gonçalves et al. [13] instead jointly model appearance and dynamics using spatio-temporal Gabor filters with different preferred spatial orientations and speeds. Neither of these approaches utilise joint statistics of filter responses.

Methods that model *local space-time structure* of dynamic textures are e.g. local binary patterns (LBP) (Zhao et al. [14]) that capture the joint binarised distribution of local neighbourhoods of pixels, either for 3D space-time volumes (VLBP) or on three orthogonal planes (LBP-TOP), where the latter reduces the computational load by considering the XY, YT, and XT planes separately. Extensions to LBP-TOP are e.g. utilising averaging and principal histogram analysis to get more reliable statistics (Ren et al. [15]) or multi-clustering of salient features to identify and remove outlier frames (AFS-TOP) (Hong et al. [16]). A related approach is multi-scale binarised statistical image features (MBSIF-TOP) introduced by Arashloo and Kittler [17], which capture local image statistics by means of *filters learned from data* by independent component analysis. Tensor dictionary learning (OTD) (Qu et al. [18]) is instead a sparse coding based approach for learning a dictionary for local space-time structure. Previous approaches using non-binary *joint histograms* for image analysis include Schiele and Crowley [19] and Linde and Lindeberg [6], but many later methods have often used either marginal histograms or relative feature strength to capture image statistics. Xu et al. [20] utilise the self-similarity of dynamic textures by creating a descriptor from the fractal dimension of motion features (DFS) and Ji et al. [21] present a method based on wavelet domain fractal analysis (WMFS).

There are also approaches combining several different descriptors such as DL-PEGASOS by Ghanem and Ahuja [22] that uses LBP, PHOG and LDS descriptors together with maximum margin distance learning or Yang et al. [23] using ensemble SVMs to combine LBP, shape-invariant co-occurrence patterns (SCOPs) and chromatic information with dynamic information represented by LDS. Qi et al. [24] present a dynamic texture descriptor leveraging deep learning to transfer prior knowledge from the image domain by extracting global features using a pretrained convolutional neural network. Compared to the time-causal scale-time kernel proposed by Koenderink [25] it should be noted that the time-causal limit kernel used in this paper is *time-recursive*, whereas no time-recursive formulation is known for the scale-time kernel.

3   Spatio-Temporal Receptive Field Model

The spatio-temporal scale-space framework and receptive field model used in this work is that of Lindeberg [2]. The axiomatically derived scale-space kernel for spatial scale s and temporal scale τ is of the form

$$T(x, y, t; \; s, \tau, u, v, \Sigma) = g(x - ut, y - vt; \; s, \Sigma) \, h(t; \; \tau) \tag{1}$$

where (x, y) denotes the image coordinates; t denotes time; $h(t; \; \tau)$ denotes a temporal smoothing kernel and $g(x - ut, y - vt; \; s, \Sigma)$ denotes a spatial affine

Gaussian kernel with spatial covariance matrix Σ that moves with image velocity (u, v). Here, we restrict ourselves to rotationally symmetric Gaussian kernels over the spatial domain and to smoothing kernels with zero image velocity leading to space-time separable receptive fields. The temporal smoothing kernel $h(t; \tau)$ used here is the time-causal kernel composed from coupling truncated exponential functions in cascade, with a composed scale-invariant limit kernel having a Fourier transform of the form [2, Eq. 38]

$$\hat{\Psi}(\omega; \tau, c) = \prod_{k=1}^{\infty} \frac{1}{1 + i\, c^{-k} \sqrt{c^2 - 1} \sqrt{\tau}\, \omega} \qquad (2)$$

where $c > 1$ is the distribution parameter for the logarithmic distribution of intermediate scale levels. For practical purposes, the limit kernel is approximated by a finite number, K, of recursive filters coupled in cascade according to [2, Sect. 6]. We here use $c = 2$ and $K \geq 7$. The time-recursive formulation means there is no need for saving a temporal buffer of previous frames — computing the scale-space representation for a new frame only requires information from the present moment and the scale-space representation for the preceding frame. The *spatio-temporal receptive fields* are in turn defined as partial derivatives of the spatio-temporal scale-space representation of a video $f(x, y, t)$

$$L_{x^{m_1} y^{m_2} t^n}(\cdot, \cdot, \cdot; s, \tau, u, v, \Sigma) = \partial_{x^{m_1} y^{m_2} t^n}(T(\cdot, \cdot, \cdot; s, \tau, u, v, \Sigma) * f(\cdot, \cdot, \cdot)) \quad (3)$$

leading to a spatio-temporal *N-jet* representation of local space-time structure

$$\{L_x, L_y, L_t, L_{xx}, L_{xy}, L_{yy}, L_{xt}, L_{yt}, L_{tt}, \ldots\}. \qquad (4)$$

We also perform scale normalisation of partial derivatives as described in [2]. A subset of receptive fields/scale-space derivative kernels can be seen in Fig. 1. For details concerning the spatio-temporal scale-space representation and the discrete implementation, we refer to [2].

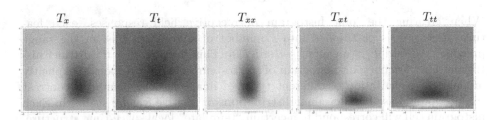

Fig. 1. Time-causal spatio-temporal scale-space derivative kernels $T_{x^m t^n}(x, t;\ s, \tau)$, with a Gaussian kernel over space and the time-causal limit kernel [2] over time, shown over a 1+1-D space-time for the space-time separable case when $v = 0$. ($s = 1$, $\tau = 1$, $K = 8$, $c = 2$) (Horizontal axis: space, $x \in [-3, 3]$. Vertical axis: time, $t \in [0, 3]$)

4   Video Descriptors

We here describe our proposed family of video descriptors. The descriptor is computed in three main steps: (i) computation of local spatio-temporal receptive field responses, (ii) dimensionality reduction with PCA and (iii) aggregating joint statistics of receptive field responses into a multidimensional histogram.

4.1   Receptive Field Responses

The first processing step is to compute spatio-temporal receptive field responses $F = [F_1, F_2, \dots F_N]$ over all individual pixels (x, y, t) in a space-time region for N scale-space derivative filters. These could include a range of different spatial and temporal scales to enable capturing image structures of different spatial extent and temporal duration. Computations are separable in all dimensions and performed frame by frame, utilising recursive smoothing along the temporal dimension. In contrast to previous methods utilising spatio-temporal filtering, such as [12, 13], our method includes a diverse group of partial derivatives from the spatio-temporal N-jet as opposed to a single filter type.

4.2   Dimensionality Reduction with PCA

When combining a large number of local image measurements, not all dimensions will carry meaningful information. For this reason, we perform dimensionality reduction with PCA of the local receptive field responses, as was empirically shown to give good results for spatial images in [6], resulting in a local feature vector $\tilde{F}(x, y, t) = [\tilde{F}_1, \tilde{F}_2, \dots \tilde{F}_M] \in \mathbb{R}^M$ $M \leq N$. The number of components M can be adapted to requirements for descriptor size and need for detail in modelling the local image structure. Dimensionality reduction can also be skipped if working with a smaller number of receptive fields.

4.3   Joint Receptive Field Histograms

When creating the joint histogram of receptive field responses, each feature dimension is partitioned into r number of equidistant bins in the range $[\text{mean}(\tilde{F}_i) - d\,\text{std}(\tilde{F}_i),\ \text{mean}(\tilde{F}_i) + d\,\text{std}(\tilde{F}_i)]$. This gives $n_{cells} = r^N$ distinct histogram bins. Such a joint histogram of spatio-temporal filter responses explicitly models the co-variation of different types of image measurements, in contrast to descriptors based on marginal distributions or relative feature strength. Each histogram cell will correspond to a certain "template" local space-time structure, similar to e.g. VLBP [14] but notably represented and computed using different primitives. The histogram descriptor thus captures the frequency of such local space-time structures in a video and the number of different "templates" will be decided by the number of receptive fields/principal components and the number of bins.

If represented naively, a joint histogram could imply a prohibitively large descriptor. However, in practise the number of *non-zero* bins can be considerably lower than the maximum number of bins, which enables utilising a computationally efficient sparse representation as outlined in [6]. Also note that although we in this work aggregate statistics over entire videos, it is straight-forward to instead compute descriptors regionally over both time and space; and thus to classify new videos after having seen only a limited number of frames.

4.4 Binary Histograms

When choosing $r = 2$ bins equivalent to a joint binary histogram, the local image structure is described by only the sign of the different image measurements [6]. This will make the descriptor invariant to uniform rescalings of the intensity values. Another attractive feature of the binary histogram is that a larger number of image measurements can be combined while still keeping down the descriptor dimensionality. Binary histograms have been proven an effective approach for other dynamic texture methods such as LBP and MBSIF-TOP. This is the descriptor version that we have chosen to investigate in this paper.

4.5 Choice of Receptive Fields and Parameters

Varying the choice of receptive fields and method parameters, gives a family of different video descriptors. In this paper, we evaluate a single member of this family: A multi-scale representation based on the set of receptive fields

$$\{L_t, L_{tt}, L_x, L_y, L_{xx}, L_{yy}, L_{xy}, L_{xt}, L_{yt}, L_{xxt}, L_{yyt}, L_{xyt}\} \tag{5}$$

with $M = 15$ principal components and $r = 2$ number of bins with d = 5. For the UCLA database, the Cartesian product of spatial scales (i.e. standard deviation for the scale-space kernel) $\sigma_s \in \{1, 2\}$ pixels and temporal scales $\sigma_\tau \in \{0.05, 0.1\}$ seconds were used, while for DynTex that has considerably higher spatial resolution, we instead used $\sigma_s \in \{2, 4\}$ pixels and $\sigma_\tau \in \{0.2, 0.4\}$ seconds.

5   Datasets

We evaluate our proposed method on several dynamic texture recognition/classification benchmarks from two widely used dynamic texture databases: UCLA and DynTex. Sample frames from these databases are shown in Fig. 2.

5.1 UCLA

The UCLA database was introduced by Soatto et al. [8] and is composed of 200 videos (160×110 pixels, 15 fps) featuring 50 different dynamic textures with 4 samples from each texture. The **UCLA50** benchmark [8] divides the 200 videos into 50 classes with one class per individual texture/scene. It should be noted

Fig. 2. Top row: Sample frames from the UCLA database. From left to right: "fire", "sea", "smoke" "waterfall", "fountain". Bottom row: Sample frames from the DynTex database. From left to right: "flags", "sea", "traffic", "escalator", "fountain".

that this partitioning is not *conceptual* in the sense of classes constituting different types of textures such as "fountains", "sea" or "flowers" but instead targets instance specific (i.e. different fountains should be separated from each other) and viewpoint specific recognition.

Since for many applications it is more relevant to recognise different dynamic texture categories, a partitioning of the UCLA dataset into conceptual classes, **UCLA9**, was introduced by Ravichandran et al. [9] with the following classes: boiling water (8), fire (8), flowers (12), fountains (20), plants (108), sea (12), smoke (4), water (12) and waterfall (16). Because of the large overrepresentation of plant videos, in the **UCLA8** benchmark those are excluded to give a less misbalanced dataset, resulting in 92 videos from 8 conceptual classes.

5.2 DynTex

A larger and more diverse dynamic texture database, **DynTex**, was introduced by Péteri et al. [26], featuring a larger variation of dynamic texture types recorded under more diverse conditions (720×576 pixels, 25 fps). From this database, three gradually larger and more challenging benchmarks have been compiled by Dubois et al. [27]. The **Alpha** benchmark includes 60 dynamic texture videos from three different classes: sea, grass and trees. There are 20 examples of each class and some variations in scale and viewpoint. The **Beta** benchmark includes 162 dynamic texture videos from ten classes: sea, vegetation, trees, flags, calm water, fountain, smoke, escalator, traffic and rotation. There are 7 to 20 examples of each class. The **Gamma** benchmark includes 264 dynamic texture videos from ten classes: flowers, sea, trees without foliage, dense foliage, escalator, calm water, flags, grass, traffic and fountains. There are 7 to 38 examples of each class and this dataset has the largest intraclass variability in terms of scale, orientation, etc.

6   Experiments

We present results both using a support vector machine (SVM) classifier and a nearest neighbour (NN) classifier, the latter to evaluate the performance also without hidden tunable parameters. For NN we use the χ^2-distance $d(x,y) = \sum_i (x_i - y_i)^2/(x_i + y_i)$ and for SVM a χ^2-kernel $e^{-\gamma d(x,y)}$. The same set of receptive fields and the same parameters (see Sect. 4) are used for all experiments and no extensive parameter tuning has been performed. For the UCLA benchmarks, we also use the non-cropped videos of size 160×110, instead of the most common setup which is to use manually extracted patches; thus our setup could be considered a slightly harder problem.

6.1   Experimental Setup and Results UCLA50

The standard test setup for the UCLA50 benchmark, which we adopt also here, is 4 fold crossvalidation where for each partitioning one of the four videos of each dynamic texture are held out for testing and the other three are used for training [8]. Test results are seen in Table 1. It can be seen that we achieve competitive results on this benchmark with three misclassified samples out of 200, giving a classification accuracy of 98.5% using an SVM classifier. Here, the best results achieved by DFS, LBP and Ensemble SVMs reach 100%. Inspecting the misclassified samples, we note that two of those are different plants from the same viewpoint being mixed up and the third one is an instance of a specific plant being misclassified as the same plant but from a different distance.

Table 1. Comparison to state-of-the-art for the UCLA benchmarks.

	UCLA8		UCLA9		UCLA50	
	SVM	NN	SVM	NN	SVM	NN
Ensemble SVMs [23]	-	-	-	-	**100.0**	-
MBSIF-TOP [17]	-	97.8	-	98.8	-	99.5
OTD [18]	**99.5**	97.0	98.2	97.5	99.8	98.5
Enhanced LBP [15]	-	-	-	98.2	-	**100.0**
Our approach	97.8	97.5	**98.6**	98.3	98.5	97.0
DFS [20]	99.2	-	97.5		89.5	**100.0**
WMFS [21]	97.0	97.2	97.1	97.0	99.8	99.1
DL-PEGASOS [22]	-	-	-	95.6		99.0
Oriented energy rep. [12]	-	-	-	-	-	81.0

6.2   Experimental Setup and Results UCLA8 and UCLA9

The standard test setup for UCLA8 and UCLA9 is to report the average accuracy over 20 random partitions, with 50% data used for training and 50% for testing (randomly bisecting each class) [22]. We use the same setup here, except that we report results as an average over 1000 trials to get more reliable statistics. It can be seen from Table 1 that our proposed approach ranks higher for these two conceptual reorganisations of the database. For UCLA9, we achieve the best result of 98.6% using an SVM classifier and the second best using a NN classifier, only surpassed by MBSIF-TOP that achieves 98.8% vs. our 98.3%. For UCLA8 we achieve 97.8% compared to the best result by OTD 99.5% using an SVM classifier, and the second best result of 97.5% vs 97.8% using a NN classifier. It can in general be noted that no single approach achieves superior performance on all three UCLA benchmarks.

A confusion matrix for UCLA9 is shown in Fig. 3, and we noted that the main cause of error for both UCLA8 and UCLA9 is confusing fire and smoke. There is indeed a similarity in dynamics between these textures in the presence of temporal intensity changes not mediated by spatial movements. Confusions between flowers and plants, as well as between fountain and waterfall, are most likely caused by similarities in the spatial appearance and the motion patterns of these dynamic texture classes.

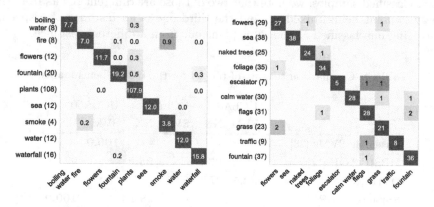

Fig. 3. Left: Confusion matrix UCLA9 averaged over trials (SVM classifier). Right: Confusion matrix DynTex Gamma leave-one-out setting (SVM classifier).

6.3   Experimental Setup and Results DynTex

For the DynTex benchmarks, the experimental setup used is leave-one-out cross-validation as in [16,17,23,24]. For this larger and more diverse database, we achieve highly satisfactory results (Table 2). Compared to other methods utilising only grey level information and the same leave-one-out experimental setup, such as AFS-TOP, LBD-TOP and MBSIF-TOP, we achieve the same or better performance on all three benchmarks except for one: when using a NN classifier

Table 2. Comparison to state-of-the-art for the DynTex benchmarks. Superscripts: *
indicates a different train-test partitioning and † the use of a nearest centroid classifier.

	Alpha		Beta		Gamma		
	SVM	NN	SVM	NN	SVM	NN	
Transfer DL [24]	**100.0**	**100.0**	**100.0**	**99.4**	*98.1*	**98.1**	Colour
Ensemble SVMs [23]	-	-	-	-	**99.5**	-	Colour
Our approach	98.3	96.7	93.2	92.6	94.3	89.4	Greyscale
MBSIF-TOP [17]	-	90.0	-	90.7	-	91.3	Greyscale
AFS-TOP [16]	98.3	91.7	90.1	86.4	94.3	89.4	Greyscale
LBP-TOP, from [24]	98.3	96.7	88.9	85.8	94.2	84.9	Greyscale
ELM [10]	-	-	93.8*	-	88.3*	-	Greyscale
2D+T curvelet [27]	-	88.0†	-	70.0†	-	68.0†	Greyscale
OTD [18]	87.8*	86.6†	76.7*	69.0†	74.8*	64.2†	Greyscale
DFS [20]	85.2*	-	76.9*	-	74.8*	-	Greyscale

on the Gamma subset MBSIF-TOP has an accuracy of 91.3% compared to our
89.4%. However, we achieve better results for the Beta subset (92.6% vs. 90.7%)
and substantially better for the Alpha subset (96.7% vs. 90.0%). Compared to
AFS-TOP we achieve the same results for the Alpha and Gamma subsets using
an SVM classifier. There is however a notable improvement for the Alpha subset using a NN classifier (96.7% vs. 91.7%) and for the Beta subset using both
classifiers (SVM: 93.2% vs. 90.1%, NN: 92.6% vs. 86.4%).

Compared to the original LBP-TOP descriptor, which could be considered
a more fair benchmark since we are benchmarking an early version of our approach, we achieve the same performance for the Alpha subset and notably better
performance on the Beta (92.6% error vs. 85.8%) and Gamma (89.4% error vs.
84.9%) subsets using a NN classifier as well as smaller improvements when using
an SVM classifier. Interestingly, this is for methods similar to ours in the sense
that they collect statistics of local space-time structures and utilise joint binary
histogram descriptors. This can be considered a strong validation that the scale-
space filters used here capture useful information.

We also show notably better results (in the order of 10–20 p.p.) than those
reported from using DFS, OTD and the 2D+T curvelet transform, but since those
use a nearest centroid classifier and a different SVM train-test partition, this
makes a direct comparison unsure. The best results reported for the three DynTex
benchmarks are from transferring deep image features [24] and the ensemble SVM
method of Yang et al. [23]. Note that both these approaches utilise colour information which can be highly discriminative for dynamic textures (our approach is
straight-forward to extend to colour, which we plan for future work). The latter
also combines several descriptors (LBP, SCOP, colour and LDS) which cannot be
directly compared to evaluating the performance of a single descriptor.

When inspecting the confusions between different classes for the DynTex benchmarks (Fig. 3), the pattern is not very clear, perhaps since this database contains larger intraclass variabilities. We note the largest ratio of misclassified samples for the escalator and traffic classes, which are also the classes with the fewest samples.

7   Summary and Discussion

We have presented a new family of video descriptors based on joint histograms of spatio-temporal receptive field responses and evaluated one member of this family on the problem of dynamic texture recognition. This is the first evaluation of using the family of *time-causal scale-space filters* derived in [2] as primitives for video analysis as well as, to our knowledge, the first video descriptor that utilises *joint statistics* of a set of "ideal" (in the sense of derived on the basis of pure mathematical reasoning) spatio-temporal scale-space filters.

Our experimental evaluation on several benchmarks from two widely used dynamic texture databases shows competitive results on the UCLA database and highly competitive results on the larger and more complex DynTex database. For the DynTex benchmarks, we interestingly show improved performance compared to methods similarly modelling statistics of local space-time structure such as local binary pattern based methods [14,15] and MBSIF-TOP [17], where the latter in contrast to our method utilises filters learned from data. This although temporal causality implies additional constraints on the feature extraction compared to allowing simultaneous access to all video frames. We consider this a strong validation that these spatio-temporal receptive fields are highly descriptive for modelling the local space-time structure, and as evidence in favour of their general applicability as primitives for video analysis.

It should be noted that the method presented here could also be implemented using a non-causal Gaussian spatio-temporal scale-space kernel, which could possibly give somewhat improved results, since at each point in time additional information from the future could also be used. However, a time delayed Gaussian kernel would imply longer temporal delays, which makes it less suited for time critical applications, as well as more computations and larger temporal buffers.

In future work [28], we will generalise the descriptor to colour by considering spatio-chromo-temporal receptive fields and complement the evaluation performed here with an investigation into which receptive field groups works best for dynamic texture recognition as well as how the number of principal components and the number of histogram bins affect the performance. We also plan to broaden the investigation to other video analysis tasks. The theoretical properties of these scale-space filters imply that they could be used to create methods provably invariant or robust to different types of natural image transformations. We see the possibility of integrating time-causal spatio-temporal receptive fields into current video analysis methods as well as using them as primitives for learning higher level features from data.

References

1. Hubel, D.H., Wiesel, T.N.: Brain and Visual Perception: The Story of a 25-Year Collaboration. Oxford University Press, Oxford (2005)
2. Lindeberg, T.: Time-causal and time-recursive spatio-temporal receptive fields. J. Math. Imaging Vis. **55**, 50–88 (2016)
3. Lindeberg, T.: Generalized Gaussian scale-space axiomatics comprising linear scale-space, affine scale-space and spatio-temporal scale-space. J. Math. Imaging Vis. **40**, 36–81 (2011)
4. Lindeberg, T.: A computational theory of visual receptive fields. Biol. Cybern. **107**, 589–635 (2013)
5. Chetverikov, D., Péteri, R.: A brief survey of dynamic texture description and recognition. In: Kurzyński, M., Puchała, E., Woźniak, M., Żołnierek, A. (eds.) Computer Recognition Systems. AINSC, vol. 30, pp. 17–26. Springer, Heidelberg (2005). doi:10.1007/3-540-32390-2_2
6. Linde, O., Lindeberg, T.: Composed complex-cue histograms: an investigation of the information content in receptive field based image descriptors for object recognition. Comput. Vis. Image Underst. **116**, 538–560 (2012)
7. Nelson, R.C., Polana, R.: Qualitative recognition of motion using temporal texture. CVGIP: Image Underst. **56**, 78–89 (1992)
8. Soatto, S., Doretto, G., Wu, Y.N.: Dynamic textures. In: IEEE International Conference on Computer Vision, vol. 2, pp. 439–446 (2001)
9. Ravichandran, A., Chaudhry, R., Vidal, R.: View-invariant dynamic texture recognition using a bag of dynamical systems. In: Computer Vision and Pattern Recognition, pp. 1651–1657 (2009)
10. Wang, L., Liu, H., Sun, F.: Dynamic texture video classification using extreme learning machine. Neurocomputing **174**, 278–285 (2016)
11. Wildes, R.P., Bergen, J.R.: Qualitative spatiotemporal analysis using an oriented energy representation. In: Vernon, D. (ed.) ECCV 2000. LNCS, vol. 1843, pp. 768–784. Springer, Heidelberg (2000). doi:10.1007/3-540-45053-X_49
12. Derpanis, K.G., Wildes, R.P.: Spacetime texture representation and recognition based on a spatiotemporal orientation analysis. IEEE Trans. Pattern Anal. Mach. Intell. **34**, 1193–1205 (2012)
13. Gonçalves, W.N., Machado, B.B., Bruno, O.M.: Spatiotemporal Gabor filters: a new method for dynamic texture recognition. arXiv preprint arXiv:1201.3612 (2012)
14. Zhao, G., Pietikainen, M.: Dynamic texture recognition using local binary patterns with an application to facial expressions. IEEE Trans. Pattern Anal. Mach. Intell. **29**, 915–928 (2007)
15. Ren, J., Jiang, X., Yuan, J.: Dynamic texture recognition using enhanced LBP features. In: IEEE International Conference on Acoustics, Speech and Signal Processing, pp. 2400–2404 (2013)
16. Hong, S., Ryu, J., Yang, H.S.: Not all frames are equal: aggregating salient features for dynamic texture classification. In: Multidimensional Systems and Signal Processing (2016). doi:10.1007/s11045-016-0463-7
17. Arashloo, S.R., Kittler, J.: Dynamic texture recognition using multiscale binarized statistical image features. IEEE Trans. Multimedia **16**, 2099–2109 (2014)
18. Quan, Y., Huang, Y., Ji, H.: Dynamic texture recognition via orthogonal tensor dictionary learning. In: IEEE International Conference on Computer Vision, pp. 73–81 (2015)

19. Schiele, B., Crowley, J.: Recognition without correspondence using multidimensional receptive field histograms. Int. J. Comput. Vis. **36**, 31–50 (2000)
20. Xu, Y., Quan, Y., Zhang, Z., Ling, H., Ji, H.: Classifying dynamic textures via spatiotemporal fractal analysis. Pattern Recogn. **48**, 3239–3248 (2015)
21. Ji, H., Yang, X., Ling, H., Xu, Y.: Wavelet domain multifractal analysis for static and dynamic texture classification. IEEE Trans. Image Process. **22**, 286–299 (2013)
22. Ghanem, B., Ahuja, N.: Maximum margin distance learning for dynamic texture recognition. In: Daniilidis, K., Maragos, P., Paragios, N. (eds.) ECCV 2010. LNCS, vol. 6312, pp. 223–236. Springer, Heidelberg (2010). doi:10.1007/978-3-642-15552-9_17
23. Yang, F., Xia, G.S., Liu, G., Zhang, L., Huang, X.: Dynamic texture recognition by aggregating spatial and temporal features via ensemble SVMs. Neurocomputing **173**, 1310–1321 (2016)
24. Qi, X., Li, C., Guoying, Z., Hong, X., Pietikäinen, M.: Dynamic texture and scene classification by transferring deep image features. Neurocomputing **171**, 1230–1241 (2016)
25. Koenderink, J.J.: Scale-time. Biol. Cybern. **58**, 159–162 (1988)
26. Péteri, R., Fazekas, S., Huiskes, M.J.: Dyntex: a comprehensive database of dynamic textures. Pattern Recogn. Lett. **31**, 1627–1632 (2010)
27. Dubois, S., Péteri, R., Ménard, M.: Characterization and recognition of dynamic textures based on the 2D+T curvelet transform. Sig. Image Video Process. **9**, 819–830 (2015)
28. Jansson, Y., Lindeberg, T.: Dynamic texture recognition using time-causal and time-recursive spatio-temporal receptive fields (2017, in preparation)

Corner Detection Using the Affine Morphological Scale Space

Luis Alvarez[✉]

Departamento de Informática y Sistemas,
Universidad de Las Palmas de Gran Canaria,
Campus de Tafira, 35017 Las Palmas de Gran Canaria, Spain
lalvarez@ulpgc.es

Abstract. We introduce a method for corner estimation based on the affine morphological scale space (AMSS). Using some explicit known formula about corner evolution across AMSS, proven by Alvarez and Morales in 1997, we define a morphological cornerness measure based on the expected evolution of an ideal corner across AMSS. We define a new procedure to track the corner motion across AMSS. To evaluate the accuracy of the method we study in details the results for a collection of synthetic corners with angles from 15 to 160°. We also present experiments in real images and we show that the proposed method can also automatically handle the case of multiple junctions.

Keywords: Affine scale space · Corner detection · Morphology

1 Introduction

Corners are very important image features used in a lot of Computer Vision tasks. In this paper we present a morphological approach based on the theoretical results introduced in [5] about the evolution of an ideal corner in the affine invariant scale space (AMSS). This scale space, which was introduced in [4], is generated by the partial differential equation

$$\frac{\partial u}{\partial t} = (\mathcal{L}(u))^{\frac{1}{3}} \tag{1}$$

where

$$\mathcal{L}(u) = \left(\frac{\partial u}{\partial x}\right)^2 \frac{\partial^2 u}{\partial y^2} - 2\frac{\partial u}{\partial x}\frac{\partial u}{\partial y}\frac{\partial^2 u}{\partial x \partial y} + \left(\frac{\partial u}{\partial y}\right)^2 \frac{\partial^2 u}{\partial r^2} \tag{2}$$

A corner is defined by a corner tip $\bar{x}_0$, an angle α and a corner bisector unit vector $\hat{u}$. In [5], authors show that under the action of AMSS, a corner tip moves in the corner bisector direction in the following way:

$$\bar{x}(t) = \bar{x}_0 + \lambda \left(\frac{4}{3}t\right)^{\frac{3}{4}} \hat{u}, \tag{3}$$

© Springer International Publishing AG 2017
F. Lauze et al. (Eds.): SSVM 2017, LNCS 10302, pp. 29–40, 2017.
DOI: 10.1007/978-3-319-58771-4_3

where

$$tan(\frac{\alpha}{2}) = \frac{1}{\lambda^2}. \tag{4}$$

The existence of a simple closed-form solution for the evolution of corners is something unique to AMSS. The evolution of corners in the linear scale spaces, or other morphological scale space as the one generated by the mean curvature motion, is much more complex and, as far as we know, there is not exist a closed-form solution in such cases. In this paper we exploit this nice behavior of AMSS to develop a robust and accurate technique to estimate corners in images. From Eq. (3) we obtain, on the one hand, that the evolution of the corner tip $\bar{x}(t)$ lies in the corner bisector and the orientation, $\hat{u}$, of the corner bisector is parallel to the image gradient in the corner tip $\bar{x}(t)$ (that is the curve normal direction), and on the other hand, for any interval $[t_0, t^*]$, the evolution of $\|\bar{x}(t) - \bar{x}(t_0)\|$ is linear with respect to $t^{\frac{3}{4}}$ for $t \in [t_0, t^*]$. Therefore we can perform a linear approximation of $\|\bar{x}(t) - \bar{x}(t_0)\|$ and the quality of such linear approximation can be used as a cornerness measure. Moreover, using Eq. (4) the slope of such linear approximation can be used to estimate the corner angle.

This paper is an extension of the work presented in [5]. The main contribution of this paper is a new method to define and track the corner evolution across AMSS using the local extrema of the operator $\mathcal{L}(u)$ defined in (2). Using this tracking procedure we define a cornerness measure based on the theoretical results introduced in [5]. We also present a detailed analysis of the associated corner detection algorithm, we study experimentally, the influence of the corner angle in the accuracy of the corner estimation and we study the application of the method to the detection of corner and multiple junctions in real images.

The rest of the paper is organized in the following way: in Sect. 2, we present some related works. In Sect. 3, we present in details the proposed corner detection algorithm. In Sect. 4, we present some experiments on synthetic and real images. In particular we use a collection of synthetic corner angles that we use to check the accuracy of the method for a range of angles. Finally, in Sect. 5, we present some conclusions.

2   Related Work

AMSS in terms of curve evolution have been introduced in [12, 13]. The existence theory of a classic affine curve evolution was completed in [6]. The level set formulation in the sense of Osher and Sethian [11] for AMSS was developed in [2–4]. More recently, in [1], the authors present an application of AMSS to the computation of affine invariant distances.

The estimation of image features in the image is a common basic step in a lot of computer vision tasks. The well-known Harris technique, [8], is the reference technique for corner estimation, it introduces a cornernes measure based on the structure tensor. More recently, a lot of attention has been devoted to the SIFT method introduced in [9] to extract image features. In [14], a generalization to the affine invariant case of SIFT method is proposed. In [7], a study about morphologically invariant descriptors is presented. In [10], a technique for corner estimation using the mean curvature scale space is proposed.

In [5], authors define an ideal corner of angle α as the following set:

$$X_\lambda = \{\bar{x} = (x, y) : y \geq \lambda^2 |x|\} \tag{5}$$

where λ is given by (4). Since Eq. (1) is morphologically invariant, the evolution of the corner X_λ is determined by any solution $u_\lambda(t, \bar{x})$ of (1) which includes X_λ as a level set of $u_\lambda(0, \bar{x})$. In particular, in [5], it is shown that for any increasing function $\phi(.)$ the following function is a solution of (1)

$$u_\lambda(t, \bar{x}) = \begin{cases} \phi\left(\left(\frac{y^2}{\lambda^2} - \lambda^2 x^2\right)^{\frac{2}{3}} - \frac{4}{3}t\right) & \text{if } \frac{y^2}{\lambda^2} - \lambda^2 x^2 \geq \left(\frac{4}{3}t\right)^{\frac{3}{2}} \\ 0 & \text{if } \frac{y^2}{\lambda^2} - \lambda^2 x^2 < \left(\frac{4}{3}t\right)^{\frac{3}{2}} \end{cases} \tag{6}$$

and then, the evolution of the corner X_λ is given by

$$X_\lambda = \left\{\bar{x} = (x, y) : y \geq \lambda\left(\lambda^2 x^2 + \left(\frac{4}{3}t\right)^{\frac{3}{2}}\right)^{\frac{1}{2}}\right\} \tag{7}$$

in particular, the tip of the corner, that we find in the direction of the corner bisector (given by $x = 0$) at each scale is provided by

$$\bar{x}(t) = \left(0, \lambda\left(\frac{4}{3}t\right)^{\frac{3}{4}}\right)$$

Since AMSS is Euclidean invariant, if the corner is centered in the point $\bar{x}_0$ and the corner bisector orientation is given by the unit vector $\hat{u}$ then, the corner evolution is given by Eq. (3).

3   Corner Estimation Algorithm Using AMSS

The proposed method for corner estimation can be divided in the following steps:

Step 1: Computation of the AMSS Scale Space. From the original image $u_0(\bar{x})$ we compute the AMSS scale space $u(t, \bar{x})$ using an explicit finite difference scheme.

Step 2: Initial Estimation of Potential Corners. We fix $t_0 \geq 0$ and we estimate an initial collection of potential corner tips $\{\bar{x}^k(t_0)\}_{k=1,\ldots,N_{t_0}}$ in the image as the local extrema (in the space variables) of the operator $(\mathcal{L}(u))^{\frac{1}{3}}(t_0, \bar{x})$. We observe that the computation of this operator is required in the AMSS estimation. Since we look for local extrema, the power $\frac{1}{3}$ is not relevant in this step. t_0 is a parameter of the algorithm and it is used to slightly smooth the image before corner estimation to avoid the computation of a lot of spurious local extrema. We point out that, in contrast to other scale spaces, using AMSS we can recover the exact position of the corners in the original image from the position of the corners in the scale $t_0 > 0$. Indeed, using Eq. (3) we obtain that

$$\bar{x}_0 = \bar{x}(t_0) - \lambda \left(\frac{4}{3}t_0\right)^{\frac{3}{4}} \hat{u}, \tag{8}$$

Step 3: Tracking of Corners Across the AMSS Scale Space. Once the original collection of potential corners $\{\bar{x}^k(t_0)\}_{k=1,\ldots,N_{t_0}}$ is estimated, we track the evolution of the corners across AMSS in the interval $[t_0, t^*]$ in the following iterative way: the interval $[t_0, t^*]$ is discretized using $\{t_n = t_0 + n \cdot \delta t\}_{n=0,\ldots,N^*}$, where δt is the time step used to compute AMSS. Then, for any $n > 0$ the position of each corner tip $\bar{x}^k(t_n)$ at the scale t_n is obtained as the extremum of the operator $(\mathcal{L}(u))^{\frac{1}{3}} (t_n, \bar{x})$ in a neighborhood of $\bar{x}^k(t_{n-1})$ following the direction of $\nabla u(t_{n-1}, \bar{x}^k(t_{n-1}))$. During this tracking procedure spurious corner sequences are removed. For instance if $(\mathcal{L}(u))^{\frac{1}{3}} (t_n, \bar{x}^k(t_n))$ changes sign or becomes too small then the corner sequence is removed.

Step 4: Linear Approximation of AMSS Corner Evolution. For each corner sequence $\{\bar{x}^k(t_n)\}_{n=0,\ldots,N^*}$, we compute a linear model (a_k, b_k) by minimizing the usual least squares approximation given by the error function

$$E(a,b) = \frac{\sum_{n=0}^{N^*} \left(\|\bar{x}^k(t_n) - \bar{x}^k(t_0)\| - (a(t_n^{\frac{3}{4}} - t_0^{\frac{3}{4}}) + b)\right)^2}{N^* + 1}, \tag{9}$$

that is, $(a_k, b_k) = \arg\min_{a,b} E(a,b)$. We observe that from the slope a_k and using the Eqs. (3) and (4) we can obtain λ_k and the corner angle. On the other hand we can compute the corner bisector unit vector $\hat{u}_k$ as a parallel vector to $x^k(t^*) - \bar{x}^k(t_0)$.

Step 5: Morphological Cornerness Measure and Corner Estimation. We point out that we can use the residual error $E(a_k, b_k)$ as a morphological cornerness measure. The lower the value of $E(a_k, b_k)$, the better the corner sequence fits the expected corner evolution. This cornerness measure is morphological in the sense that it is independent of the image grey value. It only depends on the shape of the corner evolution across AMSS. Therefore we can estimate the image corners by thresholding the residual error $E(a_k, b_k)$. In practice, we use a percentile of the values of $E(a_k, b_k)$ to estimate corners.

To represent a corner in an image we need the corner boundary lines. We observe that in our approach, for each corner, we always compute the slope parameter λ instead of the corner angle α. In the next straightforward lemma we show how to compute the corner boundary lines directly from λ.

Lemma 1. *Let $\hat{u}$ be a corner bisector and λ the slope parameter satisfying Eq. (4). Then, the vectors*

$$\hat{u}_-(\lambda) = \hat{u} - \frac{1}{\lambda^2}\hat{u}^\perp, \qquad \hat{u}_+(\lambda) = \hat{u} + \frac{1}{\lambda^2}\hat{u}^\perp,$$

are parallel to the corner boundary lines, that is, the angle between $\hat{u}$ and $\hat{u}_\pm(\lambda)$ is $\frac{\alpha}{2}$.

4   Experimental Setup

To check the accuracy of the proposed technique for a range of corners with different angles we use the collection of synthetic images of corners shown in Fig. 1. The corner angles range from 15 to 160°. In Fig. 2 we illustrate the result of the proposed technique for corner estimation for the 15° angle synthetic image. We present a zoom of the original image, the AMSS evolution for $t = 1$, the AMSS evolution for $t = 20$ and an illustration of the result of the proposed technique where we show the evolution of the corner location across AMSS for the scale interval [1,20] and the obtained corner angle obtained from the linear estimation (9). In Fig. 3 we illustrate for the 90° image the value of the operator $\mathcal{L}(u)^{\frac{1}{3}}(t, \bar{x})$ that we use as local cornerness measure to estimate and track the corner sequences.

Fig. 1. Synthetic images of corners used in the experiments. The corner angles range from 15 to 160°.

In Fig. 4 we show, for the different synthetic angle images, the evolution of $\|\bar{x}(t) - \bar{x}_0\|$ with respect to $t^{\frac{3}{4}}$ for $t \in [0, 20]$. As expected by the result presented in Eq. (3), this evolution has a linear profile where the slope depends on the corner angle (the smaller the angle, the larger the slope). We observe that for small

Fig. 2. From left to right, we present a zoom of the $15°$ angle synthetic image, the AMSS evolution for $t = 1$, the AMSS evolution for $t = 20$ and an illustration of the result of the proposed technique where whe show the evolution of the corner location across AMSS for the scale interval $[1,20]$ and the obtained corner angle obtained from the linear estimation (9).

Fig. 3. From left to right we present a zoom of the $90°$ angle image and the result of the computation of the operator $\mathcal{L}(u)^{\frac{1}{3}}(t, \bar{x})$ for $t = 0, 1, 20$.

angles, the evolution shows a linear profile after a number of iterations of AMSS. This is due to the fact that corner angles are represented as discrete synthetic images which introduce discretization errors (specially for small angles), so in this case a number of AMSS iterations are required to regularize the image corner contours. Therefore we use the AMSS evolution in $[0, t_0]$ as a regularization step. This approach presents also the advantage that we can detect multiple junctions. Indeed, using AMSS, a multiple junction is managed as a collection of corners sharing the same corner tip. As the evolution of the corners in a multiple junction moves in different directions, after a time t_0 the location of the corners will be different and then the method can detect each corner independently as different local extrema of the operator $(\mathcal{L}(u))^{\frac{1}{3}}(t_0, \bar{x})$.

In Fig. 5 we illustrate the evolution across AMSS of the value of the differential operator $(\mathcal{L}(u))^{\frac{1}{3}}$ in the corner tip for the different angles. We observe, due to the regularization effect of AMSS, an exponential decay of the evolution profile.

In Fig. 6 we illustrate the quality of the above linear approximation. We show, for the different angles, the average residual error $E(a, b)$ defined in (9) obtained using the linear approximation of $\|\bar{x}(t) - \bar{x}(t_0)\|$ with respect to $t^{\frac{3}{4}} - t_0^{\frac{3}{4}}$ for $t \in [1, 20]$. As expected (looking at the results of Fig. 4) we observe that the average residual error $E(a, b)$ is quite small (below 0.01) and the results are worse for very small or large angles where the numerical discretization to generate the synthetic image angles introduces more errors.

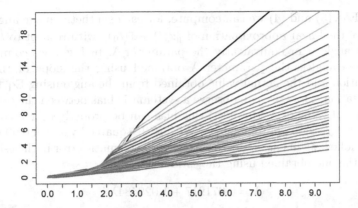

Fig. 4. For the corner images in Fig. 1 we plot the evolution of $\|\bar{x}(t) - \bar{x}_0\|$ with respect to $t^{\frac{3}{4}}$ for $t \in [0, 20]$.

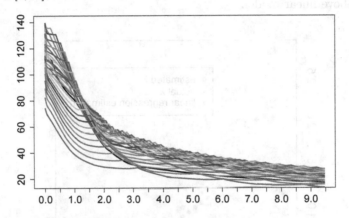

Fig. 5. For the corner images in Fig. 1 we plot the evolution of the differential operator $\mathcal{L}(u)^{\frac{1}{3}}(\bar{x}(t))$ with respect to $t^{\frac{3}{4}}$ for $t \in [0, 20]$.

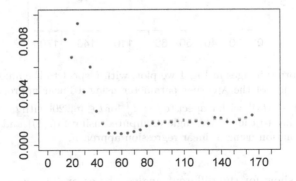

Fig. 6. For the corner images in Fig. 1 we plot, with respect to the angle (in degrees), the average residual error $E(a, b)$ defined in (9) obtained using the linear approximation of $\|\bar{x}(t) - \bar{x}(t_0)\|$ with respect to $t^{\frac{3}{4}} - t_0^{\frac{3}{4}}$ for $t \in [1, 20]$.

Using Eqs. (3) and (4) we can compute, for each synthetic image angle, from the slope of the linear approximation of $\|\bar{x}(t) - \bar{x}(t_0)\|$ with respect to $t^{\frac{3}{4}} - t_0^{\frac{3}{4}}$, the corner angle α or equivalently the parameter λ. In Fig. 7 we compare, for the range of angles, the parameter λ obtained using the slope of the linear approximation and the actual value obtained from the angle using Eq. (4). Due to discretization errors, we can observe a systematic bias between the estimation and the actual value of λ. However, this bias can be properly corrected using a basic linear regression approximation. With a "R-squared" value of 0.9998931 we obtain the following linear model to correct the systematic error in the estimation of λ from the one obtained using the estimated slope

$$\lambda = 0.071917 + 1.029484\bar{\lambda} \tag{10}$$

where $\bar{\lambda}$ represents the original estimation using the estimated slope and λ the corrected one. In Fig. 7 we also illustrate the correction in the estimation of λ using the above linear model.

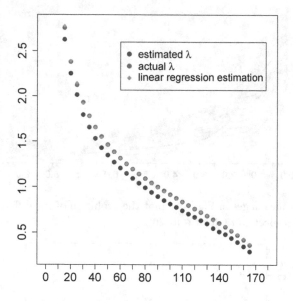

Fig. 7. For the corner images in Fig. 1 we plot, with respect to the angle (in degrees), the initial estimation of the λ corner parameter using a linear approximation of the evolution of $\|\bar{x}(t) - \bar{x}(t_0)\|$ with respect to $t^{\frac{3}{4}} - t_0^{\frac{3}{4}}$ for $t \in [t_0, 20]$ with $t_0 = 1$. The actual value of λ according to the corner angle (computed using Eq. (4)) and the correction of the initial estimation using a linear regression approach.

In Fig. 8 we show for the different angles, the error (in pixels) of the corner location estimation $\bar{x}_0$ using the proposed method for the scale interval $[1,20]$ and the error obtained using the standard Harris method with $\sigma = 1$ (the standard deviation of the Gaussian convolution kernel used to compute the structure

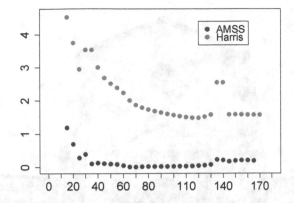

Fig. 8. For the corner images in Fig. 1 we plot, with respect to the angle (in degrees), the error (in pixels) of the corner location estimation $\bar{x}_0$ using AMSS with the scale interval $t \in [1, 20]$ and the standard Harris method.

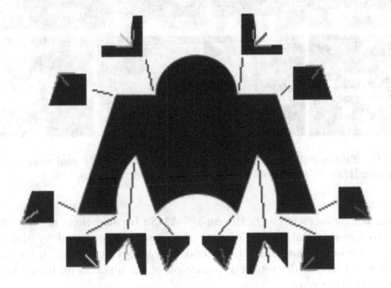

Fig. 9. We illustrate the results of the proposed method for a synthetic image including different types of corner structures using as scale interval [1,20]. We present a zoom of the corner areas where the evolution of the corner tips across AMSS and the obtained corner boundary lines are illustrated.

tensor). To estimate accurately the corner tip location in the original image from its estimation in $t_0 = 1$ we use Eq. (8). We point out that the corner estimation using AMSS is much more accurate than the one obtained by the Harris method. The main reason is that the Gaussian convolution required in Harris method moves the corners introducing errors in the corner locations. Moreover these

Fig. 10. We illustrate the results of the proposed method for a real image using as scale interval [1,20]. We also present a zoom of some corner areas.

errors can not be corrected as in the case of AMSS because there are not explicit formula to measure the corner location displacement produced by the Harris method. We observe that in both methods the errors are larger in the case of small angles where the discrete representation of the angle as an image includes large discretization errors.

In Fig. 9 we illustrate the results of the proposed method for a synthetic image including different types of corner structures.

In Fig. 10 we present an application of the proposed technique to a real image where we use a percentile of the residual average error $E(a, b)$ given by (9) to choose the most relevant corners in the image. As illustrated in the figure, the method is able to handle multiple junctions automatically without any further analysis.

5 Conclusions

In this paper we introduce a morphological cornerness measure based on the expected evolution of an ideal corner across AMSS. The main advantange of AMSS is that in this scale space we have closed-form expressions for the corner evolution and this is something unique to AMSS which allow us to develop accurate corner location estimation techniques. Moreover, using AMSS we can handle automatically more complex structures as multiple junctions. We propose a new method to track corners across AMSS based on the local extrema of the operator $\mathcal{L}(u)$ defined in (2). We present a detailed experimental study of the accuracy of the proposed method using a collection of synthetic corners using different angles. We show that the proposed method is much more accurate than the usual Harris technique. To attain such level of accuracy we use that in AMSS we can go backwards in the scale to recover the original corner location from its location at any scale (something unique to AMSS). We also present experiments in real images which show that the proposed method strongly simplifies the number of corners providing the most significant ones.

Acknowledgement. This research has partially been supported by the MINECO project reference MTM2016-75339-P (AEI/FEDER, UE) (Ministerio de Economía y Competitividad, Spain).

References

1. Alvarez, L., Cuenca, C., Esclarín, J., Mazorra, L., Morel, J.M.: Affine invariant distance using multiscale analysis. J. Math. Imaging Vis. **55**(2), 199–209 (2016)
2. Alvarez, L., Guichard, F., Lions, P.L., Morel, J.M.: Axiomatisation et nouveaux opérateurs de la morphologie mathématique. Comptes rendus de l'Académie des sciences. Série 1, Mathématique **315**(3), 265–268 (1992)
3. Alvarez, L., Guichard, F., Lions, P.L., Morel, J.M.: Axiomes et équations fondamentales du traitement d'images. (analyse multiéchelle et edp). Comptes rendus de l'Académie des sciences. Série 1, Mathématique **315**(2), 135–138 (1992)
4. Alvarez, L., Guichard, F., Lions, P.L., Morel, J.M.: Axioms and fundamental equations of image processing. Arch. Ration. Mech. Anal. **123**(3), 199–257 (1993)
5. Alvarez, L., Morales, F.: Affine morphological multiscale analysis of corners and multiple junctions. Int. J. Comput. Vis. **25**(2), 95–107 (1997)
6. Angenent, S., Sapiro, G., Tannenbaum, A.: On the affine heat equation for non-convex curves. J. Am. Math. Soc. **11**(3), 601–634 (1998)
7. Demetz, O., Hafner, D., Weickert, J.: Morphologically invariant matching of structures with the complete rank transform. Int. J. Comput. Vis. **113**(3), 220–232 (2015)
8. Harris, C., Stephens, M.: A combined corner and edge detector. In: Proceedings of Fourth Alvey Vision Conference, pp. 147–151 (1988)
9. Lowe, D.G.: Distinctive image features from scale-invariant keypoints. Int. J. Comput. Vis. **60**(2), 91–110 (2004)
10. Mokhtarian, F., Suomela, R.: Robust image corner detection through curvature scale space. IEEE Trans. Pattern Anal. Mach. Intell. **20**(12), 1376–1381 (1998)

11. Osher, S., Sethian, J.A.: Fronts propagating with curvature-dependent speed: algorithms based on Hamilton-Jacobi formulations. J. Comput. Phys. **79**(1), 12–49 (1988)
12. Sapiro, G., Tannenbaum, A.: On affine plane curve evolution. J. Funct. Anal. **119**(1), 79–120 (1994)
13. Sapiro, G., Tannenbaum, A.: Affine invariant scale-space. Int. J. Comput. Vis. **11**(1), 25–44 (1993)
14. Yu, G., Morel, J.M.: ASIFT: an algorithm for fully affine invariant comparison. Image Proces. On Line **1**, 11–38 (2011)

Nonlinear Spectral Image Fusion

Martin Benning[1($\boxtimes$)], Michael Möller[2], Raz Z. Nossek[3], Martin Burger[4], Daniel Cremers[5], Guy Gilboa[3], and Carola-Bibiane Schönlieb[1]

[1] University of Cambridge, Wilberforce Road, Cambridge CB3 0WA, UK
{mb941,cbs31}cam.ac.uk
[2] Universität Siegen, Hölderlinstraße 3, 57076 Siegen, Germany
michael.moeller@uni-siegen.de
[3] Technion IIT, Technion City, 32000 Haifa, Israel
nossekr@campus.technion.ac.il, guy.gilboa@ee.technion.ac.il
[4] Westfälische Wilhelms-Universität, Einsteinstrasse 62, 48149 Münster, Germany
martin.burger@wwu.de
[5] Technische Universität München, Boltzmannstrasse 3, 85748 Garching, Germany
cremers@tum.de

Abstract. In this paper we demonstrate that the framework of nonlinear spectral decompositions based on total variation (TV) regularization is very well suited for image fusion as well as more general image manipulation tasks. The well-localized and edge-preserving spectral TV decomposition allows to select frequencies of a certain image to transfer particular features, such as wrinkles in a face, from one image to another. We illustrate the effectiveness of the proposed approach in several numerical experiments, including a comparison to the competing techniques of Poisson image editing, linear osmosis, wavelet fusion and Laplacian pyramid fusion. We conclude that the proposed spectral TV image decomposition framework is a valuable tool for semi- and fully-automatic image editing and fusion.

Keywords: Nonlinear spectral decomposition · Total variation regularization · Image fusion · Image composition · Multiscale methods

1 Introduction

Since the rise of digital photography people have been fascinated by the possibilities of manipulating digital images. In this paper we present an image manipulation and fusion framework based on the recently proposed technique of nonlinear spectral decompositions [5,13,14] using TV regularization. By defining spectral

---

M. Benning, M. Möller and R.Z. Nossek—These authors contributed equally to this work.

Electronic supplementary material The online version of this chapter (doi:10.1007/978-3-319-58771-4_4) contains supplementary material, which is available to authorized users.

© Springer International Publishing AG 2017
F. Lauze et al. (Eds.): SSVM 2017, LNCS 10302, pp. 41–53, 2017.
DOI: 10.1007/978-3-319-58771-4_4

Fig. 1. Example of a facial image fusion result obtained by the proposed framework. The left image of Reagan and right image of Obama were used as an input, while the two middle images are synthesized using nonlinear spectral TV filters. (Color figure online)

filters that extract features corresponding to particular frequencies, we can for instance transfer wrinkles from one face to another and create visually convincing fusion results as shown in Fig. 1.

Classical multiscale methods such as Fourier analysis, sine or cosine transformations, or wavelet decompositions represent an input image as a linear superposition of a given set of basis elements. In many cases, these basis elements are given by the eigenfunctions of a suitable linear operator. For instance, the classical Fourier representation of a function as a superposition of sine and cosine functions arises from the eigenfunctions of the Laplace operator, i.e. from functions v_λ with $\|v_\lambda\| = 1$ and $\Delta v_\lambda = \lambda v_\lambda$, with periodic boundary conditions. Interestingly, the condition for v_λ being an eigenfunction can be written in terms of the regularization functional $J(v) = \frac{1}{2}\|\nabla v\|_2^2$ as

$$\lambda v_\lambda \in \partial J(v_\lambda), \tag{1}$$

where $\partial J(v) = \{p \in \mathcal{X}^* \mid J(u) - J(v) - \langle p, u-v \rangle \geq 0\}$ denotes the subdifferential of the functional $J : \mathcal{X} \to \mathbb{R}$, with $\mathcal{X}$ being a suitable function space, typically a Banach space. Since inclusion (1) makes sense for arbitrary convex regularization functions (e.g. for TV regularization), it provides a natural definition for generalizing the concept of eigenfunctions, cf. [3].

The idea of nonlinear spectral decompositions [5,13,14] (which we will recall in more detail in Sect. 3.1) is built upon the idea that an eigenfunction in the spatial domain, i.e. an element meeting (1), should be represented as a single peak in the spectral domain. Decompositions with respect to TV regularization have been shown to provide a highly image-adaptive way to represent different features and scales, see [13].

In this paper we will demonstrate that the nonlinear spectral image decomposition framework is very well suited for several challenging image fusion tasks. Our contributions include

- Proposing a nonlinear spectral image editing and fusion framework.
- Providing a robust pipeline for the automatic fusion of human faces, including face and landmark detection, registration, and segmentation.

- Illustrating state-of-the-art results evaluated against Laplacian pyramid fusion, wavelet fusion, Poisson image editing, and linear osmosis.
- Demonstrating the flexibility of the proposed framework beyond the fusion of facial images by considering applications such as object insertion and image style manipulation.

Copyright Remark: All photographs used in this paper were taken from the Wikipedia Commons page, https://commons.wikimedia.org/, or from the free images site https://commons.pixabay.com/. The photo of Barack Obama was made by Pete Souza - Creative Commons Attribution 3.0 Unported license, see https://creativecommons.org/licenses/by/3.0/deed.en.

2   Image Fusion

The most common image fusion techniques use a multiscale approach such as wavelet decompositions [30] or a Laplacian pyramid [9] to decompose two or more images, combine the decompositions differently on different scales, and reconstruct an image from the fused multiscale decomposition. Applications of the aforementioned fusion techniques include generating an all-in-focus image from a stack of differently focused images (e.g. [20]), multi- and hyperspectral imagery (cf. [1]), or facial texture transfers [28].

It was shown in [5,15] that the nonlinear spectral decomposition framework actually reduces to the usual wavelet decomposition when the TV regularization is replaced by $J(u) = \|Wu\|_1$, where W denotes the linear operator conducting the (orthogonal) wavelet transform. We, however, are going to demonstrate that the image-adaptive nonlinear decomposition approach with TV regularization is significantly better suited for image manipulation and fusion tasks.

Several other sophisticated nonlinear image multiscale decompositions have been proposed including techniques based on bilateral filtering (e.g. [12]), weighted least-squares [11], local histograms [19], local extrema [27], or Gaussian structure–texture decomposition [26]. Applications of the aforementioned methods include image equalization and abstraction, detail enhance or removal, and tone mapping/manipulation. While [26] briefly discusses applications in texture transfer, the potential of a complete image fusion by combining different frequencies of different images has not been exploited sufficiently yet.

For various image editing tasks related to inserting objects from one image g into another image f, the seminal work of Perez, Gangnet and Blake on Poisson image editing [23], provides a valuable tool. The authors proposed to minimize $E(u) = \|\nabla u - \nabla g\|^2$ subject to u coinciding with f outside of the region the object is to be inserted into.

Recent improvements of the latter have been made with osmosis image fusion, cf. [17,18]. Linear osmosis filtering for image fusion is achieved by solving a drift-diffusion PDE; here the drift vector field is constructed by combining the two vector fields $\nabla \ln(g)$ and $\nabla \ln(f)$; parts of $\nabla \ln(g)$ are inserted into $\nabla \ln(f)$, and averaged across the boundary. The initial value of the PDE is set to f, or the mean of f. A detailed description of the procedure is given in [18, Sect. 4.3]. For a general overview of image fusion techniques in different areas of application we also refer the reader to [25].

3   Nonlinear Spectral Fusion

The starting point and motivation for extending linear multiscale methods such as Fourier or wavelet decompositions into a nonlinear setting are basis elements, which often originate as eigenfunctions of a particular linear operator. As shown in Sect. 1, Fourier analysis can be recovered by decomposing a signal into a superposition of elements v_λ meeting the inclusion (1).

As mentioned in the introduction, the disadvantage of conventional decomposition techniques is the lack of adaptivity of the basis functions. In the following, we recall the definition of more general, nonlinear spectral transformations that allow to create more adaptive decompositions of images.

3.1   Nonlinear Spectral Decomposition

The idea of nonlinear spectral decompositions of [5, 13, 14] is to consider (1) for one-homogeneous functionals J (such as TV) instead of quadratic ones, which give rise to classical multiscale image representations. Since eigenvectors of one-homogeneous functionals are difficult to compute numerically (cf. [3]), the property one aims to preserve is that input data given in terms of an eigenfunction is decomposed into a single peak when being transformed into its corresponding (nonlinear) frequency representation.

Let us consider an eigenfunction $f = v_\lambda$, $\|v_\lambda\|_2 = 1$, obeying (1), and consider the behavior of the gradient flow

$$\partial_t u_{GF}(t) = -p_{GF}(t), \qquad p_{GF}(t) \in \partial J(u_{GF}(t)), \qquad u_{GF}(0) = f, \qquad (2)$$

for a one-homogeneous functional J. It follows almost directly from [3, Theorem 5] that the solution to this problem is given by

$$u_{GF}(t) = \begin{cases} (1 - t\lambda)f & \text{if } t\lambda \leq 1, \\ 0 & \text{else.} \end{cases} \qquad (3)$$

Since $u_{GF}(t)$ behaves piecewise linear in t, one can consider the second derivative to obtain a δ-peak. One defines

$$\phi_{GF}(t) = t\partial_{tt} u_{GF}(t) \qquad (4)$$

to be the spectral decomposition of the input data f, even in the case where f is not an eigenfunction of J. The additional normalization factor t admits to the reconstruction formula

$$f = \int_0^\infty \phi_{GF}(t) \, dt + \overline{f}, \qquad (5)$$

with $\overline{f} := \min_{\tilde{f} \in \text{kernel}(J)} \|\tilde{f} - f\|_2$, for arbitrary f. We refer the reader to [14] for more details on the general idea, and to [7] for a mathematical analysis of the above approach.

As we can see in (3), peaks of eigenfunctions in ϕ_{GF} appear at $t = \frac{1}{\lambda}$, i.e. earlier the bigger λ is. Therefore, one can interpret ϕ_{GF} as a wavelength decomposition, and motivate wavelength based filtering approaches of the form

$$\hat{u} = \int_0^\infty H(t) \, \phi_{GF}(t) \, dt + \overline{H} \, \overline{f}, \tag{6}$$

where the filter function H (along with the weight $\overline{H}$) can enhance or suppress selected parts of the spectrum.

As discussed in [5], there exists an alternative formulation to the gradient flow representation defined in (2). One can also consider the inverse scale space flow (see [6,8])

$$\partial_t p_{IS}(t) = f - u_{IS}(t), \quad p_{IS}(t) \in \partial J(u_{IS}(t)), \quad p_{IS}(0) = 0. \tag{7}$$

For certain regularizations J, the two approaches are provably equivalent (cf. [7]); hence, we use the approaches interchangeably based on the numerical convenience, as we also empirically observe very little difference between the numerical realisations of (2) and (7).

Note that we use the total variation as the regularizer J throughout the remainder of this paper; however, other choices for J are possible (see [5]).

3.2 Numerical Implementation

Spectral Decomposition. For the numerical implementation of our spectral image fusion we use both the gradient flow as well as the inverse scale flow formulation. The former is implemented in the exact same way as described in [14]. Formulation (7) is discretized via Bregman iterations (cf. [22]). More precisely, we compute

$$u^{k+1} = \arg\min_u \frac{\tau^{k+1}}{2}\|u - f\|_2^2 + (TV(u) - \langle p^k, u \rangle), \tag{8}$$

$$p^{k+1} = p^k + \tau^{k+1}(f - u^{k+1}), \tag{9}$$

starting with $p^0 = 0$. We then define

$$\psi^k = \begin{cases} u^1 & \text{if } k = 1, \\ u^k - u^{k-1} & \text{else,} \end{cases} \tag{10}$$

to be the frequency decomposition of the input data f.

From the optimality condition of Eq. (8) we conclude that $p^k \in \partial TV(u^k)$ for all k. Furthermore, note that Eq. (9) can be rewritten as

$$\frac{p^{k+1} - p^k}{\tau^{k+1}} = f - u^{k+1} \tag{11}$$

Fig. 2. Example of a nonlinear frequency decomposition. The left image is the input image to be decomposed, the following images illustrate selected spectral components with increasing associated frequencies. This type of decomposition is the main tool for our proposed image fusion framework.

and can therefore be interpreted as the discretization of the inverse scale space flow. In our numerical implementation we use the adaptive step size $\frac{1}{\tau^k} = 30 \cdot 0.6^{k-1}$ to better resolve significant changes of the flow. With this adaptation, we found 15 iterations to be sufficient to approximately converge to $u^{15} = f$ and to still obtain a sufficiently detailed frequency decomposition. Figure 2 illustrates a generalized frequency representation using the above method on an input image of a bee.

To solve the minimization problem of Eq. (8) numerically we use the primal-dual hybrid gradient method with diagonal preconditioning [24] and the adaptive step size rule from [16].

Image Fusion. The general idea of the spectral image fusion is to apply the nonlinear spectral image decomposition to two images or regions therein, combine the coefficients at different scales, and reconstruct an image from the fused coefficients.

Let v be a registration function that aligns a part of the second image with the location in the first image where the object is to be inserted into. Given the corresponding spectral decompositions ϕ^1 and ϕ^2, we compute the fused image u_{fused} via

$$u_{\text{fused}}(x) = \int_0^\infty H^1(x,t)\phi^1(x,t) + H^2(x+v(x),t)\phi^2(x+v(x),t) \, dt, \quad (12)$$

where the two filter functions H^1 and H^2 determine the amount of spectral information to be included in the fused image. Finally, we add a weighted linear combination of the constant parts $\overline{f^1}$ and $\overline{f^2}$ of the two input images f^1 and f^2 to u_{fused}. Note that – opposed to the original spectral representation framework from [5,13,14] – we are considering x-dependent, i.e. *spatially varying filters*, to adapt the filters in different regions of the images.

4   Results

4.1   Automatic Image Fusion of Human Faces

To illustrate the concept of using nonlinear spectral decompositions for image editing, we consider the problem of fusing two images of human faces. The latter

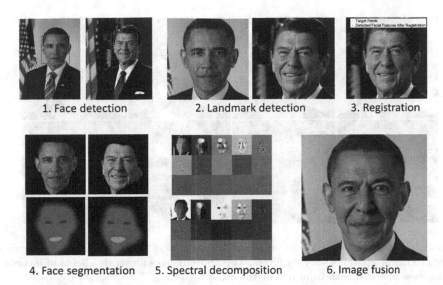

Fig. 3. Illustration of the pipeline for facial image fusion using nonlinear spectral decompositions.

has attracted quite some attention in the literature before, see e.g. [4,28]. Note that in contrast to [4,28] our fusion process does not depend on a 3d model of a face (which naturally means our framework does not handle changes of perspective).

For the presented image fusion, we have developed a fully automatic image fusion pipeline illustrated in Fig. 3. It consists of face detection using the Viola-Jones algorithm [29], facial landmark detection using [2], determining the non-rigid registration field v that has a minimal Dirichlet energy $\|\nabla v\|_2$ among all possible maps that register the detected landmarks, a face segmentation using the approach in [21] with additional information from the landmarks to distinguish between the face, mouth, and eye region, and finally the decomposition and fusion steps described in Sect. 3, where we restrict the decomposition to the regions of interest to be fused. Upon acceptance of this paper we will make the source code available in order to provide more details of the implementation.

The segmentation into the subregions allows us to define spatially varying spectral filters that treat the eye, mouth, and remaining facial regions differently, where fuzzy segmentation masks are used to blend the spectral filters from one region into the next to create smooth and visually pleasing transitions. Effects one can achieve by varying the spectral filters in the eye and mouth regions are illustrated in Fig. 4.

Figure 5 shows the filters we used to fuse the faces of the presidents Obama and Reagan for the introductory example in Fig. 1. As illustrated, the spectral filters may also differ for each of the color channels and can therefore also be applied to images decomposed into luminance and chrominance channels.

Fig. 4. The sub-segmentation of each image into a face, a mouth and an eye region allows to define spatially varying filters. The above images illustrate effects of incorporating eyes or the mouth from one or the other image.

In our examples we used the $(L, C^{G/M}, C^{R/B})$ color transform which has shown a promising performance e.g. for image demosaicking in [10]. As we can see in Fig. 5, one might want to keep more chrominance values of the target image to retain similar color impressions. Furthermore, the filter responses do not have to sum to one. In the high frequencies we keep a good amount of both images, which – in our experience – leads to sharper and more appealing results with skin-textures from both images.

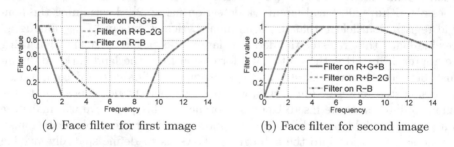

(a) Face filter for first image   (b) Face filter for second image

Fig. 5. Illustration of the fusion filters to generate the images in Fig. 1.

To illustrate the robustness of the proposed framework, we ran the fully automatic image fusion pipeline on an image set of US presidents gathered from the Wikipedia Commons page. The results are shown in the supplementary material accompanying this manuscript. The proposed nonlinear image fusion approach is robust enough to work with a great variety of different images and types of photos. The supplementary material contains further examples of fusing people with statues, and fusing a bill with a painting.

Finally, we want to highlight that the nonlinear image fusion framework has applications beyond facial image manipulation. Similar to Poisson image editing [23], one can insert objects from one image into the other by keeping low frequencies (colors and shadows) from one image and using higher frequencies (shapes and texture) from another image. Figure 6 shows an example of fusing the images of a shark and a swimmer.

Fig. 6. Inserting the shark from the left image into the middle image via spectral image fusion yields the image on the right: by keeping low frequencies from the middle image, one obtains highly believable colors in the fusion result. A smooth transition between the inserted object and the background image by a fuzzy segmentation mask (alpha-matting) was used to further avoid fusion artifacts. (Color figure online)

4.2 Comparison to Other Techniques

To illustrate the advantages of the image-adaptive nonlinear spectral decomposition we compare our algorithm to the classical multiscale methods of wavelet fusion, Laplacian pyramid fusion, and to the fotomontage techniques of Poisson image editing [23] as well as linear osmosis image editing [17,18]. We compare all methods on the challenging example of fusing a photo of Reagan with the painting of Mona Lisa, see Fig. 7. All methods use the identical registration- and segmentation-results from the automatic fusion pipeline described in Sect. 4.1. As we can see, Poisson and osmosis imaging transfer too many colors of the reference images and require more sophisticated methods for generating a guidance gradient field to also incorporate fine scale details of the target image such as the scratches on the painting. Wavelet image fusion generates unnatural colors and the Laplacian pyramid approach contains some halos. In particular, the texture of Reagans cheeks makes the Laplacian pyramid fusion look unnatural. By damping the filter coefficients of the nonlinear spectral decomposition, one can easily generate a result which is subtle enough to look realistic but still have clearly visible differences.

4.3 Artistic Image Transformations

Another application that demonstrates the variety of possibilities using nonlinear spectral decompositions for image manipulation is transforming an image such

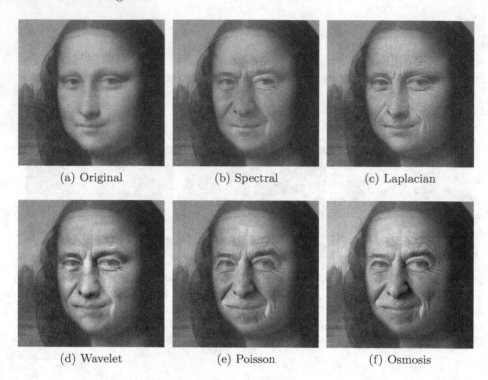

| (a) Original | (b) Spectral | (c) Laplacian |
| (d) Wavelet | (e) Poisson | (f) Osmosis |

Fig. 7. Comparing the spectral image fusion (b) for the example of injecting details from the Reagan image into the image of Mona Lisa (a) with Laplacian pyramid fusion (c), wavelet image fusion (d), Poisson editing (e), Osmosis (e). (Color figure online)

that the transformed image has a new look and feel. This means the image still keeps the same salient objects or features of the original image after the manipulation process, but they now seem as if they were composed in a different way.

As a first example we consider transferring an image of a real world scene into a painting. To accomplish the latter, we extensively enhance medium frequency bands to acquire some characteristics associated with oil paintings: a small smearing effect and high contrast between different objects. To further increase the painting effect we borrow brush stroke qualities from an actual painting (Fig. 8 left) and combine them with the original photo. The right image in Fig. 8 illustrates the result of such a procedure.

Figure 9 demonstrates a different type of manipulation enabled by nonlinear spectral decomposition. In this case we keep only very low frequencies from a fish image, and import all other frequencies from a mosaic image, leading to the impression of a fish-mosaic in the fused image.

Fig. 8. Example of transforming a photo such that it gives the impression of being an impressionist painting. Using the spectral decomposition, we extract the brush stroke features of the painting (very left) from high frequency bands at a certain area (marked in red) and embedded them into the photo image. The result is shown on the right. (Color figure online)

Fig. 9. Example of transforming ceramic art such that it gives the impression of being a mosaic. Low frequencies from the ceramic art (left) are extracted and combined with the high frequencies from the mosaic image (right).

5 Conclusions and Future Research

In this paper we demonstrated the potential of nonlinear spectral decompositions using TV regularization for image fusion. In particular, our facial image fusion pipeline produces highly realistic fusion results transferring facial details such as wrinkles from one image to another. It provides a high flexibility, leading to results superior to methods such as Poisson image editing, osmosis, wavelet fusion or Laplacian pyramids on challenging cases like the fusion of a photo and a painting. Furthermore, it easily extends to several other image manipulation tasks, including inserting objects from one image into another as well as transforming a photo into a painting.

Note that the proposed image fusion framework is not only complementary to other image fusion techniques, but can also be combined with those, e.g. by applying them on individual bands of the spectral decomposition, which is a direction of future research we would like to look into. Further directions of future research include learning a regularization that is possibly even better suited at separating facial expressions and wrinkles from the image than the total variation.

Data Statement: The corresponding programming codes are available at https://doi.org/10.17863/CAM.8305.

Acknowledgements. MBe and CBS acknowledge support from EPSRC grant EP/M00483X/1 and the Leverhulme Trust project Breaking the non-convexity barrier. MBe further acknowledges support from the Leverhulme Trust early career fellowship "Learning from mistakes: a supervised feedback-loop for imaging applications" and the Newton Trust. MM acknowledges support from the German Research Foundation (DFG) as part of the research training group GRK 1564 Imaging New Modalities. RN and GG acknowledge support by the Israel Science Foundation (grant 718/15). MBu acknowledges support by ERC via Grant EU FP 7 - ERC Consolidator Grant 615216 LifeInverse. DC acknowledges support from ERC Consolidator Grant 3D Reloaded. CBS further acknowledges support from EPSRC centre EP/N014588/1, the Cantab Capital Institute for the Mathematics of Information, and from CHiPS (Horizon 2020 RISE project grant).

References

1. Amolins, K., Zhang, Y., Dare, P.: Wavelet based image fusion techniques an introduction, review and comparison. ISPRS J. Photogramm. Remote Sens. **62**, 249–263 (2007)
2. Asthana, A., Zafeiriou, S., Cheng, S., Pantic, M.: Incremental face alignment in the wild. In: CVPR Proceedings, pp. 1859–1866 (2014)
3. Benning, M., Burger, M.: Ground states and singular vectors of convex variational regularization methods. Methods Appl. Anal. **20**(4), 295–334 (2013)
4. Blanz, V., Vetter, T.: A morphable model for the synthesis of 3D faces. In: Proceedings of the 26th Annual Conference on Computer Graphics and Interactive Techniques, pp. 187–194. ACM Press/Addison-Wesley Publishing Co. (1999)
5. Burger, M., Eckardt, L., Gilboa, G., Moeller, M.: Spectral representations of one-homogeneous functionals. In: Aujol, J.-F., Nikolova, M., Papadakis, N. (eds.) SSVM 2015. LNCS, vol. 9087, pp. 16–27. Springer, Cham (2015). doi:10.1007/978-3-319-18461-6_2
6. Burger, M., Frick, K., Osher, S.J., Scherzer, O.: Inverse total variation flow. Multiscale Model. Simul. **6**(2), 366–395 (2007)
7. Burger, M., Gilboa, G., Moeller, M., Eckardt, L., Cremers, D.: Spectral decompositions using one-homogeneous functionals (2015, submitted). http://arxiv.org/pdf/1601.02912v1.pdf
8. Burger, M., Gilboa, G., Osher, S., Xu, J.: Nonlinear inverse scale space methods. Comm. Math. Sci. **4**(1), 179–212 (2006)
9. Burt, P.J., Adelson, E.H.: A multiresolution spline with application to image mosaics. ACM Trans. Graph. (TOG) **2**(4), 217–236 (1983)
10. Condat, L., Mosaddegh, S.: Joint demosaicking and denoising by total variation minimization. In: 19th IEEE International Conference on Image Processing (ICIP), pp. 2781–2784 (2012)
11. Farbman, Z., Fattal, R., Lischinski, D., Szeliski, R.: Edge-preserving decompositions for multi-scale tone, detail manipulation. In: ACM SIGGRAPH 2008 Papers, SIGGRAPH 2008, pp. 67:1–67:10. ACM, New York (2008)
12. Fattal, R., Agrawala, M., Rusinkiewicz, S.: Multiscale shape and detail enhancement from multi-light image collections. In: ACM SIGGRAPH 2007 Papers, SIGGRAPH 2007. ACM, New York (2007)
13. Gilboa, G.: A spectral approach to total variation. In: Kuijper, A., Bredies, K., Pock, T., Bischof, H. (eds.) SSVM 2013. LNCS, vol. 7893, pp. 36–47. Springer, Heidelberg (2013). doi:10.1007/978-3-642-38267-3_4

14. Gilboa, G.: A total variation spectral framework for scale and texture analysis. SIAM J. Imaging Sci. **7**(4), 1937–1961 (2014)
15. Gilboa, G., Moeller, M., Burger, M.: Nonlinear spectral analysis via one-homogeneous functionals: overview and future prospects. J. Math. Imaging Vis. **56**(2), 300–319 (2016)
16. Goldstein, T., Esser, E., Baraniuk, R.: Adaptive primal-dual hybrid gradient methods for saddle-point problems. arXiv Preprint (2013)
17. Hagenburg, K., Breuß, M., Weickert, J., Vogel, O.: Novel schemes for hyperbolic PDEs using osmosis filters from visual computing. In: Bruckstein, A.M., Haar Romeny, B.M., Bronstein, A.M., Bronstein, M.M. (eds.) SSVM 2011. LNCS, vol. 6667, pp. 532–543. Springer, Heidelberg (2012). doi:10.1007/978-3-642-24785-9_45
18. Weickert, J., Hagenburg, K., Breuß, M., Vogel, O.: Linear osmosis models for visual computing. In: Heyden, A., Kahl, F., Olsson, C., Oskarsson, M., Tai, X.-C. (eds.) EMMCVPR 2013. LNCS, vol. 8081, pp. 26–39. Springer, Heidelberg (2013). doi:10.1007/978-3-642-40395-8_3
19. Kass, M., Solomon, J.: Smoothed local histogram filters. In: ACM SIGGRAPH 2010 Papers, SIGGRAPH 2010, pp. 100:1–100:10. ACM. New York (2010)
20. Li, S., Yang, B.: Multifocus image fusion by combining curvelet and wavelet transform. Pattern Recogn. Lett. **29**(9), 1295–1301 (2008)
21. Nieuwenhuis, C., Cremers, D.: Spatially varying color distributions for interactive multi-label segmentation. IEEE Trans. Pattern Anal. Mach. Intell. **35**(5), 1234–1247 (2013)
22. Osher, S., Burger, M., Goldfarb, D., Xu, J., Yin, W.: An iterative regularization method for total variation based image restoration. SIAM J. Multiscale Model. Simul. **4**, 460–489 (2005)
23. Pérez, P., Gangnet, M., Blake, A.: Poisson image editing. In: ACM SIGGRAPH 2003 Papers, SIGGRAPH 2003, pp. 313–318. ACM (2003)
24. Pock, T., Chambolle, A.: Diagonal preconditioning for first order primal-dual algorithms in convex optimization. In: ICCV, pp. 1762–1769 (2011)
25. Stathaki, T.: Image Fusion: Algorithms and Applications. Academic Press, Cambridge (2008)
26. Su, Z., Lu, X., Artusi, A.: A novel image decomposition approach and its applications. Vis. Comput. **29**, 1011–1023 (2013)
27. Subr, K., Soler, C., Durand, F.: Edge-preserving multiscale image decomposition based on local extrema. In: ACM SIGGRAPH Asia 2009 Papers, SIGGRAPH Asia 2009, pp. 147:1–147:9. ACM, New York (2009)
28. Thies, J., Zollhöfer, M., Nießner, M., Valgaerts, L., Stamminger, M., Theobalt, C.: Real-time expression transfer for facial reenactment. ACM Trans. Graph. (TOG), **34**(6) (2015)
29. Viola, P., Jones, M.J.: Robust real-time face detection. Int. J. Comput. Vis. **57**(2), 137–154 (2004)
30. Zeeuw, P.M.: Wavelets and Image Fusion. CWI, Amsterdam (1998)

Tubular Structure Segmentation Based on Heat Diffusion

Fang Yang[✉] and Laurent D. Cohen

CEREMADE, CNRS, UMR 7534, Université Paris Dauphine,
PSL Research University, 75016 Paris, France
yang@ceremade.dauphine.fr

Abstract. This paper proposes an interactive method for tubular structure segmentation. The method is based on the minimal paths obtained from the geodesic distance solved by the heat equation. This distance can be based both on isotropic or anisotropic metric by solving the corresponding heat equation. Thanks to the additional dimension added for the local radius around the centerline, our method can not only detect the centerline of the structure, but also extracts the boundaries of the structures. Our algorithm is tested on both synthetic and real images. The promising results demonstrate the robustness and effectiveness of the algorithm.

1 Introduction

In computer vision field, it is significant to obtain geodesic distance and geodesic lines. They play a very important role in road extraction, vessel segmentation, surface re-meshing and so on [14]. In general, the geodesic distance ϕ could be acquired via Dijkstra's method [5] or solving the Eikonal equation $\|\nabla\phi\| = \mathcal{P}$, where $\mathcal{P}$ is a potential cost function computed from the image I. The Fast Sweeping Method [23] and the Fast Marching Method [3,17] are quite often used to solve the Eikonal equation. For the extraction of the geodesic lines $\gamma^\star$ between the initial point p_{s_0} and the endpoint p_x, it can be achieved by solving an ordinary differential equation after the computation of ϕ:

$$\forall s > 0, \frac{d\gamma^\star}{ds} = -\frac{\nabla\phi}{\|\nabla\phi\|}, \gamma^\star(0) = p_x \tag{1}$$

The heat equation is a partial differential equation (PDE) that describes the evolution of the distribution of heat on a domain within time T. It has a general form:

$$\frac{\partial u}{\partial t} = \alpha\Delta u \tag{2}$$

where u stands for the heat, and α, a positive constant, represents the thermal conductivity, Δ is the Laplace operator.

In 1967, Varadhan [19] proposed a formula to approximate the geodesic distance $\phi(p_0, p_x)$ between two points p_0 and p_x on a Riemannian manifold:

$$\phi(p_0, p_x) = \lim_{t\to 0} \sqrt{-4t \log u_{p_0}(p_x, t)} \tag{3}$$

F. Lauze et al. (Eds.): SSVM 2017, LNCS 10302, pp. 54–65, 2017.
DOI: 10.1007/978-3-319-58771-4_5

where u_{p_0} the solution of Eq. (2) under the initial condition that $u_{p_0}(0) = \delta_{p_0}$ within a small time $t \to 0$.

Recently, Crane et al. [4] proposed a heat method to estimate the geodesic distance. Their approach can be divided into three steps: (1) solve Eq. (2) for some fixed time t; (2) normalize the vector field: $X = -\nabla u/|\nabla u|$; (3) solve the Poisson equation to obtain the geodesic distance: $\Delta\phi = \nabla \cdot X$. By comparing the heat method with the state-of-the-art Fast Marching Method [17], Crane et al. found that, using the heat method to obtain the geodesic distance is faster than the Fast Marching Method. This is due to the fact that steps (1) and (3) can be pre-factorized. Furthermore, the authors used a direct solver to solve the heat equation. In [15, 16], the authors prove that the sparse systems arising from the elliptic PDEs can be solved in very close to linear time.

More recently, Yang and Cohen [22] have extended and gone beyond the work of Crane et al. They introduced isotropic and anisotropic heat flows to approximate the geodesic distance by using Varadhan's formula Eq. (3). After obtaining the geodesic distance, they solve an ordinary differential equation (ODE) for backtracking the minimal path γ^*. For the isotropic case, they use Eq. (1), and for the anisotropic case, they use:

$$\forall s > 0, \frac{d\gamma^*}{ds} = -\frac{D^{-1}\nabla\phi}{\|D^{-1}\nabla\phi\|}, \gamma^*(0) = p_x \qquad (4)$$

where D is the metric tensor. It is shown in [22] that using the heat method to approximate the geodesic distance is not only fast and efficient, but also less sensitive to noise.

In the past few decades, numerous segmentation methods based on minimal paths have been proposed, such as [1–3, 10, 22].

In [22], the authors apply both isotropic and anisotropic metrics to the heat equation in order to obtain geodesic distance and curves. These curves are the centerlines of the tubular structures, and the boundaries can not be extracted at the same time. In [10], Li and Yezzi have incorporated an additional non-spatial dimension to the traditional minimal path technique [3] (where there are only spatial information). This method can measure the thickness (radius) of the structures in space. In other words, this additional dimension can help to extract the boundaries and surfaces of the structures in 2D and 3D spaces. And in the meantime, their method can also detect a precise centerline of the structures. But the potential $\mathcal{P}$ that is used in [10] is isotropic and depends on the positions. The orientations of the tubular structures are ignored. Later on, Benmansour et al. [1] have proposed an anisotropic minimal path model which also takes the additional dimension into account, so the potential depends both on the positions and the tangent directions. The way they built the metric was based on the anisotropic Optimally Oriented Flux (OOF) descriptor proposed by Law and Chung [9]. The OOF descriptor makes the propagation faster along the tubular structures. The advantage of the anisotropic model is its ability to avoid the shortcut issues effectively. Then Benmansour and Cohen have extended their method into $3D$ vessel extraction [2].

In [2,10], the authors use the Fast Marching Method to get the numerical solution of the Eikonal equation, while in this paper, we are interested in the segmentation of tubular structures by using the heat method. Here, we use the same way to construct the metric tensor as the authors do in [1,2]. This is called *2D + Radius* model in heat.

The contribution of this work is that we add a non-spatial third dimension in both isotropic and anisotropic heat diffusion to segment tubular structures. We use the OOF descriptor [9] to build the metric. Therefore, the heat method can be used to detect the centerlines and boundaries simultaneously. Besides, we use the scheme proposed in [7] to discretize the heat equation, for each image, the Laplacian operator can be precomputed. Additionally, under the same conditions, compared with the Fast Marching Method, the heat method presents good results within less time.

This paper is organized as follows: in Sect. 2, we give some background on the minimal path, the heat diffusion, and the OOF descriptor; in Sect. 3, how to construct the metric and the way to solve the heat equation are presented; in Sect. 4, we test our method on some synthetic and real data. Section 5 provides some concluding remarks and possible directions for future work.

2   Background

2.1   Minimal Paths

Given an image $I : \Omega \to \mathbb{R}^2$ and two points p_{s_0} and p_x, the geodesic γ is a curve connecting these two points that globally minimizes the following energy functional $E : \mathcal{A}_{p_{s_0}, p_x} \to \mathbb{R}^+$:

$$E(y(s)) = \int_{\Omega} \{\mathcal{P}(y(s)) + w\} ds, \quad y(s) \in \mathcal{A}p_0, p_x \qquad (5)$$

where $\mathcal{P}$ is a potential cost function computed from I, w is a positive constant that imposes regularity on the curve. $\mathcal{A}_{p_{s_0}, p_x}(s)$ is the set of all the curves linking p_{s_0} and p_x, s is the arclength.

To solve this minimalization problem, Cohen and Kimmel [3] proposed a Hamiltonian approach: Find the minimal action map $\phi : \Omega \to \mathbb{R}^2$ that solves the Eikonal equation:

$$\|\nabla \phi\| = \mathcal{P} + w \qquad (6)$$

with the boundary condition $\phi(p_{s_0}) = 0$. Popular ways to solve the Eikonal equation such as the Fast Marching [3,17] and Fast Sweeping [23] are quite often used. But these methods do not reuse information [4]: once the geodesic distance ϕ_{s_0} from the initial source point p_{s_0} is obtained, the distance from another source point p_{s_1} needs to be recomputed from scratch. According to Eq. (3), ϕ can be also approximated by the heat kernel. The advantage of using the heat kernel is that the Laplace operator could be precomputed, so that the fundamental solution of the heat equation can be acquired in a single step no matter where the initial point p_{s_0} is. In this way, the approximation of ϕ can be obtained once the heat equation is solved. Then the geodesic γ could be obtained by solving Eq. (1) or Eq. (4) depending on the heat diffusion being isotropic or anisotropic.

2.2 Isotropic and Anisotropic Heat Diffusion

Equation (2) presents a homogeneous form of heat equation. When it comes to isotropic and anisotropic heat diffusion, the heat equation could be written as:

$$\frac{\partial u}{\partial t} = k \text{div} \cdot (D \nabla u) \tag{7}$$

where k is the diffusivity, it can be a constant (as α in Eq. (2)) or a scalar function, and D can be a scalar function or a diffusion tensor. According to [20], when D is a scalar function, the heat diffusion is isotropic. And when D is a diffusion tensor, it is a tensor field of symmetric positive matrices that can encode the local orientation and anisotropy of an image [22]. Then the heat diffusion becomes anisotropic. For the 2D heat diffusion, the tensor field D can be decomposed as shown in Eq. (8):

$$D = \lambda_1 \mathbf{e}_1 \mathbf{e}_1^T + \lambda_2 \mathbf{e}_2 \mathbf{e}_2^T \tag{8}$$

λ_1 and λ_2 are the eigenvalues, $\lambda_2 \geq \lambda_1 > 0$, $\mathbf{e}_1$ and $\mathbf{e}_2$ are the corresponding orthogonal eigenvectors. A measure of the local anisotropy can be defined as $A = (\lambda_2 - \lambda_1)/(\lambda_2 + \lambda_1)$. When $\lambda_1 = \lambda_2$, the heat diffusion becomes isotropic.

The main difference between isotropic and anisotropic diffusion lies in the fact that isotropic diffusion does not include the local orientation, by using the anisotropic diffusion, heat could be more concentrated on the directions that the users design.

2.3 Optimally Oriented Flux

In order to use the relevant anisotropic heat equation, we need to find some estimates for the local orientation and scale to describe the tube-like structures. In fact, many classical enhancers like the Hessian-based vesselness mesures have been proposed [8,11]. The Hessian-based enhancers include adjacent features, while the OOF descriptor [9] avoids this problem.

Given an image $I : \Omega \to \mathbb{R}^2$, the oriented flux is the amount of the image gradient projected along the axis $\mathbf{p}$ flowing out from a $2D$ circle $\mathcal{S}_r$ at point $\mathbf{x}$ with radius r:

$$f(\mathbf{x}; r, \mathbf{p}) = \int_{\partial \mathcal{S}_r} (\nabla (G_\sigma * I)(\mathbf{x} + r\mathbf{n}) \cdot \mathbf{p})(\mathbf{p} \cdot \mathbf{n}) ds \tag{9}$$

where G_σ is a Gaussian with some variance σ, and empirically σ is set to 1. $\mathbf{n}$ is the outward unit normal of $\partial \mathcal{S}_r$. ds is the infinitesimal length on $\partial \mathcal{S}_r$. Based on the divergence theorem, the oriented flux $f(\mathbf{x}, r; \mathbf{p}) = \mathbf{p}^T \mathbf{Q}_{r,\mathbf{x}} \mathbf{p}$, where $\mathbf{Q}_{r,\mathbf{x}}$ is a symmetric matrix.

In [9], the authors only used the eigenvalues λ_i of $\mathbf{Q}_{\mathbf{x},r}$ for the vessel enhancement. In this paper, we use both the eigenvalues λ_i and the eigenvectors $\mathbf{e}_i$ of $\mathbf{Q}_{\mathbf{x},r}$ to form the diffusion tensor, thus the heat could be more concentrated on the tubular structures.

3   Construction of the Metric and Numerical Solutions of the Heat Equation

3.1   Construction of the Metric

Now we are considering building a $(d+1)$D metric, d is the dimension of the image, in our case, $d = 2$, and the $3rd$ dimension is not spatial but a radius dimension. We use the same way as described in [2] to construct the metric.

$$D(x, r) = \begin{bmatrix} \hat{D}(x,r) & \mathbf{0} \\ \mathbf{0} & \mathcal{P}_r(x,r) \end{bmatrix} \tag{10}$$

where $\hat{D}(x, r)$ is a 2×2 symmetric matrix, this entry is used to describe the spatial anisotropy. In addition, $\mathcal{P}_r(x, r)$ is the isotropic radius potential entry. For a certain scale r, the anisotropic entry $\hat{D}$ can be constructed by the eigenvalues λ_i ($i \in 1, 2$) ($\lambda_2 > \lambda_1$) and the eigenvectors $\mathbf{v}_i$ of the OOF descriptor:

$$\hat{D}(x, r) = \eta_1 (\exp{(\beta \cdot \lambda_1(x))} \mathbf{v}_1(x) \mathbf{v}_1(x)^T + \exp{(\beta \cdot \lambda_2(x))} \mathbf{v}_2(x) \mathbf{v}_2(x)^T) \tag{11}$$

The radius potential entry can be described by the eigenvalues of the OOF descriptor.

$$\mathcal{P}_r(x) = \eta_2 \exp(\beta \frac{\lambda_1(x) + \lambda_2(x)}{2}) \tag{12}$$

Here β is a constant that is controlled by the maximal spatial anisotropic ratio μ, which is defined as:

$$\mu = \max_{x,r} \sqrt{\exp(\beta \cdot (\lambda_2(x,r) - \lambda_1(x,r)))} \tag{13}$$

By choosing the maximal spatial anisotropy ratio μ, β is then fixed. $0 \leq \eta_1, \eta_2 \leq 1$ are two constants that control the space and radius speed. If we would like the heat to propagate faster on the radius dimension, we could choose a bigger $\eta_2 > \eta_1$. Empirically, in this paper, η_1 and η_2 are always set to be 1. Using Eq. (10) as the diffusion tensor in Eq. (7), the heat equation can be written as:

$$\frac{\partial u(x,r,t)}{\partial t} = \mathrm{div} \cdot (D(x,r) \nabla u(x,r,t)) \tag{14}$$

For the isotropic diffusion, the metric D becomes:

$$D(x, r) = \mathcal{P}_r(x,r) I_d \tag{15}$$

I_d is an 3×3 identity matrix.

3.2   Solving the Heat Equation

After the construction of the metric, we now solve the heat equation. Generally, the numerical approximation to the solution of the discrete heat equation could be achieved by different schemes [6,7,13,21].

Given the image $I : \Omega \rightarrow \mathbb{R}^2$, suppose that the domain is discretized into $M \times N$ grids and the scale of the third dimension $r \in [R_{min}, R_{max}]$ is K. Then the initial condition becomes: $u^0_{i,j,k} = 1, u^0_{i',j',k'} = 0, (i', j', k') \neq (i, j, k)$, and (i, j, k) is the initial point given by the users.

Numerical Solution of Isotropic Diffusion. For the isotropic diffusion, we use a backward finite differences scheme, which is also called implicit finite differences scheme. Taking the $3D$ heat equation Eq. (2) into consideration, the backward finite difference scheme would be:

$$(\mathrm{Id} - \tau \alpha \Delta)u^t = u^0 \tag{16}$$

Id is the identity matrix, τ is the diffusion time, u^t is the heat value after time τ. The Laplace operator Δ can be easily discretized as an $(N \times M \times K)^2$ block penta-diagonal sparse matrix. After the discretization of the Laplace operator Δ, the heat distribution u^t can be acquired by setting an appropriate time step τ.

Numerical Solution of Anisotropic Diffusion. For the anisotropic diffusion, we use a backward discretization scheme designed by Fehrenbach and Mirebeau [7]. The scheme is called Anisotropic Diffusion using Lattice Basis Reduction (AD-LBR). The advantages of this scheme are its non-negativity and sparsity, thus making the solution robust and fast.

For Eq. (14), the backward scheme is:

$$\frac{u^t - u^0}{\tau} = \mathrm{div} \cdot (D\nabla u^t) \tag{17}$$

To acquire the fundamental solution of Eq. (17) within a small time τ, we have:

$$(\mathrm{Id} - \tau \mathrm{div} \cdot (D\nabla))u^t = u^0 \tag{18}$$

The symmetric operator $A = \mathrm{div} \cdot (D\nabla)$, with Neumann boundary conditions, can also be defined through the identity

$$\int_\Omega u(x) \, Au(x) \, dx = \int_\Omega \nabla u(x)^{\mathrm{T}} D(x) \nabla u(x) \, dx, \tag{19}$$

for all $u \in H^1(\Omega)$. In order to discretize A, the AD-LBR approximates the contribution of each grid point $x \in \Omega$ to the r.h.s. of (19) using a sum of squared finite differences

$$\nabla u(x)^{\mathrm{T}} D(x) \nabla u(x) \approx \sum_{v \in V(x)} \omega_x(v) \left(\frac{u(x + hv) - u(x)}{h} \right)^2, \tag{20}$$

where $h > 0$ is the grid scale, $V(x)$ is a set of vectors referred to as the *stencil* of the point x, and $\omega_x(v)$ is the *weight* of the vector v at x. From these stencils and weights, the sparse symmetric matrix of A is then easily assembled. The specificity of the AD-LBR numerical scheme is that the stencils are sparse, with at most 12 elements in 3D, which limits the numerical cost of the method, and that the weights are non-negative, which guarantees discrete maximum principle as well as the robustness of the method.

The computation process involves the construction at each grid point $x \in \Omega$ of an obtuse superbase with respect to the matrix $D(x)$, which is a family $(e_i)_{i=0}^d$ of vectors with integer coordinates such that $|\det(e_1, \cdots, e_d)| = 1$ and $e_i^{\mathrm{T}} D(x) e_j \leq 0$ for all $0 \leq i < j \leq d$. The stencil is then $V(x) = \{e_i \times e_j; i \neq j\}$ and the corresponding non-negative weights are $\omega_x(e_i \times e_j) = -\frac{1}{2} e_k^{\mathrm{T}} D(x) e_l$ whenever (i, j, k, l) are pairwise distinct, $i, j, k, l \in \{0, 1, 2, 3\}$. The stencil construction is cheap and efficient thanks to arithmetic techniques, thus computation time is dominated by solving the linear systems. See [7] for details.

4   Experiments and Results

4.1   Experiment Data and Settings

We have tested our method both on synthetic and real images:

Figure 1 is an example of a noisy synthetic image (a) of size 100×100. This image is obtained by corrupting the original image with 35% pepper & salt noise. The ground truth in (d) is the original image without adding the noise. Figure 2(a) is a 300×300 vessel image and Fig. 2(e) is a 200×160 road image. The ground truth Fig. 2(d) and (h) are labelled manually.

In Fig. 3, to illustrate the advantage of anisotropic diffusion, we use a 100×100 image with a tube-like structure which has sharp corners.

Figure 4a demonstrates a medical image with a catheter. And before diffusion, to preprocess the image I, we first build a potential $\mathcal{P}$ based on the image Laplacian, then we use a sigmoid function Eq. (21) on $\mathcal{P}$.

$$I_m(x) = 1 - \frac{1}{1 + e^{\lambda(\mathcal{P}(x) - k)}} \tag{21}$$

I_m is the result after preprocessing. Here we set $\lambda = 10$ and $k = 0.5$.

For all the experiment results, the red points and blue points represent the initial points and endpoints respectively. We use the closed red curves to segment the structures boundary. And the blue curves stand for the centerlines. Moreover, the green blocks on some images are used to mark the difference between our method and the Fast Marching Method. In addition, the radius setting for Figs. 1, 2(a) and 4 ranges from 0.5 pixel to 5 pixels, and the interval is 0.5 pixel. For Figs. 2(e) and 3, the radius setting is from 1 pixel to 10, with 1 pixel interval. For the first three experiments, the same diffusion time $\tau = 0.01$ is employed.

The time consumption of the heat method is composed by two terms: the time of factorization (the disretization of the Laplacian operator) and the time of solving the heat equation. The factorization process was implemented in C++. Then we solve the heat equation under the scheme of Crane's [24]. We compare our approach with the Fast Marching implementation of Peyré *et al.* [14]. Performance was measured based on a quad core of a 2.8 GHz Intel Core i7 (Table 1).

To evaluate the performance of our method, we compute *precision* and *recall*:

$$\begin{cases} recall = \frac{TP}{TP+FN} \\ precision = \frac{TP}{TP+FP} \end{cases} \tag{22}$$

Here TP represents the segmentation part which matches the ground truth (GT), FP is the part that do not coincide with the GT, FN stands for the part that is not extracted, i.e. falsely labelled as negative.

4.2   Results and Analysis

Isotropic Diffusion on a Noisy Synthetic Image. Figure 1 is an example of a noisy synthetic image (a), with a percentage 0.35 of corrupted pixels. (d) is the ground-truth obtained by using the Fast Marching Method on the image without adding noise. From the two results (e) and (f), compared with the ground-truth (d), we can see that the heat method outperforms the Fast Marching Method, because not only the centerline but also the boundaries extracted by heat method are smoother than the ones extracted by the Fast Marching Method. Table 1 presents the *precision* and *recall* and the corresponding time consumption of these two methods. The total time of heat method is less than the Fast Marching. And the precision and recall index of heat method in higher than the Fast Marching. Additionally, the distance map obtained by Fast Marching (b) is more noisy then the one by heat diffusion (c). The distance maps (b) and (c) illustrate that the heat method is robust in noisy circumstances. This is due to the fact that the heat equation can get fast smoothing by nature. With the initial condition $u(x_0, y_0, t_0) = \delta_{x_0, y_0}(t_0)$, the heat becomes smooth as soon as $t > t_0$. Additionally, in the sense of mathematics, the solutions of the heat equation are characterized by a Gaussian kernel, this can be regarded as a blurring process. This is also the reason why the heat method can be used for filtering issues.

Table 1. Time consumption and indexes of evaluation (precision & recall)%.

Data	Heat method				Fast marching mothod		
	Factor	Solve	Precision	Recall	Time	Precision	Recall
Noisy curve	0.06 s	**0.06 s**	**94.24**	**97.58**	0.16 s	92.97	93.54
Vessel	0.48 s	**0.73 s**	89.54	**90.31**	1.18 s	**91.26**	88.62
Road	0.2 s	**0.42 s**	**93.40**	**99.82**	0.69 s	92.51	97.91

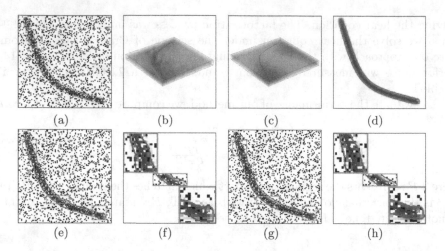

Fig. 1. Experiment on a noisy image: (a) original noisy image; (b) and (c) are the distance maps ϕ and the $3D$ minimal path between the seed point and endpoint (transparent visualization) by using the isotropic Fast Marching Method and isotropic Heat Method. (d) is the ground-truth; (e) and (g) are the results by the Fast Marching Method and Heat Method. (f) and (h) are the zoom-in results of the corresponding green boxes in (e) and (g). (Color figure online)

Isotropic Diffusion on a Vessel Image and a Road Image. Figure 2 demonstrates the experiments on a vessel image and a road image[1]. We are using the same isotropic metric for the Fast Marching Method and the heat method. For the vessel image (a), one initial point and several endpoints are selected manually. From Table 1, we can see the result by the heat method is comparable with the Fast Marching Method. First, the time consumed by both methods remains almost the same. But when we choose another source point, for the heat method, there is no need to recompute the Laplacian factor again because that the factorization is already pre-computed, which saves some time for the heat method, while for the Fast Marching, the distance must be computed entirely from scratch [4]. For the road image (e), there are many abandoned cars on both sides of the road, which may cause much influence in boundary detection. From the results (f) and (g), we can see that the boundaries (highlighted in the green rectangles) that extracted by our method show higher precision and recall. In other words, our result is less influenced by the cars than Fast Marching. In addition, our method gives a smoother result than Fast Marching.

Isotropic and Anisotropic Diffusion on a Tube-Like Structure. In Fig. 3, there is a tube-like structure with several sharp corners. Here we test the difference between isotropic and anisotropic methods. From (b), it is obvious that there is a short-cut on the way back to the initial points, in (c), the backtracking

---

[1] This image is obtained from the website of GettyImages, it is a DigitalGlobe Worldview-1 satellite image, showing abandoned cars on the road that leads to the top of the Sinjar Mountain Range.

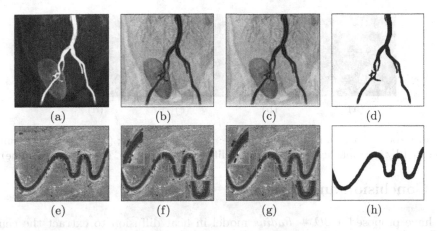

Fig. 2. Example on a medical image with several endpoints (row above) and on a road image (row below), from left to right, they are the original images, the result by the Fast Marching Method and the result by the heat method. The green rectangles illustrate the places that the heat method surpasses the Fast Marching Method. (Color figure online)

process is totally along the structure without any short-cut. This indicates that by using the anisotropic heat diffusion, the heat can be more concentrated on the direction that the users design.

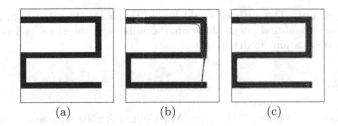

Fig. 3. Example on a tube-like structure image, (a) the original image, (b) the result by the isotropic heat method, (c) the result by the anisotropic heat method. There is a short-cut in (b). The radius becomes zero and the centerline in blue is partly superimposed on the boundary in red. In (c), the detection result of centerline and boundary is along the structure without short-cut. (Color figure online)

Diffusion on a Medical Image Within Different Time Step. The time step τ is an important factor for the heat method. It decides the time for diffusion. According to Eq. (3), the distance map ϕ could be approximated only when the diffusion time t is as small as possible. Figure 4 demonstrates the effect of diffusion time τ. Different τ are applied. From (b) to (d), τ equals to $0.1, 0.01$ and 0.001 respectively. From the results, it can be seen clearly that the longer the diffusion time is, the more the distance map gets blurred, thus leading to the shortcut on the way when backtracking to the initial point.

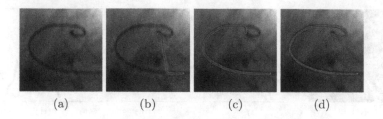

(a)   (b)   (c)   (d)

Fig. 4. Experiment on a real medical image: (a) original image; (b)–(d) are the results generated by isotropic heat diffusion with different time step τ. (Color figure online)

5   Conclusion and Prospects

We have proposed a *2D + Radius* model in heat diffusion to extract the centerlines as well as the boundaries of the tubular structures in 2D images. This model integrate the OOF descriptor and diffusion tensor. From the results, we can see that the *2D + Radius* model in heat is very robust and efficient. Besides, our model is less influenced by noise compared with the Fast Marching Method. In addition, the anisotropic diffusion does better in controlling the direction than isotropic diffusion. It is fit for detecting the very curved lines and structures.

In future, we are interested in extending this model to higher dimensions. We also would like to propose some automatic methods based on this model, in this way, we no longer need to provide the end points, which could save a lot of human interventions.

Acknowledgement. The authors would like to thank Dr. Jean-Marie Mirebeau for his fruitful discussions and suggestions on the numerical solutions of isotropic and anisotropic heat equations in 3D space.

References

1. Benmansour, F., Cohen, L.D., Law, M., Chung, A.: Tubular anisotropy for 2D vessel segmentation. In: IEEE Conference on Computer Vision and Pattern Recognition, CVPR (2009)
2. Benmansour, F., Cohen, L.D.: Tubular structure segmentation based on minimal path method and anisotropic enhancement. Int. J. Comput. Vis. **92**, 192–210 (2011)
3. Cohen, L.D., Kimmel, R.: Global minimum for active contour models: a minimal path approach. Int. J. Comput. Vis. **24**, 57–78 (1997)
4. Crane, K., Weischedel, C., Wardetzky, M.: Geodesics in heat a new approach to computing distance based on heat flow. ACM Trans. Graph. (TOG) **32**, 152 (2013)
5. Dijkstra, E.W.: A note on two problems in connexion with graphs. Numer. Math. **1**, 269–271 (1959)
6. Douglas, J., Rachford, H.H.: On the numerical solution of heat conduction problems in two and three space variables. Trans. Am. Math. Soc. **82**, 421–439 (1956)
7. Fehrenbach, J., Mirebeau, J.-M.: Sparse non-negative stencils for anisotropic diffusion. J. Math. Imaging Vis. **49**, 123–147 (2014)

8. Frangi, A.F., Niessen, W.J., Vincken, K.L., Viergever, M.A.: Multiscale vessel enhancement filtering. In: Wells, W.M., Colchester, A., Delp, S. (eds.) MICCAI 1998. LNCS, vol. 1496, pp. 130–137. Springer, Heidelberg (1998). doi:10.1007/BFb0056195
9. Law, M.W.K., Chung, A.C.S.: Three dimensional curvilinear structure detection using optimally oriented flux. In: Forsyth, D., Torr, P., Zisserman, A. (eds.) ECCV 2008. LNCS, vol. 5305, pp. 368–382. Springer, Heidelberg (2008). doi:10.1007/978-3-540-88693-8_27
10. Li, H., Yezzi, A.: Vessels as 4-D curves: global minimal 4-D paths to extract 3-D tubular surfaces and centerlines. IEEE Trans. Med. Imaging **26**, 1213–1223 (2007)
11. Lindeberg, T.: Edge detection and ridge detection with automatic scale selection. Int. J. Comput. Vis. **30**, 117–156 (1998)
12. Jean-Marie, M., Jérôme F., Laurent, R., Shaza, T.: Anisotropic diffusion in ITK. Insight J. (2015)
13. Peaceman, D.W., Rachford Jr., H.H.: The numerical solution of parabolic and elliptic differential equations. J. Soc. Ind. Appl. Math. **3**, 28–41 (1955)
14. Peyré, G., Péchaud, M., Keriven, R., Cohen, L.D.: Geodesic methods in computer vision and graphics. Found. Trends® Comput. Graph. Vis. **5**, 197–397 (2010)
15. Schmitz, P.G., Ying, L.: A fast direct solver for elliptic problems on general meshes in 2D. J. Comput. Phys. **231**, 1314–1338 (2012)
16. Schmitz, P.G., Ying, L.: A fast nested dissection solver for Cartesian 3D elliptic problems using hierarchical matrices. J. Comput. Phys. **258**, 227–245 (2014)
17. Sethian, J.A.: A fast marching level set method for monotonically advancing fronts. Proc. Nat. Acad. Sci. **93**, 1591–1595 (1996)
18. Spielman, D.A., Teng, S.-H.: Nearly-linear time algorithms for graph partitioning, graph sparsification, and solving linear systems. In: Proceedings of the Thirty-Sixth Annual ACM Symposium on Theory of Computing (2004)
19. Varadhan, S.R.S.: On the behavior of the fundamental solution of the heat equation with variable coefficients. Commun. Pure Appl. Math. **20**, 431–455 (1967)
20. Weickert, J.: Anisotropic Diffusion in Image Processing. Teubner, Stuttgart (1998)
21. Weickert, J., Scharr, H.: A scheme for coherence-enhancing diffusion filtering with optimized rotation invariance. J. Vis. Commun. Image Represent. **13**, 103–118 (2002)
22. Yang, F., Cohen, L.D.: Geodesic distance and curves through isotropic and anisotropic heat equations on images and surfaces. J. Math. Imaging Vis. **55**(2), 210–228 (2016)
23. Zhao, H.: A fast sweeping method for Eikonal equations. Math. Comput. **74**, 603–627 (2005)
24. Crane K.: Geodesic in heat. https://www.cs.cmu.edu/~kmcrane/Projects/GeodesicsInHeat/index.html
25. Peyré, G.: Numerical tours. http://www.numerical-tours.com/matlab/#fastmarching

Analytic Existence and Uniqueness Results for PDE-Based Image Reconstruction with the Laplacian

Laurent Hoeltgen[1(✉)], Isaac Harris[2], Michael Breuß[1], and Andreas Kleefeld[3]

[1] Institute for Mathematics, Brandenburg Technical University,
Platz der Deutschen Einheit 1, 03046 Cottbus, Germany
{hoeltgen,breuss}@b-tu.de
[2] Department of Mathematics, Texas A&M University, 621A Blocker Building,
3368 TAMU, College Station, TX 77843, USA
iharris@math.tamu.edu
[3] Institute for Advanced Simulation, Forschungszentrum Jülich GmbH,
Jülich Supercomputing Centre, Wilhelm-Johnen-Straße, 52425 Jülich, Germany
a.kleefeld@fz-juelich.de

Abstract. Partial differential equations are well suited for dealing with image reconstruction tasks such as inpainting. One of the most successful mathematical frameworks for image reconstruction relies on variations of the Laplace equation with different boundary conditions. In this work we analyse these formulations and discuss the existence and uniqueness of solutions of corresponding boundary value problems, as well as their regularity from an analytic point of view. Our work not only sheds light on useful aspects of the well posedness of several standard problem formulations in image reconstruction but also aggregates them in a common framework. In addition, the performed analysis guides us to specify two new formulations of the classic image reconstruction problem that may give rise to new developments in image reconstruction.

Keywords: Partial differential equations · Laplace equation · Mixed boundary conditions · Image reconstruction · Image inpainting

1 Introduction

The reconstruction of an image from a given (and potentially sparse) subset of all pixels is known as inpainting [5]. If the subset of given data is known and fixed, then the task of finding meaningful values for the remaining missing pixels is an interpolation problem. However, one could also consider a different standpoint and attempt to optimise the subset of considered pixels for a preset interpolation strategy. This reconstruction setup may be used for image compression tasks, where the goal is usually to minimise the number of known pixels while maintaining a reasonable reconstruction quality. The issue of data selection for the latter purpose turns out to be an intricate task. Selecting for instance 5% of the pixels from a 256×256 pixel image offers more than 10^{5000} possible choices.

© Springer International Publishing AG 2017
F. Lauze et al. (Eds.): SSVM 2017, LNCS 10302, pp. 66–79, 2017.
DOI: 10.1007/978-3-319-58771-4_6

For the design of a proper optimisation framework for tackling the latter problem, a good understanding of the theoretical mechanisms behind the influence of data on the final reconstruction can prove to be useful.

In general, image inpainting methods must be able to handle arbitrarily scattered data in two or sometimes even three dimensional domains. Further, reconstruction methods must also be able to handle a broad range of different codomains. These are two challenging aspects that significantly limit the choice of possible interpolation algorithms. Models for image reconstruction based on partial differential equations (PDEs) are a viable alternative to classic interpolation strategies. Partial differential equation based models deal with the task by seeking solutions of an appropriate boundary value problem. The resulting approach is very flexible and appealing since PDEs impose only very little restrictions onto the potential data and allow a thorough mathematical analysis.

In [2,8,11,16,17,19] PDE-based strategies are devised for image inpainting and compression tasks. While these works focus mostly on diffusion processes, related models for the Allen-Cahn Model are considered in [15] and the authors of [6] also analyse the Cahn-Hilliard equation. Finally, a broader discussion on fluid dynamic models for image reconstruction tasks is presented in [3]. A general introduction to inpainting methods can also be found in [4,5,20].

The previously cited works provide very successful optimisation strategies to find good data points. However, there is very little discussion on how the choice of the data influences the solutions of the underlying PDEs. Most setups consider a partial differential equation with mixed Dirichlet and Neumann boundary conditions. These boundary conditions may even evolve during an iterative process [12]. Such strategies are only well-posed if one can show that the occurring PDEs are always solvable. The simplest PDEs to be considered involve the Laplacian as differential operator. Belhachmi et al. [2] show that their solutions live in the Sobolev space H_0^1 if they have a positive capacity. In [20] the author discusses, among other formulations, the Laplace equation and requires strong regularity of the Dirichlet boundary data to show that a weak solution exists in H^1. Elaborate models often include several different boundary conditions. It is well known that the reciprocal influence of the different boundary conditions has a strong impact on the solution. The author of [21] discusses several simple examples of partial differential equations where the regularity of the solution depends on the angle at which the boundaries bearing Neumann and Dirichlet boundary conditions meet. Azzam and Kreyszig [1] impose very strong smoothness conditions on the boundary data to show existence of a solution. Hoeltgen et al. [12] extend the work of Mainberger et al. [17] by allowing fuzzy boundary conditions. A concise analysis of the impact of such design choices has not been carried out so far. Whether these fuzzy boundary conditions are favourable to the regularity of solutions is not known.

Regularity conditions, like restrictions on the angle at which the different boundary conditions meet, may assert the existence of a strong solution for mixed boundary problems but they are often not feasible for performing image processing tasks. For image reconstruction or data compression purposes the

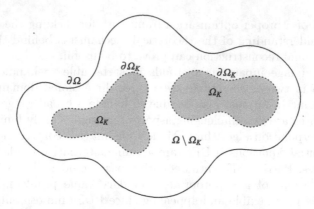

Fig. 1. Example setup considered in this paper. The set Ω_K, marked in grey, denotes known data and is used to recover the missing information on $\Omega \setminus \Omega_K$ by solving (1). Along the boundary $\partial \Omega_K$ we assume Dirichlet boundary conditions whereas $\partial \Omega \setminus \partial \Omega_K$ has Neumann conditions. Note that the set Ω_K must have positive measure but it is not necessarily connected.

assumption on boundary data needs to be that they are almost arbitrary. They may even be part of the underlying optimisation problem [2,12,16].

Let us turn to the mathematical problem formulations we deal with in this paper. Image reconstructions with the Laplace equation can be formulated as:

$$- \Delta u = 0 \text{ on } \Omega \setminus \Omega_K \quad \text{with} \quad u = f \text{ on } \partial \Omega_K, \text{ and } \partial_n u = 0 \text{ on } \partial \Omega \setminus \partial \Omega_K \quad (1)$$

where Ω is the image domain, $\Omega_K \subseteq \Omega$ the domain of known data and ∂_n represents the derivative in outer normal direction along the boundary $\partial \Omega \setminus \partial \Omega_K$ (see Fig. 1). This approach is one of the simplest, yet also one of the most successful methods for inpainting and especially compression tasks, see [18]. Problems like (1) are commonly referred to as mixed boundary value problems and in rare cases also as Zaremba's problem [22]. The existence and uniqueness of solutions has been extensively studied during the last century. A related, more general formulation as used in the work of Hoeltgen et al. [12] reads

$$c\left(x\right)\left(u\left(x\right) - f\left(x\right)\right) + \left(1 - c\left(x\right)\right)\left(-\Delta\right) u\left(x\right) = 0 \text{ on } \Omega \quad \text{and} \quad \partial_n u\left(x\right) = 0 \text{ on } \partial \Omega \quad (2)$$

for some function $c : \Omega \to \mathbb{R}$ and data f defined on the support of c. If c maps to binary values in $\{0, 1\}$, then (2) is equivalent to (1) with the Dirichlet boundary conditions specified by f at those regions where c equals 1. The non-binary formulation in (2) can be understood as a regularisation of (1) in the context of optimising the domain Ω_K for image compression tasks.

A thorough search of the relevant literature suggests that there does not exist a complete analysis on the existence and uniqueness of solutions of (1) (resp. (2)) for all possible setups that might occur in the context of image processing tasks. Nevertheless, let us emphasise that a thorough analysis on well-posedness and regularity of solutions is important for both discrete and continuous settings. In [16] it was shown that a discretised version of (1) is always solvable when there exists at least one data point in Ω_K. This result can be extended to discrete formulations of (2) by requiring that $c \not\equiv 0$, see [13]. On the other hand, if the domain Ω in (1) is the unit disc around 0 and if we seek solutions that are 0 along the boundary of this disc and 1 at the origin, then one can show that neither a strong nor a weak solution can exist [20]. However, a naive discretisation of this setup is, according to the results in [13,16], solvable. The seeming contradiction stems from the fact that a single point has Lebesgue measure 0. Belhachmi et al. [2] deal with this contradiction by requiring that the set of Dirichlet boundary data in (1) has positive capacity.

The apparent inconsistency between the continuous and discrete models seems rather unsatisfying. At first glance one does not know what a computed discrete solution corresponds to in the continuous setting. The goal of this paper is to reduce this discrepancy. We discuss several setups and provide existence and uniqueness results of solutions under suitable assumptions. These findings allow us to consider all cases related to (1) and (2) under a unified framework. To our best knowledge, the findings related to the Laplace interpolation problem (2) have not been documented before in the literature.

2 Mathematical Requirements

Most applications that solve equations of the form (1) can be modelled under the following set of assumptions (which we will silently assume to hold throughout the whole paper).

Assumption 1. *We assume the following to hold throughout the whole paper.*

1. *$\Omega \subset \mathbb{R}^2$ is an open and bounded domain with a C^∞ boundary $\partial\Omega$.*
2. *$f \colon \Omega_K \to \mathbb{R}$ is a C^∞ function containing the known data to be interpolated by the underlying PDE.*
3. *$\Omega_K \subsetneqq \Omega$ is a closed subset of Ω with positive Lebesgue measure. It represents the known data locations used to recover the missing information on $\Omega \setminus \Omega_K$. The interpolation data is given by $f(\Omega_K)$. The boundary $\partial\Omega_K$, is assumed to be C^∞, too.*

For many findings in this paper these assumptions can be weakened in various ways. However, we opt for these rather strong requirements to be able to provide a common framework in which all our results are valid. Also, for image processing tasks they do not represent severe restrictions. It is common in image processing to pre-smooth the image with a Gaussian convolution before considering the actual task. Since a Gaussian is C^∞, the same holds for the result of the convolved function, too. The smoothness of the boundary is a necessity anyway. Even the simplest PDEs usually require smooth boundaries to assert the well-posedness of a solution. Similarly, we require the set Ω_K to have positive measure to avoid ill-posed setups as the one briefly discussed in the introduction.

As already claimed, it is our goal to analyse the solutions of PDEs. In this work we consider a solution to be well-posed if it adheres to the well-posedness concept of Hadamard. The following definition from Ern and Guermond [10] suits our purpose well.

Definition 1 (Well-posedness). *Let W and V be Banach spaces equipped with norms $\|\cdot\|_W$ and $\|\cdot\|_V$, respectively. In addition, assume V to be reflexive and let A be a bounded bilinear form which maps from $W \times V$ to $\mathbb{R}$. Let F be a linear mapping from V to $\mathbb{R}$. We consider the following abstract problem formulation:*

$$find\ u \in W \quad such\ that \quad A(u,v) = F(v),\ \forall v \in V \tag{3}$$

We call this problem well-posed if the following two conditions are fulfilled.

1. *There exists a unique solution u that fulfils (3).*
2. *The following a-priori estimate holds:*

$$\exists c > 0,\ \forall F \in V',\ \|u\|_W \leqslant c\|F\|_{V'} \tag{4}$$

where V' is the dual space of V.

The previous definition reflects what one would usually expect from a reasonably formulated problem. The solution should be unique and depend continuously on the given problem data represented by the functionals F.

The forthcoming statements can be found almost verbatim in [10]. They form a fundamental part of our analysis and are listed here for the sake of completeness. We refer to their source for the detailed proofs.

Ern and Guermond [10] consider elliptic linear differential operators of the form:

$$\mathscr{L}u := -\Delta u + \mu u \tag{5}$$

over a domain $\Omega \subseteq \mathbb{R}^n$ and with $\mu \in L^\infty(\Omega, \mathbb{R})$. For given functions $h_1 \in L^2(\Omega, \mathbb{R})$ and $h_2 \in L^2(\partial\Omega, \mathbb{R})$ they analysed PDEs of the form:

$$\mathscr{L}u = h_1 \text{ on } \Omega \quad \text{and} \quad \mathscr{B}u = h_2 \text{ on } \partial\Omega \tag{6}$$

for some operator $\mathscr{B}$ that accounts for the boundary conditions. The authors discussed the following corresponding weak formulations:

Homogeneous Dirichlet Conditions: We require $u \equiv 0$ along $\partial\Omega$ and the corresponding weak formulation seeks $u \in H_0^1(\Omega)$ such that

$$\underbrace{\int_\Omega \nabla v \cdot \nabla u + \mu u v \mathrm{d}x}_{=:A(u,v)} = \int_\Omega h_1 v \mathrm{d}x, \quad \forall v \in H_0^1(\Omega) \tag{7}$$

Non-homogeneous Dirichlet Condition: We fix $u \equiv h_2$ along $\partial\Omega$ with $h_2 \in H^{\frac{1}{2}}(\partial\Omega)$. The corresponding weak formulation seeks $u := u_{h_2} + \phi$ with a lifting u_{h_2} of h_2 to $H^1(\Omega)$ and $\phi \in H_0^1(\Omega)$ such that

$$A(\phi, v) = \int_\Omega h_1 v dx - A(u_{h_2}, v), \quad \forall v \in H_0^1(\Omega) \tag{8}$$

Neumann Condition: We require $\partial_n u = n \cdot \nabla u = h_2$ along $\partial\Omega$ and require that $h_2 \in L^2(\partial\Omega)$. The corresponding weak formulation seeks $u \in H^1(\Omega)$ such that

$$A(u, v) = \int_\Omega h_1 v dx + \int_{\partial\Omega} h_2 v dS, \quad \forall v \in H^1(\Omega) \tag{9}$$

Mixed Dirichlet-Neumann Conditions: We consider a non-trivial partitioning of the form $\partial\Omega = \partial\Omega_N \cup \partial\Omega_D$ with $\partial\Omega_N \cap \partial\Omega_D = \emptyset$ and impose $u \equiv 0$ along $\partial\Omega_D$, as well as $h_2 \in L^2(\partial\Omega_N)$ and $n \cdot \nabla u = h_2$ along $\partial\Omega_N$. In this case we seek a function u in

$$H_{\partial\Omega_D}^1 := \left\{ u \in H^1(\Omega) | \ u \equiv 0 \text{ on } \partial\Omega_D \right\} \tag{10}$$

such that

$$A(u, v) = \int_\Omega h_1 v dx + \int_{\partial\Omega_N} h_2 v dS, \quad \forall v \in H_{\partial\Omega_D}^1(\Omega) \tag{11}$$

The findings concerning existence and uniqueness of solutions are summarised in the following theorem (c.f. Proposition 3.2–3.6 and Theorem 3.8 in [10]).

Theorem 1. *Let $p := \text{ess inf}_\Omega \{\mu\}$ and c_Ω the constant from the Poincaré inequality:*

$$\exists c_\Omega > 0, \forall v \in W_0^{1,2}(\Omega) : c_\Omega \|v\|_{L^2(\Omega)} \leqslant \|\nabla v\|_{L^2(\Omega)} \tag{12}$$

Then,

1. *Solving the PDE (6) is equivalent to solving the weak formulations in (7), (8), (9), and (11) with the corresponding boundary conditions.*
2. *The homogeneous and the non-homogeneous Dirichlet problem are well posed if*

$$1 + \min\left\{0, \frac{p}{c_\Omega}\right\} > 0 \tag{13}$$

3. *The Neumann problem is well-posed if $p > 0$.*
4. *The mixed Dirichlet-Neumann problem is well posed if (13) holds and if the set $\partial\Omega_D$ fulfils $\text{meas}(\partial\Omega_D) > 0$.*

In the next section we will apply the results from Theorem 1 to common use cases in image inpainting. We will see that all formulations related to (1) are indeed well-posed. The most important aspect will be the correct analysis of the boundary conditions. We also show how to cast (2) in the framework of Theorem 1 and thereby provide novel results on the well-posedness of (2). The key observation will be the relation between (2) and the Helmholtz equation.

3   Inpainting with the Laplace Equation

We remind once again, that we silently assume the setup specified in Assumption 1 at the beginning of Sect. 2. In addition to the requirements stated at the beginning of Sect. 2 we impose the following condition on the boundary data:

Assumption 2. *In addition to Assumption 1, let the following be true for the remaining part of this paper:*

4. *Whenever we are considering a problem with non-trivial mixed boundary conditions (i.e. the sets where Neumann and Dirichlet boundary conditions must hold are non-empty), then the boundary of the set of missing data $\Omega \setminus \Omega_K$ can be split into two disjoint parts $\partial\Omega \setminus \partial\Omega_K$ and $\partial\Omega_K$ and both have positive measure.*

This additional assumption prevents the Dirichlet and Neumann boundary conditions meet and thus, it prevents potential conflicting boundary conditions.

As already stated, classic Laplace interpolation solves the mixed boundary value problem in (1). Depending on the concrete size and shape of the set Ω_K it may happen that we are in either of the settings presented in Sect. 2. Let us shortly consider which cases might occur. If, for example, the set $\Omega \setminus \Omega_K$ is very small and located in the centre of our image, then we are in the presence of Dirichlet boundary conditions only. The region inside will then have to be interpolated by means of the Laplace equation with the boundary information obtained from $\partial\Omega_K$. On the other hand, if $\Omega_K = \emptyset$, then we only have to consider homogeneous Neumann boundary conditions. In the image compression context it is not uncommon that Ω_K is non-empty but significantly smaller than Ω. Then we often have to consider mixed boundary conditions. This setup considers the following boundary value problem:

$$- \Delta u = 0 \text{ on } \Omega \setminus \Omega_K \text{ with } u = f \text{ on } \partial\Omega_K \text{ and } \partial_n u = 0 \text{ on } \partial\Omega \setminus \partial\Omega_K \quad (14)$$

Let us remark, that our formulation in (14) does not fit completely into the framework for mixed boundary conditions presented in Sect. 2. Indeed in our case the Neumann conditions are homogeneous and the Dirichlet conditions are not. However, if we consider

$$- \Delta \overline{u} = \Delta f, \text{ on } \Omega \setminus \Omega_K \text{ with } \overline{u} = 0 \text{ on } \partial\Omega_K \text{ and } \partial_n \overline{u} = \partial_n f \text{ on } \partial\Omega \setminus \partial\Omega_K \quad (15)$$

then we are in the correct setup and if (15) has a unique solution $\overline{u}$, then $u := \overline{u} + f$ will clearly be a unique solution of (14).

We now formulate a first result concerning the well-posedness of the inpainting problem with the Laplacian.

Proposition 1 (Well-posedness of the inpainting problem with the Laplacian). *If all assumptions from this paper are fulfilled, then image inpainting with the Laplacian, as modelled by (1), is well posed, except when $\Omega_K = \emptyset$.*

Proof. The proof follows immediately from Theorem 1. In the case of pure Dirich-let boundary conditions we obtain a unique solution in $H^1(\Omega \setminus \Omega_K)$. Since all requirements in Theorem 1 are met by (15), it follows that its solution is unique in $H^1_{\partial\Omega\setminus\partial\Omega_K}(\Omega \setminus \Omega_K)$ and thus, also our problem in (14) has a unique solu-tion. Only the case of pure homogeneous Neumann boundary and $\Omega_K = \emptyset$ must be considered separately. Clearly, in that case any constant function will be a solution, such that we cannot assert uniqueness and therefore neither well-posedness. □

We also remark, that it may happen that the reconstruction process decouples into several sub-problems and that each subproblem is of a different kind. If, for example, the set $\Omega \setminus \Omega_K$ consists of two disjoint regions, then each region can be addressed independently of the other one. These independent regions could require Neumann boundary conditions or not, depending on whether they are placed at the vicinity of $\partial\Omega$.

Mainberger et al. [17] and later also Hoeltgen et al. [12] introduced a slightly different but interesting formulation of the mixed boundary value problem in (1). Mainberger et al. introduced the confidence function c which states whether a point is known or not and which is defined by

$$c(x) := \begin{cases} 1, & x \in \Omega_K \\ 0, & x \in \Omega \setminus \Omega_K \end{cases} \tag{16}$$

The use of the confidence function allows us rewrite (14) in a more compact functional form given by

$$c(x)(u(x) - f(x)) + (1 - c(x))(-\Delta)u(x) = 0, \quad \text{on } \Omega$$
$$\partial_n u(x) = 0, \quad \text{on } \partial\Omega \tag{17}$$

Hoeltgen et al. [12] generalised this framework and allowed c to be real-valued. In the binary setting we can either use the diffusion or the data at a given point. If c is allowed to take arbitrary values in the range $[0, 1]$ we obtain combinations between $u - f$ and $-\Delta u$. Thus, we blend the information from the data term $u - f$ with the diffused data given by $-\Delta u$. These combinations are similar to convex combinations but differ in the fact that $c(x)$ may take different values in each x. This observation has been used in [12,14] to motivate an optimal control model to tune the locations Ω_K as well as the data $f(\Omega_K)$ for PDE based image compression tasks. The authors of the latter cited works did not discuss the existence or uniqueness of solutions of (17) for arbitrarily valued functions c. However, in [13] it was shown that the discrete version of (17) imposes an upper bound of $\frac{8}{7}$ on the values of c. Interestingly, this upper bound depends on the discretisation of the Laplacian. Different discretisations yield different upper bounds. The following paragraphs consider the problem from the continuous setting. It is our goal to state conditions on the existence of a solution in a continuous formulation, which are therefore independent of the discretisation.

We state a first immediate result which asserts existence of a strong solution for a particular case in the next proposition. In this context, $\overline{\Omega}$ denotes the closure of the set Ω and $C^{k,\alpha}(\overline{\Omega})$ denotes the space of all functions which have derivatives up to order k that are continuous on $\overline{\Omega}$ and with derivatives of order k being Hölder continuous with exponent α.

Theorem 2. *Let* $0 \leqslant c(x) < 1$ *hold for all* x *in* Ω *(i.e. no pure Dirichlet boundary data), then* (17) *has a unique solution in* $C^{2,\alpha}(\overline{\Omega})$.

Proof. We reorder the terms to obtain:

$$(1 - c(x)) \Delta u(x) - c(x) u(x) = -c(x) f(x), \quad on \ \Omega$$
$$\partial_n u(x) = 0, \qquad\qquad on \ \partial\Omega \tag{18}$$

Clearly, (18) *is uniformly strongly elliptic as long as* $c(x) < 1$ *for all* x *and bounded below. In combination with our regularity assumptions on* f *and* Ω *that we imposed in this paper, it follows from Theorem 1.2, in [7] that* (18) *has a unique solution in* $C^{2,\alpha}(\overline{\Omega})$. □

As already shown in [2,17], the choice of c also has a substantial influence on the solution and in [12] it was shown that c can efficiently be optimised for image reconstruction and compression purposes. For these tasks it was essential that c maps to $\mathbb{R}$ and not just to $\{0,1\}$ or $[0,1)$. An important equivalence result for the relationship between optimising c and tuning the corresponding data f along Ω_K was subsequently shown for discrete setups in [14]. In this context it is also interesting to wonder how values of c outside of the unit interval could be interpreted in the continuous setting. A good insight might yield valuable hints on the existence and regularity of corresponding solutions.

Let us now combine the idea of a non-binary valued confidence function c with the mixed boundary value problem given in (14). We consider:

$$c(x)(u(x) - f(x)) - (1 - c(x)) \Delta u(x) = 0, \text{on } \Omega \setminus \Omega_K$$
$$u = f, \text{ on } \Omega_K \quad \text{and} \quad \partial_n u(x) = 0, \text{ on } \partial\Omega \setminus \partial\Omega_K \tag{19}$$

Equation (19) indeed generalises the previous formulation as can be seen in the next proposition.

Proposition 2. *If we define* $\Omega_K := \{x \in \Omega \mid c(x) \equiv 1\}$, *then* (19) *is equivalent to* (17) *for non-binary valued* c *and equivalent to* (14) *for binary valued* c *with range* $\{0,1\}$.

Proof. Clearly, the major difference between (19) and previous formulations lies in the distinction between the regions where $c \equiv 1$ and $c \not\equiv 1$. Otherwise they are identical. □

The following proposition shows that the considered framework is also related to the Helmholtz equation.

Proposition 3. *If the confidence function* $c\colon \Omega \to \mathbb{R}$ *is continuous, then the inpainting equation from* (19) *can be rewritten as the following inhomogeneous mixed boundary value theorem.*

$$-\Delta u\left(x\right) + \eta\left(x\right) u\left(x\right) = g\left(x\right) \quad on \quad \Omega \setminus \Omega_K$$
$$u\left(x\right) = f\left(x\right) \quad on \quad \partial\Omega_K \quad and \quad \partial_n u\left(x\right) = 0 \quad on \quad \partial\Omega \setminus \partial\Omega_K \tag{20}$$

with a continuous function η *and* g.

Proof. *Due to the intermediate value theorem and the fact that the level sets where* $c \equiv 1$ *form closed contours around the regions where* $c\left(x\right) > 1$ *we can subdivide* $\Omega \setminus \Omega_K$ *into disjoint regions where* $c < 1$ *and where* $c > 1$. *Thus, the problem decouples and allows us to discuss these two cases independently. In each case, we can divide* (19) *by* $1 - c\left(x\right)$ *and obtain the following formulation*

$$-\Delta u\left(x\right) + \eta\left(x\right) u\left(x\right) = g\left(x\right) \quad on \quad \Omega \setminus \Omega_K$$
$$u\left(x\right) = f\left(x\right), \quad on \quad \Omega_K \quad and \quad \partial_n u\left(x\right) = 0 \quad on \quad \partial\Omega \setminus \partial\Omega_K \tag{21}$$

where $\eta\left(x\right) := \frac{c(x)}{1-c(x)}$ *and* $g\left(x\right) := \eta\left(x\right) f\left(x\right)$. *Since only the values along* $\partial\Omega_K$ *are relevant for the Dirichlet boundary conditions, the claim follows.* □

Let us also briefly remark that $0 \leqslant c\left(x\right) < 1$ implies $\eta\left(x\right) \geqslant 0$ and $c\left(x\right) > 1$ implies $\eta\left(x\right) < 0$ in (20). This detail will become important in the well-posedness analysis in the forthcoming paragraphs.

The representation from (20) has a significant advantage over the original formulation in (17). The fact that we are in presence of a Helmholtz equation allows us to apply all our knowledge about this famous equation. In addition, we note that the results from Sect. 2 are applicable for its analysis. The forthcoming paragraphs will now analyse the existence of solutions of (20).

Proposition 4. *The partial differential equation stated in* (20) *corresponds to the following weak formulation:*

$$\int_{\Omega\setminus\Omega_K} \nabla W \nabla \varphi + \eta W \varphi \mathrm{d}x = \int_{\Omega\setminus\Omega_K} \Delta f \varphi \mathrm{d}x - \int_{\partial\Omega\setminus\partial\Omega_K} \varphi \partial_n f \mathrm{d}S \tag{22}$$

which needs to be solved in the space V *defined as*

$$V := \left\{ \phi \in H^1(\Omega \setminus \Omega_K) \middle| \phi \middle|_{\partial\Omega_K} \equiv 0 \right\} \tag{23}$$

Proof. *We closely follow the presentation in [9, 10]. Assume* $w \in H^2(\Omega \setminus \Omega_K)$ *solves* (20). *In a first step we perform a lifting of the boundary conditions to handle the Dirichlet data. By assumption* f *is in* $H^2(\Omega \setminus \Omega_K)$, *too. It follows that* $W := w - f$ *has 0 trace along* $\partial\Omega_K$ *and* W *solves*

$$-\Delta W + \eta W = \overbrace{g - (-\Delta f + \eta f)}^{=\Delta f} \quad on \quad \Omega \setminus \Omega_K \tag{24}$$
$$W = 0 \quad on \quad \partial\Omega_K \quad and \quad \partial_n W = -\partial_n f \quad on \quad \partial\Omega \setminus \partial\Omega_K$$

Using Green's formula and test functions $\varphi \in V$ we obtain the following functional description for the lefthand side of (24):

$$\int_{\Omega \setminus \Omega_K} (-\Delta W + \eta W) \, \varphi \, \mathrm{d}x = \int_{\Omega \setminus \Omega_K} \nabla W \nabla \varphi \, \mathrm{d}x + \int_{\Omega \setminus \Omega_K} \eta W \varphi \mathrm{d}x$$

$$+ \int_{\partial\Omega \setminus \partial\Omega_K} \varphi \partial_n f \, \mathrm{d}S - \underbrace{\int_{\partial\Omega_K} \varphi \partial_n W \, \mathrm{d}S}_{=0} \quad (25)$$

where the integral over $\partial\Omega_K$ vanishes due to our choice of the test functions. Integrating the righthand side of (24) and assembling all terms into a single expression yields the following functional equation

$$\int_{\Omega \setminus \Omega_K} \nabla W \nabla \varphi + \eta W \varphi \, \mathrm{d}x = \int_{\Omega \setminus \Omega_K} \Delta f \varphi \, \mathrm{d}x - \int_{\partial\Omega \setminus \partial\Omega_K} \varphi \partial_n f \, \mathrm{d}S \quad (26)$$

The equivalence now follows immediately from Proposition 3.6 in [10].   □

Corollary 1. *Since f is assumed to be known on Ω, Green's identities yield for the boundary integral from the righthand side of (26):*

$$\int_{\partial\Omega \setminus \partial\Omega_K} \varphi \partial_n f \, \mathrm{d}S = \int_{\Omega} \varphi \Delta f + \nabla \varphi \nabla f \mathrm{d}x \quad (27)$$

Thus, (26) can be reformulated as

$$\int_{\Omega \setminus \Omega_K} \nabla W \nabla \varphi + \eta W \varphi \mathrm{d}x = - \int_{\Omega_K} \Delta f \varphi \, \mathrm{d}x - \int_{\Omega} \nabla \varphi \nabla f \mathrm{d}x \quad (28)$$

We remark that Theorem 1 would be applicable to show the well-posedness of a solution for the weak formulation in (22) if the Poincaré constant suffices $c_\Omega > 1$ and if our function c is bounded from below by $\frac{c_\Omega}{1-c_\Omega}$. Unfortunately this lower bound cannot be determined exactly and is counter-intuitive to what we know from discrete setups. Therefore, we provide an alternative approach to show well-posedness.

Theorem 3. *There exists a compact, self-adjoint, bounded, and linear operator $B : V \to V$ such that*

$$\langle Bu, \varphi \rangle = \int_{\Omega \setminus \Omega_K} -\eta u \varphi \mathrm{d}x \quad (29)$$

holds for all u and φ in V. If the real number 1 is not an eigenvalue of this operator, then our functional equation (22) is well-posed.

Proof. From (22) and (23) in Proposition 4 it follows that our variational equation has the shape

$$A(u, \varphi) = \ell(\varphi) \quad \forall \varphi \in V \quad (30)$$

where our bilinear operator A is given by

$$A(u, \varphi) = \int_{\Omega \setminus \Omega_K} \nabla u \nabla \varphi \, dx - \int_{\Omega \setminus \Omega_K} -\eta u \varphi \, dx \qquad (31)$$

The operator A is not necessarily coercive if $\eta < 0$. However, we remark that

$$\langle u, \varphi \rangle := \int_{\Omega \setminus \Omega_K} \nabla u \nabla \varphi \, dx \qquad (32)$$

is a scalar product on V. In addition, the Riesz representation theorem asserts the existence of a linear bounded operator $B: V \rightarrow V$ such that (29) holds. Since H^1 can be embedded compactly in L^2 it follows that B is a compact and self-adjoint (η is real-valued) operator. Therefore, we may write $A(u, \varphi) = \langle (I - B)u, \varphi \rangle$ and we obtain the variational equation $(I - B)u = \ell$. From the Fredholm alternative we can now deduce that the operator $I - B$ is invertible with bounded inverse if it is injective. The latter is true when 1 is not an eigenvalue of B. Since our operator is compact, it follows that its spectrum is countable. The probability that 1 is a eigenvalue is zero, i.e. for any $c(x)$ the problem is almost surely well-posed. □

4   Conclusions and Outlook

In this work we have analysed the most common formulations occurring in PDE-based image inpainting and compression. We have shown that these formulations are well-posed if certain mild conditions are fulfilled. Such well-posedness findings are well known on the discrete side and we have now complemented the corresponding results for the continuous formulations. We think that the well-posedness results in this work pave the way for additional insights into the synergy between data value optimisation in the co-domain and the data location optimisation in the domain. While there exist some results on this for the discrete side, there are almost none for the continuous framework. In addition, the stated findings might lift certain restrictions on corresponding discrete formulations. If the continuous formulations are well-posed for almost arbitrary values of c, then this fact should carry over to discrete settings, too.

In the future we would like to use the findings from this work to analyse the well-posedness of variational settings, such as the optimal control model in [12] for which, so far, no complete analysis on the existence, uniqueness, and regularity of solutions exists. Variational models like the one in [12] use the Laplace equation as a side constraint. The results from this work yield conditions that assert that the set of feasible solutions is never empty.

References

1. Azzam, A., Kreyszig, E.: On solutions of elliptic equations satisfying mixed boundary conditions. SIAM J. Math. Anal. **13**(2), 254–262 (1982)

2. Belhachmi, Z., Bucur, D., Burgeth, B., Weickert, J.: How to choose interpolation data in images. SIAM J. Appl. Math. **70**(1), 333–352 (2009)
3. Bertalmio, M., Bertozzi, A., Sapiro, G.: Navier-stokes, fluid dynamics, and image and video inpainting. In: Proceedings of the 2001 IEEE Computer Society Conference on Computer Vision and Pattern Recognition, vol. 1, pp. 355–362. IEEE (2001)
4. Bertalmío, M., Caselles, V., Haro, G., Sapiro, G.: PDE-based image and surface inpainting. In: Paragios, N., Chen, Y., Faugeras, O. (eds.) Handbook of Mathematical Models in Computer Vision, pp. 33–61. Springer, Heidelberg (2006). doi:10.1007/0-387-28831-7_3
5. Bertalmío, M., Sapiro, G., Caselles, V., Ballester, C.: Image inpainting. In: Proceedings of the 27th Annual Conference on Computer Graphics and Interactive Techniques, pp. 417–424. ACM Press/Addison-Wesley Publishing Company (2000)
6. Bertozzi, A., Esedoglu, S., Gillette, A.: Inpainting of binary images using the Cahn-Hilliard equation. IEEE Trans. Image Proc. **16**(1), 285–291 (2007)
7. Cantrell, R.S., Cosner, C.: Spatial Ecology via Reaction-Diffusion Equations. Wiley Series in Mathematical and Computational Biology. Wiley, Hoboken (2003)
8. Chen, Y., Ranftl, R., Pock, T.: A bi-level view of inpainting-based image compression. ArXiv Report arXiv:1401.4112 (2014)
9. Dret, H.L., Lucquin, B.: Partial Differential Equations: Modeling, Analysis and Numerical Approximation. Birkhäuser, Basel (2016)
10. Ern, A., Guermond, J.L.: Theory and Practice of Finite Elements. Springer, Heidelberg (2004)
11. Galić, I., Weickert, J., Welk, M., Bruhn, A., Belyaev, A., Seidel, H.-P.: Towards PDE-based image compression. In: Paragios, N., Faugeras, O., Chan, T., Schnörr, C. (eds.) VLSM 2005. LNCS, vol. 3752, pp. 37–48. Springer, Heidelberg (2005). doi:10.1007/11567646_4
12. Hoeltgen, L., Setzer, S., Weickert, J.: An optimal control approach to find sparse data for laplace interpolation. In: Heyden, A., Kahl, F., Olsson, C., Oskarsson, M., Tai, X.-C. (eds.) EMMCVPR 2013. LNCS, vol. 8081, pp. 151–164. Springer, Heidelberg (2013). doi:10.1007/978-3-642-40395-8_12
13. Hoeltgen, L.: Optimal interpolation data for image reconstructions. Ph.D. thesis, Saarland University (2014)
14. Hoeltgen, L., Weickert, J.: Why does non-binary mask optimisation work for diffusion-based image compression? In: Tai, X.-C., Bae, E., Chan, T.F., Lysaker, M. (eds.) EMMCVPR 2015. LNCS, vol. 8932, pp. 85–98. Springer, Cham (2015). doi:10.1007/978-3-319-14612-6_7
15. Li, Y., Jeong, D., Choi, J., Lee, S., Kim, J.: Fast local image inpainting based on the Allen-Cahn model. Digit. Sig. Process. **37**, 65–74 (2015)
16. Mainberger, M., Bruhn, A., Weickert, J., Forchhammer, S.: Edge-based compression of cartoon-like images with homogeneous diffusion. Pattern Recogn. **44**(9), 1859–1873 (2011)
17. Mainberger, M., Hoffmann, S., Weickert, J., Tang, C.H., Johannsen, D., Neumann, F., Doerr, B.: Optimising spatial and tonal data for homogeneous diffusion inpainting. In: Bruckstein, A.M., Haar Romeny, B.M., Bronstein, A.M., Bronstein, M.M. (eds.) SSVM 2011. LNCS, vol. 6667, pp. 26–37. Springer, Heidelberg (2012). doi:10.1007/978-3-642-24785-9_3
18. Peter, P., Hoffmann, S., Nedwed, F., Hoeltgen, L., Weickert, J.: Evaluating the true potential of diffusion-based inpainting in a compression context. Sig. Process.: Image Commun. **46**, 40–53 (2016)

19. Schmaltz, C., Weickert, J., Bruhn, A.: Beating the quality of JPEG 2000 with anisotropic diffusion. In: Denzler, J., Notni, G., Süße, H. (eds.) DAGM 2009. LNCS, vol. 5748, pp. 452–461. Springer, Heidelberg (2009). doi:10.1007/978-3-642-03798-6_46
20. Schönlieb, C.B.: Partial Differential Equation Methods for Image Inpainting, Cambridge Monographs on Applied and Computational Mathematics, vol. 29. Cambridge University Press, Cambridge (2015)
21. Tang, C.: Mixed boundary value problems for quasilinear elliptic equations. Ph.D. thesis, Iowa State University (2013)
22. Zaremba, S.: Sur un probléme mixte relatif à l'équation de Laplace. Bulletin International de l'Académie des Sciences de Cracovie, pp. 313–344 (1910)

Combining Contrast Invariant L1 Data Fidelities with Nonlinear Spectral Image Decomposition

Leonie Zeune[1,2]([✉]), Stephan A. van Gils[1], Leon W.M.M. Terstappen[2],
and Christoph Brune[1]

[1] Department of Applied Mathematics, University of Twente, 7522 NB Enschede,
The Netherlands
{l.l.zeune,s.a.vangils,c.brune}@utwente.nl
[2] Department of Medical Cell BioPhysics, University of Twente,
7522 NB Enschede, The Netherlands
l.w.m.m.terstappen@utwente.nl

Abstract. This paper focuses on multi-scale approaches for variational methods and corresponding gradient flows. Recently, for convex regularization functionals such as total variation, new theory and algorithms for nonlinear eigenvalue problems via nonlinear spectral decompositions have been developed. Those methods open new directions for advanced image filtering. However, for an effective use in image segmentation and shape decomposition, a clear interpretation of the spectral response regarding size and intensity scales is needed but lacking in current approaches. In this context, L^1 data fidelities are particularly helpful due to their interesting multi-scale properties such as contrast invariance. Hence, the novelty of this work is the combination of L^1-based multi-scale methods with nonlinear spectral decompositions. We compare L^1 with L^2 scale-space methods in view of spectral image representation and decomposition. We show that the contrast invariant multi-scale behavior of $L^1 - TV$ promotes sparsity in the spectral response providing more informative decompositions. We provide a numerical method and analyze synthetic and biomedical images at which decomposition leads to improved segmentation.

Keywords: L^1-TV · Denoising · Scale-spaces · Nonlinear spectral decomposition · Multiscale segmentation · Eigenfunctions · Calibrable sets

1 Introduction

In imaging science, the solution of inverse problems is often addressed by the modeling and analysis of variational methods of the form:

$$\min_u \; \frac{1}{p} \, \|u - f\|^p_{L^p} + \alpha J(u) \tag{1}$$

where f denotes a noisy signal, u is a desired image function defined on Ω in $\mathbb{R}^2$. The data fidelity measures the residual in the L^p norm and J is a regularization

© Springer International Publishing AG 2017
F. Lauze et al. (Eds.): SSVM 2017, LNCS 10302, pp. 80–93, 2017.
DOI: 10.1007/978-3-319-58771-4_7

functional that has a weighting parameter $\alpha \geq 0$. In this paper, we concentrate on image denoising methods with convex and one-homogeneous regularization functionals J which can address image decomposition and segmentation adequately. More specifically, we focus on total variation regularization $J(u) = TV(u)$ and norms with $p = 1$ versus $p = 2$. One option to generate a scale-space method is a gradient flow, based on the functional (1) with initial condition $u(0, x) = f(x)$ and subdifferential inclusions forming the doubly nonlinear evolution equation:

$$0 \in \partial \|\partial_t u(t, x)\|_{L^p} + \partial J(u(t, x)). \qquad (2)$$

In the case of $p = 2$, this simplifies to well-known gradient flows of the form:

$$\partial_t u = -q(u) \quad \text{with } q \in \partial J(u). \qquad (3)$$

The regularization parameter α is now hidden in the time dependency. Corresponding inverse scale space gradient flows can be constructed via Bregman distances [1,2]. The analysis of linear eigenvalue problems and spectral decompositions, e.g. via the Fourier transform, is a well-known and widely used theory in the fields of signal, image and graph-based data processing. Due to the continuing success of nonlinear regularization functionals in imaging, there is strong interest in generalizing spectral theory to the nonlinear case. The general idea is to examine solutions to the nonlinear eigenvalue problem:

$$\lambda u \in \partial J(u). \qquad (4)$$

In [3,4], Gilboa introduced the idea of nonlinear spectral decompositions for the TV transform. By transferring solutions (eigenfunctions) of (4) to sparse peaks in a spectral domain, the idea of advanced filters, suppressing or enhancing image components similar to the Fourier transform, came about. This concept was studied for one-homogenous functionals [5–7] and scale-space flows of the form (3) with $p = 2$. In this way, a decomposition of the input signal f into significant components is possible while an exact representation of f can still be guaranteed.

For $p = 1$, the gradient flow in (2) is interesting and more challenging than for $p = 2$. Another way to obtain a forward scale-space is to construct a sequence of variational problems of the form (1) with increasing regularization parameter t_α replacing the fixed α. Here, the scale parameter t_α corresponds to the time variable t used in (2). In this paper, we will focus on this type of model particularly in view of $p = 1$. From pioneering works on nonlinear L^1 filtering [8 11], it is well known that such variational reconstruction methods share interesting multi-scale properties including contrast invariance. For this reason, L^1 data fidelities have been successfully used for advanced image reconstruction techniques [12–14], vector field estimation [15] and image decompositions regarding texture [10,16]. The special multi-scale behavior becomes clear in Fig. 1. In the $L^1 - TV$ case shown on the right, the contrast invariance leads to plateaus in the scale-space graph indicating an abrupt disappearance of TV-eigenshapes regarding the input image on the left.

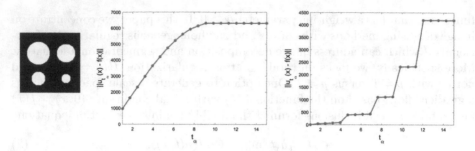

Fig. 1. *Scale-spaces.* (left) Input image f, (middle) $L^2 - TV$, (right) $L^1 - TV$.

Motivated by [9,11,17] and nonlinear spectral methods [7,18], the main goal of this work is to study L^1 versus L^2 in view of the sparsity of nonlinear spectral decompositions. Does L^1 imply sparsity and hence a more *informative spectral response*? Can we expect more *reliable image decompositions* via backtransformation facilitating improved image segmentation? What happens if complex shapes, e.g. nonconvex or *compositions of eigenfunctions*, are involved?

2   Modeling

In the following section we first give a short overview of the eigenshapes of the total variation functional and calibrable sets before we introduce the spectral framework for $L^2 - TV$ denoising in more detail. Finally, we show why a combination of the spectral framework with $L^1 - TV$ denoising seems promising and how the spectral framework can be adapted in this case.

2.1   Geometry: Eigenfunctions and Calibrable Sets

In the introduction in Fig. 1 we have already seen an input image composed of TV eigenfunctions. A general geometric description of TV eigenfunctions is given in [19–21] in terms of calibrable sets, more precisely by convex sets which are Cheeger in themself. An indicator function $\chi_C(x)$ of a convex and connected set C with finite perimeter $Per(C)$, for which C admits

$$\operatorname*{ess\,sup}_{x \in \partial C} \kappa_C(x) \leq \frac{Per(C)}{|C|} \qquad (C \text{ is Cheeger in itself})$$

where $|C|$ denotes the area and κ_C the curvature of $\partial C \in C^{1,1}$, is a solution of (4) with unit norm and therefore an eigenfunction of TV. With this geometric interpretation of eigenfunctions for TV as Cheeger sets, the role of perimeter and volume is significant for contrast invariant image decompositions. In the convex case, Duval and collaborators [17] proved that exact solutions of the $L^1 - TV$ problem are given by an morphological opening followed by a simple test over the perimeter-area ratio. This fact was first published but not proved in [22]. For more complex shapes, formed by compositions of eigenfunctions, a better understanding of the L^1 scale-space flows is therefore a very promising direction.

2.2 $L^2 - TV$ Based Spectral Analysis

The nonlinear spectral analysis framework was first introduced by Gilboa in [3,4] for the total variation regularization functional. A forward scale-space was constructed via the TV flow (3). Here, the first iterate is the original data f which is then smoothed in every time-step such that increasingly fine scales are removed. This concept was later generalized to more general one-homogenous regularization functionals $J(u)$ in [5–7]. Moreover, it was shown that the forward scale-space can also be constructed via a variational approach by iteratively solving the ROF model (1) for $p = 2$ and $J(u) = TV(u)$ using increasing regularization parameters t_α. The idea of the spectral filtering approach is to transform the signal f into a spectral domain, where both filtering of certain scales and decomposition of f into significant signals is possible. Thus, eigenfunctions will be mapped onto a peak in the spectral domain. The shape of the eigenfunction is determined by the chosen regularization functional, for $J(u) = TV(u)$ the most prominent eigenfunction is a disc with radius r surrounding the origin. In [23], Strong and Chan analyzed how the solution of the ROF model behaves for increasing t_α if f is an eigenfunction. Thus, let $f(x) = c \cdot \mathbb{1}_{B_r(0)}(x)$ be a disc of constant height c and radius r surrounding the origin and with a background of zero. Then the solution of the $L^2 - TV$ model is given as:

$$u(t_\alpha, x) = \begin{cases} \left(c - \frac{2}{r} t_\alpha\right) \cdot \mathbb{1}_{B_r(0)}(x) & \text{if } 0 \le t_\alpha < \frac{cr}{2} \\ 0 & \text{otherwise.} \end{cases} \tag{5}$$

That means that even in the noise-free case, the reconstructed solution $u(t_\alpha, x)$ never reaches the true value f and for increasing regularization parameter t_α the disc height decreases. Solutions are corrupted by a systematic contrast loss that is dependent on the regularization strength but also on the radius r and the height c of input data f. To transform such eigenfunctions to a peak in the spectral domain, Gilboa defined the spectral transform function $\phi(t, x)$ and the spectral response function $S(t)$ as:

$$\phi(t, x) = u_{tt}(t, x) \cdot t \quad \text{and} \quad S(t) = \|\phi(t, x)\|_{L^1}. \tag{6}$$

The definition of ϕ allows, under certain conditions, that the original signal f can be reconstructed via:

$$f(x) = \int_0^\infty \phi(t, x) dt + \bar{f}$$

where $\bar{f}$ is the mean of f. Filtered versions of f can be constructed by applying:

$$f_H(x) = \int_0^\infty H(t)\phi(t, x) dt + H(\infty)\bar{f}$$

where $H(t)$ is the filter function.

However, a disadvantage of the L^2 based spectral framework is ambiguity with respect to size and intensity scales. The method is not able to clearly differentiate size and intensity scales since the timepoint t_d at which a disc disappears and a peak occurs is determined by both values together.

2.3 $L^1 - TV$ Based Spectral Analysis

In the following section we want to combine the idea of nonlinear spectral TV analysis with the L^1 denoising model:

$$\min_u \ \|u - f\|_{L^1} + t_\alpha TV(u). \tag{7}$$

As mentioned earlier, this model shows very interesting multi-scale decomposition behavior and seems therefore very suitable to be combined with the spectral approach. In [9], Chan and Esedoglu showed that the behavior of solutions of the $L^1 - TV$ model if f is the TV eigenfunction $f(x) = c \cdot \mathbb{1}_{B_r(0)}(x)$ is significantly different from the L^2 case. Here, the solution is given by:

$$u(t_\alpha, x) = \begin{cases} f & \text{if } 0 \le t_\alpha < \frac{r}{2} \\ c' \cdot f \text{ with } c' \in [0,1] & \text{if } t_\alpha = \frac{r}{2} \\ 0 & \text{otherwise.} \end{cases} \tag{8}$$

An interesting observation is that the solution $u(t_\alpha, x)$ is **not** dependent on the height c of the disc but only on the radius r. That means that the $L^1 - TV$ denoising approach is contrast-invariant and therefore highly suitable for decomposing a signal f based on size scales. Note that the solution of (7) is not unique; for f defined as above and $t_\alpha = \frac{r}{2}$ there exist, for example, an infinite number of solutions.

Since the gradient flow (2) is more challenging for $p = 1$ rather than $p = 2$ (due to non-smoothness of the data-term), we construct a forward scale-space by taking a variational approach; in other words, we solve (7) for increasing regularization parameters $t_{\alpha_1} < t_{\alpha_2} < \ldots < t_{\alpha_N}$. To transform an eigenfunction of $TV(u)$ onto a peak in the spectral domain, a suitable spectral transformation function is now given by:

$$\phi(t, x) = -u_t(t, x) \text{ fulfilling } f(x) = \int_0^\infty \phi(t, x) dt + \hat{c}. \tag{9}$$

Here, the first time derivative of $u(t, x)$ is in a distributional sense and the constant $\hat{c}$ is the median of f. Since the disc's height does not decrease in every time step but remains the constant c until it immediately decreases to 0, already the first time-derivative leads to a delta peak in the spectral transform function defined via:

$$S^2(t) = \langle \phi(t, x), f(x) \rangle. \tag{10}$$

This definition was first introduced by Burger and collaborators in [6] and leads to an analogue to Parseval's identity:

$$\|f\|^2 = \langle f, f \rangle = \int_0^\infty \langle \phi(t, x), f(x) \rangle \mathrm{dt} = \int_0^\infty S^2(t) \mathrm{dt}. \tag{11}$$

The signal can be filtered based on size via:

$$f_H(x) = \int_0^\infty H(t)\phi(t, x)dt + H(\infty)\hat{c} \tag{12}$$

where $H(t)$ is again the filter function. A segmentation of objects in a certain size range (nearly independent of their intensity; only objects with intensity $\hat{c}$ cannot be found) is given by:

$$f_{\mathrm{seg},H}(x) = \left(\int_0^\infty H(t)\phi(t, x)dt > 0 \right). \tag{13}$$

Applications where this intensity-independent segmentation approach is especially helpful are described in Sect. 4.

3 Numerical Approach

The following section introduces the numerical realization of the spectral L^1-TV framework presented previously. The main component is the numerical solution of the denoising problem. To find solutions of this purely primal nonlinear minimization problem (7), we make use of the first order primal dual algorithm proposed by Chambolle and Pock [24]. As the name already suggest, the minimization scheme works with a primal dual version of (7) given by:

$$\langle \nabla u, g \rangle + \|u - f\|_{L^1} - t_\alpha \delta_P(g) \longrightarrow \min_u \max_g \tag{14}$$

where $P = \{g : \|g\|_\infty \le 1\}$ and $\delta_P(g)$ equals 0 if $g \in P$, and equals ∞ if $g \notin P$. We define $K(u) = \nabla u$, $F(u) = \|u\|_{L^1}$ and $G(u) = \|u - f\|_{L^1}$. The minimization algorithm proposed by Chambolle and Pock consists of three update steps: the first step is a dual update using the resolvent operator of F^* and the second is a primal update using the resolvent operator of G. These are followed by a simple weighting step between the previous two primal iterates. See [24] for more details. The resolvent operators for G and F^* are presented in [24, Chap. 6.2]. To construct a forward scale space, we solve the $L^1 - TV$ denoising model with increasing regularization parameter $t_{\alpha_1} < t_{\alpha_2} < \ldots < t_{\alpha_N}$ and compute the spectral transform function $\phi(t, x)$ via backward-differences and the response function $S(t)$ based on these solutions. Both the resulting primal-dual algorithm to minimize (7) and the computation of the spectral functions are embodied in Algorithm 1. Note that to receive a very high degree of convergence we needed a very large number of iterations resulting in a long computational time. With fewer iterations, the algorithm did not converge completely and eigenfunctions lost contrast altough, according to (8), this should not be the case.

Algorithm 1. First-order primal-dual algorithm to solve (7).

Parameters: data f, reg. param. $0 < t_{\alpha_1} < t_{\alpha_2} < ... < t_{\alpha_N}$, $\tau, \sigma > 0$,
　　　　$\theta \in [0, 1]$, $maxIts \in \mathbb{N}$

Initialization: $n = 0$, $u^0 = 0$, $p_0 := 0$, $\bar{u}^0 = u^0$

Iteration:

for $(i = 1 : N)$ **do**
　1. Set $\alpha = t_{\alpha_i}$.

　　while $(n < maxIts)$ **do**
　　a) $g^{n+1} = \text{Proj}_{\{\{g : \|g\|_\infty \leq 1\}\}}(g^n + \sigma \nabla \bar{u}^n)$.

　　b) $\arg_u = u^n + \tau \nabla \cdot g$.

　　c) $u^{n+1}(x) = \begin{cases} \arg_u(x) - \frac{\tau}{\alpha} & \text{if} & \arg_u(x) - f(x) > \frac{\tau}{\alpha} \\ \arg_u(x) + \frac{\tau}{\alpha} & \text{if} & \arg_u(x) - f(x) < -\frac{\tau}{\alpha} \\ f(x) & \text{if} & |\arg_u(x) - f(x)| < \frac{\tau}{\alpha} \end{cases}$.

　　d) $\bar{u}^{n+1} = u^{n+1} + \theta(u^{n+1} - u^n)$.

　　e) Set $n = n + 1$.

　　end while

　2. Set $u(t_{\alpha_i}, x) = u^n$.

　3. Set $\phi(t_{\alpha_i}, x) = u(t_{\alpha_{i-1}}, x) - u(t_{\alpha_i}, x)$.

　4. Set $S(t_{\alpha_i}) = \langle \phi(t_{\alpha_i}, x), f(x) \rangle$.

end for

return $u(t_{\alpha_1}, x), ..., u(t_{\alpha_N}, x)$, ϕ, S.

4　Results

In this section, we describe the main properties and advantages of the $L^1 - TV$ based spectral approach introduced above. We discuss both several synthetic experiments and real experiments from biological cell imaging and retina imaging. For some examples, the results are compared to results from the L^2 based spectral framework to illustrate the differences between both models. For all results, we applied the framework summarized in Algorithm 1 and cluster the spectral response function afterwards. In our experiments, we set $\tau = 0.2, \sigma = 0.625, \theta = 1$ and $maxIts = 50.000$. For synthetic datasets we used $N = 20$ linearly spaced t_{α_i} and increased N to 50 for the experimental datsets. After solving the variational model with increasing regularization parameter, we manually clustered S but comparable results can be achieved with common histogram thresholding methods such as Otsu's method, the Triangle method or methods designed for more than two classes. The different classes in the histogram are always visualized by different colors. Reconstruction of the filtered signal was performed via (12) where $H(t)$ was defined as an indicator function of the filtered time interval and the resulting signal was color-coded with the same color as in the spectral response and multiplied with the original gray values so that intensity changes in the input signal remain detectable.

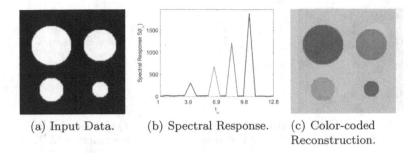

(a) Input Data.   (b) Spectral Response.   (c) Color-coded
                                                    Reconstruction.

Fig. 2. *Detection of size scales for eigenfunctions with constant intensity.* (a) Shows the original input data, (b) the resulting spectral response function of the forward $L^1 - TV$ denoising approach. Every peak in S corresponds to one disc. The color-coded reconstruction is shown in (c). (Color figure online)

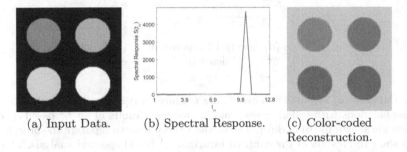

(a) Input Data.   (b) Spectral Response.   (c) Color-coded
                                                    Reconstruction.

Fig. 3. *Invariance w.r.t. to intensity scales.* (a) Shows the input data consisting of four TV eigenfunctions of similar size but various intensities. The corresponding spectral response is shown in (b). All discs vanish at the same moment, independent of their contrast. (c) The reconstruction of the peak is shown in red. (Color figure online)

Detection of Varying Eigenshapes: Size versus intensity. In this set of experiments, we focus on circular objects that are all eigenfunction of the total variation functional. The aim of these experiments is to investigate which scales can be detected and reconstructed using our method and where the differences to an L^2 based approach are. Figure 2 shows an example with four discs in front of a uniform background, all showing the same intensity level. The corresponding spectral response function (b) clearly shows the four peaks each corresponding to one disc, as can be seen in the color-coded reconstruction in (c). Since L^1 is a purely size-based approach, it decomposes these eigenfunctions clearly. The opposite case is shown in Fig. 3. Here, the input data is again composed of four discs but now with only one size and various intensity levels. Although an L^2 based approach would again show four peaks in the spectral response function due to its size/intensity ambiguity mentioned previously, we now see only one peak in the response (b). Filtering only the signal belonging to this red peak returns all four discs; see (c). This example clearly shows the contrast invariance of the L^1 data fidelity term which is a major difference between $p = 2$ and $p = 1$.

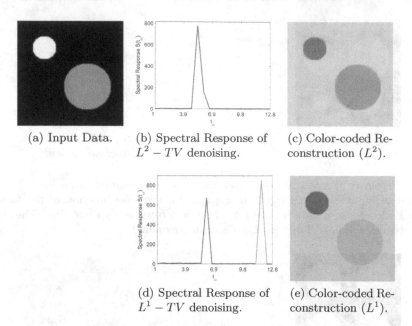

(a) Input Data.

(b) Spectral Response of $L^2 - TV$ denoising.

(c) Color-coded Reconstruction (L^2).

(d) Spectral Response of $L^1 - TV$ denoising.

(e) Color-coded Reconstruction (L^1).

Fig. 4. *Detection of size and intensity scale mixtures.* (a) Shows the input data with two eigenfunctions with differing sizes and intensities. Results of an L^2 based spectral approach are shown in (b) and (c). The method is not able to separate the objects. (d) and (e) show the results of the contrast invariant L^1 based spectral analysis. The two discs are clearly separable based on size. (Color figure online)

A direct comparison of both spectral frameworks is shown in Figs. 4 and 5. Figure 4 shows as input data (a) two discs with different sizes and intensities. From a visual perspective, this would be clearly identified as two different scales but the $L^2 - TV$ denoising approach is not able to distinguish between the objects. The scale that this approach uses is always a mixture of the size scale (small for the disc on top and large for the other one) with the intensity scale (large for the one on top and small for the second disc) and therefore it can occur that they both end up with the same "medium" scale. In the spectral domain, they are represented by one peak (b) and can therefore not be reconstructed separately. However, this is different for the contrast invariant $L^1 - TV$ approach since it is purely size based. The spectral response function shows two easily separable peaks (d) that can be reconstructed one by one (e). A similar behavior can be seen for two discs on top of each other (see Fig. 5(a)). Although these two discs are represented by two separate peaks in both approaches, the L^2 based approach mixes them if they are on top of each other. In this case, the peaks become less sparse and apart from each other (b) and in the reconstruction of the small scales (c) we see some artifacts of the larger disc (bluish ring around red disc). This is not the case for L^1. Both peaks are clearly separable (e) and the reconstruction gives a clear separation of both discs. The larger red circle in (f) is just a discretization artifact.

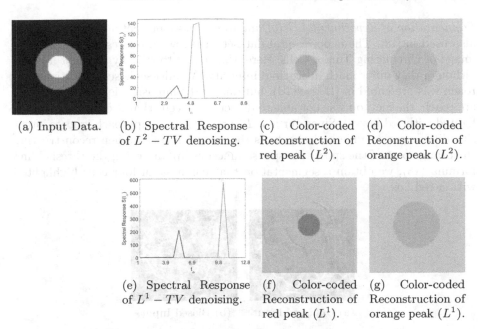

(a) Input Data.   (b) Spectral Response   (c) Color-coded   (d) Color-coded
of $L^2 - TV$ denoising.   Reconstruction of   Reconstruction of
red peak (L^2).   orange peak (L^2).

(e) Spectral Response   (f) Color-coded   (g) Color-coded
of $L^1 - TV$ denoising.   Reconstruction of   Reconstruction of
red peak (L^1).   orange peak (L^1).

Fig. 5. *Overlapping mixtures of size and intensity scales.* (a) Shows the input data with two discs with different size and intensity on top of each other. (b)–(d) shows the spectral response and the reconstructions of both peaks using an L^2 dataterm and (e)–(g) for an L^1 dataterm. In (c) we see artifacts of the larger disc already appearing at the fine scales while (f) and (g) clearly separate the two discs. (Color figure online)

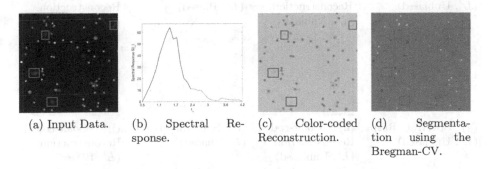

(a) Input Data.   (b) Spectral Re-   (c) Color-coded   (d) Segmenta-
sponse.   Reconstruction.   tion using the
Bregman-CV.

Fig. 6. *Segmentation of cells of multiple sizes and intensities.* (a) Shows an experimental dataset of tumor cells under a fluorescent microscope; (b) the resulting spectral response function; and (c) the color-coded reconstruction. A segmentation result taken from [18] is given in (d). Wee see that both methods can be used to obtain a multi-scale segmentation but very dim objects (red boxes) might be lost when taking an intensity based approach as in (d). In taking our purely size-based approach the dim cells are also found. (Color figure online)

Segmentation of Experimental Cell Data. In Fig. 6, we present a dataset that was
also used in [18]. The experimental dataset (a) shows a fluorescent microscopy
image of Circulating Tumor Cells. Here, the goal is to reliably segment all cells
although they differ much in size and intensity. A multi-scale segmentation approach was presented in [18], see (d), but due to the intensity dependency of this
approach, the method was not able to detect those cells that are very dim (highlighted with red boxes). Since our new L^1 based spectral approach ignores intensity differences, the method also finds the very dim cells. When reconstructing
the orange part of the spectral response function (b) and using the thresholding
formula (13), we obtain a segmentation that contains all four cells highlighted
with a red box.

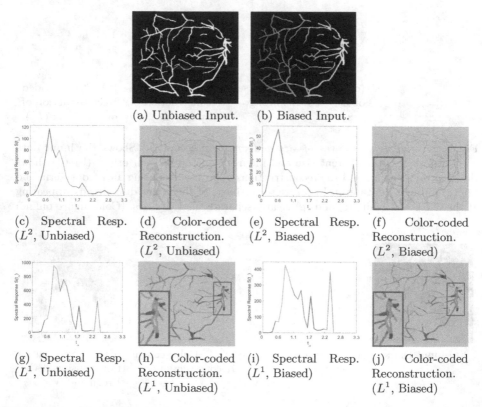

(a) Unbiased Input.   (b) Biased Input.

(c) Spectral Resp. (L^2, Unbiased)   (d) Color-coded Reconstruction. (L^2, Unbiased)   (e) Spectral Resp. (L^2, Biased)   (f) Color-coded Reconstruction. (L^2, Biased)

(g) Spectral Resp. (L^1, Unbiased)   (h) Color-coded Reconstruction. (L^1, Unbiased)   (i) Spectral Resp. (L^1, Biased)   (j) Color-coded Reconstruction. (L^1, Biased)

Fig. 7. *Decomposition of network structures without and with intensity bias.* (a) Shows
the binary input network of blood vessel [25] and (b) the same network with an intensity bias. (c)–(f) show spectral response and reconstruction results using L^2 and the
unbiased (c)–(d) resp. biased data (e)–(f). In (g)–(j), the results with L^1 are presented.
Reconstructions (d) and (f) appear very dim since vessels are not removed in one step
but are reshaped over time, resulting in a mix of (colored) scales. This is more clear in
the magnification. The turquoise part in (d) and (f) is no longer vessel-shaped but more
a roundish shadow around the original shape while the structure remains unchanged
for L^1 based reconstruction (h) and (j). This network structure is also not affected by
an intensity bias. (Color figure online)

Experimental Data of Network Structures. In Fig. 7(a), a manually segmented blood vessel network taken from the STARE dataset [25] is shown. A problem often occurring in retinal blood vessel segmentation is that small vessels are also very dim and therefore even more challenging to detect. In (b), we added an intensity bias to the original data to test whether this influences our segmentation/clustering approach or not. In (c)–(f), the spectral response functions and reconstructions for L^2 denoising are shown. We see that there are fewer clear peaks in the spectral response function, especially in the case of intensity biased input. Another problem that we observe is that the vessels are not removed while retaining their original shape but are reshaped to more circular objects. This leads to a mixing of all scales in the reconstruction and the dim appearance of the visualization. For L^1 based denoising, the spectral responses are much sparser in (h) and (j) and therefore easier to cluster. The reconstructions (g) and (j) are also much easier to interpret since the vessels are not reshaped but removed in one step based on their diameter. Thus, for both networks (even for the one with an intensity bias) we see a clear clustering of blood vessels based on size. The difference between both methods is clearly shown in the magnified box. While in the top row the largest scale is just a turquoise shadow around the thickest blood vessels, the blood vessel is clearly reconstructed in the bottom row.

5   Conclusion and Outlook

In this paper, we have described the study of contrast-invariant L^1 data fidelities for variational multi-scale methods in combination with nonlinear spectral image analysis. We have shown that the contrast invariance results in an improved sparsity of spectral responses. In comparison to standard L^2, this allows a more informative spectral image representation to be obtained. We presented a model, an efficient algorithm and numerical results. In the particular case of experimental data sets that have complex shapes and strong intensity variations of objects or the background, our method outperforms the current standard method for nonlinear spectral decomposition. For future studies, it will be important to extend the ideas to nonlocal graph-based problems such as L^1 with nonlocal TV, and further analyze the relationship of the doubly nonlinear scale-space flow to the proposed scale-space procedure.

Acknowledgements. LZ, LT, CB acknowledge support by the EUFP7 program #305341 CTCTrap and the IMI EU program #115749 CANCER-ID. CB acknowledges support for his TT position by the NWO via Veni grant 613.009.032 within the NDNS+ cluster.

References

1. Osher, S., Burger, M., Goldfarb, D., Xu, J., Yin, W.: An iterative regularization method for total variation-based image restoration. Multiscale Model. Simul. 4(2), 460–489 (2005)

2. Brune, C., Sawatzky, A., Burger, M.: Primal and dual Bregman methods with application to optical nanoscopy. Int. J. Comput. Vis. **92**(2), 211–229 (2011)
3. Gilboa, G.: A spectral approach to total variation. In: Kuijper, A., Bredies, K., Pock, T., Bischof, H. (eds.) SSVM 2013. LNCS, vol. 7893, pp. 36–47. Springer, Heidelberg (2013). doi:10.1007/978-3-642-38267-3_4
4. Gilboa, G.: A total variation spectral framework for scale and texture analysis. SIAM J. Imaging Sci. **7**(4), 1937–1961 (2014)
5. Burger, M., Eckardt, L., Gilboa, G., Moeller, M.: Spectral representations of one-homogeneous functionals. In: Aujol, J.-F., Nikolova, M., Papadakis, N. (eds.) SSVM 2015. LNCS, vol. 9087, pp. 16–27. Springer, Cham (2015). doi:10.1007/978-3-319-18461-6_2
6. Burger, M., Gilboa, G., Moeller, M., Eckardt, L., Cremers, D.: Spectral decompositions using one-homogeneous functionals. SIAM J. Imaging Sci. **9**(3), 1374–1408 (2016)
7. Gilboa, G., Moeller, M., Burger, M.: Nonlinear spectral analysis via one-homogeneous functionals: overview and future prospects. J. Math. Imaging Vis. **56**(2), 300–319 (2016)
8. Nikolova, M.: Minimizers of cost-functions involving nonsmooth data-fidelity terms. Application to the processing of outliers. SIAM J. Numer. Anal. **40**(3), 965–994 (2002)
9. Chan, T.F., Esedoglu, S.: Aspects of total variation regularized L^1 function approximation. SIAM J. Appl. Math. **65**(5), 1817–1837 (2005)
10. Aujol, J.F., Gilboa, G., Chan, T., Osher, S.: Structure-texture image decomposition-modeling, algorithms, and parameter selection. Int. J. Comput. Vis. **67**(1), 111–136 (2006)
11. Yin, W., Goldfarb, D., Osher, S.: The total variation regularized L^1 model for multiscale decomposition. Multiscale Model. Simul. **6**(1), 190–211 (2007)
12. Dong, Y., Hintermüller, M., Neri, M.: An efficient primal-dual method for L^1TV image restoration. SIAM J. Imaging Sci. **2**(4), 1168–1189 (2009)
13. Wu, C., Zhang, J., Tai, X.C.: Augmented Lagrangian method for total variation restoration with non-quadratic fidelity. Inverse Probl. Imaging **5**(1), 237–261 (2011)
14. Yuan, J., Shi, J., Tai, X.C.: A convex and exact approach to discrete constrained TV- L^1 image approximation. East Asian J. Appl. Math. **1**(02), 172–186 (2011)
15. Zach, C., Pock, T., Bischof, H.: A duality based approach for realtime TV-L^1 optical flow. In: Hamprecht, F.A., Schnörr, C., Jähne, B. (eds.) DAGM 2007. LNCS, vol. 4713, pp. 214–223. Springer, Heidelberg (2007). doi:10.1007/978-3-540-74936-3_22
16. Haddad, A.: Texture separation $BV - G$ and $BV - L^1$ models. Multiscale Model. Simul. **6**(1), 273–286 (2007)
17. Duval, V., Aujol, J.F., Gousseau, Y.: The TVL1 model: a geometric point of view. Multiscale Model. Simul. **8**(1), 154–189 (2009)
18. Zeune, L., van Dalum, G., Terstappen, L.W., van Gils, S.A., Brune, C.: Multi-scale segmentation via Bregman distances and nonlinear spectral analysis. SIAM J. Imaging Sci. **10**(1), 111–146 (2017)
19. Bellettini, G., Caselles, V., Novaga, M.: The total variation flow in R^N. J. Differ. Equ. **184**(2), 475–525 (2002)
20. Caselles, V., Chambolle, A., Novaga, M.: Uniqueness of the Cheeger set of a convex body. Pac. J. Math. **232**(1), 77–90 (2007)
21. Chambolle, A., Duval, V., Peyré, G., Poon, C.: Geometric properties of solutions to the total variation denoising problem. arXiv preprint arXiv:1602.00087 (2016)

22. Darbon, J.: Total variation minimization with L^1 data fidelity as a contrast invariant filter. In: 4th International Symposium on Image and Signal Processing and Analysis (ISpPA 2005), pp. 221–226 (2005)
23. Strong, D., Chan, T.: Edge-preserving and scale-dependent properties of total variation regularization. Inverse Probl. **19**(6), S165 (2003)
24. Chambolle, A., Pock, T.: A first-order primal-dual algorithm for convex problems with applications to imaging. J. Math. Imaging Vis. **40**(1), 120–145 (2011)
25. Hoover, A., Kouznetsova, V., Goldbaum, M.: Locating blood vessels in retinal images by piecewise threshold probing of a matched filter response. IEEE Trans. Med. Imaging **19**(3), 203–210 (2000)

An Efficient and Stable Two-Pixel Scheme for 2D Forward-and-Backward Diffusion

Martin Welk[1]([⊠]) and Joachim Weickert[2]

[1] Institute of Biomedical Image Analysis, Private University for Health Sciences, Medical Informatics and Technology, Eduard-Wallnöfer-Zentrum 1,
6060 Hall/Tyrol, Austria
martin.welk@umit.at
[2] Mathematical Image Analysis Group, Saarland University,
Campus E1.7, 66041 Saarbrücken, Germany
weickert@mia.uni-saarland.de

Abstract. Image enhancement with forward-and-backward (FAB) diffusion is numerically very challenging due to its negative diffusivities. As a remedy, we first extend the explicit nonstandard scheme by Welk et al. (2009) from the 1D scenario to the practically relevant two-dimensional setting. We prove that under a fairly severe time step restriction, this 2D scheme preserves a maximum–minimum principle. Moreover, we find an interesting Lyapunov sequence which guarantees convergence to a flat steady state. Since a global application of the time step size restriction leads to very slow algorithms and is more restrictive than necessary for most pixels, we introduce a much more efficient scheme with locally adapted time step sizes. It applies diffusive two-pixel interactions in a randomised order and adapts the time step size to the specific pixel pair. These space-variant time steps are synchronised at sync times. Our experiments show that our novel two-pixel scheme allows to compute FAB diffusion with guaranteed L^∞-stability at a speed that can be three orders of magnitude larger than its explicit counterpart with a global time step size.

1 Introduction

Partial differential equations (PDEs) and variational approaches for enhancing digital images have been investigated intensively in the last thirty years. An overview can be found e.g. in [1,12]. As continuous frameworks, these approaches excel by their concise and transparent formulation and their natural representation of rotational invariance.

However, some highly interesting models are affected by well-posedness problems, making their analysis in a continuous setting difficult. Well-posedness properties of space-discrete and fully-discrete formulations therefore receive increasing attention.

Regarding the Perona–Malik filter, a space-discrete and fully discrete theory for smooth nonnegative diffusivities was established by Weickert [12]. The corresponding explicit scheme was proven in [13] to preserve monotonicity in 1D. An extension of this analysis to singular nonnegative diffusivities was accomplished

© Springer International Publishing AG 2017
F. Lauze et al. (Eds.): SSVM 2017, LNCS 10302, pp. 94–106, 2017.
DOI: 10.1007/978-3-319-58771-4_8

by Pollak et al. [10] who verified the well-posedness of dynamical systems with discontinuous right hand sides arising from a space-discrete Perona-Malik model.

For the stabilised inverse linear diffusion process introduced by Osher and Rudin, a continuous well-posedness theory is lacking, but a stable minmod discretisation could be devised [7]. For shock filtering [5,8] which, too, is difficult to analyse in the continuous setting, discrete well-posedness results are found in [15], including an analytic solution of the corresponding dynamical system.

The *forward-and-backward (FAB) diffusion* model of Gilboa et al. [4] is another example for these difficulties. Designed for the sharpening of images, it is basically a Perona–Malik type PDE filter. However, its diffusivities take positive values in some regions and negative values in others. The absence of well-posedness results in the continuous setting is plausible given that inverse diffusion in its pure form, with negative diffusivity, is a standard example of an ill-posed problem. Experiments with standard explicit discretisations show violations of a maximum–minimum principle.

For space-discrete and fully discrete FAB diffusion some analytical results have been obtained in [14]. It was shown that space-discrete FAB diffusion is well-posed and satisfies a maximum–minimum principle if a specific nonstandard discretisation is applied at extrema. For a fully discrete 1D FAB diffusion framework with an explicit time discretisation, a maximum–minimum principle and a total variation reduction property were established. However, results for higher dimensions are still missing.

Our Contribution. In this paper, we consider the practically relevant fully discrete 2D case. We prove a maximum–minimum principle for an explicit time discretisation. By introducing a novel Lyapunov sequence – which is also interesting by itself – we prove convergence to a flat steady state. Our theoretical findings allow to devise an explicit finite difference scheme for FAB diffusion which is L^∞-stable for small positive time step sizes. Unfortunately, the time step bound is extremely small which limits the practical applicability of that scheme. However, as our analysis reveals, the small time step size is actually needed only at few locations in typical images. This motivates us to adapt the time step size locally. To obtain maximal locality and keep the diffusion interaction process as simple and transparent as possible, we split it into a sequence of two-pixel interactions. Selecting the pixel pairs randomly averages out any directional bias. Our experiments show that this gives a stable scheme for 2D FAB diffusion that is three orders of magnitude more efficient than an explicit scheme with global time step size restriction.

Structure of the Paper. In Sect. 2, we briefly review the basic ideas behind FAB diffusion. Our theoretical results for an explicit scheme with nonstandard discretisation in a two-dimensional setting are established in Sect. 3. In Sect. 4 we introduce our novel two-pixel scheme with randomised updates. Its performance is evaluated experimentally in Sect. 5. Our paper is concluded with a summary in Sect. 6.

2 Forward-and-Backward Diffusion Filtering

Forward-and-backward (FAB) diffusion filtering has been proposed by Gilboa, Sochen and Zeevi in 2002 [4]. Let a greyscale image $f : \Omega \rightarrow \mathbb{R}$ on a rectangular image domain $\Omega \subset \mathbb{R}^2$ be given. To sharpen this image, filtered versions $u(\boldsymbol{x}, t)$ of $f(\boldsymbol{x})$ are created by solving an initial–boundary value problem for the Perona-Malik type [9] PDE

$$\partial_t u = \operatorname{div}\left(g(|\boldsymbol{\nabla} u|^2)\,\boldsymbol{\nabla} u\right) \tag{1}$$

with initial condition $u(\boldsymbol{x}, 0) = f(\boldsymbol{x})$, and homogeneous Neumann boundary conditions, $\partial_{\boldsymbol{n}} u = 0$, where $\boldsymbol{n}$ denotes a vector normal to the image boundary $\partial\Omega$. Here $\boldsymbol{x}$ stands for $(x, y)^\top$. Writing partial derivatives by subscripts, we denote by $\boldsymbol{\nabla} := (\partial_x, \partial_y)^\top$ the spatial gradient and by div its corresponding divergence operator.

For the diffusivity g different models have been proposed, see for example [3,11]. Constitutive for a FAB diffusivity is that it is positive for small image gradients, while it becomes negative for larger ones. An example, adapted from [11], is

$$g(s^2) = 2\exp\left(-\frac{\kappa^2 \ln 2}{\kappa^2 - 1} \cdot \frac{s^2}{\lambda^2}\right) - \exp\left(-\frac{\ln 2}{\kappa^2 - 1} \cdot \frac{s^2}{\lambda^2}\right) \tag{2}$$

with admissible parameters $\lambda > 0$ and $\kappa > 1$. In contrast to this diffusivity, some other FAB diffusivities can also become positive again for large gradient magnitudes; see e.g. [3]. In [3] FAB diffusion has been interpreted as an energy minimisation process of a nonmonotone potential in the shape of a triple-well. FAB diffusion has also been put into relation with wavelet methods for image enhancement [6].

Beyond these works, there is not much theoretical analysis of the fully continuous FAB process documented in the literature. In particular, no existence, uniqueness and stability results have been proven. It was conjectured [4] that FAB diffusion violates a maximum–minimum principle due to the effect of negative diffusivities. In numerical experiments based on standard numerical methods, such violations were indeed observed. However, [14] brought out that using a more sophisticated space discretisation, the space-discrete process obeys the maximum–minimum principle and useful theoretical results on the space-discrete process could be established. Stability properties of fully discrete FAB diffusion were considered in [14], too, but limited to the 1D case. We will present analytical results for the 2D case in the next section.

3 Analysis of Fully Discrete FAB Diffusion in 2D

To study FAB diffusion in the fully discrete 2D case, we consider the discrete image domain $J := \{1, 2, \ldots, m\} \times \{1, 2, \ldots, n\}$. Following [14] we use a simple explicit scheme for (1) with time step size τ and grid sizes h_1 and h_2 in x- and y-direction:

$$u_{i,j}^{k+1} = u_{i,j}^k + \tau \cdot \left(\frac{g_{i+1,j}^k + g_{i,j}^k}{2} \cdot \frac{u_{i+1,j}^k - u_{i,j}^k}{h_1^2} - \frac{g_{i,j}^k + g_{i-1,j}^k}{2} \cdot \frac{u_{i,j}^k - u_{i-1,j}^k}{h_1^2} \right.$$

$$\left. + \frac{g_{i,j+1}^k + g_{i,j}^k}{2} \cdot \frac{u_{i,j+1}^k - u_{i,j}^k}{h_2^2} - \frac{g_{i,j}^k + g_{i,j-1}^k}{2} \cdot \frac{u_{i,j}^k - u_{i,j-1}^k}{h_2^2} \right). \tag{3}$$

Here, $u_{i,j}^k$ approximates u at location $((i-\frac{1}{2})h_1, (j-\frac{1}{2})h_2)$ and time $k\tau$. Further following [14], we use a nonstandard approximation for the FAB diffusivity,

$$g_{i,j}^k = g\left(\max\left(\frac{u_{i+1,j}^k - u_{i,j}^k}{h_1} \cdot \frac{u_{i,j}^k - u_{i-1,j}^k}{h_1}, 0 \right) \right.$$

$$\left. + \max\left(\frac{u_{i,j+1}^k - u_{i,j}^k}{h_2} \cdot \frac{u_{i,j}^k - u_{i,j-1}^k}{h_2}, 0 \right) \right). \tag{4}$$

In contrast to the standard approximation

$$g_{i,j}^k = g\left(\left(\frac{u_{i+1,j}^k - u_{i-1,j}^k}{2h_1} \right)^2 + \left(\frac{u_{i,j+1}^k - u_{i,j-1}^k}{2h_2} \right)^2 \right) \tag{5}$$

it offers the advantage that at extrema the gradient approximation is zero which leads to a positive FAB diffusivity. This will be essential for guaranteeing stability.

To implement homogeneous Neumann boundary conditions, we set

$$u_{0,j}^k := u_{1,j}^k, \quad u_{m+1,j}^k := u_{m,j}^k, \quad u_{i,0}^k := u_{i,1}^k, \quad u_{i,n+1}^k := u_{i,n}^k \tag{6}$$

for all indices i and j. Then (3) can be used verbatim also at boundary pixels.

3.1   Maximum–Minimum Principle

Our first result is a 2D analogue for the first statement of [14, Proposition 4], i.e. the maximum–minimum principle. The hypotheses on the grey-value range and shape of the diffusivity function g are the same as there. Our bound for τ is adapted to the 2D grid geometry.

Proposition 1. *Let an initial 2D image* $\boldsymbol{f} = (f_{i,j})$ *on* $J = \{1, 2, \ldots, m\} \times \{1, 2, \ldots, n\}$ *be given, and let the sequence of images* $\boldsymbol{u}^k = (u_{i,j}^k)$ *evolve according to (3), (4) with the initial condition* $\boldsymbol{u}^0 = \boldsymbol{f}$. *Let the grey-values* $f_{i,j}$ *be restricted to a finite interval* $[a, b]$ *of length* $R := b - a$. *Assume that there are two constants* $c_1 > c_2 > 0$ *such that the diffusivity* g *fulfils* $g(0) = c_1$, *and* $g(z) \in [-c_2, c_1]$ *for all* $z > 0$, *compare Fig. 1. Assume further that there exists an* $\omega > 0$ *such that* $g(s^2) > c_2$ *holds for all* s *with* $0 < s < \omega R$.

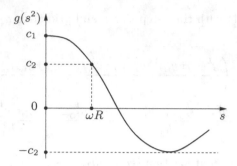

Fig. 1. Schematic view of a FAB diffusivity satisfying the conditions of Proposition 1.

Let the time step τ satisfy the inequality

$$\tau \le \vartheta := \frac{\omega^2 h_1^4 h_2^4}{2c_1(h_1^2 + h_2^2)(\omega^2 h_1^2 h_2^2 + h_1^2 + h_2^2)}. \tag{7}$$

Then u obeys the following maximum–minimum principle: If the initial signal is bounded by $f_{i,j} \in [a,b]$ for all $(i,j) \in J$, then $u_{i,j}^k \in [a,b]$ for all $(i,j) \in J$, $k \ge 0$.

The proof of this statement relies on two local properties.

Lemma 1. *Under the assumptions of Proposition 1, local maxima do not increase.*

Proof. Let $u_{i,j}^k$ be a local maximum of u^k. Then $g_{i,j}^k = c_1$, and we have that $g_{i+1,j}^k + g_{i,j}^k$ etc. are positive while $u_{i+1,j}^k - u_{i,j}^k$ etc. are negative such that all summands in the bracket on the r.h.s. of (3) are negative. This holds independent of τ.

The r.h.s. of (3) is a convex combination of $u_{i,j}^k$, $u_{i\pm1,j}^k$, $u_{i,j\pm1}^k$ if

$$1 - \frac{\tau}{2h_1^2}\left(g_{i+1,j}^k + 2g_{i,j}^k + g_{i-1,j}^k\right) - \frac{\tau}{2h_2^2}\left(g_{i,j+1}^k + 2g_{i,j}^k + g_{i,j-1}^k\right) \ge 0, \tag{8}$$

which is certainly the case if $\tau \le h_1^2 h_2^2/(2c_1(h_1^2 + h_2^2))$ (the well-known time-step limit for the standard explicit scheme in the case of nonnegative diffusivity). □

Lemma 2. *Under the assumptions of Proposition 1, a non-maximal pixel does not grow in excess of its greatest adjacent pixel within one time step.*

Proof. Let $u_{i,j}^k$ be the non-maximal pixel under consideration. Assume first that the largest grey-value among its neighbours is attained by a horizontal neighbour, say $u_{i-1,j}^k$. So $u_{i-1,j}^k$ is greater than $u_{i,j}^k$ and not less than each other neighbour of $u_{i,j}^k$.

To outline the proof first, notice that basically two situations can happen: If $u_{i,j}^k$ is only slightly smaller than $u_{i-1,j}^k$, it turns out that $u_{i,j}^k$ is "not far from maximality". In this case, its diffusivity $g_{i,j}^k$ will be positive and large enough to ensure forward diffusion (Case 1 in the following), such that again the time step limit of explicit forward diffusion applies. Otherwise, negative diffusivity may occur but at the same time there is quite some way to go before $u_{i,j}^{k+1}$ could exceed $u_{i-1,j}^k$. The overall bounds on the image contrast limit the diffusion flow and thereby the "speed" of the pixel. So one can state also in this case a time step size limit that ensures the desired inequality (Case 2). In the following, these two cases are treated exactly.

Case 1: $\frac{1}{h_1^2}(u_{i,j}^k - u_{i-1,j}^k)(u_{i+1,j}^k - u_{i,j}^k) + \frac{1}{h_2^2}(u_{i,j}^k - u_{i,j-1}^k)(u_{i,j+1}^k - u_{i,j}^k) \leq \omega^2 R^2.$

Then $g_{i,j}^k \geq c_2$, and thus $g_{i,j}^k + g_{i+1,j}^k$, $g_{i,j}^k + g_{i,j\pm1}^k \geq 0$. As a consequence, $u_{i,j}^{k+1}$ is a convex combination of $u_{i,j}^k$, $u_{i\pm1,j}^k$, $u_{i,j\pm1}^k$ if

$$1 - \frac{\tau}{2h_1^2}(g_{i+1,j}^k + 2g_{i,j}^k + g_{i-1,j}^k) - \frac{\tau}{2h_2^2}(g_{i,j+1}^k + 2g_{i,j}^k + g_{i,j-1}^k) \geq 0, \quad (9)$$

which is certainly fulfilled if $1 - \frac{4\tau c_1}{2h_1^2} - \frac{4\tau c_1}{2h_2^2} \geq 0$, i.e. $\tau \leq h_1^2 h_2^2/(2c_1(h_1^2 + h_2^2))$.

Case 2: $\frac{1}{h_1^2}(u_{i,j}^k - u_{i-1,j}^k)(u_{i+1,j}^k - u_{i,j}^k) + \frac{1}{h_2^2}(u_{i,j}^k - u_{i,j-1}^k)(u_{i,j+1}^k - u_{i,j}^k) > \omega^2 R^2.$

The difference between pixel $u_{i,j}^k$ and its greatest neighbour fulfils the inequality $u_{i-1,j}^k - u_{i,j}^k > \omega^2 R/(h_1^{-2} + h_2^{-2})$ because the contrary would imply the hypothesis of Case 1. Further, we have by the hypothesis of Case 2 that $-c_2 \leq g_{i,j}^k \leq c_2$. Together with the hypotheses from Proposition 1 on the range of g and the image range, one has

$$\begin{aligned}
-2c_2 \leq g_{i+1,j}^k + g_{i,j}^k \leq c_1 + c_2, && -R \leq u_{i+1,j}^k - u_{i,j}^k \leq R, \\
-2c_2 \leq g_{i-1,j}^k + g_{i,j}^k \leq c_1 + c_2, && 0 \leq u_{i-1,j}^k - u_{i,j}^k \leq R, \quad (10) \\
-2c_2 < g_{i,j\pm1}^k + g_{i,j}^k \leq c_1 + c_2, && -R \leq u_{i,j\pm1}^k - u_{i,j}^k \leq u_{i-1,j}^k - u_{i,j}^k.
\end{aligned}$$

Inserting this into (3) gives

$$u_{i,j}^{k+1} \leq u_{i,j}^k + \tau\left(\frac{c_1 + c_2}{2h_1^2}R + \frac{c_1 + c_2}{2h_1^2}(u_{i-1,j}^k - u_{i,j}^k) + 2\frac{c_1 + c_2}{2h_2^2}R\right), \quad (11)$$

$$u_{i-1,j}^k - u_{i,j}^{k+1} \geq (u_{i-1,j}^k - u_{i,j}^k)\left(1 - \frac{\tau(c_1 + c_2)}{2h_1^2}\right) - \frac{\tau(c_1 + c_2)R}{2}\left(\frac{1}{h_1^2} + \frac{2}{h_2^2}\right). \quad (12)$$

The r.h.s. of (12) is certainly nonnegative if

$$\tau \leq \frac{2h_1^2}{c_1 + c_2} \cdot \frac{u_{i-1,j}^k - u_{i,j}^k}{u_{i-1,j}^k - u_{i,j}^k + R(1 + 2h_1^2/h_2^2)}, \quad (13)$$

for which by our initial estimate for $u_{i-1,j}^k - u_{i,j}^k$ and monotonicity it suffices that

$$\tau \leq \frac{2\omega^2 h_1^4 h_2^4}{(c_1 + c_2)(\omega^2 h_1^2 h_2^4 + (h_2^2 + 2h_1^2)(h_1^2 + h_2^2))}. \quad (14)$$

This limit on τ ensures that the pixel under consideration cannot grow in excess of its greatest neighbour if this neighbour is a horizontal neighbour. If $u_{i,j}^k$ has its greatest neighbour in vertical direction, analogous considerations lead to a similar constraint, with h_1 and h_2 exchanged. Both bounds on τ are larger than the one of Proposition 1. □

Proof (of the Proposition). The maximum–minimum principle follows immediately from Lemmas 1 and 2 and analogous statements for local minima. □

Remark 1. Unlike in the 1D case [14, Proposition 4], the statement that an extremum may not split into two does not hold. Similar to ordinary homogeneous diffusion, a "dumbbell" configuration with a narrow ridge between two more extended plateaus can serve as a counterexample. Note that for sufficiently small grey-value differences between the ridge and the adjacent plateaus all diffusivities in this region are positive.

3.2   Strict Lyapunov Condition

The maximum–minimum principle from Proposition 1 suggests the use of the difference between global maximum and global minimum of the image as a Lyapunov function to investigate the possible convergence of discrete FAB diffusion. Our proofs from the previous subsection, however, still leave the possibility that the global maximum and minimum of the image stay constant, and different from each other, forever.

To rule out this possibility, we will refine our analysis and construct a strictly decreasing Lyapunov function by incorporating multiplicities of maxima and minima as additional information. From now on, we require that τ is strictly smaller than the bound from Proposition 1. We introduce notations for the global extremal grey-values of images with their multiplicities, and an ordering for pairs of values with multiplicities.

Definition 1. *For any image* $u = (u_{i,j})_{(i,j)\in J}$, *let* $u_{\max} := \max\limits_{i,j} u_{i,j}$, $u_{\min} := \min\limits_{i,j} u_{i,j}$ *denote its maximal and minimal grey-value, respectively, and* $n_{\max} := \#\{(i,j) \mid u_{i,j} = u_{\max}\}$, $n_{\min} := \#\{(i,j) \mid u_{i,j} = u_{\min}\}$ *their multiplicities.*

Definition 2. *Let the relation* $\prec$ *on* $\mathbb{R} \times \mathbb{N}$ *be given by*

$$(u_1, n_1) \prec (u_2, n_2) \quad :\Longleftrightarrow \quad (u_1 < u_2) \text{ or } (u_1 = u_2 \text{ and } n_1 < n_2). \tag{15}$$

Clearly, $\prec$ is a strict total order. We can now establish the maximum–minimum difference with multiplicities as Lyapunov function for discrete FAB diffusion.

Proposition 2. *Consider the fully discrete FAB diffusion (3), (4). If the time step size is chosen as* $\tau < \vartheta$ *with* ϑ *as in Proposition 1, then*

$$(u_{\max}^{k+1} - u_{\min}^{k+1}, n_{\max}^{k+1} + n_{\min}^{k+1}) \prec (u_{\max}^k - u_{\min}^k, n_{\max}^k + n_{\min}^k) \tag{16}$$

holds, unless $u_{\max}^k = u_{\min}^k$.

Proof. Let $u_{i,j}^k$ be a local maximum of $\boldsymbol{u}^k$. As in the proof of Lemma 1, we have $g_{i,j}^k = c_1$. Thus, the new value $u_{i,j}^{k+1}$ of that pixel will be a convex combination of the old grey-values of pixel (i,j) and its neighbours, with all neighbours having positive weights. Therefore, $u_{i,j}^{k+1} = u_{i,j}^k$ can happen only if all neighbours have the same value as $u_{i,j}$ in time step k. As long as not all pixels of the image have the same value, there will be at least one pixel $u_{i,j}^k = u_{\max}^k$ with a neighbour of smaller grey-value.

Following the proof of Lemma 2 we see that for $\tau < \vartheta$ the new pixel value $u_{i,j}^{k+1}$ remains strictly below the old value of its largest neighbour $u_{i-1,j}^k$. Thus, $u_{i,j}^{k+1} = u_{\max}^k$ cannot hold for a pixel with $u_{i,j}^k < u_{\max}^k$.

Combining both arguments, we see that the number of pixels attaining the value $u_{\max}^k$ decreases in time step $k+1$. As a consequence, one has $u_{\max}^{k+1} < u_{\max}^k$ (if no pixel with that value remains), or $n_{\max}^{k+1} < n_{\max}^k$ (if the maximal value remains equal).

Analogous reasoning for minima completes the proof.   □

3.3   Convergence to a Flat Steady State

An immediate consequence of Proposition 2 is the following statement.

Corollary 1. *The only fixed points of the discrete FAB diffusion process (3), (4) are the flat images given for each $\mu \in \mathbb{R}$ by*

$$u_{i,j} = \mu \quad for \ all \ (i,j) \in J. \tag{17}$$

By average grey-value invariance, the only steady state that could be reached from a given initial image $\boldsymbol{f}$ is that for which μ is the average grey value of $\boldsymbol{f}$. We will now prove convergence to this steady state.

Proposition 3. *Fully discrete FAB diffusion (3), (4) with $\boldsymbol{u}^0 = \boldsymbol{f}$ and time step size $\tau < \vartheta$ converges to the fixed point (17) where μ is the average grey value of $\boldsymbol{f}$.*

Proof. Consider the strictly decreasing (w.r.t. $\prec$) sequences $((u_{\max}^k, n_{\max}^k))_{k \in \mathbb{N}}$ and $((-u_{\min}^k, n_{\min}^k))_{k \in \mathbb{N}}$ from Proposition 2. These sequences are bounded from below by (a, N), $(-b, N)$, respectively, where $a := f_{\min}$, and $b := f_{\max}$. By an easy adaptation of the standard argument for sequences in $\mathbb{R}$ to sequences in $\mathbb{R} \times \mathbb{N}$ it follows that the sequences $(u_{\max}^k)$, $(u_{\min}^k)$ converge. Denote by $\bar{u}$, $\underline{u}$ their respective limits.

Assume $\underline{u} < \bar{u}$. By the maximum–minimum principle, $\boldsymbol{u}^k \in [a,b]^N$ holds for all k. Since $[a,b]^N$ is compact, the sequence $(\boldsymbol{u}^k)$ has a cumulation point. Because of the monotonicity of $(u_{\max}^k)$, $(u_{\min}^k)$ each cumulation point satisfies $u_{\max}^* = \bar{u}$, $u_{\min}^* = \underline{u}$.

We choose one cumulation point $\boldsymbol{u}^*$ and consider the FAB evolution $(\tilde{\boldsymbol{u}}^k)_{k \in \mathbb{N}_0}$ with initial condition $\tilde{\boldsymbol{u}}^0 = \boldsymbol{u}^*$. By Proposition 2, there exists a natural number K such that $\tilde{u}_{\max}^K = \max \tilde{\boldsymbol{u}} < \bar{u}$. Let therefore $\delta := \bar{u} - \tilde{u}_{\max}^K > 0$.

Moreover, the evolution (3), (4) satisfies a Lipschitz condition on $[a, b]^N$ with respect to the maximum norm $\| \cdot \|$, i.e.

$$\|u^k - \hat{u}^k\| < B \quad \Rightarrow \quad \|u^{k+1} - \hat{u}^{k+1}\| < LB \tag{18}$$

with some Lipschitz constant $L > 0$. Since u^* is a cumulation point of (u^k), we can choose k such that $\|u^k - u^*\| < \delta/L^K$. Consequently, $\|u^{k+K} - \tilde{u}^K\| < \delta$, and by the triangle inequality it follows that

$$u_{\max}^{k+K} \leq \tilde{u}_{\max}^K + \|u^{k+K} - \tilde{u}^K\| < \bar{u} - \delta + \delta = \bar{u}, \tag{19}$$

contradicting the convergence of $(u_{\max}^k)$ to $\bar{u}$. Thus, our assumption $\underline{u} < \bar{u}$ must be wrong, and we have $\underline{u} = \bar{u}$, i.e. convergence to a flat steady state.   □

4   An Efficient and Stable Two-Pixel Scheme

Based on the stability result from Proposition 1 it is possible to compute FAB diffusion by a stable explicit scheme. The time step size limit imposed by (7), however, is way too small for practical purposes. In fact, (7) is an *a priori* estimate for the time step size resulting from several worst-case estimates which in general apply only to a few pixel locations. The theory in Sect. 3.1 can be used to derive instead *a posteriori* estimates which allow to steer the time stepping in an adaptive way. The resulting time steps will almost always be considerably larger than (7).

To make this precise, note that (3) can be written as $u_{i,j}^{k+1} = u_{i,j}^k + \tau \dot{u}_{i,j}^k$ where the finite-difference approximation $\dot{u}_{i,j}^k$ of $\mathrm{div}(g \nabla u)$ can be computed independent of the time step size τ. To ensure that the maximum–minimum property is not violated within a time step, bounds on τ can then be derived directly from the criteria formulated in Lemmas 1 and 2 for each pixel location. First, non-enhancement of extrema is warranted for $\tau \leq \tau_{\max} := h_1^2 h_2^2/(2c_1(h_1^2 + h_2^2))$ as stated in the proof of Lemma 1. Second, local monotonicity preservation as stated in Lemma 2 can be achieved if in each time step, each non-maximal pixel is prevented from growing in excess of its largest neighbour, and each non-minimal pixel from decreasing below its smallest neighbour. Appropriate time step bounds can be computed for each pixel individually from $\dot{u}_{i,j}^k$.

Whereas these conditions could be evaluated to derive a *global* time step τ in each iteration, we obtain a higher efficiency by following a radically *localised* approach: The diffusion flow $\dot{u}_{i,j}^k$ in (3) is composed of four two-pixel flows, each between the location (i, j) and one of its neighbours. Each of these flows appears with opposite signs in the flows of its two participating pixels, which ensures that the average grey-value conservation property of the continuous diffusion process is exactly fulfilled also in its discretisation (3). In order to maintain this conservation property, we choose the two-pixel flows as the elementary units for our scheme; compare also the proceeding in [2]. Starting from an approximation u^k pertaining to evolution time $k\tau_{\max}$, a global time step of size $\tau_{\max}$ is carried out by updating two-pixel flows in random order, each one with an appropriate time step. In the case of forward diffusion the time step is chosen so that the two interacting pixels preserve their monotonicity order. In the case of backward diffusion it is chosen such that they are prevented from growing above the maximum, or decreasing below the minimum of their respective neighbourhoods. Updated values $u_{i,j}$ enter immediately the computation of other pixels. This is repeated until all flows have reached the new time level, yielding the new approximation $\boldsymbol{u}^{k+1}$.

The time step $k \mapsto k+1$ thus starts by initialising an evolution time account for each pair of neighbouring pixels, $\{(i,j),(i',j')\}$ with $(i',j') = (i+1,j)$ or $(i',j') = (i,j+1)$, as $T_{i,j;i',j'} := \tau_{\max}$. Then, the following steps are repeated until all $T_{i,j;i',j'}$ reach zero, implying that we have progressed from sync time $k\tau_{\max}$ to $(k+1)\tau_{\max}$:

1. **Random selection:** Select a two-pixel pair $\{(i,j),(i',j')\}$ randomly, with the probability of each pair to be selected being proportional to $T_{i,j;i',j'}$.
2. **Diffusivity computation:** Compute $g_{i,j}$ and $g_{i',j'}$ as in (4); let $g := \frac{1}{2}(g_{i,j} + g_{i',j'})$.
3. **Flow computation:** Compute the flow $\dot{u} := g \cdot (u_{i',j'} - u_{i,j})/h^2$, using $h = h_1$ for horizontal or $h = h_2$ for vertical neighbours.
4. **Step-size determination:** Let $\tau^* := T_{i,j;i',j'}$.
   If $g > 0$ and $\tau^* > h^2/(2g)$, reduce τ^* to $h^2/(2g)$.
   If $g < 0$ and (i,j) is not a discrete local maximum, let (i^*,j^*) be its maximal neighbour. If $u_{i,j} + \tau^*\dot{u} > u_{i^*,j^*}$, reduce τ^* to $\tau^* := (u_{i^*,j^*} - u_{i,j})/\dot{u}$.
   If $g < 0$ and (i,j) is not a discrete local minimum, let (i^*,j^*) be its minimal neighbour. If $u_{i,j} + \tau^*\dot{u} < u_{i^*,j^*}$, reduce τ^* to $\tau^* := (u_{i^*,j^*} - u_{i,j})/\dot{u}$.
   If $g < 0$ and (i',j') is not a discrete local maximum, let (i^*,j^*) be its maximal neighbour. If $u_{i',j'} - \tau^*\dot{u} > u_{i^*,j^*}$, reduce τ^* to $\tau^* := (u_{i^*,j^*} - u_{i',j'})/(-\dot{u})$.
   If $g < 0$ and (i',j') is not a discrete local minimum, let (i^*,j^*) be its minimal neighbour. If $u_{i',j'} - \tau^*\dot{u} < u_{i^*,j^*}$, reduce τ^* to $\tau^* := (u_{i^*,j^*} - u_{i',j'})/(-\dot{u})$.
5. **Two-pixel flow update:** Update $u_{i,j}$ and $u_{i',j'}$ by replacing them with the new values $\tilde{u}_{i,j} := u_{i,j} + \tau^*\dot{u}$ and $\tilde{u}_{i',j'} := u_{i',j'} - \tau^*\dot{u}$. Decrease $T_{i,j;i',j'}$ by τ^*.

This process terminates, since τ^* cannot fall below the global positive limit (7). The approximation error of our scheme can be shown to be $\mathcal{O}(\tau + h^2 + \tau/h)$. This ensures a conditionally consistent approximation to the FAB diffusion PDE if τ/h^2 is bounded by a constant when $\tau, h \to 0$. However, this is always satisfied by the stability conditions of our automatic time step size adaptation. For an efficient implementation of the algorithm, the performance of the selection in Step 1 is crucial. To this end, the bookkeeping of time step accounts $T_{i,j;i',j'}$ is done within a binary tree structure. The selection then requires logarithmic time w.r.t. the total number of pixels.

5   Experiments

Let us now evaluate our numerical algorithms. To this end we have implemented them in ANSI C and compiled the code with a GNU gcc compiler. We report

Fig. 2. Influence of the numerical scheme on the result of FAB diffusion ($\lambda = 4$, $\kappa = 2.5$, $t = 10$). **From left to right: (a)** Test image, 256×256 pixels. **(b)** Explicit scheme (3) with standard discretisation (5). Computing 1 million iterations with time step size $\tau = 10^{-5}$ requires 70 min and 13 s, while the result is unstable. **(c)** Explicit scheme (3) with nonstandard discretisation (5). Performing 1 million iterations with $\tau = 10^{-5}$ takes 66 min and 34 s. **(d)** Corresponding two-pixel scheme. We used 100 iterations with synchronisation step size $\tau_{\mathrm{max}} = 0.1$, leading to a runtime of 7.73 s. The average time step size was 0.0991.

runtimes on a single core of an Acer P 645 Laptop with an Intel® Core™ i5-5200U CPU running at 2.20 GHz. No advanced code optimisations took place.

In our first experiment we compare an implementation of our explicit scheme (3) with standard (5) or nonstandard discretisation (4) and its two-pixel variant (with nonstandard discretisation). We use the diffusivity function (2). Figure 2 shows the results for $\lambda = 4$, $\kappa = 2.5$ and stopping time $t = 10$. First, we observe that an explicit scheme with standard discretisation is unstable, even for very small time step sizes. Thus, it is not considered any further. Second, we see that an explicit scheme with nonstandard discretisation is stable for small time steps and visually equivalent to its two-pixel counterpart. However, the runtimes of both schemes differ enormously:

– **Explicit scheme (with nonstandard discretisation):**
   For the diffusivity (2) with $\lambda = 4$ and $\kappa = 2.5$, the constant ω in the time step size limit (7) is given by $\omega = 0.009568$. Together with the grid sizes $h_1 = h_2 = 1$ this yields a time step size restriction of $\tau \leq 1.14 \cdot 10^{-5}$. Choosing $\tau := 1 \cdot 10^{-5}$ requires as many as 1 million iterations to reach a stopping time of $t = 10$. The corresponding CPU time was 70 min 13 s.
– **Two-pixel scheme:**
   For the two-pixel variant of the explicit scheme with nonstandard discretisation we used a sync step size of $\tau_{\mathrm{max}} = 0.1$. Thus, only 100 sync steps are necessary to reach a stopping time of $t = 10$. This requires a CPU time of 7.73 s.

We observe that our two-pixel scheme gives a speed-up by a factor 544 !

Since the two-pixel algorithm is highly efficient, it can also be used for long term computations, arising e.g. in scale-space analysis. Figure 3 depicts the scale-space behaviour of a noisy test image when the scale-space is governed by FAB diffusion. We observe the high robustness of the FAB scale-space in spite of the

Fig. 3. Scale-space behaviour of FAB diffusion ($\lambda = 2$, $\kappa = 2.5$). **From left to right:** **(a)** Test image, 256×256 pixels. **(b)** After a diffusion time of $t = 10$. **(c)** $t = 300$. **(d)** $t = 10\,000$. All computations have been done with a two-pixel scheme with sync step size $\tau_{\max} = 0.1$.

fact that it uses negative diffusities. Moreover, the experiment confirms convergence to a flat steady state for $t \to \infty$. This is in full accordance with our theoretical results established in Sect. 3.

6   Summary and Conclusions

While backward diffusion suffers from an extremely bad reputation of being a terribly ill-posed process, we have seen in our paper that it can be turned into a highly stable evolution, provided that some essential requirements are met:

First of all, it must be stabilised at extrema in order to avoid under- and overshoots. The FAB diffusion paradigm does take care of this. Our discrete analysis is based on a FAB diffusivity that attains a positive diffusivity in zero which is larger than the moduli of all negative diffusivities. Under this mild model assumption we were able to establish a maximum–minimum principle for an explicit 2D scheme with nonstandard discretisation as well as convergence to a flat steady state, if one adheres to a very restrictive time step size limit. In order to make this concept practically viable, we came up with a novel scheme that combines several unconventional features:

- By splitting the diffusion process into a sequence of **two-pixel interactions**, we ended up with the most local scheme that is possible. The simplicity of two-pixel interactions allowed to adapt the time step size locally and use only small time steps at those locations where this is unavoidable. Although **local time step size adaptations** are uncommon in PDE-based image analysis, we have shown that they may lead to speed-ups by three orders of magnitude.
- In contrast to other splittings in the PDE-based image analysis literature which are usually synchronous, our splitting is **asynchronous**: Generating a sequence of simple two-pixel interactions turns out to be attractive, because their stability follows trivially from the stability of each two-pixel interaction.
- Introducing a **randomisation** in the order of the two-pixel diffusions removes any directional bias that is characteristic of sequential splittings which are carried out in a deterministic order.

It is our hope that our results may help to improve the reputation of backward parabolic processes, since they can offer some very attractive image enhancement properties that have hardly been explored so far, mainly because of the lack of stable numerical schemes. In our ongoing work we are also looking into extensions to other time discretisations such as (semi-)implicit schemes.

References

1. Aubert, G., Kornprobst, P.: Mathematical Problems in Image Processing: Partial Differential Equations and the Calculus of Variations. Applied Mathematical Sciences, vol. 147, 2nd edn. Springer, New York (2006)
2. Burgeth, B., Weickert, J., Tari, S.: Minimally stochastic schemes for singular diffusion equations. In: Tai, X.C., Lie, K.A., Chan, T.F., Osher, S. (eds.) Image Processing Based on Partial Differential Equations. (MATHVISUAL), pp. 325–339. Springer, Berlin (2007). doi:10.1007/978-3-540-33267-1_18
3. Gilboa, G., Sochen, N., Zeevi, Y.Y.: Image sharpening by flows based on triple well potentials. J. Math. Imaging Vis. **20**, 121–131 (2004)
4. Gilboa, G., Sochen, N.A., Zeevi, Y.Y.: Forward-and-backward diffusion processes for adaptive image enhancement and denoising. IEEE Trans. Image Process. **11**, 689–703 (2002)
5. Kramer, H.P., Bruckner, J.B.: Iterations of a non-linear transformation for enhancement of digital images. Pattern Recogn. **7**, 53–58 (1975)
6. Mrázek, P., Weickert, J., Steidl, G.: Diffusion-inspired shrinkage functions and stability results for wavelet denoising. Int. J. Comput. Vis. **64**, 171–186 (2005)
7. Osher, S., Rudin, L.: Shocks and other nonlinear filtering applied to image processing. In: Tescher, A.G. (ed.) Applications of Digital Image Processing XIV. Proceedings of SPIE, vol. 1567, pp. 414–431. SPIE Press, Bellingham (1991)
8. Osher, S., Rudin, L.I.: Feature-oriented image enhancement using shock filters. SIAM J. Numer. Anal. **27**, 919–940 (1990)
9. Perona, P., Malik, J.: Scale space and edge detection using anisotropic diffusion. IEEE Trans. Pattern Anal. Mach. Intell. **12**, 629–639 (1990)
10. Pollak, I., Willsky, A.S., Krim, H.: Image segmentation and edge enhancement with stabilized inverse diffusion equations. IEEE Trans. Image Process. **9**, 256–266 (2000)
11. Smolka, B.: Combined forward and backward anisotropic diffusion filtering of color images. In: Van Gool, L. (ed.) DAGM 2002. LNCS, vol. 2449, pp. 314–322. Springer, Heidelberg (2002). doi:10.1007/3-540-45783-6_38
12. Weickert, J.: Anisotropic Diffusion in Image Processing. Teubner, Stuttgart (1998)
13. Weickert, J., Benhamouda, B.: A semidiscrete nonlinear scale-space theory and its relation to the Perona–Malik paradox. In: Solina, F., Kropatsch, W.G., Klette, R., Bajcsy, R. (eds.) Advances in Computer Vision. (ACS), pp. 1–10. Springer, Vienna (1997). doi:10.1007/978-3-7091-6867-7_1
14. Welk, M., Gilboa, G., Weickert, J.: Theoretical foundations for discrete forward-and-backward diffusion filtering. In: Tai, X.-C., Mørken, K., Lysaker, M., Lie, K.-A. (eds.) SSVM 2009. LNCS, vol. 5567, pp. 527–538. Springer, Heidelberg (2009). doi:10.1007/978-3-642-02256-2_44
15. Welk, M., Weickert, J., Galić, I.: Theoretical foundations for spatially discrete 1-D shock filtering. Image Vis. Comput. **25**, 455–463 (2007)

Restoration and Reconstruction

Blind Space-Variant Single-Image Restoration of Defocus Blur

Leah Bar[1]([✉]), Nir Sochen[1], and Nahum Kiryati[2]

[1] Department of Applied Mathematics,
Tel-Aviv University, 69978 Tel-aviv, Israel
barleah.libra@gmail.com
[2] School of Electrical Engineering, Tel-Aviv University,
69978 Tel-aviv, Israel

Abstract. We address the problem of blind piecewise space-variant image deblurring where only part of the image is sharp, assuming a shallow depth of field which imposes significant defocus blur.

We propose an automatic image recovery approach which segments the sharp and blurred sub-regions, iteratively estimates a non-parametric blur kernel and restores the sharp image via a variational non-blind space variant method.

We present a simple and efficient blur measure which emphasizes the blur difference of the sub-regions followed by a blur segmentation procedure based on an evolving level set function.

One of the contributions of this work is the extension to the space-variant case of progressive blind deconvolution recently proposed, an iterative process consisting of non-parametric blind kernel estimation and residual blur deblurring. Apparently this progressive strategy is superior to the one step deconvolution procedure. Experimental results on real images demonstrate the effectiveness of the proposed algorithm.

Keywords: Space-variant deblurring · Blind deconvolution · Blur segmentation

1 Introduction

Most image deblurring methods rely on the standard model of a space-invariant kernel and additive noise

$$g = h * f + n. \tag{1}$$

Here h denotes a known space-invariant blur kernel, f is an ideal version of the observed image g, and n is a Gaussian noise. Blind image deblurring out of a single image is a challenging task that has received much attention and significant advances in recent years e.g. [9,12–15,17,30] and references within. The underlying assumption is that space-invariant blur is caused by an unknown kernel. Both the kernel and sharp image are recovered in the course of the blind deconvolution process. In realistic conditions however, the problem is even more

© Springer International Publishing AG 2017
F. Lauze et al. (Eds.): SSVM 2017, LNCS 10302, pp. 109–120, 2017.
DOI: 10.1007/978-3-319-58771-4_9

challenging in the sense that the blur is spatially variant. Equation (1) then takes the form

$$g(x) = \int_{\Omega} h(u, x - u) f(u) du + n, \tag{2}$$

where Ω is the image domain, x is a location in the observed image and u is a location in the ideal image f. For example, moving objects induce motion blur according to their velocity while the background stays sharp. Additionally, scenes captured with a shallow depth of field are partially defocused such that the focus varies with the distance of the object.

The problem of single image blind space-variant restoration involves blur estimation and localization with space-variant deblurring and is highly ill-posed. Some authors assume parametric kernels in motion blur [6,16,24,28] and defocus [4,19,27], and in turn limit the kernel space.

Another aspect of the problem concerns segmentation of the blurred and sharp regions. In the case of defocused images, segmentation is closely related to defocus map estimation. Most algorithms for defocus map estimation [1,10,18, 20,26,29] consist of two stages: identification of sparse defocus cues, followed by pixel-level propagation, exploiting pixel color to estimate the defocus map. Our objective is different in the sense that we attempt to recover the sharp image and accurate segmentation is not a goal by itself. For our purpose, accurate defocus map segmentation is not crucial (and quite impossible) in smooth regions.

Works closely related to our task were presented by Zhang and Cham [27] and Schelten and Roth [25]. In [27], the defocus map is estimated based on blurred edges assuming a parametric Gaussian kernel, with blur propagation. The kernel and recovered image are then calculated in an iterative fashion. The work of [25] is non-parametric hence flexible. Using the variational Bayesian method, they find the indicator function of the sharp/blurred regions and a non-parametric kernel. The sharp image is then reconstructed by non-blind space-variant deconvolution. This method is known to be computationally expensive [23].

In this paper we present a blind space-variant defocus deblurring method. Our approach consists of blur level segmentation followed by a novel progressive space-variant blind restoration, generalizing [9] for the space-variant case. The underlying model in this work is an image with a background and foreground, where one is significantly blurred by some kernel and the other is sharp. We first generalize a blur measure [2] which highlights the blur level difference between the two sub-regions. Unlike defocus map estimation, we perform single-step blur segmentation, using an evolving level set function guided by edges and image derivatives. Next, we extract the maximal rectangular blurred sub-region and start the progressive space-variant blind deblurring procedure, where the blurred rectangular sub-region is used in the kernel-estimation step. Promising results on real images demonstrate the effectiveness of the proposed algorithm.

2 Algorithmic Building Blocks

In this section, we present the algorithmic parts of the blind space-variant restoration. We then present the full progressive method.

2.1 Blur Segmentation

Consider Fig. 1. The image was synthetically blurred by an out-of-focus kernel of radius 4 within the contour. In this step we aim to extract this contour. The contour extraction procedure is based on the definition of a blur measure which can differentiate between two blur levels based on the smoothed edges of the blurry region. Generalizing [2], and inspired by the work of [8,22], we define a function E such that

$$E := \left| \log \left(\sum_i \left(\left| \frac{\partial^i g}{\partial x^i} \right| + \left| \frac{\partial^i g}{\partial y^i} \right| \right) * B_r + \varepsilon \right) \right|. \tag{3}$$

Fig. 1. Space-variant blurred image. The out-of-focus blur resides within the contour.

The index i stands for the partial derivative order of the observed image g with respect to the coordinates x and y, B_r is a ball of radius r, and ε is a small positive scalar. In the case where $i = 2$, the function represents a smoothed version of the *modified Laplacian* [22] of the observed image g. As was explained by Nayar and Nakagawa [22], although the Laplacian operator is an isotropic high pass filter, the second derivatives in the x and y directions can have opposite signs and tend to cancel each other. The modified Laplacian alleviates the problem by taking the absolute value of each partial derivative component.

This blur measure highlights the difference in gradients content between blurred and sharp regions. Particularly, since the horizontal and vertical gradients are equally weighted, this definition is more suitable to out-of-focus blur. In the case of motion blur with an arbitrary direction, gradient difference will emerge only in this particular directional derivative which is not necessarily parallel to one of the cartesian axes.

Figure 2 (left) demonstrates the blur measure with $r = 2$ pixels, where the grey levels of g are scaled to be in the range $[0, 1]$. The edge difference is exaggerated between the two regions and stretched by the log function. The blurred region turns brighter since we take the absolute value of negative quantities. The two sub-regions are now visibly distinguishable by their different gray levels.

The outcome of Chan-Vese segmentation [7] applied on E is shown on the right, and is clearly inadequate in this case. We therefore apply an alternative segmentation algorithm.

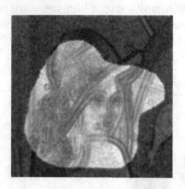

Fig. 2. Left: blur measure function, Right: outcome of Chan-Vese segmentation [7]

Let C denote the separating contour and K the edge set of the observed image g. The contour is extracted as the minimizer of the following cost function [2]:

$$
\begin{aligned}
\mathcal{F}(C,\bar{c}) = &\frac{\lambda_1}{2} \int_{\text{inside}(C) \cap K} (E - c_1)^2 dx + \frac{\lambda_2}{2} \int_{\text{outside}(C) \cap K} (E - c_2)^2 dx \\
&+ \frac{\lambda_3}{2} \int_{\text{inside}(C) \backslash K} (E - c_3)^2 dx + \frac{\lambda_4}{2} \int_{\text{outside}(C) \backslash K} (E - c_4)^2 dx \quad (4)\\
&- \oint_C |(\nabla E, \bar{n})| \, ds + \oint_C \frac{\mu}{\gamma + V_t^2 |\nabla E|^2} ds,
\end{aligned}
$$

where $\bar{c} := \{c_1, c_2, c_3, c_4\}$ is a vector denoting the average gray levels of the smoothed edges inside the contour, the edges outside the contour, the segments inside the contour and the segments outside the contour respectively. The edge set K is approximated by a continuous function v extracted by means of Mumford-Shah segmentation with the Γ-convergence method [3], where $v \approx 0$ along the edges and $v \approx 1$ within the segments. A binary edge map V_t is defined such that

$$
V_t = \begin{cases} 1, v > T, \\ 0, v \leq T, \end{cases} \quad (5)
$$

where $V_t = 1$ within the segments and $V_t = 0$ across the edges, see Fig. 3. The fifth term of Eq. (4) is a robust alignment term [11] which maximizes the projection of the gradients of E onto the curve normals. The last term is a modified geodesic active contour [5] which is a line integral of an inverse edge indicator function. This function has low values along the contour because the contribution of the original image edges is now attenuated by the binary edge map V_t.

Fig. 3. Continuous smooth edge function as was extracted from the observed image g using the Mumford-Shah segmentation. Left: edge function, Right: binary edge map

To make Eq. (4) more tractable, we implicitly represent the contour as the zero level set function $\phi : \Omega \to \mathbb{R}$ such that $C = \{x \in \Omega : \phi(x) = 0\}$. Thus we obtain

$$
\mathcal{F}(\phi, \bar{c}) = \frac{\lambda_1}{2} \int_\Omega (1-v)^2 (E-c_1)^2 H(\phi) dx + \frac{\lambda_2}{2} \int_\Omega (1-v)^2 (E-c_2)^2 (1-H(\phi)) dx
$$

$$
+ \frac{\lambda_3}{2} \int_\Omega v^2 (E-c_3)^2 H(\phi) dx + \frac{\lambda_4}{2} \int_\Omega v^2 (E-c_4)^2 (1-H(\phi)) dx
$$

$$
- \int_\Omega \left| \left(\nabla E, \frac{\nabla \phi}{|\nabla \phi|} \right) \right| |\nabla H(\phi)| dx + \int_\Omega \frac{\mu}{\gamma + V_t^2 |\nabla E|^2} |\nabla H(\phi)| dx,
$$

$$(6)$$

where H stands for the Heaviside function. The optimization is carried out by alternating between the calculation of the level set function ϕ and the vector $\bar{c}$. The implicit level set evolution takes the form

$$
\phi_t = -\frac{\delta \mathcal{F}}{\delta \phi} = - \left\{ \lambda_1 (1-v)^2 (E-c_1)^2 - \lambda_2 (1-v)^2 (E-c_2)^2 \right.
$$

$$
+ \lambda_3 v^2 (E-c_3)^2 - \lambda_4 v^2 (E-c_4)
$$

$$(7)$$

$$
\left. - \operatorname{sign} \left(\langle \nabla E, \nabla \phi \rangle \right) \nabla^2 E - \nabla \cdot \left(\frac{\mu}{\gamma + V_t^2 |\nabla E|^2} \frac{\nabla \phi}{|\nabla \phi|} \right) \right\},
$$

and the minimization of $\mathcal{F}(\phi, \bar{c})$ with respect to c_1 yields

$$
c_1 = \frac{\int (1-v)^2 E H(\phi)}{\int (1-v)^2 H(\phi)}.
$$

$$(8)$$

The constants c_2, c_3 and c_4 are calculated in the same fashion. The segmentation result is depicted in Fig. 4 where the binary edges are marked in light red.

2.2 Non-parametric Kernel Estimation

As part of the progressive algorithm, kernel estimation procedure is performed in a region contained in the blurry segment. We apply the work of Kotera et al. [13],

Fig. 4. Segmentation results of the blur measure E. The smoothed edges are marked in light red. (Color figure online)

where the sharp image f and blur kernel h are the minimizers of the functional

$$\mathcal{F}(f,h) = \frac{\gamma}{2} \int_\Omega (f*h-g)^2 dx + \alpha_f \int_\Omega |\nabla f|^p dx + \alpha_h \int_\Omega \Psi(h(x)) dx, \qquad (9)$$

where

$$\Psi(h(x)) = \begin{cases} h(x), & \text{if } h(x) > 0 \\ \infty, & \text{otherwise} \end{cases}.$$

The second term stands for the image regularizer and the third term is the L_1 regularization of the kernel h which is forced to be positive. We apply the implementation of Kotera[1] with its default parameters in all our experiments. The domain Ω is defined as a rectangle, therefore in our case we extract the maximal rectangle within the blurry segment to make use of topmost blur information. In future work this domain can be generalized to an arbitrary region of interest. The parameter p was set to 0.3. This value was used only in the kernel estimation procedure and not in the final non-blind image recovery. As was recently explained by Zon et al. [30], low dimensional or cartoon-like images are superior for kernel estimation since the estimator is directed to stronger step-edges and diverted away from weak edges which may be related to noise. We integrate this component in our progressive algorithm and use only the estimated kernel h.

2.3   Non-blind Space-Variant Deblurring

The second element of the progressive algorithm is the non-blind space-variant restoration given the blurry segment (represented by the zero level set of ϕ) and the blur kernel h. We distinguish between two cases [21]: whenever the

---

[1] http://zoi.utia.cas.cz/deconv_sparsegrad.

foreground object is out of focus and closer to the camera, there is some bleeding of the foreground to the background such that

$$g = (F_{\text{fg}} * h)(1 - \chi_{\text{bg}} * h) + F_{\text{bg}}(\chi_{\text{bg}} * h),$$

where χ_{bg} denotes the characteristics function of the background. If the foreground is in focus and is closer to the camera, there is no bleeding effect, and therefore

$$g = F_{\text{fg}}\chi_{\text{obj}} + (F_{\text{bg}} * h)(1 - \chi_{\text{obj}}),$$

where in our setting $\chi_{\text{bg}} = H(\phi)$ and $\chi_{\text{obj}} = 1 - H(\phi)$. In this work we focused on the second case but it can be easily adapted to the first one. The recovered image f is calculated by the minimization of

$$\mathcal{T}(f) = \frac{1}{2}\int_{\Omega}(f * h - g)^2 H(\phi)dx + \frac{1}{2}\int_{\Omega}(f - g)^2(1 - H(\phi))dx + \beta\int_{\Omega}|\nabla f|^p dx. \quad (10)$$

The first and second terms stand for data fidelity in the background and foreground regions respectively. The third term serves as a *global* l_p regularizer which enforces the smoothness of the recovered image and eliminates discontinuities between the sharp and blurred sub-regions. The Euler-Lagrange equation takes the form

$$\frac{\delta\mathcal{T}}{\delta f} = h(-x)(f * h - g)H(\phi) + (f - g)(1 - H(\phi)) - \beta p \nabla \cdot \left(\frac{\nabla f}{|\nabla f|^{2-p}}\right) = 0, \quad (11)$$

and it was solved by the conjugate gradients method.

3   Progressive Algorithm

We are now ready to introduce the full algorithm: first, we perform the segmentation procedure and obtain the blurry background segment $\chi_{\text{bg}} = H(\phi)$. We then start a progressive procedure as was recently introduced by Hanocka and Kiryati [9,30] for blind space-invariant restoration. From the blurry region we extract the maximal rectangular sub-region and estimate a blur kernel h_1 as was explained in Sect. 2.2. We then recover the image by the space-variant deblurring method described in Sect. 2.3 and obtain an image f_1. A blurred sub-region of f_1 is then fed again into the kernel estimation step and kernel h_2 is calculated followed by another restoration stage that yields f_2. The process lasts for few iterations, usually 2 or 3. The idea behind this approach is that the residual blur may be corrected in the second and third iterations and in turn significantly improve the restoration results. The sequence $h_1, h_2, \ldots, h_n$ ideally converges to the δ function. A detailed convergence proof can be found, for a special case, in the work of Zon et al. [30]. Here is a summary of the algorithm:

Progressive Blind Space-Variant Restoration

1. Given a blurred image g
2. Set $f_1 := g$
3. Segment the blurry region, obtain the level set function ϕ
4. Define a maximal rectangular sub-region $\mathcal{P}$ in the blurry region
5. **For** $i = 1, 2, \ldots n$
6. Estimate the blur kernel of the sub-region $\mathcal{P}(f_i)$ by solving Eq. (9) and obtain kernel h_i
7. Perform the space-variant deblurring by Eq. (11) and obtain f_{i+1}.
8. Update $g = f_{i+1}$
9. **End**

---

4   Experimental Results

In this section we demonstrate the performance of the proposed algorithm on various real images. The function E defined in Eq. (3) was taken with second and forth derivatives since the forth derivative improved the contrast between the foreground and background. The radius of the ball B_r was taken in the range 3 to 15 pixels, the threshold T of the binary edge map was 0.93, and ε was set to 0.001 in all the experiments. Color images were converted to YC_bC_r format. The E function and non-blind space-variant restoration were applied on the Y component, while the chroma components were left intact. Most of the segmentation parameters in Eq. (6) were tuned once and used in all cases: $\lambda_1 = \lambda_2 = \lambda_3 = \lambda_4 = 1$, $\gamma = 1$ and $\mu = 14$. The initial level set ϕ was the distance function of an arbitrary circle, and two or three iterations were used in the progressive loop. The regularizer weight β in (11) was manually tuned in the range $[10^{-4}, 10^{-3}]$ and p was set to 0.9 in all cases.

Consider the original image Fig. 5(a). The segmentation result on the blur measure E is shown in (b) and the extracted blurred sub-region in (c). Note that regions with no textural details are considered as background. The recovered image is shown in (f, j) and the estimated kernels in (k, l, m). The proposed algorithm is compared against the parametric kernel approach as was suggested by [27]. We manually selected the best disk kernel and applied it to our non-blind space-variant restoration algorithm (d, h). As can be seen, the estimated kernels are not pure discs and therefore the non-parametric approach (j) outperforms the parametric one (h). In addition, we show the first iteration result of our algorithm in figures (e, i). This is actually a non-parametric one step restoration approach (e.g. [25]). In this case the progressive restoration (f, j) yields a sharper image as well. More real images results are depicted in Fig. 6. As can be observed on the left column, although the segmentation is not perfectly aligned with the foreground object, it is suitable for the restoration task since the deblurring process at edgeless regions is not noticeable and the ultimate result looks natural.

(a) Original image   (b) E function   (c) Blurred sub-region

(d) Parametric kernel   (e) Proposed: step 1   (f) Proposed: step 3

(g) Original image   (h) Parametric kernel

(i) Proposed: step 1   (j) Proposed: step 3

(k) h_1 (l) h_2 (m) h_3

Fig. 5. (a) Original image; (b) Segmentation superimposed on the blur measure E; (c) Blurred rectangular sub-region; (d) Recovered image by the parametric approach; (e) Recovered image at the first iteration of the progressive method; (f) Recovered image at the third iteration of the progressive method; (g) Close-up of (a); (h) Close-up of (d); (i) Close-up of (e); (j) Close-up of (f); (k) The estimated kernel at the first progressive iteration; (l) The estimated kernel at the second progressive iteration; (m) The estimated kernel at the third progressive iteration. Image credit: Yuval Dagai.

Fig. 6. Outcome of the proposed algorithm. Left: segmentation of E function, Middle: original image, Right: recovered image by the proposed algorithm. Image credit top to bottom: Yitzhak Glick, [27], Dan Bar-Dov, [1], Nadav Cassuto.

5   Discussion

We consider the challenging problem of blind space-variant deblurring of a single image with piecewise defocus blur. The proposed algorithm consists of segmentation of the sharp and blurred regions, and progressive blind space-variant deblurring. The separating contour between the sub-regions is represented as an evolving level set and has therefore no limitation on its shape.

The segmentation is based on the definition of a blur measure which generalizes the modified Laplacian to higher derivatives and emphasizes the contrast between sharp and blurred regions. The suggested blur measure is suitable for out-of-focus blur since it takes into account horizontal and vertical gradients, but it could be adopted to other blur types. For example, for blind motion blur the blur measure could be based on a collection of different directional derivatives where the maximal contrast will emerge in the motion direction. Nevertheless, the algorithmic framework here proposed is general. The advantages of our approach rely on the progressive blind space-variant restoration process which feeds the residual blur into the blind non-parametric kernel estimation step, followed by a robust variational non-blind space variant restoration method. Experimental results on real images show that the progressive approach outperforms a single step deconvolution. For future work, we suggest additional improvement of the segmentation process by incorporating the object color into the optimization procedure as was previously performed in focus map estimation works. Furthermore, expansion of the blur measure to a general blur and multi blur sub-regions restoration could be considered as well.

References

1. Bae, S., Durand, F.: Defocus magnification. In: EUROGRAPHICS (2007)
2. Bar, L., Sochen, N., Kiryati, N.: Restoration of images with piecewise space-variant blur. In: Sgallari, F., Murli, A., Paragios, N. (eds.) SSVM 2007. LNCS, vol. 4485, pp. 533–544. Springer, Heidelberg (2007). doi:10.1007/978-3-540-72823-8_46
3. Braides, A.: Approximation of Free-Discontinuity Problems. LNM, vol. 1694. Springer, Heidelberg (1998)
4. Cao, Y., Fang, S., Wang, Z.: Digital multi-focusing from a single photograph taken with an uncalibrated conventional camera. IEEE Trans. Image Process. 22, 3703–3714 (2013)
5. Caselles, V., Kimmel, R., Sapiro, G.: Geodesic active contours. Int. J. Comput. Vis. 22, 61–79 (1997)
6. Chakrabarti, A., Zickler, T., Freeman, W.T.: Analyzing spatially-varying blur. In: CVPR (2010)
7. Chan, T., Vese, L.: Active contours without edges. IEEE Trans. Image Process. 10, 266–277 (2001)
8. Frommer, Y., Ben-Ari, R., Kiryati, N.: Adaptive shape from focus based on high order derivatives. In: Proceedings of the 26th British Machine Vision Conference (BMVC 2015) (2015)
9. Hanocka, R., Kiryati, N.: Progressive blind deconvolution. In: Azzopardi, G., Petkov, N. (eds.) CAIP 2015. LNCS, vol. 9257, pp. 313–325. Springer, Cham (2015). doi:10.1007/978-3-319-23117-4_27

10. Javaran, T.A., Hassanpour, H., Abolghasemi, V.: Automatic estimation and segmentation of partial blur in natural images. Vis. Comput. **33**, 151–161 (2017). doi:10.1007/s00371-015-1166-z
11. Kimmel, R.: Fase edge integration. In: Osher, S., Paragios, N. (eds.) Geometric Level Set Methods in Imaging Vision and Graphics. Springer, New York (2003)
12. Komodakis, N., Paragios, N.: MRF-based blind image deconvolution. In: Lee, K.M., Matsushita, Y., Rehg, J.M., Hu, Z. (eds.) ACCV 2012. LNCS, vol. 7726, pp. 361–374. Springer, Heidelberg (2013). doi:10.1007/978-3-642-37431-9_28
13. Kotera, J., Šroubek, F., Milanfar, P.: Blind deconvolution using alternating maximum a posteriori estimation with heavy-tailed priors. In: Wilson, R., Hancock, E., Bors, A., Smith, W. (eds.) CAIP 2013. LNCS, vol. 8048, pp. 59–66. Springer, Heidelberg (2013). doi:10.1007/978-3-642-40246-3_8
14. Krishnan, D., Tay, T., Fergus, R.: Blind deconvolution using a normalized sparsity measure. In: CVPR (2011)
15. Lai, W.S., Huang, J.B., Hu, Z., Ahuja, A., Yang, M.H.: A comparative study for single image blind deblurring. In: CVPR (2016)
16. Levin, A.: Blind motion deblurring using image statistics. In: Advances in Neural Information Processing Systems (NIPS 2006) (2006)
17. Levin, A., Weiss, Y., Durand, F., Freeman, W.T.: Efficient marginal likelihood optimization in blind deconvolution. In: CVPR (2011)
18. Liu, S., Zhou, F., Liao, Q.: Defocus map estimation from a single image based on two-parameter defocus model. IEEE Trans. Image Process. **25**, 5943–5956 (2016)
19. Loktyushin, A., Harmeling, S.: Automatic foreground-background refocusing. In: ICIP (2011)
20. Mahmoudpour, S., Kim, M.: Superpixel-based depth map estimation using defocus blur. In: ICIP (2016)
21. Marshall, J.A., Burbeck, C.A., Arieli, D., Rolland, J.P., Martin, K.E.: Occlusion edge blur: a cue to relative visual depth. J. Opt. Soc. Am. A **13**, 681–688 (1996)
22. Nayar, S.K., Nakagawa, Y.: Shape from focus. IEEE Trans. Pattern Anal. Mach. Intell. **16**(8), 824–831 (1994)
23. Pan, J., Hu, Z., Su, Z., Lee, H.Y., Yang, M.H.: Soft-segmentation guided object motion deblurring. In: CVPR (2016)
24. Pang, Y., Zhu, H., Li, X., Pan, J.: Motion blur detection with an indicator function for surveillance machines. IEEE Trans. Ind. Electron. **63**, 5592–5601 (2016)
25. Schelten, K., Roth, S.: Localized image blur removal through non-parametric kernel estimation. In: ICPR (2014)
26. Tiwari, J., Rai, R.K., Shrman, B.: A review on estimation of defocus blur from a single image. Int. J. Comput. Appl. **106**, 0975–8887 (2014)
27. Zhang, W., Cham, W.: Single-image refocusing and defocusing. IEEE Trans. Image Process. **21**, 873–882 (2012)
28. Zhang, Y., Hirakawa, K.: Blind deblurring and denoising of images corrupted by unidirectional object motion blur and sensor noise. IEEE Trans. Image Process. **25**, 4129–4144 (2016)
29. Zhu, X., Cohen, S., Schiller, S., Milanfar, P.: Estimating spatially varying defocus blur from a single image. IEEE Trans. Image Process. **22**, 4879–4891 (2013)
30. Zon, N., Hanocka, R., Kiryati, N.: Fast and easy blind deblurring using an inverse filter and probe (2017). arXiv:1702.01315

Denoising by Inpainting

Robin Dirk Adam, Pascal Peter$^{(\boxtimes)}$, and Joachim Weickert

Mathematical Image Analysis Group, Faculty of Mathematics and Computer Science,
Campus E1.7, Saarland University, 66041 Saarbrücken, Germany
{adam,peter,weickert}@mia.uni-saarland.de

Abstract. The filling-in effect of diffusion processes has been successfully used in many image analysis applications. Examples include image
reconstructions in inpainting-based compression or dense optic flow computations. As an interesting side effect of diffusion-based inpainting, the
interpolated data are smooth, even if the known image data are noisy:
Inpainting averages information from noisy sources. Since this effect has
not been investigated for denoising purposes so far, we propose a general
framework for denoising by inpainting. It averages multiple inpainting
results from different selections of known data. We evaluate two concrete
implementations of this framework: The first one specifies known data on
a shifted regular grid, while the second one employs probabilistic densification to optimise the known pixel locations w.r.t. the inpainting quality.
For homogeneous diffusion inpainting, we demonstrate that our regular
grid method approximates the quality of its corresponding diffusion filter.
The densification algorithm with homogeneous diffusion inpainting, however, shows edge-preserving behaviour. It resembles space-variant diffusion and offers better reconstructions than homogeneous diffusion filters.

Keywords: Diffusion · Denoising · Inpainting · Densification

1 Introduction

Image inpainting is the task of reconstructing missing image parts from available known data [2,10,17,25]. Diffusion filters have been proven to be capable
of recovering images from very sparse pixel sets in high quality [7,13,16], which
is particularly useful in the context of image compression [12,24]. This filling-in
effect has also been used successfully for more than three decades in variational
models for optic flow computation such as [14,18]. Here, dense displacement
vector fields are created by inpainting at locations where no flow can be measured and the data term vanishes. Surprisingly, these reconstructed parts of the
flow fields are often more reliable than the measured flow vectors, since the
diffusion-based inpainting solution averages information from many noisy data
in the neighbourhood [3]. One can also observe a similar effect in diffusion-based
compression applications: For low compression rates, the compressed image can
look smoother and visually more pleasing than the original.

Denoising is another classic image processing task that can be solved by diffusion. From the simple original homogeneous diffusion filter [15], a plethora

© Springer International Publishing AG 2017
F. Lauze et al. (Eds.): SSVM 2017, LNCS 10302, pp. 121–132, 2017.
DOI: 10.1007/978-3-319-58771-4_10

of fairly sophisticated approaches has evolved; see e.g. [19,27]. Although nowadays non-local denoising methods such as BM3D [9] are very popular, modern diffusion-reaction models that rely on learning yield competitive results [6]. Both the classic and the more recent diffusion-based denoising methods have in common that they approach the task by directly applying smoothing to the image. To our best knowledge, the potential denoising capabilities of diffusion-based *inpainting*, however, have not been investigated so far.

Our Contribution. In order to close this gap, we propose a general framework for *denoising by inpainting*: In order to denoise an image, we average several inpainting results that use different selections of the noisy original pixels as known data. Moreover, we introduce two different implementations of this framework that both rely on linear homogeneous diffusion inpainting, but differ w.r.t. the selection strategy for the known image points. Our investigations show that inpainting from specified points at shifted, non-overlapping regular grid positions approximates the quality of linear homogeneous diffusion. We also propose a more sophisticated probabilistic strategy inspired by the sparsification approach of Mainberger et al. [16]: It adapts the locations of known data to the image structure. Our evaluation reveals that this method possesses edge-preserving properties similar to space-variant diffusion, while using a space-invariant differential operator.

Related Work. Our work makes extensive use of diffusion filters. In particular, our implementations rely on linear homogeneous diffusion, which goes back to Iijima [15]. We also consider nonlinear isotropic diffusion, which was first introduced by Perona and Malik [19]. In contrast to linear diffusion, this filter adapts to the local image structure in order to preserve edges. After these classic models, many more have been proposed (e.g. [27]), but a full review would be beyond the scope of this work. Since we are mainly interested in gaining insight into new applications for inpainting and do not aim to produce state-of-the-art denoising results, we focus solely on linear homogeneous and nonlinear isotropic diffusion filters.

Interestingly, diffusion filtering can be related to many other types of denoising methods. For instance, Scherzer and Weickert [23] have shown connections between variational methods such as Tikhonov and Arsenin [26] or TV regularisation [22] and fully implicit time discretisations of diffusion filters. Furthermore, a large variety of diffusion filters for denoising can be interpreted as Bayesian denoising models; see e.g. [20]. Thereby, they can be seen as special cases of probabilistic approaches such as the field-of-experts model [21]. Also, relations to wavelet shrinkage have been established [28].

There are also other classes of denoising filters that we cannot discuss in detail in this work. In particular, non-local methods like BM3D [9] and its successors can be regarded as a sophisticated extension of the NL-means filter of Buades et al. [4]: Such approaches search for similar image patches and average over those to remove noise. NL-means can also be seen as a specific non-local representative of a denoising by inpainting strategy, since Buades et al. have been inspired by the exemplar-based inpainting method of Efros and Leung [10].

With respect to image inpainting, parts of our paper rely on spatial optimisation techniques. It has been shown that in cases where a sparse image representation can be chosen from the fully available original image, the selection
of known data has a significant impact on reconstruction quality [7,13,16]. In
particular, we focus on the probabilistic sparsification method by Mainberger
et al. [16] that iteratively removes image points which are easy to reconstruct. In
a broad conceptual sense, the sparsification and densification strategies that we
consider in this paper are related to the generalised cross-validation methods by
Craven and Wahba [8], since here also approximation accuracy under removal
of data is considered. However, generalised cross-validation is usually used to
determine model parameters, for instance for denoising based on wavelet shrinkage [29]. In our application, we iteratively remove known data to obtain sparse
image representations.

Organisation of the Paper. Since the concepts of diffusion-based denoising
and inpainting are integral to our work, we review them in Sect. 2. In Sect. 3 we
propose our general framework for denoising by inpainting. With an approach
based on regular masks in Sect. 4 and a densification scheme in Sect. 5, we also
present two concrete implementations of this framework. Finally, we evaluate
the new denoising methods in Sect. 6 and conclude our work with a discussion
and an outlook in Sect. 7.

2   Diffusion-Based Denoising and Inpainting

2.1   Diffusion-Based Denoising

Our goal is to apply a diffusion filter to a noisy image $f : \Omega \to \mathbb{R}$ that maps the
rectangular image domain $\Omega \subset \mathbb{R}^2$ to the grey value range $\mathbb{R}$. To this end we
start with the initial condition $u(x, y, 0) = f(x, y)$ and compute filtered versions
$\{u(x, y, t) | (x, y) \in \Omega, t \geq 0\}$ of $f(x, y)$ with diffusion time t as solutions of the
following initial boundary value problem:

$$\partial_t u = \mathrm{div}(g\,\nabla u) \quad \text{on} \quad \Omega \times (0, \infty), \tag{1}$$

$$u(x, y, 0) = f(x, y) \quad \text{on} \quad \Omega, \tag{2}$$

$$\partial_n u = 0 \quad \text{on} \quad \partial\Omega \times (0, \infty). \tag{3}$$

Here we use the outer normal vector n to the image boundary $\partial\Omega$ and the corresponding directional derivative ∂_n to specify reflecting boundary conditions. By
$\nabla = (\partial_x, \partial_y)^\top$ we denote the spatial nabla operator, and div is its corresponding divergence operator. The diffusion time t embeds the filtered images u into
a scale-space: Increasing the diffusion time simplifies the image.
The scalar-valued diffusivity $g : [0, \infty) \to (0, \infty)$ is a positive function of the
local image structure. The magnitude of g determines how much smoothing
the diffusion filter performs at a given location in the image. Three scenarios
are relevant for our paper: homogeneous, linear space-variant, and nonlinear
diffusion.

Homogeneous Diffusion. [15] uses the constant diffusivity $g = 1$. This leads to the linear diffusion equation (also known as heat equation) $\partial_t u = \Delta u$ with the Laplacian $\Delta = \partial_{xx} + \partial_{yy}$. This evolution generates the well-known Gaussian scale-space [15]. It is simple to implement and uses no additional parameters apart from t. Since homogeneous diffusion smoothes equally at all locations of the image, it is *space-invariant*. However, as it cannot distinguish between noise and edges, it also blurs semantically important image edges.

Linear Space-Variant Diffusion. [11] avoids this drawback by adapting the diffusive evolution to the *initial* image f. This can be achieved by choosing $g = g(|\nabla f|^2)$ with a decreasing diffusivity function that becomes small at edges where $|\nabla f|$ is large. An example is the Charbonnier diffusivity [5]

$$g_C(s^2) := \left(1 + \frac{s^2}{\lambda^2}\right)^{-1/2}. \tag{4}$$

Note that locations where $|\nabla f| \gg \lambda$ are regarded as edges where the diffusivity is close to 0, while we have full diffusion in regions with $|\nabla f| \ll \lambda$. Therefore, $\lambda > 0$ acts as a contrast parameter.

Nonlinear Diffusion. [19] goes one step further and chooses the diffusivity as a function of the *evolving* image $u(., t)$. Using $g = g(|\nabla u|^2)$ instead of $g = g(|\nabla f|^2)$ introduces a nonlinear feedback into the evolution. Since the evolving image becomes gradually smoother, one often obtains better denoising results than for linear space-variant diffusion.

To keep everything simple and focus on structural insights, we do not consider more advanced diffusion processes that use a diffusion tensor [27].

2.2 Diffusion-Based Inpainting

With some small modifications, the diffusion filters from the previous section can be applied to image inpainting problems. Let the original image f only be known on the *inpainting mask* $K \subset \Omega$. Our goal is to reconstruct the missing data in the *inpainting domain* $\Omega \backslash K$. We achieve this by computing the steady state $(t \to \infty)$ of the image evolution of $u(x, y, t)$ that is described by

$$\partial_t u = \operatorname{div}(g \, \nabla u) \quad \text{on} \quad \Omega \backslash K \times (0, \infty), \tag{5}$$

$$u(x, y, t) = f(x, y) \quad \text{on} \quad K \times [0, \infty), \tag{6}$$

$$\partial_n u = 0 \quad \text{on} \quad \partial\Omega \times (0, \infty). \tag{7}$$

In contrast to Eqs. (1)–(3), the diffusion PDE is only applied to the inpainting domain $\Omega \backslash K$, while Dirichlet boundary conditions fix the known data on K. This leads to a non-flat steady state. Equivalently, we can formulate the inpainting problem with the elliptic PDE

$$(1 - c(\boldsymbol{x}))Lu - c(\boldsymbol{x})(u - f) = 0 \tag{8}$$

where $Lu := \text{div}(g\,\nabla u)$, and c is a binary confidence function that is 1 on K, and 0 on $\Omega \setminus K$. Note that on $\partial\Omega$, the reflecting boundary conditions still apply. In the following sections we favour this more compact notation, and we use the term *inpainting mask* for both the set K and its associated indicator function c.

3   A General Framework for Denoising by Inpainting

In our new denoising approach we want to exploit that inpainting reconstructions are smooth, even if we apply the diffusion operator to noisy known data. Thus, given a confidence mask c as in the previous section, we expect our pixels in the inpainting domain $\Omega \setminus K$ to be more reliable than our known noisy data K.

Obviously this has the undesired effect that all noisy pixels which belong to our inpainting mask are not affected by the filter at all. To obtain a denoised image u in *all* pixels, we average n reconstructions $(v^\ell)_{\ell=0}^{n-1}$ that are computed with the same differential operator L, but with *different* inpainting masks $(c^\ell)_{\ell=0}^{n-1}$. This leads to the following general formulation:

$$(1 - c^\ell(\boldsymbol{x}))Lv^\ell - c^\ell(\boldsymbol{x})(v^\ell - f) = 0, \qquad \ell \in \{0,\ldots,n-1\}, \tag{9}$$

$$u = \frac{1}{n}\sum_{\ell=0}^{n-1} v^\ell. \tag{10}$$

Compared to standard diffusion-based denoising, we do not have to choose a diffusion time any more, since all reconstructions correspond to steady states of the n inpaintings in Eq. (9). Instead, the mask density d (the percentage of known data points) is the free parameter of our model that determines the amount of smoothing: Decreasing the mask density leads to more smoothing.

In the following, we introduce two different strategies to choose the mask locations corresponding to this density parameter. In both cases, we choose $L = \Delta$ as our differential operator, i.e. we use homogeneous diffusion inpainting.

4   Denoising with Regular Masks

For our first inpainting-based denoising model, we choose the masks as shifted versions of a regular grid. Let the spacing between known pixels in the grid be given by r in x-direction and s in y-direction. Then we have $n := r \cdot s$ ways to shift this grid in a non-overlapping way. For a discrete image with resolution $M \times N$ and grid size h, we define the space-discrete masks c^ℓ with $\ell \in \{0,\ldots,n-1\}$ by

$$c_{i,j}^{ps+q} = c^{ps+q}(ih, jh) := \begin{cases} 1 & i = p \bmod r \text{ and } j = q \bmod s, \\ 0 & \text{else.} \end{cases} \tag{11}$$

Here, $p \in \{0, r-1\}$ and $q \in \{0,\ldots,s-1\}$ are the admissible grid offsets. Each pixel in the image domain Ω is covered by exactly one mask. For our denoising model, this means that at each location the confidence in the known data is equal: We always average $n - 1$ inpainting results and the original pixel.

Experimentally, we determine that this scheme with regular masks is indeed capable of denoising, but performs slightly worse than homogeneous diffusion filtering. For a typical result see Fig. 1. However, both quantitatively and visually, the results of our regular mask inpainting approach with homogeneous diffusion appear to approximate homogeneous diffusion filtering. In the following, we justify this behaviour with considerations in the 1-D setting.

original	noisy	homog. diffusion	regular inpainting

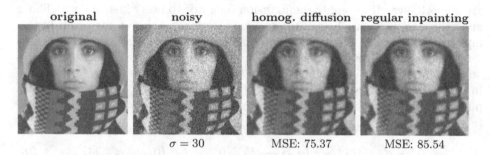

| | $\sigma = 30$ | MSE: 75.37 | MSE: 85.54 |

Fig. 1. Experiment: denoising with inpainting on regular masks versus homogeneous diffusion. For this test on *trui* with Gaussian noise ($\sigma = 30$), optimal diffusion time and grid spacing were chosen for each method respectively. We compare both methods w.r.t. the mean squared error (MSE).

1-D Analysis. Let us consider inpainting with 1-D homogeneous diffusion and regular masks with spacing n. For a pixel position i and a mask shifted by $p \in \{0, \ldots, n - 1\}$, we define the offset $\ell = |i - p| \bmod n$ relative to i. This implies that for the mask c^{ℓ} with $\ell = 0$, the location i is known. For general choices $\ell \in \{0, \ldots, n - 1\}$, the known points that are closest to i are $i - \ell$ on the left and $i + n - \ell$ on the right. Since in 1-D, inpainting with homogeneous diffusion is equivalent to linear interpolation between adjacent known points, we obtain the reconstruction v^{ℓ} at location i as

$$v_i^{\ell} = \frac{n - \ell}{n} f_{i-\ell} + \frac{\ell}{n} f_{i+n-\ell}. \tag{12}$$

Now we average our inpainting solutions $(v^{\ell})_{\ell=0}^{n-1}$ to end up with the denoised image u. This yields

$$u_i = \frac{1}{n} \sum_{\ell=0}^{n-1} v_i^{\ell} = \frac{1}{n} \sum_{\ell=0}^{n-1} \left(\frac{n - \ell}{n} f_{i-\ell} + \frac{\ell}{n} f_{i+n-\ell} \right) \tag{13}$$

$$= \frac{1}{n^2} \left(n \cdot f_i + \sum_{\ell=1}^{n-1} \ell \cdot (f_{i-n+\ell} + f_{i+n-\ell}) \right). \tag{14}$$

For the highest non-trivial regular mask density, which comes down to storing every second pixel ($n = 2$), we obtain

$$u_i = \frac{f_{i-1} + 2f_i + f_{i+1}}{4} \quad \Longleftrightarrow \quad \frac{u_i - f_i}{\tau} = \frac{f_{i+1} - 2f_i + f_{i-1}}{h^2} \qquad (15)$$

with $\tau := \frac{4}{h^2}$. Since the right equation is an explicit finite difference step of $\partial_t u = \partial_{xx} u$ with initial value f and time step size τ, this is equivalent to applying a homogeneous diffusion filter. For larger choices of n, Eq. 14 corresponds to convolving the image with a symmetric sampling of a hat function that has $2n + 1$ non-zero samples. This visually resembles Gaussian convolution.

5 Denoising with Adaptive Masks

In order to improve our denoising results compared to the non-adaptive masks from the previous section, we want to rely on *spatial mask optimisation* [7, 13, 16], a successful concept in PDE-based compression. Optimising the location of the known data can improve each individual reconstruction v^ℓ and thereby also the average u. For homogeneous diffusion inpainting, the theory of Belhachmi et al. [1] recommends to choose locations left and right of image edges. However, in images with large amounts of noise, edge detection is by no means an easy task. Moreover, we require multiple different masks for our general denoising by inpainting framework from Sect. 3.

Among the wide variety of different approaches for spatial optimisation, the probabilistic approach by Mainberger et al. [16] seems to be the most promising for our purpose: It does not rely on edge detection and contains a random component that we can use to generate different adaptive masks.

Sparsification. The original probabilistic sparsification starts with a mask that contains all image points and successively reduces the amount of known pixels until it reaches a target density d. In each iteration, it removes a fixed percentage α of known data. After inpainting with the resulting smaller mask, it adds a percentage β of the removed pixels with the highest reconstruction error back to the mask. Thus, out of $\alpha\%$ candidates, we remove the $\beta\%$ pixels that can be reconstructed best.

Unfortunately, applying sparsification directly to our denoising problem with homogeneous diffusion yields unsatisfactory results due to its local error computation: It considers the deviation of each candidate pixel from the corresponding image point in the noisy input image and preserves those candidates with the largest deviation. However, a large local difference can not only result from fine scale detail that should be preserved. Since the original data are noisy, the sparsification algorithm preserves noise that deviates from the smooth reconstruction. One solution to avoid this problem is to consider the impact of removing a single pixel on the overall reconstruction: If the noise has zero mean, computing the global error between inpainting solution and noisy image should give a better estimate to the error w.r.t. the unperturbed original. However, even with this change, sparsification selects noise pixels (see Fig. 2(b)).

The reason for this behaviour is a second source of locality: The influence of a pixel on the reconstruction result is determined by the mask density of its

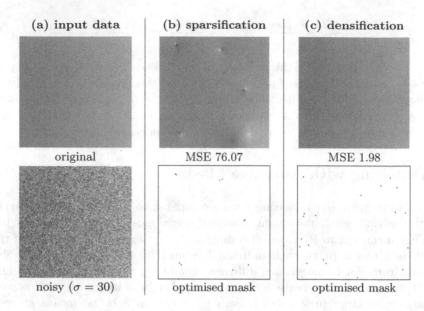

| (a) input data | (b) sparsification | (c) densification |

original   MSE 76.07   MSE 1.98

noisy ($\sigma = 30$)   optimised mask   optimised mask

Fig. 2. Experiment: densification versus sparsification. For both methods, the mask density d was optimised with a grid search w.r.t. the MSE. The noisy gradient image is not reconstructed adequately by sparsification, since it prefers to keep noisy pixels in the first iterations due to localisation. Densification does not suffer from this problem and thereby achieves a more accurate inpainting.

surroundings. This is illustrated by two extreme cases: In a mask consisting of a single pixel, its influence is truly global. It determines the average grey value of the flat steady state. In contrast, a pixel surrounded entirely by known data does not influence the inpainting at all. Since we start with a dense pixel mask in sparsification, each pixel initially has a very small influence which gradually increases the more points are removed. This leads to the preference of noisy data.

Input: Noisy image $f \in \mathbb{R}^{MN}$, number α of candidates, desired final mask density d.
Initialisation: Mask $c = 0$ is empty.
Compute:
  do
    1. Choose randomly a set $A \subset \{k \in \{1, \ldots, MN\} | c_k = 0\}$ with α candidates.
    for all $i \in A$ **do**
      2. Set temporary mask m^i such that $\forall k \in \{1, \ldots, \alpha\} \setminus \{i\} : m_k^i = c_k, m_i^i = 1$.
      3. Compute reconstruction u^i from mask m^i and image data f.
    end for
    4. Set $c = \mathrm{argmin}_{m^i} \mathrm{MSE}(u^i, f)$. This adds one mask point to c.
  while pixel density of c smaller than d.
Output: Mask c of density d.

Algorithm 1. Mask densification with global error computation.

Densification. In order to remove this second source of locality, we instead propose a densification approach in Algorithm 1. We start with an empty mask and consider α randomly selected candidates that do not belong to the mask. We then only add the single pixel that improves the overall reconstruction error w.r.t. the noisy image the most.

6   Experiments

In the following we evaluate the performance of our two approaches for denoising by inpainting from Sects. 4 and 5. We add Gaussian noise to the test images *trui*, *peppers*, and *lena* to compare our methods to diffusion filters. In order to reveal the full potential of each algorithm, we select the respective parameters such that the mean squared error (MSE) w.r.t. the ground truth is minimised. This includes the stopping time of all diffusion processes, the contrast parameter λ in the diffusivity (4) for the linear space-variant and nonlinear diffusion models, as well as the mask density for the inpainting approaches. For this optimisation, we use a straightforward grid search. For all experiments, we have fixed the number of different masks in our densification approach to $n = 128$.

The results in Fig. 1 and Table 1 confirm that our inpainting approach with regular masks approximates the quality of homogeneous diffusion filtering. It is slightly worse than its diffusion counterpart.

Our densification method, however, proves to be consistently better than denoising with homogeneous diffusion. Note that it does not only offer a better quantitative performance: Due to the preservation of edges, the results are also visually more pleasing (see Fig. 3).

Surprisingly, the densification method is even superior to linear space-variant diffusion filtering in 8 out of 9 cases considered in Table 1. In order to understand this behaviour, we should remember that the densification method achieves adaptivity by searching for the most useful pixels as inpainting data. Typically these are those pixels which are less degraded by Gaussian noise than their neighbours. Linear space-variant diffusion lacks such a mechanism to identify the most reliable pixels: All edge pixels with the same gradient magnitude are assigned the same diffusivity, regardless of their individual reliability. This explains the slightly weaker performance of linear space-variant diffusion. At the same time,

Table 1. Denoising results. We compare our two denoising by inpainting strategies (that employ homogeneous diffusion inpainting) with three diffusion filters.

Test image	Trui			Peppers			Lena		
Noise scale σ	10	20	30	10	20	30	10	20	30
Inpainting with reg. masks	27.25	56.81	85.54	35.69	65.94	97.34	44.56	91.79	134.79
Inpainting by densification	20.00	44.61	73.18	25.04	50.78	75.10	31.43	76.55	121.06
Homogeneous diffusion	24.14	49.73	75.37	32.32	60.80	89.14	43.04	89.58	131.28
Linear space-var. diffusion	19.91	46.25	73.51	25.24	52.90	82.98	32.13	77.04	126.45
Nonlinear diffusion	16.43	35.12	55.03	22.34	41.17	62.79	28.16	64.28	99.84

Fig. 3. Comparison of homogeneous diffusion (HD), linear space-variant diffusion (LS), and denoising by inpainting with densification (ID)

our model is simpler: Since it uses homogeneous diffusion, there is no need to choose a diffusivity model (e.g. Eq. 4) or the parameter λ.

Finally, comparing the densification method based on homogeneous diffusion inpainting with a nonlinear diffusion filter shows its limitations, in particular for high noise levels. This is an unfair comparison: Since the densification approach lacks a nonlinear feedback mechanism, it is not surprising that its performance is dominated by nonlinear diffusion filtering.

7 Conclusions

Our work is the first that explicitly demonstrates the denoising capabilities of PDE-based inpainting methods. In particular, implementing our general framework with adaptive inpainting masks introduces space-variant behaviour to purely homogeneous processes. The resulting densification strategy based on homogeneous diffusion inpainting does not only outperform homogeneous diffusion filtering, but even linear space-variant diffusion filters. This shows a fundamental principle for denoising that has been widely ignored: *Adaptivity in the filter model can be replaced by adaptivity of data selection.* Exploring this encouraging road further by gaining more theoretical insights is part of our ongoing work.

References

1. Belhachmi, Z., Bucur, D., Burgeth, B., Weickert, J.: How to choose interpolation data in images. SIAM J. Appl. Math. **70**(1), 333–352 (2009)
2. Bertalmío, M., Sapiro, G., Caselles, V., Ballester, C.: Image inpainting. In: Proceedings of the SIGGRApPH 2000, New Orleans, LI, pp. 417–424, July 2000
3. Bruhn, A., Weickert, J.: A confidence measure for variational optic flow methods. In: Klette, R., Kozera, R., Noakes, L., Weickert, J. (eds.) Geometric Properties from Incomplete Data, Computational Imaging and Vision, vol. 31, pp. 283–297. Springer, Dordrecht (2006)
4. Buades, A., Coll, B., Morel, J.M.: A review of image denoising algorithms, with a new one. Multiscale Model. Simul. **4**(2), 490–530 (2005)
5. Charbonnier, P., Blanc-Féraud, L., Aubert, G., Barlaud, M.: Deterministic edge-preserving regularization in computed imaging. IEEE Trans. Image Proc. **6**(2), 298–311 (1997)
6. Chen, Y., Yu, W., Pock, T.: On learning optimized reaction diffusion processes for effective image restoration. In: Proceedings of the 2015 IEEE Conference on Computer Vision and Pattern Recognition, Boston, MA, pp. 5261–5269, June 2015
7. Chen, Y., Ranftl, R., Pock, T.: A bi-level view of inpainting-based image compression. In: Proceedings of the 19th Computer Vision Winter Workshop, Křtiny, Czech Republic, pp. 19–26, February 2014
8. Craven, P., Wahba, G.: Smoothing noisy data with spline functions. Numer. Math. **31**(4), 377–403 (1978)
9. Dabov, K., Foi, A., Katkovnik, V., Egiazarian, K.: Image denoising by sparse 3-D transform-domain collaborative filtering. IEEE Trans. Image Proc. **16**(8), 2080–2095 (2007)

10. Efros, A.A., Leung, T.K.: Texture synthesis by non-parametric sampling. In: Proceedings of the Seventh IEEE International Conference on Computer Vision, Corfu, Greece, vol. 2, pp. 1033–1038, September 1999
11. Fritsch, D.S.: A medial description of greyscale image structure by gradient-limited diffusion. In: Proceedings of SPIE Visualization in Biomedical Computing 1992, vol. 1808, pp. 105–117. SPIE Press, Bellingham (1992)
12. Galić, I., Weickert, J., Welk, M., Bruhn, A., Belyaev, A., Seidel, H.P.: Image compression with anisotropic diffusion. J. Math. Imaging Vis. **31**(2–3), 255–269 (2008)
13. Hoeltgen, L., Setzer, S., Weickert, J.: An optimal control approach to find sparse data for laplace interpolation. In: Heyden, A., Kahl, F., Olsson, C., Oskarsson, M., Tai, X.-C. (eds.) EMMCVPR 2013. LNCS, vol. 8081, pp. 151–164. Springer, Heidelberg (2013). doi:10.1007/978-3-642-40395-8_12
14. Horn, B., Schunck, B.: Determining optical flow. Artif. Intell. **17**, 185–203 (1981)
15. Iijima, T.: Basic theory on normalization of pattern (in case of typical one-dimensional pattern). Bull. Electrotech. Lab. **26**, 368–388 (1962). (in Japanese)
16. Mainberger, M., Hoffmann, S., Weickert, J., Tang, C.H., Johannsen, D., Neumann, F., Doerr, B.: Optimising spatial and tonal data for homogeneous diffusion inpainting. In: Bruckstein, A.M., ter Haar Romeny, B.M., Bronstein, A.M., Bronstein, M.M. (eds.) SSVM 2011. LNCS, vol. 6667, pp. 26–37. Springer, Heidelberg (2012). doi:10.1007/978-3-642-24785-9_3
17. Masnou, S., Morel, J.M.: Level lines based disocclusion. In: Proceedings of the 1998 IEEE International Conference on Image Processing, Chicago, IL, vol. 3, pp. 259–263, October 1998
18. Nagel, H.H., Enkelmann, W.: An investigation of smoothness constraints for the estimation of displacement vector fields from image sequences. IEEE Trans. Pattern Anal. Mach. Intell. **8**, 565–593 (1986)
19. Perona, P., Malik, J.: Scale space and edge detection using anisotropic diffusion. IEEE Trans. Pattern Anal. Mach. Intell. **12**, 629–639 (1990)
20. Peter, P., Weickert, J., Munk, A., Krivobokova, T., Li, H.: Justifying tensor-driven diffusion from structure-adaptive statistics of natural images. In: Tai, X.-C., Bae, E., Chan, T.F., Lysaker, M. (eds.) EMMCVPR 2015. LNCS, vol. 8932, pp. 263–277. Springer, Cham (2015). doi:10.1007/978-3-319-14612-6_20
21. Roth, S., Black, M.J.: Fields of experts. Int. J. Comput. Vis. **82**(2), 205–229 (2009)
22. Rudin, L.I., Osher, S., Fatemi, E.: Nonlinear total variation based noise removal algorithms. Physica D **60**(1), 259–268 (1992)
23. Scherzer, O., Weickert, J.: Relations between regularization and diffusion filtering. J. Math. Imaging Vis. **12**(1), 43–63 (2000)
24. Schmaltz, C., Peter, P., Mainberger, M., Ebel, F., Weickert, J., Bruhn, A.: Understanding, optimising, and extending data compression with anisotropic diffusion. Int. J. Comput. Vis. **108**(3), 222–240 (2014)
25. Schönlieb, C.B.: Partial Differential Equation Methods for Image Inpainting. Cambridge University Press, Cambridge (2015)
26. Tikhonov, A.N., Arsenin, V.Y.: Solutions of Ill-Posed Problems. Wiley, Washington (1977)
27. Weickert, J.: Anisotropic Diffusion in Image Processing. Teubner, Stuttgart (1998)
28. Weickert, J., Steidl, G., Mrázek, P., Welk, M., Brox, T.: Diffusion filters and wavelets: what can they learn from each other? In: Paragios, N., Chen, Y., Faugeras, O. (eds.) Handbook of Mathematical Models in Computer Vision, pp. 3–16. Springer, New York (2006)
29. Weyrich, N., Warhola, G.T.: Wavelet shrinkage and generalized cross validation for image denoising. IEEE Trans. Image Proc. **7**(1), 82–90 (1998)

Stochastic Image Reconstruction from Local Histograms of Gradient Orientation

Agnès Desolneux[✉] and Arthur Leclaire

CMLA, ENS Cachan, CNRS, Université Paris-Saclay, 94235 Cachan, France
{agnes.desolneux,arthur.leclaire}@cmla.ens-cachan.fr

Abstract. Many image processing algorithms rely on local descriptors extracted around selected points of interest. Motivated by privacy issues, several authors have recently studied the possibility of image reconstruction from these descriptors, and proposed reconstruction methods performing local inference using a database of images. In this paper we tackle the problem of image reconstruction from local histograms of gradient orientation, obtained from simplified SIFT descriptors. We propose two reconstruction models based on Poisson editing and on the combination of multiscale orientation fields. These models are able to recover global shapes and many geometric details of images. They compare well to state of the art results, without requiring the use of any external database.

Keywords: Image synthesis · Reconstruction from features · SIFT · Poisson editing · Maximum entropy distributions · Exponential models

1 Introduction

Extraction of local features constitutes a first step for many image analysis tasks, e.g. image matching and rectification, object detection and tracking, image recognition, image classification, image understanding, see for instance [1] and references therein. Depending on the application, one should use local features reflecting some kind of geometric information while being invariant with respect to several image transformations. For example, in order to match two images of the same distant scene taken under different view points and different illumination conditions, one should compute local features that are invariant to homography and contrast change. It is thus an interesting question to ask how much we can retrieve from the initial image based only on these image descriptors. In other words, what information is really contained in these descriptors.

Since the pioneering work by Attneave [2], many techniques have been proposed to extract points of interest in images and information around them. Here we will only mention a few descriptors and we refer to [1,3,4] for a more comprehensive survey. An early descriptor of a patch is given by the Local Binary Descriptors [5]: it extracts the signs of difference between values of Gaussian windows applied at different locations in the patch. Perhaps one of the most famous and powerful feature extraction technique is the Scale-Invariant Feature Transform (SIFT) [3,6]. As for most image description techniques, this algorithm first

© Springer International Publishing AG 2017
F. Lauze et al. (Eds.): SSVM 2017, LNCS 10302, pp. 133–145, 2017.
DOI: 10.1007/978-3-319-58771-4_11

extracts a set of points of interest (called *keypoints*) and then computes for each keypoint a descriptor based on the local behavior of the image around this keypoint. We give a brief description of the SIFT method in Sect. 2. Another popular local descriptor is given by the histograms of gradient orientations (HOG) [7]. "Dense" HOG descriptors are obtained as quantized histograms of the gradient orientations in each patch of a non-overlapping patch set. At a higher semantic level, local image behavior can be also represented as visual words [8] which are obtained as cluster points in a feature space.

Recently, Weinzaepfel et al. [9] have raised the issue of the reconstruction from image descriptors (in particular SIFT). This work was essentially motivated by privacy issues which appear when image descriptors are clearly transmitted on an unsecured network, e.g. for image recognition or classification. Their image reconstruction method consists in pasting image parts with similar features taken from a database. This has triggered several works based on other descriptors. Vondrick et al. [10] address reconstruction from dense HOG by relying on dictionary representation of HOG and patches. Also, d'Angelo et al. [11] address reconstruction from local binary descriptors by relying on primal-dual optimization techniques. Kato and Harada address reconstruction from bag of visual words [12]. Reconstruction problems have also been addressed with methods based on neural networks [13–15]; these methods are generic and can be applied to any image representation that can be approximated by the output of a convolutional neural network (in particular HOG as suggested in [14]). Finally, generative *a contrario* models [16] have been proposed to recover an image from a set of detected features (segments for example).

In all these works, the objective is essentially to reconstruct *one* image from the descriptors. But in many cases, this description transform has no reason to be invertible: for example with the SIFT descriptors, since it does not retain information outside the SIFT cells, many images could have the same SIFT output. Thus we propose here, rather than unique reconstruction, to sample from a stochastic image model whose statistics comply with the information contained in the local descriptors. We study in particular the case of simplified SIFT transforms which extract multiscale HOG from regions around the SIFT keypoints. We will essentially propose two models that can be adapted to several transforms based on local HOG. They both rely on Poisson editing [17] which is a way to compute an image whose gradient is as close as possible to a given vector field. Also, our second model is an instance of exponential models [18,19] which provide maximum entropy stochastic models having prescribed average values for a given set of numerical features.

Our paper is organized as follows. Section 2 contains a description of the features on which our image reconstruction relies. In Sect. 3 we introduce a model (called MS-Poisson) that combines gradient orientations at different scales by solving a multiscale Poisson problem. In Sect. 4 we propose a maximum entropy model (called MaxEnt) on orientation fields which respects the statistical distribution of gradient orientation in the SIFT regions. Finally, in Sect. 5, we give and comment several reconstruction results, and compare with [9,13].

2   Overview and Notations

In all the paper we consider a gray level image $u_0 : \Omega \to \mathbb{R}$ defined on a discrete rectangle of $\mathbb{Z}^2$. The Gaussian scale-space of u_0 is denoted by $g_\sigma * u_0$ where g_σ is the Gaussian kernel of standard deviation σ. We will denote by $\mathbb{T} = \mathbb{R}/2\pi\mathbb{Z}$ the set of angles (possible orientation values).

In this paper, we propose to reconstruct an image from a simplified SIFT transform detailed below. Let us begin with a brief explanation of the main steps of the SIFT methods; for technical details we refer the reader to [20].

1. Computing SIFT keypoints:
   (a) Extract local extrema of a discrete version of $(\boldsymbol{x}, \sigma) \mapsto \sigma^2 \Delta g_\sigma * u_0(\boldsymbol{x})$.
   (b) Refine the positions of the local extrema (sub-pixel precision).
   (c) Discard extrema with low contrast and extrema located on edges.
2. Computing SIFT local descriptors associated to the keypoint $(\boldsymbol{x}, \sigma)$:
   (a) Compute one or several principal orientations θ.
   (b) For each detected orientation θ, consider a grid of 4×4 square regions around $(\boldsymbol{x}, \sigma)$. These square regions, which we call SIFT subcells are of size $3\sigma \times 3\sigma$ with one side parallel to θ. In each subcell compute the histogram of $\mathrm{Angle}(\nabla g_\sigma * u_0) - \theta$ quantized on 8 values $(k\frac{\pi}{4}, 1 \le k \le 8)$.
   (c) Normalization: the 16 histograms are concatenated to obtain a feature vector $f \in \mathbb{R}^{128}$, which is then normalized and quantized to 8-bit integers.

When computing orientation histograms in steps 2(a), 2(b), each pixel votes with a weight that depends on the value of the gradient norm at scale σ and of its distance to the keypoint center $\boldsymbol{x}$. Also in step 2(b), there is a linear splitting of the vote of an angle between the two adjacent quantized angle values.

The reconstruction method described in this paper relies on the SIFT keypoints $(\boldsymbol{x}, \sigma)$ and on 8-quantized histograms orientations of $\mathrm{Angle}(\nabla g_\sigma * u_0) - \theta$ around $\boldsymbol{x}$. In other words, we do not include the vote weights nor the normalization step 2(c).

We denote by $(s_j)_{j \in \mathcal{J}}$ the collection of SIFT subcells, $s_j \subset \Omega$. In a SIFT cell, there are 16 SIFT subcells so that different s_j can correspond to the same keypoint. We will denote by $(\boldsymbol{x}_j, \sigma_j)$ the keypoint associated to s_j, and θ_j the principal orientation. For $x \in \Omega$, we will denote by $\mathcal{J}(\boldsymbol{x}) = \{j \in \mathcal{J} \mid \boldsymbol{x} \in s_j\}$ the set of indices of SIFT subcells containing $\boldsymbol{x}$. In s_j we extract the quantized HOG H_j at scale σ_j which is identified to the piecewise constant density function

$$h_j = \sum_{\ell=1}^{8} H_j^\ell \mathbf{1}_{[\theta_j + (\ell-1)\frac{\pi}{4}, \theta_j + \ell\frac{\pi}{4}[}, \tag{1}$$

$$\text{where} \quad H_j^\ell = \frac{1}{|s_j|} \left| \left\{ \boldsymbol{x} \in s_j; \ \mathrm{Angle}(\nabla g_{\sigma_j} * u_0)(\boldsymbol{x}) - \theta_j \in [(\ell-1)\tfrac{\pi}{4}, \ell\tfrac{\pi}{4}] \right\} \right|.$$

The main purpose of this paper is to reconstruct an image whose content agrees with the multiscale HOG h_j in the SIFT subcells s_j. One main difficulty is that the gradient magnitude is *a priori* completely lost during the extraction of these features. Another issue is the fact that a point $\boldsymbol{x}$ can belong to several subcells s_j. In that case we need to find a way to combine the different information given by the histograms h_j to recover the image orientation at $\boldsymbol{x}$.

3   Poisson Reconstruction of an Image

For the first proposed reconstruction method, we define vector fields $V_j : \Omega \to \mathbb{R}^2$ that will serve as objective gradient at scale σ_j in the SIFT subcell s_j. We propose to set $V_j = w_j e^{i\gamma_j}$ where $w_j = \frac{1}{\sigma_j} \mathbf{1}_{s_j}$ (whose choice is motivated by the homogeneity argument $\nabla\left(u(\frac{\boldsymbol{x}}{\sigma})\right) = \frac{1}{\sigma}\nabla u(\frac{\boldsymbol{x}}{\sigma})$) and where γ_j is a random orientation field sampled from the probability density function h_j. In order to obtain a reconstructed image U, these objective vector fields V_j for all the scales σ_j are combined by solving a multiscale Poisson problem explained in Sect. 3.2.

3.1   Classical Poisson Reconstruction

The aim of Poisson reconstruction is to look for an image $u : \Omega \to \mathbb{R}$ whose gradient is as close as possible to an objective vector field $V = (v_1, v_2)^T : \Omega \to \mathbb{R}^2$. In the case of image editing, this technique has been proposed by Pérez et al. [17] in order to copy pieces of an image into another one in a seamless way. More precisely, the goal is to minimize the functional

$$F(u) = \sum_{\boldsymbol{x} \in \Omega} \|\nabla u(\boldsymbol{x}) - V(\boldsymbol{x})\|_2^2. \tag{2}$$

Since $F(c + u) = F(u)$ for any constant c, we can impose $\sum_{\boldsymbol{x} \in \Omega} u(\boldsymbol{x}) = 0$. If we use periodic boundary conditions for the gradient, we can solve this problem with the Discrete Fourier Transforms. Indeed, if we use the simple derivation scheme based on periodic convolutions

$$\nabla u(\boldsymbol{x}) = \begin{pmatrix} \partial_1 * u(\boldsymbol{x}) \\ \partial_2 * u(\boldsymbol{x}) \end{pmatrix} \quad \text{where} \quad \begin{cases} \partial_1 = \delta_{(0,0)} - \delta_{(1,0)} \\ \partial_2 = \delta_{(0,0)} - \delta_{(0,1)} \end{cases}, \tag{3}$$

this problem can be expressed in the Fourier domain with Parseval formula

$$F(u) = \frac{1}{|\Omega|} \sum_{\boldsymbol{\xi} \neq 0} |\widehat{\partial_1}(\boldsymbol{\xi})\widehat{u}(\boldsymbol{\xi}) - \widehat{v_1}(\boldsymbol{\xi})|_2^2 + |\widehat{\partial_2}(\boldsymbol{\xi})\widehat{u}(\boldsymbol{\xi}) - \widehat{v_2}(\boldsymbol{\xi})|_2^2. \tag{4}$$

Thus, for each $\boldsymbol{\xi}$ we have a barycenter problem which is simply solved by

$$\forall \boldsymbol{\xi} \neq 0, \quad \widehat{u}(\boldsymbol{\xi}) = \frac{\overline{\widehat{\partial_1}(\boldsymbol{\xi})}\widehat{v_1}(\boldsymbol{\xi}) + \overline{\widehat{\partial_2}(\boldsymbol{\xi})}\widehat{v_2}(\boldsymbol{\xi})}{|\widehat{\partial_1}(\boldsymbol{\xi})|^2 + |\widehat{\partial_2}(\boldsymbol{\xi})|^2}. \tag{5}$$

3.2   Multiscale Poisson Reconstruction

In order to simultaneously constrain the gradient at several scales $(\sigma_j)_{j \in \mathcal{J}}$, we propose here to consider the following multiscale Poisson energy

$$G(u) = \sum_{j \in \mathcal{J}} w(\sigma_j) \sum_{x \in \Omega} \|\nabla(g_{\sigma_j} * u)(x) - V_j(x)\|_2^2, \qquad (6)$$

where g_σ is the Gaussian kernel of standard deviation σ, $V_j = (v_{j,1}, v_{j,2})^T$ is the objective gradient at scale σ_j, and $w(\sigma_j)$ is a set of weights. In our application, since there are more keypoints in the fine scales (i.e. when σ_j is small), and since the keypoints at fine scales are generally more informative, a reasonable choice is to take all weights $w(\sigma_j) = 1$. But we keep these weights in the formula for the sake of generality.

Again, with periodic boundary conditions, this problem can be expressed in Fourier domain as

$$G(u) = \frac{1}{|\Omega|} \sum_{j \in \mathcal{J}} \sum_{\xi \neq 0} w(\sigma_j) \left(|\widehat{g}_{\sigma_j}(\xi)\widehat{\partial}_1(\xi)\widehat{u}(\xi) - \widehat{v}_{j,1}(\xi)|_2^2 + |\widehat{g}_{\sigma_j}(\xi)\widehat{\partial}_2(\xi)\widehat{u}(\xi) - \widehat{v}_{j,2}(\xi)|_2^2 \right). \qquad (7)$$

The solution is still a barycenter. It is given by (recall that $\widehat{g}_{\sigma_j}(\xi) \in \mathbb{R}$ since g_{σ_j} is even):

$$\forall \xi \neq 0, \quad \widehat{u}(\xi) = \frac{\displaystyle\sum_{j \in \mathcal{J}} w(\sigma_j)\widehat{g}_{\sigma_j}(\xi)\left(\overline{\widehat{\partial}_1(\xi)}\widehat{v}_{j,1}(\xi) + \overline{\widehat{\partial}_2(\xi)}\widehat{v}_{j,2}(\xi) \right)}{\displaystyle\sum_{j \in \mathcal{J}} w(\sigma_j)|\widehat{g}_{\sigma_j}(\xi)|^2\left(|\widehat{\partial}_1(\xi)|^2 + |\widehat{\partial}_2(\xi)|^2 \right)}. \qquad (8)$$

Notice that, depending on the finest scale, the denominator can vanish in the high frequencies because of the term $\widehat{g}_{\sigma_j}(\xi)$ (as it is the case in a deconvolution problem). Therefore, it may be useful to add a regularization term controlled by a parameter $\mu > 0$. Then, if we minimize

$$G(u) + \mu\|\nabla u\|_2^2, \qquad (9)$$

we get the well-defined solution

$$\widehat{u}(\xi) = \frac{\displaystyle\sum_{j \in \mathcal{J}} w(\sigma_j)\widehat{g}_{\sigma_j}(\xi)\left(\overline{\widehat{\partial}_1(\xi)}\widehat{v}_{j,1}(\xi) + \overline{\widehat{\partial}_2(\xi)}\widehat{v}_{j,2}(\xi) \right)}{\left(\mu + \displaystyle\sum_{j \in \mathcal{J}} w(\sigma_j)|\widehat{g}_{\sigma_j}(\xi)|^2 \right)\left(|\widehat{\partial}_1(\xi)|^2 + |\widehat{\partial}_2(\xi)|^2 \right)}. \qquad (10)$$

4   Stochastic Models for Gradient Orientations

The second reconstruction method will consist in solving a classical Poisson problem (Sect. 3.1) with one single objective gradient $V = we^{i\gamma}$ where $\gamma : \Omega \to \mathbb{T}$ is now a sample of an orientation field which is inherently designed to combine the local HOG at the scale $\sigma = 0$.

In this section, we aim at defining stochastic models of orientation fields that fit the distributions of oriented gradients in the SIFT subcells $(s_j)_{j \in \mathcal{J}}$. In contrast with the usual SIFT method, for simplicity we will consider the orientations in all subcells with the same quantization bins

$$B_\ell = [(\ell - 1)\tfrac{\pi}{4}, \ell\tfrac{\pi}{4}[, \quad (1 \leqslant \ell \leqslant 8). \tag{11}$$

We then consider for all $j \in \mathcal{J}$ and $1 \leqslant \ell \leqslant 8$, the real-valued feature function given by

$$\forall \theta \in \mathbb{T}^\Omega, \quad f_{j,\ell}(\theta) = \frac{1}{|s_j|} \sum_{x \in s_j} \mathbf{1}_{B_\ell}(\theta(x)) \tag{12}$$

We are then interested in probability distributions P on $\mathbb{T}^\Omega$ such that

$$\forall j \in \mathcal{J}, \forall \ell \in \{1, \ldots, 8\}, \quad \mathbb{E}_P(f_{j,\ell}(\theta)) = f_{j,\ell}(\theta_0), \tag{13}$$

where $\theta_0 = \mathrm{Angle}(\nabla u_0)$ is the orientation field of the original image u_0. There are many probability distributions P on $\mathbb{T}^\Omega$ that satisfy (13), and we will be mainly interested in the ones that are at the same time as "random" as possible, in the sense that they are of maximal entropy. Let us notice that the gradient orientation extracted from the MS-Poisson model (10) is not ensured to satisfy the constraints (13).

Theorem 1 [19]. *There exists a family of numbers $\lambda = (\lambda_{j,\ell})_{j \in \mathcal{J}, 1 \leqslant \ell \leqslant 8}$ such that the probability distribution*

$$dP_\lambda = \frac{1}{Z_\lambda} \exp\left(-\sum_{j,\ell} \lambda_{j,\ell} f_{j,\ell}(\theta) \right) d\theta, \tag{14}$$

where the partition function Z_λ is given by $Z_\lambda = \int_{\mathbb{T}^\Omega} \exp\left(-\sum_{j,\ell} \lambda_{j,\ell} f_{j,\ell}(\theta) \right) d\theta$, satisfies the constraints (13) and is of maximal entropy among all absolutely continuous probability distributions w.r.t. $d\theta$ satisfying the constraints (13).

Proof. This result directly follows from the general theorem given in [19]. The only difficulty is to handle the technical hypothesis of linear independence of the $f_{j,\ell}$. In our framework, the $f_{j,\ell}$ are not independent (in particular because $\sum_{\ell=1}^8 f_{j,\ell} = 1$, and also because there may be other dependencies for instance when one subcell is exactly the union of two smaller subcells). But one can still apply the theorem to an extracted linearly independent subfamily. This gives existence of the solution for the initial family $(f_{j,\ell})$ (but of course not the unicity).

One can show (see [19]) that the solutions P_λ are obtained by minimizing the smooth convex function

$$\Phi(\lambda) = \log Z_\lambda + \sum_{j,\ell} \lambda_{j,\ell} f_{j,\ell}(\theta_0). \tag{15}$$

Let us examine P_λ from closer. For that we can write

$$-\log \frac{dP_\lambda}{d\theta} - \log Z_\lambda = \sum_{j \in \mathcal{J}, 1 \leqslant \ell \leqslant 8} \lambda_{j,\ell} f_{j,\ell}(\theta) = \sum_{x \in \Omega} \varphi_{\lambda,x}(\theta(x)), \tag{16}$$

$$\text{where} \quad \varphi_{\lambda,x} = \sum_{\ell=1}^{8} \left(\sum_{j \in \mathcal{J}(x)} \frac{\lambda_{j,\ell}}{|s_j|} \right) \mathbf{1}_{B_\ell}. \tag{17}$$

This proves that under P_λ the values $\theta(x)$ are independent and have a probability distribution $\frac{1}{Z_{\lambda,x}} e^{-\varphi_{\lambda,x}}$ where $Z_{\lambda,x} = \sum_{\ell=1}^{8} \exp\left(- \sum_{j \in \mathcal{J}(x)} \frac{\lambda_{j,\ell}}{|s_j|} \right) |B_\ell|$. Therefore, the constraints (13) can be written in terms of λ as

$$\forall j, \ell, \quad \sum_{x \in s_j} \frac{1}{Z_{\lambda,x}} \exp\left(- \sum_{k \in \mathcal{J}(x)} \frac{\lambda_{k,\ell}}{|s_k|} \right) = |\{x \in s_j;\ \theta_0(x) \in B_\ell\ \}|. \tag{18}$$

Notice that this system is highly non-linear and is in general difficult to solve. However, if the SIFT subcells do not overlap (which is very rare), then the distribution on $\theta(x)$ simplifies to: the uniform distribution if x doesn't belong to any s_j, and the distribution given by the empirical quantized histogram of θ_0 on s_j if $x \in s_j$.

Now, if the SIFT subcells intersect, there is no explicit solution anymore. To cope with that, as in [18] we use a numerical scheme to find the maximum entropy distribution P_λ based on the minimization of (15). For that, we recall the gradient of $\log Z_\lambda$, obtained by differentiating the partition function:

$$\frac{\partial \log Z_\lambda}{\partial \lambda_{j,\ell}} = \frac{1}{Z_\lambda} \frac{\partial Z_\lambda}{\partial \lambda_{j,\ell}} = -\mathbb{E}_{P_\lambda}\left[f_{j,\ell}(\theta) \right]. \tag{19}$$

This expression allows us to minimize Φ with a gradient descent with constant (sufficiently small) step size, which converges [21] since Φ is a smooth convex function with Lipschitz gradient (as can be seen on the Hessian matrix).

5   Results and Discussion

In this section, for several images, we show reconstructions obtained as samples of the models proposed in the two previous sections. We also compare with other reconstruction algorithms described in [9,10] (the test images are taken from these articles).

The first model (denoted by MS-Poisson) consists in computing the solution of regularized multiscale Poisson reconstruction (10) with objective vector fields

$V_j = \frac{1}{\sigma_j} e^{i\gamma_j} \mathbf{1}_{s_j}$ where γ_j is composed of independent samples of the probability distribution h_j given by (1), that is the available HOG at scale σ_j in the sub-cell s_j. In this case, the orientation fields (γ_j) are independent. The weights are set to $w(\sigma_j) = 1$ for all j, and the regularization parameter is set to $\mu = 50$.

The second model (denoted by MaxEnt) is obtained as the solution of a classical Poisson problem associated to the objective vector field

$$V(\boldsymbol{x}) = \left(\max_{j \in \mathcal{J}(\boldsymbol{x})} \frac{1}{\sigma_j} \right) e^{i\gamma(\boldsymbol{x})} \mathbf{1}_{\mathcal{J}(\boldsymbol{x}) \neq \emptyset}. \tag{20}$$

where γ is a sample of the maximum entropy model of Sect. 4. Here again, we chose a magnitude function $|V(\boldsymbol{x})|$ that favors the locations where there is information at fine scale (note that by definition of the keypoints, $\sigma_j > 0$).

In Fig. 1 we give reconstruction results obtained with the models MS-Poisson and MaxEnt. These results show some similarity: both these algorithms are able to recover content in the SIFT subcells. They recover geometric details from the fine scale subcells while global shapes are constrained thanks to the large scale information; many objects contained in the image are easily recognizable. These reconstruction results may seem surprisingly good at first but can be explained by the fact that the local HOG in the SIFT subcells is not as sparse as one could imagine. On the left of Fig. 1 one can see that there are many keypoints in these images and in particular keypoints at fine scales which give a precise local information.

Notice that the result of MaxEnt appears a bit sharper, as expected: on the one hand, MaxEnt relies on local HOG computed at the scale of the image ($\sigma = 0$) while MS-Poisson relies on multiscale HOG, and on the other hand, MS-Poisson realizes a compromise between many objective vector fields at different scales, which introduces some blur. Of course, these algorithms cannot recover precisely the content outside the SIFT cells: this completion is essentially obtained by regularization. For example, the top of the bottle in the first row of Fig. 1 is not properly restored.

These two reconstruction methods draw a sample of a random model. But for both of them, since Poisson reconstruction is a linear operation, it is also possible to compute a reconstruction which is the expectation of these random models. It turns out that these mean images are very similar (though a bit more regular) to the random samples. In future work we will investigate the variance of these models to better explain this.

Assessing the quality of reconstruction is a very ill-posed task, in particular because (1) it is a very subjective question, (2) such a measure should be invariant to affine contrast changes, and (3) there is no information outside the SIFT subcells. In the lack of anything better, we give the values r of the normalized cross-correlation between the reconstruction and the original image (which is contrast-affine-invariant). In Fig. 1 we observe that MS-Poisson leads to much better cross-correlation values which reflects the fact that large scale contrasted regions are better retrieved (while not accounted for with MaxEnt). For that reason, in the following experiments we only show results obtained with MS-Poisson.

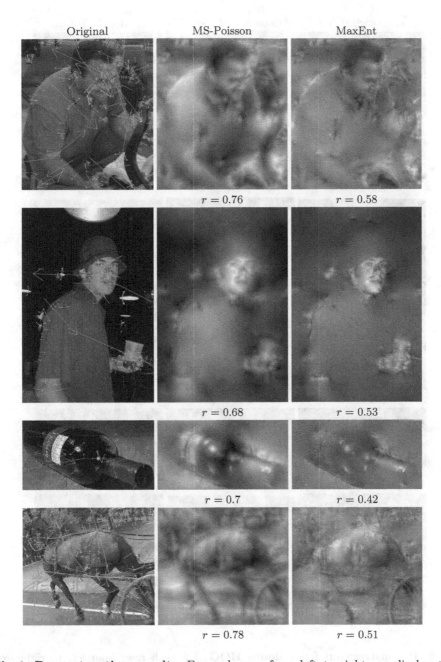

Original   MS-Poisson   MaxEnt

$r = 0.76$ $r = 0.58$

$r = 0.68$ $r = 0.53$

$r = 0.7$ $r = 0.42$

$r = 0.78$ $r = 0.51$

Fig. 1. Reconstruction results. For each row, from left to right, we display the original image with over-imposed arrows representing the keypoints (the length of the arrow is 6σ which is the half-side of the SIFT cell, and twice the size of the corresponding SIFT subcells), the reconstruction with MS-Poisson, and the reconstruction with MaxEnt. (Image Credits [10]).

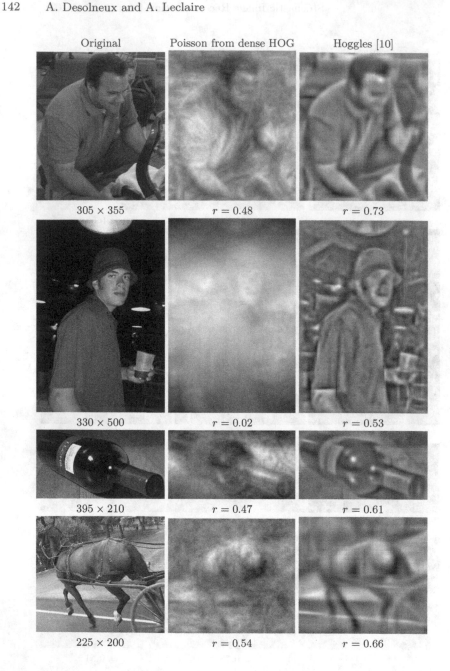

Original   Poisson from dense HOG   Hoggles [10]

305 × 355   r = 0.48   r = 0.73

330 × 500   r = 0.02   r = 0.53

395 × 210   r = 0.47   r = 0.61

225 × 200   r = 0.54   r = 0.66

Fig. 2. Reconstruction from dense HOG. For each row, from left to right we display the original image, the result of Poisson reconstruction from dense HOG (computed on 5 × 5 patches with no overlap), and the result of [10]. The levels of recovered details with the two methods are comparable. However, the result of Poisson reconstruction looks less clean because of the independent sampling of all pixels. (Image Credits [10]).

On Fig. 2, we show comparisons between the results of the Poisson reconstruction from dense HOG (computed on 5×5 non-overlapping patches), and the results of Hoggles [10]. The results of [10] look cleaner because they exploit redundancies between overlapping HOG templates (via a learned pair-dictionary representation of HOG templates and patches) whereas Poisson reconstruction only performs independent sampling of pixel orientations.

The two proposed reconstruction methods can also be applied by using the SIFT feature vectors as substitute to the input local HOG. For that, for each subcell s_j we extract the part of the descriptor that is relative to this subcell, and we normalize its sum to 1 (in order to get a probability distribution function). Such a result of SIFT reconstruction can be seen in Fig. 3. The result obtained with the SIFT descriptors retrieves the global shapes of the image but is in general less precise than the one obtained with the local HOG, because of the several normalization steps applied in SIFT.

Original   MS-Poisson from SIFT

[Weinzaepfel et al., 2011]   [Dosovitskiy & Brox, 2015]

Fig. 3. Comparison for SIFT reconstruction. In the first row we display the original image and the reconstruction results from the SIFT descriptors obtained with MS-Poisson. In the second row we display the results obtained with the methods of [9, 13]. (Color figure online) (Image Credits [9]).

In Fig. 3 we compare our reconstruction results with the methods by Weinzaepfel et al. [9] and Dosovitskiy and Brox [13]. The main difference is that our method relies only on the content provided in the SIFT subcells while these methods use an external database either to copy local information from patches with similar SIFT descriptors in [9] or to build an up-convolutional neural network for reconstruction in [13]. Thus our work has no intention to outperform these methods in terms of visual quality of reconstruction (in particular, our method has absolutely no possibility of recovering the color information). But still, one can see that MS-Poisson can recover the global shapes with no stitching artifacts (compared to [9]). However, MS-Poisson gives much blurrier results; indeed the method of [9] is able to copy patches of sharp images while the method of [13] in some sense includes a deconvolutional step through the up-convolutional network. In order to obtain sharper results, one could restrict the inner sums of the MS-Poisson energy (6) to the SIFT subcells: this new method will certainly avoid over-regularization (but the solution will not be explicit anymore).

References

1. Morel, J.M., Yu, G.: ASIFT: a new framework for fully affine invariant image comparison. SIAM J. Imaging Sci. **2**(2), 438–469 (2009)
2. Attneave, F.: Some informational aspects of visual perception. Psychol. Rev. **61**(3), 183 (1954)
3. Mikolajczyk, K., Schmid, C.: A performance evaluation of local descriptors. IEEE Trans. PAMI **27**(10), 1615–1630 (2005)
4. Tuytelaars, T., Mikolajczyk, K.: Local invariant feature detectors: a survey. Found. Trends Comput. Graph. Vis. **3**(3), 177–280 (2008)
5. Ojala, T., Pietikinen, M., Menp, T.: Multiresolution gray-scale and rotation invariant texture classification with local binary patterns. IEEE Trans. PAMI **24**(7), 971–987 (2002)
6. Lowe, D.: Distinctive image features from scale-invariant keypoints. Int. J. Comput. Vis. **60**(2), 91–110 (2004)
7. Dalal, N., Triggs, B.: Histograms of oriented gradients for human detection. In: Proceedings of the IEEE CVPR, vol. 1, pp. 886–893 (2005)
8. Sivic, J., Zisserman, A.: Video Google: a text retrieval approach to object matching in videos. In: Proceedings of the IEEE ICCV, pp. 1470–1477 (2003)
9. Weinzaepfel, P., Jégou, H., Pérez, P.: Reconstructing an image from its local descriptors. In: Proceedings of the IEEE CVPR, pp. 337–344 (2011)
10. Vondrick, C., Khosla, A., Malisiewicz, T., Torralba, A.: Hoggles: visualizing object detection features. In: Proceedings of the IEEE ICCV, pp. 1–8 (2013)
11. d'Angelo, E., Jacques, L., Alahi, A., Vandergheynst, P.: From bits to images: inversion of local binary descriptors. IEEE Trans. PAMI **36**(5), 874–887 (2014)
12. Kato, H., Harada, T.: Image reconstruction from bag-of-visual-words. In: Proceedings of the IEEE CVPR, pp. 955–962 (2014)
13. Dosovitskiy, A., Brox, T.: Inverting Visual Representations with Convolutional Networks. arXiv:1506.02753 [cs] (2015)
14. Mahendran, A., Vedaldi, A.: Understanding deep image representations by inverting them. In: IEEE CVPR, pp. 5188–5196 (2015)
15. Mahendran, A., Vedaldi, A.: Visualizing deep convolutional neural networks using natural pre-images. Int. J. Comput. Vis. **120**(3), 233–255 (2016)
16. Desolneux, A.: When the a contrario approach becomes generative. Int. J. Comput. Vis. **116**(1), 46–65 (2016)
17. Pérez, P., Gangnet, M., Blake, A.: Poisson image editing. In: ACM SIGGRAPH 2003 Papers. SIGGRAPH 2003, pp. 313–318 (2003)

18. Zhu, S., Wu, Y., Mumford, D.: Filters, random fields and maximum entropy (FRAME): towards a unified theory for texture modeling. Int. J. Comput. Vis. **27**(2), 107–126 (1998)
19. Mumford, D., Desolneux, A.: Pattern Theory: The Stochastic Analysis of Real-World Signals. A K Peters/CRC Press, Natick (2010)
20. Rey Otero, I., Delbracio, M.: Anatomy of the SIFT method. Image Process. On Line **4**, 370–396 (2014)
21. Nesterov, Y.: Introductory Lectures on Convex Optimization: A Basic Course, vol. 87. Springer, Boston (2004)

A Dynamic Programming Solution to Bounded Dejittering Problems

Lukas F. Lang[⊠]

Johann Radon Institute for Computational and Applied Mathematics,
Austrian Academy of Sciences, Altenberger Straße 69, 4040 Linz, Austria
lukas.lang@ricam.oeaw.ac.at

Abstract. We propose a dynamic programming solution to image dejittering problems with bounded displacements and obtain efficient algorithms for the removal of line jitter, line pixel jitter, and pixel jitter.

1 Introduction

In this article we devise a dynamic programming (DP) solution to dejittering problems with bounded displacements. In particular, we consider instances of the following image acquisition model. A D-dimensional image $u^\delta : \Omega \to \mathbb{R}^D$ defined on a two-dimensional domain $\Omega \subset \mathbb{R}^2$ is created by the equation

$$u^\delta = u \circ \Phi, \tag{1}$$

where $u : \Omega \to \mathbb{R}^D$ is the original, undisturbed image, $\Phi : \Omega \to \Omega$ is a displacement perturbation, and $\circ$ denotes function composition. Typically, $\Phi = (\Phi_1, \Phi_2)^\top$ is a degradation generated by the acquisition process and is considered random. In addition, u^δ may exhibit additive noise η. The central theme of this article is displacement error correction, which is to recover the original image solely from the corrupted image.

One particularly interesting class are dejittering problems. Jitter is a common artefact in digital images or image sequences and is typically attributed to inaccurate timing during signal sampling, synchronisation issues, or corrupted data transmission [10,11]. Most commonly, it is observed as *line jitter* where entire lines are mistakenly shifted left or right by a random displacement. As a result, shapes appear jagged and unappealing to the viewer. Other—equally disturbing—defects are *line pixel jitter* and *pixel jitter*. The former type is due to a random shift of each position in horizontal direction only, while the latter is caused by a random displacement in $\mathbb{R}^2$. See Fig. 1 for examples.

The problem of *dejittering* is to reverse the observed effect and has been studied in numerous works, see [4,6,7,10,11,13,15,16,18]. Recent efforts either deal with finite-dimensional minimisation problems [11,15,16] or rely on an infinite-dimensional setting [4,13,18]. Typically, variational approaches such as [4,13] are based on a linearisation of (1) and try to directly infer the true image. Alternatively, as done in [18], one can alternate between finding the displacement

© Springer International Publishing AG 2017
F. Lauze et al. (Eds.): SSVM 2017, LNCS 10302, pp. 146–158, 2017.
DOI: 10.1007/978-3-319-58771-4_12

Fig. 1. Original image, line jitter ($\rho = 4$ pixels), line pixel jitter ($\rho = 5$ pixels), pixel jitter corruption ($\rho = 5$ pixels).

and inferring the original image. Both approaches typically enforce a certain regularity of the reconstructed image.

In this article, we investigate efficient solutions to dejittering models introduced in [4, 13]. However, we assume the magnitude of each component of the displacement $x - \Phi(x)$, where $x = (x_1, x_2)^\top \in \Omega$, to be bounded by a constant $\rho > 0$. That is,

$$\|x_i - \Phi_i(x)\|_{L^\infty(\Omega)} \le \rho. \tag{2}$$

The main idea is to assume that (1) can be inverted (locally) by reconstructing the original value from a small neighbourhood. Even though not guaranteed theoretically, this approach is found to work surprisingly well for Gaussian distributed displacements of zero mean. A possible explanation is that the original value at a certain position $x \in \Omega$ is likely to occur in the close vicinity of x. Moreover, it does not require derivatives of the disturbed data, which typically occur during linearisation of (1), see [4, 13]. The obvious drawback is that $u(x)$ can only take values which appear in u^δ within a small neighbourhood of x. As a result, its capabilities are limited in the presence of noise.

We build on previous work by Laborelli [11] and Nikolova [15, 16], and utilise DP for the numerical solution. For the removal of line jitter, we extend the algorithm in [11] to include regularisation of the displacement, yielding a stabler reconstruction. In comparison to the greedy approach in [15, 16] we are able to recover a global minimiser to the one-dimensional non-linear and possibly non-convex minimisation problem formulated in Sect. 2. For the case of line pixel jitter, we rewrite the problem into a series of independent minimisation problems, each of which can be solved optimally via DP. For pixel jitter removal we follow a different strategy as the regularisation term in the considered functional prohibits a straightforward decomposition into simpler subproblems. We employ block coordinate descent, which is an iterative method and is guaranteed to converge energy-wise [2]. All of our algorithms generalise to D-dimensional images defined on $\mathbb{R}^2$. Moreover, generalisation to regularisation functionals involving

Table 1. Summary of the algorithms. m and n denote the columns and the rows of an image, respectively, $\rho \in \mathbb{N}$ is the maximum displacement, and $q \in \mathbb{N}$ is the order of the highest occurring derivative. For instance, $q = 2$ for first-order derivatives. The dimension D of the image is assumed constant.

Algorithm	Time	Memory	Comment
Line jitter	$O(mn\rho^q)$	$O(n\rho^{q-1})$	Same as [11] but with regularisation
Line pixel jitter	$O(mn\rho^q)$	$O(n\rho^{q-1})$	
Pixel jitter	$O(mn\rho^{2q})$	$O(n\rho^{2(q-1)})$	Per-iteration complexity

higher-order derivatives of the sought image and to higher-order discretisation accuracy is straightforward. Table 1 summarises the results of this work.

Notation. Let $\Omega = [0, W] \times [0, H] \subset \mathbb{R}^2$ be a two-dimensional domain. For $x = (x_1, x_2)^\top \in \mathbb{R}^2$, the p-th power of the usual p-norm of $\mathbb{R}^2$ is denoted by $\|x\|_p^p = \sum_i |x_i|^p$. For $D \in \mathbb{N}$, we denote by $u : \Omega \to \mathbb{R}^D$, respectively, by $u^\delta : \Omega \to \mathbb{R}^D$ the unknown original and the observed, possibly corrupted, D-dimensional image. A vector-valued function $u = (u_1, \ldots, u_D)^\top$ is given in terms of its components. We write $\partial_i^k u$ for the k-th partial derivative of u with respect to x_i and, for simplicity, we write $\partial_i u$ for $k = 1$. For $D = 1$, the spatial gradient of u in $\mathbb{R}^2$ is $\nabla u = (\partial_1 u, \partial_2 u)^\top$ and for $D = 3$ it is given by the matrix $\nabla u = (\partial_i u_j)_{ij}$. In the former case, its p-norm is simply $\|\nabla u\|_p$ and in the latter case it is given by $\|\nabla u\|_p^p = \sum_{j=1}^D \sum_{i=1}^2 (\partial_i u_j)^p$. For a function $f : \Omega \to \mathbb{R}^D$ and $1 \le p < \infty$ we denote the p-power of the norm of $L^p(\Omega, \mathbb{R}^D)$ by $\|f\|_{L^p(\Omega)}^p = \int_\Omega \|f(x)\|_p^p \, dx$. Moreover, $\|f\|_{L^\infty(\Omega)}$ denotes the essential supremum norm. A continuous image gives rise to a discrete representation $u_{i,j} \in \mathbb{R}^D$ of each pixel. A digital image is stored in matrix form $u \in \mathbb{R}^{m \times n \times D}$, where m denotes the number of columns arranged left to right and n the number of rows stored from top to bottom.

2   Problem Formulation

Let $u^\delta : \Omega \to \mathbb{R}^D$ be an observed and possibly corrupted image generated by (1). We aim to reconstruct an approximation of the original image $u : \Omega \to \mathbb{R}^D$. The main difficulty is that Φ^{-1} might not exist and that u^δ might exhibit noise. Lenzen and Scherzer [13] propose to find a minimising pair (u, Φ) to the energy

$$\int_\Omega \|\Phi(x) - x\|_2^2 \, dx + \alpha \mathcal{R}(u) \qquad (3)$$

such that (u, Φ) satisfies (1). Here, $\mathcal{R}(u)$ is a regularisation functional and $\alpha > 0$ is a parameter. In what follows, we consider one exemplary class of displacements which arise in dejittering problems. They are of the form

$$\Phi = \mathrm{Id} + d, \qquad (4)$$

with $d : \Omega \to \Omega$ depending on the particular jitter model. Typically, $\mathcal{R}(u)$ is chosen in accordance with d. We assume that d is Gaussian distributed around zero with σ^2 variance and whenever $x + d$ lies outside Ω we typically have $u^\delta(x) = 0$. In order to approximately reconstruct u we will assume that, for every $x \in \Omega$, there exists

$$d(x) = \arg\inf\{\|v\|_2 \mid v \in \mathbb{R}^2, u(x) = u^\delta(x - v)\}.$$

In other words, we can invert (1) and locally reconstruct u by finding d. While this requirement trivially holds true for line jitter under appropriate treatment of the boundaries, it is not guaranteed in the cases of line pixel jitter and pixel jitter. Moreover, as a consequence of (4) and (2) we have, for $i \in \{1, 2\}$,

$$\|\Phi_i(x) - x_i\|_{L^\infty(\Omega)} = \|d_i\|_{L^\infty(\Omega)} \le \rho.$$

Line Jitter. In this model, the corrupted image is assumed to be created as

$$u^\delta(x_1, x_2) = u(x_1 + d(x_2), x_2) + \eta(x_1, x_2), \tag{5}$$

where $d : [0, H] \to \mathbb{R}$ is a random displacement and $\eta : \Omega \to \mathbb{R}^D$ is typically Gaussian white noise. The corruption arises from a horizontal shift of each line by a random amount, resulting in visually unappealing, jagged shapes. Assuming zero noise, (5) can be inverted within $[\rho, W - \rho] \times [0, H]$ given d. The original image is thus given by

$$u(x_1, x_2) = u^\delta(x_1 - d(x_2), x_2). \tag{6}$$

For $\eta \not\equiv 0$ additional image denoising is required, see e.g. [17, Chap. 4] for standard methods of variational image denoising. We minimise the energy

$$\mathcal{E}^k_{\alpha,p}(d) := \alpha\|d\|^2_{L^2([0,H])} + \sum_{\ell=1}^{k} \iint_\Omega \|\partial_2^\ell u^\delta(x_1 - d(x_2), x_2)\|_p^p \, dx_1 \, dx_2, \tag{7}$$

subject to $\|d\|_{L^\infty([0,H])} \le \rho$. The first term in (7) is suitable for displacements which are Gaussian distributed around zero. It prevents the reconstruction from being fooled by dominant vertical edges and effectively removes a constant additive displacement, resulting in a centred image. The second term utilises identity (6) and penalises the sum of the magnitudes of vertical derivatives of the reconstructed image up to k-th order. Here, $\alpha \ge 0$ is a regularisation parameter and $p > 0$ is an exponent. The proposed framework for the solution of (7) is more general and allows a different exponent p_ℓ and an individual weight for each term in the sum. Moreover, any other norm of d might be considered.

We restrict ourselves to discretisations of $\mathcal{E}^1_{\alpha,p}$ and $\mathcal{E}^2_{\alpha,p}$ and assume that images are piecewise constant, are defined on a regular grid, and that all displacements are integer. Then, for every $j \in \{1, \ldots, n\}$, we seek $d_j \in \mathcal{L}$ with $\mathcal{L} := \{-\rho, \ldots, \rho\}$. By discretising with backwards finite differences we obtain

$$\mathcal{E}^1_{\alpha,p}(d) \approx \sum_{j=1}^{n} \alpha|d_j|^2 + \sum_{j=2}^{n}\sum_{i=1}^{m} \|u^\delta_{i-d_j,j} - u^\delta_{i-d_{j-1},j-1}\|_p^p, \tag{8}$$

$$\mathcal{E}^2_{\alpha,p}(d) \approx \mathcal{E}^1_{\alpha,p}(d) + \sum_{j=3}^{n}\sum_{i=1}^{m} \|u^\delta_{i-d_j,j} - 2u^\delta_{i-d_{j-1},j-1} + u^\delta_{i-d_{j-2},j-2}\|_p^p. \tag{9}$$

Line Pixel Jitter. Images degraded by line pixel jitter are generated by

$$u^\delta(x_1, x_2) = u(x_1 + d(x_1, x_2), x_2) + \eta(x_1, x_2), \tag{10}$$

where $d : \Omega \to \mathbb{R}$ now depends on both x_1 and x_2. As before, the displacement is in horizontal direction only. Images appear pixelated and exhibit horizontally fringed edges. In contrast to line jitter, in the noise-free setting one is in general not able to reconstruct the original image solely from u^δ, unless $d(\cdot, x_2) : [0, W] \to \mathbb{R}$ is bijective on $[0, W]$ for every $x_2 \in [0, H]$. As a remedy, we utilise the fact that d is assumed to be independent (in x_1) and identically Gaussian distributed around zero. The idea is that the original value $u(x_1, x_2)$, or a value sufficiently close, at (x_1, x_2) is likely be found in a close neighbourhood with respect to the x_1-direction. We assume that

$$d(x_1, x_2) = \arg\inf\{|v| \mid v \in \mathbb{R}, u(x_1, x_2) = u^\delta(x_1 - v, x_2)\} \tag{11}$$

exists and that $\|d\|_{L^\infty(\Omega)} \leq \rho$. Clearly, it is not unique without further assumptions, however, finding one d is sufficient. We utilise (11) and minimise

$$\mathcal{F}^k_{\alpha,p}(d) := \alpha\|d\|^2_{L^2(\Omega)} + \sum_{\ell=1}^{k} \iint_\Omega \|\partial_2^\ell u^\delta(x_1 - d(x_1, x_2), x_2)\|^p_p \, dx_1 \, dx_2 \tag{12}$$

subject to $\|d\|_{L^\infty(\Omega)} \leq \rho$. Again, $p > 0$ and $\alpha \geq 0$. In contrast to before, we decompose the objective into a series of minimisation problems, which then can be solved independently and in parallel by DP. To this end, let us rewrite

$$\mathcal{F}^k_\alpha(d) = \int_0^W \int_0^H \left(\alpha|d(x_1, x_2)|^2 + \sum_{\ell=1}^{k} \|\partial_2^\ell u^\delta(x_1 - d(x_1, x_2), x_2)\|^p_p \right) dx_2 \, dx_1.$$

As before we consider derivatives up to second order. Assuming piecewise constant images defined on a regular grid we seek, for each $(i, j) \in \{1, \ldots, m\} \times \{1, \ldots, n\}$, a displacement $d_{i,j} \in \mathcal{L}$ with $\mathcal{L} := \{-\rho, \ldots, \rho\}$. The finite-dimensional approximations of $\mathcal{F}^1_{\alpha,p}$ and $\mathcal{F}^2_{\alpha,p}$ hence read

$$\mathcal{F}^1_{\alpha,p}(d) \approx \sum_{i=1}^{m} \left(\sum_{j=1}^{n} \alpha|d_{i,j}|^2 + \sum_{j=2}^{n} \|u^\delta_{i-d_{i,j},j} - u^\delta_{i-d_{i,j-1},j-1}\|^p_p \right), \tag{13}$$

$$\mathcal{F}^2_{\alpha,p}(d) \approx \mathcal{F}^1_{\alpha,p}(d) + \sum_{i=1}^{m} \sum_{j=3}^{n} \|u^\delta_{i-d_{i,j},j} - 2u^\delta_{i-d_{i,j-1},j-1} + u^\delta_{i-d_{i,j-2},j-2}\|^p_p. \tag{14}$$

Pixel Jitter. An image corrupted by pixel jitter is generated by

$$u^\delta(x_1, x_2) = u(x_1 + d_1(x_1, x_2), x_2 + d_2(x_1, x_2)) + \eta(x_1, x_2), \tag{15}$$

where $d = (d_1, d_2)^\top$, $d_i : \Omega \to \mathbb{R}$, is now a vector-valued displacement. Edges in degraded images appear pixelated and fringed in both directions. Unless the displacement d is bijective from Ω to itself and $\eta \equiv 0$, there is no hope that u can be perfectly reconstructed from u^δ. However, we assume the existence of

$$d(x) = \arg\inf\{\|v\|_2 \mid v \in \mathbb{R}^2, u(x) = u^\delta(x - v)\}$$

such that $\|d_i\|_{L^\infty(\Omega)} \leq \rho$, for $i \in \{1, 2\}$. For $p > 0$ and $\alpha \geq 0$, we minimise

$$\mathcal{G}_{\alpha,p}(d) := \alpha\|d\|_{L^2(\Omega)}^2 + \int_\Omega \|\nabla(u^\delta(x - d(x)))\|_p^p \, dx$$

subject to $\|d_i\|_{L^\infty(\Omega)} \leq \rho$, $i \in \{1, 2\}$. In contrast to before, we only consider first-order derivatives of the sought image.

Assuming piecewise constant images on a regular grid and integer displacements, we seek for each $(i, j) \in \{1, \ldots, m\} \times \{1, \ldots, n\}$ an offset $d_{i,j} \in \mathcal{L}$ with $\mathcal{L} := \{-\rho, \ldots, \rho\}^2$. In further consequence, we obtain

$$\mathcal{G}_{\alpha,p}(d) \approx \sum_{i=1}^{m}\sum_{j=1}^{n} \alpha\|d_{i,j}\|_2^2 + \sum_{i=2}^{m}\sum_{j=1}^{n} \|u^\delta_{(i,j)-d_{i,j}} - u^\delta_{(i-1,j)-d_{i-1,j}}\|_p^p$$

$$+ \sum_{i=1}^{m}\sum_{j=2}^{n} \|u^\delta_{(i,j)-d_{i,j}} - u^\delta_{(i,j-1)-d_{i,j-1}}\|_p^p. \tag{16}$$

3   Numerical Solution

Dynamic Programming on a Sequence. Suppose we are given $n \in \mathbb{N}$ elements and we aim to assign to each element i a label from its associated space of labels $\mathcal{L}_i$. Without loss of generality, we assume that all $\mathcal{L}_i$ are identical and contain finitely many labels. A labelling is denoted by $x = (x_1, \ldots, x_n)^\top \in \mathcal{L}^n$, where $x_i \in \mathcal{L}$ is the label assigned to the i-th element.

Let us consider the finite-dimensional minimisation problem

$$\min_{x \in \mathcal{L}^n} \sum_{i=1}^{n} \varphi_i(x_i) + \sum_{i=2}^{n} \psi_{i-1,i}(x_{i-1}, x_i). \tag{17}$$

We denote a minimiser by x^* and its value by $E(x^*)$. Here, $\varphi_i(x_i)$ is the penalty of assigning the label $x_i \in \mathcal{L}$ to element i, whereas $\psi_{i-1,i}(x_{i-1}, x_i)$ is the cost of assigning x_{i-1} to the element $i - 1$ and x_i to i, respectively. Several minimisers of (17) might exist but finding one is sufficient for our purpose. Energies (17) typically arise from the discretisation of computer vision problems such as one-dimensional signal denoising, stereo matching, or curve detection. We refer to [5] for a comprehensive survey and to [3] for a general introduction to DP.

The basic idea for solving (17) is to restate the problem in terms of smaller subproblems. Let $|\mathcal{L}|$ denote the cardinality of $\mathcal{L}$. Then, for $j \leq n$ and $\ell \leq |\mathcal{L}|$, we define $\mathrm{OPT}(j, \ell)$ as the minimum value of the above minimisation problem (17) over the first j elements with the value of the last variable x_j being set to the ℓ-th label. That is,

$$\text{OPT}(j, \ell) := \min_{x \in \mathcal{L}^{j-1}} \sum_{i=1}^{j} \varphi_i(x_i) + \sum_{i=2}^{j} \psi_{i-1,i}(x_{i-1}, x_i).$$

Moreover, we define $\text{OPT}(0, \ell) := 0$ for all $\ell \leq |\mathcal{L}|$ and $\psi_{0,1} := 0$, and show the following recurrence:

Proposition 1. *Let $x_\ell \in \mathcal{L}$ denote the label of the j-th element. Then,*

$$\text{OPT}(j, \ell) = \varphi_j(x_\ell) + \min_{x_{j-1} \in \mathcal{L}} \{\text{OPT}(j - 1, x_{j-1}) + \psi_{j-1,j}(x_{j-1}, x_\ell)\}.$$

Proof. By induction on the elements $j \in \mathbb{N}$. Induction basis $j = 1$. Thus, $\text{OPT}(1, \ell) = \varphi_1(x_\ell)$ holds. Inductive step. Assume it holds for $j - 1$. Then,

$$\begin{aligned}
\text{OPT}(j, \ell) &= \min_{x \in \mathcal{L}^{j-1}} \sum_{i=1}^{j} \varphi_i(x_i) + \sum_{i=2}^{j} \psi_{i-1,i}(x_{i-1}, x_i) \\
&= \min_{x_{j-1} \in \mathcal{L}} \{\text{OPT}(j - 1, x_{j-1}) + \varphi_j(x_\ell) + \psi_{j-1,j}(x_{j-1}, x_\ell)\} \\
&= \varphi_j(x_\ell) + \min_{x_{j-1} \in \mathcal{L}} \{\text{OPT}(j - 1, x_{j-1}) + \psi_{j-1,j}(x_{j-1}, x_\ell)\}.
\end{aligned}$$

$\square$

It is straightforward to see that Algorithm 1 correctly computes all values of $\text{OPT}(j, \ell)$ and hence the minimum value of (17). Its running time is in $O(n|\mathcal{L}|^2)$ and its memory requirement in $O(n|\mathcal{L}|)$. Recovering a minimiser to (17) can be done either by a subsequent backward pass or even faster at the cost of additional memory by storing a minimising label x_{j-1} in each iteration.

One can generalise the algorithm to energies involving higher-order terms of $q \geq 2$ consecutive unknowns yielding a running time of $O(n|\mathcal{L}|^q)$ and a memory requirement of $O(n|\mathcal{L}|^{q-1})$. We refer to [5] for the details. The minimisation problems encountered in Sect. 2 involve terms of order at most three. It is straightforward to apply the above framework to (8), (9), (13), and (14).

Algorithm 1. Dynamic programming on a sequence.

Input: Integer n, functions φ_j and $\psi_{j-1,j}$.
Output: $E(x^*)$.
1 $B[1][\ell] \leftarrow \varphi_1(x_\ell), \forall \ell \in \mathcal{L}$;
2 **for** $j \leftarrow 2$ **to** n **do**
3   **for** $\ell \leftarrow 1$ **to** $|\mathcal{L}|$ **do**
4          $B[j][\ell] \leftarrow \varphi_j(x_\ell) + \min_{x_{j-1} \in \mathcal{L}} \{B[j - 1][x_{j-1}] + \psi_{j-1,j}(x_{j-1}, x_\ell)\}$;

5 **return** $\min_\ell B[n][\ell]$;

Energy Minimisation on Graphs. A more general point of view is to consider (17) on (undirected) graphs. Thereby, each element is associated with a vertex of the graph and one seeks a minimiser to

$$\min_{x \in \mathcal{L}^n} \sum_i \varphi_i(x_i) + \sum_{i \sim j} \psi_{i,j}(x_i, x_j). \tag{18}$$

The first term sums over all n vertices whereas the second term sums over all pairs of vertices which are connected via an edge in the graph. Such energies typically arise from the discretisation of variational problems on regular grids, such as for instance image denoising. In general, (18) is NP-hard. However, under certain restrictions on φ_i and $\psi_{i,j}$, there exist polynomial-time algorithms. Whenever the underlying structure is a tree or a sequence as above, the problem can be solved by means of DP without further restrictions. See [1] for a general introduction to the topic.

Nevertheless, many interesting problems do fall in neither category. One remedy is *block coordinate descent* [2,14] in order to approximately minimise (18), which we denote by F. The essential idea is to choose in each iteration $t \in \mathbb{N}$ an index set $\mathcal{I}^{(t)} \subset \{1, \ldots, n\}$ which contains much less elements than n, and to consider (18) only with respect to unknowns x_i, $i \in \mathcal{I}^{(t)}$. The values of all other unknowns are taken from the previous iteration. That is, one finds in each iteration

$$x^{(t)} := \arg\min_{x_i : i \in \mathcal{I}^{(t)}} F^{(t)}(x), \tag{19}$$

where $F^{(t)}$ denotes the energy in (18) with all unknowns not in $\mathcal{I}^{(t)}$ taking the values from $x^{(t-1)}$. Typically, $\mathcal{I}^{(t)}$ is chosen such that (19) can be solved efficiently. It is straightforward to see that block coordinate descent generates a sequence $\{x^{(t)}\}_t$ of solutions such that F never increases. The energy is thus guaranteed to converge to a local minimum with regard to the chosen $\mathcal{I}^{(t)}$.

We perform block coordinate descent for the solution of (16) and iteratively consider instances of (17). Following the ideas in [2,14], we consecutively minimise in each iteration over all odd columns, all even columns, all odd rows, and finally over all even rows. During minimisation the displacements of all other rows, respectively columns, are fixed. See Table 1 for the resulting algorithms.

4   Numerical Results

We present qualitative results on the basis of a test image[1] and create images degraded by line jitter, line pixel jitter, and pixel jitter by sampling displacements from a Gaussian distribution with variance $\sigma^2 = 1.5$, and rounding them to the nearest integer, see Fig. 1. Vector-valued displacements are sampled componentwise. In addition, we create instances with additive Gaussian white noise η of variance $\sigma_\eta^2 = 0.01$. We then apply to each instance the appropriate algorithm

---

[1] Taken from BSDS500 dataset at https://www.eecs.berkeley.edu/Research/Projects/CS/vision/grouping/resources.html.

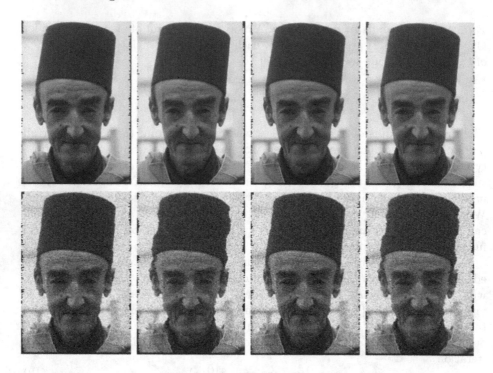

Fig. 2. Line jitter removal. Top row: minimisers of $\mathcal{E}^1_{0,0.5}$, $\mathcal{E}^2_{0,0.5}$, $\mathcal{E}^1_{0.01,0.5}$, and $\mathcal{E}^2_{0.01,0.5}$, cf. (8) and (9). Bottom row: minimisers of $\mathcal{E}^1_{0,3}$, $\mathcal{E}^2_{0,3}$, $\mathcal{E}^1_{1000,3}$, and $\mathcal{E}^2_{1000,3}$ when noise η is present in each of the four u^δ.

with varying parameters α and p, and show the results which maximise jitter removal, see Figs. 2, 3, and 4. The value of ρ is set to the maximum displacement that occurred during creation. A Matlab/Java implementation is available online.[2]

While regularisation does not seem to be crucial for line jitter removal—apart from a centred image—for line pixel jitter and pixel jitter removal it is. Moreover, including second-order derivatives in our models does not necessarily improve the result. In all cases our results indicate effective removal of jitter, even in the presence of moderate noise. However, subsequent denoising seems obligatory.

5   Related Work

Kokaram et al. [8–10] were among the first to consider line dejittering. They employed a block-based autoregressive model for grey-valued images and developed an iterative multi-resolution scheme to estimate line displacements. Subsequent drift compensation removes low frequency oscillations. Their methods seek displacements which reduce the vertical gradients of the sought image.

---

[2] https://www.csc.univie.ac.at.

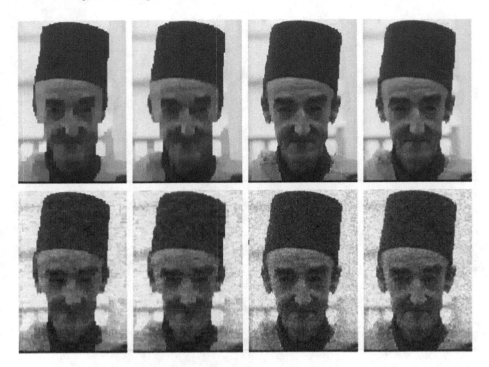

Fig. 3. Line pixel jitter removal. Top row: minimisers of $\mathcal{F}^1_{0,0.5}$, $\mathcal{F}^2_{0,0.5}$, $\mathcal{F}^1_{4,0.5}$, and $\mathcal{F}^2_{4,0.5}$, cf. (13) and (14). Bottom row: minimisers of $\mathcal{F}^1_{0,0.5}$, $\mathcal{F}^2_{0,0.5}$, $\mathcal{F}^1_{5,0.5}$, and $\mathcal{F}^2_{5,0.5}$ when noise η is present in each of the four u^δ.

For line jitter removal, a naive approach consists of fixing the first line of the image and successive minimisation of a mismatch function between consecutive lines. This greedy algorithm tends to introduce vertical lines in the reconstructed image and fails in the presence of dominant non-vertical edges [10,11]. As a remedy, Laborelli [11] proposed to apply DP and to recover a horizontal displacement for each line by minimising the sum of the pixel-wise differences between two or three consecutive lines.

Shen [18] proposed a variational model for line dejittering in a Bayesian framework and investigated its properties for images in the space of bounded variation. In order to minimise the non-linear and non-convex objective, an iterative algorithm that alternatively estimates the original image and the displacements is devised.

Kang and Shen [6] proposed a two-step iterative method termed "bake and shake". In a first step, a Perona-Malik-type diffusion process is applied in order to suppress high-frequency irregularities in the image and to smooth distorted object boundaries. In a second step, the displacement of each line is independently estimated by solving a non-linear least-squares problem. In another article [7], they investigated properties of slicing moments of images with bounded variation and proposed a variational model based on moment regularisation.

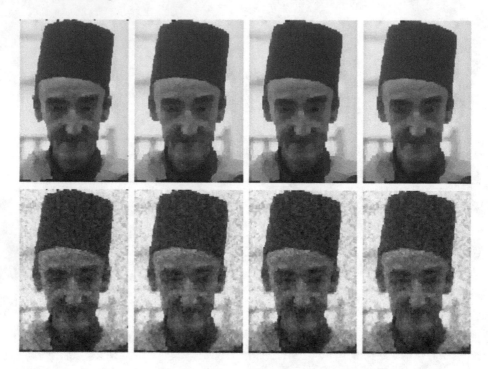

Fig. 4. Line pixel jitter removal. Top row: sequence $u^{(1)}, \ldots, u^{(4)}$, of minimisers of $\mathcal{G}_{4,0.5}$, cf. (16). Bottom row: sequence $u^{(1)}, \ldots, u^{(4)}$, of minimisers of $\mathcal{G}_{4,0.5}$ when noise η is present in u^{δ}. Results for $\alpha = 0$ are excluded due to poor quality.

In [15,16], Nikolova considered greedy algorithms for finite-dimensional line dejittering with bounded displacements. These algorithms consider vertical differences between consecutive lines up to third-order and are applicable to grey-value as well as colour images. In each step, a non-smooth and possibly non-convex function is minimised by enumeration, leading to an $O(mn\rho)$ algorithm. For experimental evaluation various error measures are discussed.

Lenzen and Scherzer [12,13] considered partial differential equations for displacement error correction in multi-channel data. Their framework is applicable to image interpolation, dejittering, and deinterlacing. For line pixel dejittering they derived gradient flow equations for a non-convex variational formulation involving the total variation of the reconstructed image.

Dong et al. [4] treated the finite-dimensional models in [15,16] in an infinite-dimensional setting. They derived the corresponding energy flows and systematically investigated their applicability for various jitter problems.

6   Conclusion

In this article we presented efficient algorithms for line jitter, line pixel jitter, and pixel jitter removal in a finite-dimensional setting. By assuming (approximate) invertibility of the image acquisition equation we were able to cast the minimisation problems into a well-known DP framework. Our experimental results indicate effective removal of jitter, even in the presence of moderate noise.

References

1. Blake, A., Kohli, P., Rother, C. (eds.): Markov Random Fields for Vision and Image Processing. MIT Press, Cambridge (2011)
2. Chen, Q., Koltun, V.: Fast MRF optimization with application to depth reconstruction. In: Proceedings of the IEEE Conference on Computer Vision and Pattern Recognition, pp. 3914–3921. IEEE, June 2014
3. Cormen, T.H., Leiserson, C.E., Rivest, R.L., Stein, C.: Introduction to Algorithms, 3rd edn. MIT Press, Cambridge (2009)
4. Dong, G., Patrone, A.R., Scherzer, O., Öktem, O.: Infinite dimensional optimization models and PDEs for dejittering. In: Aujol, J.-F., Nikolova, M., Papadakis, N. (eds.) SSVM 2015. LNCS, vol. 9087, pp. 678–689. Springer, Cham (2015). doi:10. 1007/978-3-319-18461-6_54
5. Felzenszwalb, P.F., Zabih, R.: Dynamic programming and graph algorithms in computer vision. IEEE Trans. Pattern Anal. Mach. Intell. **33**(4), 721–740 (2011)
6. Kang, S.H., Shen, J.: Video dejittering by bake and shake. Image Vis. Comput. **24**(2), 143–152 (2006)
7. Kang, S.H., Shen, J.: Image dejittering based on slicing moments. In: Tai, X.C., Lie, K.A., Chan, T.F., Osher, S. (eds.) Image Processing Based on Partial Differential Equations. Mathematics and Visualization, pp. 35–55. Springer, Heidelberg (2007)
8. Kokaram, A., Rayner, P.: An algorithm for line registration of TV images based on a 2-D AR model. In: Proceedings of Signal Processing VI, Theories and Applications, pp. 1283–1286. European Association for Signal Processing (1992)
9. Kokaram, A., Rayner, P., Van Roosmalen, P., Biemond, J.: Line registration of jittered video. In: Proceedings of the IEEE International Conference on Acoustics, Speech, and Signal Processing, vol. 4, pp. 2553–2556. IEEE Computer Society (1997)
10. Kokaram, A.C.: Motion Picture Restoration: Digital Algorithms for Artefact Suppression in Degraded Motion Picture Film and Video. Springer, London (1998)
11. Laborelli, L.: Removal of video line jitter using a dynamic programming approach. In: Proceedings of International Conference on Image Processing, (ICIP 2003), vol. 2, pp. II-331–II-334, September 2003
12. Lenzen, F., Scherzer, O.: A geometric PDE for interpolation of M-channel data. In: Tai, X.-C., Mørken, K., Lysaker, M., Lie, K.-A. (eds.) SSVM 2009. LNCS, vol. 5567, pp. 413–425. Springer, Heidelberg (2009). doi:10.1007/978-3-642-02256-2_35
13. Lenzen, F., Scherzer, O.: Partial differential equations for zooming, deinterlacing and dejittering. Int. J. Comput. Vis. **92**(2), 162–176 (2011)
14. Menze, M., Heipke, C., Geiger, A.: Discrete optimization for optical flow. In: Gall, J., Gehler, P., Leibe, B. (eds.) GCPR 2015. LNCS, vol. 9358, pp. 16–28. Springer, Cham (2015). doi:10.1007/978-3-319-24947-6_2
15. Nikolova, M.: Fast dejittering for digital video frames. In: Tai, X.-C., Mørken, K., Lysaker, M., Lie, K.-A. (eds.) SSVM 2009. LNCS, vol. 5567, pp. 439–451. Springer, Heidelberg (2009). doi:10.1007/978-3-642-02256-2_37

16. Nikolova, M.: One-iteration dejittering of digital video images. J. Vis. Commun. Image Represent. **20**, 254–274 (2009)
17. Scherzer, O., Grasmair, M., Grossauer, H., Haltmeier, M., Lenzen, F.: Variational Methods in Imaging. Applied Mathematical Sciences, vol. 167. Springer, New York (2009)
18. Shen, J.: Bayesian video dejittering by BV image model. SIAM J. Appl. Math. **64**(5), 1691–1708 (2004)

Robust Blind Deconvolution
with Convolution-Spectrum-Based Kernel
Regulariser and Poisson-Noise Data Terms

Martin Welk[✉]

Institute of Biomedical Image Analysis, Private University for Health Sciences,
Medical Informatics and Technology (UMIT),
Eduard-Wallnöfer-Zentrum 1, 6060 Hall/Tyrol, Austria
martin.welk@umit.at

Abstract. In recent work by Liu, Chang and Ma a variational blind deconvolution approach with alternating estimation of image and point-spread function was presented in which an innovative regulariser for the point-spread function was constructed using the convolution spectrum of the blurred image. Further work by Moser and Welk introduced robust data fidelity terms to this approach but did so at the cost of introducing a mismatch between the data fidelity terms used in image and point-spread function estimation. We propose an improved version of this robust model that avoids the mentioned inconsistency. We extend the model to multi-channel images and show experiments on synthetic and real-world images to compare the robust variants with the method by Liu, Chang and Ma.

1 Introduction

Since noise and blur are the two most important and ubiquitous sources of degradations in virtually all modalities of image acquisition, methods to enhance images degraded by blur have been an object of intensive research since the early times of image processing. Blur is a spatial redistribution of image intensities; in the simple case when the redistribution follows the same spatial pattern at all image locations it is modelled by convolution of the (unobservable) sharp image g with a space-invariant *point-spread function (PSF)* h as convolution kernel, i.e.

$$f = g * h + n, \tag{1}$$

where f denotes the observed degraded image, and additive noise n has been included in the model. In a similar way spatially variant blur can be modelled by replacing the convolution $*$ in (1) with a Fredholm integral operator. Methods that aim at a computational (approximate) inversion of the blur process (1) (or its more general space-variant version that we will not treat any further here) are called *deconvolution*. Two types of deconvolution problems are to be distinguished: Non-blind deconvolution assumes that the image f as well as the

© Springer International Publishing AG 2017
F. Lauze et al. (Eds.): SSVM 2017, LNCS 10302, pp. 159–171, 2017.
DOI: 10.1007/978-3-319-58771-4_13

PSF h are known, and an image u is to be found that fulfils $f \approx u * h$, such that u can be considered as an approximation of g. Blind deconvolution methods take only an image f as input and aim at reconstructing u and h at the same time. Both types of deconvolution problems are ill-posed inverse problems but of course blind deconvolution is the harder of the two.

One class of approaches to blind deconvolution are variational models that involve minimisation of an energy functional of type [2,20]

$$E(u,h) = F(f, u * h) + \alpha R_u(u) + \beta R_h(h) \qquad (2)$$

where $F(f, u * h)$ is a data fidelity term that penalises deviations from the blur equation $f = u * h$, and brings in the information of the observed image; possible choices will be discussed in more detail later in this paper. R_u and R_h are regularisers for the image and PSF, respectively, that encode assumptions on plausible images and PSFs.

Minimisation of (2) is often done by alternating minimisation, which iteratively improves estimates for u and h by minimising, respectively, the reduced functionals

$$E(u) = F(f, u * h) + \alpha R_u(u), \qquad (3)$$
$$E(h) = F(f, u * h) + \beta R_h(h). \qquad (4)$$

Note that (3) alone is just a variational model for non-blind deconvolution.

Regarding images, smoothness requirements play an important role; these can be encoded by regularisers R_u that impose increasing functions of $|\nabla u|$ at each image location as penalisers.

Whereas the suitability of this class of image regularisers is widely agreed in the field, regularisers R_h for PSFs are more difficult to formulate. Transferring the smoothness-based image regularisers to PSFs has been tried early [2,20], its success has been limited: firstly, smoothness is an adequate characterisation only of some practically relevant PSFs (such as Gaussian blur); secondly, it misses other important properties of PSFs such as locality and sparsity of support. In recent years, maximum a posteriori [7] and machine-learning approaches [13] for the regularisation of h have been proposed.

In [8] a PSF regulariser based on spectra of convolution operators was introduced, and used within an alternating optimisation approach based on an energy functional of type (2). This is an interesting new approach to the estimation of blur as it uses information from the observed image f to constrain the PSF. The data fidelity term in [8] uses classical quadratic penalisation. As it is known from the image processing literature that data fidelity terms based on less-than-quadratic penalisation allow a more robust minimisation, i.e. reduce sensitivity to extreme noise, outliers, and model violations [1,4,18,21], the authors of [9] proposed a modification of the model from [8] with these so-called robust data fidelity terms. This model, however, suffers from a mismatch between the data fidelity terms used in the image and PSF estimation.

Our Contribution. In this paper we improve the blind deconvolution model from [9] by using consistently one type of robust data fidelity term in both components of the alternating minimisation model. To this end, we modify the PSF estimation step of [9] to adopt the data fidelity term from [16] that was used in [9] only for image estimation.

To enable the processing of colour images, we state shortly multi-channel versions of the blind deconvolution model from [9] as well as of the new model. We present experiments on synthetic test images without and with noise that show the viability of the new model and illustrate the usefulness of the robust blind deconvolution models for noisy input data, and on a real-world colour image.

Structure of the Paper. The two components of alternating minimisation models as they are used in [8,9] and our new model are discussed in the next two sections: Sect. 2 recalls the image estimation models from [6,14,16] that are used in [8,9] and also in the present paper. Section 3 is devoted to PSF estimation; it recalls the PSF regularisation procedures from [8,9], and introduces our further modification of the latter model. Section 4 translates the estimation procedures to multi-channel images. Section 5 presents experimental results. Section 6 concludes the paper with a short summary and outlook.

2   Image Estimation

The estimation of the image u in the alternating minimisation of (2) is a non-blind deconvolution based on minimising (3) for which several methods exist in the literature. We recall shortly the approaches chosen in [8,9] for this purpose.

Krishnan-Fergus Method [6]. In [8] the method from [6] is used for the non-blind deconvolution step. Like the very similar method published earlier in [14], it aims at minimising a functional (3) in which the quadratic data fidelity term

$$F(f, u * h) = \int_{\Omega} \varrho(f, u * h) \, \mathrm{d}\boldsymbol{x}, \tag{5}$$

$$\varrho(f, v) \equiv \varrho_{\mathrm{quad}}(f, v) := (f - v)^2, \tag{6}$$

is combined with a regulariser R_u of type

$$R_u(u) = \int_{\Omega} |\boldsymbol{\nabla} u|^{\nu} \, \mathrm{d}\boldsymbol{x} =: \int_{\Omega} \Psi \left(|\boldsymbol{\nabla} u|^2 \right) \, \mathrm{d}\boldsymbol{x}, \tag{7}$$

where ν equals 1 in [14], and can take different discrete values in [6]; in [8] the case $\nu = 1$ is used, i.e. R_u is a total variation (TV) regulariser [12]. In [6,14] the functional $E(u)$ is rewritten using auxiliary quantities w_x, w_y into a so-called half-quadratic functional, which is then minimised by an iterative procedure that alternates between updating w_x, w_y by (nonlinear) shrinkage applied to the gradient components u_x, u_y, and updating u by a linear filter step via the Fourier domain.

Robust Regularised Richardson-Lucy Deconvolution [16]. In [9] the authors pursued the goal to introduce a robust data fidelity term $F(f, u * h)$ into the framework of [8]. In the image estimation step they decided to use the so-called robust regularised Richardson-Lucy deconvolution (RRRL) from [16] which has proven useful in several applications of non-blind deconvolution [3,11,17].

RRRL is a fixed-point iteration for a functional (3) with the robust data fidelity term

$$F(f, u * h) = \int_\Omega \Phi\big(\varrho(f, u * h)\big) \, d\boldsymbol{x}, \tag{8}$$

$$\varrho(f, v) \equiv \varrho_{\mathrm{RL}}(f, v) := v - f - f \ln \frac{f}{v}. \tag{9}$$

Note that unlike ϱ_{quad} from (6) that is related to Gaussian, Laplacean and similar symmetric additive noise types, the residual error measure ϱ_{RL} used here is related to Poisson noise and related types of noise. In (8) it is the argument to a penaliser function $\Phi : \mathbb{R}_0^+ \to \mathbb{R}_0^+$ that is assumed to increase less than linear; [16] suggests $\Phi(z) = \sqrt{z}$ or, with a numerical regularisation, $\Phi(z) = \sqrt[4]{z^2 + \varepsilon}$. For the regulariser R_u for RRRL different choices are possible, see [16], including the TV regulariser (7) with $\nu = 1$, or regularisers associated with Perona-Malik's isotropic nonlinear diffusion [10]. In [9] the TV regulariser is used, and we will follow this choice in the present paper.

3   Point-Spread Function Estimation

In this section we describe the estimation step for the PSF h in the alternating minimisation scheme. This involves, first, the specification of the PSF regulariser according to [8], and second, its minimisation in combination with a suitable data fidelity term.

For this section, we switch to a discrete setting because the formulation of the spectral decomposition in [8] is done in the finite-dimensional matrix-algebraic setting. We rewrite (4) in the discretised form

$$E(\boldsymbol{h}) := F(\boldsymbol{f}, \boldsymbol{u} * \boldsymbol{h}) + \beta R_h(\boldsymbol{h}) \tag{10}$$

with discrete images $\boldsymbol{f} = (f_{i,j})_{i,j}$, $\boldsymbol{u} = (u_{i,j})_{i,j}$ and a discrete PSF $\boldsymbol{h} = (h_{i,j})_{i,j}$. The PSF regulariser R_h and data fidelity term F will be specified in the following subsections.

3.1   Regulariser Based on Convolution Spectrum

Let us now recall the PSF regularisation approach from [8] which also underlies the work in [9] and which will also be adopted in the present paper.

To this end, we start by noticing that, for any given image $\boldsymbol{v}$, the convolution $\boldsymbol{v} * \boldsymbol{h}$ defines a linear operator on point-spread functions $\boldsymbol{h}$. For discrete $\boldsymbol{h}$ with a support of size $m_x \times m_y$, it is suggested in [8] to embed it into a larger area sized

$s_x \times s_y$ with $(s_x, s_y) \approx 1.5\,(m_x, m_y)$; assuming $n_x \times n_y$ as size of the image v and adopting the discrete convolution with zero-padding, we have the convolution operator $C^v : \mathbb{R}^{s_x \times s_y} \to \mathbb{R}^{(s_x+n_x-1) \times (s_y+n_y-1)}$, $h \mapsto v * h$. Its singular value decomposition yields $s_x s_y$ singular values $\sigma_k(v)$ whose right singular vectors can be identified with singular discrete kernels $h_k(v)$. Following the terminology of [8], one calls $\sigma_k(v)$ and $h_k(v)$ the *convolution eigenvalues* and *convolution eigenvectors* of v.

The core observation of [8], underpinned by theoretical analysis in that source, is that convolution eigenvalues of blurred images $v = u * h$ tend to be substantially smaller than those of the underlying sharp images $v = u$. In particular, the convolution eigenvectors belonging to the few smallest convolution eigenvalues $\sigma_k(u * h)$ are approximately orthogonal to h under the inner product given by convolution. In other words, $\|h_k(u*h)*h\| \approx 0$ holds for those k for which $\sigma_k(u * h) \approx 0$.

Since the convolution spectrum needs only to be computed for the blurred image, a hard regularisation approach to estimate the convolution kernel h behind the blurred image $f = g * h$ could use orthogonality of h with a suitable set of convolution eigenvectors for f directly. However, this would require a rule (such as a threshold on $\sigma_k(f)$) to determine the number of convolution eigenvectors to be used. This difficulty is avoided in [8] by using instead a soft constraint with the penaliser $\sum_{k=1}^{s_x s_y} \|h_k(f) * h\|^2 / \sigma_k(f)^2$; the weighting by inverse squared convolution eigenvalues makes the convolution eigenvectors for small convolution eigenvalues dominant in the penalisation without the need for a threshold parameter.

As a refinement to this procedure, the image f can be preprocessed by a suitable linear filter operator L. Whereas the general principle of convolution orthogonality remains valid due to the commutativity between L and the linear convolution operator, such a modification allows to re-weight the influence of different regions of the image f on the estimation of h. Following [8], we choose L as a Laplacean-of-Gaussian (LoG); this correlates with the established fact that the information in near-edge regions of a blurred image is of particular value in blur estimation, compare [19] and other works on blur estimation that exploit this property. The resulting regulariser then reads as [8]

$$R_h(h) = \sum_{k=1}^{s_x s_y} \frac{\|h_k(L(f)) * h\|^2}{\sigma_k(L(f))^2} \tag{11}$$

with the LoG operator L. Note that h enters (11) with dimensions $s_x \times s_y$; the actual minimisation, however, will be constrained to h supported on an $m_x \times m_y$ patch.

Minimisation of the regulariser R_h alone could be used to estimate h for subsequent non-blind deconvolution, but in this case no regularisation on u enters the estimation of h. Indeed, [8] states that such an approach tends to result in over-sharpened images with visible artifacts. One should therefore embed R_h into a joint functional such as (2) with alternating minimisation for u and h. To this end, $R_h(h)$ is rewritten as a quadratic form acting on kernels $h = (h_{i,j})_{i,j}$

of size $m_x \times m_y$, $R_h(\mathbf{h}) = \sum_{i,j,i',j'} H_{i,j;i',j'} h_{i,j} h_{i',j'}$ where the coefficient matrix $\mathbf{H} = (H_{i,j;i',j'})_{i,j;i',j'}$ is the Hessian

$$\mathbf{H} = \sum_{k=1}^{s_x s_y} \frac{\mathbf{C}_{m_x,m_y}^{h_k(L(\mathbf{f}))^\mathrm{T}} \mathbf{C}_{m_x,m_y}^{h_k(L(\mathbf{f}))}}{\sigma_k(L(\mathbf{f}))^2} \tag{12}$$

which can be pre-computed once for all iterations.

3.2   Robust Data Term in PSF Estimation

In [8] the regulariser (11) written with the Hessian (12) is combined with a quadratic data fidelity term to give a quadratic minimisation problem for $\mathbf{h}$. In discrete form, the quadratic data fidelity term (compare (5), (6)) reads

$$F(\mathbf{f}, \mathbf{u} * \mathbf{h}) = \sum_{i,j} \varrho(f_{i,j}, v_{i,j}) \tag{13}$$

where $\varrho \equiv \varrho_{\text{quad}}$ is given by (6), and $v_{i,j}$ by

$$\mathbf{v} = (v_{i,j})_{i,j} := \mathbf{u} * \mathbf{h}. \tag{14}$$

The minimality condition of the discrete functional $E(\mathbf{h}) = F(\mathbf{f}, \mathbf{u} * \mathbf{h}) + \beta R_h(\mathbf{h})$ composed of (13) and (11) with (12) is a linear equation system for the entries of $\mathbf{h}$,

$$\sum_{i,j} (S_{p,q;i,j} + \beta H_{p,q;i,j}) h_{i,j} = T_{p,q}, \quad \text{for all pixels } (p,q), \text{with} \tag{15}$$

$$S_{p,q;i,j} = \sum_{r,s} u_{r-i,s-j} u_{r-p,s-q}, \quad T_{p,q} = \sum_{r,s} f_{r,s} u_{r-p,s-q}. \tag{16}$$

This system, which is densely populated, due to R_h, can be solved by standard methods. Since (15) has a high condition number in some cases, regularisation by adding a multiple of the unit matrix to its coefficient matrix may be used for stabilisation.

Robust Data Term From [9]. In [9] the quadratic data fidelity term F in the PSF estimation step was replaced with a robust data fidelity term [1, 21]

$$F(\mathbf{f}, \mathbf{u} * \mathbf{h}) = \sum_{i,j} \Phi\big(\varrho(f_{i,j}, v_{i,j})\big) \tag{17}$$

where $v_{i,j}$ and $\varrho \equiv \varrho_{\text{quad}}$ are given by (14), (6), and $\Phi(z)$ is a penaliser function growing less than z. The L^1 penaliser $\Phi(z^2) = 2|z|$ (or its regularised version $\Phi(z^2) = 2\sqrt{z^2 + \varepsilon}$) is a standard choice here. The minimality condition for the so obtained non-quadratic minimisation problem is a non-linear equation system. Abbreviating

$$\varphi_{r,s} := \Phi'\big(\varrho(f_{i,j}, v_{i,j})\big), \tag{18}$$

the minimality condition system can again be written in the form (15) but

$$S_{p,q;i,j} = \sum_{r,s} \varphi_{r,s} u_{r-i,s-j} u_{r-p,s-q}, \quad T_{p,q} = \sum_{r,s} \varphi_{r,s} f_{r,s} u_{r-p,s-q} \tag{19}$$

now depend on $h_{i,j}$ via $\varphi_{r,s}$. Using this representation, [9] solved the system by iterative linearisation: Given some initial h^0, one computes for $l = 0, 1, \ldots$ the coefficients $S_{p,q;i,j}$ and $T_{p,q}$ from h^l and then solves (15) with fixed coefficients to obtain h^{l+1}. After solving the nonlinear equation system, a sparsification step is used to eliminate negative as well as small positive PSF entries; following [9], values below 0.1 times the 95%-quantile of PSF entries are set to zero.

The practical viability of this approach has been documented in [9] where experiments showed slight improvements over the method from [8]. However, from a theoretical viewpoint the combination of the L^1 fidelity term based on (6) in the PSF estimation with the one based on (9) in the image estimation breaks the unified model (2) and can only be considered as pragmatic approximation of a proper alternating minimisation of a joint energy functional, which is also righteously pointed out in the conclusion of [9].

Asymmetric Robust Data Term. To address this inconsistency in the method of [9], we combine the regulariser (11) with the a discretised version of the data fidelity term (8), (9), i.e. (17) with $\varrho \equiv \varrho_{\mathrm{RL}}$ as given by (9). As penaliser function Φ we will use in experiments $\Phi(z) = \sqrt{z}$ or an approximation thereof.

From (17), (9), (14) we compute

$$\frac{\partial}{\partial h_{p,q}} F = 2 \sum_{i,j} \Phi'\big(\varrho(f_{i,j}, v_{i,j})\big) \frac{\partial \varrho(f_{i,j}, v_{i,j})}{\partial v_{i,j}} \frac{\partial v_{i,j}}{\partial h_{p,q}}$$

$$= 2 \sum_{i,j} \Phi'\big(\varrho(f_{i,j}, v_{i,j})\big) \left(1 - \frac{f_{i,j}}{v_{i,j}}\right) u_{i-p,j-q}$$

$$= -\sum_{i,j} \frac{2\, \Phi'\big(\varrho(f_{i,j}, v_{i,j})\big)}{v_{i,j}} (f_{i,j} - v_{i,j}) u_{i-p,j-q}. \tag{20}$$

For the joint functional $E(h) = F + \beta R_h$, we obtain therefore the minimality conditions as a nonlinear equation system in the same form (15), (19) as before but with

$$\varphi_{r,s} := \frac{2\, \Phi'\big(\varrho(f_{i,j}, v_{i,j})\big)}{v_{i,j}} \tag{21}$$

instead of (18). This equation system can again be solved by iterative linearisation.

4   Multi-channel Images

Given a blurred multi-channel (such as RGB colour) image $f = (f^c)_{c \in \Gamma}$ with the channel index set Γ, it is in most cases appropriate to assume equal blur in all channels, such that one seeks a multi-channel image $\boldsymbol{u}$ and a single-channel PSF h that minimise

$$E(\boldsymbol{u}, h) = F(\boldsymbol{f}, \boldsymbol{u} * h) + \alpha R_u(\boldsymbol{u}) + \beta R_h(h), \tag{22}$$

where the single-channel data fidelity term (8) with ϱ from (6) or (9), and single-channel image regulariser $R_u(u) = \Psi(|\nabla u|^2)$ have been translated to the multi-channel setting as

$$F(\boldsymbol{f}, \boldsymbol{u} * h) = \Phi\left(\sum_{c \in \Gamma} \varrho(f^c, u^c * h)\right), \qquad R_u(\boldsymbol{u}) = \Psi\left(\sum_{c \in \Gamma} |\nabla u^c|^2\right). \tag{23}$$

By analogous derivations as in the previous sections, one obtains from (23) multi-channel minimisation methods that follow the general rule that nonlinearities are calculated by merging information from all channels, and are then applied uniformly in all channels, whereas the linear operations act separately in each channel.

Image Estimation Step. To apply this to the half-quadratic methods from [6,14], notice first that they alternate between computing auxiliary quantities w_x, w_y by a (nonlinear) shrinkage step applied to image gradients, and updating the image u in a linear step via the Fourier domain. Consequently, w_x, w_y will turn into multi-channel counterparts computed by a joint multi-dimensional shrinkage operation, whereas the Fourier step is performed channelwise.

The multi-channel version of RRRL is found in [15]; in our setting it reads as

$$(u^c)^{k+1} = \frac{h^* * \left(\Phi'(\sum_d \varrho(f^d, v^d))\frac{f^c}{v^c}\right) + \alpha\left[\mathrm{div}\left(\Psi'\left(\sum_d |\nabla u^d|^2\right)\nabla u^c\right)\right]_+}{h^* * \Phi'(\sum_d \varrho(f^d, v^d)) - \alpha\left[\mathrm{div}\left(\Psi'\left(\sum_d |\nabla u^d|^2\right)\nabla u^c\right)\right]_-} \tag{24}$$

where indices c and d refer to channels, and pixel indices i, j have been omitted.

PSF Estimation Step. In the estimation of h, operators $\boldsymbol{C^v}$ now map to a space of $|\Gamma|$ times as many dimensions than before but their convolution spectra remain to be of size $s_x s_y$, leaving the further computation of the Hessian (12) unchanged. In the equation systems of Sect. 3.2, the computation of the coefficients (16), (19) now involves a summation over channels, such as

$$S_{p,q;i,j} = \sum_{r,s}\sum_{c \in \Gamma} \varphi^c_{r,s} u^c_{r-i,s-j} u^c_{r-p,s-q}, \qquad T_{p,q} = \sum_{r,s}\sum_{c \in \Gamma} \varphi^c_{r,s} f^c_{r,s} u^c_{r-p,s-q}. \tag{25}$$

The nonlinearities $\varphi_{r,s}$ require summation over channels in the argument of Φ, such that, for the symmetric penalisers, (18) becomes uniformly for all channels

$$\varphi^c_{r,s} \equiv \varphi_{r,s} = \Phi'\left(\sum_{d \in \Gamma} \varrho(f^d_{i,j}, v^d_{i,j})\right), \qquad \varrho \equiv \varrho_{\mathrm{quad}} \text{ as in}(6), \tag{26}$$

whereas, for the asymmetric penalisers, (21) turns into

$$\varphi^c_{r,s} = \frac{2\,\Phi'\left(\sum_{d\in\Gamma}\varrho(f^d_{i,j},v^d_{i,j})\right)}{v^c_{i,j}}, \quad \varrho \equiv \varrho_{\mathrm{RL}} \text{ as in}(9). \tag{27}$$

5   Experiments

We begin by experiments on synthetic images, which allow a direct comparison of reconstructed images and PSFs with the ground truth, i.e. the original sharp image and the PSF used for its degradation. Unfortunately, quantitative measurements of PSNR or SSIM as are common for non-blind deconvolution evaluations face a difficulty in the case of blind deconvolution: As the convolution $u * h$ is invariant under opposite translations of u and h, reconstructions shifted by non-integer displacements must be treated as equally valid. In papers that do PSNR or SSIM measurements on blind deconvolution results, see [5,13], some alignment between ground truth and reconstructed images is used to compensate for such shifts; however, no discussion is provided on how the interpolation involved in alignment influences the error measures. Preliminary tests indicate that already different direction of alignment (ground truth to reconstructed image, or vice versa?) can change PSNR by more than the PSNR differences reported for different methods. We believe therefore that further work is needed to put error measurements for blind deconvolution on more solid grounds. As we cannot solve this problem within the present contribution, we restrict ourselves to visual assessments here.

Figure 1(a) shows a test image from which a blurred version, Fig. 1(b), was generated with the PSF shown in frame (g). Frames (c–f) show results of blind deconvolution with different method settings for the image and PSF estimation steps, with the corresponding reconstructed PSFs in (h–k). To ensure closeness of the results to the steady state, 300 iterations of the alternating minimisation were performed. The standard deviation in the LoG for computing the Hessian (12) was set to 2. Regularisation weights were $\alpha = 0.1$, $\beta = 10^6$ for frame (c), $\alpha = 0.003$, $\beta = 10^4$ for (d), $\alpha = 0.003$, $\beta = 10^4$ for (e), and $\alpha = 0.003$, $\beta = 3000$ for (f). The number of RRRL iterations in the image estimation of (d, e, f) was set to 300. In (e) and (f) 10 linearisation iterations were used in the PSF estimation step.

The sharpened images in Fig. 1(c–f) demonstrate that the original method from [8], (c), as well as its robustified variants from [9], (e) and the present paper, (f), achieve reasonable sharpening, with a slight advantage for the robustified methods (e, f). The combination of robust image estimation with the non-robust PSF estimation from [8] as shown in frame (d) shows no clear advantage, which is no surprise as the combination of a non-robust and robust data fidelity term is even a more blatant mismatch than that of two robust data terms in frame (e). Among the two robust methods (e), (f) there is no clear visual preference. The reconstructed PSFs (h–k) complement these findings. The robust methods yield visually the best matches (j, k) to the ground truth (g). The method from [8]

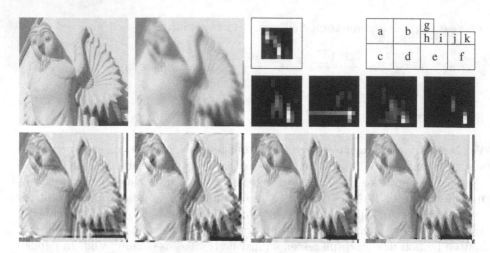

Fig. 1. (a) Test image, 128×128 pixels. (Clipped, downscaled and converted to greyscale from a photograph of the building of TU Vienna, Source of original image: https:// upload.wikimedia.org/wikipedia/commons/e/e9/TU_Bibl_01_DSC1099w.jpg, Author: Peter Haas. Available under licence CC BY-SA 3.0.) – (b) Blurred by the PSF shown in frame (g). – (c) Deblurred using the method from [8]. – (d) Deblurred using the PSF estimation from [8] with image estimation by RRRL [16]. – (e) Deblurred using the robust PSF estimation from [9] with image estimation by RRRL. – (f) Deblurred using robust PSF estimation with asymmetric penalisation (8), (9). – (g) PSF (8×8 pixels) used to generate image (b), 2.85 times enlarged. – (h–k) PSFs (13×13 pixels each) reconstructed with the images (c–f), 2.85 times enlarged.

yields an acceptable estimate (h), whereas the estimate (i) from the half-robust approach appears to be the farthest off.

In Fig. 2(a), the blurred image from Fig. 1(b) was further degraded by Gaussian noise. For this image, a non-blind RRRL deconvolution result ($\alpha = 0.01$, 300 iterations) using the ground-truth PSF is shown in Fig. 2(b). Frames (c–f, h–k) show blind deconvolution results with the same methods as in Fig. 1. Here, 300 iterations of the alternating minimisation were used (no visible changes after about 150 iterations). The standard deviation in the LoG was increased to 5 for frames (c, d, e). Regularisation weights were $\alpha = 0.1$, $\beta = 3 \cdot 10^7$ in (c), $\alpha = 0.01$, $\beta = 10^8$ in (d), $\alpha = 0.02$, $\beta = 10^5$ in (e), $\alpha = 0.01$, $\beta = 10^6$ in (f). The remaining parameters were chosen as in Fig. 1.

As can be expected, the added noise in the input image reduces the quality of deconvolution results significantly. However, it is evident that particularly the results of the fully robust methods (e, f) suffer from less ringing artifacts and noise amplification than the non-robust result (c). Among the reconstructed PSFs (h–k) the one obtained by our proposed method (k) is visually the best match to the ground truth (g).

As a real-world example, Fig. 3 presents tests on two RGB images (a, e) blurred during acquisition. The PSF estimation from [8,9] and our method (8),

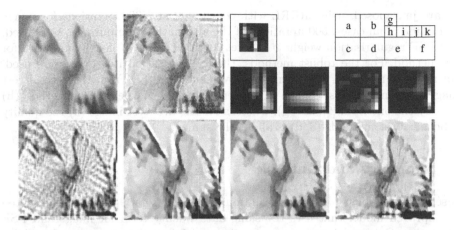

Fig. 2. (a) Blurred test image from Fig. 1(b) degraded by Gaussian noise with standard deviation 10. – (b) Non-blind RRRL deconvolution of (a) using PSF (g). – (c) Blind deconvolution using the method from [8]. – (d) Deblurred using the PSF estimation from [8] with image estimation by RRRL [16]. – (e) Deblurred using the robust PSF estimation from [9] with image estimation by RRRL. – (f) Deblurred using robust PSF estimation with asymmetric penalisation (8), (9). – (g) PSF (8 × 8 pixels) used to generate image (a), 2.85 times enlarged (same as Fig. 1(g)). – (h–k) PSFs (13 × 13 pixels each) reconstructed with the images (c–f), 2.85 times enlarged.

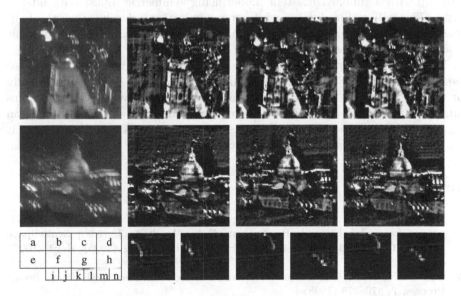

Fig. 3. (a, e) Blurred photographs, 128 × 128 pixels each (Author: Gregor Peltri). – (b, f) Deblurred using the PSF estimation from [8] and RRRL for image estimation. – (c, g) Deblurred using the robust PSF estimation from [9] and RRRL. – (d, h) Deblurred using the robust PSF estimation (8), (9) and RRRL. – (i–n) PSFs (31 × 31 pixels each, 1.93 times enlarged) for (b, f, c, g, d, h), respectively.

(9) are juxtaposed, using RRRL with $\alpha = 0.002$ and 300 iterations for image estimation in all cases. 500 iterations of the alternating minimisation were used. The PSF regularisation weight β was set to 10^5 for [8], 300 for [9] and 1000 for our method. For the robust methods, three linearisation iterations were used. Both robust methods yield some improvement over [8]. From the second test image (e), some details seem to have been recovered sharper by our method (h) than by the one from [9], see (g), whereas for the first test image (a) the quality of both robust methods (c, d) is about the same.

6 Summary and Outlook

Based on the robust blind deconvolution approach from [9], we have presented an improved model that uses the same data fidelity term for image and PSF estimation. Our model represents a consistent minimisation procedure for a joint energy functional which opens up the way for more detailed theoretical analysis in the future. We have shown by experiments the viability of our method for synthetic and real-world examples, and the advantage of the robust approaches from [9] and the present paper over their non-robust predecessor from [8] in deblurring input images with moderate noise.

From the two conflicting data fidelity terms in [9] we have favoured here the asymmetric one that is related to Poisson-type noise. It remains a desiderate to come up with a similar consistent model using symmetric robust data fidelity terms. This will require further work on minimisation procedures, as the half-quadratic approach from [6,14] underlying the image estimation in [8] is difficult to adapt to a robust setting.

Whereas for most parameters of the method heuristics yield good results, see the settings used in Sect. 5, further analysis of parameter selection, especially for the regularisation weights, remains a topic of future work. The high computational cost that is typical for blind deconvolution renders further effort on algorithmic optimisations worthwhile. As pointed out in Sect. 5, future work is also needed regarding appropriate quantitative measures for blind deconvolution.

References

1. Bar, L., Sochen, N., Kiryati, N.: Image deblurring in the presence of salt-and-pepper noise. In: Kimmel, R., Sochen, N.A., Weickert, J. (eds.) Scale-Space 2005. LNCS, vol. 3459, pp. 107–118. Springer, Heidelberg (2005). doi:10.1007/11408031_10
2. Chan, T.F., Wong, C.K.: Total variation blind deconvolution. IEEE Trans. Image Process. **7**, 370–375 (1998)
3. Elhayek, A., Welk, M., Weickert, J.: Simultaneous interpolation and deconvolution model for the 3-D reconstruction of cell images. In: Mester, R., Felsberg, M. (eds.) DAGM 2011. LNCS, vol. 6835, pp. 316–325. Springer, Heidelberg (2011). doi:10.1007/978-3-642-23123-0_32
4. Huber, P.J.: Robust Statistics. Wiley, New York (1981)

5. Köhler, R., Hirsch, M., Mohler, B., Schölkopf, B., Harmeling, S.: Recording and playback of camera shake: benchmarking blind deconvolution with a real-world database. In: Fitzgibbon, A., Lazebnik, S., Perona, P., Sato, Y., Schmid, C. (eds.) ECCV 2012. LNCS, vol. 7578, pp. 27–40. Springer, Heidelberg (2012). doi:10.1007/978-3-642-33786-4_3

6. Krishnan, D., Fergus, R.: Fast image deconvolution using hyper-Laplacian priors. In: Advances in Neural Information Processing Systems, pp. 1033–1041 (2009)

7. Levin, A., Weiss, Y., Durand, F., Freeman, W.T.: Efficient marginal likelihood optimization in blind deconvolution. In: IEEE Conference on Computer Vision and Pattern Recognition, pp. 2657–2664 (2011)

8. Liu, G., Chang, S., Ma, Y.: Blind image deblurring using spectral properties of convolution operators. IEEE Trans. Image Process. **23**, 5047–5056 (2014)

9. Moser, P., Welk, M.: Robust blind deconvolution using convolution spectra of images. In: Niel, K., Roth, P.M., Vincze, M. (eds.) 1st OAGM-ARW Joint Workshop: Vision Meets Robotics, Wels, Austria, pp. 69–78. Österreichische Computer-Gesellschaft (2016)

10. Perona, P., Malik, J.: Scale space and edge detection using anisotropic diffusion. IEEE Trans. Pattern Anal. Mach. Intell. **12**, 629–639 (1990)

11. Persch, N., Elhayek, A., Welk, M., Bruhn, A., Grewenig, S., Böse, K., Kraegeloh, A., Weickert, J.: Enhancing 3-D cell structures in confocal and STED microscopy: a joint model for interpolation, deblurring and anisotropic smoothing. Meas. Sci. Technol. **24**, 125703 (2013)

12. Rudin, L.I., Osher, S., Fatemi, E.: Nonlinear total variation based noise removal algorithms. Phys. D **60**, 259–268 (1992)

13. Schelten, K., Nowozin, S., Jancsary, J., Rother, C., Roth, S.: Interleaved regression tree field cascades for blind image deconvolution. In: IEEE Winter Conference on Applications of Computer Vision, pp. 494–501 (2015)

14. Wang, Y., Yang, J., Yin, W., Zhang, Y.: A new alternating minimization algorithm for total variation image reconstruction. SIAM J. Imaging Sci. **1**, 248–272 (2008)

15. Welk, M.: A robust variational model for positive image deconvolution. Technical report cs:1310.2085, arXiv.org (2013)

16. Welk, M.: A robust variational model for positive image deconvolution. Sig. Image Video Process. **10**, 369–378 (2016)

17. Welk, M., Raudaschl, P., Schwarzbauer, T., Erler, M., Läuter, M.: Fast and robust linear motion deblurring. Sig. Image Video Process. **9**, 1221–1234 (2015)

18. Welk, M., Theis, D., Weickert, J.: Variational deblurring of images with uncertain and spatially variant blurs. In: Kropatsch, W.G., Sablatnig, R., Hanbury, A. (eds.) DAGM 2005. LNCS, vol. 3663, pp. 485–492. Springer, Heidelberg (2005). doi:10.1007/11550518_60

19. Xu, L., Jia, J.: Two-phase kernel estimation for robust motion deblurring. In: Daniilidis, K., Maragos, P., Paragios, N. (eds.) ECCV 2010. LNCS, vol. 6311, pp. 157–170. Springer, Heidelberg (2010). doi:10.1007/978-3-642-15549-9_12

20. You, Y.L., Kaveh, M.: Anisotropic blind image restoration. In: Proceedings of the 1996 IEEE International Conference on Image Processing, Lausanne, Switzerland, vol. 2, pp. 461–464 (1996)

21. Zervakis, M.E., Katsaggelos, A.K., Kwon, T.M.: A class of robust entropic functionals for image restoration. IEEE Trans. Image Process. **4**, 752–773 (1995)

Optimal Patch Assignment for Statistically Constrained Texture Synthesis

Jorge Gutierrez[1]($\boxtimes$), Julien Rabin[2], Bruno Galerne[3], and Thomas Hurtut[1]

[1] Polytechnique Montréal, Montréal, Canada
{jorge-alberto.gutierrez-ortega,thomas.hurtut}@polymtl.ca
[2] Normandie Univ., ENSICAEN, CNRS, GREYC, Caen, France
julien.rabin@unicaen.fr
[3] Laboratoire MAP5, Université Paris Descartes and CNRS,
Sorbonne Paris Cité, Paris, France
bruno.galerne@parisdescartes.fr

Abstract. This article introduces a new model for patch-based texture synthesis that controls the distribution of patches in the synthesized texture. The proposed approach relies on an optimal assignment of patches over decimated pixel grids. This assignment problem formulates the synthesis as the minimization of a discrepancy measure between input's and output's patches through their optimal permutation. The resulting non-convex optimization problem is addressed with an iterative algorithm alternating between a patch assignment step and a patch aggregation step. We show that this model statistically constrains the output texture content, while inheriting the structure-preserving property of patch-based methods. We also propose a relaxed patch assignment extension that increases the robustness to non-stationnary textures.

Keywords: Example-based texture synthesis · Patch matching · Optimal assignment

1 Introduction

The goal of example-based texture synthesis is to generate a new texture image that reproduces the same visual characteristics as an input example without being an exact copy of it. One of the main issues is to simultaneously reproduce the global statistics of the example and the geometry of its local elements [15,16]. One can classify example-based texture synthesis methods into two categories, namely statistical matching methods and non-parametric patch-based methods.

Statistical matching methods estimate feature characteristics of the input texture to generate an output texture having the same characteristics. These features generally involve the input response to various filters whose distribution is summarized using either moments (mean value, correlation matrices, ...) or empirical distributions. In the literature, a broad range of such characteristics have been investigated such as color histograms, the Fourier modulus [10], steerable filter response histograms [6,14,22,26], and more recently occurrences in an

© Springer International Publishing AG 2017
F. Lauze et al. (Eds.): SSVM 2017, LNCS 10302, pp. 172–183, 2017.
DOI: 10.1007/978-3-319-58771-4_14

adapted patch dictionary [27, 28] or correlation matrices in convolutional neural networks [11]. By essence, these methods are successful in preserving the characteristics of interest. They perform well on stochastic textures, yet they may fail to faithfully reproduce the local elements found in more structured textures.

Patch-based methods generate a new texture by sequentially copying pieces from the example [30]. First seminal works synthesize the output texture one pixel at a time [8, 31] constraining the local coherence by choosing pixels with similar neighborhoods in the input. Subsequent contributions use patches instead of pixels as a unit of synthesis [7, 18, 20, 21]. These methods usually better succeed at reproducing the input local structures. Their success is however not guaranteed: when the input image contains constant or blurry regions, these can be indeed enlarged during the synthesis, creating "garbage regions" [1, 8, 23]. A more principled approach consists in synthesizing the output texture through the minimization of a patch-based dissimilarity texture energy [13, 19]. These methods are able to obtain high quality results for both stochastic and structured textures. Nevertheless, they still do not offer any guarantee of success, mostly because the energy does not convey any statistical matching. A first attempt to control the statistics of such patch-based synthesis is based on an empirical technique that compares the RGB histograms in order to penalize the overuse of a certain color in the output [17]. This histogram constraining technique helps to better employ the full color richness of the input. However, it requires a sequential pixel optimization, making it computationally expensive.

Over the last few years, numerical optimal transport has been shown to be a natural tool to solve efficiently optimization problems involving statistical constraints (e.g. [25]). Regarding texture synthesis, optimal transport has been used to solve the texture mixing problem using multi-histogram barycenters of steerable filter responses [26], and later for Gaussian textures [32].

The main purpose of this work is to show that numerical optimal transport is relevant for patch-based texture synthesis. Our insight for this claim is that the goal of patch-based texture synthesis algorithm is arguably to generate a new texture image whose patch distribution is the same as the input. Our main contribution is to use optimal assignment between the output and input patches. This results in a texture synthesis algorithm which enables both the reproduction of the local patterns of the input texture and the preservation of the global patch statistics (including color histogram). We also propose a relaxation of our model by allowing the assignment to vary from a permutation to an unconstrained nearest-neighbor matching.

The proposed model is first described in Sect. 2, and then the algorithm is detailed in Sect. 3 followed by an experimental validation and comparison with other methods in Sect. 4. We discuss a variant of the model in Sect. 5 in order to address some limitations.

2   Linear Patch Assignment Model

Notation. Let $u_0 : \Omega_0 \to [0,1]^3$ be the input example image and $u : \Omega \to [0,1]^3$ be the output synthesized image, both using the normalized RGB color space.

To simplify the presentation, we first consider that the pixel grids $\Omega_0 \in \mathbb{Z}^2$ and Ω have the same size, i.e. $N = |\Omega| = |\Omega_0|$. We define $\mathcal{P}(x)$ as the set of indexes of pixels in the neighborhood of x which is a square of side w ($w = 8$ in our experiments)

$$\mathcal{P}(x) = \left\{ x + t, \ t \in \{-\tfrac{w}{2}, \ldots, \tfrac{w}{2} - 1\}^2 \right\}$$

so that $p(x) = u \circ \mathcal{P}(x)$ is the patch of u in position x. The patches are extracted on sub-grids $\Omega_0^{\downarrow}$ and $\Omega^{\downarrow}$ of Ω_0 and Ω having a step size $\tfrac{w}{4}$ and size $N^{\downarrow} = |\Omega_0^{\downarrow}| = |\Omega^{\downarrow}|$. We use a symmetric boundary condition for patches of u_0 and periodic boundary condition for patches of u.

Proposed Model. Our texture synthesis approach is driven by the following optimization problem which aims at minimizing the discrepancy between the patches from the synthesized texture and patches from the example image

$$\min_{u} \ \min_{\sigma \in \Sigma_{N^{\downarrow}}} \ \sum_{x \in \Omega^{\downarrow}} \|u \circ \mathcal{P}(x) - u_0 \circ \mathcal{P} \circ \sigma(x)\|_p^r \tag{1}$$

where $\sigma : \Omega^{\downarrow} \to \Omega_0^{\downarrow}$ is a mapping between of the indexes of the patches. The most important aspect of this model is the definition of the set $\Sigma_{N^{\downarrow}}$ as the *set of permutations* of $N^{\downarrow}$ elements. The motivation is to synthesize a new texture that has the same distribution of patches as the example in order to preserve all its visual characteristics. We also consider $r = 1$ and the $\ell_{1,2}$ norm of patches, that is the sum of Euclidean norm of color coordinates

$$\|u \circ \mathcal{P}(x)\|_{1,2} = \sum_{y \in \mathcal{P}(x)} \|u(y)\|_2$$

These choices offer several advantages, resulting mainly in a separable convex optimization problem when minimizing with respect to u.

Connections with Previous Work. Problem (1) is a generic framework for texture synthesis and it is closely related to several approaches from the literature such as [13,17] inspired by the seminal work of [19]. For instance, Kwatra et al. [19] use the power $r = 0.8$ with an Euclidean norm weighted with a Gaussian falloff, and the assignment σ is not constrained to be a permutation, which results in a nearest neighbor matching. We claim that the absence of statistical constraint on the map σ is mainly responsible for the loss of features in the output textures, by discarding patches, and for the synthesis of "garbage" [8] and "blurry regions" [17], by locally repeating the same patches.

3   Algorithm

The motivation for Problem (1) is to find an image u which is pixel-wise different from the example image u_0 while having the same patch distribution. Yet Problem (1) has trivial solutions that are not relevant. For instance, using periodic boundary conditions, any circular shifting of the input image is a global minimizer. Still, as usually done for variational texture synthesis [19,22,28], we minimize the non-convex functional of Problem (1) by alternate minimization with respect to u and σ separately starting from a random image. This relies on the assumption that local minimizers of the functional provide the desired result, which is verified in practice.

More precisely, Problem (1) is convex with respect to the image u for a given σ, *i.e.* when the assignment σ between patches has been fixed: this is the *patch aggregation* step that is addressed in Sect. 3.1. In addition, the problem of finding an optimal assignment σ for a given synthesized image u is a solution of a relaxed convex problem: this is the *patch projection* step detailed in Sect. 3.2. These two steps are sequentially used in a multi-scale scheme described in Sect. 3.3.

3.1 Patch Aggregation

When the assignment σ between patches on the subgrids is fixed, optimizing the synthesized image u boils down to find

$$\operatorname*{argmin}_{u} \sum_{x \in \Omega^{\downarrow}} \|u \circ \mathcal{P}(x) - u_0 \circ \mathcal{P} \circ \sigma(x)\|_{1,2} \tag{2}$$

This is a separable convex optimization problem: each color $u(x)$ is given by

$$\operatorname*{argmin}_{u(x)} \sum_{y \in \mathcal{P}^{\downarrow}(x)} \|u(x) - u_0(\sigma(y) + x - y)\|_2 \tag{3}$$

For each pixel $x \in \Omega$, this simply corresponds to compute the color median of the 16 pixel values of patches overlapping x, located at

$$\mathcal{P}^{\downarrow}(x) = \{x + t, \ t \in \{-\tfrac{w}{2}, -\tfrac{w}{4}, 0, \tfrac{w}{4}\}^2\}$$

Our implementation solved the N problems (3) in parallel using a Douglas-Rachford splitting algorithm. Due to the lack of space, technical details are omitted and we refer to [5] for more information. We discuss in the experimental Sect. 4 the interest of this approach in comparison with other patch aggregation methods from the literature.

3.2 Optimal Patch Assignment

The output image u being fixed, an optimal assignment σ is solution of

$$\operatorname*{argmin}_{\sigma \in \Sigma_{N^{\downarrow}}} \sum_{x \in \Omega^{\downarrow}} \|u \circ \mathcal{P}(x) - u_0 \circ \mathcal{P} \circ \sigma(x)\|_{1,2} \tag{4}$$

This problem can be recast as a *linear sum assignment problem* and solved in many different ways [4]. In practice, we use the Hungarian algorithm which is very fast for small assignment problems [3] (in our setting up to images with $N = 256^2$ pixels). For synthesizing larger images or to reduce the computation time, alternative methods should be considered such as parallel implementation of the auction algorithm [29] or the approximate assignment approach using the Sliced-Wasserstein distance [26].

Algorithm 1. Optimal patch assignment texture synthesis

Input: Example texture u_0

Parameters: Number of scales: $S = 3$, patch width: $w = 8$ px,
           Iterations per scale: $\{I_s\}_{s=0}^{S-1} = \{10, 50, 50\}$

Initialization: $\{u_s\}_{s=0}^{S-1} \leftarrow$ Gaussian pyramid of u_0 (Sect.3.3)
               $u \leftarrow$ Random image with same size as u_{S-1}

for $s = S - 1$ *to 0* **do**
     for $i = 1$ *to* I_s **do**
         $\sigma \leftarrow$ Optimal assignment of patches of u to patches of u_s (Sect.3.2)
         $u \leftarrow$ Patch aggregation using σ (Sect.3.1)
         if $s \neq 0$ **then**
            $u \leftarrow$ Bilinear interpolation of u at scale $s - 1$ (Sect.3.3)

Output: Synthesized image u

3.3 Multiscale Scheme and Initialization

A common way to capture large scale correlations between characteristics in the input is to use a coarse-to-fine synthesis [18,28,31]. We apply this strategy by computing the Gaussian pyramid $\{u_s\}_{s=0}^{S-1}$ of the input image, which is composed of S images u_s computed by filtering u_0 with a Gaussian kernel with standard deviation $0.8s$ and sub-sampled with a stepsize of 2^s.

The output coarser scale $s = S - 1$ can be initialized by any image. In practice, we use a random white noise image, as done in several varational texture synthesis previous works [14,22,27]. For subsequent scales, u is first upsampled by a factor 2 using bilinear interpolation. The resulting algorithm is described in Algorithm 1. In all experiments, the patch width is fixed to $w = 8$, the number of scales is $S = 3$, and the number of iterations I_s at scale s is $\{I_s\}_{s=0}^{S-1} = \{10, 50, 50\}$.

3.4 Discussion About Output Size

For simplicity, we have assumed up to this point that the output pixel grid Ω has the same size as the input grid Ω_0, which results in defining σ as a permutation of the indexes of patches. However, in practice it is useful to synthesize output textures larger than the input. If $N^{\downarrow} = nN_0^{\downarrow}$ for some integer $n \geq 2$, a simple solution used in the experiments consists in duplicating n times the input patches. If $N^{\downarrow}$ is completely arbitrary, a usual solution is to simply crop a larger synthesized output. More relevant solutions might be obtained from bootstrapping, i.e. a random sampling of $N^{\downarrow}$ patches from the input distribution, or by considering multiple assignment. However, such a discussion is beyond the scope of this paper.

4 Experimental Results and Comparison

Figure 1 shows two synthesis results, the first having the same size as the input and the second having a double size, along with their respective assignment

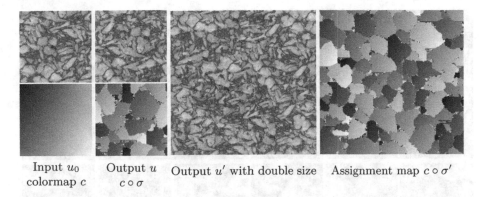

Input u_0 Output u Output u' with double size   Assignment map $c \circ \sigma'$
colormap c $c \circ \sigma$

Fig. 1. Texture synthesis with single and double size outputs u and u'. A colormap c, shown bottom-left, is used to show the corresponding assignment mappings σ and σ'. (Color figure online)

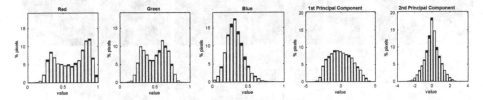

Fig. 2. RGB and patch histograms of the output u in Fig. 1. The absolute differences with the histograms from the input image u_0 are displayed in black.

maps, that correspond to the last optimal assignment σ computed during the optimization process. One can observe with the double size output that the strict assignment forces to reproduce four times the structures and colors from the input. The assignment maps demonstrate that our approach, as all patch-based methods, tends to synthesize textures that are local verbatim copies of the example.

Statistics Compliancy. The patch assignment step generates a patch distribution that is identical to the one of the input. However the patch aggregation step produces new patches and therefore the input and output patch distributions are not strictly identical. Still, to assert experimentally that these two patch distributions are really close, we propose to compare the distributions of first-order statistics between the input and the output textures. In Fig. 2 are shown RGB per-channel color distributions and 1st and 2nd principal components distributions of patches using a PCA analysis on the input patch distribution. It illustrates, as one can observe by visual inspection of Fig. 1, that the features from the two images are mostly similar.

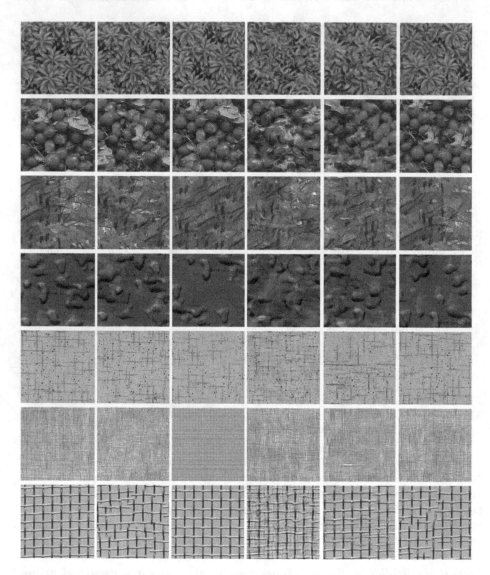

Fig. 3. Comparison of our approach with the patch-based method of Kwatra et al. [19], the two statistical matching methods of Portilla et al. [22] and Tartavel et al. [28], and the PatchMatch method of Barnes et al. [2] (with the implementation of David Tschumperlé for texture synthesis [12]). These approaches are used with the default parameters described in the respective papers.

Comparison with the State of the Art. Figure 3 shows a comparison of the results obtained using our method with the patch-based approach of Kwatra et al. [19], and the statistical matching methods of Portilla and Simoncelli [22] and Tartavel et al. [28]. The two statistical matching methods successfully preserve the color distributions. However they often fail to faithfully reproduce local structured elements. Several issues can be noticed with Kwatra et al. results. Without any statistical constraints, this method sometimes tends to *simplify* the output content. First, copy of large areas from the input may be used (first and second rows). Second, low-cost patch combination tends to be favored: constant regions therefore tend to appear (fourth row), as well as simplified characteristics (loss of whites strokes in the third example, and black spots in the fifth row). Last, when a small set of patches allows a periodic compositing, this set tends to be reused over and over (rows 6 and 7). The same issues are also raised with the non-variational state-of-the-art patch-based approach called PatchMatch [2] (see last column of Fig. 3). While our method is rather successful at both reproducing local elements and at preserving the global colors of the input, it has difficulty retaining long distance correlations on highly structured textures like in the last example of Fig. 3. The trade off between the number of scales used, the patches' width, and the size of the input, limits the scale of the structures that can be captured. Thus, compared to using patches of multiple widths for each scale (as in Kwatra et al. [19]), our single-width approach loses long-distance correlations at a specific scale. However, this also means that smaller regions are copied from the input in comparison with [19], thereby avoiding repetitive artifacts (such as the shadows in the first example) and copy of large regions (second example).

Fig. 4. Comparison of results for different values of r from left to right: r = 2, r = 0.8, r = 0.8 with Gaussian falloff weighting and r = 1 using the same random initialization. Results are quite similar, except for $r = 2$ which is noticeably less sharp.

Discussion on Patch Aggregation. As described in Sect. 3.1, once each patch of u is assigned to a patch u_0, the image u is updated by minimizing the $\ell_{1,2}$-norm, which results in computing the color median among the overlapping pixels. As a comparison, Kwatra et al. [19] use an ℓ_2-norm (with Gaussian weights) to the power $r = 0.8$, and use an iteratively reweighted least squares scheme to minimize this functional (note that this kind of methods encounter numerical issues). Figure 4 illustrates that our algorithm gives similar results when using this variant, and that simply averaging by minimizing the squared ℓ_2-norm leads naturally to blurry textures. We favored minimizing the $\ell_{1,2}$-norm since it is a well-posed convex problem.

Limitations. A limitation of our approach, due to the strict assignment constraint, is the guarantee to synthesize the same distribution of patches as in the input. Although this can be considered as an advantage in most situations, it may lead to undesired effects when inputs do not satisfy sufficiently the stationarity hypothesis.

5   Softening Statistical Constraints via Relaxed Patch Assignment

As demonstrated in the previous section, the synthesis of an image using the very same patch distribution as the one of the example image may lead to some limitations, typically when the stationarity hypothesis is false and the example contains some irrelevant features (e.g. due to illumination, scale change, or artifacts). We propose to address this problem by using soft statistical constraint in such a way that the input and output image may now have a close but different patch distribution.

5.1   Relaxed Assignment Model

We aim at defining a new synthesis model relying on a *relaxed* assignment of patches, that is, for which the one-to-one assignment constraint of Problem (1) is relaxed to enable multiple matching of some example patches. Such an idea was first proposed in [9] and refined by [24] to overcome the problem of color inconsistency in color transfer.

First, let us recall that an optimal assignment problem such as the one of Problem (4) can be recast as a Linear Sum Assignment Problem [4] of the form

$$\min_{\sigma \in \Sigma_{N^\downarrow}} \sum_{i \in \Omega^\downarrow} C_{i,\sigma(i)} = \min_{A \in \mathcal{A}} \sum_{(i,j) \in \Omega^\downarrow \times \Omega_0^\downarrow} A_{i,j} C_{i,j} \tag{5}$$

where C is a fixed cost matrix that corresponds to the distance between patches, that is, $C_{i,j} = \|u \circ \mathcal{P}(i) - u_0 \circ \mathcal{P}(j)\|_{1,2}$ and where

$$\mathcal{A} = \left\{ A \in [0,1]^{N^\downarrow \times N^\downarrow}, \ \forall i \ \sum_j A_{i,j} = 1, \ \forall j \ \sum_i A_{i,j} = 1 \right\}$$

is the set of bistochastic matrices (which is the convex hull of the set of permutation matrices).

Now, following [24], we consider the relaxed assignment problem

$$\min_{P \in \mathcal{A}_k, k \geq 0} \sum_{i,j} P_{i,j} C_{i,j} + \rho \sum_j |k_j - q_j| \tag{6}$$

where the set of relaxed assignment matrix is defined as

$$\mathcal{A}_k = \{ P \in [0,1]^{N^\downarrow \times N^\downarrow}, \ \forall i \ \sum_j P_{i,j} = 1, \ \forall j \ \sum_i P_{i,j} = k_j \}. \tag{7}$$

In this model, q_j is the desired number of matches for the example patch indexed by j and k_j is the number of times this patch is actually matched. Experiments show that the solution of this problem is a relaxed assignment, and we leave the formal proof for future work. The relaxation parameter ρ controls the soft constraint on assignment: if $\rho = 0$, the problem boils down to a nearest-neighbor matching (as done in Kwatra et al. [19]), and for large enough values of ρ, the problem is the optimal assignment problem. To sum up, this model provides relaxed assignments that range from nearest neighbor matching to optimal assignment.

5.2   Results and Discussion

Figure 5 illustrates the effect of relaxing the assignment at each iteration of Algorithm 1 using the above model. These experiments use the same random initialization and the vector q constant to 1. As expected, we observe that for

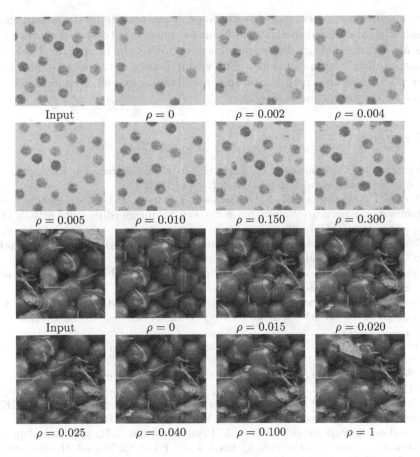

Fig. 5. Texture synthesis with relaxed assignments for different values of the relaxation parameter ρ. The value $\rho = 0$ corresponds to nearest-neighbor matching, which does not respect patch distribution. Increasing ρ gives relaxed assignment that allows for slight variation of the output patch distribution. For large values of ρ, the assignment is an optimal permutation resulting in the reproduction of characteristic of the input.

large values of ρ the relaxed matching is an optimal assignment, while small values of ρ yields relaxed assignment so that some patches of the input example may not be used.

The main practical interest of this model is that it allows for discarding some patches that may represent a rare pattern in the texture (e.g. the red dots in the first example of Fig. 5 and the green leaf of the second example). Contrarily, some other features may now be replicated (the yellow dots in the first example, some radishes in the second). However, the parameter ρ does not offer an explicit control over the structures of the input image that may disappear. A solution to achieve this goal might be to let the user define q more precisely.

6   Conclusion

A new optimal assignment model has been proposed combining the advantages of statistically constrained methods and non-parametric patch-based texture synthesis algorithms. This model can be relaxed in order to be more controllable over the output distribution of patches. The visual quality of the results encourages future work regarding computation time acceleration as well as content-oriented control for the relaxation model.

References

1. Aguerrebere, C., Gousseau, Y., Tartavel, G.: Exemplar-based texture synthesis: the Efros-Leung algorithm. IPOL **3**, 223–241 (2013)
2. Barnes, C., Shechtman, E., Finkelstein, A., Goldman, D.B., Patchmatch: A randomized correspondence algorithm for structural image editing. In: SIGGRAPH, pp. 24:1–24:11. ACM (2009)
3. Bougleux, S., Brun, L.: Linear sum assignment with edition. preprint, arXiv:1603.04380 (2016)
4. Burkard, R., Dell'Amico, M., Martello, S.: Assignment Problems. Society for Industrial and Applied Mathematics, Philadelphia (2012)
5. Combettes, P.L., Pesquet, J.C.: A Douglas rachford splitting approach to non-smooth convex variational signal recovery. IEEE J. Sel. Top. Signal Process. **1**(4), 564–574 (2007)
6. De Bonet, J.S.: Multiresolution sampling procedure for analysis and synthesis of texture images. In: SIGGRAPH, pp. 361–368. ACM (1997)
7. Efros, A.A., Freeman, W.T.: Image quilting for texture synthesis and transfer. In: SIGGRAPH, pp. 341–346. ACM (2001)
8. Efros, A.A., Leung, T.K.: Texture synthesis by non-parametric sampling. In: IEEE International Conference on Computer Vision, pp. 1033–1038 (1999)
9. Ferradans, S., Papadakis, N., Rabin, J., Peyré, G., Aujol, J.-F.: Regularized discrete optimal transport. In: Kuijper, A., Bredies, K., Pock, T., Bischof, H. (eds.) SSVM 2013. LNCS, vol. 7893, pp. 428–439. Springer, Heidelberg (2013). doi:10.1007/978-3-642-38267-3_36
10. Galerne, B., Gousseau, Y., Morel, J.-M.: Random phase textures: theory and synthesis. IEEE Trans. Image Process. **20**(1), 257–267 (2011)

11. Gatys, L., Ecker, A.S., Bethge, M.: Texture synthesis using convolutional neural networks. In: NIPS, pp. 262–270 (2015)
12. G'MIC: Greyc's magic for image computing (2016). http://gmic.eu/
13. Han, J., Zhou, K., Wei, L.-Y., Gong, M., Bao, H., Zhang, X., Guo, B.: Fast example-based surface texture synthesis via discrete optimization. Vis. Comput. **22**(9), 918–925 (2006)
14. Heeger, D.J., Bergen, J.R.: Pyramid-based texture analysis/synthesis. In: SIGGRAPH, pp. 229–238. ACM (1995)
15. Julesz, B.: Textons, the elements of texture perception, and their interactions. Nature **290**(5802), 91–97 (1981)
16. Julesz, B., Gilbert, E.N., Victor, J.D.: Visual discrimination of textures with identical third-order statistics. Biol. Cybern. **31**(3), 137–140 (1978)
17. Kopf, J., Fu, C.-W., Cohen-Or, D., Deussen, O., Lischinski, D., Wong, T.-T.: Solid texture synthesis from 2d exemplars. In: SIGGRAPH. ACM (2007)
18. Kwatra, V., Schödl, A., Essa, I., Turk, G., Bobick, A.: Graphcut textures: image and video synthesis using graph cuts. In: SIGGRAPH, pp. 277–286. ACM (2003)
19. Kwatra, V., Essa, I., Bobick, A., Kwatra, N.: Texture optimization for example-based synthesis. In: SIGGRAPH, pp. 795–802. ACM (2005)
20. Lefebvre, S., Hoppe, H.: Parallel controllable texture synthesis. In: SIGGRAPH, pp. 777–786. ACM (2005)
21. Liang, L., Liu, C., Xu, Y.-Q., Guo, B., Shum, H.-Y.: Real-time texture synthesis by patch-based sampling. ACM Trans. Graph. **20**(3), 127–150 (2001)
22. Portilla, J., Simoncelli, E.P.: A parametric texture model based on joint statistics of complex wavelet coefficients. Int. J. Comput. Vision **40**(1), 49–71 (2000)
23. Raad, L., Galerne, B.: Efros and Freeman image quilting algorithm for texture synthesis. In: IPOL (2016)
24. Rabin, J., Ferradans, S., Papadakis, N.: Adaptive color transfer with relaxed optimal transport. In: IEEE ICIP, pp. 4852–4856 (2014)
25. Rabin, J., Peyré, G.: Wasserstein regularization of imaging problem. In: IEEE ICIP, pp. 1541–1544 (2011)
26. Rabin, J., Peyré, G., Delon, J., Bernot, M.: Wasserstein barycenter and its application to texture mixing. In: Bruckstein, A.M., Haar Romeny, B.M., Bronstein, A.M., Bronstein, M.M. (eds.) SSVM 2011. LNCS, vol. 6667, pp. 435–446. Springer, Heidelberg (2012). doi:10.1007/978-3-642-24785-9_37
27. Tartavel, G., Gousseau, Y., Peyré, G.: Constrained sparse texture synthesis. In: Kuijper, A., Bredies, K., Pock, T., Bischof, H. (eds.) SSVM 2013. LNCS, vol. 7893, pp. 186–197. Springer, Heidelberg (2013). doi:10.1007/978-3-642-38267-3_16
28. Tartavel, G., Gousseau, Y., Peyré, G.: Variational texture synthesis with sparsity and spectrum constraints. JMIV **52**(1), 124–144 (2015)
29. Vasconcelos, C.N., Rosenhahn, B.: Bipartite graph matching computation on GPU. In: Cremers, D., Boykov, Y., Blake, A., Schmidt, F.R. (eds.) EMMCVPR 2009. LNCS, vol. 5681, pp. 42–55. Springer, Heidelberg (2009). doi:10.1007/978-3-642-03641-5_4
30. Wei, L.-Y., Lefebvre, S., Kwatra, V., Turk, G.: State of the art in example-based texture synthesis. In: Eurographics - State of the Art Reports (2009)
31. Wei, L.Y., Levoy, M.: Fast texture synthesis using tree-structured vector quantization. In: SIGGRAPH, pp. 479–488. ACM (2000)
32. Xia, G.-S., Ferradans, S., Peyré, G., Aujol, J.-F.: Synthesizing and mixing stationary Gaussian texture models. SIAM J. Imaging Sci. **8**(1), 476–508 (2014)

A Correlation-Based Dissimilarity Measure for Noisy Patches

Paul Riot[1]([✉]), Andrés Almansa[2], Yann Gousseau[1], and Florence Tupin[1]

[1] LTCI, Télécom ParisTech, Université Paris-Saclay, 75013 Paris, France
{paul.riot,yann.gousseau,florence.tupin}@telecom-paristech.fr
[2] MAP5, CNRS, Université Paris Descartes, 75006 Paris, France
andres.almansa@telecom-paristech.fr

Abstract. In this work, we address the problem of defining a robust patch dissimilarity measure for an image corrupted by an additive white Gaussi an noise. The whiteness of the noise, despite being a common assumption that is realistic for RAW images, is hardly used to its full potential by classical denoising methods. In particular, the L^2-norm is very widely used to evaluate distances and similarities between images or patches. However, we claim that a better dissimilarity measure can be defined to convey more structural information. We propose to compute the dissimilarity between patches by using the autocorrelation of their difference. In order to illustrate the usefulness of this measure, we perform three experiments. First, this new criterion is used in a similar patch detection task. Then, we use it on the Non Local Means (NLM) denoising method and show that it improves performances by a large margin. Finally, it is applied to the task of no-reference evaluation of denoising results, where it shows interesting visual properties. In all those applications, the autocorrelation improves over the L^2-norm.

1 Introduction

In this article, we define a new dissimilarity measure between patches from natural images that are corrupted by an additive white Gaussian noise. The common whiteness assumption, although inaccurate on processed images, is realistic on RAW images on which the denoising should preferably be performed [5]. However, most of the available algorithms do not use the white noise hypothesis to its full potential. Indeed, it is almost never enforced nor evaluated. In particular, non-local denoising methods often use the L^2-norm to compare patches and the SNR or MSE are very widely used to evaluate denoising performances. Here, we propose to evaluate patches whiteness using their autocorrelation as an alternative to the classical L^2-norm to make it more robust to noise and more discriminative. We demonstrate the potential of the proposed dissimilarity measure on three applications, namely: *(a)* similar patch detection, *(b)* non-local denoising, and *(c)* no-reference (as without oracle contrarily to SSIM or the SNR that are full-reference) denoising quality assessment.

The search for optimal dissimilarity measures between patches is not new and has already emerged in all three application areas. In a recent work [6]

© Springer International Publishing AG 2017
F. Lauze et al. (Eds.): SSVM 2017, LNCS 10302, pp. 184–195, 2017.
DOI: 10.1007/978-3-319-58771-4_15

Deledalle *et al.* use probabilistic arguments to derive optimal dissimilarity measures between noisy image patches for different kinds of noise. This leads to state of the art denoising algorithms in radar imaging, but in the case of Gaussian white noise their methodology leads to a disappointingly simple optimal measure, namely the L^2 norm, due to the agnostic statistical model that was adopted as a natural image prior. On the other hand, based on a relatively simple prior for natural image patches, Sabater *et al.* [14] propose a metric to discern similar patches from dissimilar ones that works much better for stereo vision than the L^2 norm. However this approach does not take into account the noise distribution and does not work well for noisy images.

In this work we aim to develop a dissimilarity measure that combines the advantages of both previous works. Our approach uses the autocorrelation as a measure to discriminate unstructured white noise from structured natural image features. To the best of our knowledge, only a few works proposed to take advantage of the noise statistics in this manner [1, 8–11, 13, 16]. However all these works focus on a variational formulation where a whiteness term is used to complement the data fitting and regularization terms in order to further constrain the solution to one that more closely complies with the first and second order statistics of the noise we want to estimate and remove.

Our approach is different and in a certain way more general. We propose a novel dissimilarity measure between patches whose interest in the denoising framework goes beyond the variational framework proposed in [13]. We use this measure as a substitute of the L^2-norm to more robustly identify similar patches in non-local denoising algorithms. The new dissimilarity measure improves the performances of the Non Local Means (NLM) algorithm [2] by a large margin. It can also be applied to detect similar patches in a very noisy environment. Once again, performances are improved using the autocorrelation instead of the L^2-norm.

Finally, we tackle the problem of denoising quality assessment. It is well known that the widely used SNR does not provide sufficient structural information. The SSIM presented in [17] was designed to offer a more perceptually pertinent dissimilarity measure. However, doubts can be raised regarding its relevance [7] in the context of image denoising. We propose an alternative (no-reference) way to assess the quality of image denoising, relying on the autocorrelation of the difference between patches and we show on several examples that it conveys some interesting structural information.

In the first part of this article, we explain how the autocorrelation can be used to define a new patch similarity criterion. We also explain how it can be used to perform denoising evaluation. In the second part of this work, we present a few experiments demonstrating the potential of this tool for the previously defined tasks.

2   Proposed Similarity Criterion

In the sequel we denote the noisy image by $g = f + n$ where $f \in \mathbb{R}^N$ is the noise-free image (N is the number of pixels), n is a centered white Gaussian noise of variance σ^2. The denoising task consists in computing an estimation u of the noise-free image. We call residual $R = u - g$ what was removed from the noisy image. The no-reference quality assessment task consists in determining the quality of u from a statistical analysis of the residual R.

2.1   Evaluate Whiteness with the Autocorrelation

Our goal is to enrich the L^2-norm of a noisy patch to include higher order statistics that convey more structural information. As previously stated, there exist many different tools to evaluate the whiteness [1]. Here, we chose to use the autocorrelation that allows to detect structures and dependencies.

We can define the classical autocorrelation estimator r_P on a noisy patch P of size $s \times s$ for all possible lags $(l, m) \in \{-\frac{s}{2}, ..., \frac{s}{2}\}^2$:

$$r_P(l, m) = \sum_{(x,y)} P(x, y) P(x + l, y + m) \tag{1}$$

where the indices are circular. Computed on a white noise, the $r_P(l, m)$ for $(l, m) \neq (0, 0)$ should hover around zero. On the other hand, computed on a structured image, the modulus of the autocorrelation coefficients would reach higher values showing dependencies. We note that $r_P(0, 0)$ is equal to the L^2-norm of the patch.

Choosing a circular convolution has several advantages. First, it speeds up the computation as the circular convolution can easily be computed in the Fourier domain. Second, it simplifies the calculation as every lag involves the same number of samples. Finally, it improves the estimation of the higher lags since more samples are used. Note that, in the perfect case of two identical patches corrupted with white noise, the circular convolution is harmless.

In the following, we will see how this tool can be used to enrich the L^2-norm and design a new patch dissimilarity measure as well as a new denoising evaluation method.

2.2   The Autocorrelation to Define a New Patch Dissimilarity Measure

In the non-local denoising methods, the L^2-norm of the patch difference $P_1 - P_2$ is a natural way to evaluate the distance. Indeed, supposing that the underlying noise free patches are equal, we know that $P_1 - P_2$ is a Gaussian white noise of variance $2\sigma^2$. Thus, the L^2-norm can be mathematically justified as shown in [6] as it can be directly interpreted as a generalized likelihood ratio test. However, it is not robust for strong noise levels.

When using the L^2-norm for the patch distance, it has been shown for the NLM algorithm [3] that a small patch size is optimal for low noise levels. However, when σ^2 increases the distance estimation becomes unstable on small patches and s must be increased to obtain a reliable estimate. The trade-off is that there are now less similar patches. When the signal to noise ratio is low, it has been shown in [12] that the L^2-norm often matches noise realizations over image content. This phenomenon shows that the L^2 distance is quite sensitive to the noise. Indeed, it only evaluates the energy of the patch difference $P_1 - P_2$ and does not take into account any structural information.

We show that computing the autocorrelation matrix of D is more reliable than the L^2 norm and appears to contain more structural content. This idea is applied to design a new patch dissimilarity measure using the autocorrelation estimator $r_{P_1-P_2}$ defined previously. One can note that $r_{P_1-P_2}(0,0) = ||P_1-P_2||^2$ gives the energy of $P_1 - P_2$ which is equal to the square of the L^2 norm. The other lags give information about the structural content of $P_1 - P_2$. The higher the $|r_{P_1-P_2}(l,m)|$ for $(l,m) \neq (0,0)$ are, the more structural content there is in $P_1 - P_2$, meaning that the underlying noise free patches are not similar. From there, we can design a new patch dissimilarity measure that we will refer to as Whiteness Dissimilarity Measure (WDM):

$$d_w^2(P_1, P_2) = ||r_{P_1-P_2}||_2^2. \tag{2}$$

This measure is experimentally more robust to high noise levels as it contains more structural information. It is also more reliable on big patch sizes as the autocorrelation estimation becomes more robust when more samples are available. However, we will show in the experiments that the results are also improved considering small patch sizes.

It is important to note that WDM is not a distance. Indeed, it is possible to show that it verifies the properties of non-negativity, identity of indiscernibles and symmetry. But, we can show that it does not satisfy the triangle inequality.

2.3   Denoising Evaluation Beyond the SNR

The SNR, and all its derivatives like the MSE or the PSNR, are the most commonly used metrics to evaluate and compare denoising performances. It is defined as:

$$SNR(u) = 10 \log_{10}\left(\frac{||u||^2}{||f - u||^2}\right) \tag{3}$$

Fundamentally, this measures the magnitude of the error by computing the error energy $||f - u||^2$. It is perfectly relevant from a mathematical point of view. However, it is not always informative for a visual evaluation. Indeed, it is well known not to correlate well with visual evaluation. We can also point the fact that many state of the art denoising methods are reaching very close SNR. However, some present much more visible artifacts than others. This can't be well evaluated using the SNR. This is the reason why new metrics were developed such as SSIM [17]. However, severe criticism has emerged regarding its structural properties as demonstrated in [7]. Both SSIM and the SNR use an oracle to estimate the denoising quality.

In this work, we aim at showing that the residual autocorrelation can be used as a complement to the SNR to evaluate the amount of structural content removed from the noisy image. Also, we claim that this can be linked to visual quality as it is sensitive to damaged textures and colored artifacts. On top of that, our metric is designed to work without any oracle by evaluating the residual whiteness. It also provides a local map to evaluate the denoising quality.

We propose to estimate a normalized residual autocorrelation on every patch R_k of the residual:

$$A(R_k) = \frac{\|r_{R_k}\|_2^2 - r_{R_k}(0,0)^2}{\sigma_k^4 s^2 (s^2 - 1)} \tag{4}$$

where $\sigma_k^2 = \sum_{(i,j)} R_k(i,j)^2$ is the energy of the residual estimated on the patch R_k. The normalization corresponds to the expected value of the estimator in the numerator under the hypothesis that R_k is a white Gaussian noise with zero mean and variance σ_k^2. Then, we can aggregate the $A(k)$ coefficients computed over each patch to obtain a quality map at each pixel (i,j):

$$\text{W-map}(i,j) = \frac{\sum_k \chi_k(i,j) A(R_k)}{\sum_k \chi_k(i,j)} \tag{5}$$

where $\chi_k(i,j) = 1$ if and only if (i,j) belongs to the support of R_k. This map gives a local estimate of how much structural content was removed from the image. A global score can be obtained with a simple normalized sum:

$$\text{W-score} = \frac{1}{N} \sum_{(i,j)} \text{W-map}(i,j) \tag{6}$$

with N the total number of pixels. This total score gives an estimate of the quality of denoising. When it is very close to 1, the denoising algorithm did not damage the underlying image. When it increases, it means that the residual is structured and thus some content from the image was removed. We claim that this is an interesting visual property as it is usually preferred to preserve content and only slightly denoise images, especially in the textured areas, rather than overly denoise and blur out some structural content. Also, it can be useful for later image processing tasks such as detection or recognition as we can estimate if the image content was damaged.

We note that the W-score should not be evaluated on its own as it does not contain any information on the residual energy because we removed the term $r_{R_k}(0,0)^2$. Indeed, adding a white noise to an already noisy image would lead to a perfect W-score of 1 as the residual, equal to the added noise, would be white. Thus, it should be coupled with the SNR to be properly interpreted.

We chose to remove $r_{R_k}(0,0)^2$ that contains the residual energy information because it is not clear what should be done with it. Furthermore, it is not simple to evaluate it at the same time as the other coefficients that contain a different information.

3   Experimental Results

In this section, we propose three experiments demonstrating the relevance of the proposed patch dissimilarity measure, WDM. Only a small number of visual results are shown due to length constraints, but more results are visible on the website https://wdm-ssvm2017.telecom-paristech.fr.

First, we evaluate the ability of our measure to retrieve similar patches corrupted by a strong additive white noise. Second, we show that simply replacing the L^2 norm by our measure in the Non Local Means (NLM) algorithm yields a significant performance gain. Last, the no-reference quality measure introduced in Sect. 2.3 is shown on some experiments to usefully complement the SNR.

3.1 Detecting Similar Patches with High Noise Levels

To assess the relevance of WDM to retrieve similar patches, we follow the exact same experimental protocol recently proposed in [6]. We compare the respective performances of WDM, L^1, L^2 and L^4 on a dictionary composed of 196 noise-free patches of size $s = 8$. The noise-free patches were obtained using the k-means algorithm on patches extracted from the classical Barbara image. For this experiment, it is important to have different patches in the dictionary for the probability of false alarm to be well defined. The noisy patches are noisy realizations of the noise-free patches under strong noise conditions. Here we choose a white Gaussian noise with $\sigma = 100$. This experiment is only valid for strong noise levels ($\sigma > 50$) as both criteria perform perfectly for lower noises. The dissimilarity measures are evaluated for all pairs of noisy patches. The process is repeated 20 times with independent noise realizations. Numerically, the performance of the similarity criterion is given in term of their receiver operating characteristic (ROC) curve, i.e., the curve of the probability of detection as a function of the probability of false alarm. Results are given in Fig. 1.

It clearly appears on this curve that WDM performs better than L^1, L^2 and L^4. As previously said, this is particularly true at low signal to noise ratios. Also,

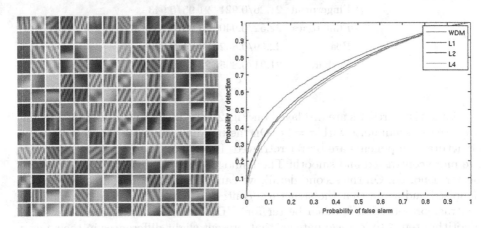

Fig. 1. (left) Patch dictionary. (right) ROC curve obtained when retrieving patches under a strong white Gaussian noise ($\sigma = 100$).

L^2 starts to match noise realizations over noise-free content after a certain noise level as shown in [12].

3.2 Improving the NLM Algorithm

The new similarity criterion defined previously can be applied to any patch based algorithm. However, for evaluation purposes we will focus on the original NLM algorithm [2]. While there are many more recent and efficient denoising methods, we believe, as it is explained in [6], that this algorithm provides a good way to compare similarity criteria. Note also that there are alternative ways to make this algorithm robust to noise, such as the PCA-based approach proposed in [15]. In this section, we will compare the use of this algorithm when using WDM and when using L^2. To limit the number of parameters, we fix a search window of size $W = 21$. To compare the results on a fair basis the bandwidth parameter h is optimized in each case to obtain the best SNR. The SNR and SSIM results for different images using different patch sizes are shown on Table 1. We can see that changing the distance from L^2 to WDM always improves the SNR by around 0.5 dB, sometimes more. The SSIM is also consistently improved.

Table 1. SNR (in dB) and SSIM performances of the NLM algorithm for L^2 and WDM patch distances with $\sigma = 25$

	L^2	WDM
Lena	22.10/0.869	22.65/0.878
Building	17.85/0.883	18.37/0.897
Mandrill	19.06/0.821	19.29/0.836
House	25.73/0.811	26.57/0.829
Fingerprint	21.26/0.921	21.95/0.943
Flintstones	22.52/0.940	23.28/0.951
Boat	22.59/0.852	23.24/0.869
Barbara	21.91/0.895	22.68/0.907

Some visual results are displayed on Fig. 2. The images were corrupted using a white Gaussian noise with $\sigma = 25$. On the building image we can note that the structural components are better retrieved. Indeed, on the first detail, the lines are more contrasted and smooth. The homogeneous parts of the image are also better denoised. On the second detail, we can see that the dark areas are better denoised and again that the structural content is better preserved. Overall, the contrast preservation is much better for WDM than for L^2. Indeed, the NLM algorithm tends to average patches that present slight differences in their mean value resulting in important losses on low frequency areas. On the contrary, simple computations can show that the WDM measure is more affected than L^2 by a constant bias, thus resulting in a smaller contrast loss.

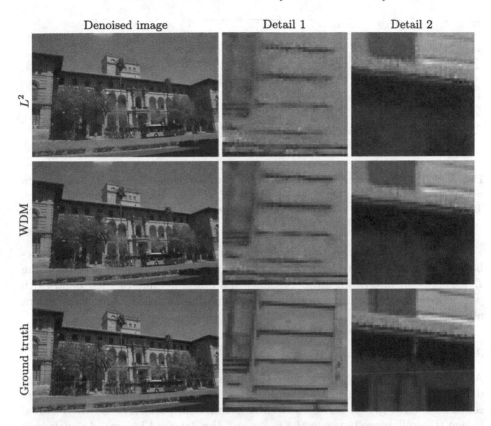

Fig. 2. Building denoising with the NLM algorithm ($s = 5$ and $W = 21$)

Improved performances are due to the fact that WDM is more robust to the noise. A good way to evaluate this claim is to test different levels of noise and compare the performances for low and high noise levels. We expect the L^2 norm to perform better on very low level noises while our measure would better suit the stronger noise levels. We show the corresponding SNR curve as a function of σ on Fig. 3(a), indeed supporting the previous claim of robustness. Those results can be further confirmed by another experiment. Using the noise free image to compute the weights and then using these weights to denoise a noisy image shows that, on the Lena image, the PSNR is better for the L^2 norm (34.66 dB) than for the WDM measure (34.57 dB). It is nevertheless interesting to note that, even in a noise free environment, the WDM distance is still relevant as it performs only very slightly worse than L^2.

Another interesting property of WDM is that it outperforms L^2 whatever the choice for s is, as can be seen on Fig. 3(c). While this was expected for large patch sizes, it is somehow surprising that this still occurs at small patch sizes (up to $s = 3$). Furthermore, the performances of WDM appear more stable with respect to the choice of s than those of L^2, in particular when s increases. This could allow further improvements for other applications that require bigger patch sizes.

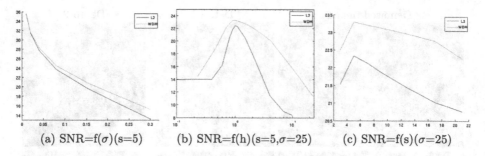

(a) SNR=f(σ)(s=5)   (b) SNR=f(h)(s=5,σ=25)   (c) SNR=f(s)(σ=25)

Fig. 3. SNR performances as a function of different parameters for the NLM algorithm using WDM and L^2 (W = 21). h was optimized to obtain the best SNR for (a) and (c). The scale is semi-log for (b) and the functions were aligned for an easier comparison.

Finally, Fig. 3(b) shows that the performances of NLM using WDM are somehow more stable with respect to the choice of the bandwidth than when using L^2. This is an interesting property since the optimal value of such bandwidth parameters can highly vary from images to images, for NLM as for more recent algorithms.

3.3   Residual Evaluation

As a last experiment, we investigate the usefulness of the quality measure introduced in Sect. 2.3, defined by Formula (6) with $s = 15$. Recall that this index relies on a local (patch-based) whiteness estimation, performed on the residual image (the difference between the noisy and the denoised image). As such, and unlike the SNR or SSIM quality measures, it may be computed without any knowledge of the noise-free image. The experiment is very simple and is only provided as a proof of concept. It consists in comparing the W-scores, as defined by Formula (6), for images having the same SNR but different visual aspects. A first example is visible on Fig. 4, where we compare (non-optimal) denoised versions of the Barbara image corrupted by a Gaussian additive noise with $\sigma = 25$. These images correspond to different denoising methods yielding relatively poor SNR (19.45 dB $\pm$ 0.05 dB). (a) and (b) were obtained with the NLM algorithm, (c) with a variationnal variant of the NLM and (d) with ROF. More examples are visible on the dedicated website.

The result (Fig. 4(a)) is relatively conservative and only a small amount of noise is removed from the noisy image. No information was removed from the image. The textures and the contrast are well preserved. As a result, no structure is detected in the residual and our criterion hovers around a value of one on the whole image. The W-score is equal to one, which is the expected score for a white residual. On the other hand, the result (Fig. 4(b)) was overly denoised, most of the textures are washed out and the final denoised image suffers heavy contrast losses. A large amount of structure was removed from the noisy image. Our evaluation criterion appears able to detect the most damaged areas (corresponding to large values of the W-map). One can note that the homogeneous

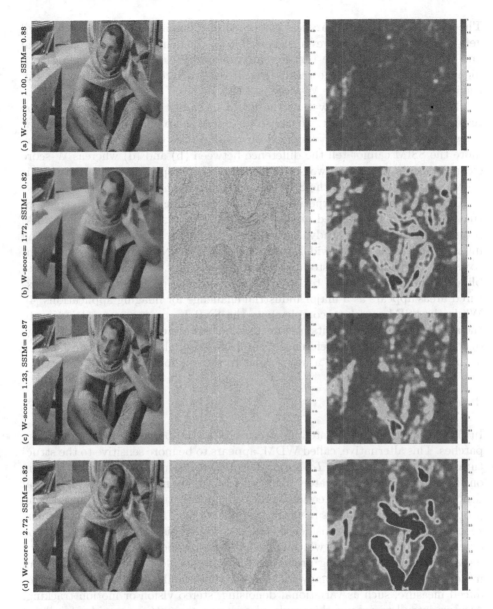

Fig. 4. Quality assessment of 4 denoising methods yielding the same SNR but different visual qualities. From left to right, denoised results, residuals, whiteness criterion maps (W-maps). (a) and (b) were obtained with the NLM algorithm, (c) with a variationnal variant of the NLM and (d) with ROF.

areas present a very low local W-map as they were well denoised. However, the textures on the clothes are completely removed and the residual is clearly correlated, as shown by the W-map. Globally, the W-score for this image is 1.72.

The result (Fig. 4(c)) appears less smoothed and damaged than (Fig. 4(b)) and gets a W-score of 1.23. However, it is visible on the denoised image, the residual and the W-map that some texture was removed on a few areas leading to a higher W-score. Finally, the result (Fig. 4(d)) clearly damaged the textures in the image. Accordingly, the W-score is 2.72.

These experiments show that the SSIM is barely able to differentiate the results (a) and (c). However, we can see on the W-map and on the residual that a few textures were locally damaged on result (c) as opposed to (a). Furthermore the SSIM cannot tell the difference between (b) and (d) whereas W-score clearly chooses (d) as the worst result. Also, the proposed quality measure is no-reference, contrarily to the SSIM that is full-reference.

Of course, this simple experiment is in no case sufficient to assess the perceptual interest of the proposed quality measure. This task deserves further work, probably through a user study. Nevertheless, we believe this measure is of strong interest. Indeed, it is now widely admitted that the SNR is in no way sufficient to assess the quality of a restoration task. In particular, it is known to be almost blind to the destruction of textured areas. Now, the preservation of such textured areas appears as a major industrial challenge for imaging applications [4]. While the SSIM somehow complements the SNR by paying more attention to the structure of the image, its usefulness is not always clear in the case of image denoising. Last, being no-reference, the proposed quality measure can be used as an objective function, in a way similar to the one followed in [13].

4   Conclusion

In this work, we have presented an alternative to the L^2 norm to compare noisy patches. This alternative, called WDM, appears to be more sensitive to the structural information than the L^2 norm. The WDM dissimilarity measure, relying on the autocorrelation operator, was applied to different tasks such as non-local denoising, similar patch detection or denoising evaluation. It showed interesting properties and performances in all those applications. This work opens many perspectives. While we only considered Gaussian white noise, the approach could be extended to other types of white noise. Also the proposed no-reference quality measure, showing promising preliminary results, would definitively deserve an in-depth validation. Last, many other applications could benefit from the introduced measure, such as variational denoising, stereo vision or motion tracking. Also we intend to extend this study in order to characterize a wider family of dissimilarity measures that are able to discriminate white noise from natural image structure.

References

1. Brunet, D., Vrscay, E.R., Wang, Z.: The use of residuals in image denoising. In: Kamel, M., Campilho, A. (eds.) ICIAR 2009. LNCS, vol. 5627, pp. 1–12. Springer, Heidelberg (2009). doi:10.1007/978-3-642-02611-9_1

2. Buades, A., Coll, B., Morel, J.M.: A review of image denoising algorithms, with a new one. Multiscale Model. Simul. **4**(2), 490–530 (2005)
3. Buades, A., Coll, B., Morel, J.M.: Non-local means denoising. Image Process. On Line **1**, 208–212 (2011)
4. Cao, F., Guichard, F., Hornung, H.: Measuring texture sharpness of a digital camera. In: IS & T/SPIE Electronic Imaging. International Society for Optics and Photonics (2009)
5. Colom, M., Buades, A., Morel, J.M.: Nonparametric noise estimation method for raw images. JOSA A **31**(4), 863–871 (2014)
6. Deledalle, C.A., Denis, L., Tupin, F.: How to compare noisy patches? patch similarity beyond Gaussian noise. Int. J. Comput. Vision **99**(1), 86–102 (2012)
7. Dosselmann, R., Yang, X.D.: A comprehensive assessment of the structural similarity index. Signal Image Video Process. **5**(1), 81–91 (2011)
8. Fehrenbach, J., Nikolova, M., Steidl, G., Weiss, P.: Bilevel image denoising using gaussianity tests. In: Aujol, J.-F., Nikolova, M., Papadakis, N. (eds.) SSVM 2015. LNCS, vol. 9087, pp. 117–128. Springer, Cham (2015). doi:10.1007/978-3-319-18461-6_10
9. Lanza, A., Morigi, S., Sgallari, F.: Variational image restoration with constraints on noise whiteness. J. Math. Imaging Vision **53**(1), 1–17 (2014)
10. Lanza, A., Morigi, S., Sgallari, F., Yezzi, A.J.: Variational image denoising based on autocorrelation whiteness. SIAM J. Imaging Sci. **6**(4), 1931–1955 (2013)
11. Lanza, A., Morigi, S., Sgallari, F., Yezzi, A.J.: Variational image denoising while constraining the distribution of the residual. Electron. Trans. Num. Anal. **42**, 64–84 (2014)
12. Lebrun, M., Buades, A., Morel, J.: A nonlocal bayesian image denoising algorithm. SIAM J. Imaging Sci. **6**(3), 1665–1688 (2013)
13. Riot, P., Almansa, A., Gousseau, Y., Tupin, F.: Penalizing local correlations in the residual improves image denoising performance. In: 2016 24th European Signal Processing Conference (EUSIPCO), pp. 1867–1871. IEEE (2016)
14. Sabater, N., Almansa, A., Morel, J.M.: Meaningful Matches in Stereovision. IEEE Trans. PAMI **34**(5), 930–942 (2011). http://hal.archives-ouvertes.fr/hal-00647995
15. Tasdizen, T.: Principal neighborhood dictionaries for nonlocal means image denoising. IEEE Trans. Image Process. **18**(12), 2649–2660 (2009)
16. Teuber, T., Remmele, S., Hesser, J., Steidl, G.: Denoising by second order statistics. Sig. Process. **92**(12), 2837–2847 (2012)
17. Wang, Z., Bovik, A.C., Sheikh, H.R., Simoncelli, E.P.: Image quality assessment: from error visibility to structural similarity. IEEE Trans. Image Process. **13**(4), 600–612 (2004)

Analysis of a Physically Realistic Film Grain Model, and a Gaussian Film Grain Synthesis Algorithm

Alasdair Newson$^{(\boxtimes)}$, Noura Faraj, Julie Delon, and Bruno Galerne

Laboratoire MAP5 (CNRS UMR 8145), Université Paris Descartes, Paris, France
alasdairnewson@gmail.com

Abstract. Film grain is a highly valued characteristic of analog images, thus realistic digital film grain synthesis is an important objective for many modern photographers and film-makers. We carry out a theoretical analysis of a physically realistic film grain model, based on a Boolean model, and derive expressions for the expected value and covariance of the film grain texture. We approximate these quantities using a Monte Carlo simulation, and use them to propose a film grain synthesis algorithm based on Gaussian textures. With numerical and visual experiments, we demonstrate the correctness and subjective qualities of the proposed algorithm.

Keywords: Film grain · Gaussian texture · Covariance · Monte Carlo simulation

1 Introduction

Film grain is the specific texture which results from the analog photographic process. This texture is highly sought after by film directors and photographers alike for its artistic qualities. Producing realistic film grain for images is therefore a crucial goal. Proposed film grain synthesis methods often rely on scanned example of film grain which is either directly blended with a given image [1,4,7], used to generate a film grain model [6,10,12,16]. Although, simple and fast, these approaches rely completely on the resolution and quality of the original scan. Furthermore, in the case where film grain is modelled as independent noise [10,16], with a variance which is dependent on the input image intensity, the grain texture is completely uncorrelated spatially, which gives a distinctly undesirable "digital" feel to the image. To tackle these issues, Newson et al. [11] proposed a physically realistic model of film grain. This made use of the Boolean model [3] from the stochastic geometry literature. In the present work, we propose an approximation of the Boolean model using Gaussian textures. The central idea is to determine the covariance of the film grain produced by the Boolean model, and impose this covariance on a white noise vector. This approach has several advantages. Firstly, once the covariance matrix is known

© Springer International Publishing AG 2017
F. Lauze et al. (Eds.): SSVM 2017, LNCS 10302, pp. 196–207, 2017.
DOI: 10.1007/978-3-319-58771-4_16

for a given image, the grain can be re-synthesized extremely quickly, since this is done by sampling a white noise vector, and multiplying it with a (very sparse) matrix. This differs from many grain synthesis algorithms which blend a fixed scan of film grain with an image. Secondly, the texture model is based on the covariance of the physically-motivated Boolean model, which means that the parameters are meaningful. From a technical point of view, for any given couple of input pixels, we determine the covariance and the expected value of the filtered Boolean model using a Monte Carlo simulation. We impose these characteristics on a Gaussian white noise to produce the output image. This paper has two main objectives. Firstly, we analyze a previously proposed, physically realistic film grain model [11], based on the Boolean model [3]. In this analysis, we consider the first and second order statistics of the grain model and propose an algorithm to determine these statistics for any given input image. These quantities are the key characteristics of film grain, therefore their theoretical calculation is of significant value. Indeed, once these quantities are known, a variety of algorithms could be proposed to exploit this information for film grain synthesis. Our second contribution is one such algorithm which simulates film grain on a given input image by imposing the previous characteristics on the output image, using a Gaussian approximation.

2   Stochastic Modelling of Film Grain

An analog film is made up of an emulsion (a gelatin) in which many microscopic silver halide crystals are suspended. These crystals are sensitive to light, which is why they are used for photography. During the exposure, when a photograph is taken, a photon may hit one of the crystals and "sensitize" it, creating a very small amount of solid silver on the crystal. The emulsion is then "developed", that is to say a chemical compound is introduced into the emulsion. This compound turns only the sensitized grains into solid silver grains, which means that the density of the grains depends on the intensity of the light (the image) which was shone upon them. A comprehensive explanation of the photographic process can be found in [9]. In order to model the previous process, Newson et al. [11] proposed to use an inhomogeneous Boolean model[1] from the stochastic geometry literature [3]. This model was also implicitly used in much of the "analog" literature concerning film grain [2,14]. In such a context, the model is defined as the union of a sequence of disks whose centers are randomly distributed in $\mathbb{R}^2$. The disks represent the silver halide grains in the film emulsion, and the density of the disks is chosen to respect the input image gray-level at each pixel. Thus, the model is defined in a *continuous* manner. Let us now formally present this model. Let u be an input image of size $m \times n$, with gray-levels normalized to the range $[0, 1)$, and let r be the radius of the disks of the Boolean model (in pixel "units"). Let $\mathcal{P} = \{z_i, \ i \in \mathbb{N}\} \subset [0, m] \times [0, n]$ be the Poisson process with intensity measure $\mu(dt) = \lambda(t)dt$. In the present context, the z_i's represent the

---

[1] Please note that the Boolean model is in fact defined in a much more general fashion, but for our purposes this definition is sufficient.

centers of the film grains. The intensity λ is defined as the following piecewise constant function

$$\lambda(x) = \frac{1}{\pi r^2} \log \frac{1}{1 - u(\lfloor x \rfloor)},$$

where $\lfloor x \rfloor$ corresponds to the pixel index p such that $x \in p + [0, 1[^2$. This manner of defining λ is chosen to ensure that within each pixel domain $p + [0, 1[^2$, the expected area of the Boolean model corresponds to the image gray-level $u(p)$, thus preserving the local "average" grey-level. Finally, let ϕ be some blurring filter (i.e. $\phi \geq 0$ and $\int_{\mathbb{R}^2} \phi = 1$).

Definition 1 (Inhomogeneous Boolean model associated with a digital image). *With the above notations, the* (inhomogeneous) Boolean model *associated with u is the random set Z that consists of the union of all the balls of radius r centered at the points z_i of the Poisson process $\mathcal{P}$, that is,*

$$Z = \bigcup_{i \in \mathbb{N}} \mathcal{B}_r(z_i) \subset \mathbb{R}^2.$$

Denoting by $\mathbb{1}_Z$ the indicator function of the Boolean model, that is, $\mathbb{1}_Z(x)$ equals 1 if $x \in Z$ and 0 otherwise, the filtered Boolean model *associated with u is the random field*

$$\phi * \mathbb{1}_Z(x) = \int_{\mathbb{R}^2} \mathbb{1}_Z(x - t)\phi(t)dt, \quad x \in \mathbb{R}^2.$$

We note that, while the digital input image u is discrete, both the Boolean model Z and the filtered Boolean model $\phi * \mathbb{1}_Z$ are defined in the continuous domain $\mathbb{R}^2$. Of course in practice, one is interested to produce a sampling of $\phi * \mathbb{1}_Z$ on a discrete grid to obtain a digital image. The first main objective of this work is the theoretical analysis of the grain model from a statistical point of view, in particular the first and second order statistics, the latter being a distinguishing feature of textures.

Proposition 1 (Expected Value and Covariance of the Filtered Boolean Model). *Consider a Boolean model Z with underlying Poisson process $\mathcal{P}$ having intensity measure $\mu : A \mapsto \int_A \lambda(t)dt$. Let ϕ represent a blurring filter. Then for all $x, y \in \mathbb{R}^2$,*

$$\mathbb{E}\left[\mathbb{1}_Z(x)\right] = 1 - \mathbb{E}\left[\mathbb{1}_{Z^c}(x)\right] = 1 - \exp\left(-\mu(\mathcal{B}_r(x))\right) \tag{1}$$

$$\mathrm{Cov}(\mathbb{1}_Z)(x, y) = \exp(-\mu(\mathcal{B}_r(x)) - \mu(\mathcal{B}_r(y)))\left(\exp(\mu(\mathcal{B}_r(x) \cap \mathcal{B}_r(y))) - 1\right). \tag{2}$$

Hence, due to the linearity of the convolution with filter ϕ, the expected value and covariance of the filtered Boolean model are given by

$$\mathbb{E}\left[\phi * \mathbb{1}_Z(x)\right] = \phi * \mathbb{E}\left[\mathbb{1}_Z\right](x) = 1 - \int_{\mathbb{R}^2} \exp(-\mu(\mathcal{B}_r(x - t)))\phi(t)dt \tag{3}$$

$$\mathrm{Cov}(\phi * \mathbb{1}_Z)(x, y) = \int_{\mathbb{R}^2} \int_{\mathbb{R}^2} \mathrm{Cov}(\mathbb{1}_Z)(x - s, y - t)\phi(s)\phi(t)dsdt. \tag{4}$$

Proof. The second part of the proposition is straightforward, so here we give a detailed proof of Eqs. (1) and (2). Let us first consider the expectation. Clearly, $\mathbb{E}\left[\mathbb{1}_Z(x)\right] = 1 - \mathbb{E}\left[\mathbb{1}_{Z^c}(x)\right]$ since $\mathbb{1}_Z(x) = 1 - \mathbb{1}_{Z^c}(x)$. Note that for any point x, $\mathbb{1}_{Z^c}(x)$ is only equal to 1 if *no* balls cover x, that is,

$$\mathbb{1}_{Z^c}(x) = \prod_{z_i \in \mathcal{P}} \mathbb{1}_{\mathcal{B}_r^c(z_i)}(x).$$

Hence one can compute $\mathbb{E}\left[\mathbb{1}_{Z^c}(x)\right]$ by invoking the following general formula. In general, for any Poisson process $\mathcal{P}$ with intensity measure Θ, and for any measurable function $f : E \to [0,1]$, one has [13, p. 65]

$$\mathbb{E}\left[\prod_{z_i \in \mathcal{P}} f(z_i)\right] = \exp\left(\int_{\mathbb{R}^2}(f-1)d\Theta\right) \tag{5}$$

In our case, we have $\Theta = \mu$ and $f(z) = \mathbb{1}_{\mathcal{B}_r^c(z)}(x) = \mathbb{1}_{\mathcal{B}_r^c(x)}(z)$, thus,

$$\mathbb{E}\left[\mathbb{1}_{Z^c}(x)\right] = \exp\left(\int_{\mathbb{R}^2}\left(\mathbb{1}_{\mathcal{B}_r^c(x)}(z) - 1\right)\lambda(z)dz\right) = \exp\left(-\mu(\mathcal{B}_r(x))\right),$$

which proves Eq. (1). Let us now turn to the computation of the covariance. Since $\mathbb{1}_{Z^c} = 1 - \mathbb{1}_Z$ and the covariance is invariant by the multiplication by -1 and the addition of a constant, one has $\mathrm{Cov}(\mathbb{1}_Z)(x,y) = \mathrm{Cov}(\mathbb{1}_{Z^c})(x,y)$. Now,

$$\mathrm{Cov}(\mathbb{1}_{Z^c})(x,y) = \mathbb{E}\left[\mathbb{1}_{Z^c}(x)\mathbb{1}_{Z^c}(y)\right] - \mathbb{E}\left[\mathbb{1}_{Z^c}(x)\right]\mathbb{E}\left[\mathbb{1}_{Z^c}(y)\right].$$

and we need to evaluate $\mathbb{E}\left[\mathbb{1}_{Z^c}(x)\mathbb{1}_{Z^c}(y)\right]$. Using the above expression of $\mathbb{1}_{Z^c}(x)$

$$\mathbb{1}_{Z^c}(x)\mathbb{1}_{Z^c}(y) = \prod_{z_j \in \mathcal{P}} \mathbb{1}_{\mathcal{B}_r^c(x) \cap \mathcal{B}_r^c(y)}(z_j)$$

Using again Eq. (5) with $f(z) = \mathbb{1}_{\mathcal{B}_r^c(x) \cap \mathcal{B}_r^c(y)}(z) = \mathbb{1}_{\mathcal{B}_r^c(x) \cap \mathcal{B}_r^c(y)}(z)$ one has

$$\mathbb{E}\left[\mathbb{1}_{Z^c}(x)\mathbb{1}_{Z^c}(y)\right] = \exp\left(\int_{\mathbb{R}^2}(\mathbb{1}_{\mathcal{B}_r^c(x) \cap \mathcal{B}_r^c(y)}(z) - 1)\,\lambda(z)\,dz\right)$$
$$= \exp(-\mu(\mathcal{B}_r(x) \cup \mathcal{B}_r(y))).$$

Hence,

$$\mathrm{Cov}(\mathbb{1}_Z)(x,y) = \exp(-\mu(\mathcal{B}_r(x) \cup \mathcal{B}_r(y))) - \exp\left(-\mu(\mathcal{B}_r(x))\right)\exp\left(-\mu(\mathcal{B}_r(y))\right)$$
$$= \exp(-\mu(\mathcal{B}_r(x)) - \mu(\mathcal{B}_r(y)))\left(\exp(\mu(\mathcal{B}_r(x) \cap \mathcal{B}_r(y))) - 1\right).$$

$\square$

Before continuing, let us summarize the theoretical results presented here. Firstly, we have shown that, in terms of covariance, the "positive" and "negative" Boolean grain models are equivalent, in other words, the covariance of the texture produced in dark regions or light regions will be symmetric with respect to the "middle" gray-level. Secondly, that this covariance is dependent on the input image gray-level, which means that methods that rely on grain scanned at a given resolution are inherently incorrect. Another remark is that in the case of the *unfiltered* Boolean model, when $||x - y|| \geq 2r$, we have $\text{Cov}(\mathbb{1}_Z(x), \mathbb{1}_Z(y)) = 0$. This is coherent with what we expect from the Boolean model, and will be useful further on. Finally, we have given the exact expression and an approximation method of the expected value and covariance of the filtered Boolean model.

3   Gaussian Approximation of the Filtered Boolean Model

The second main objective of this work is to propose an approximation of the filtered Boolean model using Gaussian textures. This requires the evaluation of the expected value and the covariance of the model for all pixels on a grid. Unfortunately, the expressions given in Eqs. (3) and (4) cannot be evaluated exactly. However, we can approximate them using a Monte Carlo integration.

3.1   Monte Carlo Integration for Approximating the Expected Value and Covariance of the Filtered Boolean Model

We will carry out two Monte Carlo integrations, one for the expected value, and one for the covariance. Let M and N be the number of samples for these Monte Carlo integrations, and $\{\xi_1 \ldots \xi_M\}$ and $\{\xi'_1 \ldots \xi'_N\}$ be two sequences of independently and identically distributed (i.i.d.) standard normal variables. Using the law of large numbers, we have

$$\frac{1}{M} \sum_{k=1}^{M} \exp[-\mu(\mathcal{B}_r(x - \xi_k))] \xrightarrow[N \to +\infty]{} \mathbb{E}[\phi * \mathbb{1}_Z^c(x)], \tag{6}$$

almost surely. This gives us a straightforward method to estimate $\mathbb{E}[\phi * \mathbb{1}_Z(x)]$. We now consider the approximation of the covariance function. Recall that the final goal of this is to create a covariance matrix which will be used to produce an output image with the same covariance as a filtered Boolean grain model.

Definition 2. *We define the approximate covariance function* $\text{Cov}_N(x, y)$ *as the approximation of* $\text{Cov}(\phi * \mathbb{1}_Z)$ *evaluated at the couple of positions* (x, y)

$$\text{Cov}_N(x, y) = \frac{1}{N^2} \sum_{k, \ell=1}^{N} \text{Cov}(\mathbb{1}_Z)(x - \xi'_k, y - \xi'_\ell). \tag{7}$$

Proposition 2. *The function* Cov_N *is symmetric, positive semidefinite, and* $\text{Cov}_N(x, y)$ *converges almost surely towards* $\text{Cov}(\phi * \mathbb{1}_Z)(x, y)$ *when* $N \to +\infty$.

Proof. The proof of symmetry is direct. For the positivity, we have to check that for every integer d, every $(\alpha_1, \ldots, \alpha_d) \in \mathbb{R}^d$ and every $(x_1, \ldots, x_d) \in (\mathbb{R}^2)^d$,

$\sum_{i,j=1}^{d} \alpha_i \alpha_j \text{Cov}_N(x_i, x_j) \geq 0$. Now, it is straightforward to show that for fixed values of $\xi'_1, \ldots, \xi'_N$,

$$\sum_{i,j=1}^{d} \alpha_i \alpha_j \text{Cov}_N(x_i, x_j) = \text{Var}\left[\sum_{i=1}^{d}\sum_{k=1}^{N} \alpha_i \mathbb{1}_Z(x_i - \xi'_k)\right] \geq 0. \tag{8}$$

As for the convergence, a direct application of the strong law of large number for u-statistics [8] shows that the part of this sum containing only couples (k, l) of distinct integers $(k \neq l)$ converges almost surely towards its expectation $\text{Cov}(\phi * \mathbb{1}_Z)(x, y)$ when $N \to +\infty$. Since the part of the sum composed of couples (k, k) is bounded by $\frac{N}{N^2}$, the whole sum converges almost surely towards the desired covariance.   □

3.2 Gaussian Texture Approximation for Grain on an Input Image

As previously mentioned, we propose to approximate analog film grain with a Gaussian texture, the latter being especially good at modeling "micro-textures" [5], of which film grain is a very good example. Recall that u denotes the input image defined over the image grid $\{0, \ldots, m-1\} \times \{0, \ldots, n-1\}$ and its associated filtered Boolean model $\phi * \mathbb{1}_Z$. By computing approximations of the expected value and covariance of this model on the grid, we can produce Gaussian vectors which approximate the filtered Boolean model. These Gaussian vectors will be the output images of our algorithm. In the following, we list the pixel coordinates as $\{p_i\}$ with $i \in \{0, \ldots, mn-1\}$, and $p_i \in \mathbb{R}^2$. Vectors and matrices will be denoted with bold font. The approximation of the expectation $\mathbb{E}[\phi * \mathbb{1}_Z(p_i)]$ on a pixel p_i of the image grid is denoted by $\hat{u}_i$ and computed thanks to the Monte Carlo integration (6)

$$\hat{u}_i = 1 - \frac{1}{M}\sum_{k=1}^{M} \exp[-\mu(\mathcal{B}_r(p_i - \xi_k))].$$

In order to compute this sum, we consider first of all the following vectors:

- $\boldsymbol{\lambda} \in \mathbb{R}^{mn}$ such that $\boldsymbol{\lambda}_i = \frac{1}{\pi r^2}\log(\frac{1}{1-u(p_i)})$;
- $\mathbf{1}$: a vector of ones.

Next, we define the matrix $\mathbf{A}^{p_i} \in \mathbb{R}^{M,mn}$, with $p_i \in \mathbb{R}^2$ such that

$$\mathbf{A}^{p_i}_{k,\ell} = \mathcal{A}(\mathcal{B}_r(p_i - \xi_k) \cap (p_\ell + [0, 1[^2)), \tag{9}$$

where $\mathcal{A}$ is the Lebesgue measure in $\mathbb{R}^2$. In other words, $\mathbf{A}^{p_i}_{k,\ell}$ is the area of the part of the disk $\mathcal{B}_r(p_i - \xi_k)$ which is contained in the pixel region $p_\ell + [0, 1[^2$. Using this matrix, one has $\mu(\mathcal{B}_r(p_i - \xi_k)) = \mathbf{A}^{p_i}_{k,.}\boldsymbol{\lambda}$, that is, computing the intensity measure of the ball $\mathcal{B}_r(p_i - \xi_k)$ boils down to a matrix-vector multiplication. Thus, the vector $\hat{\mathbf{u}}$ which approximates the expected value of the filtered Boolean model can be written

$$\hat{\mathbf{u}}_i = 1 - \frac{1}{M}\mathbf{1}^T \exp[-\mathbf{A}^{p_i}\boldsymbol{\lambda}]. \tag{10}$$

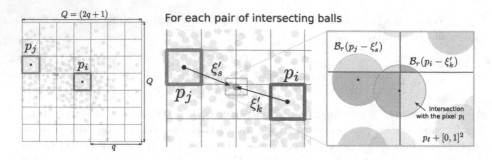

Fig. 1. Illustration of the approximation of covariance of filtered Boolean model. In this figure, we illustrate the manner in which the covariance is approximated, using a Monte Carlo simulation.

We now turn to the covariance matrix $\mathbf{C}$. The entry (i, j) of $\mathbf{C}$ is defined as the approximate covariance function evaluated at the points (p_i, p_j). In short, $\mathbf{C}_{i,j} = \text{Cov}_N(p_i, p_j)$. Similarly to the case of the expectation, we define the matrices $\mathbf{B}^{p_i}$, $\mathbf{D}^{p_j}$ and $\mathbf{D}^{p_i \cap p_j}$ (this time in $\mathbb{R}^{N^2 \times mn}$), such that, for $(k, s) \in \{0, \ldots, N-1\} \times \{0, \ldots, N-1\}$

$$\mathbf{B}^{p_i}_{k+Ns,\ell} = \mathcal{A}(\mathcal{B}_r(p_i - \xi'_k) \cap (p_\ell + [0, 1[^2))$$

$$\mathbf{D}^{p_j}_{k+Ns,\ell} = \mathcal{A}(\mathcal{B}_r(p_i - \xi'_s) \cap (p_\ell + [0, 1[^2)) \qquad (11)$$

$$\mathbf{D}^{p_i \cap p_j}_{k+Ns,\ell} = \mathcal{A}(\mathcal{B}_r(p_i - \xi'_k) \cap \mathcal{B}_r(p_i - \xi'_s) \cap (p_\ell + [0, 1[^2))$$

Finally, given these matrices, we can define the entry (i, j) of $\mathbf{C}$ as

$$\mathbf{C}_{i,j} = \frac{1}{N^2} \mathbf{1}^T \exp\left(-(\mathbf{B}^{p_i} + \mathbf{D}^{p_j})\boldsymbol{\lambda}\right) \odot \left[\exp\left(\mathbf{D}^{p_i \cap p_j}\boldsymbol{\lambda}\right) - \mathbf{1}\right], \qquad (12)$$

where $\odot$ represents the Hadamard (element-wise) vector product. Proposition 2 ensures that $\mathbf{C}$ is symmetric semi-definite positive. The covariance approximation process is illustrated in Fig. 1. An interesting feature is that we can precompute these area matrices for a given parameter set, since they are independent of the image u. Furthermore, it seems reasonable to assume that the covariance will be zero for couples (p_i, p_j) which are further apart than a certain distance, by choosing a blurring kernel ϕ with compact support. In practice, we choose a truncated Gaussian for ϕ, which is truncated at the value P_α such that, for $\xi \sim N(0, 1)$,

$$\mathbb{P}\left[\xi \in [-P_\alpha, P_\alpha]^2\right] = 1 - \alpha, \qquad (13)$$

for some small parameter α. This is the $(1 - \frac{\alpha}{2})th$ quantile of the Gaussian distribution. Now, recall that for any couple (p_i, p_j) we have

$$\mathcal{B}_r(p_i) \cap \mathcal{B}_r(p_j) = \emptyset \implies \text{Cov}(\mathbb{1}_Z(p_i), \mathbb{1}_Z(p_j)) = 0. \qquad (14)$$

This equation, combined with the fact that our Gaussians are truncated at P_α implies that for a couple (p_i, p_j) we have

$$\|p_i - p_j\|_2 > 2(P_\alpha + r) \implies \mathbf{C}_{i,j} = 0. \qquad (15)$$

Let us denote with q the maximum output pixel distance for which the covariance is non-zero. This distance is

$$q = \lfloor 2(P_\alpha + r) \rfloor. \tag{16}$$

Let $Q = (2q+1)$. For any pixel p_i, the (non-zero) covariance values are therefore limited to a square neighbourhood Ψ_{p_i} of size Q^2.

Algorithm 1. Film grain rendering algorithm with Gaussian texture.

Data: $u : \{0, 1, \ldots m - 1\} \times \{0, 1, \ldots, n - 1\} \to [0, u_{max}]$: input image
Parameters:
σ: standard deviation of the Gaussian low-pass filter
P_α: Gaussian $(1 - \alpha)$th quantile
N: number of iterations in the Monte Carlo method
Result: Image rendered with film grain

$\mathbf{X} \sim \mathcal{N}(0, \mathbf{I}^{mn,mn})$
$q = \lfloor 2(P_\alpha + r) \rfloor$
$\xi, \xi' \leftarrow$ i.i.d. r.v. with Gaussian density truncated at P_α
$\Psi_0 \leftarrow$ computeLocalNeighbourhood(q)
Load or compute the area matrices for this parameter set
$\{\mathbf{A}^0, \mathbf{B}^0, \ldots, \mathbf{D}^{\max(\Psi_0)}, \ldots, \mathbf{D}^{0 \cap \max(\Psi_0)}\} \leftarrow$ AreaMatrices(ξ, ξ', r, σ)
foreach $(i, j) \in \{0, \ldots, mn - 1\} \times \{0, \ldots, mn - 1\}$ s.t. $\mathrm{Cov}(\phi * \mathbb{1}_Z)(p_i, p_j) \neq 0$
do
 $\quad \lambda^{p_i} \leftarrow u(\Psi_{x_i})$
 $\quad \hat{\mathbf{u}}_i \leftarrow \frac{1}{M} \mathbf{A}^0 \lambda^{p_i}$
 $\quad \mathbf{C}_{p_i, p_j} = \frac{1}{N^2} \mathbf{1}^T \exp\left(-\left(\mathbf{B}^0 + \mathbf{D}^{p_j - p_i}\right) \lambda^{p_i}\right) \odot \left[\exp\left(\mathbf{D}^{0 \cap (p_j - p_i)} \lambda^{p_i}\right) - \mathbf{1}\right]$
$\mathbf{L} = \mathrm{Chol}(\mathbf{C})$
return$(\hat{\mathbf{u}} + \mathbf{L}\mathbf{X})$

Now that we have limited the extent of the covariance function, we can drastically decrease the size of the area matrices. Furthermore, these matrices only depend on the relative position of p_j with respect to p_i. Therefore, we can set p_i to be the "origin" 0 and $p_j - p_i \in \Psi_0$. In this case, we only need to calculate the matrices $\mathbf{A}^0$, $\mathbf{B}^0$, $\mathbf{D}^{p_j - p_i}$, and $\mathbf{D}^{0 \cap p_j - p_i}$. Let λ^{p_i} represent the values of λ in the neighbourhood Ψ_{p_i}. We can now rewrite the expected value and covariance using this reduced number of vectors and matrices

$$\mathbf{C}_{i,j} = \frac{1}{N^2} \mathbf{1}^T \exp\left(-\left(\mathbf{B}^0 + \mathbf{D}^{p_j - p_i}\right) \lambda^{p_i}\right) \odot \left[\exp\left(\mathbf{D}^{0 \cap (p_j - p_i)} \lambda^{p_i}\right) - \mathbf{1}\right]. \tag{17}$$

This is the final expression of the covariance matrix used in our algorithm. Once the positive semi-definite covariance matrix $\mathbf{C}$ and expected value $\hat{\mathbf{u}}$ are computed, we can easily produce Gaussian vectors with these specific expected value and covariance matrix. Indeed, consider the lower triangular matrix $\mathbf{L}$ resulting from the Cholesky decomposition of $\mathbf{C}$, such that $\mathbf{C} = \mathbf{L}\mathbf{L}^T$. For any

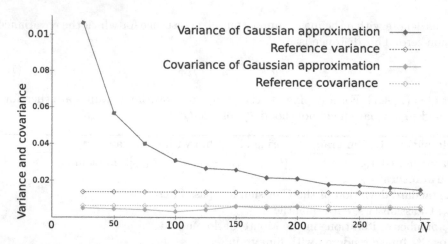

Fig. 2. Analysis of variance and covariance of the Gaussian approximation of the Boolean model. In this figure, we analyze the evolution of the variance and covariance of the Gaussian approximation of the Boolean model, as N increases. As predicted, for small values of N, the approximation is biased, due to the couples (ξ'_k, ξ'_k) in the Monte Carlo simulation. This effect diminshes as N increases.

$\mathbf{X} \in \mathbb{R}^{nm}$ following a standard Gaussian white noise, the vector $\hat{\mathbf{u}} + \mathbf{LX}$ has expected value $\hat{\mathbf{u}}$ and covariance matrix $\mathbf{C}$.

Algorithm Summary and Parameters. We now recap the full film grain synthesis algorithm. This consists of two stages: firstly the computation of the area matrices. These matrices can be pre-computed (for a given parameter set), and then stored in memory. This, in turn, requires the areas of disks and intersections of disks in the ranges of the pixels of the image grid. These areas are calculated with the geometry software CGAL [15]. The second part of the full method calculates the non-zero elements of the matrix $\mathbf{C}$, carries out the Cholesky decomposition on the latter, and then produce the output image. The complete algorithm is presented in Algorithm 1. In the experiments shown in the next section, we use the following parameters: $\sigma = 0.8$, $M = 800$, $N = 200$. The radius parameter r is varied to show different grain qualities.

4　Results

In this Section, we show some visual and numerical results of our algorithm. The first step is to verify experimentally that our Monte Carlo approach converges to the correct statistics of the Boolean model. One particular drawback of our approach is that, since we must use the same Gaussian offsets ξ'_i (in order to ensure symmetry and positive-definiteness), there is a list of couples (ξ'_k, ξ'_k) which are not i.i.d, but whose influence on the approximation diminishes as $N \to \infty$. With small values of N, this influence is significant, since the quantity $\mathrm{Cov}(\mathbb{1}_Z(p_i - \xi'_k), \mathbb{1}_Z(p_j - \xi'_k))$ (see Eq. (7)) is maximized precisely when $i = j$,

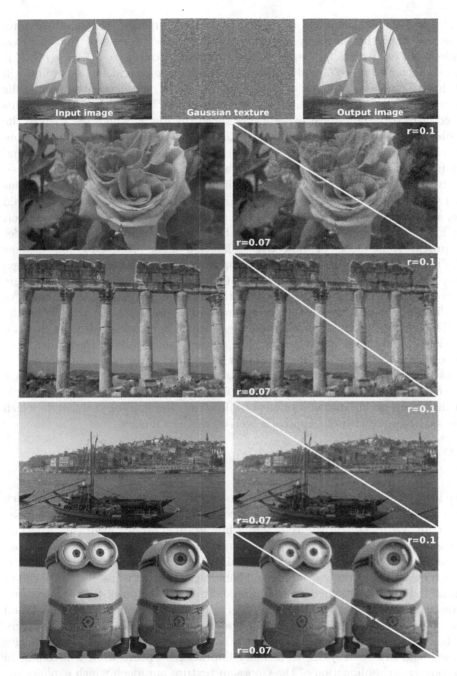

Fig. 3. Gaussian approximation of film grain. In this figure, we show a result of our film grain algorithm on several input images, in gray-scale and color. In the first example of the boat, we show the "pure" texture **LX** which is added to the image. This texture has a variance which is maximized in the areas of middling gray-level (the sky), and is minimal in the areas of extreme gray-level (the boat's sails, for example). (Color figure online)

and with small N there are not enough samples to "rectify" this bias. We note, however, that this problem is mostly restricted to the case of the *variance*. Indeed, for (x, y), s.t. $||p_i - p_j||_2 > 2r$, the quantity $\text{Cov}(\mathbb{1}_Z(p_i - \xi'_k), \mathbb{1}_Z(p_j - \xi'_k))$ is *necessarily* equal to 0. Only in the case of large zooms and/or large radii, will we have a non-zero influence of the couples (ξ'_k, ξ'_k). Thus, the convergence of the covariance is much faster, and indeed changes very little as N increases. This is confirmed by numerical experiments shown in Fig. 2, where we analyze the evolution of the values of the variance and covariance of the Monte Carlo approach, as N increases. These values are determined on a constant image, equal to 0.5 everywhere, and we compare the values to a "reference" value determined with the result of the film grain synthesis of [11]. The covariance shown is that of two vertically adjacent pixels. This gives us an idea of how large N should be, and also serves as a strong sanity check that our approach is indeed correct. In Fig. 3, we show a result of our algorithm on several input images. In order to provide some means of "objective" validation of the proposed grain, we show the result of **LX** in the middle of the top row. This represents the "pure" texture (the variance and covariance of the Gaussian approximation). This texture is coherent with what we expect, since the variance is maximal in the areas of medium gray-level, such as the sky. In areas with more extreme gray-levels, the variance is lower (the texture is smoother), which is coherent with the Boolean model. Indeed, when there are very few or very many balls in the model there is very little variation, leading to a lower value of $\mathbf{C}_{i,i}$, for any p_i in this region. This serves as a verification that the Gaussian approximation indeed displays the characteristics which we are looking for. Finally, we have shown an example of film grain on an animation image to illustrate the kind of visual style which can be achieved with our approach even on modern images.

5   Conclusion

We have presented a theoretical analysis of a physically realistic film grain model, and have derived expressions for the expected value and covariance of this model. We employ these quantities to design a film grain synthesis algorithm based on Gaussian textures. An important secondary result of this analysis is the confirmation that the covariance of film grain is dependent on the image intensity, which means that simply scanning and blending film grain is insufficient. We have presented numerical experiments which confirm that the proposed Gaussian texture accurately imitates the second-order statistics of the film grain model, and we have shown several visual results of our approach. While the proposed algorithm produces good visual results, it is as yet limited to medium-sized images (maximum 512×512) due to memory limitations. Future work will consist in proposing a simplification of the Gaussian texture approach which exploits the statistical information presented in the current work yet has reduced computational complexity.

References

1. Bae, S., Paris, S., Durand, F.: Two-scale tone management for photographic look. In: ACM Transactions on Graphics, vol. 25 (2006)
2. Bayer, B.E.: Relation between granularity and density for a random-dot model. J. Opt. Soc. Am. **54**(12), 1485+ (1964)
3. Chiu, S.N., Stoyan, D., Kendall, W.S., Mecke, J.: Stochastic Geometry and Its Applications, 3rd edn. Wiley, Hoboken (2013)
4. DxO: Dxo film pack 5 (2016). http://www.dxo.com/us/photography/photo-soft ware/dxo-filmpack
5. Galerne, B., Gousseau, Y., Morel, J.M.: Random phase textures: theory and synthesis. IEEE Trans. Image Process. **20**(1), 257–267 (2011)
6. G'MIC: Greyc's magic for image computing (2016). http://gmic.eu/
7. Grubbasoftware: Truegrain (2015). http://grubbasoftware.com/
8. Hoeffding, W.: The strong law of large numbers for u-statistics. Institute of Statistics mimeo series 302 (1961)
9. Livingston, R.: The theory of the photographic process. By C. E. Kenneth Mees. J. Phys. Chem. **49**(5), 509 (1945)
10. Moldovan, T.M., Roth, S., Black, M.J.: Denoising archival films using a learned bayesian model. In: 2006 IEEE International Conference on Image Processing, pp. 2641–2644. IEEE, October 2006
11. Newson, A., Galerne, B., Delon, J.: Stochastic modelling and realistic rendering of film grain. Technical report, Laboratoire MAP5, Université Paris Descartes, France (2016)
12. Oh, B.T., Lei, S.M., Kuo, C.C.: Advanced film grain noise extraction and synthesis for high-definition video coding. IEEE Trans. Circ. Syst. Video Technol. **19**(12), 1717–1729 (2009)
13. Schneider, R., Weil, W.: Stochastic and Integral Geometry. Springer, Heidelberg (2008)
14. Tanaka, K., Uchida, S.: Extended random-dot model. J. Opt. Soc. Am. **73**(10), 1312+ (1983)
15. The CGAL Project: CGAL User and Reference Manual. 4.9 edn. (2016). http://doc.cgal.org/4.9/Manual/packages.html
16. Yan, J.C.K.: Statistical methods for film grain noise removal and generation. Master's thesis, University of Toronto (1997)

Below the Surface of the Non-local Bayesian Image Denoising Method

Pablo Arias[1](✉) and Mila Nikolova[2]

[1] CMLA, ENS Cachan, Université Paris-Saclay, 94235 Cachan, France
`arias@cmla.ens-cachan.fr`
[2] CMLA, ENS Cachan, CNRS, Université Paris-Saclay, 94235 Cachan, France
`nikolova@cmla.ens-cachan.fr`

Abstract. The non-local Bayesian (NLB) patch-based approach of Lebrun et al. [12] is considered as a state-of-the-art method for the restoration of (color) images corrupted by white Gaussian noise. It gave rise to numerous ramifications like e.g., possible improvements, processing of various data sets and video. This article is the first attempt to analyse the method in depth in order to understand the main phenomena underlying its effectiveness. Our analysis, corroborated by numerical tests, shows several unexpected facts. In a variational setting, the first-step Bayesian approach to learn the prior for patches is equivalent to a pseudo-Tikhonov regularisation where *the regularisation parameters can be positive or negative*. Practically very good results in this step are mainly due to the aggregation stage – whose importance needs to be re-evaluated.

1 Introduction

In this paper we analyse the Non-local Bayesian (NLB) image denoising algorithm introduced by Lebrun, Buades and Morel in [12], which is based on the assumption that sets of similar patches are IID samples from a Gaussian distribution.

In recent years several works have proposed Gaussian models, or Gaussian mixture models (GMMs) as priors for image patches, achieving state-of-the-art results in image denoising and other inverse problems. In [19] a GMM with hundreds of components is used as a fixed prior for image patches. The mixture is learnt via an EM algorithm from a database of two million patches. Instead of a fixed prior [5,17] proposed to learn the GMM from the input image. Guillemot et al. [9] introduced the *covariance tree*, a hierarchical data structure capturing the covariance of image patches at several scales.

P. Arias—The work of P. Arias is funded by BPIFrance and Région Ile de France in the FUI 18 Plein Phare project. P.A. is also partly founded by the "IDI 2016" project funded by the IDEX Paris-Saclay, ANR-11-IDEX-0003-02, the Office of Naval research (ONR grant N00014-14-1-0023) and by ANR-14-CE27-001 (MIRIAM).
M. Nikolova—The work of M. Nikolova work was partially funded by the French Research Agency (ANR) under grant No ANR-14-CE27-001 (MIRIAM).

F. Lauze et al. (Eds.): SSVM 2017, LNCS 10302, pp. 208–220, 2017.
DOI: 10.1007/978-3-319-58771-4_17

The NLB algorithm differs from the previous approaches in that it does not consider a single model (GMM, covariance tree) for all image patches. Instead, there is a Gaussian model for each patch and its nearest neighbors. This is closely related to the approaches that denoise patches by applying principal component analysis (PCA) on groups of patches [6,8,15,18].

Several extensions of NLB were considered. A multiscale version was developed in [14] to handle the structured noise typical of compression artifacts. Extensions to video were proposed in [2,4]. NLB was adapted to denoise manifolds-valued images in [10]. A Bayesian hyper-prior model on the mean and the covariance in the NLB approach was proposed for inverse problems in [1].

In the NLB method, for each set of similar patches an empirical Wiener filter is used to estimate the corresponding clean patches. The denoised image results from the aggregation by averaging of these estimated patches. The Wiener filter requires to estimate the mean and the covariance matrix of the *a priori* distribution. The method consists of two steps. In the first step the statistics of the prior are estimated from the noisy patches. The second step is similar but uses the output of the first step as an oracle to estimate the *a priori* statistics.

In this work we carefully dissect the NLB algorithm, focusing on the first step which is responsible for most of the denoising. On the surface, the NLB algorithm appears as a *maximum a posteriori* (MAP) estimation of each patch. But in fact these empirical MAP estimates are poor, as a consequence of the fact that the prior covariance estimate has in general negative eigenvalues which result in an unstable filter. The success of the algorithm resides in that the aggregation phase averages out the errors of the MAP estimates, achieving similar and often better results than the ones obtained with a more standard non-negative definite estimate of the prior covariance matrix. Although the aggregation has been recognized as a good practice in patch-based denoising [13], the results presented below show that it plays a crucial role for the success of the NLB.

2   The Theory of the Algorithm

For an original gray value image $x \in \mathbb{R}^{M_1 \times M_2}$ we are given an observation contaminated with centered white normal noise n with known variance σ^2, independent of x:

$$y = x + n.$$

The approach proposed in [12] relies on the fact that natural images exhibit patch-based self-similarity, and assumes that groups of similar patches follow a normal distribution. The NLB algorithm consists in two main denoising steps: (1) compute an oracle image $\tilde{x}$ using the data y and σ^2; (2) obtain the denoised image $\hat{x}$ using the oracle $\tilde{x}$, the data y and σ^2. Each one of these steps consist of two stages: (a) denoise individually all patches using a maximum a posteriori (MAP) estimator; (b) aggregate the results of (a).

An example of the output of each step is given for the 256×256 *parrot* image, shown in Fig. 1. Some noise artifacts reside in the oracle image $\tilde{x}$. They are restored in the denoised image.

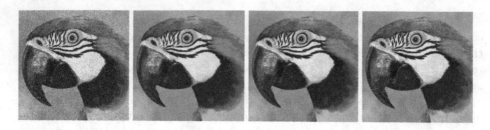

Fig. 1. From left to right: noisy image y for $\sigma = 20$; first-step denoised $\widetilde{x}$ (29.57 PSNR), denoised $\hat{x}$ (29.95 PSNR) and original image.

2.1   Bayesian Model for Patches

A patch of y (resp., x) of size $\sqrt{K} \times \sqrt{K}$ at pixel $\mathbf{i} = (i_1, i_2)$ is denoted by $\mathbf{y_i}$ (resp., $\mathbf{x_i}$). In what follows, we adopt a vector notation for patches. The likelihood of $\mathbf{x_i}$ given the observed $\mathbf{y_i}$ is

$$\mathbb{P}(\mathbf{y_i}|\mathbf{x_i}) \propto \exp\left[-\frac{\|\mathbf{x_i} - \mathbf{y_i}\|^2}{2\sigma^2}\right]. \tag{1}$$

With each patch $\mathbf{x_i}$, there is associated a set of N most similar patches $S(\mathbf{i})$ within a fixed size window. The patch $\mathbf{x_i}$ is called the reference patch. Similarity is measured with respect to the ℓ_2 distance. It is assumed that all patches in $S(\mathbf{i})$ have a normal distribution sharing the same mean $\mathbf{m_{x_i}} \in \mathbb{R}^K$ and the same covariance $C_{\mathbf{x_i}}$, see [12]. Thus

$$\mathbb{P}(\mathbf{x_i}) \propto \exp\left(-\frac{1}{2}(\mathbf{x_i} - \mathbf{m_{x_i}})^T C_{\mathbf{x_i}}^{-1}(\mathbf{x_i} - \mathbf{m_{x_i}})\right). \tag{2}$$

Using Bayes's rule, $\mathbb{P}(\mathbf{x_i}|\mathbf{y_i}) \propto \mathbb{P}(\mathbf{y_i}|\mathbf{x_i})\mathbb{P}(\mathbf{x_i})$. The MAP estimate $\hat{\mathbf{x}}_{\mathbf{i}}^{(i)}$ of the noisy reference patch $\mathbf{y_i}$,

$$\hat{\mathbf{x}}_{\mathbf{i}}^{(i)} = \arg\max_{\mathbf{x_i}} \mathbb{P}(\mathbf{x_i}|\mathbf{y_i}) = \left(I + \sigma^2 C_{\mathbf{x_i}}^{-1}\right)^{-1}\left(\mathbf{y_i} + \sigma^2 C_{\mathbf{x_i}}^{-1}\mathbf{m_{x_i}}\right)$$

is known to provide some denoising. Using that for an invertible matrix C one has $\left(I + \sigma^2 C^{-1}\right)^{-1} C^{-1} = \left(C + \sigma^2 I\right)^{-1}$ and $\sigma^2 \left(C + \sigma^2 I\right)^{-1} - I = -C\left(C + \sigma^2 I\right)^{-1}$, the MAP estimate reads also as

$$\hat{\mathbf{x}}_{\mathbf{i}} = \mathbf{m_{x_i}} + C_{\mathbf{x_i}}\left(C_{\mathbf{x_i}} + \sigma^2 I\right)^{-1}\left(\mathbf{y_i} - \mathbf{m_{x_i}}\right). \tag{3}$$

This individual MAP patch denoising is considered as the main phase of the NLB algorithm [12].

Remark 1. Extensive numerical tests reported in [11] have shown that the denoising formula (3) can be applied simultaneously to all of the N most similar patches, i.e. those belonging to $S_{\mathbf{i}}$. As a consequence the same patch $\mathbf{y_k}$ can be denoised several times, if $\mathbf{k} \in S(\mathbf{i})$ for different $\mathbf{i}$. We denote the corresponding MAP estimates as $\mathbf{x}_{\mathbf{k}}^{(i)}$.

After all patches are denoised using the local MAP estimator, an aggregation stage is applied by computing for each pixel $\mathbf{i}$ the mean over all restored patches that contain this pixel.

The main difference of the NLB method compared to other Gaussian-based models for image patches [5,17,19] is the way how the matrix $C_{\mathbf{x_i}}$ is learned from the image itself. The question is analysed in the following sections.

2.2   Learning the *A Priori* model

We have to distinguish between the first and the second steps. The number of the pixels in the square patch window is denoted by K_j and the number of similar patches by N_j, where $j = 1, 2$ indicates the step.

First Step. The N_1 patches $S_1(\mathbf{i})$ similar to the reference patch $\mathbf{y_i}$ are selected using the ℓ^2 distance between $\mathbf{y_i}$ and all patches $\mathbf{y_k}$ in a neighborhood around $\mathbf{y_i}$. Let us fix at patch $\mathbf{y_i}$ and its similar patches $\mathbf{y_k} \in S_1(\mathbf{i})$.

Since $\mathbf{x_i} \sim \mathcal{N}(\mathbf{m_{x_i}}, C_{\mathbf{x_i}})$ and $\mathbf{n_i} \sim \mathcal{N}(0, \sigma^2 I)$ and since the noise is independent from the original x, we have that $\mathbf{y_k} \sim \mathcal{N}(\mathbf{m_{x_i}}, C_{\mathbf{y_i}})$, with $C_{\mathbf{y_i}} = C_{\mathbf{x_i}} + \sigma^2 I$, for $\mathbf{y_k} \in S(\mathbf{i})$. The maximum likelihood estimates of $\mathbf{m_{x_i}}$ and $C_{\mathbf{y_i}}$ are given by the sample mean and sample covariance matrix. The ML estimate of the covariance matrix is biased. An unbiased estimator can be obtained by dividing by $N_1 - 1$ instead of N_1, yielding

$$\overline{\mathbf{y}}_\mathbf{i} = \frac{1}{N_1} \sum_{k \in S_i} \mathbf{y_k}, \quad C_{\mathbf{y_i}} = \frac{1}{N_1 - 1} \sum_{k \in S_1(\mathbf{i})} (\mathbf{y_k} - \overline{\mathbf{y}}_\mathbf{i})(\mathbf{y_k} - \overline{\mathbf{y}}_\mathbf{i})^T, \quad (4)$$

where the superscript T means transposed. Using that $C_{\mathbf{y_i}} = C_{\mathbf{x_i}} + \sigma^2 I$, the authors in [12] estimate $C_{\mathbf{x_i}}$ as

$$C_{\mathbf{x_i}} = C_{\mathbf{y_i}} - \sigma^2 I. \qquad (5)$$

This estimate is often not positive definite. There are different ways to avoid this; e.g., clipping the negative eigenvalues to zero has been used on the context of patch-based denoising in [5]. This may also have undesirable effects, see the discussion in [16, p. 406]. New facts are given in Subsect. 3.3.

In spite of the theoretical background explained above, extensive experiments in [11] have shown that using the MAP estimator yields artifacts in flat areas.

Remark 2 **(Flat areas).** *Flat areas are detected by applying a χ^2 Gaussianity test to the set of all pixels of the patches in $S(\mathbf{i})$. If a flat area is detected, the patches in $S(\mathbf{i})$ are estimated as constant patches, where the constant value is the average of all pixel values of all patches in $S(\mathbf{i})$.*

Second Step. This step is grounded on the presumption that the *oracle* estimate $\tilde{x}$ is faithful enough to provide two informations on the unknown ground truth image. These are: (1) the distances between patches in the *oracle* are well estimated, so the set of the N_2 patches similar to $\mathbf{y_i}$ is computed from the *oracle* estimate $\tilde{x}$; (2) the covariance matrices for patches provided by the *oracle* image $\tilde{x}$ are "nearly true", so these matrices are computed using only the *oracle* image.

3   An Oracle Image in the First Step

In this section we study in detail the first step of the algorithm.

3.1   Statistical Model and Filtering for 1st Step Patch Denoising

Replacing $C_{\mathbf{x_i}}$ and $\mathbf{m_{x_i}}$ in (3) by their estimates (4), we end up with the following Wiener-like filter

$$\widetilde{\mathbf{x}}_{\mathbf{k}}^{(i)} = \overline{\mathbf{y}}_{\mathbf{i}} + \left(C_{\mathbf{y_i}} - \sigma^2 I \right) C_{\mathbf{y_i}}^{-1} \left(\mathbf{y_k} - \overline{\mathbf{y}}_{\mathbf{i}} \right). \tag{6}$$

This filter is applied to all patches $\mathbf{k} \in S_1(\mathbf{i})$. After simplification, $\widetilde{\mathbf{x}}_{\mathbf{k}}^{(i)} = \mathbf{y_k} - \sigma^2 C_{\mathbf{y_i}}^{-1}(\mathbf{y_k} - \overline{\mathbf{y}}_{\mathbf{i}})$. Since $C_{\mathbf{y_i}} \succeq 0$ its eigen-decomposition is of the form

$$C_{\mathbf{y_i}} = U_{\mathbf{y_i}} \operatorname{diag}(\lambda_{\mathbf{y_i}}) U_{\mathbf{y_i}}^T. \tag{7}$$

Here $U_{\mathbf{y_i}}$ is an orthonormal matrix (i.e. it satisfies $U_{\mathbf{y_i}}^T U_{\mathbf{y_i}} = U_{\mathbf{y_i}} U_{\mathbf{y_i}}^T = I$) containing the eigenvectors of $C_{\mathbf{y_i}}$ and $\lambda_{\mathbf{y_i}} \in \mathbb{R}_{\geq 0}^K$ are the corresponding eigenvalues of $C_{\mathbf{y_i}}$ in decreasing order. The estimate of $C_{\mathbf{x_i}}$ in (5) reads as

$$C_{\mathbf{x_i}} = C_{\mathbf{y_i}} - \sigma^2 I = U_{\mathbf{y_i}} \operatorname{diag}\left(\lambda_{\mathbf{y_i}} - \sigma^2 \right) U_{\mathbf{y_i}}^T. \tag{8}$$

Thus the Wiener-like denoising in (6) can be interpreted as a filtering in the basis of the eigenvectors $U_{\mathbf{y_i}}$ of $C_{\mathbf{y_i}}$:

$$U_{\mathbf{y_i}}^T \left(\mathbf{x}_{\mathbf{k}}^{(i)} - \overline{\mathbf{y}}_{\mathbf{i}} \right) = \operatorname{diag}\left(\frac{\lambda_{\mathbf{y_i}} - \sigma^2}{\lambda_{\mathbf{y_i}}} \right) \left(U_{\mathbf{y_i}}^T \left(\mathbf{y_k} - \overline{\mathbf{y}}_{\mathbf{i}} \right) \right). \tag{9}$$

where division in the diagonal matrix is vector-wise.

A filtering of this form is stable and the learnt prior model is consistent if and only if $C_{\mathbf{y_i}} - \sigma^2 I$ has positive eigenvalues.

The Eigenvalues of the Estimated Prior Covariances $C_{\mathbf{y_i}} - \sigma^2 I$. It appears that $C_{\mathbf{y_i}} - \sigma^2 I$ nearly always has negative eigenvalues even for *non-flat* patches, whatever the level of the noise. Table 1 gives more details for five images and different values of $\sigma \in \{1, 5, 10, 20, 40\}$. The parameter choice follows the recommendations in [11]. Patches are square; for $\sigma < 20$ one takes $(K_1, N_1) = (9, 27)$ and for $20 \leq \sigma < 50$ $(K_1, N_1) = (25, 75)$; as recommended, $N_i = 3K_i$ and the search window is a square of size $\lfloor N_i/2 \rfloor$. Flat areas are detected as described in Remark 2. As in [12], with each index $\mathbf{i}$ in the image (except at the boundary) there is associated a reference patch $\mathbf{y_i}$. The set of indexes corresponding *to non-flat reference patches* is denoted by J. Column (a) contains the least eigenvalues of $C_{\mathbf{y_i}}$ for each image and for each noise level σ over all patches in the relevant set J. Since the eigenvalues are ordered decreasingly, the least one is K_1. All these least eigenvalues are much smaller that the corresponding σ^2. Column (b) shows the percentage of matrices $C_{\mathbf{y_i}} - \sigma^2 I$ over J with at least one negative eigenvalue, which also reads as $\sharp \{\mathbf{y_i}, \mathbf{i} \in J : g(\lambda_{K_1}) < 0\}$. Observe that these percentages are large, going up to 100 %. What is more, the number of negative weights in $g(\lambda_{\mathbf{y_i}})$ for non-flat reference patches is important: column (c) presents the *average* number of negative weights in $g(\lambda_{\mathbf{y_i}})$ taken over J.

Table 1. (a) The least eigenvalue of $C_{\mathbf{y}_i}$ for all reference patches in non-flat areas. (b) Percentage of reference patches $\mathbf{y}_i$ in non-flat areas with at least one negative weight in $g(\lambda_{\mathbf{y}_i})$. (c) Average number of negative weights in $g(\lambda_{\mathbf{y}_i})$ for reference patches $\mathbf{y}_i$ in non-flat areas.

		(a) $\min\limits_{\mathbf{y}_i, i \in J} \lambda_{\mathbf{y}_i}(K_1)$	(b) $\#\{\mathbf{y}_i : g(\lambda_{K_1}) < 0\}$	(c) $\overline{\#\{k \in J : g(\lambda_k) < 0\}}$
Boat (512 × 512)	$\sigma = 1$	0.087	10.25%	1.702%
	$\sigma = 5$	0.883	96.23%	40.75%
	$\sigma = 10$	3.747	99.85%	53.47%
	$\sigma = 20$	31.88	100%	55.13%
	$\sigma = 40$	122.7	100%	62.25%
Man (1024 × 1024)	$\sigma = 1$	0.059	10.37%	2.584%
	$\sigma = 5$	0.909	95.84%	41.41%
	$\sigma = 10$	3.833	99.64%	54.65%
	$\sigma = 20$	29.01	100%	56.83%
	$\sigma = 40$	134.6	100%	62.23%
Parrot (256 × 256)	$\sigma = 1$	0.051	45.43%	16.59%
	$\sigma = 5$	1.201	80.75%	29.84%
	$\sigma = 10$	4.811	93.88%	42.26%
	$\sigma = 20$	35.22	100%	48.16%
	$\sigma = 40$	134.9	100%	89.42%
Peppers (512 × 512)	$\sigma = 1$	0.126	13.48%	1.914%
	$\sigma = 5$	0.772	97.67%	46.82%
	$\sigma = 10$	3.309	99.88%	56.94%
	$\sigma = 20$	34.05	100%	56.63%
	$\sigma = 40$	127.3	100%	62.62%
Stream (512 × 512)	$\sigma = 1$	0.093	5.194%	0.856%
	$\sigma = 5$	0.942	67.77%	20.44%
	$\sigma = 10$	4.354	97.14%	39.19%
	$\sigma = 20$	29.55	100%	50.38%
	$\sigma = 40$	130.5	100%	61.69%

Consequences. Since $C_{\mathbf{x}_i} = C_{\mathbf{y}_i} - \sigma^2 I$ has negative eigenvalues it *is not a covariance matrix*, and the learned prior $\mathbb{P}(\mathbf{x}_i)$ *is not a probability*.

Table 1 shows that most of the noisy prior covariances estimated by the denoising algorithm have a large number of negative eigenvalues, and thus they have a significant impact in the pseudo-Wiener denoising in (6) and (9).

Pseudo-Tikhonov Regularization. Observe that $\widetilde{\mathbf{x}}_k^{(i)}$ in (6) is the unique stationary point of the objective F below

$$F(\mathbf{x}) = \|\mathbf{x} - \mathbf{y}_i\|^2 + \sigma^2(\mathbf{x} - \overline{\mathbf{y}}_i)^T \left(C_{\mathbf{y}_i} - \sigma^2 I\right)^{-1} (\mathbf{x} - \overline{\mathbf{y}}_i). \qquad (10)$$

Using the eigen-decomposition in (7) and the fact that $U_{\mathbf{y}_i}$ is orthonormal, F also reads as

$$F(\mathbf{x}) = \|U_{\mathbf{y}_i}^T (\mathbf{x} - \mathbf{y}_i)\|^2 + \sigma^2(\mathbf{x} - \overline{\mathbf{y}}_i)^T U_{\mathbf{y}_i} \left(\mathrm{diag}(\lambda_{\mathbf{y}_i} - \sigma^2 I)\right)^{-1} U_{\mathbf{y}_i}^T(\mathbf{x} - \overline{\mathbf{y}}_i). \quad (11)$$

We denote $\lambda_{\mathbf{y}_i} := (\lambda_1, \ldots, \lambda_K)$. Let $\mathbf{u}_{\mathbf{y}_i, k}$ stand for the kth column of $U_{\mathbf{y}_i}$. Then

$$F(\mathbf{x}) = \sum_{k=1}^{K} \left(\mathbf{u}_{\mathbf{y}_i, k}^T (\mathbf{x} - \mathbf{y}_i)\right)^2 + \beta(\lambda_k) \left(\mathbf{u}_{\mathbf{y}_i, k}^T (\mathbf{x} - \overline{\mathbf{y}}_i)\right)^2, \qquad (12)$$

where $\beta(\lambda) = \sigma^2/(\lambda - \sigma^2)$. The function $\lambda \mapsto \beta(\lambda)$ is continuous on $\mathbb{R} \setminus \{0\}$ with

$$\lim_{\lambda \searrow 0} \beta(\lambda) = -1 \quad \lim_{\lambda \nearrow \sigma^2} \beta(\lambda) = -\infty \quad \lim_{\lambda \searrow \sigma^2} \beta(\lambda) = \infty \quad \beta(2\sigma^2) = 1 \quad \lim_{\lambda \to +\infty} \beta(\lambda) = 0.$$

The objective F is a quadratic *convex-concave function*. It can be seen as a pseudo-Tikhonov regularization in the basis $U_{\mathbf{y_i}}$ where the regularization parameters $\beta(\lambda_k)$ can be positive or negative. Let us remind that classical Tikhonov regularization with all $\beta > 0$ entails oversmoothing; see e.g., [3, Sect. 3.2]. Table 1(c) shows that F in (12) has many negative regularization parameters.

Pseudo-Wiener Filtering. Equation (9) reads also as

$$U_{\mathbf{y_i}}^T \widetilde{\mathbf{x}}_k^{(i)} = \mathrm{diag}\left(\frac{\lambda_{\mathbf{y_i}} - \sigma^2}{\lambda_{\mathbf{y_i}}} \right) \left(U_{\mathbf{y_i}}^T (\mathbf{y_k} - \overline{\mathbf{y}_i}) \right) + U_{\mathbf{y_i}}^T \overline{\mathbf{y}_i}. \tag{13}$$

Since $U_{\mathbf{y_i}}$ is an orthonormal matrix, the noise statistics of $\mathbf{y_i}$ and of $U_{\mathbf{y_i}}^T \mathbf{y_i}$ are the same. The weighting coefficients in the diagonal matrix in (13) are given by a function $g : \mathbb{R}_{>0} \to \mathbb{R}$

$$g(\lambda) := (\lambda - \sigma^2)/\lambda = 1 - \sigma^2/\lambda \tag{14}$$

which is differentiable, strictly increasing with $\lim_{\lambda \searrow 0} g(\lambda) = -\infty, g(\sigma^2) = 0$ and $\lim_{\lambda \to +\infty} g(\lambda) = 1$. The weights $g(\lambda)$ are negative for $\lambda < \sigma^2$ and rapidly decrease with $\lambda \searrow 0$. This g is related to β in (12) by $g(\lambda) = (\beta(\lambda) + 1)^{-1}$.

Thus the components of $U_{\mathbf{y_i}}^T \mathbf{x}_i^{(i)}$ in (13) satisfy

$$\mathbf{u}_{\mathbf{y_i},k}^T \left(\widetilde{\mathbf{x}}_k^{(i)} - \overline{\mathbf{y}_i} \right) = g(\lambda_k) \, \mathbf{u}_{\mathbf{y_i},k}^T (\mathbf{y_k} - \overline{\mathbf{y}_i}), \quad 1 \le k \le K_1. \tag{15}$$

Figure 2 shows a sample covariance matrix $C_{\mathbf{y_i}}$ with its eigenvectors and eigenvalues $\lambda_{\mathbf{y_i}}$ for a non-flat patch of the noisy *parrot* image in Fig. 1 where $\sigma = 20$. The eigenvectors are plotted in a raster order. The weights $g(\lambda_{\mathbf{y_i}})$ in (14) are depicted in the same figure. More than half of the eigenvalues are smaller than σ^2, resulting in negative eigenvalues in $C_{\mathbf{x_i}}$ and negative filter coefficients $g(\lambda)$. The resulting filter gives large negative weights to the eigenvectors associated to the smallest eigenvalues, which look like noise with no apparent structure.

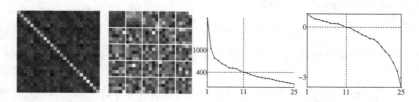

Fig. 2. For a non-flat patch in the noisy *parrot* image in Fig. 1, with $\sigma = 20$, from left to right: sample covariance matrix $C_{\mathbf{y_i}}$; its eigenvectors in raster order; the eigenvalues $\lambda_{\mathbf{y_i}}$ and the resulting weighting function $g(\lambda_{\mathbf{y_i}})$. Notice the large filter weights $g(\lambda)$ corresponding to $\lambda < \sigma^2$.

Remark 3. According to the Eckart-Young theorem, the capability of the eigenvectors of C_{y_i} to encode important features of the patch y_i decreases as the eigenvalue decreases. As far as the negative weights $g(\lambda_k)$ decrease, insignificant eigenvectors with inverted signs are amplified.

3.2 Aggregation

The process of individual patch MAP estimation terminates when all patches have been visited. A patch can be estimated multiple times using (6). The set of all MAP estimates of a patch x_k reads as $X_k := \{i \,:\, k \in S_1(i)\}$. All these patch estimates are aggregated by averaging them on their corresponding locations on the image. We denote by H the local indexes within a $\sqrt{K} \times \sqrt{K}$ patch, $H = \{h = (h_1, h_2) \,:\, 0 \le h_1, h_2 \le \sqrt{K} - 1\}$. A pixel j is contained in all the patches x_{j-h} with $h \in H$. The value of the oracle image $\widetilde{x}$ at pixel j results from averaging all estimated values for that pixel:

$$\widetilde{x}(j) = \frac{1}{A_j} \sum_{h \in H} \sum_{i \in X_{j-h}} \widetilde{x}_{j-h}^{(i)}(h), \qquad \text{with} \quad A_j = \sum_{h \in H} \sharp X_{j-h}. \tag{16}$$

There is a large variability in the aggregation weights across the image. Some patches have a high degree of self-similarity with their surroundings, and appear in many nearest neighbors sets S_1. Thus their aggregation weights A_i can be quite higher than those of other patches with singular patterns. Several patch based methods have a similar aggregation of the patch estimates [7,17,19], and it was identified in [13] as one of the key ingredients of state-of-the-art image denoising strategies.

To evaluate the impact of the different stages of the denoising algorithm, we track the non-flat patches during the denoising of the *parrot* image with $\sigma = 20$. In Fig. 3 we show the histograms of the RMSE of the non-flat patches in the input noisy image, (1) after the individual MAP estimates but before the aggregation, and (2) after their aggregation in the output oracle image. The RMSE before the aggregation (BA) is computed as

$$\text{RMSE}_{\text{BA}} = \left(\frac{1}{C} \sum_{i \in J} \sum_{k \in S_1(i)} \|\widetilde{x}_k^{(i)} - x_k\|_2^2 \right)^{\frac{1}{2}}, \tag{17}$$

where $C = \sum_{i \in J} \sharp S_1(i)$ for J the set of non-flat patches. The RMSE after the aggregation is computed similarly, with the patch of the oracle $\widetilde{x}_k$ instead of $\widetilde{x}_k^{(i)}$. The left figure corresponds to the first step of the NLB and the right to the second. It is seen that the MAP formula (6) in the first step gives quite a poor result, *with a RMSE worse than that of the noisy input image.* This is a consequence of the unreliable estimate of the covariance matrix. The aggregation stage has a crucial role to obtain the first-step denoised patch $\widetilde{x}_i$. Most of the denoising work is done during the first step of the algorithm; see also Fig. 1.

Figure 4 shows different stages of the denoising of a patch $\mathbf{y}_i$: the MAP estimate (6), the aggregation stage in (16), followed by the second step MAP and the final denoised patch $\widehat{\mathbf{x}}_i$. Figure 2 already showed that eigenvectors with small positive and also negative eigenvalues have a random structure. In Fig. 4, the significant contribution of such eigenvectors can be clearly seen: The step 1 MAP estimate before the aggregation is not better than the noisy patch. However, the aggregation of the MAP estimates yields a good approximation of the clean patch, very similar to the output after the second denoising iteration. Most of the denoising is carried out by the aggregation of the MAP estimates in the first stage.

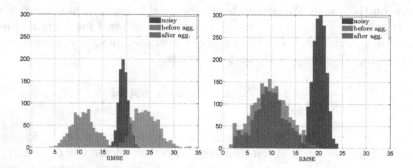

Fig. 3. Histograms of the RMSE for non-flat patches, for the *parrot* image with $\sigma = 20$.

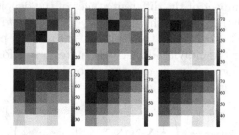

Fig. 4. Restoration of a noisy patch $\mathbf{y}_i$ of the image in Fig. 1. Top: noisy patch $\mathbf{y}_i$, step 1 MAP $\widetilde{\mathbf{x}}_i^{(i)}$, step 1 agg. $\widetilde{\mathbf{x}}_i$. Bottom: original, step 2 MAP $\widehat{\mathbf{x}}_i^{(i)}$, step 2 agg. $\widehat{\mathbf{x}}_i$.

In Fig. 5 we show all the estimates that are aggregated for two pixels in the patch shown in Fig. 4. We refer to these plots as *pixel paths*. These values correspond to the MAP estimates (Eq. (6)) of patches that contain the pixels. It is quite a general rule that a pixel has a large number of updates. The variance of the updates is huge, which results from the negative weights in the pseudo-Wiener filter. The surprising fact is that in spite of this huge variance the final value is reasonable. By manipulating the values – removing outliers based on

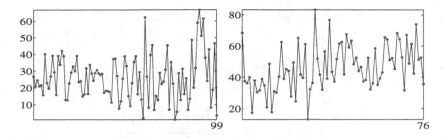

Fig. 5. *Pixel paths* for two pixels in the patch $\mathbf{y_i}$ shown in Fig. 4. These are the values that are aggregated according to (16).

the histogram – one can get better results. Since the number of updates is not known, an automatic outlier rejection does not seem simple.

3.3   The Effect of the Thresholding the Negative Weights

In the light of the results after the first step MAP estimation (Figs. 3 and 4) one is curious to better realize the role of the negative eigenvalues in the estimated matrix $C_{\mathbf{x_i}}$. A common approach is to clip negative eigenvalues to zero [5]. Our aim here is to go into the question using a family of estimates of the covariance matrix by discarding small eigenvalues in $C_{\mathbf{y_i}} - \sigma^2 I$ (see [2]):

$$C_{\mathbf{x_i}}^\tau = U_{\mathbf{y_i}} \text{diag}\left(T_\tau\left(\lambda_{\mathbf{y_i}} - \sigma^2\right)\right) U_{\mathbf{y_i}}^T, \tag{18}$$

where $\tau \in \mathbb{R}$ and $T_\tau(s) = s$ if $s \geq \tau\sigma^2$ and $T_\tau(s) = 0$ otherwise. We can then investigate the performance of the algorithm under variations of τ.

In Fig. 6 we test the estimators $C_{\mathbf{x_i}}^\tau$ for different values of τ and evaluate the PSNR on non-flat patches after the individual MAP estimation (dashed lines), and after the aggregation (continuous lines) for both denoising steps. As expected the plots become constant below $\tau = -1$, since all eigenvalues are larger than $-\sigma^2$ ($C_{\mathbf{y_i}}$ is positive definite). This is exactly the first-step MAP estimate (5) in NLB [12]. When τ increases, more and more entries in the diagonal matrix in (18) are zeroed out, together with the corresponding filter coefficients $g(\lambda_{\mathbf{y_i}})$. For τ large enough $C_{\mathbf{x_i}} \to 0$ and the MAP denoising reduces to the $\widetilde{\mathbf{x}}_k^{(i)} = \overline{\mathbf{y}}_i$. If $\tau = 0$ we recover estimator $(C_{\mathbf{y_i}} - \sigma^2)_+$ of [5].

The plot confirms the bad quality of the MAP estimates in the first denoising iteration when $\tau \leq -1$, and the impressive correction caused by the aggregation. Regarding the output of the individual MAP estimates in the first step, the best results are obtained for $\tau = 0$ (1.8 dB higher than with $\tau \leq -1$). However, this is not the case after the aggregation (continuous red curve), where slightly better results (around 0.1 dB higher) correspond to $\tau \approx 2$, and also to $\tau \approx -0.7$. The PSNRs for the second step of the algorithm are almost independent of τ. The negative eigenvalues in the first step do not have a negative effect on the performance of the whole algorithm. In fact, allowing some small negative eigenvalues seems

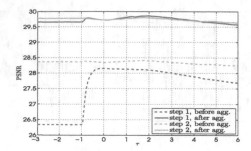

Fig. 6. PSNR of all non-flat patches after different stages of the algorithm, using the thresholded covariance matrices $C_{\mathbf{x}_i}^\tau$, as a function of τ. See text for details. (Color figure online)

slightly better than keeping all the positive eigenvalues. Although we show our analysis on a single example, we have found that this is the generally the case.

4   Second Step Denoising

The second step denoising is essentially a Wiener filter where the *a priori* statistics are estimated using the oracle image resulting from the first step. In addition, the oracle image is also used to define the set of similar patches $S_2(\mathbf{i})$. As in the first step, following Remark 1, all patches in $S_2(\mathbf{i})$ are denoised as proposed in (3). The *a priori* covariance matrix is estimated as the sample covariance matrix of the patches from the oracle image $C_{\widetilde{\mathbf{x}}_i}$, which are assumed noiseless. The coefficients of the resulting Wiener filter matrix on the basis of eigenvectors $U_{\widetilde{\mathbf{x}}_i}$ have the well-known expression $f(\lambda) = \lambda/(\lambda + \sigma^2)$.

Figure 7 shows a sample covariance matrix $C_{\widetilde{\mathbf{x}}_i}$ with its eigenvectors and eigenvalues, and the weights $f(\lambda_{\widetilde{\mathbf{x}}_i})$. The covariance matrix corresponds to the reference patch in Fig. 2. The filter weights concentrate their mass on the largest eigenvalues, which correspond to smooth eigenvalues. This is contrary to what happens in the first step, as shown in Fig. 2. Thus, unlike to the first step, eigenvectors with a random structure are much less present in the second step MAP estimates.

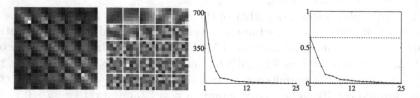

Fig. 7. For the same non-flat patch as in Fig. 2 we show, from left to right: sample covariance matrix $C_{\widetilde{\mathbf{x}}_i}$; its eigenvectors in raster order; the eigenvalues $\lambda_{\widetilde{\mathbf{x}}_i}$ and the resulting weighting function $f(\lambda_{\widetilde{\mathbf{x}}_i})$. Compare to the weights in Fig. 2.

The final denoised image is obtained by aggregation as described in Subsect. 3.2. Although the second step has a contribution to the quality of the final result, arguably most of the denoising is done in the first step, as can be seen by the Figs. 1, 3 and 4.

5 Discussion

Several patch-based methods for image denoising follow Bayesian approaches with a Gaussian (or GMM) prior for patches. The validity of the Gaussian model is questionable, but these methods produce state-of-the art results and are appealing due to their simplicity. In the case of NLB, the indefinite prior covariance estimate causes poor individual patch MAP estimates. However, they systematically lead to sets of pixel estimates whose mean (aggregate value) is visibly consistent. A good understanding of the NLB algorithm requires models that include the aggregation stage.

References

1. Aguerrebere, C., Almansa, A., Gousseau, Y., Musé, P.: A hyperprior Bayesian approach for solving image inverse problems. HAL (2016)
2. Arias, P., Morel, J.M.: Video denoising via empirical Bayesian estimation of space-time patches, January 2017, preprint. http://dev.ipol.im/pariasm/video_nlbayes/vnlb_files/vnlb_preprint.pdf
3. Aubert, G., Kornprobst, P.: Mathematical Problems in Image Processing, 2nd edn. Springer, Berlin (2006)
4. Buades, A., Lisani, J.L., Miladinović, M.: Patch-based video denoising with optical flow estimation. IEEE Trans. Image Process. 25(6), 2573–2586 (2016)
5. Chatterjee, P., Milanfar, P.: Patch-based near-optimal image denoising. IEEE Trans. Image Process. 21(4), 1635–1649 (2012)
6. Dabov, K., Foi, A., Katkovnik, V., Egiazarian, K.: BM3D image denoising with shape-adaptive principal component analysis. In: Proceedings of the Workshop on Signal Processing with Adaptive Sparse Structured Representations, pp. 1–7 (2009)
7. Dabov, K., Foi, A., Katkovnik, V., Egiazarian, K.: Image denoising by sparse 3D transform-domain collaborative filtering. IEEE Trans. IP 16(8), 2080–2095 (2007)
8. Deledalle, C.A., Salmon, J., Dalalyan, A.: Image denoising with patch based PCA: local versus global. In: Proceedings of the British Machine Vision Conference, pp. 25.1-25.10 (2011)
9. Guillemot, T., Almansa, A., Boubekeur, T.: Covariance trees for 2D and 3D processing. In: IEEE Conference on Computer Vision and Pattern Recognition, pp. 556–563 (2014)
10. Laus, F., Nikolova, M., Persch, J., Steidl, G.: A nonlocal denoising algorithm for manifold-valued images using second order statistics. SIAM J. Imaging Sci. 10, 416–448 (2017)
11. Lebrun, M., Buades, A., Morel, J.M.: Implementation of the "non-local Bayes" (NL-Bayes) image denoising algorithm. Image Process. Line 3, 1–42 (2013)
12. Lebrun, M., Buades, A., Morel, J.M.: A nonlocal Bayesian image denoising algorithm. SIAM J. Imaging Sci. 6(3), 1665–1688 (2013)

13. Lebrun, M., Colom, M., Buades, A., Morel, J.M.: Secrets of image denoising cuisine. Acta Numerica **21**, 475–576 (2012)
14. Lebrun, M., Colom, M., Morel, J.M.: The noise clinic: a blind image denoising algorithm. Image Process. Online (IPOL) **5**, 1–54 (2015)
15. Muresan, D.D., Parks, T.W.: Adaptive principal components and image denoising. In: Proceedings of the IEEE International Conference on Image Processing, vol. 1, pp. I-101–104, September 2003
16. Yaroslavsky, L.: Theoretical Foundations of Digital Imaging Using MATLAB. CRC Press, Boca Raton (2013)
17. Yu, G., Sapiro, G., Mallat, S.: Solving inverse problems with piecewise linear estimators: from Gaussian mixture models to structured sparsity. IEEE Trans. Image Process. **21**(5), 2481–2499 (2012)
18. Zhang, L., Dong, W., Zhang, D., Shi, G.: Two-stage image denoising by principal component analysis with local pixel grouping. Pattern Recogn. **43**(4), 1531–1549 (2010)
19. Zoran, D., Weiss, Y.: From learning models of natural image patches to whole image restoration. In: IEEE International Conference on Computer Vision (ICCV 2011), pp. 479–486, November 2011

Directional Total Generalized Variation Regularization for Impulse Noise Removal

Rasmus Dalgas Kongskov[✉] and Yiqiu Dong

Applied Mathematics and Computer Science at Technical University of Denmark,
Kongens Lyngby, Denmark
rara@dtu.dk

Abstract. A recently suggested regularization method, which combines directional information with total generalized variation (TGV), has been shown to be successful for restoring Gaussian noise corrupted images. We extend the use of this regularizer to impulse noise removal and demonstrate that using this regularizer for directional images is highly advantageous. In order to estimate directions in impulse noise corrupted images, which is much more challenging compared to Gaussian noise corrupted images, we introduce a new Fourier transform-based method. Numerical experiments show that this method is more robust with respect to noise and also more efficient than other direction estimation methods.

Keywords: Directional total generalized variation · Impulse noise · Variational methods · Regularization · Image restoration

1 Introduction

The use of variational methods is a successful way to improve image restoration by incorporating prior information through regularization, see e.g. [18,20,23,25]. For images corrupted by blurring and impulse noise, ℓ^1-fidelity-based variational models are effectively demonstrated their success as seen in [3,5,16,17,19,20]. In this paper, we will study restoration of impulse noise corrupted directional images.

An image $u \in \mathbb{R}^{N \times N}$ is assumed to be degraded as

$$f = \mathcal{N}(Au),$$

where A is a known blurring operator, $\mathcal{N}$ indicates degradation with impulse noise, and $f \in \mathbb{R}^{N \times N}$ is the degraded image. Impulse noise often appears due to e.g. transmission errors or malfunctioning pixels. Impulse noise is known for not degrading all image pixels, but only a part of them. The two most common types of impulse noise are salt-and-pepper noise and random-valued impulse noise. Let $\rho \in [0,1]$ be the noise-level. The model for impulse noise degradation at pixel (i,j) is

$$f_{i,j} = \begin{cases} b_{i,j}, & \text{with probability } \rho, \\ (Au)_{i,j}, & \text{with probability } 1 - \rho. \end{cases}$$

© Springer International Publishing AG 2017
F. Lauze et al. (Eds.): SSVM 2017, LNCS 10302, pp. 221–231, 2017.
DOI: 10.1007/978-3-319-58771-4_18

We assume the intensity range as $[0, 1]$. For salt-and-pepper noise, we have $b_{i,j} \in \{0, 1\}$ for all (i, j), while for random-valued impulse noise, $b_{i,j}$ is random and uniform distributed in $[0, 1]$. A variational model for restoring the impulse noise corrupted image takes the form

$$\min_u \|Au - f\|_1 + \mathcal{R}(u).$$

The choice of regularization term $\mathcal{R}$ should reflect what prior knowledge we have for the image u.

Total Variation (TV) is a very popular used regularization in image processing, which is corresponds to a piecewise constant prior [23]. The combination of ℓ^1 data-fitting and TV-regularization has been investigated for impulse noise in [5,7,16,20]. A drawback for TV-regularized methods is the so called staircasing effect, which can be successfully overcome by regularization with higher-order derivatives, e.g. Total Generalized Variation (TGV) regularization proposed in [2].

In series of applications, processing of images with a distinct main direction is typical. This could for example be different fibre materials such as carbon, glass optical fibres, see [13,24,27]. Images with a the texture following one main direction we dub directional images. Including the directional information in an image processing setting can highly improve the image quality and hence improve the material analysis.

TV-regularization has been combined with directional information for several applications and in various aspects, see [1,8–10,15,26]. Directionality has also been combined with second-order derivative regularization in [12] and with the first-order information of second-order TGV, see [11,22]. Recently in [14] a regularization method for restoring directional images has been introduced, which combines TGV with directional information estimated from the images. In [14] directional TGV (DTGV) is demonstrated to improve the quality of restorations in the case of Gaussian noise.

In this paper, we investigate DTGV-regularized variational methods for restoring impulse noise corrupted images. Under impulse noise, how to estimate the main direction is a big challenge. In order to obtain a robust direction estimation algorithm, we utilize the Fourier transform and propose a new algorithm. Numerical results show that the new direction estimation algorithm outperforms the one proposed in [14] under both impulse noise and Gaussian noise cases, and it is much more efficient due to the fast Fourier transform algorithm and non-iterative structure. With the estimated main direction, DTGV regularization is combined with the ℓ^1 data-fitting term. The minimization problem in the new variational model is solved by a primal-dual method [4]. The numerical results show that our method can successfully restore directional images by removing impulse noise and preserving the texture.

The rest of the paper is organized as follows. In Sect. 2, we briefly review DTGV regularization, and provide a new variational model for restoring directional images under impulse noise. Section 3 gives the new direction estimation algorithm, Sect. 4 gives a primal-dual algorithm for solving our restoration model. The numerical results shown in Sect. 5 demonstrate the efficiency of the new method. Finally, conclusions are drawn in Sect. 6.

2 ℓ^1-DTGV Model

In [14], the directional total generalized variaiton (DTGV) regularization, which is utilized to restore directional images, is proposed. Comparing with the TGV in [2], the idea behind DTGV relies on a change of the feasible set for the dual variable in the definition, i.e., the feasible set is turned from a spherical set into an elliptical set. This change leads to non-identical penalization along each directions. Further, in [14] it is shown that the change of the feasible set can be boiled down to the modification of the operators, which is much more implementation-friendly.

In this paper, we only consider the discrete case. Then, the discrete second order DTGV (DTGV_λ^2) of $u \in \mathbb{R}^{N \times N}$ can be written as:

$$\text{DTGV}_\lambda^2(u) = \min_{\mathbf{v} \in \mathbb{R}^{2N \times N}} \lambda_1 \sum_{i,j} |\Lambda_a R_{-\theta}(\nabla u)_{i,j} - \mathbf{v}_{i,j}|_2 + \lambda_0 \sum_{i,j} |(\widetilde{\mathcal{E}}\mathbf{v})_{i,j}|_F \quad (1)$$

where $\mathbf{v} = (v_1^\top, v_2^\top)^\top \in \mathbb{R}^{2N \times N}$ with $v_1, v_2 \in \mathbb{R}^{N \times N}$, $|\cdot|_F$ denotes Frobenius norm, and $\lambda = (\lambda_1, \lambda_2)^\top$ are positive parameters. Furthermore, the discrete gradient operator $\nabla \in \mathbb{R}^{2N \times N}$ is defined as

$$\nabla u = \begin{pmatrix} \nabla_{x_1} u \\ \nabla_{x_2} u \end{pmatrix},$$

where ∇_{x_1} and ∇_{x_2} are the derivatives along x_1 and x_2 directions, which are obtained by applying the forward finite difference scheme with symmetric boundary condition. In addition, Λ_a and R_θ are the scaling and rotation matrices

$$R_\theta = \begin{pmatrix} \cos\theta & -\sin\theta \\ \cos\theta & \sin\theta \end{pmatrix} \quad \text{and} \quad \Lambda_a = \begin{pmatrix} 1 & 0 \\ 0 & a \end{pmatrix},$$

and $\widetilde{\mathcal{E}}$ is the directional symmetrized derivative defined as:

$$(\widetilde{\mathcal{E}}\mathbf{v})_{i,j} = -\frac{1}{2}\left[\Lambda_a R_{-\theta}\begin{pmatrix} (\nabla_{x_1}^\top v_1)_{i,j} & (\nabla_{x_2}^\top v_1)_{i,j} \\ (\nabla_{x_1}^\top v_2)_{i,j} & (\nabla_{x_2}^\top v_2)_{i,j} \end{pmatrix} + \begin{pmatrix} (\nabla_{x_1}^\top v_1)_{i,j} & (\nabla_{x_1}^\top v_2)_{i,j} \\ (\nabla_{x_2}^\top v_1)_{i,j} & (\nabla_{x_2}^\top v_2)_{i,j} \end{pmatrix} R_\theta \Lambda_a\right].$$

Due to the scaling and rotation matrices, DTGV is rotationally variant, whereas TGV is rotationally invariant.

To remove impulse noise, the ℓ^1 data-fitting term in variational methods has been shown to be suitable [20]. For restoring directional images, with the prior information of the main texture direction, we combine the ℓ^1 data-fitting term with DTGV regularization and obtain the ℓ^1-DTGV model:

$$\min_{u \in \mathbb{R}^{N \times N}} \sum_{i,j} |(Au)_{i,j} - f_{i,j}| + \text{DTGV}_\lambda^2(u). \quad (2)$$

By using DTGV as regularization, the variances along the main direction θ will get more penalization than other directions.

3 Direction Estimation Algorithm

In DTGV, the directional parameter θ is very important. In [14] an algorithm for estimating the main direction from degraded images is presented, and it has been shown to work well for Gaussian noise up to a noise level around 30%. But since this algorithm has a lack of robustness with respect to high level Gaussian noise, it also cannot handle other more complicated types of noise, e.g. impulse noise. Moreover, this method requires solving a minimization problem iteratively, which reduces the computational efficiency. In this section, based on the Fourier transform we will propose a new direction estimation algorithm, which is much more robust with respect to noise and too more efficient.

The new algorithm is based on the fact that 2D Fourier basis functions can be seen as images with a significant main direction. After calculating the discrete 2D Fourier transform

$$c(\omega_1, \omega_2) = \mathcal{F}[f](\omega_1, \omega_2) = \sum_{i,j} f_{i,j} e^{-\frac{2\iota\pi}{N}(i\omega_1 + j\omega_2)} \quad \text{(imaginary unit : } \iota),$$

the magnitude of the complex coefficients, c, will provide information on the similarity between the image f and the individual directional basis-functions. If the image f indeed has one main direction, then it would resemble one or a combination of the basis-functions, and the amplitude(s) of the corresponding coefficient(s) would be relatively large. By finding the coefficients with the largest amplitude, we can obtain the main direction of the image. The Fourier based method is outlined in Algorithm 1.

Algorithm 1. Direction estimation algorithm

1: Input f.
2: Calculate Fourier transform of f: $c(\omega_1, \omega_2) = \mathcal{F}[f](\omega_1, \omega_2)$.
3: Find max-amplitude spatial frequencies: $(\omega_1^*, \omega_2^*) = \underset{(\omega_1, \omega_2)}{\mathrm{argmax}} |c(\omega_1, \omega_2)|$.
4: Estimate the direction from the spatial frequencies: $\theta = \tan^{-1}\left(\frac{\omega_2^*}{\max(\omega_1^*, \epsilon)}\right)$.
5: **return** θ.

Since a 2D Fourier transform is the only computational requirement, which can be calculated by the Fast Fourier transform, the new algorithm is highly efficient.

4 Numerical Algorithm

The objective function in (2) is convex, so convex optimization methods can be used to solve the minimization problem in (2). In this section, we apply a primal-dual method based on the work in [4] for solving (2).

According to the definition of DTGV_λ^2 in (1), we give the primal-dual formulation of (2):

$$\min_{u\in\mathcal{U},v\in\mathcal{V}} \max_{q\in\mathcal{Q},\mathbf{p}\in\mathcal{P},W\in\mathcal{W}} \langle Au-f,q\rangle + \sum_{i,j}\langle \Lambda_a R_{-\theta}[\nabla u]_{i,j} - \mathbf{v}_{i,j}, \mathbf{p}_{i,j}\rangle$$
$$+ \sum_{i,j}\langle (\tilde{\mathcal{E}}\mathbf{v})_{i,j}, W_{i,j}\rangle,$$

where $\mathcal{U}\in\mathbb{R}^{N\times N}$, $\mathcal{V}\in\mathbb{R}^{2N\times N}$, $\mathcal{Q} = \{q\in\mathcal{U} \mid |q_{i,j}|\leq 1 \text{ for } 1\leq i,j\leq N\}$, $\mathcal{P} = \{\mathbf{p}\in\mathcal{V} \mid |\mathbf{p}_{i,j}|_2\leq\lambda_1 \text{ for } 1\leq i,j\leq N\}$, $\mathcal{W} = \{W \mid W_{i,j} \text{ is a 2-by-2 symmetric matrix and } |W_{i,j}|_F\leq\lambda_0 \text{ for } 1\leq i,j\leq N\}$. This is a generic saddle-point problem, and in Algorithm 2 the primal-dual algorithm proposed in [4] is applied to solve the above optimization task.

In Algorithm 2, η is the dual step-size, τ is the primal step-size, A^* indicates the adjoint operator of A, and the projection operator is defined as

$$[\mathcal{S}_\lambda(\xi)]_{i,j} = \frac{\xi_{i,j}}{\max\left(1, \frac{|\xi_{i,j}|}{\lambda}\right)}.$$

If $\xi\in\mathcal{V}$, then $|\xi_{i,j}|$ is with 2-norm; and if $\xi\in\mathcal{W}$, then $|\xi_{i,j}|$ is with Frobenius norm.

5   Numerical Experiments

In this section, we provide numerical results to study the behavior of our method. We first compare the new direction estimation algorithm in Algorithm 1 with the one given in [14]. After this we compare our method, i.e., restoring directional images from the ℓ^1-DTGV_λ^2 model, with the one based on the ℓ^1-TGV_λ^2 model. All numerical experiments are carried out in Matlab on a laptop with a 2.9 GHz Intel Core i5 processor.

5.1   Direction Detection

Here, we use a simulated directional image as test image to compare the performance of the new direction estimation algorithm proposed in Algorithm 1 with the one from [14]. In Fig. 1 we test them on the image with up to 90% Gaussian noise, and in Fig 2 we test them on the image with up to 90% random-valued impulse noise.

Clearly, the new direction estimation algorithm is much more robust with respect to both kinds of noise. Moreover, it is much more efficient. Average time from 1000 runs on a 256×256 images is only 9 ms by the new algorithm, comparing of 407 ms by the one in [14], which is almost 45 times faster.

Algorithm 2. Primal-dual algorithm for solving ℓ^1-DTGV model

1: Require f, A, λ, a, θ and tol.

2: Estimate Lipschitz constant L, e.g. using power-method for A.

3: Initialize $u^0 = 0$, $\bar{u}^0 = 0$, $\mathbf{p}^0 = 0$, $q^0 = 0$, $\mathbf{v}^0 = 0$, $\bar{\mathbf{v}}^0 = 0$, $w^0 = 0$, $e^0 = 0$, $\eta < \frac{1}{\sqrt{L}}$, $\tau < \frac{1}{\sqrt{L}}$.

4: **while** $e^k >$ tol **do**

$$\mathbf{p}^{k+1} = \arg\max_{\mathbf{p} \in \mathcal{P}} \left\langle \widetilde{\nabla} \bar{u}^k - \bar{\mathbf{v}}^k, \mathbf{p} \right\rangle - \frac{1}{2\eta} \|\mathbf{p} - \mathbf{p}^k\|_2^2$$

$$= \mathcal{S}_{\lambda_1}\left(\mathbf{p}^k + \eta\left(\widetilde{\nabla}\bar{u}^k - \bar{\mathbf{v}}^k\right)\right)$$

$$W^{k+1} = \arg\max_{W \in \mathcal{W}} \left\langle \widetilde{\mathcal{E}}\bar{\mathbf{v}}^k, W \right\rangle - \frac{1}{2\eta}\|W - W^k\|_F^2$$

$$= \mathcal{S}_{\lambda_0}\left(W^k + \eta\widetilde{\mathcal{E}}\bar{\mathbf{v}}^k\right)$$

$$q^{k+1} = \arg\max_{q \in \mathcal{Q}} \left\langle A\bar{u}^k - f, q \right\rangle - \frac{1}{2\eta}\|q - q^k\|_2^2$$

$$= \mathcal{S}_1\left(q^k + \eta(A\bar{u}^k - f)\right)$$

$$u^{k+1} = \arg\min_{u \in \mathcal{U}} \left\langle Au, q^{k+1} \right\rangle + \left\langle \widetilde{\nabla}u, \mathbf{p}^{k+1} \right\rangle + \frac{1}{2\tau}\|u - u^k\|_2^2$$

$$= u^k + \tau\left(\widetilde{\mathrm{div}}\,\mathbf{p}^{k+1} - A^*q^{k+1}\right)$$

$$\mathbf{v}^{k+1} = \arg\min_{\mathbf{v} \in \mathcal{V}} -\left\langle \mathbf{v}, \mathbf{p}^{k+1} \right\rangle + \left\langle \widetilde{\mathcal{E}}\mathbf{v}, W^{k+1} \right\rangle + \frac{1}{2\tau}\|\mathbf{v} - \mathbf{v}^k\|_2^2$$

$$= \mathbf{v}^k + \tau\left(\mathbf{p}^{k+1} + \widetilde{\mathrm{div}}\,W^{k+1}\right)$$

$$\bar{u}^{k+1} = 2u^{k+1} - u^k$$

$$\bar{\mathbf{v}}^{k+1} = 2\mathbf{v}^{k+1} - \mathbf{v}^k$$

$$e^{k+1} = \frac{\|u^k - u^{k+1}\|_2}{\|u^k\|_2}$$

end while

5: **return** u^{k+1}.

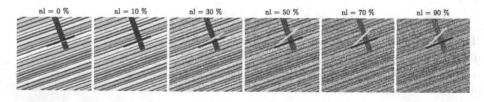

Fig. 1. Estimating the main direction in the test images with additive Gaussian noise ("nl" denotes the noise level). The colored lines indicates the estimated direction by using the method in [14] (red) and the new method (blue). (Color figure online)

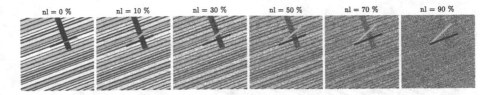

Fig. 2. Estimating the main direction in the test images with random-valued impulse noise ("nl" denotes the noise level). The colored lines indicates the estimated direction by using the method in [14] (red) and the new method (blue). (Color figure online)

5.2   Image Denosing and Deblurring

In this section, we examine the difference between using TGV^2_λ and DTGV^2_λ as regularizers combined with a ℓ^1-data fidelity term for restoring images corrupted by impulse noise.

In DTGV, except the main direction parameter θ, there are another three parameters: the scaling parameter a and the regularization parameter $\lambda = (\lambda_0, \lambda_1)$. The scaling parameter a demonstrates to what extent the textures in images following the main direction. If $a = 1$, DTGV becomes identical to the rotation invariant TGV. Due to the good performance of the direction estimation algorithm, as suggested in [14] we choose a relatively small, saying $a < 0.3$. In addition, same as the TGV in [2], we fix the ratio $\frac{\lambda_0}{\lambda_1}$ as 2, which commonly yeilds good restoration results. All the numerical results shown here are the ones with the highest peak-signal-to-noise-ratio (PSNR) values after adjusting the parameters λ_1 and $a \in (0, 0.3)$.

The first denoising experiment is using a 512×512 test image, which is corrupted by the salt-and-pepper noise with the noise level as 30%, 50% and 70%, respectively. In Fig. 3 the restored results from both regularizers are presented. It is obvious that the DTGV reglurizer provides better results, and the improvement of the PSNR values is even more than 10 dB. But in the dark region perpendicular to the main direction we see some artifacts from the DTGV regularization. It is due to the diffusion of the different intensities along the main direction.

In the second denoising experiment, a real bamboo image is used (253×253 pixels). In this image the main direction varies smoothly throughout the image within a range of about $15°$. Here, we test our method and the one based on ℓ^1-TGV model for removing random valued impulse noise, which is much more difficult than the salt-and-pepper noise. The best-PSNR results are shown in Fig. 4. As seen restoring a real image with random-valued impulse noise is a harder problem for both methods, but the improvement of using DTGV is again clear, both visually and quantitively. Since in the DTGV regularizer we only consider one main direction, the variation of the directional is not taken into account, which leads to some line artifacts.

The deblurring and denoising experiment is also with the bamboo image. Here, we consider the Gaussian blurring with standard deviation $\sigma = 2$ and the

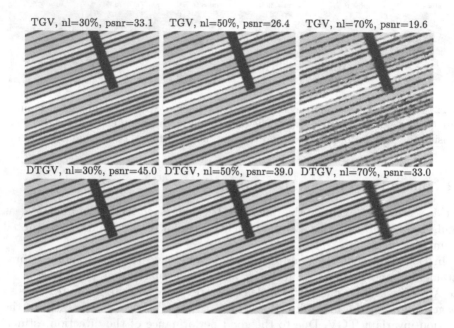

Fig. 3. Denoising results from the salt-and-pepper noise corrupted images.

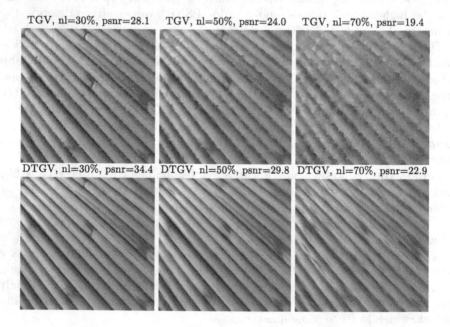

Fig. 4. Denoising results for a real image corrupted by random-valued impulse noise.

TGV, nl=30%, psnr=34.0   TGV, nl=50%, psnr=29.7   TGV, nl=70%, psnr=22.1

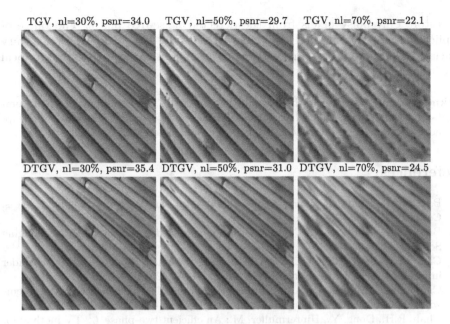

Fig. 5. Restoration results for blur images with random-valued impulse noise.

random valued impulse noise. The best-PSNR results are shown in Fig. 5. Our method with DTGV regularization gives the highest PSNR values in all three different noise level cases. The visual difference also can be observed, especially in high noise level cases.

6 Conclusions

In this paper, we apply a recently proposed directional regularization, DTGV, on image restoration under impulse noise. By combining DTGV with ℓ^1 data-fitting term, we give a new ℓ^1-DTGV variational model. In order to estimate the main direction directly from impulse noise corrupted images, which is much more challenging than Gaussian noise case, we propose a new direction estimation algorithm based on the Fourier transform. The new algorithm is much more robust with respect to the noise, and furthermore also much more efficient than a previously suggested algorithm in [14]. The numerical results show that our DTGV-regularized method improve the TGV-based method on restoring impulse-noise-corrupted directional images significantly. Hence, there is a high advantage of incorporating the direction information into the regularization for directional image restoration.

In order to further improve the restoration results, especially in high noise level cases, in the future we intend to extend our method to the two-phase approach, referring to the work in [3,5,6,21]. That is, in the first phase we distinguish the noisy pixels, and then in the second phase we utilize the variational method to restore only noisy pixels from the detected noise-free pixels. The range of applications for this method could be extended by letting the direction vary spatially, which would require a reliable, e.g. adaptive, way to estimate local directions.

Acknowledgments. The authors would like to thank the reviewers for their comments and suggestions, which has helped to improve this article. The work was supported by Advanced Grant 291405 from the European Research Council.

References

1. Bayram, I., Kamasak, M.E.: A directional total variation. Eur. Signal Process. Conf. **19**(12), 265–269 (2012)
2. Bredies, K., Kunisch, K., Pock, T.: Total generalized variation. SIAM J. Imaging Sci. **3**(3), 492–526 (2010)
3. Cai, J.F., Chan, R.H., Nikolova, M.: Fast two-phase image deblurring under impulse noise. J. Math. Imaging Vis. **36**(1), 46–53 (2010)
4. Chambolle, A., Pock, T.: A first-order primal-dual algorithm for convex problems with applications to imaging. J. Math. Imaging Vis. **40**(1), 120–145 (2011)
5. Chan, R.H., Dong, Y., Hintermuller, M.: An efficient two-phase L^1-TV method for restoring blurred images with impulse noise. IEEE Trans. Image Process. **19**(7), 1731–1739 (2010)
6. Chan, R.H., Ho, C.W., Nikolova, M.: Salt-and-pepper noise removal by median-type noise detectors and detail-preserving regularization. IEEE Trans. Image Process. 14(10), 1479–1485 (2005)
7. Dong, Y., Hintermüller, M., Neri, M.: An efficient primal-dual method for L^1TV image restoration. SIAM J. Imaging Sci. **2**(4), 1168–1189 (2009)
8. Easley, G.R., Labate, D., Colonna, F.: Shearlet-based total variation diffusion for denoising. IEEE Trans. Image Process. **18**(2), 260–268 (2009)
9. Estellers, V., Soatto, S., Bresson, X.: Adaptive regularization with the structure tensor. IEEE Trans. Image Process. **24**(6), 1777–1790 (2015)
10. Fei, X., Wei, Z., Xiao, L.: Iterative directional total variation refinement for compressive sensing image reconstruction. Signal Process. Lett. IEEE **20**(11), 1070–1073 (2013)
11. Ferstl, D., Reinbacher, C., Ranftl, R., Ruether, M., Bischof, H.: Image guided depth upsampling using anisotropic total generalized variation. Proc. IEEE International Conference on Computer Vision, pp. 993–1000 (2013)
12. Hafner, D., Schroers, C., Weickert, J.: Introducing maximal anisotropy into second order coupling models. Ger. Conf. Pattern Recognit. **9358**, 79–90 (2015)
13. Jespersen, K.M., Zangenberg, J., Lowe, T., Withers, P.J., Mikkelsen, L.P.: Fatigue damage assessment of uni-directional non-crimp fabric reinforced polyester composite using X-ray computed tomography. Compos. Sci. Technol. **136**, 94–103 (2016)
14. Kongskov, R.D., Dong, Y., Knudsen, K.: Directional Total Generalized Variation Regularization. submitted (2017). http://arxiv.org/abs/1701.02675
15. Lefkimmiatis, S., Roussos, A., Maragos, P., Unser, M.: Structure tensor total variation. SIAM J. Imaging Sci. **8**(2), 1090–1122 (2015)
16. Ma, L., Ng, M., Yu, J., Zeng, T.: Efficient box-constrained TV-type-l1 algorithms for restoring images with impulse noise. J. Comput. Math. **31**(3), 249–270 (2013)

17. Ma, L., Yu, J., Zeng, T.: Sparse representation prior and total variation-based image deblurring under impulse noise. SIAM J. Imaging Sci. 6(4), 2258–2284 (2013)
18. Mumford, D., Shah, J.: Optimal approximations by piecewise smooth functions and associated variational problems. Commun. Pure Appl. Math. 42(5), 577–685 (1989)
19. Nikolova, M.: Minimizers of cost-functions involving nonsmooth data-fidelity terms. Application to the processing of outliers. Siam J. Numer. Anal. 40(3), 965–994 (2003)
20. Nikolova, M.: A variational approach to remove outliers and impulse noise. J. Math. Imaging Vis. 20(1–2), 99–120 (2004)
21. Nikolova, M., Chan, R.H., Cai, J.F.: Two-phase approach for deblurring images corrupted by impulse plus Gaussian noise. Inverse Probl. Imaging 2(2), 187–204 (2008)
22. Ranftl, R., Gehrig, S., Pock, T., Bischof, H.: Pushing the limits of stereo using variational stereo estimation. IEEE Intell. Veh. Symp. Proc. 1, 401–407 (2012)
23. Rudin, L.I., Osher, S., Fatemi, E.: Nonlinear total variation based noise removal algorithms. Phys. D Nonlinear Phenom. 60(1–4), 259–268 (1992)
24. Sandoghchi, S.R., Jasion, G.T., Wheeler, N.V., Jain, S., Lian, Z., Wooler, J.P., Boardman, R.P., Baddela, N.K., Chen, Y., Hayes, J.R., Fokoua, E.N., Bradley, T., Gray, D.R., Mousavi, S.M., Petrovich, M.N., Poletti, F., Richardson, D.J.: X-ray tomography for structural analysis of microstructured and multimaterial optical fibers and preforms. Opt. Express 22(21), 26181 (2014)
25. Tikhonov, A.N., Arsenin, V.I.: Solutions of ill-posed problmes. Winston, Philadelphia (1977)
26. Turgay, E., Akar, G.B.: Directionally adaptive super-resolution. In: 2009 16th IEEE International Conference on Image Processing vol. 1, 1201–1204 (2009)
27. Zhang, Z., Hartwig, G.: Relation of damping and fatigue damage of unidirectional fibre composites. Int. J. Fatigue 24(7), 713–718 (2002)

Tomographic Reconstruction

A Novel Convex Relaxation for Non-binary Discrete Tomography

Jan Kuske[1(✉)], Paul Swoboda[2], and Stefania Petra[1]

[1] MIG, Institute of Applied Mathematics, Heidelberg University,
Heidelberg, Germany
jan.kuske@iwr.uni-heidelberg.de
[2] Institute of Science and Technology (IST) Austria, Klosterneuburg, Austria

Abstract. We present a novel convex relaxation and a corresponding inference algorithm for the non-binary discrete tomography problem, that is, reconstructing discrete-valued images from few linear measurements. In contrast to state of the art approaches that split the problem into a continuous reconstruction problem for the linear measurement constraints and a discrete labeling problem to enforce discrete-valued reconstructions, we propose a joint formulation that addresses both problems simultaneously, resulting in a tighter convex relaxation. For this purpose a constrained graphical model is set up and evaluated using a novel relaxation optimized by dual decomposition. We evaluate our approach experimentally and show superior solutions both mathematically (tighter relaxation) and experimentally in comparison to previously proposed relaxations.

1 Introduction

We study the discrete tomography problem, that is reconstructing a discrete-valued image from a small number of linear measurements (tomographic projections), see Fig. 1 for an illustration. The main difficulty in reconstructing the original image is that there are usually far too few measurements, making the problem ill-posed. Hence, it is common to search for a discrete-valued image that (i) satisfies the measurements and (ii) minimizes an appropriate energy function.

More generally, the discrete tomography problem can be regarded as reconstructing a *discrete-valued synthesis/analysis-sparse* signal from few measurements which is observed by *deterministic* sensors A. This is, in turn, a special instance of the compressed sensing problem [7], for which it has been shown that discreteness constraints on the possible values of the reconstructed function can significantly reduce the number of required measurements [10].

Acknowledgments: We gratefully acknowledge support by the DFG (German Science Foundation), Grant GRK 1653. This work is partially funded by the European Research Council under the European Unions 7th Framework Programme (FP7/2007-2013)/ERC grant agreement no 616160. The authors would like to thank Vladimir Kolmogorov for helpful discussions.

F. Lauze et al. (Eds.): SSVM 2017, LNCS 10302, pp. 235–246, 2017.
DOI: 10.1007/978-3-319-58771-4_19

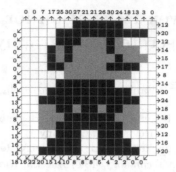

Fig. 1. Examplary discrete tomography example on three-valued image (white = 0, gray = 1, black = 2) with three projection directions: horizontal, vertical and diagonal (right upper to lower left). Horizontal sums are written on the right, vertical sums on the top and diagonal sums on the left and bottom.

However, the discreteness constraint leads to great computational challenges. Simple outer convex relaxations coming from continuous scenarios are doomed to fail, as they will not output discrete solutions, unless the signal sparsity satisfies favourable relations and A is well-conditioned on the class of sparse signals, e.g. a random matrix. In fact, in most practical scenarios the projection matrices fall short of assumptions that underlie rigorous compressed sensing theory (like e.g. the restricted isometry property [7]), and standard algorithms from the continuous ℓ_1-setting cannot be applied any more. Rounding continuous solutions will on the other hand render the solutions infeasible for the measurement constraints.

Therefore, algorithms exploiting the *combinatorial structure* of the discrete tomography problem are necessary to successfully exploit discreteness as prior knowledge and to reduce the number of required measurements.

Related Work. Several algorithms have been proposed to solve the discrete tomography problem. Among them are (i) linear programming-based algorithms [9,17], (ii) belief propagation [8], (iii) network flow techniques [3], (iv) convex-concave programming [14,19] (v) evolutionary algorithms [2] and other heuristic algorithms [4,6,11,12]. Not all approaches are applicable to the general discrete tomography problem we treat here: algorithms [6,8,9,11,12,17] only support binary labels, while [3,4] solves only the feasiblity problem and does not permit any energy. Algorithms [14,19] are applicable to the setting we propose but are purely primal algorithms and do not output dual lower bounds (which we do). Hence, one cannot judge proximity of solutions computed by [14,19] to global optimal ones, prohibiting its use in branch and bound. In case convex relaxations were considered [3,9,17,19], they were less tight than the one we propose, leading to inferior dual bounds.

Contribution. We propose the (to our knowledge) first LP-based algorithm for the non-binary discrete tomography problem. In particular, we

– recast the discrete tomography problem as a Maximum-A-Posteriori inference problem in a graphical model with additional linear constraints coming from the tomographic projections in Sect. 2,

- construct higher order factors in the graphical model such that a feasible solution to the higher order factors coincides with solutions feasible for the tomographic projections and
- present an efficient exact algorithm for solving the special case when exactly one ray constraint is present and the energy factorizes as a chain (such a problem will be called a one-dimensional discrete tomography problem) in Sect. 3,
- decompose the whole problem into such subproblems and solve this decomposition with bundle methods in Sect. 4.

Our approach leads to significantly tighter bounds as compared to generalising previously proposed relaxations to the non-binary case, see Proposition 1 in Sect. 4 and experiments in Sect. 5. Code and datasets are available on GitHub[1].

Notation. Let $[a, b] = \{a, \ldots, b\}$ be the set of natural numbers between a and b. For $x \in \mathbb{R}$ we denote by $\lfloor x \rfloor$ and $\lceil x \rceil$ the floor and ceiling function.

2   Problem Statement

The discrete tomography problem we study consists in finding a discrete labeling $x \in \{0, 1, \ldots, k-1\}^n$ such that (i) tomographic projection constraints given by $Ax = b$ with $A \in \{0,1\}^{m \times n}, b \in \mathbb{N}^m$ are fulfilled and (ii) x minimizes some *energy* $E : \{0, 1, \ldots, k-1\}^n \to \mathbb{R}$. We assume that E factorizes according to a pairwise graphical model: given a graph $G = (V, E)$, together with a *label space* $\mathcal{X}_V := \prod_{u \in V} \mathcal{X}_u, \mathcal{X}_u := \{0, 1 \ldots, k-1\} \; \forall u \in V$, the energy is a sum of *unary potentials* $\theta_u : \mathcal{X}_u \to \mathbb{R} \; \forall u \in V$ and *pairwise* ones $\theta_{uv} : \mathcal{X}_u \times \mathcal{X}_v \to \mathbb{R} \; \forall uv \in E$. The full problem hence reads

$$\min_{x \in \mathcal{X}_V} E(x) := \sum_{u \in V} \theta_u(x_u) + \sum_{uv \in E} \theta_{uv}(x_u, x_v) \quad \text{s.t.} \quad Ax = b. \tag{1}$$

For the discrete tomography problem we usually choose G to be a grid graph corresponding to the pixels of the image to be reconstructed, zero unary potentials $\theta_u \equiv 0 \; \forall u \in V$, **as no local information about the image values is known**, and pairwise potentials $\theta_{uv} = g(x_u - x_v)$ penalize intensity transitions, e.g. $g(\cdot) = |\cdot|$ (TV) or $g(\cdot) = \min(1, |\cdot|)$ (Potts). Such choice of pairwise potentials assigns small energy to labelings x with a regular spatial structure.

3   One-Dimensional Non-binary Discrete Tomography

A natural decomposition of the discrete tomography problem (1) consists of (i) considering a subproblem for each ray constraint separately and (ii) joining them together via Lagrangian variables. We will study the first aspect below and the second one in the next section. In particular, let $U = \{u_1, \ldots, u_n\} \subseteq V$ be

---

[1] https://github.com/pawelswoboda/LP_MP

the variables from a single ray constraint $x_{u_1} + \ldots + x_{u_n} = b$ corresponding to a row of the projection matrix A in (1). Assume that pairwise potentials form a chain, i.e. they are $\theta_{u_i u_{i+1}}$, $i = 1, \ldots, n-1$. The *one-dimensional discrete tomography problem* is

$$\min_{(x_1,\ldots,x_n) \in \mathcal{X}_U} \sum_{u \in U} \theta_u(x_u) + \sum_{i \in [n-1]} \theta_{u_i, u_{i+1}}(x_{u_i}, x_{u_{i+1}})$$

$$\text{s.t.} \sum_{u \in U} x_u = b. \tag{2}$$

We present an exact linear programming relaxation and an efficient message-passing routine to solve (2) below.

3.1   Linear Programming Model

The one-dimensional discrete tomography subproblem (2) could naively be solved by dynamic programming by going over all variables $u_1, \ldots, u_n$ sequentially. This however would entail quadratic space complexity in the number of nodes in U, as the state space for variable u_i would need to include costs for all possible labels x_{u_i} and all values of the intermediate sum $\sum_{j=1}^{i-1} x_{u_j}$. The latter sum can have $1 + \sum_{j=1}^{i-1}(|\mathcal{X}| - 1)$ possible values. To achieve a better space complexity, we will recursively (i) equipartition variables $u_1, \ldots, u_n$, (ii) define LP-subproblems in terms of so-called *counting factors* which are exact on each subpartition and (iii) join them together to eventually obtain an exact LP-relaxation for (2). Our approach is inspired by [16].

Partition of Variables. Given the nodes $u_1, \ldots, u_n$, we choose an equipartition $\Pi_1 = \{u_1, \ldots, u_{\lfloor n/2 \rfloor}\}$ and $\Pi_2 = \{u_{\lfloor n/2 \rfloor+1}, \ldots, u_n\}$. We recursively equipartition Π_1 into $\Pi_{1,1}$ and $\Pi_{1,2}$ and do likewise for Π_2. For $u_1, \ldots, u_8$ we obtain a recursive partitioning as in Fig. 2.

Counting Factors. Given an interval, a *counting factor* holds the states of its left and right end and the value of the intermediate sum.

Definition 1 (Counting label space). *The counting label space for interval* $[i, j]$ *is* $\mathcal{X}_{i:j} := \mathcal{X}_{u_i} \times \mathcal{S}_{i:j} \times \mathcal{X}_{u_j}$ *with* $\mathcal{S}_{i:j} = \{0, 1, \ldots, 1 + \sum_{l=i+1}^{j-1}(|\mathcal{X}_{u_l}| - 1)\}$ *holding all possible intermediate sums. A counting label* $x_{i:j}$ *consists of the three components* $(x_{u_i}, s_{i:j}, x_{u_j})$: *its left endpoint label* x_{u_i}, *intermediate sum* $s_{i:j} :=$ $x_{u_{i+1}} + \ldots + x_{u_{j-1}}$ *and right endpoint label* x_{u_j}.

See again Fig. 2 for the exemplary case $U = \{u_1, \ldots, u_8\}$.

For interval $[i, j]$ there are $|\mathcal{X}_{i:j}| = |\mathcal{X}_{u_i}| \cdot |\mathcal{X}_{u_j}| \cdot |\mathcal{S}_{i:j}|$ distinct counting labels. We associate to each counting factor *counting marginals* $\mu_{i:j}$ satisfying $\{\mu_{i:j} \in \mathbb{R}_+^{|\mathcal{X}_{i:j}|} : \sum_{x_{i:j} \in \mathcal{X}_{i:j}} \mu_{i:j}(x_{i:j}) = 1\}$.

Assuming an uniform label space $|\mathcal{X}_u| = k$ $\forall u \in V$, the total space complexity of all counting factors is $O(k^3 \cdot n \cdot \log(n))$, hence subquadratic in the number of nodes in U.

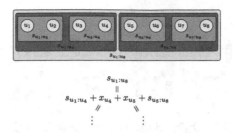

$$s_{u_1:u_8}$$
$$\parallel$$
$$s_{u_1:u_4} + x_{u_4} + x_{u_5} + s_{u_5:u_8}$$
$$\diagup\diagup \qquad\qquad \diagdown\diagdown$$
$$\vdots \qquad\qquad\qquad \vdots$$

Fig. 2. *Partition of variables:* The chain of variables $U = \{u_1, \ldots, u_8\}$ (red boxes) is first partitioned into $\Pi_1 = \{u_1, u_2, u_3, u_4\}, \Pi_2 = \{u_5, u_6, u_7, u_8\}$ (blue boxes), and then into $\Pi_{1,1} = \{u_1, u_2\}, \Pi_{1,2} = \{u_3, u_4\}, \Pi_{2,1} = \{u_5, u_6\}, \Pi_{2,2} = \{u_7, u_8\}$ (green boxes). *Counting sums:* The topmost sum $s_{u_1:u_8} = x_{u_2} + \ldots + x_{u_7}$ is composed of sums $s_{1:4}$ for partition Π_1 and $s_{5:8}$ for Π_2. Subsums are generated recursively for $s_{1:4}$ and $_{5:8}$ again. (Color figure online)

Joining Counting Factors. Assume the partitioning of variables has produced two adjacent subsets $\Pi = \{u_i, \ldots, u_j\}$ and $\Pi' = \{u_{j+1}, \ldots, u_l\}$, which were constructed from their common subset $\Pi \cup \Pi' \subseteq U$. The associated three counting factors with marginals $\mu_{i:j}, \mu_{j+1:l}$ and $\mu_{i:l}$ introduced above shall be consistent with respect to each other.

Definition 2 (Label consistency). *Label $x_{i:l} \in \mathcal{X}_{i:l}$, $x_{i:j} \in \mathcal{X}_{i:j}$ and $x_{j+1:l}$ are consistent with each other, denoted by $x_{i:j}, x_{j+1:l} \sim x_{i:l}$ iff (i) left endpoint labels of $x_{i:j}$ and $x_{i:l}$ match, (ii) right endpoint labels of $x_{j+1:l}$ and $x_{i:l}$ match and (ii) intermediate sums match $s_{i:l} = s_{i:j} + x_{u_j} + x_{u_{j+1}} + s_{j+1:l}$.*

We enforce this by introducing a *higher order marginal* $\mu_{i:j:l} \in \mathbb{R}_+^{\mathcal{X}_{i:j} \times \mathcal{X}_{j+1:l}}$ to bind together $\mu_{i:j}, \mu_{j+1:l}$ and $\mu_{i:l}$.

$$\sum_{x_{j+1:l}} \mu_{i:j:l}(x_{i:j}, x_{j+1:l}) = \mu_{i:j}(x_{i:j}) \qquad \forall x_{i:j} \in \mathcal{X}_{i:j} \quad (3)$$

$$\sum_{x_{i:j}} \mu_{i:j:l}(x_{i:j}, x_{j+1:l}) = \mu_{j+1:l}(x_{j+1:l}) \qquad \forall x_{j+1:l} \in \mathcal{X}_{j+1:l} \quad (4)$$

$$\sum_{x_{i:j}, x_{j+1:l} \sim x_{i:l}} \mu_{i:j:l}(x_{i:j}, x_{j+1:l}) = \mu_{i:l}(x_{i:l}) \qquad \forall x_{i:l} \in \mathcal{X}_{i:l} \quad (5)$$

The recursive arrangement of counting factors is illustrated in Fig. 3.

Remark 1. The constraints between $\mu_{i:j:l}$ and $\mu_{i:j}$ and $\mu_{j+1:l}$ are analogous to the marginalization constraints between pairwise and unary marginals in the local polytope relaxation for pairwise graphical models [18]. The constraints between $\mu_{i:j:l}$ and $\mu_{i:l}$ however are different. Hence, specialized efficient solvers for inference in graphical models cannot be applied.

Costs. Above we have described the polytope for the one-dimensional discrete tomography problem (2). The LP-objective consists of vectors $\theta_{i:j}$ for each

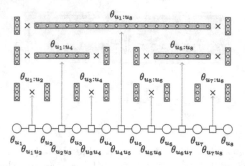

Fig. 3. Illustration of the tree construction used for solving the one-dimensional tomography problem (2) with $\ell = 3$, i.e. three labels. On the bottom is the original chain, above it are three layers of counting factors. Each counting factor keeps track of the label x_u (left vertical bar), x_v (right vertical bar) and the intermediate sum $\sum_{w \in U:u<w<v} x_w$ (middle horizontal bar).

counting marginal and $\theta_{i:j:l}$ for each higher order marginal. Accounting for the pairwise costs in (2) we set $\theta_{i:j}(x_{i:j}) := \begin{cases} \theta_{u_i u_j}(x_{u_i}, x_{u_j}), & i+1 = j \\ 0, & \text{otherwise} \end{cases}$ for the counting factors and for the higher order factors we set $\theta_{i:j:l}(x_{i:j}, x_{j+1:l}) := \theta_{u_j u_{j+1}}(x_{u_j}, x_{u_{j+1}})$. For the projection constraint in (2) we set costs of the top counting marginal as $\theta_{1:n}(x_{1:n}) := \begin{cases} 0, & x_{u_1} + s_{1:n} + x_{u_n} = b \\ \infty, & \text{otherwise} \end{cases}$.

3.2 Message Passing Algorithm

Above we have introduced a linear program formulation for the one-dimensional discrete tomography problem (2). While it is possible to solve it with a standard LP-solver, doing so would be slow. As the counting factors and the higher order marginals connecting them form a tree, it is possible to devise a message passing algorithm optimizing (2) exactly. First, this implies that the linear programming relaxation for (2) is exact, as message passing amounts to optimizing the Lagrangian dual of this same relaxation. Second, marginals do not need to be held explicitly, holding messages is enough. The size of all messages equals the size of all counting factors, hence giving again subquadratic space complexity.

Message passing for (2) is detailed in Algorithm 1. It proceeds by first computing *up messages* from adjacent fine subsets to coarser subsets (i.e. going up the tree in Fig. 3) and afterwards computing *down messages* from coarse subsets to their equipartition (i.e. going down the tree in Fig. 3). Messages reparametrize costs of counting and higher order factors.

Reparametrization. Let indices $i < j < l$ be given, where $[i : j]$, $[j + 1 : l]$ and $[i : l]$ are subsets generated by the recursive partitioning. Let messages $\phi_{i:j:l}^{\leftarrow}, \phi_{i:j:l}^{\rightarrow}, \phi_{i:j:l}^{\uparrow}$ correspond to constraints (3), (4) and (5) respectively. Messages ϕ act on (reparametrize) costs θ as

$$\theta^{\phi}_{i:j:l}(x_{i:j}, x_{j+1:l}) \mathrel{+}= \phi^{\leftarrow}_{i:j:l}(x_{i:j}) \qquad\qquad \theta^{\phi}_{i:j}(x_{i:j}) \mathrel{-}= \phi^{\leftarrow}_{i:j:l}(x_{i:j}) \qquad (6)$$

$$\theta^{\phi}_{i:j:l}(x_{i:j}, x_{j+1:l}) \mathrel{+}= \phi^{\rightarrow}_{i:j:l}(x_{j+1:l}) \qquad \theta^{\phi}_{j+1:l}(x_{j+1:l}) \mathrel{-}= \phi^{\rightarrow}_{i:j:l}(x_{j+1:l}) \qquad (7)$$

$$\theta^{\phi}_{i:j:l}(x_{i:j}, x_{j+1:l}) \mathrel{+}= \phi^{\uparrow}_{i:l}(x_{i:l}) \qquad\qquad \theta^{\phi}_{i:l}(x_{i:l}) \mathrel{-}= \phi^{\uparrow}_{i:j:l}(x_{i:l}) \qquad (8)$$

Algorithm 1. Message passing for one-dimensional discrete tomography

---

1 **Up messages:**
2 **for** $[i, j] \cup [j + 1, l] = [i, l] \in \Pi$ *in ascending order* **do**
3      $\phi^{\leftarrow}_{i:j:l} = \theta_{i:j}$
     $\phi^{\rightarrow}_{i:j:l} = \theta_{j+1:l}$ // Send messages to higher order counting factor $\theta^{\phi}_{i:j:l}$
4      $\phi^{\uparrow}_{i:j:l}(x_{i:l}) = \min\limits_{x_{i:j}, x_{j+1:l} \sim x_{i:l}} \theta^{\phi}_{i:j:l}(x_{i:j}, x_{j+1:l})$ // Send message from higher
    // order to counting factor $\theta^{\phi}_{i:l}$
5 **end**
6 $x^*_{1:n} \in \arg\min_{x_{1:n} \in \mathcal{X}_{1:n}} \theta_{1:n}(x_{1:n})$;   // optimum of top counting factor
7 **Down messages:**
8 **for** $[i, j] \cup [j + 1, l] = [i, l] \in \Pi$ *in descending order* **do**
9      $\phi^{\uparrow}_{i:j:l} = \theta_{i:j:l}$;   // Send message to higher order factor
10      $x^*_{i:j}, x^*_{j+1:l} \in \arg\min\limits_{x_{i:j}, x_{j+1:l} \sim x^*_{i:l}} \theta^{\phi}_{i:j:l}(x_{i:j}, x_{j+1:l})$;   // compute optimal labels
11 **end**

Fast Message Computation. Naively computing one up messages would result in time complexity $O(\ell^5 \cdot n^2)$, which would make the algorithm prohibitively slow. We will describe a fast message computation technique for (3), which uses the structure of the corresponding linear constraints (5) and relies on the latent factorization of $\theta^{\phi}_{i:j:l}$. Specifically, when we fix the endpoints x_{u_i}, x_{u_j} of interval $[i, j]$ and $x_{u_{j+1}}, x_{u_l}$ of $[j + 1, l]$, (3) becomes

$$\phi^{\uparrow}_{i:j:l}(x_{i:l}) = \min_{s_{i:j} + s_{j+1:l} = s_{i:l} - x_{u_j} - x_{u_j}} \theta_{u_j, u_{j+1}}(x_{u_j}, x_{u_{j+1}}) + \phi^{\leftarrow}_{i:j}(x_{i:j}) + \phi^{\rightarrow}_{j+1:l}(x_{j+1:l}), \quad (9)$$

Problem (9) is an instance of the min-sum convolution problem: Given $a, b \in \mathbb{R}^n$, compute $c \in \mathbb{R}^{2n-1}$, where $c_i = \min_{j \le i}(a_j + b_{i-j})$. This can be seen by replacing $\phi^{\leftarrow}$ by a, $\phi^{\rightarrow}$ by b and noting that $\theta_{u_j, u_{j+1}}$ is a constant, as x_{u_j} and $x_{u_{j+1}}$ were fixed. For the min-sum convolution problem efficient algorithms [5] were proposed with expected running time $O(n \log(n))$ under the assumption that sorting a and b results in permutations occurring with uniform probability. Problem (9) can be efficiently computed by performing $O(\ell^4)$ min-sum convolutions (one convolution for every choice of endpoints).

Remark 2 (Comparison to [16]). While our approach for solving (2) is inspired by [16], it is notably different: (i) our model includes pairwise potentials forming a chain, while [16] assumes that pairwise potentials do not occur between neighboring subsets. This necessitates to store left and right endpoints in counting factors. (ii) [16] optimizes a different objective: they solve the sum-product version of (2) (i.e. they exchange min by + and + by · in (2)). This allows [16] to use fast Fourier transforms for message computations, instead of the harder min-sum convolution problems.

4   Discrete Tomography Graphical Model

The discrete tomography problem (1) consists of m = #rows(A) distinct one-dimensional subproblems (2). We connect all subproblems (2) via Lagrangian variables into one large problem. This procedure is called dual decomposition, see [15] for an introduction. Specifically, in our discrete tomograpy problems subproblems only share variables $v \in V$, but not edges $e \in E$ (shared edges can be handled analogously). Then for each node $u \in V$ which participates in the i-th subproblem, we introduce the Lagrangian variable $\lambda_{i,u} \in \mathbb{R}^{|\mathcal{X}_u|}$. The i-th subproblem then consists of solving (2) with the subset of variables U_i, where the unary potentials are the Lagrangian variables $\theta_u = \lambda_{i,u}$. We denote its energy by $E_i(\cdot|\lambda_i)$. The overall problem is

$$\max_{\lambda_1,\ldots,\lambda_m} \sum_{i=1}^{m} \min_{x \in \mathcal{X}_{U_i}} E_i(x|\lambda_i) \quad \text{s.t.} \quad \sum_i \lambda_{i,u} \equiv 0 \quad \forall u \in V. \tag{CTG}$$

An exemplary 4×4 model with eight subproblems coming from two projection directions can be seen in Fig. 4.

Optimization of Relaxation (CTG). To maximize (CTG) we use the bundle solver ConicBundle[2] to find optimal Lagrangian variables λ and Algorithm 1 to find solutions to the one-dimensional subproblems. The bundle method will only give us a dual lower bound to the value of the optimal reconstruction.

Primal Solution. To obtain a feasible reconstruction, we solve a reduced problem by excluding labels with high cost: Given dual variables λ_i, let x^* be the optimal solution to the i-th subproblem on variables $U_i \subseteq V$. For each label $x_u \in \mathcal{X}_u, u \in U_i, x_u \neq x_u^*$ we compute the energy $x'^* \in \arg\min_{\{x' \in \mathcal{X}_U : x_u = x'_u\}} E_i(x'|\lambda_i)$ of the minimal reconstruction for subproblem i when the label at u is fixed to x_u (this value can be read off from the reparametrization output by Algorithm 1). Only if the gap $E_i(x'^*|\lambda_i) - E_i(x^*|\lambda_i)$ is smaller than some given threshold, we consider the label x_u. We construct the discrete tomograpy problem on this reduced set of possible labelings and solve the problem with CPLEX [1].

Comparison to Previously Used Relaxation. It can be shown that the algorithms in [3,9,17,19] use the following relaxation.

$$\begin{aligned}
&\min_{\mu \geq 0} \sum_{u \in V} \langle \theta_u, \mu_u \rangle + \sum_{uv \in E} \langle \theta_{uv}, \mu_{uv} \rangle \\
&\text{s.t.} \sum_{x_u \in \mathcal{X}_u} \mu_u(x_u) = 1 \quad \forall u \in V \\
&\qquad \sum_{x_u \in \mathcal{X}_u} \mu_{uv}(x_u, x_v) = \mu_v(x_v) \quad \forall x_v \in \mathcal{X}_v \\
&\qquad \sum_{x_v \in \mathcal{X}_v} \mu_{uv}(x_u, x_v) = \mu_u(x_u) \quad \forall x_u \in \mathcal{X}_u \\
&\qquad \sum_{u \in V} A_{iu} \cdot \left(\sum_{x_u \in \mathcal{X}_u} x_u \cdot \mu_u(x_u) \right) = b_i \quad i = 1, \ldots, m.
\end{aligned} \tag{STD}$$

---

[2] https://www-user.tu-chemnitz.de/~helmberg/ConicBundle/.

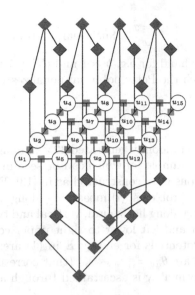

Fig. 4. Illustration of a complete graphical model for the discrete tomography problem with projections along rows and columns of the underlying 4×4 grid. Graphical model consisting of submodel for energy E in (1), indicated by unary (circles) and pairwise (red rectangles) potentials on the 4×4 grid, and counting factors (blue diamond) for the projection constraints $Ax = b$ using the tree construction above the grid (horizontal projection) and below (vertical projection). The higher order potentials are left out for the sake of clarity of presentation. (Color figure online)

This relaxation (STD) is the straightforward generalization of the local polytope relaxation [18] to the discrete tomography problem. The only difference are the linear constraints in the last line of (STD). When specialized to the one-dimensional discrete tomography problem (2), the difference between (STD) and our approach is: for (STD) the tomographic projections are directly enforced through the unary marginals $\mu_u, u \in \mathsf{V}$ instead of enforcing them through the counting factors and higher order ones as we did in Sect. 3. This more simplistic relaxation (STD) is however less tight.

Proposition 1. *Relaxation* (STD) *is less tight than* (CTG).

Proof. Relaxation (STD) is equivalent to applying it to each tomographic projection separately and then joining every subproblem by Lagrangian variables as we did with our approach above (CTG), see [15, Sect. 1.6]. Hence, it is enough to show that (STD) is not tight in the one-dimensional case (2). We give a counterexample. Assume $\mathcal{X}_u = \{0, 1\} \; \forall u \in U$ and we are given Potts pairwise potentials $\theta_{uv}(x_u, x_v) = \begin{cases} 0, & x_u = x_v \\ 1, & x_u \neq x_v \end{cases}$ and zero unary potentials $\theta_u \equiv 0$. Set unary marginals $\mu_u(1) = \frac{b}{|U|}$ and $\mu_u(0) = 1 - \mu_u(1) \; \forall u \in U$ and pairwise marginals as $\mu_{uv}(x_u, x_v) = \begin{cases} \mu_u(x_u), & x_u = x_v \\ 0, & x_u \neq x_v \end{cases}$. Such marginals are feasible to (STD), yet give cost 0. On the other hand for e.g. $b = 1$ and $|U| > 1$ there must be at least one label transition, which the Potts potential penalizes with cost 1.   □

5   Experiments

Test Images. We used 200 randomly generated 32×32 images with three distinct intensity values $\{0, 1, 2\}$, examples of which can be seen in Fig. 5. Matrices A for the tomographic projections were constructed as in [13]. For each test image we consider two tomographic problems: (i) measuring along horizontal and vertical directions or (ii) measuring along horizontal, vertical and two diagonal directions (left upper to right lower and left lower to right upper corner). This gives 400 test problems in total. Potentials for energy E in (1) are: unary potentials are zero, while pairwise ones are $\theta_{uv} = |x_u - x_v|$ (that corresponds to TV). Due to integrality of all costs, optimality is ascertained through a duality gap <1.

Fig. 5. These images are examples from our testset of 200 images with size 32×32. Black represents value 0, gray 1 and white 2.

Algorithms. We identify our solvers by a prefix **{CTG|STD}** depending on whether (CTG) or (STD) is solved and by a suffix **{CB|relax|BB}** depending on whether ConicBundle, CPLEX [1] or CPLEX with branch and bound enabled was utilized. This gives in total 5 solvers: **CTG_CB**, **CTG_relax**, **CTG_BB**, **STD_relax** and **STD_BB**. We set a timelimit of 1 h for all algorithms.

Unfortunately, CPLEX cannot solve problems larger than 32×32. When solving the relaxation (CTG), it already consumes multiple GB of memory for 32×32 images. Solving (STD) on the other hand leads to low memory consumption, but CPLEX takes too much time for larger problems (>1 h). Hence, to have a baseline, we stick to 32×32 images.

Results. We have proved in Proposition 1 that relaxation (STD) is less tight than our relaxation (CTG). In fact, the first line in Table 2 shows that this occurs 350 times. Furthermore, our tighter relaxation also actually helps in giving optimality certificates. In Table 1 we confirm this numerically: **STD_relax** can provide optimality certificates 53 times, while **CBC_CB** and **CTG_relax** can do so in total 205 times. Interestingly, when using the branch and bound capabilities of CPLEX, the picture changes and **STD_BB** outperforms **CTG_BB**. This is probably due to the fact that CPLEX can solve the underlying relaxation (STD) much faster than (CTG). We conjecture that the picture will change if the more efficient implementation **CBC_CB** is used as a bounds provider inside a branch and bound solver. This is however outside the scope of our work.

In Fig. 6 we give a detailed plot on how much our relaxation (CTG) improved upon (STD).

Also, our relaxation helps in reconstructing the signal. Out of 238 instances, where our heuristic could find an optimal integral solution (third line in Table 2) there were 12 cases, where only our heuristic could do so (second line in Table 2).

Table 1. Number of instances where duality gap <1 (optimality).

	STD relax	STD BB	CTG CB	CTG relax	CTG BB
Duality gap "<1"	53	243	178	154	182
				205	

Table 2. Comparison of bounds and primal solutions obtained by (STD) or (CTG).

	#Instances
(CTG) > (STD) (our relaxation yields **strictly better** lower bound)	350
Our heuristic **(only)** found **optimal** integral solution	12
Our heuristic found **optimal** integral solution	238

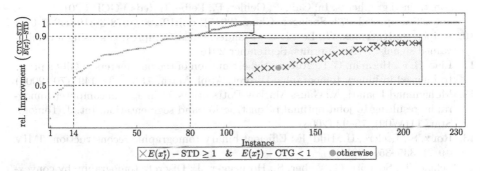

Fig. 6. Comparison of lower bounds (STD) and (CTG). We show relative improvement $(CTG)\text{-}(STD)/_{E(x^*)-(STD)}$ on all problems, where we knew by either method the true optimal solution $E(x^*)$, but where (STD) is not tight ($(STD) < E(x^*)$). Lower bound (STD) was computed by **STD_relax**, while (CTG) was computed by **CTG_CB** and **CTG_relax**. A marker close to zero means no improvement and close to one means our relaxation solved the instance exactly. We marked points with a blue cross if only (CTG) but not (STD) achieved a duality gap <1, i.e. optimality, and used a red circle otherwise. For almost all instance we have an improvement of 0.5 and for more than half of the instances an improvement of 0.9. (Color figure online)

6 Conclusion

We have proposed a novel convex relaxation and an accompanying algorithm for the non-binary discrete tomography problem. We have showed theoretically and empirically that our novel relaxation is tighter than the traditionally used relaxation. Solving our new relaxation helps in decoding tomographic reconstructions.

References

1. IBM ILOG CPLEX Optimizer. http://www-01.ibm.com/software/integration/optimization/cplex-optimizer/
2. Batenburg, K.J.: An evolutionary algorithm for discrete tomography. Discret. Appl. Math. **151**(1), 36–54 (2005)
3. Batenburg, K.J.: A network flow algorithm for reconstructing binary images from continuous X-rays. JMIV **30**(3), 231–248 (2008)
4. Batenburg, K.J., Sijbers, J.: DART: a practical reconstruction algorithm for discrete tomography. IEEE TIP **20**(9), 2542–2553 (2011)
5. Bussieck, M., Hassler, H., Woeginger, G.J., Zimmermann, U.T.: Fast algorithms for the maximum convolution problem. Oper. Res. Lett. **15**, 1–5 (1994)
6. Carvalho, B.M., Herman, G.T., Matej, S., Salzberg, C., Vardi, E.: Binary tomography for triplane cardiography. In: Kuba, A., Šáamal, M., Todd-Pokropek, A. (eds.) IPMI 1999. LNCS, vol. 1613, pp. 29–41. Springer, Heidelberg (1999). doi:10.1007/3-540-48714-X_3
7. Foucart, S., Rauhut, H.: A Mathematical Introduction to Compressive Sensing. Birkhäuser, Basel (2013)
8. Gouillart, E., Krzakala, F., Mzard, M., Zdeborov, L.: Belief-propagation reconstruction for discrete tomography. Inverse Prob. **29**(3), 035003 (2013)
9. Kappes, J.H., Petra, S., Schnörr, C., Zisler, M.: TomoGC: binary tomography by constrained graphcuts. In: Gall, J., Gehler, P., Leibe, B. (eds.) GCPR 2015. LNCS, vol. 9358, pp. 262–273. Springer, Cham (2015). doi:10.1007/978-3-319-24947-6_21
10. Keiper, S., Kutyniok, G., Lee, D.G., Pfander, G.E.: Compressed sensing for finite-valued signals. ArXiv e-prints, September 2016
11. Liao, H.Y., Herman, G.T.: Automated estimation of the parameters of Gibbs priors to be used in binary tomography. Discret. Appl. Math. **139**(1–3), 149–170 (2004)
12. Mohammad-Djafari, A.: Gauss-Markov-Potts priors for images in computer tomography resulting to joint optimal reconstruction and segmentation. Int. J. Tomogr. Stat. **11**(W09), 76–92 (2008)
13. Roux, S., Leclerc, H., Hild, F.: Efficient binary tomographic reconstruction. JMIV **49**(2), 335–351 (2014)
14. Schüle, T., Schnörr, C., Weber, S., Hornegger, J.: Discrete tomography by convex-concave regularization and D.C. programming. Discret. Appl. Math. **151**, 229–243 (2005)
15. Sontag, D., Globerson, A., Jaakkola, T.: Introduction to dual decomposition for inference. In: Optimization for Machine Learning. MIT Press (2011)
16. Tarlow, D., Swersky, K., Zemel, R.S., Adams, R.P., Frey, B.J.: Fast exact inference for recursive cardinality models. In: UAI (2012)
17. Weber, S., Schnörr, C., Hornegger, J.: A linear programming relaxation for binary tomography with smoothness priors. In: IWCIA (2003)
18. Werner, T.: A linear programming approach to max-sum problem: a review. IEEE TPAMI **29**(7), 1165–1179 (2007)
19. Zisler, M., Petra, S., Schnörr, C., Schnörr, C.: Discrete tomography by continuous multilabeling subject to projection constraints. In: Rosenhahn, B., Andres, B. (eds.) GCPR 2016. LNCS, vol. 9796, pp. 261–272. Springer, Cham (2016). doi:10.1007/978-3-319-45886-1_21

Image Reconstruction by Multilabel Propagation

Matthias Zisler[1(✉)], Freddie Åström[1], Stefania Petra[2], and Christoph Schnörr[1]

[1] Image and Pattern Analysis Group, Heidelberg University, Heidelberg, Germany
zisler@math.uni-heidelberg.de
[2] Mathematical Imaging Group, Heidelberg University, Heidelberg, Germany

Abstract. This work presents a non-convex variational approach to joint image reconstruction and labeling. Our regularization strategy, based on the KL-divergence, takes into account the smooth geometry on the space of discrete probability distributions. The proposed objective function is efficiently minimized via DC programming which amounts to solving a sequence of convex programs, with guaranteed convergence to a critical point. Each convex program is solved by a generalized primal dual algorithm. This entails the evaluation of a proximal mapping, evaluated efficiently by a fixed point iteration. We illustrate our approach on few key scenarios in discrete tomography and image deblurring.

1 Introduction

Optimal partition of image data into multiple discrete classes, each representing some semantic information is a relevant problem not only in visual scene understanding but also in, e.g., discrete tomography. A class, or label, in these examples may include sky, road, person and various tissue types such as bone or soft tissue. In addition to be defined from a finite set of image labels, discrete tomography data must first be reconstructed from few discrete projections (data measurements) which constitutes a highly ill-posed problem.

In this work, we propose to jointly solve the labeling problem while enforcing a linear constraint systems, such as the one stemming from discrete tomography. Our smooth variational formulation enables efficient inference of the otherwise NP-hard constrained multilabeling problem. We formulate the objective in a general setting and propose a regularization strategy taking into account the smooth geometry on the space of discrete probability distributions, induced by the Fisher-Rao metric. We focus on the key applications of non-binary discrete tomography (e.g., non-destructive material testing [1]) and deblurring and denoising with joint labeling. As illustrated in Fig. 1 our framework can accurately reconstruct and label severely blurred and noisy data.

Related Work. To avoid the combinatorial nature of discrete optimization problems, it is common to use convex relaxations to approximate the integrality constraints [2–5]. However, convex relaxation is loose in connection with a weak

Acknowledgments: We gratefully acknowledge support by the German Science Foundation, grant GRK 1653.

F. Lauze et al. (Eds.): SSVM 2017, LNCS 10302, pp. 247–259, 2017.
DOI: 10.1007/978-3-319-58771-4_20

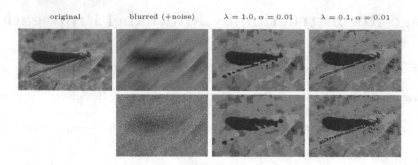

original   blurred (+noise) $\lambda = 1.0, \alpha = 0.01$ $\lambda = 0.1, \alpha = 0.01$

Fig. 1. Reconstruction and labeling with our proposed model (3) of a severely blurred and noisy image of an insect with discrete label set $\mathcal{L} = \{\blacksquare, \blacksquare, \blacksquare, \blacksquare, \blacksquare, \blacksquare\}$. In both cases our model can reconstruct fine details present in the original image (see [8]). For the experimental setup we refer to Sect. 4. (Color figure online)

data term, and the performance of the required rounding step (post-processing), projecting the solution of the relaxed problem to the set of feasible solutions, is hard to control. Non-convex approaches perform rounding or discretization already during optimization. On the other hand, these formulations are sensitive to initialization. Recently, a continuous, smooth non-convex approach to image labeling was introduced in [6] which avoids many of the aforementioned drawbacks (see also [7]). In particular, the labeling is initialized with the uninformative barycentric coordinates of the probability simplex but still avoid poor local minima. The underlying mechanism, which governs the inference process, is the evolution of a Riemannian gradient flow defined on the manifold of row-stochastic matrices which terminates at a labeling. Inspired from this work we formulate our constrained labeling problem as an optimization problem enforcing spatial consistency via discrete probability distributions, which entail the joint reconstruction and labeling. The ability of the present approach to simultaneously perform rounding and optimization is a significant conceptual difference to all approaches based on convex relaxations.

Constraining the solution of an inverse problem to piece-wise constant regions motivates the use of sparsifying priors, such as total variation (TV) based energy formulations [9]. However, applying the TV prior component-wise on the simplex variables, e.g., as done in [10] does not respect the geometry of the underlying probability distributions. To overcome this shortcoming, we propose to exploit the Kullback-Leibler (KL) divergence to enforce spatially consistent assignments. Our approach is motivated from the fact that the KL-divergence locally approximates the squared geodesic distance when considering the probability simplex as a Riemanian manifold endowed with the Fisher-Rao metric [11,12]. Note that we use the same strategy from [10] to obtain a meaningful dataterm for the constraint labeling problem.

Contributions and Organization. Section 2 gives an overview of the constrained multilabeling problem. This section also introduces our *non-convex* approach which reconstructs an image and simultaneously enforces spatially coherent labeling by our novel regularizer. Our optimization problem is formulated in the framework of difference of convex function (DC) programming in Sect. 3, which comes along with a convergence guarantee. Furthermore we evaluate the generalized proximal mapping of our proposed regularizer by an fixed point iteration rather then solving a large non-linear system of equations. This strategy is numerically efficient even for larger problem instances. In Sect. 4 we compare our approach on few problem instances and Sect. 5 concludes the paper.

Basic Notation. Operations and functions are applied component-wise to vectors $v, w \in \mathbb{R}^n$ and matrices i.e., $vw = (\dots, v_i w_i, \dots)$. The KL-divergence is defined by $\mathrm{KL}(x, y) = \langle x, \log(x/y) \rangle$ for stochastic vectors as well as row-stochastic matrices where $\langle \cdot, \cdot \rangle$ denotes the Euclidean scalar product. Moreover we set $\mathbb{1} = (1, 1, \dots, 1)^T$.

2 Constrained Multilabeling, Model and Relaxation

Problem Statement. Consider the linear system of equations

$$Au = b, \quad u_i \in \mathcal{L} \quad \forall i = 1, \dots, N, \tag{1}$$

where the solution is constrained to a discrete set $\mathcal{L}$ of labels. Note in the general setting this integer constraint formulation leads to NP hard problems. Furthermore, we assume that there are less measurements b than pixels $m \ll N$ and hence the inverse problem is ill-posed and requires prior knowledge (regularization). A common choice is the Potts model [13], $\|\nabla u\|_0 := |\{i \,|\, (\nabla u)_i \neq 0\}|$ for sparse gradient regularization which favours piecewise constant images. This gives the problem

$$\min_u \lambda \cdot \|\nabla u\|_0 \quad \text{s.t.} \quad Au = b \ \wedge \ u_i \in \mathcal{L} \quad \forall i = 1, \dots, N \tag{2}$$

and we refer to (2) as a *constrained multilabeling problem* with Potts regularization. From the viewpoint of graphical models, the system of affine subspace constraints induce (very) high-order potentials. This high-order interaction induced by the non-local constraints results in a non-standard labeling problem that is intractable for large problem sizes. Therefore, we instead adopt the strategy of solving a sequence of convex relaxations in order to minimize a non-convex energy, which properly approximates the original problem.

Model and Relaxation. We relax the hard assignment of a label from a given set $\mathcal{L} := \{c_1, \dots, c_K\}$ of priors to each pixel $i \in [N] = \{1, 2, \dots, N\}$ to discrete probability distributions $z \in \mathcal{G} = \{z \in [0, 1]^{N \times K} : \langle z_i, \mathbb{1} \rangle = 1, \ \forall i \in [N]\}$ and $(z_{ik})_{k=1}^K$ is the distribution describing the assignment in pixel i.

Energy. We propose the non-convex energy

$$\min_{z \in \mathcal{G}} J(z), \qquad J(z) = \lambda R_{\mathcal{G}}(z) - \alpha \langle z, \log(z) \rangle + D(z) \tag{3}$$

which consists of three basic building blocks detailed below: (i) regularization for spatial coherence controlled by parameter $\lambda \geq 0$, (ii) an entropy term enforcing an unique decision with weight $\alpha \geq 0$ and (iii) a dataterm. For convex relaxations [3–5], a rounding scheme is generally required to obtain an integral solution. In our case, however, the concave entropy term promotes an integral solution.

Dataterm. We consider two cases of the dataterm: *separable* and *non-separable*. The separable case refers to problem where noisy image data u_i^0 is directly observed. We introduce a distance function $d_{\mathcal{L}}$ measuring the similarity to the priors $c_k \in \mathcal{L}, k \in [K]$, resulting in the dataterm

$$D_{\text{unary}}(z, S) = \langle z, S \rangle \quad \text{where} \quad S_{ik} := d_{\mathcal{L}}(u_i^0, c_k). \tag{4}$$

We introduce the assignment operator $\mathrm{P}_{\mathcal{L}}(z) = zc$ where $c = (c_1, \ldots, c_K)^T$, which assigns to each pixel i a convex combination of labels in terms of the distribution z_i. The non-separable case refers to problems where image data u_i^0 *cannot* be directly observed since it is the solution of the inverse problem (1). As a consequence, we instead minimize the distance $d(A\mathrm{P}_{\mathcal{L}}(z), b)$, ($u = \mathrm{P}_{\mathcal{L}}(z)$ in (1)) between the forward projection A and given measurements b. In [10] it was shown that if $D(z) = D(\mathrm{P}_{\mathcal{L}}(z))$ is defined over the assigned solution $\mathrm{P}_{\mathcal{L}}(z)$ one is required to introduce, e.g., a concave self-assignment term. Accordingly, we define the dataterm

$$D_{\text{inverse}}(z, A, b) = d(A\mathrm{P}_{\mathcal{L}}(z), b) + \langle z, (\mathrm{P}_{\mathcal{L}}(z)\mathbb{1}_K^T - \mathbb{1}_N c^T)^2 \rangle, \tag{5}$$

for non-separable inverse labeling problems. Note that when the self-assignment term in (5) is constrained to the simplex, then the vertices of the simplex become its minima. The entropy term (3), which has the same minimzers as the self-assignment term, enforces integral solutions, while the self-assignment term in (5) has a meaningful descent direction w.r.t. to the labels (pushing the assignment $\mathrm{P}_{\mathcal{L}}(z)$ towards the label values c_k). Furthermore, the linearization of the self-assignment term in a point z^0 resembles D_{unary} with $u^0 = \mathrm{P}_{\mathcal{L}}(z^0)$ and is the squared Euclidean norm.

Regularizer. To enforce spatial coherence over pixel-wise probability distributions Zach et al. [2] regularize each individual layer z_k to get a convex relaxation of the Potts model. A tighter relaxation is obtained by regularizing across the layers [3,4]. However, these works employ Euclidean norms that disregard the underlying geometry of the discrete probability distributions and hence necessitate an additional re-projection step onto the simplex.

Instead, we propose a regularizer $R_{\mathcal{G}}(z)$ (see (3)) which respects the underlying geometry of the probability simplex by coupling probability distributions across layers via the KL divergence. Our regularizer is defined as

$$R_{\mathcal{G}}(z) := \sum_{i=1}^{N} \sum_{j \in \mathcal{N}(i)} \frac{1}{N_s} \mathrm{KL}(z_i, z_j) \quad \text{where} \quad N_s := |\mathcal{N}(i)|. \tag{6}$$

which enforces spatial coherence by pairwise interactions in neighborhoods $\mathcal{N}(i)$ induced by the underlying grid-graph of the image.

It is well-known that the KL divergence locally approximates the *squared* geodesic distance on the probability simplex equipped with the Fisher-Rao metric [11]. In this sense, (6) naturally respects the information geometric properties of the underlying manifold. Furthermore, for this particular manifold, our formulation *without* approximation of the quadratic geodesic distance would correspond to a *non-local* extension of a quadratic regularizer in the framework of [14]. We have

Lemma 1 (Basic properties). *Let $z \in \mathcal{G}$ and define $R_{\mathcal{G}}(z)$ by (6). Then*

1. *$R_{\mathcal{G}}(z)$ is a convex function*
2. *$R_{\mathcal{G}}(z)$ is the KL-divergence between z_i and the geometric mean of the vectors z_j indexed by $j \in \mathcal{N}(i)$,*

$$R_{\mathcal{G}}(z) = \sum_{i=1}^{N} KL(z_i, gm(\{z_j\}_{j \in \mathcal{N}(i)})), \quad gm(\{z_j\}_{j \in \mathcal{N}(i)}) := \prod_{j \in \mathcal{N}(i)} z_j^{\frac{1}{N_s}}. \quad (7)$$

Proof. Assertion 1 follows from the joint convexity of the KL-divergence [15]. The second claim can be seen by

$$R_{\mathcal{G}}(z) = \sum_{i=1}^{N} \sum_{j \in \mathcal{N}(i)} \frac{1}{N_s} \langle z_i, \log(\frac{z_i}{z_j}) \rangle = \sum_{i=1}^{N} \langle z_i, \log(\prod_{j \in \mathcal{N}(i)} (\frac{z_i}{z_j})^{\frac{1}{N_s}}) \rangle \quad (8a)$$

$$= \sum_{i=1}^{N} \langle z_i, \log(z_i^{N_s \frac{1}{N_s}} \prod_{j \in \mathcal{N}(i)} (z_j^{\frac{1}{N_s}})^{-1}) \rangle = \sum_{i=1}^{N} KL(z_i, \prod_{j \in \mathcal{N}(i)} z_j^{\frac{1}{N_s}}) \quad (8b)$$

□

Next we reformulate the objective function (3) as a difference of convex (DC) program [16] and work out a corresponding optimization algorithm.

3 Optimization

DC Programming. A large subclass of non-convex objective functions are DC functions which can be (locally) minimized by DC Programming [16]. The basic form of a DC program is given by

$$z^* = \arg\min_{z} g(z) - h(z), \quad (9)$$

where $g(z)$ and $h(z)$ are proper, lower semicontinuous, convex functions. There exists a simplified version of the DC algorithm [17] for minimizing (9) which guarantees convergence to a critical point by starting with $z^0 \in \text{dom}(g)$ and then alternatingly applying the updates $v^n \in \partial h(z^n)$ and $z^{n+1} \in \partial g^*(v^n)$ until a termination criterion is reached, where g^* denotes the Legendre-Fenchel conjugate [18] of g.

Algorithm 1. Iterated Primal Dual Algorithm

Init: choose the barycenter for $z^0 \in \mathcal{G}$, $q^0 \in \mathrm{dom}(D^*)$ and $\tau, \sigma > 0$
while *not converged* **do**
    Set $\hat{z} = z^l$
    while *not converged* **do**

$$z^{n+1} = \arg\min_{z \in \mathcal{G}} \lambda R_\mathcal{G}(z) + \langle z, A^* q^n - \nabla h(\hat{z}) \rangle + \frac{1}{\tau} \mathrm{KL}(z, z^n) \qquad (11)$$

$$q^{n+1} = \arg\min_q D^*(q) - \langle q, A(2z^{n+1} - z^n) \rangle + \frac{1}{2\sigma} \|q - q^n\|_2^2 \qquad (12)$$

        $n \leftarrow n+1$
    $l \leftarrow l+1$
Output: $z^* = z^l$

To apply the DC algorithm to our non-convex energy $J(z)$ in (3), we rewrite $J(z) = g(z) - h(z)$ as a DC function. We set $h_{\mathrm{unary}}(z) = \alpha \langle z, \log(z) \rangle$ for the case of a separable dataterm and $h_{\mathrm{inverse}}(z) = \alpha \langle z, \log(z) \rangle - \langle z, (\mathrm{P}_\mathcal{L}(z) \mathbb{1}_K^T - \mathbb{1}_N c^T)^2 \rangle$ for the non-separable case since the entropy and the self assignment term are concave. We denote by $g(z) = \lambda R_\mathcal{G}(z) + D(z)$ the remaining convex terms from (3), where $D(z)$ corresponds to the convex part of (5). The DC algorithm results in the fixed point iteration

$$z^{n+1} = \arg\min_{z \in \mathcal{G}} \lambda R_\mathcal{G}(z) + D(z) - \langle z, \nabla h(z^n) \rangle, \qquad (10)$$

where the gradient $\nabla h(z)$ for the separable case is given by $\nabla h_{\mathrm{unary}}(z) = \alpha(\log(z) + \mathbb{1}_N \mathbb{1}_K^T)$ and in the non-separable case by $\nabla h_{\mathrm{inverse}}(z) = \alpha(\log(z) + \mathbb{1}_N \mathbb{1}_K^T) - (\mathrm{P}_\mathcal{L}(z) \mathbb{1}_K^T - \mathbb{1}_N c^T)^2$. We refer to [10] for the gradient of the second term of $\nabla h_{\mathrm{inverse}}(z)$.

Solving the Fixed Point Iteration. Algorithm 1 solves the fixed point iteration (10) iteratively using the generalized primal dual algorithm [19].

Primal Update. The primal update step (11) requires to evaluate the generalized proximal operator of the regularizer (6). We rewrite (11) as

$$z^{n+1} = \arg\min_{z \in \mathcal{G}} R_\mathcal{G}(z) + \frac{1}{\lambda \tau} \mathrm{KL}(z, p), \qquad (13)$$

where the argument $p \in \mathcal{G}$ is given by the non-linear gradient descent step

$$p = \arg\min_{z \in \mathcal{G}} \langle z, A^* q^n - \nabla h(\hat{z}) \rangle + \frac{1}{\tau} \mathrm{KL}(z, z^n) \qquad (14a)$$

$$= \frac{z^n \exp(-\tau(A^* q^n - \nabla h(\hat{z})))}{\langle z^n, \exp(-\tau(A^* q^n - \nabla h(\hat{z}))) \rangle}. \qquad (14b)$$

Note that the argmin induces normalization of p, thus $p \in \mathcal{G}$.

Theorem 1 below states that evaluating the proximal mapping (13) can be done approximately by an efficient fixed point iteration rather then solving a large non-linear equation system (optimality conditions). Even for larger problem instances, this fixed point iteration evaluates the proximal mapping very efficiently. Specifically, in our numerical experiments we observed convergence within few iterations and we initialize with p for warm start. Due to the fact that the variation in (7) with respect to geometric averaging is significantly smaller than in the first argument of the KL-divergence (see [6]), we have

Theorem 1 (Evaluation of the proximal mapping). *Let $p \in \mathcal{G}$ be fixed and define $R_{\mathcal{G}}(z)$ by (6), then the fixed point iteration converges for every $z^0 \in \mathcal{G}$*

$$z_i^{m+1} = \arg\min_{z \in \mathcal{G}} KL(z_i, gm(\{z_j^m\}_{j \in \mathcal{N}(i)})) + \frac{1}{\tau\lambda} KL(z_i, p_i), \quad \forall i \in [N]. \quad (15)$$

Proof. We evaluate the fixed point iteration (15) and obtain

$$z_i^{m+1} = \frac{(p_i)^{\frac{1}{1+\tau\lambda}} gm(\{z_j^m\}_{j \in \mathcal{N}(i)})^{\frac{\tau\lambda}{1+\tau\lambda}}}{\langle (p_i)^{\frac{1}{1+\tau\lambda}}, gm(\{z_j^m\}_{j \in \mathcal{N}(i)})^{\frac{\tau\lambda}{1+\tau\lambda}} \rangle} \quad \forall i \in [N], \quad (16)$$

Without loss of generality we skip the intermediate normalizations and normalize only the *last* iterate since the normalization of the intermediate steps cancel out. This yields the fixed point iteration with $p \in \mathcal{G}$ fixed and initial point $z^0 \in \mathcal{G}$

$$z_i^{m+1} = (p_i)^{\frac{1}{1+\tau\lambda}} gm(\{z_j^m\}_{j \in \mathcal{N}(i)})^{\frac{\tau\lambda}{1+\tau\lambda}}. \quad (17)$$

Taking the logarithm of (17), substituting $u^m = \log(z^m)$ and $r = \log(p)$, gives

$$u_i^{m+1} = \frac{1}{1+\tau\lambda} r_i + \frac{\tau\lambda}{1+\tau\lambda} \sum_{j \in \mathcal{N}(i)} \frac{1}{N_s} u_j^m. \quad (18)$$

Rewriting the neighborhood interactions by the associated stochastic matrix Q, with $Q_{ij} := 1/N_s$ for $j \in \mathcal{N}(i)$ and 0 otherwise, we get the explicit expression

$$u^{m+1} = \frac{1}{1+\tau\lambda} r + \underbrace{\frac{\tau\lambda}{1+\tau\lambda} Q}_{:=\tilde{P}} u^m = \frac{1}{1+\tau\lambda} \sum_{l=0}^{m} \tilde{P}^l r + \tilde{P}^{m+1} u_0. \quad (19)$$

Since Q, per definition, is a stochastic matrix and $\tau\lambda(1+\tau\lambda)^{-1} < 1$ it follows that $\lim_{m\to\infty} \tilde{P}^m = 0$ thus $|\lambda_i| < 1$ holds for all eigenvalues from $\tilde{P}$ and $(I - \tilde{P})$ is invertible. This implies that the geometric series of the matrix $\tilde{P}$ converges to

$$u = \lim_{m\to\infty} u^m = \frac{1}{1+\tau\lambda} (I - \tilde{P})^{-1} r. \quad (20)$$

Resubstitute the continuous functions $z = \exp(u)$, $r = \log(p)$ into (20) and normalization finally gives

$$z^* = \frac{\exp\left(\frac{1}{1+\tau\lambda}(I - \tilde{P})^{-1} \log(p)\right)}{\langle \exp\left(\frac{1}{1+\tau\lambda}(I - \tilde{P})^{-1} \log(p)\right), \mathbb{1}\rangle}, \quad (21)$$

which yields the limit point z^* independent from the starting point z^0.   □

Dual Update. Due to the convexity of D and the standard Euclidean proximal mapping, the dual step can be evaluated in a straightforward manner.

Parameter Selection. Following the parameter selection of [19, Example 7.2] we set $\tau = \sqrt{K}/L_{12}^2$ in the primal update and $\sigma = 1/\sqrt{K}$ in the dual update. Note that this parameter configuration implies that the condition $\sigma\tau \leq \|A\|^2$ holds, where operator norm of A is given by $L_{12} = \|A\| = \sup_{\|x\|_1 \leq 1} \|Ax\|_2 = \max_j \|A_j\|_2$ with respect to the mixed $L_1 - L_2$-norm. This stems from the fact that, in the primal, the negative entropy is 1-strongly convex with respect to the L_1-norm when restricted to the simplex, which induce our KL-divergence.

4   Experiments

In this section we evaluate our proposed model (3) for separable and non-separable dataterms. We used a 3×3 neighborhood system in all experiments. To guarantee fully discrete solutions we use only a simple pixelwise maximum likelihood (argmax) rounding scheme. We avoid numerical issues when evaluating the KL-divergences by adopting the renormalization strategy from [6].

Parameter Influence. This experiment shows the influence of the regularization parameter λ and discretization parameter α. We generated random color noise u^0 and used the dataterm $D_{\text{unary}}(z, S) = \langle z, S \rangle$ (4) with $S_{ik} = d(u_i^0, c_k) = \|u_i^0 - c_k\|_2^2$ where the labels $c_k \in \mathcal{L} = \{\blacksquare, \blacksquare, \blacksquare\}$. Figure 2 shows that larger λ acts as a smoothing parameter enforcing larger constant regions, whereas α favors consistency over the discrete label space, i.e., the data range. The presence of the entropy term is promoting an integral solution as illustrated in the left most-column. In this experiment no rounding was applied.

Interface Propagation. In this example we illustrate the information propagation in the case when the dataterm is uninformative. We use the same model configuration and $\mathcal{L}$ as the in previous experiment with $\lambda = 10$ and $\alpha = 1$.

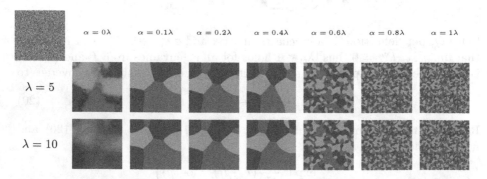

Fig. 2. Random color noise, see top left corner, is labeled with $\mathcal{L} = \{\blacksquare, \blacksquare, \blacksquare\}$ with varying regularization parameter λ and discretization parameter α. (Color figure online)

Fig. 3. The evolution of the interfaces are shown for increasing iteration number with the label set $c_k \in \mathcal{L} = \{\blacksquare, \blacksquare, \blacksquare\}$. The interfaces are propagated uniformly from the three seed-pixels into the uninformative image until they meet in a triple junction. (Color figure online)

We set the input data u^0 to a constant gray image with three seed pixels: one ($\blacksquare$)-pixel in the top left corner, one ($\blacksquare$)-pixel in the bottom left corner and one ($\blacksquare$)-pixel in the middle of the right edge. Figure 3 displays the evolution of the interfaces for increasing iterations. We see that the information given by the three seed-pixels is uniformly propagated into the image until the interfaces meet in a triple junction which demonstrates uniform propagation speeds. In this experiment no rounding was applied.

Joint Deblurring and Labeling. We used the non-separabel dataterm D_{inverse} (5) implemented by the L_1-norm and the self-assignment term was extended component-wise to each color channel. The label set $\mathcal{L} = \{\blacksquare, \blacksquare, \blacksquare, \blacksquare, \blacksquare, \blacksquare\}$ was generated by K-means clustering with 6 cluster of the original image seen in Fig. 1. The same figure shows the reconstruction of a severe blurred picture of an insect (motion blur of 65 pixel length) and joint labeling with two different parameter configurations: high regularization and low regularization. In a more challenging setting we additionally corrupt 50% pixels of the blurred image with random colors drawn from a uniform distribution. In both cases we reconstruct fine details of the original image.

Discrete Tomography Reconstruction. The reconstruction problem in discrete tomography aims to recover an image $u \in \mathbb{R}^N$ from a small number of possibly noisy measurements $b = Au + \nu \in \mathbb{R}^m$. The latter correspond to line integrals that sum up all absorptions over each ray transmitted through the object. A given projection matrix $A \in \mathbb{R}^{m \times N}$ encodes the imaging geometry, here we used the parallel beam setup. The width of the sensor-array was set 1.5 times the image size, so that every pixel intersects with a least a single projection ray. We used the non-separabel dataterm D_{inverse} (5) implemented by the indicator function to enforce the constraints (see [10] for details). We compare our model to state-of-the-art approaches for non-binary discrete tomography in limited angles scenarios. Specifically, we considered DART [20], the energy minimization method from Varga et al. [21] (Varga) and [10] (LayerTV) with a layer-wise total variation regularizer.

Setup. For the evaluation we measured the relative pixel error, that is the relative number of erroneously reconstructed pixels as compared to the groundtruth. We tried to use the default parameters of the competing approaches as proposed by

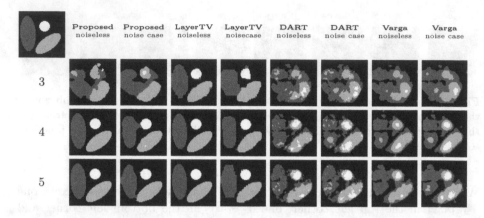

Fig. 4. Visual results of experiment with ellipses phantom.

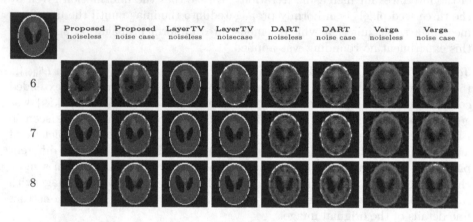

Fig. 5. Visual results of experiment with Shepp-Logan phantom.

their authors. However, the test-datasets differ in size, we slightly adjusted the parameters to get best results for every algorithm and problem instance.

Results. In Figs. 5 and 4 the proposed approach gives perfect reconstructions with a low number of projection angles in the noiseless case and also returns high-quality reconstructions in the presence of noise, only LayerTV needs one projection less however a non-trivial rounding strategy is used. This is depicted in Fig. 6 for the Shepp-Logan phantom from 7 projections where LayerTV clearly gives a non-integral solution and requires a special rounding strategy to obtain a meaningful reconstruction, further details are given in the caption. Figure 7 shows the numerical evaluation of the approaches for increasing (but small) numbers of projections, in the noiseless case (filled markers) and in the noisy case (non-filled markers), with Poisson noise $SNR = 20$ dB.

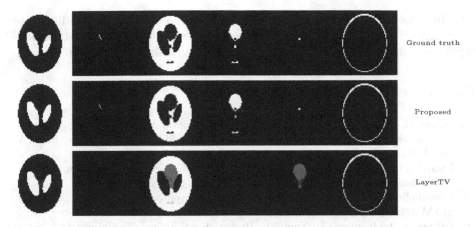

Fig. 6. Reconstruction of the Shepp-Logan phantom from 7 projections, where the indicator variables z^k are shown for each layer $k \in [K]$ from left to right. White denotes the selected label. The LayerTV produces a non-integral solution with a convex combination of the labels - illustrating the need for rounding, whereas our proposed model directly gives an unique labeling.

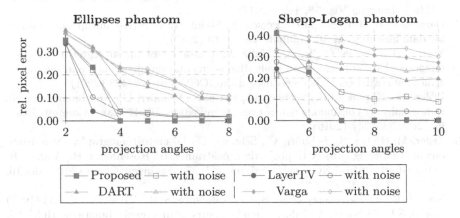

Fig. 7. Relative pixel error compared to the number of projections. In the Shepp-Logan phantom LayerTV can reconstruct the phantom with one less projection, however a special rounding strategy is performed to obtain a meaningful solution.

5   Conclusion

In this work we presented a novel variational approach to joint image reconstruction and labeling. Opposed to state of the art reconstruction algorithms which use intra layer coupling strategies, or basic Euclidean inter layer coupling, we have instead derived the first inter layer coupling which preserves the information geometric properties of the underlying statistical manifold. Additionally, we have shown that the evaluation of a generalized proximal mapping, relying on the

KL-divergence, can be efficiently evaluated. The numerical evaluation illustrate the competitiveness of our approach compared to state of the art discrete tomography reconstruction and deblurring and denoising with joint labeling.

References

1. Hanke, R., Fuchs, T., Uhlmann, N.: X-ray based methods for non-destructive testing and material characterization. Nucl. Instrum. Methods Phys. Res. Sect. A: Accel. Spectrom. Detect. Assoc. Equip. **591**(1), 14–18 (2008)
2. Zach, C., Gallup, D., Frahm, J., Niethammer, M.: Fast global labeling for real-time stereo using multiple plane sweeps. In: VMV, pp. 243–252 (2008)
3. Chambolle, A., Cremers, D., Pock, T.: A convex approach to minimal partitions. SIAM J. Imaging Sci. **5**(4), 1113–1158 (2012)
4. Lellmann, J., Kappes, J., Yuan, J., Becker, F., Schnörr, C.: Convex multi-class image labeling by simplex-constrained total variation. In: Tai, X.-C., Mørken, K., Lysaker, M., Lie, K.-A. (eds.) SSVM 2009. LNCS, vol. 5567, pp. 150–162. Springer, Heidelberg (2009). doi:10.1007/978-3-642-02256-2_13
5. Lellmann, J., Schnörr, C.: Continuous multiclass labeling approaches and algorithms. SIAM J. Imaging Sci. **4**(4), 1049–1096 (2011)
6. Åström, F., Petra, S., Schmitzer, B., Schnörr, C.: Image labeling by assignment. J. Math. Imaging Vis. **58**, 1–28 (2017)
7. Bergmann, R., Fitschen, J.H., Persch, J., Steidl, G.: Iterative multiplicative filters for data labeling. Int. J. Comput. Vis., 1–19 (2017)
8. Martin, D., Fowlkes, C., Tal, D., Malik, J.: A database of human segmented natural images and its application to evaluating segmentation algorithms and measuring ecological statistics. In: Proceedings of the ICCV, pp. 416–423 (2001)
9. Zisler, M., Kappes, J.H., Schnörr, C., Petra, S., Schnörr, C.: Non-binary discrete tomography by continuous non-convex optimization. IEEE Trans. Comput. Imaging **2**(3), 335–347 (2016)
10. Zisler, M., Petra, S., Schnörr, C., Schnörr, C.: Discrete tomography by continuous multilabeling subject to projection constraints. In: Rosenhahn, B., Andres, B. (eds.) GCPR 2016. LNCS, vol. 9796, pp. 261–272. Springer, Cham (2016). doi:10.1007/978-3-319-45886-1_21
11. Kass, R.E.: The geometry of asymptotic inference. Stat. Sci. **4**(3), 188–234 (1989)
12. Amari, S.I., Cichocki, A.: Information geometry of divergence functions. Bull. Pol. Acad. Sci.: Tech. Sci. **58**(1), 183–195 (2010)
13. Potts, R.B.: Some generalized order-disorder transformations. Math. Proc. Camb. Philos. Soc. **48**, 106–109 (1952)
14. Weinmann, A., Demaret, L., Storath, M.: Total variation regularization for manifold-valued data. SIAM J. Imaging Sci. **7**(4), 2226–2257 (2014)
15. Cover, T., Thomas, J.: Elements of Information Theory, 2nd edn. Wiley, Hoboken (2006)
16. Pham Dinh, T., El Bernoussi, S.: Algorithms for solving a class of nonconvex optimization problems. Methods of subgradients. In: Hiriart-Urruty, J.B. (ed.) Fermat Days 85: Mathematics for Optimization. North-Holland Mathematics Studies, vol. 129, pp. 249–271. North-Holland, Amsterdam (1986)
17. Pham-Dinh, T., Hoai An, L.: Convex analysis approach to D.C. programming: theory, algorithms and applications. Acta Math. Vietnam. **22**(1), 289–355 (1997)
18. Rockafellar, R.T., Wets, R.J.B.: Variational Analysis. Springer, Heidelberg (2009)

19. Chambolle, A., Pock, T.: On the ergodic convergence rates of a first-order primal-dual algorithm. Math. Program. **159**(1), 253–287 (2016)
20. Batenburg, K., Sijbers, J.: DART: a practical reconstruction algorithm for discrete tomography. IEEE Trans. Image Process. **20**(9), 2542–2553 (2011)
21. Varga, L., Balázs, P., Nagy, A.: An energy minimization reconstruction algorithm for multivalued discrete tomography. In: 3rd International Symposium on Computational Modeling of Objects Represented in Images, Italy, pp. 179–185 (2012)

User-Friendly Simultaneous Tomographic Reconstruction and Segmentation with Class Priors

Hans Martin Kjer[✉], Yiqiu Dong, and Per Christian Hansen

Department of Applied Mathematics and Computer Science,
Technical University of Denmark, Kongens Lyngby, Denmark
hmkj@dtu.dk

Abstract. Simultaneous Reconstruction and Segmentation (SRS) strategies for computed tomography (CT) present a way to combine the two tasks, which in many applications traditionally are performed as two successive and separate steps. A combined model has a potentially positive effect by allowing the two tasks to influence one another, at the expense of a more complicated algorithm. The combined model increases in complexity due to additional parameters and settings requiring tuning, thus complicating the practical usability. This paper takes it outset in a recently published variational algorithm for SRS. We propose a simplification that reduces the number of required parameters, and we perform numerical experiments investigating the effect and the conditions under which this approach is feasible.

1 Introduction

Inverse problems – such as reconstruction problems in CT imaging – cannot be solved without regularization, i.e., incorporation of some prior information. Such priors are often very generic in nature, e.g., they express knowledge of the smoothness of the solution; in the filtered back projection algorithm we discard high-frequency components. Such generic approaches are often fast and they can be applied to a broad class of reconstruction problems. But their disadvantage is that they fail to incorporate more specific priors about the object under reconstruction, and they also fail to incorporate knowledge about how the result is further used in the data analysis process.

This work considers an algorithm [8] that incorporates priors about the absorption coefficients of the materials that constitute the object. Such priors have a strong stabilizing effect on the reconstruction, meaning that we can handle more noisy and/or more underdetermined problems than without the priors. At the same time, the algorithm – in addition to the reconstructed image – also produces a segmented image suited for further data analysis in post-processing steps (automatic identification of geometric structure or interest points, quantification of qualitative material parameters, etc.).

A classical approach to segmentation of CT reconstructions is to first compute a reconstructed image by means of a standard algorithm, say, filtered back

© Springer International Publishing AG 2017
F. Lauze et al. (Eds.): SSVM 2017, LNCS 10302, pp. 260–270, 2017.
DOI: 10.1007/978-3-319-58771-4_21

projection, and then apply segmentation to this image. A danger of this approach is that reconstruction errors propagate in an undesirable way to the segmentation. The advantage of a joint reconstruction–segmentation algorithm is that we avoid this type of error propagation.

There are several methods presented in the literature that perform *simultaneous reconstruction and segmentation* (SRS) in different forms. In some cases it is proposed to find a reconstruction that is equivalent to a segmentation, i.e., a reconstruction into discrete intensities [1,5]. However, such simplification may not be acceptable in all scenarios. Alternatively, some authors suggests to incorporate shape-based priors into the reconstruction algorithm via level-set segmentation [7,10]. In applications within, e.g., material science where the objects are much less geometrically constrained than biomedical/anatomical scenarios, it may be difficult to initialize the estimate of the shape and make such a segmentation work properly. Other authors choose an intensity-based way of specifying the prior, i.e., assuming knowledge about the material types present and their respective attenuation properties [8,9].

No matter the type of segmentation strategy, the problem is often non-convex. A general strategy for obtaining a solution is to iteratively alter between solving the reconstruction subproblem and the segmentation subproblem separately, letting one influence the solution of the other.

This work builds on [8,9] that use a variational formulation for the SRS problem. In short, the reconstruction model consists of a data-fitting term and a so-called class-fitting term where we fit the segmentation to the classes given as a prior, and regularization is applied only to the segmentation subproblem. The segmentation is intensity-based and assumes prior knowledge about the correct number K of classes or materials present in the object and their respective attenuation coefficients. The latter are modeled as Gaussian distributions $\mathcal{N}(\mu_k, \sigma_k^2)$, where μ_k is the expected value of the coefficient, and σ_k^2 is the variance. The segmentation is regularized with a Total Variation (TV) metric to impose that materials are supposed to be spatially coherent within each region. One difficulty with this approach is that the σ_k's are typically not known a priori, which renders this method difficult to use in practice.

Here we propose to simplify the SRS algorithm from [8]. We impose the assumption that all class priors have the same variance $\bar{\sigma}^2$, which reduces the number of parameters, and we consider this variance as an unknown that is determined from the data by our algorithm. As we will show, this results in a third term in the above-mentioned reconstruction model. Our contribution is to explore the effect of introducing this joint variance estimate in the SRS algorithm. Using numerical experiments, we test the performance on different simulated phantoms, investigating the consequences and the conditions where the proposed simplification is beneficial.

2   The New Reconstruction Model and the Algorithm

2.1   The Reconstruction Model

Here we briefly describe the new reconstruction model, and we refer to the original works [8,9] for additional details. A strong familiarity with the terminology of CT imaging and the mathematical basics of tomographic reconstruction is assumed, see, e.g. [3].

The SRS model encompasses both reconstruction and segmentation. Here, an intensity-based classifier with neighborhood dependence is used, which fits neatly into a variational Bayesian model formulation. The premise is that we allow the segmentation to provide the necessary regularization of the reconstruction.

The forward problem takes the form $\mathbf{A}x = b$, where $x \in \mathbb{R}^N$ represents the image of attenuation coefficients, $\mathbf{A} \in \mathbb{R}^{M \times N}$ is the system matrix for the CT scanner, and $b \in \mathbb{R}^M$ contains the measured data. Given the intensity of a pixel x_j, it is possible to calculate a probability δ_{jk} of this value belonging to class k of the material, with $k = 1, 2, \ldots, K$. Moreover we associate a Gaussian intensity distribution $\mathcal{N}(\mu_k, \bar{\sigma}^2)$ with each class, and we assume that K and $\mu_1, \mu_2, \ldots, \mu_K$ are known a priori – while the joint variance $\bar{\sigma}^2$ is unknown. Defining $\delta_k = \{\delta_{1k}, \delta_{2k}, \ldots, \delta_{Nk}\}$, we use a regularization term $\mathcal{R}(\delta_k)$ in the form of neighborhood regularization which models that the different materials appear in spatially coherent regions.

Originating from the classic variational Bayesian formulation of the CT reconstruction problem, the reconstruction model takes the form

$$(x^*, \delta^*, \bar{\sigma}^*) = \underset{x, \delta, \bar{\sigma}}{\operatorname{argmin}} \left(\lambda_{\text{data}} \|\mathbf{A}x - b\|_2^2 + \lambda_{\text{class}} \sum_{k=1}^{K} \mathcal{R}(\delta_k) \right.$$
$$\left. - \sum_{j=1}^{N} \log \left[\sum_{k=1}^{K} \frac{\delta_{jk}}{\sqrt{2\pi}\bar{\sigma}} \exp \left(-\frac{(x_j - \mu_k)^2}{2\bar{\sigma}^2} \right) \right] \right). \tag{1}$$

Here we introduced the following terminology:

- $\delta \in \mathbb{R}^{N \times K}$ is a matrix where each element δ_{jk} represents the probability of pixel j belonging to class k, with the constraints

$$\sum_{k=1}^{K} \delta_{jk} = 1, \qquad \delta_{jk} \geq 0. \tag{2}$$

- $\mu \in \mathbb{R}_+^K$ is the vector of known mean attenuation coefficients.
- $\bar{\sigma} \in \mathbb{R}_+$ is the joint standard deviation of the μ_k's.
- λ_{data} is a regularization parameter representing the amount of trust in the measured data.
- λ_{class} is a regularization parameter representing the strength of the regularization.

Segmentation: The matrix δ contains the probabilities of a pixel belonging to a certain class. In the segmentation, denoted by $L \in \mathbb{N}^N$, the assignment is done by evaluating which of the classes that has the greatest probability for each pixel:

$$l_j := \underset{k}{\mathrm{argmax}} \, (\delta_{jk}), \, \forall j. \tag{3}$$

2.2 Related Work

In the work of Romanov et al. [8], each class has an individual standard deviation σ_k, assuming that all σ_k's can be specified a priori. Arguably, the mean attenuation coefficients of various materials are often easy to assume known for CT problems, as it is more or less possible to look them up. However, the variances are difficult to know a priori. Further, having individual σ_k's may not be necessary; the numerical experiments in [8] show that one joint standard deviation is sufficient. The algorithm in [8] includes two stages, and the purpose of the second stage – which uses a slightly different model – is basically to verify the result of the first stage. In this paper, we only consider the first stage, and all our numerical comparisons are restricted to this stage.

In the work of Van De Sompel and Brady [9], the class prior parameters (i.e., the μ_k's and σ_k's) were also individual for each class. They proposed to include a third subproblem in the SRS formulation to compute these parameters. In our experience it is cumbersome to get that approach to work properly, and this could explain why neither experiments nor results of that approach were reported in the original publication.

In summary, the novelty of this work lies in the assumption of a joint estimate $\bar{\sigma}$ for the class prior standard deviation, which is computed from the given data. Thus we include a third subproblem in the model, similar to [9], but we assume that the mean attenuation coefficients are known and fixed.

2.3 The Optimization Algorithm

We solve the minimization problem in (1) by using an iterative algorithm where we alternate between subproblems where we solve for one unknown, while the others are kept fixed.

Subproblem 1. Here we consider the computation of the reconstruction x^* while the segmentation and class priors are assumed fixed, using the same simplification of the model as introduced in [8]:

$$x^* = \underset{x}{\mathrm{argmin}} \left(\lambda_{\mathrm{data}} \|\mathbf{A}\,x - b\|_2^2 + \sum_{j=1}^{N} \frac{(x_j - \hat{\mu}_j)^2}{2\hat{\sigma}_j^2} \right). \tag{4}$$

The first term is the classic least squares data fitting term, and the second term is the segmentation influence where the following simplifications have been introduced:

$$\hat{\mu}_j = \sum_{k=1}^{K} \delta_{jk}\mu_k, \qquad \hat{\sigma}_j^2 = \sum_{k=1}^{K} \left(\delta_{jk}(\bar{\sigma}^2 + \mu_k^2) \right) - \hat{\mu}_j^2. \tag{5}$$

The pixel-wise bulk statistics $\hat{\mu}_j$ and $\hat{\sigma}_j^2$ are averages of the class prior parameters weighted by the current belief in each class (i.e., the class probability). With those assumptions, (4) is a linear least-squares problem which can be solved efficiently using the classical CGLS algorithm.

Subproblem 2. Here the reconstruction and class priors are fixed while we compute the segmentation or, more specifically, the class probabilities δ^*:

$$\delta^* = \underset{\delta}{\mathrm{argmin}} \left(\lambda_{\mathrm{class}} \sum_{k=1}^{K} \mathcal{R}(\delta_k) - \sum_{j=1}^{N} \log \left[\sum_{k=1}^{K} \delta_{jk} w_{jk} \right] \right), \tag{6}$$

in which

$$w_{jk} = \frac{1}{\sqrt{2\pi}\bar{\sigma}} \exp \left(-\frac{(x_j - \mu_k)^2}{2\bar{\sigma}^2} \right).$$

The first term is the regularization imposing a neighborhood dependence on the class probabilities δ_{jk}. We use Total Variation (TV) regularization, which is equivalent to the 1-norm of the gradient magnitude for the k'th prior class. When using the forward finite difference approximation, the function takes the form

$$\mathcal{R}_{\mathrm{TV}}(\delta_k) = \sum_{j \in \mathcal{J}} \sqrt{(-\delta_{jk} + \delta_{j'k})^2 + (-\delta_{jk} + \delta_{j''k})^2}, \tag{7}$$

where $\mathcal{J}$ represent the pixel indices of the image domain, while j' and j'' denote neighbor pixels in the horizontal and vertical directions. At the boundary of the image domain, the value of the nearest pixel is repeated.

Due to the constraints (2) it is recommended to compute δ^* using the Frank-Wolfe algorithm [2] or a similar conditional gradient method. A small constant, $\epsilon = 10^{-3}$, is added to Eq. 7, in order to make the function differentiable at all points.

Subproblem 3. Here the reconstruction and segmentation are fixed, while the class prior standard deviation $\bar{\sigma}$ is computed:

$$\bar{\sigma}^* = \underset{0.1 > \bar{\sigma} > 0}{\mathrm{argmin}} - \sum_{j=1}^{N} \log \left[\sum_{k=1}^{K} \frac{\delta_{jk}}{\sqrt{2\pi}\bar{\sigma}} \exp \left(-\frac{(x_j - \mu_k)^2}{2\bar{\sigma}^2} \right) \right] \tag{8}$$

With the constraints on δ_{jk} (Eq. 2) and the limitations on $x_j = [0,1]$ and $\mu_k = [0,1]$, the problem can be solved within the specified bounds, with a constrained optimization method, e.g., the interior-point algorithm [4] using the implementation in Matlab.

3   Simulation Experiments

The numerical experiments are not meant to compare the performance of the proposed SRS algorithm against classic or competing reconstruction methods. For such a comparison, we refer to [8]. Instead, the purpose is to investigate the effect of introducing the joint class prior standard deviation $\bar{\sigma}$. Recall that in the approach of [8] the user was forced to choose the σ_k's. The question is then whether our approach is able to compete against the original approach.

We perform numerical experiments using different simulated phantoms of varying difficulty. Experiments on real data are considered out of scope for this initial study. We use the optimal settings (i.e., manually chosen regularization parameters) for each phantom type, and we compare the following two versions of the SRS algorithm:

1. The *baseline method* where we specify a joint $\bar{\sigma}_\mathrm{B}$ for all classes.
2. The *proposed new method* where $\bar{\sigma}$ is computed from the data (from an initial guess provided by the user).

Scanner Set-Up. A 2D CT scanning scenario is simulated using the function `paralleltomo` from the AIR Tools package [6], which emulates a system with a parallel-beam geometry. The phantoms are generated in a square domain of 64×64 pixels, i.e., $N = 64^2 = 4096$ unknowns.

The detector has full coverage of the object at any given projection angle. Using a detector pixel spacing of 1 image pixel, the required number of detectors is therefore $N_\mathrm{dect} = \lceil \sqrt{2N} \rceil = 91$. The X-ray projections are $6°, 12°, \ldots, 180°$, for a total of $N_\mathrm{proj} = 30$ projections. Thus, the amount of data is $M = N_\mathrm{dect} \cdot N_\mathrm{proj} = 91 \cdot 30 = 2730$, and the under-determined rate of this system is $M/N = 0.67$.

Gaussian noise e is added to the simulated data to further represent imperfect data-acquisition. The noise level $\eta = \|e\|_2 / \|\mathbf{A}\, x^\mathrm{GT}\|_2$, where x^GT denotes the true object, is set to either 0.01 or 0.05, depending on the experiment and phantom.

Phantoms. Three different types of phantoms are used for the experiments, each representing an object with different challenging aspects. An instantiation of each phantom type and their respective correct segmentation is shown in Fig. 4 (top row). The various relevant algorithmic settings are listed in Table 1.

Table 1. Settings for experiments.

Phantom	λ_data	λ_class	$\bar{\sigma}_\mathrm{B}$	μ	η
Grains	0.1	2.2	0.05	$\{0, \frac{1}{(K-1)}, \frac{2}{(K-1)}, \ldots, \frac{(K-1)}{(K-1)}\}$	0.05
4-phase	20	0.5	0.05	$\{0, 0.33, 0.66, 1\}$	0.01
3-phase	100	0.4	0.05	$\{0.1, 0.2, 0.525\}$	0.01

The **grains** phantom has $K = 8$ classes appearing as single homogeneous regions with straight-line interfaces. It is a relatively easy phantom for the SRS algorithm to handle, as it is possible to run a high weighting on the regularization without risking that small features are eroded.

The **4-phase** phantom contains a background and three additional classes that appear in multiple homogeneous regions, each of which is varying in size and has irregular boundaries. This phantom is more challenging as too much regularization will tend to erode small regions.

The **3-phase** phantom is composed of $K = 3$ classes, where one is the background and the other two appear as multiple overlapping blob-like regions. All the materials have smoothly varying intensities (which are not Gaussian distributed). This makes the problem even more challenging, as the classes are not fully separable by intensity only, and since the specified class prior Gaussian assumption does not fit the distribution of intensities. Therefore, we choose a lower noise level for the experiments with this phantom.

Three different experimental set-ups are used in order to explore various aspects of the SRS algorithm.

Experiment 1. We run the baseline method and the proposed method with initial values $\bar{\sigma} = \{0.01, 0.03, 0.05, 0.07, 0.09\}$, using all three phantoms. This is repeated 10 times using different initializations of the random noise e. The purpose of this experiment is two-fold. One is to explore the influence of the initial $\bar{\sigma}$ for the proposed method on different types of problems. It is important to see if the performance is stable over different initializations, as it would otherwise be an important parameter for the user to choose in practical applications. Secondly, the experiment serves to compare the overall performance against the baseline method.

Experiment 2. We run 50 repetitions using both the baseline method and the proposed method (with initial $\bar{\sigma} = 0.05$) on the **grains** phantom with different noise initializations. This experiment allows us to see the variation in the performance.

Experiment 3. This experiment serves to show how $\bar{\sigma}$ evolves during the iterations. Using 4 different initializations of the **grains** phantom, we run the proposed method with initial $\bar{\sigma} = \{0.01, 0.03, 0.05, 0.07, 0.09\}$.

Algorithm. The SRS algorithm consists of three individual optimization steps within each iteration of the entire algorithm, and in each step we need solve one subproblem as described in Sect. 2.3. That results in several additional optimizer settings, which are described here.

The stopping criterion for the outer iterations is

$$\frac{\|x^{n+1} - x^n\|_2}{\|x^n\|_2} \leq 10^{-3},$$

where n counts the iterations, plus a maximum of 20 iterations. The stopping criterion for the CGLS algorithm is that the change in the independent variable drops below 10^{-4} plus a maximum of 2500 iterations.

The Frank-Wolfe algorithm for updating the segmentation uses a convergence tolerance of $5 \cdot 10^{-5}$ for the change in the norm of the independent variable, plus a maximum number of 25000 iteration. Each iteration of this algorithm contains an optimization for the step-size. This was done using Matlab's built-in `fminbnd` function, with a tolerance of 10^{-5} for the change in the step-size. The Frank-Wolfe step is the most time-consuming part of the SRS algorithm, and changes in its settings and parameters typically have the greatest impact on the computing time.

The optimization for the third subproblem was done using Matlab's built-in `fmincon` function with default settings (i.e., the interior point algorithm with 1000 iterations maximum).

Evaluation. As all the experiments are simulated problems, we have the luxury of knowing both the underlying true image x^{GT} and its segmentation L^{GT}, which allows us to define error measures for the reconstruction and the segmentation

$$x_{\mathrm{Err}} = \frac{\|x^{\mathrm{GT}} - x^*\|_2^2}{\|x^{\mathrm{GT}}\|_2^2}, \qquad L_{\mathrm{Err}} = \frac{1}{N} \sum_{j=1}^{N} \mathcal{I}(l_j^{\mathrm{GT}} \neq l_j^*), \tag{9}$$

where $\mathcal{I}$ is a logical indicator function.

4   Results and Discussion

The performance results of Experiment 1 are summarized in Fig. 1 which shows that, compared with the baseline method, the proposed new method provides comparable results with respect to reconstruction errors and segmentation errors.

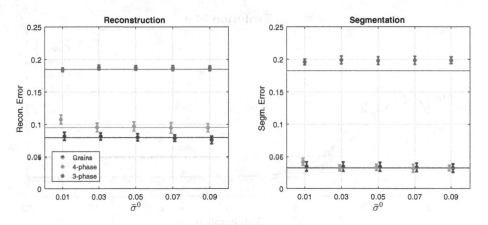

Fig. 1. Experiment 1: Illustration of the difference between using an optimal fixed $\bar{\sigma}_{\mathrm{B}}$ in the baseline algorithm (solid line) versus various initial $\bar{\sigma}$'s for the proposed new algorithm (error bars). The solid line is drawn at the average of the repeated baseline experiments. The error bars show the mean $\pm$ one standard deviation of 10 repeated experiments with different noise realization.

Moreover, obviously the numerical results by our method are very robust with respect to the initial value $\bar{\sigma}$.

The histograms of reconstruction and segmentation errors for Experiment 2 are shown in Fig. 2. The correlation coefficient between the errors for the two methods is ≈ 0.9, for both the reconstruction and the segmentation errors. It further shows that, for different realizations of the noise with the same noise level, our method performs similarly as the baseline method.

Figure 3 illustrates the evolution of $\bar{\sigma}$ during the SRS optimization algorithm, applied to 4 different realizations of the **grains** phantom. Observe that it is the variation within the random instances of the phantom that provides most

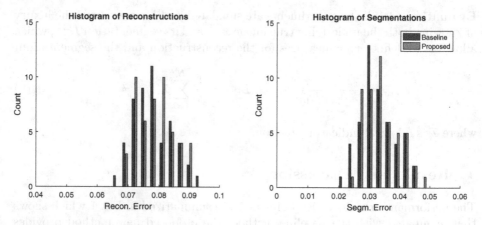

Fig. 2. Experiment 2: Histogram of reconstruction and segmentation errors for both methods tested on an instantiation of the **grains** phantom.

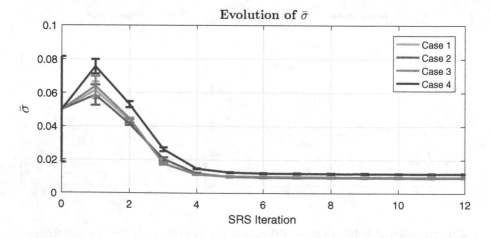

Fig. 3. Experiment 3: The evolution of $\bar{\sigma}$ for four different random realizations of the **grains** phantom. Each line shows the average $\bar{\sigma}^n \pm$ one standard deviation across all experiments with different initial $\bar{\sigma}^0$'s.

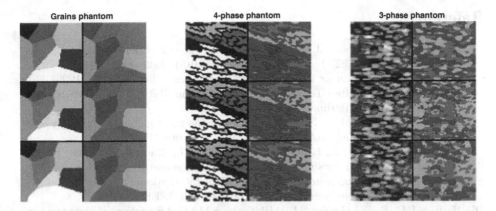

Fig. 4. The worst case for each phantom type. Respectively, the reconstruction (left) and segmentation (right) of the ground truth object (top), the baseline experiment (middle) and the worst case experiment with the proposed method (bottom).

variation in the results, while the choice of the initial $\bar{\sigma}$ has little influence. The shown trend for $\bar{\sigma}$ was similar in the other phantoms as well.

Finally, the qualitative differences between the two methods are illustrated in Fig. 4. The worst case is shown for each phantom type, meaning the case from Experiment 1 where the proposed method had the largest error, i.e., $x_{Err} + L_{Err}$ relative to the baseline experiment.

Generally, using the proposed variant of the SRS algorithm we observe that the errors for both reconstruction and segmentation are slightly larger than the baseline algorithm (Fig. 1), but qualitatively the results are similar (Fig. 4). Moreover, the choice of the initial $\bar{\sigma}$ has little influence on the convergence and the result (Fig. 3). In summary, for the type of applications where an assumption of equal class variance is appropriate it seems feasible to use our proposed method. Arguably, the minor decrease in accuracy is justified by the gained simplicity of having fewer required parameters.

5   Conclusion

We proposed a user-friendly approach for simultaneous tomographic reconstruction and segmentation strategies by using intensity-based classifiers, which requires fewer input parameters comparing with the existing method in [8]. In our new method, we use a joint standard deviation $\bar{\sigma}$ which is computed as part of the reconstruction problem. Our numerical experiments show that the results for the simplified algorithm are comparable to the ones with the best selected $\bar{\sigma}$, and that the proposed new method is robust with respect to the initialization.

Acknowledgments. This work is supported by Advanced grant no. 291405 "High-Definition Tomography" from the European Research Council.

References

1. Batenburg, K.J., Sijbers, J.: DART: a practical reconstruction algorithm for discrete tomography. IEEE Trans. Image Process. **20**(9), 2542–2553 (2011)
2. Bertsekas, D.P.: Nonlinear Programming. Athena Scientific, Belmont (1999)
3. Buzug, T.M.: Computed Tomography: From Photon Statistics to Modern Cone-Beam CT. Springer, Berline (2008)
4. Byrd, R.H., Hribar, M.E., Nocedal, J.: An interior point algorithm for large-scale nonlinear programming. SIAM J. Optim. **9**(4), 877–900 (1999)
5. Depypere, M., Nuyts, J., Laperre, K., Carmeliet, G., Maes, F., Suetens, P.: The minimal entropy prior for simultaneous reconstruction and segmentation of in vivo microCT trabecular bone images. In: 2009 IEEE International Symposium on Biomedical Imaging: From Nano to Macro, pp. 586–589. IEEE (2009)
6. Hansen, P.C., Saxild-Hansen, M.: AIR Tools - a MATLAB package of algebraic iterative reconstruction methods. J. Comput. Appl. Math. **236**(8), 2167–2178 (2012)
7. Ramlau, R., Ring, W.: A Mumford-Shah level-set approach for the inversion and segmentation of X-ray tomography data. J. Comput. Phys. **221**(2), 539–557 (2007)
8. Romanov, M., Dahl, A.B., Dong, Y., Hansen, P.C.: Simultaneous tomographic reconstruction and segmentation with class priors. Inverse Prob. Sci. Eng. **24**(8), 1432–1453 (2015)
9. Van de Sompel, D., Brady, M.: Simultaneous reconstruction and segmentation algorithm for positron emission tomography and transmission tomography. In: Proceedings of the 5th IEEE International Symposium on Biomedical Imaging: From Nano to Macro, pp. 1035–1038. IEEE (2008)
10. Yoon, S., Pineda, A.R., Fahrig, R.: Simultaneous segmentation and reconstruction: a level set method approach for limited view computed tomography. Med. Phys. **37**(5), 2329–2340 (2010)

An Optimal Transport-Based Restoration Method for Q-Ball Imaging

Thomas Vogt$^{(\boxtimes)}$ and Jan Lellmann

Institute of Mathematics and Image Computing (MIC),
University of Lübeck, Lübeck, Germany
{vogt,lellmann}@mic.uni-luebeck.de

Abstract. We propose a variational approach for edge-preserving total variation (TV)-based regularization of Q-ball data from high angular resolution diffusion imaging (HARDI). While total variation is among the most popular regularizers for variational problems, its application to orientation distribution functions (ODF), as they naturally arise in Q-ball imaging, is not straightforward. We propose to use an extension that specifically takes into account the metric on the underlying orientation space. The key idea is to write the difference quotients in the TV seminorm in terms of the Wasserstein statistical distance from optimal transport. We combine this regularizer with a matching Wasserstein data fidelity term. Using the Kantorovich-Rubinstein duality, the variational model can be formulated as a convex optimization problem that can be solved using a primal-dual algorithm. We demonstrate the effectiveness of the proposed framework on real and synthetic Q-ball data.

Keywords: Variational methods · Total variation · Q-ball imaging · Wasserstein distance

1 Introduction

Overview. In Q-ball imaging, one considers data $f : \Omega \to \mathcal{P}(\mathbb{S}^2)$ given on an open, bounded, connected image domain $\Omega \subset \mathbb{R}^d$ with values in the space of *Borel probability measures* $\mathcal{P}(\mathbb{S}^2)$ over the two-dimensional unit sphere $\mathbb{S}^2 \subseteq \mathbb{R}^3$. For each $x \in \Omega$, the value $f_x := f(x)$ is a Borel probability measure on $\mathbb{S}^2$. In particular, we have $f_x(A) \in [0,1]$ for each Borel subset $A \subset \mathbb{S}^2$ and $f_x(\mathbb{S}^2) = 1$. We consider a variational approach for restoring noisy Q-ball data,

$$\inf_{u:\Omega \to \mathcal{P}(\mathbb{S}^2)} \int_\Omega \delta(f_x, u_x) \, dx + R(u),$$

with an appropriately chosen pointwise distance $\delta(\cdot, \cdot)$ (Fig. 1). This has applications in the field of medical fiber tractography of cerebral white matter based on data that is obtained from diffusion-weighted (DW) magnetic resonance imaging (MRI) or, more precisely, high angular resolution diffusion imaging (HARDI) [23].

© Springer International Publishing AG 2017
F. Lauze et al. (Eds.): SSVM 2017, LNCS 10302, pp. 271–282, 2017.
DOI: 10.1007/978-3-319-58771-4_22

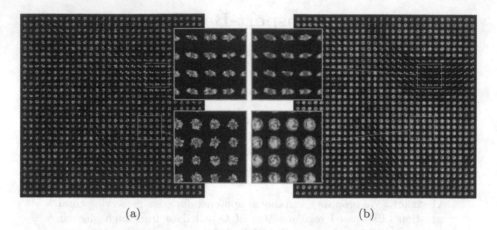

(a)   (b)

Fig. 1. Q-ball image of the corpus callosum, reconstructed from HARDI data of the human brain [20], (a) with added white Gaussian noise and (b) our TV-based reconstruction using a Wasserstein-1 data term. Noise is reduced substantially, while regions with isotropic diffusion are accurately restored or preserved.

In this work, we focus on edge-preserving total variation (TV) regularization, i.e., $R(u)$ should encourage gradient sparsity. To this end, we adapt a specialized formulation of TV that takes the metric on the space $\mathbb{S}^2$ into account. Similarly, for the metric $\delta(\cdot, \cdot)$, we focus on the Wasserstein-1-distance from the theory of optimal transport [24].

Motivation: Q-Ball Imaging. In medical applications, the diffusivity of water in tissues that exhibit fibrous microstructures, such as muscle fibres or axons in cerebral white matter, contains valuable information about the fiber architecture in the living organism. *Diffusion-weighted* (DW) magnetic resonance imaging (MRI) is well-established as a way of measuring the main diffusion directions by consecutively applying six or more magnetic field gradients. In *diffusion tensor imaging* (DTI) [2], few measurements are combined to extract the main diffusion direction which provides sufficient information in the case of well-aligned fiber directions. However, crossing and branching of fibers at a scale smaller than the voxel size, also called intra-voxel orientational heterogeneity (IVOH), often occurs in human cerebral white matter due to the relatively large (millimeter-scale) voxel size of DW-MRI data. Therefore, DTI data is insufficient for accurate fiber tract mapping in regions with complex fiber crossings.

High angular resolution diffusion imaging (HARDI) [22] allows for more accurate restoration of IVOH by increasing the number of applied magnetic field gradients. A widely used reconstruction scheme for HARDI data is *Q-ball imaging* [23] where the quantity of interest is the marginal probability of diffusion in a given direction, the *orientation distribution function* (ODF) [1]. However, the high angular resolution results in a larger amount of noise. Consequently, HARDI data is a particularly interesting target for postprocessing in terms of denoising and regularization [6].

Contribution. We propose a non-parametric Wasserstein-total variation regularizer for Q-ball data. Our approach is based on the observation that the regularizer in [14] amounts to a Wasserstein-based distance on the jump set. We supply the necessary theory and formally prove this connection (Sect. 2). We derive an efficient numerical formulation (Sect. 3) as a primal-dual saddle-point problem involving only convex functions. Applications to synthetic and real-world data show significant reduction of noise as well as qualitatively convincing results (Sect. 4).

Related Models. There are approaches that apply TV regularization directly to the HARDI signal $S(q)$ [13,16]. These approaches are not applicable to the ODFs of the Q-ball model which our model is aimed at. Other TV models depend on a specific parametrization of the ODFs by spherical harmonics [4,18]. In contrast, our proposed model does not depend on the specific parametrization of ODFs.

In [25], Mumford-Shah and Potts functionals are defined for manifold-valued images introducing an edge-preserving model for Q-ball data equipped with the Fisher-Rao metric following [5,10,11]. However, the Fisher-Rao metric does not take the manifold structure of $\mathbb{S}^2$ into consideration and is not amenable to biological interpretations [17].

Our work is based on [14], where the authors derive a total variation regularizer for probability measures as a convex relaxation scheme regularization of manifold-valued images. An extension of the Kantorovich-Rubinstein formulation of the Wasserstein distance that our saddle-point formulation makes use of has been applied in [15] to the simpler problem of real-valued image denoising.

Our proposed method incorporates a TV model that does not depend on the specific parametrization of the ODFs. It is based on data fidelity and regularization terms that take the manifold structure of $\mathbb{S}^2$ into account, without reducing the ODF model to a simpler statistical interpretation. Furthermore, the model can be efficiently implemented using state-of-the-art primal-dual methods.

2   A W_1-TV_{W_1} Functional for Q-Ball Data

A straightforward approach to denoising probability distributions is to apply a Rudin-Osher-Fatemi (ROF) model, based on the L^2 norm on $L^2(\mathbb{S}^2)$ and a suitable extension of the total variation (TV) regularizer, to the probability density functions:

$$\inf_{u:\Omega\to\mathcal{P}(\mathbb{S}^2)}\int_\Omega\int_{\mathbb{S}^2}(f_x(z)-u_x(z))^2\,dz\,dx+\lambda TV(u) \tag{1}$$

However, this does not allow singular measures for u_x and does not account for the (Riemannian) manifold structure of $\mathbb{S}^2$: as long as the supports of u_x and f_x do not intersect, the local cost in the data term does not depend on the relative orientation of the modes (peaks) of u_x and f_x in $\mathbb{S}^2$.

The Metric Space $(\mathcal{P}(\mathbb{S}^2), W_1)$. In order to account for the manifold structure of $\mathbb{S}^2$, we equip $\mathcal{P}(\mathbb{S}^2)$ with the Wasserstein-1-metric

$$W_1(\mu, \mu') := \inf \left\{ \int_{\mathbb{S}^2 \times \mathbb{S}^2} d_{\mathbb{S}^2}(x, y) \, d\gamma(x, y) : \ \gamma \in \mathcal{P}(\mathbb{S}^2 \times \mathbb{S}^2), \ \pi_1\gamma = \mu, \pi_2\gamma = \mu' \right\}$$

that is well-known from the theory of optimal transport [24]. Here $\pi_i\gamma$ denotes the i-th marginal of the measure γ that is supported on the product space $\mathbb{S}^2 \times \mathbb{S}^2$, i.e., $\pi_1\gamma(A) := \gamma(A \times \mathbb{S}^2)$ and $\pi_2\gamma(B) := \gamma(\mathbb{S}^2 \times B)$. By $d_{\mathbb{S}^2}(\cdot, \cdot)$ we refer to the geodesic distance metric on the Riemannian manifold $\mathbb{S}^2$.

Data Term. Using this natural distance, we consider functionals of the form

$$\inf_{u:\Omega \to \mathcal{P}(\mathbb{S}^2)} W_1(f_x(z), z_x(z)) + R(u).$$

If one discretizes the space of probability measures $\mathcal{P}(\mathbb{S}^2)$ using discrete probability measures on a set of points $z^1, \ldots, z^l \in \mathbb{S}^2$, a naive implementation of W_1 requires to discretize the transport plan γ using l^2 points, which quickly becomes prohibitively large. Fortunately, W_1 is particularly well-suited for efficient implementation due to the Kantorovich-Rubinstein duality [12]:

$$W_1(\mu, \mu') = \sup \left\{ \int_{\mathbb{S}^2} p \, d(\mu - \mu') : p \in \mathrm{Lip}_1(\mathbb{S}^2) \right\}, \tag{2}$$

where we denote by $\mathrm{Lip}_1(\mathbb{S}^2)$ the space of Lipschitz-continuous functions on $\mathbb{S}^2$ with Lipschitz-constant not larger than 1.

Regularization. We claim that if one chooses the W_1 metric for the data term, the regularizer R should also be modified accordingly. In order to motivate this, we consider what the intended behavior of R should be on "cartoon-like" functions $u : \Omega \to \mathcal{P}(\mathbb{S}^2)$ that only take two different values: let

$$u(x) = \begin{cases} u^+, & x \in U, \\ u^-, & x \in \Omega \setminus U, \end{cases} \tag{3}$$

for some fixed set $U \subset \Omega$ with smooth boundary ∂U, and $u^+, u^- \in \mathcal{P}(\mathbb{S}^2)$. Assuming for a moment that u^+ and u^- have a density, classical vector-valued TV assigns to such u a penalty of $\mathcal{H}^{d-1}(\partial U) \cdot \|u^+ - u^-\|_2$, where the $(d-1)$-dimensional Hausdorff measure $\mathcal{H}^{d-1}(\partial U)$ is the length or area of the jump set. Similarly to the data term, we propose to replace the suboptimal 2-norm by the Wasserstein distance, i.e., we require

$$R(u) = \mathcal{H}^{d-1}(\partial U) \cdot W_1(u^+, u^-) \tag{4}$$

instead. We consider the following formulation for the regularizer R.

Definition 1. *For a function* $u : \Omega \to \mathcal{P}(\mathbb{S}^2)$, *we define*

$$\mathrm{TV}_{W_1}(u) := \sup \left\{ \int_{\Omega} \langle -\operatorname{div} p(x, \cdot), u_x \rangle \, dx : \right.$$

$$\left. p \in C_c^1(\Omega \times \mathbb{S}^2; \mathbb{R}^d), \ p(x, \cdot) \in \mathrm{Lip}_1(\mathbb{S}^2; \mathbb{R}^d) \right\}, \quad (5)$$

where $\langle g, \mu \rangle := \int_{\mathbb{S}^2} g(z) \, d\mu(z)$ *whenever* μ *is a measure on* $\mathbb{S}^2$ *and* g *is a real- or vector-valued function on* $\mathbb{S}^2$. *The divergence* $\operatorname{div} p(x, \cdot)$ *is understood to be taken in the variable* x *only, and pointwise in the second argument.*

Note that the Lipschitz constraint in (5) can be efficiently implemented as a pointwise constraint on the norm of $\nabla_z p(x, z)$. The formulation is a special case of the one proposed in [14] in the context of approximating manifold-valued variational problems. However, the authors did not include any precise results about correctness in the functional-analytic setting.

We now supply the proof that this functional has the desired property (4):

Proposition 1. *Assume that* U *is compactly contained in* Ω *with* C^2*-boundary* ∂U. *Let* $u^+, u^- \in \mathcal{P}(\mathbb{S}^2)$ *and let* $u : \Omega \to \mathcal{P}(\mathbb{S}^2)$ *be defined as in (3). Then*

$$\mathrm{TV}_{W_1}(u) = \mathcal{H}^{d-1}(\partial U) \cdot W_1(u^+, u^-).$$

Proof. Let $p : \Omega \times \mathbb{S}^2 \to \mathbb{R}^d$ satisfy the constraints in (5) and denote by ν the outer unit normal of ∂U. The set Ω is bounded, u^+, u^- are probability measures, and $\|\operatorname{div} p\|_{C^0(\Omega \times \mathbb{S}^2)} < \infty$ holds due to the regularity assumptions on p, therefore the following integrals converge absolutely. Using Fubini's and Gauss's theorem, we compute

$$\int_{\Omega} \langle -\operatorname{div} p(x, \cdot), u_x \rangle \, dx$$

$$= \int_{\mathbb{S}^2} \int_U -\operatorname{div} p(x, z) \, dx \, du^-(z) + \int_{\mathbb{S}^2} \int_{\Omega \setminus U} -\operatorname{div} p(x, z) \, dx \, du^+(z)$$

$$\stackrel{\text{Gauss}}{=} \int_{\mathbb{S}^2} \int_{\partial U} p(x, z) \cdot \nu(x) \, d\mathcal{H}^{d-1}(x) \, d(u^+ - u^-)(z)$$

$$= \int_{\partial U} \left[\int_{\mathbb{S}^2} p(x, z) \cdot \nu(x) \, d(u^+ - u^-)(z) \right] d\mathcal{H}^{d-1}(x)$$

$$\leq \int_{\partial U} W_1(u^+, u^-) \, d\mathcal{H}^{d-1}(x) = \mathcal{H}^{d-1}(\partial U) W_1(u^+, u^-).$$

For the inequality, we used that $z \mapsto p(x, z)$ is 1-Lipschitz; therefore $z \mapsto p(x, z) \cdot \nu(x)$ is 1-Lipschitz as well and fulfills the constraints in the dual definition of W_1 in (2). Taking the supremum over p as in (5), we arrive at

$$\mathrm{TV}_{W_1}(u) \leq \mathcal{H}^{d-1}(\partial U) W_1(u^+, u^-).$$

For the reverse inequality, let $\tilde{p} \in \mathrm{Lip}_1(\mathbb{S}^2)$. By the assumption on ∂U, the unit normal field ν is continuously differentiable. Since U is also compactly contained in Ω, there is an extension $\tilde{\nu} \in C_c^1(\Omega)$ of ν onto all of Ω. Now $p(x, z) := \tilde{p}(z)\tilde{\nu}(x)$ has the properties required in (5) and hence, by the same computation as above,

$$
\begin{aligned}
\mathrm{TV}_{W_1}(u) &\geq \int_\Omega \langle -\operatorname{div} p(x, \cdot), u_x \rangle \, dx \\
&= \int_{\partial U} \left[\int_{\mathbb{S}^2} \tilde{p}(z) \, d(u^+ - u^-)(z) \right] \|\nu(x)\|_2^2 \, d\mathcal{H}^{d-1}(x) \\
&= \mathcal{H}^{d-1}(\partial U) \int_{\mathbb{S}^2} \tilde{p}(z) \, d(u^+ - u^-)(z).
\end{aligned}
$$

Taking the supremum over all $\tilde{p} \in \mathrm{Lip}_1(\mathbb{S}^2)$ and using the characterization (2) of W_1 shows the desired reverse inequality and concludes the proof. $\square$

Complete $W_1 - \mathrm{TV}_{W_1}$ Model. Given a noisy reference image $f : \Omega \to \mathcal{P}(\mathbb{S}^2)$, we propose to solve the variational minimization problem

$$
\inf_{u:\Omega \to \mathcal{P}(\mathbb{S}^2)} \int_\Omega W_1(f_x, u_x) \, dx + \lambda \mathrm{TV}_{W_1}(u) \tag{6}
$$

using the definitions of $W_1(\cdot, \cdot)$ and $\mathrm{TV}_{W_1}(u)$ in (2) and (5). As argued above, this naturally penalizes jumps in u by the Wasserstein distance of the left and right limit, correctly taking the metric structure of $\mathbb{S}^2$ into account both in the data term as well as in the regularizer.

We remark that the requirement (4) does not define the regularizer uniquely. However, as shown above, setting $R = \mathrm{TV}_{W_1}$ satisfies the requirement, has a compact representation and can be efficiently implemented using (2).

3   Numerical Scheme

We closely follow the discretization scheme in [14] in order to formulate the problem in a saddle-point form that is amenable to standard primal-dual algorithms.

Discretization. We assume a d-dimensional image domain Ω that is discretized using n points $x^1, \ldots, x^n \in \Omega$. Differentiation in Ω is done on a staggered grid with Neumann boundary conditions such that the dual operator to the differential operator D is the negative divergence with vanishing boundary values.

The model is not only valid for the manifold $\mathbb{S}^2$, therefore we state the setting in full generality: We assume that the image takes values in the space of probability measures on an s-dimensional manifold $\mathcal{M}$ that is discretized using l points $z^1, \ldots, z^l \in \mathcal{M}$. If $u, v \in \mathbb{R}^{n,l}$ are the discretizations of functions on $\Omega \times \mathcal{M}$, i.e. $u_k^i \approx u(x^i, z^k)$, we define an L^2-inner product by

$$
\langle u, v \rangle_b := \sum_{i,k} b_k u_k^i v_k^i
$$

using the weights vector $b \in \mathbb{R}^l$ to account for the volume element at each $z^k \in \mathcal{M}$. Gradients of functions on $\mathcal{M}$ are defined on a staggered grid of m points $y^1, \ldots, y^m \in \mathcal{M}$, such that each y^j has r neighboring points $\mathcal{N}_j \subset \{1, \ldots, l\}$, $\#\mathcal{N}_j = r$, among the z^k so that the gradient $g \in \mathbb{R}^{m,s}$ of a function $p \in \mathbb{R}^l$ (i. e. $p_k \approx p(z^k)$) on the manifold $\mathcal{M}$ is encoded by

$$A^j g^j = B^j P^j p, \text{ for each } j \in \{1, \ldots, m\}.$$

The matrices $P^j \in \{0, 1\}^{r,l}$, $A^j \in \mathbb{R}^{s,s}$ and $B^j \in \mathbb{R}^{s,r}$ tie g^j to the gradient of p on the manifold $\mathcal{M}$; for details we refer the reader to [14].

Discretized $W_1 - \mathrm{TV}_{W_1}$ Model. Based on the above discretization, we can formulate saddle point forms for (6) and (1) that allow to apply a primal-dual first-order method such as [3]. In the following, the input or reference image is given by $f \in \mathbb{R}^{l,n}$ and the dimensions of the primal and dual variables are

$$u \in \mathbb{R}^{l,n}, \quad p \in \mathbb{R}^{l,d,n}, \quad g \in \mathbb{R}^{n,m,s,d}, \quad p_0 \in \mathbb{R}^{l,n}, \quad g_0 \in \mathbb{R}^{n,m,s}.$$

Note that, for $\min\{d, s\} \leq 2$ (in particular for $\mathcal{M} = \mathbb{S}^2$), explicit formulas for the orthogonal projections on the spectral norm balls are available. These projections appear in the proximal steps due to the spectral norm constraints on g (denoted by $\| \cdot \|_\sigma$).

Saddle-Point Form with Wasserstein Data Term. Using a W_1 data term, the problem's saddle point form reads

$$\min_{u} \max_{p,g} \quad W_1(u, f) + \langle Du, p \rangle_b$$

$$\text{s.t.} \quad u^i \geq 0, \ \langle u^i, b \rangle = 1, \ A^j g_t^{ij} = B^j P^j p_t^i, \ \|g^{ij}\|_\sigma \leq \lambda \ \forall i, j, t$$

or, again applying the Kantorovich-Rubinstein duality (2) to the data term,

$$\min_{u} \max_{p,g,p_0,g_0} \quad \langle u - f, p_0 \rangle_b + \langle Du, p \rangle_b$$

$$\text{s.t.} \quad u^i \geq 0, \ \langle u^i, b \rangle = 1 \ \forall i,$$

$$A^j g_t^{ij} = B^j P^j p_t^i, \ \|g^{ij}\|_\sigma \leq \lambda \ \forall i, j, t,$$

$$A^j g_0^{ij} = B^j P^j p_0^i, \ \|g_0^{ij}\|_2 \leq 1 \ \forall i, j.$$

The equality constraints can be included into the objective function by introducing suitable Lagrange multipliers.

Saddle Point Form with Quadratic Data Term. For comparison, we also implemented the quadratic model (1) using $\mathrm{TV} = \mathrm{TV}_{W_1}$. The quadratic data term can be implemented using the saddle point form

$$\min_{u} \max_{p,g} \quad \langle u - f, u - f \rangle_b + \langle Du, p \rangle_b$$

$$\text{s.t.} \quad u^i \geq 0, \ \langle u^i, b \rangle = 1, \ A^j g_t^{ij} = B^j P^j p_t^i, \ \|g^{ij}\|_\sigma \leq \lambda \ \forall i, j, t.$$

4   Experimental Results

We implemented our method in Python 3.5 using NumPy 1.11, PyCUDA 2016.1.2 and CUDA 7.5. The examples were computed on an Intel Xeon X5670 2.93 GHz with 24 GB of memory and an NVIDIA GeForce GTX 480 graphics card with 1,5 GB of dedicated video memory. For each step in the primal-dual algorithm, a set of kernels was launched on the GPU, while the primal-dual gap was computed on the CPU.

Synthetic 1D Images. The synthetic images were generated using the Multi-Tensor Simulation framework `dipy.sims.voxel` included in the Dipy project [9]. The choice of generation parameters as well as the addition of complex Gaussian noise follow the description in [7].

Unimodals. A first impression of the different behavior of the W_1 data term compared to a standard L^2 data term is given in Fig. 2, where very high regularization parameters λ force the model to produce constant images. The linearly changing unimodal orientation distribution is blurred by the L^2 data term, whereas the W_1 data term tends to concentrate the mass close to the median diffusion direction. Here, the ODF is called unimodal if there is one main diffusion direction even though, due to the symmetric structure of diffusion ODFs, an unimodal ODF has two modes (on opposite sites of the sphere).

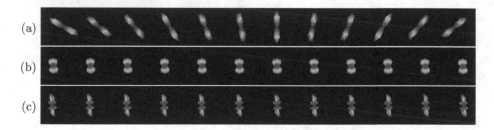

Fig. 2. (a) is a 1D image of synthetic unimodal ODFs where the main diffusion direction's angle varies linearly from left to right. This image is strongly regularized (large λ) using (b) an L^2 data term ($\lambda = 2$) and (c) a W_1 data term ($\lambda = 10$). The L^2 data term prefers a blurred mixture of diffusion directions whereas W_1 concentrates the mass close to the median diffusion direction.

A similar experiment (Fig. 3) demonstrates that the behavior of the W_1 model is preferable if the main diffusion directions of the unimodal ODFs underlie random distortion (noise). The ground truth consists of 12 identical unimodal ODFs, while the main diffusion directions have been randomly distorted in the input image following a Gaussian distribution on the angle with 20° standard deviation.

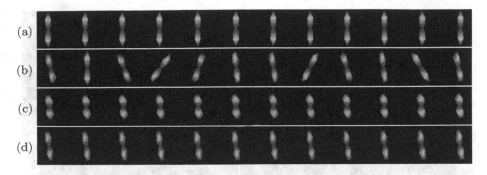

Fig. 3. Synthetic 1D Q-ball image of unimodal ODFs. (a) ground truth with constant modes and (b) noisy image with distorted diffusion directions. The noisy image was denoised using (c) a quadratic data term ($\lambda = 0.85$) and (d) the Wasserstein-1 data term ($\lambda = 2.5$). The directional noise causes blurring in the L^2 case, whereas the W_1 data term keeps the mass concentrated: The entropy of the original data is 2.267 compared to 2.336 (L^2) and 2.279 (W_1).

The regularization parameter λ was chosen so that the W_1 distance to the ground truth is minimized. Both models reduce the distortion significantly: While the distances of the noisy image to the ground truth are 1.368 with respect to W_1, the distances of the regularized images are 0.727 (W_1 model) and 0.621 (L^2 model).

However, using the W_1 models results in improved tightness (lower entropy) of the ODFs, which is particularly promising in the context of fiber tractography, where a precise localization of the main diffusion directions is necessary for accurately tracing fine structures.

Bimodals and Edge Preservation. The next example (Fig. 4) is inspired by [25], where a similar 1D image is used for demonstration of edge preservation properties. Six voxels of the ground truth are chosen to be bimodal ODFs with the two main diffusion directions separated by 55°. The remaining six voxels are almost uniform ODFs (unimodal ODFs with almost uniform distribution of eigenvalues corresponding to the main diffusion directions). As both models use the proposed TV_{W_1} regularizer, the edge is preserved and a piecewise constant image is produced in both cases.

However, just as classical ROF models tend to reduce jump sizes across edges, and lose contrast, the result produced using the L^2 model exhibits bimodal ODFs on both sides of the jump and the tightness of the original bimodals gets lost.

Real-World Example – Human Brain HARDI Data. In order to demonstrate the applicability of our method to real-world problems, we applied it to a 2D slice from the human brain HARDI data set from [20] that contains part of the corpus callosum. To fit the HARDI data to the Q-ball ODF model, we used a spherical harmonic reconstruction model from [1] as implemented in Dipy's `CsaOdfModel`. We added Gaussian noise following the process in [7]. For a 2D

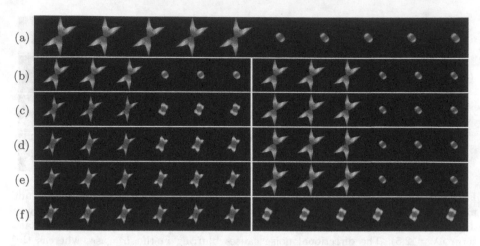

Fig. 4. Synthetic 1D Q-ball image of bimodal and almost uniform ODFs: The (a) original data was denoised (b)–(f) using an L^2 data term (left) and a W_1 data term (right) for increasing values of λ (on the left-hand side $\lambda = 0.05, 0.55, 1.05, 1.55, 2.05$ and on the right-hand side $\lambda = 0.05, 1.35, 2.65, 3.95, 5.25$). Both models preserve the edge. However, as is known from classical ROF models, the L^2 data term produces a gradual transition – i. e., contrast loss – towards the constant image, while the W_1 data term exhibits a sudden phase transition.

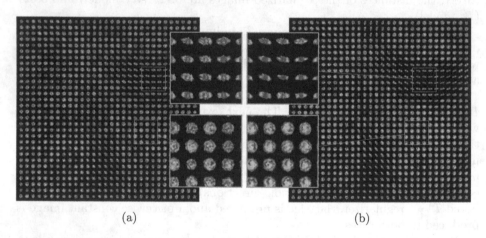

(a)   (b)

Fig. 5. Q-ball image of the corpus callosum, reconstructed from HARDI data of the human brain [20], with added white Gaussian noise and our TV-based reconstruction using (a) a quadratic data term ($\lambda = 0.11$) and (b) a Wasserstein-1 data term ($\lambda = 0.9$). The noise is reduced perceivably in both cases, but the quadratic data term tends to blur the diffusion direction (loss of contrast).

slice of 30×30 voxels, run times are appx. 28 min for the Wasserstein data term and 16 min for the quadratic data term. That's after the relative primal-dual gap is brought down to values in the order of 10^{-6} (deviation from global minimum less than 0.001 %). The regularization parameter λ was manually chosen based on visual inspection. However, optimization of λ with respect to the distance from the ground truth leads to similar results.

Figure 1 shows that the W_1 model succeeds at reducing the overall noise level. A comparison between the results produced by the L^2 and the W_1 model is shown in Fig. 5. While both models successfully reduce the noise, an overall blurring effect is more evident in the L^2 case – in line with our observations on the synthetic images discussed above.

5   Conclusion

We proposed a combined W_1–TV$_{W_1}$ variational model for restoring Q-ball data with values on the unit sphere $\mathbb{S}^2$, which properly takes the metric on $\mathbb{S}^2$ into account, both in the data term as well as in the regularizer.

We demonstrated that our proposed model exhibits classical properties of TV regularization schemes, including preservation of edges and formation of piecewise constant regions. In connection with an L^2 data term, basic properties of ROF models, such as a loss of contrast, can be replicated. The proposed combined W_1–TV$_{W_1}$ model is more robust, respects the metric on the original range $\mathbb{S}^2$ and better preserves unimodal distributions.

The model does not require symmetry of Q-ball data on the sphere, and therefore could be easily adapted to novel asymmetric ODF approaches [8,19]. Moreover, the approach is easily extendable to images with values in the probability space over a different manifold, or even a metric space, as they appear for example in statistical models of computer vision [21].

Despite a relatively efficient implementation using standard primal-dual algorithms, numerical performance is still limited by the high dimensionality of the problem even for small images. Developing specialized numerical methods, as well as a quantitative evaluation as a preprocessing step for fiber tractography, is subject to further work.

References

1. Aganj, I., Lenglet, C., Sapiro, G.: ODF reconstruction in Q-Ball imaging with solid angle consideration. In: Proceedings of the IEEE International Symposium on Biomedical Imaging, ISBI 2009, pp. 1398–1401 (2009)
2. Basser, P.J., Mattiello, J., LeBihan, D.: MR diffusion tensor spectroscopy and imaging. Biophys. J. 66(1), 259–207 (1994)
3. Chambolle, A., Pock, T.: A first-order primal-dual algorithm for convex problems with applications to imaging. J. Math. Imaging Vis. 40(1), 120–145 (2011)
4. Chen, Y., Guo, W., Zeng, Q., Liu, Y.: A nonstandard smoothing in reconstruction of apparent diffusion coefficient profiles from diffusion weighted images. Inverse Prob. Imaging 2(2), 205–224 (2008)
5. Cheng, J., Ghosh, A., Jiang, T., Deriche, R.: A Remannian framework for orientation distribution function computing. Med. Image Comput. Comput. Assist. Interv. 2009 12(1), 911–918 (2009)

6. Delputte, S., Dierckx, H., Fieremans, E., D'Asseler, Y., Achten, R., Lemahieu, I.: Postprocessing of brain white matter fiber orientation distribution functions. In: ISBI 2007, pp. 784–787 (2007)

7. Descoteaux, M., Angelino, E., Fitzgibbons, S., Deriche, R.: Apparent diffusion coefficients from high angular resolution diffusion imaging: estimation and applications. Magn. Reson. Med. **56**(2), 395–410 (2006)

8. Ehricke, H.H., Otto, K.M., Klose, U.: Regularization of bending and crossing white matter fibers in MRI Q-ball fields. Magn. Reson. Imaging **29**(7), 916–926 (2011)

9. Garyfallidis, E., Brett, M., Amirbekian, B., Rokem, A., Van Der Walt, S., Descoteaux, M., Nimmo-Smith, I., Contributors, D.: Dipy, a library for the analysis of diffusion MRI data. Front. Neuroinf. **8**(8), 1–17 (2014)

10. Goh, A., Lenglet, C., Thompson, P., Vidal, R.: A nonparametric Riemannian framework for processing High Angular Resolution Diffusion Images (HARDI). In: CVPR 2009, pp. 2496–2503 (2009)

11. Goh, A., Lenglet, C., Thompson, P.M., Vidal, R.: A nonparametric Riemannian framework for processing high angular resolution diffusion images and its applications to ODF-based morphometry. Neuroimage **56**(3), 1181–1201 (2011)

12. Kantorovich, L.V., Rubinshten, G.Sh.: On a functional space and certain extremum problems. Dokl. Akad. Nauk SSSR **115**, 1058–1061 (1957)

13. Kim, Y., Thompson, P.M., Vese, L.A.: HARDI data denoising using vectorial total variation and logarithmic barrier. Inverse Prob. Imaging **4**(2), 273–310 (2010)

14. Lellmann, J., Strekalovskiy, E., Koetter, S., Cremers, D.: Total variation regularization for functions with values in a manifold. In: 2013 IEEE International Conference on Computer Vision, pp. 2944–2951 (2013)

15. Lellmann, J., Lorenz, D.A., Schönlieb, C., Valkonen, T.: Imaging with Kantorovich-Rubinstein discrepancy. SIAM J. Imaging Sci. **7**(4), 2833–2859 (2014)

16. McGraw, T., Vemuri, B., Ozarslan, E., Chen, Y., Mareci, T.: Variational denoising of diffusion weighted MRI. Inverse Prob. Imaging **3**(4), 625–648 (2009)

17. Ncube, S., Srivastava, A.: A novel Riemannian metric for analyzing HARDI data. In: Proceedings of the SPIE 7962, Id. 79620Q (2011)

18. Ouyang, Y., Chen, Y., Wu, Y.: Vectorial total variation regularisation of orientation distribution functions in diffusion weighted MRI. Int. J. Bioinform. Res. Appl. **10**(1), 110–127 (2014)

19. Reisert, M., Kellner, E., Kiselev, V.G.: About the geometry of asymmetric fiber orientation distributions. IEEE Trans. Med. Imaging **31**(6), 1240–1249 (2012)

20. Rokem, A., Yeatman, J., Pestilli, F., Wandell, B.: High angular resolution diffusion MRI. Stanford Digital Repository (2013). http://purl.stanford.edu/yx282xq2090

21. Srivastava, A., Jermyn, I.H., Joshi, S.H.: Riemannian analysis of probability density functions with applications in vision. In: CVPR 2007, pp. 1–8 (2007)

22. Tuch, D.S., Reese, T.G., Wiegell, M.R., Makris, N., Belliveau, J.W., Wedeen, V.J.: High angular resolution diffusion imaging reveals intravoxel white matter fiber heterogeneity. Magn. Reson. Med. **48**(4), 577–582 (2002)

23. Tuch, D.S.: Q-ball imaging. Magn. Reson. Med. **52**(6), 1358–1372 (2004)

24. Villani, C.: Optimal Transport: Old and New. Grundlehren der mathematischen Wissenschaften, vol. 338. Springer, Berlin (2009)

25. Weinmann, A., Demaret, L., Storath, M.J.: Mumford-Shah and potts regularization for manifold-valued data. J. Math. Imaging Vis. **55**, 428 (2016)

Nonlinear Flows for Displacement Correction and Applications in Tomography

Guozhi Dong[1(✉)] and Otmar Scherzer[1,2]

[1] Computational Science Center, University of Vienna,
Oskar-Morgenstern-Platz 1, 1090 Wien, Austria
{guozhi.dong,otmar.scherzer}@univie.ac.at
[2] Johann Radon Institute for Computational and Applied Mathematics (RICAM),
Austrian Academy of Sciences, Altenbergerstrasse 69, 4040 Linz, Austria

Abstract. In this paper we derive nonlinear evolution equations associated with a class of non-convex energy functionals which can be used for correcting displacement errors in imaging data. We show a preliminary convergence result of a relaxed convexification of the non-convex optimization problem. Some properties on the behavior of the solutions of these filtering flows are studied by numerical analysis. At the end, we provide examples for correcting angular perturbations in tomographical data.

Keywords: Non-convex regularization · Nonlinear flow · Displacement correction · Radon transform · Angular perturbation

1 Introduction

In this paper, we are investigating variational methods and partial differential equations for filtering displacement errors in imaging data. Such types of errors appear when measurement data are *sampled* erroneously. In this work we consider measurement data u^δ, which are considered perturbations of an ideal function u at random sampling locations $(x_1 + d_i(x_i), x_2)$: That is,

$$u^\delta(\mathbf{x}) = u(x_1 + d_i(x_i), x_2), \text{ for } \mathbf{x} = (x_1, x_2) \in \mathbb{R}^2. \tag{1}$$

A particular case of a displacement error $x_1 \to d_1(x_1)$ appears in Computerized Tomography (here the x_1-component denotes the X-ray beam direction (θ below)) when the angular sampling is considered erroneous. In this case the recorded data are

$$y^\delta(\theta, l) = R[f](\theta + d_1(\theta), l). \tag{2}$$

Here $R[f]$ denotes the *Radon transform* or *X-ray transform* of the function f, and θ and l denote the beam direction and beam distance, respectively.

Displacement errors of the form $d_2(x_2)$ are jittering errors, and the filtering and compensation of such has been considered in [3,6,11,12,15].

© Springer International Publishing AG 2017
F. Lauze et al. (Eds.): SSVM 2017, LNCS 10302, pp. 283–294, 2017.
DOI: 10.1007/978-3-319-58771-4_23

Our work is motivated by [7,8], where partial differential equations for denoising image data destructed by *general* sampling errors of the form

$$u^\delta(\mathbf{x}) = u(\mathbf{x} + \mathbf{d}) \text{ with } \mathbf{d} : \mathbb{R}^2 \to \mathbb{R}^2,$$

have been stated. The nonlinear evolution equations have been derived by mimicking a convex semi-group for a non-convex energy. The PDEs from [7,8] revealed properties similar to the mean curvature motion equation [4,5]. In comparison to [7,8], here, we are considering displacement errors in the x_1-component only.

The paper is organized as follows: In Sect. 2, we review the state of the art of non-convex regularization models for sampling error corrections: In particular, we comment on algorithms for recovering different types of displacements in a discrete setting. In Sect. 3, we consider nonlinear filtering flows motivated from non-convex regularization energies. For these flows we present numerical experiments, which suggest particular properties of the PDEs. Finally, we present an application of the novel filtering techniques for correcting tomographical image data with errors in the beam directions.

2   Non-convex Regularization Models

We study the following problem: Let $i \in \{1, 2\}$ be fixed. Given noisy image data u^δ, the goal is to simultaneously recover the ideal function u and the displacement d_i satisfying (1). Figure 1 shows the effect of the two different displacement errors d_1 and d_2 on some image data, respectively. The two displacement errors result in image data with orthogonal visual perturbations.

To this end we consider the following optimization problem:

$$\min_{d_i} \quad \mathcal{J}_i(d_i | u^\delta) := \left\| \partial_i^k u^\delta(x_1 - d_i(x_i), x_2) \right\|, \\ \text{such that } |d_i| \leq M. \tag{3}$$

Here $\|\cdot\|$ denotes some proper quasi-norm or norm of functions $v : \mathbb{R}^2 \to \mathbb{R}$ and the choice of $k \in \mathbb{N}$ depends on the a-priori information on regularity of the function u.

Below, we are considering *discrete* and *continuous* optimization formulations of Problem (3).

- In the discrete optimization problem, $d_i(x) \in \mathbb{Z}$ denotes the pixel displacements of columns $(i = 1)$ and rows $(i = 2)$, respectively. The image data u can be represented as a matrix with non-negative integer values, that is $u \in \mathbb{N}_0^{l \times n}$, where each matrix entry denotes the discrete image intensity of the image data at a position $(c, r) \in \{1, \ldots, l\} \times \{1, \ldots, n\}$. Moreover, the derivatives are considered in the sense of finite differences.
- In a continuous formulation, $d_i \in \mathbb{R}$ and the image is considered a function $u : \mathbb{R}^2 \to \mathbb{R}$.

For $i = 2$, the discrete optimization problem (3) has been investigated in [11,12] and the continuous optimization problem has been studied in [3,15].

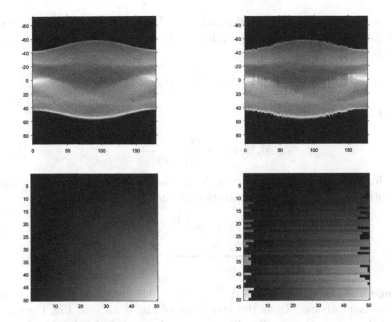

Fig. 1. Top: Non-disturbed and angular disturbed sinogram of the Shepp-Logan phantom (in the notation of the Radon transform $x_1 = \theta$ *and* $x_2 = l$). Bottom: Original and jittered image. The two different kinds of errors results appear as visually complementary data perturbations. This observation is the basis of regularization methods (6), where jittering is corrected by regularizing in x_2 direction and tomographic problems are corrected by filtering in x_1 direction.

2.1 Discrete Optimization Algorithms

The computational complexity of the discrete optimization algorithms varies significantly for solving the discrete Problem (3) with $i = 1$ and $i = 2$.

- Nikolova [11,12] introduced a highly efficient optimization algorithm with exhaustive search for the case $i = 2$. The complexity is $\mathcal{O}(Mn)$ for $u \in \mathbb{N}_0^{l \times n}$.
- For $i = 1$ the discrete optimization problem (3) is an *assignment* problem. Even the simplified problem of alignment of the columns in each of the $\lfloor \frac{l}{M} \rfloor$ non-intersecting sub-blocks has already an exponential complexity $\mathcal{O}((M!)^{\lfloor \frac{l}{M} \rfloor})$ by exhaustive search.

  We note that the complexity of assignment problems depends on the properties of the given cost functionals. For linear assignment problem (see e.g. [1]), the Hungarian algorithm [9] has a complexity $\mathcal{O}(l^3)$. However, nonlinear assignment problems [14], such as Problem (3), are usually *NP-hard*.

2.2 Continuous Models

The discrete optimization algorithm for solving Problem (3) can be used to correct for large displacement errors. Small (including subpixel) displacement errors can be corrected for by using partial differential equations: If the displacement d_i is small, following [3,8], we consider a first order approximation of the continuous data $u : \mathbb{R}^2 \to \mathbb{R}$. Then

$$u^\delta(\mathbf{x}) = u(x_1 + d_i(x_i), x_2) \approx u(\mathbf{x}) + d_i(x_i)\partial_1 u(\mathbf{x}), \qquad (4)$$

such that

$$d_i(x_i) \approx \frac{u^\delta(\mathbf{x}) - u(\mathbf{x})}{\partial_1 u(\mathbf{x})}. \qquad (5)$$

We aim for simultaneous minimizing the displacement error d_i and maximizing the smoothness of u by the minimization of the functional

$$\mathcal{F}(u; u^\delta) := \underbrace{\frac{1}{2} \int_{\mathbb{R}^2} \frac{(u(\mathbf{x}) - u^\delta(\mathbf{x}))^2}{(\partial_1 u(\mathbf{x}))^2} d\mathbf{x}}_{=:\mathcal{D}_2(u, u^\delta)} + \alpha \underbrace{\frac{1}{p} \int_{\mathbb{R}^2} (\partial_i^k u(\mathbf{x}))^p d\mathbf{x}}_{=:\mathcal{R}_{i,k,p}(u)}, \qquad (6)$$

with some fixed parameter $\alpha > 0$. Our particular choice of the regularization functional is motivated from the structure of the data (see Fig. 1), where we observed that correcting for line jittering requires regularization in x_2-direction and angular displacements require regularization in x_1-direction.

The functional $\mathcal{F}$ is non-convex with respect to u and has a singularity when $\partial_1 u$ vanishes. For the practical minimization we consider an approximation consisting of a sequence of convex minimization problems:

$$\begin{cases} u_0 = u^\delta, \\ u_m := \arg\min_u \mathcal{F}_\varepsilon^c(u; u_{m-1}) \text{ for all } m \in \mathbb{N}, \end{cases} \qquad (7)$$

where $\epsilon > 0$ is a small real number, and $\{\mathcal{F}_\varepsilon^c(\cdot; u_{m-1})\}_{m \in \mathbb{N}}$ is the set of convex functionals defined by

$$\mathcal{F}_\varepsilon^c(u; u_{m-1}) := \frac{1}{2} \int_{\mathbb{R}^2} \frac{(u(\mathbf{x}) - u_{m-1}(\mathbf{x}))^2}{(\partial_1 u_{m-1}(\mathbf{x}))^2 + \varepsilon} d\mathbf{x} + \alpha \mathcal{R}_{i,k,p}(u). \qquad (8)$$

In the following we give a convergence result inspired from [2] on the relaxed formulation (8), which might give some intuition to the solution of (6).

Theorem 1. *Let $p \in \{1, 2\}$, $k \in \{1, 2\}$, $\varepsilon > 0$, and let $\{u_m\}_{m \in \mathbb{N}}$ be the sequence of minimizers from (7).*

1. *The sequences $(\mathcal{F}_\varepsilon^c(u_m, u_{m-1}))_{m \in \mathbb{N}}$ and $(\mathcal{R}_{i,k,p}(u_m))_{m \in \mathbb{N}}$ both are monotonically decreasing.*
2. *If there exist a constant $C > 0$ and if $\sup\{\|\partial_1 u_m\|_{L^\infty} : m \in \mathbb{N}_0\} = C < \infty$, then*

$$\|u_m - u_{m-1}\|_{L^2} \to 0, \text{ as } m \to \infty.$$

Proof. From the definition of $\mathcal{F}_\varepsilon^c$ in (8) it follows that $\mathcal{F}_\varepsilon^c(u, u_m)$ is proper, strictly convex, and lower semi-continuous for every $m \in \mathbb{N}$. Thus there exists an unique minimizer u_{m+1} minimizing $\mathcal{F}_\varepsilon^c(u, u_m)$.

We are able to infer the following inequalities

$$0 \leq \mathcal{F}_\varepsilon^c(u_{m+1}, u_m) \leq \mathcal{F}_\varepsilon^c(u_m, u_m) = \alpha \mathcal{R}_{i,k,p}(u_m) \leq \mathcal{F}_\varepsilon^c(u_m, u_{m-1}),$$

and

$$\mathcal{R}_{i,k,p}(u_{m+1}) \leq \frac{\mathcal{F}_\varepsilon^c(u_{m+1}, u_m)}{\alpha} \leq \frac{\mathcal{F}_\varepsilon^c(u_m, u_m)}{\alpha} = \mathcal{R}_{i,k,p}(u_m),$$

which shows that both $(\mathcal{F}_\varepsilon^c(u_m, u_{m-1}))_{m \in \mathbb{N}}$ and $(\mathcal{R}_{i,k,p}(u_m))_{m \in \mathbb{N}}$ are non-negative and monotonically decreasing.

For the second statement,

$$\frac{1}{2} \int_{\mathbb{R}^2} \frac{(u_m - u_{m-1})^2}{|\partial_1 u_{m-1}|^2 + \varepsilon} = \mathcal{F}_\varepsilon^c(u_m, u_{m-1}) - \mathcal{F}_\varepsilon^c(u_m, u_m)$$
$$\leq \mathcal{F}_\varepsilon^c(u_m, u_{m-1}) - \mathcal{F}_\varepsilon^c(u_{m+1}, u_m).$$

From the uniform boundedness assumption of $\{u_m\}$ it follows that

$$\frac{1}{2(C^2 + \varepsilon)} \|u_m - u_{m-1}\|_{L^2}^2 \leq \mathcal{F}_\varepsilon^c(u_m, u_{m-1}) - \mathcal{F}_\varepsilon^c(u_{m+1}, u_m).$$

Since the sequence $\{\mathcal{F}_\varepsilon^c(u_m, u_{m-1})\}_{m \in \mathbb{N}}$ is bounded from below and monotonically decreasing it follows that $\|u_m - u_{m-1}\|_{L^2} \to 0$. $\qquad \square$

Identifying $\Delta t = \alpha$, the formal optimality condition for (8) characterizes the solution of (7) by

$$\begin{cases} \dfrac{u_m - u_{m-1}}{\Delta t} = (|\partial_1 u_{m-1}|^2 + \varepsilon)(-1)^{k-1}\partial_i^k \left(\dfrac{\partial_i^k u_m}{|\partial_i^k u_m|^{2-p}} \right), \\ u_0 = u^\delta. \end{cases} \tag{9}$$

On the other hand, if $\partial_1 u(\mathbf{x})$ is relatively large, the estimate of the displacement by the error measure in (5) is unrealistic, and a least squares error measure $(u(\mathbf{x}) - u^\delta(\mathbf{x}))^2$ might be more efficient. To be able to compensate for relatively large and small displacement errors simultaneously, and utilize the previous analysis, we, therefore, propose to use the geometric mean of the two error measures

$$\mathcal{D}_1(u, u^\delta) := \frac{1}{2} \int_{\mathbb{R}^2} \frac{(u(\mathbf{x}) - u^\delta(\mathbf{x}))^2}{|\partial_1 u(\mathbf{x})|} d\mathbf{x}. \tag{10}$$

In this case we end up with the following variational model

$$\mathcal{F}(u; u^\delta) := \mathcal{D}_1(u, u^\delta) + \alpha \mathcal{R}_{i,k,p}(u). \tag{11}$$

We can proceed in a similar way, and identifying $\Delta t = \alpha$ again, the iterative convex relaxation of functional (11) will give (12) similarly to (9)

$$\begin{cases} \dfrac{u_m - u_{m-1}}{\Delta t} = (|\partial_1 u_{m-1}| + \varepsilon)\, (-1)^{k-1} \partial_i^k \left(\dfrac{\partial_i^k u_m}{\left|\partial_i^k u_m\right|^{2-p}} \right), \\[4mm] u_0 = u^\delta. \end{cases} \tag{12}$$

3   Nonlinear Flows

Let $i,\ k,\ p,\ q \in \{1,2\}$ be fixed and assume that u^δ is given. u_m solving (9) (corresponding to $q = 2$), (12) (corresponding to $q = 1$) can be considered a numerical approximation of the flow

$$\begin{cases} \dot{u} = (-1)^{k-1} |\partial_1 u|^q\, \partial_i^k \left(\dfrac{\partial_i^k u}{\left|\partial_i^k u\right|^{2-p}} \right) & \text{in } \mathbb{R}^2 \times (0, \infty), \\[4mm] u = u^\delta \text{ in } \mathbb{R}^2 \times \{0\} \end{cases} \tag{13}$$

at time $t = m\Delta t$. Here $u = u(\mathbf{x}, t)$ and $\dot{u}$ denotes the derivative of u with respect to t. We also can consider (13) as the flow according to the non-convex functional $\mathcal{F}$ given in (6) or (11) (depend on the choice of q).

Remark 2. *In practical simulations the unbounded domain $\mathbb{R}^2$ is replaced by $\Omega = (0,1)^2$ and the flow is associated with boundary conditions:*

$$\partial_i^{2l-1} u = 0, \text{ on } \{0,1\} \times (0,1), \text{ for all } l = 1, \ldots, k \text{ and for } i = 1;$$
$$\partial_i^{2l-1} u = 0, \text{ on } (0,1) \times \{0,1\}, \text{ for all } l = 1, \ldots, k \text{ and for } i = 2.$$

The case of $i = 2$ has been considered in [3].

When $i = 1$, the right hand side of (13) only involves partial derivatives of u with respect to x_1, such that it reduces to a system of independent equations defined for the functions $u(\cdot, x_2)$ for every $x_2 \in (0,1)$.

3.1   Properties of the Flows

In the following, we present some numerical simulations with (13).

– For $i = 1$ (13) reads as follows

$$\dot{u} = (-1)^{k-1} |\partial_1 u|^q\, \partial_1^k \left(\dfrac{\partial_1^k u}{\left|\partial_1^k u\right|^{2-p}} \right). \tag{14}$$

Figure 2 shows numerical simulations of (14) for different choices of k and p with $q = 2$. In all test cases the initial data u^δ is a function representing a narrow white strip on a black background. We visualize the solutions at

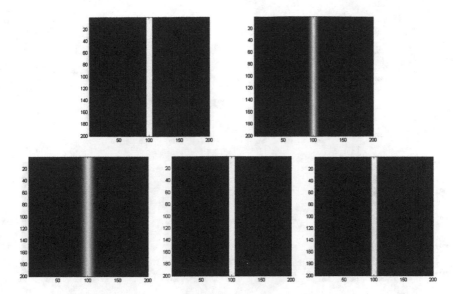

Fig. 2. The solutions of the PDEs (14) with $q = 2$ at time $t = 10^{-6}$. From top to bottom, and from left to right, the images are corresponding to the initial value u^δ and the results of the evolution with various parameters: $k = 1, p = 2$; $k = 2, p = 2$; $k = 1, p = 1$; $k = 2, p = 1$ in (14). We consider the x_1 lines are discretized with mesh size $\Delta x_1 = 0.1$.

$t = 10^{-6}$ with identical time unit. We observe diffusion of the white strip for all choices of k and p except in the case $k = 1, p = 1$, with $q = 2$.

We emphasis that when $k = 1, p = 2$ and $q = 2$ (14) reads as follows

$$\dot{u} = |\partial_1 u|^2 \, \partial_1^2 u = \frac{\partial_1((\partial_1 u)^3)}{3}, \tag{15}$$

of which the differential operator on the right-hand side is a one dimensional *p-Laplacian* with $p = 4$ (see [16] for some regularity properties, where they have a general result for *p-Laplacian* in $\mathbb{R}^n$). Hence the Eq. (15) is nothing but a system of independent one dimensional *p-Laplacian* flow, of which the equilibrium (stationary point) is a function of the form $\tilde{u} = c_1(x_2; u^\delta)x_1 + c_2(x_2; u^\delta)$, where $c_1(x_2; u^\delta)$ and $c_2(x_2; u^\delta)$ are functions independent of the x_1 variable.

- For $i = 2$ (13) reads as follows

$$\dot{u} = (-1)^{k-1} |\partial_1 u|^q \, \partial_2^k \left(\frac{\partial_2^k u}{|\partial_2^k u|^{2-p}} \right). \tag{16}$$

We investigate the long time behavior of the solution of Eq. (16) initialized with some curved interface data u^δ. The numerical results are presented in Fig. 3. We find that the curved interface evolves into a vertical line (for all cases of k and p, with $q = 2$, we have tested), which we assume to be a general analytical property of the PDEs.

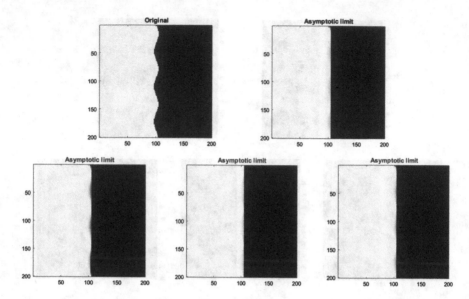

Fig. 3. The long time behaviors of the PDEs in (16) with $q = 2$. From top to bottom, and from left to right, the images are corresponding to the initial value u^δ and the results of the evolution with $q = 2$ and various parameters: $k = 1, p = 2$; $k = 2, p = 2$; $k = 1, p = 1$; $k = 2, p = 1$ in (16).

3.2   Angular Correction in Tomography

Now, we are applying the displacement correction methods for problems arising in tomography. As data we consider angular disturbed sinograms of the Radon transform of 2D images and the final goal is to reconstruct the corresponding attenuation coefficients. If the sinogram is recorded with angular perturbations, without further processing, application of the inverse Radon transform may produce outliers in the reconstruction (see Fig. 4). As a test image we use the Shepp-Logan phantom of size 128×128, and discretize the angular axis of the sinogram domain $[0, \pi)$ with uniform step size $\frac{1}{90}\pi$. The synthetic data are generated by evaluating the Radon transform along the line in direction $\hat{\theta} = \theta + d_1(\theta)$. The (inverse) Radon transforms are implemented with the Matlab toolbox.

In the first series of experiments (see Fig. 5), we allow the random perturbations on the beam directions to be $d_1(\theta) \in [0, \frac{1}{30}\pi]$, which is relatively small. The correction process consists of a coupled steps: in the first step we apply the nonlinear flows to the erroneous sinogram; then we apply inverse Radon transform to the results from the first step. In the example shown in Fig. 5 these sampling errors do not cause significant mismatch in the reconstruction.

Although the flows in (14) are suitable for correcting small displacement errors, they may not be very qualified for the data with larger displacement errors

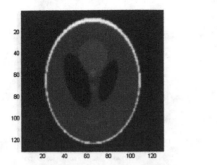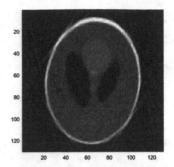

Fig. 4. Left: Phantom image. Right: A direct reconstruction with a filter backprojection (FBP) algorithm from an angular perturbed sinogram (see Fig. 1).

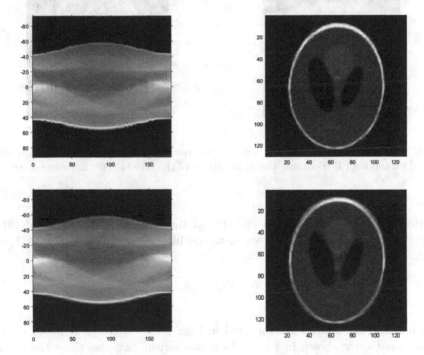

Fig. 5. Top Left: Sinogram with relatively small angular error $(d_1(\theta) \in [0, \frac{1}{30}\pi])$. Top Right: Direct reconstruction with a FBP algorithm.Bottom: The applications of the flow (14) for angular correction with parameter settings $k = 1, p = 2$ and $q = 2$.

and with additive noise. In the latter case, the recorded sinogram is considered to be

$$y^\delta(\theta, l) = R[f](\theta + d_1(\theta), l) + \eta, \tag{17}$$

where η denotes some additive noise. Here the filtering by the flow defined in (13) with $q = 1$ outperforms the filtering by the flow with $q = 2$. In the numerical

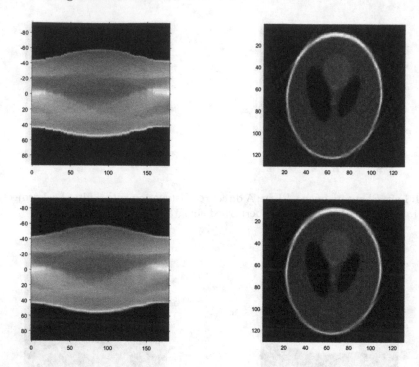

Fig. 6. Top: The results obtained with an heuristic discrete optimization algorithm method for solving (3). Bottom: The applications of the flow (18) for angular correction.

experiments, we tested with an example of the angular perturbation $d_1(\theta) \in [0, \frac{1}{18}\pi]$ (see Fig. 1). For $q = 1$ we show the filtering by (13) with $k = 1$ and $p = 2$. That is, we use the equation

$$\dot{u} = |\partial_1 u| \, \partial_1^2 u, \tag{18}$$

for filtering.

Our numerical results are reported in Figs. 6 and 7, which is based on the displacement error shown in Fig. 1. As a comparison, we also show the results when Problem (3) is considered a discrete optimization problem and is solved with a heuristic discrete optimization algorithm, which is generalized from [12]. The right one on the top of Fig. 6 shows the final result, having no preference against standard FBP. The bottom images in Fig. 6 show the results which are obtained by applying the nonlinear flow (18) for correcting the unknown angular perturbations. In this example, the nonlinear flows have a better performance in comparing with the heuristic discrete optimization algorithm. From the results shown in Fig. 7, we find that the proposed equation (18) is able to correcting the angle displacement error and denoise simultaneously.

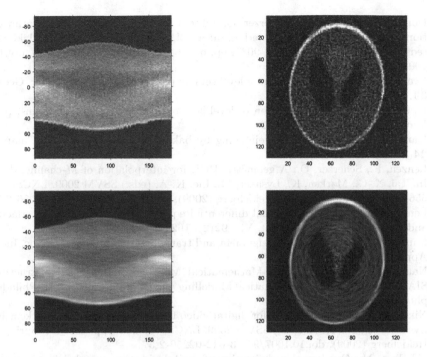

Fig. 7. The applications of the flow (18) for angular correction from data containing both displacement and additive errors.

4   Conclusion

In this paper, we have considered two families of nonlinear flows for correcting two different kinds of displacement errors. Our numerical analysis revealed interesting properties on the behavior of the solutions of the PDEs, which should be confirmed by further theoretical studies in the future. We have also presented some applications to tomography, where the novel PDEs are able to correct for angular displacement errors. Some other application area of our methods are electron tomography in single particle analysis [10, 13].

Acknowledgements. The authors thank the reviewers for some helpful comments. The work of OS has been supported by the Austrian Science Fund (FWF): Geometry and Simulation, project S11704 (Variational methods for imaging on manifolds), and Interdisciplinary Coupled Physics Imaging, project P26687-N25.

References

1. Burkard, R., Dellamico, M., Martello, S.: Assignment problems, revised reprint. Other Titles in Applied Mathematics. SIAM, Philadelphia (2009). Revised edition
2. Chan, T., Mulet, P.: On the convergence of the lagged diffusivity fixed point method in total variation image restoration. SIAM J. Numer. Anal. **36**(2), 354–367 (1999)

3. Dong, G., Patrone, A.R., Scherzer, O., Öktem, O.: Infinite dimensional optimization models and PDEs for dejittering. In: Aujol, J.-F., Nikolova, M., Papadakis, N. (eds.) SSVM 2015. LNCS, vol. 9087, pp. 678–689. Springer, Cham (2015). doi:10.1007/978-3-319-18461-6_54

4. Evans, L.C., Spruck, J.: Motion of level sets by mean curvature. I. J. Differ. Geom. **33**, 635–681 (1991)

5. Evans, L.C., Spruck, J.: Motion of level sets by mean curvature. II. Trans. Am. Math. Soc. **330**, 321–332 (1992)

6. Kang, S.H., Shen, J.: Video dejittering by bake and shake. Image Vis. Comput. **24**(2), 143–152 (2006)

7. Lenzen, F., Scherzer, O.: A geometric PDE for interpolation of M-channel data. In: Tai, X.-C., Mørken, K., Lysaker, M., Lie, K.-A. (eds.) SSVM 2009. LNCS, vol. 5567, pp. 413–425. Springer, Heidelberg (2009). doi:10.1007/978-3-642-02256-2_35

8. Lenzen, F., Scherzer, O.: Partial differential equations for zooming, deinterlacing and dejittering. Int. J. Comput. Vis. **92**(2), 162–176 (2011)

9. Munkres, J.: Algorithms for assignment and transportation problems. J. Soc. Indu. Appl. Math. **5**(1), 32–38 (1957)

10. Natterer, F., Wübbeling, F.: Mathematical Methods in Image Reconstruction. SIAM Monographs on Mathematical Modelling and Computation. SIAM, Philadelphia (2001)

11. Nikolova, M.: Fast dejittering for digital video frames. In: Tai, X.-C., Mørken, K., Lysaker, M., Lie, K.-A. (eds.) SSVM 2009. LNCS, vol. 5567, pp. 439–451. Springer, Heidelberg (2009). doi:10.1007/978-3-642-02256-2_37

12. Nikolova, M.: One-iteration dejittering of digital video images. J. Vis. Commun. Image Represent. **20**, 254–274 (2009)

13. Öktem, O.: Mathematics of electron tomography. In: Scherzer, O. (ed.) Handbook of Mathematical Methods in Imaging, pp. 937–1031. Springer, New York (2015)

14. Voss, S.: Heuristics for nonlinear assignment problems. In: Pardalos, P.M., Pitsoulis, L. (eds.) Nonlinear Assignment Problems, Algorithms and Applications. Combinatorial Optimization, vol. 7, pp. 175–215, Kluwer Academic Publishers (2000)

15. Shen, J.: Bayesian video dejittering by BV image model. SIAM J. Appl. Math. **64**(5), 1691–1708 (2004)

16. Uhlenbeck, K.: Regularity for a class of non-linear elliptic systems. Acta Math. **138**(1), 219–240 (1977)

Performance Bounds for Cosparse Multichannel Signal Recovery via Collaborative-TV

Lukas Kiefer and Stefania Petra$^{(\boxtimes)}$

MIG, Institute of Applied Mathematics, Heidelberg University,
Heidelberg, Germany
petra@math.uni-heidelberg.de

Abstract. We consider a new class of regularizers called collaborative total variation (CTV) to cope with the ill-posed nature of multichannel image reconstruction. We recast our reconstruction problem in the analysis framework from compressed sensing. This allows us to derive theoretical measurement bounds that guarantee successful recovery of multichannel signals via CTV regularization. We derive new measurement bounds for two types of CTV from Gaussian measurements. These bounds are proved for multichannel signals of one and two dimensions. We compare them to empirical phase transitions of one-dimensional signals and obtain a good agreement especially when the sparsity of the analysis representation is not very small.

1 Introduction

To tackle the problem of reconstructing an undersampled multi-channel signal $u = (u^1, \ldots, u^c) \in \mathbb{R}^{n \times c}$ from linear measurements simultaneously in all c channels we employ collaborative total variation (CTV) regularization. CTV was introduced in [1] in order to unify several vectorial TV models proposed in the literature that not only depend on the coupling of the spatial derivatives but also on the coupling of (spectral, color) channels. In fact, intra-image (co-)sparsity and inter-channel similarity are important prior knowledge for image reconstruction. CTV is a promising tool to exploit such structure. The authors in [1] define CTV from a 3D data structure of the gradient: one dimension corresponding to the pixels, one dimension for derivatives, and one dimension for the channels and then penalize this structure using a different norm along each dimension. Depending on the type of these norms, different properties of the regularization (e.g. smoothness, correlated channel) are obtained.

We further consider two types of measurements for multichannel signal:

(i) *full linear measurements across all channels*, described by

$$M \operatorname{vec}(u) = b, \tag{1}$$

in terms of a full Gaussian measurement matrix $M \in \mathbb{R}^{m \times cn}$, and

© Springer International Publishing AG 2017
F. Lauze et al. (Eds.): SSVM 2017, LNCS 10302, pp. 295–307, 2017.
DOI: 10.1007/978-3-319-58771-4_24

(ii) *separable channel-wise measurements*, described by $Au = (Au^1, \ldots, Au^c)$ or equivalently

$$M_A \operatorname{vec}(u) = b_A, \quad M_A = \operatorname{diag}(\underbrace{A, \ldots, A}_{c \text{ times}}), \tag{2}$$

with a block diagonal $M_A \in \mathbb{R}^{m \times cn}$ containing c copies of a Gaussian matrix $A \in \mathbb{R}^{m \times n}$.

We theoretically investigate the performance of our multichannel image reconstruction problem

$$\min_{u \in \mathbb{R}^{n \times c}} \operatorname{CTV}(u) \quad \text{subject to} \quad M \operatorname{vec} u = b, \tag{3}$$

from full Gaussian measurements (i), and experimentally from separable channel-wise measurements (ii). Even though we consider here Gaussian measurements only, our analysis is motivated by spectral computed tomography (CT) [2,3] that has lately attracted considerable attention, due to its capability in identifying and discriminating materials. Also the newly developed photon-counting sensors can acquire X-ray intensity data in different energy levels. Moreover, in spectral CT an image can be sparsely represented in each of the multiple energy channels and is highly correlated among energy channels.

Our performance guarantees build on techniques of compressed sensing [4] for characterizing the phase transitions of convex optimization problems in recovering undersampled structured signals from Gaussian measurements.

Contribution, Related Work. This line of work contributes to the theory of vectorial total variation minimization by providing a bound on the number of Gaussian random measurements in order to recover a gradient sparse multichannel signal via collaborative total variation [1]. Our analysis is based on estimating Gaussian widths of descent cones [4,5] of a CTV-norm at the (co-)sparse multichannel signal to be recovered, similarly to [6]. This results in *nonuniform recovery guarantees*: for a fixed a (co-)sparse multichannel signal (with respect to the discrete gradient) we provide bounds that guarantee that the given multichannel signal is recovered via CTV with high probability. This is in contrast to uniform recovery bounds which are often based on the null space property or the restricted isometry property [4].

2 Collaborative Total Variation

We consider collaborative total variation (CTV) introduced in [1], that induce various types of vectorial TV terms for multichannel signals by choosing specific *collaborative norms* that act specifically on the space of image gradients, i.e. $\| \cdot \|_{CTV} : \mathbb{R}^{p \times d \times c} \to \mathbb{R}$.

Consider the one-dimensional discrete derivative operator $\mathbf{d} : \mathbb{R}^N \to \mathbb{R}^{N-1}$, $(\mathbf{d})_{ij} = -1$ if $i = j$, $(\mathbf{d})_{ij} = 1$ if $j = i + 1$ and $(\mathbf{d})_{ij} = 0$ otherwise. For

$n = N \times N$ and multichannel square images the discrete gradient operator $\mathbf{D} : \mathbb{R}^{n \times c} \to \mathbb{R}^{(n-N) \times 2 \times c}$ writes

$$(\mathbf{D}u)_{::k} = \left((\mathbf{d} \otimes I_N)u^k \ (I_N \otimes \mathbf{d})u^k\right), \quad \forall k \in [c], \tag{4}$$

where $\otimes$ stands for the Kronecker product and $I_N \in \mathbb{R}^{N \times N}$ for the identity matrix. The 3D data structure of the gradient is organized in pixel slices $X_{i::} \in \mathbb{R}^{2 \times c}$, derivative slices $X_{:j:} \in \mathbb{R}^{(n-N) \times c}$ and channel slices $X_{::k} \in \mathbb{R}^{(n-N) \times 2}$ with $i \in [n - N]$, $j \in \{1, 2\}$ and $k \in [c]$.

Definition 1. *Let* $\| \cdot \|_a : \mathbb{R}^p \to \mathbb{R}$ *be any vector norm and* $\| \cdot \|_b : \mathbb{R}^{d \times c} \to \mathbb{R}$ *be any matrix norm. The* collaborative norm *of* $B \in \mathbb{R}^{p \times d \times c}$ *is given by*

$$\| \cdot \|_{b,a} : \mathbb{R}^{p \times d \times c} \to \mathbb{R}, \qquad \|B\|_{b,a} = \|v\|_a,$$

where $v \in \mathbb{R}^p$ *is entry-wise defined by* $v_i = \|B_{i::}\|_b$ *for* $i \in [p]$. *We denote by* $\mathbb{B}_{b,a}$ *the closed unit ball with respect to a given collaborative norm, i.e.*

$$\mathbb{B}_{b,a} = \{B \in \mathbb{R}^{p \times d \times c} \ : \ \|B\|_{b,a} \leq 1\}.$$

For $p, q, r \in [1, \infty]$, the notation $\ell_{p,q,r}$ stands for the collaborative norm $\| \cdot \|_{a,b}$ where $\| \cdot \|_b$ is the mixed matrix norm $\ell_{p,q}$ induced by the ℓ_p- and ℓ_q-norm and $\| \cdot \|_a$ is the ℓ_r-norm. Then the collaborative total variation is defined as $\mathrm{CTV}(\cdot) = \|\mathbf{D} \cdot \|_{\ell_{p,q,r}}$ with $\mathbf{D}$ from (4). We restrict our attention to three collaborative norms corresponding to $\ell_{1,1,1}$, $\ell_{2,1,1}$ and $\ell_{\infty,1,1}$. Given $B \in \mathbb{R}^{p \times d \times c}$, they read

$$\|B\|_{1,1,1} = \sum_{i=1}^{p} \sum_{j=1}^{d} \sum_{k=1}^{c} |B_{ijk}|, \tag{5}$$

$$\|B\|_{2,1,1} = \sum_{i=1}^{p} \sum_{j=1}^{d} \left(\sum_{k=1}^{c} B_{ijk}^2\right)^{\frac{1}{2}}, \tag{6}$$

$$\|B\|_{\infty,1,1} = \sum_{i=1}^{p} \sum_{j=1}^{d} \max_{k \in [c]} |B_{ijk}|. \tag{7}$$

We collect two properties of collaborative norms regarding their dual norms and their subdifferential that are both theoretically and algorithmically relevant. Both results are taken from [1].

Theorem 1 (Dual norms of collaborative norms, [1, Theorem 1]). *Let* $\| \cdot \|_{b^*}$ *and* $\| \cdot \|_{a^*}$ *be the dual norms to* $\| \cdot \|_b$ *and* $\| \cdot \|_a$. *If* $\|w\|_{a^*}$ *only depends on the absolute values of* w_i, *then the dual norm to* $\| \cdot \|_{b,a}$ *at the point* $B \in \mathbb{R}^{p \times d \times c}$ *is given by* $\|v^*\|_{a^*}$, *where* $v^* \in \mathbb{R}^p$ *is entry-wise defined by* $v_i^* = \|B_{i::}\|_{b^*}$.

Theorem 2 (Subdifferential of collaborative norms, [1, Theorem 2]). *Let* $B \in \mathbb{R}^{p \times d \times c}$ *and* $\| \cdot \|_{b,a}$ *be defined as in Theorem 1. Then the subdifferential of* $\| \cdot \|_{b,a}$ *at* B *is given by*

$$\partial(\|B\|_{b,a}) = \left\{A \in \mathbb{R}^{p \times d \times c} : \|A\|_{b^*,a^*} \leq 1 \text{ and } \langle B, A \rangle = \|B\|_{b,a}\right\}.$$

3   Cosparse Recovery via CTV

Let $M \in \mathbb{R}^{m \times nc}$ be a measurement matrix and $\Omega : \mathbb{R}^{n \times c} \to \mathbb{R}^{p \times d \times c}$ be a 3D array-valued analysis operator. Then our reconstruction problem reads

$$\hat{u} = \text{argmin}_{z \in \mathbb{R}^{n \times c}} \|\Omega z\|_{\ell_{p,q,r}} \quad \text{subject to} \quad M \text{ vec}(z) = b, \tag{8}$$

or, if we are given corrupted measurements $b = M \text{ vec}(u) + e$, $\|e\|_2 \leq \eta$,

$$\hat{u} = \text{argmin}_{z \in \mathbb{R}^{n \times c}} \|\Omega z\|_{\ell_{p,q,r}} \quad \text{subject to} \quad \|M \text{ vec}(z) - b\|_2 \leq \eta. \tag{9}$$

For the special cases of $\| \cdot \|_{\ell_{p,q,r}} = \| \cdot \|_{1,1,1}$ and $\| \cdot \|_{\ell_{p,q,r}} = \| \cdot \|_{\infty,1,1}$ we provide results concerning measurement bounds that ensure robustness of (9) similarly to the ones given in [6] for the single channel ℓ_1-approach. To this end, we define an index set similar to the notion of cosupport.

Definition 2. *Let* $u \in \mathbb{R}^{n \times c}$ *and* $\Omega : \mathbb{R}^{n \times c} \to \mathbb{R}^{p \times d \times c}$ *a 3D array-valued analysis operator. We define the index set* $\Lambda \subset [p]$ *by*

$$\Lambda := \{i \in [p] : (\Omega u)_{i::} = 0\}. \tag{10}$$

Below, we state our main result in terms of Definition 2 and a generic analysis operator Ω, that will be further specialized to the discrete image gradient.

Theorem 3. *Let* $\Omega : \mathbb{R}^{n \times c} \to \mathbb{R}^{p \times d \times c}$ *be a 3D array-valued analysis operator and* $u \in \mathbb{R}^{n \times c}$ *with* $\Lambda \subset [p]$ *from (10). For a random draw* $M \in \mathbb{R}^{m \times nc}$ *of a Gaussian matrix, let noisy measurements* $b = M \text{ vec}(u) + e$ *be given with* $\|e\|_2 \leq \eta$ *and* $\varepsilon \in (0,1)$. *If*

$$\frac{m^2}{m+1} \geq \left(\sqrt{nc - \frac{\mathbb{E}[\|(\Omega G)_\Lambda\|_{q,1,1}]^2}{\max_{z \in \mathbb{B}_{\|\cdot\|_F}} \|\Omega z\|_{q,1,1}^2}} + \sqrt{2 \ln(\varepsilon^{-1})} + \tau \right)^2, \tag{11}$$

where G *denotes a* $n \times c$-*dimensional Gaussian random matrix, then with probability at least* $1 - \varepsilon$ *any minimizer* $\hat{u}$ *of (9) with* $q \in \{1, \infty\}$ *will satisfy* $\|u - \hat{u}\|_F \leq \frac{2\eta}{\tau}$.

The l.h.s. in (11) is approximately m (especially for large m) and the r.h.s. is a bound on m for robust signal reconstruction via (9). The quantity ε controls the probability of the event $\|u - \hat{u}\|_F \leq \frac{2\eta}{\tau}$, where η is the given noise level and τ is a bound on the "restricted" smallest singular value of M, see (13) below. From the proof of Theorem 3 it also follows that the r.h.s. in (11) in an upper bound on the *minimal* number of measurements that guarantee exact recovery from noiseless measurements. In order to derive explicit measurement bounds for a given analysis operator Ω, we now estimate the expected value and the max-term in formula (11).

3.1   Gaussian Width Framework

We first collect preparatory results for the proof of Theorem 3. We define for a fixed collaborative norm $\| \cdot \|_{CTV}$ and analysis operator Ω the *descent cone* of CTV($\cdot$) at a point $x \in \mathbb{R}^{n \times c}$,

$$T(u) := \text{cone}\{z - u : \|\Omega z\|_{CTV} \leq \|\Omega u\|_{CTV}\} \tag{12}$$

and its intersection with the Frobenius unit sphere $\mathcal{T}(u) := T(u) \cap S_F^{n \times c}$. The importance of the set $\mathcal{T}(u)$ is clarified through the next result that guarantees robustness of (9).

Lemma 1 [4, Theorem 4.36]. *Let $u \in \mathbb{R}^{n \times c}$. If*

$$\inf_{v \in \mathcal{T}(u)} \|M \text{ vec}(v)\|_2 \geq \tau \tag{13}$$

for some $\tau > 0$, then a minimizer $\hat{u}$ of (9) with $b = M \text{ vec}(u) + e$ satisfies $\|u - \hat{u}\|_F \leq \frac{2\eta}{\tau}$.

We estimate the probability of the event (13) given a Gaussian measurement matrix M with the help of Gordon's escape through a mesh theorem. In order to formulate the latter, we define the *Gaussian width* of a subset C of $\mathbb{R}^{n \times c}$ [5] through

$$\omega(C) = \mathbb{E}[\sup_{z \in C} \langle G, z \rangle],$$

where G is a $n \times c$ Gaussian random matrix.

Theorem 4 (Gordon's escape through a mesh, [4, Theorem 9.21]). *Let M be a $m \times nc$ Gaussian random matrix and $T \subset S_F^{n \times c}$. Then, for $t > 0$,*

$$\mathbb{P}\left(\inf_{v \in T} \|M \text{ vec}(v)\|_F > E_m - \omega(T) - t\right) \geq 1 - \exp\left(\frac{-t^2}{2}\right),$$

where $E_m := \mathbb{E}[\|G\|_F] \geq m/\sqrt{m+1}$ for a m-dimensional standard Gaussian random vector G.

Endowed with Lemma 1 and Theorem 4, we are left to estimate the Gaussian width of $\mathcal{T}(u)$. Here we use a classic result from [7, Proposition 10.2, Proposition 4.1] specialized to our definition of $\omega(\mathcal{T}(u))$: For a Gaussian random matrix G it is

$$\omega(\mathcal{T}(u)) \leq \inf_{t \geq 0} \mathbb{E}\left[\text{dist}\left(G, t\partial\|\Omega \cdot \|_{CTV}(u)\right)\right]. \tag{14}$$

3.2   Nonuniform Recovery Guarantees for CTV

In this section, we prove Theorem 3. First, we upper bound the right hand side of (14) for $T(u)$ in (12), where $\|\Omega u\|_{CTV} := \|\Omega u\|_{\ell_{p,q,r}}$.

Lemma 2. *Let $\Omega : \mathbb{R}^{n\times c} \to \mathbb{R}^{p\times d\times c}$ be a 3D array-valued analysis operator, G an $n \times c$-dimensional Gaussian random matrix and $u \in \mathbb{R}^{n\times c}$. Then*

$$\inf_{t\geq 0} \mathbb{E}\left[\text{dist}\left(G, t\partial\|\Omega\cdot\|_{\ell_{p,q,r}}(u)\right)\right]^2 \leq nc - \frac{\omega\left(\partial\|\Omega\cdot\|_{\ell_{p,q,r}}(u)\right)^2}{\max\limits_{z\in\mathbb{B}_{\|\cdot\|_F}}\|\Omega z\|^2_{\ell_{p,q,r}}}. \tag{15}$$

Proof. Similarly to [6, Lemma 1] using the chain rule for subdifferentials, Theorem 2 and Theorem 1 and replacing the ℓ_1-norm by a generic collaborative norm $\|\cdot\|_{\ell_{p,q,r}}$.

Proof of Theorem 3. Let $q \in \{1,\infty\}$ and $q^* := 1$ if $q = \infty$ and $q^* := \infty$ if $q = 1$. We deduce from (14) and (15)

$$E_m - \omega(\mathcal{T}(u)) - t \geq E_m - \sqrt{nc - \frac{\omega\left(\partial\|\Omega\cdot\|_{q,1,1}(u)\right)^2}{\max\limits_{z\in\mathbb{B}_{\|\cdot\|_F}}\|\Omega z\|^2_{q,1,1}}} - t. \tag{16}$$

Theorem 2 and the subdifferential chain rule imply that for all $z \in \partial\|\Omega\cdot\|_{q,1,1}(u)$ there exists some $\alpha \in \mathbb{R}^{p\times d\times c}$ such that

$$z = \Omega^\top\alpha, \quad \|\alpha\|_{q^*,\infty,\infty} \leq 1 \text{ and } \langle\alpha, \Omega u\rangle = \|\Omega u\|_{q,1,1}.$$

The latter one implies

$$\sum_{i\in[p]}\sum_{j\in[d]}\sum_{k\in[c]}\alpha_{ijk}(\Omega u)_{ijk} = \sum_{i\in[p]}\sum_{j\in[d]}\|(\Omega u)_{ij:}\|_q$$

$$= \sum_{i\in\Lambda^c}\sum_{j\in[d]}\|(\Omega u)_{ij:}\|_q + \sum_{i\in\Lambda}\sum_{j\in[d]}\underbrace{\|(\Omega u)_{ij:}\|_q}_{=0} = \sum_{i\in\Lambda^c}\sum_{j\in[d]}\|(\Omega u)_{ij:}\|_q.$$

Considering the two cases separately we have for all $i \in \Lambda^c$:

$$\text{for } q = 1, \qquad \alpha_{ijk} = \text{sign}(\Omega u)_{ijk},$$

$$\text{for } q = \infty, \qquad \alpha_{ijk} = \begin{cases} \text{sign}(\Omega u)_{ijk}, & \text{if } k \in \text{argmax}_\gamma |(\Omega u)_{ij\gamma}|, \\ 0, & \text{otherwise.} \end{cases}$$

Hence, the Gaussian width satisfies

$$\omega(\partial\|\Omega\cdot\|_{q,1,1}(u)) = \mathbb{E}[\max_{z\in\partial\|\Omega\cdot\|_{q,1,1}(u)}\langle G, z\rangle]$$

$$= \mathbb{E}[\langle\Omega G, \alpha_{(\Lambda^c::)}\rangle] + \mathbb{E}[\max_{\alpha_\Lambda\in\mathbb{B}_{\|\cdot\|_{q^*,\infty,\infty}}}\langle\Omega G, \alpha_{(\Lambda::)}\rangle].$$

The first summand is the expected value of a linear combination of standard Gaussians, hence it equals zero. Thus,

$$\omega(\partial\|\Omega\cdot\|_{q,1,1}(u)) = \mathbb{E}[\max_{\alpha_\Lambda\in\mathbb{B}_{\|\cdot\|_{q^*,\infty,\infty}}}\langle\Omega G, \alpha_{(\Lambda::)}\rangle] = \mathbb{E}[\|(\Omega G)_{(\Lambda::)}\|_{q,1,1}].$$

Combining this with (16) and using $E_m \geq m/\sqrt{m+1}$ we get

$$E_m - \omega\left(\mathcal{T}(u)\right) - t \geq \frac{m}{\sqrt{m+1}} - \sqrt{n - \frac{\mathbb{E}[\|\Omega_\Lambda g\|_{q,1,1}]^2}{\max\limits_{z \in \mathcal{B}_{\|\cdot\|_F}} \|\Omega z\|_{q,1,1}^2}} - t.$$

The choice of $t = \sqrt{2\ln(\varepsilon^{-1})}$ and m from (11) give us

$$E_m - \omega\left(\mathcal{T}(u)\right) - \sqrt{2\ln(\varepsilon^{-1})} \geq \tau.$$

Consequently, we have

$$\mathbb{P}\left(\inf_{v \in \mathcal{T}(u)} \|M \operatorname{vec}(v)\|_F \geq \tau\right) \geq \mathbb{P}\left(\inf_{v \in \mathcal{T}(u)} \|M \operatorname{vec}(v)\|_F \geq E_m - \omega\left(\mathcal{T}(u)\right) - \sqrt{2\ln(\varepsilon^{-1})}\right)$$

$$\geq 1 - \exp\left(-\frac{\left(\sqrt{2\ln(\varepsilon^{-1})}\right)^2}{2}\right) = 1 - \varepsilon,$$

where the second inequality stems from Theorem 4. Lemma 1 concludes the proof.

3.3   Explicit Bounds for the Finite Difference Operator

Here we make explicit the general analysis operator Ω. We consider the one- and two-dimensional difference operators for the recovery of multichannel one- and two-dimensional signals.

Multichannel One-Dimensional Signal Recovery
Case $\ell_{\infty,1,1}$: The expectation in (11) reads

$$\mathbb{E}[\|\mathbf{d}_\Lambda G\|_{\infty,1,1}] = \sum_{i \in \Lambda} \mathbb{E}[\max_{k \in [c]} \{|G_{i+1,k} - G_{ik}|\}].$$

We set $Y_{ik} := |G_{i+1,k} - G_{ik}|$ and note that for a fixed i $(Y_{ik})_{k \in [c]}$ are iid half-normal distributed random variables, see [8, Sect. 2.2.2 ff.]. Thus, the cumulative distribution function (cdf) of $\max_{k \in [c]} Y_{ik}$ satisfies

$$F_{\max\limits_{k \in [c]} Y_{ik}}(t) = \mathbb{P}(\max_{k \in [c]} Y_{ik} \leq t) = \mathbb{P}(Y_{i1} \leq t, \ldots, Y_{ic} \leq t)$$

$$= \prod_{k \in [c]} \mathbb{P}(Y_{ik} \leq t) = \mathbb{P}(Y_{i1} \leq t)^c = F_{Y_{i1}}(t)^c,$$

i.e., the cdf of $\max_{k \in [c]} Y_{ik}$ is the c-th power of the cdf of the half-normal distribution. Due to [8, Eq. (2.14)], it is $F_{Y_{i1}}(t) = \operatorname{erf}(\frac{t}{2})$ where erf denotes the error function [9]. Consequently, we have

$$\mathbb{E}[\max_{k \in [c]} Y_{ik}] = \int_0^\infty 1 - F_{\max\limits_{k \in [c]} Y_{ik}}(t) \, \mathrm{d}t - \int_{-\infty}^0 F_{\max\limits_{k \in [c]} Y_{ik}}(t) \, \mathrm{d}t$$

$$= \int_0^\infty 1 - F_{\max\limits_{k \in [c]} Y_{ik}}(t) \, \mathrm{d}t = \int_0^\infty 1 - F_{Y_{i1}}(t)^c \, \mathrm{d}t$$

$$= \int_0^\infty 1 - \operatorname{erf}(\tfrac{t}{2})^c \, \mathrm{d}t. \tag{17}$$

The value of (17) can be explicitly computed for $c = 2$ and equals

$$\int_0^\infty 1 - \mathrm{erf}(\tfrac{t}{2})^2 \; dt = 2\sqrt{\frac{2}{\pi}}.$$

Therefore, and since the range of erf is $[0,1]$, we can lower bound (17) for $c \geq 2$ by $2\sqrt{\frac{2}{\pi}}$. Thus, for $c \geq 2$ we derive the estimation

$$\mathbb{E}[\|\mathbf{d}_\Lambda G\|_{\infty,1,1}] = \sum_{i \in \Lambda} \mathbb{E}[\max_{k \in [c]} \{ \; |G_{i+1,k} - G_{ik}| \}] \geq \sum_{i \in \Lambda} 2\sqrt{\frac{2}{\pi}} = 2\sqrt{\frac{2}{\pi}} \cdot |\Lambda| . \quad (18)$$

For $z \in \mathbb{B}_{\|\cdot\|_F}$ it holds

$$\|\mathbf{d}z\|_{\infty,1,1} = \sum_{i=1}^{n-1} \max_{k \in [c]} |z_{i+1,k} - z_{ik}| \leq \sum_{i=1}^{n-1} \sum_{k=1}^{c} |z_{i+1,k} - z_{ik}|$$

$$\leq \sum_{k=1}^{c} 2\|z_{:,k}\|_1 = 2\|z\|_{1,1} \leq 2\sqrt{cn}\|z\|_F \leq 2\sqrt{cn}.$$

Hence, $\max_{z \in \mathbb{B}_{\|\cdot\|_F}} \|\mathbf{d}z\|_{\infty,1,1} \leq 2\sqrt{cn}$.

Case $\ell_{1,1,1}$: Concerning $\|\mathbf{d}z\|_{1,1,1}$, the same approximations as for $\ell_{\infty,1,1}$ still apply, thus $\|\mathbf{d}z\|_{1,1,1} \leq 2\sqrt{cn}$. Furthermore, from the properties of the half-normal distribution we get

$$\mathbb{E}[\|(\mathbf{d}G)_\Lambda\|_{1,1,1}] = \sum_{i \in \Lambda} \sum_{k \in [c]} \mathbb{E}[|G_{i+1,k} - G_{ik}|] = \sum_{i \in \Lambda} \sum_{k \in [c]} \frac{2}{\sqrt{\pi}} + \frac{2}{\sqrt{\pi}} = |\Lambda| \, c \frac{4}{\sqrt{\pi}}.$$

Inserting the above estimations from above (11) yields the next result.

Theorem 5. *Let* $\mathbf{d} : \mathbb{R}^{n \times c} \to \mathbb{R}^{(n-1) \times c}$, $c \geq 2$ *be the one-dimensional finite difference operator,* $q \in \{1, \infty\}$ *and* $u \in \mathbb{R}^{n \times c}$ *with* $|\Lambda| = n - 1 - s$, *where* Λ *is defined by* (10). *For a random draw* $M \in \mathbb{R}^{m \times nc}$ *of a Gaussian matrix, let noisy measurements* $b = M \, \mathrm{vec}(u) + e$ *be given with* $\|e\|_2 \leq \eta$ *and* $\varepsilon \in (0,1)$. *If*

$$\frac{m^2}{m+1} \geq \begin{cases} \left(\left(\sqrt{n \left(c - \frac{2}{\pi c} \left(1 - \frac{1}{n} - \frac{s}{n} \right)^2 \right)} \right) + \sqrt{2 \ln(\varepsilon^{-1})} + \tau \right)^2 & \text{for } q = \infty, \\[4mm] \left(\left(\sqrt{n \left(c - \frac{c}{\pi} \left(1 - \frac{1}{n} - \frac{s}{n} \right)^2 \right)} \right) + \sqrt{2 \ln(\varepsilon^{-1})} + \tau \right)^2 & \text{for } q = 1, \end{cases} \quad (19)$$

then with probability at least $1 - \varepsilon$ *any minimizer* $\hat{u}$ *of* (9) *with* $\|\cdot\|_{CTV} = \|\mathbf{d}\cdot\|_{q,1,1}$ *satisfies* $\|u - \hat{u}\|_F \leq \frac{2\eta}{\tau}$.

Multichannel Image Recovery

Case $\ell_{\infty,1,1}$: Deriving the estimations for $\mathbb{E}[\|\mathbf{D}_\Lambda G\|_{\infty,1,1}]$ and $\max\limits_{z\in\mathbb{B}_{\|\cdot\|_F}} \|\mathbf{D}z\|_{\infty,1,1}$ is completely analogous to case of the one-dimensional finite difference operator. The results read

$$\mathbb{E}[\|\mathbf{D}_\Lambda G\|_{\infty,1,1}] \geq 4\sqrt{\frac{2}{\pi}} \cdot |\Lambda| \quad \text{and} \quad \max_{z\in\mathbb{B}_{\|\cdot\|_F}} \|\mathbf{D}z\|_{\infty,1,1} \leq 4\sqrt{cN}.$$

Case $\ell_{1,1,1}$: Deriving the estimations for $\mathbb{E}[\|\mathbf{D}_\Lambda G\|_{1,1,1}]$ and $\max\limits_{z\in\mathbb{B}_{\|\cdot\|_F}} \|\mathbf{D}z\|_{1,1,1}$ is analogous to the one-dimensional case. The results read

$$\mathbb{E}[\|(\mathbf{D}G)_\Lambda\|_{1,1,1}] = |\Lambda|\, c\frac{4}{\sqrt{\pi}} \quad \text{and} \quad \max_{z\in\mathbb{B}_{\|\cdot\|_F}} \|\mathbf{D}z\|_{1,1,1} \leq 4\sqrt{cN}.$$

Inserting these estimations from into (11) gives the next result.

Theorem 6. *Let* $\mathbf{D}: \mathbb{R}^{n\times c} \to \mathbb{R}^{(n-N)\times 2\times c}$ *be the finite difference operator,* $q \in \{1,\infty\}$ *and* $u \in \mathbb{R}^{n\times c}$, $n = N^2$ *with* $|\Lambda| = n - N - s$, *where* Λ *is defined by (10). For a random draw* $M \in \mathbb{R}^{m\times nc}$ *of a Gaussian matrix, let noisy measurements* $b = M\,\mathrm{vec}(u) + e$ *be given with* $\|e\|_2 \leq \eta$ *and* $\varepsilon \in (0,1)$. *If*

$$\frac{m^2}{m+1} \geq \begin{cases} \left(\sqrt{N^2\left(c - \frac{2}{\pi c}\left(1 - \frac{1}{N} - \frac{s}{N^2}\right)^2\right)} + \sqrt{2\ln(\varepsilon^{-1})} + \tau\right)^2 & \text{for } q = \infty, \\ \left(\sqrt{N^2\left(c - \frac{c}{\pi}\left(1 - \frac{1}{N} - \frac{s}{N^2}\right)^2\right)} + \sqrt{2\ln(\varepsilon^{-1})} + \tau\right)^2 & \text{for } q = 1, \end{cases} \tag{20}$$

then with probability at least $1-\varepsilon$ *any minimizer* $\hat{u}$ *of (9) with* $\|\cdot\|_{CTV} = \|\mathbf{D}\cdot\|_{q,1,1}$ *satisfies* $\|u - \hat{u}\|_F \leq \frac{2\eta}{\tau}$.

4 Numerical Optimization

To solve (8) we apply the Chambolle-Pock optimization scheme [10]. The iteration reads

$$u^{k+1} = u^k - \tau(M^\top y^k - \mathbf{div}\,z^k),$$
$$\overline{u}^{k+1} = 2u^{k+1} - u^k,$$
$$y^{k+1} = y^k + \sigma(M\overline{u}^{k+1} - b),$$
$$z^{k+1} = \mathrm{Proj}_{\mathbb{B}_{\|\cdot\|_{CTV_*}}}(z^k + \sigma \mathbf{d}\overline{u}^{k+1})$$

where all variables are column-wise vectorized and $\tau, \sigma > 0$. Convergence [10] is ensured if $\sigma\tau(\|M\|_2^2 + \|\mathbf{d}\|_2^2) \leq \sigma\tau(\|M\|_2^2 + 12) < 1$ holds. For different choices of CTV, we have to adjust the z-update by utilizing the correct projection that can be derived by Theorem 1 and Theorem 2, see [1].

5   Experiments

Phase Transitions for CTV Regularization. Here we demonstrate that one can undersample a cosparse multichannel signal and yet reconstruct it accurately via (3). We estimate empirically the precise limits to such undersampling and compare them to the theoretically derived measurement bounds from Theorem 5. In particular, we consider multichannel one-dimensional signals and set $\Omega = \mathbf{d}$. The CTV's are induced by (5)–(7). To separate successful from unsuccessful reconstruction we define a reconstruction to be successful if the relative ℓ_2-error $E_{\ell_2} \leq 10^{-5}$, as done in [6]. We generated 100 test multichannel signals for each sparsity parameter s, $s = |\Lambda^c|$ and sampled them by full linear Gaussian

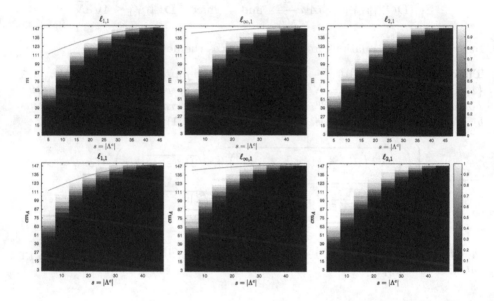

Fig. 1. Empirical phase transitions for various CTV regularizers applied to one-dimensional multichannel signals. The red lines correspond to the theoretical bounds in Theorem 5. Top row: recovery probability from full Gaussian measurement matrices $M \in \mathbb{R}^{m \times 150}$ across channels. Bottom row: recovery probability by separable channel-wise measurements M_A, that correspond to block matrices $M = \mathrm{diag}(A, \ldots, A)$ with Gaussian $A \in \mathbb{R}^{m_A \times 50}$. Even though full measurements across carry more information, we observe no significant difference in recovery probabilities between the two row. Empirical phase transitions for various CTV regularizers applied to one-dimensional multichannel signals. The red lines correspond to the theoretical bounds in Theorem 5. Top row: recovery probability from full Gaussian measurement matrices $M \in \mathbb{R}^{m \times 150}$ across channels. Bottom row: recovery probability by separable channel-wise measurements M_A, that correspond to block matrices $M = \mathrm{diag}(A, \ldots, A)$ with Gaussian $A \in \mathbb{R}^{m_A \times 50}$. Even though full measurements across carry more information, we observe no significant difference in recovery probabilities between the two row. (Color figure online)

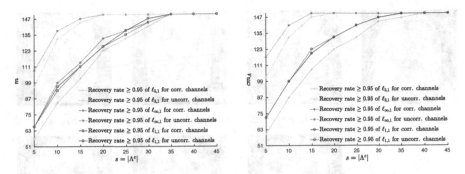

Fig. 2. Curves corresponding to 95% exact recovery. The dotted curves correspond to signals with completely uncorrelated channels. Left panel: full Gaussian measurements across all channel with $M \in \mathbb{R}^{m \times 150}$. Right panel: separate channel-wise measurements via block matrices M_A with Gaussian $A \in \mathbb{R}^{m_A \times 50}$.

measurements $M \in \mathbb{R}^{m \times nc}$ (1 across all channels. We solved (8) per tuple (m, s), $s = |\Lambda^c|$ and determined the ratio of successful recoveries. The ranges of values were chosen as $s = 5, 10, \ldots 45$ and $m = 3, 6, \ldots 150$. The signals $x \in \mathbb{R}^{50 \times 3}$ were generated randomly along the lines of [11, Sect. 2.2] and by stapling the resulting intra-channel s-cosparse signals. Furthermore, we superimpose the measurement bounds derived in Theorem 5 (omitting terms of lower order) to the corresponding plots in the top row of Fig. 1. In the same way, we derived empirical phase transitions for measurement matrices $M_A = \operatorname{diag}(A, \ldots, A)$ in block form, see (2). We refer to Fig. 1 for the discussion of the results. Figure 2 shows empirical measurement bounds corresponding to 95% recovery rates. Furthermore, Fig. 2 illustrates how CTV (5)–(7) affects recovery of channel correlated and channel uncorrelated cosparse signals in terms of number of measurements. Signals with uncorrelated channels, have the same cosparsity as the correlated ones, but jumps occur at different spatial positions. The number of measurements can be kept at minimum if for correlated channel signals we use CTV defined via the $\ell_{2,1}$- and the $\ell_{\infty,1}$-norm, while for uncorrelated channel signals one should use the $\ell_{1,1}$-CTV regularizer. This is in agreement with the experiments in [1].

Multichannel Image CTV Reconstruction. For the choice $\Omega = \mathbf{D}$, CTV's defined by (5)–(7) and the practical relevant case of separable channel-wise measurements M_A, see (1), the recovery by (3) is demonstrated in Fig. 3. It shows a phantom head image with correlated color channels and its reconstructions for $m_A = 280$ and $m_A = 310$ Gaussian measurements *per channel* respectively. From [12, Proposition 4.3 and Lemma 4.7] we derive a measurement bound for the corresponding separate intra-channel ℓ_0-problems: $310 \leq m_A \leq 368$. The results show that we come close to this interval using the CTV $\ell_{2,1,1}$-regularizer. The image is reconstructed from 310 measurements; even for 280 measurements, the result is optically acceptable.

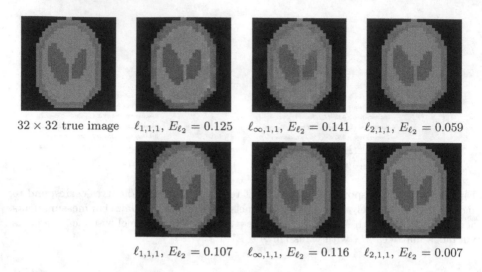

32×32 true image $\ell_{1,1,1},\ E_{\ell_2} = 0.125$ $\ell_{\infty,1,1},\ E_{\ell_2} = 0.141$ $\ell_{2,1,1},\ E_{\ell_2} = 0.059$

$\ell_{1,1,1},\ E_{\ell_2} = 0.107$ $\ell_{\infty,1,1},\ E_{\ell_2} = 0.116$ $\ell_{2,1,1},\ E_{\ell_2} = 0.007$

Fig. 3. First row: $m_A = 280$ Gaussian measurements. Second row: $m_A = 310$ Gaussian measurements. The examples reflect the trend of the previous phase transitions in Figs. 1 and 2: $\ell_{2,1,1}$ is superior to $\ell_{1,1,1}$ and $\ell_{\infty,1,1}$ given correlated channels. (Color figure online)

6   Conclusion

We have presented results on the nonuniform recovery from Gaussian random measurements of cosparse multichannel signals with respect to the one- and two-dimensional difference operators. In particular, we derived a measurement bound that estimates the allowed undersampling of multichannel cosparse signals such that regularization via collaborative total variation (CTV) succeeds. The derived bounds are quite accurate when the sparsity of the analysis representation of the multichannel signal is not very small. Moreover, we demonstrated empirically that separable channel-wise Gaussian measurements are equivalent to using full Gaussian measurements across all channels.

References

1. Duran, J., Möller, M., Sbert, C., Cremers, D.: Collaborative total variation: a general framework for vectorial TV models. SIAM J. Imaging Sci. **9**(1), 116–151 (2016)
2. Shikhaliev, P., Fritz, S.: Photon counting spectral CT versus conventional CT: comparative evaluation for breast imaging application. Phys. Med. Biol. **56**(7), 1905–1930 (2011)
3. Semerci, O., Hao, N., Kilmer, M., Miller, E.: Tensor-based formulation and nuclear norm regularization for multienergy computed tomography. IEEE Trans. Image Process. **23**(4), 1678–1693 (2014)
4. Foucart, S., Rauhut, H.: A Mathematical Introduction to Compressive Sensing. Birkhäuser, Basel (2013)

5. Chandrasekaran, V., Recht, B., Parrilo, P., Willsky, A.: The convex geometry of linear inverse problems. Found. Comput. Math. **12**(6), 805–849 (2012)
6. Kabanava, M., Rauhut, H., Zhang, H.: Robust analysis ℓ_1-recovery from Gaussian measurements and total variation minimization. Eur. J. Appl. Math. **26**(06), 917–929 (2015)
7. Amelunxen, D., Lotz, M., McCoy, M., Tropp, J.: Living on the edge: phase transitions in convex programs with random data. Inf. Inference **3**(3), 224–294 (2014)
8. Ahsanullah, M., Kibria, B., Shakil, M.: Normal and Student's t Distributions and Their Applications. Atlantis Studies in Probability and Statistics. Atlantis Press, Paris (2014)
9. Cody, W.J.: Rational Chebyshev approximations for the error function. Math. Comput. **23**(107), 631–637 (1969)
10. Chambolle, A., Pock, T.: A first-order primal-dual algorithm for convex problems with applications to imaging. J. Math. Imaging Vis. **40**(1), 120–145 (2011)
11. Nam, S., Davies, M.E., Elad, M., Gribonval, R.: The cosparse analysis model and algorithms. Appl. Comput. Harmon. **34**(1), 30–56 (2013)
12. Deniţiu, A., Petra, S., Schnörr, C., Schnörr, C.: Phase transitions and cosparse tomographic recovery of compound solid bodies from few projections. Fundam. Inform. **135**(1–2), 73–102 (2014)

Simultaneous Reconstruction and Segmentation of CT Scans with Shadowed Data

François Lauze[1]([✉]) [iD], Yvain Quéau[2], and Esben Plenge[1]

[1] Department of Computer Science, Universtity of Copenhagen,
Copenhagen, Denmark
francois@di.ku.dk
[2] Computer Vision Group, TU München, Munich, Germany

Abstract. We propose a variational approach for simultaneous reconstruction and multiclass segmentation of X-ray CT images, with limited field of view and missing data. We propose a simple energy minimisation approach, loosely based on a Bayesian rationale. The resulting non convex problem is solved by alternating reconstruction steps using an iterated relaxed proximal gradient, and a proximal approach for the segmentation. Preliminary results on synthetic data demonstrate the potential of the approach for synchrotron imaging applications.

1 Introduction

X-ray Computerised Tomography (CT) attempts at reconstructing a 3D structure from a set of planar projections that consist of attenuated measurements of X-rays across an object. In many domains, especially material sciences and geosciences, this reconstructed structure is often a building block for segmentation, which is further used to analyse some physical properties of the sample, such as porosity and tortuosity, or to perform some numerical simulations. Traditionally, and because of its low cost, Filtered Back Projection reconstruction (FBP) is performed, followed by segmentation. This has the disadvantage to propagate reconstruction errors in the segmentation. Other approaches have thus been proposed that do not decouple these steps. Discrete tomography [1] reconstructs an image with a small finite number of values, while Yoon et al. reconstruct a segmented image, using a level set approach [12]. In this work we follow a simultaneous reconstruction and segmentation (SRS) approach to produce both reconstructed image and its segmentation. This approach was first proposed by van Sompel and Brady [10], using a Hidden Markov Measure Field Model (HMMFM). Another was proposed by Ramlau and Ring in [8]. Romanov et al. [9] assumed that information about the segmentation is known in the form of prior knowledge on the parameters of a Gaussian Mixture Model for intensity distribution, and some partial convexification is performed. A Potts-Model based algorithm was proposed by Storah et al. in [11]. The present work is somewhat similar, though we place ourselve in a limited Field of View situation, where the detector extent is less than the object diameter. Algebraic Reconstruction

© Springer International Publishing AG 2017
F. Lauze et al. (Eds.): SSVM 2017, LNCS 10302, pp. 308–319, 2017.
DOI: 10.1007/978-3-319-58771-4_25

Techniques (ART) are know to perform properly ([7], Chap. VI), though an extra difficulty is that the signal may be *partially* blocked at certain angles, a situation somewhat similar, but not identical to limited-angle tomography. FBP solvers can also reasonably deal with limited field of view by proper extension of the sinogram data (see also [7], Chap. VI), however, noise is still propagated and the presence of holes in the sinogram produces potentially severe streak artifacts in the reconstruction affecting thereafter the segmentation quality. One of the reasons for these streak artifacts is the fact that the absence of measurements is interpreted as a zero-measurement in FBP. Ongoing work on extending microlocal analysis [5] from the limited angle problem to this type of sinogram missing data is also providing clues on potential singularities arising from them.

This work is targeted towards Synchrotron X-Ray tomography, as often the case in material science. This means a simple, parallel beam geometry. We come back to the SRS problem where we attempt to estimate all parameters during the reconstruction and segmentation process. A clear modelling of what is available allows to properly take into account missing data, both for FoV and unrecorded data. Spatial regularisation, via Total Variation minimisation, and positivity constraints reduce noise and artifacts, providing an inpainting-like mechanism for the missing data. We couple it to a segmentation term which, in the reconstruction phase, also acts as a reaction towards specific values. Because out of the FoV, reconstructed values are not reliable, the segmentation is run only inside the FoV.

The paper is organised as follows. Section 2 formalises SRS with limited field of view and occluding geometry as a Bayesian inference problem. This yields an energy-minimisation formulation which is numerically tackled in Sect. 3. Starting from a rough initial reconstruction and segmentation obtained by standard methods, the proposed algorithm iteratively refines the reconstruction, given the current segmentation, and then the segmentation, given the current reconstruction. Both these steps are efficiently achieved by lagged proximal iterations. The preliminary results presented in Sect. 4 confirm that this joint approach is promising, in comparison with the standard sequential strategy.

2 Statement of the Problem

For a monochromatic X-ray travelling along a line L, Lambert-Beer's law asserts that

$$I_L = I_0 \exp\left(-\int_L f(x)\,dx\right) \iff y_L := \log\frac{I_0}{I_L} = \int_L f(x)\,dx \qquad (2.1)$$

where I_0 is the initial intensity and f the attenuation coefficient function. Recovering f accounts thus to solving (2.1) for f when we have observed $(y_L)_L$. More precisely, the *Radon transform* $R : L^1(\mathcal{D}) \to L^1(\mathbb{S}^1 \times \mathbb{R})$ of a function f is defined as

$$Rf(\theta, s) = \int_{\theta^\perp} f(s\theta + y)\,dy, \quad \theta \in \mathbb{S}^1, s \in \mathbb{R}. \qquad (2.2)$$

with $\mathcal{D}$ a bounded domain of $\mathbb{R}^2$, $\mathbb{S}^1$ the unit circle of $\mathbb{R}$, and $\theta^\perp$ the line orthogonal to θ. The well celebrated inversion formula proven by Radon in 1917 states that when f is smooth with compact support, it can be recovered from its Radon transform by the *inverse Radon transform*:

$$f(x) = \frac{1}{4\pi^2} \int_{\mathbb{S}^1} \int_{-\infty}^{\infty} \frac{\frac{\partial}{\partial s} Rf(\theta, t)}{x \cdot \theta - t} \, dt d\theta. \tag{2.3}$$

This inversion is however ill-posed, and in our setting, we observe only $Rf(\theta, s)$ for values (θ, s) in a potentially complex sub-domain of $\mathbb{S}^1 \times \mathbb{R}$, as illustrated in Fig. 2. Filtered backprojection (FBP) is used to stabilise the inverse Radon transform, and relatively simple tricks can deal with the limited Field of View problem in the (FBP) settings. The shadowing caused by the presence of metallic bars induces however serious artifacts in FBP. This has motivated us to follow a discrete, direct approach.

Notations. We start by introducing notations used in the sequel. In the 2-dimensional setting, the sought function f can be viewed as a discrete $N \times N \to \mathbb{R}$ image x on a regular square grid, called *tomogram* and represented as a vector of $\mathbb{R}^{N^2}$. It is assumed to be large enough to cover the object we want to image. Each x_n, $n = 1 \ldots N^2$, satisfies

$$x_{\min} \leq x_n \leq x_{\max} \tag{2.4}$$

with $x_{\min} \geq 0$, $x_{\max} \leq +\infty$. This is a simple box constraint and we denote by $\mathcal{C}$ the box $[x_{\min}, x_{\max}]^{N^2}$. In the 3D setting, x would be a $N \times B \times P$ discrete image, with similar box constraints. Yet, in this preliminary work we restrict ourselves to the 2D case.

Because we are in the parallel beam geometry setting, each angular projection is inherently 2D to 1D. Assume ℓ directions and a detector array of length d with M elements, where d is larger that the diameter of the object under scrutiny. Our aim is to recover the image $\mathbf{x}$ from samples of the Radon transform of the underlying attenuation function f, which form an $\ell \times M$ discrete image called *sinogram*, and represented as a vector $y \in \mathbb{R}^{\ell M}$. The corresponding projection matrix/discrete Radon Transform $\mathbf{R}$ is thus an element of $\mathbb{R}^{\ell M \times N^2}$ such that the sinogram is obtained as

$$y = \mathbf{R}x. \tag{2.5}$$

This is a discrete analogue to the standard FBP setting. We choose here a simple model where entry $\mathbf{R}_{ij}$ represents the contribution of grid element j to the line-ray encoded by i, as for instance the length of the intersection of this line and the grid element. Other less local representations can be chosen, see [4] for instance, for discussions on the generation of the discrete Radon transform matrices.

When the detector array has a length d' smaller than the object diameter, some parts of the object are not traversed by X-rays, or these rays are not

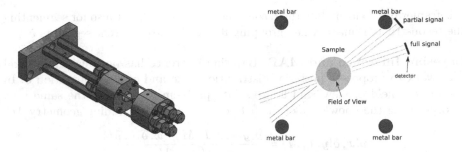

Fig. 1. Acquisition setup. Left: device holding the sample to be imaged. Right: limited Field of View and obstacle.

recorded. If assuming the same resolution as for building $\mathbf{R}$, the resulting projection matrix $\mathbf{Q}$ is made of a subset of lines of $\mathbf{R}$. With m rays recorded per view, $\mathbf{Q}$ is a $\mathbb{R}^{\ell m \times N^2}$ matrix obtained from $\mathbf{R}$ by a linear projector $\mathbf{P}_F \in \mathbb{R}^{\ell m \times \ell M}$. The reduced sinogram $\mathbf{y}_F$ is $\mathbf{y}_F = \mathbf{P}_F \mathbf{y}$.

In the situation described in Fig. 1, the geometry of the missing data in the sinogram will vary according to the ratio between bar radius and detector extent. This is easily computed by projecting orthogonally the disks along the detector, at each angle. Figure 2 illustrates this in two extreme cases, a very large and a very narrow detector.

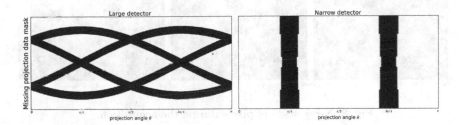

Fig. 2. Sinogram geometry induced by the occluding geometry of the bars of Fig. 1.

Each point in the sinogram corresponds to a unique angle and detector position and thus to a line of the projection matrix. Lines corresponding to missing data points in the sinogram space should also be removed from the projection matrix. This can be modelled as another projector $\mathbf{P}_M \subset \mathbb{R}^{S \times \ell m}$ with $S \leq \ell m$, and the predicted incomplete sinogram data $\mathbf{y}$ can be written as

$$\mathbf{y} = \mathbf{P}_M \mathbf{y}_F = \mathbf{P}_M \mathbf{P}_F \mathbf{R} \mathbf{x} = \mathbf{A} \mathbf{x}. \tag{2.6}$$

where $\mathbf{A}$ is of size $S \times N^2$. If the field of view is limited or if the geometry induces occlusions, then $S < N^2$ and the image $\mathbf{x}$ cannot be recovered directly from the sinogram $\mathbf{y}$ by inverting $\mathbf{A}$. It is necessary to introduce additional constraints: the Bayesian framework provides a natural framework for such a task. We thus use this framework to formulate the reconstruction problem, but also for segmenting the reconstructed image **x** i.e., grouping its pixels into different segments $\boldsymbol{\delta}$.

Bayesian Inference and MAP. Bayesian inference has been used in several SRS work to propose a posterior distribution of $\boldsymbol{x}$ and of a segmentation $\boldsymbol{\delta}$. In the limited field of view, and limited data problem we proceed the same way, incorporating the knowledge of the field of view F and occluding geometry M.

$$p(\boldsymbol{x}, \boldsymbol{\delta}|\boldsymbol{y}, F, M) = \frac{p(\boldsymbol{y}|\boldsymbol{x}, \boldsymbol{\delta}, F, M)p(\boldsymbol{x}, \boldsymbol{\delta}|F, M)}{p(\boldsymbol{y}|F, M)}$$

$$\propto p(\boldsymbol{y}|\boldsymbol{x}, F, M)p(\boldsymbol{x}, \boldsymbol{\delta}|F, M) \tag{2.7}$$

The likelihood term $p(\boldsymbol{y}|\boldsymbol{x}, F, M)$ expresses how the observed sinogram data may deviate from the one predicted in (2.6). The conditional prior $p(\boldsymbol{x}, \boldsymbol{\delta}|F, M)$ links image values, segmentation and geometry of the field of view and occluding data. There is in general no hope to get a proper reconstruction out of the field of view. This is what Fig. 3, which records the amount of recorded X-rays beams crossing each pixel, illustrates.

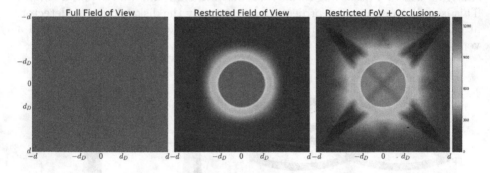

Fig. 3. X-ray visits of pixels during the acquisition.

It makes clear that between full field of view and restricted field of view (left and centre image), a large amount of information is lost, while this loss is much more moderate between centre and right image (restricted field of view and occluding geometry), and thus suggests that if a restricted field of view reconstruction is possible, then with proper priors, a reconstruction is also possible with (moderate) occluding geometry. So in order to reconstruct a tomogram and segment it, we choose a joint prior on $(\boldsymbol{x}, \boldsymbol{\delta})$ independent of M, i.e., we assume $p(\boldsymbol{x}, \boldsymbol{\delta}|F, M) = p(\boldsymbol{x}, \boldsymbol{\delta}|F)$. We may want to factorise it further by writing $p(\boldsymbol{x}, \boldsymbol{\delta}|F) = p(\boldsymbol{x}|\boldsymbol{\delta}, F)p(\boldsymbol{\delta}|F) = p(\boldsymbol{\delta}|\boldsymbol{x}, F)p(\boldsymbol{x}|F)$, but the unfactorised expression keeps the symmetry between $\boldsymbol{\delta}$ and **x**.

A Maximum a Posteriori approach leads to minimisation of the neg-log-posterior

$$(\boldsymbol{x}^*, \boldsymbol{\delta}^*) = \operatorname{argmin}_{\boldsymbol{x}, \boldsymbol{\delta}} - \log p(\boldsymbol{y}|\boldsymbol{x}, F, M) - \log p(\boldsymbol{x}, \boldsymbol{\delta}|F). \tag{2.8}$$

Sinogram noise in X-ray tomography is usually modelled as Poisson, and in the high number of X-rays quanta, the limiting distribution can be considered Gaussian [4], hence a least-squares term can be chosen for the first component in (2.8). The joint prior encodes both priors on x and δ on F as well as their mutual dependence. We propose a discrete TV prior for x, with box-positivity constraints. For the interplay between x and δ, a simple Pott's model term is used. And for the prior on δ, we ask smoothness of the segments within a HMMFM framework. For that purpose write $\delta = (v, c)$ where $v : F \to \Delta_K$ is the label field, Δ_K is the standard simplex of $\mathbb{R}^K$ where K is the number of labels (supposed to be known in advance), $v_n = (v_{n1}, \ldots, v_{nK}) \in \Delta_k \iff v_{nk} \geq 0$, $k = 1 \ldots K$ and $\sum_{k=1}^{K} v_{nk} = 1$. A discrete squared-gradient magnitude is used for regularisation of v. Putting all pieces together, we obtain the following cost function:

$$\mathcal{E}(x, c, v; y) = \frac{1}{2}\|Ax - y\|_2^2 + \alpha J_F(x) + \frac{\beta}{2}\left(\lambda \sum_{n \in F} \sum_{k=1}^{K} v_{nk}(x_n - c_k)^2 + \frac{1}{2}\|Dv\|_2^2\right),$$

$$0 \leq x_{\min} \leq x_n \leq x_{\max} \leq +\infty, \quad v_n \in \Delta_K. \tag{2.9}$$

In this expression, $c \in \mathbb{R}^K$ is the vector of mean segment values, $J_F(x)$ is the discrete TV-semi norm of x over F, D is a matrix representing the finite differences stencil used to approximate the gradient, and α, β and λ are user-defined hyper-parameters that need to be tuned appropriately.

3   Optimisation

The cost function is convex in x, in v and in c, but not jointly convex in x, v, c. We propose to optimise it iteratively by alternating between updates of x, v and c. We first describe updates for the different arguments, from the simplest to the most complex one. Then we describe the full algorithm. As segmentation is difficult to obtain without reconstruction, a few iterations of a TV-reconstruction algorithm, followed by a K-means segmentation, are performed prior to start the joint optimisation. These iterations are actually simplifications of the joint optimisation when one or the other arguments are known.

3.1   The Problem in c

The problem in c is classical and trivial: each c_k is given by

$$c_k = \frac{\sum_{n=1}^{N^2} v_{nk} x_n}{\sum_{n=1}^{N^2} v_{nk}}. \tag{3.1}$$

3.2   The Problem in v

Call $U_K = \Delta_K^F$ the set of functions from F to Δ_K. After simplification of (2.9), the part of the cost function of interest in v is $\mathcal{F}(v) = \frac{1}{2}\|Dv\|_2^2 + \lambda \langle g, v \rangle + \iota_{U_K}(v)$

Algorithm 1. Sketch of the full algorithm.

Input: Sinogram y, field of view F, sinogram mask M, number of classes K, weight
   parameters α, β, λ, ART parameter $\rho \in (0,2)$, maximum number of iterations L_{RS}.
Output: Reconstruction x and segmentation $(\mathbf{v}, \mathbf{c})$ of x on F.
Initialisation: Run approximate reconstruction to produce x^0. Run a K-means or
   Otsu clustering to produce $(\mathbf{c}^0, \mathbf{v}^0)$ from x^0 and F.
   for $i = 0$ to L_{RS} **do**
      ▷ **Solution in x**
      Solve for x^{i+1} from x^i, $\mathbf{c}^i$ and $\mathbf{v}^i$.
      ▷ **Solution in c**
      Solve for $\mathbf{c}^{i+1}$ from x^{i+1} and $\mathbf{v}^i$.
      ▷ **Solution in v**
      Solve for $\mathbf{v}^{i+1}$ from x^{i+1} and $\mathbf{c}^{i+1}$.
   end for

with $\mathbf{g} = \left((x - c_1)^2, \ldots, (x - c_K)^2\right)^T$, $\langle -, - \rangle$ is the Euclidean inner product on
$\mathbb{R}^{N^2 K}$ and ι_{U_K} the indicator function of U_K incorporating the constraints on $\mathbf{v}$.
We write $h(\mathbf{v}) = \frac{1}{2}\|\mathbf{D}\mathbf{v}\|_2^2 + \lambda \langle \mathbf{g}, \mathbf{v} \rangle$. A classical solution is the proximal method
which consists in computing $\mathbf{v}^{i+1}$ iteratively, by using the following lagged
j-iterations:

$$\mathbf{v}^{j+1} = \text{prox}_{t_i \mathcal{F}}(\mathbf{v}^j) = \text{argmin}_{\mathbf{v} \in U_K} \left\{ h(\mathbf{v}) + \frac{1}{2t_i}\|\mathbf{v} - \mathbf{v}^j\|_2^2 \right\}$$

$$= \mathcal{P}_{U_k}\left(\mathbf{v}^j - t_i \tilde{\nabla} h(\mathbf{v}^{j+1})\right) \tag{3.2}$$

with t_i a diminishing gradient step, constant over a sweep i and set to $t_i = 1/(1+i)$, and $\tilde{\nabla} h(\mathbf{v}^{j+1})$ the subgradient of h at $\mathbf{v}^{j+1}$ [3]. As h is in fact smooth,
the subgradient is just its usual gradient $\nabla h(\mathbf{v}^{j+1})$: $\nabla h(\mathbf{v}) = \mathbf{D}^T \mathbf{D} \mathbf{v} + \lambda \mathbf{g}$ with
$-\mathbf{D}^T \mathbf{D}$ a discrete "vector Laplacian". In practice replace it by the two-steps
method

$$\tilde{\mathbf{v}}^{j+1} = \left(\mathbf{D}^T \mathbf{D} + t_j^{-1} id_F\right)^{-1} \left(t_j^{-1} \mathbf{v}^j - \lambda \mathbf{g}\right) \tag{3.3}$$

$$\mathbf{v}^{j+1} = \mathcal{P}_{U_K}\left(\tilde{\mathbf{v}}^{j+1}\right). \tag{3.4}$$

Reflective boundary conditions are used to solve (3.3) while the projection
onto U_K can for instance be implemented using classical simplex projection
algorithms.

3.3   The Problem in x

With $\mathbf{c}$ and $\mathbf{v}$ fixed, the problem in x still presents two difficulties that pre-
vent a direct approach: (1) the TV-seminorm term $J_F(\mathbf{x})$ and the size of the
matrix $\mathbf{A}$. Row/block of rows action methods and iterated proximal algorithms
provide a way to deal with it, following [6]. Before describing it, we rewrite the
segmentation term in a more compact way.

Let $\Pi_F : \boldsymbol{x} \mapsto \boldsymbol{x}_{|F}$ the restriction to F. Let also N_F denote the amount of pixels in the field of view F, so that Π_F can be identified with a projection $\mathbb{R}^{N^2} \to \mathbb{R}^{N_F}$. Then

$$\frac{1}{2} \sum_{n \in F} \sum_{k=1}^{K} \mathbf{v}_{nk} \left(x_n - c_k \right)^2 = \frac{1}{2} \| \mathbf{V} \Pi_F \boldsymbol{x} - L(\mathbf{V}, \mathbf{c}) \|_2^2 \qquad (3.5)$$

where we have set $\mathbf{V} = (\mathbf{V}_1, \ldots, \mathbf{V}_K)^T$ with $\mathbf{V}_k = \mathrm{diag}(\mathbf{v}_{1k}, \ldots, \mathbf{v}_{nk})^{\frac{1}{2}}$ and $L(\mathbf{V}, c) = \left((c_1 \mathbf{V}_1 1_{N_F})^T, \ldots, (c_K \mathbf{V}_K 1_{N_F})^T \right)^T$, $1_{N_F} = (1, \ldots, 1)^T \in \mathbb{R}^{N_F}$. Note that $\mathbf{V}^T \mathbf{V} = \mathrm{id}_{\mathbb{R}^{N_F}}$. Dividing $\mathbf{A}$ in p blocks (one per viewing angle, if the view is non-empty), we have

$$\mathcal{E}(\boldsymbol{x}) = \sum_{q=1}^{p} \frac{1}{2} \| \mathbf{A}_q \boldsymbol{x} - \boldsymbol{y}_q \|_2^2 + \alpha J_F(\boldsymbol{x}) + \frac{\beta \lambda}{2} \| \mathbf{V} \boldsymbol{x} - L(\mathbf{V}, \mathbf{c}) \|_2^2 \qquad (3.6)$$

where we abusively denote $\mathbf{V} := \mathbf{V} \Pi_F$ for sake of compactness.

We write $\mathcal{E}(\boldsymbol{x}) = \sum_{q=1}^{p+2} f_q(\boldsymbol{x})$ with

$$f_q(\boldsymbol{x}) = \frac{1}{2} \| \mathbf{A}_q \boldsymbol{x} - \boldsymbol{y}_q \|_2^2, \quad q = 1 \ldots p \qquad (3.7)$$

$$f_{p+1}(\boldsymbol{x}) = \alpha J_F(\boldsymbol{x}), \qquad (3.8)$$

$$f_{p+2}(\boldsymbol{x}) = \frac{\beta \lambda}{2} \| \mathbf{V} \boldsymbol{x} - L(\mathbf{V}, \mathbf{c}) \|_2^2. \qquad (3.9)$$

Using one of the schemes (RIPG-I or RIPG-II) from [6], we obtain the following iterative scheme. With $\rho \, in \,]0, 2[$ and an initial estimate set for the i-th sweep, a full update on $\boldsymbol{x}^i$ is given as follows.
Set $\boldsymbol{x}_i^0 = \boldsymbol{x}^i$. Then for $q = 1$ up to $p + 2$:

$$\mathbf{z}^q = \mathrm{prox}_{t_i f_q}(\boldsymbol{x}_i^q)$$
$$\boldsymbol{x}_i^{q+1} = \mathcal{P}_C(\rho \mathbf{z}^q + (1 - \rho) \boldsymbol{x}_i^q)$$

and set $\boldsymbol{x}^{i+1} = \boldsymbol{x}_i^{p+2}$. The first p steps are updates from the Radon transform, step $p + 1$ is a TV regularisation, while the last step is a reaction towards the current segmentation. $\mathcal{P}_C$ is the box constraint projection from (2.4).

The proximality operators for the first p equations and the last one have the form $\mathrm{prox}_{t\phi}(\boldsymbol{x})$ where $\phi(\boldsymbol{x})$ is quadratic, $\phi(\boldsymbol{x}) = \frac{\delta}{2} \| \mathbf{H} \boldsymbol{x} - \mathbf{z} \|_2^2$ with $\mathbf{H} \in \mathbb{R}^{L \times N^2}$ and $\mathbf{z} \in \mathbb{R}^L$. By definition of the prox operator, one has

$$\mathrm{prox}_{t\phi}(\boldsymbol{x}) = \underset{\mathbf{u} \in \mathbb{R}^{N^2}}{\mathrm{argmin}} \left\{ \frac{t\delta}{2} \| \mathbf{H} \mathbf{u} - \mathbf{z} \|_2^2 + \frac{1}{2} \| \mathbf{u} - \boldsymbol{x} \|_2^2 \right\}. \qquad (3.10)$$

Writing the normal equations, one get

$$\mathrm{prox}_{t\phi}(\boldsymbol{x}) = \left(\mathbf{H}^T \mathbf{H} + \frac{1}{t\delta} \mathrm{id}_{\mathbb{R}^{N^2}} \right)^{-1} \left(\mathbf{H}^T \mathbf{z} + \frac{1}{t\delta} \boldsymbol{x} \right). \qquad (3.11)$$

Using the classical relation valid for all $\tau \notin \mathrm{spec}(\mathbf{MM}^T) \cup \{0\}$ and all $\mathbf{M} \in \mathbb{R}^{n \times m}$,

$$\left(\mathbf{M}^T \mathbf{M} + \tau \mathrm{id}_{\mathbb{R}^m}\right)^{-1} \mathbf{M}^T = \mathbf{M}^T \left(\mathbf{MM}^T + \tau \mathrm{id}_{\mathbb{R}^n}\right)^{-1} \qquad (3.12)$$

Eq. (3.11) can be rewritten as

$$\mathrm{prox}_{t\phi}(\boldsymbol{x}) = \boldsymbol{x} - \mathbf{H}^T \left(\mathbf{HH}^T + \frac{1}{t\delta}\mathrm{id}_{\mathbb{R}^L}\right)^{-1} (\mathbf{H}\boldsymbol{x} - \mathbf{z}) \qquad (3.13)$$

and $\mathbf{H}^T \left(\mathbf{HH}^T + \frac{1}{t\delta}\mathrm{id}_{\mathbb{R}^n}\right)^{-1}$ is a regularised or damped pseudoinverse of $\mathbf{H}$. We use it for the first p equations with $\mathbf{H} = \mathbf{A}_q$, $\delta = 1$, $t = t_i$. This correspond to a block-damped ART approach. With a standard discretization of the Radon transform, the image resolution being given by detector resolution, $\mathbf{A}_q \mathbf{A}_q^T$ is at most (and most often) tridiagonal, its values can be cached for reuse in subsequent updates.

A FISTA scheme [2] is used for the TV-regularization proximal step originbating from decomposition (3.8) (see also discussion in [6]).

For the segmentation reaction equation, $\mathbf{H} = \mathbf{V}\Pi_F$ and $\mathbf{H}^T\mathbf{H} = \Pi_F^T \mathbf{V}^T \mathbf{V} \pi_F = \Pi_F^T \Pi_F$ and $\boldsymbol{y} = \Pi_F^T \Pi_F \boldsymbol{x}$ is given by $\boldsymbol{y}_s = \boldsymbol{x}_s$ if $s \in F$ and $\boldsymbol{y}_s = 0$ if not. The proximal calculation is actually straightforward. Pixels out of F are not modified (in accordance of course with our prior hypothesis and the form (2.9) of the cost function), while in F, they are updated via the simple formula: the s-component of $\boldsymbol{z}^q$ is given by

$$\boldsymbol{z}_s^q = \frac{\sum_{k=1}^K \mathbf{v}_{sk}\mathbf{c}_k + (t_i\beta\lambda)^{-1} (\boldsymbol{x}_i^q)_s}{1 + (t_i\beta\lambda)^{-1}} \qquad (3.14)$$

4   Experiments

To evaluate our variational SRS strategy, we consider the synthetic dataset from Fig. 4. We created a 2D tomogram of size $N \times N$ with $N = 300$, containing

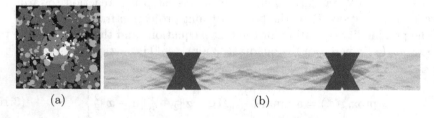

(a)   (b)

Fig. 4. Dataset used for evaluation. (a) Ground truth image, of size 1000×1000. The field of view is indicated by the central circle. (b) Sinogram computed from (a), of size 720×282, with missing data and additive, zero-mean, Gaussian noise (with standard deviation equal to 1% of the signal amplitude.

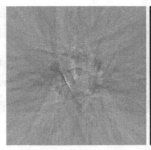

Fig. 5. Left: FBP reconstruction result, in the case where the sinogram does not contain missing data. Although it is quite sensitive to noise, the reconstruction is satisfactory and can be used for segmentation. Middle: same, when the sinogram contains missing data. Right: K-means segmentation applied to the middle reconstruction, which is not informative.

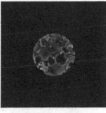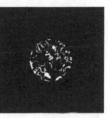

RMSE = 58.37 $\tau = 0.81$

Fig. 6. Initial 3D-reconstruction and segmentation. From left to right: TV-reconstruction of the image; absolute difference between (a) and ground truth (Fig. 4-a): black is 0, white is 255, and RMSE is the root mean square error; K-means Otsu clustering obtained from (a); classification map, where black indicates good classification, white indicates bad classification, and τ is the rate of good classification. Sharp structures are not very well recovered, and small areas are badly segmented.

randomly generated circular patterns. To simulate various materials, each circular pattern was attributed one out of $K = 3$ scalar values within the set $\{0, 128, 255\}$. From this tomogram, we generated the corresponding sinogram using $l = 720$ directions (corresponding to a equally reparted 1D slices at every angle of 0.25 rad within $[0, \pi]$). To simulate limited field of view, only the central part of the tomogram is considered for reconstruction and segmentation, leading to a sinogram of size 720×282. Gaussian noise was then added to the sinogram. Eventually, some measurements in the sinogram were set to the null value, in order to simulate occluding geometry.

Figure 5 shows that standard FBP is not only sensitive to noise, but also efficient only when there is no missing data in the sinogram. This justifies the need for a joint reconstruction and segmentation strategy, instead of a sequential treatment.

Figure 6 presents our initial guess for the reconstruction (TV-reconstruction, without segmentation) and for the segmentation (K-means applied to the

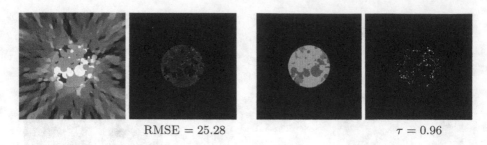

RMSE = 25.28 $\tau = 0.96$

Fig. 7. Top: 3D-reconstruction and segmentation after 500 iterations, with the same convention as in Fig. 6. At convergence, fine structures are recovered and small areas are finely segmented.

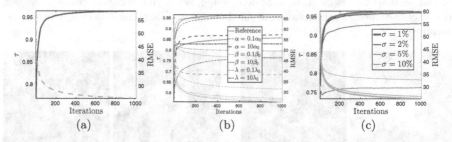

(a)   (b)   (c)

Fig. 8. (a) Evolution of the RMSE on the reconstructed image, and of the good classification rate on the segmentation, as functions of the iteration. As the iterations go, both the 3D-reconstruction and the segmentation are improved. (b) Evaluation of the reconstruction and the segmentation as functions of iterations, for different sets of model parameters (noise level: $\sigma = 1\%$). (c) Ditto, with increasing noise level (the same reference parameters are used in all four experiments).

TV-reconstruction result). The results are already much better than the standard FBP approach of Fig. 5, but thin structures are missed by the TV-reconstruction, which biases the subsequent segmentation.

Starting from this initial guess, we let our SRS algorithm iteratively refine the reconstruction and segmentation for 500 iterations, which required around 10 mn of computation on a recent I7 processor with 32 GB of RAM, using non-parallelised Python codes. Figure 7 shows that the final reconstruction and segmentation are much more accurate than the initial result from Fig. 6. By plotting the evolution of the reconstruction and segmentation error as functions of the iteration number (Fig. 8-a), we observe that most of the gain is achieved during the first iterations, a $\tau = 90\%$ segmentation accuracy being reached after only 50 iterations. This indicates that accurate results can be expected within a reasonable time, which could be further reduced using parallelisation. Next, we question in Fig. 8-b, c the robustness of our method to the choice of parameters and to increasing noise level. The method is quite sensitive to the choice of parameters, but the same set of parameters can be used for a reasonable range of noise (here, it is only with $\sigma = 10\%$ that the reference set of parameters is inappropriate).

5 Conclusion

In this paper we proposed a joint image reconstruction and segmentation for Limited Field of View shadowed tomographic data. Data shadowing/occlusion makes it difficult, if not impossible, to recover a tomogram using the classical filtered backprojection approach. However, we showed that from an inverse problem viewpoint, when the amount of missing data is reasonable due to the shadowing effect, recovery is possible and by coupling it with segmentation, we avoid resolution loss in the latter stage.

Other types of segmentations can be used, the main memory and time bottleneck is the reconstruction part, though some method modifications may allow for a high degree of parallelism with reasonable block reconstruction approaches which open for fast GPU implementations. Investigating such acceleration techniques would be particularly worthwile regarding real-world applications to synchrotron imaging, which involve tremendous amount of data.

Aknowledgement. F. Lauze acknowledges funding from the Innovation Fund Denmark and Mærsk Oil and Gas A/S, for the P^3 Project. E. Plenge acknowledges funding from EUs 7FP under the Marie Skodowska-Curie grant (agreement no 600207), and from the Danish Council for Independent Research (grant ID DFF5054-00218).

References

1. Batenburg, K.J., Sijbers, J.: DART: a practical reconstruction algorithm for discrete tomography. IEEE Trans. Image Process. **20**(9), 2542–2553 (2011)
2. Beck, A., Teboulle, M.: Fast gradient-based algorithms for constrained total variation image denoising and deblurring problems. IEEE TIP **18**(11), 2419–2434 (2009)
3. Bertsekas, D.: Incremental proximal methods for large scale convex optimization. Math. Program. Ser. B **129**, 163–195 (2011)
4. Buzug, T.: Computed Tomography: From Photon Statistics to Modern Cone Beam CT. Springer, Heidelberg (2008)
5. Frickel, J., Quinto, E.T.: Characterization and reduction of artifacts in limited angle tomography. Inverse Probl. **29**(12) (2013)
6. Andersen, M.S., Hansen, P.C.: Generalized row action methods for tomographic imaging. Numer. Algorithms **67**, 121–144 (2014)
7. Natterer, F.: The Mathematics of Computerized Tomography, vol. 32. SIAM, Philadelphia (1986)
8. Ramlau, R., Ring, W.: A Mumford-Shah approach for contour tomography. J. Comput. Phys. **221**(2), 539–557 (2007)
9. Romanov, M., Dahl, A.B., Dong, Y., Hansen, P.C.: Simultaneous tomographic reconstruction and segmentation with class priors. Inverse Probl. Sci. Eng. **24**(8) (2016)
10. van de Sompel, D., Brady, M.: Simultaneous reconstruction and segmentation algorithm for positron emission tomography and transmission tomography. In: Proceedings of the 2008 International Symposium on Biomedical Imaging (2008)
11. Storah, M., Weinmann, A., Frickel, J., Unser, M.: Joint image reconstruction and segmentation using the Potts model. Inverse Probl. **2**(32) (2015)
12. Yoon, S., Pineda, A.R., Fahrig, R.: Simultaneous segmentation and reconstruction: a level set method approach for limited view computed tomography. Med. Phys. **37**(5), 2329–2340 (2010)

Segmentation

Graphical Model Parameter Learning
by Inverse Linear Programming

Vera Trajkovska[1]([✉]), Paul Swoboda[2], Freddie Åström[1], and Stefania Petra[3]

[1] Image and Pattern Analysis Group, Heidelberg University, Heidelberg, Germany
vera.trajkovska@iwr.uni-heidelberg.de
[2] Institute of Science and Technology, Klosterneuburg, Austria
[3] Mathematical Imaging Group, Heidelberg University, Heidelberg, Germany

Abstract. We introduce two novel methods for learning parameters of graphical models for image labelling. The following two tasks underline both methods: (i) perturb model parameters based on given features and ground truth labelings, so as to exactly reproduce these labelings as optima of the local polytope relaxation of the labelling problem; (ii) train a predictor for the perturbed model parameters so that improved model parameters can be applied to the labelling of novel data. Our first method implements task (i) by inverse linear programming and task (ii) using a regressor e.g. a Gaussian process. Our second approach simultaneously solves tasks (i) and (ii) in a joint manner, while being restricted to linearly parameterised predictors. Experiments demonstrate the merits of both approaches.

1 Introduction

Graphical models are nowadays widely applied in computer vision due to the growing interest of describing and understanding visual scenes. One often formulates maximum a posteriori (MAP) tasks which assign predefined discrete labels associated with the scene information to the image data. This inference problem is well studied, see e.g. [1] for a recent comprehensive account.

However, it is well known that the performance of any MAP formulation depends on pre-specified, often heuristically determined, set of model parameters which are thought to reflect the data. To overcome this problem, we present a framework that *learns* model parameters θ which collect the function values of the unary and pairwise potentials θ^i, θ^{ij} of the discrete graphical model

$$E_\theta(x) = \sum_{i \in \mathcal{V}} \theta^i(x_i) + \sum_{ij \in \mathcal{E}} \theta^{ij}(x_i, x_j) \tag{1}$$

defined on a graph $\mathcal{G} = (\mathcal{V}, \mathcal{E})$, where $\mathcal{V}$ and $\mathcal{E}$ are the node and edge set of $\mathcal{G}$. The energy function E_θ evaluates assignment of labels x_i from a predefined

Acknowledgments: VT and FÅ gratefully acknowledge support by the German Science Foundation, grant GRK 1653.

© Springer International Publishing AG 2017
F. Lauze et al. (Eds.): SSVM 2017, LNCS 10302, pp. 323–334, 2017.
DOI: 10.1007/978-3-319-58771-4_26

label set $\mathcal{L} = (1, \ldots, L)$ to every node $i \in \mathcal{V}$. The optimisation problem defined in (1) is in general NP-hard, therefore one often formulates instead the standard linear program (LP) relaxation which enforces consistency of unary and pairwise variables enclosed in μ via the local polytope $\mathcal{L}_\mathcal{G}$. This gives the minimisation problem

$$\min_{\mu \in L_\mathcal{G}} \langle \theta, \mu \rangle, \tag{2}$$

where $\langle \cdot, \cdot \rangle$ denotes the Euclidean inner product. For background reading on (1) and (2) we refer to [2,3].

Contribution, Organisation. Our objective is to develop an energy-based framework for learning parameters of a graphical model (1). We present two methods further abbreviated as **invLPA** and **LA**.

In the first method (invLPA) we exploit *inverse linear programming* [4,5] in Sect. 2 to compute for each training image $k \in [N]$ a perturbation θ^k of an initial model parameter $\hat{\theta}$, obtained with any other learning method, so that the relaxed problem (2) attains a (global) minimum at each ground truth labelling μ^{*k}. Ground trough labelings must satisfy

$$\mu^{*k} \in \arg\min_{\mu \in L_\mathcal{G}} \langle \hat{\theta} + \theta^k, \mu \rangle, \quad k \in [N], \tag{3}$$

for the *corrected* model parameter $\hat{\theta} + \theta^k$. In this way, individual model parameter perturbations can be computed, i.e. task (i), whenever ground-truth data become available, and can be subsequently used to predict using a linear or nonlinear regressor, i.e. task (ii), novel model parameters $\theta = \theta(w)$ that are parameterised by a vector w. We demonstrate invLPA experimentally in Sect. 4.

In Sect. 3 we introduce the second method (LA) via the *ansatz*

$$\min_{w \in \mathbb{R}^d} \sum_{k \in [N]} \|x^k(w) - x^{*k}\|_1 \quad \text{subject to} \quad x^k(w) \in \arg\min E_{\theta^k(w)}(x), \tag{4}$$

in order to determine model parameters $\theta = \theta(w)$ in terms of a parameter vector $w \in \mathbb{R}^d$ so that the labellings x^k, obtained by minimising the functional (1) for N training images $k \in [N]$, fit given ground truth labelings x^{*k}. In Sect. 3, we work out a convex relaxation of the non-convex bilevel optimisation problem (4) based (a) on the LP relaxation (2) and (b) on the most common case of *linearly* parameterised local potentials $\theta^i(w_u), \theta^{ij}(w_p)$ by a corresponding vector w_u and w_p, respectively.

A major difference between the methods invLPA and LA is the linearity of the parameterisation in LA. This linearity assumption is essential to come up with a tight convex relaxation that can directly utilise established inference solvers for subproblems of the overall learning problem. By contrast, invLPA is more flexible in that as any more sophisticate model parameter predictor can be used for the model parameter prediction task (ii). Working out method LA, on the other hand, enables us to reconsider the most common approach for structured prediction. Both methods as well as comparison to other learning methods are demonstrated in Sect. 4. We conclude in Sect. 5.

Remark. To simplify the exposition, we confine ourselves in this paper to *binary* labelling problems. The extension to the non-binary case is straightforward.

2   Inverse Linear Programming Approach (invLPA)

Here we present method invLPA. We first estimate corrected model parameters $\tilde{\theta}^k := \hat{\theta} + \theta^k$ given k ground truth labelings μ^{*k} by computing perturbations θ^k of initial model parameters $\hat{\theta}$, i.e. task (i), followed by a prediction step which yields the final model parameters, i.e. task (ii).

2.1   Model Parameter Perturbation

For this method we consider $L_{\mathcal{G}}$, in (2), to be defined by the so called minimal representation [2] i.e., $\mu_i = \mathbb{P}(x_i = 1)$, $\mu_{ij} = \mathbb{P}(x_i = 1 \wedge x_j = 1)$, $i \in \mathcal{V}, ij \in \mathcal{E}$. We write these local polytope constraints as $A\mu \geq b$ and $\mu \geq 0$. Furthermore, we define dual variables ν and ν_μ corresponding to the local polytope constraints. Then the Karush-Kuhn-Tucker (KKT) [6] optimality conditions

$$A^\top \nu + \nu_\mu = \theta, \qquad 0 \leq \nu \perp A\mu - b \geq 0, \qquad 0 \leq \nu_\mu \perp \mu \geq 0 \qquad (5)$$

connect μ with the dual variables. We show below how we obtain the perturbations θ of the initial potentials $\hat{\theta}$ so that the relaxed labelling problem (2) attains for $\tilde{\theta} = \hat{\theta} + \theta$ the given ground truth labelling μ^* as a global minimiser.

Proposition 1. *Let $n = |\mathcal{V}|, m = |\mathcal{E}|$ and $\hat{\theta} \in \mathbb{R}^{n+m}$ be a given model parameter. Suppose the local polytope based on the minimal problem representation is given by $L_{\mathcal{G}} = \{\mu \in \mathbb{R}_+^{n+m} : A\mu \geq b\}$. Let $\mu^* \in \{0,1\}^n$ be a given binary ground truth labelling. Then the minimal ℓ_1-norm perturbation $\theta \in \mathbb{R}^{n+m}$ of $\hat{\theta}$ such that $\mu^* \in \arg\min\{\langle \hat{\theta} + \theta, \mu \rangle : \mu \in L_{\mathcal{G}}\}$ is a solution to the linear program*

$$\min_{\theta, \nu_\mu, \nu} \|\theta\|_1 \quad s.t. \quad A^\top \nu + \nu_\mu = \hat{\theta} + \theta \qquad (6a)$$

$$\theta \in \mathbb{R}^{n+m}, \; \nu_\mu \in \mathbb{R}_+^{n+m}, \; \nu \in \mathbb{R}_+^{\dim(b)}, \; \nu_{\mathcal{I}} = 0, \; (\nu_\mu)_{\mathcal{J}} = 0, \qquad (6b)$$

$$\mathcal{I} = \{i \in [\dim(b)] : (A\mu^* - b)_i > 0\}, \; \mathcal{J} = \{j \in [n+m] : \mu_j^* > 0\}. \qquad (6c)$$

Proof. The minimal norm perturbation θ can be found by replacing θ by $\hat{\theta} + \theta$ and μ by μ^* in (5), and by determining along with θ optimal dual variables ν^*, ν_μ^* through solving (6a), subject to the constraints (6b) and (6c) induced by the complementary slackness conditions (5) and the ground truth labelling μ^*.

Remark. Problem (6) can be recast as a linear programm.

2.2 Model Parameter Prediction

We computed above the corrected potentials $\tilde{\theta}$ from the given ground truth labelings. Here we use these perturbed potentials to predict new potentials based on novel data features. In principle any prediction method can be used in this step. Here we consider linear least-squares (LS), a linear sparsifying ℓ_1-norm approach (L1), and a Gaussian process as a nonlinear regression method (NL). For the case of linear fitting in LS and L1, we assume that the potentials θ depend linearly on some vector w, $\theta(w)$. The predictor is defined in terms of parameter vector w and given feature vectors f^k, see below.

Least-Squares Fitting: We set up an over constrained system and solve

$$\min_w \sum_{k \in [N]} |\langle f^k, w \rangle - \tilde{\theta}^k(w)|^2. \tag{7}$$

ℓ_1-norm Fitting: In addition to the smooth least-squares approach, we also apply the sparse regularisation approach

$$\min_{w,s_k} \|w\|_1 + \lambda \sum_{k \in [N]} |s_k|, \quad \langle f^k, w \rangle - s_k = \tilde{\theta}_k(w), \quad k \in [N], \quad \lambda > 0. \tag{8}$$

Nonlinear Prediction (Gaussian Regression [7]):

$$\bar{\theta}(f) := k_N(f)^\top \left(K(F) + \sigma_n^2 I \right)^{-1} \tilde{\theta} \qquad (\sigma_n^2 \text{ is a parameter}) \tag{9a}$$

$$= \sum_{k \in [N]} w_k(F, \tilde{\theta}) k(f^k, f), \qquad w(F, \tilde{\theta}) := \left(K(F) + \sigma_n^2 I \right)^{-1} \tilde{\theta}, \tag{9b}$$

where $K(F) = \left\{ k(f^k, f^j) \right\}_{k,j \in [N]}$ is the kernel matrix evaluated on a set of training feature vectors for the standard Gaussian symmetric kernel function. $k_N(f)$ evaluates this kernel function at any novel feature vector f (not yet specified) and all given feature vectors (train data).

3 Linearly Parameterised Joint Learning Approach (LA)

We now develop the linearised approach LA. First, a relaxation of (4) is worked out, followed by an optimisation approach. We note that in this section we use the overcomplete representation [2] of the local polytope constraints, as opposed to the minimal representation used in Sect. 2.

3.1 Model Parameter Perturbation

We start with the primal-dual pair of LP's

Primal: **Dual:**

$$\min_{\mu \geq 0} \langle \theta, \mu \rangle \quad \text{s.t.} \quad A\mu = 0, \ \mu_0 = 1; \qquad \max_{\psi, \phi} \psi \quad \text{s.t.} \quad \theta - A^\top \phi - e_0 \psi \geq 0, \tag{10}$$

where the primal vector μ is augmented by the scalar variable μ_0 as first component which enforces the mass constraints $\sum_{x_i \in \{0,1\}} \mu_i(x_i) - \mu_0 = 0$, $i \in \mathcal{V}$ as a part of the system $A\mu = 0$, in addition to the usual consistency constraints defining the local polytope. Likewise, the vector ϕ together with a scalar variable $\psi \in \mathbb{R}$ forms the dual variables[1], and $e_0 = (1, 0, \ldots, 0)^\top$ is the corresponding unit vector. The primal is equivalent to (2) with the usual local polytope constraints but in a slightly different form. The dual is just the reparameterised formulation of the relaxed labelling problem over the local polytope [3]. Accordingly we define reparameterised potentials as $\theta_{w,\phi} := \theta(w) - A^\top \phi$. Let $\hat{\mu}$ be optimal for the primal. The complementary slackness conditions state that $\exists (\hat{\psi}, \hat{\phi})$ dual variables such that

$$\hat{\mu}_i(x_i) > 0 \qquad \Longrightarrow \qquad \theta^i_{w,\hat{\phi}}(x_i) = 0, \tag{11a}$$

$$\hat{\mu}_{ij}(x_i, x_j) > 0 \qquad \Longrightarrow \qquad \theta^{ij}_{w,\hat{\phi}}(x_i, x_j) = 0, \tag{11b}$$

$$\hat{\mu}_0 > 0 \qquad \Longrightarrow \qquad \hat{\psi} = \theta^0 + \sum_{i \in \mathcal{V}} \hat{\phi}_i. \tag{11c}$$

The third implication is always satisfied if ψ is set accordingly. Let μ^* and x^* be the unique optimal pair corresponding to the ground truth labelling. The uniqueness assumption is crucial in the whole formulation of the problem. From the uniqueness and the first two implications we have

$$\begin{aligned} \theta^i_{w,\phi}(x_i^*) = 0, \\ \theta^i_{w,\phi}(1 - x_i^*) \geq \varepsilon, \end{aligned} \quad \text{and} \quad \begin{aligned} \theta^{ij}_{w,\phi}(x_i^*, x_j^*) = 0, \\ \theta^{ij}_{w,\phi}(x_i, x_j) \geq \varepsilon, \quad \forall (x_i, x_j) \neq (x_i^*, x_j^*), \end{aligned} \tag{12}$$

for some $\varepsilon > 0$ and all $i \in \mathcal{V}$, $ij \in \mathcal{E}$. Using an additional vector $s \geq 0$ of slackness variables in order to turn the inequalities in (12) to equations, we finally arrive at the problem

$$\min_{w, \phi, s \geq 0} \langle \mu^*, s \rangle, \quad \langle \mu^*, s \rangle = \sum_{i \in \mathcal{V}} s_i(x_i^*) + \sum_{ij \in \mathcal{E}} s_{ij}(x_i^*, x_j^*) \quad \text{s.t.}$$

$$\theta^i_{w,\phi}(x_i^*) - s_i(x_i^*) = 0, \qquad \theta^i_{w,\phi}(1 - x_i^*) - s_i(1 - x_i^*) = \varepsilon, \tag{13}$$

$$\theta^{ij}_{w,\phi}(x_i^*, x_j^*) - s_{ij}(x_i^*, x_j^*) = 0, \qquad \theta^{ij}_{w,\phi}(x_i, x_j) - s_{ij}(x_i, x_j) = \varepsilon,$$

$\forall (x_i, x_j) \neq (x_i^*, x_j^*)$ and some $\varepsilon > 0$ and all $i \in \mathcal{V}$, $ij \in \mathcal{E}$. Regarding the formulation (13) above we aim at penalising the slackness variables s. Since $\theta(w)$ is depending linearly on w the problem (13) above is a (large scale) LP.

3.2 Model Parameter Prediction

The large scale LP in (13) cannot be solved with standard LP solvers due to the large problem sizes. Therefore we propose to split the optimisation problem into labelling and parameter estimation subproblems. We restrict ourselves

---

[1] We do not denote the dual variables by ν, as in the preceding section, due to the slightly different LP formulation (10).

to linearly dependent potentials $\theta = (\theta^i, \theta^{ij})^\top$ with $w = (w_u, w_p)^\top$ to use off-the-shelf inference solvers for the labelling subproblems. We solve the labelling subproblems with QPBO [8], which are subsequently fused by Lagrange multipliers. Now, to derive a tractable optimisation problem, we modify the linearly parameterised local potentials to read

$$\tilde{\theta}^i(w; x_i) := \begin{pmatrix} -\varepsilon \mathbb{1}_{\{x_i^*=1\}} \\ \langle w_u, f^i \rangle - \varepsilon \mathbb{1}_{\{x_i^*=0\}} \end{pmatrix},$$

$$\tilde{\theta}^{ij}(w; x_i, x_j) := \begin{pmatrix} \langle w_p^{00}, f^{ij} \rangle - \varepsilon \mathbb{1}_{\{(x_{ij}^*)\neq(0,0)\}} & \langle w_p^{01}, f^{ij} \rangle - \varepsilon \mathbb{1}_{\{(x_{ij}^*)\neq(0,1)\}} \\ \langle w_p^{10}, f^{ij} \rangle - \varepsilon \mathbb{1}_{\{(x_{ij}^*)\neq(1,0)\}} & \langle w_p^{11}, f^{ij} \rangle - \varepsilon \mathbb{1}_{\{(x_{ij}^*)\neq(1,1)\}} \end{pmatrix}, \quad (14)$$

where f^i, f^{ij} denote arbitrary unary and pairwise feature vectors extracted at pixel $i \in \mathcal{V}$ and edge $ij \in \mathcal{E}$, and with $\mathbb{1}_{\text{predicate}} = 1$ if predicate is true and $\mathbb{1}_{\text{predicate}} = 0$ otherwise. Based on the new redefined reparameterised potentials $\tilde{\theta}_{w,\phi}$ in (14), we rewrite (13) as

$$\min_{w,\phi,s} \langle \mu^*, s \rangle \quad \text{s.t.} \quad \tilde{\theta}_{w,\phi} - s = 0. \quad (15)$$

The dual of (15) with respect to ϕ and s and fixed w now reads

$$\max_{\mu} \langle -\tilde{\theta}_w, \mu \rangle \quad \text{s.t.} \quad (16a)$$

$$\sum_{x_j \in \{0,1\}} \mu_{ij}(x_i, x_j) - \mu_j(x_i) = 0, \qquad \sum_{x_i \in \{0,1\}} \mu_{ij}(x_i, x_j) - \mu_j(x_j) = 0, \quad (16b)$$

$$\mu_i(x_i) - \mu_i^*(x_i) \geq 0, \qquad \qquad \mu_{ij}(x_i, x_j) - \mu_{ij}^*(x_i, x_j) \geq 0, \quad (16c)$$

and $\forall i \in \mathcal{V}, \forall ij \in \mathcal{E}$. We can bring the above defined constraints to the usual local polytope constraints by shifting μ to $\mu - \mu^*$ and consequently adding $\langle \tilde{\theta}_w, \mu^* \rangle$ to the dual objective term. We are now ready to formulate the final saddle point problem, taking into account a collection of N training samples we have

$$\min_{w} L(w), \qquad L(w) = \sum_{k \in [N]} \max_{\mu \in L_{\mathcal{G}}} \left\{ \langle -\tilde{\theta}_w^k, \mu \rangle + \langle \tilde{\theta}_w^k, \mu^{*k} \rangle \right\}. \quad (17)$$

Close connection to structural Support Vector Machine (SVM) [9,10] can be observed if we consider our objective (17) as minimising a loss function. Our ε parameter in (12) and (14) has the same role as the slack variables in structural SVM. Rather than optimising the slack variables we set ϵ appropriately beforehand and then minimise the loss function directly.

3.3 Optimisation

We address minimisation of (17) via a smoothed version of the subgradient method, known as the deflected subgradient method [11–13]. In the deflected subgradient method the sequence of subgradients $(g^{(k)})_{k\geq 0}$ is replaced by

---

Algorithm 1. Deflected subgradient algorithm with Polyak stepsize

---

input : $k = 1$, $w^{(1)} = 0$, $h^{(0)} = 0$, $\overline{L} = 0.1$, $L(w^{(1)}) = \infty$, $\epsilon_1 = 10^{-5}$, $\epsilon_2 = 10^{-6}$,
$\qquad n = 40$

1 **while** $L(w^{(k)}) - \overline{L} > \epsilon_2$ **do**

2 $\quad$ Obtain $\mu^{w^{(k)}}$ with QPBO [8] and compute $L(w^{(k)})$;

3 $\quad$ $L_{min} = \min_{i \in [k]} \{ L(w^{(i)}) \}$;

4 $\quad$ **if** $L(w^{(k)}) < \overline{L}$ **then** $\overline{L} = L(w^{(k)}) - \epsilon_1$;

5 $\quad$ Choose $g^k \in \partial_w L(w^{(k)})$ from (18) and (19) ;

6 $\quad$ $h^{(k)} = g^{(k)} + \beta^k h^{(k-1)}$, $\beta^k = \max\{0, -1.5 \frac{g^{(k)}(h^{(k-1)})^\top}{\|h^{(k-1)}\|^2}\}$;

7 $\quad$ **if** $\|h^{(k)}\| < \epsilon_2$ **then** break ;

8 $\quad$ $w^{(k+1)} = w^{(k)} - \alpha_k h^{(k)}$, $\alpha_k = \frac{L(w^{(k)}) - \overline{L}}{\|h^{(k)}\|^2}$;

9 $\quad$ $k \leftarrow k + 1$;

10 $\quad$ **if** $\mod(k, n) = 0 \land L_{min} \geq \overline{L} + \epsilon_1$ **then** $\overline{L} = \frac{\overline{L} + L_{min}}{2}$;

11 **return** $w^{(k)}$

$(h^{(k)})_{k \geq 0} = g^{(k)} + \beta^k h^{(k-1)}$, with β^k chosen as suggested by [13], to obtain a smoother sequence of updates $(w^{(k)})_{k \geq 0}$ and faster convergence. The deflected subgradient method is in general used with a (modified) Polyak step size [14] that significantly speeds up the subgradient method. Hence, rather than using the common "divergent series" approach with a diminishing step size α_k satisfying $\sum_{k \geq 0} \alpha_k = \infty$, we apply the adaptive step size $\frac{1}{\|g^{(k)}\|^2} (L(w^{(k)}) - \overline{L})$ due to Polyak, where $\overline{L}$ is adapted to compensate for not knowing the optimal value L^*. Alternative strategies for adaption could be applied [15, Sect. 3.2]. The pseudocode is given in Algorithm 1. Under standard assumptions and an appropriate choice of parameters, convergence can be guaranteed. We refer to [12, Theroem 3.10, Theroem 3.11, Theroem 3.12] for a convergence analysis. Concerning the choice of a subgradient in line 5 of Algorithm 1 we remark that it can be computed by

$$\partial_{w_u} L(w) \ni \sum_{i \in \mathcal{V}} f^i \cdot (-\mu_i^w(1) + \mu_i^*(1)) \tag{18}$$

$$\partial_{w_p} L(w) \ni \sum_{ij \in \mathcal{E}} f^{ij} \cdot (-\mu_{ij}^w(0,0) + \mu_{ij}^*(0,0) - \mu_{ij}^w(0,1) + \mu_{ij}^*(0,1) - \mu_{ij}^w(1,0)$$
$$+ \mu_{ij}^*(1,0) - \mu_{ij}^w(1,1) + \mu_{ij}^*(1,1)), \tag{19}$$

where μ^w is a solution to the labelling subproblem in (17).

4   Experiments

We validate both methods by:

$\quad$ (a) *Learning unary potentials* under a fixed Ising prior and (b) *learning pairwise potentials* with very weak unary terms for a scenario where any standard

(a)  (b)

Fig. 1. Filter masks for computing feature vectors, (a) unary and (b) pairwise. (a) After correlating an input image with the filter masks, the resulting values were encoded for each pixel by stacking corresponding unit-vectors. This resulted in feature vectors $f^i \in \mathbb{R}^{97}$. (b) After correlating an input image with the filters masks we extract feature vectors f^i, for every pixel i. We define pairwise features $f^{ij} := \{k(f^l, f^k)\}_{k,l \in \mathcal{N}(i) \cup \mathcal{N}(j)}$ where each entry is a Gaussian kernel, with variance $\sigma = 0.4$. $\mathcal{N}(i)$ and $\mathcal{N}(j)$ are 4-neighbourhoods for pixels i and j. The filters in (a) and (b) were chosen naturally so as to capture the particular structure of the random lines images Figs. 2(b) and 3(b) respectively.

regulariser, e.g. an Ising prior, would certainly fail. (c) Jointly learning unary and pairwise terms using LA. We demonstrate LA on the Weizmann horse dataset [16] and compare results with a standard linear SVM trained on the unary data. (d) Learning pairwise terms using invLPA, and (e) comparison to two other learning methods from [17], one with margin based loss and one with likelihood based loss function.

4.1 Random Lines: Learning Unary and Pairwise Potentials

(a) Learning Unary Potentials. Here we learn unary potentials while we fix the pairwise potentials to an Ising prior. We define unary features using the correlation output of 8 binary filter masks, see Fig. 1(a) applied to the images in Fig. 2(b) generated by a random line process.

We compare our proposed approach with a state of the art logistic classifier (L), where regularisation is applied as a post-processing step.

Results. Figure 2 illustrates our obtained results, see caption for further comments. To evaluate the resulting labelling we use the percentage of mislabelled pixels defined as $\frac{\sum_p (I(p) = I_{gt}(p))}{0.01|p|}$ where I is the final segmented image, I_{gt} the ground truth segmentation and $|p|$ the number of pixels in the image. Recovery errors are shown and discussed in Table 1(a).

(b) Learning Pairwise Potentials. In the scenario of noisy input data, see Fig. 3(b), we learn pairwise potentials with weak unary potentials, i.e. for unaries we use only single pixel comparison to a fixed threshold, 0.5 in our case. The pairwise features f^{ij}, $ij \in \mathcal{E}$ are defined using image correlation with 10 image filter masks, see Fig. 1(b) for details.

Results. Figure 3 shows the resulting segmentations and Table 1(b) shows the corresponding error values. We refer to respective caption for a discussion.

4.2 Weizmann Horse Dataset

Experimental Setup. The Weizmann horse dataset [16] contains 327 images of horses with different poses, shades and background including ground truth

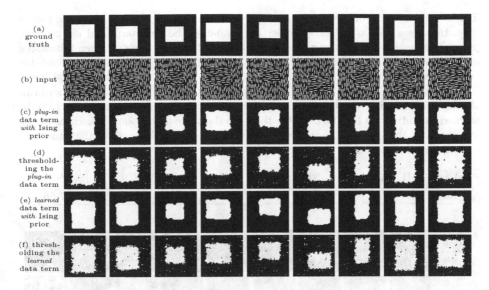

Fig. 2. Exemplary images from the test dataset (a,b) chosen at random. Segmentation results when using a linear classifier trained offline using logistic regression with (c) and without additional regularisation (d), in comparison to method invLPA with (e) and without regularizer (f). The final results improve *only* for invLPA that learns *in conjunction* with the regulariser.

segmentations. We randomly divide each of the 5 color type image groups into train, (70%) and test (30%) datasets. We use SLIC [18] superpixels to process the image data, a common approach to reduce the problem size, and benefit from the rich superpixel structure when extracting features.

- Our unary feature vector, $f^u \in \mathbb{R}^{21}$, is comprised of (1) the logarithm of the eigenvalues of the covariance region (superpixel) descriptor [19], (2) mean CIELAB and RGB color values of pixels in superpixel and (3) the center coordinates of each superpixel.
- Our pairwise feature vector, $f^p \in \mathbb{R}^6$, is composed of (1) the multivariate Hellinger distance between empirical Gaussian distributions measured both in the RGB and CIELAB space, respectively, (2) the Log-Euclidean distance between the covariance descriptors defined in the unary term and (3) the quadratic chi squared distances [20], defined using histograms on the RGB, CIELAB space and SIFT histograms.

We remark that more powerful *engineered* feature representations may improve the segmentation results, however as we show in the evaluation: given inexact potentials our proposed framework *learns* a more descriptive representation, thus improving the final segmentation result. In order to further improve the numerical efficiency we group superpixels into nonlocal neighbourhoods where each group contains the closest three layer neighbours relative to the reference superpixel. In addition to using the percentage of mislabelled pixels we also use the percentage of mislabelled foreground pixels $100\frac{\text{Area}(F \cap F_{gt})}{\text{Area}(F \cup F_{gt})}$, see [21], where F

Table 1. Evaluation of method invLPA for (a) learning unary and (b) pairwise potentials. In (a) we train a logistic classifier (L) offline on the data term and use an Ising prior. The resulting error shown in column In(L) is further improved when initialising invLPA with this trained data term via logistic regression. We use the three prediction methods from Sect. 2.2 LS (linear least squares fitting), L1 (ℓ_1-regularised linear fitting) and NL (Gaussian process). Our second method LA from Sect. 3 outperforms the logistic classifier too. For (b) we initialise the pairwise potentials for invLPA by learned potentials via LA, In(LA). We then use the same prediction methods as in (a). We conclude that invLPA *always improves* on the error of the method that was used to initialise the potentials.

(a)	In(L)	LS	L1	NL	LA		(b)	In(LA)	LS	L1	NL
% mis	2.44	2.42	2.44	**2.00**	2.02		% mis	7.59	**7.48**	7.59	7.56

Fig. 3. Random line process images. Segmentation results (c) when applying the learned regularizer to the noisy input data (b). The results show that the regularizer *captures* and *preserves* to some extent the random image structure, unlike any standard prior that cannot discriminate foreground lines from noise. E.g. a tuned Ising prior results in constant images.

is the foreground mask of the segmented image and F_{gt} is the foreground mask of the ground truth segmentation.

Validation and Method Comparison. LA which jointly learns unary and pairwise potentials, is compared to a linear SVM [22] trained on the corresponding unary features. Moreover, these learned unaries are transferred (and kept fixed) to invLPA, while the pairwise potentials are used as initialisation. We compare our LA method where we minimise a loss function based on MAP estimate to two other methods for learning parameters of graphical models from [17] with different types of loss function, one based on maximum posterior marginal (MPM) estimates, clique logistic loss (Marg) and one based on maximum likelihood estimation (MLE), surrogate likelihood loss, (Lik). These two loss function were the best performing from the two different types of loss functions as reported in [17] on the horse dataset. We adopt the parameters and inference used in [17].

Results. Evaluations are reported in Table 2(a,b) and Fig. 4. We clearly see that LA outperforms the linear SVM. InvLPA always performs as well or better as the method that initialises the potentials (here LA). We conclude that our framework is a competitive learning method compared to [17].

Table 2. Results of invLPA (a) and LA (b) on the horse dataset. (a) In(LA) stands for initialisation with LA for invLPA. The error of In(LA) is further improved by invLPA where the prediction task is accomplished by LS, L1 and NL. (b) Results of jointly learning unary and pairwise potentials via LA from Sect. 3 compared to a linear SVM and two learning methods from [17], Marg and Lik, see text for details. We note that even if invLPA is initialised by the same potentials of LA the numbers under In(LA) in (a) and LA (b) differ due to the inexact conversion we used from minimal to overcomplete representation for the local polytope constraints, in order to be able to use the same inference method (QPBO) as in (b).

(a)	In(LA)	LS	L1	NL	(b)	LA	SVM	Marg	Lik
% mis	25.1	23.8	25.1	**20.4**	% mis	18.7	46.4	**17.4**	22.0
% mis fg	**43.7**	44.5	**43.7**	51.2	% mis fg	41.5	53.5	**36.6**	52.0

Fig. 4. Segmentations on a subset of the test horse dataset. Mislabelled pixels are shown in red. Overall our method (b) has approximately the same performance as Marg (c). In the first image our method beats Marg, but in the third one Marg shows better performance. On the other hand, Lik (d) fails on some images. (Color figure online)

5 Conclusion

We introduced two methods for learning graphical model parameters applied to image labelling. The invLPA method computes corrections of initial model parameters so that given ground truth labelings are matched exactly. These corrections are computed by solving a linear program, separately (or in parallel) for every ground truth labelling. Assuming the specific case of linearly parameterised local potentials, a second method is proposed that resembles structured prediction and exhibits competitive performance. Moreover, the invLPA method always improves the potentials initialised by other method.

References

1. Kappes, J., Andres, B., Hamprecht, F., Schnörr, C., Nowozin, S., Batra, D., Kim, S., Kausler, B., Kröger, T., Lellmann, J., Komodakis, N., Savchynskyy, B., Rother, C.: A comparative study of modern inference techniques for structured discrete energy minimization problems. Int. J. Comput. Vis. **115**(2), 155–184 (2015)

2. Wainwright, M.J., Jordan, M.I.: Graphical Models, Exponential Families, and Variational Inference. Now Publishers Inc., Breda (2008)

3. Werner, T.: A linear programming approach to max-sum problem: a review. IEEE Trans. Pattern Anal. Mach. Intell. **29**(7), 1165–1179 (2007)

4. Zhang, J., Liu, Z.: Calculating some inverse linear programming problems. J. Comput. Appl. Math. **72**(2), 261–273 (1996)

5. Ahuja, R., Orlin, J.: Inverse optimization. Oper. Res. **49**(5), 771–783 (2001)

6. Kuhn, H.W., Tucker, A.W.: Nonlinear programming. In: 2nd Berkeley Symposium on Mathematical Statistics and Probability, pp. 481–492 (1951)

7. Rasmussen, C., Williams, C.: Gaussian Processes for Machine Learning. MIT Press, Cambridge (2006)

8. Kolmogorov, V., Rother, C.: Minimizing non-submodular functions with graph cuts - a review. IEEE Trans. Pattern Anal. Mach. Intell. **29**(7), 1274–1279 (2007)

9. Finley, T., Joachims, T.: Training structural SVMs when exact inference is intractable. In: Proceedings of the ICML, pp. 304–311 (2008)

10. Tsochantaridis, I., Hofmann, T., Joachims, T., Altun, Y.: Support Vector Machine Learning for Interdependent and Structured Output Spaces. In: ICML, pp. 104–111 (2004)

11. d'Antonio, G., Frangioni, A.: Convergence analysis of deflected conditional approximate subgradient methods. SIAM J. Optim. **20**(1), 357–386 (2009)

12. Guta, B.: Subgradient optimization methods in integer programming with an application to a radiation therapy problem. Technical report, TU Kaiserslautern (2003)

13. Camerini, P., Fratta, L., Maffioli, F.: On improving relaxation methods by modified gradient techniques. In: Balinski, M.L., Wolfe, P. (eds.) Nondifferentiable Optimization. Mathematical Programming Studies, vol. 3, pp. 26–34. Springer, Heidelberg (1975)

14. Polyak, B.: Minimization of unsmooth functionals. U.S.S.R. Comput. Math. Math. Phys. **9**, 14–29 (1969)

15. Bertsekas, D.: Convex Optimization Algorithms. Athena Scientific, Belmont (2015)

16. Borenstein, E., Sharon, E., Ullman, S.: Combining top-down and bottom-up segmentation. In: CVPRW, p. 46 (2004)

17. Domke, J.: Learning graphical model parameters with approximate marginal inference. IEEE Trans. Pattern Anal. Mach. Intell. **35**(10), 2454–2467 (2013)

18. Achanta, R., Shaji, A., Smith, K., Lucchi, A., Fua, P., Susstrunk, S.: SLIC superpixels compared to state-of-the-art superpixel methods. IEEE Trans. Pattern Anal. Mach. Intell. **34**(11), 2274–2282 (2012)

19. Tuzel, O., Porikli, F., Meer, P.: Region covariance: a fast descriptor for detection and classification. In: Leonardis, A., Bischof, H., Pinz, A. (eds.) ECCV 2006. LNCS, vol. 3952, pp. 589–600. Springer, Heidelberg (2006). doi:10.1007/11744047_45

20. Pele, O., Werman, M.: The quadratic-chi histogram distance family. In: Daniilidis, K., Maragos, P., Paragios, N. (eds.) ECCV 2010. LNCS, vol. 6312, pp. 749–762. Springer, Heidelberg (2010). doi:10.1007/978-3-642-15552-9_54

21. Bertelli, L., Yu, T., Vu, D., Gokturk, B.: Kernelized structural SVM learning for supervised object segmentation. In: CVPR, pp. 2153–2160 (2011)

22. Suykens, J.A.K., Vandewalle, J.: Least squares support vector machine classifiers. Neural Process. Lett. **9**(3), 293–300 (1999)

A Fast MBO Scheme
for Multiclass Data Classification

Matt Jacobs[(✉)]

University of Michigan, Ann Arbor, USA
majaco@umich.edu

Abstract. We describe a new variant of the MBO scheme for solving the semi-supervised data classification problem on a weighted graph. The scheme is based on the minimization of the graph heat content energy. The resulting algorithms guarantee dissipation of the graph heat content energy for an extremely wide class of weight matrices. As a result, our method is both flexible and unconditionally stable. Experimental results on benchmark machine learning datasets show that our approach matches or exceeds the performance of current state-of-the-art variational methods while being considerably faster.

1 Introduction

Classifying high dimensional data is one of the central problems in machine learning and computer vision. The graphical approach to these problems builds a weighted graph from the data set and searches for an optimal partitioning of the vertices into distinct classes. The search is driven by the goal of minimizing the total weight of cut edges between adjacent vertices in different classes. To avoid trivial solutions, it is necessary to impose certain constraints or penalties on the segmentations. For example, one may penalize solutions that do not give a reasonably uniform distribution of vertices among the different classes. In general, solving graph partitioning problems with combinatorial penalties, such as the normalized cut [12] or Cheeger cut [3], is known to be NP-hard. The essential difficulty stems from the fact that one is attempting to minimize a non-convex objective function. Nonetheless, approximate solutions have been calculated using spectral clustering (for example [12,21]) and more recently, fast implementations of gradient descent [2,10].

In this paper we consider the semi-supervised learning (SSL) data classification problem. In the SSL setting, the number of classes is known and a certain training subset of the data is provided with the ground truth classification. The objective is to then classify the remaining points using the training data. The SSL problem is highly amenable to variational methods. The training data can be incorporated into norm or linear type penalty terms that are much easier to solve than the combinatorial penalties of the unsupervised methods mentioned above. Recent results in SSL have shown that variational methods are competitive with artificial neural networks, while requiring far less training data and computation time to obtain high quality solutions [9].

© Springer International Publishing AG 2017
F. Lauze et al. (Eds.): SSVM 2017, LNCS 10302, pp. 335–347, 2017.
DOI: 10.1007/978-3-319-58771-4_27

We approach the SSL problem using a variational model based on the weighted graph cut. We then solve the model using a scheme closely related to the MBO algorithm. The MBO algorithm was introduced by Merriman, Bence and Osher in [14] as an efficient algorithm for generating mean curvature flow of an interface. The algorithm alternates between solving a linear diffusion equation and pointwise thresholding. In Euclidean space, mean curvature flow arises as gradient descent for minimal partition problems. Thus, it is naturally connected to segmentation e.g. via the Mumford-Shah functional [16] and the many other models it inspired (see Chap. 25 in [19] for an exhaustive reference). As a result, MBO type schemes have been used to solve a number of segmentation problems. The authors of [7] derived an MBO scheme from the Ginzburg-Landau energy to solve the piecewise constant Mumford-Shah functional. Building on the approach of [7], the authors of [9] introduced a multiclass version of the Ginzburg-Landau energy on graphs and derived an MBO scheme for solving the SSL problem.

Recent theoretical developments in threshold dynamics [5,6,8] have led to vast generalizations of the original MBO algorithm. The key to these new developments is the heat content energy, which gives a non-local approximation to the perimeter of a set [1,15]. Generalizations of the heat content form a family of energies, essentially indexed by diffusion kernels, that are Lyapunov functionals for MBO type algorithms [6]. These energies give a natural and principled way to extend MBO schemes to a wide variety of situations, including segmentation problems on graphs.

This work represents the first exploration and extension of the theory developed in [5,6,8] to problems in machine learning and graph partitioning. Our main contribution is two new MBO schemes for the SSL problem, GHCMBO and GHCMBOS, based on the graph heat content energy (GHC) introduced in [8]. Our resulting schemes are novel in several ways. They generalize and simplify previous graph MBO schemes [9,13], allowing virtually any graph diffusion process. GHC is a Lyapunov functional for our algorithms, thus we can guarantee unconditional stability and convergence to a local minimum. We find that our methods match or exceed the accuracy of other state-of-the-art variational methods for SSL, while being much faster, more flexible, and easier to code.

2 Background and Notation

2.1 The Graphical Model

We consider the SSL data classification problem over the structure of an undirected weighted graph $G = (\mathcal{V}, W)$. $\mathcal{V}$ is the set of data points, and the weight matrix $W : \mathcal{V} \times \mathcal{V} \to \mathbb{R}$ is a symmetric matrix that describes the connection strength between any two points.

The datasets we consider in this work are collections of real vectors embedded in a high dimensional Euclidean space. A key assumption of machine learning is that the data is concentrated near a low dimensional manifold. Our goal is to reflect this manifold structure in our choice of weight matrix. Ideally, we would like to weight points based on the geodesic distances between them, however this information is not readily available to us and would lead to a very dense weight matrix. Instead, we assume that the manifold is locally Euclidean, and only compute the k nearest neighbors of each point in the Euclidean metric. Computing just a small fraction of the distances ensures that W will be a sparse matrix, which will be essential for the fast performance of our algorithms.

Under these assumptions a popular choice for the nearest neighbor weights are the Zelnick-Manor and Perona (ZMP) weight functions [22]:

$$W(x, y) = \exp\left(\frac{-d_E(x, y)^2}{\sigma(x)\sigma(y)}\right) \tag{1}$$

where d_E is the Euclidean distance and $\sigma(x), \sigma(y)$ are local scaling parameters for x, y respectively. We will construct our weight matrices using the ZMP weights, where we set $\sigma(x) = d_E(x, x_r)$ where x_r is the rth nearest neighbor of x. To recover a symmetric matrix we simply set $W(x, y) \leftarrow \max(W(x, y), W(y, x))$.

It will be useful for us to have a notion of an approximate geodesic distance between points in the graph that are not nearest neighbors. With the structure of the weight matrix, we may compute approximations to the geodesic distance by traversing through paths in the graph. Let a path p in the graph be a sequence of vertices $\{x_1, \ldots, x_s\}$ such that $W(x_i, x_{i+1}) \neq 0$ for every $1 \leq i \leq s - 1$. Let the length $\ell_q(p)$ of a path be

$$\ell_q(p) = \left(\sum_{1 \leq i \leq s-1} (-\log(W(x_i, x_{i+1})))^{q/2}\right)^{1/q} = \left[\sum_{1 \leq i \leq s-1} \left(\frac{d_E(x_i, x_{i+1})}{\sqrt{\sigma(x)\sigma(y)}}\right)^q\right]^{1/q} \tag{2}$$

Let $\pi(x, y)$ be the set of all paths from x to y. Then the q-geodesic distance between x and y, denoted $d_{G,q}(x, y)$, may be defined as

$$d_{G,q}(x, y) = \min_{p \in \pi(x,y)} \ell_q(p) \tag{3}$$

Given any subset $S \subset V$ the distance $d_{G,q}(x, S) = \min_{z \in S} d_{G,q}(x, z)$ may be efficiently computed using Dijkstra's algorithm.

2.2 Semi-supervised Data Classification

Given a set of data points V, a fixed collection of labels $\{1, \ldots, N\}$, and a fidelity subset $F \subset V$ of points whose labels are known, the semi-supervised data classification problem asks to correctly label the remaining points in $V \backslash F$. Any solution of the problem is a partition $\Sigma = (\Sigma_1, \ldots, \Sigma_N)$ of V where Σ_i is the set of points that are assigned label i. An N-phase partition of V may be represented as a function $u : V \to \{e_1, \ldots, e_N\}$ where $e_i \in \mathbb{R}^N$ is the ith standard basis vector. The convex relaxation of this space is the set of functions $u : V \to S_N$, where S_N is the simplex

$$S_N = \{p \in [0, 1]^N : \sum_{i=1}^{N} p_i = 1\} \tag{4}$$

A point $\mathbf{p} \in \mathcal{S}_N$ can be interpreted as a vector of probabilities, where p_i gives the confidence that a point should be assigned label i. We will denote the ground truth segmentation of the points as the function $\mathbf{u}^*$.

Variational approaches solve the problem by finding minimizers of energies of the form

$$E(\mathbf{u}) = R(\mathbf{u}) + \text{Fid}(\mathbf{u}). \tag{5}$$

Here R is a regularizing term that is typically some relaxation of the weighted graph cut (6), and Fid is a term that incorporates the fidelity data F.

$$\text{Cut}(\boldsymbol{\Sigma}) = \frac{1}{2} \sum_{i=1}^{N} \sum_{x \in \Sigma_i} \sum_{y \notin \Sigma_i} W(x, y). \tag{6}$$

Given some constants $f_i(x)$, we will assume throughout that $\text{Fid}(\mathbf{u})$ has the linear structure (7). We will address the connection between the coefficients $f_i(x)$ and the fidelity set F in Sect. 3.2.

$$\text{Fid}(\mathbf{u}) = \sum_{i=1}^{N} \sum_{x \in \mathcal{V}} f_i(x) u_i(x) \tag{7}$$

3   The MBO Scheme

There are many possible relaxations of the weighted graph cut (6). Our approach is to model the graph cut with the graph heat content energy (GHC) introduced in [8]. The graph heat content is a family of energies indexed by the class of affinity matrices, symmetric non-negative matrices $A : \mathcal{V} \times \mathcal{V} \to \mathbb{R}$. Every affinity matrix induces a (potentially unnormalized) diffusion process on the graph. Given an affinity matrix A, the graph heat content of a function $\mathbf{u} : \mathcal{V} \to \mathcal{S}_N$ is

$$\text{GHC}(\mathbf{u}) = \frac{1}{2} \sum_{i=1}^{N} \sum_{x,y \in \mathcal{V}} A(x, y) u_i(x)(1 - u_i(y)). \tag{8}$$

If the affinity matrix A is the weight matrix W then GHC is a relaxation of the graph cut.

GHC is based on the continuum heat content energy (HC) defined in [6]. Given a nonnegative convolution kernel K, the heat content of a function on the m-dimensional torus, $\mathbf{u} : \mathbb{T}^m \to \mathcal{S}_N$ is

$$\text{HC}_\epsilon(\mathbf{u}) = \frac{1}{\epsilon} \sum_{i=1}^{N} \int_{\mathbb{T}^m} \int_{\mathbb{R}^m} u_i(x)(1 - u_i(x + \epsilon z)) K(z) dz dx. \tag{9}$$

In the special case that $\mathbf{u}$ is a partition, the term inside the sum measures the amount of heat that diffuses out of phase i in time ϵ under the diffusion generated by K. For small values of ϵ, the amount of heat that escapes is proportional to the perimeter of phase i. Thus, the heat content gives a non-local approximation to total variation on partitions. In fact, the authors of [6] show that the approximation of the heat content to total variation becomes exact in the limit. As $\epsilon \to 0$, the energy $\mathrm{HC}_\epsilon(\mathbf{u})$ Gamma converges in $L^1(\mathbb{T}^m)$ to $\sum_{i=1}^N \|\nabla u_i\|$ when $\mathbf{u}$ is a partition and to ∞ otherwise. This makes the heat content energy a natural choice for segmentation problems.

3.1   MBO via Linearization of the Heat Content

We now derive an MBO scheme for minimizing energies of the form

$$E(\mathbf{u}) = \mathrm{GHC}(\mathbf{u}) + \mathrm{Fid}(\mathbf{u}) \tag{10}$$

following the approach developed in [6] for the continuum heat content. The connection to the MBO algorithm can be seen by considering the variations of GHC at a configuration $\mathbf{u}$ in the direction of φ. Using the quadratic structure of GHC we obtain:

$$\mathrm{GHC}(\mathbf{u}+\varphi) = \mathrm{GHC}(\mathbf{u}) + \frac{1}{2}\sum_{i=1}^N \sum_{x\in\mathcal{V}} \varphi_i(x) \sum_{y\in\mathcal{V}} A(x,y)\Big((1-2u_i(y)) - \varphi_i(y)\Big). \tag{11}$$

When A is positive semi-definite (PSD), the quadratic form $-\varphi_i^T A\varphi_i$ is negative for all $\varphi_i : \mathcal{V} \to \mathbb{R}$, thus combining (11) with the linearity of Fid we may conclude:

$$E(\mathbf{u}+\varphi) - E(\mathbf{u}) \le \mathrm{Fid}(\varphi) + \frac{1}{2}\sum_{i=1}^N \sum_{x\in\mathcal{V}} \varphi_i(x) \sum_{y\in\mathcal{V}} A(x,y)(1-2u_i(y)). \tag{12}$$

The right hand side of Eq. (12) is the linearization of E at the function $\mathbf{u}$. The inequality implies that we may obtain a configuration of lower energy, $\mathbf{u}+\varphi$, by minimizing the linearization over valid directions φ. The only constraint on φ is that $\mathbf{u} + \varphi$ must be an element of the domain of E, i.e. $\mathbf{u}(x) + \varphi(x) \in \mathcal{S}_N$ for all x. This allows us to easily solve the right hand side of (12), and we see that the minimizer $\mathbf{u} + \varphi$ is actually a partition where each phase is given by:

$$\Sigma_i = \{x \in \mathcal{V} : i = \operatorname*{arg\,min}_{1\le j\le N} f_j(x) - \psi_j(x)\} \tag{13}$$

where $\psi_j(x) = \sum_{y\in\mathcal{V}} A(x,y)u_j(y)$ is the diffusion value of u_j at x.

Iterating the minimization procedure (12–13) leads to Algorithm 1, GHCMBO, which is a graph analogue of the MBO scheme of alternating diffusion with pointwise thresholding. Each iteration dissipates GHC and the configuration space is compact, thus the algorithm must converge to a fixed point. In fact, fixed points of (12) are necessarily local minima of the energy. This guarantee of energy dissipation and convergence represents a significant theoretical advancement over previous graph MBO schemes for the SSL problem [9,13].

Algorithm 1. GHCMBO

The $(n + 1)^{\text{th}}$ partition Σ^{n+1} is obtained from the nth partition Σ^n as follows:

1. Diffusion by A:

$$\psi_i^{n+1}(x) = \sum_{y \in \Sigma_i^n} A(x, y) \quad \text{for} \quad 1 \le i \le N \tag{14}$$

2. Thresholding:

$$\Sigma_i^{n+1} = \{x \in \mathcal{V} : i = \underset{1 \le j \le N}{\arg\min} f_j(x) - \psi_j^{n+1}(x)\} \quad \text{for} \quad 1 \le i \le N \tag{15}$$

In addition to the favorable theoretical properties, GHCMBO is extremely fast. At every step the configuration is a partition, thus computing the vector $\boldsymbol{\psi}^{n+1}(x) = (\psi_1^{n+1}(x), \dots, \psi_N^{n+1}(x))$ requires just $\deg_0(x)$ additions, where $\deg_0(x)$ counts the number of nonzero entries of A in row x. As a result, when A is sparse, each iteration has low computational complexity. Furthermore, the step sizes of the scheme are very large, allowing for rapid convergence. The combination of simple computations and large step sizes makes GHCMBO significantly faster than other state-of-the-art methods (cf. timings in Tables 2, 3, 4, 5 and 6).

To adapt GHCMBO to the problem at hand, we need to construct a PSD affinity matrix A that is related to the weighted graph structure $G = (\mathcal{V}, W)$. The simplest choice is to take $A = W^2$. Another possible choice is the graph heat kernel $H_t = e^{-tL}$, where L is the symmetric normalized graph Laplacian and $t > 0$. However, this adds a parameter t, and the heat kernel is typically not sparse. Previous graph MBO schemes [9,13] have been restricted to diffusion by the heat equation and associated kernels. In addition to energy dissipation, one of the chief advantages of our approach is the ability to more freely choose a diffusion generated by a sparse matrix while avoiding extra parameters.

A natural question to ask is when can W itself be chosen for A. W is a desirable choice, as W is the sparsest matrix that still retains the full structure of the graph. Furthermore, when $A = W$ the graph heat content is a relaxation of the weighted graph cut. In general, one cannot expect that W as constructed in (1) will be positive semi-definite. An example in [8] (with no fidelity term) shows that for a given binary partition and a very natural nonnegative but not positive semi-definite weight matrix, GHCMBO gets trapped in a 2-periodic loop between two different configurations. One of the configurations has a higher energy than the other, thus there are cases where A is not PSD and GHCMBO both increases the energy and gets stuck in a non-productive loop.

It is possible however, to modify the algorithm so that the energy is guaranteed to decrease for a much wider class of matrices. In [8] it was shown that one can guarantee dissipation of GHC for any affinity matrix A by computing convolutions slightly more often. In particular, this implies that we may take $A = W$. The key feature of this new scheme, GHCMBOS, is that only one phase is allowed to shrink at a time. Although GHCMBOS has a more restrictive update rule, arguments in [8] show that the algorithm does not terminate prematurely. If the diagonal entries of A are strictly positive, every fixed point of GHCMBOS is a fixed point of GHCMBO. We describe GHCMBOS in Algorithm 2 below.

Algorithm 2. GHCMBOS

The $(n+1)^{\text{th}}$ partition Σ^{n+1} is obtained from the nth partition Σ^n by a sequence of substeps $\Sigma^{n,\ell}$ indexed by $\ell \in \{1, \ldots, N\}$. Define $\Sigma^{n,0} := \Sigma^n$ and $\Sigma^{n+1} := \Sigma^{n,N}$, then $\Sigma^{n,\ell}$ is obtained from $\Sigma^{n,\ell-1}$ as follows:

1. Diffusion by A:

$$\psi_i^{n,\ell}(x) = \sum_{y \in \Sigma_i^{n,\ell-1}} A(x,y) \quad \text{for} \quad 1 \leq i \leq N \tag{16}$$

2. Restricted Thresholding:

$$\Sigma_\ell^{n,\ell} = \{x \in \Sigma_\ell^{n,\ell-1} : \ell = \arg\min_{1 \leq j \leq N} f_j(x) - \psi_j^{n,\ell}\} \tag{17}$$

$$\Sigma_i^{n,\ell} = \Sigma_i^{n,\ell-1} \cup \{x \in \Sigma_\ell^{n,\ell-1} : i = \arg\min_{1 \leq j \leq N} f_j(x) - \psi_j^{n,\ell}\} \quad \text{for} \quad i \neq \ell \tag{18}$$

Although GHCMBOS appears to require more computation than GHCMBO, the increase in complexity is modest. At the ℓth substep, calculations (16–18) are only necessary for $x \in \Sigma_\ell^{n,\ell-1}$. Thus, the complexity of a full step of GHCMBOS is comparable to the complexity of a step of GHCMBO. In our experiments GHCMBOS runs faster than GHCMBO (see Sect. 4). The sparsity of W as compared to W^2 offsets any potential increase in complexity.

3.2 A Fidelity Term Based on Graph Geodesics

Thus far, we have not described how to construct $\text{Fid}(\mathbf{u}) = \sum_{i=1}^{N} \sum_{x \in \mathcal{V}} f_i(x) u_i(x)$ from the fidelity data F. The simplest way is to impose a penalty on points whose labeling differs from the ground truth labeling, $\mathbf{u}^*$, on F. Thus, we may take $f_i(x) = \lambda(1 - u_i^*(x))$ for $x \in F$ and zero for all other x. When λ is taken to infinity, the fidelity term becomes a hard constraint. We can easily incorporate the hard constraint into the minimization algorithms GHCMBO and GHCMBOS by simply not updating the points in the fidelity set.

If $\text{Fid}(\mathbf{u})$ is only active on fidelity nodes, the ground truth labeling $\mathbf{u}^*$ may be difficult to find in the energy landscape, especially when the size of F is very small compared to $\mathcal{V}$. For example, if F is small, then the global minimum of the energy will be near a partition that assigns all points outside of the fidelity set to the same label. For this reason, we introduce a fidelity term that is active on all of the nodes. Our approach is inspired by the region force in [20].

There, the authors introduce a linear penalty term where $f_i(x)$ is based on the diffusion distance [4] between x and elements of the fidelity set with labeling i.

Our fidelity term instead uses the graph geodesic distance defined in Eq. (3). For nodes in the fidelity set we use the hard constraint described above. For $x \notin F$, and some positive constant τ we take

$$f_i(x) = -\tau \exp(-d_{G,2}(x, F_i)^2). \tag{19}$$

where F_i is the set of fidelity points labeled i. We find that our fidelity term outperforms the diffusion distance fidelity term of [20]. On the MNIST data set, the initialization produced by labeling $x \in V \setminus F$ according to $i(x) = \arg\min_j f_j(x)$ is much closer to the ground truth labeling, when using (19) instead of the term in [20] (see Table 4).

4   Experimental Results

We test the two variants of our scheme GHCMBO and GHCMBOS with the fidelity term (19). In GHCMBO we take $A = W^2$, and in GHCMBOS we take $A = W$. For all experiments we set $\tau = 0.1$ in the fidelity term. Non-fidelity nodes $x \in V \setminus F$ are initialized by assigning x to phase $i(x) = \arg\min_{1 \leq j \leq N} f_j(x)$. The algorithm stops whenever a fixed point is reached. On average, convergence requires between 10 to 30 iterations depending on the size of V and F. On all datasets, we chose the nearest neighbor and weight matrix scaling parameters k and r experimentally. To the best of our knowledge, there is no simple and principled way of choosing these values beyond experimentation. Choosing suboptimal k and r has a modest impact – about a 0.2–1.5% drop in accuracy.

We test our algorithm on several benchmark machine learning datasets: Three Moons, MNIST, Opt-Digits, and COIL. All experiments were run using C code on a single core of an Intel i5-4250U processor at 1.30 GHz with 4 GB RAM. k-nearest neighbors were calculated using the kd-tree code in the VLFeat library. Table 1 shows the timing information for VLFeat. All of our subsequent timing results for GHCMBO and GHCMBOS include the time it takes to calculate the fidelity coefficients $f_i(x)$ and run the iterations (14–15) or (16–18). For every dataset we averaged our results over 100 trials at different fixed fidelity set sizes. In each trial, the points in the fidelity set were chosen at random and the number of points in each class was allowed to be random.

Table 1. Benchmark datasets

Dataset	Dimension	Points	Classes	W construction timing (s)
Three Moons	100	1,500	3	0.025
MNIST	784	70,000	10	149.04
Opt-Digits	64	5620	10	2.03
COIL	241	1500	6	0.33

We compare our results to previous graph MBO schemes (MBO eigenvectors [9], HKPR1/2 MBO [13]) and the total variation based convex method (TVRF [20]). The results reported for the other methods are taken from their respective papers (hence the blank entries in certain columns).

4.1 Three Moons

The Three Moons synthetic data set consists of three half circles embedded into $\mathbb{R}^{100}$ with Gaussian noise. The standard construction is built from circles centered at $(0,0), (3,0), (1.5, 0.4)$ with radii of $1, 1$, and 1.5 respectively. The first two half circles lie in the upper half plane, while the third circle lies in the lower half plane. The circles are then embedded into $\mathbb{R}^{100}$ by setting the remaining 98 coordinates to zero. Finally, Gaussian noise with mean zero and standard deviation 0.14 is added to each of the 100 coordinates.

We construct the dataset by sampling 500 points from each of the three circles, for a total of 1500 points. The weight matrix was built using the 15 nearest neighbors with local scaling by the 7th nearest neighbor. We tested fidelity sets of size 25, 50 and 75. Results for this dataset are recorded in Table 2. GHCMBO and GHCMBOS outperform the methods of [20] and are comparable to the accuracy of [9]. Both of our methods are nearly two orders of magnitude faster than [9].

Table 2. Three Moons

Method	$|F| = 25$	$|F| = 50$	$|F| = 75$	Timing (ms)
TVRF [20]	96.4%	98.2%	98.6%	–
MBO eigenvectors [9]	–	–	**99.12%**	344
GHCMBO	97.45%	98.61%	98.94%	4.1
GHCMBOS	**97.81%**	**98.93%**	99.08%	3.1

4.2 MNIST

MNIST is a database of 70,000 grayscale 28×28 pixel images of handwritten digits (0–9). Each of the digits is centered and size normalized. We combine them to create a single set of 70,000 images to test against. We perform no preprocessing on the images.

The weight matrix is calculated using the 15 nearest neighbors with local scaling based on the 7th nearest neighbor. We tested fidelity sets of size 150, 300, 450 and 2500. Results for this dataset are recorded in Table 3. GHCMBO outperforms all of the other methods while being 1.8 to 4 orders of magnitude faster. GHCMBOS is even faster than GHCMBO, but is less accurate at the smaller fidelity set sizes.

Table 3. MNIST

Method	$|F| = 150$	$|F| = 300$	$|F| = 450$	$|F| = 2500$	Timing (s)
TVRF [20]	94.6%	96.6%	96.8%	–	61
HKPR1 MBO [13]	–	–	–	97.52%	22.3
HKPR2 MBO [13]	–	–	–	97.48%	4,428
MBO eigenvectors [9]	–	–	–	96.91%	1,699
GHCMBO	**95.97%**	**96.81%**	**97.09%**	**97.54%**	0.30
GHCMBOS	92.91%	95.33%	96.32%	97.27%	0.17

Table 4. Comparing Fidelity terms on MNIST

Method	$|F| = 150$	$|F| = 300$	$|F| = 450$	Timing (s)
Fidelity only [20]	35.5%	52.3%	71.5%	0.4
Fidelity only (19)	**84.93%**	**88.61%**	**90.90%**	0.13

In Table 4 we compare our fidelity term (19) with the diffusion distance fidelity term used in [20]. Each point is labeled according to $i(x) = \arg\min_j f_j(x)$ and then the accuracy is measured without running any further algorithms. Our fidelity term is significantly more accurate than the fidelity term in [20].

4.3   Opt-Digits

Opt-Digits is a database of 5620 handwritten digits [11]. The data is recorded as an 8×8 integer matrix, where each element is between 0 and 16.

We construct the weight matrix using the 15 nearest neighbors and local scaling by the 7th nearest neighbor. We tested fidelity sets of size 50, 100, and 150. Results for this dataset are recorded in Table 5. Our methods are comparable or superior to the results of [20].

Table 5. Opt-Digits

Method	$|F| = 50$	$|F| = 100$	$|F| = 150$	Timing (ms)
TVRF [20]	**95.9%**	97.2%	**98.3%**	–
GHCMBO	95.68%	**97.63%**	98.10%	15.4
GHCMBOS	94.20%	96.30%	97.28%	11.0

4.4   COIL

The Columbia Object Image Library (COIL-100) is a database of 128×128 pixel color images of 100 different objects photographed at various different angles [17]. In [18] the authors processed the COIL images to create a more difficult benchmark set. The red channel of each image is downsampled to 16×16 pixels by averaging over blocks of 8×8 pixels. The images are then further distorted and downsampled to create 241 dimensional feature vectors. Then 24 of the objects are randomly selected and randomly partitioned into 6 different classes. Discarding 38 images from each class leaves 250 images per class for a total of 1500 points.

We construct the weight matrix using the 4 nearest neighbors and local scaling by the 4th nearest neighbor. We tested fidelity sets of size 50, 100, and 150. Results for this dataset are recorded in Table 6. Both GHCMBO and GHCMBOS considerably outperform all of the other methods. In addition, our approaches are anywhere from 200 to nearly 100,000 times faster than the other methods.

Table 6. COIL

Method	$|F| = 50$	$|F| = 100$	$|F| = 150$	Timing (ms)
TVRF [20]	80.3%	90.0%	91.7%	–
MBO eigenvectors [9]	–	–	91.46%	220
HKPR1 MBO [13]	–	–	91.09%	1,000
HKPR2 MBO [13]	–	–	91.23%	92,000
GHCMBO	**83.01%**	92.24%	94.30%	1.00
GHCMBOS	82.96%	**92.30%**	**94.34%**	0.76

5 Conclusion

We have presented two MBO schemes, GHCMBO and GHCMBOS, for solving the SSL problem on a weighted graph. Our schemes are based on the graph heat content energy (GHC) and the theory developed in the series of papers [5,6,8]. We solve the SSL problem by minimizing an energy that combines GHC with a linear fidelity term based on graph geodesics, inspired by the region force in [20]. GHC depends on the choice of affinity matrix A, which induces a diffusion process on the graph. If A is PSD then GHCMBO decreases the energy at every step, while GHCMBOS minimizes the energy for all affinity matrices. Our approach considerably generalizes and simplifies previous SSL graph MBO schemes [9,13]. The guarantee of energy dissipation and convergence to local minima is a new and important theoretical advance for SSL graph MBO schemes.

Experimental results on benchmark datasets show that both GHCMBO and GHCMBOS produce results with comparable or superior accuracy to other state-of-the-art methods [9,13,20]. In addition, our schemes were considerably faster. Our slower algorithm, GHCMBO, was nearly two orders of magnitude faster than [9,13,20] on every dataset. Our algorithms are so fast because we are free to choose diffusions generated by extremely sparse matrices, and take very large step sizes through the configuration space.

Unlike the basic MBO scheme, the new variants discussed in this paper extend to very general multiphase situations where the interaction between each phase pair may be treated differently. In a future work we plan to apply this idea to the SSL problem, using the fidelity data to learn the most favorable set of pairwise interactions.

Acknowledgments. The author is grateful to Selim Esedoğlu for helpful comments and suggestions. The author was supported by NSF DMS-1317730.

References

1. Alberti, G., Bellettini, G.: A non-local anisotropic model for phase transitions: asymptotic behavior of rescaled energies. Eur. J. Appl. Math. **9**, 261–284 (1998)
2. Bresson, X., Chan, T., Tai, X., Szlam, A.: Multi-class trans- ductive learning based on l1 relaxations of cheeger cut and mumford-shah-potts model. J. Math. Imaging Vis. **49**(1), 191–201 (2013)
3. Cheeger, J.: A lower bound for the smallest eigenvalue of the Laplacian. In: Problems in Analysis, pp. 195–199 (1970)
4. Coifman, R.R., Lafon, S., Lee, A.B., Maggioni, M., Nadler, B., Warner, F., Zucker, S.W.: Geometric diffusions as a tool for harmonic analysis and structure definition of data: diffusion maps. PNAS **102**, 7426–7431 (2005)
5. Elsey, M., Esedoğlu, S.: Threshold dynamics for anisotropic surface energies. Technical report, UM (2016). Under review
6. Esedoğlu, S., Otto, F.: Threshold dynamics for networks with arbitrary surface tensions. Commun. Pure Appl. Math. **68**(5), 808–864 (2015)
7. Esedoğlu, S., Tsai, Y.-H.: Threshold dynamics for the piecewise constant Mumford-Shah functional. J. Comput. Phys. **211**(1), 367–384 (2006)
8. Esedoğlu, S., Jacobs, M.: Convolution kernels, and stability of threshold dynamics methods. Technical report, University of Michigan (2016)
9. Garcia-Cardona, C., Merkurjev, E., Bertozzi, A.L., Flenner, A., Percus, A.G.: Multiclass data segmentation using diffuse interface methods on graphs. IEEE Trans. Pattern Anal. Mach. Intell. **36**(8), 1600–1613 (2014)
10. Hein, M., Setzer, S.: Beyond spectral clustering - tight relaxations of balanced graph cuts. In: Advances in Neural Information Processing Systems 24 (NIPS) (2011)
11. Kaynak, C.: Methods of combining multiple classifiers and their applications to handwritten digit recognition. Master's thesis, Institute of Graduate Studies in Science and Engineering, Bogazici University (1995)
12. Malik, J., Shi, J.: Normalized cuts and image segmentation. IEEE Trans. Pattern Anal. Mach. Intell. **22**(8), 888–905 (2000)
13. Merkurjev, E., Bertozzi, A., Chung, F.: A semi-supervised heat kernel pagerank MBO algorithm for data classification (2016, submitted)
14. Merriman, B., Bence, J.K., Osher, S.J.: Diffusion generated motion by mean curvature. In: Taylor, J. (ed.) Proceedings of the Computational Crystal Growers Workshop, pp. 73–83. AMS (1992)
15. Miranda, M., Pallara, D., Paronetto, F., Preunkert, M.: Short-time heat flow and functions of bounded variation in $\mathbb{R}^N$. Ann. Fac. Sci. Toulouse Math. **16**(1), 125–145 (2007)
16. Mumford, D., Shah, J.: Optimal approximations by piecewise smooth functions and associated variational problems. Commun. Pure Appl. Math. **42**, 577–685 (1989)

17. Nene, S.A., Nayar, S.K., Murase, H.: Columbia object image library (coil-100). Technical report, Columbia University (1996)
18. Zien, A., Chapelle, O., Scholkopf, B.: Semi-Supervised Learning. The MIT Press, Cambridge (2006)
19. Scherzer, O. (ed.): Handbook of Mathematical Methods in Imaging. Springer, Heidelberg (2011)
20. Yin, K., Tai, X.-Y., Osher, S.J.: An effective region force for some variational models for learning and clustering. Technical report, UCLA (2016)
21. Yu, S.X., Shi, J.: Multiclass spectral clustering. In: Ninth IEEE International Coference on Computer Vision, vol. 1, pp. 313–319, October 2003
22. Zelnik-Manor, L., Perona, P.: Self-tuning spectral clustering. In: Advances in Neural Information Processing Systems (2004)

Convex Non-Convex Segmentation over Surfaces

Martin Huska[2], Alessandro Lanza[1], Serena Morigi[1(✉)], and Fiorella Sgallari[1]

[1] Department of Mathematics, University of Bologna, Bologna, Italy
{alessandro.lanza2,serena.morigi,fiorella.sgallari}@unibo.it
[2] Department of Mathematics, University of Padova, Padova, Italy
martin@math.unipd.it

Abstract. The paper addresses the segmentation of real-valued functions having values on a complete, connected, 2-manifold embedded in $\mathbb{R}^3$. We present a three-stage segmentation algorithm that first computes a piecewise smooth multi-phase partition function, then applies clusterization on its values, and finally tracks the boundary curves to obtain the segmentation on the manifold. The proposed formulation is based on the minimization of a Convex Non-Convex functional where an ad-hoc non-convex regularization term improves the treatment of the boundary lengths handled by the ℓ_1 norm in [2]. An appropriate numerical scheme based on the Alternating Directions Methods of Multipliers procedure is proposed to efficiently solve the nonlinear optimization problem. Experimental results show the effectiveness of this three-stage procedure.

Keywords: Manifold segmentation · Images on manifold · ADMM · Convex non-convex strategy

1 Introduction

Segmentation is an important aspect in the understanding and analysis of images. It involves separating an image into K disjoint regions that are homogeneous according to a certain feature such as intensity or texture, to identify more meaningful high level information in the image.

In 3D surface analysis, segmentation techniques can also be used to detect certain special parts of the given surface. Applications range from reading barcodes printed or etched onto object surfaces, to structure detection in 3D medical imaging, or even identification and tracking of features in sequences of textured triangle meshes. In a more general context, we consider the segmentation of a real-valued function f defined on a complete, connected, 2-manifold $\mathcal{M}$ embedded in $\mathbb{R}^3$. Since the 2-manifold is not restricted to be a parametric manifold, but rather a more generic arbitrary topology manifold, the well-known successful methods for image segmentation [2,3,9] can not be directly exploited. To take

Electronic supplementary material The online version of this chapter (doi:10.1007/978-3-319-58771-4_28) contains supplementary material, which is available to authorized users.

© Springer International Publishing AG 2017
F. Lauze et al. (Eds.): SSVM 2017, LNCS 10302, pp. 348–360, 2017.
DOI: 10.1007/978-3-319-58771-4_28

into account the geometry of the manifold itself, popular variational formulations for image segmentation in the Euclidean space $\mathbb{R}^n$, have been adapted and generalized on surfaces. The segmentation model first introduced by Chan and Vese [3] for images has been proposed for surfaces in [14] and [13]. However, in [13] the number of parts has to be chosen a priori, and the model relies on a TV penalty which is less sparsity promoting with respect to the non-convex penalty here proposed.

In this work we introduce a new framework for segmentation of manifolds based on scalar-valued features which exploits global or local shape information represented by a generic real-valued function $f : \mathcal{M} \to \mathbb{R}$ defined on a 2-manifold $\mathcal{M}$, to infer a decomposition of $\mathcal{M}$ in salient parts. The basic step in the proposed framework is represented by the solution of the following variational model:

$$\min_u \mathcal{J}(u; \lambda, \eta, a),$$

$$\mathcal{J}(u; \lambda, \eta, a) := \frac{\lambda}{2} \int_{\mathcal{M}} (u - f)^2 \, d\mathcal{M} + \frac{\eta}{2} \int_{\mathcal{M}} |\nabla_w u|^2 \, d\mathcal{M} + \int_{\mathcal{M}} \phi\left(|\nabla_w u|; a\right) \, d\mathcal{M},$$

$$(1)$$

where $\lambda > 0, \eta \geq 0$ are regularization parameters, $\nabla_w u$ is the intrinsic (Riemannian) gradient defined on $\mathcal{M}$ and $d\mathcal{M}$ is the manifolds element measure, while $| \cdot |$ is the Riemannian norm, $u : \mathcal{M} \to \mathbb{R}$ represents the manifold-valued partition function, and $\phi(\cdot; a) : [0, +\infty) \to \mathbb{R}$ is a parameterized, non-convex penalty function with parameter $a \geq 0$, which controls the degree of non-convexity and will be referred to as the *concavity parameter*. The functional is composed by the sum of smooth convex (quadratic) terms and a non-smooth non-convex regularization term designed for penalizing simultaneously the non-smoothness of the inner regions and the length of the segmented boundaries. Thus the functional $\mathcal{J}$ in (1) is non-smooth and can be convex or non-convex depending on the parameters λ, η and a. We are interested in solving the segmentation problem via construction and then optimization of the Convex Non-Convex (CNC) functional $\mathcal{J}$ in (1). From the seminal works in [1], and [10] for CNC image denoising, very interesting developments have been presented by Selesnik and others for different purposes, see [4, 6–8] for more details. The attractiveness of such CNC approach resides in its ability to promote sparsity more strongly than it is possible by using only convex terms while at the same time maintaining convexity of the total optimization problem, so that well-known reliable convex minimization approaches can be used to compute the (unique) solution.

A first contribution of this paper is the derivation of conditions that ensure the functional $\mathcal{J}$ in problem (1) is convex – despite the regularization term being nonconvex. The inclusion of the manifold's geometry is done by characterizing the convexity parameter a locally. Therefore the model (1) has a unique global minimizer. In this paper, as a second contribution, we propose a three-stage variational segmentation method inspired by the piecewise smoothing proposal in [2] which is a convex variant of the classical Mumford-Shah model. In the first stage an approximate solution u^* to the optimization problem (1) is computed. Once u^* is obtained, then in the second stage the segmentation is done by thresholding u^* into different parts. The thresholds can be given by the users or can be obtained automatically using any clustering methods, such as for example the K-means algorithm. As discussed in [2], this allows for a K-phase segmentation ($K \geq 2$) by choosing ($K - 1$) thresholds after u^* is computed in the first stage. In contrast, many multiphase methods require K to be given in advance which implies that if K changes, the minimization problem has to be solved again. Finally, a contour track phase is computed to extract boundary curves delimiting the segmented regions on the manifold.

This work is organized as follows. In Sect. 2 we characterize the non-convex penalty functions $\phi(\,\cdot\,;a)$ considered in the above model. In Sect. 3 we provide a sufficient condition for strict convexity of the cost functional in (1) and in Sect. 4 we illustrate in detail the Alternating Directions Methods of Multipliers (ADMM)-based numerical algorithm used to compute approximate solutions of (1). Some segmentation results are illustrated in Sect. 5. Conclusion are drawn in Sect. 6.

2   Non-convex Penalty Functions

In this section we characterize the non-convex penalty functions $\phi(\,\cdot\,;a)$ used in (1). We denote the sets of non-negative and positive real numbers as $\mathbb{R}_+ := \{\, t \in \mathbb{R} : t \geq 0 \,\}$ and $\mathbb{R}_+^* := \{\, t \in \mathbb{R} : t > 0 \,\}$, respectively. Analogously to [4,6,7], we consider parameterized penalty functions $\phi(t;a) : \mathbb{R}_+ \to \mathbb{R}_+$ such that for any value of the parameter $a \in \mathbb{R}_+$ the following assumptions are satisfied:

(A1) $\phi(t;a) \in \mathcal{C}^2(\mathbb{R}_+)$ (ϕ twice continuously differentiable in t on $\mathbb{R}_+$)

(A2) $\phi'(t;a) > 0 \quad \forall t \in \mathbb{R}_+$ (ϕ strictly increasing in t on $\mathbb{R}_+$)

(A3) $\phi''(t;a) \leq 0 \quad \forall t \in \mathbb{R}_+$ (ϕ concave in t on $\mathbb{R}_+$)

(A4) $\phi(0;a) = 0, \; \phi'(0^+;a) = 1,$ (ϕ, ϕ', ϕ'' normalization)
$\inf_{t \in \mathbb{R}_+} \phi''(t;a) = \phi''(0^+;a) = -a\,.$

We remark that a represents a scalar indicator of the "degree of concavity" of the penalty function ϕ, thus justifying the name *concavity parameter*. Moreover, we set $\phi(t;0) := t$, such that the ℓ_1-norm penalty is recovered as a special case of $\phi(\cdot;a)$ when $a = 0$. We refer to [4,7] for a detailed discussion on commonly used penalty functions satisfying assumptions (A1)–(A4) above, such as

$$\phi_{\log}(t;a) = \frac{\log(1 + at)}{a}, \; \phi_{\mathrm{rat}}(t;a) = \frac{t}{1 + at/2}, \; \phi_{\mathrm{atan}}(t;a) = \frac{\mathrm{atan}\left(\frac{1+2at}{\sqrt{3}}\right) - \frac{\pi}{6}}{a\sqrt{3}/2}.$$

$$(2)$$

In Fig. 1 we show the plots of these penalty functions, for three different values $a \in \{2, 3, 4\}$ of the concavity parameter.

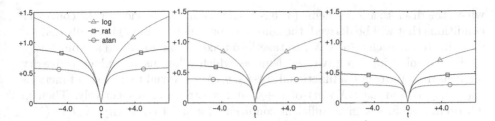

Fig. 1. Plots of the penalty functions $\phi_{\log}(t; a), \phi_{\mathrm{rat}}(t; a), \phi_{\mathrm{atan}}(t; a)$ defined in (2), for different values of the concavity parameter a: $a = 2$ (left), $a = 3$ (center), $a = 4$ (right).

3 Convexity Analysis

In this section we seek for a sufficient condition on the parameters $\lambda > 0, \eta, a \geq 0$, such that the objective functional $\mathcal{J}(\,\cdot\,; \lambda, \eta, a)$ in (1) is strictly convex. At this aim we introduce some basic notations and the discretization of problem (1). Let the manifold $\mathcal{M}$ embedded in $\mathbb{R}^3$ be well represented by a piecewise linear approximation, i.e. triangulation, we assume that the manifold is sampled at n points and represented by a mesh $\Omega := (V, T)$, where $V = \{X_i\}_{i=1}^n \in \mathbb{R}^{n \times 3}$ is the set of vertices, and $T \in \mathbb{N}^{n_T \times 3}$ is the graph connectivity matrix. The direct connection between the neighbors X_i and X_j is referred as edge e_{ij} and thus the whole set $E = \{e_{ij}\} \subseteq V \times V$. For each vertex X_i, we denote by $N(X_i) = \{X_j : e_{ij} \in E\}$ its 1-ring neighborhood, defined as the set of incident vertices to X_i, and by N_i the corresponding ordered set of vertex indices. Then $v_i = |N(X_i)|$ is the so-called valence of vertex X_i. The scalar functions $f, u \colon \Omega \to \mathbb{R}$, are sampled over the vertices V of the mesh Ω. Denoting by $f_i := f(X_i)$, and analogously by $u_i := u(X_i), i = 1, \ldots, n$, the sampled functions are represented by vectors $u, f \in \mathbb{R}^n$. At each vertex X_i, the 1-ring neighborhood $N(X_i)$ defines v_i discrete directional derivatives, each calculated along a different direction identified by the edges $e_{ij}, j = 1, \ldots, v_i$ and defined as follows

$$\left. \frac{\partial u}{\partial e_{ij}} \right|_{X_i} \approx w_{ij}(u_j - u_i), \qquad w_{ij} := w(X_i, X_j) = \frac{1}{|e_{ij}|}. \tag{3}$$

The intrinsic gradient $\nabla_w u$ of u in (1) evaluated at vertex X_i is a vector in the tangent space $T_{X_i}\mathcal{M}$, whose magnitude can be approximated as follows

$$\|(\nabla_w u)_i\|_2 = \sqrt{\sum_{j \in N_i} w_{ij}^2 (u_j - u_i)^2}. \tag{4}$$

We are now ready to rewrite $\mathcal{J}$ in (1) in discrete vector-indexed form:

$$\begin{aligned} \mathcal{J}(u; \lambda, \eta, a) &= \sum_{i=1}^n \frac{\lambda}{2} (u_i - f_i)^2 + \sum_{i=1}^n \frac{\eta}{2} \left[\sum_{j \in N_i} w_{ij}^2 (u_j - u_i)^2 \right] \\ &+ \sum_{i=1}^n \phi \left(\sqrt{\sum_{j \in N_i} w_{ij}^2 (u_j - u_i)^2}; a_i \right), \end{aligned} \tag{5}$$

where the discretization scheme (4) has been used in (5). In view of the convexity conditions that will be derived, the convexity parameter a in (1) is locally defined as a_i in (5) for each vertex X_i, to take into account the manifold's geometry.

In the following, we give two lemmas which allow us to reduce convexity analysis from the original functional $\mathcal{J}(\,\cdot\,;\lambda,\eta,a)$ of n variables to easier functions $f_v(\,\cdot\,;\lambda,\eta,a)$ and $g_v(\,\cdot\,;\lambda,\eta,a)$ of $v+1$ and v variables, respectively. Then in Theorem 1 we finally give sufficient conditions for strict convexity of $\mathcal{J}$ in (5).

Lemma 1. *Let* $f_v(\,\cdot\,;\lambda,\eta,a)\colon \mathbb{R}^{v+1} \to \mathbb{R}$ *be the function defined by*

$$f_v(x_0, x_1, \ldots, x_v; \lambda, \eta, a) := \frac{\lambda}{2} \sum_{j=0}^{v} \frac{1}{v_j + 1} x_j^2 + \frac{\eta}{2} \sum_{j=1}^{v} w_{0j}^2 (x_j - x_0)^2$$

$$+ \phi\left(\sqrt{\sum_{j=1}^{v} w_{0j}^2 (x_j - x_0)^2} \,; a \right). \tag{6}$$

Then, the functional $\mathcal{J}(\,\cdot\,;\lambda,\eta,a) : \mathbb{R}^n \to \mathbb{R}$ *defined in (5) is strictly convex if all the functions* $f_{v_i}(\,\cdot\,;\lambda,\eta,a_i) : \mathbb{R}^{v_i+1} \to \mathbb{R}$, $i = 1,\ldots,n$, *are strictly convex.*

Proof. The functional $\mathcal{J}$ in (5) can be rewritten in the following equivalent form:

$$\mathcal{J}(u;\lambda,\eta,a) = \mathcal{A}(u) + \sum_{i=1}^{n} f_{v_i}(u_i, u_{N_i(1)}, \ldots, u_{N_i(v_i)}; \lambda, \eta, a_i), \tag{7}$$

where $\mathcal{A}(u)$ is an affine function of u and the function f_v is defined in (6). We remark that the generic i-th term of the last two sums in (5) involves $v_i + 1$ different vertices and that, globally, the last two sums involve the generic i-th vertex $v_i + 1$ times. Since the affine function $\mathcal{A}(u)$ does not affect convexity, we can conclude that the functional $\mathcal{J}$ in (7) - or, equivalently, in (5) - is strictly convex if all the functions f_{v_i} in (7) are strictly convex.   □

Lemma 2. *The function* $f_v(\,\cdot\,;\lambda,\eta,a) : \mathbb{R}^{v+1} \to \mathbb{R}$ *defined in (6) is strictly convex if the function* $g_v(\,\cdot\,;\lambda,\eta,a) : \mathbb{R}^v \to \mathbb{R}$ *defined by*

$$g_v(y_1, \ldots, y_v; \lambda, \eta, a) = \frac{1}{2}\left(\eta + \frac{\lambda}{\kappa}\right) \sum_{j=1}^{v} y_j^2 + \phi\left(\sqrt{\sum_{j=1}^{v} y_j^2}\,; a\right) \tag{8}$$

is strictly convex, where

$$\kappa = (1 + \tilde{v})\lambda_1, \tag{9}$$

with $\tilde{v} := \max_j v_j$, *and* λ_1 *is the largest eigenvalue of matrix* $Q \in \mathbb{R}^{(v+1)\times(v+1)}$ *defined as*

$$Q = \begin{bmatrix} \sum w_i^2 & -w_1^2 & -w_2^2 & -w_3^2 & \cdots & -w_v^2 \\ -w_1^2 & w_1^2 & 0 & 0 & \cdots & 0 \\ -w_2^2 & 0 & w_2^2 & 0 & \cdots & 0 \\ -w_3^2 & 0 & 0 & w_3^2 & \cdots & 0 \\ \vdots & \vdots & \vdots & \vdots & \ddots & 0 \\ -w_v^2 & 0 & 0 & 0 & 0 & w_v^2 \end{bmatrix}. \tag{10}$$

where $(w_1, w_2, \ldots, w_v)^T \in \mathbb{R}^v$ *are the weights defined in (3) associated with a generic vertex in V of valence v.*

The proof is provided as supplementary material.

Theorem 1. *Let the function* $\phi(\,\cdot\,;a) : \mathbb{R}_+ \to \mathbb{R}$ *satisfy assumptions (A1)–(A4) in Sect. 2. Then, a sufficient condition for functional* $\mathcal{J}(\,\cdot\,;\lambda,\eta,a)$ *in (5) to be strictly convex is that the parameters* (λ,η,a) *satisfy:*

$$a_i < \eta + \frac{\lambda}{\kappa_i} \quad \Longleftrightarrow \quad a_i = \tau_c \left(\eta + \frac{\lambda}{\kappa_i} \right), \quad \tau_c \in [0,1), \tag{11}$$

for every $i \in \{1, \dots, n\}$, *with* κ_i *defined in (9).*

Proof. Based on Lemmas 1–2, the functional $\mathcal{J}(\,\cdot\,;\lambda,\eta,a)$ is strictly convex if all the functions $g_{v_i}, i \in \{1, \dots, n\}$, defined in (8) are strictly convex. Then, based on Proposition 2 in [4], the statement (11) follows.   □

We conclude by highlighting some properties of functional $\mathcal{J}$ in (5).

Definition 1. *Let* $Z : \mathbb{R}^n \to \mathbb{R}$ *be a (not necessarily smooth) function. Then, Z is said to be* μ-*strongly convex iff there exists a constant* $\mu > 0$, *called the modulus of strong convexity of Z, such that function* $Z(x) - \frac{\mu}{2} \|x\|_2^2$ *is convex.*

Proposition 1. *Let* $\phi(\,\cdot\,;a) : \mathbb{R}_+ \to \mathbb{R}$ *be a penalty function as defined in (2) and let the parameters* (λ,η,a) *satisfy condition (11). Then, the functional* $\mathcal{J}(\,\cdot\,;\lambda,\eta,a)$ *in (5) is proper, continuous, bounded from below by zero, coercive and* μ-*strongly convex with* μ *equal to*

$$\mu = \lambda + \min_{i=1,\dots,n} \{\kappa_i(\eta - a_i)\}. \tag{12}$$

Remark: *Note that* μ *is not necessarily maximal.*

The proof is provided in the supplementary material.

4 Applying ADMM to the Proposed CNC Model

In this section, we illustrate the ADMM-based iterative algorithm used to compute minimizers of our discrete objective functional $\mathcal{J}$ in (5) in case that parameters λ, η, a satisfy condition (11), such that $\mathcal{J}$ is strictly convex.

Let us first introduce sparse matrix representations of the discrete gradient and divergence operators to speed up the computations. In particular, the discrete gradient operator is represented by the matrix $M \in \mathbb{R}^{(\hat{v}n) \times n}, M = (M_1^T, M_2^T, \dots, M_{\hat{v}}^T)^T$, where $\hat{v}$ denotes the maximum valence in Ω and each sub-matrix $M_j \in \mathbb{R}^{n \times n}, j = 1, \dots, \hat{v}$, represents the linear operator which simultaneously computes the j-th directional derivative at all vertices, that is

$$(M_j)_{ik} = \begin{cases} w_{iz} & \text{for } k = z \\ -w_{iz} & \text{for } k = i, \quad z = N_i(j). \\ 0 & \text{otherwise} \end{cases} \tag{13}$$

At the i-th row of M_j, corresponding to the j-th directional derivative at the i-th vertex, the only non-zero elements are the one on the main diagonal and the one corresponding to the j-th neighbor of the i-th vertex. Thus, each sub-matrix M_j has exactly $2n$ non-zero elements. In addition, we have $M^T M = (M_1^T M_1 + M_2^T M_2 + \ldots + M_{\hat{v}}^T M_{\hat{v}})$. To proceed with ADMM on triangular mesh surfaces, we introduce the auxiliary variable $t \in \mathbb{R}^{\hat{v}n}$, and reformulate problem (5) in the equivalent form:

$$\{u^*, t^*\} \leftarrow \arg\min_{u,t} \left\{ \frac{\lambda}{2}\|u - f\|_2^2 + \sum_{i=1}^{n}\left[\frac{\eta}{2}\|t_i\|_2^2 + \phi(\|t_i\|_2; a_i)\right]\right\} \quad (14)$$

$$\text{subject to}: \quad t = Mu, \quad (15)$$

where $t_i := \left((M_1 u)_i, (M_2 u)_i, \ldots, (M_{v_i} u)_i\right)^T \in \mathbb{R}^{v_i}$ represents the discrete gradient of u at vertex X_i. To solve problem (14)–(15), we define the augmented Lagrangian functional

$$\mathcal{L}(u, t; \rho; \lambda, \eta, a) = \frac{\lambda}{2}\|u - f\|_2^2 + \sum_{i=1}^{n}\left[\frac{\eta}{2}\|t_i\|_2^2 + \phi(\|t_i\|_2; a_i)\right]$$

$$- \langle \rho, t - Mu \rangle + \frac{\beta}{2}\|t - Mu\|_2^2, \quad (16)$$

where $\beta > 0$ is a scalar penalty parameter and $\rho \in \mathbb{R}^{\hat{v}n}$ is the vector of Lagrange multipliers associated with the linear constraint $t = Mu$ in (15). We then consider the following saddle-point problem:

$$\text{Find} \quad (u^*, t^*; \rho^*) \in \mathbb{R}^n \times \mathbb{R}^{\hat{v}n} \times \mathbb{R}^{\hat{v}n}$$

$$\text{s.t.} \quad \mathcal{L}(u^*, t^*; \rho; \lambda, \eta, a) \leq \mathcal{L}(u^*, t^*; \rho^*; \lambda, \eta, a) \leq \mathcal{L}(u, t; \rho^*; \lambda, \eta, a)$$

$$\forall (u, t; \rho) \in \mathbb{R}^n \times \mathbb{R}^{\hat{v}n} \times \mathbb{R}^{\hat{v}n}. \quad (17)$$

Given the previously computed (or initialized for $k = 0$) vectors $u^{(k)}$ and $\rho^{(k)}$, the k-th iteration of the proposed ADMM-based iterative scheme applied to the solution of the saddle-point problem (16)–(17) reads as follows:

$$t^{(k+1)} \leftarrow \arg\min_{t \in \mathbb{R}^{\hat{v}n}} \mathcal{L}(u^{(k)}, t; \rho^{(k)}; \lambda, \eta, a) \quad (18)$$

$$u^{(k+1)} \leftarrow \arg\min_{u \in \mathbb{R}^n} \mathcal{L}(u, t^{(k+1)}; \rho^{(k)}; \lambda, \eta, a) \quad (19)$$

$$\rho^{(k+1)} \leftarrow \rho^{(k)} - \beta\left(t^{(k+1)} - Mu^{(k+1)}\right) \quad (20)$$

In the following we show in detail how to solve the two minimization sub-problems (18) and (19) for the primal variables t and u, respectively.

Although the minimization sub-problems are all strictly convex and admit a unique solution, convergence of the overall ADMM algorithm is clearly not guaranteed. We postpone the analysis of convergence of the proposed ADMM scheme to a future extended version of this work.

4.1   Solving the Sub-problem for t

The minimization sub-problem for t in (18) can be rewritten as follows:

$$t^{(k+1)} \leftarrow \arg \min_{t \in \mathbb{R}^{\hat{v}n}} \left\{ \sum_{i=1}^{n} \left[\frac{\eta}{2} \|t_i\|_2^2 + \phi(\|t_i\|_2; a_i) \right] + \frac{\beta}{2} \left\| t - r^{(k+1)} \right\|_2^2 \right\} \quad (21)$$

where constant terms have been omitted and where the vector $r^{(k+1)} \in \mathbb{R}^{\hat{v}n}$ is constant with respect to the optimization variable t and is given by:

$$r^{(k+1)} = Mu^{(k)} + \frac{1}{\beta} \rho^{(k)}. \quad (22)$$

The minimization problem in (21) rewritten in component-wise (vertex-by-vertex) form, is equivalent to the following n independent lower dimensional problems:

$$t_i^{(k+1)} \leftarrow \arg \min_{t_i \in \mathbb{R}^{v_i}} \left\{ \phi(\|t_i\|_2; a_i) + \frac{\eta}{2} \|t_i\|_2^2 + \frac{\beta}{2} \left\| t_i - r_i^{(k+1)} \right\|_2^2 \right\}, \quad (23)$$

with $i = 1, \ldots, n$, $r_i^{(k+1)} := \left(Mu^{(k)} \right)_i + \left(\rho^{(k)} \right)_i / \beta$ and $\left(Mu^{(k)} \right)_i, \left(\rho^{(k)} \right)_i \in \mathbb{R}^{v_i}$ denote the discrete gradient and the associated vector of Lagrange multipliers at vertex X_i, respectively, with valence v_i.

Since we are imposing that condition (11) is satisfied, such that the original functional $\mathcal{J}(u; \lambda, \eta, a)$ in (1) is strictly convex, we aim at avoiding non-convexity of the ADMM sub-problems (23). In the first part of Proposition 2 below, we give necessary and sufficient conditions for strict convexity of the cost functions in (23). In particular, based on (25)–(26), we can state that the problems in (23) are strictly convex if and only if the following conditions hold:

$$\beta > \max_{i=1,\ldots,n} a_i - \eta. \quad (24)$$

In case conditions in (24) are satisfied, the unique solutions of the strictly convex problems in (23) can be obtained by the soft-thresholding operator defined in (28)–(29). We remark that the nonlinear equation in (29) can be solved up to a sufficient accuracy by very few steps of the iterative Newton method.

Proposition 2. *Let $\eta, a \geq 0, \beta > 0$ and $r \in \mathbb{R}^v$ be given constants, and let $\phi(\cdot; a) : \mathbb{R}_+ \to \mathbb{R}$ be a function satisfying assumptions (A1)–(A4) in Sect. 2. Then, the function*

$$\theta(x) := \phi(\|x\|_2; a) + \frac{\eta}{2} \|x\|_2^2 + \frac{\beta}{2} \|x - r\|_2^2, \quad x \in \mathbb{R}^v, \quad (25)$$

is strictly convex if and only if the following condition holds:

$$\beta > a - \eta. \quad (26)$$

Moreover, in case that (26) holds, the strictly convex minimization problem

$$\arg \min_{x \in \mathbb{R}^v} \theta(x) \tag{27}$$

admits the unique solution $x^* \in \mathbb{R}^v$ given by the following shrinkage operator:

$$x^* = \xi^* r, \quad \text{with } \xi^* \in [0, 1[, \text{ and} \tag{28}$$

(a) $\xi^* = 0$ if $\|r\|_2 \le \dfrac{1}{\beta}$

(b) $\xi^* \in]0, 1[$ unique solution of :   (29)
    $\phi'(\|r\|_2 \xi; a) + \|r\|_2 ((\eta + \beta)\xi - \beta) = 0$ otherwise.

The proof is provided in the supplementary material.

4.2   Solving the Sub-problem for u

The minimization sub-problem for u in (19) can be rewritten as follows:

$$u^{(k+1)} \leftarrow \arg \min_{u \in \mathbb{R}^n} \left\{ \frac{\lambda}{2} \|u - f\|_2^2 + \langle \rho^{(k)}, Mu \rangle + \frac{\beta}{2} \|t^{(k+1)} - Mu\|_2^2 \right\}, \tag{30}$$

where constants have been omitted. The quadratic minimization problem (30) has first-order optimality conditions which lead to the following linear system:

$$\left(I + \frac{\beta}{\lambda} M^T M \right) u = f + \frac{\beta}{\lambda} M^T \left(t^{(k+1)} - \frac{1}{\beta} \rho^{(k)} \right). \tag{31}$$

Since the product $M^T M$ is symmetric and the ratio $\frac{\beta}{\lambda}$ is positive, the $n \times n$ coefficient matrix of the linear system (31) is symmetric pos. semi definite and highly sparse. Hence, (31) admits a unique solution obtained very efficiently by the iterative (preconditioned) conjugate gradient method.

5   Experimental Results

In this section we describe the experimental results which assess the performance of the proposed segmentation algorithm where in (1) we used the $\phi_{\log}$ penalty function defined in (2). For what concerns the ADMM, the parameter β is chosen according to condition (24), and the ADMM iterations are terminated as soon as the relative change between two successive iterates satisfies

$$err := \|u^{(k)} - u^{(k-1)}\|_2 \, / \, \|u^{(k-1)}\|_2 < 10^{-4}. \tag{32}$$

All reported images were created by the software ParaView and its VTK reader, which natively interpolates the false colors sampled over vertices.

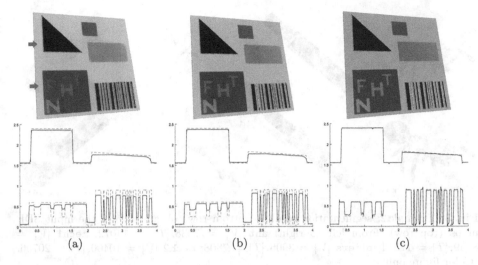

Fig. 2. Example 1: (a) Convex regime for $\tau_c = 0$, (b) CNC regime for $\tau_c = 0.99$, (c) Non-convex regime for $\tau_c = 100$. Boundary contours detected by the third stage of the segmentation algorithm are overimposed for three different partitions. (Color figure online)

Example 1. In our first example, we consider an image function defined on a smooth manifold, a plane, discretized by a mesh of resolution $|V| = 85709$ and $|T| = 171356$. We investigate the usefulness of the considered model both in the convex, CNC and non-convex regimes. In particular, the convex case corresponds to the classical TV-L$_2$ model introduced for image denoising in [11], and is obtained by setting $\tau_c = 0$ in (11), the CNC model is given for $\tau_c = 0.99$ thus maximizing the non-convexity of the penalty term while preserving the overall convexity of the functional $\mathcal{J}$. Finally, for $\tau_c = 100$ we get a strictly non-convex model solved by the same ADMM procedure. We set the regularization parameter $\eta = 0$ and the fidelity parameter λ in the range $[500, 700]$. The input image textured on the plane was corrupted by an additive white Gaussian noise with standard deviation $\sigma = 5 \times 10^{-2}$. The results u^* of the first phase of our segmentation algorithm are shown in Fig. 2 top row, and the associated values along the two lines indicated by red arrows are illustrated in Fig. 2, bottom row. The original intensity values are plotted in red dashed line. For the convex regime in Fig. 2(a) we can observe the typical behavior of TV-L$_2$ model: corners are smoothed and the contrast is decreased. The algorithm is stopped after 59 iterations, with a Root Mean Square Error (RMSE) of 18.88, with respect to the uncorrupted textured image plane. The CNC regime in Fig. 2(b) presents sharper edges and the loss of contrast is decreased. The number of iterations needed for convergence was 55 and RMSE = 13.20. The non-convex regime produces the result shown in Fig. 2(c), with RMSE = 4.19. In this case the algorithm did not converge to the given threshold within the maximum number of iterations 500. Results in Fig. 2 indicate that higher quality restorations can be achieved by

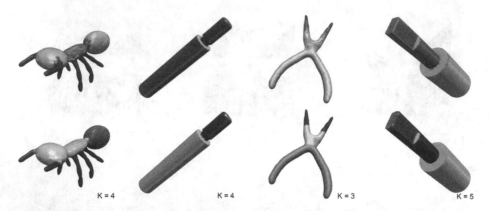

Fig. 3. Example 2: segmentation results (bottom row) obtained from the input SDF maps (top row). From left to right: ant $|V| = 7038, |T| = 14072$; mech1 $|V| = 8759, |T| = 17514$; pliers $|V| = 3906, |T| = 7808$; mech2 $|V| = 10400, |T| = 20796$. (Color figure online)

pushing model (1) beyond its convexity limits, however the numerical convergence is affected by the non-convexity of the functional $\mathcal{J}$.

Example 2. In the second example, we aim to segment a 2-manifold into K disjoint regions that are homogeneous according to a certain feature, in this context represented by the thickness map of the object, computed on the mesh by the so-called Shape Diameter Function (SDF) with the method proposed in [5]. The real-valued SDFs are shown in Fig. 3 top. We applied our algorithm in the CNC regime, namely with $\tau_c = 0.99, \lambda = \{50, 100, 30, 100\}$ and $\eta = 10$, which produced the partition function. Afterwards, the simple thresholding is used in order to clusterize the object into K homogeneously thick parts. The segmented parts, together with the number of partitions K on bottom right, are shown in Fig. 3 bottom, using false colors. We conclude this example presenting an empirical investigation on the numerical convergence of the proposed ADMM-based minimization scheme. By the way of illustration, in Fig. 4 we report the convergence plots concerning the ant model. The plots in Fig. 4 (left column) show the relative change err defined in (32) and the functional values over the iterations in the CNC regime, whereas the right column of Fig. 4 shows the same quantities for the non-convex regime. The plots reported, and the similar results obtained for the other 2-manifolds, confirm that the numerical convergence in the non-convex regime is slower than in the CNC regime.

Example 3. In this example we show how the salient parts are nicely identified by the boundary tracking in the third phase of the segmentation algorithm. In Fig. 5 we show the segmentation of a real-valued function on the mesh hand, $|V| = 26422, |T| = 52840$; which has been corrupted by an additive Gaussian noise with $\sigma = 10^{-2}$. From left to right: the input noisy data, the result u^* of the ADMM algorithm using $\lambda = 200$ and $\eta = 4$, the boundary curves overimposed to

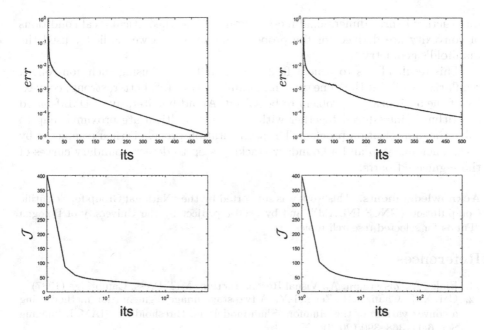

Fig. 4. Example 2: top: relative errors over iterations for **ant** mesh in CNC (left) and non-convex (right) regimes in logarithmic scale in y-axis. bottom: corresponding values of $\mathcal{J}$ in (5) with logarithmic scale of x-axis.

Fig. 5. Example 3: noisy textured mesh, result of the ADMM algorithm, segmented parts in false colors with overimposed the boundary curves, detailed zoom. (Color figure online)

the clusterization of u^*, and a zoomed detail. The boundaries between the segmented parts (black solid line) is detected and then smoothed by projecting the boundary vertices onto the cubic spline obtained by least-squares approximation (white solid line).

6   Conclusions

In this work we presented a new variational CNC model for multiphase segmentation of real-valued functions on manifolds, where a non-convex regularization term allows for penalizing the non-smoothness of the inner segmented parts and preserves the length of the boundaries. The CNC strategy is generalized for unstructured three dimensional meshes/graphs, and theoretical local conditions of convexity are derived for the proposed model where we explicitly used the manifold's geometry.

This result allows to benefit from the advantages of using such non-convex regularizer while, at the same time, maintaining strict (or, better, strong) convexity of the optimization problem to be solved. An ad hoc iterative ADMM-based algorithm is introduced together with a specific multivariate proximal map to solve the minimization problem. The segmentation process is then completed by a thresholding step and a boundary tracking step to detect boundary curves of the segmented parts.

Acknowledgements. This work was supported by the "National Group for Scientific Computation (GNCS-INDAM)" and by ex60% project by the University of Bologna "Funds for selected research topics".

References

1. Blake, A., Zisserman, A.: Visual Reconstruction. MIT Press, Cambridge (1987)
2. Cai, X.H., Chan, R.H., Zeng, T.Y.: A two-stage image segmentation method using a convex variant of the Mumford-Shah model and thresholding. SIAM J. Imaging Sci. **6**(1), 368–390 (2013)
3. Chan, T., Vese, L.: Active contours without edges. IEEE Trans. Image Process. **10**, 266–277 (2001)
4. Chen, P.Y., Selesnick, I.W.: Group-sparse signal denoising: non-convex regularization, convex optimization. IEEE Trans. Signal Process. **62**, 464–3478 (2014)
5. Huska, M., Morigi, S.: A meshless strategy for shape diameter analysis. Vis. Comput. **33**(3), 303–315 (2017)
6. Lanza, A., Morigi, S., Sgallari, F.: Convex image denoising via non-convex regularization. In: Aujol, J.-F., Nikolova, M., Papadakis, N. (eds.) SSVM 2015. LNCS, vol. 9087, pp. 666–677. Springer, Cham (2015). doi:10.1007/978-3-319-18461-6_53
7. Lanza, A., Morigi, S., Sgallari, F.: Convex image denoising via non-convex regularization with parameter selection. J. Math. Imaging Vis. **56**(2), 195–220 (2016)
8. Lanza, A., Morigi, S., Selesnick, I., Sgallari, F.: Nonconvex nonsmooth optimization via convex-nonconvex majorization-minimization. Numerische Math. (2016). doi:10.1007/s00211-016-0842-x
9. Mumford, D., Shah, J.: Optimal approximations by piecewise smooth functions and associated variational problems. Commun. Pure Appl. Math. **42**(5), 577–685 (1989)
10. Nikolova, M.: Estimation of binary images by minimizing convex criteria. In: Proceedings of the IEEE International Conference on Image Processing, vol. 2, pp. 108–112 (1998)
11. Rudin, L.I., Osher, S., Fatemi, E.: Nonlinear total variation based noise removal algorithms. Phys. D **60**(1–4), 259–268 (1992)
12. Tai, X.C., Duan, Y.: Domain decomposition methods with graph cuts algorithms for total variation minimization. Adv. Comput. Math. **36**(2), 175–199 (2012)
13. Wu, C., Zhang, J., Duan, Y., Tai, X.-C.: Augmented Lagrangian method for total variation based image restoration and segmentation over triangulated surfaces. J. Sci. Comput. **50**(1), 145–166 (2012)
14. Zhang, J., Zheng, J., Wu, C., Cai, J.: Variational mesh decomposition. ACM Trans. Graph. **31**(3), 21:1–21:14 (2012)

Numerical Integration of Riemannian Gradient Flows for Image Labeling

Fabrizio Savarino[(✉)], Ruben Hühnerbein, Freddie Åström, Judit Recknagel, and Christoph Schnörr

Image and Pattern Analysis Group, RTG 1653,
Heidelberg University, Heidelberg, Germany
{fabrizio.savarino,freddie.astroem}@iwr.uni-heidelberg.de

Abstract. The image labeling problem can be described as assigning to each pixel a single element from a finite set of predefined labels. Recently, a smooth geometric approach was proposed [2] by following the Riemannian gradient flow of a given objective function on the so-called assignment manifold. In this paper, we adopt an approach from the literature on uncoupled replicator dynamics and extend it to the geometric labeling flow, that couples the dynamics through Riemannian averaging over spatial neighborhoods. As a result, the gradient flow on the assignment manifold transforms to a flow on a vector space of matrices, such that parallel numerical update schemes can be derived by established numerical integration. A quantitative comparison of various schemes reveals a superior performance of the adaptive scheme originally proposed, regarding both the number of iterations and labeling accuracy.

Keywords: Image labeling · Assignment manifold · Riemannian gradient flow · Replicator equation · Multiplicative updates

1 Introduction

Overview, Motivation. The image labeling problem can be described as assigning to each pixel a single element from a finite set of predefined labels. Usually, this is done by finding optima of a globally defined objective function which evaluates the quality of labelings. In general the problem of computing globally optimal labels is NP-hard. Therefore, various relaxations are used to yield a computationally feasible problem [7].

In [2] a smooth geometric approach is proposed on the manifold of row-stochastic matrices with full support, called the *assignment manifold* and denoted by $\mathcal{W} \subset \mathbb{R}^{m \times n}$ (for details see Sect. 2). Their approach is as follows. The assignment manifold $\mathcal{W}$ is turned into a Riemannian manifold by the Fisher Rao

Acknowledgments: We gratefully acknowledge support by the German Science Foundation, grant GRK 1653.

F. Lauze et al. (Eds.): SSVM 2017, LNCS 10302, pp. 361–372, 2017.
DOI: 10.1007/978-3-319-58771-4_29

(information) metric (cf. [5]). The i-th element of a given label set $\mathcal{L} = \{l_1, \ldots l_n\}$ is identified with the i-th corner of the standard simplex, i.e. l_i is identified with the i-th standard unit vector $e_i \in \mathbb{R}^n$. For a chosen distance function, the distance information between the image data and predefined labels $\mathcal{L}$ is collected into distance matrix D. This matrix is lifted onto the manifold $\mathcal{W}$ and denoted by L. Riemannian means (also called Karcher means) are used to transform the lifted distance information L into a similarity matrix S, which induces regularizing dependencies between labels assigned to pixels within a spatial neighbourhood. For a more detailed introduction of the assignment filter we refer again to [2].

The quality of an assignment $W \in \mathcal{W}$ is measured by the correlation with the similarity matrix $S(W) \in \mathcal{W}$. Using the standard inner product $\langle \cdot, \cdot \rangle$ on $\mathbb{R}^{m \times n}$, the corresponding objective function is given by

$$J: \mathcal{W} \to \mathbb{R}, \quad W \mapsto J(W) := \langle W, S(W) \rangle. \tag{1.1}$$

Finding an optimal assignment corresponds to solving the nonlinear smooth optimization problem $\max_{W \in \mathcal{W}} J(W)$. Their optimization approach is to maximize the objective function by following the *Riemannian gradient ascent flow* on the manifold $\mathcal{W}$,

$$\dot{W}(t) = \nabla_{\mathcal{W}} J(W(t)), \quad W(0) = \frac{1}{n} \mathbb{E}, \tag{1.2}$$

where $\mathbb{E}$ is the matrix containing one in every entry. This constitutes an unbiased initialization in every row i at the barycenter of the respective simplex. Due to the specific choice of the Fisher Rao metric, the gradient flow (1.2) can be rewritten as a *coupled non-linear* system of replicator equations for each row W_i, with $i \in [m] := \{1, \ldots, m\}$, given by

$$\dot{W}_i(t) = W_i(t) \cdot \nabla_i J(W(t)) - \langle W_i(t), \nabla_i J(W(t)) \rangle W_i(t), \tag{1.3}$$

where $\nabla_i J(W) = \left(\frac{\partial}{\partial W_{i1}} J(W), \ldots, \frac{\partial}{\partial W_{in}} J(W) \right)$ is the Euclidean gradient and '$\cdot$' denotes the componentwise multiplication of two vectors.

In [2, Sect. 3] an *explicit Euler method* is used to approximate the integral curve of the gradient flow with the *adaptive step-size* of the i-th row explicitly chosen as

$$h_i^{(k)} = \frac{1}{\langle W_i^{(k)}, \nabla_i J(W^{(k)}) \rangle}, \quad W_i^{(k+1)} = \frac{W_i^{(k)} \cdot \nabla_i J(W^{(k)})}{\langle W_i^{(k)}, \nabla_i J(W^{(k)}) \rangle}, \quad i \in [m], \tag{1.4}$$

which results in a multiplicative update scheme for $W_i^{(k)}$. This scheme is then further simplified by approximating the Euclidean gradient with the similarity matrix $\nabla_i J(W) \approx S_i(W)$. An obvious advantage of this update formula is that it is easy to implement and computationally cheap. As demonstrated in [2] this numerical scheme achieved good performance on some academical examples, despite its simplicity.

On the other hand, this numerical scheme *only works for this particular setting*: choice of the Fisher Rao metric, explicit Euler updates with a specific step-size rule, the particular objective function J and the gradient approximation $\nabla_i J(W) \approx S_i(W)$. As a result, if any of these ingredients is changed, the proposed scheme of [2] is not applicable anymore.

Contribution. In this paper we propose a more principled approach in terms of a top down numerical framework. To this end, we generalize the *transformation* of the uncoupled replicator equation from [3] to gradient flows *of arbitrary objective functions on any Riemannian manifold*. This transformation is then applied to the assignment manifold. The main idea is to transform the gradient flow from the assignment manifold $\mathcal{W}$ onto a vector subspace $T^m \subset \mathbb{R}^{m \times n}$ of $m \times n$ matrices, using a diffeomorphism $\exp_C \colon T^m \to \mathcal{W}$ (see Fig. 1). This transformation ensures that the corresponding numerical solution of the gradient flow, computed on T^m, evolves on the assignment manifold $\mathcal{W}$. In this framework, the numerical algorithm can be flexibly chosen and adapted for any objective function and any Riemannian metric on the assignment manifold.

As a second contribution, we use our framework for generating and comparing various multiplicative update schemes, their efficiency regarding the number of iterations, and how they effect the labeling accuracy.

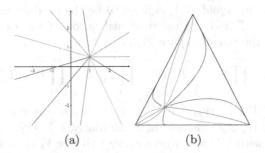

(a)   (b)

Fig. 1. Illustration of the transformation map. For $m = 1$, rays in T originating from a point $x \in T$ (a) are mapped by $\exp_C$ to curves on the simplex (b) starting at $p = \exp_C(x)$. This curves are first-order approximation of the geodesics at p (see Sect. 2).

2   Preliminaries: The Assignment Manifold

We briefly introduce the notation and geometric setting of the assignment manifold from [2]. Let $m, n \in \mathbb{N}_{>0}$. The standard inner product on $\mathbb{R}^n$ as well as on $\mathbb{R}^{m \times n}$ is denoted by $\langle \cdot, \cdot \rangle$ and $\mathbb{1} = (1, 1, \dots, 1)^\top \in \mathbb{R}^n$. Let $\Delta_n = \{p \in \mathbb{R}^n : p_i \geq 0 \text{ for } i = 1, \dots, n, \langle p, \mathbb{1} \rangle = 1\}$ be the probability simplex of dimension $n - 1$. The relative interior of the simplex

$$S := \mathrm{rint}(\Delta_n) = \{p \in \Delta_n : p_i > 0 \text{ for } i = 1, \dots, n\} \qquad (2.1)$$

is a smooth manifold of dimension $n - 1$ with a global chart and an $n - 1$ dimensional constant tangent space

$$T_p S = \{v \in \mathbb{R}^n : \langle v, \mathbb{1} \rangle = 0\} =: T \subset \mathbb{R}^n. \qquad (2.2)$$

There is an orthogonal decomposition $\mathbb{R}^n = T \oplus \mathbb{R}\mathbb{1}$ with respect to $\langle \cdot, \cdot \rangle$ together with the linear projection map onto T given by

$$\pi \colon \mathbb{R}^n \to T, \quad x \mapsto \pi[x] := \left(I - \tfrac{1}{n}\mathbb{1}\mathbb{1}^\top\right)x. \tag{2.3}$$

$\mathcal{S}$ equipped with the Fisher Rao metric becomes a Riemannian manifold. The Fisher Rao metric at $p \in \mathcal{S}$ is given by

$$g_p^{\mathcal{S}} \colon T \times T \to \mathbb{R}, \qquad g_p^{\mathcal{S}}(u,v) = \langle u, \mathrm{Diag}(\tfrac{1}{p})v \rangle, \qquad u, v \in T. \tag{2.4}$$

Since there is a global chart for $\mathcal{S}$ and constant tangent space T, the tangent bundle is trivial $T\mathcal{S} \cong \mathcal{S} \times T$. In order to assure closed form solutions to Riemannian means, the exponential map of $\mathcal{S}$ is approximated in [2] by the so-called *lifting map*

$$\exp \colon T\mathcal{S} = \mathcal{S} \times T \to \mathcal{S}, \quad (p, u) \mapsto \exp_p(u) = \frac{pe^u}{\langle p, e^u \rangle}, \tag{2.5}$$

where e^u is the componentwise exponential. Although, $\exp_p \colon T \longrightarrow \mathcal{S}$ is a diffeomorphism for every $p \in \mathcal{S}$, it is not the exponential map of the Riemannian manifold. However, according to [2, Proposition 3.1] it provides a first-order approximation of the geodesics at $p \in \mathcal{S}$.

The *assignment manifold* $\mathcal{W}$ is defined to be the product manifold given by (2.6). Using $T_p\mathcal{S} = T$ and the usual identification of the tangent space of a product manifold, the tangent space $T_W\mathcal{W}$ of $\mathcal{W}$ at $W \in \mathcal{W}$ is

$$\mathcal{W} := \prod_{i=1}^m \mathcal{S}, \qquad T_W\mathcal{W} = \prod_{i=1}^m T_{W_i}\mathcal{S} = \prod_{i=1}^m T =: T^m. \tag{2.6}$$

An element $W = (W_1, \ldots, W_m)^\top \in \mathcal{W} \subset \mathbb{R}^{m \times n}$ is a $m \times n$ matrix with $W\mathbb{1} = \mathbb{1}$, where the i-th row W_i is an element of $\mathcal{S}$. Similarly, $V = (V_1, \ldots, V_m)^\top \in T^m \subset \mathbb{R}^{m \times n}$ is a matrix with $V\mathbb{1} = 0$, where every i-th row V_i is an element of T. In the following this identification of $\mathcal{W}$ and T^m as subsets of $\mathbb{R}^{m \times n}$ is used.

There is again an orthogonal decomposition $\mathbb{R}^{m \times n} = T^m \oplus \{\lambda^\top \mathbb{E} : \lambda \in \mathbb{R}^m\}$ with respect to $\langle \cdot, \cdot \rangle$, where $\mathbb{E} \in \mathbb{R}^{m \times n}$ is the matrix with $\mathbb{E}_{ij} = 1$ for all entries. The orthogonal projection map onto T^m is given by

$$\Pi \colon \mathbb{R}^{m \times n} \to T^m, \quad X \mapsto \Pi[X] := (\pi[X_1], \ldots, \pi[X_m])^\top, \tag{2.7}$$

with π due to (2.3), and where X_i denotes the i-th row of the matrix $X \in \mathbb{R}^{m \times n}$.

The Fisher Rao metric on every component $\mathcal{S}$ induces a product metric and turns $\mathcal{W}$ into a Riemannian manifold. At $W \in \mathcal{W}$ and for $U, V \in T^m$, this Riemannian metric $g_W^{\mathcal{W}}$ is given by

$$g_W^{\mathcal{W}}(U, V) = \sum_{k=1}^m g_{W_k}^{\mathcal{S}}(U_k, V_k) = \sum_{k=1}^m \langle U_k, \mathrm{Diag}(\tfrac{1}{W_k})V_k \rangle,$$

where W_k, V_k and U_k again denote the k-th row of the matrices W, V and U. The mapping (2.5) naturally extends to $\mathcal{W}$ by (we reuse the symbol exp)

$$\exp \colon \mathcal{W} \times T^m \to \mathcal{W}, \quad (W, V) \mapsto \exp_W(V) = \left(\exp_{W_1}(V_1), \ldots, \exp_{W_m} V_m\right).$$

The map $\exp_W \colon T^m \to \mathcal{W}$ is a diffeomorphism for every $W \in \mathcal{W}$.

3   Transformation of the Gradient Flow

3.1   General Approach: Isometric Manifolds

Before we present the result of this section, we briefly review some basic concepts of differential geometry, based on [1,8].

Let (M, g^M) be a Riemannian manifold and $f : M \to \mathbb{R}$ a smooth function. Using the standard identification $T_r \mathbb{R} = \mathbb{R}$ for $r \in \mathbb{R}$, the Riemannian gradient $\nabla_M f(x)$ of f at $x \in M$ can be defined as the unique element of $T_x M$ satisfying

$$g_x^M(\nabla_M f(x), v) = Df(x)[v], \quad \forall v \in T_x M, \tag{3.1}$$

where $Df(x) : T_x M \to T_{f(x)} \mathbb{R} = \mathbb{R}$ is the differential of f.

Let (N, g^N) be another Riemannian manifold. The *pullback* of the Riemannian metric g^N via a smooth map $F : M \to N$ at $p \in M$ is denoted as $F^* g_p^N : T_p M \times T_p M \to \mathbb{R}$ and defined by

$$\left(F^* g^N\right)_p (v, u) = g_{F(p)}^N \left(DF(p)[v], DF(p)[u]\right), \quad u, v \in T_p M. \tag{3.2}$$

In general, $F^* g^N$ need not be positive definite and hence may not be a Riemannian metric. If $F : M \to N$ is an immersion, however, then $g^M := F^* g^N$ is a Riemannian metric.

An *isometry* is a diffeomorphism $F : (M, g^M) \to (N, g^N)$ between Riemannian manifolds with $F^* g^N = g^M$. Using standard arguments from differential geometry we have the following.

Lemma 1. *Let* $F : (M, g^M) \to (N, g^N)$ *be an isometry between two Riemannian manifolds and* $f : N \to \mathbb{R}$ *as well as* $\bar{f} : M \to \mathbb{R}$ *be smooth real valued functions with* $\bar{f} = f \circ F$, *i.e. the diagram commutes. Then the Riemannian gradients of* f *and* $\bar{f}$ *are related for every* $x \in M$ *by* $\nabla_N f(F(x)) = DF(x)[\nabla_M \bar{f}(x)]$.

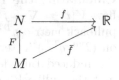

An immediate consequence of the previous lemma is the following.

Proposition 1. *Suppose* (M, g^M) *and* (N, g^N) *are isometric Riemannian manifolds with isometry* $F : M \to N$. *Let* $f : N \to \mathbb{R}$ *be a smooth function and set* $\bar{f} = f \circ F : M \to \mathbb{R}$. *Furthermore, let* $C \subset \mathbb{R}$ *be an open interval with* $0 \in C$. *Then* $\gamma : C \to N$ *with* $\gamma(0) = y_0$ *solves (3.3)(a) if and only if the curve* $\eta : C \to M$ *with* $\gamma = F \circ \eta$ *and* $\eta(0) = F^{-1}(y_0)$ *solves (3.3)(b).*

$$\text{(a)} \quad \dot{\gamma}(t) = \nabla_N f(\gamma(t)) \qquad \text{(b)} \quad \dot{\eta}(t) = \nabla_M \bar{f}(\eta(t)). \tag{3.3}$$

3.2   Application to the Assignment Manifold

Transformation for the Assignment Manifold. The idea of transforming a gradient flow on $\mathcal{W}$ onto a vector space is as follows. Set $C := \frac{1}{n} \mathbb{E} \in \mathcal{W}$, i.e. every row $C_i = \frac{1}{n}\mathbb{1} \in \mathcal{S}$ is the barycenter of the simplex. The tangent space $T_C \mathcal{W} = T^m \subset \mathbb{R}^{m \times n}$ is a vector subspace and itself a smooth manifold. Using the diffeomorphism $\exp_C \colon T^m \to \mathcal{W}$, we turn T^m into a Riemannian manifold through the pullback metric $g^{T^m} := \exp_C^* g^{\mathcal{W}}$. By construction, $\exp_C$ is an isometry between (T^m, g^{T^m}) and $(\mathcal{W}, g^{\mathcal{W}})$.

Suppose now $f \colon \mathcal{W} \to \mathbb{R}$ is a smooth function and set $\bar{f} := f \circ \exp_C \colon T^m \to \mathbb{R}$. Let $\nabla_{\mathcal{W}} f$ and $\nabla_{T^m} \bar{f}$ denote the Riemannian gradient of $(\mathcal{W}, g^{\mathcal{W}})$ and (T^m, g^{T^m}) respectively. Then we can transform the gradient flow of f due to Proposition 1.

Corollary 1. *Given the setting above, the curve $t \mapsto W(t) \in \mathcal{W}$ with $W(0) = C$ solves the gradient flow (3.4)(a) if and only if the curve $t \mapsto V(t) \in T^m$ with $V(0) = 0$ and $W(t) = \exp_C\big(V(t)\big)$ solves the gradient flow (3.4)(b).*

$$\text{(a)} \quad \dot{W}(t) = \nabla_{\mathcal{W}} f(W(t)) \qquad \text{(b)} \quad \dot{V}(t) = \nabla_{T^m} \bar{f}\big(V(t)\big). \tag{3.4}$$

Remark 1. The above construction works in general. One can choose any Riemannian metric on $\mathcal{S}$, define the induced product metric on $\mathcal{W}$ and then turn $\exp_C$ into an isometry by using the pullback metric on T^m.

Corollary 1 enables the transformation of the Riemannian gradient flow (1.2), which has the form (3.4)(a), to a flow of the form (3.4)(b) on the vector space $T^m \subset \mathbb{R}^{m \times n}$, to which standard numerical methods can be applied. Furthermore, this formulation ensures that the corresponding flow in terms of $W(t)$ always stays on the assignment manifold, and that there is no need for projecting onto the simplex after a numerical integration step.

Calculating the Riemannian Gradient. In order to compute the gradient flow $\dot{V}(t) = \nabla_{T^m} \bar{f}$ of a pullback function $\bar{f} = f \circ \exp_C$ with respect to the pullback metric $g^{T^m} = \exp_C^* g^{\mathcal{W}}$, we express the Riemannian gradient $\nabla_{T^m} \bar{f}$ on (T^m, g^{T^m}) in terms of the Euclidean gradients $\nabla \bar{f}$ and ∇f with respect to the induced Euclidean structure of $T^m, \mathcal{W} \subset \mathbb{R}^{m \times n}$. To this end, we express first the pullback metric g^{T^m} in terms of the canonical inner product $\langle \cdot, \cdot \rangle$ on $T^m \subset \mathbb{R}^{m \times n}$.

Lemma 2. *Let $U, V \in T^m$. For any $X \in T^m$, the pullback metric g^{T^m} on T^m is given by $g_X^{T^m}(U, V) = \langle U, D\exp_C(X)[V] \rangle$.*

Proof. Set $W = \exp_C(X)$. It follows from the proof of [2, Proposition 3.1] that the differential of the lifting map $\exp_{C_i} \colon T \to \mathcal{S}$ onto the simplex is given by $D\exp_{C_i}(X_i) = \text{Diag}(W_i) - W_i W_i^\top$ with $W_i = \exp_{C_i}(X_i)$ for all $i = 1, \ldots, m$. A short calculation using this explicit formula and the orthogonal projection $\pi \colon \mathbb{R}^n \to T$ given by (2.3) shows $\pi \circ \text{Diag}(\frac{1}{W_i}) \circ D\exp_{C_i}(X_i)[V_i] = V_i$. Insertion into the definition of the pullback metric g^{T^m} proves the statement. $\qquad\square$

Lemma 3. *The Euclidean gradients of $\bar{f} = f \circ \exp_C$ and f at $X \in T^m$ are related by $\nabla \bar{f}(X) = D\exp_C(X)\big[\nabla f\big(\exp_C(X)\big)\big]$.*

Proof. With $W = \exp_C(X)$, we have for all $V \in T^m$

$$\langle \nabla \bar{f}(X), V \rangle = D\bar{f}(X)[V] = Df(W)[D\exp_C(X)[V]]$$
$$= \langle \nabla f(W), D\exp_C(X)[V] \rangle = \langle D\exp_C(X)[\nabla f(W)], V \rangle,$$

where the last equality holds due to the symmetry of $D\exp_C(X)$ with respect to the Euclidean metric on $\mathbb{R}^{m \times n}$. Thus, $\nabla \bar{f}(X) = D\exp_C(X)[\nabla f(W)]$. $\square$

Lemma 4. *Given the setting above, the Riemannian gradient of $\bar{f} : T^m \to \mathbb{R}$ with respect to g^{T^m} is given by $\nabla_{T^m} \bar{f}(X) = \nabla f(\exp_C(X))$.*

Proof. Let $X \in T^m$. Due to the formula of Lemma 2, we have

$$D\bar{f}(X)[V] = g_X^{T^m}(\nabla_{T^m}\bar{f}(X), V) = \langle D\exp_C(X)[\nabla_{T^m}\bar{f}(X)], V \rangle, \qquad (3.5)$$

for all $V \in T^m$. Using the induced inner product on $T^m \subset \mathbb{R}^{m \times n}$ yields the Euclidean gradient $\nabla \bar{f}(X)$ with $D\bar{f}(X)[V] = \langle \nabla \bar{f}(X), V \rangle$ for all $V \in T^m$. Combining these two equations gives $\langle \nabla \bar{f}(X), V \rangle = \langle D\exp_C(X)[\nabla_{T^m}\bar{f}(X)], V \rangle$ for all $V \in T^m$ and therefore $D\exp_C(X)[\nabla_{T^m}\bar{f}(X)] = \nabla \bar{f}(X)$. By Lemma 3

$$D\exp_C(X)[\nabla_{T^m}\bar{f}(X)] = \nabla \bar{f}(X) = D\exp_C(X)[\nabla f(\exp_C(X))]$$

and the statement follows, since $D\exp_C(X)$ is a vector space isomorphism. $\square$

Now we return to the objective function (1.1) from [2], given by $J(W) = \langle W, S(W) \rangle$ for $W \in \mathcal{W}$. We are prepared to use the transformed gradient flow for solving the maximization problem $\max_{W \in \mathcal{W}} J(W)$. Applying Corollary 1 to the gradient flow (1.2) on $\mathcal{W}$ yields the flow $\dot{V} = \nabla_{T^m} \bar{J}(V(t))$ on the tangent space, with $\bar{J} = J \circ \exp_C$. Due to Lemma 4, we further have $\dot{V}(t) = \nabla J(\exp_C(V(t)))$. It remains to compute the Euclidean gradient $\nabla J(W) \in T^m$.

Lemma 5. *The Euclidean gradient of $J : \mathcal{W} \to \mathbb{R}$ with $J(W) = \langle W, S(W) \rangle$ is given by*

$$\nabla J(W) = \Pi[S(W)] + DS(W)^* \circ \Pi[W],$$

where $DS(W)^*$ is the adjoint linear map of $DS(W) : T^m \to T^m$ with respect to the Euclidean inner product $\langle \cdot, \cdot \rangle$ on T^m, and $\Pi : \mathbb{R}^{m \times n} \to T^m$ is the orthogonal projection given by (2.7).

Proof. A smooth curve $\gamma : (-\epsilon, \epsilon) \to \mathcal{W}$ with $\gamma(0) = W, \dot{\gamma}(0) = V \in T^m$ gives

$$DJ(W)[V] = \frac{d}{dt} J(\gamma(t))\Big|_{t=0} = \langle \dot{\gamma}(t), S(\gamma(t)) \rangle\Big|_{t=0} + \langle \gamma(t), \frac{d}{dt} S(\gamma(t)) \rangle\Big|_{t=0}$$
$$= \langle V, S(W) \rangle + \langle W, DS(W)[V] \rangle.$$

Using the projection $\Pi : \mathbb{R}^{m \times n} \to T^m$, we decompose W and $S(W)$ into $W = \Pi[W] + U_W$ and $S(W) = \Pi[S(W)] + U_S$, with $U_W, U_S \in (T^m)^{\perp}$. Due to $V, DS(W)[W] \in T^m$ these orthogonal decompositions give

$$\langle V, S(W) \rangle + \langle W, DS(W)[V] \rangle = \langle V, \Pi[S(W)] \rangle + \langle \Pi[W], DS(W)[V] \rangle$$
$$= \langle V, \Pi[S(W)] \rangle + \langle DS(W)^* \circ \Pi[W], V \rangle,$$

where $DS(W)^*$ is the adjoint linear map of $DS(W)$. Thus, we have $DJ(W)[V] = \langle \Pi[S(W)] + DS(W)^* \circ \Pi[W], V \rangle$, $\forall V \in T^m$, which proves the claim. $\square$

Summing up, we obtain the explicit form of the flow (3.4)(b) in the specific case $\bar{f} = \bar{J} = J \circ \exp_C$.

Theorem 1. *Solving the gradient flow* (1.2) *from* [2] *is equivalent to* $W(t) = \exp_C(V(t))$, *where* $V(t)$ *solves*

$$\dot{V}(t) = \nabla J\big(W(t)\big) = \Pi\big[S(W)\big] + DS(W)^* \circ \Pi[W], \qquad V(0) = 0. \qquad (3.6)$$

4   Numerical Approach

Multiplicative Update Formulae. The reformulation of the gradient flow on the tangent space enables the application of a broad range of numerical schemes. We discretize the transformed flow using explicit Runge–Kutta methods [6, Chap. II.2]. A general iteration step for each row $i = 1, \ldots, m$ reads

$$V_i^{(k+1)} = V_i^{(k)} + h^{(k)} P_i^{(k)}, \quad W_i^{(k+1)} = \exp_{C_i}\big(V_i^{(k+1)}\big) = \frac{W_i^{(k)} e^{h^{(k)} P_i^{(k)}}}{\langle W_i^{(k)}, e^{h^{(k)} P_i^{(k)}} \rangle}, \tag{4.1}$$

where $h^{(k)} \in \mathbb{R}_{>0}$ denotes the step-size and $P_i^{(k)}$ the direction in the k-th iteration. We point out the similarity to the multiplicative updates (1.4) and the ability to modify them, through the choice of a numerical integration method represented by $P_i^{(k)}$ of (4.1).

Assignment Normalization. Let $W(t) \in \mathcal{W}$ be a smooth curve solving the gradient flow (1.2). Based on [2, Conjecture 3.1], every row $W_i(t) \in \mathcal{S}$ of this solution curve is expected to approach some vertex of the simplex for $t \to \infty$. As a consequence, all but one entry of $W_i(t)$ approach 0 as $t \to \infty$. However, the numerical computations also have to evolve on $\mathcal{W}$, i.e. all entries of $W(t)$ have to be positive all the time. Since, there is a difference between mathematical and numerical positivity, we adopt the strategy in [2] to avoid these numerical problems. This is done by restricting the discrete flow of every row $W_i(t)$ onto the ε -simplex $\Delta_\varepsilon := \{p \in \Delta_n : p_i \geq \varepsilon \text{ for } i = 1, \ldots, n\}$ through a normalization step (cf. [2, Sect. 3.3.1]), after each iteration.

Let $V(t) \in T^m$ be the solution of the transformed gradient flow and $W(t) = \exp_C(V(t))$. The convergence of each $W_i(t) \in \mathcal{S}$, $i \in [m]$ to some vertex of the simplex translates to the convergence of each $V_i(t) \in T$, $i \in [m]$ to infinity in a certain direction, as depicted in Fig. 1. In order to normalize $W(t)$, we restrict each $V_i(t)$ to the closed ball $B_R(0) \subset T^m$ of radius $R > 0$ centered at 0. This can be seen as a smooth approximation of the ε-simplex by choosing the radius R such that the image of the sphere $\partial B_R(0)$ under $\exp_C$ intersects Δ_ε at the vertices (Fig. 2c).

As shown in [4], the normalization in [2] dramatically influences the discrete flow. Therefore, it is expected that the normalization on the tangent space influences the discrete flow as well. In this paper, however, we investigate the flow up to the smooth ε boundary for $\varepsilon = 10^{-10}$ (Fig. 2c) and leave a numerical analysis of the flow *on* this boundary for follow-up work.

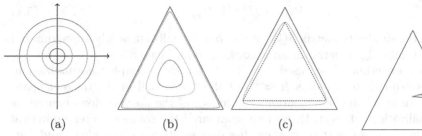

Fig. 2. Assignment Normalization on the Tangent Space. Illustration of how balls centered at 0 on the tangent space T (a) are mapped by each component of $\exp_C \colon T^m \to \mathcal{W}$ onto the simplex (b) in order to smoothly approximate the ε-simplex Δ_ε (c dashed line).

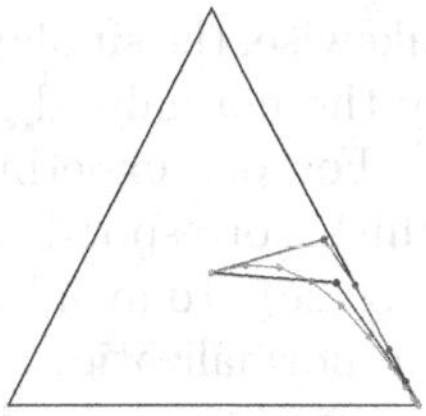

Fig. 3. Typical stepsizes. Manifold approach: red line. Tangent space: green line step length 1, blue line step length 5. (Color figure online)

5 Experiments

In this section we investigate the influence of the discretization method and the specific choice of the step-size in [2], by comparing it to our approach using a more accurate discretization. In [2], an adaptive step-size for the i-th row $W_i^{(k)}$ in the k-th iteration is explicitly set to $h_i^{(k)}$ given by (1.4) in order to arrive at the multiplicative update scheme (1.4) for numerically integrating the gradient flow (1.3). At first glance, this choice seems rather non-intuitive: During the initial phase of the iteration, when W_i and S_i are *uncorrelated*, then $\langle W_i^{(k)}, S_i(W^{(k)}) \rangle \approx 0$ and the step-sizes are *large*, whereas if they are *correlated*, then the step-sizes are *small* and slow down the convergence of the algorithm.

Our focus in this paper is on the *initial phase of the iteration where by far the most assignments of labels emerge*: Do the aggressive step-sizes (1.4) affect the quality of the resulting labeling?

Set-Up and Implementation. For this assessment, we chose an academical labeling scenario depicted by Fig. 4. The color image comprised 256 colors which also served as labels $\mathcal{C} = \{c_1, \ldots, c_{256}\}$. By shuffling colors at randomly chosen pixel locations we created a noisy version as input for the different methods. The labeling task is to recover the ground truth image. The success of this task is measured by the percentage of correctly labeled pixels.

In order to compare impartially the discretization methods we also used the simplified gradient on the tangent space $\nabla J(W) \approx \Pi[S(W)]$ (cf. [2, Sect. 3.3.3]). The main intuition behind this simplification is that the similarity matrix $S(W)$ is the result of averaging over spatial neighborhoods and therefore is expected to change slowly, i.e. $DS(W) \approx 0$. Due to this assumption and in view of Theorem 1 the transformed flow simplifies to

$$\dot{V}(t) = \Pi\big[S(W(t))\big]. \tag{5.1}$$

Likewise, the similarity matrix $S(W)$ is computationally efficiently approximated by the normalized geometric mean according to [2, Lemma 3.3].

For our experiments we used $\varepsilon = 10^{-10}$ for the ε-simplex normalization, which corresponds to a radius $R \approx 23$ of the closed ball in the tangent space (Fig. 2c). To avoid the aforementioned influence of the *discrete* flows caused by the normalization (cf. Sect. 4), we only compared the solutions after numerical integration *up to the first time where the flow meets the ε-simplices and normalization occurs* (cf. Fig. 2). Due to this termination criterion not all the rows $W_i^{(k)} \in \mathcal{S}$ may have converged to a vertex of the respective simplex.

After termination of every discretization method, we do the following to obtain an unique labeling as output. At every pixel i, we choose label $c_{k_i} \in \mathcal{C}$ with k_i the column index of the maximum entry of $W_i = (W_{i1}, \dots, W_{i256})$.

For the integration of the gradient flow (5.1) on the tangent space, we considered the common *explicit Euler method*, which reads

$$V_i^{(k+1)} = V_i^{(k)} + h^{(k)} \Pi\big[S(W^{(k)})\big], \tag{5.2}$$

and *Heun's method*, which reads

$$\tilde{V}_i^{(k+1)} = V_i^{(k)} + h^{(k)} \Pi\big[S(W^{(k)})\big],$$
$$V_i^{(k+1)} = V_i^{(k)} + \frac{h^{(k)}}{2}\big(\Pi\big[S(W^{(k)})\big] + \Pi\big[S(\tilde{W}^{(k+1)})\big]\big). \tag{5.3}$$

In both cases we us the initial value $V^{(0)} = 0$. For more details about these methods, we refer e.g. to [6, Chap. II.2].

Results. Figure 4 and Table 1 summarize our quantitative findings. The approach [2] ('manifold approach') is compared to the two schemes (5.2) and (5.3) ('tangent space approach') using three different stepsizes for each, and three different scales for spatial regularization (neighbourhood size $|\mathcal{N}_\varepsilon|$ for geometric averaging). During all experiments the selectivity parameter ρ ([2, Sect. 3.1]) for scaling the distance matrix is chosen to be constant. Observations:

(i) Despite early termination after first-time hitting the ε-simplex boundary, $\geq 93\%$ *correct* decisions are made by *all* methods, for a reasonable strength of regularization ($\geq 5 \times 5$ neighbourhoods). The performance is slightly inferior for weak regularization (3×3 neighbourhood), due to the influence of noise. It also deteriorates for larger spatial scales, because then signal structure is regarded as noise, too (compare the slightly decreasing performance of 7×7 vs. 5×5).

(ii) Although the manifold approach takes the *minimal* number of updates (listed as numbers in brackets) due to the aggressive adaptive stepsizes (1.4), it performed *best*!

Observation (ii) is our major – somewhat surprising – finding: A more careful numerical evolution and integration of the Riemannian gradient flow does *not*

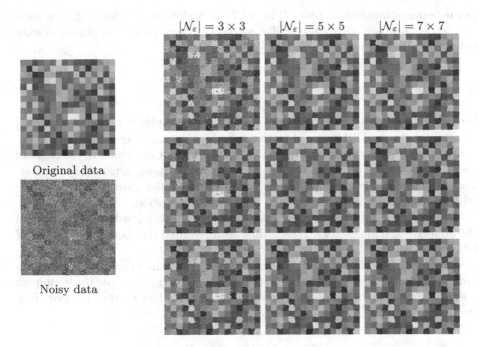

Fig. 4. Step-size influence on labeling. First row: method from [2]. Second row: Explicit Euler method on the tangent space with constant step-size 1. Third row Heun's method on the tangent space with step-size 1. All experiments where done with $\rho = 0.1$. (Color figure online)

Table 1. Labeling performance of geometric flows. The table displays for each integration method the percentages of correctly labeled pixels and the number of iterations in parentheses until the first normalization occurs. h_{adapt} denotes the adaptive step-sizes of [2] given by (1.4). We compare h_{adapt} with constant step-sizes on the tangent space with length $h_{\mathrm{const}}^1 = 1$, $h_{\mathrm{const}}^5 = 5$ and $h_{\mathrm{const}}^{10} = 10$. For an interpretation of the parameters ρ and $|\mathcal{N}_\varepsilon|$, we refer to [2, Sect. 3.1]. See Sect. 5, paragraph 'Results', for a discussion of the table.

$\rho = 0.1$		Manifold approach	Tangent space approach					
			Explicit Euler			Heun's method		
Step-size		h_{adapt}	h_{const}^1	h_{const}^5	h_{const}^{10}	h_{const}^1	h_{const}^5	h_{const}^{10}
Neighborhood size $|\mathcal{N}_\varepsilon|$	3×3	87,7	90,6	89,4	89,0	91,1	91,0	91,3
		(2)	(24)	(5)	(3)	(24)	(5)	(3)
	5×5	95,1	93,7	94,0	94,2	93,6	93,5	93,4
		(3)	(24)	(5)	(3)	(24)	(5)	(3)
	7×7	94,9	93,5	93,8	94,0	93,3	92,9	93,3
		(3)	(26)	(6)	(3)	(25)	(6)	(3)

pay in terms of labeling accuracy (Fig. 3)! This validates the claim of [2] that their geometric approach yields robust flows towards high-quality labelings, despite being overall non-convex.

6   Conclusion

We generalized the transformation of the uncoupled replicator equation from [3] to gradient flows of arbitrary objective functions on any Riemannian manifold. This transformation was then applied to the assignment manifold, to reformulate the gradient flow of [2] for image labeling on a vector space, amenable to numerical integration. This enables the generation of parallel multiplicative update schemes using etablished methods of numerical integration.

A comparison of various update schemes reveales a remarkable efficiency of the adaptive scheme used in [2] regarding *both* required number of iterations and labeling accuracy.

Our further work will study a major extension of the present framework, in order to address the open point: How to cope with the flow *on* the ε-simplex boundary in a *continuous and efficient* manner, similar to the 'interior' flow studied in this paper.

References

1. Absil, P.-A., Mathony, R., Sepulchre, R.: Optimization Algorithms on Matrix Manifolds. Princeton University Press, Princeton, Woodstock (2008)
2. Åström, F., Petra, S., Schmitzer, B., Schnörr, C.: Image labeling by assignment. J. Math. Imaging Vis. **58**(2), 211–238 (2017)
3. Ay, N., Erb, I.: On a notion of linear replicator equations. J. Dyn. Differ. Equ. **17**(2), 427–451 (2005)
4. Bergmann, R., Fitschen, J.H., Persch, J., Steidl, G.: Iterative multiplicative filters for data labeling. Int. J. Comput. Vis. 1–19 (2017). http://dx.doi.org/10.1007/s11263-017-0995-9
5. Burbea, J., Rao, C.R.: Entropy differential metric, distance and divergence measures in probability spaces: a unified approach. J. Multivar. Anal. **12**, 575–596 (1982)
6. Hairer, E., Nørsett, S.P., Wanner, G.: Solving Ordinary Differential Equations I. Springer Series in Computational Mathematics, vol. 8, 2nd edn. Springer, Berlin (1993)
7. Kappes, J.H., Andres, B., Hamprecht, F.A., Schnörr, C., Nowozin, S., Batra, D., Kim, S., Kausler, B.X., Kröger, T., Lellmann, J., Komodakis, N., Savchynskyy, B., Rother, C.: A comparative study of modern inference techniques for structured discrete energy minimization problems. IJCV **155**(2), 155–184 (2015)
8. Lee, J.M.: Introduction to Smooth Manifolds. Springer, New York (2003)

MAP Image Labeling Using Wasserstein Messages and Geometric Assignment

Freddie Åström$^{(\boxtimes)}$, Ruben Hühnerbein, Fabrizio Savarino, Judit Recknagel, and Christoph Schnörr

Image and Pattern Analysis Group, RTG 1653,
Heidelberg University, Heidelberg, Germany
`freddie.astroem@iwr.uni-heidelberg.de`

Abstract. Recently, a smooth geometric approach to the image labeling problem was proposed [1] by following the Riemannian gradient flow of a given objective function on the so-called assignment manifold. The approach evaluates user-defined data term and additionally performs Riemannian averaging of the assignment vectors for spatial regularization. In this paper, we consider more elaborate graphical models, given by both data and pairwise regularization terms, and we show how they can be evaluated using the geometric approach. This leads to a novel inference algorithm on the assignment manifold, driven by local Wasserstein flows that are generated by pairwise model parameters. The algorithm is massively edge-parallel and converges to an integral labeling solution.

Keywords: Image labeling · Graphical models · Message passing · Wasserstein distance · Assignment manifold · Riemannian gradient flow · Replicator equation · Multiplicative updates

1 Introduction

Overview. Let $\mathcal{G} = (\mathcal{V}, \mathcal{E})$ denote a grid graph embedded into the image domain $\Omega \subset \mathbb{R}^2$. Vertices $i, j, \ldots \in \mathcal{V}$ index grid positions. A random variable $x_i \in \mathcal{X}$ is assigned to each position i, which takes values in a finite set $\mathcal{X}$ of so-called labels. *Image labeling* commonly denotes the minimization problem

$$\min_{x \in \mathcal{X}^{|\mathcal{V}|}} E(x), \qquad E(x) = \sum_{i \in \mathcal{V}} E_i(x_i) + \sum_{ij \in \mathcal{E}} E_{ij}(x_i, x_j) \qquad (1.1)$$

for a given objective function that comprises local functions E_i, E_{ij}, which define a data term and a regularizer, respectively. The data term is typically based on local predictors of the labels, that are trained offline based on observed image features. The latter pairwise terms measure the similarity of labels assigned to adjacent pixel positions and thus enforce spatially smooth label assignments.

The image labeling problem covers a broad range of applications. Accordingly, methods for approximately solving the combinatorial problem (1.1) have attracted a lot of research activities – see [7] for a recent survey.

© Springer International Publishing AG 2017
F. Lauze et al. (Eds.): SSVM 2017, LNCS 10302, pp. 373–385, 2017.
DOI: 10.1007/978-3-319-58771-4_30

The basic *convex relaxation* of (1.1) is based on a reformulation of the objective function in terms of local vectors

$$\theta_i = \big(\theta_i(x_i)\big)_{x_i \in \mathcal{X}} \in \mathbb{R}^{|\mathcal{X}|}, \qquad \theta_{ij} = \big(\theta_{ij}(x_i, x_j)\big)_{x_i, x_j \in \mathcal{X}} \in \mathbb{R}^{|\mathcal{X}|^2}, \qquad (1.2)$$

whose components are equal to the function values $E_i(x_i), E_{ij}(x_i, x_j)$. Defining in a similar way local indicator vectors $\mu_i \in \{0,1\}^{|\mathcal{X}|}, \mu_{ij} \in \{0,1\}^{|\mathcal{X}|^2}$ yields the linear representation $E_i(x_i) = \langle \theta_i, \mu_i \rangle$ and $E_{ij}(x_i, x_j) = \langle \theta_{ij}, \mu_{ij} \rangle$. Collecting all local terms into vectors θ and μ, respectively, and relaxing the integrality constraint, yields the so-called *local polytope relaxation* [14,16]

$$\min_{\mu} \langle \theta, \mu \rangle \quad \text{subject to} \quad \mu \in \mathcal{P}, \qquad \mathcal{P} = \Big\{ \mu \colon \sum_{x_i \in \mathcal{X}} \mu_{ij}(x_i, x_j) = \mu_j(x_j), \quad (1.3a)$$

$$\sum_{x_j \in \mathcal{X}} \mu_{ij}(x_i, x_j) = \mu_i(x_i), \quad \mu_{ij} \geq 0, \quad \mu_i \in \Delta_c, \quad \forall i \in \mathcal{V}, \forall ij \in \mathcal{E} \Big\}, \quad (1.3b)$$

where $\Delta_c \subset \mathbb{R}^c, c = |\mathcal{X}|$ denotes the $(c-1)$-dimensional probability simplex. It is well known [17] that this relaxation is only exact for *acyclic* graphs $\mathcal{G}$. For cyclic graphs and image grid graphs, in particular, minimizers $\mu^* \notin \{0,1\}^{\dim(\mu)}$ are not integral, in general. As a consequence, some rounding method is applied to μ^* as postprocessing.

The recent work [1] proposed a *smooth non-convex* approach to the image labeling problem. It is entirely defined in terms of local vectors $W_i \in \text{rint}(\Delta_c)$, $i \in \mathcal{V}$ that live on the relative interior of the simplex which is turned into a simple manifold (see Sect. 2). These vectors are determined by local information, analogous to the data terms $E_i(x)$ of (1.1). In addition, spatial regularization is enforced by computing Riemannian means of the vectors W_i within a local neighborhood around each pixel location i. By construction, the algorithm returns *integral* solutions that make a postprocessing step obsolete. The work [2] studies the multiplicative numerical scheme used in [1], along with a variant, and provides a convergence analysis.

Contribution. The objective of the present paper is to adopt and extend the approach of [1] in order to evaluate established graphical models of the form (1.1), which abound in the literature. This raises the question as to how to take into account the regularizing terms of (1.1). This will be accomplished (i) by regularized Wasserstein distances between adjacent assignment vectors $W_i, W_j, ij \in \mathcal{E}$ (these vectors replace μ_i, μ_j in our approach) that are directly based on the given model parameters θ_{ij}, and (ii) by evolving the corresponding Riemannian gradient on the assignment manifold, as proposed in [1]; see Fig. 1 for an illustration. The resulting approach adds a novel inference algorithm for the image labeling problem to the literature [7]. It may be seen as a sparse interior point algorithm that is exact on acyclic graphs (Lemma 1), and simultaneously performs relaxation and rounding to integrality in a smooth geometric fashion on cyclic graphs. See the Remarks 1, 2 and Sect. 3 for additional detailed comments that classify and position our work.

Related Work. Optimal transport and the Wasserstein distance have become a major tool of image modeling and analysis [8]. Regarding the finite-dimensional formulation in terms of linear programs, we apply the standard device of enhancing convexity through entropic regularization, which increases smoothness in the dual domain. We refer e.g. to [13] and [3, Ch. 9] for basic related work and the connection to matrix scaling algorithms and the history. A smoothed version of the basic Sinkhorn algorithm has become popular in machine learning due to [4], and smoothed Wasserstein distances have been comprehensively investigated in [5,10] for computing Wasserstein barycenters and interpolation. Our approach to image labeling, in conjunction with the geometric approach of [1], is novel.

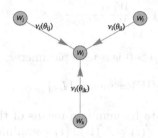

Fig. 1. Illustration of a key aspect of our approach for a given graph $\mathcal{G} = (\mathcal{V}, \mathcal{E})$. Marginals $W_v \in \mathcal{S}$, $v \in \{i, j, k, l\} \subset \mathcal{V}$ assigned to pixel positions v evolve on the assignment manifold $\mathcal{S}$. Regularization parameters θ_e, $e \in \{ij, ik, il\} \subset \mathcal{E}$ of a given graphical model define Wasserstein distances between pairs of marginals that are incident to edge e. These distances generate *Wasserstein messages* $\nu_v(\theta_e)$ that drive the evolution of W_i, in addition to ordinary local data terms based on observed data.

Organization. Section 2 introduces components of the approach of [1] on which our approach is based on. Our approach is detailed in Sect. 3. Numerical experiments validate and illustrate our approach in Sect. 4.

Basic Notation. $\langle \cdot, \cdot \rangle$ denotes the canonical inner product inducing the Euclidean norm $\|v\| = \langle v, v \rangle^{1/2}$ for vectors or the Frobenius norm $\|A\|_F = \langle A, A \rangle^{1/2}$ in the cases of matrices. $\mathbb{1} = (1, 1, \dots, 1)^\top$ of appropriate dimension. Functions apply componentwise to vectors, e.g. $e^v = (e^{v_1}, \dots, e^{v_n})^\top$. The componentwise multiplication of vectors is denoted as $p \cdot q = (p_1 q_1, \dots, p_n q_n)^\top$. Likewise, we write $\frac{q}{p} := p^{-1} \cdot q$ for the componentwise subdivision by a strictly positive vectors. The set $\mathcal{L}_c = \{e_1, \dots, e_c\}$ collects the c unit vectors as extreme points of the probability simplex $\Delta_c = \{p \in \mathbb{R}_+^c : \langle \mathbb{1}, p \rangle = 1\}$. The indicator function of a closed convex set C is denoted by $\delta_C(x) = 0$ if $x \in C$, and $\delta_C(x) = +\infty$ otherwise. We set $n = |\mathcal{V}|$ and $[c] = \{1, 2, \dots, c\}$ for $c \in \mathbb{N}$.

2   Image Labeling on the Assignment Manifold

We collect components of the approach [1] that are required to introduce our approach in Sect. 3.

Analogous to the vectors μ_i of (1.3), the basic variables are vectors $W_i \in \mathcal{S} :=$ rint(Δ_c), $i \in \mathcal{V}$, with $\mathcal{S}$ denoting the relative interior of the probability simplex equipped with the Fisher-Rao metric. A label is assigned to pixel i whenever the vectors W_i are ε-close to some unit vector from the set $\mathcal{L}_c$.

Let f_i, $i \in \mathcal{V}$ denote observed data and f_j^*, $j \in [c]$ given labels. The choice of a distance function $d(\cdot, \cdot)$ defines the distance vectors

$$D_i = \left(d(f_i, f_1^*), \ldots, d(f_i, f_c^*)\right)^\top \in \mathbb{R}^c \tag{2.1}$$

and in turn the likelihood vectors

$$L_i(W_i) = \exp_{W_i}(-U_i/\rho) := \frac{W_i \cdot e^{-U_i/\rho}}{\langle W_i, e^{-U_i/\rho}\rangle} \in \mathcal{S}, \qquad U_i = D_i - \frac{1}{c}\langle \mathbb{1}, D_i\rangle \mathbb{1}, \quad (2.2)$$

at every pixel $i \in \mathcal{V}$, where $\rho > 0$ is a user parameter. Next similarity vectors

$$S_i(W) = \text{mean}_{\mathcal{S}}\{L_j\}_{j \in \overline{\mathcal{N}}(i)} \tag{2.3}$$

are computed as approximate Riemannian means of the likelihood vectors over *closed* local neighborhoods $\overline{\mathcal{N}}(i) = \mathcal{N}(i) \cup \{i\}$ containing the center pixel i. The matrix $W \in \mathcal{W} \in \mathbb{R}^{n \times c}$ collects the vectors W_i as row vectors and is an element of the so-called assignment manifold $\mathcal{W} = \mathcal{S} \times \cdots \times \mathcal{S}$ ($n = |\mathcal{V}|$ times). Similarly, the vectors $S_i(W)$ are collected as rows of the similarity matrix $S(W) \in \mathcal{W}$.

The counterpart of the convex relaxation (1.3) for determining a labeling is the smooth non-convex problem

$$\sup_{W \in \mathcal{W}} J(W), \quad J(W) = \langle S(W), W\rangle, \quad \dot{W}(t) = \nabla_{\mathcal{W}}J(W), \quad W(0) = \frac{1}{c}\mathbb{1}\mathbb{1}^\top, \quad (2.4)$$

together with the Riemannian gradient flow on the right-hand side of (2.4): The objective is to determine the assignment matrix W so as to maximize the correlation (inner product) with the similarity matrix, that incorporates the given data and spatial regularization depending on W, too.

Numerical approximations of the gradient flow (2.4) yield assignment vectors W_i, $i \in \mathcal{V}$ that are ε-close to some unit vector from the set $\mathcal{L}_c$, which holds in all experiments. For further details we refer to [1]. A postprocessing step for rounding, as with the convex approach (1.3), is *not* required.

3   Application to Graphical Models

Our approach to the evaluation of a given graphical model of the form (1.1), using the geometric approach of Sect. 2, involves the steps: (1) smooth approximation of the LP relaxation (1.3), (2) adopting the geometry of the assignment manifold, and (3) labeling through numerical optimization. Finally, (4), we reconsider and discuss again Fig. 1.

(1) Smooth Approximation of the LP Relaxation. Setting

$$\mathcal{P}_\mathcal{V} = \{\mu_\mathcal{V} = (\mu_1, \ldots, \mu_n) \colon \mu_i \in \Delta_c, \, i \in \mathcal{V}\}, \tag{3.1a}$$

$$\Pi(\mu_i, \mu_j) = \{\mu_{ij} \geq 0 \colon \mu_{ij} \text{ satifies the marginal. constraints (1.3)}\} \tag{3.1b}$$

we rewrite problem (1.3) in the form

$$\min_{\mu_\mathcal{V} \in \mathcal{P}_\mathcal{V}} \Big(\sum_{i \in \mathcal{V}} \langle \theta_i, \mu_i \rangle + \sum_{ij \in \mathcal{E}} \min_{\mu_{ij} \in \Pi(\mu_i, \mu_j)} \langle \theta_{ij}, \mu_{ij} \rangle \Big), \tag{3.2}$$

which involves the local Wasserstein distances

$$d_W(\mu_i, \mu_j; \theta_{ij}) = \min_{\mu_{ij} \in \Pi(\mu_i, \mu_j)} \langle \theta_{ij}, \mu_{ij} \rangle, \quad ij \in \mathcal{E}. \tag{3.3}$$

Lemma 1. *Problems (3.2) and (1.3) are equivalent, that is (3.2) is the convex local polytope relaxation of the graphical model (1.1).*

Proof. This follows from the equation

$$\min_{\mu \in \mathcal{P}} \langle \theta, \mu \rangle = \min_{\mu \in \mathcal{P}} \big(\langle \theta_\mathcal{V}, \mu_\mathcal{V} \rangle + \langle \theta_\mathcal{E}, \mu_\mathcal{E} \rangle \big) \tag{3.4a}$$

$$= \min_{\mu_\mathcal{V}} \big(\langle \theta_\mathcal{V}, \mu_\mathcal{V} \rangle + \min_{\mu_\mathcal{E}} \sum_{ij \in \mathcal{E}} (\langle \theta_{ij}, \mu_{ij} \rangle + \delta_{\Pi(\mu_i, \mu_j)}(\mu_{ij})) \tag{3.4b}$$

where $\mu_\mathcal{E} = (\ldots, \mu_{ij}, \ldots)$ and similarly $\theta_\mathcal{E}$ collect the local vectors indexed by edges, analogous to $\mu_\mathcal{V}$ given by (3.1a) and $\theta_\mathcal{V}$ for the vertices.   □

Using the entropy function $H(\mu_{ij}) = -\sum_{x_i, x_j} \mu_{ij}(x_i, x_j) \log \mu_{ij}(x_i, x_j)$, where μ satisfies (3.1), our approach is to smooth the convex but non-smooth (piecewise-linear) local functions $d_W(\mu_i, \mu_j; \theta_{ij})$ by entropy regularization,

$$d_{W,\tau}(\mu_i, \mu_j; \theta_{ij}) = \min_{\mu_{ij} \in \Pi(\mu_i, \mu_j)} \{\langle \theta_{ij}, \mu_{ij} \rangle - \tau H(\mu_{ij})\}, \quad ij \in \mathcal{E}, \quad \tau > 0, \tag{3.5}$$

and to minimize the resulting *smooth convex* functional

$$\min_{\mu_\mathcal{V} \in \mathcal{P}_\mathcal{V}} E_\tau(\mu_\mathcal{V}), \qquad E_\tau(\mu_\mathcal{V}) = \Big\{ \sum_{i \in \mathcal{V}} \langle \theta_i, \mu_i \rangle + \sum_{ij \in \mathcal{E}} d_{W,\tau}(\mu_i, \mu_j; \theta_{ij}) \Big\} \tag{3.6}$$

by adopting and suitably extending the geometric approach of Sect. 2.

Remark 1. The role of smoothing employed here should *not* be merely considered as a pure *numerical* techniqe (cf. e.g. [9]) for handling the non-smooth convex programs (1.3) and (3.2), because solving the *non-tight* relaxation (1.3) is *not* our focus. Rather, we are interested in approximately solving the original combinatorial labeling problem (1.1), which will be achieved by applying a geometric optimization strategy to (3.6) that converges to *integer-valued* solutions, i.e. labelings. Thus, smoothing in the case of (3.6) is a strategy for taming the combinatorial labeling problem, that is *independently* applied and does *not* conflict with the geometric numerical strategy for computing integral (non-fuzzy) labelings.

(2) Geometric Minimization Approach. In this section, we will consider (i) the computation of the partial gradients $\nabla_{\mu_i} E_\tau(\mu_\mathcal{V})$ and (ii) a natural way for incorporating this information into the geometric approach of Sect. 2.

Regarding (i), we use the following classical result, which is an extension of Danskin's theorem due to Rockafellar.

Theorem 1 [6,11]. *Let $f(z) = \max_{w \in W} g(z, w)$, where W is compact and the function g is differentiable and $\nabla_z g(z, w)$ depending continuously on (z, w). If in addition $g(z, w)$ is convex in z, and if $\bar{z}$ is a point such that $\arg\max_{w \in W} g(\bar{z}, w) = \{\bar{w}\}$, then f is differentiable at $\bar{z}$ with*

$$\nabla f(\bar{z}) = \nabla_z g(\bar{z}, \bar{w}). \tag{3.7}$$

We apply Theorem 1 to the function $d_{W,\tau}$ of (3.6). To this end, let

$$A \colon \mathbb{R}^{c^2} \to \mathbb{R}^c, \quad A\mu_{ij} = \begin{pmatrix} \mu_i \\ \mu_j \end{pmatrix} \tag{3.8}$$

denote the linear mapping so that (3.8) is equal to the marginalizations constraints (3.1b). Furthermore, we introduce the projection

$$\Pi_0 \colon \mathbb{R}^c \to T\mathcal{S}, \quad \Pi_0(v) = (I - \frac{1}{c}\mathbb{1}\mathbb{1}^\top), \qquad T\mathcal{S} = \{v \in \mathbb{R}^c \colon \langle \mathbb{1}, v \rangle = 0\} \tag{3.9}$$

onto the tangent space of the manifold $\mathcal{S}$ of Sect. 2, i.e. the subspace of zero-mean vectors (which does not depend on a base point of $\mathcal{S}$).

Corollary 1. *Let μ_i, μ_j be given. Then the gradient $\nabla d_{W,\tau}(\mu_i, \mu_j; \theta_{ij})$ of the function (3.5) is given by the unique solution $(\bar{\nu}_i, \bar{\nu}_j)$ of the equation*

$$\begin{pmatrix} \mu_i \\ \mu_j \end{pmatrix} = A \exp\left[\frac{1}{\tau}\left(A^\top \begin{pmatrix} \bar{\nu}_i \\ \bar{\nu}_j \end{pmatrix} - \theta_{ij}\right)\right], \qquad \bar{\nu}_i, \bar{\nu}_j \in T\mathcal{S}. \tag{3.10}$$

Proof. The function $d_{W,\tau}$ is defined by the convex problem

$$d_{W,\tau}(\mu_i, \mu_j; \theta_{ij}) = \min_{\mu_{ij}} \left(\langle \theta_{ij}, \mu_{ij} \rangle + f_\tau(\mu_{ij})\right) \quad \text{s.t.} \quad A\mu = \begin{pmatrix} \mu_i \\ \mu_j \end{pmatrix} \tag{3.11}$$

with $f_\tau(\mu_{ij}) = -\tau H(\mu_{ij}) + \delta_{\mathbb{R}_+^{c^2}}(\mu_{ij})$ and dual problem

$$\max_{\nu_i, \nu_j} g(\mu_i, \mu_j, \nu_i, \nu_j) = \max_{\nu_i, \nu_j} \left[\langle \mu_i, \nu_i \rangle + \langle \mu_j, \nu_j \rangle - f_\tau^*\left(A^\top \begin{pmatrix} \nu_i \\ \nu_j \end{pmatrix} - \theta_{ij}\right)\right] \tag{3.12}$$

and convex conjugate function $f_\tau^*(\nu_{ij}) = \tau \sum_{x_i, x_j} e^{\frac{\nu_{ij}(x_i, x_j) - \tau}{\tau}}$. Compactness of the set of maximizers follows from the continuity of f_τ^* (closed level sets) and $\lim_{\tau \to 0} f_\tau^*(\nu_{ij}) = \delta_{\mathbb{R}^{c^2}}(\nu_{ij})$, and uniqueness is due to the constraint $\nu_i, \nu_j \in T\mathcal{S}$, which removes the ambiguity $(\nu_i + c\mathbb{1}, \nu_j - c\mathbb{1})$ in the argument of f_τ^* of (3.12), for arbitrary constants $c \in \mathbb{R}$. Since g is linear in μ_i, μ_j, Theorem 1 applies, and Eq. (3.7) becomes (3.10), where we omitted the immaterial scaling factor caused by τ in the numerator of f_τ^*. $\qquad\square$

We wish to point out that strong duality between the primal (3.11) and its dual (3.12) holds since μ_i in fact are $W_i \in \mathcal{W}, i \in \mathcal{V}$ which are strictly positive.

It remains to explain how we apply the geometric approach from Sect. 2.

For clarity, we adopt the corresponding notation and replace in the remainder of this paper the local vectors μ_i by W_i, $i \in \mathcal{V}$.

Equation (2.2) defines likelihood vectors $L_i(W_i) = \exp_{W_i}\left(-\Pi_0(D_i)/\rho\right)$ in terms of some vector of distances D_i of the data point f_i to given labels. Since the local energy $\langle \theta_i, \mu_i \rangle$ plays a similar role in the functional (3.6), i.e. measuring a local distance to the labels, it is natural to project the gradient to the tangent space and to define the likelihood vectors

$$L_i(W_i) = \exp_{W_i}\left(-\Pi_0(\theta_i)/\rho\right) = \exp_{W_i}(-\theta_i/\rho), \qquad i \in \mathcal{V}, \qquad (3.13)$$

where the projection can be omitted because the mapping $\exp_{W_i}$ defined by (2.2) is invariant against the addition of constant vectors $c\mathbb{1}$, $c \in \mathbb{R}$.

Regarding the pairwise energy terms of (3.6), we proceed in a similar way. For every edge $ij \in \mathcal{E}$, we determine the gradient of the corresponding summand, given by the solution $(\bar{\nu}_i, \bar{\nu}_j)$ to (3.10) (with μ_i, μ_j on the left-hand side replaced by W_i, W_j) and define the likelihood vectors

$$L_{ij;i}(W_i) = \exp_{W_i}(-\bar{\nu}_i/\tau), \qquad L_{ij;j}(W_j) = \exp_{W_j}(-\bar{\nu}_j/\tau), \qquad ij \in \mathcal{E}. \quad (3.14)$$

At this point, we have taken into account the *pairwise* parameters of the graphical model (1.1), and we continue with adapting the final steps of the approach proposed in [1]. Assuming an *arbitrary but fixed orientation* for every edge (i.e. $ij \in \mathcal{E}$ implies $ji \notin \mathcal{E}$), we define for every node i the sets of neighbors of i given by edges *incoming* and *outgoing* to/from i,

$$I(i) = \{j \in \mathcal{V}: ji \in \mathcal{E}\}, \qquad O(i) = \{j \in \mathcal{V}: ij \in \mathcal{E}\}. \qquad (3.15)$$

Then, based on the likelihood vectors associated with each node i,

$$\mathcal{L}_i(W) = \{L_i(W_i)\} \cup \left(\cup_{j \in I(i)} L_{ji;i}(W_j)\right) \cup \left(\cup_{j \in O(i)} L_{ij;i}(W_j)\right), \quad i \in \mathcal{V}, \quad (3.16)$$

we compute analogous to (2.3) the similarity vectors

$$S_i(W) = \mathrm{mean}_{\mathcal{S}}\big(\mathcal{L}_i(W)\big)\big/\langle \mathbb{1}, \mathrm{mean}_{\mathcal{S}}(\mathcal{L}_i(W))\rangle, \quad i \in \mathcal{V} \qquad (3.17)$$

and solve the optimization problem (2.4).

Remark 2. The reader may wonder: Why do we not simply encode the pairwise energy terms $E_{ij}(x_i, x_i)$ by $\langle W_i, \theta_{ij}W_j \rangle$ and generate likelihood vectors by the corresponding partial gradients $\theta_{ij}W_j$ and $\theta_{ij}^\top W_i$? The reason is that this would closely correspond to the naive mean field approach to labeling, which is plagued by the local minima problem, as the generally *non-convex* quadratic form $\langle W_i, \theta_{ij}W_j \rangle$ indicates. By contrast, our approach couples the marginals W_i, W_j in terms of the given parameters θ_{ij} through the *convex local* smoothed Wasserstein distance $d_{W,\tau}(W_i, W_j; \theta_{ij})$.

(3) Numerical Optimization. Defining the local model parameter matrices

$$\Theta_{ij} \in \mathbb{R}^{c \times c}, \quad E(\Theta_{ij}) = e^{\frac{-\Theta_{ij}}{\tau}}, \quad (\Theta_{ij})_{kl} = \theta_{ij}(x_k, x_l), \quad x_k, x_l \in \mathcal{X}, \quad (3.18)$$

where the edge-indexed matrix θ_{ij} is not necessarily symmetric, Eq. (3.10) takes the form $\begin{pmatrix} W_i \\ W_j \end{pmatrix} = \mathrm{Diag}(e^{\frac{\nu_i}{\tau}})E(\Theta_{ij})\,\mathrm{Diag}(e^{\frac{\nu_j}{\tau}})$, where $\mathrm{Diag}(\cdot)$ denotes the diagonal matrix with the argument vector as entries. The vectors $\bar{\nu}_i, \bar{\nu}_j$ can be determined by Sinkhorn's algorithm, up to a common multiplicative constant. Setting

$$v_i := e^{\frac{\nu_i}{\tau}}, \qquad v_j := e^{\frac{\nu_j}{\tau}}, \qquad (3.19)$$

the corresponding fixed point iterations read

$$v_i^{(k+1)} = \frac{W_i}{E(\Theta_{ij})\left(\frac{W_j}{E(\Theta_{ij})^\top v_i^{(k)}}\right)}, \qquad v_j^{(k+1)} = \frac{W_j}{E(\Theta_{ij})^\top \left(\frac{W_i}{E(\Theta_{ij})v_j^{(k)}}\right)}, \quad (3.20)$$

which are iterated until $\|v_i^{(k+1)} - v_i^{(k)}\| \leq 10^{-16}$, $\|v_j^{(k+1)} - v_j^{(k)}\| \leq 10^{-16}$, which for a reasonable range of $\Theta_{ij} \in [0,1]^{c \times c}$ happens quickly after few iterations. Denoting the iterates after convergence by $v_i^{(\infty)}, v_j^{(\infty)}$, resubstitution into (3.19) and projection onto $T\mathcal{S}$ using (3.9) gives the vectors

$$\bar{\nu}_i = \tau \Pi_0(\log v_i^{(\infty)}), \qquad \bar{\nu}_j = \tau \Pi_0(\log v_j^{(\infty)}). \qquad (3.21)$$

which are used to compute the edge likelihood vectors (3.14). These likelihood vectors together with the corresponding vectors (3.13) generated by the data term define (3.16) and in turn the similarity vectors (3.17), which are integrated into the multiplicative scheme of [1] to evolve the marginals by

$$W_i^{(k+1)} = (W_i^{(k)} \cdot S_i(W^{(k)}))/\langle W_i, S_i(W^{(k)}) \rangle, \qquad i \in \mathcal{V}, \quad \forall j, k \in \mathcal{N}(i). \quad (3.22)$$

We adopt the following approximations from [1]: In case an entry of $W_i^{(k+1)}$ drops below $\varepsilon = 10^{-10}$, we set $W_i^{(k+1)} = \varepsilon$ and hence let ε play the role of 0. Furthermore, we approximate the Riemannian mean by the geometric mean, which due to [1, Prop. 3.1] provides a closed form first-order approximation of the geodesics of $\mathcal{S}$ in terms of the mapping $\exp_{W_i}(\cdot)$ defined by (2.2). Finally, we terminate the update scheme (3.22) when the average of the entropies of $W_i^{(k+1)}$ over $i \in \mathcal{V}$ drops below 10^{-3}.

Wasserstein Messages. The rationale behind (3.14) becomes more apparent when rewriting the fixed point Eq. (3.20) *after* convergence in the form

$$v_i^{(\infty)} = W_i/(E(\Theta_{ij})v_j^{(\infty)}), \qquad v_j^{(\infty)} = W_j/(E(\Theta_{ij})^\top v_i^{(\infty)}). \qquad (3.23)$$

This shows that the variables $\bar{\nu}_i, \bar{\nu}_j$ which generate the likelihood vectors (3.14), are *passed along the edges indicent to pixel i* (see Fig. 1). Taking

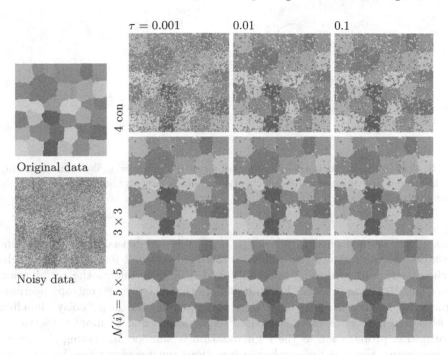

Fig. 2. A 4-connected neighborhood denotes the pixels $(x \pm 1, y)$ and $(x, y \pm 1)$ for image coordinates (x, y) at i, and 3×3 and 5×5 mean fully connected neighborhoods with 9 and 25 pixels involved in geometric averaging (cf. (3.17)). For $\rho = 1$, we see that the regularization changes slowly within each scale $\mathcal{N}$ with increasing τ, and increasing the neighborhood sizes increases the spatial regularization.

the log of both sides of the first equation results due to (3.21) in $\overline{\nu}_i = \tau \Pi_0 \left(\log W_i - \log(E(\Theta_{ij}) v_j^{(\infty)}) \right)$, and in a similar expression for $\overline{\nu}_j$. Comparing this to the general formula for solving Eq. (2.2) for U_i due to [1, App. B.2], $U_i = \rho \Pi_0 (\log W_i - \log L_i)$, suggests to identify likelihood vectors that are generated along the edges, as given by (3.14).

Since $\overline{\nu}_i, \overline{\nu}_j$ are the dual variables corresponding to the local marginalization constraints of (1.3) resp. (3.1b), we call these vectors *Wasserstein messages*, in view of the established message passing schemes [17] that aim at solving the dual LP of (1.3) by fixed point iteration. Unlike the latter schemes, our approach satisfies the marginalization constraints *all the time* during the numerical optimization process, rather than only after convergence to a fixed point (provided this happens with common belief propagation on an acyclic graph).

4   Experiments

Parameter Influence, Convergence Rate. In order to better assess the parameter influence we defined 35 unit vectors, each corresponding to one label, encoded on the simplex. This assures that the unary (or distance function,

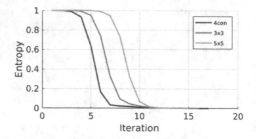

Fig. 3. Entropy as a function of iterations for $\tau = 0.1$ and $\rho = 1$. With an increasing neighborhood size we observe slower convergence which, however, gives a more spatially coherent labeling, as seen in Fig. 2.

cmp. (2.1)) defined as $d(f_i, f_j^*) = \|f_i - f_j^*\|_1$ is not biased towards any single label. Figure 2 shows the influence, for fixed $\rho = 0.2$ for increasing neighborhood size and increasing selectivity τ. In all experiments the termination criteria of 10^{-3} was reached. Figure 3 depicts that the average entropy decrease rapidly for smaller neighborhood sizes. This is reflected in a "noisy" labeling as seen in Fig. 2 since noise is treated as structure due to more conservative information propagation as the regularization is smaller. Increasing the neighborhood size increases the number of iterations until convergence, because the algorithm resolves the 'label competition' through stronger geometric averaging, which results in a smoother labeling. Overall, however, the number of iterations is small.

Inference on Cyclic Graphs. We focus next on the performance of our approach for difficult inference problems on cyclic graphs. To this end, we considered the binary labeling problem on the triangle with three nodes as minimal complete graph, together with many instances of model parameters where the convex LP relaxation (1.3) *fails completely*: It returns the fractional solution $(1/2, 1/2)$ as optimal extreme point of the local polytope for *every* node, which

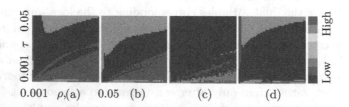

Fig. 4. Energy values for optima computed for the 'frustrated triangle' problem, for various values of τ and ρ. Dark blue color indicates that the globally optimal integral solution was found. The results indicate the existence of an optimal parameter regime for all problem instances. White color indicates that the convergence rate slowed down significantly. The panel labels correspond to the ones in Table 1. (Color figure online)

thus necessitates a postprocessing step to find the optimal binary 0/1 solution, that is equivalent to the original combinatorially hard problem.

Table 1 shows some instances of unary potentials that we used, together with the pairwise potential $\left(\begin{smallmatrix} 0 & -0.1 \\ -0.1 & 0 \end{smallmatrix}\right)$ that favors different labels on adjacent nodes. The latter is impossible on a triangle, which explains the difficulty of this labeling problem. Table 1 shows the energy LP_{frac} of the convex relaxation as lower bound, together with the energy LP_{int} of the optimal binary labeling, determined by exhaustive search.

It is clear that our geometric approach can only find a local binary optimum for this NP-hard problem. Figure 4 shows for 4 problem instances the "energy landscape" resulting after convergence, for varying values of the parameters τ and λ, where the lowest energy corresponding to LP_{int} is encoded with blue. Table 1 displays in the rightmost column the energy within the blue region, which confirms that the optimal *binary* solution was found *without rounding*. The shape of the energy landscape looked roughly the same for all problem instances. A better understanding of how to find parameter values corresponding to the blue region in applications, will be the subject of future work.

Table 1. Unary potentials for the 'frustrated triangle' problem constructed such that the LP relaxation yields a fractional solution $(1/2, 1/2)$ at each vertex. The three right-most columns show the energies LP_{frac} of the LP relaxation, the energy LP_{int} of the globally optimal integral solution, and the energy obtained with our geometric approach within the blue region of parameter values, as displayed by Fig. 4.

	Unary	LP_{frac}	LP_{int}	Geometric
(a)	(0.13, 0.10, 0.86, 0.95, 1.03, 1.06)	1.77	1.79	1.79
(b)	(1.68, 1.67, 0.10, 0.16, 1.21, 1.27)	2.75	2.78	2.78
(c)	(0.99, 0.90, 1.49, 1.46, 0.10, 0.16)	2.25	2.26	2.26
(d)	(1.53, 1.49, 0.10, 0.12, 0.25, 0.19)	1.54	1.58	1.58
(e)	(0.10, 0.10, 1.49, 1.40, 0.86, 0.93)	2.14	2.16	2.16
(f)	(1.08, 0.94, 0.12, 0.10, 1.12, 1.14)	1.95	1.96	1.96

Denoising by Labeling. We competitively compared the performance of our approach for the labeling problem depicted by Fig. 5, using a standard data term together with an Ising prior. To this end, we also evaluated the mean field method [14] and loopy belief propagation [15] (Loopy-BP) based on the UGM package [12], and local rounding was used for these methods as a post-processing step to obtain an integral solution. Figure 5 shows the visual reconstruction as well as the corresponding energy values and percentage of correct labels, which reveals a superior performance of our approach.

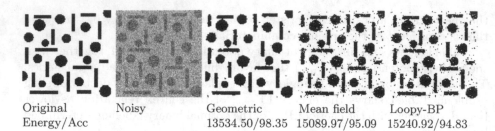

Original	Noisy	Geometric	Mean field	Loopy-BP
Energy/Acc		13534.50/98.35	15089.97/95.09	15240.92/94.83

Fig. 5. Noisy binary image recovery. Compared to standard message passing algorithms, our geometric approach shows competitive performance regarding both optimal energy and labeling accuracy. The parameter configuration was $\tau = 0.05$ and $\lambda = 1$, and a 4 connectivity neighborhood was used for geometric spatial regularization.

5   Conclusion

We presented a novel approach which evaluate established graphical models in a smooth geometric setting. Taking into account pairwise potentials, we formulated a novel inference algorithm that propagates "Wasserstein messages" along edges. These messages are lifted to the assignment manifold and drive a Riemannian gradient flow, that terminates at an integral labeling. Our work adds a new inference method to the literature, that simultaneously performs relaxation and rounding to integrality in a smooth geometric fashion.

Acknowledgments. We gratefully acknowledge support by the German Science Foundation, grant GRK 1653.

References

1. Åström, F., Petra, S., Schmitzer, B., Schnörr, C.: Image labeling by assignment. J. Math. Imaging Vis. **58**(2), 211–238 (2017)
2. Bergmann, R., Fitschen, J.H., Persch, J., Steidl, G.: Iterative multiplicative filters for data labeling. Int. J. Comput. Vis. 1–19 (2017). http://dx.doi.org/10.1007/s11263-017-0995-9
3. Brualdi, R.: Combinatorial Matrix Classes. Cambridge University Press, Cambridge (2006)
4. Cuturi, M.: Sinkhorn Distances: Lightspeed Computation of Optimal Transport. In: Proceedings of the NIPS (2013)
5. Cuturi, M., Peyré, G.: A smoothed dual approach for variational wasserstein problems. SIAM J. Imag. Sci. **9**(1), 320–343 (2016)
6. Danskin, J.: The theory of max min with applications. SIAM J. Appl. Math. **14**, 641–664 (1966)
7. Kappes, J., Andres, B., Hamprecht, F., Schnörr, C., Nowozin, S., Batra, D., Kim, S., Kausler, B., Kröger, T., Lellmann, J., Komodakis, N., Savchynskyy, B., Rother, C.: A comparative study of modern inference techniques for structured discrete energy minimization problems. Int. J. Comput. Vis. **115**(2), 155–184 (2015)

8. Kolouri, S., Park, S., Thorpe, M., Slepcev, D., Rohde, G.: Transport-based analysis, modeling, and learning from signal and data distributions (2016). preprint: https://arxiv.org/abs/1609.04767
9. Nesterov, Y.: Smooth minimization of non-smooth functions. Math. Program. Ser. A **103**, 127–152 (2005)
10. Peyré, G.: Entropic approximation of wasserstein gradient flows. SIAM J. Imag. Sci. **8**(4), 2323–2351 (2015)
11. Rockafellar, R.: On a special class of functions. J. Opt. Theor. Appl. **70**(3), 619–621 (1991)
12. Schmidt, M.: UGM: Matlab code for undirected graphical models, January 2017
13. Schneider, M.: Matrix scaling, entropy minimization, and conjugate duality (II): the dual problem. Math. Program. **48**, 103–124 (1990)
14. Wainwright, M., Jordan, M.: Graphical models, exponential families, and variational inference. Found. Trends Mach. Learn. **1**(1–2), 1–305 (2008)
15. Weiss, Y.: Comparing the mean field method and belief propagation for approximate inference in MRFs. In: Advanced Mean Field Methods: Theory and Practice, pp. 229–240. MIT Press (2001)
16. Werner, T.: A linear programming approach to max-sum problem: a review. IEEE Trans. Patt. Anal. Mach. Intell. **29**(7), 1165–1179 (2007)
17. Yedidia, J., Freeman, W., Weiss, Y.: Constructing free-energy approximations and generalized belief propagation algorithms. Trans. I. Theor. **51**(7), 2282–2312 (2005)

Multinomial Level-Set Framework for Multi-region Image Segmentation

Tammy Riklin Raviv[✉]

Electrical and Computer Engineering and the Zlotowski Center for Neuroscience,
Ben-Gurion University of the Negev, Beer-Sheva, Israel
rrtammy@ee.bgu.ac.il

Abstract. We present a simple and elegant level-set framework for multi-region image segmentation. The key idea is based on replacing the traditional regularized Heaviside function with the multinomial logistic regression function, commonly known as Softmax. Segmentation is addressed by solving an optimization problem which considers the image intensities likelihood, a regularizer, based on boundary smoothness, and a pairwise region interactive term, which is naturally derived from the proposed formulation. We demonstrate our method on challenging multi-modal segmentation of MRI scans (4D) of brain tumor patients. Promising results are obtained for image partition into the different healthy brain tissues and the malignant regions.

1 Introduction

Image segmentation is a fundamental computer vision problem, having a great importance in numerous application domains including astrophysics, security, autonomous vehicles, manufacturing quality control, biomedical imaging analysis and many others. The variety of existing image segmentation approaches consider a piecewise smoothness model of an image, as presented in a seminal work by Mumford and Shah [9], and aim to cluster image pixels (or voxels) into semantic regions based on their spatial relations and low-level features (e.g. intensity, texture) similarities. The proposed manuscript refers to the level-set framework [10], which is a widely used, unsupervised technique, for image segmentation that can be applied to multi-dimensional data in a straight forward manner and naturally accounts for different segmentation topologies.

Multi-region image segmentation can be, in practice, considered as a series of object-background seperation steps, carried out in an hierarchical or one-against-all manners. This, however, requires accounting for the possible heterogeneity of the current-step background, which may include several objects to be further segmented. In the inspiring work of Zhu and Yuille [16] a much more powerful approach was suggested. The main concept was the introduction of a *region competition* mechanism to the co-segmentation of an entire image into multiple regions. This 'pictorial' terminology refers to the process of membership assignment of pixels that are in the interface of two or more neighboring regions. This is addressed by constraining the sum of membership probabilities

© Springer International Publishing AG 2017
F. Lauze et al. (Eds.): SSVM 2017, LNCS 10302, pp. 386–395, 2017.
DOI: 10.1007/978-3-319-58771-4_31

for each pixel to one, thus circumventing the occurrence of 'overlaps' or 'vacuums'. In a later work by Brox and Weickert [2] this concept was formalized using a level-set framework, such that each region is represented by a different level-set function and a coupled curve evolution process, that enforces the constraint of disjoint regions. Pohl et al. [11] suggested an hierarchical segmentation scheme in which brain MRI scans are first parcellated into different tissues, e.g. gray matter (GM), white matter (WM), Cerebrospinal fluid (CSF) and then each tissue is partitioned into anatomical regions.

A more economical multi-region level-set framework was proposed by Vese and Chan [15]. They showed that a binary tree of $\log M$ level-set functions is sufficient for the semantic partition of an image into M regions. Recently, in [6], a smart mathematical representation of a level-set function, based on Voronoi implicit interface method [14] allowed a multi-region segmentation with only a single level-set function.

In this framework we do use M level-set functions for the segmentation of M regions. Yet, unlike the multiphase segmentation approach of Jung et al. [7], that is based on the phase transition model of Modica and Mortola, we do not use sinusoidal potentials. Inspired by [12,13] that replaced the traditional regularized Heaviside function, suggested by [3] with a logistic regression (LR) function that converts the level-set functions into probability maps, we introduce the multinomial LR (Softmax function) into the level-set formulation. There are several benefits for using an LR function, rather than a scaled arctangent function (as in [3]) or a sinc function (as in [7]). First, it has some desirable mathematical properties, e.g. its first derivatives are symmetrical and can be represented by the product of two LR functions. It also has appealing interpretation being related to the Boltzmann distribution. In probability theory, the output of the softmax function is used to represent a categorical distribution - that is, a probability distribution over M different possible outcomes. In the context of the proposed framework, the Softmax function ties together all level-set functions, such that the pixels (voxels) membership probabilities are always summed to one and no vacuums or overlaps occur when choosing the most probable regions. The Softmax formulation allows to accommodate cases where three or more region boundaries co-intersect in a straightforward and elegant manner. In fact, all regions 'take part' in the segmentation of each of them. It turns out that when differentiating the resulting level-set functional to derive the gradient descent equations, some nice properties are obtained, including the 'appearance' of a pairwise region interaction term. Therefore, each region 'competes' with every other region with no additional overhead.

The proposed framework is conceptually novel, mathematically elegant and robust with only two parameters to tune. While we consider the main contribution as theoretical we chose to exemplify our method for the challenging problem of multi-modal MRI segmentation of brain tumor patients. Specifically we consider the segmentation of healthy brain tissues (WM, GM, CSF) and the malignant regions. These images are considered difficult to segment due to the diffused boundaries of the malignant regions and the significant deformation of healthy brain tissues that are pushed away by the tumor.

The rest of the paper is organized as follows. Section 2 presents the underlying probabilistic model principles and introduces the multinomial LR function in a level-set functional. The proposed mathematical formulation yields an elegant derivation of the respective gradient descent equations, detailed in Sect. 2.3. Segmentation of 3D brain MRI scans are demonstrated in 3. We conclude in Sect. 4.

2   Multi-region Level-Set Framework

2.1   Problem Formulation

Our goal is to partition an image $I \colon \Omega \to \mathbb{R}^3$ or a set of related images (RGB channels, multi-modal MRI images) $\mathcal{I} \colon \Omega \to \mathbb{R}^4$, into M disjoint regions: $\omega_1, \ldots, \omega_M$, such that $\omega_i \cap \omega_j = \emptyset$ for each $i \neq j$, and $\bigcup_{i=1}^{M} \omega_i = \Omega$ where ω_M is the background.

Alternatively, we can define a labeling function (segmentation) Γ that assines labels $1, \ldots M$ to the image voxels $\mathbf{x}$, where a label m by a one-hot vector $[0, \ldots, 0, 1, 0, \ldots, 0]$ such the 1 is located at the $m - s$ entry. Considering a generative probabilistic segmentation model, we assume that Γ generates the observed image $\mathcal{I}$ with probability $\mathcal{P}(\mathcal{I}|\Gamma; \{\theta_m\}_{m=1}^{M})$, where θ_m are the parameters that model the intensity distribution of a region m in $\mathcal{I}$. We further assume that the image intensities of each region can be modeled by a multivariate normal distribution, therefore $\theta_m = \{\mu_m, \sigma_m, c_m\}$, denoting the means vector, the covariance matrix and the component proportion, respectively.

To address the segmentation problem, we jointly optimize for the segmentations Γ and the model parameters $\theta = \{\theta_1, \ldots, \theta_m\}$

$$\{\hat{\theta}, \hat{\Gamma}\} = \arg\max_{\{\theta, \Gamma\}} \log \mathcal{P}(\mathcal{I}, \Gamma; \theta) \tag{1}$$

$$= \arg\max_{\{\theta, \Gamma\}} \left[\log \mathcal{P}(\mathcal{I}|\ \Gamma; \theta) + \log \mathcal{P}(\Gamma)\right]. \tag{2}$$

We propose to alternate between estimating the maximum a posteriori (MAP) segmentations and updating the model parameters. For given model parameters, the segmentations can be estimated by solving the following MAP problem:

$$\hat{\Gamma} = \arg\max_{\Gamma} \left[\log \mathcal{P}(I|\Gamma; \theta) + \log \mathcal{P}(\Gamma)\right], \tag{3}$$

where $\log \mathcal{P}(I|\Gamma; \theta)$ is the image likelihood term and $\log \mathcal{P}(\Gamma)$ can be defined as the functional regularizer. We then fix $\hat{\Gamma}$ and estimate the model parameters θ by a Maximum Likelihood (ML) problem:

$$\hat{\theta} = \arg\max_{\theta} \log \mathcal{P}(I|\ \Gamma, \theta) \tag{4}$$

2.2   Probabilistic Level-Set Framework

We use $\phi_1 \dots \phi_{M-1}$ level-set functions to partition the image, where $\phi_m \colon \Omega \to \mathbb{R}$. For the case where $M = 2$ (object/background segmentation) the arctangent sigmoid proposed in [3] as a regularized Heaviside function, is replaced by the standard LR sigmoid, as in [12,13]:

$$H_\epsilon(\phi) = \frac{1}{2}\left(1 + \tanh\left(\frac{\phi}{2\epsilon}\right)\right) = \frac{1}{1 + e^{-\phi/\epsilon}}, \tag{5}$$

Using the log-odds formulation instead of the conventional signed distance function (SDF), the level-set function can be redefined as follows:

$$\phi(\mathbf{x}) \triangleq \epsilon \operatorname{logit}(p) = \epsilon \, \log \frac{p(\mathbf{x} \in w)}{1 - p(\mathbf{x} \in \omega)} = \epsilon \, \log \frac{p(\mathbf{x} \in \omega)}{p(\mathbf{x} \in \Omega \setminus \omega)}. \tag{6}$$

By simple algebraic manipulations on Eqs. (5–6), $H_\epsilon(\phi)$ can be written as:

$$H_\epsilon(\phi(\mathbf{x})) = \frac{1}{1 + p(\mathbf{x} \in \Omega \setminus \omega)/p(\mathbf{x} \in \omega)} = p(\mathbf{x} \in \omega), \tag{7}$$

The function H_ϵ maps the values of ϕ into probabilities. In other words, $H_\epsilon(\phi(\mathbf{x}))$ can be considered as the probability that a voxel $\mathbf{x}$ is part of the object. Note that for the boundary voxels, $\{\mathbf{x}_B\} \triangleq \{\mathbf{x} \in \Omega | \phi(\mathbf{x}) = 0\}$, $H_\epsilon(\phi(\mathbf{x}_B)) = 0.5$. We can equivalently say that $\{\mathbf{x}_B\}$ are assigned to the object region with probability 0.5, i.e. there is maximum uncertainty to whether these voxels are assigned to the foreground or to the background. Figure 1 presents the main concept.

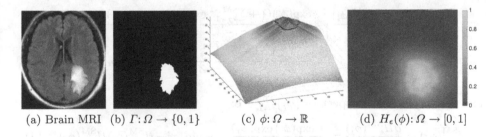

(a) Brain MRI   (b) $\Gamma \colon \Omega \to \{0,1\}$ (c) $\phi \colon \Omega \to \mathbb{R}$ (d) $H_\epsilon(\phi) \colon \Omega \to [0,1]$

Fig. 1. (a) A 2D slice of a brain MRI scan (FLAIR) of a glioma patient. The tumor boundary is marked in red. (b) Binary (hard) segmentation of the tumor. (c) A sign distance function (SDF) of the binary image. The zero level-set, which partitions the function into a background regions (below zero) and foreground (above zero) is marked in black. (d) A probabilistic map presenting the soft segmentation corresponding to (b). The value at each voxel represents the probability that this voxel belongs to the object (tumor area). The probabilistic map is generated by applying a logistic regression sigmoid (Eq. 7) to the SDF shown in (c). (Color figure online)

2.3   Multi-region Segmentation

We now generalize the binary segmentation framework presented above to multi-region segmentation. Following the log-odd formulation [1,12] we define:

$$\phi_i \triangleq \log \frac{p(\mathbf{x} \in \omega_i)}{p(\mathbf{x} \in \omega_M)}. \tag{8}$$

By definition,

$$p_i \triangleq p(\mathbf{x} \in \omega_i) = \frac{\exp(\phi_i)}{Z} = \frac{\exp(\phi_i)}{1 + \sum_{j=1}^{M-1} \exp(\phi_j)}, \tag{9}$$

$$p_M \triangleq \frac{1}{Z} = \frac{1}{1 + \sum_{j=1}^{M-1} \exp(\phi_j)}. \tag{10}$$

therefore,

$$1 - p_i = \frac{1 + \sum_{j=1}^{M-1} \exp(\phi_j) - \exp(\phi_i)}{Z} = \frac{1 + \sum_{j=1,j \neq i}^{M-1} \exp(\phi_j)}{Z} \triangleq \bar{p}_i \tag{11}$$

We define a smooth Heaviside function using the multinomial LR function (Softmax function), see [1]:

$$H_\epsilon^{\mathrm{SM}}(\phi_i) \triangleq p_i = \frac{\exp(\phi_i)}{Z} \tag{12}$$

Thus,

$$\delta_i^{\mathrm{SM}}(\phi_i) = \frac{\partial H_\epsilon^{\mathrm{SM}}(\phi_i)}{\partial \phi_i} = \frac{\exp(\phi_i)(1 + \sum_{j=1}^{M-1} \exp(\phi_j)) - \exp(\phi_i) \exp(\phi_i)}{Z^2} \tag{13}$$

$$= \frac{\exp(\phi_i)}{Z} \cdot \frac{1 + \sum_{j=1,j \neq i}^{M-1} \exp(\phi_j)}{Z} = p_i \bar{p}_i$$

The derivatives with respect to $\{\phi_i\}_{i=1}^M$ are:

$$\delta_{j,i}^{\mathrm{SM}}(\phi_j) = \frac{\partial H_\epsilon^{\mathrm{SM}}(\phi_j)}{\partial \phi_i} = \frac{-\exp(\phi_i) \exp(\phi_j)}{Z^2} = -p_i p_j = -H_\epsilon^{\mathrm{SM}}(\phi_i) H_\epsilon^{\mathrm{SM}}(\phi_j). \tag{14}$$

$$\delta_{M,i}^{\mathrm{SM}}(\phi_j) = \frac{\partial H_\epsilon^{\mathrm{SM}}(\phi_M)}{\partial \phi_i} = \frac{-\exp(\phi_i)}{Z^2} = -p_i p_M = -H_\epsilon^{\mathrm{SM}}(\phi_i) H_\epsilon^{\mathrm{SM}}(\phi_M). \tag{15}$$

The term $-H_\epsilon^{\mathrm{SM}}(\phi_i) H_\epsilon^{\mathrm{SM}}(\phi_j)$ is exactly the repulsive pairwise region interaction term, where two regions in the image compete. Deriving the gradient descent equation of the image likelihood term, for example, (see below) one gets a nice intuitive expression.

2.4 Image Likelihood Term

The image likelihood term E_{IL} in a level-set function can be derived from the left hand term of Eq. (3) i.e., $E_{IL} \propto -\log \mathcal{P}(I|\phi_1, \ldots \phi_{M-1}; \theta)$ Assuming normal distribution of the image intensities within each region, i.e. $\theta_i = \{\mu_i, \sigma_i, c_i\}$,, an energy function of a multi-label cost functional will look as follows:

$$
E_{IL}(\phi_1, \ldots \phi_{M-1}) = -\sum_{i=1}^{M-1} \int_{\Omega} \left[p(\mathbf{x} \in \omega_i) \log G(I; \theta_i) + p(\mathbf{x} \notin \omega_i) \log G(I; \theta_M) \right] d\mathbf{x}
$$

$$
= -\sum_{i=1}^{M-1} \int_{\Omega} \left[\frac{\exp(\phi_i)}{Z} \log G(I; \theta_i) + \frac{1}{Z} \log G(I; \theta_M) \right] d\mathbf{x}. \tag{16}
$$

Using the first variation of Eq. 16 and the Euler-Lagrange equations, the gradient descent term, associated with the image likelihood term, of each level-set function ϕ_i gets the following form:

$$
\frac{\partial \phi_i}{\partial t}^{IL} = \sum_{j=1, j\neq i}^{M} H_\epsilon^{SM}(\phi_i) H_\epsilon^{SM}(\phi_j) \log p(I; \theta_j) + H_\epsilon^{SM}(\phi_i)\left(1 - H_\epsilon^{SM}(\phi_i)\right) \log p(I; \theta_i)
$$

$$
= \sum_{j=1}^{M} \delta_{j,i}^{SM} \log p(I; \theta_j), \tag{17}
$$

where, $\delta_{i,i}^{SM} \triangleq \delta_i^{SM}$.

2.5 Smoothness Term Regularizer

The smoothness term associated with each level-set function takes the following form:

$$
E_{REG}(\phi_i) = \int_{\Omega} |\nabla H_\epsilon^{SM}(\phi_i(\mathbf{x}))| d\mathbf{x}, \tag{18}
$$

The respective gradient descent equation gets the following form:

$$
\frac{\partial \phi_i}{\partial t}^{REG} = H_\epsilon^{SM}(\phi_i)\left(1 - H_\epsilon^{SM}(\phi_i)\right) \operatorname{div}\left(\frac{\nabla \phi_i}{|\nabla \phi_i|}\right) = \delta_{i,i}^{SM}(\phi_i)\operatorname{div}\left(\frac{\nabla \phi_i}{|\nabla \phi_i|}\right) \tag{19}
$$

2.6 Multinomial Level-Set Algorithm

The proposed method is fully automatic and completely unsupervised, i.e. no prior is available. The first phase of the algorithm is therefore unsupervised clustering of the image regions, based on its intensities, using expectation maximization (EM) [4]. The EM algorithm results in $M-1$ likelihood maps, $G(I; \theta_i)$ where $G\colon \Omega \to [0,1]$. A label m is assigned to an image pixel (or voxel) $\mathbf{x}$ if the maximum value of $G\big(I(\mathbf{x}); \theta_i\big)$ is obtained for $i = m$. Once the image pixels are labeled, one can generate $M - 1$ SDFs, each is associated with a level-set function. The algorithm is then carried out, where at each step the intensity distribution parameters are re-estimated (for each region separately) following an update of each of the level-set functions $\phi_1 \ldots \phi_{M-1}$ using gradient descent equations of the form:

$$\frac{\partial \phi_i}{\partial t} = \sum_{j=1}^{M} \delta_{j,i}^{\mathrm{SM}} \log p(I; \theta_j) + \delta_{i,i}^{\mathrm{SM}} \mathrm{div}\big(\frac{\nabla \phi_i}{|\nabla \phi_i|}\big) \tag{20}$$

3   Experimental Results

We tested our method using multi-modal, longitudinal MR brain scans of low and high-grade glioma patients (human adults). The raw data of this experiment is from the Brain Tumor Segmentation (BRATS) challenge [8]. All segmentation processes are done in 3D. We present 2D slices of the obtained 3D segmentations for better visualization.

3.1   Qualitative Assessment

The proposed segmentation famework is visually demonstrated in Fig. 2. The upper row presents an axial brain slice of high grade glioma patient scanned with four different imaging modalities (T1, T1Gad, T2, Flair) along with manual annotation of the tumor region and the surrounding edema (right-most image). Manual segmentation of the healthy tissues is not available. The second row presents soft segmentation (probability maps) obtained by the proposed method, of four main brain regions of interest: WM, GM, CSF and tumor. The right-hand-side figure presents the label map (hard segmentation) generated from the soft segmentation maps. To segment the tumor itself into two regions we used the tumor boundaries obtained by the proposed automatic segmentation for initialization. We then further segmented the image into tumor, tumor core and healthy tissues (modelled by a mixture of multivariate Gaussians). Figure 3 visually demonstrates the proposed automatic segmentation and manual labeling of both the entire tumor region including the edema (red outline) and the tumor core (blue outline) for brain scans of four modalities of a 3D scan of high-grade glioma patient.

3.2   Quantitative Assessment

We use manual annotations made by clinical experts to test the segmentation to qualitatively asses the segmentation. Specifically, we use Dice scores [5] to quantify the mismatches between the automatic segmentations obtained by the proposed method and the expert segmentation considered as gold standard. Let S_A and S_M be two binary label maps defining the automatic and the manual

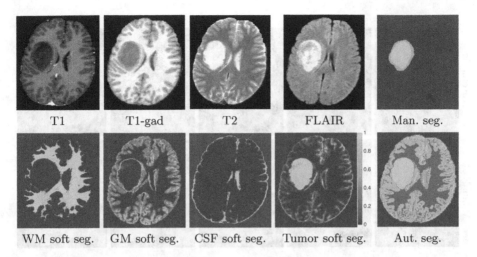

Fig. 2. Upper row: Axial brain slice of low grade glioma patient scanned with four different imaging modalities (T1, T1Gad, T2, Flair). The right most image presents manual annotation done by a clinical expert of the tumor region (yellow) and the surrounding edema (green-yellow). Manual segmentation of the healthy tissues is not available. Lower row: Soft segmentations (probability maps) of four main brain regions: WM (sky blue), GM (orange), CSF (green) and tumor (yellow). The right-most image presents the label map (hard segmentation) generated from the soft segmentation maps. The raw data of this experiment is from the Brain Tumor Segmentation (BRATS) challenge (http://www.imm.dtu.dk/projects/BRATS2012) organized by B. Menze, A. Jakab, S. Bauer, M. Reyes, M. Prastawa, and K. Van Leemput. (Color figure online)

segmentation of a particular ROI. The Dice score $D_{\text{DICE}} \in [0,1]$ measures the overlap between S_A and S_M :

$$D_{\text{DICE}} = \frac{2|S_A \cap S_M|}{|S_A| + |S_M|}. \tag{21}$$

Tumor segmentation results of 3D brain scans of high-grade (HG) and low-grade (LG) glioma patients are presented in Table 1.

Table 1. Dice scores obtained for tumor segmentation of high-grade (HG) and low-grade (LG) glioma patients multi-modal 3D bain scans.

Scan Idx.	Dice score
LG0002	0.9142
LG0011	0.7293
HG002	0.8333
HG003	0.6964

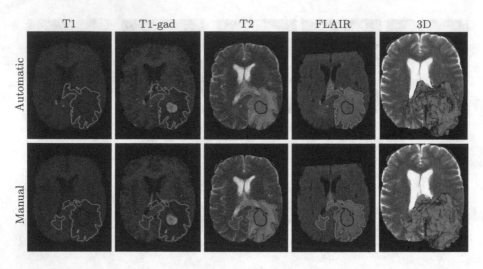

Fig. 3. Axial brain slice of high grade glioma patient along with the proposed 3D multi-modal co-segmentation (upper row) and manual (lower row) segmentation of the entire tumor including the surrounding edema (red outlines) and the tumor core (blue outline) across 4 modalities. The 3D view is shown with a Flair scan using a different axial slice. The raw data of this experiment is from the Brain Tumor Segmentation (BRATS) challenge. (Color figure online)

4   Conclusion

A novel concept for multi-region image segmentation using level-sets is presented. Specifically, establishing our framework on a generative probabilistic model, we use the multinomial LR sigmoid as a key component in a level-set functional. Pairwise region interaction term is naturally derived using the proposed formulation.

Image segmentation is exemplified for multi-modal MRI scans (4D data) of brain tumor patients. These images are considered difficult to segment because of the diffused boundaries of the malignant regions and the significant deformation of healthy brain tissues due to the tumor.

While the segmentation results are very promising, given the challenging segmentation task we aimed to address, the main strength of the proposed framework, in our opinion, is the conceptually novel theoretical formulation in its mathematical elegance. Segmentation is carried out in a completely unsupervised manner where neither a training set nor any form of prior is required. Note that the method is robust with only two parameters to tune: namely, the slope of the multinomial LR sigmoid and the size of the gradient descent update step. Nevertheless, we believe that the underlying mathematical derivation can elaborate a variety of segmentation problems, of different imaging modalities and domains, in which (but not limited to) top-down information is available and essential.

References

1. Bishop, C.M.: Pattern Recognition and Machine Learning. Springer, New York (2006)
2. Brox, T., Weickert, J.: Level set segmentation with multiple regions. IEEE Trans. Image Process. **15**(10), 3213–3218 (2006)
3. Chan, T., Vese, L.: Active contours without edges. IEEE Trans. Image Process. **10**(2), 266–277 (2001)
4. Dempster, A., Laird, N., Rubin, D.: Maximal likelihood form incomplete data via the EM algorithm. Proc. Roy. Stat. Soc. **39**, 1–38 (1977)
5. Dice, L.: Measure of the amount of ecological association between species. Ecology **26**(3), 29–302 (1945)
6. Dubrovina-Karni, A., Rosman, G., Kimmel, R.: Multi-region active contours with a single level set function. IEEE Trans. Pattern Anal. Mach. Intell. **37**(8), 1585–1601 (2015)
7. Jung, Y.M., Kang, S.H., Shen, J.: Multiphase image segmentation via modicamortola phase transition. SIAM J. Appl. Math. **67**(5), 1213–1232 (2007)
8. Menze, B., Jakab, A., Bauer, S., Kalpathy-Cramer, J., Farahani, K., Kirby, J., et al.: The multimodal brain tumor image segmentation benchmark (BRATS). IEEE Trans. Med. Imaging **34**(10), 1993–2024 (2015)
9. Mumford, D., Shah, J.: Optimal approximations by piecewise smooth functions and associated variational problems. Commun. Pure Appl. Math. **42**, 577–684 (1989)
10. Osher, S., Sethian, J.: Fronts propagating with curvature-dependent speed: algorithms based on Hamilton-Jacobi formulations. J. Comput. Phys. **79**, 12–49 (1988)
11. Pohl, K., Bouix, S., Nakamura, M., Rohlfing, T., McCarley, R., Kikinis, R., Grimson, W., Shenton, M., Wells, W.: A hierarchical algorithm for MR brain image parcellation. IEEE Trans. Med. Imaging **26**(9), 1201–1212 (2007)
12. Pohl, K., Fisher, J., Bouix, S., Shenton, M., McCarley, R., Grimson, W., Kikinis, R., Wells, W.: Using the logarithm of odds to define a vector space on probabilistic atlases. Med. Image Anal. **11**(6), 465–477 (2007)
13. Riklin Raviv, T., Van Leemput, K., Menze, B., Wells, W., Golland, P.: Segmentation of image ensembles via latent atlases. Med. Image Anal. **14**(5), 654–665 (2010)
14. Saye, R., Sethian, J.: The Voronoi implicit interface method for computing multiphase physics. PNAS **108**(49), 19498–19503 (2011)
15. Vese, L., Chan, T.: A multiphase level set framework for image segmentation using mumford and shah model. Int. J. Comput. Vis. **50**(3), 271–293 (2002)
16. Zhu, S., Yuille, A.: Region competition: unifying snakes, region growing, and bayes/MDL for multiband image segmentation. IEEE Trans. Pattern Anal. Mach. Intell. **18**(9), 884–900 (1996)

Local Mean Multiphase Segmentation
with HMMF Models

Jacob Daniel Kirstejn Hansen$^{(\boxtimes)}$ and François Lauze ⓘ

Department of Computer Science, University of Copenhagen, Copenhagen, Denmark
`{jdkh,francois}@di.ku.dk`

Abstract. This paper presents two similar multiphase segmentation methods for recovery of segments in complex weakly structured images, with local and global bias fields, because they can occur in some X-ray CT imaging modalities. Derived from the Mumford-Shah functional, the proposed methods assume a fixed number of classes. They use local image average as discriminative features. Region labels are modelled by Hidden Markov Measure Field Models. The resulting problems are solved by straightforward alternate minimisation methods, particularly simple in the case of quadratic regularisation of the labels. We demonstrate the proposed methods' capabilities on synthetic data using classical segmentation criteria as well as criteria specific to geoscience. We also present a few examples using real data.

1 Introduction

Image segmentation remains a fundamental task in Image Analysis, often used as a mandatory preprocessing step for further analysis. The large variety of sources and contents has generated a myriad of approaches, from simple clustering to more sophisticated ones. Our field of application is the analysis of X-ray computerised micro or nanotomograph (X-ray μCT or nCT) of geological samples. While these samples are essentially made of homogeneous materials, with edges and flat surfaces, they are not too structured in terms of shapes. Figure 1 illustrates two typical examples, with different resolutions. Such an image can be modelled as a function $u : \Omega \subset \mathbb{R}^d \to \mathbb{R}$, with $d = 2, 3$

$$u = L \left(\sum_{i=1}^{n} \alpha_i \chi_{\Omega_i} \right) + \eta \tag{1.1}$$

where $\Omega_1, \ldots \Omega_n$ are the different segments, α_i their intensity. L models blur and resolution effect, such as partial volume; η contains noise and bias field. In high-photon-count synchrotron imaging, the noise can be considered as Gaussian, but still depends on the underlying intensity [3].

A wealth of methods for multiphase image segmentation are based on variational models, especially the classical Mumford-Shah (MS) functional [11]. The MS model is region-based and copes with non stationarity in segments by proposing a cartoon-representation of the image data:

© Springer International Publishing AG 2017
F. Lauze et al. (Eds.): SSVM 2017, LNCS 10302, pp. 396–407, 2017.
DOI: 10.1007/978-3-319-58771-4_32

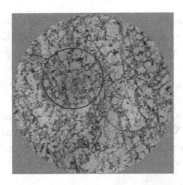 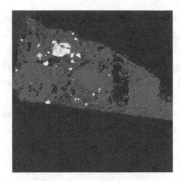

Fig. 1. Two (slices) of tomograms with internal reference names (irn): Hod chalk #16 [13] and WIG1T #156 respectively. A bias field is clearly present in the first image.

$$\mathcal{E}(c, \Gamma; u) = \frac{1}{2} \int_{\Omega} (c - u)^2 \, d\boldsymbol{x} + \frac{\nu}{2} \int_{\Omega \backslash \Gamma} |\nabla c|^2 \, d\boldsymbol{x} + \mu \ell(\Gamma), \qquad (1.2)$$

with Γ a hypersurface in Ω (i.e., 1D when $d = 2$, 2D when $d = 3$) such that $\Omega \backslash \Gamma$ is a disjoint union of regions $\Omega_1 \sqcup \cdots \sqcup \Omega_{n(\Gamma)}$, the number of classes n being determined by Γ, and $\ell(\Gamma)$ is the Hausdorff measure of Γ. At optimality, the model provides segment boundaries and a simplified representation c of the input image u.

The optimisation of Γ is a complex task and has led to many approaches and simplifications. The Chan and Vese formulation [5] assumes a two-segment model and piecewise constant c. Although the model has been extended to multiple classes, it cannot cope with local or global bias fields, or more complex non-stationarity in u. For complex non-stationarity and potential transparency-like effects, such as in X-ray imaging, an inpainting-based approach was proposed in [9]. This approach, however, is limited to two phases and relatively simple content. Bias field problems are well known in the MRI community, see for instance [15]. In contrast to our additive representation, these bias fields are multiplicative.

An approach more relevant to our work is [16] that presents a global, a regularisation, and a local term model with level sets, but is limited to two phases. It is also worth mentioning the work of [8] for two-phase segmentation and bias field estimation. Our methods do not attempt to estimate the bias field, but deal with it implicitely. Closest to our model is the work of [2], that we will use in the next section.

To cope with a higher, but fixed number n of segments, binary labelling is used: let $\mathcal{B}_n = \{e_1, \ldots, e_n\}$ be the standard basis vector of $\mathbb{R}^n$. Then a labelling function $\mathbf{v} = (\mathbf{v}_1, \ldots, \mathbf{v}_n) : \Omega \to \mathcal{B}_n$ is defined by $\mathbf{v}(\boldsymbol{x}) = e_i$ iff $\boldsymbol{x} \in \Omega_i$, and optimisation is performed on $\mathbf{v}$ instead of Γ:

$$\mathcal{E}(c, \mathbf{v}; u) = \frac{1}{2} \sum_{i=1}^{n} \int_{\Omega_i} (c - u)^2 \mathbf{v}_i \, d\boldsymbol{x} + \frac{\nu}{2} \sum_{i=1}^{n} \int_{\Omega_i} |\nabla c|^2 \, d\boldsymbol{x} + \mu \int |D\mathbf{v}|. \quad (1.3)$$

The presence of the operator L in the image model (1.1) makes soft labelling more appropriate in our setting. The concept of soft labelling is formalised in Marroquin's Hidden Markov Measure Field Models (HMMFM) [10]. This formalisation replaces $\mathcal{B}_n$ by its convex hull $\Delta_n = \{(s_1, \ldots, s_n) : \forall i, s_i \geq 0, \sum_i s_i = 1\}$, also used in [4] for their relaxation approach, which we use in one of our proposed models.

The rest of the paper is organised as follows: In Sect. 2 we derive two models, differing in their label regularisation term. We propose minimisation algorithms in Sect. 3. Then we demonstrate their capabilities experimentally in Sect. 4. We conclude and discuss future work in the last section.

2   Derivation of the Model

As noted by Brox et al. [2], in their two-phase approach, the minimiser c of (1.2) on segment Ω_i is the Tikhonov regularisation of u on Ω_i and satisfies the equation

$$\frac{c - u}{\nu} = \Delta c$$

and approximates the solution at time $t = \nu$ of the diffusion equation $c_t = \Delta c$ with initial value $c_0 = u$. Following [14], one can replace the regularisation term $\frac{\nu}{2} \int_{\Omega_i} |\nabla c|^2 \, d\boldsymbol{x}$ by an infinite regulariser $\frac{1}{2} \sum_{n=1}^{\infty} \frac{\nu^n}{n!} \int_{\Omega_i} |D^n c|^2$. The corresponding minimiser is the solution of the diffusion equation for all $\nu > 0$. These solutions can be approximated by Gaussian convolution, i.e., $c \approx g_{\sqrt{\nu}} * u$ On Ω_i. This opens the way for other smoothing kernels, in particular simple rotationally symmetric nearest neighbours (NN) kernels h_ρ (moving average) with radius $\rho > 0$. In the sequel g will denote one of these kernels. Kernel parameters, i.e., standard deviation σ for a Gaussian kernel, or the radius ρ for the NN-kernel, are linked to the variation of the unknown bias field. Following the discussion above, we replace c in (1.3) by a smoothing c_i of u on Ω_i and attempt to minimise instead

$$\mathcal{E}(\mathbf{v}; u) = \frac{1}{2} \sum_{i=1}^{n} \int_{\Omega} (c_i - u)^2 \mathbf{v}_i \, d\boldsymbol{x} + \frac{\mu}{2} \sum_{i=1}^{n} \int_{\Omega} |D\mathbf{v}_i| \tag{2.1}$$

with

$$c_i(\boldsymbol{x}) = \frac{(u\mathbf{v}_i) * g(\boldsymbol{x})}{\mathbf{v}_i * g(\boldsymbol{x})}, \quad \boldsymbol{x} \in \operatorname{supp} \mathbf{v}_i. \tag{2.2}$$

Energy (2.1) depends only on the labelling function $\mathbf{v}$, though in a complicated way in the local average (2.2). The gradient for the data term of (2.1) can be derived easily, but the resulting object is rather complex. This can be replaced by a "Chan-Vese"-like trick. Indeed, for $\boldsymbol{x} \in \Omega_i$, $c_i(\boldsymbol{x})$ is the minimizer of $d \mapsto g * \left[(u - d)^2 \mathbf{v}_i\right](\boldsymbol{x})$ as shown by a direct calculation. We can rewrite the variational segmentation problem (2.1) as the optimisation of

$$\mathcal{E}_{TV}(\mathbf{c}, \mathbf{v}) = \frac{1}{2} \sum_{i=1}^{n} \int_{\Omega} g * \left[(u - c_i(\boldsymbol{x}))^2 \mathbf{v}_i \right] (\boldsymbol{x}) \, d\boldsymbol{x} + \frac{\mu}{2} \sum_{i=1}^{n} \int_{\Omega} |D\mathbf{v}_i| \qquad (2.3)$$

$$\mathbf{v}(\boldsymbol{x}) \in \Delta_n \text{ (a.e)}$$

with $\mathbf{c} = (c_1 \ldots, c_n)$, and $c_i : D_i \supset \text{supp } \mathbf{v}_i \to \mathbb{R}$. The relaxation of the perimeter term used in [4] is very tight and often produces almost binary label fields $\mathbf{v}$. While this may be desirable in many situations, this can be a drawback, especially when partial volume effects have strong influence, as this is often the case in our 3D micro-CT applications, where a posterior probability may be better than a hard assignment. To avoid this relaxation behaviour, we replace the perimeter term by a quadratic one:

$$\mathcal{E}_Q(\mathbf{c}, \mathbf{v}) = \frac{1}{2} \sum_{i=1}^{n} \int_{\Omega} g * \left[(u - c_i(\boldsymbol{x}))^2 \mathbf{v}_i \right] (\boldsymbol{x}) \, d\boldsymbol{x} + \frac{\mu}{2} \sum_{i=1}^{n} \int_{\Omega} |D\mathbf{v}_i|^2 \, d\boldsymbol{x} \quad (2.4)$$

under the same HMMFM constraint on $\mathbf{v}$.

3   Optimisation

To optimise segmentation functionals (2.3) and (2.4), we use an approach where updates on $\mathbf{c}$ and $\mathbf{v}$ are computed alternately. The same general framework is used for both approaches.

Algorithm 1. Sketch of the algorithms.

Input: Input image volume u, number of classes n, weight parameter μ, kernel g and
   maximum number of iterations L_{RS}.
Output: Segmentation $(\mathbf{v}, \mathbf{c})$ of u.
Initialisation: Run a K-means or Otsu clustering to produce $(\mathbf{c}^0, \mathbf{v}^0)$ from u. For
   (2.3), an extra variable $\bar{\mathbf{v}}^0$ is initialised as $\mathbf{v}^0$ and dual variable $\boldsymbol{\xi}$ is initialised as 0,
   see below.
   for $r = 0$ to L_{RS} **do**
     ▷ **Solution in c**
       Solve for $\mathbf{c}^{r+1}$ from u and $\mathbf{v}^r$.
     ▷ **Solution in v**
       Solve for $\mathbf{v}^{r+1}$ from u and $\mathbf{c}^{r+1}$.
   end for

3.1   Update for c

Because of their very definitions, updates of the different local functions $c_1, \ldots, c_n$ are computed via (2.2).

3.2   Update for v

To compute an update of the HMMFM variable $\mathbf{v}$ for (2.3), we use the framework of [4] and a proximal method for (2.4). In the sequel, we denote by $\mathcal{L}_n := \mathcal{L}(\Omega, \Delta_n)$

the set of HMMFM $\Omega \to \Delta_n$ with proper regularity: $\mathcal{L}(\Omega, \Delta_n) \subset W^{1,2}(\Omega, \mathbb{R}^n)$ (resp. $\subset BV(\Omega, \mathbb{R}^n)$) for functional (2.4) (resp. (2.3)).

We first compute the gradient (in the $L^2(\Omega)$ sense) of the shared data term:

$$\mathbf{v} \mapsto \mathcal{E}_D(\mathbf{c}, \mathbf{v}) = \frac{1}{2} \sum_{i=1}^{n} \int_{\Omega} g * \left[(u - c_i(\boldsymbol{x}))^2 \mathbf{v}_i \right] (\boldsymbol{x}) \, d\boldsymbol{x}. \tag{3.1}$$

This term is linear in $\mathbf{v}$, thus equal to its differential and the gradient is obtained by adjunction, via the easily shown rule

$$\langle g * u, v \rangle_{L^2(\Omega)} = \langle u, \breve{g} * (v \chi_\Omega) \rangle_{L^2(\mathbb{R}^2)} \tag{3.2}$$

with $\breve{g}(t) = g(-t)$. Both Gaussian and NN-kernels are even: $\breve{g} = g$. Note also that if supp $u \subset \Omega$, the adjunction rule (3.2) simplifies to

$$\langle g * u, v \rangle_{L^2(\Omega)} = \langle u, \breve{g} * (v \chi_\Omega) \rangle_{L^2(\Omega)}. \tag{3.3}$$

We use these properties to rewrite $d_\mathbf{v} \mathcal{E}_D . \mathbf{w} = \mathcal{E}_D(\mathbf{w}, \mathbf{c})$ as

$$\mathcal{E}_D(\mathbf{c}, \mathbf{w}) = \frac{1}{2} \sum_{i=1}^{n} \langle \mathbf{w}_i, u^2 g * \chi_\Omega - 2ug * c_i + g * c_i^2 \rangle_{L^2(\Omega)},$$

for a $\mathbf{w} = (\mathbf{w}_1, \dots, \mathbf{w}_n)$ with support in Ω. The sought gradient is thus

$$\nabla_\mathbf{v} \mathcal{E}_D = \frac{1}{2} \left(u^2 g * \chi_\Omega - 2ug * c_i + g * c_i^2 \right)_{i=1}^{n}. \tag{3.4}$$

Quadratic Regularised Functional. Functional (2.4) is differentiable with respect to $\mathbf{v}$, with a gradient given by

$$\nabla_\mathbf{v} \mathcal{E}_Q = \nabla_\mathbf{v} \mathcal{E}_D - \mu \Delta \mathbf{v} \tag{3.5}$$

with Δ a vector Laplacian and assuming null Neumann boundary conditions on $\partial \Omega$. An update for a current value $\mathbf{v}^r$ at iteration r is computed in two steps. In the sequel, t_r is a descent step that may or may not depend on r. We in fact decrease it in our implementation, $t_r = C/r$ for a constant C.

1. Implicit descent step: $\overline{\mathbf{v}^r} = \mathbf{v}^r - t_r \left(\nabla_\mathbf{v} \mathcal{E}_Q - \nu \Delta \overline{\mathbf{v}^r} \right)$, i.e. we solve the following equation

$$\left(-\nu \Delta + t_r^{-1} \mathrm{id} \right) \overline{\mathbf{v}^{r+1}} = t_r^{-1} \mathbf{v}_r - \nabla_\mathbf{v} \mathcal{E}_D. \tag{3.6}$$

2. Projection:

$$\mathbf{v}^{r+1} = \mathcal{P}_{\mathcal{L}_n} \left(\overline{\mathbf{v}^r} \right). \tag{3.7}$$

This is a variation over an incremental proximal step, the reader is referred to [1]. Numerically, a 4-points stencil is used to discretise the Laplacian and we perform one sweep of a Jacobi solver per update. The orthogonal projection operator $\mathcal{P}_{\mathcal{L}_n}$ projects each $\mathbf{v}(\boldsymbol{x})$ on the standard simplex. We use the classical algorithm from [7].

Total-Variation Regularised Functional. Functional (2.3) is not differentiable with respect to $\mathbf{v}$ and the optimisation in $\mathbf{v}$ from (3.6) is replaced by the primal dual step of [4]. We recall it for the reader's convenience. In a continuous setting, the total variation is defined by duality. The local convex envelope of [4]

$$J(\mathbf{v}) = \sup\left\{ -\int_{\Omega} \sum_{i=1}^{n} \mathbf{v}_i \mathrm{div}\xi_i \ : \ \boldsymbol{\xi} \in C_c^{\infty}(\Omega, \mathbb{R}^{n \times d}, \boldsymbol{\xi}(x) \in K, \forall x \in \Omega \right\}$$

with $K = \{\mathbf{q} \in \mathbb{R}^{n \times d} : |q_i - q_j| <= 1, \forall i < j\}$ gives in fact the proper representation of the TV-norm of the HMMFM $\mathbf{v}$, due to a convexity argument.

The primal variable at iteration r is $\mathbf{v}^r$, used with the extra one $\bar{\mathbf{v}}^r$, while the dual variable is $\boldsymbol{\xi}^r$. We update them as follows. Set $\boldsymbol{\xi}_0^r = \boldsymbol{\xi}^r$, $\mathbf{v}_0^r = \mathbf{v}^r$ and $\bar{\mathbf{v}}_0^r = \bar{\mathbf{v}}^r$. Then we run I iterations

$$\boldsymbol{\xi}_{i+1}^r = \mathcal{P}_K \left(\boldsymbol{\xi}_i^r + \tau_r \nabla \bar{\mathbf{v}}_i^r \right) \tag{3.8}$$

$$\mathbf{v}_{i+1}^r = \mathcal{P}_{\mathcal{L}_n} \left(\mathbf{v}_i^r + t_r \left(\mathrm{div}\boldsymbol{\xi}_{i+1}^r - \nabla_{\mathbf{v}} \mathcal{E}_D \right) \right) \tag{3.9}$$

$$\bar{\mathbf{v}}_{i+1}^r = 2\mathbf{v}_{i+1}^r - \mathbf{v}_i^r. \tag{3.10}$$

and set $\boldsymbol{\xi}^{r+1} = \boldsymbol{\xi}_I^r$, $\mathbf{v}^{r+1} = \mathbf{v}_I^r$ and $\bar{\mathbf{v}}^{r+1} = \bar{\mathbf{v}}_I^r$. We set $I = 3$ as it provides the best results. Numerically, forward differences are used for the gradient ∇, and the numerical divergence is defined by duality. In contrast to the quadratic regularization method, the descent step parameter t_r and ascent step parameter τ_r are kept fixed.

4   Experimental Validation

There is no ground truth segmentation available on real tomograms. Therefore we present and evaluate results on a synthetic volume that we call SYN250 in the sequel. It simulates a porous medium, i.e., a medium which contains voids. It has a background class (void) and three non-background classes, simulating three different materials in a sample. Four segments are thus expected.

Noise is then added to it. A global bias field is added, resulting in the test volume SYN250$_{\text{global}}$. A per-segment bias field is also added to SYN250$_{\text{global}}$, resulting in the second test volume SYN250$_{\text{local}}$. We describe below how we have generated them, the evaluation methodology used, and the parameter selection.

All results have been obtained on a personal computer with a 4th generation Intel Core i7-4910MQ CPU, at 2.90 GHz, 32 GB DDR3 1600 Mhz RAM, and Ubuntu vivid, 15.04 operating system.

4.1   Synthetic Datasets

Clean Data. It consists of randomly distributed balls on a 3D volume of size $250 \times 250 \times 250$ voxels. Radii range from 3 to 10 voxels, uniformly distributed as well as the centre locations. Intensity values follow known material class distributions, and the sampling is stopped when a background to material ratio is reached. Ball overlap is allowed to complicate the geometry of the data.

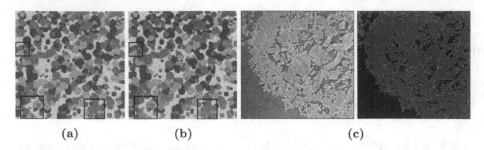

(a)   (b)   (c)

Fig. 2. The synthetic datasets with global (a) and global + class bias fields (b), $SYN250_{global}$ and $SYN250_{class}$ respectively. Each red square highlights significant differences between the two. In the largest square, an entire class has been cancelled out, due to the class bias fields. (c) shows the segmentation result, using the proposed method with $\mu = 25$ and kernel size $= 256$, of a real 2-phase tomogram (irn: Chalk P3 1.1.3C), of dimensions $800 \times 800 \times 256$, with added bias field, inducing intensity variations between -10% and 20% of the original intensity range. (Color figure online)

Bias Field and Noise. Global bias fields are added as 3rd degree polynomials with random coefficients scaled to cover a given percentage of the intensity range. Per-segment bias fields are generated the same way. Gaussian white noise is added with a standard deviation up to 15% of the intensity range. Bias field and noise is added to the ground truth.

4.2   Performance Criteria

We report primarily Sørensen-Dice (DSC) index. True positive rate (TPR/sensitivity), true negative rate (TNR/specificity), and positive predictive value (PPV/precision) are computed. Also, porosity (amount of background in material), pore network connectivity, which summarises the background class/void inside the material: largest connected pore network divided by the total pore size. Porosity ratio (Por. ratio) is the ratio between measured porosity and the ground truth porosity. Connectivity ratio (Con. ratio) does the same for connectivity.

These parameters describe properties of the pore space, and are essential for the correctness of future geophysical applications, like fluid simulation studies. A detailed explanation of these two parameters can be found in [12].

Measurements of TPR, TNR, and PPV have been computed for each class individually. To account for class distribution, a weighted sum is used, with weights corresponding to the ground truth class distributions. A unique DSC score formed by averaging the different class versus class is reported.

The running time T is an important factor for the method. All experiments run five iterations of Algorithm 1. We also experimented with up to 100 iterations for all the relevant iterative methods. They showed a slight improvement in segmentation results, but at the cost of a large running time.

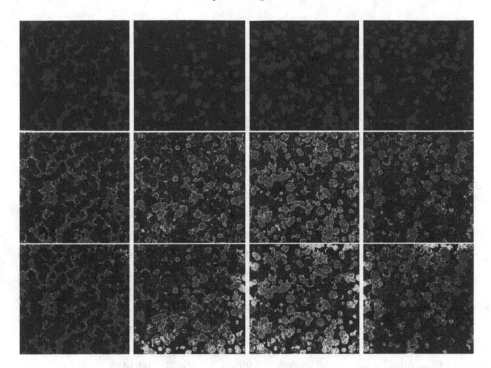

Fig. 3. Segmentation of $\text{SYN250}^3_{\text{global}}$ (row 2) and $\text{SYN250}^3_{\text{local}}$ (row 3), using the proposed method. Row 1 is ground truth. Each column corresponds to a class.

4.3 Methods

In the sequel, method (2.4) is referred to as Tikhonov, (2.3) as TV. We also use the piecewise constant Mumford-Shah method of [4] as PCMS. We compare with Otsu and Dual filtering (Dual filter) methods used in [12].

4.4 Results

Segmentation results of the simulated data are visualised in Fig. 3, using Tikhonov and NN-kernels. It clearly illustrates the difficulty of a visual evaluation, due to the complexity of the data, and the necessity of objective criteria.

We started by estimating parameters of the methods to provide the best DSC score. Both Tikhonov and TV include kernel parameters and smoothness versus data fidelity weight parameters. For a Gaussian kernel, the kernel parameter is its standard deviation σ, while for the NN-kernel, it is the radius ρ. Table 1 shows the best parameters for the DSC score of the $\text{SYN250}_{\text{global}}$ dataset. The methods show comparable behaviours in terms of kernel parameters and smoothness weights. They are slightly suboptimal for $\text{SYN250}_{\text{local}}$, but with a DSC score difference less than 0.05%.

Next, we compare DSC, TPR, TNR, PPV for the $\text{SYN250}_{\text{global}}$ dataset in Table 2 for our methods and the other test methods. Running time is also

Table 1. Best parameters for the variants of the proposed method, run on SYN250$_{\text{global}}$.

Method	Kernel parameter	$\dfrac{1}{\mu}$
Tikhonov NN	53	91
Tikhonov Gaussian	55	89
TV NN	102	4
TV Gaussian	172	4

Table 2. DSC, TPR, TNR, PPV, and T values for the segmentation results of SYN250$_{\text{global}}$, using the selected methods.

Method	Kernel	DSC	TPR	TNR	PPV	T (s)
Tikhonov	NN	**0.991576**	**0.98018**	**0.99504**	**0.98606**	90.10
Tikhonov	Gaussian	0.991422	0.97975	0.99497	0.98587	162.92
TV	NN	0.956096	0.89397	0.97732	0.93107	228.28
TV	Gaussian	0.956050	0.89389	0.97729	0.93097	311.28
Method	-	DSC	TPR	TNR	PPV	T (s)
PCMS	-	0.958090	0.88087	0.98259	0.94811	114.96
Otsu	-	0.894342	0.78868	0.93196	0.80911	**2.02**
Dual filter	-	0.954899	0.90980	0.96833	0.91485	16.51

reported in the same table. The same is done for the SYN250$_{\text{local}}$ dataset in Table 3. We now report geological relevant criteria, in Table 4 for SYN250$_{\text{global}}$ and in Table 5 for SYN250$_{\text{local}}$.

For both datasets, Tikhonov methods perform better than the others with a slight advantage on all the criteria used. For DSC, TPR, TNR, PPV, there is a slight advantage to the NN-kernel, while Gaussian seems slightly better for connectivity measurements, though, the difference is not significant. All methods present degraded performances when per-segment bias fields are applied. This is of course to be expected. Figure 2a and b illustrate that in that situation, it seems that some spatially closed segments merge.

Our proposed method has also been validated on real experimental data in Fig. 2c for a high resolution 2-phased setting and Fig. 4 for a low resolution 3-phased setting. In both cases a $[-10, 20]\%$ bias field was added. From visual inspection, the results are very satisfying in both cases.

Generally the smoothness to data fidelity weight μ has the biggest impact on the results, and this is of course expected. We optimised for it directly, but other methods, such as Hansen's L-curve [6] could be considered.

The extend of the kernel was related to the rate of convergence, larger kernels converging faster. Of course, choosing a kernel size approaching the dimensions of the image will result in a Chan-Vese/piecewise constant-like behaviour and not remove the bias field properly. Choosing too small a kernel produces similarly

Table 3. DSC, TPR, TNR, PPV, and T values for the segmentation results of SYN250$_{local}$, using the selected methods.

Method	Kernel	DSC	TPR	TNR	PPV	T (s)
Tikhonov	NN	**0.978750**	**0.95435**	**0.98884**	**0.96224**	76.60
Tikhonov	Gaussian	0.977205	0.95039	0.98801	0.95997	160.85
TV	NN	0.940032	0.86449	0.96659	0.89872	224.71
TV	Gaussian	0.939879	0.86027	0.96764	0.90113	305.83
Method	-	DSC	TPR	TNR	PPV	T (s)
PCMS	-	0.941654	0.84959	0.97265	0.91403	108.18
Otsu	-	0.888680	0.77736	0.92772	0.79739	**1.89**
Dual filter	-	0.937939	0.87588	0.95904	0.88345	15.44

Table 4. Porosity, connectivity and their respective ratios to the same measures for the ground truth, run on SYN250$_{global}$, using the selected methods.

Method	Kernel	Porosity	Por. ratio	Connectivity	Con. ratio
Ground truth	-	*0.249998*	*1.0*	*0.999617*	*1.0*
Tikhonov	NN	**0.248629**	**0.994523**	0.998814	0.999197
Tikhonov	Gaussian	0.248567	0.994272	**0.998851**	**0.999234**
TV	NN	0.237072	0.948296	0.990781	0.991160
TV	Gaussian	0.237048	0.948198	0.990785	0.991164
Method	-	Porosity	Por. ratio	Connectivity	Con. ratio
PCMS	-	0.233670	0.934685	0.997779	0.998161
Otsu	-	0.228024	0.912102	0.980602	0.980978
Dual filter	-	0.228537	0.914155	0.996137	0.996519

Table 5. Porosity, connectivity and their respective ratios to the same measures for the ground truth, run on SYN250$_{local}$, using the selected methods.

Regularizer	Kernel	Porosity	Por. ratio	Connectivity	Con. ratio
Ground truth	-	*0.249998*	*1.0*	*0.999617*	*1.0*
Tikhonov	NN	**0.250620**	**1.002488**	0.998527	0.998909
Tikhonov	Gaussian	0.250724	1.002902	**0.998541**	**0.908923**
TV	NN	0.243557	0.974236	0.994584	0.994966
TV	Gaussian	0.242811	0.971251	0.995116	0.995498
Method	-	Porosity	Por. ratio	Connectivity	Con. ratio
PCMS	-	0.239993	0.959977	0.998053	0.998436
Otsu	-	0.234354	0.937422	0.979921	0.980297
Dual filter	-	0.236129	0.944522	0.996227	0.996609

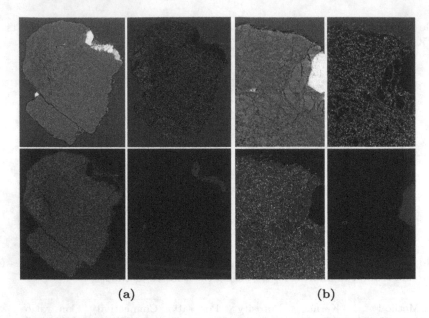

Fig. 4. Segmentation of a real 3-class dataset (irn: Hod chalk #16 from the North Sea Basin) using the proposed method. Size $= 256 \times 1025 \times 825$. $\nu = 300$, kernel size $= 512^3$.

poor results because the underlying image structure is not represented well. Kernel extents should be related to the frequency/scale of the bias field. Priori knowledge of this scale could be obtained by considerations of the physics of the measurement device, as well as prior knowledge of the material content.

5   Conclusion

In this paper we have proposed two multiphase segmentation methods that cope with noise and bias fields for complex low structured volumes, especially targeted to μCT and nanoCT used in geology. Based on the Mumford-Shah functional, they discriminate regions based on local averages of their contents. Using HMMFM and with Tikhonov regularisation or TV regularisation, they provide spatially coherent class posteriors of voxels. The methods are easy to implement and reasonably fast, though we have not optimised for running time. Their running time performances could be greatly improved by proper parallelisation.

We have investigated the methods on synthetic datasets via Gaussian- and NN-kernels. They appear robust to parameter variation. They show similar results, though with an advantage to NN-kernels and quadratic regularisation. We have validated them using some classical segmentation validation criteria as well as more specific criteria used in geoscience. In a future work, we will investigate means for estimating the kernel extent and develop parallel code.

Acknowledgements. J. Hansen and F. Lauze acknowledge funding from the Innovation Fund Denmark and Mærsk Oil and Gas A/S, for the P^3 Project. We thank Henning Osholm Sørensen for giving us access to the experimental tomography data.

References

1. Bertsekas, D.: Incremental proximal methods for large scale convex optimization. Math. Program. Ser. B. **129**, 163–195 (2011)
2. Brox, T., Cremers, D.: On local regions models and a statistical interpretation of the piecewise smooth Mumford-Shah functional. Int. J. Comput. Vis. **84**, 184–193 (2009)
3. Buzug, T.N.: Computed Tomography from Photon Statistics to Modern Cone Beam CT. Springer, Berlin (2008)
4. Chambolle, A., Cremers, D., Pock, T.: A convex approach to minimal partitions. SIAM J. Imaging Sci. **5**(4), 1113–1158 (2012)
5. Chan, T.F., Vese, L.A.: Active contours without edges. Trans. Image Process. **10**(2), 266–277 (2001)
6. Hansen, P.C., O'Leary, D.P.: The use of the L-curve in the regularization of discrete ill-posed problems. SIAM J. Sci. Comput. **14**(6), 1487–1503 (1993)
7. Held, M., Crowder, P.W.W.: Validation of subgradient optimization. Math. Program. **6**, 62–88 (1974)
8. Huang, C., Zeng, L.: An active contour model for the segmentation of images with intensity inhomogeneities and bias field estimation. PloS One **10**(4), e0120399 (2015)
9. Lauze, F., Nielsen, M.: From inpainting to active contours. Int. J. Comput. Vis. **79**(1), 31–43 (2008)
10. Marroquin, J.L., Santana, E.A., Botello, S.: Hidden Markov measure field models for image segmentation. IEEE Trans. Pattern Anal. Mach. Intell. **25**(11), 1380–1387 (2003)
11. Mumford, D., Shah, J.: Optimal approximations by piecewise smooth functions and associated variational problems. Commun. Pure Appl. Math. **42**(5), 577–685 (1989)
12. Müter, D., Pedersen, S., Sørensen, H.O., Feidenhans'L, R., Stipp, S.L.S.: Improved segmentation of X-ray tomography data from porous rocks using a dual filtering approach. Comput. Geosci. **49**, 131–139 (2012)
13. Müter, D., Sørensen, H.O., Jha, D., Harti, R., Dalby, K.N., Suhonen, H., Feidenhans, R., Engstrøm, F., Stipp, S.L.S.: Resolution dependence of petrophysical parameters derived from X-ray tomography of chalk. Appl. Phys. Lett. **105**, 4 (2014)
14. Nielsen, M., Florack, L., Deriche, R.: Regularization, scale-space, and edge detection filters. J. Math. Imaging Vis **7**, 201 307 (1997)
15. Pham, D.L., Prince, J.L.: Adaptive fuzzy segmentation of magnetic resonance images. IEEE Trans. Med. Imaging **18**(9), 737–752 (1999)
16. Wang, X.-F., Huang, D.-S., Xu, H.: An efficient local chan-vese model for image segmentation. Pattern Recognit. **43**(3), 603–618 (2010)

An Efficient Lagrangian Algorithm
for an Anisotropic Geodesic
Active Contour Model

Günay Doğan[1,2]([✉])

[1] Theiss Research, La Jolla, CA 92037, USA
g.dogan@theissresearch.org
[2] National Institute of Standards and Technology, Gaithersburg, MD 20899, USA

Abstract. We propose an efficient algorithm to minimize an anisotropic surface energy generalizing the Geodesic Active Contour model for image segmentation. In this energy, the weight function may depend on the normal of the curve/surface. Our algorithm is Lagrangian, but nonparametric. We only use the node and connectivity information for computations. Our approach provides a flexible scheme, in the sense that it allows to easily incorporate the generalized gradients proposed recently, especially those based on the H^1 scalar product on the surface. However, unlike these approaches, our scheme is applicable in any number of dimensions, such as surfaces in 3d or 4d, and allows weighted H^1 scalar products, with weights may depending on the normal and the curvature. We derive the second shape derivative of the anisotropic surface energy, and use it as the basis for a new weighted H^1 scalar product. In this way, we obtain a Newton-type method that not only gives smoother flows, but also converges in fewer iterations and much shorter time.

1 Introduction

Finding the boundaries of objects or regions in images is a fundamental problem in computer vision. Active contour methods proposed in the eighties have been a very successful approach to solve this problem. One of the pioneering methods of this approach is the Geodesic Active Contour (GAC) model by Caselles et al. In [4], they propose finding the boundaries as curves Γ that correspond to the minima of a weighted length integral

$$J_{GAC}(\Gamma) = \int_{\Gamma} \rho(|\nabla I(x)|)d\sigma, \tag{1}$$

where $\rho(s) = (1 + s^2/\lambda^2)^{-1}$, $\lambda > 0$ and $I : \mathcal{D} \subset \mathbb{R}^2 \to \mathbb{R}$ is the smoothed image intensity function. Later Caselles et al. extend this to 3d in [5] to extract surfaces in volumetric images.

Following [4], many extensions and intricate energies were proposed to address the challenges of the segmentation problem. However the model (1)

© Springer International Publishing AG 2017
F. Lauze et al. (Eds.): SSVM 2017, LNCS 10302, pp. 408–420, 2017.
DOI: 10.1007/978-3-319-58771-4_33

has maintained its value and is still widely used. In this paper, we consider an anisotropic variant of (1) in a more general setting

$$J(\Gamma) = \int_{\Gamma} g(x, n) d\sigma, \tag{2}$$

where Γ is an $(d$-1$)$-dimensional surface in a d-dimensional space. The energy $J(\Gamma)$ is an anisotropically weighted surface integral. The weight function g depends on the normal n of the surface Γ, as well as the spatial coordinates x of the surface. This variation has found application in edge integration [15] and variational stereo [10,11,14].

To devise minimization schemes for (2), we need to compute deformation velocities V to evolve the surface Γ in a way that will decrease its energy. A crucial step for this is to quantify the effect of a candidate velocity V on the energy $J(\Gamma)$. For this, we use the concept of shape derivatives [8], which we define in Sect. 2. The shape derivative of $J(\Gamma)$ with respect to a velocity V is given by $dJ(\Gamma; V) = \int_{\Gamma} (g\kappa + \partial_n g + \mathrm{div}_{\Gamma}(g_y)_{\Gamma}) V d\sigma$, where $V = V \cdot n$ and κ is the mean curvature of Γ, g_y denotes the derivative of g with respect to the normal variable, div_{Γ} is the tangential divergence operator defined in Sect. 2. This has been known in the area of geometric flows [7], but was recently rederived in computer vision literature using method of moving frame [12] and level set formalism [21]. If we choose

$$V = -(g\kappa + \partial_n g + \mathrm{div}_{\Gamma}(g_y)_{\Gamma}), \tag{3}$$

we ensure $dJ(\Gamma; V) \leqslant 0$, hence energy decrease for $J(\Gamma)$. This choice commonly used in computer vision corresponds to using an L^2 metric for the velocity space. Recently H^1 metric has been proposed by Charpiat et al. [6] and Sundaramoorthi et al. [23]. When applied to the surface energy (2), this corresponds to the following velocity equation

$$\alpha_0 \Delta_{\Gamma} V + V = -(g\kappa + \partial_n g + \mathrm{div}_{\Gamma}(g_y)_{\Gamma}), \tag{4}$$

where $\alpha_0 \geqslant 0$ is a constant and Δ_{Γ} denotes the tangential Laplacian operator defined in Sect. 2. This equation yields spatially coherent velocities, therefore smoother evolutions. In [6,23], the H^1 metric is considered in 2d for curves only and a numerical solution is proposed by turning it into an ODE and computing the solution with a convolution.

In this paper, we will consider the weak form of a more general version of (4)

$$\langle \alpha \nabla_{\Gamma} V, \nabla_{\Gamma} \phi \rangle + \langle \beta V, \psi \rangle = -\langle g\kappa, \phi \rangle - \langle \partial_n g, \phi \rangle + \langle (g_y)_{\Gamma}, \nabla_{\Gamma} \phi \rangle, \ \forall \phi \in H^1(\Gamma), \tag{5}$$

where $\alpha = \alpha(x, n, \kappa) \geqslant 0$, $\beta = \beta(x, n, \kappa) \geqslant 0$ and ∇_{Γ} denotes the tangential gradient defined in 2. This more general velocity equation provides new opportunities to compute better descent velocities for (2). In particular, we can derive the second shape derivative of (2) and leverage (5) to implement Newton-type minimization schemes (see [1] for a trust-region-Newton method). *The second shape derivative of (2) is the first contribution of this paper (see [13] for GAC* energy (1)), and it will enable us to achieve faster convergence, and robustness to varying image conditions.

We will also propose a Lagrangian computational scheme based on the finite element method (FEM) to compute the velocity V from (5) and to deform the surface Γ with V decreasing its energy $J(\Gamma)$. *This FEM-based velocity scheme is the main contribution of our paper and has the following advantages*:

- The scheme is applicable in any number of dimensions including surface in 3d and 4d, unlike the schemes proposed in [6,23], applicable in 2d only.
- The weights α, β in (5) are not constant as in [6,23]. They can in fact be more general functions and depend on the position x, the normal n and the mean curvature κ of the surface Γ, and we exploit this to implement fast Newton-type minimization schemes.
- Although the scheme is Lagrangian, it is nonparametric, that is, we do not parametrize the surface Γ. We only work with the list of simplices that represent Γ. This greatly simplifies the implementation.
- To compute the velocity V using (5), we only need first derivatives g_x, g_y of g. This is in contrast to the previous approaches [10,14] that use (3) within a level set framework. They need to account for the term $\text{div}_\Gamma(g_y)_\Gamma$, which requires second derivatives of g. As level set discretization of this term is very tedious, it is often ignored.

2   Shape Derivatives of the Energy

We use the concept of shape derivatives to understand the change in the energy induced by a given velocity field V. Once we have the means to evaluate how any given velocity V affects the energy, we will be able to choose a descent velocity from the space of admissible velocities, namely a velocity that decreases the energy for a given surface Γ.

Before we start deriving the shape derivatives of (2). We need some definitions and concepts from differential geometry. We denote the outer unit normal, the scalar (total or mean) curvature and the curvature vector of surface $\Gamma \in C^2$ by n, κ, $\boldsymbol{\kappa}(:= \kappa n)$ respectively. For given functions $f, w \in C^2(\mathcal{D})$ on image domain $\mathcal{D}$, we define the tangential gradient $\nabla_\Gamma f = (\nabla f - \partial_n f n)|_\Gamma$, tangential divergence $\text{div}_\Gamma w = (\text{div} w - n \cdot Dw \cdot n)|_\Gamma$, tangential Laplacian $\Delta_\Gamma f = (\Delta f - n \cdot D^2 f \cdot n - \kappa \partial_n f)|_\Gamma$. We define the *shape derivative* of energy $J(\Gamma)$ at Γ with respect to velocity field V as the limit $dJ(\Gamma; V) = \lim_{t \to 0} \frac{1}{t}(J(\Gamma_t) - J(\Gamma))$, where $\Gamma_t = \{x(t, X) : X \in \Gamma\}$ is the deformation of Γ by V via equation $\frac{dx}{dt} = V(x(t)), x(0) = X$ [8,20]. For a surface-dependent function $\psi(\Gamma)$, the *material derivative* $\dot{\psi}(\Gamma; V)$ and the *shape derivative* $\psi'(\Gamma; V)$ at Γ in direction V are defined as follows [20, Def. 2.85,2.88]:

$$\dot{\psi}(\Omega; V) = \lim_{t \to 0} \frac{1}{t}(\psi(x(t, \cdot), \Gamma_t) - \psi(\cdot, \Gamma_0)), \quad \psi'(\Gamma; V) = \dot{\psi}(\Gamma; V) - \nabla_\Gamma \psi \cdot V.$$

The 2nd shape derivatives defined as: $\psi''(\Gamma; V, W) = (\psi'(\Gamma; V))'(\Gamma; W)$, and $d^2 J(\Gamma; V, W) = d(dJ(\Gamma; V))(\Gamma; W)$.

With these definitions, we can now calculate the shape derivative of the weighted surface energy (2). In the following, V denotes $\mathbf{V} \cdot n$ the normal component of the vector velocity.

Lemma 1 [13, Sect. 3]. *The shape derivative $n'(\Gamma; \mathbf{V})$ of the normal n of the surface Γ in direction $\mathbf{V}$ is given by $n' = n'(\Gamma; \mathbf{V}) = -\nabla_\Gamma V$.*

Theorem 1 [20, Sect. 2.33]. *Let $\psi = \psi(x, \Gamma)$ be given so that $\dot{\psi}(\Gamma; \mathbf{V})$, $\psi'(\Gamma; \mathbf{V})$ exist. Then $J(\Gamma) = \int_\Gamma \psi(x, \Gamma) d\sigma$ is shape differentiable and we have $dJ(\Gamma; \mathbf{V}) = \int_\Gamma \psi'(\Gamma; \mathbf{V}) d\sigma + \int_\Gamma (\partial_\nu \psi + \kappa \psi) V d\sigma$.*

Notice that the shape derivative depends only on the normal component V of $\mathbf{V}$. Therefore, from this point on, we work with scalar velocities V so that $\mathbf{V} = V n$.

Theorem 2. *Let $\psi = \psi(x, \Gamma)$ be given so that $\psi'(\Gamma; V)$, $\psi''(\Gamma; V, W)$ exist. Then, the 2nd shape derivative of $J(\Gamma) = \int_\Gamma \psi(x, \Gamma) d\sigma$ with respect to V, W is*

$$d^2 J(\Gamma; V, W) = \int_\Gamma \psi''(\Gamma; V, W) d\sigma + \int_\Gamma \psi \nabla_\Gamma V \cdot \nabla_\Gamma W + (\kappa^2 - \Sigma \kappa_i^2) \psi V W d\sigma$$

$$+ \int_\Gamma (\partial_n \psi'(\Gamma; W) + \kappa \psi'(\Gamma; W)) V + (\partial_n \psi'(\Gamma; V) + \kappa \psi'(\Gamma; V)) W d\sigma.$$

In the following, g_x, g_y denote the derivatives of $g(x, n)$ with respect to the first variable x and the second variable n respectively.

Proposition 1. *The shape derivative of (2) at Γ with respect to V is*

$$dJ(\Gamma; V) = \int_\Gamma (\kappa g + \partial_n g) V - g_y \cdot \nabla_\Gamma V d\sigma = \int_\Gamma (\kappa g + \partial_n g + \mathrm{div}_\Gamma (g_y)_\Gamma) V d\sigma.$$

Proof. We use Theorem 1 with $\psi = g(x, n)$. Then $\psi'(\Gamma; V) = g_y \cdot n' = -g_y \cdot \nabla_\Gamma V$ using Lemma 1. We also need to compute the normal derivative of $g(x, n)$. We have $\partial_n \psi = \partial_n(g(x, n)) = \partial_n g + g_y^T \partial_n n = \partial_n g$ (note $\partial_n n = 0$). We substitute $\psi', \partial_n \psi$ in Theorem 1 $\Rightarrow dJ(\Gamma; V) = \int_\Gamma (\kappa g + \partial_n g) V - g_y \cdot \nabla_\Gamma V d\sigma$.

We apply the tangential Green's formula to the last term of the integral, and use the identity $\mathrm{div}_\Gamma(\boldsymbol{\omega})_\Gamma = \mathrm{div}_\Gamma(\boldsymbol{\omega}) - \kappa \boldsymbol{\omega} \cdot n$ [8, Chap. 8] to obtain the result.

Proposition 2. *The 2nd shape deriv. $d^2 J(\Gamma; V, W)$ of (2) w.r.t. velocities V, W*

$$d^2 J = \int_\Gamma \nabla_\Gamma V \cdot ((g - g_y \cdot n) Id + g_{yy}) \cdot \nabla_\Gamma W d\sigma + \int_\Gamma \left(\frac{\partial^2 g}{\partial n^2} + 2\kappa \frac{\partial g}{\partial n} + (\kappa^2 - \sum \kappa_i^2) g \right) V W d\sigma$$

$$- \int_\Gamma (\kappa g_y - g_y^T \nabla_\Gamma n + n^T g_{xy}^T) \cdot (\nabla_\Gamma W V + \nabla_\Gamma V W) d\sigma.$$

Proof. $\psi = g(x, n)$ in Theorem 2 $\Rightarrow \partial_n \psi = \partial_n g, \partial_{nn} \psi = \partial_{nn} g, \psi'(\Gamma; V) = -g_y \cdot \nabla_\Gamma V$,

$$\psi''(\Gamma; V, W) = -(g_y)' \cdot \nabla_\Gamma V - g_y \cdot (\nabla_\Gamma V)' = \nabla_\Gamma V \cdot g_{yy} \cdot \nabla_\Gamma W - g_y \cdot n \nabla_\Gamma V \cdot \nabla_\Gamma W$$

$$= \nabla_\Gamma V \cdot (g_{yy} - g_y \cdot n \, Id) \cdot \nabla_\Gamma W$$

$$\partial_n \psi'(\Gamma; V) = -\partial_n g_y \cdot \nabla_\Gamma V - g_y \cdot \partial_n \nabla_\Gamma V = -(g_{yx} n) \cdot \nabla_\Gamma V - g_y \cdot (-\nabla_\Gamma n \nabla_\Gamma V)$$

$$= (g_y^T \nabla_\Gamma n - n^T g_{yx}^T) \nabla_\Gamma V,$$

since $\partial_n \nabla_\Gamma V = -\nabla_\Gamma n \nabla_\Gamma V$. Substitute deriv.s of ψ in Theorem (2), and reorganize.

3   The Minimization Algorithm

Given shape derivatives of surface energy (2) in Sect. 2, we can develop
an iterative minimization algorithm to compute minimal surfaces as follows:

choose an initial surface Γ^0.
repeat
    compute the descent velocity $\boldsymbol{V}^k$.
    choose step size τ^k.
    update the surface points $\boldsymbol{X}^{k+1} = \boldsymbol{X}^k + \tau^k \boldsymbol{V}^k$, $\forall \boldsymbol{X}^k \in \Gamma^k$.
until stopping criterion is satisfied.

This is a well-known approach. However, realizing an effective algorithm that will
always converge, with a small number of iterations and a small computational
cost, is not straight-forward. One needs to design the three main components of
the algorithm carefully to ensure effectiveness for a diverse set of image inputs.
These are: *stopping criterion, step size τ^k selection,* and *the gradient descent
velocity $\boldsymbol{V}^k$*. Wrong stopping criteria may lead to premature termination of iterations or no convergence. The selection of the step sizes has an impact on convergence as well. Cautious small steps at each iteration can ensure convergence,
but may result in too many iterations and long computation times, whereas
large steps can enable fast convergence, but might miss the local minima that
we need to capture. Moreover, in some iteration schemes, large step sizes can
create instabilities in the surface evolution, manifested as noisy or oscillatory
geometric patterns on the surface. We describe our solutions for these below.

Step Size Selection: Minimization problems of this type have traditionally
been formulated as surface evolution problems with fixed step sizes. However,
with fixed steps, one may miss the minima, or the iterations may not converge.
For this reason, we use the Armijo criterion [13,18] to select a step $10^{-4} \leqslant \tau^k \leqslant$
1 ensuring energy decrease at iteration k. Our initial candidate for a step at
iteration k is $\min(2\tau^{k-1}, \tau_{\max}^k)$ where is $\tau_{\max}^k$ is a safe-guard maximum step that
can be taken at iteration k and we set $\tau^0 = 0.01$. We accept and use the step τ^k
if it satisfies the following energy decrease condition,

$$J(\Gamma^{k+1}) < J(\Gamma^k) + \eta\tau^k dJ(\Gamma^k; V^k), \qquad (6)$$

where is η a small positive number, $\eta = 10^{-3}$ in our experiments. If condition (6)
is not satisfied, we reduce this step (divide by two) until it is satisfied.

Since our goal is to reach a *local* minimum of (2), we do not want to move
the surface Γ too much at each iteration (not to miss a minimum). Therefore, we
impose an iteration-dependent max step $\tau_{\max}^k$, based on the maximum displacement Γ can take without missing an important feature of energy landscape. If δ_I
is the image-dependent bound on the displacement we allow, then the maximum
step is given by $\tau_{\max}^k = \delta_I / \max(V)$, in which the bound δ_I can be set to the average width of a valley of the energy weight $g(x, n)$ or the average edge width of the
image function $I(x)$. In our examples, we used $\delta_I = 2\sigma$, where σ is the standard

deviation of Gaussian $G_\sigma(x)$ applied to the image $I(x)$ to define the isotropic edge indicator function $g(x) = 1/(1+|\nabla G_\sigma * I(x)|^2/\lambda^2), \lambda = \frac{1}{4}\max|\nabla G_\sigma * I| > 0$.

Stopping Criterion: In finite-dimensional optimization, the iterations are stopped when the norm of the energy gradient is below a given threshold. A typical choice for this norm is the Euclidean norm. This is not applicable to the shape gradient, because it is a mapping defined on the surface, and the surface itself changes through the iterations. To address these issues, we use the L^2 norm $\|G\|_{L^2(\Gamma)} = \left(\int_\Gamma |G|^2 d\sigma\right)^{1/2}$ of the shape gradient $G = g\kappa + \partial_n g + \text{div}_\Gamma(g_y)_\Gamma$ and accompanying shape gradient thresholds $\varepsilon_{abs}, \varepsilon_{rel}$ to realize a stopping criterion. If we require the pointwise value $|G(x)|$ of the shape gradient at the optimal surface Γ^* to be a small fraction of a pointwise maximum value $G_{max} \approx \max_{x \in D, n \in S^1} |G(x,n)|$, then the following threshold for the L^2 norm can be used

$$\|G\|_{L^2(\Gamma)} < (\varepsilon_{abs} + \varepsilon_{rel} G_{max})|\Gamma|^{1/2}. \tag{7}$$

In our experiments, we set $\varepsilon_{abs} = 0.1, \varepsilon_{rel} = 0.01$, and use the quantity $\max|g|/\delta_I$ as an indicator of the scale of G_{max}. In addition to the stopping criterion (7), we monitor the energy change. If step size selection cannot provide an acceptable step τ^k satisfying (6) before convergence (7), then we check energy change in recent iterations. If the change has been very small, i.e. $|J(\Gamma^k) - \overline{J}| < \varepsilon_J|\overline{J}|$ then we terminate iterations. We set $\varepsilon_J = 10^{-4}$, and $\overline{J} = \frac{1}{n_J}\sum_{l=1}^{n_J} J(\Gamma^l)$ is the average energy for the last $n_J = 5$ iterations.

A Simple Descent Velocity: An obvious choice that is commonly used in literature is to set the velocity equal to the negative shape gradient

$$V = -G = -(g\kappa + \partial_n g + \text{div}_\Gamma(g_y)_\Gamma). \tag{8}$$

This clearly is a descent velocity as $dJ(\Gamma; V) = \int_\Gamma GV d\sigma = -\int_\Gamma G^2 d\sigma \leqslant 0$. The velocity (8) was used in [10, 14, 15] for energy minimization. There are two downsides to (8): (1) The curvature term $g\kappa$ makes the geometric evolution unstable, requires very small steps. (2) The term $\text{div}_\Gamma(g_y)_\Gamma$ requires two derivatives on data function g and is very tedious to discretize when expanded explicitly.

The first downside can be alleviated by pursuing a *semi-implicit stepping scheme*. We recall the identities, $\kappa = -\Delta_\Gamma X$, $\kappa = \kappa \cdot n$, $V = Vn$, relating the position vector X, the scalar and vector curvatures κ, κ, the scalar and vector velocities V, V. Then instead of using the following explicit update sequence at each iteration, $\kappa^k = -\Delta_\Gamma X^k \rightarrow \kappa^k = \kappa^k \cdot n^k \rightarrow V^k = -(g\kappa^k + f(\Gamma^k)) \rightarrow V^k = V^k n^k \rightarrow X^{k+1} = X^k + \tau^k V^k$ $(f(\Gamma) := \partial_n g + \text{div}_\Gamma(g_y)_\Gamma)$, we keep $\kappa^{k+1}, \kappa^{k+1}, V^{k+1}, V^{k+1}$ as unknowns to be evaluated at the next iteration. But this requires us solve the following system of equations at each iteration to compute the velocity from the known points X^k and normals n^k of the current surface Γ^k: $V^{k+1} - V^{k+1}n^k = 0$,

$$\kappa^{k+1} - \tau\Delta_\Gamma V^{k+1} = -\Delta_\Gamma X^k, \kappa^{k+1} - \kappa^{k+1} \cdot n^k = 0, V^{k+1} + g\kappa^{k+1} = -f^k. \tag{9}$$

This semi-implicit scheme is unconditionally stable, i.e. no stability bound imposed on step size τ^k, but it requires more computation per iteration as we handle a larger number of unknowns at each iteration, and solve a large system of equations, in contrast to the simple update sequence ($\boldsymbol{X}^k \to \kappa^k \to \kappa^k \to V^k \to \boldsymbol{V}^k \to \boldsymbol{X}^{k+1}$) in the explicit scheme.

The 2nd downside can be alleviated by writing velocity eqn $V = -G$ in weak form: multiply with a smooth test function ϕ defined on Γ, integrate over Γ

$$\langle V, \phi \rangle = -\langle G, \phi \rangle = -\langle g\kappa + \partial_n g, \phi \rangle + \langle g_y, \nabla_\Gamma \phi \rangle, \tag{10}$$

where $\langle u, v \rangle = \int_\Gamma uv \, d\sigma$ is the L^2 scalar product on Γ. To obtain (10), we use Green's identity $\int_\Gamma v \operatorname{div}_\Gamma \boldsymbol{w} d\sigma = -\int_\Gamma \boldsymbol{w} \cdot \nabla_\Gamma v d\sigma$ for integration by parts. Unlike strong form (8), weak form (10) does not require additional derivatives of g_y.

Better Descent Velocities: The velocity computed with Eq. (10) is the L^2 gradient descent velocity (as we use the L^2 scalar product on Γ on the left hand side of (10)). We can choose to use other scalar products to define other gradient descent velocities [2, 6, 22, 23]. These velocities can have desirable properties, such as smoother surface evolution, faster convergence. To realize such a framework, we choose a generic scalar product $b(\cdot, \cdot)$ inducing a Hilbert space $B(\Gamma)$ on Γ. Then velocity V computed by the *generalized velocity equation*

$$b(V, \phi) = -\langle G, \phi \rangle = -\langle g\kappa + \partial_n g, \phi \rangle + \langle g_y, \nabla_\Gamma \phi \rangle, \quad \forall \phi \in B(\Gamma), \tag{11}$$

is a descent velocity, because it satisfies $dJ(\Gamma; V) = -\langle G, V \rangle = -b(V, V) \leqslant 0$. Two possible options for the scalar product are L^2 and weighted H^1:

$$\langle V, W \rangle_{L^2} = \langle V, W \rangle = \int_\Gamma VW \, d\sigma, \quad \langle V, W \rangle_{H^1} = \langle \alpha \cdot \nabla_\Gamma V, \nabla_\Gamma W \rangle + \langle \beta V, W \rangle,$$

where $\alpha(x, \Gamma), \beta(x, \Gamma)$ are spatially-varying weight functions, and may depend on the geometry, e.g. normal, curvature, of Γ as well. The function $\alpha : \mathbb{R}^d \times \Gamma \to \mathbb{R}^{d \times d}$ is a positive definite matrix-valued, and $\beta : \mathbb{R}^d \times \Gamma \to \mathbb{R}$ is a positive scalar-valued. The H^1 scalar product with constant weight functions was used in [6, 23]. Our framework, in contrast, enables us to use general non-constant weight functions, which can also depend on the geometry of Γ. This offers more flexibility in the choice of gradient descent velocities.

A particularly useful choice is based on the shape Hessian of the surface energy, derived in Sect. 2. If we compute the velocity V using the Newton's method, solving equation, $d^2 J(\Gamma; V, \phi) = -dJ(\Gamma; \phi) (= -\langle G, \phi \rangle)$, $\forall \phi \in B(\Gamma)$, we find that this velocity leads to faster convergence, quadratic close to the minimum. One easily sees that the 2nd shape derivative

$$d^2 J(\Gamma; V, W) = \langle \alpha \cdot \nabla_\Gamma V, \nabla_\Gamma W \rangle + \langle \beta V, W \rangle - \langle \gamma \cdot \nabla_\Gamma V, W \rangle - \langle \gamma \cdot \nabla_\Gamma W, V \rangle, \tag{12}$$

is similar to a weighted H^1 scalar product, when $\alpha(x, \Gamma) = (g - g_y \cdot n)Id + g_{yy}$, $\beta(x, \Gamma) = \partial_{nn} g + 2\kappa \partial_n g + (\kappa^2 - \sum \kappa_i^2)g$, $\gamma(x, \Gamma) = \kappa g_y - g_y^T \nabla_\Gamma n + n^T g_{xy}^T$.

The shape Hessian (12) however is not a proper scalar product, and it cannot be used with the generalized velocity Eq. (11) to compute descent velocities, because it is not positive definite. Still, we can try to use it to create a custom scalar product based on (12) to achieve improved convergence. For this, we propose the thresholded coefficients

$$\alpha_+ = (g - g_y \cdot n)_+ Id + g_{yy}, \quad \beta_+ = \left(\partial_{nn}g + 2\kappa\partial_n g + (\kappa^2 - \sum \kappa_i^2)g\right)_+,$$

where $f_+ = \max(f, \varepsilon)$ with $\varepsilon = 1$ for β_+, $\varepsilon = \min(g)$ for α_+ in our implementation, and g is designed so that the Hessian matrix function g_{yy} is positive semidefinite. Then by neglecting the last two terms in (12), we obtain the following weighted H^1 scalar product

$$\langle V, W \rangle_{H^1} = \langle \alpha_+ \cdot \nabla_\Gamma V, \nabla_\Gamma W \rangle + \langle \beta_+ V, W \rangle, \tag{13}$$

which acts like a preconditioner on the velocity and results in smoother surface evolutions and convergence in fewer iterations compared to the L^2 velocity (8).

4 Lagrangian Discretization

The minimization algorithm developed so far is in the continuous mathematical realm, and cannot yet be used to compute numerical minima for energy (2). For the actual computation, we need a discrete representation of the surface; moreover, a discretization of the energy (2), and all the relationships used in a minimization iteration: the step size condition (6), the stopping criterion (7), the velocity Eq. (11). The original algorithm for GAC model [4,5] relied on a Eulerian level set representation of the surface, and the minimization was carried out as a level set evolution with fixed step size. The discretization was by finite differences on the image grid. This can have high computational cost if all the grid points are evaluated as unknowns in the iterations. In this work, we opt for a Lagrangian discretization of the problem for its efficiency and the flexibility it offers to realize an effective shape optimization algorithm.

Discretization of the Geometry: We discretize the surface as a set of simplices $\{\Gamma_i^h\}_{i=1}^m$, namely, line segments making up polygonal curves in 2d, and triangulated surfaces in 3d. The simplices provide a basis for discretization of the minimization equations as well. This simplicial discretization is compact and efficient; a collection of curves used to segment a megapixel image can be represented with only a few hundred nodes, providing orders of magnitude reduction in the number of variables compared to a Eulerian representation.

We can tune the efficiency of the surface representation even further by implementing spatial adaptivity. More nodes are used to increase surface resolution in complicated parts of the geometry or the image, and fewer nodes in flat areas. To manage this dynamically through the evolution of Γ, we use geometrically-consistent surface refinement and coarsening operations [3]. For a line segment, refinement introduces a new node in the middle, and projects it along the normal to match curvature. For a triangle, we use longest-edge bisection approach [19]. Coarsening is just an undo operation for refinement. These adaptations are executed at the end of each iteration to ensure accuracy before the next iteration.

Finite Element Method for Velocity: We use the simplicial discretization $\{\Gamma_i^h\}_{i=1}^{n_\Gamma}$ of the approximate surface Γ^h to introduce a finite element (FE) discretization of the velocity equations. We choose a set of piecewise linear nodal basis functions $\{\phi_i\}_{i=1}^{m}$ defined on surface elements. The function ϕ_i satisfies $\phi_i(x_i) = 1$ on i^{th} node x_i of Γ^h, but $\phi_i(x_j) = 0$ on the other nodes $x_j, j \neq i$. We use $\{\phi_i\}$ as test functions in the generalized velocity Eq. (11):

$$b(V, \phi_i) = -\langle G, \phi_i \rangle = -\langle g\kappa + \partial_n g, \phi_i \rangle - \langle g_y, \nabla_\Gamma \phi_i \rangle, \quad i = 1, \ldots, m.$$

Similarly, we take the geometric relationships $\kappa = -\Delta_\Gamma X, \kappa = \kappa \cdot n, V = Vn$, multiply by ϕ_i, integrate on Γ^h, and write them in weak form: $\langle \kappa, \phi_i \rangle = \langle \nabla_\Gamma X, \nabla_\Gamma \phi_i \rangle$, $\langle \kappa, \phi_i \rangle = \langle \kappa \cdot n, \phi_i \rangle$, $\langle V, \phi_i \rangle = \langle V, \phi_i \cdot n \rangle$, where ϕ_i is the vector-valued test functions, e.g. $\phi_i = (\phi_i, \phi_i)$ in 2d. We also expand all the critical quantities in terms $\{\phi_i\}_{i=1}^{m}$, so that they are represented by coefficient vectors $\kappa = \sum_{j=1}^{m} \mathbf{k}_j \phi_j = \mathbf{k}_j \phi_j$, $\kappa = \mathbf{k}_j \phi_j$, $V = \mathbf{v}_j \phi_j$, $V = \mathbf{v}_j \phi_j$. In this way, we obtain discretized equations in matrix form: $\mathbf{Ak} = \mathbf{Mx}$, $\mathbf{Mk} = \mathbf{Nk}$, $\mathbf{Bv} = \mathbf{g}$, $\mathbf{Mv} = \mathbf{Nv}$, where $\mathbf{A}_{ij} = \langle \nabla_\Gamma \phi_i, \nabla_\Gamma \phi_j \rangle$, $\mathbf{M}_{ij} = \langle \phi_i, \phi_j \rangle$, $\mathbf{B}_{ij} = \langle \alpha_+ \cdot \nabla_\Gamma \phi_i, \nabla_\Gamma \phi_j \rangle + \langle \beta_+ \phi_i, \phi_j \rangle$, $\mathbf{N}_{ij}^k = \langle \phi_i, \phi_j n_k \rangle$, $\mathbf{g}_i = -\langle g\kappa + \partial_n g, \phi_i \rangle - \langle g_y, \nabla_\Gamma \phi_i \rangle$, and vector versions $\mathbf{A}, \mathbf{M}$.

The matrices $\mathbf{A}, \mathbf{M}, \mathbf{B}$ consist of tridiagonal blocks in 2d, and they can be inverted in $O(m)$ time. In 3d, they are sparse matrices, and can still be inverted efficiently using a sparse direct solver or the conjugate gradient algorithm. Given the current surface nodes $\mathbf{x} = \{x_i \in \Gamma^h\}_{i=1}^{m}$, we solve for the discrete velocity $\mathbf{v}$ with the explicit sequence $\mathbf{k} = \mathbf{A}^{-1}\mathbf{Mx} \to \mathbf{k} = \mathbf{M}^{-1}\mathbf{Nk} \to \mathbf{v} = \mathbf{B}^{-1}\mathbf{g} \to \mathbf{v} = \mathbf{M}^{-1}\mathbf{NV}$. The semi-implicit equations (9) are discretized similarly, then solved as a coupled system of equations with a much larger coefficient matrix.

Adaptivity of Discretization: The central concern for the quality of the discretization is accuracy, specifically, how faithfully it captures the geometry, and how well it resolves important features in the image, meanwhile maintaining efficiency as well. Thus we aim to keep accuracy within a reasonable range, not too low or too high. We use two separate criteria for judging the accuracy:

(1) *Geometry*: Measure geometric discretization error with $\max_{\Gamma_i^h} |\kappa| |\Gamma_i^h|^2$ in 2d, $\max_{\Gamma_i^h} \frac{|n_i - n_j|}{h} |\Gamma_i^h|^2$ in 3d (n_j is the normal of the neighbor element).

(2) *Data*: To see how well the element Γ_i^h resolves the data func. $g(x, n)$, compare low and high order quadrature approximations of the local integral $\int_{\Gamma_i^h} g(x, n) d\sigma$. Mesh elements are refined if one of two errors is large, coarsened if both are low.

An additional and critical adaptivity criterion is how well we are approximating the shape gradient G, key to velocity computations (11), step size selection (6), and stopping criterion (7). Ideally, the optimization iterations would converge to the optimal surface Γ^*, and we would have the shape gradient $|G(x)| \approx 0, \forall x \in \Gamma^*$. In practice, the energy, the shape gradient, and the velocity will be from different discretizations, and thus may be *inconsistent*. This typically manifests itself with step size selection failures close to the minimum.

When this occurs, we identify 10% elements with largest G value, refine them, restart shape optimization to ensure convergence with satisfactory accuracy.

We also enable topological adaptivity in 2d, e.g. merging, splitting of curves, based on intersection detection and local surgery to reconnect curves [9,16,17].

5 Numerical Experiments

We test our algorithm with synthetic and real image examples in 2d and 3d. We set $g(x, n) = 1/(1 + |\nabla G_\sigma * I(x)|^2/\lambda^2)$, $\lambda = \frac{1}{4} \max |\nabla G_\sigma * I| > 0$ and $\sigma = 2$ pixels in the Gaussian $G_\sigma(x)$. We minimize (2) using L^2 velocity (8), and the weighted H^1 velocity using (13) (subject to a maximum iteration number of 1000).

We first evaluate the two velocities and our numerical algorithm on two clean synthetic images. The merit of these two images is that it enables us to evaluate the sensitivity of our algorithm with respect to image resolution, thereby the sharpness of the image gradient at the object boundary. For this, we generate the same image at resolutions of $200^2, 400^2, 800^2, 1600^2$ pixels. We examine the number of iterations, the number of energy evaluations, and the actual running times from the velocities (see Fig. 1). We find that H^1 velocity gives superior results in all these cases. It is robust with respect to image resolution, whereas the performance of L^2 velocity deteriorates as the resolution increases. At highest resolution, L^2 does not converge and stops at the maximum iteration number.

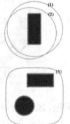

resolution	200	400	800	1600
(1) $\mathbf{L^2}$	27, 29, 0.4s	83, 87, 1.2s	299, 319, 4.6s	1000, 1286, 15.4s
$\mathbf{H^1}$	25, 26, 0.2s	41, 42, 0.3s	81, 82, 0.6s	153, 154, 1.1s
(2) $\mathbf{L^2}$	52, 57, 0.7s	169, 176, 2.4s	665, 706, 9.1s	1000, 1337, 14.3s
$\mathbf{H^1}$	27, 28, 0.2s	57, 65, 0.4s	90, 91, 0.7s	184, 190, 1.3s
(3) $\mathbf{L^2}$	145, 184, 2.3s	462, 592, 7.8s	1000, 1138, 16.1s	1000, 1377, 14.2s
$\mathbf{H^1}$	119, 180, 1.3s	101, 108, 1.0s	286, 383, 2.9s	645, 925, 8.3s

Fig. 1. L^2 and H^1 velocities used to segment two synthetic images of increasing resolution (top right), starting with the different initial curves (1), (2), (3) (yellow), converging to the (red) boundary curves. Iteration numbers, energy evaluations and actual timings (seconds) are compared. (Color figure online)

Next we evaluate our algorithm with real image examples (see Fig. 2). We examine the quality of the segmentation, and report the number of iterations, the number of energy evaluations, and the actual running times. We find that our observations from synthetic examples are repeated on the real examples as well. The L^2 velocity takes much longer than the weighted H^1 velocity, both in terms of iteration numbers and running times.

Finally, we test our algorithm on synthetic 3d examples (see Fig. 3). We verify that our discrete representation can be successfully used to segment 3d objects

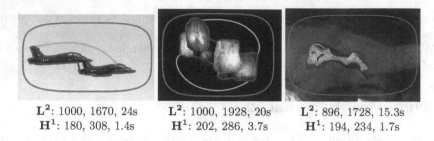

L²: 1000, 1670, 24s   **L²**: 1000, 1928, 20s   **L²**: 896, 1728, 15.3s
H¹: 180, 308, 1.4s   **H¹**: 202, 286, 3.7s   **H¹**: 194, 234, 1.7s

Fig. 2. L^2 and H^1 velocities used to segment three example images. The optimization starts with the yellow curves, and converges to the cyan final curve with L^2 velocity, and red curve with H^1 velocity. Iteration numbers, energy evaluations and actual timings (seconds) are reported and compared for each example. L^2 velocity terminates by reaching the maximum (1000) number of iterations in examples 1, 2. (Color figure online)

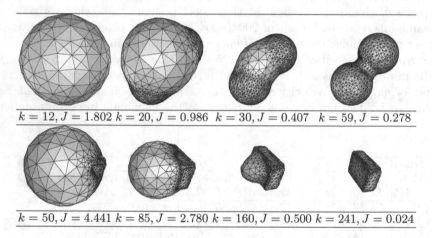

$k = 12, J = 1.802$ $k = 20, J = 0.986$ $k = 30, J = 0.407$ $k = 59, J = 0.278$

$k = 50, J = 4.441$ $k = 85, J = 2.780$ $k = 160, J = 0.500$ $k = 241, J = 0.024$

Fig. 3. Iterations from segmentations of two synthetic 3d objects using weighted H^1 velocity. Note the spatial adaptivity of the triangulated surface adjusting to the objects.

with weighted H^1 descent velocities of the surface energy (2). These examples also demonstrate the spatial adaptivity of the triangulated surface mesh. We start the optimization with coarse meshes. These meshes are then adapted and refined as the geometry gets more complicated and as the algorithm senses more details of the data through the iterations. The final objects are captured in good detail without resorting to an excessively refined mesh.

6   Conclusion

We propose a new minimization algorithm for a more general anisotropic version (2) of the Geodesic Active Contour model [4,5,10,12,14] in any number of dimensions, supporting alignment penalties on the normal of the surface, in addition to isotropic image-based penalties. The first variation of this energy, used to develop minimization algorithms, is already known. We derive the second variation or second shape derivative, and use it to develop a Newton-type shape optimization algorithm that results in smoother descent velocities, and converges in fewer iterations and in less time. The Newton-type minimization algorithm is more robust; it exhibits consistent convergence behavior for increasing resolution of the same image, with sharper gradients, whereas the performance of the commonly-used L^2 velocity deterioriates.

We use a Lagrangian (not Eulerian e.g. level sets) discretization of the geometry, namely, polygonal curves in 2d and triangulated surfaces in 3d, for computational efficiency and ease of implementation. Our representation is adaptive and captures the objects in the image accurately, but economically, adding more nodes and resolution only when necessary (see Fig. 3). The velocity equations are discretized using the Finite Element Method, which can be solved efficiently, in linear time with respect to number of nodes in the case of 2d polygonal curves. Unlike previous approaches [6, 23], our discretization can handle and compute a variety of generalized descent velocities, including L^2, H^1 and Newton, for any number of dimensions, 2d, 3d, 4d.

Acknowledgement. This work was performed under the financial assistance award 70NANB16H306 from the U.S. Department of Commerce, National Institute of Standards and Technology.

References

1. Bar, L., Sapiro, G.: Generalized newton-type methods for energy formulations in image processing. SIAM J. Imaging Sci. **2**(2), 508–531 (2009)
2. Baust, M., Yezzi, A., Unal, G., Navab, N.: Translation, scale, and deformation weighted polar active contours. J. Math. Imaging Vis. **44**(3), 354–365 (2012)
3. Bonito, A., Nochetto, R.H., Pauletti, M.S.: Geometrically consistent mesh modification. SIAM J. Numer. Anal. **48**(5), 1877–1899 (2010)
4. Caselles, V., Kimmel, R., Sapiro, G.: Geodesic active contours. IJCV **22**(1), 61–79 (1997)
5. Caselles, V., Kimmel, R., Sapiro, G., Sbert, C.: Minimal surfaces: a geometric three-dimensional segmentation approach. Numer. Math. **77**(4), 423–451 (1997)
6. Charpiat, G., Maurel, P., Pons, J.P., Keriven, R., Faugeras, O.: Generalized gradients: priors on minimization flows. IJCV **73**(3), 325–344 (2007)
7. Deckelnick, K., Dziuk, G., Elliott, C.M.: Computation of geometric partial differential equations and mean curvature flow. Acta Numer. **14**, 139–232 (2005)
8. Delfour, M.C., Zolésio, J.P.: Shapes and Geometries. Advances in Design and Control. SIAM, Philadelphia (2001)
9. Delingette, H., Montagnat, J.: Shape and topology constraints on parametric active contours. Comput. Vis. Image Underst. **83**(2), 140–171 (2001)
10. Faugeras, O., Keriven, R.: Variational principles, surface evolution, PDE's, level set methods and the stereo problem. IEEE Trans. Image Process. **7**, 336–344 (1998)
11. Goldlücke, B., Magnor, M.: Space-time isosurface evolution for temporally coherent 3D reconstruction. In: CVPR I, pp. 350–355, June 2004

12. Goldlücke, B., Magnor, M.: Weighted minimal hypersurfaces and their applications in computer vision. In: Pajdla, T., Matas, J. (eds.) ECCV 2004. LNCS, vol. 3022, pp. 366–378. Springer, Heidelberg (2004). doi:10.1007/978-3-540-24671-8_29

13. Hintermüller, M., Ring, W.: A second order shape optimization approach for image segmentation. SIAM J. Appl. Math. **64**(2), 442–467 (2003/04)

14. Jin, H., Soatto, S., Yezzi, A.J.: Multi-view stereo beyond lambert. In: CVPR (1), pp. 171–178. IEEE Computer Society (2003)

15. Kimmel, R., Bruckstein, A.: Regularized Laplacian zero crossings as optimal edge integrators. IJCV **53**(3), 225–243 (2003)

16. Lachaud, J.O., Montanvert, A.: Deformable meshes with automated topology changes for coarse-to-fine 3D surface extraction. Med. Image Anal. **3**(2), 187–207 (1999)

17. McInerney, T., Terzopoulos, D.: T-snakes: topology adaptive snakes. Med. Image Anal. **4**(2), 73–91 (2000)

18. Nocedal, J., Wright, S.J.: Numerical Optimization. Springer Series in Operations Research. Springer, New York (1999)

19. Schmidt, A., Siebert, K.: Design of Adaptive Finite Element Software. Springer, Berlin (2005)

20. Sokołowski, J., Zolésio, J.P.: Introduction to Shape Optimization. Springer Series in Computational Mathematics, vol. 16. Springer, Berlin (1992)

21. Solem, J.E., Overgaard, N.C.: A geometric formulation of gradient descent for variational problems with moving surfaces. In: Kimmel, R., Sochen, N.A., Weickert, J. (eds.) Scale-Space 2005. LNCS, vol. 3459, pp. 419–430. Springer, Heidelberg (2005). doi:10.1007/11408031_36

22. Sundaramoorthi, G., Yezzi, A., Mennucci, A.: Coarse-to-fine segmentation and tracking using sobolev active contours. PAMI **30**(5), 851–864 (2008)

23. Sundaramoorthi, G., Yezzi, A., Mennucci, A.C.: Sobolev active contours. IJCV **73**(3), 345–366 (2007)

A Probabilistic Framework for Curve Evolution

Vedrana Andersen Dahl[✉] and Anders Bjorholm Dahl

Department of Applied Mathematics and Computer Science,
Technical University of Denmark, Kongens Lyngby, Denmark
{vand,abda}@dtu.dk

Abstract. In this work, we propose a nonparametric probabilistic framework for image segmentation using deformable models. We estimate an underlying probability distributions of image features from regions defined by a deformable curve. We then evolve the curve such that the distance between the distributions is increasing. The resulting active contour resembles a well studied piecewise constant Mumford-Shah model, but in a probabilistic setting. An important property of our framework is that it does not require a particular type of distributions in different image regions. Additional advantages of our approach include ability to handle textured images, simple generalization to multiple regions, and efficiency in computation. We test our probabilistic framework in combination with parametric (snakes) and geometric (level-sets) curves. The experimental results on composed and natural images demonstrate excellent properties of our framework.

1 Introduction

A well studied variational approach to image segmentation is the Mumford-Shah model [10], often combined with a level-set curve representation [11]. Especially the two-phase piecewise constant case has been extensively studied. The goal is to partition the image into two regions, each represented by a single intensity value. The curve evolution algorithm proposed by Chan and Vese [3,4] estimates the mean intensities of image regions. The curve is then evolved depending on whether intensities under the curve lie closer to one, or the other, estimated mean.

Our segmentation approach is strongly inspired by [3,4] and a related model from [13,15]. Like them, we obtain an estimate on image regions, followed by the deformation of the curve. However, instead of operating on pixel intensities, we estimate the underlying distribution of image features. By doing so, we obtain a pixel-wise probability of belonging to one, or the other, region, and we subsequently use those probabilities for deforming the curve.

An important property of our segmentation model is that we estimate the underlying distributions without making any assumptions, e.g. assuming it to be unimodal. Instead, our model uses distributions that are learned and dynamically adapted in a nonparametric way. In this aspect, our work resembles curve evolution proposed in [9], where they evolve the curve by assuming that segmented regions are homogeneous. We assume that regions have different distributions.

© Springer International Publishing AG 2017
F. Lauze et al. (Eds.): SSVM 2017, LNCS 10302, pp. 421–432, 2017.
DOI: 10.1007/978-3-319-58771-4_34

Furthermore, we perform averaging on clusters of image patches and are therefore able to handle textured regions. The typical approach to texture segmentation involves mapping the image to a texture descriptor space. Here the assumption is that descriptors within textures are similar while they differ between textures. Such an approach was already suggested by [4] using texture orientation, and has been extended in [12] with the structure tensor. For better performance, the scale of the structure tensor is automatically estimated in [2], while [1] utilizes diffusion.

More recently [7] suggested to use sparse dictionaries together with an user-initiated active contour. Another patch-based approach [14] uses a patch subspace model for active contours. For each segment they learn a set of orthonormal basis vectors, and use this for modeling image patches and evolving the curve.

Our texture model was introduced in [5,6]. In this approach, clustering of image patches allows for computation of pixel-wise probabilities, which then deform the curve. In the work presented here, we formulate a more general histogram-based framework for using empirical probabilities in both intensity-based and texture-based deformable models. This study also brings the mathematical foundations which prove the correctness of our approach.

2   Method

We consider an image where the task is to separate the foreground from the background, and we use subscripts F and B for the corresponding image entities, such as for the image domain Ω consisting of Ω_F and Ω_B. At the same time, a curve C divides the image into inside and outside region, and for those regions we use subscripts in and out. In few places we use the set notation, where $\Omega_{\text{in}\cap\text{F}}$ is a part of the foreground region which is inside the curve.

The terms we use for image regions are chosen for the simplicity of the presentation, but the models we describe do not rely on any special topology of the object or the curve, and can handle a general two-phase segmentation.

The segmentation energy E should be defined such that the desired segmentation has a minimal energy. Segmentation is obtained by moving the curve to minimize the energy, and the essence of the approach is in deriving suitable curve deformation forces $F = -\nabla E$.

The contributions to the segmentation energy may be divided into an external energy and an internal energy. The external energy is determined by the image and is the focus of our upcoming method description.

The internal energy is determined solely by the shape of the curve. A typical choice is a length of the curve $E_{\text{int}} = \alpha \int_C ds$, here weighted with parameter α. This discourages stretching of the curve with the force $F_{\text{int}} = -\alpha\kappa N$ where N denotes an outward unit normal, and κ is the signed curvature. Those regulatory forces are the key to success of deformable models. Therefore, even though expressions presented below show only external contributions, bear in mind that those are supplemented by internal forces.

2.1 Inspiration

Before defining our segmentation energy and curve deformation, we revise two models which inspired this work.

An external energy closely related to the two-phase piecewise constant Mumford-Shah model is

$$E_{\text{ext}} = \int_{\Omega_{\text{in}}} (I - m_{\text{in}})^2 \, dx + \int_{\Omega_{\text{out}}} (I - m_{\text{out}})^2 \, dx \tag{1}$$

where I is an image intensity as a function of the pixel position, while m_{in} and m_{out} are mean intensities of the inside and the outside region. This energy finds the best (in a squared-error sense) piecewise constant approximation of I. An evolution that will contract a curve toward a minimum is derived in [3] as

$$F_{\text{ext}} = \frac{1}{2}(m_{\text{in}} - m_{\text{out}}) \left(I - m_{\text{in}} + I - m_{\text{out}} \right) N. \tag{2}$$

A different energy proposed by [15] uses the distance between estimated mean intensities as a measure of region separation

$$E_{\text{ext}} = -\frac{1}{2}(m_{\text{in}} - m_{\text{out}})^2. \tag{3}$$

The corresponding flow, similar to (2) but with area normalization (we use A for areas of the regions), is

$$F_{\text{ext}} = (m_{\text{in}} - m_{\text{out}}) \left(\frac{I - m_{\text{in}}}{A_{\text{in}}} + \frac{I - m_{\text{out}}}{A_{\text{out}}} \right) N. \tag{4}$$

In case of an image truly consisting of two regions of constant intensity, the minimizer is the same for the two energy functions. However, under noise or blurred boundaries (2) minimizes the intra-region variance while (4) maximizes the inter-region difference.

2.2 Probability Framework

Let us first explain the probability framework on a simple intensity-based example. Assume that foreground region contains pixels with intensities that follow one discrete probability distribution, while background intensities follow another distribution. In our examples intensities are from $K = \{1, \ldots, 256\}$.

Given an arbitrary curve, we can extract the absolute histogram of the inside and the outside region. Dividing those by the areas inside and outside the curve respectively, we obtain normalized frequencies $f_{\text{in}}(k)$ and $f_{\text{out}}(k)$. Those empirical probabilities will (to some degree, depending on the position of the curve) reflect the difference between the foreground and the background distributions.

If we consider a pixel of intensity $k \in K$, the probability of it belonging to the inside distribution is

$$p_{\text{in}}(k) = \frac{1}{Z} f_{\text{in}}(k), \tag{5}$$

where a normalization constant $Z(k) = f_{\text{in}}(k) + f_{\text{out}}(k)$ ensures that probabilities sum to 1.

Consider constructing a probability image P_{in} from the image I by replacing each pixel values k with $p_{\text{in}}(k)$, for all $k \in K$. This is illustrated for three images in Fig. 1. In the first image the foreground and the background regions follow two non-overlapping distributions. This demonstrates a situation where P_{in} is an excellent indicator of foreground-background segmentation. The second image shows two overlapping, but rather different distributions. Here P_{in} is still a good indicator for segmentation, especially if combined with some regularization. The last image shows two similar distributions, which is a challenging situation and motivates our patch-based approach in Sect. 2.5.

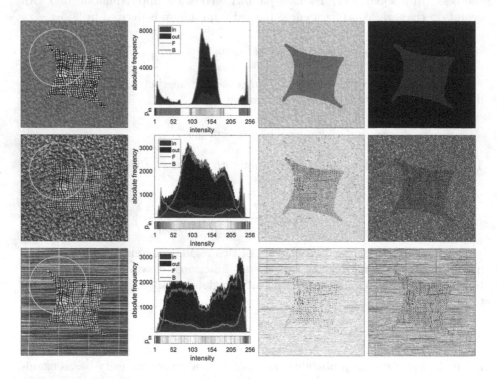

Fig. 1. Distributions of intensity values for the three input images show in the *left column*. The absolute histograms (*second column*) of each image are divided into inside and outside part according to the separation indicated on the input by the green curve. Foreground and background histograms are added as curves for comparison. The colored bars under the histograms show p_{in} in shades of blue for values under 0.5, white for 0.5 and red for values above 0.5. (The same color scheme is used throughout the paper.) *Third column* shows P_{in} computed for inside-outside separation indicated on the input image by the green curve, while the *rightmost column* shows the probability image when the curve aligns with the boundary between the foreground and the background. (Color figure online)

2.3   Fundamentals

Let us demonstrate two statements on probability distributions which are fundamental for our approach.

Statement 1 (Maximal distance). *Assume that f_F and f_B are probability distribution functions of foreground and background regions. A curve partitions the image in outside and inside, such that the induced subregions (e.g. $\Omega_{in \cap F}$) are representative. The total variation distance*

$$D(f_{in}, f_{out}) = \frac{1}{2} \sum_K |f_{in}(k) - f_{out}(k)| \tag{6}$$

is largest if the curve is aligned with the boundary between foreground and background.

Proof. Notice that f_{in} is a mixture density, i.e. a convex combination of f_F and f_B with the coefficients given by the proportions of foreground and background inside the curve, and similar is valid for f_{out}. We introduce convex weights $\lambda = A_{in \cap B}/A_{in}$ and $\mu = A_{out \cap F}/A_{out}$ and write

$$f_{in} = (1 - \lambda)f_F + \lambda f_B$$
$$f_{out} = \mu f_F + (1 - \mu)f_B. \tag{7}$$

Consequently, the distance between f_{in} and f_{out} is smaller than the distance between f_F and f_B. More precisely, we have

$$D(f_{in}, f_{out}) = |1 - \lambda - \mu| \frac{1}{2} \sum_K |f_F(k) - f_B(k)| \tag{8}$$

which is maximal when $\lambda = \mu = 0$ corresponding to $\Omega_{in} = \Omega_F$ and $\Omega_{out} = \Omega_B$ (or the flipped solution for $\lambda = \mu = 1$). $\square$

Note that the distance between the normalized histograms for arbitrary pixel partitioning may be larger than this limit, if the separation in inside and outside is systematic. In the third case on Fig. 1, such situation would occur if inside contains all low-intensity pixels from both foreground and background. However, a curve should be rather convoluted to allow for such not-representative partitioning.

Statement 2 (Maximization). *Consider two empirical probability distribution functions (normalized histograms) f_{in} and f_{out} obtained by collecting intensity values inside and outside the curve. Assume there is a pixel with intensity $\hat{k}$ in the outside region and $f_{in}(\hat{k}) > f_{out}(\hat{k})$. The total variation distance*

$$D(f_{in}, f_{out}) = \frac{1}{2} \sum_K |f_{in}(k) - f_{out}(k)|. \tag{9}$$

will increase if we move this pixel from outside to inside.

Proof. Values for normalized histograms after the move are

$$f'_{\text{in}}(k) = \frac{A_{\text{in}}}{A_{\text{in}}+1} f_{\text{in}}(k) + \frac{1}{A_{\text{in}}+1}\delta(k-\hat{k})$$

$$f'_{\text{out}}(k) = \frac{A_{\text{out}}}{A_{\text{out}}-1} f_{\text{out}}(k) - \frac{1}{A_{\text{out}}-1}\delta(k-\hat{k}). \tag{10}$$

We consider the sign of differences $(f_{\text{in}}(k) - f_{\text{out}}(k))$ and $(f'_{\text{in}}(k) - f'_{\text{out}}(k))$. For $k = \hat{k}$ the difference is, and will remain, positive. All negative differences will stay negative, while some positive differences for $k \neq \hat{k}$ might become negative. This allows us to partition K in three subsets

$$K^{++} = \{k \mid f_{\text{in}}(k) > f_{\text{out}}(k) \text{ and } f'_{\text{in}}(k) \geq f'_{\text{out}}(k)\}$$
$$K^{+-} = \{k \mid f_{\text{in}}(k) > f_{\text{out}}(k) \text{ and } f'_{\text{in}}(k) < f'_{\text{out}}(k)\} \tag{11}$$
$$K^{-} = \{k \mid f_{\text{in}}(k) \leq f_{\text{out}}(k)\}.$$

Furthermore, we define a sum $S_{\text{in}}^{++} = \sum_{K^{++}} f_{\text{in}}(k)$ and similar sums for S_{in}^{+-}, S_{in}^{-}, S_{out}^{++}, S_{out}^{+-} and S_{out}^{-}.

The total variation distance before the move now reduces to

$$D(f_{\text{in}}, f_{\text{out}}) = \frac{1}{2}\left(S_{\text{in}}^{++} - S_{\text{out}}^{++} + S_{\text{in}}^{+-} - S_{\text{out}}^{+-} + S_{\text{out}}^{-} - S_{\text{in}}^{-}\right) = S_{\text{out}}^{-} - S_{\text{in}}^{-}, \tag{12}$$

where last equality uses the fact that values of f_{in} and f_{out} sum to 1. For the total variation distance after the move we have

$$D(f'_{\text{in}}, f'_{\text{out}}) = \frac{1}{2}\left(\frac{A_{\text{in}}S_{\text{in}}^{++}}{A_{\text{in}}+1} - \frac{A_{\text{out}}S_{\text{out}}^{++}}{A_{\text{out}}-1} + \frac{1}{A_{\text{in}}+1} + \frac{1}{A_{\text{out}}-1} + \right.$$
$$\left. + \frac{A_{\text{out}}S_{\text{out}}^{+-}}{A_{\text{out}}-1} - \frac{A_{\text{in}}S_{\text{in}}^{+-}}{A_{\text{in}}+1} + \frac{A_{\text{out}}S_{\text{out}}^{-}}{A_{\text{out}}-1} - \frac{A_{\text{in}}S_{\text{in}}^{-}}{A_{\text{in}}+1}\right)$$
$$= \frac{A_{\text{out}}}{A_{\text{out}}-1}\left(S_{\text{out}}^{+-} + S_{\text{out}}^{-}\right) - \frac{A_{\text{in}}}{A_{\text{in}}+1}\left(S_{\text{in}}^{+-} + S_{\text{in}}^{-}\right) \tag{13}$$

Comparing (12) to (13), and after removing inequalities which hold due to change in areas, we are left with needing to establish

$$\frac{A_{\text{in}}}{A_{\text{in}}+1}S_{\text{in}}^{+-} < \frac{A_{\text{out}}}{A_{\text{out}}-1}S_{\text{out}}^{+-}. \tag{14}$$

This is a consequence of $\hat{k} \notin K^{+-}$, (10) and (11). □

Statement 2 shows that moving pixels according to the difference of normalized histograms increases the distance between the distributions, while Statement 1 claims that under the assumption of representative sub-regions this leads to foreground–background segmentation. If we assure that the curve is relatively smooth (regularized), this assumption will hold.

2.4   Probabilities for Curve Evolution

Inspired by the insights presented in Sect. 2.3 we propose external forces for curve evolution

$$F_{\text{ext}} = (P_{\text{in}} - P_{\text{out}})N, \tag{15}$$

where empirical probabilities P_{in} and P_{out} are estimated from inside and outside regions as in Sect. 2.2. Note that by using $(p_{\text{in}} - p_{\text{out}})$ instead of $(f_{\text{in}} - f_{\text{out}})$ we still move the curve in the correct direction, but we eliminate the effect of the overall pixel frequency. We plan to investigate the relationship between the two flows in the future work. Let us comment on a couple of aspects of our probabilistic approach.

First, the computation of P_{in} from the curve may be implemented in terms of a linear mapping. To see this, consider ordering image pixels in some way, e.g. column-wise, and defining a binary matrix $\mathbf{B}$ by $b_{ik} = 1$ if a pixel i has an intensity value k, and 0 otherwise. Consider also a binary inside-outside mask defined by the curve, and unfolded using the same ordering as with image pixels. We denote this vector $\mathbf{c}_{\text{in}}$. The product $\mathbf{B}^{\mathsf{T}}\mathbf{c}_{\text{in}}$ contains an absolute histogram of the inside region. We have

$$\mathbf{f}_{\text{in}} = \frac{\mathbf{B}^{\mathsf{T}}\mathbf{c}_{\text{in}}}{A_{\text{in}}} \quad \text{and} \quad \mathbf{f}_{\text{out}} = \frac{\mathbf{B}^{\mathsf{T}}(1 - \mathbf{c}_{\text{in}})}{A_{\text{out}}}. \tag{16}$$

The bold font indicates a vector, but its elements are values of $f_{\text{in}}(k)$. After element-wise normalization of vector elements we have a vector $\mathbf{p}_{\text{in}}$ containing probabilities $p_{\text{in}}(k)$. The product $\mathbf{B}\mathbf{p}_{\text{in}}$ now contains elements of P_{in}, which only need to be arranged in the image grid.

Said in other words, a biadjacency matrix encoding a pixel–value relation defines a mapping from the image domain to the intensity domain and back. This is useful for an efficient implementation of our deformable model, and is important since many iterations might be needed during evolution.

The second aspect to mention is the discrete nature of our model. For an image with continuous intensities, e.g. from the interval $[0, 1]$ our approach still applies provided that we perform a suitable binning of pixels values. In the upcoming text we take this strategy a step further.

2.5   Patch-Based Probabilities

Looking back at the third case in Fig. 1 we notice that a distribution of image features might be a better descriptor for image regions. To use a frequency approach, we first decide on a suitable binning strategy. For this we extract M-by-M patches from the image I, choose a number of bins, and perform k-means clustering. We use Euclidian distance on vectors obtained by collecting patch intensities e.g. column-wise. This gives us a set of cluster centers (we call this a *dictionary*) and every cluster center can be rearranged on a grid and visualized as an image patch. Furthermore, for every patch from the image I we know which cluster it belongs to. This can be represented as an assignment image S, which contains a bin number assigned to the central pixel of each image patch. (We reserve the value 0 for pixels at image boundary.)

We may proceed as if S is an intensity image, illustrated in the first part of Fig. 2. The probability of each patch is concentrated in a central pixel which creates abrupt changes in the probability image. One may argument for filtering P_{in} with M-by-M kernel, to dissolve each probability across a whole patch. Instead, we propose a solution which is better for an accurate placement of the segmentation boundary.

The final improvement in our patch-based probability model is motivated by the realization that some of the dictionary elements represent a spacial transition between the foreground and the background. We therefore allow that pixels in the dictionary patches have individual probabilities. In other words, the histogram now contains M^2 values per cluster, and it makes sense to visualize it as a collection of patches. To estimate a histogram we locate all image patches clustered together under a dictionary element, and for every pixel position within the patch we count how many times it appears inside (or outside) the curve. Dictionary probabilities computed in this way are shown in Fig. 2, third column. When going back from dictionary probabilities to the image, for every image pixel we consider all histogram values it contributed to, and average their contributions.

It is worth mentioning that calculation of the probability image from a curve still may be implemented in terms of a linear mapping. The biadjacency matrix $\mathbf{B}$ should now represent the relation between image pixels and dictionary pixels. Each row of $\mathbf{B}$ corresponds to a pixel from the image, while columns correspond to pixels in the dictionary (unwrapped in some order). The computation of dictionary probabilities is still obtain through multiplication with $\mathbf{B}^{\mathrm{T}}$. For computation of image probabilities note that elements of $\mathbf{B}\mathbf{p}_{\text{in}}$ need to be divided with sum of rows from $\mathbf{B}$. The elements of P_{in} are therefore given by the product $\mathrm{diag}(\mathbf{B}\mathbf{1})^{-1}\mathbf{B}\mathbf{p}_{\text{in}}$.

In other words, also when using patch probabilities, we can efficiently compute probabilities using a biadjacency matrix $\mathbf{B}$. And since $\mathbf{B}$ does not change with curve evolution, it is enough to construct it just once, after clustering.

2.6   Multi-phase Segmentation

Our probabilistic framework can rather straightforwardly handle multiple phases. Given a partitioning of the image in multiple regions, we can compute normalized frequencies corresponding to the inside of each region. This leads to a set of probability images P_j, one for each region. A parametric curve will then be moved according to (15), but where we compare the probabilities for the two regions the curve is dividing.

In case of a geometric curve, we adopt a strategy of using one level-set for each phase. For an evolution without a vacuum or overlap, we use an additional transformation of probability images as described in [6]. This is applied for each phase, and transforms J probabilities (one for each phase) into two, one for the phase in question and another for all other phases.

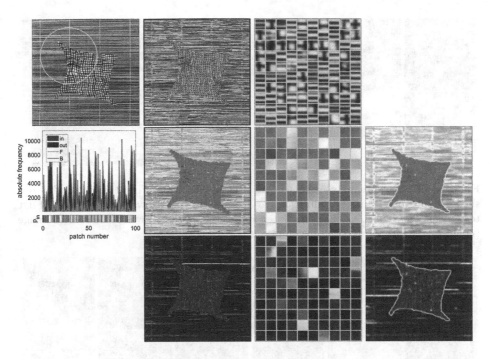

Fig. 2. Distribution of patches for a textured image. *First row* shows an input image (*left*), an assignment image (*middle*) and a dictionary containing 100 patches obtained from the image (*right*). The size of the image is 640-by-640 pixels, and patches are 11-by-11 pixels. *Second row* shows histograms for patch centers (*left*) and P_{in} using a central-pixel approach, for inside indicated by the green curve (*middle left*). The histogram appears ragged due to lack of obvious sorting of the clusters. The colored bar below the histogram indicates p_{in} for each patch center. Also in *second row*, dictionary probabilities (*middle right*) and P_{in} (*right*) using a patch-probabilities approach are shown. *Last row* shows similar results but for inside being the foreground region of the image. Note that probabilities indicate that some patches often appear on the boundary between foreground and background. (Color figure online)

3 Results and Discussion

In our current implementation the initialization is provided as a curve (usually a small circle) vaguely outlining a region in the image. It is our experience that even a weak initialization leads to a reasonable estimate of probability densities for different image regions – see a small test in Fig. 3.

The effect of the regularization parameter α is shown in Fig. 4. In the case of intensity-based segmentation, a strong regularization is needed for good results. This might have an undesirable effect where the boundary between foreground and background has a high curvature. With the patch-based model we can use a weaker regularization and obtain a more accurate segmentation result.

We have implemented our approach as both a parametric (snakes [8]) and geometric (level-sets [11]) deformable model. In Fig. 5 we compare the two

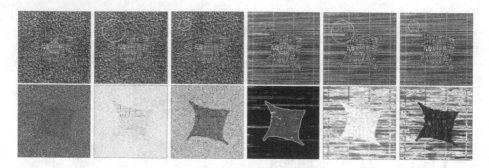

Fig. 3. Initialization analysis shown on two images from Figs. 1 and 2. *Top row* shows input images and initialization curves. *Bottom row* shows calculated P_{in}. First test image (*columns 1–3*) uses the intensity-based approach, while the second image (*columns 4–6*) uses the patch distributions.

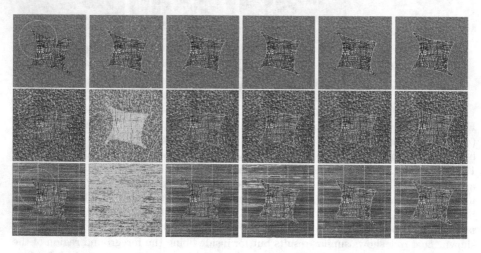

Fig. 4. Effect of regularization on results for images from Figs. 1 and 2. *First column* shows input image and curve initialization. *Columns 2–5* show converged results of intensity based segmentation with $\alpha = 0$, $\alpha = 1$, $\alpha = 2$, and $\alpha = 5$ respectively. *Rightmost column* brings results of the patch-based approach, with dictionary containing 1554 image patches of size 7-by-7, and with $\alpha = 0$ for the first two rows and $\alpha = 1$ for the last.

implementations on a pair of natural images. When the foreground consists of a single object, the results obtained with the two curve representations are comparable, with level-sets being slightly more prone to noise. When an image contains multiple foreground regions, level-sets are capable of adapting the topology and capturing multiple foreground objects. The snakes approach is constrained by a single curve topology and does not capture the additional foreground regions. Furthermore, the presence of foreground regions outside the curve makes the probability estimation more blurry.

Fig. 5. Snakes and level-set segmentations of natural images. *First column*: initialization. *Columns 2–3*: results using level-sets and the final P_{in}. *Columns 4–5*: results using snakes and the final P_{in}. Patches of size 3-by-3 are used for the top image and 7-by-7 for the bottom image. Both dictionaries contain 1554 patches. Regularization parameters are $\alpha = 2$ for the level-set model and $\alpha = 1$ for the snakes model, but those cannot be directly compared due to differences in implementation.

Results of a single multi-phase segmentation are shown in Fig. 6.

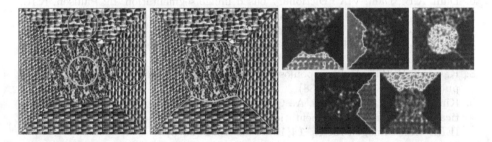

Fig. 6. Segmentation using a multiphase level-set method. Big images shows the initialization and the obtained result. Remaining images show the pixel-wise probabilities of the five regions. A dictionary contains 1554 9-by-9 patches and $\alpha = 2$.

4   Conclusion

We reformulate the established deformable models for image segmentation in a probabilistic framework. The similarity of our framework with the deformation model presented in (3) and (4) lies in obtaining region estimates by averaging, and then moving the curve to increase the distance between those estimates. While they estimate intensity means, we estimate intensity distributions. Averaging is also fundamental for the model in (1) and (2), and additional similarity to our model is that pixel move to the image region to which they fit better. While they use a difference between pixel intensity and an estimated mean as a measure of fit, we use probabilities. In both cases, moving pixels will improve the current estimate of the region property.

Just like those established models, our approach is simple, based on counting and averaging, and with an efficient implementation. Still, the model is very powerful and provides good segmentation. We believe that our framework would be a useful addition to the family of deformable models.

References

1. Brox, T., Rousson, M., Deriche, R., Weickert, J.: Colour, texture, and motion in level set based segmentation and tracking. Image Vis. Comput. **28**(3), 376–390 (2010)
2. Brox, T., Weickert, J.: A TV flow based local scale estimate and its application to texture discrimination. J. Vis. Commun. Image Represent. **17**(5), 1053–1073 (2006)
3. Chan, T., Vese, L.: An active contour model without edges. In: Nielsen, M., Johansen, P., Olsen, O.F., Weickert, J. (eds.) Scale-Space 1999. LNCS, vol. 1682, pp. 141–151. Springer, Heidelberg (1999). doi:10.1007/3-540-48236-9_13
4. Chan, T.F., Vese, L.A.: Active contours without edges. IEEE Trans. Image Process. **10**(2), 266–277 (2001)
5. Dahl, A.B., Dahl, V.A.: Dictionary snakes. In: International Conference on Pattern Recognition (ICPR), pp. 142–147. IEEE (2014)
6. Dahl, A.B., Dahl, V.A.: Dictionary based image segmentation. In: Paulsen, R.R., Pedersen, K.S. (eds.) SCIA 2015. LNCS, vol. 9127, pp. 26–37. Springer, Cham (2015). doi:10.1007/978-3-319-19665-7_3
7. Gao, Y., Bouix, S., Shenton, M., Tannenbaum, A.: Sparse texture active contour. IEEE Trans. Image Process. **22**(10), 3866–3878 (2013)
8. Kass, M., Witkin, A., Terzopoulos, D.: Snakes: active contour models. Int. J. Comput. Vis. **1**(4), 321–331 (1988)
9. Kim, J., Fisher, J.W., Yezzi, A., Çetin, M., Willsky, A.S.: A nonparametric statistical method for image segmentation using information theory and curve evolution. IEEE Trans. Image Process. **14**(10), 1486–1502 (2005)
10. Mumford, D., Shah, J.: Optimal approximations by piecewise smooth functions and associated variational problems. Commun. Pure Appl. Math. **42**(5), 577–685 (1989)
11. Osher, S., Sethian, J.A.: Fronts propagating with curvature-dependent speed: algorithms based on Hamilton-Jacobi formulations. J. Comput. Phys. **79**(1), 12–49 (1988)
12. Rousson, M., Brox, T., Deriche, R.: Active unsupervised texture segmentation on a diffusion based feature space. In: IEEE Conference on Computer Vision and Pattern Recognition (CVPR), vol. 2, pp. II-699. IEEE (2003)
13. Tsai, A., Yezzi Jr., A., Willsky, A.S.: Curve evolution implementation of the Mumford-Shah functional for image segmentation, denoising, interpolation, and magnification. IEEE Trans. Image Process. **10**(8), 1169–1186 (2001)
14. Wang, J., Chan, K.L.: Incorporating patch subspace model in Mumford-Shah type active contours. IEEE Trans. Image Process. **22**(11), 4473–4485 (2013)
15. Yezzi Jr., A., Tsai, A., Willsky, A.: A statistical approach to snakes for bimodal and trimodal imagery. In: International Conference on Computer Vision (ICCV), vol. 2, pp. 898–903. IEEE (1999)

Convex and Non-Convex Modeling and Optimization in Imaging

Denoising of Image Gradients and Constrained Total Generalized Variation

Birgit Komander$^{(\boxtimes)}$ and Dirk A. Lorenz

TU Braunschweig, Braunschweig, Germany
{b.komander,d.lorenz}@tu-braunschweig.de

Abstract. We derive a denoising method that uses higher order derivative information. Our method is motivated by work on denoising of normal vectors to the image which then are used for a better denoising of the image itself. We propose to denoise image gradients instead of image normals, since this leads to a convex optimization problem. We show how the denoising of the image gradient and the image itself can be done simultaneously in one optimization problem. It turns out that the resulting problem is similar to total generalized variation denoising, thus shedding more light on the motivation of the total generalized variation penalties. Our approach, however, works with constraints, rather than penalty functionals. As a consequence, there is a natural way to choose one of the parameters of the problems and we motivate a choice rule for the second involved parameter.

1 Introduction

In the paper from 2004, Lysaker et al. [1] proposed an image denoising technique in two steps. First, they used a total variation filter to smooth the normal vectors of the level-sets of a given noisy image. If u_0 is the given image and $n_0 = \nabla u_0 / |\nabla u_0|$ are the corresponding normals, the denoised normals have been obtained by minimizing

$$\int |\nabla n| + \tfrac{\lambda}{2} \int |n - n_0|$$

with respect to the constraint $|n| = 1$. As a second step, they tried to find a surface to fit these smoothed normal vectors. The first problem is highly non-linear and non-convex and [1] derive a descent method by driving a dynamic version of the Euler-Lagrange equation to steady state. Also the step to recover the image with known normals proposed in [1] uses this technique. In [2] a similar idea has been applied for a problem of deflectometric surface measurements where the measurement device does not only produces approximate point coordinates but also approximate surface normals. It turned out that the incorporation of surface normals results in a fairly non-linear problem. Switching from surface normals to image gradients, however, turns out to lead to a linear problem.

Here we propose a similar technique, where, in the first attempt, we use gradient vectors of the noisy input image instead of normal vectors. The advantage

© Springer International Publishing AG 2017
F. Lauze et al. (Eds.): SSVM 2017, LNCS 10302, pp. 435–446, 2017.
DOI: 10.1007/978-3-319-58771-4_35

of using gradient vectors instead of normal vector is that the resulting optimization problems are convex, as we will see at the beginning of Sect. 2. We observe that denoising of image gradient and the image itself in two stages is neither a satisfactory denoising method, nor necessary, as one can do both steps in just one minimization problem. We will derive this minimization problem and then observe that we obtain a problem which can be seen as a constrained version of the successful total generalized variation (TGV) method [3], thus linking the old idea of denoising of image normals to the recent idea of TGV denoising. This approach gives a new view on the nature of the TGV method and the constrained version allows for a noise-driven choice of the two involved parameters. Our approach bears similarities with the denoising by sparse vector fields in [4] which focuses on image compression.

The paper is organized as follows. Throughout Sect. 2, we will develop the first sequential approach to an optimization problem, which will combine the sequential problems into one problem that will handle both, the denoising of gradients and image, in order to get a descent result of the removing of noise from the image. After the formulation of the denoising problem, we will see, that our proposed technique, termed constrained total generalized variation (CTGV) is similar to the TGV denoising. The TGV method uses an optimization formulation with weighted penalty terms in the objective functional. We will also discuss the choice of the constraint parameters. In Sect. 3 we derive an algorithm for the CTGV problem, show some results in Sect. 4, and finally draw some conclusions.

2   Constrained Total Generalized Variation

The model for the input image u_0 is given by $u_0 = u^\dagger + \eta$, where $u^\dagger$ is the ground truth image and η the noise. For the moment, we consider the noise power $\|\eta\|_2$ to be known. The goal is to remove the noise in order to obtain a close approximation to $u^\dagger$.

Let us consider that, in addition to u_0, we know $\delta_1 = \|\eta\|_2$ and $D^\dagger := \nabla u^\dagger$, i.e. the gradient of the noise-free image. Then, a denoising problem could be formed by minimizing a norm distance over u between ∇u and $D^\dagger$ subject to the constraint that u is close to u_0.

A natural choice for the distance from ∇u to $D^\dagger$ is similar to total variation, i.e. we use the Euclidean norm for the gradient in combination with the one-norm which leads to the mixed norm

$$\|D\|_{2,1} = \int \|D(x)\|_2 \mathrm{d}x.$$

Hence, the optimization problem writes as

$$\min_u \|\nabla u - D^\dagger\|_{2,1} \quad s.t. \quad \|u - u_0\|_2 \le \delta_1. \tag{1}$$

As can be seen in the results in Sect. 4, this allows for remarkably good reconstructions. However, most of the times we do not have any informations about $D^\dagger$. In that case, we could use the idea of Lysaker et al. [1] and compute a good approximation D of $D^\dagger$ by denoising the gradients $D_0 := \nabla u_0$ as a first step. In a second step, we could solve (1) with the estimated D instead of $D^\dagger$.

To denoise the gradient vectors we solve

$$\min_D F(D) \quad s.t. \quad \|D - D_0\|_{2,1} \le \delta_2$$

and need a smoothness penalty F for the gradient vectors. Naturally, a norm of a derivative of the gradient can be used. A first candidate could be the Jacobian of the gradient, i.e.

$$J(\nabla u) = \begin{pmatrix} \partial_x(\partial_x u) & \partial_y(\partial_x u) \\ \partial_x(\partial_y u) & \partial_y(\partial_y u) \end{pmatrix},$$

which amounts to the Hessian of u which is symmetric as soon as u is twice continuously differentiable. However, notice that the Jacobian of an arbitrary vector field is not necessarily symmetric and hence using $F(D) = \|J(D)\|$ seems unnatural. Instead, we could use the symmetrized Jacobian,

$$\mathcal{E}(D) = \begin{pmatrix} \partial_x D_1 & \frac{1}{2}(\partial_y D_1 + \partial_x D_2) \\ \frac{1}{2}(\partial_y D_1 + \partial_x D_2) & \partial_y D_2 \end{pmatrix},$$

where D_1 and D_2 are the parts of D corresponding to the partial derivatives in directions x and y. Note that for twice continuously differentiable u we have that

$$\mathcal{E}(\nabla u) = J(\nabla u) = \mathrm{Hess}(u),$$

i.e. in both cases we obtain the Hessian of u.

Hence, we can denoise the image gradient by solving

$$\min_D \|\mathcal{E}(D)\|_{2,1} \quad s.t \quad \|D - D_0\|_{2,1} \le \delta_2 \tag{2}$$

and then use the result D instead of $D^\dagger$ in (1) to obtain a denoised image. However, it turned out that this method does not lead to good results (not shown here due to space limitations). In view of this, we propose to combine problems (1) and (2) into one optimization problem to still take advantage of the idea of denoising of image gradients to denoise the image itself. This leads to

$$\min_{u,D} \|\mathcal{E}(D)\|_{2,1} \quad s.t \quad \|u - u_0\|_2 \le \delta_1,$$
$$\|\nabla u - D\|_{2,1} \le \delta_2. \tag{3}$$

The first constraint is the same as in (1) and the second constraint differs only in that it uses the gradient ∇u of the denoised image instead of ∇u_0.

Let us take a closer look at (3): If we reformulate the problem with penalization instead of constraints, we obtain

$$\min_{u,D} \|\mathcal{E}(D)\|_{2,1} + \tfrac{\beta_1}{2}\|u - u_0\|_2^2 + \beta_0\|\nabla u - D\|_{2,1}.$$

Rearranging terms and using different weights, we obtain exactly the optimization problem

$$\min_{u} \tfrac{1}{2}\|u - u_0\|_2^2 + \mathrm{TGV}_\alpha(u) \tag{4}$$

from [3,5] with the total generalized variation penalty

$$\mathrm{TGV}_\alpha(u) = \min_{D} \; \alpha_1\|\nabla u - D\|_{2,1} + \alpha_0\|\mathcal{E}(D)\|_{2,1}. \tag{5}$$

As we can see, the same terms occur in (5) and (3). The difference is that (3) uses a formulation with constraint functions instead of weighted penalty functions within the objective functional.

Consequently, we define the constrained total generalized variation (CTGV) as

$$\mathrm{CTGV}_\delta(u) = \min_{D} \; \|\mathcal{E}(D)\|_{2,1} \quad s.t. \quad \|\nabla u - D\|_{2,1} \leq \delta \tag{6}$$

and problem (3) becomes

$$\min_{u} \; \mathrm{CTGV}_{\delta_2}(u) \quad s.t. \quad \|u - u_0\|_2 \leq \delta_1. \tag{7}$$

Lemma 1. *The functionals* TGV *and* CTGV *are equivalent in the sense that for any u it holds that for any $\alpha > 0$ there exists $\delta > 0$ such that each minimizer D_α of the* $\mathrm{TGV}_\alpha(u)$ *minimization problem is also a minimizer of the* $\mathrm{CTGV}_\delta(u)$ *minimization problem and vice versa.*

Proof. Results like this that relate solution for penalized and constrained problems are fairly common, see e.g. [6], but we give the short proof for completeness. Consider $\alpha_0 = 1$ and $\alpha_1 = \alpha$. Let D_α be a minimizer of the TGV functional (5), i.e. $\mathrm{TGV}_{1,\alpha}(u) = \|\mathcal{E}(D_\alpha)\|_{2,1} + \alpha\|\nabla u - D_\alpha\|_{2,1}$. Then it is clear that for $\delta(\alpha) = \|\nabla u - D_\alpha\|_{2,1}$ we have that D_α is feasible and also optimal for (6).

Conversely, if $\alpha(\delta)$ is the Lagrange multiplier for the constraint in (6) and D^δ is optimal there, then D^δ is also optimal for the problem (5) with $\alpha_1 = \alpha(\delta)$ and $\alpha_0 = 1$. $\qquad\square$

Lemma 2. *The* TGV *denoising problem* (4) *and the* CTGV *denoising problem* (7) *are equivalent in the sense that for any minimizer u_α of* (4) *there exists δ_1, δ_2 such that u_α is a solution of* (7). *Conversely, for any δ_1, δ_2 such that the constraints in* (7) *are active for a minimizer u_δ there exist α_0, α_1 such that u_δ is a solution of* (4).

Proof. The proof is similar to the one of lemma 1: Assume that u_α is a solution of (4) and D_α is a corresponding optimal vector field. Now set $\delta_1 = \|u_\alpha - u_0\|_2$ and $\delta_2 = \|\nabla u_\alpha - D_\alpha\|_{2,1}$. Then the pair (u_α, D_α) is feasible and optimal for (7).

Conversely, if (u_δ, D_δ) is optimal for (7) with active constraints, set α_0 and α_1 to the respective Lagrange multipliers and observe that then (u_δ, D_δ) is optimal for (4). $\qquad\square$

To solve problem (7) (or (3)) we reformulate it as a convex-concave saddle point problem. One way to do so is, similarly to [5], to introduce a block operator and two dual variables and write

$$\min_{u,D} \max_{p,q} \left\langle \begin{pmatrix} \nabla & -I \\ 0 & \mathcal{E} \end{pmatrix} \begin{pmatrix} u \\ D \end{pmatrix}, \begin{pmatrix} p \\ q \end{pmatrix} \right\rangle + \mathcal{I}_{\|\cdot-u_0\|_2 \leq \delta_1}(u)$$
$$- \left(\mathcal{I}_{\|\cdot\|_{2,\infty} \leq \delta_2}(q) + \delta_2 \|p\|_{2,\infty} \right), \tag{8}$$

where $\mathcal{I}_C(x)$ is an indicator function of a set C.

Applying, for example, the primal-dual algorithm from [7] to this problem would lead to iterates which are neither primal, nor dual feasible. In order to avoid this circumstance, we reformulate the optimization problem by defining a variable $\psi := \nabla u - D$. Thus, the denoising problem writes as

$$\min_{u,\psi} \|\mathcal{E}(\nabla u - \psi)\|_{2,1} \quad s.t \quad \|u - u_0\|_2 \leq \delta_1,$$
$$\|\psi\|_{2,1} \leq \delta_2. \tag{9}$$

As shown in the next section, this formulation saves one dual variable in comparison to (3) and also, the primal-dual method from [7] ensures primal and dual feasibility.

Next, we take a look at the constraint parameters and how to choose them. When we go back to the model of the given noisy image, $u_0 = u^\dagger + \eta$, we should consider that the output image of the denoising process should not differ any more from $u^\dagger$ than the input u_0. Hence, we can choose

$$\delta_1 := \|u_0 - u^\dagger\|_2 = \|\eta\|_2. \tag{10}$$

Thus, the first constraint parameter is the noise power and relies on an estimate of this quantity.

For the choice of the second parameter δ_2 we observe the following:

Lemma 3. *Let*

$$u^{\text{TV}} \in \arg\min \|\nabla u\|_{2,1} \quad s.t \quad \|u - u_0\|_2 \leq \delta_1.$$

Then it holds

$$\delta_2 = \|\nabla u_0\|_{2,1} \implies u_0 \text{ is a solution of (7)}$$
$$\delta_2 = \|\nabla u^{\text{TV}}\|_{2,1} \implies u^{\text{TV}} \text{ is a solution of (7)}$$

Finally, for $\delta_2 = 0$ we obtain that

$$\arg\min\{\text{CTGV}_0(u) \mid \|u - u_0\| \leq \delta_1\} = \arg\min\{\|\text{Hess}(u)\|_{2,1} \mid \|u - u_0\| \leq \delta_1\}.$$

Proof. For the first assertion observe that the pair $(u, \psi) = (u_0, \nabla u_0)$ is feasible for the problem (9) with objective equal to zero, hence optimal. Similarly, for the second claim $(u, \psi) = (u^{\text{TV}}, \nabla u^{\text{TV}})$ is feasible with zero objective. Lastly, when $\delta_2 = 0$, we get $\nabla u = D$ and the statement follows from $\mathcal{E}(\nabla u) = \text{Hess}(u)$. □

In other words: The choice $\delta_2 = \text{TV}(u_0)$ leads to no denoising, while $\delta_2 = \text{TV}(u^{\text{TV}})$ does not do denoising beyond the TV-denoising. Finally, $\delta_2 = 0$ is denoising with a pure second-order objective. Similarly, one sees that for $\delta_2 \geq \text{TV}(u^{\text{TV}})$ one still gets u^{TV} as an optimal solution, since $(u^{\text{TV}}, \nabla u^{\text{TV}})$ is still feasible. Moreover, one suspects that in this parameter regime multiple solutions exist (as every pair $(u, \nabla u)$ which is feasible leads to a zero objective). As a consequence, one should choose the value of δ_2 between 0 and $\text{TV}(u^{\text{TV}})$ to see denoising beyond TV-denoising. In the experiments below, we will see that a simple choice $\delta_2 = \text{TV}(u^{\text{TV}})/2$ leads to good results.

3   Algorithms

We formulate the problem (9) in primal form as $\min_{u,\psi} F(u,\psi) + G(K(u,\psi))$, and derive the dual problem and saddle point formulation together with update functions as follows:

The functional $F(u,\psi)$ is

$$F(u,\psi) = \mathcal{I}_{\|\cdot - u_0\|_2 \leq \delta_1}(u) + \mathcal{I}_{\|\cdot\|_{2,1} \leq \delta_2}(\psi),$$

while $G(w) = \|w\|_{2,1}$. The Fenchel-Rockefellar dual of G is

$$G^*(v) = \mathcal{I}_{\|\cdot\|_{2,\infty} \leq 1}(v).$$

Thus, the saddle point formulation is

$$\min_{u,\psi} \max_{v} \left\langle K\begin{pmatrix} u \\ \psi \end{pmatrix}, v \right\rangle + F(u,\psi) - G^*(v)$$

$$= \min_{\substack{\|u-u_0\|_2 \leq \delta_1 \\ \|\psi\|_{2,1} \leq \delta_2}} \max_{\|v\|_{2,\infty} \leq 1} \left\langle K\begin{pmatrix} u \\ \psi \end{pmatrix}, v \right\rangle,$$

where $K = \mathcal{E}\begin{pmatrix} \nabla & -I \end{pmatrix}$, hence, $K^* = \begin{pmatrix} \nabla^* \\ -I \end{pmatrix}\mathcal{E}^*$. The dual problem reads as

$$\max_{v} -F^*(-K^*v) - G^*(v)$$

and the dual function of $F(u,\psi)$ is

$$F^*(s,\phi) = \sup_{u,\psi} \langle s,u \rangle + \langle \phi,\psi \rangle - \left(\mathcal{I}_{\|\cdot - u_0\|_2 \leq \delta_1}(u) + \mathcal{I}_{\|\cdot\|_{2,1} \leq \delta_2}(\psi)\right)$$

$$= \sup_{\substack{\|u-u_0\|_2 \leq \delta_1 \\ \|\psi\|_{2,1} \leq \delta_2}} \langle s,u \rangle + \langle \phi,\psi \rangle = \sup_{\substack{\|w\|_2 \leq \delta_1 \\ \|\psi\|_{2,1} \leq \delta_2}} \langle s,w \rangle + \langle s,u_0 \rangle + \langle \phi,\psi \rangle$$

$$= \delta_1 \|s\|_2 + \langle s,u_0 \rangle + \delta_2 \|\phi\|_{2,\infty},$$

hence, the dual optimization problem is

$$\max_{v} -\delta_1 \|\nabla^*\mathcal{E}^*v\|_2 + \langle \nabla^*\mathcal{E}^*v, u_0 \rangle - \delta_2 \|\mathcal{E}^*v\|_{2,\infty} - \mathcal{I}_{\|\cdot\|_{2,\infty} \leq 1}(v). \tag{11}$$

Together, we can write down the update functions for iteration n via proximal mappings

$$\begin{pmatrix} u^{n+1} \\ \psi^{n+1} \end{pmatrix} = \text{prox}_{\tau F}\left(\begin{pmatrix} u^n \\ \psi^n \end{pmatrix} - \tau K^* v^n\right),$$

$$v^{n+1} = \text{prox}_{\sigma G^*}\left(v^n + \sigma K(2u^{n+1} - u^n - (2\psi^{n+1} - \psi^n))\right).$$

These proximal mappings reduce to projections,

$$u^{n+1} = \text{proj}_{\|\cdot - u_0\|_2 \leq \delta_1}\left(u^n - \tau \nabla^* \mathcal{E}^* v^n\right),$$

$$\psi^{n+1} = \text{proj}_{\|\cdot\|_{2,1} \leq \delta_2}\left(\psi^n + \tau \mathcal{E}^* v^n\right),$$

$$v^{n+1} = \text{proj}_{\|\cdot\|_{2,\infty} \leq 1}\left(v^n + \sigma \mathcal{E}(\nabla(2u^{n+1} - u^n) - (2\psi^{n+1} - \psi^n))\right).$$

This results in Algorithm 1.

Algorithm 1. Constrained TGV

Input : Noisy image u_0, constraint parameters δ_1, δ_2
Output: Denoised image u
Initialization: $u^0 \leftarrow u_0$, $\psi^0 \leftarrow \text{proj}_{\|\cdot\|_{2,1} \leq \delta_1}(\nabla u_0)$, $v^0 \leftarrow 0$.
repeat
$\quad u^{n+1} \leftarrow \text{proj}_{\|\cdot - u_0\|_2 \leq \delta_1}\left(u^n - \tau \nabla^* \mathcal{E}^* v^n\right)$
$\quad \psi^{n+1} \leftarrow \text{proj}_{\|\cdot\|_{2,1} \leq \delta_2}\left(\psi^n + \tau \mathcal{E}^* v^n\right)$
$\quad v^{n+1} \leftarrow \text{proj}_{\|\cdot\|_{2,\infty} \leq 1}\left(v^n + \sigma \mathcal{E}(\nabla(2u^{n+1} - u^n) - (2\psi^{n+1} - \psi^n))\right)$
until *convergence of* u^{n+1};
return u^{n+1}

Due to the projections in the iteration we see, looking at the primal problem (9) and the dual problem (11), that all iterates are primal and dual feasible and hence, we can use the following primal-dual gap

$$\text{gap}(u, \psi, v) = \|\mathcal{E}(\nabla u - \psi)\|_{2,1} + \delta_1 \|\nabla^* \mathcal{E}^* v\|_2 - \langle \nabla^* \mathcal{E}^* v, u_0\rangle + \delta_2 \|\mathcal{E}^* v\|_{2,\infty} \tag{12}$$

as a stopping criterion.

4 Results

In this section we want to take a closer look at CTGV-denoised images in comparison to other known techniques. We tested our proposed method with different images and changing noise level and image sizes (Table 1).

All images have gray values in the range $[0, 1]$ and we used additive Gaussian noise with a scaling factor c_η, i.e., $\eta = \texttt{randn}(\texttt{size}(u_0)) \cdot c_\eta$.

Throughout, we assume that $\delta_1 = \|\eta\|_2$ is known (which is not an unreasonable assumption since the noise level can be estimated from the noisy image alone and there exists routines that do so with reasonable accuracy).

Table 1. Comparison of PSNR values for TV-denoised images with and without known true gradients and CTGV-denoised images.

	TV with $D = D^\dagger$			TV with $D = 0$			CTGV		
	c_η $= 0.1$	c_η $= 0.25$	c_η $= 0.5$	c_η $= 0.1$	c_η $= 0.25$	c_η $= 0.5$	c_η $= 0.1$	c_η $= 0.25$	c_η $= 0.5$
Affine (64×64)	43.26	39.39	33.13	27.65	22.68	19.22	30.99	25.71	21.16
Affine (128×128)	45.18	37.56	32.81	30.27	25.17	21.51	33.82	26.86	24.37
Affine (256×256)	50.84	43.02	38.90	33.67	28.63	24.99	37.01	31.21	27.28
Eye (128×128)	45.03	37.41	32.66	27.83	24.20	21.77	28.71	25.19	23.39
Eye (256×256)	50.29	42.47	38.35	28.67	25.58	23.16	29.34	26.76	25.03
Eye (512×512)	53.81	46.68	40.69	30.83	27.74	25.36	31.86	29.05	27.43
Barbara (128×128)	44.78	37.15	32.40	25.06	21.01	18.43	25.52	21.19	18.85
Barbara (256×256)	49.95	42.13	38.00	26.25	22.62	20.09	26.68	23.05	20.77
Barbara (512×512)	53.50	46.38	40.39	24.88	22.33	20.66	25.11	22.48	21.10
Cameraman (128×128)	45.11	37.49	32.74	26.54	22.34	19.77	26.25	22.20	19.47
Cameraman (256×256)	50.25	42.44	38.31	27.28	23.36	20.92	27.03	22.85	20.58
Cameraman (512×512)	53.97	46.84	40.85	29.96	26.05	23.42	30.39	26.15	23.40

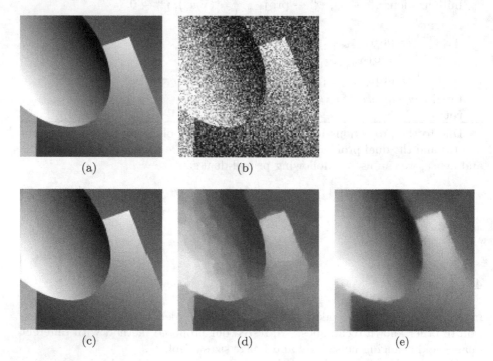

Fig. 1. Denoising of the affine image (128×128 pixels). Ground truth (a), noisy image wit $c_\eta = 0.25$ (b), TV with $D = \nabla u^\dagger$ (c), TV with $D = 0$ (d), CTGV (e)

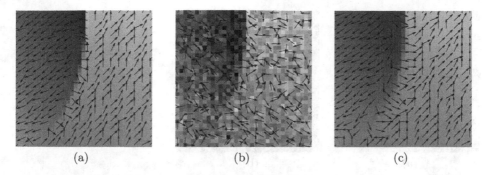

Fig. 2. Visualization of normalized image gradients. Clean image (a), noisy image (b), CTGV denoised image (c)

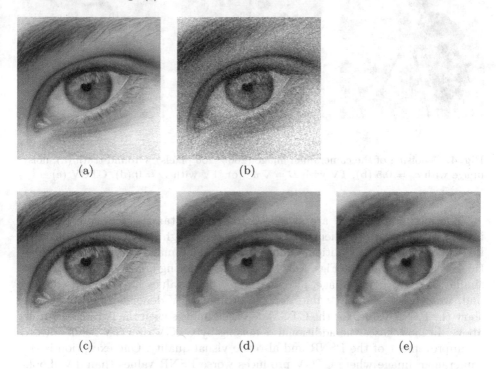

Fig. 3. Denoising of the eye image (256×256 pixels). Ground truth (a), noisy image with $c_\eta = 0.1$ (b), TV with $D = \nabla u^\dagger$ (c), TV with $D = 0$ (d), CTGV (e)

As a gold standard we denoised the images u_0 with the method (1), i.e. we used the gradient $D^\dagger = \nabla u^\dagger$ as proxy in the total variation penalty. Second, we calculated TV denoised images u^{TV} and finally we performed CTGV denoising with additional parameter

$$\delta_2 = \frac{\|\nabla u^{\mathrm{TV}}\|_{2,1}}{2}. \tag{13}$$

Fig. 4. Denoising of the cameraman image (256×256 pixels). Ground truth (a), noisy image with $c_\eta = 0.5$ (b), TV with $D = \nabla u^\dagger$ (c), TV with $D = 0$ (d), CTGV (e)

The methods we used are as follows: The gold standard method, i.e. solving (1) with the true gradient $D^\dagger := \nabla u^\dagger$, leads to high PSNR values. This is to be expected since the additional information of true image gradients is unrealistic. As can be seen in the Figs. 1, 3, 4 and 5, the resulting images look remarkably similar to the original image, although noisy pixel values have been used. Second, we listed the PSNR values for the ordinary TV-denoising and finally we show the PSNR values for the CTGV-denoised images with the parameters from above. In most cases the additional denoising by CTGV over TV leads both to an improvement of the PSNR and also the visual quality. One exception is the cameraman image where CTGV produces worse PSNR values than TV. Looking at Fig. 4 we may argue that this is due to the fact that this image does not contain too many smoothly varying regions but many sharp transitions so that the TV denoising already does a good job.

Finally observe that the improvement from TV to CTGV (and also the worsening in case of the cameraman) is consistent over all image sizes and noise levels, which indicates that at least scaling the parameter δ_2 according to (13) is more or less correct.

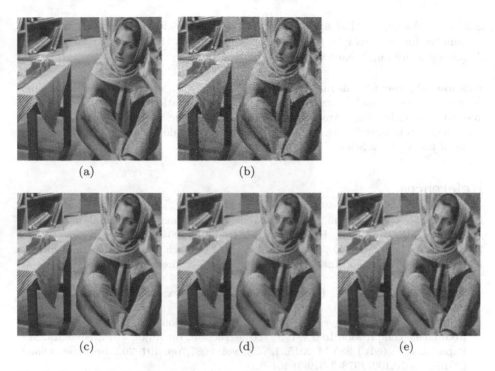

Fig. 5. Denoising of the barbara image (512×512 pixels). Ground truth (a), noisy image with $c_\eta = 0.1$ (b), TV with $D = \nabla u^\dagger$ (c), TV with $D = 0$ (d), CTGV (e)

While the PSNR values of CTGV denoising are almost always higher than the values of TV denoising, they do not came close to the gold standard of using the correct image gradients. On the other hand, Fig. 2 shows that the CTGV produces images gradients which are indeed close to the true gradients. This may indicate that the dependence of the denoising result is sensitive to small errors in the estimated gradients.

5   Conclusion

We provided a new view on the total generalized variation penalty by relating it to the older idea of denoising of image normals. Our derivation leads to the CTGV denoising which is a formulation with constraints rather than penalties. The new method is equivalent to the TGV denoising method in the sense that there exists an implicit mapping between the parameters of one method to the parameters of the other method which leads to equal minimizers. We derive a heuristic rule to choose the two parameters based on the estimated noise level on the TV denoising image. Numerical results indicate that the heuristic indeed yields better results as pure TV denoising but the results of CTGV denoising are closer to TV denoising than to the gold-standard of using the correct image gradients. We expect that a more sophisticated heuristic for the choice of the δ_2 parameter for the error in the image gradient exists that leads to even better denoising results and leave this to future work.

Acknowledgement. This material was based upon work supported by the National Science Foundation under Grant DMS-1127914 to the Statistical and Applied Mathematical Sciences Institute. Any opinions, findings, and conclusions or recommendations expressed in this material are those of the author(s) and do not necessarily reflect the views of the National Science Foundation.

References

1. Lysaker, M., Osher, S., Tai, X.C.: Noise removal using smoothed normals and surface fitting. IEEE Trans. Img. Proc. **13**(10), 1345–1357 (2004)
2. Komander, B., Lorenz, D., Fischer, M., Petz, M., Tutsch, R.: Data fusion of surface normals and point coordinates for deflectometric measurements. J. Sens. Sens. Syst. **3**, 281–290 (2014)
3. Bredies, K., Kunisch, K., Pock, T.: Total generalized variation. SIAM J. Imaging Sci. **3**(3), 492–526 (2010)
4. Brinkmann, E.-M., Burger, M., Grah, J.: Regularization with sparse vector fields: from image compression to TV-type reconstruction. In: Aujol, J.-F., Nikolova, M., Papadakis, N. (eds.) SSVM 2015. LNCS, vol. 9087, pp. 191–202. Springer, Cham (2015). doi:10.1007/978-3-319-18461-6_16
5. Knoll, F., Bredies, K., Pock, T., Stollberger, R.: Second order total generalized variation (TGV) for MRI. Magn. Reson. Med. **65**(2), 480–491 (2011)
6. Lorenz, D.A., Worliczek, N.: Necessary conditions for variational regularization schemes. Inverse Prob. **29**, 075016 (2013)
7. Chambolle, A., Pock, T.: A first-order primal-dual algorithm for convex problems with applications to imaging. J. Math. Imaging Vis. **40**(1), 120–145 (2011)

Infimal Convolution Coupling
of First and Second Order Differences
on Manifold-Valued Images

Ronny Bergmann[1], Jan Henrik Fitschen[1(✉)], Johannes Persch[1],
and Gabriele Steidl[1,2]

[1] Department of Mathematics, University of Kaiserslautern, Kaiserslautern, Germany
{bergmann,fitschen,persch,steidl}@mathematik.uni-kl.de
[2] Fraunhofer ITWM, Kaiserslautern, Germany

Abstract. Recently infimal convolution type functions were used in regularization terms of variational models for restoring and decomposing images. This is the first attempt to generalize the infimal convolution of first and second order differences to manifold-valued images. We propose both an extrinsic and an intrinsic approach. Our focus is on the second one since the summands arising in the infimal convolution lie on the manifold themselves and not in the higher dimensional embedding space. We demonstrate by numerical examples that the approach works well on the circle, the 2-sphere, the rotation group, and the manifold of positive definite matrices with the affine invariant metric.

Keywords: Infimal convolution · TGV · Higher order differences · Restoration of manifold-valued images · Decomposition of manifold-valued images

1 Introduction

Variational methods have gained a lot of interest in image processing in recent years due to their flexibility to model a large variety of tasks and their efficiency in computing. Typically, such models consist of a data fitting term and a regularization term also known as prior. In this paper we restrict our attention to least squares data fitting terms. Starting with methods having first order derivatives in their regularization term like the total variation (TV) [24], higher order derivatives were incorporated into the approach to cope with the staircasing effect caused by TV regularization and to better adapt to specific applications. Besides additive coupling of higher order derivatives, see, e.g., [20], their infimal convolution (IC) [14] or their total generalized variation (TGV) [13] were proposed in the literature. In many applications such as image denoising the combination of first and second order differences by IC or TGV shows better results than just the additive coupling, see, e.g., [25,26]. In the following we are mainly interested in the IC regularization approach. The IC of two functions $F_i \colon \mathbb{R}^N \to \mathbb{R} \cup \{+\infty\}$, $i = 1, 2$, is defined by

© Springer International Publishing AG 2017
F. Lauze et al. (Eds.): SSVM 2017, LNCS 10302, pp. 447–459, 2017.
DOI: 10.1007/978-3-319-58771-4_36

$$(F_1 \square F_2)(u) = \inf_{u=v+w} \{F_1(v) + F_2(w)\} = \inf_v \{F_1(v) + F_2(u-v)\}. \qquad (1)$$

If F_i, $i = 1, 2$, are proper, convex, lower semi-continuous and $F_i(u) = F_i(-u)$, then $F_1 \square F_2$ is also proper, convex, lower semi-continuous and the infimum is attained [21]. A prominent example is the IC of a function F_1 with the squared Euclidean norm, known as Moreau-Yosida envelope of F_1. In various applications, the individual IC components v and w are of interest, e.g., in motion separation [17] or crack detection [9]. The IC of the TV functional with other functionals, which are often concatenations of norms and certain linear operators, was used for texture-structure or line-point separation [4,15,27].

With the emerging possibilities to capture different modalities of data, image processing methods are transferred to the case where the measurements (pixels) take values on Riemannian manifolds. Examples are Interferometric Synthetic Aperture Radar (InSAR) with values on the circle $\mathbb{S}^1$, directional data on the 2-sphere $\mathbb{S}^2$, electron backscatter diffraction (EBSD) with data on quotient manifolds of SO(3) or diffusion tensor magnetic resonance imaging (DT-MRI), where each measurement is a symmetric positive definite 3×3 matrix.

Recently, the TV regularization has been generalized to Riemannian manifolds [16,18,29,33]. In [6,11,12] the model was updated by second order differences where the coupling was realized in an additive manner. For the special case of DT-MRI, i.e., symmetric positive definite matrices, another approach using tensor calculus resulting in the Frobenius norm instead of a distance on the Riemannian manifold was investigated in [28] and extended to a TGV approach in [31].

In this paper we make a first proposal how to modify the IC of TV-like terms with first and second order differences to manifold-valued images. The special IC leading to Moreau-Yosida envelopes on manifolds was considered, e.g., in [5]. A straightforward idea is to embed the d-dimensional manifold into $\mathbb{R}^n$, $n > d$, so that Euclidean arithmetic can be applied, and to add a constraint that the resulting image values have to lie on the manifold. Due to the constraint the problem becomes often non-convex. For the TV regularization such an embedding idea was applied, e.g., in [22]. First, we study how this embedding approach can be generalized to the IC regularization in the manifold-valued setting. A drawback of this extrinsic method is that the IC components live in the higher dimensional embedding space and not on the manifold. This makes their interpretation and visualization difficult. Therefore we propose an intrinsic model where all actors remain on the manifold. The main question is how to replace the addition in (1) with a suitable operation on manifolds. Here we make use of the midpoints of geodesics. We apply a gradient descent algorithm for the minimization and provide the necessary ingredients for the algorithm.

The outline of the paper is as follows: We give a brief review of existing first and second order models in the Euclidean as well as manifold-valued setting in Sect. 2. In Sect. 3 we propose an extrinsic IC model. Our main contribution is the introduction of an intrinsic IC model together with the quantities to run a gradient descent minimization algorithm in Sect. 4. Finally, Sect. 5 contains a first collection of numerical examples. Conclusions and an outlook to future work is given in Sect. 6.

2   Functionals with First and Second Order Differences

In this section, we briefly recall the functionals with first and second order differences we are interested in. We start with real-valued images since this is important for the extrinsic approach, and continue with the manifold-valued setting required for our intrinsic model. In the rest of this paper, let $\mathcal{G} := \{1, \ldots, N_1\} \times \{1, \ldots, N_2\}$ denote the pixel grid of an image of size $N_1 \times N_2$ and let $N := N_1 N_2$.

Real-Valued Images. Let $u: \mathcal{G} \to \mathbb{R}$ be a gray-value image. We use forward differences in horizontal and vertical directions in the discrete isotropic TV term

$$\mathrm{TV}(u) := \sum_{p \in \mathcal{G}} \sqrt{\sum_{q \in \mathcal{N}_p} (u_q - u_p)^2}, \tag{2}$$

where $\mathcal{N}_p := \{p + (0,1), p + (1,0)\} \cap \mathcal{G}$. We define central horizontal second order differences

$$d_{2,\mathrm{h}}(u_p) := \begin{cases} |u_{p-(1,0)} - 2u_p + u_{p+(1,0)}|, & p_1 \in \{2, \ldots, N_1 - 1\}, \\ 0, & \text{else}, \end{cases}$$

and similarly in vertical direction by replacing $(1,0)$ by $(0,1)$ and p_1, N_1 by p_2, N_2. We use them in the functional

$$\mathrm{TV}_2(u) := \sum_{p \in \mathcal{G}} \sqrt{d_{2,\mathrm{h}}^2(u_p) + d_{2,\mathrm{v}}^2(u_p)}.$$

Instead of coupling the TV and TV_2 terms in an additive way and minimizing for a given $f: \mathcal{G} \to \mathbb{R}$ the functional

$$E_{\mathrm{Add}}(u) := \frac{1}{2} \|f - u\|_2^2 + \alpha \left(\beta \, \mathrm{TV}(u) + (1 - \beta) \, \mathrm{TV}_2(u) \right), \tag{3}$$

we are interested in

$$E_{\mathrm{IC}}(u) := \frac{1}{2} \|f - u\|_2^2 + \alpha \min_{u = v + w} \left(\beta \, \mathrm{TV}(v) + (1 - \beta) \, \mathrm{TV}_2(w) \right), \tag{4}$$

where $\alpha > 0$ and $\beta \in [0,1]$. In various applications the summands v and w appearing in the IC decomposition are of interest on their own. To make them unique, e.g., the mean value of v could be fixed.

Manifold-Valued Images. Let $\mathcal{M}$ be a connected, complete d-dimensional Riemannian manifold. By $T_x \mathcal{M}$ we denote the tangent space of $\mathcal{M}$ at $x \in \mathcal{M}$ with the Riemannian metric $\langle \cdot, \cdot \rangle_x$. Let $\gamma_{\widehat{x,y}}$ be a geodesic connecting $x, y \in \mathcal{M}$

and dist: $\mathcal{M} \times \mathcal{M} \to \mathbb{R}_{\geq 0}$ the geodesic distance on $\mathcal{M}$. By $\mathcal{M}^N$ we denote the product manifold with usual product distance. Instead of gray-value images, we consider images $u: \mathcal{G} \to \mathcal{M}$ with values on a manifold. Replacing the absolute differences in the TV term (2) by distances on the manifold we get

$$\text{TV}(u) := \sum_{p \in \mathcal{G}} \sqrt{\sum_{q \in \mathcal{N}_p} \text{dist}^2(u_q, u_p)}.$$

Observing that in the Euclidean case the second order difference of $x, y, z \in \mathbb{R}^d$ can be rewritten as $x - 2y + z = 2(\frac{1}{2}(x + z) - y)$, we define a counterpart for $x, y, z \in \mathcal{M}$ as follows [6]: let $\mathcal{C}_{x,z}$ be the set of mid points $\gamma_{\widehat{x,z}}(\frac{1}{2})$ of all geodesics joining x and z. Note that the geodesic γ is unique on manifolds with non positive curvature, i.e., Hadamard manifolds. Then we define

$$d_2(x, y, z) := \min_{c \in \mathcal{C}_{x,z}} \text{dist}(c, y).$$

Using this definition as before for the rows and columns of u, we get

$$d_{2,\text{h}}(u_p) := \begin{cases} d_2(u_{p+(1,0)}, u_p, u_{p-(1,0)}), & p_1 \in \{2, \ldots, N_1 - 1\} \\ 0, & \text{else,} \end{cases}$$

and similarly for the vertical differences. We set

$$\text{TV}_2(u) := \sum_{p \in \mathcal{G}} \sqrt{d_{2,\text{h}}^2(u_p) + d_{2,\text{v}}^2(u_p)}.$$

Note that for Hadamard manifolds, in contrast to the TV functional, the TV_2 functional is not convex. The additive model

$$E_{\text{Add}}(u) := \frac{1}{2} \sum_{p \in \mathcal{G}} \text{dist}(f_p, u_p)^2 + \alpha \left(\beta \, \text{TV}(u) + (1 - \beta) \, \text{TV}_2(u) \right)$$

was used in [6] for the denoising of manifold-valued images $f: \mathcal{G} \to \mathcal{M}$ and with a slight modification for inpainting in [12]. We are interested in an IC approach similar to (2).

3   Extrinsic Infimal Convolution Model

Recall that by Whitney's theorem [34] every smooth d-dimensional manifold can be smoothly embedded into an Euclidean space of dimension $n = 2d$. Moreover, by Nash's theorem [19] every Riemannian manifold can be isometrically embedded into an Euclidean space of suitable dimension. In applications we will deal with spheres $\mathbb{S}^d$ with natural embedding into $\mathbb{R}^{d+1}$, $SO(3)$ with embedding into $\mathbb{R}^9$ if considered as 3×3 matrices or into $\mathbb{R}^4$ via the quaternion representation. Further, symmetric positive definite $r \times r$ matrices can be embedded into $\mathbb{R}^{r^2}$. Based on an appropriate embedding of $\mathcal{M}$ into $\mathbb{R}^n$ we suggest to minimize the following functional over $\mathbb{R}^{nN}$:

$$E_{\mathrm{IC}}^{\mathrm{ext}}(u) := \frac{1}{2}\|f - u\|_2^2 + \alpha\left(\beta\,\mathrm{TV}\,\square(1 - \beta)\,\mathrm{TV}_2\right)(u) \quad \text{s.t.} \quad u \in \mathcal{M}^N.$$

Under the assumption that $\mathcal{M}$ is closed, we directly get the existence of a global minimizer by the coercivity and lower semi-continuity of the functional. Due to the constraint, the functional is in general not convex. In various applications we are searching for minimizers $v, w \in \mathbb{R}^{nN}$ of

$$\mathcal{E}^{\mathrm{ext}}(v, w) := \frac{1}{2}\|f - v - w\|_2^2 + \alpha\left(\beta\,\mathrm{TV}(v) + (1 - \beta)\,\mathrm{TV}_2(w)\right) \text{ s.t. } v + w \in \mathcal{M}^N$$

and set finally $u := v + w$. We apply an ADMM to minimize the above functional. The algorithm can be implemented in a straightforward way, where one step requires the orthogonal projection onto the respective manifold. For the manifold of positive definite matrices the resulting problems are convex and convergence follows by standard arguments. It was shown in [23] based on [3] that convergence for compact manifolds as $\mathrm{SO}(n)$ or $\mathbb{S}^n$ can be achieved, at least for fixed Lagrangian multipliers, by adding proximal terms to the minimization problems inside the ADMM. We note that convergence of the ADMM for special non-convex functionals was also addressed in [32], but the assumptions of that paper do not fit into our setting.

4   Intrinsic Infimal Convolution Model

In the extrinsic model the IC components v and w live in the embedding space. Next we propose a model where they are also elements of the manifold. We start with an intuitive example of an $\mathbb{S}^1$-valued image in Fig. 1. Here points in the embedding space $\mathbb{R}^2$ can still be visualized (middle, right image). The decomposition into constant and "cyclic linear" parts, which approximate geodesics, is nicely visible in the intrinsic model (left, middle image).

To set up our model we realize that in the Euclidean setting the IC of two one-homogeneous functions as TV and TV_2 can be rewritten as

$$F_1\square F_2(u) = \frac{1}{2}\inf_{u = \frac{1}{2}(v + w)}\{F_1(v) + F_2(w)\}. \tag{5}$$

Now we may consider the "midpoint infimal convolution" of $F_i\colon \mathcal{M} \to \mathbb{R}$, $i = 1, 2$, given by

$$F_1\square_m F_2(u) := \inf_{u \in \mathcal{C}_{v,w}}\{F_1(v) + F_2(w)\},$$

and using $F_1 := \mathrm{TV}$ and $F_2 := \mathrm{TV}_2$ we define the following functional on $\mathcal{M}^N$:

$$E_{\mathrm{IC}}^{\mathrm{int}}(u) := \frac{1}{2}\,\mathrm{dist}^2(u, f) + \alpha\left(\beta\,\mathrm{TV}\,\square_m(1 - \beta)\,\mathrm{TV}_2\right)(u).$$

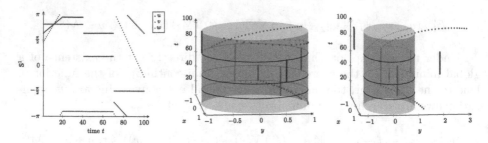

Fig. 1. Decomposed $\mathbb{S}^1$-valued signal by intrinsic ($\alpha = 0.005$, $\beta = 0.2$) and extrinsic ($\alpha = 0.03$, $\beta = \frac{1}{3}$) IC approaches. Left: Piecewise linear signal u (black) determined by its angles in $[-\pi, \pi)$ and its decomposition into v (red) w (blue) via the intrinsic IC model. Middle: Same signal embedded into $\mathbb{R}^2$, where the horizontal axis switches to the vertical one. Right: Result of the extrinsic IC model in the embedding space $\mathbb{R}^2$ (with scaling (4)). (Color figure online)

More precisely, we are interested in minimizing the slightly different functional

$$\mathcal{E}^{\text{int}}(v, w) = \frac{1}{2} \sum_{p \in \mathcal{G}} \text{dist}^2(\gamma_{v_p, \widehat{w_p}}(\tfrac{1}{2}), f_p) + \alpha \left(\beta \, \text{TV}(v) + (1 - \beta) \, \text{TV}_2(w)\right)$$
$$= \frac{1}{2} \sum_{p \in \mathcal{G}} \mathrm{d}_2^2(v_p, f_p, w_p) + \alpha \left(\beta \, \text{TV}(v) + (1 - \beta) \, \text{TV}_2(w)\right). \tag{6}$$

Here, $\gamma_{v, \widehat{w}}(\tfrac{1}{2})$ addresses the midpoint of the geodesic having smallest distance from f, and we finally set $u := \gamma_{v, \widehat{w}}(\tfrac{1}{2})$.

In order to apply a gradient descent algorithm, we smooth these terms as follows:

$$\text{TV}_\varepsilon(v) := \sum_{p \in \mathcal{G}} \sqrt{\sum_{q \in \mathcal{N}_p} \text{dist}^2(v_p, v_q) + \varepsilon^2},$$
$$\text{TV}_{2, \varepsilon}(w) := \sum_{p \in \mathcal{G}} \sqrt{\mathrm{d}_{2, \mathrm{h}}^2(w_p) + \mathrm{d}_{2, \mathrm{v}}^2(w_p) + \varepsilon^2}, \quad \varepsilon > 0. \tag{7}$$

We denote the functional (4) with these smoothed terms by $\mathcal{E}_\varepsilon^{\text{int}}$. Now the gradient descent algorithm consists of the following iterations:

$$v^{(k+1)} = \exp_{v^{(k)}}\left(-\tau_k \nabla_v \mathcal{E}_\varepsilon^{\text{int}}(\cdot, w^{(k)})(v^{(k)})\right),$$
$$w^{(k+1)} = \exp_{w^{(k)}}\left(-\tau_k \nabla_w \mathcal{E}_\varepsilon^{\text{int}}(v^{(k)}, \cdot)(w^{(k)})\right), \tag{8}$$

where $\tau_k := \rho^l s$, $s \in \mathbb{R}_{>0}$, $\rho \in (0, 1)$, and $l \in \mathbb{N}$ is the smallest integer such that the Armijo condition with $c \in (0, 1)$ is satisfied:

$$\mathcal{E}_\varepsilon^{\text{int}}(v^{(k)}, w^{(k)}) - c\rho^l \sqrt{\|\nabla_v \mathcal{E}_\varepsilon^{\text{int}}(\cdot, w^{(k)})(v^{(k)})\|_{v^{(k)}} + \|\nabla_w \mathcal{E}_\varepsilon^{\text{int}}(v^{(k)}, \cdot)(w^{(k)})\|_{w^{(k)}}^2}$$

$$> \mathcal{E}_\varepsilon^{\text{int}}\left(\exp_{v^{(k)}}\left(-\tau_k \nabla_v \mathcal{E}_\varepsilon^{\text{int}}(\cdot, w^{(k)})(v^{(k)})\right), \exp_{w^{(k)}}\left(-\tau_k \nabla_w \mathcal{E}_\varepsilon^{\text{int}}(v^{(k)}, \cdot)(w^{(k)})\right)\right).$$

Using [1, Proposition 4.2], it can be proved that the sequence $(v^{(k)}, w^{(k)})_{k \in \mathbb{N}}$ generated by (4) converges to a critical point of $\mathcal{E}^{\text{int}}$.

To obtain the gradients in (4) we need to compute the gradients of all the involved summands. Using that $\nabla_\mathcal{M} \text{dist}^2(\cdot, y)(x) = -2 \log_x y$ we give their explicit expression:

(i) *Summands in the data fitting term:* Let $\gamma_{\widehat{x,z}}(t)$ be the geodesic whose midpoint $c(x, z) := \gamma_{\widehat{x,z}}(\frac{1}{2})$ has smallest distance to f. Then we obtain for $\text{d}_2^2(x, f, z) = \text{dist}^2(c(x, z), f)$ by the chain rule

$$\nabla_\mathcal{M} \text{d}_2^2(\cdot, f, z)(x) := \sum_{j=1}^d \left\langle -2 \log_{c(x,z)} f, D_x c(\cdot, z)[\Xi_j(\tfrac{1}{2})] \right\rangle_{c(x,z)} \Xi_j(0)$$

and similarly for z. Here $\{\Xi_1(0), \ldots, \Xi_d(0)\}$ denotes an orthonormal basis of $T_x \mathcal{M}$, $\{\Xi_1(t), \ldots, \Xi_d(t)\}$ its parallel transport along $\gamma_{\widehat{x,z}}(t)$, and $D_x c(\cdot, z)$ is the derivative of $c(\cdot, z)$ in x whose derivation is given in detail in [6].

(ii) *Summands in* TV_ε: Let $p \in \mathcal{G}$, then we have for all $q \in \mathcal{G}$ such that $p \in \mathcal{N}_q$,

$$\nabla_{v_p}\left(\sqrt{\sum_{r \in \mathcal{N}_p} \text{dist}^2(v_p, v_r) + \varepsilon^2}\right) = \sum_{r \in \mathcal{N}_p} \frac{-\log_{v_p} v_r}{\sqrt{\sum_{r \in \mathcal{N}_p} \text{dist}^2(v_p, v_r) + \varepsilon^2}}$$

$$\nabla_{v_p}\left(\sqrt{\sum_{r \in \mathcal{N}_q} \text{dist}^2(v_q, v_r) + \varepsilon^2}\right) = \frac{-\log_{v_p} v_q}{\sqrt{\sum_{r \in \mathcal{N}_q} \text{dist}^2(v_q, v_r) + \varepsilon^2}}.$$

(iii) *Summands in* $\text{TV}_{2,\varepsilon}$: Let $c_h(w_p)$, and $c_v(w_p)$ be the midpoints of the shortest geodesic joining $w_{p-(1,0)}, w_{p+(1,0)}$, and $w_{p-(0,1)}, w_{p+(0,1)}$, respectively. Then we have

$$\nabla_{w_p}\left(\sqrt{\text{d}_{2,h}^2(w_p) + \text{d}_{2,v}^2(w_p)}\right) = \frac{-\left(\log_{w_p} c_h(w_p) + \log_{w_p} c_v(w_p)\right)}{\sqrt{\text{d}_{2,h}^2(w_p) + \text{d}_{2,v}^2(w_p) + \varepsilon^2}}.$$

For the horizontal neighbors $w_p, w_q := w_{p+(1,0)}, w_{q+(1,0)}$ we obtain

$$\nabla_{w_p}\left(\sqrt{\text{d}_{2,h}^2(w_q) + \text{d}_{2,v}^2(w_q)}\right) = \frac{1}{2} \frac{\nabla_\mathcal{M} \text{d}_2^2(\cdot, w_q, w_{q+(1,0)})(w_p)}{\sqrt{\text{d}_{2,h}^2(w_q) + \text{d}_{2,v}^2(w_q) + \varepsilon^2}}$$

and similarly in the case where w_q is a right neighbor of w_p and for the vertical neighborhoods.

5   Numerical Results

In this section we demonstrate the performance of the proposed models. We start with a noise-free $\mathbb{S}^2$-valued signal to illustrate the decomposition for the intrinsic model and its interpretation. In a second example we look at denoising of a signal in SPD(2) and the resulting decomposition. Finally we show a real-world application, namely denoising of electron backscatter diffraction (EBSD) data, i.e., SO(3)-valued images.

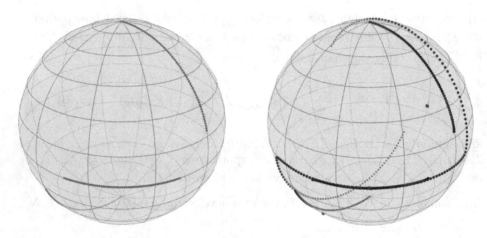

Fig. 2. Decomposition of a signal f of(192) samples (left) into two parts: a part v (red) consisting of three nearly constant parts (small TV value) and a nearly piecewise geodesic curve (small (TV$_2$) value) part w (blue). The mid point signal u (black) nearly reconstructs f (green). (Color figure online)

$\mathbb{S}^2$-**Valued Data.** Let $\mathcal{M}$ be the two-dimensional sphere. We take a signal along three geodesics being great arcs from the north pole to the equator, along the equator, and further to the south pole. The segments are shortened to $\frac{1}{5}$, $\frac{3}{20}$, and $\frac{1}{5}$ of a circle, respectively. Hence we obtain three geodesic segments with jumps in between, see Fig. 2 (left). We apply the IC model (4) with $\alpha = \frac{11}{100}, \beta = \frac{1}{11}$. The result u approximates f and its decomposition into v and w yields signals that are nearly piecewise constant and piecewise geodesic, respectively.

SPD(2)-**Valued Data.** Figure 3 shows results for denoising a signal with values on the manifold of positive definite 2×2 matrices. We created a signal u_0 as the midpoint of a signal with four constant parts and one with two geodesic parts. We apply the additive model (2) and the IC model (4) to a noisy version f of this signal. The results shown in Fig. 3 are optimized with respect to the mean squared error $\epsilon := \frac{1}{|\mathcal{G}|} \sum_{p \in \mathcal{G}} \text{dist}^2(u_p, u_{0,p})$. The parameters $\alpha\beta$ and $\alpha(1 - \beta)$ are chosen by a grid search, for the additive model on $\{0, \frac{1}{100}, \ldots, 1\}$. For the

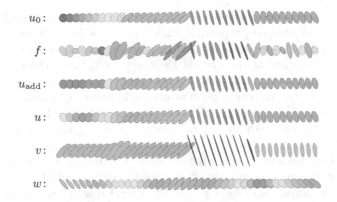

Fig. 3. Denoising of a SPD(2) valued signal f. The reconstruction with the intrinsic IC model yields $u = c(v, w)$, with piecewise constant part v and geodesic part w. An additive coupling of TV and TV_2 in (2) leads to u_{add}. (Color figure online)

IC model $\alpha\beta$ is optimized on $\{\frac{1}{10}, \frac{2}{10}, \dots, 1\}$ and $\alpha(1 - \beta)$ on $\{\frac{1}{2}, 1, \dots, 5\}$. The reconstruction from the IC model u with parameters $\alpha = 4.5, \beta = \frac{1}{9}$ achieves an error of $\epsilon = 0.0269$, while the additive model u_{add} with $\alpha = 0.46$ and $\beta = 1$ only obtains an error of $\epsilon = 0.0316$. Also visually the result of the IC model is better, in particular the smooth parts. Looking at the components v and w, we see the decomposition into a piecewise constant and a geodesic component.

SO(3)-Valued Data. EBSD aims at an analysis of the crystal structure of crystalline materials, see [2]. It is a fundamental task in material science since the

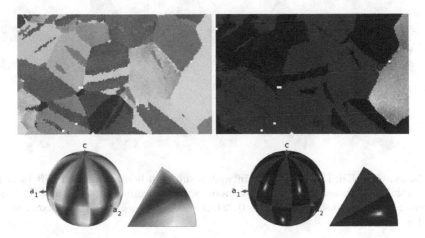

Fig. 4. The raw EBSD data of a Magnesium sample, the colorization of the sphere used to assign to each rotation a certain color according to the mapping $SO(3)/S \ni m \mapsto m^{-1}(0, 0, 1)^T \in \mathbb{S}^2/S$ and the colorization of a spherical triangle. Left: standard colormap, right: stretched colormap to handle individual grains. (Color figure online)

microscopic structure affects macroscopic attributes of materials such as ductility, electrical and lifetime properties. EBSD provides for each position on the surface of a specimen a so-called Kikuchi pattern, which allows the identification of the orientation of the crystal (SO(3) value). Since the crystal lattice possesses certain symmetries, it is invariant under its specific finite symmetry group $S \subset SO(3)$, i.e., the orientation at each grid point $i \in \mathcal{G}$ is only given as an equivalence class $[f_i] = \{f_i s \mid s \in S\} \in SO(3)/S$, $f_i \in SO(3)$. EBSD images usually consist of regions with similar orientations called grains. Figure 4 displays a typical EBSD image of a Magnesium specimen from the software package MTEX [7]. This software package is also used for handling and color visualizing the data. For certain macroscopic properties the pattern of orientations within single grains is important, see e.g., [8,30]. EBSD images are often corrupted by noise so that denoising techniques have to be applied. Figure 5 displays a single grain. Since the rotations vary little within a single grain, we treat the data as SO(3)-valued and apply a stretched colorization in Fig. 4 (right). Within this single grain there also occurs an edge, a so-called subgrain boundary. Thus, when denoising such kind of data, it is necessary to smooth out the noise and at the same time preserve subgrain boundaries. Figure 5 shows the results for the extrinsic and intrinsic model. For this example we restrict the pixel grid $\mathcal{G}$ to the pixels that belong to the grain. Both methods show good denoising results. Nevertheless, the intrinsic approach illustrates the components better.

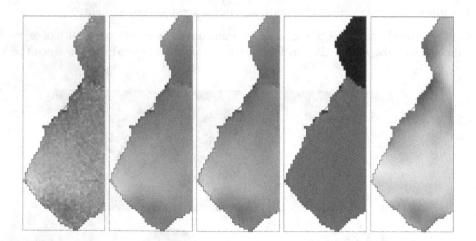

Fig. 5. Denoised EBSD data of a grain with a subgrain boundary. From left to right: noisy grain, result u using the extrinsic model with embedding into $\mathbb{R}^9$ ($\alpha = 0.03$, $\beta = \frac{1}{3}$), result of the intrinsic model ($\alpha = 0.024$, $\beta = 0.25$), i.e., u and its two components v and w.

6   Conclusion and Outlook

We proposed extrinsic and intrinsic variational models for the restoration of manifold-valued images with IC regularization terms consisting of first and second order differences. In contrast to the extrinsic model, the IC components of the intrinsic model are again values on the manifold. Indeed, we have thought about other IC models where the decomposition components remain on the manifold. Another approach could be given for Lie groups when replacing the addition in the IC term by the group operation. We have not considered this model here since it fits only for the rotation group. The gradient descent minimization is very slow. To handle large images we have to think about the construction of accelerated algorithms as those in [10]. Moreover, the handling of other functions than just first and second order differences is part of our future work.

Acknowledgements. Funding by the German Research Foundation (DFG) within the project STE 571/13-1 & BE 5888/2-1 and within the Research Training Group 1932, project area P3, is gratefully acknowledged. Furthermore, G. Steidl acknowledges the support by the German Federal Ministry of Education and Research (BMBF) through grant 05M13UKA (AniS).

References

1. Absil, P.-A., Mahony, R., Sepulchre, R.: Optimization Algorithms on Matrix Manifolds. Princeton University Press, Princeton (2009)
2. Adams, B.L., Wright, S.I., Kunze, K.: Orientation imaging: the emergence of a new microscopy. J. Metall. Mater. Trans. A **24**, 819–831 (1993)
3. Attouch, H., Bolte, J., Redont, P., Soubeyran, A.: Proximal alternating minimization and projection methods for nonconvex problems: an approach based on the Kurdyka-Lojasiewicz inequality. Math. Oper. Res. **35**(2), 438–457 (2010)
4. Aujol, J.-F., Gilboa, G., Chan, T., Osher, S.: Structure-texture image decomposition – modelling, algorithms and parameter selection. Int. J. Comput. Vision **67**(1), 111–136 (2006)
5. Azagra, R.D., Ferrera, C.J.: Inf-convolution and regularization of convex functions on Riemannian manifolds of nonpositive curvature. Revista matemática Complutense **19**(2), 323–345 (2006)
6. Bačák, M., Bergmann, R., Steidl, G., Weinmann, A.: A second order non-smooth variational model for restoring manifold-valued images. SIAM J. Sci. Comput. **38**(1), A567–A597 (2016)
7. Bachmann, F., Hielscher, R.: MTEX - MATLAB toolbox for quantitative texture analysis (2005–2016). http://mtex-toolbox.github.io/
8. Bachmann, F., Hielscher, R., Jupp, P.E., Pantleon, W., Schaeben, H., Wegert, E.: Inferential statistics of electron backscatter diffraction data from within individual crystalline grains. J. Appl. Crystallogr. **43**, 1338–1355 (2010)
9. Balle, F., Eifler, D., Fitschen, J.H., Schuff, S., Steidl, G.: Computation and visualization of local deformation for multiphase metallic materials by infimal convolution of TV-type functionals. In: Aujol, J.-F., Nikolova, M., Papadakis, N. (eds.) SSVM 2015. LNCS, vol. 9087, pp. 385–396. Springer, Cham (2015). doi:10.1007/978-3-319-18461-6_31

10. Bergmann, R., Chan, R.H., Hielscher, R., Persch, J., Steidl, G.: Restoration of manifold-valued images by half-quadratic minimization. Inverse Prob. Imaging **10**(2), 281–304 (2016)

11. Bergmann, R., Weinmann, A.: Inpainting of cyclic data using first and second order differences. In: Tai, X.-C., Bae, E., Chan, T.F., Lysaker, M. (eds.) EMM-CVPR 2015. LNCS, vol. 8932, pp. 155–168. Springer, Cham (2015). doi:10.1007/978-3-319-14612-6_12

12. Bergmann, R., Weinmann, A.: A second order TV-type approach for inpainting and denoising higher dimensional combined cyclic and vector space data. J. Math. Imaging Vis. **55**(3), 401–427 (2016)

13. Bredies, K., Kunisch, K., Pock, T.: Total generalized variation. SIAM J. Imaging Sci. **3**(3), 492–526 (2010)

14. Chambolle, A., Lions, P.-L.: Image recovery via total variation minimization and related problems. Numer. Math. **76**(2), 167–188 (1997)

15. Donoho, D.L., Kutyniok, G.: Geometric separation using a wavelet-shearlet dictionary. In: SampTA 2009 (2009)

16. Giaquinta, M., Mucci, D.: Maps of bounded variation with values into a manifold: total variation and relaxed energy. Pure Appli. Math. Q. **3**(2), 513–538 (2007)

17. Holler, M., Kunisch, K.: On infimal convolution of TV-type functionals and applications to video and image reconstruction. SIAM J. Imaging Sci. **7**(4), 2258–2300 (2014)

18. Lellmann, J., Strekalovskiy, E., Koetter, S., Cremers, D.: Total variation regularization for functions with values in a manifold. In: IEEE ICCV, pp. 2944–2951 (2013)

19. Nash, J.: The imbedding problem for Riemannian manifolds. Ann. Math. **63**(1), 20–63 (1956)

20. Papafitsoros, K., Schönlieb, C.B.: A combined first and second order variational approach for image reconstruction. J. Math. Imaging Vis. **2**(48), 308–338 (2014)

21. Rockafellar, R.T.: Convex Analysis. Princeton University Press, Princeton (1970)

22. Rosman, G., Tai, X.-C., Kimmel, R., Bruckstein, A.M.: Augmented-Lagrangian regularization of matrix-valued maps. Methods Appl. Anal. **21**(1), 121–138 (2014)

23. Rosman, G., Wang, Y., Tai, X.-C., Kimmel, R., Bruckstein, A.M.: Fast regularization of matrix-valued images. In: Bruhn, A., Pock, T., Tai, X.-C. (eds.) Efficient Algorithms for Global Optimization Methods in Computer Vision. LNCS, vol. 8293, pp. 19–43. Springer, Heidelberg (2014). doi:10.1007/978-3-642-54774-4_2

24. Rudin, L., Osher, S., Fatemi, E.: Nonlinear total variation based noise removal algorithms. Physica D **60**(1), 259–268 (1992)

25. Setzer, S., Steidl, G.: Variational methods with higher order derivatives in image processing. In: Approximation XII: San Antonio 2007, pp. 360–385 (2008)

26. Setzer, S., Steidl, G., Teuber, T.: Infimal convolution regularizations with discrete ℓ_1-type functionals. Commun. Math. Sci. **9**(3), 797–827 (2011)

27. Starck, J.-L., Elad, M., Donoho, D.L.: Image decomposition via the combination of sparse representations and a variational approach. IEEE Trans. Image Process. **14**(10), 1570–1582 (2005)

28. Steidl, G., Setzer, S., Popilka, B., Burgeth, B.: Restoration of matrix fields by second order cone programming. Computing **81**, 161–178 (2007)

29. Strekalovskiy, E., Cremers, D.: Total variation for cyclic structures: Convex relaxation and efficient minimization. In: IEEE CVPR , pp. 1905–1911. IEEE (2011)

30. Sun, S., Adams, B., King, W.: Observation of lattice curvature near the interface of a deformed aluminium bicrystal. Philos. Mag. A **80**, 9–25 (2000)

31. Valkonen, T., Bredies, K., Knoll, F.: Total generalized variation in diffusion tensor imaging. SIAM J. Imaging Sci. **6**(1), 487–525 (2013)
32. Wang, Y., Yin, W., Zeng, J.: Global convergence of ADMM in nonconvex nonsmooth optimization. ArXiv preprint arXiv:1511.06324 (2015)
33. Weinmann, A., Demaret, L., Storath, M.: Total variation regularization for manifold-valued data. SIAM J. Imaging Sci. **7**(4), 2226–2257 (2014)
34. Whitney, H.: Differentiable manifolds. Ann. Math. **37**(3), 645–680 (1936)

Optimal Transport for Manifold-Valued Images

Jan Henrik Fitschen[1], Friederike Laus[1(✉)], and Bernhard Schmitzer[2]

[1] Department of Mathematics, University of Kaiserslautern, Kaiserslautern, Germany
{fitschen,friederike.laus}@mathematik.uni-kl.de
[2] Institute for Computational and Applied Mathematics,
University of Münster, Münster, Germany
schmitzer@uni-muenster.de

Abstract. We introduce optimal transport-type distances for manifold-valued images. To do so we lift the initial data to measures on the product space of image domain and signal space, where they can then be compared by optimal transport with a transport cost that combines spatial distance and signal discrepancy. Applying recently introduced 'unbalanced' optimal transport models leads to more natural results. We illustrate the benefit of the lifting with numerical examples for interpolation of color images and classification of handwritten digits.

1 Introduction

The optimal transport (OT) problem has found various applications in signal and image processing, computer vision and machine learning [7,8,13,15]. In imaging applications one typically faces two problems: Standard OT can only compare measures of equal mass which is often an unnatural assumption. Further, the involved discretized transport problems are very high-dimensional and challenging to solve. The former problem has for instance been addressed by the Hellinger-Kantorovich (HK) distance (or Wasserstein-Fisher-Rao distance) [5,10,12], which allows to compare 'unbalanced' measures of different mass. This metric does not only extend to measures of different total mass, but yields often also more reasonable results on balanced measures by removing artifacts where small portions of mass would otherwise have to be moved very far. For numerically solving OT problems a broad family of methods has been devised, such as the network simplex [1] or a fluid-dynamic formulation [3]. Another choice is the entropy regularization technique and the Sinkhorn scaling algorithm [7], which has been extended to 'unbalanced' problems in [6].

The OT distance – and the HK distance – induce a metric on non-negative, scalar signals. Recently, the question how to define meaningful transport-type metrics on multi-channel data has arisen. For instance, in [8] OT has been extended to RGB color images, and in [15] so-called TL^p-distances are introduced, a transport-type metric over vector valued signals. It is illustrated that these distances remain sensitive to high-frequency signal oscillations, but are at the same time robust to deformations such as translations, thus uniting the advantages of L^p and Wasserstein distances. In both approaches the original

© Springer International Publishing AG 2017
F. Lauze et al. (Eds.): SSVM 2017, LNCS 10302, pp. 460–472, 2017.
DOI: 10.1007/978-3-319-58771-4_37

non-scalar data is transformed to a non-negative scalar measure on the product space of image domain and signal space, where it can be compared in a classical OT framework.

Contribution and Outline. In this article we build on the work of [8] and present a framework for transport-type metric on multi-channel and manifold valued data. Also in our approach, signals will be lifted to measures on the product space of image domain and signal space, and then compared with transport-type metrics, using a cost function combining spatial distance and signal discrepancy. For comparison we use the HK distance, which can compare non-normalized images and yields more natural assignments. To solve the resulting, high-dimensional optimization problems we employ efficient diagonal scaling algorithms based on entropy regularization [6] that generalize the well-known Sinkhorn algorithm.

In our numerical examples, we apply our framework to color images in different color spaces by defining three lifting models with different interpretations of the mass and signal component and show that they are adapted for different types of images. The geodesic structure of the OT and HK distances can be used to compute image interpolations. For this we propose a back projection map that takes an intermediate lifted measures back to an intermediate manifold valued image. To showcase the potential for machine learning applications, we further apply the idea to classification of handwritten digits of the MNIST database. The sample data is initially scalar and no lifting would be required. We demonstrate that lifting, based on features extracted from the scalar data, yields improved performance.

The article is organized as follows: In Sect. 2 we introduce the generic mathematical framework of our model. Section 3 discusses discretization and optimization. Application of our model to color images and the MNIST handwritten digits database with corresponding numerical results are presented in Sect. 4.

Relation to [8] *and* [15]. The framework presented in this article is more general compared than the approach of [8] and our optimization scheme extends to more complex signal spaces. Relative to [15] we use unbalanced transport for comparison and introduce the back projection map. Moreover, [15] mostly uses a fixed reference measure with constant density for lifting. We put more emphasis on this choice, in particular we extract the measure from the signal, which is an important part of our model. Conversely, for the MNIST example we propose that the signal can be extracted from the measure.

2   Unbalanced Transport for Manifold-Valued Signals

2.1   Wasserstein and Hellinger-Kantorovich Distances

Let $X \subset \mathbb{R}^d$ be the image domain, e.g. $[0,1]^2$, and $\mathcal{M}$ the signal space, e.g. an appropriate color space. Further, let $d_X(x_0, x_1) = \|x_0 - x_1\|_2$ be the Euclidean distance on X and let $d_{\mathcal{M}}$ be a suitable metric on $\mathcal{M}$. We denote by $\mathcal{Y} = X \times \mathcal{M}$

the product space which we endow with the metric $d_{\mathcal{Y}}^2((x_0, m_0), (x_1, m_1)) = d_X^2(x_0, x_1) + \lambda^2 \cdot d_{\mathcal{M}}^2(m_0, m_1)$, where $\lambda \geq 0$ is a relative weighting parameter. We assume that X, $\mathcal{M}$ and $\mathcal{Y}$ are compact, complete and equipped with their Borel σ-algebras. For a measurable space Z (for example X, $\mathcal{Y}$ or $\mathcal{Y} \times \mathcal{Y}$), we denote by $\mathcal{P}(Z)$ the set of non-negative Radon measures over Z and by $\mathcal{P}_1(Z) \subset \mathcal{P}(Z)$ the set of probability measures. The Dirac delta at $z \in Z$ is denoted by δ_z. For two measurable spaces Z_1, Z_2, a measure $\mu \in \mathcal{P}(Z_1)$ and a measurable map $f \colon Z_1 \to Z_2$, the *push-forward* (or image measure) $f_{\#}\mu$ of μ under f is given by $(f_{\#}\mu)(\sigma) = \mu(f^{-1}(\sigma))$ for all measurable sets $\sigma \subset Z_2$.

Let $\mathrm{pr}_{Z,0} \colon Z^2 \to Z$, $(z_0, z_1) \mapsto z_0$ and similarly $\mathrm{pr}_{Z,1}(z_0, z_1) = z_1$ be projections from Z^2 to the first and second component. For a measure $\pi \in \mathcal{P}(Z^2)$ the first and second marginal are then given by $\mathrm{pr}_{Z,i\sharp}\pi$, $i \in \{0, 1\}$ respectively.

Let $\mu_i \in \mathcal{P}_1(X)$, $i \in \{0, 1\}$. The set

$$\Pi_X(\mu_0, \mu_1) = \left\{ \pi \in \mathcal{P}(X^2) \colon \mathrm{pr}_{X,i\sharp}\pi = \mu_i \text{ for } i \in \{0, 1\} \right\} \quad (2.1)$$

is called the set of *transport plans* between μ_0 and μ_1. Every $\pi \in \Pi_X(\mu_0, \mu_1)$ describes a rearrangement of the mass of μ_0 into μ_1. The *2-Wasserstein distance* over X between μ_0 and μ_1 is given by

$$d_{W,X}^2(\mu_0, \mu_1) = \inf_{\pi \in \Pi_X(\mu_0, \mu_1)} \int_{X^2} d_X^2(x_0, x_1) \, \mathrm{d}\pi(x_0, x_1). \quad (2.2)$$

This means we are looking for the cheapest plan π, where the cost of moving one unit of mass from x_0 to x_1 is given by $d_X^2(x_0, x_1)$. The Wasserstein distance $d_{W,X}$ is a metric over $\mathcal{P}_1(X)$, for a thorough introduction to this topic we refer to [16].

The distance $d_{W,X}$ only allows comparison between normalized measures: otherwise $\Pi_X(\mu_0, \mu_1)$ is empty and $d_{W,X}(\mu_0, \mu_1) = +\infty$. This is remedied by the Hellinger-Kantorovich distance, as introduced e.g. in [12], which allows creation and annihilation of mass and hence induces a (finite) metric over all non-negative measures $\mathcal{P}(X)$. For a parameter $\kappa > 0$ the Hellinger-Kantorovich distance is given by [12, Sects. 6–7]

$$d_{HK,X}^2(\mu_0, \mu_1) = \kappa^2 \inf_{\pi \in \mathcal{P}(X^2)} \sum_{i=0}^{1} \mathrm{KL}(\mathrm{pr}_{X,i\sharp}\pi | \mu_i) + \int_{X^2} c_{X,\kappa}(x_0, x_1) \, \mathrm{d}\pi(x_0, x_1) \quad (2.3)$$

where

$$c_{X,\kappa}(x_0, x_1) = \begin{cases} -\log\left([\cos(d_X(x_0, x_1)/\kappa)]^2\right) & \text{if } d_X(x_0, x_1) < \kappa \cdot \frac{\pi}{2} \\ +\infty & \text{else,} \end{cases} \quad (2.4)$$

and $\mathrm{KL}_X(\mu|\nu)$ denotes the Kullback-Leibler (KL) divergence from ν to μ. Compared to (2.2) the constraint $\mathrm{pr}_{X,i\sharp}\pi = \mu_i$, $i \in \{0, 1\}$ is relaxed. The plan π can now be any non-negative measure and the discrepancy between $\mathrm{pr}_{X,i\sharp}\pi$ and μ_i is penalized by the KL divergence. This implies in particular that $d_{HK,X}(\mu_0, \mu_1)$ is finite when $\mu_0(X) \neq \mu_1(X)$. Additionally, the cost d_X^2 is replaced by $c_{X,\kappa}$.

Note that $c_{X,\kappa}(x_0, x_1) = +\infty$ if $d_X(x_0, x_1) \geq \kappa \cdot \pi/2$. Thus, beyond this distance no transport occurs and mass growth completely takes over. The precise form of $c_{X,\kappa}$ is determined by an equivalent fluid-dynamic-type formulation [12]. The parameter κ balances between transport and mass changes. As $\kappa \to 0$, $d_{HK,X}/\kappa$ converges towards the Hellinger distance, which is purely local and does not involve transport. For $\kappa \to \infty$ one finds $d_{HK,X}(\mu_0, \mu_1) \to d_{W,X}(\mu_0, \mu_1)$ [12, Sect. 7.7].

When (X, d_X) is a length space, this holds for $(\mathcal{P}_1(X), d_{W,X})$ as well. Let μ_0, $\mu_1 \in \mathcal{P}_1(X)$ and let π be a corresponding minimizer of (2.2). A geodesic between μ_0 and μ_1 can be reconstructed from π. Intuitively, a mass particle at $\pi(x_0, x_1)$ has to travel with constant speed along the geodesic from x_0 to x_1 (which is a straight line in $\mathbb{R}^d$). This can be formalized as follows: for $t \in [0, 1]$ let

$$\gamma_t \colon X \times X \to X, \qquad (x_0, x_1) \mapsto (1 - t) \cdot x_0 + t \cdot x_1. \tag{2.5}$$

That is, $t \mapsto \gamma_t(x_0, x_1)$ describes the geodesic between x_0 and x_1 in X. Then a geodesic between μ_0 and μ_1 is given by

$$[0, 1] \ni t \mapsto \mu_t = \gamma_{t\#}\pi. \tag{2.6}$$

This is the *displacement interpolation* [16] between μ_0 and μ_1. It often provides a more natural interpolation than the naive linear trajectory $[0, 1] \ni t \mapsto (1-t) \cdot \mu_0 + t \cdot \mu_1$. The famous Benamou-Brenier formula [3] is an equivalent fluid-dynamic-type reformulation of (2.2) directly in terms of finding the displacement interpolation.

Similarly, $(\mathcal{P}(X), d_{HK,X})$ is a length space and geodesics can be constructed from optimal couplings π in (2.3). The construction is more involved, since particles change their mass and speed while travelling. We refer to [12, Part II] for a detailed elaboration of $d_{HK,X}$ geodesics. There also is a fluid-dynamic-type formulation for $d_{HK,X}$ [5,10,12], in which mass changes are penalized by the Hellinger (or Fisher-Rao) distance. This equivalence determines the precise form of (2.4). An illustration of displacement interpolations is given in Fig. 1.

2.2   Manifold-Valued Images, Lifted Measures and Distances

Next, we extend the transport-type metrics to $\mathcal{M}$-valued signals. First, observe that in complete analogy to Sect. 2.1, $\Pi_{\mathcal{Y}}$, $KL_{\mathcal{Y}}$ and $c_{HK,\mathcal{Y}}$ can be defined over the metric space $(\mathcal{Y}, d_{\mathcal{Y}})$. Consequently, the Wasserstein distance $d_{W,\mathcal{Y}}$ and Hellinger-Kantorovich distance $d_{HK,\mathcal{Y}}$ can be constructed over $\mathcal{P}_1(\mathcal{Y})$ and $\mathcal{P}(\mathcal{Y})$. For example, for $\nu_0, \nu_1 \in \mathcal{P}_1(\mathcal{Y})$ we find

$$d_{W,\mathcal{Y}}^2(\nu_0, \nu_1) = \inf_{\pi \in \Pi_{\mathcal{Y}}(\nu_0,\nu_1)} \int_{\mathcal{Y}^2} d_{\mathcal{Y}}^2((x_0, m_0), (x_1, m_1)) \, d\pi((x_0, m_0), (x_1, m_1)). \tag{2.7}$$

Now, the key is to lift the original $\mathcal{M}$-valued signals over X to non-negative measures on the product space $\mathcal{Y} = X \times \mathcal{M}$, where they can then be compared with $d_{W,\mathcal{Y}}$ and $d_{HK,\mathcal{Y}}$. Let $f_i \colon X \to \mathcal{M}$, $i \in \{0, 1\}$ be two (measurable)

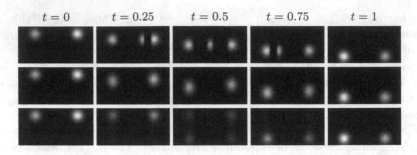

$$t = 0 \qquad t = 0.25 \qquad t = 0.5 \qquad t = 0.75 \qquad t = 1$$

Fig. 1. Geodesics in $(\mathcal{P}_1(X), d_{W,X})$ and $(\mathcal{P}(X), d_{HK,X})$. *Top row:* Wasserstein geodesic between two pairs of Gaussians with different mass. To compensate the local difference, mass is sent from the right to the left. *Middle row:* Hellinger-Kantorovich geodesic for $\kappa = 60$. The mass difference between upper and lower Gaussians is compensated locally by creating and shrinking mass, leading to a more natural interpolation. Note that the left and right Gaussian are travelling at slightly different speeds and are slightly ellipsoidal during transport, which is characteristic for d_{HK} geodesics. *Bottom row:* d_{HK} geodesic for $\kappa = 16$. A lot of the differences between the two images is now compensated purely by growth and shrinkage of mass.

$\mathcal{M}$-valued images that we want to compare and let $\mu_i \in \mathcal{P}(X)$ be two corresponding measures. The choice of the measures μ_i is an important part of the model and we will describe this choice in detail for each model in Sect. 4.1.

From the pairs (f_i, μ_i), $i \in \{0, 1\}$, we generate two measures on $\mathcal{Y}$ as follows:

$$\nu_i = F_{i\#}\mu_i, \quad \text{where } F_i \colon X \to \mathcal{Y}, \quad x \mapsto \big(x, f_i(x)\big) \qquad (2.8)$$

For example, if $\mu_0 = \delta_x$ then $\nu_0 = \delta_{(x, f_0(x))}$. That is, a Dirac measure at $x \in X$ is lifted to a Dirac at $(x, f_0(x)) \in \mathcal{Y}$. The signal f_i becomes encoded in the position of the mass of ν_i (i.e. we only 'care' about the values of f_i μ_i-a.e.).

Let $F \colon (x_0, x_1) \mapsto \big(F_0(x_0), F_1(x_1)\big) = \big((x_0, f_0(x_0)), (x_1, f_1(x_1))\big)$. It is then a simple exercise to show that $F_{\#}\Pi_X(\mu_0, \mu_1) = \Pi_{\mathcal{Y}}(F_{0\#}\mu_0, F_{1\#}\mu_1)$. Consequently, for lifted measures $\nu_i = F_{i\#}\mu_i$ the lifted Wasserstein distance can be written as

$$d_{W,\mathcal{Y}}^2(\nu_0, \nu_1) = \inf_{\pi \in \Pi_X(\mu_0, \mu_1)} \int_{X^2} \big(d_X^2(x_0, x_1) + \lambda^2 d_{\mathcal{M}}^2\big(f_0(x_0), f_1(x_1)\big)\big) \, \mathrm{d}\pi(x_0, x_1).$$

$$(2.9)$$

This implies that the lifted distance $d_{W,\mathcal{Y}}$ between lifted signals can be computed by a transport problem over X, where the transport cost between x_0 and x_1 not only depends on the spatial distance $d_X(x_0, x_1)$, but also on the 'signal distance' $d_{\mathcal{M}}(f_0(x_0), f_1(x_1))$. An analogous interpretation holds for the lifted Hellinger-Kantorovich distance. The authors of [15] provide some intuition for lifted distances $(\mathcal{Y}, d_{W,\mathcal{Y}})$ and show that (2.9) defines a distance over (signal,measure)-pairs (f, μ). We will illustrate these lifted distances and demonstrate their benefit for meaningful image registration and enhanced classification scores for various example models throughout Sect. 4.

Again, in analogy to Sect. 2.1, when $(\mathcal{Y}, d_{\mathcal{Y}})$ is a length space, so are $(\mathcal{P}_1(\mathcal{Y}), d_{W,\mathcal{Y}})$ and $(\mathcal{P}(\mathcal{Y}), d_{HK,\mathcal{Y}})$. Accordingly, for two marginals $\nu_0, \nu_1 \in \mathcal{P}_1(\mathcal{Y})$ (or

$\mathcal{P}(\mathcal{Y})$) one can construct geodesics $t \mapsto \nu_t$ similar to (2.6) (or for d_{HK}). The main difference is that the map γ_t, describing geodesics in X, (2.5) has to be replaced by geodesics on $(\mathcal{Y}, d_{\mathcal{Y}})$. In the lifted geodesics, mass is travelling both in spatial direction X as well as the 'signal' direction $\mathcal{M}$.

We want to use such geodesics to interpolate between pairs of signals (f_i, μ_i) that we lift to measures ν_i via (2.8), $i \in \{0, 1\}$. However, an intermediate point ν_t, $t \in (0, 1)$ on the geodesic between ν_0 and ν_1, cannot always be written as a lifting of an intermediate pair (f_t, μ_t). Intuitively, this is because at time t several mass particles might occupy the same spatial location $x \in X$, but at different signal positions $m, m' \in \mathcal{M}$ and such a constellation cannot be obtained by a push-forward from $\mathcal{P}(X)$ as in (2.8). We propose to resolve such overlaps by picking for each location in $x \in X$ the barycenter $\overline{m} \in \mathcal{M}$ w.r.t. $d_{\mathcal{M}}$ of all signal values m and m' that can be found at this location. Let $\rho \in \mathcal{P}_1(\mathcal{M})$ describe a signal distribution of lifted mass particles in $\mathcal{Y}$ 'over' a given location $x \in X$. The barycenter of ρ is defined as

$$\mathrm{Bar}(\rho) = \operatorname*{argmin}_{\overline{m} \in \mathcal{M}} \int_{\mathcal{M}} d_{\mathcal{M}}^2(\overline{m}, m) \, d\rho(m). \tag{2.10}$$

In this article we assume that a unique minimizer exists. When $\mathcal{M}$ is a convex subset of $\mathbb{R}^n$ the barycenter is given by the center of mass. To construct (f, μ) from a given $\nu \in \mathcal{P}(\mathcal{Y})$ we first set

$$\mu = \mathsf{P}_{\#}\nu \quad \text{where} \quad \mathsf{P} \colon \mathcal{Y} \to X, \quad (x, m) \mapsto x. \tag{2.11}$$

That is, at every point $x \in X$, μ gathers all the mass of ν in the fibre $\{x\} \times \mathcal{M}$. Then, by the disintegration theorem [2, Thm. 5.3.1], there is a family of probability measures ρ_x for all $x \in X$ (unique μ-a.e.) such that we can write

$$\int_{\mathcal{Y}} \phi(x, m) \, d\nu(x, m) = \int_X \left(\int_{\mathcal{M}} \phi(x, m) \, d\rho_x(m) \right) d\mu(x) \tag{2.12}$$

for any measurable $\phi \colon \mathcal{Y} \to [0, +\infty]$. ρ_x can be thought of as describing how the mass of ν in the fibre $\{x\} \times \mathcal{M}$ is distributed. Now, we set $f(x) = \mathrm{Bar}(\rho_x)$, which is well-defined μ-almost everywhere. This signal f is the best point-wise approximation of the lifted measure ν in the sense of (2.10). We call (f, μ) the *back projection* of ν. Note that if ν is in fact a lifting of some (f, μ), then $\rho_x = \delta_{f(x)}$ μ-a.e. and (f, μ) are recovered (μ-a.e.) by back projection.

3   Discretization and Optimization

For our numerical experiments we assume that all measures μ_i are concentrated on a discrete Cartesian pixel grid $\mathbf{X} = \{x_1, \ldots, x_N\} \subset X \subset \mathbb{R}^2$ and we only care about the values of signals f_i on $\mathbf{X}$. Thus, all feasible π in (2.9) are concentrated on $\mathbf{X}^2$ and (2.9) becomes a finite dimensional problem. It can be written as

$$d_{W,\mathcal{Y}}^2(F_{0\#}\mu_0, F_{1\#}\mu_1) = \inf_{\boldsymbol{\pi} \in \boldsymbol{\Pi}(\mu_0, \mu_1)} \langle \boldsymbol{d}, \boldsymbol{\pi} \rangle, \text{where } \langle \boldsymbol{d}, \boldsymbol{\pi} \rangle \stackrel{\text{def.}}{=} \sum_{j,k=1}^{N} d_{j,k} \, \pi_{j,k}, \tag{3.1}$$

with discrete vectors $\boldsymbol{\mu}_i \in \mathbb{R}^N$, $(\boldsymbol{\mu}_i)_j = \mu_i(\{x_j\})$, discrete couplings $\boldsymbol{\Pi}(\boldsymbol{\mu}_0, \boldsymbol{\mu}_1) = \{\boldsymbol{\pi} \in \mathbb{R}_+^{N \times N} : \boldsymbol{\pi} \mathbf{1} = \boldsymbol{\mu}_0, \boldsymbol{\pi}^\top \mathbf{1} = \boldsymbol{\mu}_1\}$ and $\boldsymbol{d}_{j,k} = d_X^2(x_j, x_k) + \lambda^2 d_{\mathcal{M}}^2(f_0(x_j),$ $f_1(x_k))$. Here, $\mathbf{1} \in \mathbb{R}^N$ is the vector with all entries being 1, $\boldsymbol{\pi} \mathbf{1}$, $\boldsymbol{\pi}^\top \mathbf{1}$ give the column and row sums of $\boldsymbol{\pi}$, which is the discrete equivalent of $\mathrm{pr}_{X, i\sharp} \pi$. Similarly, since $\mathrm{KL}(\mu|\nu) = +\infty$ if $\mu \not\ll \nu$, all feasible π in the unbalanced problem (2.3) are concentrated on $\mathbf{X}^2$. The discrete unbalanced equivalent of (2.9) becomes

$$d_{HK,\mathcal{Y}}^2(F_{0\#}\mu_0, F_{1\#}\mu_1) = \kappa^2 \inf_{\boldsymbol{\pi} \in \mathbb{R}_+^{N \times N}} \mathbf{KL}(\boldsymbol{\pi}\,\mathbf{1}|\boldsymbol{\mu}_0) + \mathbf{KL}(\boldsymbol{\pi}^\top \mathbf{1}|\boldsymbol{\mu}_1) + \langle \boldsymbol{c}, \boldsymbol{\pi} \rangle, \quad (3.2)$$

where $\boldsymbol{c}_{j,k} = c_{HK,\mathcal{Y}}((x_j, f_0(x_j)), (x_k, f_1(x_k)))$, analogous to $\boldsymbol{d}$, and $\mathbf{KL}$ is the discrete Kullback-Leibler divergence. Note that this approach does not require discretization of the signal space $\mathcal{M}$. Once an optimal $\boldsymbol{\pi}$ for the finite dimensional problems (3.1) or (3.2) is obtained, it can be used to construct the geodesic between $F_{0\#}\mu_0$ and $F_{1\#}\mu_1$ with the lifted variants of (2.6) (or for d_{HK}), see above. These geodesics consist of a finite number of Dirac measures travelling smoothly through $\mathcal{Y}$.

Now, we describe the discretized back projection. To generate an intermediate image (f_t, μ_t), living on the discrete grid $\mathbf{X}$, we proceed as follows: the mass of any travelling Dirac at location $(x, m) \in \mathcal{Y}$ is distributed to the closest four pixels in $\mathbf{X}$ according to bilinear interpolation. In this way, we obtain for each pixel $x_j \in \mathbf{X}$ a total mass, corresponding to $\mu_t(\{x_j\}) = (\boldsymbol{\mu}_t)_j$, (2.11), and a distribution over $\mathcal{M}$, corresponding to ρ_x, (2.12). The barycenter of this distribution, (2.10), yields the discrete backprojected signal $f_t(x_j)$.

To solve problems (3.1) and (3.2) we employ the entropy regularization approach for optimal transport [7] and unbalanced transport [6]. For a (small) positive parameter $\varepsilon > 0$ we regularize the problems by adding the term $\varepsilon \cdot \mathbf{KL}(\boldsymbol{\pi}|\boldsymbol{I})$, where $\boldsymbol{I} \in \mathbb{R}^{N \times N}$ is the matrix with all entries being 1 and by a slight abuse of notation $\mathbf{KL}$ denotes the discrete KL-divergence extended to matrices. The regularized variant of (3.1) can be solved with the Sinkhorn algorithm [7], the regularized version of (3.2) with a slightly more general (but equally simple) scaling algorithm [6]. In our examples, N is of the order of 10^4, hence working on the full grid $\mathbf{X} \times \mathbf{X}$ is infeasible. To obtain good approximations to the original problems (3.1) and (3.2) we want to choose a small ε, which leads to several numerical issues. To remedy these problems we employ the numerical scheme described in [14]. In particular this allows setting ε small enough to make the induced entropic smoothing practically negligible and uses sparse approximations of $\mathbf{X}^2$ to reduce the required memory and runtime.

In [8] a Benamou-Brenier-type formula [3] was used to solve problem (2.7) for RGB-images (cf. Sect. 4.1) with a particular formulation that required only three points to discretize $\mathcal{M}$ (corresponding to three color channels). However, it would be challenging to generalize this approach to other, higher-dimensional $\mathcal{M}$, since it would entail discretizing the high-dimensional space $\mathcal{Y} = X \times \mathcal{M}$.

4   Examples and Numerical Results

4.1   Color Images

Let $\mathbf{X} \subset \mathbb{R}^2$ be the discrete image domain (cf. Sect. 3) and let $g \colon \mathbf{X} \to \mathcal{C}$ be a color image, where $\mathcal{C}$ is either the RGB or HSV color space (for details on the color spaces we refer to [9]). In the following, we present three different ways how to choose $\mathcal{M}$ and how to generate the pair (f, μ) from g. In the first two models μ takes the form $\mu = \sum_{x \in \mathbf{X}} w(x) \cdot \delta_x$, so μ can be specified by fixing the weighting function $w \colon \mathbf{X} \to \mathbb{R}_+$.

rgb-cube: Let $\mathcal{C} = [0,1]^3$ be the RGB color space. In this model we choose $\mathcal{M} = \mathcal{C}$ and $d_{\mathcal{M}}$ is the Euclidean distance on $\mathcal{M}$. We set $f = g$ and $w(x) = 1$ for all $x \in \mathbf{X}$, i.e. μ is the 'uniform' counting measure over the pixels. So every pixel gets lifted to a point determined by its RGB values with mass 1.

hsv-disk: Let $\mathcal{C} = S^1 \times [0,1]^2$ represent the HSV color space and let $g = (h, s, v)$ be a triplet of functions specifying hue, saturation and value of each pixel. In this model we choose $\mathcal{M} = S^1 \times [0,1]$ and set $f = (h, s)$ and $w = v$. For $(h_0, s_0), (h_1, s_1) \in \mathcal{M}$ the metric is given by

$$d_{\mathcal{M}}^2((h_0, s_0), (h_1, s_1)) = \left\| \begin{pmatrix} s_0 \cos(h_0) \\ s_0 \sin(h_0) \end{pmatrix} - \begin{pmatrix} s_1 \cos(h_1) \\ s_1 \sin(h_1) \end{pmatrix} \right\|_2^2,$$

which is the Euclidean distance in polar coordinates. In this model, hue and saturation of each pixel are transformed into lifted coordinates and the value channel is transformed into mass. Black pixels are not assigned any mass. This model is suited for scenarios where intensity puts the emphasis on certain details, e.g. bright objects on a dark background.

rgb-triple: Let again $\mathcal{C} = [0,1]^3$ be the RGB color space. This model requires a slight extension of the lifting framework and (2.8), as every pixel is transformed into three Dirac masses. As in rgb-cube we choose $\mathcal{M} = [0,1]^3$. Let $g = (\mathsf{r}, \mathsf{g}, \mathsf{b})$ be a function triplet specifying an RGB image. We define the lifted measure as

$$\nu = \sum_{x \in \mathbf{X}} \mathsf{r}(x) \cdot \delta_{(x,(1,0,0)^\top)} + \mathsf{g}(x) \cdot \delta_{(x,(0,1,0)^\top)} + \mathsf{b}(x) \cdot \delta_{(x,(0,0,1)^\top)}.$$

To reconstruct a color image from a (discrete) measure $\nu \in \mathcal{P}(\mathcal{Y})$ we map a Dirac $\rho \cdot \delta_{(x,(z_1,z_2,z_3))}$ to the color $(\mathsf{r}, \mathsf{g}, \mathsf{b}) = (\rho z_1, \rho z_2, \rho z_3)$. This is a reformulation of the color transport model of [8] in our framework. It is particularly suited in cases where we want to model additive mixing of colors. In Fig. 2 we visualize geodesics in $(\mathcal{M}, d_{\mathcal{M}})$ for the models rgb-cube and hsv-disk in the RGB cube and the HSV cylinder. For example, the trajectory from blue to red in both models goes via pink, as expected. But the precise transition varies. Figure 3 shows the transport between simple mixtures of Gaussians of different colors to illustrate the behavior of our model. The first two rows show how the weighting between color transport and spatial transport influences the result. The third row depicts the result of the back projection in case of superposition of two Gaussians. Finally, in the last two rows the fundamentally different behavior of

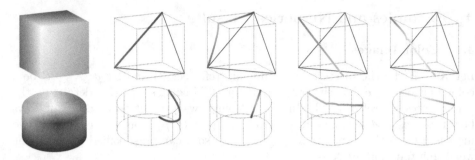

Fig. 2. Geodesics in the models rgb-cube (second and fourth column) and hsv-disk (third and fifth column), visualized in the RGB cube (top) and the HSV cylinder (bottom). Trajectories from 'red' $(r, g, b) = (1, 0, 0)$ to 'blue' $(r, g, b) = (0, 0, 1)$ (second and third column) and from 'pink' $(r, g, b) = (1, 0, 1)$ to 'green' $(r, g, b) = (\frac{1}{2}, 1, 0)$ (fourth and fifth column). (Color figure online)

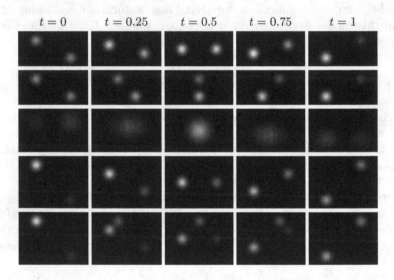

Fig. 3. Back projection of several geodesics between mixtures of Gaussians in $d_{W,y}$ for the color model hsv-disk (and rgb-triple, last row). *First row:* $\lambda \approx 0$, transport cost depends essentially only on spatial location, regardless of colors. *Second row:* with $\lambda = 50$ a more natural color assignment is obtained. *Third row:* 'collision' of a blue and a red Gaussian results in a pink Gaussian via back projection. *Fourth and fifth row:* comparison between color models: hsv-disk gradually interpolates the hue, rgb-triple decomposes each pixel into elementary colors and rearranges these components. (Color figure online)

the models hsv-disk and rgb-triple is visible, here the rgb-triple model leads to a division of color into the single color channels.

Next, we provide three examples for real images in Fig. 4. The examples are chosen in order to illustrate which model is suited best for which kind of images.

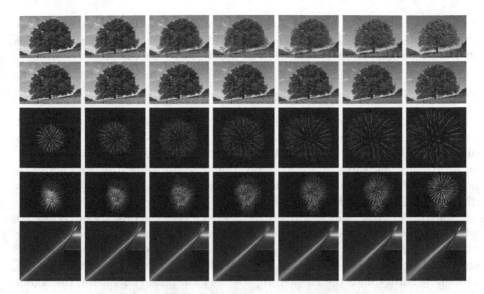

Fig. 4. Transport of 'real' images. *First two rows:* Transport between two photos of trees in different seasons using the rgb-cube model for the whole image and for the color only. *Third and fourth row:* Transport of firework images using the hsv-disk model. The hsv-diskmodel is advantageous here since there are large dark parts that get a small weight in this model. *Fifth row:* Transport between two images showing the spectrum of light using the rgb-triple model. Due to the decomposition of the spectrum with the prism the rgb-triple model is a natural choice for this example. (Color figure online)

For standard photographies, the rgb-cube model is suited best. As an example, we show in the top row the interpolation between two photos of a tree, taken in summer and autumn.[1] For the second row we use the same optimal π, but during interpolation mass particles only travel in signal direction, staying at the same spatial location. Thus, only the color is transformed while the geometry of the image remains fixed (cf. [15]). Both cases yield realistic interpolations, despite slight artifacts in the first row. This is expected, as optimal transport does not explicitly enforce spatial regularity of the optimal matching. For geometrically aligned images as in our example, these artifacts can be removed in a local post-processing step. Future work will include studying additional terms to enforce more spatially regular interpolations between images with substantially different geometries. In the hsv-disk model, the mass of a pixel depends on its intensity. As a consequence, the model is well suited for images showing bright objects on a dark background. An example for such kind of images are fireworks, and the third and fourth row Fig. 4 show the results obtained by transporting such images in the hsv-disk model. In both cases, color and shape are nicely interpolated during the transport. In the rgb-triple model, each color channel is treated separately, which allows the mass to travel through the channels. Such a color decomposition

---

[1] The tree images were kindly provided by Dr. J. Hagelüken.

naturally occurs in the spectral decomposition of light. The fifth row of Fig. 4 gives the interpolation between an image with pure white light and an image showing the single colors of the spectrum obtained with a prism.[2]

4.2 MNIST Handwritten Digits

In this section we present an example for a machine learning application on the MNIST handwritten digits dataset [11]. The dataset consists of 28×28 pixel gray level images of handwritten digits $\{0, 1, \ldots, 9\}$, which we interpret as probability measures in $\mathcal{P}_1(X)$. Note that despite using d_{HK} we choose to normalize all images before comparison because we do not want *global* mass differences to influence the distance, but only *local* discrepancies.

Since the original samples already lie in $\mathcal{P}_1(X)$, they can directly be compared with $d_{W,X}$ or $d_{HK,X}$. A priori, there is no need for a signal manifold $\mathcal{M}$ or lifting. Nevertheless, for an image $\mu \in \mathcal{P}_1(X)$, we propose to interpret a locally smoothed Hessian of the image as $\mathbb{R}^{2 \times 2} = \mathcal{M}$-valued signal f, metrized by the Frobenius norm. Since the Hessian represents local image curvature, the signal f can be thought of as encoding the local orientation of the lines in μ. We demonstrate that by using this additional information, the lifted distances $d_{W,y}$ and $d_{HK,y}$ can discriminate more accurately between different digits. Figure 5 shows the improved performance in nearest neighbour retrieval and a clearer class separation in a multi-dimensional scaling representation. Note that both the lifting, as well as switching from standard to unbalanced transport improve the performance. The approach to generate the signal f from μ can be seen as complimentary to the color models (Sect. 4.1) and illustrates the flexibility of the lifting approach.

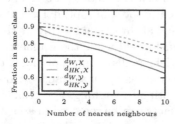 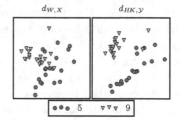

Fig. 5. *Left:* Nearest neighbour retrieval on MNIST dataset with various transport-type metrics. We randomly selected 20 samples from each class and computed the metric matrix. The plot shows the fraction of samples from the same class among the closest n neighbours w.r.t. different metrics. Using the Hellinger-Kantorovich metric improves performance relative to the Wasserstein metric; lifting the images improves performance over the standard comparison. *Right:* 2-d classical multi-dimensional scaling projection [4] of $d_{W,X}$ and $d_{HK,y}$ for classes '5' and '9'. (Color figure online)

---

[2] The images were kindly provided by N. Spiker.

5   Conclusion

Standard transport-type distances are limited to scalar non-negative measures. We presented a lifting procedure to allow comparison of non-scalar signals. The method is generic and flexible, as illustrated by our examples: we computed interpolations of images over different color spaces and demonstrated the benefit of the lifted distances for classification in a simple machine learning example. Future work comprises the study of more complex signal manifolds, such as spheres and SPD matrices, as well as the computation of corresponding barycenters.

Acknowledgements. Funding by the German Research Foundation (DFG) within the Research Training Group 1932 "Stochastic Models for Innovations in the Engineering Sciences", project area P3, is gratefully acknowledged.

References

1. Ahuja, R.K., Magnanti, T.L., Orlin, J.B.: Network Flows: Theory, Algorithms, and Applications. Prentice-Hall Inc., Upper Saddle River (1993)
2. Ambrosio, L., Gigli, N., Savaré, G.: Gradient Flows in Metric Spaces and in the Space of Probability Measures. Springer Science & Business Media, Heidelberg (2006)
3. Benamou, J.D., Brenier, Y.: A computational fluid mechanics solution to the Monge-Kantorovich mass transfer problem. Numer. Math. **84**(3), 375–393 (2000)
4. Borg, I., Groenen, P.J.F.: Modern Multidimensional Scaling. Springer Series in Statistics, 2nd edn. Springer, New York (2005)
5. Chizat, L., Peyré, G., Schmitzer, B., Vialard, F.X.: An interpolating distance between optimal transport and Fisher-Rao metrics. Found. Comput. Math. (2016)
6. Chizat, L., Peyré, G., Schmitzer, B., Vialard, F.X.: Scaling algorithms for unbalanced transport problems. http://arxiv.org/abs/1607.05816 (2016)
7. Cuturi, M.: Sinkhorn distances: lightspeed computation of optimal transport. In: Advances in Neural Information Processing Systems. pp. 2292–2300 (2013)
8. Fitschen, J.H., Laus, F., Steidl, G.: Transport between RGB images motivated by dynamic optimal transport. J. Math. Imaging Vis. **56**, 409–429 (2016)
9. Gonzalez, R.C., Woods, R.E., Eddins, S.L.: Digital Image Processing using MATLAB, vol. 2. Gatesmark Publishing, Knoxville (2009)
10. Kondratyev, S., Monsaingeon, L., Vorotnikov, D.: A new optimal transport distance on the space of finite Radon measures (2015). http://arxiv.org/abs/1505.07746
11. Lecun, Y., Bottou, L., Bengio, Y., Haffner, P.: Gradient-based learning applied to document recognition. Proc. IEEE **86**(11), 2278–2324 (1998)
12. Liero, M., Mielke, A., Savaré, G.: Optimal entropy-transport problems and a new Hellinger-Kantorovich distance between positive measures. ArXiv Preprint arXiv:1508.07941 (2015)
13. Rubner, Y., Tomasi, C., Guibas, L.J.: The earth mover's distance as a metric for image retrieval. Int. J. Comput. Vis. **40**(2), 99–121 (2000)

14. Schmitzer, B.: Stabilized sparse scaling algorithms for entropy regularized transport problems (2016). https://arxiv.org/abs/1610.06519
15. Thorpe, M., Park, S., Kolouri, S., Rohde, G.K., Slepčev, D.: A transportation L^p distance for signal analysis (2016). https://arxiv.org/abs/1609.08669
16. Villani, C.: Optimal Transport Old and New. Grundlehren der Mathematischen Wissenschaften. Springer, Heidelberg (2009)

Time Discrete Extrapolation
in a Riemannian Space of Images

Alexander Effland[1]([✉]), Martin Rumpf[1], and Florian Schäfer[2]

[1] Institute for Numerical Simulation, Universität Bonn, Bonn, Germany
{alexander.effland,martin.rumpf}@ins.uni-bonn.de
[2] California Institute of Technology, Pasadena, USA
florian.schaefer@caltech.edu

Abstract. The Riemannian metamorphosis model introduced and analyzed in [7,12] is taken into account to develop an image extrapolation
tool in the space of images. To this end, the variational time discretization for the geodesic interpolation proposed in [2] is picked up to define a
discrete exponential map. For a given weakly differentiable initial image
and a sufficiently small initial image variation it is shown how to compute a discrete geodesic extrapolation path in the space of images. The
resulting discrete paths are indeed local minimizers of the corresponding
discrete path energy. A spatial Galerkin discretization with cubic splines
on coarse meshes for image deformations and piecewise bilinear finite
elements on fine meshes for image intensity functions is used to derive
a fully practical algorithm. The method is applied to real images and
image variations recorded with a digital camera.

Keywords: Image extrapolation · Shape space · Elastic registration ·
Exponential map

1 Introduction

Riemannian geometry has influenced imaging and computer vision tremendously
in the past decades. In particular, many methods in image processing have ben-
efited from concepts emerging from Riemannian geometry like geodesic curves,
the logarithm, the exponential map, and parallel transport. For example, when
considering the space of images as an infinite-dimensional Riemannian manifold,
the exponential map of an input image w.r.t. an initial variation corresponds to
an image extrapolation in the direction of this infinitesimal variation. In particular, the large deformation diffeomorphic metric mapping (LDDMM) framework
proved to be a powerful tool underpinned with the rigorous mathematical theory of diffeomorphic flows. In fact, Dupuis et al. [3] showed that the resulting
flow is actually a flow of diffeomorphism. Trouvé [10] exploited Lie group methods to construct a distance in the space of deformations. Vialard et al. [13,14]
studied methods from optimal control theory to accurately estimate this initial
momentum and to relate it to the Hamiltonian formulation of the geodesic flow.
Furthermore, they used the associated Karcher mean to compute intrinsic means

© Springer International Publishing AG 2017
F. Lauze et al. (Eds.): SSVM 2017, LNCS 10302, pp. 473–485, 2017.
DOI: 10.1007/978-3-319-58771-4_38

of medical images. Lorenzi and Pennec [6] applied the LDDMM framework to compute geodesics and parallel transport using Lie group methods.

The metamorphosis model [7,12] generalizes the flow of diffeomorphism approach allowing for intensity variations along transport paths and associated a corresponding cost functional with these variations. In [11], Trouvé and Younes rigorously analyzed the local geometry of the resulting Riemannian manifold and proved the existence of geodesic curves for square-integrable images and the (local) existence as well as the uniqueness of solutions of the initial value problem for the geodesic equation in the case of images with square-integrable weak derivatives. Holm et al. [4] studied a Lagrangian formulation for the metamorphosis model and proved existence both for the boundary value and the initial value problem in the case of measure-valued images.

In [2], a variational time discretization of the metamorphosis model based on a sequence of simple, elastic image matching problems was introduced and Γ-convergence to the time continuous metamorphosis model was proven. Furthermore, using a finite element discretization in space a robust algorithm was derived.

Here, we pick up this approach and use it to develop a discrete exponential map in the space of images. In fact, the Euler-Lagrange equations of the discrete path energy proposed in [2] give rise to a set of equations, which characterize time steps of a discrete initial value problem for a given initial image and a given initial image variation. A straightforward treatment, for instance via a Newton scheme, would lead to higher order derivatives of image functions concatenated with diffeomorphic deformations, which are both theoretically and numerically very difficult to treat. We show how to avoid these difficulties using a proper transformation of the defining Euler-Lagrange equations via integral transformations, integration by parts, and suitable choices of test functions, and reduce the number of unknowns. To this end, we derive a fixed point algorithm based on a suitable variant of the Euler-Lagrange equations.

The paper is organized as follows: In Sect. 2, we briefly recall the metamorphosis model in the time continuous and time discrete setting, respectively. Departing from the Euler-Lagrange equations of a time discrete geodesic, a single time step of the discrete exponential map is derived in Sect. 3. Then the discrete geodesic shooting relies on the iterative application of the one step extrapolation. In Sect. 4, the associated Euler-Lagrange equations are rewritten as a fixed point problem. Using suitable discrete ansatz spaces an efficient and stable algorithm is derived in Sect. 5. Finally, numerical results for different applications are presented in Sect. 6.

2   Review of the Metamorphosis Model and Its Time Discretization

In this section, we briefly recall in a non-rigorous fashion the Riemannian geometry of the space of images based on the flow of diffeomorphism and its extension, the metamorphosis model. For a detailed exposition of these models we refer to [1,3,4,7,11,12].

Throughout this paper, we suppose that the image domain $\Omega \subset \mathbb{R}^n$ for $n \in \{2, 3\}$ has Lipschitz boundary. For a flow of diffeomorphism $\phi(t) : \bar{\Omega} \to \mathbb{R}^n$ for $t \in [0, 1]$ driven by the *Eulerian velocity* $v(t) = \dot{\phi}(t) \circ \phi^{-1}(t)$ we take into account a quadratic form L subjected to certain growth and consistency conditions, which can be considered as a Riemannian metric on the space of diffeomorphisms and thus on the space of diffeomorphic transformations $u(t) = u_0 \circ \phi^{-1}(t)$ of a given reference image u_0. Based on these ingredients one can define the associated *(continuous) path energy*

$$\widetilde{\mathcal{E}}[(\phi(t))_{t \in [0,1]}] = \int_0^1 \int_\Omega L[v, v] \, dx \, dt.$$

By construction, this model comes with the brightness constancy assumption in the sense that the material derivative $\frac{D}{\partial t} u = \dot{u} + v \cdot \nabla u$ vanishes along the motion paths. Contrary to this, the metamorphosis approach allows for image intensity variations along motion paths and penalizes the integral over the squared material derivative as an additional term in the metric. Hence, the *path energy* in the metamorphosis model for an image curve $u \in L^2((0, 1), L^2(\Omega))$ and $\delta > 0$ is defined as

$$\mathcal{E}[u] := \int_0^1 \inf_{(v,z)} \int_\Omega L[v, v] + \frac{1}{\delta} z^2 \, dx \, dt, \tag{1}$$

where the infimum is taken over all pairs $(v, z) \in H_0^{2m}(\Omega, \mathbb{R}^n) \times L^2(\Omega, \mathbb{R})$ which fulfill the transport equation $\frac{D}{\partial t} u = \dot{u} + v \cdot \nabla u = z$. Here, we consider $L[v, v] := Dv : Dv + \gamma \Delta^m v \cdot \Delta^m v$ with $\gamma > 0$ and $2m > 1 + \frac{n}{2}$, where we use the notation $A : B = \text{tr}(A^T B)$. To formulate this rigorously, one has to take into account the weak material derivative $z \in L^2((0, 1), L^2(\Omega))$ defined via the equation $\int_0^1 \int_\Omega \eta z \, dx \, dt = - \int_0^1 \int_\Omega (\partial_t \eta + \text{div}(v\eta)) u \, dx \, dt$ for all $\eta \in C_c^\infty((0, 1) \times \Omega)$. Geodesic curves are defined as minimizers of the path energy (1). Under suitable assumptions, one can prove the existence of a *geodesic curve* in the class of all regular curves with prescribed initial and end image. For the definition of regular curves and the existence proof we refer to [11].

In what follows, we consider the time discretization of the path energy (1) proposed in [2] adapted to the slightly simpler transport cost $L[\cdot, \cdot]$. To this end, we define for arbitrary images $u, \tilde{u} \in L^2(\Omega)$ the *time discrete matching energy*

$$\mathcal{W}[u, \tilde{u}] := \min_{\phi \in \mathcal{A}} \left\{ \mathcal{W}^D[u, \tilde{u}, \phi] := \int_\Omega |D\phi - \mathbb{1}|^2 + \gamma |\Delta^m \phi|^2 + \frac{1}{\delta} (\tilde{u} \circ \phi - u)^2 \, dx \right\}, \tag{2}$$

which is composed of a rescaled thin plate regularization term (first two terms) and a quadratic $L^2(\Omega)$-mismatch measure (cf. [2, (6.2)]). Here, we define the *set of admissible deformations* $\mathcal{A} := \{\phi \in H^{2m}(\Omega, \Omega) : \phi - \mathbb{1} \in H_0^{2m}(\Omega, \Omega)\}$.

Using the direct method in the calculus of variations it is easy to show that for $u \in L^2(\Omega)$ and $2m - \frac{n}{2} > 1$, which ensures the continuity of the deformations via Sobolev embedding, there exists a constant $C_{\mathcal{W}} > 0$ that solely depends on γ, δ, Ω and m, such that for every $\tilde{u} \in L^2(\Omega)$ with $\|\tilde{u} - u\|_{L^2(\Omega)} \leq C_{\mathcal{W}}$ there is a minimizing deformation $\phi \in \mathcal{A}$ for $\mathcal{W}$, i.e. $\mathcal{W}[u, \tilde{u}] = \mathcal{W}^D[u, \tilde{u}, \phi]$, and ϕ is a $C^1(\Omega)$-diffeomorphism.

Following the general approach for the variational time discretization of geodesic calculus in [9] and the particular discretization of the metamorphosis model in [2], we define the discrete path energy $\mathbf{E}_K$ on a sequence of $K + 1$ images $(u_0, \ldots, u_K) \in (L^2(\Omega))^{K+1}$ with $K \geq 2$ as the weighted sum of the discrete matching energy evaluated at consecutive images, i.e.

$$\mathbf{E}_K[u_0, \ldots, u_K] := K \sum_{k=1}^{K} \mathcal{W}[u_{k-1}, u_k]. \tag{3}$$

Then, a $(K+1)$-tuple $(u_0, \ldots, u_K) \in (L^2(\Omega))^{K+1}$ with given images u_0 and u_K is defined to be a *discrete geodesic curve* connecting s u_0 and u_K if it minimizes $\mathbf{E}_K$ w.r.t. all other $(K + 1)$-tuples with u_0 and u_K fixed. It is shown in [2] that a suitable extension of the discrete path energy $\mathbf{E}_K$ Γ-convergences to the continuous path energy $\mathcal{E}$. Let us finally mention that neither the matching deformation in (2) nor the discrete geodesic curve defined as the minimizer of (3) for given input images u_0 and u_K are necessarily unique.

3   The Time Discrete Exponential Map

Before we define the discrete exponential map let us briefly recall the definition of the continuous exponential map on a Riemannian manifold. Let $y : [0, 1] \to \mathcal{M}$ be the unique geodesic curve for a prescribed initial position $y(0) = y_A$ and an initial velocity $\dot{y}(0) = v$ on a Riemannian manifold $(\mathcal{M}, g)$. The exponential map is then defined as $\exp_{y_A}(v) = y(1)$. Furthermore, one easily checks that $\exp_{y_A}(\frac{k}{K}v) = y(\frac{k}{K})$ for $0 \leq k \leq K$. We refer to the textbook [5] for a detailed discussion of the (continuous) exponential map. Now, we ask for a time discrete counterpart of the exponential map in the metamorphosis model. To this end, we consider an image u_0 as the initial data and a second image u_1 such that $\zeta_1 = u_1 - u_0$ represents a small variation of the image u_0. This variation ζ_1 is the discrete counterpart of the infinitesimal variation given by the velocity v in the continuous case. For varying values of $K \geq 2$ we now ask for a discrete geodesic $(u_0, u_1, \ldots, u_K)$ defined as the minimizer of the discrete path energy (3). For simplicity, let us suppose that this discrete geodesic curve is unique, which is indeed true for short discrete geodesics. Based on our above observation for the continuous exponential map we then define $\mathrm{EXP}_*^k(\,\cdot\,)$ as the discrete counterpart of $\exp_*(\frac{k}{K} \cdot)$, i.e. we set

$$\mathrm{EXP}_{u_0}^k(\zeta_1) := u_k$$

for $k = 1, \ldots, K$. The definition of the exponential map $\mathrm{EXP}_{u_0}^k(\zeta_1)$ does not depend on the number of time steps K. Indeed, if $(u_0, u_1, u_2, \ldots, u_K)$ is a discrete geodesic, then $(u_0, u_1, u_2, \ldots, u_k)$ with $k \leq K$ is also a geodesic. Taking into

Fig. 1. Schematic drawing of $\mathrm{EXP}_{u_0}^k(\zeta_1)$, $k = 1, \ldots, K$, the input data is highlighted in red. (Color figure online)

account $k = 2$ we immediately observe that the sequence of discrete exponential maps $(\mathrm{EXP}_{u_0}^k(\zeta_1))_{k=1,\ldots}$ can iteratively be defined as follows

$$\mathrm{EXP}_{u_0}^k(\zeta_1) = u_k := \mathrm{EXP}_{u_{k-2}}^2(\zeta_{k-1}) \qquad (4)$$

for $k \geq 2$, where $\zeta_{k-1} = u_{k-1} - u_{k-2}$, and for the sake of completeness we define $\mathrm{EXP}_{u_0}^0(\zeta_1) = u_0$ and $\mathrm{EXP}_{u_0}^1(\zeta_1) = u_1 = u_0 + \zeta_1$. Thus, it essentially remains to compute EXP^2 for a given input image u_{k-2} and an image variation $\zeta_{k-1} = u_{k-1} - u_{k-2}$ (see Fig. 1). For a detailed discussion of the discrete exponential map in the simpler model of Hilbert manifolds we refer to [9]. The particular challenge here is that the matching energy $\mathcal{W}$ cannot be evaluated directly, but requires to solve the variational problem (2) for the matching deformation.

There are two major restrictions regarding the input images u_0 and u_1: we require input images with square-integrable weak derivatives and we assume that the initial variation is sufficiently small in $L^2(\Omega)$. Both properties are kept along the extrapolated image sequence, i.e. $\mathrm{EXP}_{u_0}^k(u_1 - u_0) \in H^1(\Omega)$ for any $k \geq 1$ and $u_{k-1} - u_{k-2}$ for $k \geq 2$ will remain small provided that ζ_1 is small.

Hence, in what follows we consider images in $H^1(\Omega)$ and define for any $k \geq 2$ $u_k := \mathrm{EXP}_{u_{k-2}}^2(\zeta_{k-1})$ as the (unique) image in $H^1(\Omega)$ such that

$$u_{k-1} = \underset{u \in H^1(\Omega)}{\mathrm{argmin}} \ \underset{\phi_{k-1}, \phi_k \in \mathcal{A}}{\min} \ \mathcal{W}^D[u_{k-2}, u, \phi_{k-1}] + \mathcal{W}^D[u, u_k, \phi_k]. \qquad (5)$$

For the sake of simplicity, we restrict to the first step in the iterative computation of the discrete exponential map with $k = 2$. Given $u_0, u_1 \in H^1(\Omega)$ the first order optimality conditions for (5) for $u_2 \in H^1(\Omega)$ and $\phi_1, \phi_2 \in \mathcal{A}$ read as

$$\int_\Omega (u_1 \circ \phi_1 - u_0) v \circ \phi_1 - (u_2 \circ \phi_2 - u_1) v \, \mathrm{d}x = 0, \qquad (6)$$

$$\int_\Omega 2D\phi_1 : D\psi + 2\gamma \Delta^m \phi_1 \cdot \Delta^m \psi + \frac{2}{\delta}(u_1 \circ \phi_1 - u_0)(\nabla u_1 \circ \phi_1) \cdot \psi \, \mathrm{d}x = 0, \qquad (7)$$

$$\int_\Omega 2D\phi_2 : D\psi + 2\gamma \Delta^m \phi_2 \cdot \Delta^m \psi + \frac{2}{\delta}(u_2 \circ \phi_2 - u_1)(\nabla u_2 \circ \phi_2) \cdot \psi \, \mathrm{d}x = 0 \qquad (8)$$

for all $v \in H^1(\Omega)$ and all $\psi \in H_0^{2m}(\Omega)$ for $2m - \frac{n}{2} > 2$.

Next, we reformulate (8), remove the dependency on the unknown function u_2 and in addition restrict to function evaluations of u_1 and thereby avoid evaluations of derivatives of u_1. Under the assumptions that (6) and (7) hold true,

$\partial \Omega \in C^{4m}$ and for $u_0, u_1, u_2 \in L^{\infty}(\Omega) \cap H^1(\Omega)$ Eq. (8) is equivalent to

$$\int_{\Omega} 2\gamma \Delta^m \phi_2 \cdot \Delta^m \psi + 2D\phi_2 : D\psi \, dx$$

$$= \int_{\Omega} 2\gamma \Delta^m \phi_1 \cdot \Delta^m (((D\phi_2)^{-1}\psi) \circ \phi_1) + 2D\phi_1 : D(((D\phi_2)^{-1}\psi) \circ \phi_1)$$

$$- \frac{(u_1 \circ \phi_1 - u_0)^2}{\delta \det D\phi_1} \left((D\phi_2)^{-T} : (D^2\phi_2(D\phi_2)^{-1}\psi) - (D\phi_2)^{-T} : D\psi \right) \circ \phi_1 \, dx. \quad (9)$$

The proof of this reformulation is based on a repeated application of the transformation formula and a regularity result for polyharmonic equations (see the Appendix A). We will use it to define a fully discrete fixed point iteration to compute the deformation ϕ_2 numerically. Once ϕ_2 is available the image u_2 can be calculated via the equation

$$u_2 = \left(\frac{u_1 - u_0 \circ \phi_1^{-1}}{\det(D\phi_1) \circ \phi_1^{-1}} \right) \circ \phi_2^{-1} + u_1 \circ \phi_2^{-1}, \quad (10)$$

which directly follows from (6) by the transformation rule taking into account the diffeomorphism property of ϕ_2. Here, the first summand reflects the intensity modulation along the geodesic, the second summand quantifies the contribution due to the transport.

Concerning a theoretical foundation of this approach, it can be shown that there exists a solution (u_2, ϕ_1, ϕ_2) to the system of Eqs. (6), (7) and (8) for image pairs (u_0, u_1) provided that u_0 and u_1 are bounded in $H^1(\Omega)$ and sufficiently close in $L^2(\Omega)$. This does not necessarily imply that for given u_0 and u_1 the resulting discrete path (u_0, u_1, u_2) is the unique discrete geodesic connecting u_0 and u_2. However, if the images u_0 and u_1 are sufficiently close in $H^1(\Omega)$, then a unique discrete geodesic connecting u_0 and u_2 exists. Existence can be established using a variant of the above fixed point argument and uniqueness under the stronger assumptions can be established by an implicit function theorem argument (cf. the corresponding proof for the discrete exponential map on Hilbert manifolds given in [9]). The presentation of the proofs goes beyond the scope of this paper.

4   Fixed Point Formulation

In what follows, we introduce a spatial discretization scheme as well as an algorithm to compute the discrete exponential map based on the time discrete operator $\text{EXP}^2_{u_0}(u_1 - u_0)$ for given images u_0 and u_1. Let us recall that the computation of EXP^k for $k > 2$ requires the iterative application of EXP^2 as defined in (4). In explicit, we ask for a numerical approximation of the matching deformations ϕ_1, ϕ_2 and the current succeeding image $u_2 = \text{EXP}^2_{u_0}(u_1 - u_0)$ along the (extrapolated) discrete path. Here, we restrict to two dimensional images and for the sake of simplicity we assume that the image domain is the unit square, i.e. $\Omega = (0,1)^2$. Conceptually, the generalization to three dimensions is straightforward. As a simplification for the numerical implementation, we restrict to the case $m = 1$ despite the theoretical requirement that $m > 1 + \frac{n}{4} = \frac{3}{2}$.

To set up the fixed point iteration in light of (9) we define a nonlinear operator $\mathcal{T} : \mathcal{A} \to H^{-2m}(\Omega)$ and a linear operator $\mathcal{R} : \mathcal{A} \to H^{-2m}(\Omega)$ with

$$\mathcal{T}[\phi](\psi) = \int_\Omega -2\gamma D\Delta\phi_1 : (D((D\phi)^{-1}\psi) \circ \phi_1) - 2\Delta\phi_1 \cdot ((D\phi)^{-1}\psi) \circ \phi_1$$
$$- \frac{(u_1 \circ \phi_1 - u_0)^2}{\delta \det D\phi_1} ((D\phi)^{-T} : (D^2\phi(D\phi)^{-1}\psi) - (D\phi)^{-T} : D\psi) \circ \phi_1 \, dx$$

$$\mathcal{R}[\phi](\psi) = \int_\Omega 2\gamma \Delta^m\phi \cdot \Delta^m\psi + 2D\phi : D\psi \, dx$$

for all $\psi \in H_0^{2m}(\Omega)$. The linear operator $\mathcal{R}$ has a bounded inverse by means of the Lax-Milgram theorem. Thus, we can rewrite (9) as a fixed point equation as follows

$$\phi_2 = (\mathcal{R}^{-1} \circ \mathcal{T})[\phi_2] \tag{11}$$

and more explicitly $\mathcal{T}[\phi_2](\psi) = \mathcal{R}[\phi_2](\psi)$ for all test functions $\psi \in H_0^{2m}(\Omega)$. A core property of this formulation is that it does not require any evaluation of image intensity gradients. To improve the stability of the numerical algorithm with respect to the evaluation of the first integrand of $\mathcal{T}[\phi](\psi)$ we additionally rewrite this expression by making use of $A : B = \text{tr}(A^T B)$ as follows

$$\int_\Omega D\Delta\phi_1 : D((D\phi)^{-1}\psi) \circ \phi_1) \, dx$$
$$= \int_\Omega ((D\phi)^{-T} \circ \phi_1)D\Delta\phi_1 : D(\psi \circ \phi_1) + D\Delta\phi_1 : D((D\phi)^{-1} \circ \phi_1)(\psi \circ \phi_1) \, dx.$$

5 Space Discretization

We use different discrete ansatz spaces for the deformations and the images reflecting the different regularity requirements of the fixed point formulation (11). As the discrete ansatz space for the deformations we choose the conforming space of cubic splines $\mathcal{S}_H \subset C^2(\Omega)$ in order to evaluate weak derivatives up to third order. Furthermore, this already ensures smoothness of the deformations independent of the regularization energy. Here, $H = 2^{-N}$ with $N \in \mathbb{N}$ denotes the grid size of the underlying uniform and quadratic mesh. The associated basis functions are vector-valued B-splines. Moreover, we only impose the Dirichlet boundary condition $\Phi = \mathbb{1}$ on $\partial\Omega$ instead of the stronger boundary conditions $\Phi - \mathbb{1} \in H_0^2(\Omega)$ for the discrete deformations $\Phi \in \mathcal{S}_H$ since we experimentally observed that these Dirichlet boundary conditions appear to be sufficient to reliably compute proper deformations. The gray value images are approximated via finite element functions in the space $\mathcal{V}_h$ of piecewise bilinear and globally continuous functions on Ω with input intensities in the range $[0,1]$. The underlying grid consists of uniform quadratic cells with mesh size $h = 2^{-M}$

with $M \in \mathbb{N}$ and $M > N$. We take into account the usual Lagrange basis functions and represent image intensities by functions $\mathbf{U} \in \mathcal{V}_h$. In our numerical experiments we set $M = N + 1$.

Now, we are in the position to define spatially discrete counterparts of the operators involved in the fixed point iteration. We apply a Gaussian quadrature of order 5 on both meshes. For the fully discrete counterparts of the operators $\mathcal{T}$ and $\mathcal{R}$ one gets

$$\mathbf{T}[\boldsymbol{\Phi}](\boldsymbol{\Psi}) = \sum_{c_H, q_H} \omega_{q_H}^{c_H} \Big(-2\gamma((D\boldsymbol{\Phi})^{-T} \circ \boldsymbol{\Phi}_1(\mathbf{x}_{q_H}^{c_H})) D\Delta\boldsymbol{\Phi}_1(\mathbf{x}_{q_H}^{c_H}) : D(\boldsymbol{\Psi} \circ \boldsymbol{\Phi}_1(\mathbf{x}_{q_H}^{c_H}))$$
$$-2\gamma D\Delta\boldsymbol{\Phi}_1(\mathbf{x}_{q_H}^{c_H}) : D((D\boldsymbol{\Phi})^{-1} \circ \boldsymbol{\Phi}_1(\mathbf{x}_{q_H}^{c_H}))(\boldsymbol{\Psi} \circ \boldsymbol{\Phi}_1(\mathbf{x}_{q_H}^{c_H}))$$
$$-2\Delta\boldsymbol{\Phi}_1(\mathbf{x}_{q_H}^{c_H}) \cdot ((D\boldsymbol{\Phi})^{-1}\boldsymbol{\Psi}) \circ \boldsymbol{\Phi}_1(\mathbf{x}_{q_H}^{c_H}) \Big)$$
$$-\sum_{c_h, q_h} \frac{\omega_{q_h}^{c_h}}{\delta} \frac{(\mathbf{U}_1 \circ \boldsymbol{\Phi}_1(\mathbf{x}_{q_h}^{c_h}) - \mathbf{U}_0(\mathbf{x}_{q_h}^{c_h}))^2}{\det D\boldsymbol{\Phi}_1(\mathbf{x}_{q_h}^{c_h})}$$
$$\cdot ((D\boldsymbol{\Phi})^{-T} : (D^2\boldsymbol{\Phi}(D\boldsymbol{\Phi})^{-1}\boldsymbol{\Psi}) - (D\boldsymbol{\Phi})^{-T} : D\boldsymbol{\Psi}) \circ \boldsymbol{\Phi}_1(\mathbf{x}_{q_h}^{c_h}),$$
$$\mathbf{R}[\boldsymbol{\Phi}](\boldsymbol{\Psi}) = \sum_{c_H, q_H} \omega_{q_H}^{c_H} \big(2\gamma\Delta\boldsymbol{\Phi}(\mathbf{x}_{q_H}^{c_H}) \cdot \Delta\boldsymbol{\Psi}(\mathbf{x}_{q_H}^{c_H}) + 2D\boldsymbol{\Phi}(\mathbf{x}_{q_H}^{c_H}) : D\boldsymbol{\Psi}(\mathbf{x}_{q_H}^{c_H}) \big)$$

for $\boldsymbol{\Psi} \in \mathcal{S}_H$ with $\boldsymbol{\Psi} = 0$ on $\partial\Omega$. Here, we sum over all grid cells c_H of the spline mesh and all local quadrature points within these cells indexed by q_H with respect to the deformation energy and over all grid cells c_h of the finer finite element mesh and all local quadrature points within these cells indexed by q_h. Here, $(\omega_{q_H}^{c_H}, \mathbf{x}_{q_H}^{c_H})$ and $(\omega_{q_h}^{c_h}, \mathbf{x}_{q_h}^{c_h})$ are the pairs of quadrature weights and points on the spline mesh and the finite element mesh, respectively. Moreover, we set $\mathbf{U}_i = \mathcal{I}_h(u_i)$ for $i = 0, 1$ with $\mathcal{I}_h$ representing the Lagrange interpolation on $\mathcal{V}_h$.

Finally, one obtains the following fixed point iteration to compute the spatially discrete deformation $\boldsymbol{\Phi}_2$

$$\boldsymbol{\Phi}^{j+1} = \big(\mathbf{R}^{-1} \circ \mathbf{T}\big)[\boldsymbol{\Phi}^j]$$

for all $j \geq 0$ and initial data $\boldsymbol{\Phi}^0 = \mathbb{1}$. The application of $\mathbf{R}^{-1}$ requires the solution of the associated linear system of equations. In a preparatory step, the deformation $\boldsymbol{\Phi}_1 \in \operatorname{argmin}_{\boldsymbol{\Phi} \in \mathcal{S}_H} \mathbf{W}^D[\mathbf{U}_0, \mathbf{U}_1, \boldsymbol{\Phi}]$, which is used in the first step of a time discrete geodesic shooting, is calculated using a Fletcher-Reeves nonlinear conjugate gradient descent multilevel scheme with an Armijo step size control.

Then, the deformation in the current step is computed using the aforementioned fixed point iteration, which is stopped if the L^∞-difference of the deformations in two consecutive iterations is below the threshold value THRESHOLD $= 10^{-12}$. To compute $\mathbf{U}_2$, we employ the spatially discrete analog of the update formula (10)

$$\mathbf{U}_2(\mathbf{x}) = \left(\frac{\mathbf{U}_1 - \mathbf{U}_0 \circ \boldsymbol{\Phi}_1^{-1}}{\det(D\boldsymbol{\Phi}_1) \circ \boldsymbol{\Phi}_1^{-1}} \right) \circ \boldsymbol{\Phi}_2^{-1}(\mathbf{x}) + \mathbf{U}_1 \circ \boldsymbol{\Phi}_2^{-1}(\mathbf{x}). \tag{12}$$

Here, we evaluate (12) at all grid nodes of the finite element grid. To compute approximate inverse deformations $\mathbf{\Phi}_i^{-1} \in \mathcal{S}_H$, $i \in \{1,2\}$, all cells of the grid associated with $\mathcal{S}_H$ are traversed and the deformed positions $\mathbf{\Phi}_i(\mathbf{x}_j)$ for all vertices $\mathbf{x}_j$, $j \in \{1,\ldots,4\}$, of the current element are computed. Then, we use a bilinear interpolation of these deformed positions to define an approximation of $\mathbf{\Phi}_i^{-1}(x)$ for $x \in \Omega$. Furthermore, we explicitly ensure the boundary condition $\mathbf{\Phi}_i^{-1}(x) = x$ for $x \in \partial\Omega$.

In our numerical experiments on real image data, we observed slight local oscillations emerging from the inexact evaluation of the expression $\mathbf{U}_1(\mathbf{x}) - \mathbf{U}_0 \circ \mathbf{\Phi}_1^{-1}(\mathbf{x})$ in the quadrature of the intensity modulation. Since the calculation of EXP^k requires a recursive application of EXP^2, these oscillations turn out to be sensitive to error propagation, and it is advantageous to apply in each step a post-processing by an anisotropic diffusion filtering (see [8]). Alternatively, one could replace the squared weak material derivative by a term $((1 - \frac{\sigma^2}{2}\Delta)z)^2$ for a small filter width $\sigma \ll 1$.

6 Numerical Results

In this section, we present applications of the fully discrete exponential map proposed in Sect. 4. In all computations, we used the parameters $\gamma = 10^{-4}$ and $\delta = 10^{-2}$.

In [2, Fig. 6.2], a geodesic sequence between two female portrait paintings[1] was computed using the finite element discretization for both the images and the deformations on the same grid. The image resolution is 257×257 ($M = 8$). We recomputed this geodesic sequence $(\tilde{\mathbf{U}}_0, \tilde{\mathbf{U}}_1, \ldots, \tilde{\mathbf{U}}_{16})$ with $K = 16$ for the discrete function spaces $\mathcal{V}_h$ and $\mathcal{S}_H$ with $N = 7$, the resulting sequence is shown in the first row of Fig. 2 with framed input images $\tilde{\mathbf{U}}_0$ and $\tilde{\mathbf{U}}_{16}$. Afterwards, a discrete exponential shooting was computed with an initial image $\mathbf{U}_0$ and an initial variation $\mathbf{U}_1 - \mathbf{U}_0$ taken from this geodesic sequence. In the fourth and fifth row, the discrete motion field $\mathbf{v}_k = \frac{1}{\tau}(\mathbf{\Phi}_k - \mathbb{1})$, which significantly alters in time, and the intensity modulation $\mathbf{I}_k = \mathbf{U}_k \circ \mathbf{\Phi}_k - \mathbf{U}_{k-1}$ (postprocessed via anisotropic diffusion) are shown, respectively. Furthermore, Fig. 3 illustrates the effect of the anisotropic diffusion filtering on the intensity modulation for $k \in \{4,8\}$.

Figure 4 depicts a picture detail of the discrete exponential map for time steps $k = 0,1,2,4,8,16$ applied to two pairs of photos of human faces with a resolution of 1025×1025 of the full images. The red boxes indicate input images (first and third row). The input pictures are consecutive photos of a series at 5 and 7 fps, respectively, taken with a digital camera. Due to the higher resolution texture of the images the intensity modulations tend to slightly stronger local oscillations, which are damped with a slightly stronger anisotropic

---

[1] First painting by A. Kauffmann (public domain, see http://commons.wikimedia. org/wiki/File:AngelikaspsKauffmannsps-spsSelfspsPortraitsps-sps1784.jpg), second painting by R. Peale (GFDL, see http://en.wikipedia.org/wiki/File:MaryspsDenison. jpg).

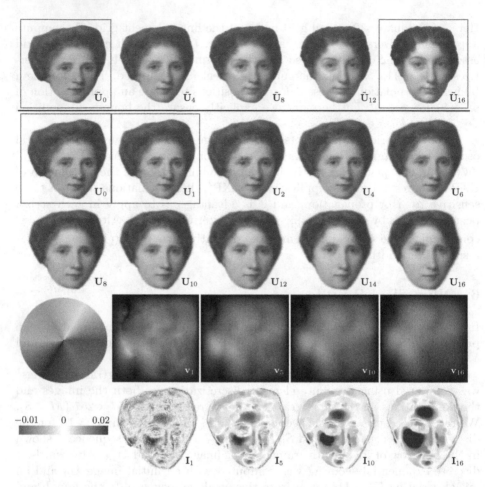

Fig. 2. The first row depicts distinct images of the discrete geodesic sequence associated with the input images $\tilde{\mathbf{U}}_0$ and $\tilde{\mathbf{U}}_{16}$ (in red boxes). The discrete exponential map for distinct time steps is shown in the second and third row, where the input images $\mathbf{U}_0$ and $\mathbf{U}_1$ coincide with $\tilde{\mathbf{U}}_0$ and $\tilde{\mathbf{U}}_1$ from the geodesic sequence, respectively. In addition, the corresponding discrete velocity field as well as the intensity modulation (fourth and fifth row) are shown. (Color figure online)

diffusion filtering. We observe that small initial variations result in a nonlinear deformation of the lips (first row) and of the lips, the cheeks and the eyes (third row), respectively. Furthermore, the textures are reliably transported along the sequence. The second and fourth row depict the color coded time varying velocity fields.

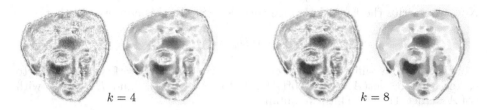

Fig. 3. Comparison of the intensity modulations in the application shown in Fig. 2 in the case of no post-processing (left) and with the implemented post processing via anisotropic diffusion filtering (right) for $k = 4$ (first image pair) and $k = 8$ (second image pair). (Color figure online)

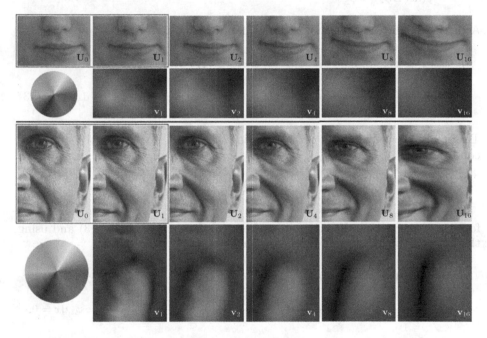

Fig. 4. First/third row: picture details of $\mathrm{EXP}^k_{\mathbf{U}_0}(\mathbf{U}_1 - \mathbf{U}_0)$ applied to two pairs of photos of human faces for the time steps $k = 0, 1, 2, 4, 8, 16$. Second/fourth row: the associated discrete velocity fields $\mathbf{v}_k$. (Color figure online)

A   Appendix

Here, we derive Eq. (9) from the system of Euler-Lagrange equations (6), (7) and (8). By using the transformation formula the energy $\mathcal{W}^D$ can be rewritten as follows

$$\mathcal{W}^D[u_1, u_2, \phi_2] = \int_\Omega |D\phi_2 - \mathbb{1}|^2 + \gamma|\Delta^m \phi_2|^2 + \frac{1}{\delta} \frac{(u_2 - u_1 \circ \phi_2^{-1})^2}{\det(D\phi_2) \circ \phi_2^{-1}} \, \mathrm{d}x.$$

Now we rewrite the Euler-Lagrange equation (8). To this end, we use that

$$\partial_{\phi_2}\phi_2^{-1}(\psi) = -((D\phi_2)^{-1}\psi) \circ \phi_2^{-1},$$

which follows by differentiating $(\phi_2 + \epsilon\psi) \circ (\phi_2 + \epsilon\psi)^{-1} = \mathbb{1}$ with respect to ϵ, and that $\partial_A \det(A)(B) = \operatorname{cof}(A) : B$ for $A \in GL(n)$ and $B \in \mathbb{R}^{n,n}$ with $\operatorname{cof} A = (\det A)A^{-T}$. Thus, we obtain

$$\int_\Omega 2D\phi_2 : D\psi + 2\gamma\Delta^m\phi_2 \cdot \Delta^m\psi + \frac{2}{\delta}(u_2 - u_1 \circ \phi_2^{-1})\frac{(\nabla u_1 \cdot (D\phi_2)^{-1}\psi) \circ \phi_2^{-1}}{\det(D\phi_2) \circ \phi_2^{-1}}$$

$$+ \frac{(u_2 - u_1 \circ \phi_2^{-1})^2}{\delta(\det D\phi_2)^2 \circ \phi_2^{-1}}\left(\operatorname{cof} D\phi_2 : (D^2\phi_2(D\phi_2)^{-1}\psi) - \operatorname{cof} D\phi_2 : D\psi\right) \circ \phi_2^{-1}\,\mathrm{d}x = 0.$$

A further application of the transformation formula with respect to ϕ_2 yields

$$\int_\Omega 2D\phi_2 : D\psi + 2\gamma\Delta^m\phi_2 \cdot \Delta^m\psi + \frac{2}{\delta}(u_2 \circ \phi_2 - u_1)\nabla u_1 \cdot (D\phi_2)^{-1}\psi$$

$$+ \frac{1}{\delta}\frac{(u_2 \circ \phi_2 - u_1)^2}{\det D\phi_2}\left(\operatorname{cof} D\phi_2 : (D^2\phi_2(D\phi_2)^{-1}\psi) - \operatorname{cof} D\phi_2 : D\psi\right)\,\mathrm{d}x = 0. \quad (13)$$

To remove the dependency of the function u_2 above, we employ the pointwise condition

$$u_2 \circ \phi_2 - u_1 = \frac{u_1 - u_0 \circ \phi_1^{-1}}{\det(D\phi_1) \circ \phi_1^{-1}}$$

for a.e. $x \in \Omega$, which directly follows from (6). Inserting this in (13) and using the integral transformation formula we achieve

$$\int_\Omega 2D\phi_2 : D\psi + 2\gamma\Delta^m\phi_2 \cdot \Delta^m\psi + \frac{2}{\delta}(u_1 \circ \phi_1 - u_0)(\nabla u_1 \cdot (D\phi_2)^{-1}\psi) \circ \phi_1$$

$$+ \frac{1}{\delta}\frac{(u_1 \circ \phi_1 - u_0)^2}{\det D\phi_1}\left(\frac{\operatorname{cof} D\phi_2 : (D^2\phi_2(D\phi_2)^{-1}\psi) - \operatorname{cof} D\phi_2 : D\psi}{\det D\phi_2}\right) \circ \phi_1\,\mathrm{d}x = 0.$$

Here, we take into account the identity $\operatorname{cof}(A) = \det(A)A^{-T}$. Next, we consider the test function $\zeta := ((D\phi_2)^{-1}\psi) \circ \phi_1$ in (7). To justify this, we need a regularity result for polyharmonic PDEs to show $\zeta \in H_0^{2m}(\Omega)$. Inserting ζ into (7) we get

$$-\int_\Omega \frac{2}{\delta}(u_1 \circ \phi_1 - u_0)(\nabla u_1 \cdot (D\phi_2)^{-1}\psi) \circ \phi_1\,\mathrm{d}x$$

$$= \int_\Omega 2\gamma\Delta^m\phi_1 \cdot \Delta^m(((D\phi_2)^{-1}\psi) \circ \phi_1) + 2D\phi_1 : D(((D\phi_2)^{-1}\psi) \circ \phi_1)\,\mathrm{d}x.$$

By adding this identity to the above equation we finally obtain (9).

References

1. Beg, M.F., Miller, M.I., Trouvé, A., Younes, L.: Computing large deformation metric mappings via geodesic flows of diffeomorphisms. Int. J. Comput. Vis. **61**(2), 139–157 (2005)
2. Berkels, B., Effland, A., Rumpf, M.: Time discrete geodesic paths in the space of images. SIAM J. Imaging Sci. **8**(3), 1457–1488 (2015)
3. Dupuis, P., Grenander, U., Miller, M.I.: Variational problems on flows of diffeomorphisms for image matching. Q. Appl. Math. **56**, 587–600 (1998)
4. Holm, D., Trouvé, A., Younes, L.: The Euler-Poincaré theory of metamorphosis. Q. Appl. Math. **67**, 661–685 (2009)
5. Klingenberg, W.P.A.: Riemannian Geometry. de Gruyter Studies in Mathematics, vol. 1, 2nd edn. Walter de Gruyter & Co., Berlin (1995)
6. Lorenzi, M., Pennec, X.: Geodesics, parallel transport & one-parameter subgroups for diffeomorphic image registration. Int. J. Comput. Vis. **105**(2), 111–127 (2013)
7. Miller, M.I., Younes, L.: Group actions, homeomorphisms, and matching: a general framework. Int. J. Comput. Vis. **41**(1–2), 61–84 (2001)
8. Perona, P., Malik, J.: Scale-space and edge detection using anisotropic diffusion. IEEE Trans. Pattern Anal. Mach. Intell. **12**(7), 629–639 (1990)
9. Rumpf, M., Wirth, B.: Variational time discretization of geodesic calculus. IMA J. Numer. Anal. **35**(3), 1011–1046 (2015)
10. Trouvé, A.: Diffeomorphisms groups and pattern matching in image analysis. Int. J. Comput. Vis. **28**(3), 213–221 (1998)
11. Trouvé, A., Younes, L.: Local geometry of deformable templates. SIAM J. Math. Anal. **37**(1), 17–59 (2005)
12. Trouvé, A., Younes, L.: Metamorphoses through Lie group action. Found. Comput. Math. **5**(2), 173–198 (2005)
13. Vialard, F.-X., Risser, L., Rueckert, D., Cotter, C.J.: Diffeomorphic 3D image registration via geodesic shooting using an efficient adjoint calculation. Int. J. Comput. Vis. **97**, 229–241 (2012)
14. Vialard, F.-X., Risser, L., Rueckert, D., Holm, D.D.: Diffeomorphic atlas estimation using geodesic shooting on volumetric images. Ann. BMVA **2012**, 1–12 (2012)

On a Projected Weiszfeld Algorithm

Sebastian Neumayer[1], Max Nimmer[1,2]([⊠]), Gabriele Steidl[1,3],
and Henrike Stephani[3]

[1] Department of Mathematics, University of Kaiserslautern, Kaiserslautern, Germany
{sneumaye,nimmer,steidl}@mathematik.uni-kl.de
[2] Leibniz Institute of Photonic Technology (IPHT), Jena, Germany
[3] Fraunhofer Institute for Industrial Mathematics (ITWM), Kaiserslautern, Germany
henrike.stephani@itwm.fraunhofer.de

Abstract. Weiszfeld's method provides an efficient way for computing the weighted median of anchor points $p_j \in \mathbb{R}^n$, $j = 1, \ldots, M$, i.e., the minimizer of $\sum_{j=1}^{M} w_j \|x - p_j\|_2$. In certain applications as in unmixing problems it may be required that x lies in addition in a specific set. In other words we have to deal with a constrained median problem. In this paper we are concerned with closed convex sets lying in a hyperplane of $\mathbb{R}^n$ as e.g., the linearly transformed probability simplex. We propose a projected version of the Weiszfeld algorithm to find the minimizer of the constrained median problem and prove the convergence of the algorithm. Here the main contribution is the appropriate handling of iterates taking values in the set of anchor points. A first artificial example shows that the model produces promising results in the presence of different kinds of noise.

Keywords: Median · Projected Weiszfeld algorithm · Spectral demixing

1 Introduction

For a given set of pairwise distinct points $P := \{p_j \in \mathbb{R}^n : j = 1, \ldots, M\}$, called anchor points, the weighted median is defined as a minimizer of

$$\sum_{j=1}^{M} w_j \|x - p_j\|_2, \tag{1}$$

where the weights $w_j > 0$ count for example how often the different points appear. The problem is known under different names like Steiner problem, Fermat-Weber problem, Fermat-Torricelli problem or geometric median. It is easy to check that in the case $w_i > \sum_{j \neq i} w_j$ the minimizer is given by p_i, but in general it is not a point of P. The coincidence with one of the anchor points is a key requirement of diverse modified spatial vector median definitions as the '(extended) vector median filter' [2], the '(generalized) vector directional filter' and the 'directional distance filter' [8,18]. In general there does not exist a closed expression for the median in more than one dimension. In two dimensions, the

© Springer International Publishing AG 2017
F. Lauze et al. (Eds.): SSVM 2017, LNCS 10302, pp. 486–497, 2017.
DOI: 10.1007/978-3-319-58771-4_39

minimizer is known for three and four points. If the three points span a triangle with angles smaller than 120°, then the median is the Steiner or Torricelli point from which the given points can be seen under an angle of 120°. If one angle of the triangle is larger than 120°, then the median is just that point. For four points spanning a convex quadrangle the median is the intersection of its diagonals. If their convex hull is a triangle, the median is the inner point.

For more general cases there exist several methods to compute the weighted median such as second order cone programming via interior point methods [13,21], the alternating direction method of multipliers and the parallel proximal point algorithm [7,16] the primal-dual interior point method [1] or Newton methods combined with an active set approach [6,15]. One of the best known algorithms for solving the median problem is the Weiszfeld algorithm which goes back to the Hungarian mathematician A. Vazsonyi [20]. The algorithm has inspired and still causes a lot of work on related problems and methods. In [11,12] it was recognized that the original convergence proof of Weiszfeld fails if an iterate produced by the algorithm belongs to the anchor set P. It was shown in [5] that the set of starting points which leads to such a situation is denumerable supposed that the affine hull of P is the whole $\mathbb{R}^n$. For bypassing the anchor points the most natural way is to define an appropriate descent direction of the functional in those points [14,19]. For modifications of the algorithm in connection with the robust principle/independent component analysis we refer to [10]. Local and asymptotic convergence rates of the Weiszfeld algorithm were given in [9] and a non-asymptotic sublinear convergence rate was proved in [3]. The very good performance of Weiszfeld's algorithm in comparison with the PPXA was shown by numerical examples in [16]. A good reference on past and ongoing research is [3], see also the references therein.

In some applications it may be desirable that the minimizer of (1) fulfills additional constraints, e.g., lies in a given convex set. So far we have only found the preprint [17] which adapts the Weiszfeld algorithm in some way to such a setting, where the authors suppose that the constraining set has an interior. In this paper, we are interested in sets $\mathcal{C}$ which are subsets of hyperplanes of $\mathbb{R}^n$ and consequently do not have an interior. The aim of this paper is the construction of a Weiszfeld-like algorithm for the constrained median problem and to give a convergence proof. If the iterates do not get stuck in an anchor point, the ordinary Weiszfeld step can just be accomplished by an orthogonal projection step. The main work is required for the treatment of anchor point iterates.

The outline of the paper is as follows: Since the initial idea to have a look at constrained median problems came from the task of robust unmixing we start by explaining the relation and setting up the model in Sect. 2. The main contribution of this paper is the derivation of a projected Weiszfeld algorithm in Sect. 3, where we add an additional data term with a discrete frame operator for additional flexibility. Taking special care of iterates which get stuck in an anchor point we prove the convergence of the algorithm in Sect. 4. We provide a small numerical example in Sect. 5 and show directions of future research in Sect. 6.

2   Constrained Median and Unmixing Problems

The initial idea to deal with constrained median problems came from robust hyperspectral unmixing. For example, it arises in the sorting of different kinds of plastic mixtures in waste treatment. Figure 1 shows three samples of plastics, pure polyethylen and polystyrol on top and a polluted mixture of them on the bottom. We are interested in the computation of the ratio of the mixture from a hyperspectral image in which we are given a rough estimate which pixels belong to the mixture, enclosed by the red line in the image. Consequently, there are many outlier spectra in the given data, which favors a median approach over, e.g., a least squares approach.

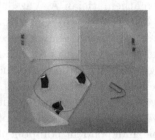

Fig. 1. Polyethylen and polystyrol samples (top) and a polluted mixture of them (bottom).

We briefly describe how the unmixing problem can be treated as a constrained median problem. Let $S \in \mathbb{R}^{d,n}$, $d \geq n$ be a given matrix with full column rank. Assume that we are given M points $\{q_j \in \mathbb{R}^d : j = \ldots, M\}$ which are noisy samples of a wanted convex combination of the columns of S. For example, these columns of S could be known spectra of basic materials and the q_j are spectra of a mixed material recorded at several points. We are interested in the mixture coefficients $\hat{x}$

$$\hat{x} = \arg\min_{x \in \Delta_n} \sum_{j=1}^{M} w_j \|Sx - q_j\|_2, \tag{2}$$

where $\Delta_n := \{x \in \mathbb{R}^n_{\geq 0} : \langle x, 1_n \rangle = 1\}$ denotes the probability simplex and 1_n the vector with n entries 1.

Using the QR decomposition $S = QR$ with an orthogonal matrix $Q \in R^{d,d}$ and $R := \begin{pmatrix} \tilde{R} \\ 0 \end{pmatrix}$, where $\tilde{R} \in \mathbb{R}^{n,n}$ is an invertible upper triangular matrix, the objective in problem (2) can be rewritten as

$$\sum_{j=1}^{M} w_j \|Sx - q_j\|_2 = \sum_{j=1}^{M} w_j \|QRx - q_j\|_2 = \sum_{j=1}^{M} w_j \|Rx - Q^{\mathsf{T}} q_j\|_2.$$

Let p_j be the vector consisting of the first n components of $Q^\mathsf{T} q_j$, $j = 1, \ldots, M$. Then problem (2) becomes

$$\hat{x} = \tilde{R}^{-1} \operatorname*{arg\,min}_{x \in \tilde{R}\Delta_n} \sum_{j=1}^{M} w_j \|x - p_j\|_2. \tag{3}$$

This is a constrained weighted median problem, where the set $\tilde{R}\Delta_n$ is a closed convex set in the hyperplane $\{x \in \mathbb{R}^n : \langle x, \tilde{R}^{-\mathsf{T}} 1_n \rangle = 1\}$.

In this paper we consider the following more general setting. Let $f \in \mathbb{R}^m$ and $K \in \mathbb{R}^{m,n}$, $m \geq n$ fulfill

$$K^\mathsf{T} K = I_n,$$

i.e., the rows of K form a Parseval frame. Let $P := \{p_j \in \mathbb{R}^n : j = \ldots, M\}$ be a set of pairwise different points and $w_j > 0$, $j = 1, \ldots, M$. The case of multiple points p_j can be included by updating the corresponding weights w_j with respect to their number. By $\emptyset \neq C \subseteq \mathbb{R}^n$ we denote a closed, convex set where we assume that aff C is a hyperplane in $\mathbb{R}^n$ with normal vector $\xi \in \mathbb{R}^n$, $\|\xi\|_2 = 1$, i.e.,

$$\operatorname{aff} C = \{x \in \mathbb{R}^n : \langle \xi, x \rangle = c\} \tag{4}$$

for a constant $c \in \mathbb{R}$. Further we suppose that the points p_j are either not contained in C or are in ri C, but not on the boundary of C. We consider the constrained median problem

$$\operatorname*{arg\,min}_{x \in C} E(x) := \frac{\lambda}{2} \|Kx - f\|_2^2 + \sum_{j=1}^{M} w_j \|x - p_j\|_2. \tag{5}$$

If $\lambda \neq 0$, the frame analysis term is strictly convex and the problem has a unique solution. If $\lambda = 0$ we assume in the rest of this paper that the points in P are not aligned. Then we can show similarly as in [21] with the slight modification due to the constraint that (5) has a unique minimizer.

3 Projected Weiszfeld Algorithm

In this section we deduce a modified Weiszfeld algorithm to find the minimizer of (5). By Fermat's rule we know that $\hat{x} = \operatorname{arg\,min}_{x \in C} E(x)$ if and only if

$$0 \in \partial E(\hat{x}) + N_C(\hat{x}), \tag{6}$$

where $N_C(\hat{x}) := \{p \in \mathbb{R}^n : \langle p, x - \hat{x} \rangle \leq 0 \; \forall x \in C\}$ denotes the normal cone of C in $\hat{x}$ and $\partial E(\hat{x}) := \{p \in \mathbb{R}^n : E(x) \geq E(\hat{x}) + \langle p, x - \hat{x} \rangle\}$ the subdifferential of E in $\hat{x}$, see [4, Proposition 4.7.2]. In particular, (6) can only be fulfilled if $\hat{x} \in C$ since otherwise $N_C(\hat{x}) = \emptyset$. Moreover, note that for $\hat{x} \in \operatorname{ri} C$,

$$N_C(\hat{x}) = \{\alpha \xi : \alpha \in \mathbb{R}\}. \tag{7}$$

Using the variational inequality of the orthogonal projection $P_{\mathcal{C}} : \mathbb{R}^n \to \mathcal{C}$ we see that (6) is fulfilled if and only if there exists $p \in \partial E(\hat{x})$ such that

$$\hat{x} = P_{\mathcal{C}}(\hat{x} - \gamma p) \tag{8}$$

for arbitrary $\gamma > 0$. Depending on the differentiability properties of E we distinguish two cases. Note that it is always required that $\hat{x} \in \mathcal{C}$.

Case 1. If $\hat{x} \notin P$, then the subdifferential consists of the single point $\partial E(\hat{x}) = \{\nabla E(\hat{x})\} = \{G(\hat{x})\}$ with

$$G(\hat{x}) = \lambda K^{\mathsf{T}}(K\hat{x} - f) + \sum_{j=1}^{M} w_j \frac{\hat{x} - p_j}{\|\hat{x} - p_j\|_2}$$

$$= \underbrace{(\lambda + \sum_{j=1}^{M} \frac{w_j}{\|\hat{x} - p_j\|_2})}_{s(\hat{x})}\hat{x} - \left(\lambda K^{\mathsf{T}}f + \sum_{j=1}^{M} w_j \frac{p_j}{\|\hat{x} - p_j\|_2}\right).$$

Choosing $\gamma := s(\hat{x})^{-1}$ in (8) we see that the minimizer is the fixed point of

$$\hat{x} = P_{\mathcal{C}}(\hat{x} - s(\hat{x})^{-1}G(\hat{x})).$$

Case 2. If $\hat{x} = p_k$ for some $k \in \{1, \ldots, M\}$, then

$$\partial E(p_k) = \lambda(p_k - K^{\mathsf{T}}f) + \sum_{\substack{j=1 \\ j \neq k}}^{M} w_j \frac{p_k - p_j}{\|p_k - p_j\|_2} + B_{w_k}(0) = G_k + B_{w_k}(0),$$

where $B_{w_k}(0)$ denotes the ball centered at zero with radius w_k and

$$G_k := \lambda(p_k - K^{\mathsf{T}}f) + \sum_{\substack{j=1 \\ j \neq k}}^{M} w_j \frac{p_k - p_j}{\|p_k - p_j\|_2}.$$

Note that $p_k \in \mathcal{C}$ and by assumption on P then $p_k \in \mathrm{ri}(\mathcal{C})$ so that $N_{\mathcal{C}}(p_k)$ is given by (7). Hence we see that (6) is fulfilled if and only if there exists $\alpha \in \mathbb{R}$ such that $G_k + \alpha\xi \in B_{w_k}(0)$. This is the case if and only if there exists $\alpha \in \mathbb{R}$ such that

$$w_k^2 \geq \|G_k + \alpha\xi\|^2 = \|G_k\|^2 + 2\alpha\langle G_k, \xi\rangle + \alpha^2 = (\alpha + \langle G_k, \xi\rangle)^2 + \|G_k\|^2 - \langle G_k, \xi\rangle^2$$

which is true if and only if $\|G_k\|^2 - \langle G_k, \xi\rangle^2 \leq w_k^2$. The vector

$$v := \langle G_k, \xi\rangle\xi - G_k \tag{9}$$

is orthogonal to ξ and has squared norm $\|v\|^2 = \|G_k\|^2 - \langle G_k, \xi\rangle^2$. If condition (8) is not fulfilled, the vector in $\partial E(p_k)$ which has minimal distance from $N_{\mathcal{C}}(p_k)$ is given by

$$G_k + w_k \frac{v}{\|v\|_2}.$$

Setting

$$G(x) := \begin{cases} \lambda(x - K^T f) + \sum_{j=1}^{M} w_j \frac{x-p_j}{\|x-p_j\|_2} & \text{if } x \notin P, \\ 0 & \text{if } x = p_k \in P, \ \|G_k\|^2 - \langle G_k, \xi \rangle^2 \le w_k^2, \\ G_k + w_k \frac{v}{\|v\|_2}, & \text{if } x = p_k \in P, \ \|G_k\|^2 - \langle G_k, \xi \rangle^2 > w_k^2. \end{cases}$$

and

$$s(x) := \begin{cases} \lambda + \sum_{j=1}^{M} \frac{w_j}{\|x-p_j\|_2} & \text{if } x \notin P, \\ \lambda + \sum_{\substack{i=1 \\ i \ne k}}^{M} \frac{w_j}{\|p_k-p_j\|_2} & \text{if } x = p_k \in P, \end{cases}$$

the considerations in both cases lead to Algorithm 1.

Algorithm 1. Projected Weiszfeld Algorithm

Input: ξ normal of aff $\mathcal{C}$, $x^{(0)} \in \mathcal{C}$; $w_j > 0$; $p_j \in \mathbb{R}^n$, $j = 1, \ldots, M$ pairwise distinct,
    not aligned and not boundary points of $\mathcal{C}$
r = 0
repeat
    $x^{(r+\frac{1}{2})} := x^{(r)} - s(x^{(r)})^{-1} G(x^{(r)})$
    if $x^{(r)} \notin P$ **then**
        $x^{(r+1)} := P_{\mathcal{C}}(x^{(r+\frac{1}{2})})$
    else if $x^{(r)} = p_k \in P$ **then**
        $x^{(r+1)} := \lambda_k P_{\text{aff}\,\mathcal{C}}(x^{(r+\frac{1}{2})}) + (1 - \lambda_k)p_k$
        where $\lambda_k := \max \{\lambda \in [0,1] : \lambda P_{\text{aff}\,\mathcal{C}}(x^{(r+\frac{1}{2})}) + (1-\lambda)p_k \in \mathcal{C}\}$
    $r \to r + 1;$
until a stopping criterion is reached

Remark 1 (Interpolation Step in Algorithm 1). If $P_{\text{aff}\mathcal{C}}(x^{(r+\frac{1}{2})}) \in \mathcal{C}$, then $\lambda_k = 1$ and the "else" step in Algorithm 1 is again just the orthogonal projection onto $\mathcal{C}$. Otherwise, the above interpolation must be computed. If we restrict ourselves to subsets $\{x \in \mathbb{R}^n : \langle x, \xi \rangle = c, \ Ax \le b\}$ as in the demixing problem (3), then the interpolation step can by easily computed since λ has obviously to fulfill

$$\lambda(AP_{\text{aff}\,\mathcal{C}}(x^{(r+\frac{1}{2})}) - Ap_k) + Ap_k \le b.$$

Thus, if $\mathcal{I}$ denotes the indices $l \in \{1, \ldots, n\}$ for which $AP_{\text{aff}\,\mathcal{C}}(x^{(r+\frac{1}{2})}) > b_l$, then

$$\lambda_k = \min_{l \in \mathcal{I}} \frac{(b - Ap_k)_l}{(AP_{\text{aff}\mathcal{C}}(x^{(r+\frac{1}{2})}) - Ap_k)_l}.$$

4 Convergence Analysis

The overall analysis follows the path in [14,16] where we have to take the additional projection/interpolation and particularly the treatment of iterates taking values in the anchor set into account.

Lemma 1. *Let $\{x^{(r)}\}_r$ be the sequence generated by Algorithm 1.*

(i) *If $x^{(r+1)} = x^{(r)}$, i.e., $x^{(r)}$ is a fixed point of the iteration operator, then $x^{(r)}$ is a minimizer of E over $\mathcal{C}$ and conversely.*

(ii) *If $x^{(r+1)} \neq x^{(r)}$, then $E(x^{(r+1)}) < E(x^{(r)})$.*

Proof

(i) The first assertion follows from the above considerations in Case 1/2. Keep in mind that if $x^{(r)} \in P$ is a fixed point, we have $P_{\mathcal{C}} = P_{\text{aff}\,\mathcal{C}}$ since this point is in the relative interior.

(ii) Let $x^{(r+1)} \neq x^{(r)}$. To show the second assertion we distinguish two cases.

Case 1. Let $x^{(r)} \notin P$. This case follows mainly the lines in the above papers, so we abbreviate the derivation. Then we have some useful formulas: Using that for $a \geq 0, b > 0$ it holds $a - b \leq (a^2 - b^2)/(2b)$. Setting $a := \|x^{(r+1)} - p_j\|_2$ and $b := \|x^{(r)} - p_j\|_2$ we see that

$$E(x^{(r+1)}) - E(x^{(r)})$$

$$\leq \sum_{j=1}^{M} \left(\frac{w_j}{2\|x^{(r)} - p_j\|_2} (\|x^{(r+1)} - p_j\|_2^2 - \|x^{(r)} - p_j\|_2^2) \right) + \frac{\lambda}{2}(\|Kx^{(r+1)} - f\|_2^2 - \|Kx^{(r)} - f\|_2^2).$$

Using $\|u - v\|_2^2 - \|w - v\|_2^2 = 2\langle u - w, u - v \rangle - \|u - w\|_2^2$ we get

$$E(x^{(r+1)}) - E(x^{(r)}) < \left\langle x^{(r+1)} - x^{(r)}, \sum_{j=1}^{M} \frac{w_j}{\|x^{(r)} - p_j\|}(x^{(r+1)} - p_j) + \lambda K^T(Kx^{(r+1)} - f) \right\rangle.$$

Since $K^T K = I$ and by definition of $s(x)$ it holds that

$$E(x^{(r+1)}) - E(x^{(r)}) < \langle x^{(r+1)} - x^{(r)}, s(x^{(r)})(x^{(r+1)} - (x^{(r)} - s(x^{(r)})^{-1}G(x^{(r)})))\rangle.$$

$$= s(x^{(r)})\langle x^{(r+1)} - x^{(r)}, x^{(r+1)} - x^{(r+\frac{1}{2})}\rangle \leq 0, \qquad (10)$$

where the last inequality follows since $x^{(r+1)}$ is the orthogonal projection of $x^{(r+\frac{1}{2})}$ onto $\mathcal{C}$.

Case 2. Let $x^{(r)} = p_k \in P$. We directly conclude

$$\|G_k\|^2 - \langle G_k, \xi \rangle^2 > w_k^2.$$

By the same conclusions as in Case 1 with $x^{(r)} = p_k$ and a separate handling of the k-th summand we arrive instead of (10) at

$$E(x^{(r+1)}) - E(x^{(r)}) < w_k \|x^{(r+1)} - p_k\|_2 + s(p_k)\langle x^{(r+1)} - p_k, x^{(r+1)} - (p_k - s(p_k)^{-1}G_k)\rangle.$$

The second summand on the right-hand side can be rewritten as

$$s(p_k)\langle x^{(r+1)} - p_k, x^{(r+1)} - \big(p_k - s(p_k)^{-1}\underbrace{(G_k + w_k \frac{v}{\|v\|})}_{G(p_k)}\big)\rangle - \langle x^{(r+1)} - p_k, w_k \frac{v}{\|v\|_2}\rangle.$$

Using that $x^{(r+1)} = \lambda_k P_{\text{aff}\,C}\big(p_k - s(p_k)^{-1}G(p_k)\big) + (1-\lambda_k)p_k$ and the variational inequality of the orthogonal projection we see that the first summand is not positive. Therefore we obtain

$$E(x^{(r+1)}) - E(x^{(r)}) < w_k\|x^{(r+1)} - p_k\|_2 - w_k\langle x^{(r+1)} - p_k, \frac{v}{\|v\|_2}\rangle. \qquad (11)$$

The orthogonal projection of a point x onto aff C is given by $x + (c - \langle x,\xi\rangle)\xi$ with the constant c defined in (4). Consequently we get

$$x^{(r+1)} - p_k = \lambda_k\big(-s(p_k)^{-1}G(p_k) + \big(c - \langle p_k - s(p_k)^{-1}G(p_k), \xi\rangle\big)\xi\big)$$

and since $p_k \in C$ further

$$x^{(r+1)} - p_k = \lambda_k s(p_k)^{-1}\big(\langle G(p_k),\xi\rangle\xi - G(p_k)\big).$$

Now we can compute

$$\|x^{(r+1)} - p_k\|_2^2 = \lambda_k^2 s(p_k)^{-2}\big(\|G(p_k)\|^2 - \langle G(p_k),\xi\rangle^2\big)$$
$$= \lambda_k^2 s(p_k)^{-2}\big(\|G_k\|_2^2 + 2w_k\langle G_k, \frac{v}{\|v\|_2}\rangle + w_k^2 - \langle G_k,\xi\rangle^2\big)$$

and

$$\langle x^{(r+1)} - p_k, \frac{v}{\|v\|_2}\rangle = -\lambda_k s(p_k)^{-1}\langle G(p_k), \frac{v}{\|v\|_2}\rangle = -\lambda_k\Big(s(p_k)^{-1}\langle G_k, \frac{v}{\|v\|_2}\rangle + w_k\Big).$$

By definition of v in (9) we get

$$\langle G_k, \frac{v}{\|v\|_2}\rangle = \langle G_k, \frac{\langle G_k,\xi\rangle\xi - G_k}{(\|G_k\|^2 - \langle G_k,\xi\rangle^2)^{\frac{1}{2}}}\rangle = \frac{\langle G_k,\xi\rangle^2 - \|G_k\|^2}{(\|G_k\|^2 - \langle G_k,\xi\rangle^2)^{\frac{1}{2}}}$$
$$= -(\|G_k\|^2 - \langle G_k,\xi\rangle^2)^{\frac{1}{2}} =: -a.$$

Plugging this into (11) we obtain

$$E(x^{(r+1)}) - E(x^{(r)}) < \frac{\lambda_k w_k}{s(p_k)}\Big(\big(\|G_k\|_2^2 - 2w_k\,a + w_k^2 - \langle G_k,\xi\rangle^2\big)^{\frac{1}{2}} + -a + w_k\Big)$$
$$= \frac{\lambda_k w_k}{s(p_k)}\big(|w_k - a| + (w_k - a)\big).$$

Since we have by the assumption for Case 2 that $w_k < a$ the right-hand side becomes zero and we are done. $\qquad \square$

Lemma 2. *Let $p_k \in C$ with $p_k \notin \arg\min_x E(x)$. Then the whole sequence $\{x^{(r)}\}_{r\in\mathbb{N}}$ generated by Algorithm 1 cannot converge to p_k.*

Proof. Let $T : \mathcal{C} \to \mathcal{C}$ be given by

$$T(x) := P_{\mathcal{C}}(x - s(x)^{-1}G(x)). \tag{12}$$

We only have finitely many points in P. Hence, since p_k is not a fixed point, Alg. 1 becomes the Picard iteration of the operator T after sufficiently many iterations or gets stuck at a different element of P. In the later case the sequence does not converge to p_k and we are done. Therefore we can restrict our attention to (12).

We show that there exist $\epsilon_k > 0$ such that

$$\lim_{x^{(r)} \to p_k} \frac{\|T(x^{(r)}) - p_k\|_2}{\|x^{(r)} - p_k\|_2} = 1 + \epsilon_k. \tag{13}$$

We notice that for $x \in \mathcal{C}$ sufficiently near to p_k the operator T can be written as

$$T(x) = x - s(x)^{-1}G(x) - (\langle x - s(x)^{-1}G(x), \xi \rangle - c)\xi$$
$$= x - s(x)^{-1}G(x) + \langle s(x)^{-1}G(x), \xi \rangle \xi$$

since in a small enough ball around $p_k \in \operatorname{ri}\mathcal{C}$ we have $P_{\mathcal{C}} = P_{\mathrm{aff}\mathcal{C}}$. Therefore

$$T(x) - p_k = s(x)^{-1}\tilde{G}(x) + \langle s(x)^{-1}G(x), \xi \rangle \xi$$
$$= \|x - p_k\|_2 (\|x - p_k\|_2 s(x))^{-1}(\tilde{G}(x) + \langle G(x), \xi \rangle \xi),$$

where

$$\tilde{G}(x) := \lambda(K^{\mathrm{T}}f - p_k) + \sum_{j \neq k} \frac{w_j(p_j - p_k)}{\|x - p_j\|_2}.$$

Consequently, we obtain

$$\frac{\|T(x) - x\|_2}{\|x - p_k\|_2} = (\|x - p_k\|_2 s(x))^{-1}\|\tilde{G}(x) + \langle G(x), \xi \rangle \xi\|_2.$$

Since $\|x - p_k\|_2 s(x) = \|x - p_k\|_2(\lambda + \sum_{j \neq k} \frac{w_j}{\|x - p_j\|_2}) + w_k$ and $\langle x - p_k, \xi \rangle / \|x - p_k\| = 0$ we get

$$\lim_{x^{(r)} \to p_k} \frac{\|T(x^{(r)}) - p_k\|_2}{\|x^{(r)} - p_k\|_2} = w_k^{-1}\| - G_k + \langle G_k, \xi \rangle \xi\|_2 = w_k^{-1}\|v\|_2.$$

By assumption on p_k there exists $\epsilon_k > 0$ such that $\|v\|_2 = (1 + \epsilon_k)w_k$. This implies (13).

From (13) we see immediately that the sequence $\{x^{(r)}\}_r$ cannot converge to p_k. $\qquad\square$

Now the convergence of the projected Weiszfeld algorithm can be shown similarly as in [16]. To make the paper self contained we add the proof with the necessary slight modifications.

Theorem 1. *Let $\hat{x} = \arg\min_{x \in \mathcal{C}} E(x)$. Then, for any $x^{(0)} \in \mathcal{C}$, the sequence $\{x^{(r)}\}_r$ generated by Algorithm 1 converges to $\hat{x}$.*

Proof. If f $x^{(r)} = \hat{x}$ for some r we are done by Lemma 1. Assume now that $\{x^{(r)}\}_r$ is an infinite sequence. By Lemma 1 and since E is coercive we know that $\{x^{(r)}\}_r$ is bounded. Hence there exists a convergent subsequence $\{x^{(r_j)}\}_j$ of $\{x^{(r)}\}_r$. Let $\lim_{j\to\infty} x^{(r_j)} = \tilde{x}$. It remains to show that $\tilde{x} = \hat{x}$. Since $\{E(x^{(r)})\}_r$ is monotone decreasing and bounded, it is convergent, say $\lim_{r\to\infty} E(x^{(r)}) = M$. Thus,

$$M = \lim_{j\to\infty} E(x^{(r_j)}) = \lim_{j\to\infty} E(x^{(r_j+1)}) = \lim_{j\to\infty} E(T(x^{(r_j)})),$$

where T is the iteration operator in (12). We distinguish two cases.

Case 1. If $\tilde{x} \notin P$, then T is continuous at $\tilde{x}$, i.e. $\lim_{j\to\infty} T(x^{(r_j)}) = T(\tilde{x})$. By continuity of E we obtain $M = E(\tilde{x}) = E(T(\tilde{x}))$. By Lemma 1 this is only possible if $\tilde{x} = \hat{x}$.

Case 2. Assume that $\tilde{x} = p_k \in P$ and $\tilde{x} \neq \hat{x}$. By Lemma 2, the whole sequence $\{x^{(r)}\}_r$ cannot converge to p_k. Therefore, there exist (one or more) subsequences converging to some points $p_j \neq p_k$. (Convergence of subsequences to points not contained in P is not possible since by the above considerations the only other cluster point could be $\hat{x}$, but $M = E(\hat{x}) < E(p_k) = M$ is a contradiction.) Thus, for a small enough constant $\varepsilon > 0$, all but a finite number of points lie within ε-balls around some points $p_j \in P$. Here, we choose $\varepsilon < \min_{i\neq j} \|p_i - p_j\|/3$ which implies that there is an index $n(\varepsilon) \in \mathbb{N}$ such that all $x^{(r)}$, $r \geq n(\varepsilon)$, lie within these balls. Then, there exits an infinite number of indices $s \geq n(\varepsilon)$ with $\|x^{(s+1)} - x^{(s)}\| > \varepsilon$. By the proof of Lemma 1 we have

$$E(x^{(s+1)}) - E(x^{(s)}) \leq -\sum_{j=1}^{M} \frac{w_j}{2\|x^{(s)} - p_j\|}\|x^{(s+1)} - x^{(s)}\|_2^2 < -\frac{w_k}{2\varepsilon}\varepsilon^2.$$

This is a contradiction to the convergence of $E(x^{(r)})$.   □

5   A Toy Example

In this section we compare our model

$$\text{(I)}\quad \arg\min_{x\in\Delta} \sum_{j=1}^{M} \|Sx - q_j\|_2,$$

with the following ones:

$$\text{(II)}\quad \arg\min_{x\geq 0} \sum_{j=1}^{M} \|Sx - q_j\|_2, \qquad \text{(III)}\quad \arg\min_{x\in\Delta} \sum_{j=1}^{M} \|Sx - q_j\|_2^2,$$

$$\text{(IV)}\quad \arg\min_{x\in\Delta} \sum_{j=1}^{M} \|x - y_j\|_2, \qquad \text{(V)}\quad \arg\min_{x} \sum_{j=1}^{M} \|x - z_j\|_2,$$

where $y_j := \arg\min_{x \geq 0} \|Sx - q_j\|_2^2$, $j = 1, \ldots, M$ and $z_j := \arg\min_{x \in \Delta} \|Sx - q_j\|_2^2$, $j = 1, \ldots, M$. In the toy example we consider a mixing matrix $S \in \mathbb{R}^{224,7}$, which contains 7 spectra from the USGS spectral library[1]. The ground truth $x^* \in \Delta_7$ was chosen randomly. We are mainly interested in the robustness of the models. To this end, for the mixture x^*, the points q_j, $j = 1, \ldots, 100$ were chosen as noisy versions of Sx^* corrupted by three different kinds of noise. For the first experiment we added white Gaussian noise with standard deviation 0.1. In the second case, we perturbed the data white Gaussian noise with standard deviation 0.03 and only 55 values q_j were taken from the appropriate mixture, while the other 45 ones were chosen from three random other mixtures. We call this corruption "cluster + Gaussian". In a third setting we corrupted the data by 45% impulse noise, i.e., in 45% of the pixels the spectra were replaced with random values between 0 and 0.5.

The experiments were repeated 4000 times. The average error $\|x^* - \hat{x}\|_2$ over these runs is reported in Table 1. For the "cluster + Gaussian" perturbation our model gives the best results. Clearly, for pure Gaussian noise, the least squares model (III) is better suited. For impulse noise, the constrained least squares approach coupled with the median (V) performs best. However, also for the these cases our approach gives reasonable results.

Table 1. Average error for several demixing methods.

	I	II	III	IV	V
Gaussian	0.0314	0.0364	0.0304	0.0522	0.0447
Cluster + Gaussian	0.0785	0.0789	0.1336	0.1050	0.0997
Impulse	0.0510	0.4040	0.2919	0.0721	0.0264

6   Conclusions

We proposed a projected Weiszfeld algorithm which finds the point in a convex bounded set of a hyperplane in $\mathbb{R}^n$ having the smallest weighted sum of Euclidean distances to a given set of anchor points. We proved the convergence of the algorithm. We are completely aware there exists a huge amount of literature on hyperspectral unmixing with and without knowing the matrix S. Although problems of this kind were the starting point of our considerations, the focus of this paper is on the exact formulation of a Weiszfeld-type algorithm in the presence of constraints such that the algorithm can theoretically not collapse in an anchor point. The application to real-world unmixing problems is a topic of our future research. It is further of interest if accelerations as those proposed, e.g., in [3] carry over to the constrained setting. Moreover the incorporation of other linear operators K than just frame operators and the comparison and coupling with other algorithms will be addressed in a forthcoming paper.

---

[1] Available from http://speclab.cr.usgs.gov/spectral-lib.html.

References

1. Andersen, K.D., Christiansen, E., Conn, A.R., Overton, M.L.: An efficient primal-dual interior-point method for minimizing a sum of Euclidean norms. SIAM J. Sci. Comput. **22**(1), 243–262 (2000)
2. Astola, J., Haavisto, P., Neuvo, Y.: Vector median filters. Proc. IEEE **78**(4), 678–689 (1990)
3. Beck, A., Sabach, S.: Weiszfelds method: old and new results. J. Optim. Theory Appl. **164**(1), 1–40 (2015)
4. Bertsekas, D.P., Nedić, A., Ozdaglar, A.E.: Convex Analysis and Optimization. Athena Scientific, Belmont (2003)
5. Brimberg, J.: The Fermat-Weber location problem revisited. Math. Program. **71**, 71–76 (1995)
6. Calamai, P.H., Conn, A.R.: A projected Newton method for l_p norm location problems. Math. Program. **38**(1), 75–109 (1987)
7. Combettes, P.L., Pesquet, J.C.: A proximal decomposition method for solving convex variational inverse problems. Inverse Prob. **24**(6), 065014 (2008)
8. Karakos, D., Trahanias, P.E.: Generalized multichannel image-filtering structures. IEEE Trans. Image Process. **6**(7), 1038–1044 (1997)
9. Katz, I.N.: Local convergence in Fermat's problem. Math. Program. **6**(1), 89–104 (1974)
10. Keeling, S.L., Kunisch, K.: Robust ℓ_1 approaches to computing the geometric median and principal and independent components. J. Math. Imaging Vis. **56**(1), 99–124 (2016)
11. Kuhn, H.W.: A note on Fermat's problem. Math. Program. **4**, 98–107 (1973)
12. Kuhn, H.W., Kuenne, R.E.: An efficient algorithm for the numerical solution of the generalized Weber problem in spatial economics. J. Reg. Sci. **4**(2), 21–33 (1962)
13. Nesterov, Y., Nemirovskii, A.: Interior-Point Polynomial Algorithms in Convex Programming, vol. 13. Society for Industrial and Applied Mathematics (SIAM), Philadelphia (1994)
14. Ostresh, L.M.: On the convergence of a class of iterative methods for solving the Weber location problem. Oper. Res. **26**(4), 597–609 (1978)
15. Overton, M.L.: A quadratically convergent method for minimizing a sum of Euclidean norms. Math. Program. **27**(1), 34–63 (1983)
16. Setzer, S., Steidl, G., Teuber, T.: On vector and matrix median computation. J. Comput. Appl. Math. **236**(8), 2200–2222 (2012)
17. Torres, G.A.: A Weiszfeld-like algorithm for a Weber location problem constrained to a closed and convex set. arXiv preprint arXiv:1204.1087 (2012)
18. Trahanias, P.E., Venetsanopoulos, A.N.: Vector directional filters - a new class of multichannel image processing filters. IEEE Trans. Image Process. **2**(4), 528–534 (1993)
19. Vardi, Y., Zhang, C.H.: A modified Weiszfeld algorithm for the Fermat-Weber location. Math. Program. **90**, 559–566 (2001)
20. Weiszfeld, E.: Sur le point pour lequel les sommes des distances de n points donnés et minimum. Tôhoku Math. J. **43**, 355–386 (1937)
21. Welk, M., Weickert, J., Becker, F., Schnörr, C., Feddern, C., Burgeth, B.: Median and related local filters for tensor-valued images. Sig. Process. **87**(2), 291–308 (2007)

A Unified Framework for the Restoration of Images Corrupted by Additive White Noise

Alessandro Lanza[1], Federica Sciacchitano[2], Serena Morigi[1(✉)], and Fiorella Sgallari[1]

[1] Department of Mathematics, University of Bologna, Bologna, Italy
{alessandro.lanza2,serena.morigi,fiorella.sgallari}@unibo.it
[2] Department of Mathematics, University of Genova, Genova, Italy
sciacchitano@dima.unige.it

Abstract. We propose a robust variational model for the restoration of images corrupted by blur and the general class of additive white noises. The solution of the non-trivial optimization problem, due to the non-smooth non-convex proposed model, is efficiently obtained by an Alternating Directions Method of Multipliers (ADMM), which in particular reduces the solution to a sequence of convex optimization sub-problems. Numerical results show the potentiality of the proposed model for restoring blurred images corrupted by several kinds of additive white noises.

Keywords: Variational image restoration · Additive white noise · Total Variation · Non-convex non-smooth optimization · ADMM

1   Introduction

During the image acquisition and transmission processes, degradation effects such as those due to blur and noise always occur. One of the main goals of image processing is to eliminate these unwanted effects and to recover *clean* images from the acquired blurred and noisy images. Over the years, one of the most studied class of noises is that of additive, independent identically distributed (in short i.i.d.) noises, which affect all the pixels by independent random corruptions coming from the same distribution [3]. This class includes important noises such as those characterized by Gaussian [12], uniform [5], Laplacian [11] and Cauchy [13] distributions, which can be found in many applications, such as e.g. medical and astronomic imaging [3]. For any of these noise distributions, ad hoc variational models have been devised in the past for image restoration; see [3]. However, in many practical applications it is difficult to know a priori the noise distribution and, in any case, the noise might be the outcome of several sources thus giving raise to mixed noise models [4] with very specific/complex distributions.

To overcome these inherent difficulties, in this paper we propose a robust variational model aimed at restoring images corrupted by blur and by the generic wide class of additive white - or uncorrelated - noises [3], which include i.i.d noises

© Springer International Publishing AG 2017
F. Lauze et al. (Eds.): SSVM 2017, LNCS 10302, pp. 498–510, 2017.
DOI: 10.1007/978-3-319-58771-4_40

as a particular case and whose precise definition will be given later. Without loss of generality, we consider grayscale images with a square $d \times d$ domain. The discrete model of the image degradation process we consider in this paper reads

$$g = Ku + n, \tag{1}$$

where $u, n, g \in \mathbb{R}^{d^2}$ represent vectorized forms of the unknown uncorrupted image, unknown noise realization and observed corrupted image, respectively, and where $K \in \mathbb{R}^{d^2 \times d^2}$ is a known linear blurring operator. Given K and g, and under the assumption that the additive noise process is white, our goal is to solve the ill-conditioned - or even singular, depending on K - inverse problem of recovering an as accurate as possible estimate u^* of the unknown clean image u.

The proposed variational model is as follows:

$$u^* \leftarrow \arg\min_{u \in \mathcal{W}_\alpha} \mathrm{TV}(u), \qquad \mathrm{TV}(u) := \sum_{i=1}^{d^2} \|(\nabla u)_i\|_2, \tag{2}$$

where $\mathrm{TV}(u)$ is the discrete Total Variation semi-norm of image u and $(\nabla u)_i \in \mathbb{R}^2$ denotes the discrete gradient of image u at pixel i. We chose the TV regularizer for its popularity but any other regularizer could be used as well, such as nonlocal TV [6], TV_p [15] or fractional TV [10]. The key novelty behind our proposal is the feasible set $\mathcal{W}_\alpha$, referred as the *whiteness set*, that will be defined in Sect. 3. Coarsely speaking, $\mathcal{W}_\alpha$ contains restored images u for which the associated residue images $Ku - g$ resemble the realization of a white noise process.

Recently, a few variational methods have been proposed for the restoration of white noise-corrupted images by explicitly using soft/hard whiteness constraints. In [8] the authors proposed a denoising model containing a penalty term aimed at promoting whiteness of the residue image. Then, another approach has been proposed in [9] to handle also blur, based on a hard whiteness constraint in the frequency domain. Both these previous works highlight how, by explicitly forcing whiteness of the residue image, very high quality restorations can be achieved especially for textured images. However, in [8,9] only white Gaussian noise has been considered, whereas in this paper we propose a hard whiteness constraint which allows to deal effectively with the generic class of additive white noises, at the same time retaining the desirable high capability of restoring textures.

The proposed model (2) is non-smooth due to the objective function and non-convex due to the whiteness constraint. To compute the solution of this non-trivial optimization problem we propose an ADMM-based [16] algorithm which reduces the solution to a sequence of convex optimization sub-problems.

The paper is organized as follows. In Sect. 2 we introduce the distributions related to the important cases of additive white noises considered in this paper. In Sect. 3 we define the whiteness set. The ADMM-based algorithm used to solve our model is illustrated in Sect. 4 and numerical results are presented in Sect. 5. Conclusions are drawn in Sect. 6.

2   Additive White Noises

In this section, we characterize the distributions of the additive white noise models considered in this paper.

A commonly used paradigm for image restoration is the probabilistic Maximum A Posteriori (MAP) approach [3]: the restored image is obtained as the maximizer of the posterior probability of the unknown clean image u given the observed image g and the blurring operator K, considered as a deterministic parameter. In formulas:

$$u^* \leftarrow \arg \max_{u \in \mathbb{R}^{d^2}} \Pr(u|g; K) = \arg \min_{u \in \mathbb{R}^{d^2}} \{-\log \Pr(u) - \log \Pr(g|u; K)\}, \quad (3)$$

where (3) follows by applying the Bayes' rule, by dropping the *evidence* term $\Pr(g)$ since it does not depend on u, and by reformulating maximization as a minimization of the negative logarithm. The two terms $\Pr(u)$ and $\Pr(g|u; K)$ represent the *prior* and the *likelihood*, respectively [7]. Choosing a TV prior and replacing the suitable noise model in the likelihood, the MAP inference formula in (3) turns into an unconstrained variational model of the form

$$u^* \leftarrow \arg \min_{u \in \mathbb{R}^{d^2}} \{\mathrm{TV}(u) + \mu \mathcal{F}(u, g)\}, \quad (4)$$

where the TV regularization term enforces certain prior information on the clean image u, namely sparsity of gradient magnitudes, the fidelity term $\mathcal{F}(u, g)$ enforces closeness of Ku^* to g according to the noise model, and μ is a positive regularization parameter balancing the two terms.

Some important examples of distributions of additive white noises are the uniform, the Gaussian, the Laplacian and the Cauchy. For an overview of these models we refer the reader to [2,3,5,11–14] and the references therein. For each of the mentioned noise distributions, in Table 1 we report the probability density function (pdf), the variance and the associated fidelity term $\mathcal{F}(u, g)$ one obtains by applying the MAP derivation above.

Since in our assumptions (see Sect. 3) the variance has to be finite, from now on we consider a modified version of the Cauchy distribution: the truncated Cauchy distribution with scale parameter $\gamma > 0$, [1], whose pdf reads as

$$p(x) = \left(2\gamma \arctan(L/\gamma) \left(1 + (x/\gamma)^2\right)\right)^{-1} \text{ if } |x| \leq L, \quad p(x) = 0 \text{ if } |x| > L,$$

where $L > 0$ defines the finite support $[-L, L]$ of the pdf. Note that it is reasonable to consider the truncated version of the Cauchy pdf since in practice the range of images is always a finite interval, in our case $[0, 1]$. However, for this distribution the fidelity term is unknown and it will be matter of future studies.

To highlight the differences between the considered distributions, in Fig. 1 we show the pdfs of the Uniform, Gaussian, Laplace and Cauchy distributions with zero-mean and unit-variance. Comparing the pdfs, we can see that Cauchy pdf has the highest tails, which means that for large values the density approaches zero slower than the other distributions, i.e. rare events have the probability to occur more often. Therefore, Cauchy is the most impulsive among the considered noises, Laplace is more impulsive than Gaussian and the uniform pdf has no tails.

Table 1. Common additive (zero-mean) white noise distributions and some properties.

Distribution	pdf $p(x)$	Variance	Fidelity $\mathcal{F}(u,g)$
Uniform	$\dfrac{1}{2a}\chi_{[-a,a]}(x)$	$a^2/3$	$\imath_{[-a,a]}\left(\|Ku-g\|_\infty\right)$
Gaussian	$\dfrac{1}{\sqrt{2\pi\sigma^2}}\exp\left(-\dfrac{x^2}{2\sigma^2}\right)$	σ^2	$\|Ku-g\|_2^2$
Laplace	$\dfrac{1}{2b}\exp\left(-\dfrac{|x|}{b}\right)$	$2b^2$	$\|Ku-g\|_1$
Cauchy	$\dfrac{1}{\pi}\dfrac{\gamma}{\gamma^2+x^2}$	Not finite	$\sum_i \log\left(\gamma^2+(Ku-g)_i^2\right)$

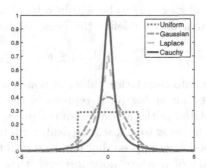

Fig. 1. Plots of zero-mean, unit-variance pdfs for the distributions in Table 1.

3   Whiteness Constraints

Given a single realization $n := \{\, n[i,j] \in \mathbb{R} : i,j = 1,\ldots,d \,\} \in \mathbb{R}^{d\times d}$ of a white noise process, the *sample auto-correlation* of n is a function r_n mapping all the possible lags $(l,m) \in \Theta := \{-(d-1),\ldots,d-1\}^2$ into a scalar value given by

$$r_n[l,m] := \frac{1}{d^2}\left(n \star n\right)[l,m] = \frac{1}{d^2}\left(n' * n\right)[l,m]$$

$$= \frac{1}{d^2}\sum_{i,j=1}^{d} n[i,j]\,n[i+l,j+m], \quad (l,m) \in \Theta, \tag{5}$$

where $\star$ and $*$ denote the 2-D discrete correlation and convolution operators, respectively, and where $n'[i,j] = n[-i,-j]$. Clearly, for (5) being defined for all lags $(l,m) \in \Theta$, the noise realization n must be padded with at least $d-1$ samples in all directions, in other words boundary conditions for the noise realization have to be chosen. In this paper, we assume that the noise process is periodic, such that $\star$ and $*$ in (5) indicate circular correlation and convolution, respectively. This assumption yields symmetry properties of the sample auto-correlation function, such that in the rest of the paper we consider the restriction of the sample auto-correlation function to the subset $\overline{\Theta} := \{0,\ldots,d-1\}^2$ of Θ.

It can be proved that, with the further assumption that the noise process is ergodic [7], the sample auto-correlation r_n is a good estimate of the so-called *ensemble auto-correlation* ρ_n. In particular, for a white noise process we have:

$$\lim_{d \to \infty} r_n[l, m] = \rho_n[l, m] = \begin{cases} \sigma_n^2 & \text{for } (l, m) = (0, 0) \\ 0 & \text{for } (l, m) \in \overline{\Theta}_0 := \overline{\Theta} \setminus \{0, 0\}, \end{cases} \tag{6}$$

where the first equality in (6) comes from the ergodicity assumption and the second equality represents the formal definition of a white noise process, with σ_n denoting the standard deviation of the white noise process distribution. A set of white noise realizations can thus be defined in the spatial domain by constraining the values of r_n in (5) to lie within a band around the theoretical limit given in (6). In particular, we define the *noise whiteness set* as follows:

$$W_\alpha := \{ n \in \mathbb{R}^{d \times d} : -w_\alpha \leq r_n[l, m] \leq w_\alpha \ \forall (l, m) \in \overline{\Theta}_0 \}. \tag{7}$$

We notice that only the auto-correlation values at non-zero lags are constrained. In fact, the auto-correlation at lag $(0, 0)$ represents the variance of the noise process, which is not related to the whiteness of the process. The positive scalar w_α, referred to as the *whiteness bound*, will be dealt with in the next subsection.

In our restoration model, we impose that the residue of the restoration $Ku - g$ resembles the realization of a white noise process, that is the residue image belongs to the whiteness set W_α defined in (7). Hence, the *whiteness set* in our model (2) takes the form

$$\mathcal{W}_\alpha := \{ u \in \mathbb{R}^{d^2} : -w_\alpha \leq \frac{((Ku - g) \star (Ku - g))[l, m]}{d^2} \leq w_\alpha \ \forall (l, m) \in \overline{\Theta}_0 \}. \tag{8}$$

3.1 Whiteness Bounds

We formulate the following conjecture to characterize the distribution of the sample auto-correlation values which holds for any type of white noise distributions considered in this paper: as the dimension d tends to ∞, for any non-zero lag pair (l, m) the sample auto-correlation $r_n[l, m]$ of the realization $n \in \mathbb{R}^{d \times d}$ of a white ergodic noise process with finite variance σ_n^2 distributes as a zero-mean Gaussian with standard deviation $\sigma_r = \sigma_n^2 / \sqrt{N}$, where $N = d^2$ is the number of samples in the realization. This conjecture was proved experimentally through a Monte Carlo simulation, a theoretical proof will be considered in future work. Based on this conjecture, it is reasonable to set the whiteness bound in (8) as

$$w_\alpha = \alpha \sigma_r, \tag{9}$$

where the whiteness coefficient $\alpha > 0$ allows to set the probability that the sample auto-correlation at any given non-zero lag pair falls inside the whiteness set. We remark that the choice of the whiteness coefficient α should not depend on the value of σ_r and, hence, on the number of pixels N or the value of the noise standard deviation σ_n.

4   Applying ADMM to the Proposed Model

In this section, we illustrate the ADMM-based [16] iterative algorithm used to numerically solve the proposed constrained minimization problem (2) with the feasible set $\mathcal{W}_\alpha$ defined in (8).

Towards this aim, first we resort to the variable splitting technique and introduce three auxiliary variables $r \in V$, $s \in V$ and $t \in Q$, with $V := \mathbb{R}^{d^2}$ and $Q := \mathbb{R}^{2d^2}$, such that model (2) is rewritten in the following equivalent form:

$$\{u^*, t^*, r^*, s^*\} \;\leftarrow\; \arg\min_{u,t,r,s} \left\{ \sum_{i=1}^{d^2} \| t_i \|_2 + \imath_{\mathcal{B}}(r, s) \right\}$$

$$\text{s.t.}: \quad t = Du, \; r = Ku - g, \; s = Ku - g, \tag{10}$$

where $D := (D_h^T, D_v^T)^T \in \mathbb{R}^{2d^2 \times d^2}$, $t_i := \left((D_h u)_i, (D_v u)_i \right)^T \in \mathbb{R}^2$ represents the discrete gradient of image u at pixel i, and D_h, D_v represent the horizontal and vertical first order finite difference operators. $\imath_{\mathcal{B}}$ is the indicator function of the feasible set $\mathcal{B}$ for the variables r and s defined by

$$\mathcal{B} := \left\{ (r, s) \in V \times V: \; -w_\alpha d^2 \leq r \star s \leq w_\alpha d^2 \right\}, \tag{11}$$

where $\imath_{\mathcal{B}}(r, s)$ takes the value 0 for $(r, s) \in \mathcal{B}$ and $+\infty$ otherwise.

The auxiliary variable t is introduced to transfer the discrete gradient operator $(\nabla u)_i$ out of the non-differentiable term $\| \cdot \|_2$. The variables r and s play the role of the restoration residue $Ku - g$ within the whiteness constraint (8) so that constraint (11) is now imposed on r and s.

To solve (10), we define the augmented Lagrangian functional

$$\mathcal{L}(u, t, r, s; \lambda_t, \lambda_r, \lambda_s) \;=\; \sum_{i=1}^{d^2} \| t_i \|_2 + \imath_{\mathcal{B}}(r, s)$$

$$- \langle \lambda_t, t - Du \rangle + \frac{\beta_t}{2} \| t - Du \|_2^2$$

$$- \langle \lambda_r, r - (Ku - g) \rangle + \frac{\beta_{rs}}{2} \| r - (Ku - g) \|_2^2$$

$$- \langle \lambda_s, s - (Ku - g) \rangle + \frac{\beta_{rs}}{2} \| s - (Ku - g) \|_2^2, \tag{12}$$

where $\beta_t, \beta_{rs} > 0$ are scalar penalty parameters and $\lambda_t \in Q$, $\lambda_r, \lambda_s \in V$ are the vectors of Lagrange multipliers associated with the linear constraints in (10). We used a common penalty parameter β_{rs} for the variables r and s since they represent the same quantity, namely the restoration residue.

Given the previously computed (or initialized for $k = 0$) vectors u^k, r^k, s^k, λ_t^k, λ_r^k and λ_s^k, the k-th iteration of the proposed ADMM-based iterative scheme [16] applied to the solution of the saddle-point problem related to the functional (12) reads as follows:

$$t^{k+1} \quad \leftarrow \quad \arg\min_{t \in Q} \; \mathcal{L}(u^k, t, r^k, s^k; \lambda_t^k, \lambda_r^k, \lambda_s^k) \tag{13}$$

$$r^{k+1} \quad \leftarrow \quad \arg\min_{r \in V} \; \mathcal{L}(u^k, t^{k+1}, r, s^k; \lambda_t^k, \lambda_r^k, \lambda_s^k) \tag{14}$$

$$s^{k+1} \quad \leftarrow \quad \arg\min_{s \in V} \; \mathcal{L}(u^k, t^{k+1}, r^{k+1}, s; \lambda_t^k, \lambda_r^k, \lambda_s^k) \tag{15}$$

$$u^{k+1} \quad \leftarrow \quad \arg\min_{u \in V} \; \mathcal{L}(u, t^{k+1}, r^{k+1}, s^{k+1}; \lambda_t^k, \lambda_r^k, \lambda_s^k) \tag{16}$$

$$\begin{pmatrix} \lambda_t^{k+1} \\ \lambda_r^{k+1} \\ \lambda_s^{k+1} \end{pmatrix} \leftarrow \begin{pmatrix} \lambda_t^k - \beta_t \left(t^{k+1} - Du^{k+1} \right) \\ \lambda_r^k - \beta_{rs} \left(r^{k+1} - (Ku^{k+1} - g) \right) \\ \lambda_s^k - \beta_{rs} \left(s^{k+1} - (Ku^{k+1} - g) \right) \end{pmatrix}. \tag{17}$$

In the following subsections we show how to solve the four minimization sub-problems for the primal variables t, r, s and u, respectively. Although the minimization sub-problems are all strictly convex and admit a unique solution, convergence of the overall ADMM algorithm is clearly not guaranteed. We postpone the analysis of convergence of the proposed ADMM scheme to a future extended version of this work.

4.1 Solving the Sub-problem for t

The minimization sub-problem for t in (13) can be written as follows:

$$t^{k+1} \leftarrow \arg\min_{t \in Q} \left\{ \sum_{i=1}^{d^2} \|t_i\|_2 - \langle \lambda_t^k, t - Du^k \rangle + \frac{\beta_t}{2} \left\| t - Du^k \right\|_2^2 \right\}, \tag{18}$$

and the solution is obtained by the following closed-form shrinkage operators:

$$t_i^{k+1} = \max \left\{ \|q_i^k\|_2 - \frac{1}{\beta_t}, 0 \right\} \frac{q_i^k}{\|q_i^k\|_2}, \quad i = 1, \ldots, d^2, \tag{19}$$

where $0 \cdot (0/0) = 0$ is assumed, and the constant vectors $q_i^k \in \mathbb{R}^2$ are defined as

$$q_i^k := \left(Du^k \right)_i + \frac{1}{\beta_t} \left(\lambda_t^k \right)_i, \quad i = 1, \ldots, d^2. \tag{20}$$

The overall cost of this subproblem is linear in the number of pixels d^2.

4.2 Solving the Sub-problems for r

The minimization sub-problem for r in (14) is as follows:

$$r^{k+1} \quad \leftarrow \quad \arg\min_{r \in V} \left\{ \iota_B(r, s^k) - \langle \lambda_r^k, r - (Ku^k - g) \rangle + \frac{\beta_{rs}}{2} \left\| r - (Ku^k - g) \right\|_2^2 \right\}$$

$$\leftarrow \quad \arg\min_{r \in \mathcal{B}_r^k} \left\{ \frac{1}{2} \left\| r - v_r^k \right\|_2^2 \right\}, \tag{21}$$

that is, the solution r^{k+1} of (21) is given by the Euclidean projection of the constant (with respect to the optimization variable r) vector

$$v_r^k := Ku^k - g + \frac{1}{\beta_{rs}} \lambda_r^k \qquad (22)$$

onto the convex feasible set

$$\mathcal{B}_r^k := \left\{ r \in V \colon\; -w_\alpha d^2 \le r \star s^k \le w_\alpha d^2 \right\}. \qquad (23)$$

An efficient solver for the quadratic problem (21)–(23) is given in Sect. 4.5.

4.3 Solving the Sub-problems for s

The minimization sub-problem for s in (15) is as follows:

$$s^{k+1} \;\leftarrow\; \arg\min_{s \in V} \left\{ \imath_{\mathcal{B}}(r^{k+1}, s) - \left\langle \lambda_s^k, s - \left(Ku^k - g \right) \right\rangle + \frac{\beta_{rs}}{2} \left\| s - \left(Ku^k - g \right) \right\|_2^2 \right\}$$

$$\leftarrow \arg\min_{s \in \mathcal{B}_s^k} \left\{ \frac{1}{2} \left\| s - v_s^k \right\|_2^2 \right\}, \qquad (24)$$

that is, the solution s^{k+1} of (24) is given by the Euclidean projection of the constant (with respect to the optimization variable s) vector

$$v_s^k := Ku^k - g + \frac{1}{\beta_{rs}} \lambda_s^k \qquad (25)$$

onto the convex feasible set

$$\mathcal{B}_s^k := \left\{ s \in V \colon\; -w_\alpha d^2 \le r^{k+1} \star s \le w_\alpha d^2 \right\}. \qquad (26)$$

An efficient solver for the quadratic problem (24)–(26) is given in Sect. 4.5.

4.4 Solving the Sub-problem for u

The minimization sub-problem for u in (16) can be re-written as follows:

$$u^{k+1} \;\leftarrow\; \arg\min_{u \in V} \left\{ \; - \left\langle \lambda_t^k, t^{k+1} - Du \right\rangle + \frac{\beta_t}{2} \left\| t^{k+1} - Du \right\|_2^2 \right.$$

$$- \left\langle \lambda_r^k, r^{k+1} - (Ku - g) \right\rangle + \frac{\beta_{rs}}{2} \left\| r^{k+1} - (Ku - g) \right\|_2^2$$

$$\left. - \left\langle \lambda_s^k, s^{k+1} - (Ku - g) \right\rangle + \frac{\beta_{rs}}{2} \left\| s^{k+1} - (Ku - g) \right\|_2^2 \right\}$$

The above quadratic minimization problem can be solved for u^{k+1} by computing the solution of the following $d^2 \times d^2$ linear system:

$$\left(D^T D + 2\frac{\beta_{rs}}{\beta_t} K^T K \right) u \;=\; D^T \left(t^{k+1} - \frac{1}{\beta_t} \lambda_t^k \right)$$

$$+ \frac{\beta_{rs}}{\beta_t} K^T \left(r^{k+1} + s^{k+1} - \frac{1}{\beta_{rs}} \lambda_r^k - \frac{1}{\beta_{rs}} \lambda_s^k + 2g \right). \qquad (27)$$

The coefficient matrix of the linear system in (27) is symmetric positive definite, highly sparse and, under the assumption of periodic boundary conditions for u, block-circulant with circulant blocks. Hence, at each ADMM iteration the linear system in (27) can be solved by one forward and one inverse FFT, each at a cost of $O(d^2 \log d^2)$. We remark that symmetric or anti-symmetric boundary conditions could be assumed as well, thus simply replacing FFT with fast cosine or sine transforms and retaining the same computational complexity.

4.5   Computing Projection

In this subsection, we are interested in solving efficiently quadratic programs of the form of the sub-problems for r and s. Let $v \in V$ and $m \in V$ be given (vectorized) images and $b \in \mathbb{R}_+$ a given scalar positive bound. We want to solve:

$$x^* = \arg \min_{x \in \mathcal{S}_x} \left\{ \frac{1}{2} \|x - v\|_2^2 \right\}, \tag{28}$$

where $\mathcal{S}_x \subseteq V$ is the convex feasible set

$$\mathcal{S}_x = \{ x \in V : \ -b \leq m \star x \leq b \}, \tag{29}$$

with $\star$ denoting the 2-D circular correlation operator.

In order to solve (28), we use the ADMM procedure. By introducing the auxiliary variable $y \in V$, (28) can be rewritten in the following equivalent form:

$$\{x^*, y^*\} = \arg \min_{x,y \in V} \left\{ \imath_{\mathcal{S}_y}(y) + \frac{1}{2} \|x - v\|_2^2 \right\} \text{ s.t. } : \ y = Mx, \tag{30}$$

where $\mathcal{S}_y \subseteq V$ is the convex feasible set

$$\mathcal{S}_y = \{ y \in V : \ -b \leq y \leq b \}, \tag{31}$$

and $M \in \mathbb{R}^{d^2 \times d^2}$ is the matrix associated with the linear operator corresponding to the circular correlation with the image m. To solve (30)–(31), we define the augmented Lagrangian functional

$$\mathcal{L}_p(x, y; \lambda_p) = \imath_{\mathcal{S}_y}(y) + \frac{1}{2} \|x - v\|_2^2 - \langle \lambda_p, y - Mx \rangle + \frac{\beta_p}{2} \|y - Mx\|_2^2, \tag{32}$$

where $\beta_p > 0$ is a scalar penalty parameter and $\lambda_p \in V$ is the vector of Lagrange multipliers associated with the system of linear constraints in (30).

A standard ADMM iterative procedure can be applied to solve (32).

5   Experimental Results

We carry out a preliminary experimental evaluation of the proposed TV-W restoration model when applied to images synthetically corrupted by space-invariant Gaussian blur and additive white noise of different types among uniform (AWUN), Gaussian (AWGN), Laplacian (AWLN) and truncated Cauchy

(AWCN). We consider the test images geometry and skyscrapers shown in the first column of Fig. 2, which contain flat regions, neat edges and textures. In accordance with the degradation model (1), the corrupted images input to restoration are obtained by blurring the original image (the blur kernel is created through the MATLAB command fspecial('Gaussian',band,sigma)) and then adding a realization of white noise with standard deviation σ_n. For each example, we compare the performance of our TV-W model with that of the variational model having the same TV regularizer and a suitable fidelity term according to the noise type - see Table 1 - referred to generically as TV-F model. In particular, for AWGN-corrupted images we solved the TV-ℓ_2 model by the ADMM algorithm contained in the software package freely available at http://www.caam.rice.edu/~optimization/L1/ftvd/v4.0/. For AWLN-corrupted images, we solved the TV-ℓ_1 model by implementing the ADMM algorithm presented in [17], for AWCN-corrupted images we used the code provided by the authors of [13], while for AWUN-corrupted images we implemented an ad hoc ADMM-based algorithm. For all the examples, the regularization parameter of the TV-F model has been hand-tuned so that the solution satisfies the discrepancy principle, that is the variance of the residue image must be equal to the variance σ_n^2 of the synthetically added noise. In the interest of a fair comparison, for all the examples in our TV-W model we set the standard deviation σ_r of the residue image auto-correlation - see the definition of σ_r in Sect. 3.1 - by taking the true value σ_n^2 of the noise variance. For what concerns the computation of the whiteness bound by (9), numerical tests indicated that the performance of TV-W are quite robust to choices of the whiteness coefficient α. Hence, we fixed $\alpha = 2.5$ for all the experiments. We used the following parameters for the ADMM algorithm: $\beta_t = 200, \beta_{rs} = 150, \beta_p = 1$. Finally, since the TV-W model is non-convex, it is also worth mentioning that we set the constant image with gray level equal to the average of the observed corrupted image g as the initial iterate of the ADMM algorithm.

The quality of the corrupted and restored images is measured by the Blurred Signal-to-Noise Ratio (BSNR) and the Improved Signal-to-Noise Ratio (ISNR):

$$\text{BSNR}(u,g) = 10\log_{10}\frac{\|Ku - E[Ku]\|_2^2}{\|Ku - g\|_2^2}, \quad \text{ISNR}(u,g,u^*) = 10\log_{10}\frac{\|g - u\|_2^2}{\|u^* - u\|_2^2},$$

where $u, g, u^* \in \mathbb{R}^{d^2}$ are the uncorrupted, corrupted and restored images, respectively, and where $E[Ku]$ represents the mean gray level of image Ku. The ISNR provides a measure of the quality of the restored image: a high ISNR value indicates that u^* is an accurate approximation of u.

In Table 2 we report the restoration results obtained for the test images geometry and skyscrapers corrupted by different Gaussian blurs, namely with kernels defined by parameters band $= 7$, sigma $= 1.5$ for geometry and band $= 5$, sigma $= 1.5$ for skyscrapers, and by AWUN, AWGN, AWLN, AWCN with standard deviations $\sigma_n \in \{5, 10\}$. In the columns labeled TV-F and TV-W we report the ISNR values achieved by the compared models. For TV-W we also display, in parenthesis, the standard deviation (or, better, the l_2-norm) of the residue image, in formulas $\|Ku^* - g\|_2$. From the results in Table 2, we can state

Table 2. Restoration results.

Image	Noise	$\sigma_n = 5$			$\sigma_n = 10$		
		BSNR	TV-F	TV-W	BSNR	TV-F	TV-W
Geometry	AWUN	19.55	3.10	4.98 (5.04)	13.54	2.26	4.91 (10.03)
	AWGN	19.54	2.42	5.02 (5.04)	13.54	1.08	5.04 (10.03)
	AWLN	19.57	3.14	5.01 (5.03)	13.55	1.44	4.96 (10.00)
	AWCN	19.60	4.26	6.09 (5.01)	13.57	3.78	6.89 (9.99)
Skyscrapers	AWUN	18.39	1.40	1.92 (5.06)	12.37	1.14	1.44 (10.09)
	AWGN	18.37	1.14	1.88 (5.07)	12.35	0.63	1.47 (10.09)
	AWLN	18.40	1.46	1.88 (5.07)	12.38	0.84	1.45 (10.09)
	AWCN	18.26	2.04	2.48 (5.19)	12.26	1.54	2.36 (10.20)

Fig. 2. Visual results for the geometry (top row) and skyscrapers (bottom row) images. From left to right: original, corrupted (Laplace noise with $\sigma_n = 10$ for geometry, Cauchy noise with $\sigma_n = 10$ for skyscrapers), restored by TV-F, restored by TV-W.

that the proposed general-purpose TV-W model significantly outperforms the specific TV-F models for all the considered examples. In particular, it improves the ISNR of about 3dB and 0.5dB on average for the geometry and skyscrapers images, respectively. It is also worth noting that the standard deviations of the residue images of the TV-W model are always approximately equal to the standard deviation of the noise corruption, even if no explicit constraint on this quantity is contained in the whiteness set $\mathcal{W}_\alpha$ in (8).

Overall, these preliminary results indicate that the proposed TV-W model holds the potential not only for dealing effectively with unknown noise distributions but also for yielding restorations of higher quality than those obtainable by noise-specific models, especially for images containing textures. To provide further evidence of that, in Fig. 2 we report some visual restoration results for both the test images `geometry` and `skyscrapers`, from which it is clear how the TV-W model yields higher quality restoration of textures.

6 Conclusions

We presented a new robust variational model for the restoration of images corrupted by blur and by the general class of additive white noises, which holds the potential for effectively restoring images corrupted by noises with unknown distributions. In the proposed constrained model, the feasible set contains restored images u such that the associated residue images $Ku - g$ resemble the realization of a white noise process. We obtain a non-smooth non-convex model that is solved by an efficient ADMM-based algorithm which reduces the solution to a sequence of convex optimization sub-problems. Experimental comparisons with the variational models having suitable fidelity terms, demonstrate the effectiveness of the proposed model, especially for textured images. The proposed method can be used in conjunction with any regularization operator other than TV. Future work will investigate how this could improve the overall performance.

Acknowledgements. This work was supported by the "National Group for Scientific Computation (GNCS-INDAM)" and by ex60% project by the University of Bologna "Funds for selected research topics".

References

1. Ben-Israel, A.: A concentrated cauchy distribution with finite moments. Ann. Oper. Res. **208**(1), 147 153 (2013)
2. Bouman, C., Sauer, K.: A generalized Gaussian image model for edge-preserving MAP estimation. IEEE Trans. Image Process. **2**(3), 296–310 (1993)
3. Bovik, A.C.: Handbook of Image and Video Processing. Academic Press, Cambridge (2010)
4. Lanza, A., Morigi, S., Sgallari, F., Wen, Y.W.: Image restoration with Poisson-Gaussian mixed noise. Comput. Methods Biomech. Biomed. Eng.: Imaging Vis. **2**(1), 12–24 (2013)
5. Clason, C.: L^∞ fitting for inverse problems with uniform noise. Inverse Prob. **28**(10), 104007 (2012)
6. Gilboa, G., Osher, S.: Nonlocal operators with applications to image processing. Multiscale Model. Simul. **7**(3), 1005–1028 (2009)
7. Keren, D., Werman, M.: Probabilistic analysis of regularization. IEEE Trans. Pattern Anal. Mach. Intell. **15**(10), 982–995 (1993)
8. Lanza, A., Morigi, S., Sgallari, F., Yezzi, A.J.: Variational image denoising based on autocorrelation whiteness. SIAM J. Imaging Sci. **6**(4), 1931–1955 (2013)
9. Lanza, A., Morigi, S., Sgallari, F.: Variational image restoration with constraints on noise whiteness. J. Math. Imaging Vis. **53**(1), 61–77 (2015)
10. Chan, R.H., Lanza, A., Morigi, S., Sgallari, F.: An adaptive strategy for the restoration of textured images using fractional order regularization. Numer. Math.: Theory Methods Appl. **6**(1), 276–296 (2013)

11. Nikolova, M.: A variational approach to remove outliers and impulse noise. J. Math. Imaging Vis. **20**(1), 99–120 (2004)
12. Rudin, L., Osher, S., Fatemi, E.: Nonlinear total variation based noise removal algorithms. Phys. D **60**(1–4), 259–268 (1992)
13. Sciacchitano, F., Dong, Y., Zeng, T.: Variational approach for restoring blurred images with cauchy noise. SIAM J. Imaging Sc. **8**(3), 1894–1922 (2015)
14. Widrow, B., Kollár, I.: Quantization Noise: Roundoff Error in Digital Computation, Signal Processing, Control, and Communications. Cambridge University Press, New York (2008)
15. Lanza, A., Morigi, S., Sgallari, F.: Constrained TV_p-ℓ_2 model for image restoration. J. Sci. Comput. **68**(1), 64–91 (2016)
16. Boyd, S., Parikh, N., Chu, E., Peleato, B., Eckstein, J.: Distributed optimization and statistical learning via the alternating direction method of multipliers. Found. Trends Mach. Learn. **3**(1), 1–122 (2011)
17. Wu, C., Zhang, J., Tai, X.C.: Augmented lagrangian method for total variation restoration with non-quadratic fidelity. Inverse Probl. Imaging **5**(1), 237–261 (2011)

Learning Filter Functions in Regularisers by Minimising Quotients

Martin Benning[1], Guy Gilboa[2], Joana Sarah Grah[1(✉)],
and Carola-Bibiane Schönlieb[1]

[1] Department of Applied Mathematics and Theoretical Physics,
University of Cambridge, Centre for Mathematical Sciences, Wilberforce Road,
Cambridge CB3 0WA, UK
{mb941,jg704,cbs31}@cam.ac.uk
[2] Electrical Engineering Department, Technion - Israel Institute of Technology,
Technion City, 32000 Haifa, Israel
guy.gilboa@ee.technion.ac.il

Abstract. Learning approaches have recently become very popular in the field of inverse problems. A large variety of methods has been established in recent years, ranging from bi-level learning to high-dimensional machine learning techniques. Most learning approaches, however, only aim at fitting parametrised models to favourable training data whilst ignoring misfit training data completely. In this paper, we follow up on the idea of learning parametrised regularisation functions by quotient minimisation as established in [3]. We extend the model therein to include higher-dimensional filter functions to be learned and allow for fit- and misfit-training data consisting of multiple functions. We first present results resembling behaviour of well-established derivative-based sparse regularisers like total variation or higher-order total variation in one-dimension. Our second and main contribution is the introduction of novel families of non-derivative-based regularisers. This is accomplished by learning favourable scales and geometric properties while at the same time avoiding unfavourable ones.

Keywords: Regularisation learning · Non-linear eigenproblem · Sparse regularisation · Generalised inverse power method

1 Introduction

Learning approaches for variational regularisation models constitute an active area of current research. In so-called bi-level learning approaches [8,14], for instance, one seeks to minimise a cost functional subject to a variational minimisation problem usually consisting of a data fidelity term and a regularisation term. Application of such models range from learning of suitable regularisation parameters to learning the correct operator or entire model, strongly dependent on the type of the underlying problem. In [9], the authors compared performance of Total Variation (TV), Infimal Convolution TV (ICTV) and second-order Total

© Springer International Publishing AG 2017
F. Lauze et al. (Eds.): SSVM 2017, LNCS 10302, pp. 511–523, 2017.
DOI: 10.1007/978-3-319-58771-4_41

Generalised Variation (TGV^2) regularisers combined with both L_1 and L_2 cost functions for denoising of 200 images of the BSDS300 dataset measured by SSIM, PSNR and an objective value. There was no unique regulariser that always performed best. The images in the above-mentioned dataset differ from each other significantly enough such that advantages of the different regularisers become apparent for images with different prominent features such as sharp edges or piecewise linear regions.

Another approach to variational regularisation learning is dictionary learning [7]. In this approach the basic paradigm is that local image regions (patches) can be composed based on a linear combination of very few atoms from some dictionary. The dictionary could be global, for example wavelets or DCT-based, and in those cases a basis. However, it was revealed that tailored dictionaries to the specific image (or class of images), which are overcomplete, outperform the global dictionaries. These dictionaries are typically learned from the noisy image itself using algorithms such as K-SVD [1] based on orthogonal-matching-pursuit (OMP). Recent studies have shown relations between convolutional neural nets and convolutional sparse coding [17]. One can conceptually perceive our proposed convolution filter set $\{h_i\}$, which defines the target-specific regulariser, as a small dictionary which is learned based on a few positive and negative image examples.

Learning approaches for variational regularisation models are aiming to design appropriate regularisation and customise it to particular structures present in the image. A somewhat separate route is the mathematical analysis of model-based regularisation, aiming at understanding the main building-blocks of existing regularisers to pave the path for designing new ones. In [2], for instance, the concept of ground states, singular values and singular vectors of regularisation functionals has been introduced, enabling the computation of solutions of variational regularisation schemes that can be reconstructed perfectly (up to a systematic bias).

In [3] a new model motivated by generalised, non-linear Eigenproblems has been proposed to learn parametrised regularisation functions. As a novelty, both wanted and unwanted outcomes are incorporated in the model by integrating the former in the numerator and the latter in the denominator:

$$\hat{h} \in \operatorname*{arg\,min}_{\substack{\|h\|_2=1 \\ \mathrm{mean}(h)=0}} \frac{J(u^+; h)}{J(u^-; h)}, \quad J(u; h) = \|u * h\|_1, \tag{1}$$

where h is a parametrisation of a regularisation functional J and u^+ and u^- are desired and undesired input signals, respectively.

The basic idea underlying the model in [3] is optimisation of a quotient with respect to a convolution kernel parametrising certain regularisation functionals. In the paper, the authors investigate the same regularisation function, which is the one-norm of a signal convolved with a kernel h both in the numerator and denominator. In the former, the input is a desirable signal, i.e. a function, which is preferred to be sparse once convolved with the kernel, whereas the latter is a signal to be avoided, yielding a large one-norm once convolved. In [3], the undesirable signal has only been chosen to be pure noise or a noisy version of the desired input signal. In this work, however, we are also going to use clean signals as undesirable signals, with specific geometric properties or scales one wants to avoid. In Sect. 4 we are going to see that this will enable us to derive tailored filters superior to those derived merely from desirable fitting data.

2 The Proposed Learning Model

In order to be able to incorporate multiple input functions, different regularisation functionals and multi-dimensional filter functions, we generalise the model in [3] as follows:

$$\hat{h} \in \arg\min_{\substack{\|h\|_2=1 \\ \mathrm{mean}(h)=0}} \frac{\frac{1}{M} \sum_{i=1}^{M} \sum_{k=1}^{K} J(u_i^+; h_k)}{\frac{1}{N} \sum_{j=1}^{N} \sum_{k=1}^{K} J(u_j^-; h_k)}, \quad J(u; h) = \|u * h\|_1. \tag{2}$$

Now, $\hat{h} = (\hat{h}_1, \ldots, \hat{h}_K)$, where $\hat{h}_k \in \mathbb{R}^n$ for all $k \in \{1, \ldots, K\}$, is a combination of multiple filter functions. The signals $u^+, u^- \in \mathbb{R}^m$ are one-dimensional or two-dimensional images written as a column vector. In the following section we want to describe how we want to solve (2) numerically.

2.1 Numerical Implementation

Viewing the quotients in (1) and (2) as generalised Rayleigh quotients, we observe that we deal with the (numerical) solution of generalised Eigenvalue problems. In order to solve (1) and (2) with the same algorithm, we write down an abstract algorithm for the solution of

$$\hat{h} \in \arg\min_h \left\{ \frac{F(h)}{G(h)} \quad \text{subject to} \quad \|h\|_2 = 1 \quad \text{and} \quad \mathrm{mean}(h) = 0 \right\}. \tag{3}$$

The optimality condition of (3) is given via $0 \in \partial F(\hat{h}) - \hat{\mu} \, \partial G(\hat{h})$, where $\partial F(\hat{h})$ and $\partial G(\hat{h})$ denote the subdifferential of F and G at $\hat{h}$, respectively, and $\hat{\mu} = F(\hat{h})/G(\hat{h})$. Note that the Lagrange multipliers for the constraints are zero by the same argumentation as in [18, Sect. 2], and can therefore be omitted.

In [13] the authors have proposed a generalised inverse power method to tackle problems of the form (3). We, however, follow [5] and use a modification with added penalisation of the squared two-norm between h and the previous iterate, to guarantee coercivity (and therefore existence and uniqueness of the solution) of the main update. The proposed algorithm for solving (3) therefore reads as

$$\begin{cases} h^{k+\frac{1}{2}} &= \underset{\text{mean}(h)=0}{\arg\min} \left\{ F(h) - \mu^k \langle h - h^k, s^k \rangle + \| h - h^k \|_2^2 \right\} \\ \mu^{k+1} &= \dfrac{F(h^{k+\frac{1}{2}})}{G(h^{k+\frac{1}{2}})} \\ s^{k+1} &\in \partial G(h^{k+\frac{1}{2}}) \\ h^{k+1} &= \dfrac{h^{k+\frac{1}{2}}}{\left\| h^{k+\frac{1}{2}} \right\|_2} \end{cases} \tag{4}$$

Similar to [3] we are using the CVX MATLAB® software for disciplined convex programming [12]. Due to the non-convexity of the overall problem and the resulting dependence on random initialisations of the filter, we re-initialise h and iterate (4) 100 times. As also explained in [3], reconstruction of a noisy signal in order to test the behaviour of the optimal filter is obtained by solving the following constrained optimisation problem:

$$\hat{u} = \underset{u \in \mathbb{R}^m}{\arg\min} \, J(u; \hat{h}) \qquad \text{subject to} \quad \| u - f \|_2 \leq \eta \sigma \sqrt{m}, \tag{5}$$

where f is the sum of u^+ and Gaussian noise with zero mean and variance σ^2, η is a weighting factor and m is the number of elements of u^+.

Remark. In the setting of [3], there is indeed an even more efficient way of finding suitable filter functions h. Simplifying the model to a variant without the need of having a negative input function u^- yields the same results, which is a clear indicator that in the above-mentioned framework the numerator plays a dominant role. In fact, varying model (1) by replacing the one-norm in the denominator by $\|h\|_2$ returns exactly the same solutions. However, we would like to stress that the denominator is going to play a more important role in our extended model, since we are able to incorporate more than one input function u^-, especially ones which are different from pure noise. In fact, one can think of a large variety of undesired input signals such as specific textures and shapes.

Despite existing convergence results previously stated in [13] and [5] we want to briefly state a simplified convergence result for global convergence of Algorithm 4 in the following.

2.2 A Brief Convergence Analysis

Following [4, Sect. 3.2], we show two results that are essential for proving global convergence of Algorithm (4): a descent lemma and a bound of the subgradient by the iterates gap. We start with the sufficient decrease property of the objective.

Lemma 1. *Let F and G be proper, lower semi-continuous and convex functions. Then the iterates of Algorithm (4) satisfy*

$$\mu^{k+\frac{1}{2}} + \frac{1}{G(h^{k+\frac{1}{2}})} \| h^{k+\frac{1}{2}} - h^k \|^2 \leq \mu^k,$$

if we further assume $G(h^{k+\frac{1}{2}}) \neq 0$ for all $k \in \mathbb{N}$.

Proof. From the first equation of Algorithm (4) we observe

$$F(h^{k+\frac{1}{2}}) + \|h^{k+\frac{1}{2}} - h^k\|_2^2 \leq F(h^k) + \mu^k \langle s^k, h^{k+\frac{1}{2}} - h^k \rangle$$
$$\leq F(h^k) + \mu^k \left(G(h^{k+\frac{1}{2}}) - G(h^k) \right)$$
$$= \mu^k G(h^{k+\frac{1}{2}}),$$

due to the convexity of G. If we divide by $G(h^{k+\frac{1}{2}})$ on both sides of the equation, we obtain

$$\mu^{k+\frac{1}{2}} + \frac{1}{G(h^{k+\frac{1}{2}})} \|h^{k+\frac{1}{2}} - h^k\|^2 \leq \mu^k,$$

which concludes the proof.   □

In order to further prove a bound of the subgradient by the iterates gap, we assume that G is smooth and further has a Lipschitz-continuous gradient ∇G. We want to point out that this excludes choices for G such as in (1) and (2), as the one-norm is neither smooth nor are its subgradients Lipschitz-continuous. A remedy here is the smoothing of the one-norms in (1) and (2). If we replace the one-norm(s) in the denominator with Huber one-norms, i.e. we replace the modulus in the one-norm with the Huber function

$$\phi_\gamma(x) = \begin{cases} \frac{x^2}{2}, & |x| \leq \gamma \\ \gamma \left(|x| - \frac{\gamma}{2} \right), & |x| > \gamma \end{cases},$$

we can achieve smoothness and Lipschitz-continuity of the gradient, where the Lipschitz parameter depends on the smoothing parameter γ. We want to note that for γ small enough we have not seen any significant difference in numerical performance between using the one-norm or its Huber counterpart.

Lemma 2. *Let F and G be proper, lower semi-continuous and convex functions, and let G be differentiable with L-Lipschitz-continuous gradient, i.e. $\|\nabla G(h_1) - \nabla G(h_2)\|_2 \leq L\|h_1 - h_2\|_2$ for all h_1 and h_2 and a fixed constant L. Then the iterates of Algorithm (4) satisfy*

$$\|r^{k+\frac{1}{2}} - \mu^{k+\frac{1}{2}} \nabla G(x^{k+\frac{1}{2}})\|_2 \leq (2 + C^{k+\frac{1}{2}} L)\|h^{k+\frac{1}{2}} - h^k\|_2,$$

for some constant $C^{k+\frac{1}{2}}$, $r^{k+\frac{1}{2}} \in \partial F(h^{k+\frac{1}{2}})$ and $\mu^{k+\frac{1}{2}} := \mu^{k+1} = F(h^{k+\frac{1}{2}})/ G(h^{k+\frac{1}{2}})$.

Proof. This follows almost instantly from the optimality condition and the Lipschitz-continuity of ∇G. We obtain

$$r^{k+\frac{1}{2}} - \mu^k \nabla G(h^k) = 2(h^k - h^{k+\frac{1}{2}}), \tag{6}$$

for $r^{k+\frac{1}{2}} \in \partial F(h^{k+\frac{1}{2}})$, as the optimality condition of the first sub-problem of (4) - note that we can omit the zero-mean constraint with a similar argumentation as earlier. Hence, we obtain

$$\|r^{k+\frac{1}{2}} - \mu^{k+\frac{1}{2}} \nabla G(x^{k+\frac{1}{2}})\|_2 = \|r^{k+\frac{1}{2}} - \mu^k \nabla G(x^k) + \mu^k \nabla G(x^k) - \mu^{k+\frac{1}{2}} \nabla G(x^{k+\frac{1}{2}})\|_2$$

$$= \|2(h^k - h^{k+\frac{1}{2}}) + \mu^k \nabla G(x^k) - \mu^{k+\frac{1}{2}} \nabla G(x^{k+\frac{1}{2}})\|_2$$

$$\leq 2\|h^{k+\frac{1}{2}} - h^k\|_2 + C^{k+\frac{1}{2}} \|\nabla G(x^{k+\frac{1}{2}}) - \nabla G(x^k)\|_2$$

thanks to (6) and the triangle inequality. The constant $C^{k+\frac{1}{2}}$ equals either μ^k or $\mu^{k+\frac{1}{2}}$, depending on whether $\|\mu^{k+\frac{1}{2}} \nabla G(x^{k+\frac{1}{2}}) - \mu^k \nabla G(x^k)\|_2 \leq \mu^{k+\frac{1}{2}}$ $\|\nabla G(x^{k+\frac{1}{2}}) - \nabla G(x^k)\|_2$ or $\|\mu^{k+\frac{1}{2}} \nabla G(x^{k+\frac{1}{2}}) - \mu^k \nabla G(x^k)\|_2 \leq \mu^k \|\nabla G(x^{k+\frac{1}{2}}) - \nabla G(x^k)\|_2$. Using the Lipschitz-continuity of G then yields

$$\|r^{k+\frac{1}{2}} - \mu^{k+\frac{1}{2}} \nabla G(x^{k+\frac{1}{2}})\|_2 \leq 2\|h^{k+\frac{1}{2}} - h^k\|_2 + C^{k+\frac{1}{2}} L\|h^{k+\frac{1}{2}} - h^k\|_2$$

$$= (2 + C^{k+\frac{1}{2}} L)\|h^{k+\frac{1}{2}} - h^k\|_2.$$

This concludes the proof.   □

Under the additional assumption that the function F/G satisfies the Kurdyka-Łojasiewicz property (cf. [15,16]) we can now use Lemmas 1 and 2 to show finite length of the iterates (4) similar to [4, Theorem 1], following the general recipe of [4, Sect. 3.2]. Note that we further have to substitute $h^{k+\frac{1}{2}} = \|h^{k+\frac{1}{2}}\|_2 h^{k+1}$ in order to also show global convergence of the normalised iterates.

3   Reproducing Standard Sparse Penalties

In this section we want to demonstrate that we are able to reproduce standard first- and second-order total variation regularisation penalties in 1D.

Figure 1 shows results for different sizes of the kernel h. In all experiments the filter function is indeed resembling a two-point stencil functioning as a finite differences discretisation of TV. This is expected as the desired input function is a TV Eigenfunction.

In Fig. 2 (a) we can reproduce a filter resembling a second-order derivative. This is indeed expected as we choose three different piecewise-linear functions as desired input signals. The reconstruction in (b) is performed according to (5).

In a more sophisticated example, we mimic a TV-TV^2 infimal convolution model, where we are given a known decomposition $u^+ = v + w$, i.e. u^+ consists of a smooth part v and a piecewise constant part w. When minimising

$$\frac{\|h_1 * v\|_1 + \|h_2 * w\|_1}{\|h_1 * u^-\|_1 + \|h_2 * u^-\|_1},$$

with respect to h_1 and h_2, we indeed obtain two filters resembling a second- and first-order derivative, respectively (cf. Fig. 3).

4   Novel Sparse Filters

In this section we derive a new family of regularisers not necessarily related to derivatives in contrast to the total variation. They have the interesting property of reconstructing piecewise-constant both vertical and horizontal lines in the corresponding null-spaces. Consequently, we are able to almost perfectly reconstruct those types of images and obtain better denoising results compared to standard TV denoising. In [10], a definition of desirable features of a regulariser, which is adapted for a specific type of images, is given. It is suggested that in the ideal case, all instances belonging to the desired clean class should be in the null-space of the regulariser (see [10, Sect. 2] and also compare [6]). This is exactly what we obtain in the following.

In Fig. 4, a new family of diagonal regularisers is established for piecewise-constant images with stripes in both vertical and horizontal direction. For denoising purposes, those filters yield superior results over TV denoising as they additionally avoid loss of contrast, which would occur when performing TV denoising for these examples. The reason for that is simply that if we consider a 2×2 diagonal-shaped filter $h = [1, -1; -1, 1]$ in the variational problem (5), we can expect both horizontal and vertical stripes to be in its null-space. Therefore, we obtain perfect shape preservation for any regularisation parameter η. Note that 1-pixel-thick stripes are in the null-space as well (cf. Fig. 5 (left), where $f - u = 0$).

In Fig. 5 (centre) we can observe that rectangles are also well preserved with this filter. For better performance, however, one could additionally use a contrast preserving mechanism such as Bregman iteration or as in our case low-pass filtering. On the right, Fig. 5 illustrates how the diagonal filter is capable of removing diagonal structures in an image.

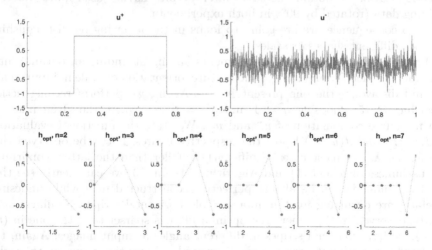

Fig. 1. Optimal filters in 1D setting for different sizes of h. Top: u^+ (left) and u^- (right). Bottom: Optimal filters choosing $n \in \{2, 3, \ldots, 7\}$ (from left to right).

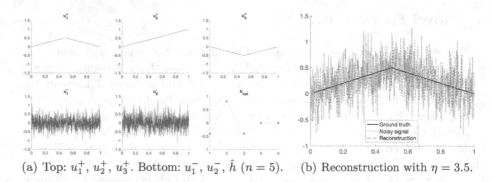

(a) Top: u_1^+, u_2^+, u_3^+. Bottom: u_1^-, u_2^-, $\hat{h}$ ($n = 5$).   (b) Reconstruction with $\eta = 3.5$.

Fig. 2. 1D result for multiple piecewise-linear input functions u_i^+ and noisy signals u_j^-.

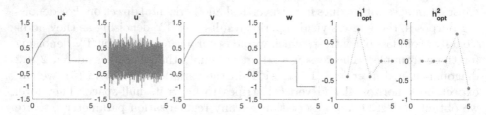

Fig. 3. 1D infimal convolution result for two filters ($n = 5$) and known decomposition $u^+ = v + w$. From left to right: u^+, u^-, v, w, $\hat{h}_1$, $\hat{h}_2$.

However, for denoising tasks this filter is not optimal. For images that do not consist exclusively of horizontal or vertical stripes it produces undesired artefacts in the reconstruction such as additional thin stripes in horizontal and vertical direction. Also, we obtain the same filter despite having used quite different training data (rotated by 90°) in both experiments.

As a consequence, we are going to focus in the following on distinguishing between different shapes or scales.

Figure 6 shows a variety of experiments aiming at finding an optimal filter function $\hat{h}$, which favours the specific texture, orientation or scale in input image u^+ and disfavours the one present in u^-. Again, we perform reconstruction according to (5) choosing $\eta = 1$ and $\sigma^2 = 0.005$, where the given image f is a noise-free combination of u^+ and u^-. We state the functional evaluations of $J(u^+; \hat{h})$ and $J(u^-; \hat{h})$ below the respective figures. It can be observed that the former are in most cases significantly smaller than the latter, confirming the usefulness of model (1) and Algorithm (4). In (a), we can clearly see that the left-hand-side can be almost perfectly reconstructed in $\hat{u}$ while undesired artefacts are occurring for the unfavourable horizontal stripes. Similar results can be observed in (b), where the optimal filter is sparser than the one in (a). In (c), we have diagonal stripes in different angles as input images. Again, the left-hand side is almost perfectly reconstructed whereas the stripes on the right-hand side appear blurred. In (d), the diagonal stripes are only one pixel thick

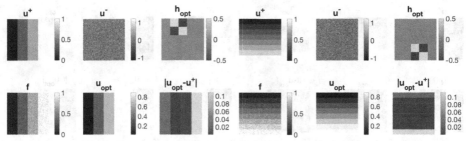

(a) Optimal filter and reconstruction for thick vertical stripes.

(b) Optimal filter and reconstruction for thin horizontal stripes.

Fig. 4. Experiments for 2D piecewise-constant images. Top: u^+ (ground truth for reconstruction), u^- (pure Gaussian noise, $\sigma = 0.3$), $\hat{h}$. Bottom: Noisy image f (Gaussian noise added to u^+, $\sigma^2 = 0.005$), reconstruction $\hat{u}$ ($\eta = 1$), absolute difference between reconstruction and ground truth.

and hence the appearance of the filter changes significantly. The regulariser is able to reconstruct the left-hand side of f very well. We exchange u^+ and u^- in (e) and (f). First, the circle is the desired and the square is the undesired input signal. The opposite case holds true for example (f). Here, again the diagonal-shaped filter performs best and blurs the circular structure enforcing edges in vertical and horizontal direction.

Sometimes it is necessary to find suitable filters by increasing their size, as can be seen in Fig. 7(a). On the right-hand side we can see the optimal filter calculated assuming a size of 5×5. By increasing the size slightly to 7×7, we obtain a much more reasonable filter being able to recover the circles. The filter itself almost resembles a circle with a radius of three pixels. In (b), given the ground truth image on the top left and four rotated versions of it in angles between 0 and 45° as favourable input as well as five noise signals as negative input, we obtain the filter on the bottom right, which performs surprisingly well at denoising the image on the top right.

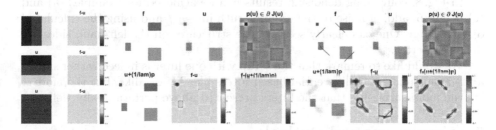

Fig. 5. The stripe images are in the novel diagonal filter's null-space (left). Rectangles can be well preserved (centre) and thin diagonal structures can be removed (right).

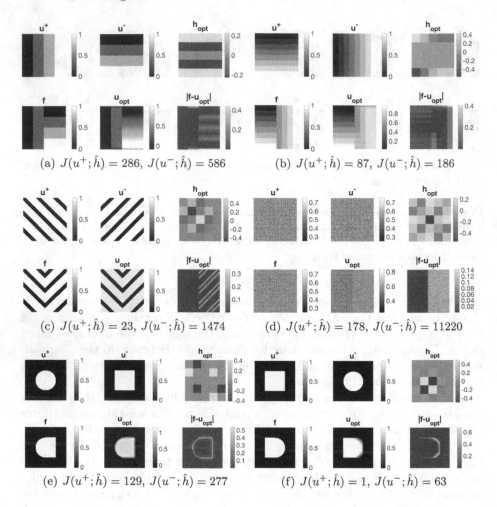

Fig. 6. Our learning framework facilitates distinguishing shapes, angles and scales.

In Fig. 8, convincing denoising results can be achieved for examples (a) and (c) in Fig. 6, adding noise to the ground truth image f and using the calculated optimal filter. One can clearly see that the structures on the left-hand sides are denoised better.

We would like to remark that the setup with one filter is indeed rather simple and cannot mimic 2D differential-based filters like TV or alike, but therefore it is even more surprising that the filters presented above perform really well.

5   Conclusions and Outlook

Starting from the model in [3], we derived a more generalised formulation suitable for minimisation with respect to multi-dimensional filter functions. In addition, our flexible framework allows for multiple desired and undesired input signals.

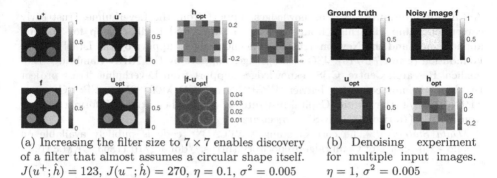

(a) Increasing the filter size to 7×7 enables discovery of a filter that almost assumes a circular shape itself. $J(u^+; \hat{h}) = 123$, $J(u^-; \hat{h}) = 270$, $\eta = 0.1$, $\sigma^2 = 0.005$

(b) Denoising experiment for multiple input images. $\eta = 1$, $\sigma^2 = 0.005$

Fig. 7. Further experiments: Increasing filter size and number of input images.

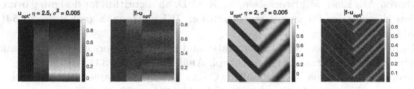

Fig. 8. Denoising performance of filters in Fig. 6 (a) and (c).

We were able to reproduce different common first- and second-order regularisers such as TV and TV^2 in the 1D case. Furthermore, we created a new family of non-derivative-based regularisers suitable for specific types of images. Also, we showed that specific shapes such as diagonal stripes can be eliminated while applying such parametrised regularisers. In addition, we believe that our learning approach is suitable for distinguishing between different shapes, scales and textures. A great advantage and novelty is that we are able to include both favourable and unfavourable input signals in our framework.

Regarding numerical implementation, we would like to stress that for computational simplicity in combination with the CVX framework we have only considered Dirichlet boundary conditions so far, but will use different boundary conditions (like the more suitable Neumann boundary conditions) in the future.

We further assume that the ansatz of filter functions respectively convolutions as parametrisations for the regularisers is too generic especially for denoising tasks. It will be interesting to look into dictionary-based sparsity approaches, and to then learn basis functions with the presented quotient model.

Moreover, future work might include applications in biomedical imaging such as reconstruction in CT or MRI as well as denoising or object detection in light microscopy images. In [19], the authors present a multiscale segmentation method for circulating tumour cells, where they are able to detect cells of different sizes. Using our model, we believe that shape or texture priors incorporated in sparsity-based regularisers could be well improved. One possible application could be mitotic cell detection (cf. [11]).

Acknowledgements.. MB acknowledges support from the Leverhulme Trust early career fellowship "Learning from mistakes: a supervised feedback-loop for imaging applications" and the Newton Trust. GG acknowledges support by the Israel Science Foundation (grant 718/15). JSG acknowledges support by the NIHR Cambridge Biomedical Research Centre. CBS acknowledges support from Leverhulme Trust project Breaking the non-convexity barrier, EPSRC grant EP/M00483X/1, EPSRC centre EP/N014588/1, the Cantab Capital Institute for the Mathematics of Information, and from CHiPS (Horizon 2020 RISE project grant).

Data Statement. The corresponding MATLAB® code is publicly available on Apollo - University of Cambridge Repository (https://doi.org/10.17863/CAM.8419).

References

1. Aharon, M., Elad, M., Bruckstein, A.: K-SVD: an algorithm for designing overcomplete dictionaries for sparse representation. IEEE Trans. Signal Process. **54**(11), 4311–4322 (2006)
2. Benning, M., Burger, M.: Ground states and singular vectors of convex variational regularization methods. Methods Appl. Anal. **20**(4), 295–334 (2013)
3. Benning, M., Gilboa, G., Schönlieb, C.-B.: Learning parametrised regularisation functions via quotient minimisation. PAMM **16**(1), 933–936 (2016)
4. Bolte, J., Sabach, S., Teboulle, M.: Proximal alternating linearized minimization for nonconvex and nonsmooth problems. Math. Program. **146**(1–2), 459–494 (2014)
5. Bresson, X., Laurent, T., Uminsky, D., Brecht, J.V.: Convergence and energy landscape for Cheeger cut clustering. In: Advances in Neural Information Processing Systems (2012)
6. Brox, T., Kleinschmidt, O., Cremers, D.: Efficient nonlocal means for denoising of textural patterns. IEEE Trans. Image Process. **17**(7), 1083–1092 (2008)
7. Bruckstein, A.M., Donoho, D.L., Elad, M.: From sparse solutions of systems of equations to sparse modeling of signals and images. SIAM Rev. **51**(1), 34–81 (2009)
8. De Los Reyes, J.C., Schönlieb, C.-B.: Image denoising: learning the noise model via nonsmooth PDE-constrained optimization. Inverse Probl. Imaging **7**(4), 1139–1155 (2013)
9. De Los Reyes, J.C., Schönlieb, C.-B., Valkonen, T.: Bilevel parameter learning for higher-order total variation regularisation models. J. Math. Imaging Vis., 1–25 (2016)
10. Gilboa, G.: Expert regularizers for task specific processing. In: Kuijper, A., Bredies, K., Pock, T., Bischof, H. (eds.) SSVM 2013. LNCS, vol. 7893, pp. 24–35. Springer, Heidelberg (2013). doi:10.1007/978-3-642-38267-3_3
11. Grah, J.S., Harrington, J., Koh, S.B., Pike, J., Schreiner, A., Burger, M., Schönlieb, C.-B., Reichelt, S.: Mathematical Imaging Methods for Mitosis Analysis in Live-Cell Phase Contrast Microscopy. arXiv preprint arXiv:1609.04649 (2016)
12. Grant, M., Boyd, S.: CVX: Matlab software for disciplined convex programming, version 2.1 (2016). http://cvxr.com/cvx
13. Hein, M., Bühler, T.: An inverse power method for nonlinear eigenproblems with applications in 1-spectral clustering and sparse PCA. In: Advances in Neural Information Processing Systems (2010)
14. Kunisch, K., Pock, T.: A bilevel optimization approach for parameter learning in variational models. SIAM J. Imaging Sci. **6**(2), 938–983 (2013)

15. Kurdyka, K.: On gradients of functions definable in o-minimal structures. Annales de l'institut Fourier **48**(3), 769–783 (1998)
16. Łojasiewicz, S.: Une propriété topologique des sous-ensembles analytiques réels. In: Les Équations aux Dérivées Partielles, pp. 87–89 (1963)
17. Papyan, V., Romano, Y., Elad, M.: Convolutional Neural Networks Analyzed via Convolutional Sparse Coding. arXiv preprint arXiv:1607.08194 (2016)
18. Schmidt, M.F., Benning, M., Schönlieb, C.-B.: Inverse Scale Space Decomposition. arXiv preprint arXiv:1612.09203 (2016)
19. Zeune, L., van Dalum, G., Terstappen, L., van Gils, S.A., Brune, C.: Multiscale Segmentation via Bregman Distances and Nonlinear Spectral Analysis. arXiv preprint arXiv:1604.06665 (2016)

Bregman-Proximal Augmented Lagrangian Approach to Multiphase Image Segmentation

Jing Yuan[1(✉)], Ke Yin[2], Yi-Guang Bai[1], Xiang-Chu Feng[1],
and Xue-Cheng Tai[3]

[1] School of Mathematics and Statistics, Xidian University, Xi'an, China
{jyuan,xcfeng}@xidian.edu.cn
[2] Center for Mathematical Sciences, Huazhong University of Science and Technology,
Wuhan, China
kyin@hust.edu.cn
[3] Mathematics Department, University of Bergen, Bergen, Norway
tai@math.uib.no

Abstract. This work studies the optimization problem of assigning multiple labels with the minimum perimeter, namely Potts model, in the spatially continuous setting. It was extensively studied within recent years and used to many different applications of image processing and computer vision, especially image segmentation. The existing convex relaxation approaches use total-variation functionals directly encoding perimeter costs, which result in pixelwise simplex constrained optimization problems and can be efficiently solved under a primal-dual perspective in numerics. Among most efficient approaches, such challenging simplex constraints are tackled either by extra projection steps to the simplex set at each pixel, which requires intensive simplex-projection computations, or by introducing extra dual variables resulting in the dual optimization-based *continuous max-flow formulation* to the studied convex relaxed Potts model. However, dealing with such extra dual flow variables needs additional loads in both computation and memory; particularly for the cases with many labels. To this end, we propose a novel optimization approach upon the *Bregman-Proximal Augmented Lagrangian Method (BPALM)*, for which the Bregman distance function, instead of the classical quadratic Euclidean distance function, is integrated in the algorithmic framework of Augmented Lagrangian Methods. The new optimization method has significant numerical advantages; it naturally avoids extra computational and memory burden in enforcing the simplex constraints and allows parallel computations over different labels. Numerical experiments show competitive performance in terms of quality and significantly reduced memory load compared to the state-of-the-art convex optimization methods for the convex relaxed Potts model.

1 Introduction

The multi-labeling problem in image processing and computer vision [18] was extensively studied, which searches the optimal labeling $l \in l_1, \ldots, l_n$ of image pixel. Computing such optimal labeling function with respect to some energy

© Springer International Publishing AG 2017
F. Lauze et al. (Eds.): SSVM 2017, LNCS 10302, pp. 524–534, 2017.
DOI: 10.1007/978-3-319-58771-4_42

functional is an important mathematical strategy to model a wide range of applications, e.g. image segmentation [5,17], 3D reconstruction [12] etc. In this work, we focus on the Potts model which minimizes the total perimeter of all the labelled regions and corresponds to a practically important special case of Markov Random Fields (MRFs) when in a discrete graph setting [16]. For more than two labels, solvng such typical MRF optimization problems is NP hard, where only provably good approximate solutions are guaranteed, for example, via α-expansion or $\alpha - \beta$ swap [5] and some LP relaxations [13,23]. Major drawbacks of such discrete optimization methods, however, exist: first, implementing computations and storages over graphs often consumes a high computer memory, especially for 3D or 4D image grids; second, the results are often biased by the discrete graph grid and cause metrication errors, while reducing such visual artifacts requires either adding more neighbour nodes [4,11] or applying high-order clique [10], both introduce extra computation and memory burden.

Based on the works of [8,17,20,27], the convex optimization-based methods have been proposed to study the same Potts model in the spatially continuous setting, which tries to partition the image domain Ω into n disjoint subdomains:

$$\min_{\{\Omega_i\}_{i=1}^n} \sum_{i=1}^n \int_{\Omega_i} \rho(l_i, x)\, dx + \lambda \sum_{i=1}^n |\partial\Omega_i| \tag{1}$$

$$\text{s.t.} \quad \cup_{i=1}^n \Omega_i = \Omega, \quad \Omega_k \cap \Omega_l = \emptyset,\, \forall k \neq l \tag{2}$$

where $|\partial\Omega_i|$ measures the perimeter of each disjoint subdomain Ω_i, $i = 1\ldots n$. The function $\rho(l_i, x), i = 1\ldots n$, evaluates the performance of assigning the label l_i to each pixel x. Clearly, Potts model favors the labeling with 'tight' boundaries.

Let $u_i(x), i = 1\ldots n$, denote the indicator function of the disjoint subdomain Ω_i, i.e. $u_i(x) = 1, i = 1\ldots n$, when $x \in \Omega_i$, or zero otherwise. Then the perimeter of each disjoint subdomain can be computed by

$$|\partial\Omega_i| = \int_\Omega |\nabla u_i|\, dx, \quad i = 1\ldots n. \tag{3}$$

Therefore, the spatially continuous Potts model (1) can be reformulated as

$$\min_{u_i(x)\in\{0,1\}} \sum_{i=1}^n \int_\Omega \{u_i(x)\rho(l_i, x) + \lambda|\nabla u_i|\}\, dx, \quad \text{s.t.} \quad \sum_{i=1}^n u_i(x) = 1,\, \forall x \in \Omega \tag{4}$$

where the constraints on $u_i(x)$, $i = 1\ldots n$, corresponds to the condition (2) of segmented regions. The optimization model (4) is obviously nonconvex and challenging due to the binary configuration of each function $u_i(x) \in \{0,1\}$.

The proposed *convex relaxed Potts model* [1,8,15,25] relax such binary constraints to the convex interval $[0,1]$ and approximates (4) by

$$\min_{u\in S} \sum_{i=1}^n \int_\Omega u_i(x)\, \rho(l_i, x)\, dx + \alpha \sum_{i=1}^n \int_\Omega |\nabla u_i|\, dx \tag{5}$$

where S is the convex constraint such that $u(x) := (u_1(x), \ldots, u_n(x)) \in \triangle_+$ and $\triangle_+$ is the simplex set, i.e.

$$\text{for } \forall x \in \Omega, \quad \sum_{i=1}^{n} u_i(x) = 1; \quad u_i(x) \in [0,1], \quad i = 1 \ldots n. \tag{6}$$

The computation result of the convex relaxed Potts model (5) gives rise to a cut of the continuous image domain Ω with multiple phases. Many convex optimization approaches to (5) were proposed, e.g. [1,8,15,20,25,27], using the standard primal-dual convex optimization theories [3], and achieved great advantages in numerical practices. Most works, e.g. [14,15,27], proposed to directly solve (5) in a functional splitting style, which explores alternating the projection to such pointwise simplex set (6) and tackling the total-variation-like function term at each iteration. In [8,19], the authors introduced another relaxation based on a multi-layered configuration, which was shown to be tighter. A more complex constraint on the dual variable p is given to avoid multiple countings. In addition, a PDE-based projection-descent scheme was applied to achieve its minimum. In contrast to [1,8,14,15,19,25,27] avoided directly tackling the convex relaxed Potts problem (5), but solved its equivalent dual model:

$$\max_{q_i \in C_\alpha} \int_\Omega \left\{ \min \left(\rho(l_1, x) + \text{div } q_1 \ldots \rho(l_n, x) + \text{div } q_n \right) \right\} dx. \tag{7}$$

where $\text{div } q_i$, $i = 1 \ldots n$, solves the dual formulation of the associated total-variation function and the convex set C_α is defined as $|q_i(x)| \leq \alpha$ for each $i = 1 \ldots n$. Interestingly, the final result labeling functions $u_i(x)$, $i = 1 \ldots n$, are just the optimum multipliers to the dual energy function of (7) [1,25]. [1] showed that the nonsmooth dual formulation (7) can be well approximated by the maximization of a smooth energy function with $s > 0$, i.e.

$$\max_{p_i \in C_\lambda} -s \int_\Omega \left\{ \log \sum_{i=1}^{n} \exp(\frac{-\rho_i - \text{div } q_i}{s}) \right\} dx. \tag{8}$$

Such a smooth dual model (8) approaches (7) with a smooth maximum-entropy regularizer and can be solved efficiently by a simple and reliable algorithmic scheme due to its smoothness and convexity. [25] actutally reformulated (7) by

$$\max_{p_s, p, q} \min_{u} \int_\Omega \left\{ (1 - \sum_{i=1}^{n} u_i) p_s + \sum_{i=1}^{n} u_i p_i + \sum_{i=1}^{n} u_i \text{ div } q_i \right\} dx \tag{9}$$

subject to $p_s(x)$ is free, $p_i(x) \leq \rho(\ell_i, x)$ and $q_i \in C_\alpha$, $i = 1 \ldots n$; where the first and second term of (9) imply the pixelwise simplex constraints on the labeling functions (6). With helps of the introduced extra 'flow' variables $p_s(x)$ and $p_i(x)$ in (9), [25] re-organized (9) and solved the convex relaxed Potts problem (5) by the so-called continuous max-flow model, based on the classical augmented lagrangian method, where a linear equality constraint of flow-balance at each image pixel was discovered in the spatially continuous setting.

Clearly, effectively handling the pixelwise simplex constraints (6) is the key step of solving the convex relaxed Potts problem (5): at each iteration, [8, 15, 19, 27] explicitly computed the projection to the constraint set at each pixel; in contrast, [25] implemented such projections implicitly by introducing the extra dual 'flow' variables, which successfully avoided all the computing steps w.r.t. the projections to a simplex set and resulted in an efficient algorithm using the classical augmented lagrangian method; however, when the total number of labels or the image size is big, it is expected that such introduced dual 'flow' variables dramatically increase both memory and computation burden so as to store and update such additional dual 'flow' variables at each iteration.

1.1 Contributions

In this work, we propose a novel optimization approach to the convex relaxed Potts model (5) upon a new optimization framework using the *Bregman Proximal Augmented Lagrangian Method (BPALM)* which essentially utilizes the general Bregman distance function, instead of the classical quadratic Euclidean distance, for updating the dual multipliers, therefore enjoys great numerical advantages. In comparison to [8, 15, 19, 27], the introduced algorithm successfully avoids explicit computation of projections to the simplex at each pixel, which essentially reduces extra computations; in contrast to the recently proposed continuous max-flow method [24–26], the new algorithm does not require additional flow variables to implicitly enforce such pixelwise simplex constraints, hence essentially decreases the required memory load for computing, particularly for the cases with a big number of labels or large image scale. Experiments showed our new algorithm reached a comparatively faster convergence rate than the proposed continuous max-flow algorithm [25]; and used much less memory load!

2 Bregman Proximal Optimization Method

In this section, we introduce a novel method, under the optimization framework of *Bregman Proximal Augmented Lagrangian Method (BPALM)* [9, 22], to solve the dual convex relaxed Potts model (7). It follows the algorithmic framework of the classical Augmented Lagrangian Method (ALM), but applies the general Bregman distance function, e.g. the entropy Kullback-Leibler distance, for updating dual multipliers. The proposed optimization method converges to the optimum multipliers to (7) which just corresponds to the optimum labeling functions to the convex relaxed Potts problem (5).

Classical Augmented Lagrangian Method to (5). As in [25], we can re-organize the equivalent primal-dual formulation (9) to (5) as follows:

$$\max_{p_s,p,q} \min_u \left\{ L(p_s, p, q, u) := \int_\Omega p_s \, dx + \sum_{i=1}^n \int_\Omega u_i (\operatorname{div} q_i - p_s + p_i) \, dx \right\} \quad (10)$$

$$\text{s.t.} \quad p_i(x) \le \rho(\ell_i, x), \quad |q_i(x)| \le \alpha; \quad i = 1 \dots n$$

Minimizing (10) over the labeling function $u(x)$ first results in an equivalent flow-maximization problem, i.e. the so-called continuous max-flow model [25]:

$$\max_{p_s, p, q} \int_\Omega p_s \, dx \tag{11}$$

subject to

$$|q_i(x)| \leq \alpha, \quad p_i(x) \leq \rho(\ell_i, x), \quad i = 1 \ldots n; \tag{12}$$

$$\big(\operatorname{div} q_i - p_s + p_i\big)(x) = 0, \quad i = 1, \ldots, n. \tag{13}$$

In view of the linear equality constraints (13), the energy function of (10) is the Lagrangian function to the continuous max-flow model (11), and the computed labeling function u is just the optimum multiplier function to such linear equality constraints (13) [25]. Given the classical framework of the ALM (21) and (22), we define the augmented Lagrangian function (20) w.r.t. the Lagrangian function $L(p_s, p, q, u)$ of (10) such that

$$\tilde{L}_c(p_s, p, q, u) := L(p_s, p, q, u) - \frac{c}{2}\|\operatorname{div} q_i - p_s + p_i\|^2;$$

the classical ALM, therefore, results in the so-called *continuous max-flow algorithm* [25] (see Algorithm 1).

Algorithm 1. Classical Augmented Lagrangian Method Based Algorithm

Initialize all the variables (p_s, p, q, u); for each k-th iteration, perform the following steps until convergence:

– Maximize $\tilde{L}_{c^k}(p_s, p, q, u)$ over the flow variables p_s, p and q respectively by

$$p_s^{k+1} := \arg\max_{p_s} \tilde{L}_{c^k}(p_s, p^k, q^k, u^k); \tag{14}$$

$$p^{k+1} := \arg\max_{p} \tilde{L}_{c^k}(p_s^{k+1}, p, q^k, u^k), \quad \text{s.t. (12)}; \tag{15}$$

$$q^{k+1} := \arg\max_{q} \tilde{L}_{c^k}(p_s^{k+1}, p^{k+1}, q, u^k), \quad \text{s.t. (12)}; \tag{16}$$

which can be solved approximately by one iteration of projected gradient.
– Update the labeling function u by

$$u_i^{k+1} = u_i^k - c^k\big(\operatorname{div} q_i^{k+1} - p_s^{k+1} + p_i^{k+1}\big), \tag{17}$$

for $i = 1, \ldots, n$.

Bregman Proximal Augmented Lagrangian Method (BPALM). In order to introduce the new optimization method to (5), now we consider the following primal-dual optimization problem which generalizes the optimization problem (7) studied in this paper:

$$\min_{u \in C_u} \max_{p \in C_p} L(p, u) = f(p) + \langle u, G(p)\rangle \tag{18}$$

where the function $f(p)$ is convex, $G(p)$ is a linear function, C_u and C_p are the respective constraints on u and p. Clearly, when there is no constraint on u, i.e. C_u is the whole domain space of u (often a Hilbert space), minimizing (18) over u gives the following constrained maximization problem

$$\max_{q \in C_p} f(p), \quad \text{s.t. } G(p) \equiv 0. \tag{19}$$

Then the classical ALM can be applied to solve such linear constrained optimization problem (19) using the following augmented Lagrangian function:

$$\tilde{L}_c(p, u) = f(p) + \langle u, G(p) \rangle - \frac{c}{2}\|G(p)\|^2; \tag{20}$$

and boils down to two subsequent steps at each k-th iteration:

$$p^{k+1} = \arg\max_{p \in C_p} \tilde{L}_{c^k}(p, u^k), \tag{21}$$

$$u^{k+1} = u^k - c^k G(p^{k+1}), \tag{22}$$

where $c_k > 0$ is the step-size at k-th iteration.

Especially, [22] showed the above classical augmented Lagrangian function $\tilde{L}_{c^k}(p, u^k)$ (20) at each k-th iteration can be viewed as a proximal to u^k [7,21]

$$\tilde{L}_{c^k}(p, u^k) = \min_u \left\{ f(p) + \langle u, G(p) \rangle + \frac{1}{2c^k}\|u - u^k\|^2 \right\}, \tag{23}$$

hence the two optimization steps (21)–(22) of the classical ALM are just the two optimization steps over the primal and dual variables p and u respectively! In this way, [22] further demonstrated the quadratic Euclidean distance function defining such classical augmented Lagrangian function (23) can be replaced by the generalized Bregman distance function [6]

$$D_g(u, u^k) = g(u) - g(u^k) - \langle \partial g(u^k), u - u^k \rangle, \tag{24}$$

where $g(x)$ is a differentiable and strictly convex function.

Clearly, the Bregman distance (24) provides a quite general conception on the proximity measurement: for example, the function $g(x) = \frac{1}{2}\|x\|^2$ just gives the often-used squared Euclidean distance $\frac{1}{2}\|x - y\|^2$; the entropy function for the vector $x := (x_1, \ldots, x_n) \in (\mathbb{R}^+)^n$

$$g(x) = \sum_i (x_i \log x_i - x_i)$$

results in the generalized *Kullback-Leibler* divergence of two vectors $x, y \in (\mathbb{R}^+)^n$ such that

$$D_g(x, y) = \sum_{i=1}^n \left(x_i \log(x_i/y_i) - x_i + y_i \right), \tag{25}$$

see also [2] for the definitions of more Bregman distances.

On the other hand, such Bregman distance function can deal with the constraint $u \in C_u$ much easier, which, then, gives rise to a generalized version of ALM, namely the *Bregman Proximal Augmented Lagrangian Method (BPALM)* in this paper. Given the Lagrangian function $L(p, u)$ in (18) and Bregman distance function (24), its generalized augmented Lagrangian function at k-th iteration can be essentially obtained as follows [6]:

$$L_{c^k}(p, u^k) := \min_{u \in C_u} \left\{ f(p) + \langle u, G(p) \rangle + \frac{1}{c^k} D_g(u, u^k) \right\}. \tag{26}$$

By simple computation, the so-called *BPALM* algorithm just iterates the following two subsequent steps at each k-th iteration:

$$p^{k+1} = \arg\max_{p \in C_p} f(p) + \frac{1}{c^k} g^* [\partial g(u^k) - c^k G(p)], \tag{27}$$

$$u^{k+1} = \partial g^{-1} [\partial g(u^k) - c^k G(p^{k+1})], \tag{28}$$

where $g^*(\cdot)$ is the conjugate of the convex function $g(u)$ such that $g^*(q) = \max_u \{\langle u, q \rangle - g(u)\}$. In this paper, we focus on the *Kullback-Leibler (KL)* distance (25) based *BPALM* to solve the convex relaxed Potts problem (5).

Bregman Proximal Augmented Lagrangian Method to (5). Considering (7), the convex relaxed Potts problem (5) can be equally expressed as

$$\min_{u \in S} \max_{|q_i(x)| \leq \alpha} L(q, u) = \int_\Omega \sum_{i=1}^n u_i \left(\rho_i + \text{div } q_i \right) dx. \tag{29}$$

where S is pixelwise simplex constraints as defined in (6).

For any two functions $u(x), v(x) \in S$, we use the Kullback-Leibler distance function (25)

$$KL(u, v) = \int_\Omega \sum_{i=1}^n u_i \log(\frac{u_i}{v_i}) dx,$$

to measure their entropy proximity/distance within a simplex set. Then, we can define the corresponding augmented Lagrangian function (26) such that

$$L_{c^k}(q, u^k) = \min_{u \in S} L(q, u) + \frac{1}{c^k} KL(u, u^k) \tag{30}$$

$$= -c \int_\Omega \log \left\{ \sum_{i=1}^n u_i^k \exp \left(- \frac{\rho_i + \text{div } q_i}{c} \right) \right\} dx, \tag{31}$$

where $c^k > 0$ is the step-size at k-th iteration. This generates novel *BPALM* algorithmic steps (27) and (28) for solving (5) (see also Algorithm 2).

Note: Comparing to the classical ALM based algorithm (Algorithm 1), it is easy to see that the new KL-distance based *BPALM* gives rise to the new algorithm (Algorithm 2) using much less variables. In contrast, the classical ALM based

---

Algorithm 2. Bregman Proximal Augmented Lagrangian Method Based Alg.

Initialize $u^i(x) \in (0, 1)$ $\forall x \in \Omega$ and q_i, for each $k = 1, \ldots$, perform the following steps:

- Maximize over the flows q by

$$q_i^{k+1} := \arg \max_{|q_i(x)| \leq \alpha} L_c(q_{j<i}^{k+1}, q_i, q_{j>i}^k, u^k); \qquad (32)$$

which can be solved approximately by one iteration of projected gradient.
- Update the message function u by

$$u_i^{k+1} := \frac{u_i^k \exp(-G_i^{k+1}/c)}{\sum_{j=1}^n u_j^k \exp(-G_j^{k+1}/c)}, \qquad (33)$$

where for $\forall x \in \Omega$

$$G_i^{k+1}(x) = (\rho_i + \operatorname{div} q_i^{k+1})(x).$$

---

algorithm is actually obtained from the primal-dual model (9) (equivalent to (10)) which essentially applies the additional flow variables $p_s(x)$ and $p_i(x)$, $i = 1 \ldots n$, to force the lableing functions $u_i(x)$, $i = 1 \ldots n$, within the pixelwise simplex set S; in practical computation, the labeling functions $u_i(x)$, $i = 1 \ldots n$, initially do not satisfy the simplex constraint at each pixel, but its optimization orbit $u^k(x)$ is forced to finally fall into such pixelwise simplex constraint, i.e. an outer projection orbit. Yet, the new *BPALM* based algorithm comes from an equivalent optimization formulation (29) and omitts using the extra flow variables $p_s(x)$ and $p_i(x)$, $i = 1 \ldots n$, where the KL-proximal optimization of (30) generates an optimization orbit $u^k(x)$, $k = 1 \ldots$, which exactly locates inside the pixelwise simplex constraint at each iteration, i.e. an inner projection orbit. Obviously, the new *BPALM* algorithm (Algorithm 2) requires less memory load and less computation steps at each iteration; this provides many advantages in numerics, especially while the total number of labels or the image size becomes big. We will show this in the following experiment section.

3   Experiments

In this section, we make experiments to validate and compare the two algorithms of Algorithms 1 and 2 to the convex relaxed Potts problem (5), which are both obatined from an ALM-like optimization framework but with different distance metrics, i.e. the quadratic Euclidean distance and KL distance. Distinct from the state-of-the-art methods [8,15,19,27], both algorithms do not require explicitly computing the projection to the simplex set at each pixel, hence need less computation load.

Examples are given in Fig. 1, where we have used the Mumford-Shah data term $\rho_i(x) = |I(x) - \ell_i|^2$, $i = 1, \ldots, n$. The initialization of the classical ALM algorithm (Algorithm 1) is $u_l(x) = 1$ and $u_{i \neq j}(x) = 0$ $i = 1 \ldots n$, when $\rho_j(x)$

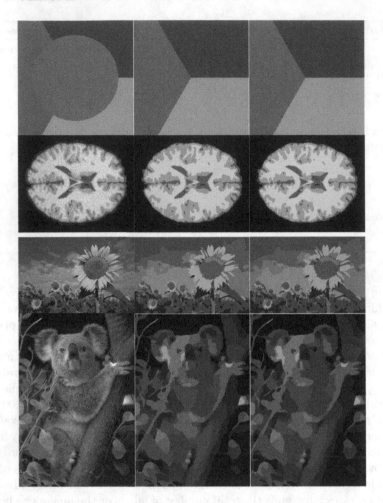

Fig. 1. Each row (from left to right): the input image, results by the classical ALM (Algorithm 1), results by the new *BPALM* (Algorithm 2). For all the experiments, we use the same parameters for both algorithms: 1st row (inpainting in gray area), $(\alpha, n) = (0.03, 3)$; 2nd row, $(\alpha, n) = (0.04, 4)$; 3rd row, $(\alpha, n) = (0.047, 10)$; 4th row, $(\alpha, n) = (0.02, 8)$.

is the minimum of all $\rho_i(x)$ $i = 1 \ldots n$; and the initialization of the Bregman proximal augmented Lagrangian algorithm (Algorithm 2) is $u_i(x) = 1/n$, $i = 1 \ldots n$, i.e. all labeling functions are initialized with equal value $1/n$. As we see, both algorithms of Algorithms 1 and 2 obtained equally good solutions. This is expected as both of them should theoretically converge to the same result.

In our experiments, both algorithms reached convergence using a wide range of step-size $c > 0$. For convergence measure, we find a good estimate of the final energy E^* by solving the problem with over 2000 iterations, and the convergence evaluation at each iteration k is then measured by $\epsilon = \frac{E^k - E^*}{E^*}$. For the three experiments (see Fig. 1) and the chosen precision $\epsilon \leq 10^{-4}$, both the total number of iterations to reach convergence and memory load are evaluated for comparison, see Table 1; the proposed *BPALM* Algorithm 2 obtained a relatively faster convergence along with much less memory burden!

Table 1. Compare both algorithms of Algorithms 1 and 2: for the last three different experiments (see Fig. 1) with the precision $\epsilon \leq 10^{-4}$; for each experiment, both the total iteration numbers and memory load are evaluated for comparison. As we see, Algorithm 2 reached convergence with less iterations and memory burden!

	Brain $\epsilon \leq 10^{-4}$	Flower $\epsilon \leq 10^{-4}$	Bear $\epsilon \leq 10^{-4}$
Algorithm 1	62 iter., 56.9 MB	147 iter., 136.3 MB	133 iter., 75.7 MB
Algorithm 2	55 **iter., 40.2 MB**	135 **iter., 86.5 MB**	128 iter., **52.3 MB**

4   Conclusions

In this paper, we introduce and study a novel Bregman-proximal ALM to solve the convex relaxed Potts model (5) which has essentially many applications in image processing and computer vision. Comparing to the classical ALM based algorithm, i.e. the continuous max-flow algorithm, the new *BPALM* based algorithm obtains comparatively faster convergence, and requires much less memory load due to omitting extra flow variables to enforce the pixelwise simplex constraint. Under the perspective of the introduced *BPALM*, it is expected that the other different Bregman distance functions from different convex functions can be used to generate new algorithmic schemes, for example $g(v) = -\log(v)$, with applications to many other problems in image processing and computer vision.

References

1. Bae, E., Yuan, J., Tai, X.C.: Global minimization for continuous multiphase partitioning problems using a dual approach. Technical report CAM09-75, UCLA, CAM, September 2009
2. Banerjee, A., Merugu, S., Dhillon, I.S., Ghosh, J.: Clustering with bregman divergences. J. Mach. Learn. Res. **6**, 1705–1749 (2005)
3. Bertsekas, D.P.: Nonlinear Programming. Athena Scientific, Belmont (1999)
4. Boykov, Y., Kolmogorov, V.: Computing geodesics and minimal surfaces via graph cuts. In: ICCV 2003, pp. 26–33 (2003)
5. Boykov, Y., Veksler, O., Zabih, R.: Fast approximate energy minimization via graph cuts. IEEE Trans. Pattern Anal. Mach. Intell. **23**, 1222–1239 (2001)
6. Bregman, L.M.: The relaxation method of finding the common point of convex sets and its application to the solution of problems in convex programming. USSR Comput. Math. Math. Phys. **7**, 200–217 (1967)
7. Censor, Y.A., Zenios, S.A.: Parallel Optimization: Theory, Algorithms and Applications. Oxford University Press, Oxford (1997)

8. Chambolle, A., Cremers, D., Pock, T.: A convex approach for computing minimal partitions. Technical report TR-2008-05, Department of Computer Science, University of Bonn, Bonn, Germany, November 2008
9. Iusem, A.N., Svaiter, B.F., Teboulle, M.: Entropy-like proximal methods in convex programming. Math. Oper. Res. **19**(4), 790–814 (1994)
10. Kohli, P., Kumar, M.P., Torr, P.H.S.: p^3 and beyond: move making algorithms for solving higher order functions. IEEE Trans. Pattern Anal. Mach. Intell. **31**(9), 1645–1656 (2009)
11. Kolmogorov, V.: What metrics can be approximated by geo-cuts, or global optimization of length/area and flux. In: ICCV, pp. 564–571 (2005)
12. Kolmogorov, V., Zabih, R.: Multi-camera scene reconstruction via graph cuts. In: Heyden, A., Sparr, G., Nielsen, M., Johansen, P. (eds.) ECCV 2002. LNCS, vol. 2352, pp. 82–96. Springer, Heidelberg (2002). doi:10.1007/3-540-47977-5_6
13. Komodakis, N., Tziritas, G.: Approximate labeling via graph-cuts based on linear programming. Pattern Anal. Mach. Intell. **29**, 1436–1453 (2007)
14. Lellmann, J., Becker, F., Schnörr, C.: Convex optimization for multi-class image labeling with a novel family of total variation based regularizers. In: ICCV, pp. 646–653 (2009)
15. Lellmann, J., Kappes, J., Yuan, J., Becker, F., Schnörr, C.: Convex multi-class image labeling by simplex-constrained total variation. Technical report, HCI, IWR, University Heidelberg, IWR, University Heidelberg, November 2008
16. Li, S.Z.: Markov Random Field Modeling in Image Analysis. Springer-Verlag New York, Inc., Secaucus (2001)
17. Nikolova, M., Esedoglu, S., Chan, T.F.: Algorithms for finding global minimizers of image segmentation and denoising models. SIAM J. App. Math. **66**(5), 1632–1648 (2006)
18. Paragios, N., Chen, Y., Faugeras, O.: Handbook of Mathematical Models in Computer Vision. Springer-Verlag New York, Inc., Secaucus (2005)
19. Pock, T., Chambolle, A., Bischof, H., Cremers, D.: A convex relaxation approachfor computing minimal partitions. In: CVPR, Miami, Florida (2009)
20. Pock, T., Schoenemann, T., Graber, G., Bischof, H., Cremers, D.: A convex formulation of continuous multi-label problems. In: Forsyth, D., Torr, P., Zisserman, A. (eds.) ECCV 2008. LNCS, vol. 5304, pp. 792–805. Springer, Heidelberg (2008). doi:10.1007/978-3-540-88690-7_59
21. Rockafellar, R.T.: Convex Analysis. Princeton Mathematical Series, vol. 28. Princeton University Press, Princeton (1970)
22. Teboulle, M.: Entropic proximal mappings with applications to nonlinear programming. Math. Oper. Res. **17**(3), 670–690 (1992)
23. Wainwright, M., Jaakkola, T., Willsky, A.: Map estimation via agreement on (hyper)trees: message-passing and linear programming approaches. IEEE Trans. Inf. Theory **51**, 3697–3717 (2002)
24. Yuan, J., Bae, E., Tai, X.C.: A study on continuous max-flow and min-cut approaches. In: CVPR, San Francisco, USA (2010)
25. Yuan, J., Bae, E., Tai, X.-C., Boykov, Y.: A continuous max-flow approach to potts model. In: Daniilidis, K., Maragos, P., Paragios, N. (eds.) ECCV 2010. LNCS, vol. 6316, pp. 379–392. Springer, Heidelberg (2010). doi:10.1007/978-3-642-15567-3_28
26. Yuan, J., Bae, E., Tai, X.-C., Boykov, Y.: A spatially continuous max-flow and min-cut framework for binary labeling problems. Numerische Mathematik **126**(3), 559–587 (2014)
27. Zach, C., Gallup, D., Frahm, J.-M., Niethammer, M.: Fast global labeling for real-time stereo using multiple plane sweeps. In: Vision, Modeling and Visualization Workshop (VMV) (2008)

Optical Flow, Motion Estimation and Registration

A Comparison of Isotropic and Anisotropic Second Order Regularisers for Optical Flow

Daniel Maurer$^{(\boxtimes)}$, Michael Stoll, Sebastian Volz,
Patrick Gairing, and Andrés Bruhn

Computer Vision and Intelligent Systems Group,
Institute for Visualization and Interactive Systems,
University of Stuttgart, 70569 Stuttgart, Germany
{maurer,stoll,volz,gairing,bruhn}@vis.uni-stuttgart.de

Abstract. In variational optical flow estimation, second order regularisation plays an important role, since it offers advantages in the context
of non-fronto-parallel motion. However, in contrast to first order smoothness constraints, most second order regularisers are limited to isotropic
concepts. Moreover, the few existing anisotropic concepts are lacking
a comparison so far. Hence, our contribution is twofold. (i) First, we
juxtapose general concepts for isotropic and anisotropic second order
regularization based on direct second order methods, infimal convolution techniques, and indirect coupling models. For all the aforementioned
strategies suitable optical flow regularisers are derived. (ii) Second, we
show that modelling anisotropic second order smoothness terms gives an
additional degree of freedom when penalising deviations from smoothness. This in turn allows us to propose a novel anisotropic strategy
which we call double anisotropic regularisation. Experiments on the two
KITTI benchmarks show the qualitative differences between the different
strategies. Moreover, they demonstrate that the novel concept of double
anisotropic regularisation is able to produce excellent results.

Keywords: Higher order regularisation · Variational methods · Optical
flow

1 Introduction

Due to their intrinsic capability to fill-in missing information from the neighbourhood, variational methods are among the most popular techniques in computer
vision. In particular, they are often applied in the context of ill-posed problems,
where regularisation is needed to provide meaningful results. One of such problems is the estimation of the optical flow. Thereby, the task is to compute the
displacement vector field between two consecutive frames of an image sequence.
While many variational optical flow methods rely on first order smoothness terms
[3,18,27,32,34], approaches based on second order regularisation have recently
gained more and more attention [1,7,11,23,28]. In particular in scenes with ego

© Springer International Publishing AG 2017
F. Lauze et al. (Eds.): SSVM 2017, LNCS 10302, pp. 537–549, 2017.
DOI: 10.1007/978-3-319-58771-4_43

motion, they allow to estimate piecewise affine flow fields which cannot be captured adequately by first order smoothness terms; see e.g. [23].

However, compared to other applications such as denoising or stereo reconstruction, second order smoothness terms are still used comparably seldom for computing the optical flow. Hence, in the following, we give a brief overview over existing strategies to model second order smoothness terms that is not restricted to the task of optical flow estimation only. We thereby focus on local strategies, i.e. smoothness terms that do not make use of larger neighbourhoods; cf. [22]. In general, these strategies can be roughly divided into three classes:

Direct Approaches. The probably most intuitive way to model second order smoothness assumptions is to penalise second order derivatives of the sought functions directly. We will refer to the corresponding methods as direct approaches. Such methods include e.g. the Hessian [7,13,16,26,29], the Laplacian [5,16] and operators based on decorrelated second order derivatives [28]. However, this does not allow to model discontinuities in the first order derivatives, and hence does not preserve jumps equally well as first order approaches.

Combined Approaches. In order to tackle this problem, direct first and second order regularisers can be combined. This can be done in two ways. On the one hand, both regularisers can be applied at the same time. Thereby, switching can be realised with a spatially adaptive weights [15]. On the other hand, one can additively split the unknowns in two or more layers and apply a separate regularisation to each of the layers in terms of an infimal convolution [4]. This, however, requires to cope with additional unknowns.

Indirect Approaches. A third class is given by indirect approaches, which can often be interpreted as coupling models. These approaches are typically realised using auxiliary functions which approximate first order derivatives, and regularisers that enforce smoothness assumptions on these auxiliary functions. This in turn allows to model discontinuities in both first and second order derivatives. Such methods include e.g. the total generalised variation (TGV) [1,2] and its variants [8,10,11,21,23]. To the same group one may also count overparametrised approaches [19], which approximate a second order regularisation by introducing an affine-parametrisation of the unknowns and using a first order regularisation of the coefficients. However, as shown in [28] this is not fully equivalent to second order regularisation.

A second important concept in the modelling of smoothness terms besides the consideration of higher order regularisers is the use of directional information. Such anisotropic strategies have proven to be beneficial not only in the context of first order regularisers [18,27,32,34], but also w.r.t. second order smoothness terms [8,10,15,21]. Lenzen *et al.* [15] embedded such concepts in a combined approach, where image information is used to steer the directions. Regarding indirect approaches, Ranftl *et al.* [21], Ranftl [23] and Ferstl *et al.* [8] introduced similar concepts into the coupling term, which connects the auxiliary functions and the first order derivatives. Recently, Hafner *et al.* [10] extended this work by introducing the anisotropy not only in the coupling term but also in the smoothness term, which enforces directional smoothness on the auxiliary functions.

Please note that, from all the above mentioned approaches only the works [1,7,11,19,23,28] have been proposed in the context of optical flow estimation and only one of them [23] makes use of anisotropic strategies. Moreover, as observed in [14], introducing anisotropic concepts in higher order smoothness terms allows to choose different penalisation strategies related to different degrees of anisotropy – in contrast to the first order case. Hence, not only the question persists which of the three aforementioned classes performs best in the context of optical flow estimation, but also which degree of anisotropy is most suitable when modelling second order smoothness terms for this task.

Contributions. In our paper, we address both questions. On the one hand, we investigate and compare representative approaches of the three abovementioned classes and demonstrate the benefits of introducing anisotropic concepts in each of these classes. On the other hand, we propose a novel anisotropic second order regularisation strategy that exceeds existing optical flow regularisers regarding the degree of anisotropy. Results for the KITTI benchmark confirm our findings.

Organisation. In Sect. 2 we introduce our variational framework based on the recent work of Demetz et al. [7]. In Sect. 3 we then discuss one representative isotropic regularisation technique for each of the three classes and derive our anisotropic counterparts. After briefly sketching the minimisation in Sect. 4, we present a qualitative and quantitative evaluation of the introduced regularisers in Sect. 5. Finally, we conclude with a summary in Sect. 6.

2   Variational Model for Optical Flow

Let us start by introducing our baseline approach. To this end, we consider the recent method Demetz et al. [7] that explicitly models local illumination changes in terms of a set of coefficient fields. Given two consecutive frames I_0, $I_1 : \Omega \to \mathbb{R}$ of an image sequence, the method seeks to compute both the flow field $\mathbf{w} = (u, v)^\top : \Omega \to \mathbb{R}^2$ and the set of coefficients $\mathbf{c} = (c_0, \dots, c_{N-1})^\top : \Omega \to \mathbb{R}^N$ as minimiser of the following energy functional:

$$E(\mathbf{w}, \mathbf{c}) = \int_\Omega D(\mathbf{w}, \mathbf{c}) + \beta \cdot R_{\text{illum}}(\mathbf{c}) + \alpha \cdot R_{\text{flow}}(\mathbf{w}) \, d\mathbf{x}, \tag{1}$$

where $\mathbf{x} = (x, y)^\top \in \Omega$ denotes the location within a rectangular image domain Ω. It consists of a data term D, a regulariser R_{illum} for the coefficients as well as a regulariser R_{flow} for the flow field. The parameters α and β allow to steer the relative impact of the terms.

The data term consists of an illumination compensated brightness and gradient constancy assumption. It reads

$$D(\mathbf{w}, \mathbf{c}) = \Psi_D \left((I_1(\mathbf{x} + \mathbf{w}) - \Phi(I_0(\mathbf{x}), \mathbf{c}))^2 \right)$$
$$+ \gamma \cdot \Psi_D \left(\|\nabla I_1(\mathbf{x} + \mathbf{w}) - \nabla \Phi(I_0(\mathbf{x}), \mathbf{c})\|_2^2 \right) \tag{2}$$

where $\Psi_D(s^2) = 2\epsilon^2 \sqrt{1 + s^2/\epsilon^2}$ is the Charbonnier penaliser [6], γ is a weighting parameter and $\Phi(I, \mathbf{c})$ is a parametrised brightness transfer function. In contrast to [7] we choose a normalised affine brightness transfer function given by

$$\Phi(I, \mathbf{c}) = I + \sum_{i=0}^{1} c_i \cdot \phi_i(I), \quad \text{with} \quad \phi_0(I) = \frac{I}{n_0}, \quad \text{and} \quad \phi_1(I) = \frac{1}{n_1}, \qquad (3)$$

where n_0 and n_1 are normalisation factors such that $\|\phi_i(I)\|_2 = \left(\int \phi_i^2(I) \, dI \right)^{\frac{1}{2}} = 1$. Typically, such an affine basis is sufficient, since it can handle most illumination changes, while offering a lower complexity compared to a learned basis as in [7].

Regarding the coefficient regulariser R_{illum} we follow the original work and apply anisotropic first order regularisation [34]. The corresponding smoothness term can essentially be derived from Eq. (6) by replacing the flow field u, v with the coefficients field c_0, c_1. The main focus of the following section, however, lies on the comparison of different first and second order strategies for R_{flow}.

3 Flow Regularisers

3.1 First Order Regularisation

Isotropic. Since the seminal work of Horn and Schunck [12] first order regularisers have a long tradition. Even today, such regularisers are still frequently used; see e.g. [24]. A well-known isotropic variant is given by [3]:

$$R_{\text{1-iso}}(\mathbf{w}) = \Psi \left(|\nabla u|^2 + |\nabla v|^2 \right) . \qquad (4)$$

where Ψ is a penaliser function that allows to preserve discontinuities in the flow field, e.g. $\Psi(s^2) = 2\epsilon^2 \sqrt{1 + s^2/\epsilon^2}$ [6]. This type of smoothness term also comprises the well-known total variation regularisation (TV) [25,33].

Anisotropic. In order to improve the performance at object boundaries, i.e. by smoothing along object edges but not across them, several anisotropic extensions have been proposed. Going back to the work of Nagel and Enkelmann [18], the idea is to exploit directional information to steer the smoothing [27,31,32,34]. Let us first rewrite Eq. (4) using the unit vectors $\mathbf{e}_1 = (1, 0)^\top$ and $\mathbf{e}_2 = (0, 1)^\top$:

$$R_{\text{1-iso}}(\mathbf{w}) = \Psi \left(\sum_{l=1}^{2} \left(\mathbf{e}_l^\top \nabla u \right)^2 + \left(\mathbf{e}_l^\top \nabla v \right)^2 \right) . \qquad (5)$$

Here, $\mathbf{e}_l^\top \nabla u$ and $\mathbf{e}_l^\top \nabla v$ are the directional derivatives $\partial_{\mathbf{e}_l} u$ and $\partial_{\mathbf{e}_l} v$, respectively. By replacing the unit vectors $\mathbf{e}_1$, $\mathbf{e}_2$ with locally varying directions $\mathbf{r}_1$, $\mathbf{r}_2$, which form an orthonormal basis, *and* by applying the penalisation to both directions separately, we obtain the anisotropic counterpart of Eq. (4) given by [27,34]:

$$R_{\text{1-aniso}}(\mathbf{w}) = \sum_{l=1}^{2} \Psi_l \left(\left(\mathbf{r}_l^\top \nabla u \right)^2 + \left(\mathbf{r}_l^\top \nabla v \right)^2 \right) . \qquad (6)$$

Please note that this model comprises the complementary regulariser from [34]. For determining the local directions $\mathbf{r}_1$, $\mathbf{r}_2$, one can use the eigenvectors of either the structure tensor [27] or the regularisation tensor [34].

3.2   Direct Second Order Regularisation

Isotropic. The probably most intuitive way to model second order smoothness assumptions is to penalise the second order derivatives of the flow directly. A prominent isotropic example is based on the Hessian [7]

$$R_{2\text{-iso}}(\mathbf{w}) = \Psi\left(\|\mathcal{H}u\|_F^2 + \|\mathcal{H}v\|_F^2\right),\tag{7}$$

where $\|\cdot\|_F$ is the Frobenius norm, and $\mathcal{H}u$ and $\mathcal{H}v$ is the Hessian of u and v, respectively. It is also used in denoising [16,26] and shape from shading [29]. Other matrix norms generalising the Frobenius norm, e.g. l_p-norms [26] $(p = 1)$ or Schatten$_p$-norms [13] $(p = 1, 2, \infty)$ have been considered as well.

Anisotropic. Let us now derive the corresponding anisotropic counterpart. As for the first order case we rewrite the isotropic regulariser using $\mathbf{e}_1$, $\mathbf{e}_2$:

$$R_{2\text{-iso}}(\mathbf{w}) = \Psi\left(\sum_{l=1}^{2}\sum_{k=1}^{2}\left(\mathbf{e}_k^\top \mathcal{H}u\,\mathbf{e}_l\right)^2 + \left(\mathbf{e}_k^\top \mathcal{H}v\,\mathbf{e}_l\right)^2\right)\tag{8}$$

where $\mathbf{e}_k^\top \mathcal{H}u\,\mathbf{e}_l$ and $\mathbf{e}_k^\top \mathcal{H}v\,\mathbf{e}_l$ are the second order directional derivatives $\partial_{\mathbf{e}_k\mathbf{e}_l}u$ and $\partial_{\mathbf{e}_k\mathbf{e}_l}v$, respectively. Once again we replace the unit vectors $\mathbf{e}_1$, $\mathbf{e}_2$ with the locally varying directions $\mathbf{r}_1$, $\mathbf{r}_2$. As observed in [14] in the context of denoising, now two possibilities arise how to penalise the directional derivatives. One can either penalise the directions $\mathbf{r}_k$ jointly or penalise all the directional derivatives separately. Please note that this constitutes a substantial difference to the first order case, where both options coincide. The first case leads to

$$R_{2\text{-aniso-single}}(\mathbf{w}) = \sum_{l=1}^{2}\Psi_l\left(\sum_{k=1}^{2}\left(\mathbf{r}_k^\top \mathcal{H}u\,\mathbf{r}_l\right)^2 + \left(\mathbf{r}_k^\top \mathcal{H}v\,\mathbf{r}_l\right)^2\right),\tag{9}$$

which we will refer to as the *single anisotropic* case. The latter case yields

$$R_{2\text{-aniso-double}}(\mathbf{w}) = \sum_{l=1}^{2}\sum_{k=1}^{2}\Psi_{l,k}\left(\left(\mathbf{r}_k^\top \mathcal{H}u\,\mathbf{r}_l\right)^2 + \left(\mathbf{r}_k^\top \mathcal{H}v\,\mathbf{r}_l\right)^2\right),\tag{10}$$

which we will denote as the *double anisotropic* case. To the best of our knowledge, both anisotropic variants have not been used in the context of optical flow so far.

3.3   Combined Approaches

Isotropic. As a representative for the class of combined regularisers we consider an infimal convolution approach. To this end, we combine the direct first and second order regularisers from Sects. 3.1 and 3.2 with a weight λ, respectively. Hence, using $\mathbf{w}_i = (u_i, v_i)^\top$ with $i = \{1, 2\}$, we obtain for the isotropic case

$$R_{\text{inf-iso}}(\mathbf{w}) = \inf_{\mathbf{w}_1 + \mathbf{w}_2 = \mathbf{w}} \left\{ \Psi \left(|\nabla u_1|^2 + |\nabla v_1|^2 \right) + \lambda \cdot \Psi \left(\|\mathcal{H}u_2\|_F^2 + \|\mathcal{H}v_2\|_F^2 \right) \right\}. \quad (11)$$

Anisotropic. Combining the single anisotropic direct first order and second order regularisers from Eqs. (6) and (9) yields

$$R_{\text{inf-aniso-single}}(\mathbf{w}) = \inf_{\mathbf{w}_1 + \mathbf{w}_2 = \mathbf{w}} \left\{ \sum_{l=1}^{2} \Psi_l \left(\left(\mathbf{r}_l^\top \nabla u_1 \right)^2 + \left(\mathbf{r}_l^\top \nabla v_1 \right)^2 \right) \right.$$

$$\left. + \lambda \cdot \sum_{l=1}^{2} \Psi_l \left(\sum_{k=1}^{2} \left(\mathbf{r}_k^\top \mathcal{H}u_2\, \mathbf{r}_l \right)^2 + \left(\mathbf{r}_k^\top \mathcal{H}v_2\, \mathbf{r}_l \right)^2 \right) \right\}. \quad (12)$$

which resembles the combined approach for scalar-valued denoising from [15]. Analogously, the double anisotropic case is given by

$$R_{\text{inf-aniso-double}}(\mathbf{w}) = \inf_{\mathbf{w}_1 + \mathbf{w}_2 = \mathbf{w}} \left\{ \sum_{l=1}^{2} \Psi_l \left(\left(\mathbf{r}_l^\top \nabla u_1 \right)^2 + \left(\mathbf{r}_l^\top \nabla v_1 \right)^2 \right) \right.$$

$$\left. + \lambda \cdot \sum_{l=1}^{2} \sum_{k=1}^{2} \Psi_{l,k} \left(\left(\mathbf{r}_k^\top \mathcal{H}u_2\, \mathbf{r}_l \right)^2 + \left(\mathbf{r}_k^\top \mathcal{H}v_2\, \mathbf{r}_l \right)^2 \right) \right\}. \quad (13)$$

As before, we are not aware of any optical flow methods where such anisotropic infimal convolution regularisers have been applied.

3.4 Indirect Second Order Regularisation

Isotropic. Finally, as a representative for the class of indirect second order methods, we consider an isotropic coupling approach. It consists of two terms: a coupling term that models the similarity of the gradient to an auxiliary function and a smoothness term that enforces smoothness on this auxiliary function [1]:

$$R_{\text{c-iso}}(\mathbf{w}) = \inf_{\mathbf{a}, \mathbf{b}} \left\{ \Psi \left(|\nabla u - \mathbf{a}|^2 + |\nabla v - \mathbf{b}|^2 \right) + \lambda \cdot \Psi \left(\|\mathcal{J}\mathbf{a}\|_F^2 + \|\mathcal{J}\mathbf{b}\|_F^2 \right) \right\}. \quad (14)$$

Here, $\mathbf{a} = (a_1, a_2)^\top$ and $\mathbf{b} = (b_1, b_2)^\top$ are the auxiliary vector fields that approximate the gradients ∇u and ∇v, respectively, $\mathcal{J}\mathbf{a}$ and $\mathcal{J}\mathbf{b}$ denote the Jacobians of $\mathbf{a}$ and $\mathbf{b}$, and λ serves as weighting parameter. This type of smoothness term comprises the well-known total generalised variation regulariser (TGV) [2].

Anisotropic. First rewriting the isotropic case using the unit vectors $\mathbf{e}_1$, $\mathbf{e}_2$

$$R_{\text{c-iso}}(\mathbf{w}) = \inf_{\mathbf{a}, \mathbf{b}} \left\{ \Psi \left(\sum_{l=1}^{2} \left(\mathbf{e}_l^\top (\nabla u - \mathbf{a}) \right)^2 + \left(\mathbf{e}_l^\top (\nabla v - \mathbf{b}) \right)^2 \right) \right.$$

$$\left. + \lambda \cdot \Psi \left(\sum_{l=1}^{2} \sum_{k=1}^{2} \left(\mathbf{e}_k^\top \mathcal{J}\mathbf{a}\, \mathbf{e}_l \right)^2 + \left(\mathbf{e}_k^\top \mathcal{J}\mathbf{b}\, \mathbf{e}_l \right)^2 \right) \right\}, \quad (15)$$

and then introducing the directions $\mathbf{r}_1$, $\mathbf{r}_2$ with separate penalisation yields the single anisotropic case which is a vector-valued extension of the anisotropic coupling model of Hafner *et al.* [10] proposed in the context of focus fusion. It reads

$$
R_{\text{c-aniso-single}}(\mathbf{w}) = \inf_{\mathbf{a},\mathbf{b}} \left\{ \sum_{l=1}^{2} \Psi_l \left(\left(\mathbf{r}_l^\top (\nabla u - \mathbf{a}) \right)^2 + \left(\mathbf{r}_l^\top (\nabla v - \mathbf{b}) \right)^2 \right) \right.
$$
$$
\left. + \lambda \cdot \sum_{l=1}^{2} \Psi_l \left(\sum_{k=1}^{2} \left(\mathbf{r}_k^\top \mathcal{J} \mathbf{a}\, \mathbf{r}_l \right)^2 + \left(\mathbf{r}_k^\top \mathcal{J} \mathbf{b}\, \mathbf{r}_l \right)^2 \right) \right\}. \quad (16)
$$

The corresponding double anisotropic regulariser reads

$$
R_{\text{c-aniso-double}}(\mathbf{w}) = \inf_{\mathbf{a},\mathbf{b}} \left\{ \sum_{l=1}^{2} \Psi_l \left(\left(\mathbf{r}_l^\top (\nabla u - \mathbf{a}) \right)^2 + \left(\mathbf{r}_l^\top (\nabla v - \mathbf{b}) \right)^2 \right) \right.
$$
$$
\left. + \lambda \cdot \sum_{l=1}^{2} \sum_{k=1}^{2} \Psi_{l,k} \left(\left(\mathbf{r}_k^\top \mathcal{J} \mathbf{a}\, \mathbf{r}_l \right)^2 + \left(\mathbf{r}_k^\top \mathcal{J} \mathbf{b}\, \mathbf{r}_l \right)^2 \right) \right\}, \quad (17)
$$

where $\mathbf{r}_k^\top \mathcal{J} \mathbf{a}\, \mathbf{r}_l$ and $\mathbf{r}_k^\top \mathcal{J} \mathbf{b}\, \mathbf{r}_l$ can be considered to be an approximation of the directional derivative $\mathbf{r}_k^\top \mathcal{H} u\, \mathbf{r}_l$ and $\mathbf{r}_k^\top \mathcal{H} v\, \mathbf{r}_l$, respectively. Also for the anisotropic coupling models we are not aware of any optical flow method that makes use of such regularisers. Regarding the anisotropic coupling term, [23] is close in spirit.

4   Minimisation

In order to minimise the non-convex energy functional in Eq. (1), we follow [7] and employ an incremental coarse-to-fine approach based on two nested fixed point iterations; see also [3]. Hence, we must solve a differential formulation of the original energy on each resolution level k for the unknown increments $\mathbf{dw}^k$, $\mathbf{dc}^k$. The differential formulation for the data term is derived by a linearisation w.r.t. to the unknown increments and introducing an additional constraint normalisation as in [34]. In case of the smoothness term the differential formulation follows directly from the definition of the increments. To compute the increments on level k, we discretise the Euler-Lagrange equations of the differential energy. In case of first order divergence expressions we apply the discretisation from [30]. Regarding the second order divergence equivalents as well as the remaining derivatives we use standard finite differences. As solver for the inner fixed point iteration we apply a cascadic multicolour variant of the SOR method.

5   Experiments

For evaluating the performance of our different regularisers, we focussed on the KITTI Flow 2012 [9] and Flow 2015 [17] benchmark. The corresponding sequences contain a large amount of highly non-fronto-parallel motion. To keep

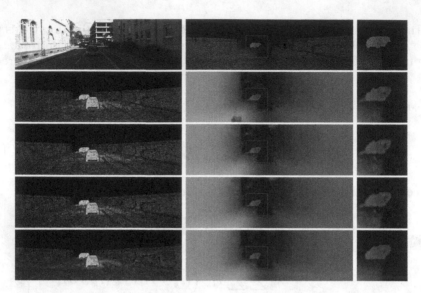

Fig. 1. Training sequence #166 of the KITTI Flow 2015 benchmark [17]. Best viewed electronically. **First row**: Reference frame, ground truth. **Second row**: Bad pixel visualisation and computed flow for the first order anisotropic regulariser. **Third row**: Double anisotropic direct second order regulariser. **Fourth row**: Double anisotropic infimal convolution regulariser. **Fifth row**: Double anisotropic coupling regulariser.

the number of adjustable parameters small, we set most parameters fixed and only optimised the weights α, β, γ and λ. Regarding the penaliser functions Ψ_* for the flow regulariser, we chose the Charbonnier penaliser [6] with $\epsilon = 0.01$.

First vs. Second Order. In our first experiment, we demonstrate the advantage of second order regularisation over first order regularisation when it comes to the estimation of non-fronto-parallel motion. Therefore, we used an exemplary training sequence of the KITTI 2015 benchmark and computed the flow with all double anisotropic second order variants as well as with an anisotropic first order regulariser. The results in terms of both a bad pixel and a flow visualisation are depicted in Fig. 1. Due to the ego-motion of the camera, especially the pixels at the image boundary exhibit a large non-fronto-parallel motion which is not captured well with the first order regulariser (second row). Nevertheless, it recovers quite sharp motion discontinuities. In contrast, the smoothness weight α of the direct second order (third row) as well as of the infimal convolution approach (fourth row) had to be chosen rather small to obtain a good result. This in turn leads to noisy areas that are clearly visible in the flow field. The coupling model does not show this drawback (fifth row). It yields a result which is sharp at motion discontinuities, but smooth in homogeneous flow regions.

Table 1. Average endpoint error (AEE), percentage of erroneous pixels (BP), endpoint error > 3px, and runtimes for the different regularisers on the KITTI Flow 2012 [9] and KITTI Flow 2015 [17] OCC-training sets (all regions).

			KITTI '12		KITTI '15		
			AEE	BP	AEE	BP	Runtime
Direct	First order	Isotropic	4.39	16.53	12.88	29.87	22 s
Direct	First order	Anisotropic	4.26	16.25	12.45	28.94	23 s
Direct	Second order	Isotropic	2.75	10.07	11.40	24.61	26 s
Direct	Second order	Single anisotropic	2.35	9.84	10.60	24.29	33 s
Direct	Second order	Double anisotropic	2.32	9.73	10.49	24.05	33 s
Inf-conv	Second order	Isotropic	2.30	9.66	9.60	23.61	43 s
Inf-conv	Second order	Single anisotropic	2.30	9.64	9.45	23.30	51 s
Inf-conv	Second order	Double anisotropic	2.28	9.58	9.38	23.00	52 s
Coupling	Second order	Isotropic	**2.18**	9.65	9.24	22.90	65 s
Coupling	Second order	Single anisotropic	2.20	**9.57**	9.07	22.37	65 s
Coupling	Second order	Double anisotropic	2.20	**9.57**	**8.98**	**22.27**	96 s

Quantitative Evaluation. In our second experiment, we used the complete KITTI 2012 and 2015 training data sets to evaluate the performance of all regularisers from Sect. 3. Therefore, we first optimised the four model parameters w.r.t. the percentage of erroneous pixels (BP) using downhill simplex on a small subset of the training data and then evaluated common error metrics on the complete training data set – including the average endpoint error (AEE); see Table 1. In accordance with our first experiment, we see that second order regularisation is beneficial in the presence of non-fronto-parallel motion. One can also see, that introducing a higher degree of anisotropy allows to further reduce the errors. In particular, for the direct second order model this is obvious. The best performance is achieved with the double anisotropic coupling model.

Penalisation Strategies. Up to now, we have restricted our choice of the penaliser functions Ψ_* to the Charbonnier penaliser. Hence, in our third experiment, we consider our best method – the double anisotropic coupling model – and analyse different penalisation strategies. To this end, we compare different combinations of the edge-enhancing Perona-Malik penaliser (PM) [20] $\Psi(s^2) = \lambda^2 \log\left(1 + s^2/\lambda^2\right)$ and the edge-preserving Charbonnier penaliser (Ch) [6]. The results in Table 2 show that choosing the leading penalisers Ψ_1 and $\Psi_{1,1}$ to be edge-enhancing works best. Only regarding the AEE of the KITTI 2015 benchmark, pure edge-preserving regularisation allows to achieve better results.

Table 2. Comparison of different penalisers for the double anisotropic coupling model.

Coupling term		Smoothness term				KITTI Flow '12		KITTI Flow '15	
Ψ_1	Ψ_2	$\Psi_{1,1}$	$\Psi_{1,2}$	$\Psi_{2,1}$	$\Psi_{2,2}$	AEE	BP	AEE	BP
Ch	Ch	Ch	Ch	Ch	Ch	2.20	9.57	**8.98**	22.27
PM	Ch	Ch	Ch	Ch	Ch	2.10	9.46	9.19	21.98
		PM	Ch	Ch	Ch	**2.05**	**9.33**	9.14	**21.82**
		PM	PM	Ch	Ch	2.07	9.37	9.15	21.83
		PM	PM	PM	Ch	2.10	9.53	9.17	21.90

Comparison to the Literature. Finally, in our fourth experiment, we compare our double anisotropic coupling model to current optical flow methods from the literature. To this end, we submitted results to the KITTI 2012 and 2015 benchmark. In Tables 3 and 4, we listed all non-anonymous pure two-frame optical flow methods that do not make use of additional information, such as stereo images, extra time-frames, semantic information or assume an underlying epipolar geometry. As one can see, our novel regulariser allows to obtain excellent results. In particular, it significantly outperforms all other variational approaches including BTF-ILLUM (isotropic direct second order [7]), TGV2ADCSIFT (isotropic second order coupling [1]), and NLTGV-SC (non-local second order coupling

Table 3. Comparison of pure two-frame optical flow methods for the KITTI 2012 test sequences. Superscripts denote the rank of each method in the corresponding column.

Method	Out-Noc	Out-All	Avg-Noc	Avg-All
PatchBatch	5.29%[1]	14.17%[8]	1.3 px[1]	3.3 px[5]
Our method	**5.57%**[2]	**10.71%**[2]	**1.3 px**[1]	**2.8 px**[1]
DDF	5.73%[3]	14.18%[9]	1.4 px[6]	3.4 px[6]
PH-Flow	5.76%[4]	10.57%[1]	1.3 px[1]	2.9 px[3]
FlowFields	5.77%[5]	14.01%[7]	1.4 px[6]	3.5 px[7]
CPM-Flow	5.79%[6]	13.70%[6]	1.3 px[1]	3.2 px[4]
NLTGV-SC	5.93%[7]	11.96%[4]	1.6 px[13]	3.8 px[9]
DDS-DF	6.03%[8]	13.08%[5]	1.6 px[13]	4.2 px[11]
TGV2ADCSIFT	6.20%[9]	15.15%[11]	1.5 px[9]	4.5 px[12]
DiscreteFlow	6.23%[10]	16.63%[12]	1.3 px[1]	3.6 px[8]
BTF-ILLUM	6.52%[11]	11.03%[3]	1.5 px[9]	2.8 px[1]
DeepFlow2	6.61%[12]	17.35%[14]	1.4 px[6]	5.3 px[13]
Data-Flow	7.11%[13]	14.57%[10]	1.9 px[15]	5.5 px[14]
DeepFlow	7.22%[14]	17.79%[15]	1.5 px[9]	5.8 px[15]
EpicFlow	7.88%[15]	17.08%[13]	1.5 px[9]	3.8 px[9]

Table 4. Comparison of pure two-frame optical flow methods for the KITTI 2015 test sequences. Superscripts denote the rank of each method in the corresponding column.

Method	FI-bg	FI-fg	FI-all
PatchBatch	$19.98\%^1$	$30.24\%^5$	$21.69\%^1$
DDF	$20.36\%^3$	$29.69\%^3$	$21.92\%^2$
Our method	$\mathbf{20.01\%^2}$	$\mathbf{32.82\%^6}$	$\mathbf{22.14\%^3}$
DiscreteFlow	$21.53\%^4$	$26.68\%^1$	$22.38\%^4$
CPM-Flow	$22.32\%^5$	$27.79\%^2$	$23.23\%^5$
Full-Flow	$23.09\%^6$	$30.11\%^4$	$24.26\%^6$
EpicFlow	$25.81\%^7$	$33.56\%^7$	$27.10\%^7$
DeepFlow	$27.96\%^8$	$35.28\%^8$	$29.18\%^8$

[22]). This confirms once more the benefits of our double anisotropic coupling model.

6 Conclusion

In this paper, we juxtaposed several isotropic and anisotropic second order regularisation strategies for variational optical flow methods. In particular, we showed how different anisotropic variants can be derived from a single isotropic smoothness term, and how modelling a higher degree of anisotropy in terms of a double anisotropic model can further improve the quality. Experiments with the recent KITTI 2012 and 2015 benchmark not only showed favourable results, but also demonstrated that double anisotropic second order coupling models are among the state-of-the-art in variational motion estimation.

Acknowledgements. We thank the German Research Foundation (DFG) for financial support within project B04 of SFB/Transregio 161.

References

1. Braux-Zin, J., Dupont, R., Bartoli, A.: A general dense image matching framework combining direct and feature-based costs. In: Proceedings of International Conference on Computer Vision, pp. 185–192 (2013)
2. Bredies, K., Kunisch, K., Pock, T.: Total generalized variation. SIAM J. Imaging Sci. **3**(3), 492–526 (2010)
3. Brox, T., Bruhn, A., Papenberg, N., Weickert, J.: High accuracy optical flow estimation based on a theory for warping. In: Pajdla, T., Matas, J. (eds.) ECCV 2004. LNCS, vol. 3024, pp. 25–36. Springer, Heidelberg (2004). doi:10.1007/978-3-540-24673-2_3
4. Chambolle, A., Lions, P.-L.: Image recovery via total variation minimization and related problems. Numer. Math. **76**(2), 167–188 (1997)

5. Chan, T., Marquina, A., Mulet, P.: High-order total variation-based image restoration. SIAM J. Sci. Comput. **22**(2), 503–516 (2000)
6. Charbonnier, P., Blanc-Féraud, L., Aubert, G., Barlaud, M.: Deterministic edge-preserving regularization in computed imaging. IEEE Trans. Image Process. **6**(2), 298–311 (1997)
7. Demetz, O., Stoll, M., Volz, S., Weickert, J., Bruhn, A.: Learning brightness transfer functions for the joint recovery of illumination changes and optical flow. In: Fleet, D., Pajdla, T., Schiele, B., Tuytelaars, T. (eds.) ECCV 2014. LNCS, vol. 8689, pp. 455–471. Springer, Cham (2014). doi:10.1007/978-3-319-10590-1_30
8. Ferstl, D., Reinbacher, C., Ranftl, R., Rüther, M., Bischof, H.: Image guided depth upsampling using anisotropic total generalized variation. In: Proceedings of International Conference on Computer Vision, pp. 993–1000 (2013)
9. Geiger, A., Lenz, P., Urtasun, R.: Are we ready for autonomous driving? The KITTI vision benchmark suite. In: Proceedings of IEEE Conference on Computer Vision and Pattern Recognition, pp. 3354–3361 (2012)
10. Hafner, D., Schroers, C., Weickert, J.: Introducing maximal anisotropy into second order coupling models. In: Gall, J., Gehler, P., Leibe, B. (eds.) GCPR 2015. LNCS, vol. 9358, pp. 79–90. Springer, Cham (2015). doi:10.1007/978-3-319-24947-6_7
11. Hewer, A., Weickert, J., Scheffer, T., Seibert, H., Diebels, S.: Lagrangian strain tensor computation with higher order variational models. In: Proceedings of British Machine Vision Conference, pp. 129.1–129.10 (2013)
12. Horn, B., Schunck, B.: Determining optical flow. Artif. Intell. **17**, 185–203 (1981)
13. Lefkimmiatis, S., Ward, J.P., Unser, M.: Hessian Schatten-norm regularization for linear inverse problems. IEEE Trans. Image Process. **22**(5), 1873–1888 (2013)
14. Lellmann, J., Morel, J.-M., Schönlieb, C.-B.: Anisotropic third-order regularization for sparse digital elevation models. In: Kuijper, A., Bredies, K., Pock, T., Bischof, H. (eds.) SSVM 2013. LNCS, vol. 7893, pp. 161–173. Springer, Heidelberg (2013). doi:10.1007/978-3-642-38267-3_14
15. Lenzen, F., Becker, F., Lellmann, J.: Adaptive second-order total variation: an approach aware of slope discontinuities. In: Kuijper, A., Bredies, K., Pock, T., Bischof, H. (eds.) SSVM 2013. LNCS, vol. 7893, pp. 61–73. Springer, Heidelberg (2013). doi:10.1007/978-3-642-38267-3_6
16. Lysaker, M., Lundervold, A., Tai, X.C.: Noise removal using fourth-order partial differential equation with applications to medical magnetic resonance images in space and time. IEEE Trans. Image Process. **12**(12), 1579–1590 (2003)
17. Menze, M., Geiger, A.: Object scene flow for autonomous vehicles. In: Proceedings of IEEE Conference on Computer Vision and Pattern Recognition, pp. 3061–3070 (2015)
18. Nagel, H.-H., Enkelmann, W.: An investigation of smoothness constraints for the estimation of displacement vector fields from image sequences. IEEE Trans. Patt. Anal. Mach. Intell. **8**(5), 565–593 (1986)
19. Nir, T., Bruckstein, A.M., Kimmel, R.: Over-parameterized variational optical flow. Int. J. Comput. Vis. **76**(2), 205–216 (2008)
20. Perona, P., Malik, J.: Scale space and edge detection using anisotropic diffusion. IEEE Trans. Pattern Anal. Mach. Intell. **2**, 629–639 (1990)
21. Ranftl, R., Gehrig, S., Pock, T., Bischof, H.: Pushing the limits of stereo using variational stereo estimation. In: IEEE Intelligent Vehicles Symposium, pp. 401–407 (2012)

22. Ranftl, R., Bredies, K., Pock, T.: Non-local total generalized variation for optical flow estimation. In: Fleet, D., Pajdla, T., Schiele, B., Tuytelaars, T. (eds.) ECCV 2014. LNCS, vol. 8689, pp. 439–454. Springer, Cham (2014). doi:10.1007/978-3-319-10590-1_29

23. Ranftl, R.: Higher-Order Variational Methods for Dense Correspondence Problems. Ph.D thesis. Graz University of Technology, Austria (2014)

24. Revaud, J., Weinzaepfel, P., Harchaoui, Z., Schmid, C.: EpicFlow: Edge-preserving interpolation of correspondences for optical flow. In: Proceedings of IEEE Conference on Computer Vision and Pattern Recognition, pp. 1164–1172 (2015)

25. Rudin, L., Osher, S., Fatemi, E.: Nonlinear total variation based noise removal algorithms. Physica D **60**, 259–268 (1992)

26. Scherzer, O.: Denoising with higher order derivatives of bounded variation and an application to parameter estimation. Computing **60**(1), 1–27 (1998)

27. Sun, D., Roth, S., Lewis, J.P., Black, M.J.: Learning optical flow. In: Forsyth, D., Torr, P., Zisserman, A. (eds.) ECCV 2008. LNCS, vol. 5304, pp. 83–97. Springer, Heidelberg (2008). doi:10.1007/978-3-540-88690-7_7

28. Trobin, W., Pock, T., Cremers, D., Bischof, H.: An Unbiased second-order prior for high-accuracy motion estimation. In: Rigoll, G. (ed.) DAGM 2008. LNCS, vol. 5096, pp. 396–405. Springer, Heidelberg (2008). doi:10.1007/978-3-540-69321-5_40

29. Vogel, O., Bruhn, A., Weickert, J., Didas, S.: Direct shape-from-shading with adaptive higher order regularisation. In: Sgallari, F., Murli, A., Paragios, N. (eds.) SSVM 2007. LNCS, vol. 4485, pp. 871–882. Springer, Heidelberg (2007). doi:10.1007/978-3-540-72823-8_75

30. Weickert, J., Welk, M., Wickert, M.: L^2-Stable nonstandard finite differences for anisotropic diffusion. In: Kuijper, A., Bredies, K., Pock, T., Bischof, H. (eds.) SSVM 2013. LNCS, vol. 7893, pp. 380–391. Springer, Heidelberg (2013). doi:10.1007/978-3-642-38267-3_32

31. Weickert, J., Schnörr, C.: A theoretical framework for convex regularizers in PDE-based computation of image motion. Int. J. Comput. Vision **45**(3), 245–264 (2001)

32. Werlberger, M., Trobin, W., Pock, T., Wedel, A., Cremers, D., Bischof, H.: Anisotropic Huber-L^1 optic flow. In: Proceedings of British Machine Vision Conference (2009)

33. Zach, C., Pock, T., Bischof, H.: A duality based approach for realtime TV-L^1 optical flow. In: Proceedings of German Pattern Recognition, pp. 214–223 (2007)

34. Zimmer, H., Bruhn, A., Weickert, J.: Optic flow in harmony. Int. J. Comput. Vis. **93**(3), 368–388 (2011)

Order-Adaptive Regularisation for Variational Optical Flow: Global, Local and in Between

Daniel Maurer$^{(\boxtimes)}$, Michael Stoll, and Andrés Bruhn

Computer Vision and Intelligent Systems Group,
Institute for Visualization and Interactive Systems,
University of Stuttgart, 70569 Stuttgart, Germany
{maurer,stoll,bruhn}@vis.uni-stuttgart.de

Abstract. Recent approaches for variational motion estimation typically either rely on first or second order regularisation strategies. While first order strategies are more appropriate for scenes with fronto-parallel motion, second order constraints are superior if it comes to the estimation of affine flow fields. Since using the wrong regularisation order may lead to a significant deterioration of the results, it is surprising that there has not been much effort in the literature so far to determine this order automatically. In our work, we address the aforementioned problem in two ways. (i) First, we discuss two anisotropic smoothness terms of first and second order, respectively, that share important structural properties and that are thus particularly suited for being combined within an order-adaptive variational framework. (ii) Secondly, based on these two smoothness terms, we develop four different variational methods and with it four different strategies for adaptively selecting the regularisation order: a global and a local strategy based on half-quadratic regularisation, a non-local approach that relies on neighbourhood information, and a region based method using level sets. Experiments on recent benchmarks show the benefits of each of the strategies. Moreover, they demonstrate that adaptively combining different regularisation orders not only allows to outperform single-order strategies but also to obtain advantages beyond the ones of a frame-wise selection.

Keywords: Higher order regularisation · Variational methods · Optical flow

1 Introduction

Regularisation plays a central role in the design of variational methods for optical flow estimation. By assuming the desired flow field to be smooth or piecewise smooth one actually models an implicit propagation of information from the neighbourhood. This so called filling-in effect offers two important advantages. On the one hand, it helps to resolve potential ambiguities in the data term due to a non-unique matching cost. On the other hand, it allows to obtain dense and accurate results even in case of noise or missing information.

© Springer International Publishing AG 2017
F. Lauze et al. (Eds.): SSVM 2017, LNCS 10302, pp. 550–562, 2017.
DOI: 10.1007/978-3-319-58771-4_44

While many classical optical flow approaches resort to first order regularisation [3,7,20,26,28], recent tasks related to automotive data [5,12,23] and aerial images [17] have shown that also second order smoothness terms can be useful. For instance, they allow to estimate piecewise affine flow fields resulting from a moving camera. However, second order priors also have a drawback. They are less suited to estimate fronto-parallel motion, since they are likely to misinterpret local fluctuations as affine motion (regularisation order vs. robustness).

This fact is also reflected in all standard benchmarks. While leading methods in the automotive KITTI 2012 [14] and KITTI 2015 [19] benchmarks make use of second order smoothness terms, the best performing approaches on the synthetic MPI Sintel [8] and Middlebury [2] benchmark rely on first order priors. Evidently, it would be desirable to develop an adaptive variational model that globally or locally selects the most appropriate regularisation order. This would not only enable us to obtain good results independent of the benchmark, it would also allow us to apply the corresponding approach to a broader range of applications.

Related Work. The simplest way to improve the performance of a variational optical flow method is the user-based selection of the most appropriate regularisation order [24]. This, however, requires prior knowledge on the underlying application which might not be available beforehand. Moreover, such a hand-tuned strategy focusses on the entire application and hence does not allow to choose the most suitable order in a scene-wise or even pixel-wise manner.

A more advanced selection strategy is implicitly realised by so-called coupling models such as the total generalised variation (TGV) [5] and its non-local variant (NLTGV) [23]. Originally proposed in the context of denoising [6], the key idea of such models is to introduce auxiliary functions that approximate first order derivatives while imposing smoothness on these auxiliary functions themselves. Due to this design, coupling models allow the preservation of motion discontinuities in both the original and the auxiliary function. This in turn comes down to edge-preserving first and second order regularisation, respectively. Although this strategy alleviates the overfitting problem, it can be observed for benchmarks with mainly fronto-parallel motion (Middlebury, MPI Sintel) that the performance of coupling models cannot keep up with the one of pure first order regularisers. This clearly shows that there is room for improvement when it comes to the design of adaptive schemes for selecting the regularisation order.

The only explicit order-adaptive approach that we found in the optical flow literature is the method of Volz et al. [25]. However, instead of selecting the spatial regularisation order, the method determines the trajectoral one. Moreover, the approach is based on fitting polynomial approximations to the results of a preliminary run. In that sense, the selection process is not really self contained.

Finally, the work that we consider most similar in spirit to our method is the approach of Lenzen et al. [18]. Although the approach has been proposed in the context of denoising, the underlying variational model adaptively combines a direct first and second order regulariser. Thereby the switching between the two regularisers is steered by local image information. While adapting the regularisation order to the underlying image may be useful in the context of denoising, one should keep in mind that we are actually interested in motion estimation. Hence, slopes in the image are typically unrelated to slopes in the flow field.

Contributions. In our paper we address all the aforementioned shortcomings: Based on two recent anisotropic first and second order regularisers [15, 28] we derive a general strategy for variational methods, that allows to adapt the regularisation order automatically during the estimation. This strategy that is based on the structural similarity of first order priors and second order coupling models not only allows to combine the advantages of both regularisation orders, it is also solution-driven in that sense that the decision on the regularisation order relies exclusively on the approximation quality of the resulting flow field. Based on this strategy, we propose four variational methods with a different degree of adaptation, ranging from a frame-wise adaptation to a pixel-wise selection. In this context, we also introduce concepts for spatially regularising the decision process in terms of a non-local neighbourhood or a global smoothness term. Finally, we demonstrate the usefulness of the proposed adaptation strategies by providing results for all major benchmarks. These results not only show the clear advantages of the global selection strategy compared to a standard single-order regularisation, it also make explicit that a local selection strategy can be very beneficial if it is combined with some form of spatial coherence.

Organisation. In Sect. 2 we introduce the general variational framework and discuss the two underlying smoothness terms. In Sect. 3 we then derive our novel order-adaptive regularisation scheme and present four models differing in their degree of adaptation. While a brief sketch on the minimisation is given in Sect. 4, Sect. 5 provides a qualitative and quantitative evaluation of the proposed methods. Finally, we conclude the paper with a summary in Sect. 6.

2   Variational Model

Let us start by reviewing the traditional framework for variational optical flow computation. In order to estimate the optical flow $\mathbf{u} = (u, v)^\top : \Omega \to \mathbb{R}^2$, defined on the rectangular image domain $\Omega \subset \mathbb{R}^2$, one typically minimises an energy functional of the following form

$$E(\mathbf{u}) = D(\mathbf{u}) + \alpha \cdot R(\mathbf{u}), \tag{1}$$

which consists of two terms: a data term D and a regularisation term R. While the data term assumes constancy on certain image features, the regularisation term helps to overcome possibly ambiguous solutions of the data term. The weighting parameter α allows to adjust the relative impact of both terms.

Data Term. Regarding the data term one often makes use of illumination invariant constancy assumptions which are penalised in a statistically robust way. In our case, we follow the work of [9], which combines a separately robustified brightness and gradient constancy assumption. Let $I_0, I_1 : \Omega \to \mathbb{R}$ denote two subsequent images obtained from an original image sequence via convolution with a spatial Gaussian of standard deviation σ. Then the data term is given by

$$D(\mathbf{u}) = \int_{\Omega} \Psi_D \left((I_1(\mathbf{x}+\mathbf{u}) - I_0(\mathbf{x}))^2 \right) + \gamma \cdot \Psi_D \left(\|\nabla I_1(\mathbf{x}+\mathbf{u}) - \nabla I_0(\mathbf{x})\|_2^2 \right) d\mathbf{x}, \quad (2)$$

where $\mathbf{x} = (x, y)^\top \in \Omega$ denotes the location, γ is a weighting parameter to balance the two assumptions and $\Psi_D(s^2) = 2\epsilon^2\sqrt{1 + s^2/\epsilon^2}$ is chosen to be the sub-quadratic Charbonnier penaliser [10].

Regularisation Term. For the regularisation term R one typically employs either a first or a second order smoothness assumption. In the following, we will discuss two recent anisotropic smoothness terms of first and second order, respectively, that could potentially be used. We have selected these two terms because they share important structural properties and are thus particularly suited for being combined in our order-adaptive framework later on.

Our choice for the first order smoothness term is the anisotropic complementary regulariser of Zimmer *et al.* [28]

$$R_1(\mathbf{u}) = \int_{\Omega} S_1(\mathbf{u}) \, d\mathbf{x} = \int_{\Omega} \sum_{l=1}^{2} \Psi_l \left(\left(\mathbf{r}_l^\top \nabla u\right)^2 + \left(\mathbf{r}_l^\top \nabla v\right)^2 \right) d\mathbf{x}. \quad (3)$$

Here, $\mathbf{r}_1(\mathbf{x})$, $\mathbf{r}_2(\mathbf{x})$ denote two orthonormal vectors obtained as the eigenvectors of the regularisation tensor [28], which can be seen as a generalisation of the structure tensor [13] to arbitrary constancy assumptions. Following [25], we choose $\Psi_1(s^2) = \epsilon^2 \log\left(1 + s^2/\epsilon^2\right)$ to be the edge-enhancing Perona-Malik penaliser [22] and $\Psi_2(s^2) = 2\epsilon^2\sqrt{1 + s^2/\epsilon^2}$ to be the edge-preserving Charbonnier penaliser [10].

Regarding the second order regularisation model we choose the recent anisotropic coupling model of Hafner *et al.* [15] that has been proposed in the context of focus fusion, but that has not been considered for optical flow computation so far. It can be seen as an anisotropic variant of TGV [6] and is given by

$$R_2(\mathbf{u}) = \int_{\Omega} \inf_{\mathbf{a},\mathbf{b}} \left\{ S_2(\mathbf{u},\mathbf{a},\mathbf{b}) + \beta \cdot S_{\mathsf{aux}}(\mathbf{a},\mathbf{b}) \right\} d\mathbf{x}. \quad (4)$$

It consists of two terms: a coupling term S_2 that connects the gradients ∇u and ∇v of the flow to auxiliary functions $\mathbf{a}(\mathbf{x})$ and $\mathbf{b}(\mathbf{x})$ via

$$S_2(\mathbf{u},\mathbf{a},\mathbf{b}) = \sum_{l=1}^{2} \Psi_l \left(\left(\mathbf{r}_l^\top (\nabla u - \mathbf{a})\right)^2 + \left(\mathbf{r}_l^\top (\nabla v - \mathbf{b})\right)^2 \right), \quad (5)$$

and a smoothness term S_{aux} that enforces smoothness on these auxiliary functions themselves

$$S_{\mathsf{aux}}(\mathbf{a},\mathbf{b}) = \sum_{l=1}^{2} \Psi_l \left(\sum_{k=1}^{2} \left(\mathbf{r}_k^\top \mathcal{J}\mathbf{a}\,\mathbf{r}_l\right)^2 + \left(\mathbf{r}_k^\top \mathcal{J}\mathbf{b}\,\mathbf{r}_l\right)^2 \right). \quad (6)$$

Here $\mathcal{J}\mathbf{a}$ and $\mathcal{J}\mathbf{b}$ denote the Jacobian of $\mathbf{a}$ and $\mathbf{b}$, respectively, and the parameter β allows to adjust the smoothness of the auxiliary functions.

Let us point out the strong similarity between the first order model S_1 and the coupling term S_2. While the first order model assumes the directional derivatives in r_1- and r_2-direction to be similar to zero, the coupling term assumes them to be similar to auxiliary functions, which should be smooth by themselves. This in turn makes the energies of both terms comparable and, consequently, makes them ideal candidates for a combination within our order-adaptive framework.

3   Order-Adaptive Regularisation

In this section we introduce our novel order-adaptive regularisation model, that combines the advantages of both first and second order regularisation. We will present four variants which differ in their degree of adaptivity, which ranges from a global (frame-wise) to a local (pixel-wise) adaptation.

Global Adaptive Scheme. To derive our order-adaptive scheme step-by-step we start with a simple combination of the previous introduced first and second order regularisation strategies, which reads

$$R\left(\mathbf{u}\right) = \int_\Omega \inf_{\mathbf{a},\mathbf{b}} \left\{ S_1\left(\mathbf{u}\right) + S_2(\mathbf{u},\mathbf{a},\mathbf{b}) + \beta \cdot S_{\mathsf{aux}}(\mathbf{a},\mathbf{b}) \right\} d\mathbf{x}. \tag{7}$$

To render this combination frame-wise adaptive, we introduce a global weighting parameter $c \in [0, 1]$ and a selection term $\phi_\lambda\left(c\right)$ similar in spirit to half-quadratic regularisation [4]:

$$R\left(\mathbf{u}, c\right) = \int_\Omega \inf_{\mathbf{a},\mathbf{b}} \left\{ c \cdot S_1\left(\mathbf{u}\right) + (1-c) \cdot S_2(\mathbf{u},\mathbf{a},\mathbf{b}) + \beta \cdot S_{\mathsf{aux}}(\mathbf{a},\mathbf{b}) + \phi_\lambda\left(c\right) \right\} d\mathbf{x}. \tag{8}$$

Let us now derive a suitable selection term $\phi_\lambda\left(c\right)$ that allows for a meaningful selection of the regularisation order. In this context, we will also motivate why the convex combination only includes S_1 and S_2 and not S_{aux}. Evidently, when deciding on the regularisation order, the question arises which model fits better: a constant model or an affine model. This question is answered by a comparison of the average energies related to S_1 and S_2. Since the affine model S_2, however, includes the constant model S_1 one should only prefer the model S_2 if it yields a minimum average benefit T compared to the model S_1. This avoids overfitting to small fluctuations. Formulating this requirement in terms of a differentiable sigmoid function, we propose to determine the weighting parameter as

$$c = \frac{1}{1 + e^{-\Delta/\lambda}} \quad \text{with} \quad \Delta = T + \frac{1}{|\Omega|} \int_\Omega S_2 - S_1\, d\mathbf{x}, \tag{9}$$

where λ allows to adjust the slope, i.e. the sensitivity of the sigmoid function. As desired, c approaches 1 if the average gain $\frac{1}{|\Omega|} \int_\Omega S_1 - S_2\, d\mathbf{x} \ll T$ and c approaches 0 if the average gain $\frac{1}{|\Omega|} \int_\Omega S_1 - S_2\, d\mathbf{x} \gg T$.

What remains to be done is to derive a selection term that models the desired behaviour. To this end, we take a look at the derivative $\frac{\partial R}{\partial c} = 0$, which reads

$$0 = \int_\Omega S_1\left(\mathbf{u}\right) - S_2(\mathbf{u},\mathbf{a},\mathbf{b}) + \phi_\lambda'\left(c\right)\, d\mathbf{x}. \tag{10}$$

By rewriting Eq. (9) as

$$\int_\Omega S_1\left(\mathbf{u}\right) - S_2\left(\mathbf{u}, \mathbf{a}, \mathbf{b}\right) dx = |\Omega| \left(\lambda \cdot \ln\left(\frac{1}{c} - 1\right) + T\right), \tag{11}$$

and plugging this into in Eq. (10) we obtain

$$\phi'_\lambda\left(c\right) = -\lambda \cdot \ln\left(\frac{1}{c} - 1\right) - T. \tag{12}$$

Integrating both sides then yields the desired selection term

$$\phi_\lambda\left(c\right) = \lambda \left(\ln\left(1 - c\right) - c \cdot \ln\left(\frac{1}{c} - 1\right)\right) - Tc + C. \tag{13}$$

Finally, to obtain a more transparent write up of the model, we choose the integration constant $C = T$ and introduce

$$\phi\left(c\right) = \frac{\phi_\lambda\left(c\right) - \left(1 - c\right) \cdot T}{\lambda} = \ln\left(1 - c\right) - c \cdot \ln\left(\frac{1}{c} - 1\right). \tag{14}$$

This allows us to rewrite the new regulariser as

$$R_{\text{global}}\left(\mathbf{u}, c\right) = \int_\Omega \inf_{\mathbf{a}, \mathbf{b}} \Big\{c \cdot S_1\left(\mathbf{u}\right) + \left(1 - c\right) \cdot \left(S_2(\mathbf{u}, \mathbf{a}, \mathbf{b}) + T\right)$$
$$+ \beta \cdot S_{\text{aux}}(\mathbf{a}, \mathbf{b}) + \lambda \cdot \phi\left(c\right) \Big\} \, dx, \tag{15}$$

which can be regarded as a combination of a first order regulariser and a second order regulariser with activation cost T, subject to a selection term with weight λ.

Local Adaptive Scheme. Analogous to the global adaptive scheme, we can derive a local adaptive variant. The main difference is that we replace the weighting parameter c with a spatially varying weighting function $c_{\text{local}} : \Omega \to [0, 1]$ that is determined based on the *local* energy difference via

$$c_{\text{local}} = \frac{1}{1 + e^{-\Delta/\lambda}} \quad \text{with} \quad \Delta = T + S_2 - S_1. \tag{16}$$

The corresponding local adaptive regulariser reads

$$R_{\text{local}}\left(\mathbf{u}, c_{\text{local}}\right) = \int_\Omega \inf_{\mathbf{a}, \mathbf{b}} \Big\{c_{\text{local}} \cdot S_1\left(\mathbf{u}\right) + \left(1 - c_{\text{local}}\right) \cdot \left(S_2\left(\mathbf{u}, \mathbf{a}, \mathbf{b}\right) + T\right)$$
$$+ \beta \cdot S_{\text{aux}}\left(\mathbf{a}, \mathbf{b}\right) + \lambda \cdot \phi\left(c_{\text{local}}\right) \Big\} \, dx. \tag{17}$$

A similar weighting strategy has been used in [27] to locally decide between two different constancy assumptions in the data term.

Non-local Adaptive Scheme. Besides the local and global adaptation scheme we also propose a variant that takes a neighbourhood into account, when deciding on the regularisation order. It is given by

$$R_{\text{nonlocal}}\left(\mathbf{u}, c_{\text{nl}}\right) = \int_{\Omega} \inf_{\mathbf{a},\mathbf{b}} \left\{ \bar{c}_{\text{nl}} \cdot S_1\left(\mathbf{u}\right) + \left(1 - \bar{c}_{\text{nl}}\right) \cdot \left(S_2\left(\mathbf{u}, \mathbf{a}, \mathbf{b}\right) + T\right) \right.$$
$$\left. + \beta \cdot S_{\text{aux}}\left(\mathbf{a}, \mathbf{b}\right) + \lambda \cdot \phi\left(c_{\text{nl}}\right) \right\} d\mathbf{x}, \quad (18)$$

where

$$\bar{c}_{\text{nl}}(\mathbf{x}) = \frac{1}{|\mathcal{N}(\mathbf{x})|} \int_{\mathcal{N}(\mathbf{x})} c_{\text{nl}}(\mathbf{y}) \, d\mathbf{y}. \quad (19)$$

Here $\mathcal{N}(\mathbf{x})$ denotes the rectangular shaped neighbourhood around $\mathbf{x}$ and $|\mathcal{N}(\mathbf{x})|$ is the size of the neighbourhood, so that $\frac{1}{|\mathcal{N}(\mathbf{x})|} \int_{\mathcal{N}(\mathbf{x})} 1 \, d\mathbf{y} = 1$. Please note that only locations inside the image domain contribute to the neighbourhood, i.e. $|\mathcal{N}(\mathbf{x})|$ becomes smaller towards image boundaries.

When minimising (18) w.r.t. c_{nl} this yields

$$c_{\text{nl}} = \frac{1}{1 + e^{-\Delta/\lambda}} \quad \text{with} \quad \Delta = \int_{\mathcal{N}(\mathbf{x})} \frac{1}{|\mathcal{N}(\mathbf{y})|} \left(T + S_2 - S_1\right) d\mathbf{y}, \quad (20)$$

At locations where all neighbourhoods have equal size this further simplifies to

$$c_{\text{nl}} = \frac{1}{1 + e^{-\Delta/\lambda}} \quad \text{with} \quad \Delta = T + \frac{1}{|\mathcal{N}(\mathbf{x})|} \int_{\mathcal{N}(\mathbf{x})} \left(S_2 - S_1\right) d\mathbf{y}. \quad (21)$$

Region Adaptive Scheme. As a final variant we propose a level-set-based approach. It replaces the selection cost term ϕ with a spatial smoothness term. Let $z : \Omega \to \mathbb{R}$ be a level-set function and let $c_{\text{region}}(z)$ denote a differential sigmoid function that approximates the Heavyside function

$$c_{\text{region}}(z) = \frac{1}{1 + e^{-z/\lambda}}. \quad (22)$$

The region adaptive scheme then reads

$$R_{\text{region}}\left(\mathbf{u}, z\right) = \int_{\Omega} \inf_{\mathbf{a},\mathbf{b}} \left\{ c_{\text{region}}(z) \cdot S_1\left(\mathbf{u}\right) + \left(1 - c_{\text{region}}(z)\right) \cdot \left(C_2\left(\mathbf{u}, \mathbf{a}, \mathbf{b}\right) + T\right) \right.$$
$$\left. + \beta \cdot S_{\text{aux}}\left(\mathbf{a}, \mathbf{b}\right) + \theta \cdot |\nabla c_{\text{region}}(z)| \right\} d\mathbf{x}. \quad (23)$$

Let us point out that this scheme comes with a slight drawback regarding the computational effort. While all previous approaches allow to estimate the weighting parameter/function in closed form, this is not possible for the region adaptive scheme. The reason is the spatial smoothness term, which requires to evolve the underlying level-set function z; see e.g. [1,11].

4   Minimisation

To minimise the non-convex energy functional (1) we derive the associated Euler-Lagrange equations and solve them by means of an incremental coarse-to-fine fixed point iteration [7]. Thereby, we compute on each resolution level a flow increment **du** and the increments **da**, **db** of the auxiliary functions. In this context, we apply a constraint normalisation to the linearised constancy assumptions as proposed in [28]. We then solve the resulting non-linear system of equations at each level as a series of linear systems of equations by keeping the non-linear expressions from the data and smoothness term fixed. As solver for each linear system of equations we apply a cascadic multicolour variant of the SOR method. In case of the global, local and non-local scheme we update the weighting parameter c, the weighting functions c_{local} and $c_{\text{nl}}/\bar{c}_{\text{nl}}$ in the same fashion as the non-linear expressions. To this end, we explicitly evaluate the corresponding equations (9), (16), and (19) and (20), respectively. Since the level-set function z cannot be evaluated in closed form, we employ an explicit scheme for its computation based on an upwind discretisation [21].

5   Experiments

Comparison of Selection Strategies. In our first experiment, we investigate the performance of our novel order-adaptive regularisers. Therefore, we created a set of synthetic image sequences that contain fronto-parallel motion, affine motion, or a combination of both; see Fig. 1. In order to visually assess the order selection quality of the different regularisers, we made use of the gradient magnitude of the ground truth flow. It yields small values for fronto-parallel motion and large values for affine motion and thus may serve as a rough indicator which type of motion is present. The gradient magnitude as well as the computed weighting maps c of the different selection schemes are depicted in Fig. 2. It shows the image-wise adaptation of the global approach as well as the pixel-wise adaptation of the other schemes. Moreover, one can see that the local approach exhibits a noisy selection behaviour which is less prominent in the approaches that consider neighbourhood information or spatial smoothness. Finally, one can observe that first order regularisation is preferred at motion discontinuities, while in other regions the order depends on the local fit; see Eqs. (16), (21), (22).

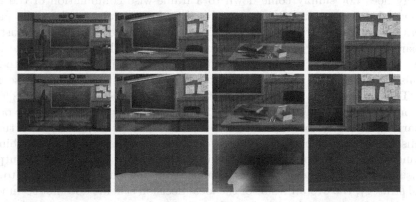

Fig. 1. Synthetic *Classroom* sequences. **From left to right**: Sequence 1 to 4. **First row**: First frame. **Second row**: Second frame. **Third row**: Ground truth flow field.

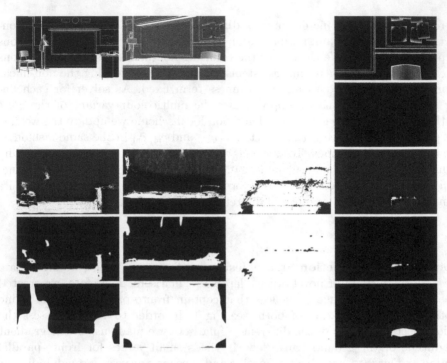

Fig. 2. Comparison of the adaptation behaviour of the proposed approaches in terms of the weighting map c. **From left to right:** Sequence 1 to 4. **From top to bottom:** Gradient magnitude of the ground truth flow field, global approach, local approach, non-local approach (window size 3×3) and region-based approach.

The corresponding quantitative evaluation in terms of the average endpoint error is given in Table 1. For each of the models the parameters have been optimised *jointly* for all sequences. As one can see, both single-order approaches are already outperformed by the global selection strategy. Please note that this strategy does not simply come down to a frame-wise combination of the first and second order results. On the one hand, it has to rely on the same parameters for both regularisation orders, since the energy of both terms must be comparable to allow for a reasonable decision. On the other hand, the selection of the regularisation order can be applied level-wise during the coarse-to-fine optimisation, since this allows to correct less reliable decisions from coarse grid data. This also explains why even w.r.t. to the individual error scores, the global decision strategy is sometimes able to outperform the results of the single-order regularisers. Please also note that the pure second order regulariser is actually an anisotropic variant of TGV [6]. This demonstrates that explicitly combining first and second order smoothness terms in an adaptive manner allows to outperform such implicit strategies based on robust coupling terms. In contrast to the global strategy, the overall result of the local decision scheme does not seem very convincing. However, a closer look at the individual error values reveals that this strategy actually provides the best results for three out of four sequences. The

Table 1. Comparison of different regularisation strategies for the four synthetic *Classroom* sequences in terms of the average endpoint error (AEE) and runtime.

		Seq. 1	Seq. 2	Seq. 3	Seq. 4	Avg.	Runtime
First order		0.129	0.358	2.038	**0.088**	0.653	17 s
Second order		0.141	0.370	0.669	0.102	0.321	75 s
Adaptive order	Global	0.141	0.365	0.667	0.095	0.317	100 s
Adaptive order	Local	**0.111**	**0.260**	1.115	**0.088**	0.393	105 s
Adaptive order	Non-local	0.116	0.275	0.737	0.095	**0.307**	120 s
Adaptive order	Region	0.125	0.366	**0.662**	0.098	0.313	180 s

Table 2. Comparison of different regularisation strategies for the four standard benchmarks in terms of the average endpoint error (AEE) and the bad pixel error (BP).

		Middlebury (AEE)	Sintel (AEE)	KITTI '12 (BP)	KITTI '15 (BP)
First order		0.213	4.327	18.026	30.053
Second order		0.222	6.518	9.461	22.736
Adaptive order	Global	0.211	4.213	9.423	22.424
Adaptive order	Local	0.211	**4.082**	11.537	24.938
Adaptive order	Non-local	0.211	4.145	9.468	**22.158**
Adaptive order	Region	**0.208**	4.358	**9.415**	22.343

main problem lies in the noisy selection behaviour which results from the pixelwise decision process. The best overall performance is provided by the non-local strategy and the region-based method. They combine the flexibility of the local strategy with the robustness of the global method.

Comparison on Benchmark Data. In our second experiment we compare the four novel regularisers using recent optical flow benchmarks. To this, end, we computed results for the training data sets of the Middlebury [2], the KITTI 2012 [14], the KITTI 2015 [19] and the MPI Sintel [8] benchmark. We optimised the parameters for all sequences of a benchmark jointly, but for the benchmarks themselves separately using the provided training data. The corresponding results are listed in Table 2. On the one hand, it becomes explicit that the order-adaptive strategies successfully combine the benefits of pure first and second order regularisation methods. In most cases they even outperform the best single-order result. On the other hand, the tendency of the different strategies confirms our observations from the first experiment. While the local approach can yield very good results (Sintel), it suffers from noisy decisions at the same time (KITTI 2012 and KITTI 2015). In contrast, the non-local scheme and the region-based scheme perform best. Also the global selection strategy performs surprisingly well due to its robustness. Please note that by optimising the activation cost T jointly with the other parameters, the resulting decision scheme may favour a certain regularisation order depending on the training data. However, the decision schemes still allow to choose between both regularisation orders which significantly differs from just learning the regularisation order.

Comparison to the Literature. In our final experiment, we compare our results to the ones from the literature. To this end, we submitted the results of our non-local method to the aforementioned benchmarks. As expected, we obtain similar results as comparable first order methods (e.g. Zimmer *et al.* [28]) in the Middlebury and the Sintel benchmark (Rank 30 and 54) and even better results than comparable second order methods (e.g. Demetz *et al.* [12], Ranftl *et al.* [23]) for the KITTI 2012 and KITTI 2015 benchmark (Rank 26 and 25). This confirms that adaptively selecting the regularisation order is indeed worthwhile.

6   Conclusion

In this paper we have investigated the usefulness of adaptively selecting the regularisation order in variational optical flow estimation. In this context, we have proposed four different selection strategies and with it four novel order-adaptive regularisers that adaptively combine two anisotropic smoothness terms of first and second order, respectively. Thereby, we proposed a local and a global selection strategy as well as a non-local and a region-based variant. While the global selection strategy turned out to be highly robust at the expense of being less adaptive, the local approach allowed a flexible point-wise selection at the expense of producing noisy decisions. By imposing some form of spatial regularity, i.e. neighbourhood information or a spatial smoothness term, we finally succeeded to combine the advantages of both strategies. These considerations were confirmed by our experiments. They showed that adaptively combining different regularisation orders not only allows to outperform single-order strategies but also that in-frame-adaptivity can be useful if the decision process is regularised.

Acknowledgements. We thank the German Research Foundation (DFG) for financial support within project B04 of SFB/Transregio 161.

References

1. Amiaz, T., Kiryati, N.: Piecewise-smooth dense optical flow via level sets. Int. J. Comput. Vis. **68**(2), 111–124 (2006)
2. Baker, S., Scharstein, D., Lewis, J.P., Roth, S., Black, M.J., Szeliski, R.: A database and evaluation methodology for optical flow. Int. J. Comput. Vis. **92**(1), 1–31 (2011)
3. Black, M.J., Anandan, P.: The robust estimation of multiple motions: parametric and piecewise-smooth flow fields. Comput. Vis. Image Underst. **63**(1), 75–104 (1996)
4. Blake, A., Zisserman, A.: Visual Reconstruction. MIT Press, Cambridge (1987)
5. Braux-Zin, J., Dupont, R., Bartoli, A.: A general dense image matching framework combining direct and feature-based costs. In: Proceedings of the International Conference on Computer Vision, pp. 185–192 (2013)
6. Bredies, K., Kunisch, K., Pock, T.: Total generalized variation. SIAM J. Imaging Sci. **3**(3), 492–526 (2010)

7. Brox, T., Bruhn, A., Papenberg, N., Weickert, J.: High accuracy optical flow estimation based on a theory for warping. In: Pajdla, T., Matas, J. (eds.) ECCV 2004. LNCS, vol. 3024, pp. 25–36. Springer, Heidelberg (2004). doi:10.1007/978-3-540-24673-2_3

8. Butler, D.J., Wulff, J., Stanley, G.B., Black, M.J.: A naturalistic open source movie for optical flow evaluation. In: Fitzgibbon, A., Lazebnik, S., Perona, P., Sato, Y., Schmid, C. (eds.) ECCV 2012. LNCS, vol. 7577, pp. 611–625. Springer, Heidelberg (2012). doi:10.1007/978-3-642-33783-3_44

9. Bruhn, A., Weickert, J.: Towards ultimate motion estimation: combining highest accuracy with real-time performance. In: Proceedings of the International Conference on Computer Vision, pp. 749–755 (2005)

10. Charbonnier, P., Blanc-Féraud, L., Aubert, G., Barlaud, M.: Deterministic edge-preserving regularization in computed imaging. IEEE Trans. Image Process. 6(2), 298–311 (1997)

11. Cremers, D., Soatto, S.: Motion competition: a variational approach to piecewise parametric motion segmentation. Int. J. Comput. Vis. 62(3), 249–265 (2005)

12. Demetz, O., Stoll, M., Volz, S., Weickert, J., Bruhn, A.: Learning brightness transfer functions for the joint recovery of illumination changes and optical flow. In: Fleet, D., Pajdla, T., Schiele, B., Tuytelaars, T. (eds.) ECCV 2014. LNCS, vol. 8689, pp. 455–471. Springer, Cham (2014). doi:10.1007/978-3-319-10590-1_30

13. Förstner, W. Gülch, E.: A fast operator for detection and precise location of distinct points, corners and centres of circular features. In: Proceedings of the ISPRS Intercommission Conference on Fast Processing of Photogrammetric Data, pp. 281–305 (1987)

14. Geiger, A., Lenz, P., Urtasun, R.: Are we ready for autonomous driving? The KITTI vision benchmark suite. In: Proceedings of the IEEE Conference on Computer Vision and Pattern Recognition, pp. 3354–3361 (2012)

15. Hafner, D., Schroers, C., Weickert, J.: Introducing maximal anisotropy into second order coupling models. In: Gall, J., Gehler, P., Leibe, B. (eds.) GCPR 2015. LNCS, vol. 9358, pp. 79–90. Springer, Cham (2015). doi:10.1007/978-3-319-24947-6_7

16. Horn, B., Schunck, B.: Determining optical flow. Artif. Intell. 17, 185–203 (1981)

17. Kuschk, G., Cremers, D.: Fast and accurate large-scale stereo reconstruction using variational methods. In: Proceedings of the ICCV Workshops, pp. 1–8 (2013)

18. Lenzen, F., Becker, F., Lellmann, J.: Adaptive second-order total variation: an approach aware of slope discontinuities. In: Kuijper, A., Bredies, K., Pock, T., Bischof, H. (eds.) SSVM 2013. LNCS, vol. 7893, pp. 61–73. Springer, Heidelberg (2013). doi:10.1007/978-3-642-38267-3_6

19. Menze, M., Geiger, A.: Object scene flow for autonomous vehicles. In Proceedings of the IEEE Conference on Computer Vision and Pattern Recognition, pp. 3061–3070 (2015)

20. Nagel, H.-H., Enkelmann, W.: An investigation of smoothness constraints for the estimation of displacement vector fields from image sequences. IEEE Trans. Pattern Anal. Mach. Intell. 8(5), 565–593 (1986)

21. Osher, S., Sethian, J.A.: Fronts propagating with curvature-dependent speed: algorithms based on Hamilton-Jacobi formulations. J. Comput. Phys. 79(1), 12–49 (1988)

22. Perona, P., Malik, J.: Scale space and edge detection using anisotropic diffusion. IEEE Trans. Pattern Anal. Mach. Intell. 2, 629–639 (1990)

23. Ranftl, R., Bredies, K., Pock, T.: Non-local total generalized variation for optical flow estimation. In: Fleet, D., Pajdla, T., Schiele, B., Tuytelaars, T. (eds.) ECCV 2014. LNCS, vol. 8689, pp. 439–454. Springer, Cham (2014). doi:10.1007/978-3-319-10590-1_29
24. Vogel, C., Roth, S., Schindler, K.: An evaluation of data costs for optical flow. In: Weickert, J., Hein, M., Schiele, B. (eds.) GCPR 2013. LNCS, vol. 8142, pp. 343–353. Springer, Heidelberg (2013). doi:10.1007/978-3-642-40602-7_37
25. Volz, S., Bruhn, A., Valgaerts, L., Zimmer, H.: Modeling temporal coherence for optical flow. In: Proceedings of the International Conference on Computer Vision (2011)
26. Weickert, J., Schnörr, C.: A theoretical framework for convex regularizers in PDE-based computation of image motion. Int. J. Comput. Vis. 45(3), 245–264 (2001)
27. Xu, L., Jia, J., Matsushita, Y.: Motion detail preserving optical flow estimation. IEEE Trans. Pattern Anal. Mach. Intell. 34, 1744–1757 (2012)
28. Zimmer, H., Bruhn, A., Weickert, J.: Optic flow in harmony. Int. J. Comput. Vis. 93(3), 368–388 (2011)

Transport Based Image Morphing
with Intensity Modulation

Jan Maas[1], Martin Rumpf[2], and Stefan Simon[2(✉)]

[1] Institute of Science and Technology Austria, Klosterneuburg, Austria
jan.maas@ist.ac.at
[2] Institute for Numerical Simulation, Universität Bonn, Bonn, Germany
martin.rumpf@ins.uni-bonn.de, s6stsimo@uni-bonn.de

Abstract. We present a generalized optimal transport model in which the mass-preserving constraint for the L^2-Wasserstein distance is relaxed by introducing a source term in the continuity equation. The source term is also incorporated in the path energy by means of its squared L^2-norm in time of a functional with linear growth in space. This extension of the original transport model enables local density modulations, which is a desirable feature in applications such as image warping and blending. A key advantage of the use of a functional with linear growth in space is that it allows for singular sources and sinks, which can be supported on points or lines. On a technical level, the L^2-norm in time ensures a disintegration of the source in time, which we use to obtain the well-posedness of the model and the existence of geodesic paths. The numerical discretization is based on the proximal splitting approach [18] and selected numerical test cases show the potential of the proposed approach. Furthermore, the approach is applied to the warping and blending of textures.

Keywords: Optimal transport · Texture morphing · Generalized Wasserstein distance · Proximal splitting

1 An Optimal Transport Model with Source Term

In the last decade optimal transport became a very popular tool in image processing and image analysis [18], where the quadratic Wasserstein distance is applied for instance in non-rigid image registration and warping. It was also used to robustly measure distances between images or to segment and classify images [17]. Driven by applications for instance in imaging [2,3,21] there is a strong demand to develop robust and efficient algorithms to compute optimal transport geodesics, such as the entropic regularization [4,16] or the sparse multiscale approach [22].

Electronic supplementary material The online version of this chapter (doi:10.1007/978-3-319-58771-4_45) contains supplementary material, which is available to authorized users.

© Springer International Publishing AG 2017
F. Lauze et al. (Eds.): SSVM 2017, LNCS 10302, pp. 563–577, 2017.
DOI: 10.1007/978-3-319-58771-4_45

In their groundbreaking paper Benamou and Brenier [1] reformulated (for numerical purposes) the problem of optimal transport first considered by Monge and then relaxed by Kantorovich in a continuum mechanical framework describing the evolution of the mass distribution in time. This reformulation turned out to be the geodesic equation on the L^2 Wasserstein space. For an underlying flow of a density θ with Eulerian velocity v one considers the path energy

$$\mathcal{E}[\theta, v] = \int_0^1 \int_D \theta |v|^2 \, dx \, dt, \tag{1}$$

where $D \subset \mathbb{R}^d$ is assumed to be a closed, bounded convex domain with Lipschitz boundary. Then the quadratic Wasserstein distance $W_2[\theta_A, \theta_B]$ between two probability density function θ_A and θ_B can be computed by minimizing $\mathcal{E}$ over all density functions $\theta : [0, 1] \times D \to \mathbb{R}$ and velocity fields $v : [0, 1] \times D \to \mathbb{R}^d$ subject to the continuity equation $\partial_t \theta + \text{div}(\theta v) = 0$ and the constraints $\theta(0) = \theta_A$ and $\theta(1) = \theta_B$. Here the continuity equation enforces $\theta(t)$ to remain in the space of probability densities. In applications such as image registration or image morphing, input images are frequently not of the same mass. Thus, a contrast modulation on the input images is required before an optimal match between the input images can be computed. But, even if the total mass of the input images coincides, the incorporation of local intensity modulation is desirable to cope with the variability of natural images and to avoid "artificial" long range transport just for the purpose of mass redistribution between totally independent image structures.

Recently, several optimal transport models [8, 13–15, 19] have been proposed, which relax the mass preserving condition and incorporate a source term in the transport model to allow arbitrary input measures. To this end one introduces a source term $z : [0, 1] \times D \to \mathbb{R}$ in the modified continuity equation

$$\partial_t \theta + \text{div}(\theta v) = z. \tag{2}$$

This source terms has then to be incorporated in the path energy via a suitable penalty term, which represents the cost of mass production. Here, we propose the following generalized action functional

$$\mathcal{E}_\delta[\theta, v, z] = \int_0^1 \int_D \theta |v|^2 \, dx \, dt + \frac{1}{\delta} \int_0^1 \left(\int_D r(z) \, dx \right)^2 \, dt \tag{3}$$

subject to the relaxed continuity Eq. (2) and the constraints $\theta(0) = \theta_A$ and $\theta(1) = \theta_B$, where $r : \mathbb{R} \to \mathbb{R}$ is a non-negative, convex function satisfying $r(0) = 0$ and the linear growth condition $r(s) \leq C(1 + |s|)$ for all $s \in \mathbb{R}$. Cases of interest in our considerations are $r(s) = |s|$ corresponding to the L^1 norm in space or more appropriate in imaging applications a Huber norm in space with $r(s) = \frac{1}{2\beta} s^2$ for $|s| \leq \beta$ and $|s| - \frac{\beta}{2}$ else for some $\beta > 0$. In this model $\delta > 0$ denotes a penalty parameter which allows to grade the mass modulation rate. It is desirable to allow also for singular sources which are supported on line segments of points in space. The linear growth property will ensure that singular source terms are admissible.

For this model existence of a shortest (geodesic) paths given by a minimizer of the cost functional $\mathcal{E}_\delta$ existed. To prove this the appropriate framework is that of Radon measures and a suitable decomposition of the measures for mass, momentum and source term into absolutely continuous and orthogonal parts with respect to the Lebesgue measure. Since these decompositions are not unique, it is useful to require 1-homogeneity of the integrands for the singular measures, which ensures that the definition of the energy functionals does not depend on the decomposition. In particular, we will observe that our class of models allows singular sources. Furthermore, the L^2-norm in time provides an equi-integrability estimate, which guarantees compactness in the space of curves of Radon measures and is thus essential to establish existence of a minimizer.

The flow formulation (1) has been used in [1] primarily to compute optimal transport geodesics numerically with an augmented Lagrangian approach. In [18] it was shown that a proximal splitting algorithm leads to an equivalent optimization method. We will extend this approach to derive a suitable numerical discretization of our model.

This paper is organized as follows: First, in Sect. 2 we give an overview of recent developments on optimal transport models with source term. In Sect. 3 we rigorously define the generalized optimal transport model and establish the existence of optimal transport geodesics. Then we propose in Sect. 4 an efficient numerical scheme via proper adaptation of the proximal splitting method. Finally, in Sect. 5 we present results and discuss properties of the generalized model.

2   Related Work on Optimal Transport with Source Term

In very recent years there has been a lot of activity on the extension of optimal transport distances to spaces of densities or measures with possibly different masses, which we here briefly summarize and point out differences to our model. A so-called partial optimal transport model was proposed by Caffarelli and McCann [5] and analyzed by Figalli [12]. By relaxing the marginal constraint in the Kantorovich formulation, they ask for the optimal transport of a fixed fraction of some initial to a final density function. Note that there is actually no source term involved, but one is rather interested in the geometry of the subsets which are actually transported.

Furthermore, there are generalized transport distances which are closely related to the Benamou-Brenier formulation and based on a minimization of a path energy subject to the continuity equation with source term. Picolli and Rossi [19, 20] considered minimizer of the path energy

$$\mathcal{E}_{L^1} = \int_0^1 \int_D \theta |v|^2 \, dx \, dt + \left(\int_0^1 \int_D |z| \, dx \, dt \right)^2$$

subject to Eq. (2). They prove for absolutely continuous measures θ and absolutely continuous sources z with respect to the Lebesque measure that this geodesic formulation corresponds to solving the problem

$$\inf_{\tilde{\theta}_A, \tilde{\theta}_B : |\tilde{\theta}_A| = |\tilde{\theta}_B|} |\tilde{\theta}_A - \theta_A| + |\tilde{\theta}_B - \theta_B| + W_2(\tilde{\theta}_A, \tilde{\theta}_B).$$

Instead of the squared L^1 norm, Maas et al. [15] choose as penalization of the source term the squared L^2 norm:

$$\mathcal{E}_{L^2} = \int_0^1 \int_D \theta |v|^2 \, dx \, dt + \int_0^1 \int_D |z|^2 \, dx \, dt.$$

Chizat et al. [8] and Liero et al. [14] proposed an interpolating distance between the Wasserstein distance and the Fisher-Rao distance by minimizing the energy

$$\mathcal{E}_{WF} = \int_0^1 \int_D \theta(|v|^2 + \alpha(z)) \, dx \, dt$$

subject to the continuity equation $\partial_t \theta + \mathrm{div}(\theta v) = \theta z$. Note that the source term in this model is integrated w.r.t. to the measure given by θ. Furthermore, in [7] a static Kantorovich formulation is derived and it is shown that the distance in [19,20] arises as a special case.

At first glance, the distances obtained by minimizing the energies $\mathcal{E}_{L^1}$ and $\mathcal{E}_{L^2}$ seem to be very similar to our proposed energy (3). The difference becomes crucial when properly extending the energies to the space of Radon measures. In fact, a penalization of the source term squared L^2 norm does not allow singular sources which are for instance concentrated on lines of points, whereas such sources are possible in our model as it will be demonstrated in Sect. 4. However, choosing a penalization in the L^1 norm in space-time does not guarantee that the resulting minimizing measure is actually a curve in time in the space of Radon measures. Indeed, the generalized Benamou and Brenier model (3) allows for singular measures as source terms, which are for instance concentrated on lower dimensional sets.

3   Variational Formulation for the Generalized Transport Model

Here, we formulate a measure-valued setup for the energy in (3) as well as for the continuity equation with source term (2). We follow the lines of [9] and the treatment of the source term in the L^2-norm in space-time presented in [15].

First, we apply the change of variables $(\theta, v) \mapsto (\theta, m = \theta v)$ already used by Benamou and Brenier [1]. Instead of the pair (θ, v) we consider the pair (θ, m), where m denotes the momentum, such that the integrand $|v|^2 \theta$ pointwise transforms into

$$\Phi(\theta, m) = \begin{cases} \frac{|m|^2}{\theta} & \text{if } \theta > 0, \\ 0 & \text{if } (\theta, m) = 0, \\ +\infty & \text{otherwise.} \end{cases}$$

with the advantage that Φ is lower-semicontinuous, convex and 1-homogeneous.

A generalized continuity equation $\partial_t \mu + \mathrm{div}(\nu) = \zeta$ in terms of measure-valued quantities, namely mass $\mu \in \mathscr{M}^+([0,1] \times D)$, momentum $\nu \in \mathscr{M}([0,1] \times D; \mathbb{R}^d)$, and source term $\zeta \in \mathscr{M}([0,1] \times D)$ and for given boundary values $\mu_0 = \mu_A$ and $\mu_1 = \mu_B$ is defined in the sense of distributions, by testing against all space-time test functions $\eta \in C^1([0,1] \times D)$:

$$0 = \int_0^1 \left[\int_D \partial_t \eta(t,x) \, \mathrm{d}\mu_t(x) + \int_D \nabla \eta(t,x) \cdot \mathrm{d}\nu_t(x) + \int_D \eta(t,x) \, \mathrm{d}\zeta_t(x) \right] \mathrm{d}t$$
$$- \int_D \eta(1,x) \, \mathrm{d}\mu_B(x) + \int_D \eta(0,x) \, \mathrm{d}\mu_A(x). \tag{4}$$

We will consider curves of measures on D instead of just measures on the product space $[0,1] \times D$ as the proper measure theoretic setup for the continuity equation with source term. Further, we denote the set of all solutions of the weak continuity equation with source term by $\mathcal{CE}[0,1]$.

Next, we define the energy (3) in terms of measures. To this end we decompose for each $t \in [0,1]$ the triple $(\mu_t, \nu_t, \zeta_t) \in \mathscr{M}^+(D) \times \mathscr{M}(D; \mathbb{R}^d) \times \mathscr{M}(D)$ using the Lebesgue decomposition theorem. Thus, we can rigorously define the total energy functional $\mathcal{E}_\delta$ (cf. 3) for measures $(\mu, \nu, \zeta) \in \mathscr{M}^+([0,1] \times D) \times \mathscr{M}([0,1] \times D; \mathbb{R}^d) \times \mathscr{M}([0,1] \times D)$ using these decompositions. Finally, following [15], we obtain the following existence result for minimizing paths.

Theorem 1 (Existence of geodesics). *Let $\delta \in (0,\infty)$ and take $\mu_A, \mu_B \in \mathscr{M}^+(D)$. Then there exists a minimizer $(\overline{\mu}_t, \overline{\nu}_t, \overline{\zeta}_t)_{t \in [0,1]}$ of the energy $\mathcal{E}_\delta$ subject to the weak continuity Eq. (4). Moreover, this defines a metric $\mathcal{W}_\delta$ on $\mathscr{M}^+(D)$, and the associated curve $(\overline{\mu}_t)_{t \in [0,1]}$ is a constant speed geodesic for $\mathcal{W}_\delta$, i.e.,*

$$\mathcal{W}_\delta[\overline{\mu}_s, \overline{\mu}_t] = |s - t| \mathcal{W}_\delta[\mu_A, \mu_B]$$

for all $s, t \in [0,1]$.

The proof of this theorem with an additional representation formula for the generalized Wasserstein distance is given in the supplementary material accompanying this paper.

4   Proximal Splitting Algorithm

In this section we derive a numerical scheme to compute geodesics for our new distance for $d = 2$. To this end, we will adapt the proximal splitting algorithm, which was proposed by Papadakis et al. [18] for the classical L^2 optimal transport problem. In detail, the constraint optimization problem is first rewritten as a non-constraint minimization problem adding the indicator function of the set of solutions of the continuity equation $\mathcal{CE}[0,1]$ to the cost functional. Then, the proximal splitting algorithm yields a solution scheme, which only requires to solve a space-time elliptic problem and to project pointwise onto a convex set. The resulting algorithm is equivalent to the augmented Lagrangian approach in

[1]. Different from [1,18] we will use a finite element discretization instead of finite differences.

Let us briefly recall the definition and the basic properties of a proximal mapping (see for instance [6,18]). In the following, let $(X.\| \cdot \|_X)$ be a Hilbert space and $f : X \to \mathbb{R} \cup \{\infty\}$ a convex and lsc function. Then the proximal mapping of f is defined as

$$\text{prox}_f(x) = \underset{y \in X}{\text{argmin}} f(y) + \frac{1}{2}\|x - y\|^2.$$

In the sequel it will be important to compute the proximal mapping of the indicator function

$$\mathcal{I}_K(x) = \begin{cases} 0 & \text{if } x \in K, \\ +\infty & \text{if } x \notin K. \end{cases}$$

of a convex set $K \subset X$, which is just given by $\text{prox}_{\mathcal{I}_K}(x) = \text{proj}_K(x)$, where proj_K is the orthogonal projection on K with respect to the norm $\| \cdot \|_X$. Now, we suppose that D is a polygonal domain and consider a tetrahedral mesh S_h with grid size h for the space time domain $[0,1] \times D$, which is generated from a triangular mesh for the domain D via subdivision of prisms $(k\,h,(k+1)h) \times T$ (with T being a triangle) into 3 tetrahedrons such that the resulting tetrahedral mesh is an admissible triangulation in space time. On this triangulation we define finite element spaces

$V^1(S_h) = \{\phi_h : [0,1] \times D \to \mathbb{R} : \phi_h \text{ continuous and piecewise linear on elements in } S_h\}$,
$V^0(S_h) = \{\theta_h : [0,1] \times D \to \mathbb{R} : \theta_h \text{ piecewise constant on elements in } S_h\}$.

This allows us define discretization

$$\theta_h \in V^0(S_h), \quad m_h \in \left(V^0(S_h)\right)^d, \quad z_h \in V^1(S_h),$$

for the measures for mass, momentum and source, respectively. Furthermore, we will use the notation $p_h = (\theta_h, m_h) \in V^0(S_h)^{d+1}$. For a triple $(\theta_h, m_h, z_h) \in V_h^0(S_h) \times V_h^0(S_h)^d \times V_h^1(S_h)$ we choose a weighted L^2 norm

$$\|(\theta_h, m_h, z_h)\| := \left(\int_0^1 \int_D |\theta_h|^2 + |m_h|^2 + \frac{1}{\delta}|z_h|^2 \, dx \, dt\right)^{\frac{1}{2}},$$

which can be computed exactly by choosing a quadrature rule of at least second order. In correspondence to the weak formulation (4) the set of discrete solutions of a continuity equation is defined as follows:

Definition 1. *Let $\theta_A, \theta_B \in V^0(S_h)$ be given. Then, the set $\mathcal{CE}_h$ of solutions of a weak continuity equation with source term and boundary values θ_A, θ_B is given by all triples $(\theta_h, m_h, z_h) \in V_h^0(S) \times V_h^0(S)^d \times V_h^1(S)$ satisfying*

$$\int_0^1 \int_D \theta_h \partial_t \phi_h + m_h \nabla_x \phi_h + z\phi_h \, dx \, dt = \int_D \phi_h(1)\theta_B - \phi_h(0)\theta_A \, dx \quad \forall \phi_h \in V^1(S_h).$$

Note that we used Neumann boundary condition in space. The approach can easily be adopted in case of Dirichlet or periodic boundary conditions.

Now, we can state a discrete version of the minimization problem:

$$\inf_{(\theta_h, m_h, z_h) \in \mathcal{CE}_h} \left(\int_0^1 \int_D \Phi(\theta_h, m_h) \, dx \, dt + \frac{1}{\delta} \int_0^1 \left(\int_D \mathcal{R}_h(z_h) \, dx \right)^2 dt \right),$$

where $\mathcal{R}_h[z_h]$ denotes a suitable interpolation of $r(z_h)$. Here, we define $\mathcal{R}_h[z_h](t, x)$ as the piecewise affine interpolation of $r(z_h((k-1)h, \cdot))$ on the triangle T for $(t, x) \in (kh, (k+1)h) \times T$ (one of the prisms underlying the tetrahedral grid). Numerically, we are not able to treat singular measures as presented in Sect. 3. Our concrete choices of $r(s)$, which coincide with $|s|$ for large s allow to approximate such measures in the source term cost supported on the union of the support of basis functions. Thus point or line sources are numerically treated via sources with support thickness $2h$. To apply a proximal splitting algorithm, we split the functional into

$$F_1(\theta_h, m_h, z_h) := F_{\text{trans}}(\theta_h, m_h) + \frac{1}{\delta} F_{\text{source}}(z_h)$$

with $F_{\text{trans}}(\theta_h, m_h) := \int_0^1 \int_D \Phi(\theta_h, m_h) \, dx \, dt$, $F_{\text{source}}(z_h) := \int_0^1 \left(\int_D \mathcal{R}_h[z_h] \, dx \right)^2 dt$,

$$F_2(\theta_h, m_h, z_h) := \mathcal{I}_{\mathcal{CE}_h}(\theta_h, m_h, z_h).$$

Next, let us compute the proximal mappings of F_1 and F_2.

Proximal Map of F_2. The computation of the proximal mapping of the indicator function of $\mathcal{CE}_h$ requires the orthogonal projection of a point $(p_h = (\theta_h, m_h), z_h) \in V^0(S)^{d+1} \times V^1(S)$ onto $\mathcal{CE}_h$, i.e. we ask for $(p_h^*, z_h^*) \in \text{argmin}_{(q_h, w_h) \in \mathcal{CE}_h} \|(p_h, z_h) - (q_h, w_h)\|^2$. The associated Lagrangian is given by

$$L[(q_h, w_h), \psi_h] = \|(p_h, z_h) - (q_h, w_h)\|^2 - \int_0^1 \int_D q_h \cdot \nabla_{(t,x)} \psi_h + w_h \psi_h \, dx \, dt + \int_D \psi_h(1) \theta_B - \psi_h(0) \theta_A \, dx,$$

with a Lagrange multiplier $\psi_h \in V^1(S_h)$. In terms of this Lagrangian the projection problem can be written as a saddle point problem, where as ask for $(p_h^*, z_h^*, \phi_h^*) \in V^0(S)^{d+1} \times V^1(S) \times V^1(S)$, such that

$$L[(p_h^*, z_h^*, \phi_h^*)] = \min_{(q_h, w_h) \in V_h^0(S)^{d+1} \times V_h^1(S)} \max_{\psi_h \in V_h^1(S)} L[(q_h, w_h, \psi_h)].$$

The Euler-Lagrange equations corresponding to this saddle point problem are given by

$$\int_0^1 \int_D p_h^* \cdot \nabla_{(t,x)} \psi_h + z_h^* \psi_h \, dx \, dt = \int_D \psi_h(1) \, \theta_B - \psi_h(0) \, \theta_A \, dx \quad \forall \psi_h \in V_h^1(S) \quad (5)$$

$$\int_0^1 \int_D q_h \cdot \nabla_{(t,x)} \phi_h^* \, dx \, dt = \int_0^1 \int_D 2(p_h^* - p_h) \, q_h \, dx \, dt \quad \forall q_h \in V_h^0(S)^{d+1} \quad (6)$$

$$\int_0^1 \int_D \phi_h^* w_h \, dx \, dt = \int_0^1 \int_D \frac{2}{\delta}(z_h^* - z_h) \, w_h \, dx \, dt \quad \forall w_h \in V_h^1(S) \quad (7)$$

Testing Eq. (6) with $q_h = \nabla_{(t,x)} \psi_h$ and then using Eq. (5) gives

$$\int_0^1 \int_D \frac{1}{2} \nabla_{(t,x)} \phi_h^* \cdot \nabla_{(t,x)} \psi_h \, dx \, dt = \int_0^1 \int_D (p_h^* - p_h) \cdot \nabla_{(t,x)} \psi_h \, dx \, dt$$

$$= \int_D \psi_h(1) \theta_B - \psi_h(0) \theta_A \, dx - \int_0^1 \int_D z_h^* \psi_h + p_h \cdot \nabla_{(t,x)} \psi_h \, dx \, dt$$

Hence, by using Eq. (7) ($z_h^* = z_h + \frac{\delta}{2} \phi_h^*$) we obtain

$$\int_0^1 \int_D \frac{1}{2} \nabla_{(t,x)} \phi_h^* \nabla_{(t,x)} \psi_h + \frac{\delta}{2} \phi_h^* \psi_h \, dx \, dt = \int_D \psi_h(1) \theta_B - \psi_h(0) \theta_A \, dx$$

$$- \int_0^1 \int_D z_h \psi_h + p_h \nabla_{(t,x)} \psi_h \, dx \, dt$$

for all $\psi_h \in V_h^1(S)$.

After computing ϕ_h the solution of the projection problem is given by

$$p_h^* = p_h + \frac{1}{2} \nabla_{(t,x)} \phi_h^*, \quad z_h^* = z_h + \frac{\delta}{2} \phi_h^*.$$

Proximal Map of F_1. The transport term F_{trans} does only depend on θ_h and m_h and can be treated exactly as for classical optimal transport. Since we observe pointwise that $\Phi^* = \mathcal{I}_K$ is an indicator function of the convex set

$$K = \left\{ (\theta, m) \; : \; \theta + \frac{|m|^2}{4} \leq 0 \right\},$$

(see [1]) we can use Moreau's identity and get

$$\text{prox}_\Phi (\theta, m) = (\theta, m) - \text{prox}_{\Phi^*} (\theta, m) = (\theta, m) - \text{proj}_K (\theta, m).$$

The projection onto K can be computed separately on each tetrahedron of the simplicial mesh S_h due to the choice of our finite element spaces with $p_h \in V^0(S_h)^{d+1}$.

We note that for a source term in L^2 both in space and time we easily get a pointwise update

$$\text{prox}_{\frac{\gamma}{\delta} |\cdot|^2} (z) = \underset{w}{\text{argmin}} \frac{1}{\delta} |w|^2 + \frac{1}{\delta} |w - z|^2 = \frac{1}{1 + \gamma} z.$$

Following the computation in [11] we also get a pointwise update for the proximal operator of the source term in $L^1(L^1)$, which is given by

$$\text{prox}_{\frac{\gamma}{\delta} |z|} (z) = \begin{cases} 0, & \text{if } |z| \leq \frac{\gamma}{2} \\ z - \frac{\gamma}{2} sgn(z), & \text{else.} \end{cases}$$

Thus, a numerical scheme for a source term in $L^1(L^1)$ would be as simple as for a source term in $L^2(L^2)$, but existence of geodesics is not guaranteed.

In case of a linear growth function $r(\cdot)$ the minimization problem only decouples in time but not in space. Hence, for each discrete time step k we have to solve

$$\underset{w_h}{\operatorname{argmin}} \frac{\gamma}{\delta} \left(\int_D \mathcal{R}_h[w_h](kh, x) \, dx \right)^2 + \frac{1}{2\delta} \int_D |w_h(kh, x) - z_h(kh, x)|^2 \, dx.$$

For a source term in $L^2(L^1)$ the minimization problem is well defined, but since $r(z) = |z|$ is not differentiable it is not clear how to find the minimizer. Therefore we restrict our numerical computations to the case of r being the Huber function and use a gradient descent to compute this minimum.

Douglas-Rachford Splitting Algorithm. Finally, to solve the minimization problem

$$(p_h^*, z_h^*) \in \underset{(q_h, w_h) \in V^0(S)^{d+1} \times V^1(S)}{\operatorname{argmin}} F_1(q_h, w_h) + F_2(q_h, w_h)$$

we apply the Douglas-Rachford splitting algorithm [10], which is given by the iteration

$$(q_h^n, w_h^n) = \operatorname{prox}_{\gamma F_2}((p_h^{n-1}, z_h^{n-1})),$$
$$(p_h^n, z_h^n) = (p_h, z_h)^{n-1} + \alpha \left(\operatorname{prox}_{\gamma F_1}(2(q_h^n, w_h^n) - (p_h, z_h)^{n-1}) - (q_h, w_h)^n \right),$$

for an initial value (p_h^0, z_h^0) and a step size weight α have to be chosen. It is guaranteed that for $\gamma > 0$ and $\alpha \in (0, 2)$ the sequence (p_h^n, z_h^n) as well as $(q_h^n, w_h)^n$ converges to a solution of the minimization problem.

5   Numerical Results

We have applied the proposed scheme for the optimal transport with source term for different sets of (θ_A, θ_B), which we show in the accompanying figures always from left $(\theta(0) = \theta_A)$ to right $(\theta(1) = \theta_B)$. In all computations $D = (0, 1)^2$ and the grid size is $h = 2^{-7}$. Recall, that the Huber function is given by $r(s) = \frac{1}{2\beta} s^2$ for $|s| \leq \beta$ and $|s| - \frac{\beta}{2}$, where we choose $\beta = 10^{-4}$. At first, we demonstrate that the density function r for the source term is the right choice to deal with approximations of singular measures as source terms. To this end, we consider in Fig. 1 measures θ_A and θ_B supported on a thin rectangular strip with constant but different density. The proposed model with the L^2–Huber $[L^2(H)]$ type cost functional $\int_0^1 (\int_D r(\theta) \, dx)^2 \, dt$ for the source term is able to generate the required singular measure and the Wasserstein geodesic is just given by a blending of the two measure θ_A and θ_B. The generating of singular sources is not possible for an L^2 type cost functional in space time $[L^2(L^2)]$, which was proposed in [15]. Indeed, chosen the cost functional $\int_0^1 \int_D z^2 \, dx \, dt$ for the same data, the generation of mass via the source term takes place on a thick super set of the rectangular strip and is then transported toward to strip. We also observe a similar effect for absolutely continuous measures. In Fig. 2 we compare the

$L^2(H)$ and the $L^2(L^2)$ source term for geodesics connecting differently scaled characteristic functions of a square. Again, the resulting geodesic for the $L^2(H)$-model is given by a blending of the two measure θ_A and θ_B, whereas in the $L^2(L^2)$ the additional mass in image u_B is generated from a bigger support. Figure 3 shows a plot of $t \mapsto \int_D |z(t, \cdot)| \, dx$ for both models underlining the equidistribution of the source in time for the $L^2(H)$ model. Let us remark, that numerical diffusion in particular on coarse meshes leads to a blurring effect for the source term at discontinuities of the density which is then accompanied by minor transport to compensate for this diffusion.

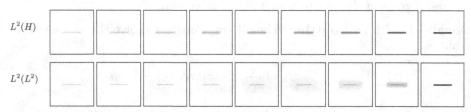

Fig. 1. Optimal transport geodesic between approximations of singular measures with different intensity. Here the source term parameter is $\delta = 10^0$.

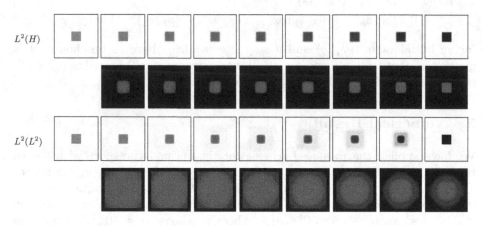

Fig. 2. Optimal transport geodesic and corresponding source terms between two characteristic functions of squares with different intensity. Here the source term parameter is $\delta = 10^0$.

Next, we investigate the effect of the source term parameter δ for the $L^2(H)$ model. In Fig. 4 we choose as input data θ_A at time $t = 0$ a characteristic function of a square and as input data θ_B at time $t = 1$ the same measure density with an additional characteristic function of a translated square of the same size. Now, optimizing the connecting path with respect to the generalized Wasserstein distance there is a competition between the curve which simply blends the second square and a curve which transports part of the second square and blends of remaining non transported measure. This balance between both processes depends on δ. In the limit $\delta \to 0$ transport becomes cheaper, which

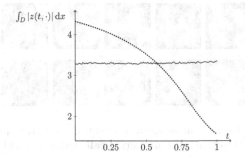

Fig. 3. Distribution of the L^1-norm of the source term in time for the example in Fig. 2. (continuous line: $L^2(H)$, dotted line: $L^2(L^2)$)

is reflected by the computational results for small δ. In contrast for $\delta \to \infty$ transport becomes expensive and a simple blending can be observed for large values of δ in Fig. 4. A similar effect is shown in Fig. 5, where the a bump function in the center of a periodic cell is transported to a splitted bump function in the corners applying periodic boundary conditions.

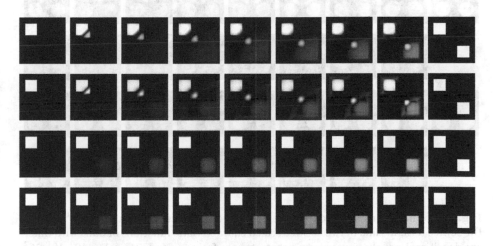

Fig. 4. Generalized Wasserstein geodesic between a scaled characteristic functions on a square and two differently scaled characteristic functions of squares of the same size. The dependance on the source term parameter is shown for the $L^2(H)$ model. From top to bottom $\delta = 10^{-2}, 10^{-1}, 10^0, 10^1$.

In Fig. 6 another type of interaction between generation and transport of mass is shown. The initial images at time $t = 0$ consists of three scaled characteristic functions of balls, where one of this balls has smaller density value. The final image at time $t = 1$ is based on the identical geometric configuration, but with swapped densities. Depending on the parameter δ a certain amount of mass is

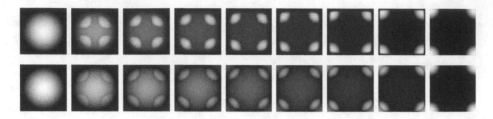

Fig. 5. Generalized Wasserstein geodesic connecting two translated bump functions are computed. The bump functions are periodically extended and $\delta = 10^{-2}$ (top) and $\delta = 10^{0}$ (bottom).

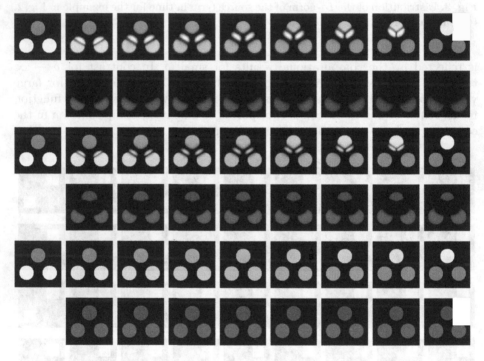

Fig. 6. Optimal transport geodesic with corresponding distribution of the L^1-norm of the source term in time between three scaled characteristic functions of balls with different densities. Here the source term parameter are from top to bottom $\delta = 10^0, 10^1, 10^2$.

transported from the two balls with higher intensity in the image at time $t = 0$. At the same time a blending of the transported masses as a compensation for the non balanced total mass can be observed. Figure 7 shows plots of the functions $t \mapsto \int_D |z(t, \cdot)| \, dx$, $t \mapsto \int_D z^+(t, \cdot) \, dx$, and $t \mapsto \int_D |z^-(t, \cdot)| \, dx$ for the different values of δ.

A striking observation in Fig. 3 and Fig. 7 is that $t \mapsto \int_D |z(t, \cdot)| \, dx$ is approximately constant in time for the $L^2(H)$ model. This is in constrast to the $L^2(L^2)$ model as indicated in Fig. 3.

$$\int_D |z(t,\cdot)|\,\mathrm{d}x$$
$$\int_D z^+(t,\cdot)\,\mathrm{d}x$$
$$\int_D z^-(t,\cdot)\,\mathrm{d}x$$

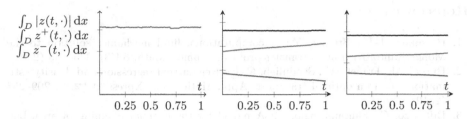

0.25 0.5 0.75   1   0.25 0.5 0.75   1   0.25 0.5 0.75   1

Fig. 7. Distribution of the L^1-norm of the source term in time for the example in Fig. 6 for $\delta = 10^0, 10^1, 10^2$.

Finally Figs. 8 and 9 depict examples for images of wood texture and marble texture. Generalized Wasserstein geodesics in case of the $L^2(H)$ cost functional are shown.

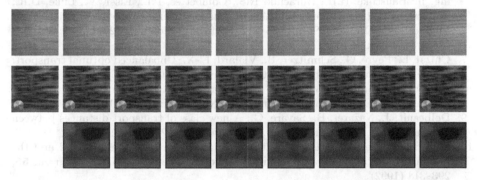

Fig. 8. Optimal transport geodesic between wood textures (top). Here the source term parameter is $\delta = 10^0$. Further the corresponding momentum (middle) and source term (bottom) are depicted.

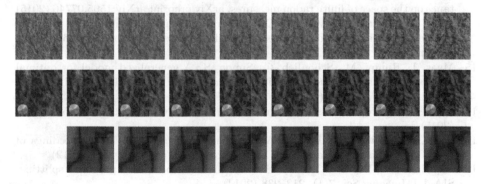

Fig. 9. Optimal transport geodesic between marble textures (top). Here the source term parameter is $\delta = 10^{-2}$. Further the corresponding momentum (middle) and source term (bottom) are depicted.

References

1. Benamou, J.-D., Brenier, Y.: A computational fluid mechanics solution to the Monge-Kantorovich mass transfer problem. Numer. Math. **84**(3), 375–393 (2000)
2. Burger, M., Franek, M., Schönlieb, C.-B.: Regularized regression and density estimation based on optimal transport. Appl. Math. Res. eXpress **2012**(2), 209–253 (2012)
3. Buttazzo, G., Santambrogio, F.: A model for the optimal planning of an urban area. SIAM J. Math. Anal. **37**(2), 514–530 (2005)
4. Carlier, G., Duval, V., Peyré, G., Schmitzer, B.: Convergence of entropic schemes for optimal transport, gradient flows. arXiv preprint arXiv:1512.02783 (2015)
5. Caffarelli, L.A., McCann, R.J.: Free boundaries in optimal transport and monge-ampere obstacle problems. Ann. Math. **171**, 673–730 (2010)
6. Combettes, P.L., Pesquet, J.-C.: Proximal splitting methods in signal processing. In: Bauschke, H.H., Burachik, R.S., Combettes, P.L., Elser, V., Luke, D.R., Wolkowicz, H. (eds.) Fixed-Point Algorithms for Inverse Problems in Science and Engineering. SOA, vol. 49, pp. 185–212. Springer, Heidelberg (2011). doi:10.1007/978-1-4419-9569-8_10
7. Chizat, L., Peyré, G., Schmitzer, B., Vialard, F.-X.: Unbalanced optimal transport: geometry and kantorovich formulation. arXiv preprint arXiv:1508.05216 (2015)
8. Chizat, L., Schmitzer, B., Peyré, G., Vialard, F.-X.: An interpolating distance between optimal transport, Fischer-Rao. arXiv preprint arXiv:1506.06430 (2015)
9. Dolbeault, J., Nazaret, B., Savaré, G.: A new class of transport distances between measures. Calc. Var. Partial Differ. Equ. **34**(2), 193–231 (2009)
10. Eckstein, J., Bertsekas, D.P.: On the douglas-rachford splitting method and the proximal point algorithm for maximal monotone operators. Math. Program. **55**, 293–318 (1992)
11. Esser, E.: Applications of lagrangian-based alternating direction methods and connections to split Bregman. CAM Rep. **9**, 31 (2009)
12. Figalli, A.: The optimal partial transport problem. Arch. Ration. Mech. Anal. **195**(2), 533–560 (2010)
13. Kondratyev, S., Monsaingeon, L., Vorotnikov, D.: A new optimal transport distance on the space of finite radon measures. arXiv preprint arXiv:1505.07746 (2015)
14. Liero, M., Mielke, A., Savaré, G.: Optimal transport in competition with reaction: the Hellinger-Kantorovich distance and geodesic curves. Preprint no. 2160, WIAS (2015)
15. Maas, J., Rumpf, M., Schönlieb, C., Simon, S.: A generalized model for optimal transport of images including dissipation and density modulation. ESAIM Math. Model. Numer. Anal. **49**(6), 1745–1769 (2015)
16. Peyré, G.: Entropic Wasserstein gradient flows. arXiv preprint arXiv:1502.06216 (2015)
17. Peyré, G., Fadili, J., Rabin, J.: Wasserstein active contours. In: Proceedings of IEEE International Conference on Image Processing, pp. 2541–2544 (2012)
18. Papadakis, N., Peyré, G., Oudet, E.: Optimal transport with proximal splitting. SIAM J. Imaging Sci. **7**(1), 212–238 (2014)
19. Piccoli, B., Rossi, F.: On properties of the generalized Wasserstein distance. arXiv preprint arXiv:1304.7014 (2013)
20. Piccoli, B., Rossi, F.: Generalized Wasserstein distance and its application to transport equations with source. Arch. Ration. Mech. Anal. **211**, 335–358 (2014)

21. Rubner, Y., Tomasi, C., Guibas, L.J.: The earth mover's distance as a metric for image retrieval. Int. J. Comput. Vis. **40**(2), 99–121 (2000)
22. Schmitzer, B.: A sparse multi-scale algorithm for dense optimal transport. arXiv preprint arXiv:1510.05466 (2015)

Vehicle X-ray Scans Registration:
A One-Dimensional Optimization Problem

Abraham Marciano[1,2]([✉]), Laurent D. Cohen[1], and Najib Gadi[2]

[1] Université Paris-Dauphine, PSL Research University, CNRS, UMR 7534,
CEREMADE, 75016 Paris, France
marciano@ceremade.dauphine.fr
[2] Smiths Detection, 94405 Vitry-sur-Seine, France

Abstract. Over the years, image registration has been largely employed in medical applications, robotics and geophysics. More recently, it has increasingly drawn attention of security and defense industries, particularly aiming at threat detection automation. This paper first introduces a short overview of mathematical methods for image registration, with a focus on variational approaches. In a second part, a specific registration task is presented: the optimal alignment between X-ray scans of an inspected vehicle and an empty reference of the same car model. Indeed, while being scanned by dedicated imaging systems, the car speed is not necessarily constant which may entail non-rigid deformations in the resulting image. The paper simply addresses this issue by applying a rigid transform on the reference image before using the variational framework solved in one dimension. For convergence and speed purposes, line-search techniques and a multiscale approach are used.

Keywords: Image registration · Variational approach · One-dimensional optimization

1 Introduction

Due to the recent global context, security has increasingly become a top priority for governments and agencies all around the world. Meanwhile, larger amounts of data have to be processed in more limited periods of time. Thus, the switch to automation of threat targeting constitutes a crucial step.

The vision industry has significantly been impacted by this move and must address new problems, often by resorting to widely used techniques such as image registration. As defined by Modersitzki et al. [1–3], it consists in finding a "reasonable" transformation applied on a template image T to get an optimal alignment with a reference image R.

In this paper, we present a challenging registration task: aligning top-view scans of a car under inspection and an empty reference of the same model. The obvious purpose of this process is to automatically identify added objects in a vehicle and target potential security threats or contraband goods. Though, for X-ray imaging systems such as Smiths Detection HCVL, the car is trailed by a mechanism pushing its rear wheels so

© Springer International Publishing AG 2017
F. Lauze et al. (Eds.): SSVM 2017, LNCS 10302, pp. 578–589, 2017.
DOI: 10.1007/978-3-319-58771-4_46

that the speed may not be constant over time. This imperfection often gives non-rigid deformations in the resulting image (see Fig. 1) due to "over-sampling" (car deceleration) or "sub-sampling" (car acceleration) of the scanned object.

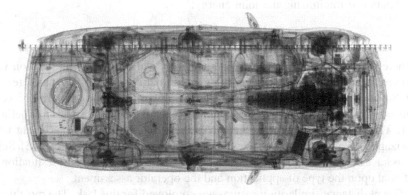

Fig. 1. Top-view scan of a vehicle. The spare wheel shows a non-rigid deformation as a result of the car slowdown during the scanning process.

Note that deforming potential threats in the image is not desirable for further recognition tasks. Thus, we consider the current inspection scan as the static image R and the empty reference image from our database as the moving template T (such that R does not undergo any non-linear warping).

The paper first gives an overview of the general non-rigid registration problem formulated in the variational framework. Parametric and non-parametric methods are detailed along with their numerical resolution. We will also show that, when applied to our registration problem, these schemes fail to yield a consistent transform with respect to the reference image or by violating the car's intrinsic rigidity.

In Sect. 3, we will demonstrate that the composition of a rigid transform followed by a one-dimensional optimization scheme applied on T gives a valid solution. An explicit formulation of the problem is given in detail as well as its numerical framework.

2   Problem Setup and Non-linear Methods Overview

2.1   Mathematical Problem Setup

As mentioned, given R and T, respectively a reference image and a template image, we aim at finding a transformation on T such that the warped template matches the reference as closely as possible [1–3]. Generally, R and T are defined as d-dimensional images $R, T : \Omega \to \mathbb{R}$, $\Omega \in \,]0, 1[^d$ (normalized coordinates). The transformation is expressed by $u : \Omega \to \mathbb{R}^d$, commonly referred to as the displacement field applied on each position $x \in \Omega$ in T.

Hence, for a particular $x \in \Omega$, $T(x)$ corresponds to the grayscale value of T at x and we wish to find u so that $T(x + u)$ is similar to $R(x)$ (see [4, 5] e.g.). Since our images are 2D, we take $d = 2$.

The unified non-linear registration framework is formulated as follows [2]: find a transformation u minimizing the joint energy:

$$J(u) = D(T(u), R) + \alpha S(u) \tag{1}$$

Where $T(u)$ denotes the transformed image with value $T(x + u)$ at location x, and D represents the data fitting term, quantifying the similarity between $T(u)$ and R (external force). Since optimizing D turns to an ill-posed problem, a regularizer term S has been introduced. It refers directly to the "reasonable" aspect of the transformation as defined in Sect. 1. The smoothing parameter α controls the strength of the displacement field u regularization, ensuring its smoothness during deformation (internal force) [2–5]. Several methods have been developed to estimate a proper α (see [2, 6]), but in most situations it is conditional upon the type of application and the operator assessment.

Different distance/similarity measures are employed for this task. The most popular is the *sum of differences* distance (SSD) whereas the *normalized-cross-correlation* (NCC) is also widely used for monomodal registration problems. The *mutual information* distance (MI) is dedicated to the registration of images obtained with different modalities (e.g. CT and MRI) [3, 7]. More sophisticated measures have also been developed in the last decade, such as the *normalized gradient fields* (NGF) (see [7, 8]). In this paper the SSD distance is preferred for its simplicity and efficiency to solve our monomodal registration issue.

Likewise, several regularizers are outlined in the state of the art literature. The next sub-section gives more details about the different smoothing techniques. Note that the main constraint in the selection of similarity measures or regularizers is the existence of a Gâteaux derivative for the optimization scheme to be used later [4].

2.2   Methods Overview

Landmark-based registration is widely adopted in medical applications for instance [9]. The displacement field is first evaluated on identified points (landmarks), followed by a TPS (*thin-plate-spline*) interpolation yielding a dense estimation of u (see [3]).

Still, an accurate automatic detection of landmarks remains a challenging task (see [9] e.g.). In this paper, the focus is therefore given on intensity-based methods which fall into two categories:

- Parametric techniques: the transformation is restricted to a known parametric model. The optimization process aims at automatically identifying the optimal parameters of u. Non-linear techniques resort to a linear combination of a small set of basis functions (B-spline, *free-form deformations* – FFD methods). See [3, 7] for a complete overview of PIR methods (Parametric Image Registration). For these techniques, the parametrization itself implicitly integrates a strong regularizer, especially for low dimensional transformation spaces ($S(u) = 0$). Yet, a Tychonov smoothing term may also be employed [3].

- Non-parametric techniques: The transformation is no longer parametrized. The optimization processes over the displacement field u itself making the regularization term $S(u)$ essential. *L2 norm*-based models such as curvature [5], fluid [10] and elastic [11] regularizers are the most widespread (see [3] or [7] for a complete overview). For NPIR (Non-Parametric Image Registration) methods, discretization is regularizer-dependent. Different schemes can be adopted such as nodal, centered or staggered grids. See [3, 7] for more details about discretization and interpolation issues.

  Thirion's demons popular method [12] derives from optical flow techniques with a diffusion-like regularizer [1, 5]. It is especially useful for high dimensional and computationally demanding non-linear problems [5].

  Models with rigidity or volume-preserving constraints have also proven their efficiency. Yet, they are beyond the scope of this paper. See [13–15] for further details.

2.3 Numerical Resolution

Modersitzki [3, 7] proposes a unified numerical optimization framework to minimize (1). Both NPIR and PIR are solved by a quasi-Gauss-Newton descent method [16]. The gradient $\nabla J(u)$ and Hessian $H(u)$ of $J(u)$ are computed (the Hessian is often approximated). The descent direction $dd = H(u)^{-1}\nabla J(u)$ is calculated at each iteration. Also, Armijo's line-search backtracking method is employed to get an optimal step size for each update of u [3, 16]. In general, minimization is stopped whenever the variation of the transformation $\|\nabla u\|_2$ falls below a pre-set tolerance threshold ϵ. See [3] for more details about the stopping criterion.

A multi-level strategy is also used. It yields a smoother objective function at coarser levels, hence easier to minimize. Thus, the resulting displacement field constitutes a good initialization for the finer level and local minima issues can be overcome [2, 3].

Alternative optimization paradigms have also been proposed for computationally expensive cases. The *l*-BFGS approximates the inverse of the Hessian using an initial guess H_0 and a sequence composed of descent directions and gradients [16]. Trust-region methods are quite popular as well since they can achieve fast quadratic convergence [16]. See [3] for further details and [17] for a more advanced overview of variational methods and their numerical frameworks.

2.4 Tests on Our Images

In this example, the inspection of the front part of a given vehicle is considered (Fig. 2 (a)). A corresponding empty reference scan from the same model is used for registration (from a different car, Fig. 2(b)). Major visual differences are easily identified at the rear-view mirrors, front wheels, the gearbox, the steering wheel, a few liquid tanks and the battery. Figure 2 represents the reference and template images after pose estimation (rigid registration, see Sect. 3.4 for further details). Two methods are tested in this part: B-spline registration and Thirion's demons method.

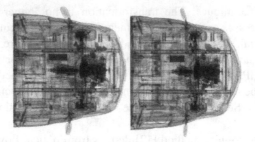

Fig. 2. (a) Empty reference of a vehicle front part; (b) Front part under inspection after pose estimation

Figure 3 shows some results obtained via the demons method with two different smoothing parameters and a multi-level approach. Note that green and pink colors depict respectively the differences originating from the moving template *T* and image *R* under inspection (as defined in Sect. 1).

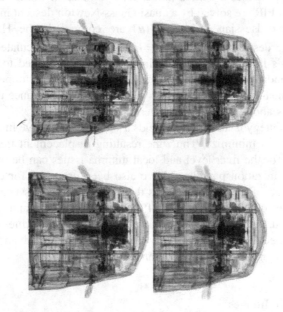

Fig. 3. Demons registration results (resulting T_{final} and overlay of T_{final} and R) with a smoothing parameter of 0.5 (top) and 2 (bottom) (Color figure online)

B-spline registration is also tested with a multiscale approach and a "thin sheet of metal" smoothness penalty set to 0.01 and 0.1 (Fig. 4).

Besides computational cost considerations (B-spline registration can be significantly time-consuming), these standard methods do not achieve accurate registration for the particular case addressed here. See Fig. 10 for the resulting SSD distances of

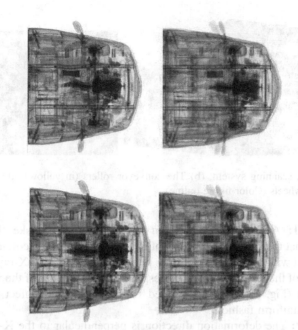

Fig. 4. B-spline registration results (resulting T_{final} and overlay of T_{final} and R) with a smoothing parameter of 0.01 (top) and 0.1 (bottom)

each method. In fact, the vehicle's rigidity along with the mechanical process behind the non-rigid deformation have to be taken into account. The idea is to simplify the optimization problem by moving from a 2-dimensional to a one-dimensional scheme. More particularly, the displacement field has to be constrained to the longitudinal direction and must remain uniform along the car's width. The next section outlines the motivations and numerical aspects of our method.

3 Registering with a One-Dimensional Optimization Scheme

3.1 Introduction to Our Registration Problem

In HCVL X-ray imaging systems, an inspected vehicle is trailed by a conveyor facility via rollers pushing on its back wheels (Fig. 5). The conveyor speed is meant to be constant and fixed to 12 m/min. Though, the car often rolls off the trailer equipment as a result of shocks between the conveyor rollers and the wheels. The vehicle speed undergoes disturbances affecting the scanning process: a slowdown (resp. acceleration) implies a local "over-sampling" (resp. "sub-sampling") in specific regions of the car (see Fig. 1).

Let's consider two X-ray images of the same car model (not necessarily the same vehicle): we assume that pose estimation has already been performed such that both images were linearly registered through a rigid transform. We formulate two strong hypothesis:

Fig. 5. (a) HCVL scanning system; (b) The conveyor rollers (in yellow) applying a pushing force on the rear wheels (Color figure online)

- **Hypothesis 1:** A *columnwise-constant deformation*. We make the reasonable assumption that the field of displacement is uniform along each column. In fact, the car is scanned with a constant sampling rate while entering the X-ray beam line so each column of the resulting image corresponds to a lateral cut of the vehicle scan at a given time (Fig. 6). Thus, any speed disturbance would affect each separate column in a uniform fashion.
- **Hypothesis 2:** The deformation direction is perpendicular to the X-ray beam line (the vertical component of u is null). This assumption is an accurate approximation since the car can hardly strive from the conveyor during scanning (Fig. 6).

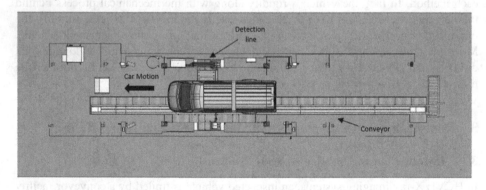

Fig. 6. Top-view description of the HCVL system

3.2 Method Outline

Let's formulate the 1D optimization problem. Given two images R and T, pose estimation is performed by applying a rigid transform on T. For notation simplification, we keep using T to designate the moving image following this pre-processing warping.

We define x and y as the horizontal and vertical coordinates of $x \in \Omega$:

$$x = (x, y) \tag{2}$$

Similarly, the displacement field:

$$u = \big(u_x(x, y), u_y(x, y)\big) \tag{3}$$

Hypothesis 1 implies that

$$u_x(x, y) = u_x(x) \tag{4}$$

And **Hypothesis 2** yields

$$u_y(x, y) = 0 \tag{5}$$

Eventually, combining (5) and (4) gives:

$$u = (u_x(x), 0). \tag{6}$$

With an *SSD* distance and a regularizer of the form: $S(u) = \frac{1}{2}\|\nabla u\|_2^2$, (1) becomes:

$$\text{Find } u \text{ minimizing } J(u) = \frac{1}{2}\|T(u) - R\|_2^2 + \frac{1}{2}\alpha\|\nabla u\|_2^2 \tag{7}$$

On the basis of (6), (7) turns to a one-dimensional optimization problem that can be solved via simple descent techniques.

3.3 Numerical Resolution

For a given column index x, (7) is equivalent to:

Find $u_x(x)$ minimizing

$$J(u_x(x)) = \frac{1}{2}\|T(u_x(x)) - R\|_2^2 + \frac{1}{2}\alpha\left\|\frac{\partial u_x(x)}{\partial x}\right\|_2^2 \tag{8}$$

A first-degree descent scheme would be relevant for this 1D optimization problem (low complexity). We resort to the gradient descent method, in combination Armijo's backtracking line search method [16]. We evolve the following equation with Dirichlet boundary conditions:

$$\frac{\partial u_x(x)}{\partial t} = -\nabla J(u_x(x)) \, for \, x \in \Omega \backslash \partial\Omega \, with \, u_x(x) = 0 \, for \, x \in \partial\Omega \tag{9}$$

The gradient of $J(u_x(x))$ is computed from (8):

$$\nabla J(u_x(x)) = \frac{\partial T(x + u_x(x))}{\partial u_x} (T(x + u_x(x)) - R(x)) - \alpha \frac{\partial^2 u_x(x)}{\partial x^2} \qquad (10)$$

By abuse of notation: $T(x + u_x(x))$ corresponds to the column of T at $x + u_x(x)$. We note $X = x + u_x(x)$ such that $\frac{\partial T(x + u_x(x))}{\partial u_x} = \frac{\partial T(x + u_x(x))}{\partial X}$, referring to the gradient of T at $x + u_x(x)$. We get the final expression:

$$\nabla J(u_x(x)) = \frac{\partial T(x + u_x(x))}{\partial X} (T(x + u_x(x)) - R(x)) - \alpha \frac{\partial^2 u_x(x)}{\partial x^2} \qquad (11)$$

A multi-scale approach is used to speed up the registration process and in order to avoid convergence at local minima. Thereby, the displacement $u_x^{(p)}$ obtained at level p gives a strong initialization for the displacement estimate $u_x^{(p-1)}$ for the finer level $p - 1$. The number of levels is fixed to $l = 4$.

Empirically, a smoothing parameter set to $\alpha = 0.5$ for all scales yields accurate and stable results. The stopping criterion is analogous to the method described in Sect. 2.3 with a chosen threshold $\epsilon = 1$.

At the end, an estimate of T transformed via the optimal displacement field u^* is calculated using linear or cubic interpolation (both techniques give similar results in our case).

3.4 Experimental Results on Scan Images

Our method is applied on the example of Sect. 2.4. Figure 7 displays T and R prior to rigid registration. In a first stage, a rigid transform is automatically computed using SURF [18] feature points matching and RANSAC filtering [19]. The transform applied on T gives a pose estimation between both images. See Fig. 8 for a visual description of alignment before and after pose estimation. This pre-processing step is often necessary to rectify slight differences of car positioning or geometry variations between separate X-ray systems (at different sites).

Our multiscale one-dimensional minimization scheme yields the following image T_{final} with the corresponding columnwise-constant displacement field u^*(Fig. 9).

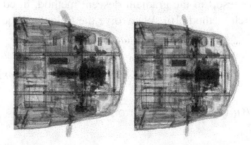

Fig. 7. (a) Empty reference of a vehicle front part; (b) Front part under inspection

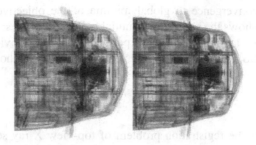

Fig. 8. (a) Overlay of both images before pose estimation; (b) Overlay following pose estimation by rigid registration

Fig. 9. (a) Resulting image; (b) Displacement field; (c) Overlay of R and T_{final}

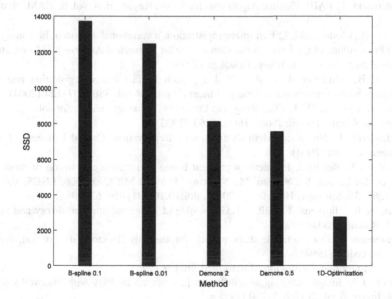

Fig. 10. SSD distances reached for each method (with its corresponding smoothing parameter)

After reaching convergence to global minima of the objective function (8), the resulting alignment shows the vanishing of initial major differences: the mirrors as well as the battery or the steering wheel align perfectly (Fig. 9). Obviously, our method achieves the lowest SSD cost in comparison with the different methods tested (Fig. 10).

4   Conclusion

This paper addresses the registration problem of top-view X-ray scans from two different vehicles of the same model. It especially aims at dealing with non-linear deformations induced by possible speed variations of the vehicle during scanning.

A simple and intuitive solution is described: in a first stage, a pose estimation between both scans is performed. Then, assuming that the field of displacement is columnwise-constant and parallel to the car's motion, a one-dimensional optimization scheme is formulated. It is solved by well-known descent techniques in combination with Armijo's backtracking method and a multiscale approach. Both visual and numerical results presented in this paper demonstrate the necessity for our method as well as its high performances in terms of registration accuracy.

References

1. Haber, E., Heldmann, S., Modersitzki, J.: A computational framework for image-based constrained registration. Linear Algebra Appl. **431**(3), 459–470 (2009)
2. Haber, E., Modersitzki, J.: A multilevel method for image registration. SIAM J. Sci. Comput. **27**(5), 1594–1607 (2006)
3. Modersitzki, J.: FAIR: Flexible Algorithms for Image Registration, vol. 6. SIAM, New Delhi (2009)
4. Fischer, B., Modersitzki, J.: Fast image registration: a variational approach. In: Psihoyios, G. (ed.) Proceedings of the International Conference on Numerical Analysis and Computational Mathematics, pp. 69–74. Wiley, Hoboken (2003)
5. Fischer, B., Modersitzki, J.: A unified approach to fast image registration and a new curvature based registration technique. Linear Algebra Appl. **380**, 107–124 (2004)
6. Haber, E., Ascher, U.M., Oldenburg, D.: On optimization techniques for solving nonlinear inverse problems. Inverse Probl. **16**(5), 1263 (2000)
7. Modersitzki, J.: Numerical Methods for Image Registration. Oxford University Press on Demand, Oxford (2004)
8. Haber, E., Modersitzki, J.: Intensity gradient based registration and fusion of multi-modal images. In: Larsen, R., Nielsen, M., Sporring, J. (eds.) MICCAI 2006. LNCS, vol. 4191, pp. 726–733. Springer, Heidelberg (2006). doi:10.1007/11866763_89
9. Crum, W.R., Hartkens, T., Hill, D.L.G.: Non-rigid image registration: theory and practice. Br. J. Radiol. (2004)
10. Christensen, G.E.: Deformable shape models for anatomy (Doctoral dissertation, Washington University) (1994)
11. Broit, C.: Optimal registration of deformed images (1981)
12. Thirion, J.P.: Image matching as a diffusion process: an analogy with Maxwell's demons. Med. Image Anal. **2**(3), 243–260 (1998)

13. Haber, E., Modersitzki, J.: Numerical methods for volume preserving image registration. Inverse Probl. **20**(5), 1621 (2004)
14. Modersitzki, J.: FLIRT with rigidity—image registration with a local non-rigidity penalty. Int. J. Comput. Vis. **76**(2), 153–163 (2008)
15. Staring, M., Klein, S., Pluim, J.P.: Nonrigid registration using a rigidity constraint. In: Medical Imaging, p. 614413. International Society for Optics and Photonics, March 2006
16. Nocedal, J., Wright, S.: Numerical Optimization. Springer Science and Business Media, New York (2006)
17. Chumchob, N., Chen, K.: A robust multigrid approach for variational image registration models. J. Comput. Appl. Math. **236**(5), 653–674 (2011)
18. Bay, H., Tuytelaars, T., Gool, L.: SURF: speeded up robust features. In: Leonardis, A., Bischof, H., Pinz, A. (eds.) ECCV 2006. LNCS, vol. 3951, pp. 404–417. Springer, Heidelberg (2006). doi:10.1007/11744023_32
19. Fischler, M.A., Bolles, R.C.: Random sample consensus: a paradigm for model fitting with applications to image analysis and automated cartography. Commun. ACM **24**(6), 381–395 (1981)

Evaluating Data Terms
for Variational Multi-frame Super-Resolution

Kireeti Bodduna[✉] and Joachim Weickert

Mathematical Image Analysis Group, Faculty of Mathematics and Computer Science,
Saarland University, 66041 Saarbrücken, Germany
{bodduna,weickert}@mia.uni-saarland.de

Abstract. We present the first systematic evaluation of the data terms for multi-frame super-resolution within a variational model. The various data terms are derived by permuting the order of the blur-, downsample-, and warp-operators in the image acquisition model. This yields six different basic models. Our experiments using synthetic images with known ground truth show that two models are preferable: the widely-used warp-blur-downsample model that is physically plausible if atmospheric blur is negligible, and the hardly considered blur-warp-downsample model. We show that the quality of motion estimation plays the decisive role on which of these two models works best: While the classic warp-blur-downsample model requires optimal motion estimation, the rarely-used blur-warp-downsample model should be preferred in practically relevant scenarios when motion estimation is suboptimal. This confirms a widely ignored result by Wang and Qi (2004). Last but not least, we propose a new modification of the blur-warp-downsample model that offers a very significant speed-up without substantial loss in the reconstruction quality.

Keywords: Super-resolution · Variational methods · Inverse problems

1 Introduction

Generating high resolution (HR) images is one of the main objectives of photography. These images show more details of the scene which is crucial for many applications such as surveillance, medical or satellite imaging. Instead of opting for expensive high precision optics, the other way is to enhance the resolution after capturing. While there exist methods to enhance the resolution of a single image [9,12,23], which is referred to as single-frame super-resolution, a more common technique is to acquire several low resolution (LR) images of the same scene and combine the information from them into a single HR image. This process is known as super-resolution (SR) reconstruction.

Super-resolution is an inverse problem where we are trying to recover the unknown HR image. Given N LR images $\left\{ \boldsymbol{f}_L^k \right\}_{k=1}^{N}$ of resolution $N_L = L_1 \times L_2$, we want to find a HR image $\boldsymbol{f}_H$ of resolution $N_H = H_1 \times H_2$ where $N_H = N_L \times z$

© Springer International Publishing AG 2017
F. Lauze et al. (Eds.): SSVM 2017, LNCS 10302, pp. 590–601, 2017.
DOI: 10.1007/978-3-319-58771-4_47

(z is the zoom factor). This HR image f_H should minimize the following energy function:

$$E(f_H) = \sum_{k=1}^{N} |P_k(f_H) - f_L^k|^2 \qquad (1)$$

where $P_k(f_H)$ is the projection of the HR image onto the LR scale and $|.|$ denotes the Euclidean norm. The projection operator $P_k(f_H)$ is modeled by a sequence of linear transformations: Blurring, motion warping and downsampling are the three operators that describe the relation between the HR scene and the LR realizations of the scene. The order of these operators is decided keeping in mind the image acquisition procedure. The procedure of acquiring digital images is modeled as follows [8]:

$$f_L^k = DB_{cam}W_kB_{atmp}f_H + e_k \qquad (2)$$

The HR scene f_H undergoes an atmospheric blurring matrix B_{atmp} (size: $N_H \times N_H$) first. The objects in the scene are assumed to be moving with the camera as the frame of reference. This motion is modeled by a warping operator W_k (size: $N_H \times N_H$). The moving objects then undergo a blurring due to the point spread function (PSF) of the camera is modeled by B_{cam} (size: $N_H \times N_H$). Finally the HR scene is downsampled by the camera detector system which is modeled with the help of the operator D (size: $N_L \times N_H$). An additive noise vector e_k of size N_L is assumed. This entire process leads to a single LR realization f_L^k of size N_L. It should be mentioned that the blurring and the downsampling operators do not have an index k as the atmospheric conditions and the camera conditions are assumed to be same for all the LR realizations.

The seminal work on multi-frame super-resolution goes back to Tsai et al. [20]. The standard observational model for SR reconstruction that is widely followed [1,2,5,7,10,11,13–16,18,19,24] was first proposed and represented in a matrix-vector formulation by Elad et al. [6]:

$$f_L^k = DBW_kf_H + e_k \qquad (3)$$

One can see that the atmospheric blurring operator from Eq. 1 has been dropped. Dealing with an extra blurring matrix might be a bit cumbersome both with respect to the number of parameters in the model and the computational burden. Also, on the other hand it is not a bad assumption to assume that the camera blur is the dominant one amongst the two type of blurs, especially in cases where images are obtained from microscopes.

Our Contribution. Evaluating the SR observational models that either deviate or do not deviate from the image acquisition process in terms of ordering of the operators, is still an open research field. Very few works [18,21,25] have concentrated their research on this particular problem. Variational models are known for the many degrees of freedom they provide while modeling various problems. In this work, we make use of this liberty provided by variational models to systematically evaluate the different SR data terms. These different SR data terms are derived by modifying the image acquisition model but are mathematically still plausible. We only focus on the data term as the discussions for the smoothness terms are similar to that of other applications like image denoising and optic flow. Finally, we also propose a new modified observational model which helps to save a lot of computational time.

Paper Structure. The outline of this paper is as follows: We propose various SR observational models and introduce the optic flow method used in calculating the warping matrix in Sect. 2. The experiments and discussions on the results from the experiments are presented in Sect. 3. We consolidate the conclusions from the performed experiments and discussions in Sect. 4.

2   Modeling and Theory

2.1   Optic Flow

The warping matrix in Eq. 2 represents the displacements that the objects in the HR scene have undergone before being captured as a LR image by the camera. We make use of a simplified version of the popular optic flow method by Brox et al. [4] to estimate this matrix (we omit gradient constancy and just consider grey value constancy). This method is designed specifically for handling large displacements by using a theory of multi-scale warping. Also, the method does not assume a particular type of motion and hence it is a very good fit for estimating the warping matrix. We consider one of the LR images to be the reference image. The warping matrix is calculated for every reference image - LR image pair. In the following we briefly sketch the main ideas behind this optic flow method.

Let $\boldsymbol{x} := (x, y, t)^T$ denote the position vector and $\boldsymbol{w} = (u, v, 1)^T$ the unknown displacement vector field. Penalizing the deviations from the grey value constancy and enabling interaction between pixels can be modeled by the following continuous energy functional:

$$E(u, v) = \int_{\Omega} \left(\Psi(|f(\boldsymbol{x} + \boldsymbol{w}) - f(\boldsymbol{x})|^2 + \alpha_{OF}(\Psi(|\boldsymbol{\nabla}u|^2 + |\boldsymbol{\nabla}v|^2)) \right) d\boldsymbol{x} \qquad (4)$$

where Ω is the image domain, f denotes the image sequence and $\boldsymbol{\nabla}$ represents a spatio-temporal gradient. To tackle the effect of outliers on a quadratic energy, an increasing convex function $\Psi(s^2)$ is applied for a robust convex energy functional such as $\Psi(s^2) = \sqrt{s^2 + \epsilon^2}$ with a small positive constant ϵ required for retaining the convex property of the energy functional after the application of Ψ. Moreover, α_{OF} is the regularization parameter. The goal is to find a $\boldsymbol{w}$ which minimizes the above energy functional.

The multi-scale warping approach is integrated in the Euler-Lagrange equations of the above energy functional. It involves a downsampling operation, which allows linearisation of the grey value constancy assumption, thus leading to a linear system of equations. More specific details about the parameters and the optic flow method itself can be found in the paper by Brox et al. [4].

2.2 Evaluated SR Observational Models

In this section, we propose the super-resolution observational models that deviate from the image acquisition procedure mentioned in Eq. 2. These Models 1–6 are specified in Table 1. The modifications that lead to the deviations from the imaging physics are a combination of dropping one of the blurring operators and permuting the operators. It should be mentioned that the warping and blurring matrices are space variant and hence none of the three operators (blur, warp and downsample) commute with each other. This also assures that none of the proposed models are equivalent to each other. The aim is to test which of the models gives the best SR reconstruction results.

Table 1. Proposed SR observational models along with the mean squared error (MSE) values of the obtained reconstructed SR image for TS1 using flows F1 and F2. The optimized parametric values are also shown.

#	Observational model	MSE (F1)	MSE (F2)	σ (F1)	σ (F2)	α (F1)	α (F2)
1	$DBW_k f_H = f_L^k$	**103.26**	170.11	0.57	0.59	0.002	0.006
2	$DW_k B f_H = f_L^k$	121.76	171.27	0.65	0.61	0.004	0.005
3	$BDW_k f_H = f_L^k$	120.63	193.23	0.63	0.65	0.009	0.06
4	$W_k DB f_H = f_L^k$	116.46	164.15	0.57	0.51	0.0008	0.0004
5	$BW_k D f_H = f_L^k$	120.12	173.93	0.58	0.55	0.0004	0.0007
6	$W_k BD f_H = f_L^k$	121.91	173.51	0.61	0.56	0.0008	0.0005

For the evaluation of different observational models, we embed them in a variational framework. As mentioned in Sect. 1, we capitalized on the flexibility of the variational models for evaluating different data terms. Let us consider Model 1. The energy that has to minimized in order to obtain an SR image using the standard observational model (Model 1) is given by

$$E(f_H) = \frac{1}{2} \sum_{k=1}^{N} |DBW_k f_H - f_L^k|^2 + \frac{1}{2}\alpha |A_1 f_H|^2 \qquad (5)$$

where A_1 is a discrete approximation of the gradient. A higher value of α would give rise to an SR image with a smoother gradient. The Euler-Lagrange equation of this energy functional is given by

$$\sum_{k=1}^{N} W_k^T B^T D^T (DBW_k f_H - f_L^k) - \alpha |A_2 f_H| = 0 \qquad (6)$$

where A_2 is the discrete approximation of the Laplacian. We have used a Gaussian blurring kernel throughout this paper to model the blurring operator B. Since B describes a space invariant Gaussian blur, the transposed matrix

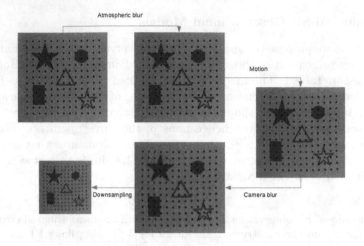

Fig. 1. Generation of Test Set 1 (TS1).

B^T is the same as B. The matrix D^T is the upsampling operator while D is the downsampling operator. For mathematical consistency, D^T and D should be implemented with the same interpolation technique. We have used the area based interpolation technique for upsampling and downsampling processes. The matrix W_k represents the forward warping matrix while W_k^T denotes backward warping. We have implemented warping using bilinear interpolation.

We use a gradient descent scheme with parameters τ (the time step size) and ℓ_{max} (the number of iterations) to solve the Euler-Lagrange equations of all the proposed models in Table 1. The gradient descent scheme applied to the Euler-Lagrange equation of the standard model is given by

$$f_H^{\ell+1} = f_H^\ell + \tau\left(\alpha A_2 f_H^\ell - \sum_{k=1}^{N} W_k^T B^T D^T (DBW_k f_H^\ell - f_L^k)\right). \qquad (7)$$

3   Experiments

3.1   Image Datasets

To evaluate the performance of the methods mentioned in Table 1, we have generated two LR test image sequences. More specifically, we have simulated the image acquisition process of a HR scene on two ground truth HR images. The *shapes* image has a texture background taken from the texture image database of the Massachusetts Institute of Technology which is available at the following link: http://vismod.media.mit.edu/vismod/imagery/VisionTexture/vistex. html. We refer to the 'shapes' image sequence as Test Set 1 (TS1). The second image sequence which is composed of self generated text is referred to as Test Set 2 (TS2). The ground truth of both image sequences is a 512×512 greyscale image. Figure 1 shows the generation of the image sequence TS1 from

(a) Original Image　　(b) Area upsampled refer- (c) Model 1 (MSE: 103.26)
　　　　　　　　　　　ence frame

Fig. 2. SR reconstructed image of TS1 using F1 as optic flow.

its ground truth. We have simulated a deformation type of motion with sub-pixel displacements using a combination of sine and cosine waves with randomly selected amplitude. It is well known that sub-pixel displacements are a require-ment for super-resolution [17]. The ground truth image in TS2 undergoes a similar degradation process but without atmospheric blur. A zooming factor of $z = 3$ was used in both image datasets.

3.2 Parameters

Optic Flow Parameters: The model parameters are α_{OF} (smoothness/ regu-larization parameter for optic flow) and σ_{OF} (Gaussian pre-smoothing standard deviation). We have assumed a scenario where the ground truth optic flow is not available (which is generally the case) for selecting the optic flow parameters. Hence, we select sub-optimal optic flow model parameters by confirming visually that the images are properly registered. The numerical parameters are η (down-sampling factor), η_1 (we use 10 inner fixed point iterations), η_2 (10 outer fixed point iterations) and ω (we select 1.95 for the SOR over-relaxation parameter). For evaluation purposes, we consider the same optic flow parameters for different data terms used for a particular image dataset.

SR Parameters: We have optimized the two model parameters α (for regu-larization) and σ (standard deviation of the Gaussian kernel for blurring) with respect to the mean squared error (MSE) as the ground truth SR image is avail-able. This helps in evaluating the performance of different SR data terms. The numerical parameters are ℓ_{max} and τ. A decay of the norm of the residue by a factor of 10^{-5} was used as the stopping criterion for iterations. We also utilize a Fast Explicit Diffusion (FED) scheme [22] to accelerate the explicit gradient descent scheme. We observed that $\tau = 0.1$ was a stable time step size for all the proposed observational models through backtracking search.

It should be mentioned that modifications of the variational SR reconstruc-tion method we used are definitely possible. For better results, we can use more complex optic flow models, anisotropic blurring kernels, robust data terms, discontinuity-preserving anisotropic smoothness terms and more sophisticated interpolation strategies. However, the aim of our work is to compare the performance of the data terms. To this very end, we keep things simple by assuming a noise-free scenario. For comparison purposes, we have integrated all our models on a common platform. It uses the same variational framework and default parameter settings for the optic flow algorithm.

Both image sequences had 13 images and we have used the last image as the reference image in both cases. An area upsampled reference image was used as an initialisation for the solution of the gradient descent scheme.

3.3   Results and Discussion

As explained in Sect. 3.2, we have selected the optic flow parameters by confirming that the images are properly registered, assuming the real world scenario where the ground truth flow is not known. To emphasize the importance of a good optic flow for super-resolution, we have performed the experiments on TS1 using two different sets of optic flow parametric values. The first set of optic flow parameters with $\eta = 0.5, \sigma_{OF} = 0.3, \alpha_{OF} = 8.0$ is represented as F1. The optic flow parametric set $\eta = 0.5, \sigma_{OF} = 0.3, \alpha_{OF} = 30.0$ is denoted by F2. We have selected the parametric values of F2 such that the corresponding image registration was inferior when compared to the image registration with F1. It should be remembered that TS1 is generated by simulating both atmospheric blur and camera blur. From Table 1, we can conclude two things from the reported MSE values. Firstly, the best SR reconstructed image using F1 is better than the best SR reconstructed image using F2. This is not a surprising result since better optic flow leads to better image registration and hence a better reconstructed SR image. Secondly, the ranking of the data terms with respect to the MSE value has changed with change in optic flow. This is more surprising than the first conclusion. With a better optic flow, the standard SR observational model (Model 1) gives the best results by a fair margin. If the optic flow is bad (F2), this is no longer the case. Thus, this experiment emphasizes the importance of optic flow in both quality of the reconstructed image and the ranking of the data terms. Figure 2 shows the reconstructed image of TS1 using F1 and Model 1.

From the above discussion, we could think that, to conclude correctly about the ranking of the proposed SR observational models in Table 1, the ground truth optic flow has to be used. Hence for TS2, we have used both ground truth (GT) optic flow and sub-optimal optic flow (SOF) with $\eta = 0.9, \alpha_{OF} = 15.0, \sigma_{OF} = 0.3$. One needs to remember that TS2 has been generated without simulating atmospheric blur. This is the general case scenario where camera blur is dominant over atmospheric blur. Table 2 shows the MSE values of the reconstructed SR image of TS2 while Fig. 3 shows the reconstructed images. We can conclude that the standard observational model gives the best results for the ground truth optic flow. This is similar to the observation in the previous experiment where Model 1 gave the best results for better optic flow F1. On using SOF as the optic flow parametric values, Model 2 gave the best results. It can be observed that the error in the best reconstructed image using GT is much smaller than the error

Table 2. Proposed SR observational models along with the MSE values of the obtained reconstructed SR image for TS2 using both ground truth (GT) and sub-optimal flow (SOF). The optimized parametric values are also shown.

#	Observational model	MSE (GT)	MSE (SOF)	σ (GT)	σ (SOF)	α (GT)	α (SOF)
1	$DBW_k f_H = f_L^k$	**10.85**	**173.18**	0.34	0.42	0.0002	0.003
2	$DW_k B f_H = f_L^k$	**23.42**	**162.86**	0.35	0.45	0.0005	0.002
3	$BDW_k f_H = f_L^k$	77.92	248.38	0.50	0.55	0.0009	0.005
4	$W_k DB f_H = f_L^k$	250.35	294.00	0.31	0.33	0.001	0.0006
5	$BW_k D f_H = f_L^k$	422.82	451.70	0.42	0.43	0.002	0.001
6	$W_k BD f_H = f_L^k$	423.52	451.91	0.42	0.43	0.002	0.002

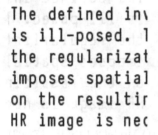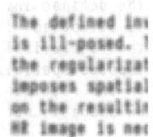

The defined inv
is ill-posed. 1
the regularizat
imposes spatial
on the resultir
HR image is nec

The defined in\
is ill-posed. 1
the regularizat
imposes spatial
on the resultir
HR image is nec

The defined in\
is ill-posed. 1
the regularizat
imposes spatial
on the resultir
HR image is nec

(a) Original Image   (b) Area upsampled reference image   (c) Model 1 (GT, 10.85)

The defined in\
is ill-posed. 1
the regularizat
imposes spatial
on the resultir
HR image is nec

The defined in\
is ill-posed. 1
the regularizat
imposes spatial
on the resultir
HR image is nec

The defined in\
is ill-posed. 1
the regularizat
imposes spatial
on the resultir
HR image is nec

(d) Model 2 (GT, 23.42)   (e) Model 1 (SOF, 173.18)   (f) Model 2 (SOF, 162.86)

Fig. 3. SR reconstructed images of TS2 along with MSE and flow.

in the best reconstructed image using SOF. This reinforces the critical nature of motion estimation in SR reconstruction. The main reason behind Models 1 and 2 performing better is that they are the closest to the image acquisition model in Eq. 2. In other words, the only manipulation they undergo while they are derived from the image acquisition model is dropping one of the blur operators but they do not undergo any swapping of operators like in Models 3–6. The lesson to be learnt from this experiment is that the observational model needs to stay as close as possible to the imaging physics. Now, is this a trivial result? We will be answering this question shortly.

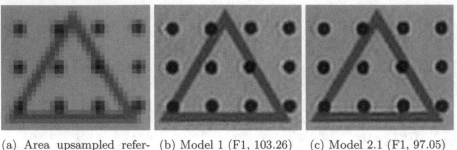

(a) Area upsampled refer- (b) Model 1 (F1, 103.26)   (c) Model 2.1 (F1, 97.05)
ence image

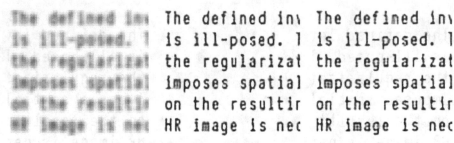

(d) Area upsampled refer- (e) Model 2 (SOF, 162.86) (f) Model 2.1 (SOF, 172.03)
ence image

Fig. 4. SR reconstructed images of TS1 and TS2 using Model 2.1.

Zhang et al. [25] and Rockefort et al. [18] have discussed the application of
both observational Models 1 and 2 but only when affine motion is assumed.
Wang et al. [21] provide a short but insightful work. They also discuss Models
1 and 2 in the case where camera blur is dominant over atmospheric blur. They
do not have constraints on the type of motion. With the help of simple counter
arguments based on the theory of operator commutability, they prove that, in
the case where motion has to be estimated from the LR images (similar to the
case where sub-optimal flow has been used for TS2), SR reconstruction using
Model 1 introduces a systematic error. Model 2 does not introduce this error
and hence it should be preferred over Model 1. The other case is the one where
the motion between the HR scenes is known (similar to the case where we have
used ground truth flow). In such a case Model 1 gives better results than Model
2 as there is no systematic error. Wang et al. also support their arguments with
experimental validations. One can see that by observing the MSE values and the
reconstructed images of TS2, the experimental validations of [21] are confirmed.
However, by using a multi-scale warping approach, we have employed a more
advanced variational motion estimation method than the one [3] by Wang et al.
[21]. This still doesn't guarantee that the standard observational model performs
better. Also, they discard the smoothness term in evaluating Models 1 and 2.
Thus, with our experiments, we can additionally conclude that inclusion of a

regularization term does not change the ranking of the models with respect to SR reconstruction. One could expect to reduce this performance gap between the two Models 1–2 by using even better optic flow.

Thus, going back to the unanswered question above, it is not confirmed that if we deviate from the image acquisition process but still follow a mathematically plausible observational model, we are bound to get worse results. The arguments in the above paragraph support this statement. In such a case it is really necessary that one verifies all mathematically plausible models. Thus, our contribution of evaluating all the six models is not a trivial experiment. However, it turned out that Models 3–6 are outperformed by Models 1–2.

Eventhough Model 2 does not outperform Model 1 by a large margin (while using sub-optimal flow), when we retrospect the reported works on super-resolution after [21] was reported, it is surprising that in most of the works the standard observational model has been used [1,2,10,11,14,15,24]. Model 2 has not been considered as a possible observational model.

3.4 More Efficient Model

Now we propose another mathematically plausible model derived from Model 2 and discuss what could be the advantages of using it. The following is the representation of what we denote as Model 2.1: $Bf_H = W_k^T D^T f_L^k$. It is clear that it is dervied from Model 2 as the ordering of operators is the same. However, it is definitely different from Model 2 itself as warping and downsampling are interpolation operations. Interpolation in general is not an invertible operation. This model also deviates from the imaging physics but is still a mathematically plausible model. The gradient descent of the Euler-Lagrange equation corresponding to the energy using Model 2.1 in the data term, is given by:

$$f_H^{\ell+1} = f_H^\ell + \tau(\alpha A_2 f_H^\ell - (N B^T B f_H^\ell - C)) \tag{8}$$

where $C = \sum_{k=1}^N B^T W_k^T D^T f_L^k$ can be precomputed. Such a precomputation is not possible with Model 2.

Figure 4 shows the reconstructed images using Model 2.1. The parameters $\sigma = 0.64, \alpha = 0.006$ were selected for TS1 and $\sigma = 0.59, \alpha = 0.002$ were selected for TS2 after optimizing for the MSE with respect to the ground truth SR image. We can conclude from the Fig. 4 that the reconstructed HR images obtained using Model 2.1 are not far off from Models 1 and 2 in terms of image reconstruction quality. However, it was observed that because of being able to pre-compute C, the gradient descent of Model 2.1 is twenty-five times faster for TS1 and eighteen times faster for TS2 when compared to the gradient descent schemes of Models 1 and 2 respectively. This can be a decisive advantage in time critical applications.

4   Conclusion and Outlook

Super-resolution requires to model three physical penomena: blur, warp, and downsample. In our paper, we have performed the first systematic evaluation of the influence of the order of these three operators on the result of a variational super-resolution model. This has led to the surprising result that it is not always the physically most plausible and most widely used model which performs best in a practical setting when motion estimation may suffer from errors. Thus, it is worthwhile to consider also alternative models. Moreover, we saw that closely related models can lead to algorithms with strongly differing efficiency: By reformulating the blur-warp-downsample model we managed to come up with a novel model that was 18–25 times more efficient. These insights emphasize the fundamental importance of careful model design.

A possible future work would be to confirm the evaluation performed in this paper also for the case of color images. We are also going to apply our super-resolution algorithms to real world images from biophysics that suffer from severe noise and the absence of ground truth data.

References

1. Babacan, S., Molina, R., Katsaggelos, A.: Variational Bayesian super resolution. IEEE Trans. Image Process. **20**(4), 984–999 (2011)
2. Belekos, S., Galatsanos, N., Katsaggelos, A.: Maximum a posteriori video super-resolution using a new multichannel image prior. IEEE Trans. Image Process. **19**(6), 1451–1464 (2010)
3. Black, M., Anandan, P.: A framework for robust estimation of optical flow. In: Proceedings of the Fourth International Conference on Computer Vision, pp. 231–236. IEEE Computer Society Press, Berlin, Germany, May 1993
4. Brox, T., Bruhn, A., Papenberg, N., Weickert, J.: High accuracy optical flow estimation based on a theory for warping. In: Pajdla, T., Matas, J. (eds.) ECCV 2004. LNCS, vol. 3024, pp. 25–36. Springer, Heidelberg (2004). doi:10.1007/978-3-540-24673-2_3
5. Chaudhuri, S.: Super-Resolution Imaging. Springer, New York (2001)
6. Elad, M., Feuer, A.: Restoration of a single superresolution image from several blurred, noisy, and undersampled measured images. IEEE Trans. Image Process. **6**(12), 1646–1658 (1997)
7. Elad, M., Hel-Or, Y.: A fast super-resolution reconstruction algorithm for pure translational motion and common space-invariant blur. IEEE Trans. Image Process. **10**(8), 1187–1193 (2001)
8. Farsiu, S., Robinson, M.D., Elad, M., Milanfar, P.: Fast and robust multi-frame super resolution. IEEE Trans. Image Process. **13**(10), 1327–1364 (2004)
9. Glasner, D., Shai, B., Irani, M.: Super-resolution from a single image. In: Proceedings of the Twelfth International Conference on Computer Vision, pp. 349–356. IEEE, Kyoto, Japan, September 2009
10. He, H., Kondi, L.: An image super-resolution algorithm for different error levels per frame. IEEE Trans. Image Process. **15**(3), 592–603 (2006)
11. Li, X., Hu, Y., Gao, X., Tao, D., Ning, B.: A multi-frame image super-resolution method. Sig. Process. **90**(2), 405–414 (2010)
12. Marquina, A., Stanley, J.: Image super-resolution by TV-regularization and Bregman iteration. Springer J. Sci. Comput. **37**(3), 367–382 (2008)
13. Milanfar, P.: Super-Resolution Imaging. CRC Press, Boca Raton (2010)

14. Mitzel, D., Pock, T., Schoenemann, T., Cremers, D.: Video super resolution using duality based TV-L1 optical flow. In: Denzler, J., Notni, G., Süße, H. (eds.) DAGM 2009. LNCS, vol. 5748, pp. 432–441. Springer, Heidelberg (2009). doi:10.1007/978-3-642-03798-6_44

15. Ng, M., Shen, H., Lam, E., Zhang, L.: A total variation regularization based super-resolution reconstruction algorithm for digital video. EURASIP J. Adv. Sig. Process. 1, 1–6 (2007)

16. Nguyen, N., Milanfar, P., Golub, G.: Efficient generalized cross-validation with applications to parametric image restoration and resolution enhancement. IEEE Trans. Process. 10(9), 1299–1308 (2001)

17. Park, S., Park, M., Kang, M.: Super-resolution image reconstruction: a technical overview. IEEE Sig. Process. Mag. 20(3), 21–36 (2003)

18. Rochefort, G., Champagnat, F., Besnerais, G.L., Giovannelli, J.: An improved observation model for super-resolution under affine motion. IEEE Trans. Image Process. 15(11), 3325–3337 (2006)

19. Tian, J., Ma, K.: A survey on super-resolution imaging. Sig. Image Video Process. 5(3), 329–342 (2011)

20. Tsai, R., Huang, T.: Multiframe image restoration and registration. Adv. Comput. Vis. Image Process. 1(2), 317–339 (1984)

21. Wang, Z., Qi, F.: On ambiguities in super-resolution modeling. IEEE Sig. Process. Lett. 11(8), 678–681 (2004)

22. Weickert, J., Grewenig, S., Schroers, C., Bruhn, A.: Cyclic schemes for PDE-based image analysis. Int. J. Comput. Vis. 118(3), 275–299 (2016)

23. Yang, J., Wright, J., Huang, T., Ma, Y.: Image super-resolution via sparse representation. IEEE Trans. Image Process. 19(11), 2681–2873 (2010)

24. Zhang, L., Zhang, H., Shen, H., Li, P.: A super-resolution reconstruction algorithm for surveillance images. Sig. Process. 90(3), 848–859 (2010)

25. Zhang, X., Jiang, J., Peng, S.: Commutability of blur and affine warping in super-resolution with application to joint estimation of triple-coupled variables. IEEE Trans. Image Process. 21(4), 1796–1808 (2012)

Compressed Motion Sensing

Robert Dalitz[1], Stefania Petra[1(✉)], and Christoph Schnörr[2]

[1] MIG, Institute of Applied Mathematics, Heidelberg University,
Heidelberg, Germany
robert.dalitz@iwr.uni-heidelberg.de, petra@math.uni-heidelberg.de
[2] IPA, Institute of Applied Mathematics, Heidelberg University,
Heidelberg, Germany
schnoerr@math.uni-heidelberg.de

Abstract. We consider the problem of sparse signal recovery in *dynamic* sensing scenarios. Specifically, we study the recovery of a sparse *time-varying* signal from linear measurements of a *single* static sensor that are taken at two different points in time. This setup can be modelled as observing a single signal using two different sensors – a real one and a virtual one induced by signal motion, and we examine the recovery properties of the resulting combined sensor. We show that not only can the signal be uniquely recovered with overwhelming probability by linear programming, but also the correspondence of signal values (signal motion) can be established between the two points in time. In particular, we show that in our scenario the performance of an undersampling static sensor is doubled or, equivalently, that the number of sufficient measurements of a static sensor is halved.

1 Introduction

Overview, Motivation. On of the most common scenarios of compressed sensing concerns the unique recovery of a sparse vector $x \in \mathbb{R}^n$ from $m < n$ linear measurements by ℓ_1-norm minimization,

$$\min_{x \in \mathbb{R}^n} \|x\|_1 \quad \text{subject to} \quad Ax = b_x, \tag{1}$$

based on suitable conditions on the sensor matrix A [3]. In this paper, we extend this scenario in that x undergoes some unknown transformation,

$$y = T(x), \tag{2}$$

and then is observed once more by the *same* sensor: $Ay = b_y$. The corresponding extension of (1) reads

$$\min_{x,y \in \mathbb{R}^n} \left\| \begin{pmatrix} x \\ y \end{pmatrix} \right\|_1 \quad \text{subject to} \quad \begin{pmatrix} A & 0 \\ 0 & A \end{pmatrix} \begin{pmatrix} x \\ y \end{pmatrix} = \begin{pmatrix} b_x \\ b_y \end{pmatrix}. \tag{3}$$

Acknowledgments. We gratefully acknowledge support by the German Science Foundation, grant GRK 1653.

F. Lauze et al. (Eds.): SSVM 2017, LNCS 10302, pp. 602–613, 2017.
DOI: 10.1007/978-3-319-58771-4_48

This formulation, however, merely doubles the number of measurements to $2m$ and the number of variables to be recovered to $2n$. Additionally, it has the weakness that the additional m linear measurements are not independent.

On the other hand, if the transformation T of (2) was *known*, then the number of variables to be recovered remains n, because the *same* vector x is observed in two different ways. Moreover, suppose the measurements (2) of the transformed vector can be approximated by $A(T)x \approx AT(x)$ in terms of a *virtual* sensor $A(T)$ (regarded as a function of T), then the number of measurements is *effectively* doubled to $2m$ and the recovery problem reads

$$\min_{x \in \mathbb{R}^n} \|x\|_1 \quad \text{subject to} \quad \begin{pmatrix} A \\ A(T) \end{pmatrix} x = \begin{pmatrix} b_x \\ b_y \end{pmatrix}. \tag{4}$$

The key questions addressed in this paper are: How much can we gain from (4) relative to (1), under suitable assumptions from the viewpoint of compressed sensing? How can we cope with the unknown transformation T and recover it at the same time? Since T is usually a transformation of x between two subsequent points in time, we call (4) the *compressed motion sensing (CMS)* problem.

To approach this problem, we consider as a first step the following specific variant of (4): The vector x results from a discretization of a continuous medium observed on a grid graph, that covers a bounded Euclidean domain $\Omega \subset \mathbb{R}^{\dim}$, $\dim \in \{2, 3\}$. A concrete example is the setup of [7] related to the imaging in experimental fluid dynamics, where every component $x_i \in \{0, 1\}$, $i \subset [n]$ indicates the absence or presence of a particle in a turbulent fluid. We adopt this scenario which is sufficient for our purpose to introduce the CMS problem.

Assuming a sufficiently fine spacing of the vertices i of the grid graph, any transformation $T \colon \Omega \to \Omega$ can be approximated by a permutation

$$y = Px, \qquad x \in \{0, 1\}^n, \tag{5}$$

which represents the motion of particles on the grid graph. As a consequence, the specific version of the *CMS sensor* of (4), that we study in this paper, reads

$$B := \begin{pmatrix} A \\ AP \end{pmatrix} \in \mathbb{R}^{2m \times n}. \qquad \text{(CMS sensor)} \tag{6}$$

Specifically, we are concerned with the following **objectives** of showing that:

1. the CMS sensor (6) effectively doubles the number of measurements and turns a poor sensor into a stronger one;
2. the vector $x \in \{0, 1\}^n$ can be recovered uniquely;
3. the transformation (5) in terms of the permutation matrix P can be *jointly* determined as well, together with x, by linear programming.

Points (1)–(3) are illustrated in Fig. 1 where $\Omega \subset \mathbb{R}^2$ is a square domain, uniformly tesselated by square pixels, and the sensor matrix A encodes sums of pixel values along all image rows and columns – cf. Fig. 2 and Eq. (7), also called projections. This simple setup of orthogonal projections is a classical scenario of discrete tomography [4] and severely ill-posed. As Fig. 1 illustrates, however, our results show that even on the basis of such a poor sensor matrix A, the corresponding CMS sensor (5) enables to infer unique recovery and correspondence (motion) information (5) within a certain sparsity regime. In other words, *our approach turns a poor sensor into a stronger one*, while using overall the *same number* of $2m$ measurements.

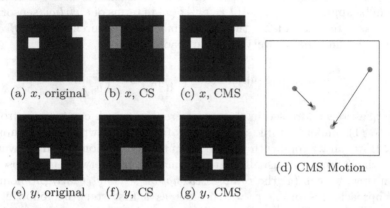

(a) x, original   (b) x, CS   (c) x, CMS

(d) CMS Motion

(e) y, original   (f) y, CS   (g) y, CMS

Fig. 1. Recovery of two sparse subsequent 6×6 vectors x (a) and y (e) by standard CS recovery via (1) and by compressed motion sensing (CMS), respectively, based on a sensor matrix A with projects along two orthogonal directions (rows and columns). Standard CS recovery (b, f) by solving (1) fails due to poor sensor properties of A, despite low sparsity. Using the same number of measurements the CMS sensor (6) leads to unique recovery (c, g) and correspondence (motion) information (d) so that $y = Px$.

Related Work. Our work builds on [7] where the connection between tomographic particle imaging and compressed sensing was established, along with an average case analysis of recovery conditions for *static* scenarios. In this paper, we establish the extension to more realistic *dynamic* scenarios. Applications include, in particular, the two-frame analysis of tomographic particle image sequences in experimental fluid dynamics (cf. Fig. 5).

Related other work includes [8] on the application of compressed sensing techniques to scene reconstruction in computer vision from multiple perspective views. The transformations are naturally restricted to low-dimensional Euclidean and affine transforms, and the recovery problem amounts to alternatingly minimizing a *non-convex* objective function. Our approach can deal with a significantly larger class of transformations and solve the *joint* problem of reconstruction and transformation estimation *globally optimal* by linear programming.

Our 'discretize-then-optimize' strategy adopted in this paper relates our recovery problem to *discrete optimal transport* [12]. The authors of [2] study *regularized* discrete optimal transport in connection with color transfer between natural images, where regularization enforces *spatially smooth* displacements. In this paper, we establish uniqueness of both recovery and displacements between particles solely based on a large subclass of one-to-one grid transformations, that includes also *non-smooth* displacement fields encountered in various applications.

A *continuous* variational approach based on optimal transport to object recovery from multiple tomographic measurements is studied in [1]. The numerical implementation of the approach seems to suffer from severe issues of numerical sensitivity and stability, and has only be applied to solid bodies of simple shapes. Related very interesting work, with a focus on dynamic tomography in experimental fluid dynamics, was published recently [9,10]. The authors adopt too a continuous PDE-based approach (iteratively linearized Monge-Ampère equation) which may lead to a more economical problem parametrization and enables, in particular, to take into account physical fluid flow models. On the other hand, a performance analysis is only provided for simple 1D settings or a single particle in 2D, and additional rectifying filters are needed if the approach is not discretized on a sufficiently fine grid.

Outside the field of mathematics, highly engineered state-of-the-art approaches to particle matching and tomographic recovery in experimental fluid dynamics, that require parameter tuning and do not provide any recovery guarantees, include [5,6,11].

2   Sparse Recovery Guarantees

In this section, we address objectives 1 and 2 as discussed in Sect. 1 and analyze sparse recovery of the vector x by compressed motion sensing. We adopt the scenario of [7].

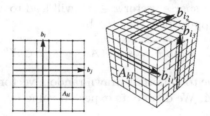

Fig. 2. LEFT: Imaging geometry with d^2 cells and $2d$ projection rays (here: $d = 6$) for problems of spatial dimension $D = 2$. RIGHT: Imaging geometry with d^3 cells and $3d^2$ rays (here: $d = 7$) for problems of spatial dimension $D = 3$. The corresponding sensor matrices A are given by (7).

We consider both dim $= 2$ and dim $= 3$ spatial dimensions. Figure 2 depicts the incidence geometry of the sensor A in terms of orthogonal projection rays The corresponding sensor matrices A are

$$A = \begin{pmatrix} \mathbb{1}_d^\top \otimes I_d \\ I_d \otimes \mathbb{1}_d^\top \end{pmatrix} \quad \text{if dim} = 2, \qquad A = \begin{pmatrix} \mathbb{1}_d^\top \otimes I_d \otimes I_d \\ I_d \otimes \mathbb{1}_d^\top \otimes I_d \\ I_d \otimes I_d \otimes \mathbb{1}_d^\top \end{pmatrix} \quad \text{if dim} = 3, \ (7)$$

where the number d of pixels or voxels along each coordinate direction serves as discretization parameter.

We assume that

$$x \in \mathcal{X}_s^n := \{z \in \{0,1\}^n : |\mathrm{supp}(z)| = s\} \tag{8}$$

is a uniformly drawn s-sparse vector and $P \in \Pi_n$ is a uniformly drawn permutation matrix. We next provide a *sufficient* condition in terms of sparsity s for unique recovery of $x \in \mathcal{X}_s^n$ via

$$\min_{z \in \mathbb{R}^n} \|z\|_1 \quad \text{subject to} \quad \begin{pmatrix} A \\ AP \end{pmatrix} z = \begin{pmatrix} Ax \\ APx \end{pmatrix}, \quad z \geq 0. \tag{9}$$

Since the columns of $B = \begin{pmatrix} A \\ AP \end{pmatrix}$ in (6) sum up to a constant the nonnegative constraints in (9) are self-regularizing.

Remark 1. Indeed, all elements z that satisfy $Bz = Bx$ have equal ℓ_1-norm

$$\|z\|_1 = \mathbb{1}_n^\top z = \frac{1}{2\dim} \mathbb{1}_{2m}^\top Bz = \frac{1}{2\dim} \mathbb{1}_{2m}^\top Bx = const.$$

Thus, in our setting, enforcing sparsity by ℓ_1-regularization (4) would be redundant. For sparse recovery we just need to take nonnegativity into account.

We next provide an average case analysis that guarantees unique recovery of a uniformly distributed random vector $x \in \mathcal{X}_s^n$ as the unique *nonnegative* of $Bz = Bx$. We closely follow [7] wherein the provided guarantees rest upon the following observation: A sparse vector $x \in \mathcal{X}_s^n$ will lead to a sparse measurement vector $b := Ax$. The support of b, denoted by

$$I_s := \mathrm{supp}(b) = \mathrm{supp}(Ax), \quad x \in \mathcal{X}_s^n \tag{10}$$

is a random variable due to uniformly drawn random vectors x and the incidence geometry encoded by A. We denote its expected value by

$$m_s := \mathbb{E}\big[|I_s|\big] \leq m. \tag{11}$$

After removing the $m - |I_s|$ redundant rows from A, corresponding to zero-components of b, we may also remove every column corresponding to cells (pixels, voxels) that are met by any ray corresponding to a removed row. We denote the index set of the remaining columns by

$$J_s := [n] \setminus \{j \in [n] : A_{ij} > 0, \forall i \in [m] \setminus I_s\}. \tag{12}$$

The resulting "effective" number $|J_s|$ of columns is a random variable with expected value denoted by

$$n_s := \mathbb{E}\big[|J_s|\big]. \tag{13}$$

For highly sparse scenarios with a very small sparsity s, every non-zero component of x creates multiple non-zero entries in b, because every cell (pixel, voxel) intersects with multiple projection rays. As a consequence, the ratio $\frac{m_s}{n_s}$ is larger than 1. This ratio decreases with increasing s and in particular defines a critical maximal value

$$s_{\mathrm{crit}} := \min\left\{s \in [n]: m_s/n_s \geq 1\right\}. \tag{14}$$

In [7], the authors computed the expected values m_s and n_s which enables to solve numerically (14) for s_{crit}. In addition, concentration inequalities were established that bound deviations of $|I_s|, |J_s|$ from their expected values m_s, n_s. In this work, we confine ourselves to computing m_s and n_s for the compressed motion sensor (6) and apply the previous considerations to the system $Bx = b$, with $b := Bx$ and $x \in \mathcal{X}_s^n$.

Lemma 1. *Let $X \in \mathcal{X}_s^n$ and $\mathcal{P} \in \Pi_n$ be independent and uniformly distributed random variables of s-sparse vectors $x \in \mathcal{X}_s^n$ and permutation matrices $P \in \Pi^n$. Then $Y = \mathcal{P}X \in \mathcal{X}_s^n$ is also uniformly distributed.*

Proof. Let $x, y \in \mathcal{X}_s^n$ be any realizations. Then there are $s!(n-s)!$ permutations P mapping x_S to y_S: $y = Px$. Denote this set by $\Pi^n(x; y)$ and count combinations of its elements with possible x from $\mathcal{X}_s^n$. ∎

Proposition 1. *Let the effective number of rows and columns of the sensor matrix (6) be indexed by*

$$I_s := supp(Bx), \quad x \in \mathcal{X}_s^n \qquad\qquad |I_s| \in [2m], \tag{15a}$$
$$J_s := [n] \setminus \{j \in [n]: B_{ij} > 0, \forall i \in [2m] \setminus I_s\}, \qquad |J_s| \in [n]. \tag{15b}$$

Assume the s-sparse vector $x \in \mathcal{X}_s^n$ is uniformly drawn. Then

$$m_s = \mathbb{E}\big[|I_s|\big] = 2\dim \cdot d^{\dim-1}\left(1 - \left(1 - \frac{1}{d^{\dim-1}}\right)^s\right), \tag{16a}$$

$$n_s = \mathbb{E}\big[|J_s|\big] = d^{\dim}\left(1 + \sum_{k=1}^{2\dim}(-1)^k \binom{2\dim}{k}\left(1 - \frac{k(d-1)+1}{d^{\dim}}\right)^s\right). \tag{16b}$$

Proof. The proof basically generalizes the reasoning of [7, Lemma 5.1, Proposition 5.3] to the CMS matrix (6). Due to lack of space, we skip the details.

∎

As a result, the reconstruction of a random s-sparse nonnegative vector x will be based on a reduced linear system restricted to the rows I_s and the columns J_s. Dimensions of reduced systems will be the same for most random sets $S = supp(x) \subset J_s$ with $|S| = s$. Consequently, a sufficient condition that guarantees unique recovery of $x \in \mathcal{X}_s$ via

$$\text{find} \quad z \geq 0 \quad \text{subject to} \quad Bz = Bx, \tag{17}$$

is that the coefficient matrices B_{I_s,J_s} of the reduced systems are of full rank and overdetermined. B_{I_s,J_s} is on average overdetermined if the sparsity s is chosen according to (14), where s_{crit} solves

$$m_s = n_s, \tag{18}$$

with m_s, n_s defined in (16a) and (16b). Solving (18) for s_{crit} results in a curve that depends on the problem size d only, and is illustrated in Fig. 3a. To determine this curve we used a standard numerical root finding algorithm in order to compute the corresponding solution of (18) for each d in the plotted range.

Concerning the second issue, the full rank of B_{I_s, J_s}, we can resort to small random perturbations of the non-zero entries of A in (7), and thus preserving the sparse structure that encodes the underlying incidence relation of the sensor B. As a consequence the dimension of the reduced systems of a perturbed system does not change.

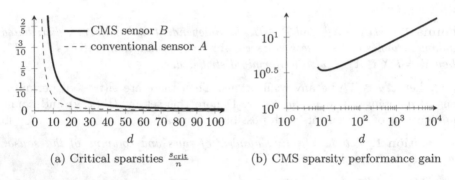

(a) Critical sparsities $\frac{s_{\text{crit}}}{n}$ (b) CMS sparsity performance gain

Fig. 3. Critical sparsity values $\frac{s_{\text{crit}}}{n}$ that enable with high probability unique recovery of s-sparse nonnegative vectors whenever $s \leq s_{\text{crit}}$, using sensor (7) for dim = 3 and the corresponding CMS sensor B in (a). Plot (b) shows the factor $\frac{s_{\text{crit}}^A}{s_{\text{crit}}}$ between the two functions in (a), that is the **theoretical sparsity performance gain of CMS**. This curve reaches a minimum of 3.4 and becomes larger than 17 for $d \geq 10^4$

The perturbed matrix $\tilde{A}$ is computed by uniformly perturbing the non-zero entries $A_{ij} > 0$ to obtain $\tilde{A}_{ij} \in [A_{ij} - \varepsilon, A_{ij} + \varepsilon]$, and by normalizing subsequently all column vectors of $\tilde{A}$ such that they all sum up to a constant e.g. equal to dim. We then define the "perturbed" CMS sensor as the CMS sensor (6) corresponding to $\tilde{A}$, i.e.

$$\tilde{B} := \begin{pmatrix} \tilde{A} \\ \tilde{A}P \end{pmatrix} \in \mathbb{R}^{2m \times n}. \tag{19}$$

We next give a sufficient condition that guarantees uniqueness of a nonnegative and sparse enough vector sampled by a CMS sensor of the form (19).

Proposition 2. *There exists a perturbed matrix $\tilde{A}$ that has the same structure as A from (7) such that the perturbed system $\tilde{B}z = \tilde{B}x$, with $\tilde{B}$ defined as in (19), admits unique recovery of s-sparse nonnegative vectors $x \in \mathcal{X}_s$ with high probability, i.e. the set*

$$\{z \in \mathbb{R}^n : \tilde{B}z = \tilde{B}x, z \geq 0\} \tag{20}$$

is a singleton with high probability, if s satisfies condition $s \leq s_{crit}$, *where* s_{crit}
solves (18).

Proof. Analogously to [7, Proposition 5.10].

3   Joint Reconstruction and Motion Estimation

Displacement Estimation. We consider first the problem of determining the
displacement mapping $P \in \Pi^n(x;y)$ from a *known* $x \in \mathcal{X}_s^n$ to a *known* $y \in$
$\mathcal{X}_s^n$ (the joint problem is addressed below). Recall the particle imaging setup
illustrated in Fig. 2: Every component $x_i, y_i \in \{0,1\}, i \in [n]$ indicates the absence
or presence of a particle in a cell. We assume that the n cells have an arbitrarily
fixed order and define the two support sets

$$S_x := \text{supp}(x), \quad S_y := \text{supp}(y). \tag{21}$$

The displacement corresponds to s moving particles and becomes an one-to-one
assignment between the s cells in S_x and S_y. We associate with the assignment
of $j \in S_x$ to $i \in S_y$ the cost C_{ij}. Then the *linear assignment* problem reads

$$\min_{P \in \mathcal{P}^n} \text{tr}(C^\top P) \quad \text{subject to} \quad Px = y, P^\top x = y, P \geq 0, \tag{22}$$

where $\mathcal{P}^n := \{P \in \mathbb{R}_+^{n \times n}: P\mathbb{1} = \mathbb{1}, P^\top \mathbb{1} = \mathbb{1}\}$ is the Birkhoff polytop. This linear
program is also a special case of the Kantorovich formulation of the *discrete
optimal transport* problem [12]. $C \in \mathbb{R}_+^{n \times n}$ is the cost matrix related to the
"energy" needed to move particles in x to y. It can be chosen based on physical
prior knowledge about the scenario at hand – see Sect. 4.

Solving the Joint Problem. We now address the problem of *jointly* estimating
x, y and the displacement between x and y in terms of $P \in \Pi^n(x;y)$ restricted
to the supports (21). We define the assignment matrix $D \in \{0,1\}^{n \times n}$ as

$$D_{S_y, S_x} := P_{S_y, S_x} \in \Pi_s \quad \text{and} \quad D_{S_y^c, S_x^c} := 0. \tag{23}$$

Our approach is based on merging the CMS problem (4) with the linear
assignment problem (22) into a single optimization problem, which reads

$$\min_{x,y,P} \text{tr}\left(C^\top P\right) \quad \text{subject to} \quad Ax = b_x, Ay = b_y, x, y \geq 0, \tag{24}$$
$$Px = y, P^\top y = x, P \geq 0.$$

Note that problem (24) is *block biconvex*: for each fixed (x,y) problem (24) is
convex w.r.t. P, and it is also convex w.r.t. (x,y) for any fixed P. Rather than
considering a block coordinate descent approach that sequentially updates the
two blocks of variables (x,y) and P via proximal minimization, see e.g. [13],
we replace the non-convex constraints $Px = y$, $P^\top y = x$ and solve instead the
linear program

$$\min_{x,y,D} \text{tr}\left(C^\top D\right) \quad \text{subject to} \quad Ax = b_x, Ay = b_y, x, y \geq 0, \tag{25}$$
$$D\mathbb{1} = y, D^\top \mathbb{1} = x, D \geq 0.$$

Proposition 3. *Assume that $x, y \in \mathcal{X}_s^n$ and $P \in \Pi^n(x; y)$. Set $S_x = supp(x)$, $S_y = supp(y)$. Consider D from (23). If (x, y, D) is a solution of (24), then (x, y, D) is also a solution of (25). Likewise, a solution (x, y, D) of (25) is also a solution of (24).*

Proof. We have $Dx = D_{S_x} x_{S_x} = D\mathbb{1} = y$, $D^\top y = D_{S_y}^\top y_{S_y} = D^\top \mathbb{1} = x$ and hence (x, y, D) is feasible for both (24) and (25). $\qquad\square$

Hence, the optimal assignment D between $x, y \in \mathcal{X}_s^n$ is a sparse matrix with s nonzero entries, that equals a permutation matrix when restricted to the support of x and y.

Corollary 1. *Consider $x \in \mathcal{X}_s$ that is mapped to $y = Px$ via $P \in \Pi_n(x; y)$. Then there exists a perturbation $\tilde{A}$ of A from (7) and a cost matrix $C \in \mathbb{R}_+^{n \times n}$ such that we can exactly recover x and y and the assignment matrix $D \in \{0, 1\}^{n \times n}$ from (23) with $y = Dx$ and $D_{S_y, S_x} := P_{S_y, S_x} \in \Pi_s$ with high probability by solving problem (25), specialized to*

$$\min_{u,v,D} tr\left(C^\top D\right) \quad \text{subject to} \quad \tilde{A}u = \tilde{A}x, \tilde{A}v = \tilde{A}y, u, v \geq 0,$$

$$D\mathbb{1} = y, D^\top \mathbb{1} = x, D \geq 0, \tag{26}$$

provided that $s \leq s_{crit}$, with s_{crit} solving (18).

Proof. By Proposition 2 there exists $\tilde{A}$ such that $x \in \mathcal{X}_s$ is the unique nonnegative solution of

$$\tilde{B}u = \begin{pmatrix} \tilde{A} \\ \tilde{A}P \end{pmatrix} u = \begin{pmatrix} \tilde{A} \\ \tilde{A}P \end{pmatrix} x = \begin{pmatrix} \tilde{A}x \\ \tilde{A}y \end{pmatrix}. \tag{27}$$

By Proposition 3 (x, y, D) with $D_{S_y, S_x} = P_{S_y, S_x} \in \Pi_s$ and $D_{S_y^c, S_x^c} := 0$ is a (vertex) solution of (26) for an appropriate $C \in \mathbb{R}_+^{n \times n}$.

The next section shows that in practice a perturbation of A is not necessary.

4 Experiments

In this section we empirically validate the previous theoretical results and illustrate the performance of the CMS approach in practice. We are concerned with the following issues:

(1) the exact recovery of sparse vectors $x \in \mathcal{X}_s$ by linear programming (17) when the CMS sensor B combines a poor tomographic sensor A (7) with a random permutation;

(2) the assignment matrix D from (23) in terms of the permutation matrix $P \in \Pi_n(x; y)$ can be jointly determined as well, together with x and y, by linear programming (25).

Exact Recovery of Sparse Vectors. We assess the sufficient sparsity s_{crit} (14) derived via Proposition 1 that induces overdetermined reduced systems and guarantees unique nonnegative recovery via a *perturbation* of CMS, see Proposition 2. Here we consider a CMS sensor B (6) that incorporates the *unperturbed* tomographic sensor A (7). Numerical experiments show that no perturbation of A is necessary in practice. We consider the particle recovery problem in three dimensions (dim = 3). For a fixed d, we vary the sparsity s in order to determine empirically the *critical* sparsity that guarantees unique recovery of s-sparse vectors sampled by B via (17). For each d and s, we generate a permutation matrix P uniformly at random as part of the CMS sensor B and a random binary signal $x \in \mathcal{X}_s^n$ with uniform support. Form $b = Bx$ we recover $\hat{x}$ by solving the LP (17). If the recovery error $\|x - \hat{x}\|_2 < 10^{-8}$, we declare recovery successful. We repeat this experiment 200 times and count the success ratio, plotted in Fig. 4.

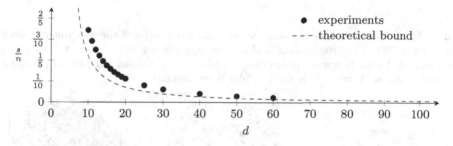

Fig. 4. Experimental validation of the derived recovery guarantee from Proposition 1 for dim = 3. The empirical relative sparsity $\frac{s}{n}$ (black dots) that separates recovery from nonrecovery together with the *sufficient* theoretical sparsity bound s_{crit} (14) for comparison. We note that perturbation of A in view of Proposition 2 was not necessary, but critical when using only the static sensor A according to [7].

Joint Recovery and Motion Estimation. The minimal example shown in Fig. 1 already illustrates the potential of CMS. More realistic scenarios are shown in Fig. 5 using a cost matrix filled with Euclidean distances between grid nodes. The underlying motion was generated by discretizing a turbulent random vector field to grid positions in order to be captured by a permutation.

The critical role of the cost matrix via (25) is illustrated in Fig. 6. We generate a vector field $y \in \mathbb{R}^3$ from $x \in \mathbb{R}^3$ by

$$y = \begin{pmatrix} \cos(\alpha) & \sin(\alpha) & 0 \\ -\sin(\alpha) & \cos(\alpha) & 0 \\ 0 & 0 & 1 \end{pmatrix} x + \begin{pmatrix} 0 \\ 0 \\ v_z \end{pmatrix} \tag{28}$$

with $\alpha = \mathrm{rad}(5v_z)$. This represents a rotation around and a constant shift along the z-axis. $v_z \in \mathbb{N}$ is the vertical velocity on a voxel basis. In addition to an Euclidean cost matrix, we define a cost matrix that penalizes particles that do not move along their orbit around the z-axis, i.e.

$$C_{i,j} = \min_z \left\{ \|z - w_j\|_2^2 : \left\| \begin{pmatrix} z_1 \\ z_2 \end{pmatrix} \right\| = \left\| \begin{pmatrix} w_{i,1} \\ w_{i,2} \end{pmatrix} \right\| \right\} \tag{29}$$

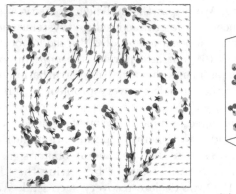
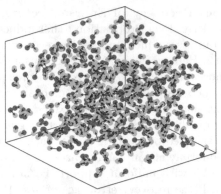

(a) CMS recovery of 80 particles on a 256 × 256 grid.

(b) CMS recovery of 500 particles on a 256 × 256 × 256 grid.

Fig. 5. Exact CMS recovery of particles (blue and red dots) and the assignment (black arrows) via (25). The true motion is shown as gray arrows. (a) Sensor A from (7) is complemented with two more projections at 45 and 135° to define CMS. In (b) the 3 projection sensor A from (7) is used. (Color figure online)

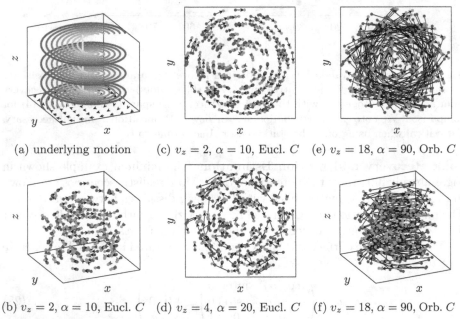

(a) underlying motion   (c) $v_z = 2$, $\alpha = 10$, Eucl. C (e) $v_z = 18$, $\alpha = 90$, Orb. C

(b) $v_z = 2$, $\alpha = 10$, Eucl. C (d) $v_z = 4$, $\alpha = 20$, Eucl. C (f) $v_z = 18$, $\alpha = 90$, Orb. C

Fig. 6. Vortex motion (28) in a $257 \times 257 \times 257$ volume with additional vertical shift v_z (a) and recovered assignments by CMS (b)–(f). Recovery of particles and assignment is exact when the cost matrix C is Euclidean, if displacements are small, i.e. $v_z = 2$ and $\alpha = 10$ (b), (c). After increasing both, recovery with an Euclidean C fails (d), but CMS is still capable of recovering the correct motion by using a different cost matrix (29) called *Orbit* C here. Even for comparably large displacements the CMS recovery is perfect (e), (f).

with voxel locations $w_i \in \mathbb{Z}^3$. The result for 200 moving particles according to (28) and different values of velocity v_z are shown in Fig. 6. Using (29) perfect motion recovery is possible even for large displacements. This shows the flexibility of our framework in incorporating motion priors.

5 Conclusion

We introduced "Compressed Motion Sensing", a novel framework the exploits sparsity for recovery within dynamic scenarios. We gave theoretical recovery guarantees and validated them experimentally. The approach can be flexibly adapted to a broad range of applications that involve physical prior knowledge. Besides signal reconstruction, motion is recovered too, by using in a cost-effective way undersampled measurements of a single sensor at multiple points in time.

References

1. Abraham, I., Abraham, R., Bergounioux, M., Carlier, G.: Tomographic reconstruction from a few views: a multi-marginal optimal transport approach. Appl. Math. Optim. **75**(1), 55–73 (2017)
2. Ferradans, S., Papadakis, N., Peyré, G., Aujol, J.: Regularized discrete optimal transport. SIAM J. Imaging Sci. **7**(3), 1853–1882 (2014)
3. Foucart, S., Rauhut, H.: A Mathematical Introduction to Compressive Sensing. Springer, Heidelberg (2013)
4. Herman, G.T., Kuba, A.: Discrete Tomography: Foundations Algorithms and Applications. Birkhäuser, Basel (1999)
5. Lynch, K.P., Scarano, F.: An efficient and accurate approach to MTE-MART for time-resolved tomographic PIV. Exp. Fluids **56**(3), 1–16 (2015)
6. Novara, M., Batenburg, K.J., Scarano, F.: Motion tracking-enhanced MART for tomographic PIV. Meas. Sci. Technol. **21**(3), 035401 (2010)
7. Petra, S., Schnörr, C.: Average case recovery analysis of tomographic compressive sensing. Linear Algebra Appl. **441**, 168–198 (2014)
8. Puy, G., Vandergheynst, P.: Robust image reconstruction from multiview measurements. SIAM J. Imaging Sci. **7**(1), 128–156 (2014)
9. Saumier, L., Khouider, B., Agueh, M.: Optimal transport for particle image velocimetry. Commun. Math. Sci. **13**(1), 269–296 (2015)
10. Saumier, L., Khouider, B., Agueh, M.: Optimal transport for particle image velocimetry: real data and postprocessing algorithms. SIAM J. Appl. Math. **75**(6), 2495–2514 (2015)
11. Schanz, D., Gesemann, S., Schröder, A.: Shake-the-box: lagrangian particle tracking at high particle image densities. Exp. Fluids **57**(70), 1–27 (2016)
12. Villani, C.: Optimal Transport: Old and New. Grundlehren der mathematischen Wissenschaften. Springer, Heidelberg (2009)
13. Xu, Y., Yin, W.: A block coordinate descent method for regularized multiconvex optimization with applications to nonnegative tensor factorization and completion. SIAM J. Imaging Sci. **6**(3), 1758–1789 (2013)

A Unified Hyperelastic Joint Segmentation/Registration Model Based on Weighted Total Variation and Nonlocal Shape Descriptors

Noémie Debroux and Carole Le Guyader[(✉)]

Laboratoire de Mathématiques, Normandie Université, INSA de Rouen,
685 Avenue de l'Université, 76801 Saint-Etienne-du-Rouvray Cedex, France
{noemie.debroux,carole.le-guyader}@insa-rouen.fr

Abstract. In this paper, we address the issue of designing a unified variational model for joint segmentation and registration in which the shapes to be matched are viewed as hyperelastic materials, and more precisely, as Saint Venant-Kirchhoff ones. The dissimilarity measure relates local and global (or region-based) information, since relying on weighted total variation and on a nonlocal shape descriptor inspired by the Chan-Vese model for segmentation. Theoretical results emphasizing the mathematical and practical soundness of the model are provided, among which relaxation, existence of minimizers, analysis of two numerical methods of resolution, asymptotic results and a Γ-convergence property.

Keywords: Segmentation · Registration · Nonlinear elasticity · Saint Venant-Kirchhoff material · Quasiconvexity · Relaxation · Weighted BV space · Piecewise constant Mumford-Shah model · Nonlocal operators · Γ-convergence · Asymptotic results

1 Introduction

While segmentation aims to partition a given image into significant constituents and identify structures such as homogeneous regions or edges in order to quantify information (see [2, Chap. 4] for instance or [28, Part II], for a relevant analysis of this problem), registration, given two images called Template and Reference, consists of determining an optimal diffeomorphic transformation (or deformation) φ that maps the structures visible in the Template into the corresponding ones in the Reference. This latter technique is encountered in the domain of

N. Debroux and C. Le Guyader—The project is co-financed by the European Union with the European regional development fund (ERDF, HN0002137) and by the Normandie Regional Council via the M2NUM project. The authors would like to thank Dr. Caroline Petitjean (LITIS, Université de Rouen, France) for providing the cardiac cycle MRI images.

F. Lauze et al. (Eds.): SSVM 2017, LNCS 10302, pp. 614–625, 2017.
DOI: 10.1007/978-3-319-58771-4_49

shape tracking, multi-modality fusion to facilitate diagnosis and treatment planning [26], progression disease evaluation, shape averaging [25], etc.

We refer the reader to [26] for an extensive overview of existing registration techniques in a systematic manner. The sought deformation φ is seen as the optimal solution of a specifically designed cost function, the problem being mathematically hard to solve due to its ill-posedness, to the involved non-linearity, to its non-convexity and to its versatile formulation. As structure/salient component/shape/geometrical feature matching and intensity distribution comparison rule registration, it sounds relevant to intertwine the segmentation and registration tasks into a single framework: accurate segmented structures allow to drive the registration process correctly providing then a reliable deformation field between the encoded structures, whilst the difficulty of weak edge segmentation can be overcome thanks to registration. The idea of combining segmentation and registration is not new. Prior related works suggest to perform these two processes simultaneously: [27, 29] (in a level set framework), [17] (registration is achieved using the transfer of edges based on the Active Contour Without Edges ACWE model [9]), [18] (model based on metric structure comparison), [1, 15] (active contour framework combined with dense deformation fields of optical flow), [14] (Mumford-Shah type free discontinuity problem to match edges and normals), [16, 21, 22] (joint phase field segmentation and registration models). The scope of the proposed work is thus to address the issue of designing a theoretically well-posed joint segmentation registration model in a variational formulation, capable of handling large deformations and providing a reliable matching of the structures encoded in the Reference and in the Template. While the former goal is achieved working within the hyperelastic framework, the latter is accomplished by devising an original dissimilarity measure based on weighted total variation (ensuring edge mapping) and a region-based criterion, so combining local and nonlocal structure comparison.

To summarize, the novelty of the paper rests upon: (i) an original modelling involving the stored energy function of a Saint Venant-Kirchhoff material, weighted total variation and a region-based criterion; (ii) the introduction of a relaxed problem for which theoretical results are provided; (iii) the derivation of two numerical methods of resolution: a first one based on the dual formulation of weighted total variation and on a decoupling principle yielding asymptotic results, and a second one, original and based on the approximation of the weighted total variation by a sequence of integral operators involving a differential quotient and a suitable sequence of radial mollifiers. This work falls within the continuation of [21, 22] but includes novel aspects both in the modelling (with the integration of a region-based criterion entailing substantial modifications in the mathematical proofs) and in the design of the algorithm (introduction of a nonlocal operator), giving in practice more accurate segmentation and registration results in comparison to [21] (exhaustively exemplified in [13] empirically/visually, and by computing comparison criteria such as the Dice coefficient or the mutual information to assess the segmentation and registration accuracy), and yielding a decomposition of the Reference into a simplified version and an oscillatory part.

2   Mathematical Modelling

2.1   Depiction of the Model

Let Ω be a connected bounded open subset of $\mathbb{R}^2$ of class $\mathcal{C}^1$. Let us denote by $R : \bar{\Omega} \to \mathbb{R}$ the Reference image assumed to be sufficiently smooth and by $T : \bar{\Omega} \to \mathbb{R}$ the Template image. For theoretical and numerical purposes, we assume that T is compactly supported on Ω to ensure that $T \circ \varphi$ is always defined and we assume that T is Lipschitz continuous. It can thus be considered as an element of the Sobolev space $W^{1,\infty}(\mathbb{R}^2)$. Let $\varphi : \bar{\Omega} \to \mathbb{R}^2$ be the sought deformation. A deformation is a smooth mapping that is orientation-preserving and injective, except possibly on $\partial\Omega$. The deformation gradient is $\nabla\varphi : \bar{\Omega} \to M_2(\mathbb{R})$, the set $M_2(\mathbb{R})$ being the set of real square matrices of order 2. The deformation φ is seen as the optimal solution of a specifically designed cost function comprising a regularization on φ prescribing the nature of the deformation, and a term measuring alignment or how the available data are exploited to drive the registration process. To allow large deformations, the shapes to be warped are viewed as isotropic, homogeneous, hyperelastic materials, and more precisely as Saint Venant-Kirchhoff ones [10]. This outlook dictates the design of the regularization on φ which is thus based on the stored energy function of a Saint Venant-Kirchhoff material.

We recall that the right Cauchy-Green strain tensor (interpreted as a quantifier of the square of local change in distances due to deformation) is defined by $C = \nabla\varphi^T\nabla\varphi = F^T F$. The Green-Saint Venant strain tensor is defined by $E = \dfrac{1}{2}(C - I)$. Associated with a given deformation φ, it is a measure of the deviation between φ and a rigid deformation. We also need the following notations: $A : B = \operatorname{tr} A^T B$, the matrix inner product and $||A|| = \sqrt{A : A}$, the related matrix norm (Frobenius norm). The stored energy function of a Saint Venant-Kirchhoff material is defined by $W_{SVK}(F) = \widehat{W}(E) = \dfrac{\lambda}{2}(\operatorname{tr} E)^2 + \mu \operatorname{tr} E^2$, λ and μ being the Lamé coefficients. To ensure that the distribution of the deformation Jacobian determinants does not exhibit too large contractions or too large expansions, we complement the stored energy function W_{SVK} by the term $(\det F - 1)^2$ controlling that the Jacobian determinant remains close to 1. (Note that the stored energy function W_{SVK} alone lacks a term penalizing the determinant: it does not preclude deformations with negative Jacobian. The expression of its quasiconvex envelope is more complex since involving explicitly the singular values of F. Also, when they are all lower than 1, the quasiconvex envelope equals 0, which shows bad behavior under compression). Therefore, the regularization can be written, after intermediate computations, as $W(F) = \beta(||F||^2 - \alpha)^2 - \frac{\mu}{2}(\det F)^2 + \mu(\det F - 1)^2 + \frac{\mu(\lambda+\mu)}{2(\lambda+2\mu)}$, where α and β depend on λ and μ. Although meaningful, function W takes on a drawback since it is not quasiconvex (see [11, Chap. 9] for a complete review of this notion), which raises an issue of a theoretical nature since we cannot obtain the weak lower semi-continuity property. The idea is thus to replace W by its quasicon-

vex envelope defined by $QW(\xi) = \begin{cases} W(\xi) & \text{if } ||\xi||^2 \geq 2\dfrac{\lambda + \mu}{\lambda + 2\mu}, \\ \Psi(\det \xi) & \text{if } ||\xi||^2 < 2\dfrac{\lambda + \mu}{\lambda + 2\mu}, \end{cases}$ and Ψ, the

convex mapping such that $\Psi : t \mapsto -\dfrac{\mu}{2}t^2 + \mu\,(t-1)^2 + \dfrac{\mu(\lambda + \mu)}{2(\lambda + 2\mu)}$ (see [21] for the derivation).

The regularizer is now complemented by a dissimilarity measure inspired by the unification model of image segmentation (geodesic active contours [8] and piecewise-constant Mumford-Shah model [19]) and image denoising (Rudin-Osher-Fatemi model [24]) into a global minimization framework introduced by Bresson et al. [7]. In that purpose, let $g : \mathbb{R}^+ \to \mathbb{R}^+$ be an edge detector function satisfying $g(0) = 1$, g strictly decreasing and $\lim\limits_{r \to +\infty} g(r) = 0$. From now on, we set $g := g(|\nabla R|)$ and for theoretical purposes, we assume that $\exists c > 0$ such that $0 < c \leq g \leq 1$ and that g is Lipschitz continuous (in fact, we need g to belong to the global Muckenhoupt class of weight functions for technical purposes, which is ensured here. See [4, p. 1] for the theoretical definition). Following Baldi [4], we denote by $BV(\Omega, g)$ the set of functions $u \in L^1(\Omega, g)$ (set of all functions u that are integrable with respect to the measure $g\,dx$) such that

$$\sup \left\{ \int_\Omega u \operatorname{div} \Psi \, dx \, , |\Psi| \leq g \text{ e., } \Psi \in \operatorname{Lip}_0(\Omega, \mathbb{R}^2) \right\} \tag{1}$$

is finite, with $\operatorname{Lip}_0(\Omega, \mathbb{R}^2)$ the space of Lipschitz functions with compact support. We denote by $\operatorname{var}_g u$ the quantity (1).

Remark 1. In [4], Baldi defines the BV-space taking as test functions elements of $\operatorname{Lip}_0(\Omega, \mathbb{R}^2)$. Classically in the literature, the test functions are chosen in $\mathcal{C}_c^1(\Omega, \mathbb{R}^2)$. It can be proved that these two definitions coincide thanks to density results and mollification.

To get a clearer picture of the meaning of (1), we give the following result:

Remark 2. Taken from [4, Remark 10]
Given a weight w sufficiently smooth, if E is a regular bounded open set in $\mathbb{R}^2$, with boundary of class $\mathcal{C}^2$, then $|\partial E|(\Omega, w) = \operatorname{var}_w \chi_E = \int_{\Omega \cap \partial E} w \, dH^1$, which can be interpreted in the case where $w = g$ as a new definition of the curve length with a metric that depends on the Reference image content.

Equipped with this material, we propose introducing as dissimilarity measure the following functional:

$$W_{fid}(\varphi) = \operatorname{var}_g T \circ \varphi + \frac{\nu}{2} \int_\Omega (T \circ \varphi(x) - R(x))^2 \, dx$$

$$+ a \int_\Omega \left[(c_1 - R(x))^2 - (c_2 - R(x))^2 \right] T \circ \varphi(x) \, dx, \tag{2}$$

with $c_1 = \frac{\int_\Omega R(x) H_\varepsilon (T \circ \varphi(x) - \rho) \, dx}{\int_\Omega H_\varepsilon (T \circ \varphi(x) - \rho) \, dx}$ and $c_2 = \frac{\int_\Omega R(x) (1 - H_\varepsilon (T \circ \varphi(x) - \rho)) \, dx}{\int_\Omega (1 - H_\varepsilon (T \circ \varphi(x) - \rho)) \, dx}$ — we dropped the dependency on φ to lighten the expressions —, H_ε denoting a regularization of the Heaviside function and $\rho \in [0, 1]$ being a fixed parameter allowing to partition $T \circ \varphi$ in two phases and yielding a binary version of the Reference. ρ can be estimated by analyzing the Reference histogram to discriminate two relevant regions or phases. This proposed functional emphasizes the link between the geodesic active contour model [8] and the ACWE model: if $\tilde{T}$ is the characteristic function of the set Ω_C, bounded subset of Ω with regular boundary, $\text{var}_g \tilde{T}$ is a new definition of the length of $\mathcal{C}$ with a metric depending on the Reference content (so minimizing this quantity is equivalent to locating the curve on the boundary of the shape contained in the Reference), while $\int_\Omega \left[(c_1 - R(x))^2 - (c_2 - R(x))^2 \right] \tilde{T}(x) \, dx$ approximates R in the L^2 sense by two regions Ω_C and $\Omega \backslash \Omega_C$ with two values c_1 and c_2.

In the end, the global minimization problem (QP) is stated by:

$$\inf_{\varphi \in \mathcal{W} = \text{Id} + W_0^{1,4}(\Omega, \mathbb{R}^2)} \bar{I}(\varphi) = W_{fid}(\varphi) + \int_\Omega QW(\nabla \varphi) \, dx.$$

Also, we denote by (P) the minimization problem phrased in terms of W, and by I the related functional.

2.2   Theoretical Results

We prove that the infimum of (QP) is attained and relate the minimum of (QP) to the infimum of (P). Note that one always has $\inf(QP) \leq \inf(P)$.

Theorem 1. *Existence of minimizers. The infimum of (QP) is attained. Let us assume that $T \in W^{2,\infty}(\mathbb{R}^2)$. Let $\bar{\varphi}$ be a minimizer of (QP). Then there exists a sequence $\{\varphi_n\}_{n=1}^\infty \subset \text{Id} + W_0^{1,4}(\Omega, \mathbb{R}^2)$ such that $\varphi_n \rightharpoonup \bar{\varphi}$ in $W^{1,4}(\Omega, \mathbb{R}^2)$ as $n \to +\infty$ and $\int_\Omega \frac{\nu}{2}(T \circ \varphi_n - R)^2 + a \left[(c_1^n - R)^2 - (c_2^n - R)^2 \right] T \circ \varphi_n + W(\nabla \varphi_n) \, dx \to \int_\Omega \frac{\nu}{2}(T \circ \bar{\varphi} - R)^2 + a \left[(\bar{c}_1 - R)^2 - (\bar{c}_2 - R)^2 \right] T \circ \bar{\varphi} + QW(\nabla \bar{\varphi}) \, dx$. If moreover $\nabla \varphi_n$ strongly converges to $\nabla \bar{\varphi}$ in $L^1(\Omega, M_2(\mathbb{R}))$, then one has $I(\varphi_n) \to \bar{I}(\bar{\varphi})$, yielding $\min(QP) = \inf(QP) = \inf(P)$.*

Proof. We refer the reader to [13].

We now investigate two numerical methods for the resolution of (QP).

3   Numerical Methods of Resolution

3.1   Auxiliary Variables and Quadratic Penalization

Motivated by a prior related work by Negrón Marrero [20] dedicated to the analysis of a numerical method for problems in nonlinear elasticity, we propose introducing a related decoupled problem involving two auxiliary variables - $\tilde{T}$ simulating $T \circ \varphi$ and V simulating $\nabla \varphi$ (the underlying idea being to remove the nonlinearity in the derivatives of φ) - and L^2/L^1 penalizations. This decoupled problem is defined by:

$$\inf_{\bar{W} \times \chi} \bar{I}_\gamma(\varphi, V, \tilde{T}) = \mathrm{var}_g \tilde{T} + \frac{\nu}{2} \int_\Omega (T \circ \varphi - R)^2 \, dx$$

$$+ a \int_\Omega \left[(c_1 - R)^2 - (c_2 - R)^2 \right] \tilde{T} \, dx + \int_\Omega QW(V) \, dx$$

$$+ \gamma \| T \circ \varphi - \tilde{T} \|_{L^1(\Omega)} + \frac{\gamma}{2} \| V - \nabla\varphi \|^2_{L^2(\Omega, M_2(\mathbb{R}))}, \qquad (3)$$

with $\bar{W} = \left\{ \varphi \in \mathrm{Id} + W_0^{1,2}(\Omega, \mathbb{R}^2) \right\}$ and $\chi = \left\{ V \in L^4(\Omega, M_2(\mathbb{R})), \tilde{T} \in BV (\Omega, g) \right\}$. This problem corresponds in fact to the conversion of the original problem phrased in terms of φ, V and $\tilde{T}$ under equality constraints $V = \nabla\varphi$ a.e. and $T \circ \varphi = \tilde{T}$ a.e., into an unconstrained minimization problem via quadratic and L^1 penalizations. The following asymptotic result holds:

Theorem 2. *Asymptotic result.*
Let (γ_j) be an increasing sequence diverging to $+\infty$. Let also $\left(\varphi_k^{\gamma_j}, V_k^{\gamma_j}, \tilde{T}_k^{\gamma_j} \right)$ be a minimizing sequence of (3) associated with γ_j. Then there exists a subsequence of it denoted by $\left(\varphi_{N(\gamma_{\varsigma(j)})}^{\gamma_{\varsigma(j)}}, V_{N(\gamma_{\varsigma(j)})}^{\gamma_{\varsigma(j)}}, \tilde{T}_{N(\gamma_{\varsigma(j)})}^{\gamma_{\varsigma(j)}} \right)$ and a minimizer $\bar{\varphi}$ of $\bar{I}$ such that
$$\lim_{j \to +\infty} \bar{I}_{\gamma_{\varsigma(j)}} \left(\varphi_{N(\gamma_{\varsigma(j)})}^{\gamma_{\varsigma(j)}}, V_{N(\gamma_{\varsigma(j)})}^{\gamma_{\varsigma(j)}}, \tilde{T}_{N(\gamma_{\varsigma(j)})}^{\gamma_{\varsigma(j)}} \right) = \bar{I}(\bar{\varphi}).$$

Proof. We refer the reader to [13].

Remark 3. When applying the direct method of the calculus of variations to problem (3) for fixed $\gamma = \gamma_j$, we obtain the boundedness of the minimizing component $V_k^{\gamma_j}$ in $L^4(\Omega, M_2(\mathbb{R}))$, which allows to extract a weakly converging subsequence still denoted by $V_k^{\gamma_j}$. Unfortunately, we cannot say anything about the behaviour of $\det V_k^{\gamma_j}$, preventing us from obtaining any minimizer existence result. That is the reason why the previous asymptotic result involves for each γ_j a minimizing sequence associated with the decoupled problem.

We introduce an algorithm based on the following alternative framework. We first solve $\inf_{\tilde{T}} E(\tilde{T}) = \mathrm{var}_g \tilde{T} + a \int_\Omega \left[(c_1 - R)^2 - (c_2 - R)^2 \right] \tilde{T} \, dx + \gamma \| T \circ \varphi - \tilde{T} \|_{L^1(\Omega)}$ for large enough γ and fixed φ, using the dual formulation of the weighted total variation. Then we solve for fixed $\tilde{T}$ the problem in (φ, V) using implicit and semi-implicit finite difference schemes. We refer the reader to [21] for numerical details of the implementation : although the work proposed in [21] differs in some parts from the proposed model, the derivation of the equations as well as their discretization can be adapted from [21]. A remarkable result relating again registration and segmentation is stated next.

Theorem 3. *Suppose that $g \in [0,1]$, $R \in [0,1]$ and that $T \circ \varphi$ is a characteristic function of a bounded open subset $\widehat{\Omega} \subset \Omega$ with boundary of class C^2 — with the assumptions on T, it is not theoretically the case—. Then for any c_1, c_2, a, γ, if $0 \le u \le 1$ is a minimizer of E, for almost every $\kappa \in [0,1]$, the characteristic function $\chi_{\widehat{\Omega}(\kappa)=\{x \,|\, u(x) > \kappa\}}$ is a global minimizer of E.*

Proof. We refer the reader to [13].

In practice, it means that once $\tilde{T}$ is computed, for almost every $\kappa \in [0,1]$, the characteristic function $\chi_{\{x \,|\, \tilde{T}(x) > \kappa\}}$ provides a segmentation of the Reference image.

3.2   Nonlocal Operator

Inspired by prior related works by Aubert and Kornprobst [3], Boulanger and co-authors [5] (in which the authors address the question of the calculus of variations for nonlocal functionals), Dávila [12] and Ponce [23] dedicated to expressing the semi-norms of the Sobolev spaces and the BV space thanks to a nonlocal operator, we introduce the sequence $\{\rho_n\}_{n \in \mathbb{N}}$ of radial mollifiers satisfying: $\forall n \in \mathbb{N}$, $\forall x \in \mathbb{R}^2$, $\rho_n(x) = \rho_n(|x|)$; $\forall n \in \mathbb{N}$, $\rho_n \ge 0$; $\forall n \in \mathbb{N}$, $\int_{\mathbb{R}^2} \rho_n(x)\,dx = 1$; $\forall \delta > 0$, $\lim\limits_{n \to +\infty} \int_\delta^{+\infty} \rho_n(r) r\,dr = 0$. Then the following approximation result holds:

Theorem 4. *Let $\Omega \subset \mathbb{R}^2$ be an open bounded set with Lipschitz boundary and let $f \in BV(\Omega, g) \subset BV(\Omega)$ (as $0 < c \le g \le 1$ everywhere). Consider $\{\rho_n\}$ defined previously. Then*

$$\lim_{n \to +\infty} \int_\Omega g(x) \left[\int_\Omega \frac{|f(x) - f(y)|}{|x - y|} \rho_n(x - y)\,dy \right] dx$$

$$= \left[\frac{1}{|S^1|} \int_0^{2\pi} \left| e. \binom{\cos(\theta)}{\sin(\theta)} \right| d\theta \right] var_g\, f = K_{1,2}\, var_g\, f,$$

with e being any unit vector of $\mathbb{R}^2$ and S^1 being the unit sphere in $\mathbb{R}^2$.

Proof. The proof is based on the adaptations of Lemmas [12, 2–3] considering the measures $\mu_i = g(x) \left(\int_\Omega \frac{|f(x) - f(y)|}{|x - y|} \rho_i(x - y)\,dy \right) dx$.

In our work, we use this characterization to approximate the weighted total variation. We propose minimizing the following functional:

$$\inf_{\varphi \in \mathrm{Id} + W_0^{1,4}(\Omega, \mathbb{R}^2)} \left\{ E_n(\varphi) = a \int_\Omega \left[(c_1 - R)^2 - (c_2 - R)^2 \right] T \circ \varphi\,dx \right.$$

$$+ \frac{1}{K_{1,2}} \int_\Omega g(x) \left[\int_\Omega \frac{|T \circ \varphi(y) - T \circ \varphi(x)|}{|x - y|} \rho_n(x - y)\,dy \right] dx$$

$$\left. + \frac{\nu}{2} \|T \circ \varphi - R\|_{L^2(\Omega)}^2 + \int_\Omega QW(\nabla\varphi)\,dx \right\}. \qquad \text{(NLP)}$$

We first state the existence of minimizers for this functional E_n for every $n \in \mathbb{N}^*$.

Theorem 5. *Existence of minimizers for E_n.*
Problem (NLP) admits at least one solution.

Proof. The proof is rather classical. The proper feature is obtained thanks to the following result by Bourgain, Brezis and Mironescu [6].

Proposition 1. *Taken from [6]*
Assume $1 \leq p < \infty$ and $u \in W^{1,p}(\Omega)$, and let $\rho \in L^1(\mathbb{R}^N)$, $\rho \geq 0$. Then

$$\int_\Omega \int_\Omega \frac{|u(x) - u(y)|^p}{|x - y|^p} \rho(x - y) \, dx \, dy \leq C \, \|u\|^p_{W^{1,p}(\Omega)} \, \|\rho\|_{L^1(\mathbb{R}^N)},$$

where $\|u\|_{W^{1,p}(\Omega)}$ denotes the classical semi-norm and C depends only on p and Ω.

An important Γ-convergence result highlighting the interest of this numerical method is given next.

Theorem 6. *Γ-convergence.*
Let $\{\bar{\varphi}_n\}_n \in Id + W_0^{1,4}(\Omega, \mathbb{R}^2)$ be a sequence of minimizers of E_n. Then there exist a subsequence still denoted by $\{\bar{\varphi}_n\}_n$ and $\bar{\varphi} \in Id + W_0^{1,4}(\Omega, \mathbb{R}^2)$ a minimizer of $\bar{I}$ such that $\bar{\varphi}_n \underset{n \to +\infty}{\rightharpoonup} \bar{\varphi}$ in $W^{1,4}(\Omega, \mathbb{R}^2)$. If we assume that $g \in \mathcal{C}^1(\bar{\Omega})$ with $\|\nabla g\|_{\mathcal{C}^0(\bar{\Omega})} = k < +\infty$, then one has $\lim_{n \to +\infty} E_n(\bar{\varphi}_n) = \bar{I}(\bar{\varphi})$.

Proof. The loss of symmetry in the expression of the nonlocal component (due to the g component) raises a technical difficulty. To overcome this issue, an additional assumption is set on g in order to use Taylor's expansion and to recover then some symmetry.
We first extract a subsequence weakly converging to $\bar{\varphi}$ in $W^{1,4}(\Omega, \mathbb{R}^2)$. We then easily show that $\limsup_{n \to +\infty} E_n(\bar{\varphi}_n) \leq \bar{I}(\bar{\varphi})$. It remains to be proved that $\bar{I}(\bar{\varphi}) \leq \liminf_{n \to +\infty} E_n(\bar{\varphi}_n)$. Due to compactness properties and the analysis done in the proof of the existence of minimizers for E_n, it suffices to prove that $var_g \, T \circ \bar{\varphi} \leq \liminf_{n \to +\infty} \frac{1}{K_{1,2}} \int_\Omega g(x) \left[\int_\Omega \frac{|T \circ \bar{\varphi}_n(y) - T \circ \bar{\varphi}_n(x)|}{|x-y|} \rho_n(|x - y|) \, dy \right] dx.$
We refer the reader to [13] for additional details.

The numerical treatment of the non local operator is dictated by the following theoretical result, based again on a splitting method.

Theorem 7. *Let $\tilde{T}$ and V be two auxiliary variables simulating respectively $T \circ \varphi$ and $\nabla \varphi$. Let us introduce the new decoupled problem (NLDP) defined by*

$$\inf_{\substack{\varphi \in Id + W_0^{1,2}(\Omega, \mathbb{R}^2) \\ (V, \tilde{T}) \in L^4(\Omega, M_2(\mathbb{R})) \times BV(\Omega, g)}} \left\{ E_{n,\gamma}(\varphi, V, \tilde{T}) = \frac{\nu}{2} \|T \circ \varphi - R\|^2_{L^2(\Omega)} + \int_\Omega QW(V) \, dx \right.$$

$$+ \frac{1}{K_{1,2}} \int_\Omega g(x) \left[\int_\Omega \frac{|\tilde{T}(y) - \tilde{T}(x)|}{|x - y|} \rho_n(x - y) \, dy \right] dx + \gamma \|\tilde{T} - T \circ \varphi\|_{L^1(\Omega)}$$

$$\left. + a \int_\Omega [(c_1 - R)^2 - (c_2 - R)^2] \, T \circ \varphi \, dx + \frac{\gamma}{2} \|V - \nabla \varphi\|^2_{L^2(\Omega, M_2(\mathbb{R}))} \right\}. \quad \text{(NLDP)}$$

Assume that $g \in C^1(\bar{\Omega})$ with $\|\nabla g\|_{C^0(\bar{\Omega})} = k < +\infty$. Let (γ_j) be an increasing sequence of positive real numbers such that $\lim\limits_{j \to +\infty} \gamma_j = +\infty$ with $\gamma_0 > 4a\|R$ $\|^2_{L^\infty(\Omega)}$. Let (n_l) be a sequence of natural integers such that $\lim\limits_{l \to +\infty} n_l = +\infty$ and for all $l \in \mathbb{N}^*$, there exists $\varphi_l \in Id + W_0^{1,4}(\Omega, \mathbb{R}^2)$ s. t. $\bar{I}(\varphi_l) \leq \inf\limits_{\varphi \in Id + W_0^{1,4}(\Omega, \mathbb{R}^2)}$

$\bar{I}(\varphi) + \frac{1}{l}$ and $\forall n \in \mathbb{N}, n \geq n_l \Rightarrow \left| \frac{1}{K_{1,2}} \int_\Omega g(x) \left[\int_\Omega \frac{|T \circ \varphi_l(y) - T \circ \varphi_l(x)|}{|y - x|} \rho_n(x - y) \right. \right.$

$\left. \left. dy \right] dx - var_g(T \circ \varphi_l) \right| \leq \frac{1}{l}$ since $T \circ \varphi_l \in BV(\Omega, g)$. Let also $(\varphi_k(n_l, \gamma_j),$

$V_k(n_l, \gamma_j), \tilde{T}_k(n_l, \gamma_j))$ be a minimizing sequence of (NLDP) with $\gamma = \gamma_j$ and $n = n_l$. Then there exists a subsequence denoted by $\left(\varphi_{N(n_{\psi(l)}, \gamma_{\zeta(j)})}(n_{\psi(l)}, \gamma_{\zeta(j)}), \right.$ $V_{N(n_{\psi(l)}, \gamma_{\zeta(j)})} n_{\psi(l)}, \gamma_{\zeta(j)}), \ \tilde{T}_{N(n_{\psi(l)}, \gamma_{\zeta(j)})}(n_{\psi(l)}, \gamma_{\zeta(j)}) \right)$ of $(\varphi_k(n_l, \gamma_j), V_k(n_l, \gamma_j),$ $\tilde{T}_k(n_l, \gamma_j))$ and a minimizer $\bar{\varphi}$ of $\bar{I}$ such that

$$\lim_{l \to +\infty} \lim_{j \to +\infty} E_{n_{\psi(l)}, \gamma_{\zeta(j)}} \left(\varphi_{N(n_{\psi(l)}, \gamma_{\zeta(j)})}(n_{\psi(l)}, \gamma_{\zeta(j)}), V_{N(n_{\psi(l)}, \gamma_{\zeta(j)})}(n_{\psi(l)}, \gamma_{\zeta(j)}), \right.$$

$$\left. \tilde{T}_{N(n_{\psi(l)}, \gamma_{\zeta(j)})}(n_{\psi(l)}, \gamma_{\zeta(j)}) \right) = \bar{I}(\bar{\varphi}).$$

Proof. We refer the reader to [13].

A numerical implementation of this nonlocal model is analyzed in [13]. In the next section, we focus on the results obtained with the method depicted in Subsect. 3.1.

4   Numerical Experiments on Real Data

Medical illustrations are now presented: for the mapping of a tore to an MRI scan of human brain (128×192) involving large deformations, and on MRI images of a cardiac cycle (150×150), the Reference corresponding to end diastole and the Template, to end systole. In both cases, the deformation remains mechanically meaningful (positivity of the Jacobian). The obtained results outperform those in [21] both in terms of segmentation and registration accuracy with in particular, the capture of small details, and in the restitution of a more faithful simplified version of the Reference image. These elements are corroborated visually first, and by the computation of the Dice coefficient and the mutual information, demonstrating that the inclusion of nonlocal information provides better results. An exhaustive analysis and a systematic comparison with prior related works can be found in [13]. For both applications, the ranges of the parameters are the same. Parameter ν balancing the fidelity term is between 2 and 10, while parameter a is between 40 and 100. The Lamé coefficient λ is set to 10 (it has no physical meaning but is related to Poisson's ratio, measure of Poisson's effect which can be regarded as the ability of a material compressed in one direction to expand in the other direction - this choice of λ is not physically inconsistent), while the coefficient μ (measuring rigidity) is between 1000 and 3500 and γ is close to 80000. At last, the introduced model is highly non convex (yielding potentially many local minima), but in practice nevertheless, the algorithm has the tendency to compute a global minimizer.

4.1   Slice of a Human Brain

We first applied the algorithm to a slice of a human brain data with complex topologies *(courtesy of Laboratory Of Neuro-Imaging, UCLA)*. The results are satisfactory since the deformed Template matches very well the convolutions of the brain and the segmentation of the Reference goes well inside the concavities (Fig. 1).

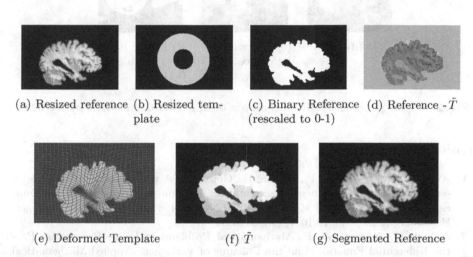

(a) Resized reference (b) Resized tem- (c) Binary Reference (d) Reference -$\tilde{T}$
                    plate   (rescaled to 0-1)

   (e) Deformed Template   (f) $\tilde{T}$ (g) Segmented Reference

Fig. 1. Mapping of a tore to a slice of a human brain, $\rho = 0.5$, $\mu = 1000$, $\min\{\det \nabla \varphi\} = 0.0445$.

4.2   Cardiac MRI Images

To assess the accuracy of the algorithm in handling large deformations, we present an experiment on cardiac MRI images (Fig. 2).

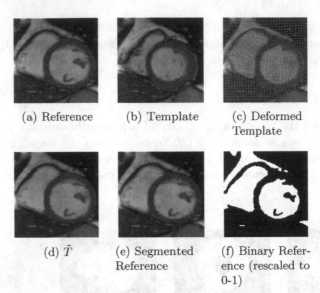

(a) Reference   (b) Template   (c) Deformed Template

(d) $\tilde{T}$ (e) Segmented Reference   (f) Binary Reference (rescaled to 0-1)

Fig. 2. Mapping of cardiac MRI images, $\rho = 0.05$, $\mu = 3500$, $\min\{\det \nabla\varphi\} = 0.0245$.

References

1. An, J., Chen, Y., Huang, F., Wilson, D., Geiser, E.: A variational PDE based level set method for a simultaneous segmentation and non-rigid registration. In: Duncan, J.S., Gerig, G. (eds.) MICCAI 2005. LNCS, vol. 3749, pp. 286–293. Springer, Heidelberg (2005). doi:10.1007/11566465_36
2. Aubert, G., Kornprobst, P.: Mathematical Problems in Image Processing: Partial Differential Equations and the Calculus of Variations. Applied Mathematical Sciences. Springer, Heidelberg (2001)
3. Aubert, G., Kornprobst, P.: Can the nonlocal characterization of Sobolev spaces by Bourgain et al. be useful for solving variational problems? SIAM J. Numer. Anal. **47**(2), 844–860 (2009)
4. Baldi, A.: Weighted BV functions. Houst. J. Math. **27**(3), 683–705 (2001)
5. Boulanger, J., Elbau, P., Pontow, C., Scherzer, O.: Non-local functionals for imaging. In: Bauschke, H.H., Burachik, R.S., Combettes, P.L., Elser, V., Russell Luke, D., Wolkowicz, H. (eds.) Fixed-Point Algorithms for Inverse Problems in Science and Engineering, pp. 131–154. Springer, New York (2011)
6. Bourgain, J., Brezis, H., Mironescu, P.: Another look at Sobolev spaces. In: Menaldi, J.L., Rofman, Sulem, A. (eds.) Optimal Control and Partial Differential Equations, in honour of Professor Alain Bensoussan's 60th Birthday, pp. 439–455 (2001)
7. Bresson, X., Esedoḡlu, S., Vandergheynst, P., Thiran, J.P., Osher, S.: Fast global minimization of the active contour/snake model. J. Math. Imaging Vis. **68**, 151–167 (2007)
8. Caselles, V., Kimmel, R., Sapiro, G.: Geodesic active contours. Int. J. Comput. Vis. **22**(1), 61–87 (1993)
9. Chan, T., Vese, L.: Active contours without edges. IEEE Trans. Image Process. **10**(2), 266–277 (2001)

10. Ciarlet, P.: Elasticité Tridimensionnelle. Masson, Paris (1985)
11. Dacorogna, B.: Direct Methods in the Calculus of Variations, 2nd edn. Springer, Heidelberg (2008)
12. Dávila, J.: On an open question about functions of bounded variation. Calc. Var. Partial Differ. Equ. **15**(4), 519–527 (2002)
13. Debroux, N., Le Guyader, C.: A joint segmentation/registration model based on a nonlocal characterization of weighted total variation and nonlocal shape descriptors, in preparation
14. Droske, M., Rumpf, M.: Multiscale joint segmentation and registration of image morphology. IEEE Trans. Pattern Anal. Mach. Intell. **29**(12), 2181–2194 (2007)
15. Gorthi, S., Duay, V., Bresson, X., Cuadra, M.B., Castro, F.J.S., Pollo, C., Allal, A.S., Thiran, J.P.: Active deformation fields: dense deformation field estimation for atlas-based segmentation using the active contour framework. Med. Image Anal. **15**(6), 787–800 (2011)
16. Han, J., Berkels, B., Droske, M., Hornegger, J., Rumpf, M., Schaller, C., Scorzin, J., Urbach, H.: Mumford-Shah model for one-to-one edge matching. IEEE Trans. Image Process. **16**(11), 2720–2732 (2007)
17. Le Guyader, C., Vese, L.: A combined segmentation and registration framework with a nonlinear elasticity smoother. Comput. Vis. Image Underst. **115**(12), 1689–1709 (2011)
18. Lord, N., Ho, J., Vemuri, B., Eisenschenk, S.: Simultaneous registration and parcellation of bilateral hippocampal surface pairs for local asymmetry quantification. IEEE Trans. Med. Imaging **26**(4), 471–478 (2007)
19. Mumford, D., Shah, J.: Optimal approximations by piecewise smooth functions and associated variational problems. Commun. Pure Appl. Anal. **42**, 577–685 (1989)
20. Negrón Marrero, P.: A numerical method for detecting singular minimizers of multidimensional problems in nonlinear elasticity. Numer. Math. **58**, 135–144 (1990)
21. Ozeré, S., Gout, C., Le Guyader, C.: Joint segmentation/registration model by shape alignment via weighted total variation minimization and nonlinear elasticity. SIAM J. Imaging Sci. **8**(3), 1981–2020 (2015)
22. Ozeré, S., Le Guyader, C.: A joint segmentation-registration framework based on weighted total variation and nonlinear elasticity principles. In: 2014 IEEE International Conference on Image Processing (ICIP), pp. 3552–3556 (2014)
23. Ponce, A.C.: A new approach to Sobolev spaces and connections to Γ-convergence. Calc. Var. Partial Differ. Equ. **19**(3), 229–255 (2004)
24. Rudin, L., Osher, S., Fatemi, E.: Nonlinear total variation based noise removal algorithms. Phys. D **60**(1–4), 259–268 (1992)
25. Rumpf, M., Wirth, B.: A nonlinear elastic shape averaging approach. SIAM J. Imaging Sci. **2**(3), 800–833 (2009)
26. Sotiras, A., Davatzikos, C., Paragios, N.: Deformable medical image registration: a survey. IEEE Trans. Med. Imaging **32**(7), 1153–1190 (2013)
27. Vemuri, B., Ye, J., Chen, Y., Leonard, C.: Image registration via level-set motion: applications to atlas-based segmentation. Med. Image Anal. **7**(1), 1–20 (2003)
28. Vese, L., Le Guyader, C.: Variational Methods in Image Processing. Chapman & Hall/CRC Mathematical and Computational Imaging Sciences Series. Taylor & Francis, Abingdon (2015)
29. Yezzi, A., Zollei, L., Kapur, T.: A variational framework for joint segmentation and registration. In: Math Methods Biomed Image Analysis, IEEE-MMBIA, pp. 44–51 (2001)

3D Vision

Adaptive Discretizations for Non-smooth Variational Vision

Virginia Estellers[✉] and Stefano Soatto

UCLA Vision Lab, Los Angeles, USA
virginia.estellers@gmail.com

Abstract. Variational problems in vision are solved numerically on the pixel lattice because it provides the simplest computational grid to discretize the input images, even though a uniform grid seldom matches the complexity of the solution. To adapt the complexity of the discretization to the solution, it is necessary to adopt finite-element techniques that match the resolution of piecewise polynomial bases to the resolving power of the variational model, but such techniques have been overlooked for nonsmooth variational models. To address this issue, we investigate the pros and cons of finite-element discretizations for nonsmooth variational problems in vision, their multiresolution properties, and the optimization algorithms to solve them. Our 2 and 3D experiments in image segmentation, optical flow, stereo, and depth fusion reveal the conditions where finite-element can outperform finite-difference discretizations by achieving significant computational savings with a minor loss of accuracy.

1 Discretizations for Non-smooth Models in Vision

Many inference tasks in vision are formulated as variational optimization problems that estimate a function over the image plane. This variational approach is more robust and accurate than sparse feature techniques because it exploits all the information in the input images to estimate a solution at pixel resolution. With standard discretizations this produces optimization problems with as many variables as image pixels, require regularization to resolve undeterminations, and limit the deployment of variational models in resource-constrained systems.

Variational techniques solve vision problems by (i) designing cost functionals that describe the properties of the solution, (ii) discretizing the continuous model into the digital domain, and (iii) developing numerical algorithms to minimize it. While research has recently focused on modeling and optimization with non-smooth regularizers like TV and robust ℓ_1-norm data penalties, the choice of discretization of non-smooth variational models has received less attention. Most algorithms are implemented on the pixel lattice with finite-difference (FD) approximations of spatial derivatives. This makes the implementation simple but inefficient in flat areas because the discretization is not adapted to the resolution power of the model or the complexity of the solution. To investigate the effects of the discretizations on variational vision, we introduce alternative finite-element (FE) discretizations that match the complexity of the unknown solution, instead

F. Lauze et al. (Eds.): SSVM 2017, LNCS 10302, pp. 629–642, 2017.
DOI: 10.1007/978-3-319-58771-4_50

of the input data, and reduce the computational cost of the optimization. The discretizations are adapted to the variational model and follow a multiscale construction that mimics multiresolution optimization of non-convex problems. Our goal is to investigate the integration of FE techniques with the optimization algorithms used in vision for non-differentiable functionals and raise awareness of their advantages and drawbacks with three contributions: (i) introduction of adaptive multi-resolution discretizations for a wide class of non-smooth vision problems, (ii) adaptation of the optimization algorithms developed for non-smooth variational models to FE discretizations, (iii) experimentally investigation of the pros and cons of FE discretizations in common 2 and 3D vision problems.

2   Related Methods

FE techniques [23] are common in graphics and computational sciences [1,2] because they parametrize surfaces of arbitrary topology and can model discontinuities. The inverse nature of vision poses a challenge to these techniques because the differentiability of the functions are unknown and must be inferred from data. As a result FE techniques in vision have largely focused on smooth vartiational [8] or PDE models for image diffusion [28,29], segmentation [26,27], or optical flow estimation [24,25]. Only [9,10] explicitly use FE techniques for nonsmooth variational problems in vision, but resort to complex polynomial bases that are expensive to evaluate and refine. We investigate simpler FE discretizations with lower computational cost.

In 3D vision, the surface reconstruction techniques [3–5] resort to similar principles to handle large volumes by constructing basis functions over octrees at multiple resolutions but limit their optimization to least-squares problems and rely on octree grids adapted to the input pointcloud, not the reconstructed surface, that reproduce the noise and artifacts of the input data. Our FE discretization adapts to the complexity of the unknown solution, not the input data, and seamlessly merge with the optimization algorithms [6,7] used for variational 2 and 3D vision models.

Loosely related are kernel and parametric models designed for specific applications. Wavelets in image reconstruction lead to similar coefficient-based parametrizations but depend on uniform discretizations of the pixel grid. The flow and stereo methods [11–14] estimate multiple parametric models on the pixel grid or its super-pixelization [15] but are only adapted to the input image, not to the solution. In active contours segmentation, narrow-band implementations implicitly create a non-uniform discretization of the domain and implement PDE models limited by slow descent algorithms. Compared to these techniques, we handle a broader range of applications and optimizations.

3   A Wide Range of Target Problems

We target variational models of the form

$$\min_u \int_\Omega [\alpha f(u) + g(\nabla u)]dx, \tag{1}$$

where α is a scalar parameter, f is a data-dependent functional, and g is a regularization functional. The unknown function $u : \Omega \to \mathbb{R}$ is defined over the domain $\Omega \subset \mathbb{R}^d$ and resctricted to the space of bounded variation $BV(\Omega)$. To illustrate its applicability, we choose 4 sample problems with different model and optimization complexities: segmentation, optical flow, stereo, and depth fusion.

Image segmentation partitions the domain of an image I into homogeneous regions. A popular model [16,17] for binary segmentation finds the indicator function u that partitions I into two regions with mean intensities μ_1, μ_2 solving

$$\min_{0 \le u \le 1} \int_\Omega \alpha[(I - \mu_1)^2 - (I - \mu_2)^2]u + |\nabla u| \quad R_1 = \{x | u(x) > \frac{1}{2}\}, \ R_2 = \Omega \setminus R_1, \tag{2}$$

and thresholding u to binarize the solution of the convex optimization problem. The resolution necessary for the indicator function u is lower than the resolution of the image because we are only interested on its zero-level set and, where we need a fine spatial resolution with a coarse discretization for the rest of Ω.

In optical flow estimation, the unknown of the problem is a vector field $\boldsymbol{u} = (u, v)$ that describes the apparent motion of pixels between two consecutive image frames I_1, I_2. A common formulation [18,19] as an optimization problem

$$\min_u \int_\Omega \alpha |I_1(x) - I_2(x + \boldsymbol{u})|_\epsilon + |\nabla u| + |\nabla v| \quad |z|_\epsilon = \begin{cases} \frac{1}{2\epsilon}|z|^2 & \text{if } |z| \le \epsilon \\ |z| - \frac{\epsilon}{2} & \text{otherwise} \end{cases}, \tag{3}$$

contains a data term $|I_1(x) - I_2(x + \boldsymbol{u})|_\epsilon$ that measures pixel correspondences with the Huber-loss function $|\cdot|_\epsilon$ and a regularizer $|\nabla u| + |\nabla v|$ that penalizes large gradients of the flow. The data term is usually substituted by a convex approximation $f_l(\boldsymbol{u}) = |b + a \cdot \boldsymbol{u}|_\epsilon$ that linearizes the image around the current flow estimate $\boldsymbol{u}_l$. The optimization is then solved as a sequence of convex problems

$$\boldsymbol{u}_{l+1} \leftarrow \min_u \int \alpha f_l(\boldsymbol{u}) + |\nabla u| + |\nabla v| \quad f_l(\boldsymbol{u}) = |I_1(x) - I_2(x + \boldsymbol{u}_l) + \nabla I_2(x + \boldsymbol{u}_l)(\boldsymbol{u} - \boldsymbol{u}_l)|_\epsilon$$

The regularizer is a critical part of the model because it resolves the ambiguities of the data term in flat regions, where a flow estimate at pixel resolution relies on the regularizer to resolve the excessive degrees of freedom of pixel discretizations.

A similar model can be applied in stereo reconstruction to estimate the 3D geometry of a scene from a pair of images with different vantage points. A depth parametrization describes the scene geometry visible from the image pair and confines the optimization variable to the image domain Ω to formulates the problem as the estimation of the depth map u by solving the optimization

$$\min_u \int \alpha |I_2(\omega(u)) - I_1|_\epsilon + |\nabla u| \quad \omega = \pi \circ g_r \circ \pi^{-1}, \tag{4}$$

where the domain warping ω back-projects image pixels from I_1 onto the surface and then projects them onto I_2 with the relative camera pose change g_r. The dependency on u in the data term is again substituted by a convex approximation

$f_l(u) = |b+au|_\epsilon$ that linearizes the warping around the current u_l and the original problem is solved by the sequence

$$u_{l+1} \leftarrow \min_u \int \alpha f_l(\boldsymbol{u}) + |\nabla u| \quad f_l(u) = |I_2(\omega(u_l)) - I_1 + \frac{\partial I_2(\omega(u))}{\partial u}(u - u_l)|_\epsilon.$$

The TV regularizer penalizes large variations in depth and is again the key to the resolution of the undetermined data term in flat regions. The smoothness imposed by the regularizer can also be obtained with an adaptive discretization.

The optimization problem (1) has also been used to estimate a single surface from a collection of partial and noisy measuremets [20–22]. We adopt the model of [22] to make no assumptions on the topology of the scene and estimate a signed-distance representation u of the surface from a collection of depth maps described by truncated distance functions and combined into a histogram of distance functions $h: \Omega \to \mathbb{R}^L$ over the volume. The reconstruction solves

$$\min_u \int_\Omega \alpha \sum_{i=1}^{L} h_i |u - b_i| + |\nabla u|, \tag{5}$$

where $b_i, h_{,i}$ are the center and count of i-th histogram bin [22]. The regularizer $|\nabla u|$, is necessary to resolve indeterminations in the histograms caused by either overlapping noisy depth maps or undersampled depth areas or holes. Similar to segmentation, a fine discretization is only necessary close to the surface.

4   Adaptive Piecewise Polynomial Basis

FE methods approximate a PDE solution by a linear combination $u(x) = \sum_i^n c_i \phi_i(x)$ of basis functions, $\phi_i: \Omega \to \mathbb{R}$, and substitute the original PDE with a system of algebraic equations in the basis coefficients $\boldsymbol{c} = [c_1, \ldots, c_n]$. When we apply this paradigm to our problem, we approximate the minimization over the function space $BV(\Omega)$ by a minimization over the space of coefficients $\boldsymbol{c} \in \mathbb{R}^n$.

The resolution and smoothness of the discretization is determined by the shape of the basis functions, while its computational cost by their evaluation. This guides our choice of discretization: first, the basis functions must have non-uniform resolution to represent both sharp edges and smooth regions at a minimal cost; second, they must have non-trivial derivatives ∇u; and they must be compactly supported to evaluate u fast. We thus propose a piecewise polynomial basis over elements with minimal support and analytic derivatives.

We review the basic properties of FE discretizations [23] with triangular elements, and sketch their extension to quad- and octrees. Each tessellation offers different properties: Delaunay triangulations avoid the skinny triangles that make FE discretizations unstable and can match discontinuities in ∇u with the edges of the triangulation; while quad- and octree tesselations reduce the cost of evaluation but constrain the discontinuities of ∇u to be axis-aligned.

4.1   Triangular Linear Finite Elements

A linear function of two variables, $a_1x_1 + a_2x_2 + a_0$, is uniquely determined by its values on the 3 vertices of a non-degenerate triangle K. The set of these functions thus defines a functional space $\mathbb{P}^1(K)$ of dimension 3 over the triangle. Given two triangles K_1, K_2 with a common edge, a piecewise linear function $u \in \mathbb{P}^1(K_i)$ uniquely determined by its values at the 4 vertices of the triangles is continuous across them; these functions thus form a functional space of dimension 4. Repeating this procedure for a triangulation of Ω with n vertices $\mathcal{K}$, we obtain a function that is linear on each triangle, continuous in Ω, and uniquely determined by its values on the triangulation vertices $v_1, \ldots, v_n$. These functions define a vector space V_T of continuous piecewise linear functions known as triangular linear finite elements.

The space V_T has dimension n and a basis formed by the set of unique continuous piecewise linear function that verify $\phi_i(v_j) = \delta_{ij}$. These functions are compactly supported, have integrable derivatives discontinuous at edges, and can be constructed from a reference element $\hat{K}$ that decouples the analytic properties of the basis from the geometry of the triangulation. The reference element is the triangle with vertices $(0,0),(1,0),(0,1)$ and basis functions

$$\hat{\phi}_1(\xi,\eta) = 1 - \xi - \eta \qquad \hat{\phi}_2(\xi,\eta) = \xi \qquad \hat{\phi}_3(\xi,\eta) = \eta. \tag{6}$$

We can map any triangle $K \in \mathcal{K}$ with vertices $(x_1,y_1),(x_2,y_2),(x_3,y_3)$ bijectively into $\hat{K}$ with the affine transform

$$\begin{bmatrix} x \\ y \end{bmatrix} = F_K(\xi,\eta) = \begin{pmatrix} x_2 - x_1 & x_3 - x_1 \\ y_2 - y_1 & y_3 - y_1 \end{pmatrix} \begin{bmatrix} \xi \\ \eta \end{bmatrix} + \begin{bmatrix} x_1 \\ y_1 \end{bmatrix} = B_K \begin{bmatrix} \xi \\ \eta \end{bmatrix} + \begin{bmatrix} x_1 \\ y_1 \end{bmatrix}. \tag{7}$$

and evaluate the i-th basis function of triangle K, ϕ_i^K, and its derivatives by

$$\phi_i^K = \hat{\phi}_i \circ F_K^{-1} \qquad\qquad \nabla\phi_i^K = B_K^{-T}(\hat{\nabla}\hat{\phi}_i \circ F_K^{-1}), \tag{8}$$

where $\nabla\phi_i^K = B_K^{-T}\hat{\nabla}\hat{\phi}_i$ as $\hat{\nabla}\hat{\phi}_i = [\frac{\partial\hat{\phi}_i}{\partial\xi}, \frac{\partial\hat{\phi}_i}{\partial\eta}]$ is constant for linear elements.

4.2   Finite Elements Over Quad- and Octrees

When the elements of the tessellation are the rectangular cells of a quadtree, the same argument shows that $\mathbb{Q}^1 = \{a_0 + a_1\xi + a_2\eta + a_3\xi\eta | \ a_0, \ldots, a_3 \in \mathbb{R}\}$ defines a polynomial space of dimension 4 where each element is uniquely determined by its values on the vertices of the cell. In this case, the reference element $\hat{K}$ is the square with vertices $(\pm1, \pm1)$ and basis functions

$$\hat{\phi}_1 = \frac{1}{4}(1-\xi)(1-\eta) \quad \hat{\phi}_2 = \frac{1}{4}(1+\xi)(1-\eta) \quad \hat{\phi}_3 = \frac{1}{4}(1+\xi)(1+\eta) \quad \hat{\phi}_4 = \frac{1}{4}(1-\xi)(1+\eta).$$

The affine transform (9) maps the reference space $\mathbb{Q}^1$ into any quadtree cell K to define a polynomial space $\mathbb{Q}^1(K) = \{\hat{q} \circ F_K^{-1} | \hat{q} \in \mathbb{Q}^1\}$ of dimension 4 and basis $\phi_i^K = \hat{\phi}_i \circ F_K^{-1}$.

$$\begin{bmatrix} x \\ y \end{bmatrix} = F_K(\xi,\eta) = \frac{1}{2}\begin{pmatrix} \Delta_x & 0 \\ 0 & \Delta_y \end{pmatrix}\begin{bmatrix} \xi \\ \eta \end{bmatrix} + \begin{bmatrix} x_c \\ y_c \end{bmatrix} = B_K\begin{bmatrix} \xi \\ \eta \end{bmatrix} + \begin{bmatrix} x_c \\ y_c \end{bmatrix} \quad \begin{array}{l} (x_c, y_c) \text{ cell center} \\ \Delta_x \times \Delta_y \text{ cell size} \end{array} \tag{9}$$

Gluing together the spaces over each cell, we obtain the space of continuous piece-wise polynomial functions over a quadtree grid V_Q. This construction extends to 3D domains by defining a polynomial space with three reference variables $(\xi, \nu, \eta) \in [-1, 1]^3$ and mapping the resulting polynomial space to each cell in an octree tessellation.

4.3   Adaptive Multiresolution

Many variational models in vision, e.g., optical flow or stereo, are not convex problems guaranteed to convergence to a global minimum and require multires-olution strategies to guide the optimization algorithm to a local minimum rel-evant at multiple scales. In FD discretizations, this is achieved by solving the optimization problem over a pyramid of uniform grids of increasing resolutions, initializing the minimization at finer grids with the solution from coarser grids and exponentially increasing the memory and computational costs of the dis-cretization regardless of the complexity of the solution.

In FE discretizations, it is possible to only increase the cost of multiresolution representations when the solution requires it. To this purpose, we locally increase the spatial resolution of FE discretizations by subdividing only the elements that require higher spatial resolution and updating their basis functions. Following this principle, we initialize the discretization with a uniform FE tessellation $\mathcal{K}^0$, basis function $V^0 = \{\phi_1^0, \ldots, \phi_n^0\}$, $c^0 = 0$, and alternate between:

1. Solve $\min_{u \in \text{span } V^l} \int_\Omega \alpha f(u) + g(\nabla u)$ initializing $u = \sum_{i \in V^{l-1}} c_i^{l-1} \phi_i^{l-1}$.
2. Refine the elements in $\mathcal{K}^l$ where the objective function evaluated at u^l exceeds threshold δ to define a finer tessellation $\mathcal{K}^{l+1}$ and basis functions V^{l+1}.

The process stops when the resolution of the pixels is reached. At each level, the optimization converges with only a few iterations because the algorithm is initialized close to the optimum, as in multiresolution FD pyramids, but is more efficient because the number of minimization variables – basis functions– only increases if the representation of the solution at finner scales requires it: flat areas keep a coarse-element discretization while discontinuities are resolved at finer scales. See Fig. 1(m)–(n) in our Experiments.

The refinement criteria tries to minimize the objective function by increasing the resolution of the discretization in areas where the data term or the regular-izer are large, i.e., the estimated solution violates the model assumptions. We thus consider the variational model as ground-truth to compute the error of our discretization; this refinement criterion is similar to the one used in computa-tional science even though vision models are not as accurate and reliable. We choose this criterion to estimate the discretization because it is the only one consistent with the solution of the proposed model, choosing of a model is a dif-ferent question. In particular, we set threshold δ to fix the number of elements N in the final discretization when we refine the same percentage p at each level. In quadtrees, for instance, $N = 2^{D_0}(1 + 3p)^{D-D_0}$ is a function of the depths D_0, D of quadtrees matching the resolution of the initial tessellation and pixel grids, and δ is the $1 - p$ percentile of the objective over the elements.

5   Minimization

FE discretizations are designed to solve PDEs by approximating them with an algebraic system of equations in the basis coefficients. Applied to our variational problem (1), FE solvers must first derive the Euler-Lagrange PDE that characterizes the minimum and are limited to differentiable functionals incompatible with most vision models. For this reason, we resort to algorithms developed in vision for non-differentiable functionals.

To this purpose, we use quadrature to approximate the integral with the sum

$$\int_\Omega [\alpha f(u(x)) + g(\nabla u(x))]\, dx \approx \sum_{k=1}^m w_k\, [\alpha f(u(x_k)) + g(\nabla u(x_k))] \qquad (10)$$

where $x_k \in \mathbb{R}^d$ are quadrature points and $w_k > 0$ quadrature weights. As the objective functional only depends on the value of u at quadrature points, it is convenient to define the variable $\boldsymbol{u} = [u(x_1), \ldots, u(x_m)] = P\boldsymbol{c} \in \mathbb{R}^m$, where the k-th row of matrix P is $[\phi_1(x_k) \ldots \phi_n(x_k)] \in \mathbb{R}^{1 \times n}$. Similarly, the gradient of u at the quadrature points satisfies $[\nabla u(x_1), \ldots, \nabla u(x_m)] = N\boldsymbol{c} \in \mathbb{R}^m$, where the k-th row of matrix $N \in \mathbb{R}^{dm \times n}$ is $[\nabla \phi_1(x_k) \ldots \nabla \phi_n(x_k)]$, and the optimization problem

$$\min_u \underbrace{\sum_{k=1}^m \alpha w_k f(u(x_k))}_{F(P\boldsymbol{c})} + \underbrace{\sum_{k=1}^m w_k g(\nabla u(x_k))}_{G(N\boldsymbol{c})} = \min_c\ F(P\boldsymbol{c}) + G(N\boldsymbol{c}). \qquad (11)$$

has the standard form of many convex minimization problems solved with splitting techniques. Among them, we adopt a primal-dual formulation and rewrite (11) as the saddle-point problem with dual variables $\boldsymbol{\lambda} \in \mathbb{R}^m$, $\boldsymbol{\nu} \in \mathbb{R}^{dm}$

$$\max_{\boldsymbol{\lambda},\, \boldsymbol{\nu}} \min_c\ -F^*(\boldsymbol{\lambda}) - G^*(\boldsymbol{\nu}) + \langle \boldsymbol{\lambda}, P\boldsymbol{c} \rangle + \langle \boldsymbol{\nu}, N\boldsymbol{c} \rangle, \qquad (12)$$

where * denotes the convex conjugate and $\langle \cdot, \cdot \rangle$ the Euclidean scalar product. We then solve (12) with algorithm [7] as the sequence of proximal problems and updates

$$\boldsymbol{\lambda}^{n+1} \leftarrow \min_{\boldsymbol{\lambda}}\ \sigma F^*(\boldsymbol{\lambda}) + \frac{1}{2}\|\boldsymbol{\lambda} - (\boldsymbol{\lambda}^n + \sigma P\bar{\boldsymbol{c}}^n)\|^2 \qquad (13)$$

$$\boldsymbol{\nu}^{n+1} \leftarrow \min_{\boldsymbol{\nu}}\ \sigma G^*(\boldsymbol{\nu}) + \frac{1}{2}\|\boldsymbol{\nu} - (\boldsymbol{\nu}^{n+1} + \sigma N\bar{\boldsymbol{c}}^n)\|^2 \qquad (14)$$

$$\boldsymbol{c}^{n+1} = \boldsymbol{c}^n - \tau(N^*\boldsymbol{\nu}^{n+1} + P^*\boldsymbol{\lambda}^{n+1}), \quad \bar{\boldsymbol{c}}^n = 2\boldsymbol{c}^n - \boldsymbol{c}^{n-1}. \qquad (15)$$

The minimization is efficient because we find simple closed-form solutions for (13)–(14) similar to the ones in FD discretizations that now parallelize over quadrature points instead of pixels. Experiments show that 3-, 4, and 8-point quadrature over triangular, quad- and octree elements produce accurate approximations, see Fig. 2.

Minimization in λ. We solve the proximal problem that updates λ through Moreau's identity, solving the minimization problem

$$y^* = \arg\min_{y} F(y) + \frac{\sigma}{2}\|y - \frac{\hat{\lambda}}{\sigma}\|^2 = \min_{y} \sum_{k=1}^{m} \alpha w_k f(y_k) + 0.5\sigma(y_k - \frac{\hat{\lambda}_k}{\sigma})^2. \tag{16}$$

and updating the dual variable $\lambda = \hat{\lambda} - \sigma y^*$ accordingly. The objective function in the minimization in y is decoupled in of its components y_k with a different term and thus the solution minimizes independently each of these terms, that is,

$$\min_{y_k} \alpha w_k f(y_k) + 0.5\sigma(y_k - \frac{\hat{\lambda}_k}{\sigma})^2. \tag{17}$$

As the function f is convex, the minimizers are the zeros of the subgradient of the objective function with respect to each y_k. The resulting equations, after basic manipulations, directly provide the closed-form solutions and the following dual updates:

$$\text{segmentation } \lambda_k = \alpha w_k[\mu_1^2 + \mu_2^2 + (\mu_2 - \mu_1)I(x_k)] \tag{18}$$

$$\text{stereo } \lambda_k = \begin{cases} \alpha w_k a_k & \text{if } a_k\hat{\lambda}_k + \sigma b_k > \alpha a_k^2 + \sigma\epsilon \\ -\alpha w_k a_k & \text{if } a_k\hat{\lambda}_k + \sigma b_k < -(\alpha a_k^2 + \sigma\epsilon) \\ \frac{\alpha a_k}{\rho_k}[a_k\hat{\lambda}_k + w_k\sigma b_k] & \text{otherwise} \end{cases} \tag{19}$$

$$\text{optical flow } \boldsymbol{\lambda}_k = \begin{cases} \alpha w_k \boldsymbol{a}_k & \text{if } \boldsymbol{a}_k^T\hat{\boldsymbol{\lambda}}_k + \sigma b_k > \alpha|\boldsymbol{a}_k|^2 + \sigma\epsilon \\ -\alpha w_k \boldsymbol{a}_k & \text{if } \boldsymbol{a}_k^T\hat{\boldsymbol{\lambda}}_k + \sigma b_k < -(\alpha|\boldsymbol{a}_k|^2 + \sigma\epsilon) \\ \hat{\boldsymbol{\lambda}}_k - \sigma M_k(\hat{\boldsymbol{\lambda}}_k - \frac{\alpha w_k b_k}{\epsilon}\boldsymbol{a}_k) & \text{otherwise} \end{cases} \tag{20}$$

$$\text{depth fusion } \lambda_k = \text{median}(\hat{\lambda}_k - \sigma b_1, \ldots, \hat{\lambda}_k - \sigma b_L, W_{1k}, \ldots, W_{Lk}) \tag{21}$$

where $W_{ik} = \alpha w_k[\sum_{j=1}^{i} h_i(x_k) - h_i(x_k)]$, the sub-index k indicates the components associated with the quadrature point x_k, a and b are the variables in the linearization of stereo and flow, and the 2×2 matrix $M_k = [\sigma I_2 + \frac{\alpha w_k}{\epsilon}\boldsymbol{a}_k\boldsymbol{a}_k^T]^{-1}$ is inverted analytically.

Minimization in ν. Let $\hat{\nu} = \nu^n + \sigma N\bar{c}^n$ and recall that the conjugate of a norm is the indicator of its dual unit ball, the minimization in ν for (2), (4)–(5) and each flow component in (3) decouples in each quadrature point and simplifies to

$$\min_{\nu} \sum_{k=1}^{m} \sigma g^*(\nu_k) + \frac{1}{2}|\nu_k - \hat{\nu}_k|^2 = \min_{|\nu_k| < w_k} \sum_{k=1}^{m} \frac{1}{2}|\nu_k - \hat{\nu}_k|^2 \Rightarrow \nu_k = \frac{w_k}{\max(\,w_k, |\hat{\nu}_k|\,)}\hat{\nu}_k.$$

6   Experimental Results

Our experiments are designed to compare discretizations, not variational models or optimization algorithms. To this purpose, we implement the segmentation, stereo, flow and depth-fusion models of Sect. 3 and the optimization algorithm [7] with our FE and the standard FD discretizations and multiresolution pyramids. Models and algorithm are chosen for their prevalence, not to top the state-of-the-art of each application.

Since the pixel grid defines the finest resolution to do inference from the input images, the performance of FD discretizations at pixel grid defines the gold standard in terms of accuracy. We use standard metrics in each application: angular error (ae) in flow, relative root mean-square (rms) error in stereo, and visual inspection in segmentation and depth fusion. To compare time performance, we implement all the algorithms in python and run them on a CPU Intel $i7$ at 2.6 GHz with the same number of warps, iterations, and image pyramids in FD discretizations and FE refinement levels. We investigate the speed, accuracy, and limitations of each discretization in Figs. 1, 2, 3, 4 and 5.

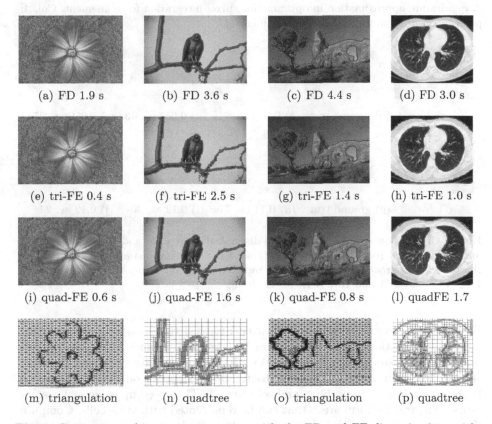

(a) FD 1.9 s   (b) FD 3.6 s   (c) FD 4.4 s   (d) FD 3.0 s

(e) tri-FE 0.4 s   (f) tri-FE 2.5 s   (g) tri-FE 1.4 s   (h) tri-FE 1.0 s

(i) quad-FE 0.6 s   (j) quad-FE 1.6 s   (k) quad-FE 0.8 s   (l) quadFE 1.7

(m) triangulation   (n) quadtree   (o) triangulation   (p) quadtree

Fig. 1. Comparison of image segmentation with the FD and FE discretizations with triangular (tri-FE) and rectangular (quad-FE) elements. The contours of the segmentation are in blue. The tessellations of FE discretizations in row 4 adapt to the image structures and speed-up ×2–×3 the optimization. (Color figure online)

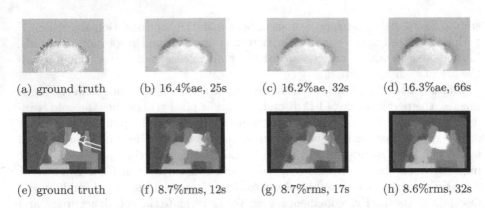

(a) ground truth   (b) 16.4%ae, 25s   (c) 16.2%ae, 32s   (d) 16.3%ae, 66s

(e) ground truth   (f) 8.7%rms, 12s   (g) 8.7%rms, 17s   (h) 8.6%rms, 32s

Fig. 2. Effects of quadrature approximations in optimization, element refinement, and relative error. Col. 2: quadrature approximation in optimization and refinement. Col. 3: quadrature approximation in optimization, pixel integration for refinement. Col. 4: pixel integration in optimization and refinement.

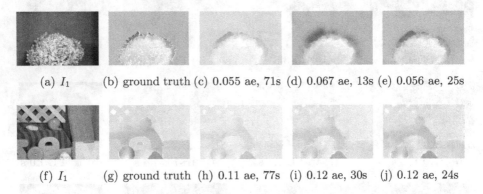

(a) I_1 (b) ground truth (c) 0.055 ae, 71s (d) 0.067 ae, 13s (e) 0.056 ae, 25s

(f) I_1 (g) ground truth (h) 0.11 ae, 77s (i) 0.12 ae, 30s (j) 0.12 ae, 24s

Fig. 3. Optical flow estimation with FD discretization (col. 3) and triangular (col. 4) and quadrilateral (col. 5) FE discretizations. FE discretizations are 2–3 times faster than the FD approach for a loss of 0.01 radians of angular error, or relative errors of 15% (FD) and 21% and 16% (FE) for Hydrangea.

Speed. Our discretization with quadtree FEs is 3 times faster than a FD for image segmentation, 0.6–2 times faster for stereo, 3–5 times faster for optical-flow, and 4–5 faster for depth fusion. With FE triangulations, the speed gains are similar. The gain in speed from our discretization depends on the complexity of both the minimization problem and solution. (1) The speed up is larger for solutions with large uniform areas that can be represented with large cells. Compare the segmentations of Fig. 1(i)–(j), where the complexity of the image is transferred into the tessellation and computational cost. (2) The speed-up is lower for image segmentation and depth fusion problems that only benefit from the adaptivity of discretization, while flow and stereo also benefit from an adaptive multiresolution to amortize the overheads of constructing FE tessellations.

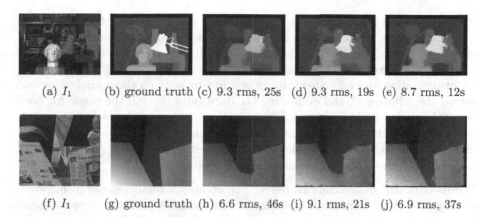

(a) I_1 (b) ground truth (c) 9.3 rms, 25s (d) 9.3 rms, 19s (e) 8.7 rms, 12s

(f) I_1 (g) ground truth (h) 6.6 rms, 46s (i) 9.1 rms, 21s (j) 6.9 rms, 37s

Fig. 4. Depth-from-stereo estimation with FD (column 3) and triangular (column 4) and quadrilateral (column 5) FE discretizations. FE are 2 time faster than the FDs for a loss in accuracy below 3% in the relative RMS error.

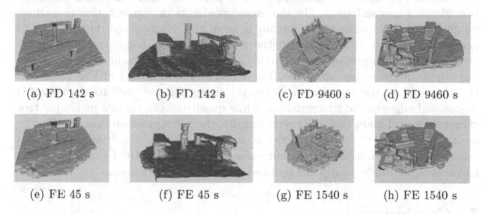

(a) FD 142 s   (b) FD 142 s   (c) FD 9460 s   (d) FD 9460 s

(e) FE 45 s   (f) FE 45 s   (g) FE 1540 s   (h) FE 1540 s

Fig. 5. Surfacsses reconstructed from 14 and 24 depth maps of a small outdoor scene (left) and a tabletop model (right). FD and FE reconstructions have comparable qualities, but the FE is 3 and 6 times faster because the optimization problem is smaller and the histograms are only computed at quadrature points.

Accuracy. The gains in speed come with a loss in accuracy: 0.01–0.02 radians of angular error in optical flow (15–20% of relative error), below 3% of relative root-mean-square error in stereo, and small perturbations of the contours in image segmentation and fusion. The results of FE discretizations are thus qualitatively similar to the FD ones but tend to blurr sharp transitions in u; this causes small artifacts in the estimated flow and stereo results of Figs. 3 and 4 but has minimal impact on segmentation depth-map fusion Figs. 1 and 5 as u is post-processed to extract its zero-level set.

Quadrature is accurate for the regularizer because we constrain the solution to the span of a spline basis, but is only a valid approximation for the integration of the data term if large FE cells correspond to flat regions in the image plane or volume, while discontinuities in u are supported by fine elements. Figure 2 compares the evaluation of the data term over all the image pixels with different quadrature approximations: using quadrature to both compute the integral in the optimization and refinement, using quadrature only on the optimization but not on the refinement, and evaluating the data term over all the pixels for both the optimization and refinement. The experiment shows that quadrature speeds optimization with a small accuracy loss and the refinement process partitions elements with large objective values, caused by either large errors in the forward model (data term) or sharp transitions in u (regularizer).

Trade-Offs. FE discretizations reduce the computational cost of optimization as they reduce the number of variables but introduce a data-structure overhead by tessellating of the image domain into elements. When the information in the data term is uniformly distributed, like in flow or stereo problems, FE discretizations results in larger accuracy losses or reduced speed ups because the optimal tessellation approaches a uniform grid. For problems where the input information clusters in small areas, like the image gradients in segmentation or surface patches in depth fusion, the speed up is large and compensates for any loss of accuracy that can be corrected in the post-processing that extracts the zero-level set of u. This property is of particular interest for 3D reconstruction where large uniform grids are unfeasible. The memory requirements of FE discretizations depend on the tessellation. Delaunay triangulations need to store the 2D points and edges of the triangulation, while quadtrees can encode its simple tree structure with binary codes. Experimentally, the refinement process of triangles is unable to align the discontinuities in u to the edges of the triangles without creating skewer triangles that compromise the stability of the FE discretization as we must estimate jointly the optimal u and its discretization.

7   Conclusions

The discretization of variational problems has received little attention in vision as the pixel lattice offers an obvious computational grid that, if not efficient, is simple and accurate. As a result, when accuracy and not speed or memory is the bottleneck, finite-difference are better discretizations for variational models. Finite element discretizations suit problems where the information in the input data is spatially sparse as they allow for multiresolution optimizations that allocates resources adaptively to match the complexity of the solution. This is important for 3D problems like surface reconstruction or image segmentation, but offers limited benefits for 2D problems like optical flow or stereo that are described by matching pixels of uniform lattices.

Acknowledgements. This research was partially funded by SNSF grant P300P2-161038, NSF grant 442511-SS-22001 and AFOSR grant FA9550-15-1-0229.

References

1. Les, P., Wayne, T.: The Nurbs Book. Springer, Berlin (1997)
2. Sederberg, T.W., Zheng, J., Sewell, D., Sabin, M.: Non-uniform recursive subdivision surfaces. In: SIGGRAPH, pp. 387–394 (1998)
3. Kazhdan, M., Hoppe, H.: Screened poisson surface reconstruction. ACM Trans. Graph. **32**, 1–13 (2013)
4. Calakli, F., Taubin, G.: SSD: smooth signed distance surface reconstruction. Comput. Graph. Forum **30**, 1993–2002 (2011)
5. Ummenhofer, B., Brox, T.: Global, dense multiscale reconstruction for a billion points. In: CVPR (2015)
6. Combettes, P.L., Pesquet, J.-C.: Proximal splitting methods in signal processing. In: Bauschke, H.H., Burachik, R.S., Combettes, P.L., Elser, V., Luke, D.R., Wolkowicz, H. (eds.) Fixed-Point Algorithms for Inverse Problems in Science and Engineering. SOA, vol. 49, pp. 185–212. Springer, New York (2011). doi:10.1007/978-1-4419-9569-8_10
7. Chambolle, A., Pock, T.: A first-order primal-dual algorithm for convex problems with applications to imaging. J. Math. Imaging Vis. **40**, 120–145 (2010)
8. Balzer, J., Morwald, T.: Isogeometric finite-elements methods and variational reconstruction tasks in vision – a perfect match. In: CVPR, pp. 1624–1631 (2012)
9. Morwald, T., Balzer, J., Vincze, M.: Direct optimization of T-splines based on Multiview Stereo. In: 2014 2nd International Conference on 3D Vision (3DV) (2014)
10. Estellers, V., Scott, M., Tew, K., Soatto, S.: Robust poisson surface reconstruction. In: Aujol, J.-F., Nikolova, M., Papadakis, N. (eds.) SSVM 2015. LNCS, vol. 9087, pp. 525–537. Springer, Cham (2015). doi:10.1007/978-3-319-18461-6_42
11. Cremers, D., Soatto, S.: Motion competition: a variational approach to piecewise parametric motion segmentation. IJCV **62**, 249–265 (2004)
12. Nir, T., Bruckstein, A., Kimmel, R.: Over-parameterized variational optical flow. IJCV **76**(2), 205–216 (2008)
13. Sun, D., Sudderth, E.B., Black, M.J.: Layered segmentation and optical flow estimation over time. In: CVPR, pp. 1768–1775, June 2012
14. Yang, J., Li, H.: Dense, accurate optical flow estimation with piecewise parametric model. In: CVPR, pp. 1019–1027 (2015)
15. Vogel, C., Schindler, K., Roth, S.: Piecewise rigid scene flow. In: ICCV, pp. 1377–1384 (2013)
16. Chan, T.F., Esedoglu, S., Nikolova, M.: Algorithms for finding global minimizers of image segmentation and denoising models. SIAM J. Appl. Math. **66**, 1632–1648 (2006)
17. Goldstein, T., Bresson, X., Osher, S.: Geometric applications of the split Bregman method: segmentation and surface reconstruction. J. Sci. Comput. **45**, 272–293 (2009)
18. Wedel, A., Pock, T., Zach, C., Bischof, H., Cremers, D.: An improved algorithm for TV-L^1 optical flow. In: Cremers, D., Rosenhahn, B., Yuille, A.L., Schmidt, F.R. (eds.) Statistical and Geometrical Approaches to Visual Motion Analysis. LNCS, vol. 5604, pp. 23–45. Springer, Heidelberg (2009). doi:10.1007/978-3-642-03061-1_2
19. Sun, D., Roth, S., Black, M.J.: Secrets of optical flow estimation and their principles. In: CVPR, pp. 2432–2439, June 2010
20. Zach, C., Pock, T., Bischof, H.: A globally optimal algorithm for robust TV-L1 range image integration. In: ICCV, pp. 1–8 (2007)

21. Merrell, P., Akbarzadeh, A., Wang, L., Mordohai, P., Frahm, J.M., Yang, R., Nistér, D., Pollefeys, M.: Real-time visibility-based fusion of depth maps. In: ICCV (2007)
22. Graber, G., Pock, T., Bischof, H.: Online 3D reconstruction using convex optimization. In: ICCV Work 2011, pp. 708–711 (2011)
23. Hughes, T.J.R.: The Finite Element Method: Linear Static and Dynamic Finite Element Analysis. Courier Corporation, North Chelmsford (2012)
24. Kirchner, H., Niemann, H.: Finite element method for determination of optical flow. Pattern Recogn. Lett. 13, 131–141 (1992)
25. Cohen, I., Herlin, I.: Non uniform multiresolution method for optical flow computation. In: Berger, M.O., Deriche, R., Herlin, I., Jaffré, J., Morel, J.M. (eds.) ICAOS 1996. LNCIS, vol. 219, pp. 315–322. Springer, Heidelberg (1996). doi:10.1007/3-540-76076-8_144
26. Schnörr, C.: A study of a convex variational diffusion approach for image segmentation and feature extraction. J. Math. Imaging Vis. 8, 271–292 (1998)
27. Yaacobson, F., Givoli, D.: An adaptive finite element procedure for the image segmentation problem. Int. J. Numer. Methods Biomed. Eng. 14, 621–632 (1998)
28. Preußer, T., Rumpf, M.: An adaptive finite element method for large scale image processing. J. Vis. Commun. Image Represent. 11, 183–195 (2000)
29. Bänsch, E., Mikula, K.: A coarsening finite element strategy in image selective smoothing. Comput. Vis. Sci. 1, 53–61 (1997)

The Hessian of Axially Symmetric Functions on SE(3) and Application in 3D Image Analysis

Michiel H.J. Janssen[✉], Tom C.J. Dela Haije, Frank C. Martin, Erik J. Bekkers, and Remco Duits

Department of Mathematics and Computer Science, Eindhoven University of Technology, Eindhoven, The Netherlands
M.H.J.Janssen@tue.nl

Abstract. We propose a method for computation of the Hessian of axially symmetric functions on the roto-translation group $SE(3)$. Eigendecomposition of the resulting Hessian is then used for curvature estimation of tubular structures, similar to how the Hessian matrix of 2D or 3D image data can be used for orientation estimation. This paper focuses on a new implementation of a Gaussian regularized Hessian on the roto-translation group. Furthermore we show how eigenanalysis of this Hessian gives rise to exponential curve fits on data on position and orientation (e.g. orientation scores), whose spatial projections provide local fits in 3D data. We quantitatively validate our exponential curve fits by comparing the curvature of the spatially projected fitted curve to ground truth curvature of artificial 3D data. We also show first results on real MRA data. Implementations are available at: http://lieanalysis. nl/orientationscores.html.

1 Introduction

The Hessian matrix of 2D or 3D image data is commonly used to analyze the local structure of the data. Eigendecomposition of the Hessian matrix is common for orientation estimation and ridge detection, and eigenvalues have been used in features such as vesselness [8]. We aim to extend such techniques to functions on positions and orientations $\mathbb{R}^3 \times S^2$ which can be identified with axially symmetric functions on the 3D roto-translation group $SE(3)$. This paper focuses on the implementation of the Hessian of real-valued axially symmetric functions on $SE(3)$.

Data on positions and orientations can be obtained in several different settings. Here we focus on orientation scores, where data is obtained from 3D data by an invertible wavelet-type transformation [9]. Other options include liftings [2,12], and diffusion-weighted MRI [10]. In general $U(\mathbf{x}, \mathbf{n}) : \mathbb{R}^3 \times S^2 \to \mathbb{R}$ is to be considered a probability density of finding a local oriented structure (i.e. an elongated structure) at position $\mathbf{x} \in \mathbb{R}^3$ with orientation $\mathbf{n} \in S^2$.

Just as in 2D and 3D data, eigendecomposition of the Hessian produces the directions of principle curvature with corresponding curvature values. When

© Springer International Publishing AG 2017
F. Lauze et al. (Eds.): SSVM 2017, LNCS 10302, pp. 643–655, 2017.
DOI: 10.1007/978-3-319-58771-4_51

considering 3D data the eigenvector with smallest eigenvalue is often used to find the orientation of a line structure. When considering the direction of a structure in the extended space of positions and orientations this does not only give us information about spatial orientation of the structure but also about the change in orientation which is directly related to curvature. This technique has already been used for curvature estimation of blood vessels in 2D data [1], and here we extend this technique to 3D.

Local curve optimization that accounts for local curvature via spiral fits has been proposed in [11], where a more complex model of neighboring curves is fitted. We have a simpler curve fit model (e.g. we do not account for fanning out). Our model has the advantage that we obtain curve fits as exact solutions of Euler-Lagrange equations and use the full-distribution on $\mathbb{R}^3 \times S^2$ instead of only relying on the principle eigenvector of the diffusion tensor.

Regarding the implementation of the Hessian matrix, we rely on Gaussian derivatives. For angular derivatives, finite derivatives were used in other works [5]. On the sphere S^2, limited amount of samples due to computation time and non uniform sampling can cause problems such as bias towards sampled orientations and additional numerical blur. Furthermore, adding regularization is not trivial when using finite differences and such implementations do not allow us to calculate derivatives at orientations which do not lie on the sampling grid. Especially this last shortcoming is problematic in practice. To solve this problem we express our spherical data in spherical harmonics after which the computation of the Gaussian Hessian is exact.

Theory on how eigenanalysis of the Hessian relates to exponential curve fits can be found in [6], where orientation estimation was extended to the space of positions and orientations $\mathbb{R}^3 \times S^2$. There a Hessian on the extended space $SE(3)$ was used but no details on implementation were given. The key objective of this article is to present a new algorithm for calculating the Hessian of axially symmetric functions on $SE(3)$ via spherical harmonics. This is useful for exponential curve fits and curvature estimation of elongated structures (e.g. vessels) in 3D data. Furthermore, we address validation of the exponential curve fits and the induced curvature measurements. First we provide background theory in Sect. 2, followed by a discussion of the discrete implementation of the Hessian in Sect. 3. Then we include the algorithm for curvature estimation in Sect. 4. Finally we quantitatively validate our method on artificial 3D data with ground truth curvatures and show first results on real MRA data in Sect. 5.

2   Theory

2.1   Embedding of $\mathbb{R}^3 \times S^2$ Data in SE(3)

When processing data on positions and orientations it is often necessary to equip the domain with a structure that links the data across different orientation channels, in such a way that a notion of alignment between local orientations is taken into account. This is achieved by embedding data on positions and orientations into the roto-translation group $SE(3) = \mathbb{R}^3 \rtimes SO(3)$, with group product $g_1 g_2 = (\mathbf{x}_1, \mathbf{R}_1)(\mathbf{x}_2, \mathbf{R}_2) = (\mathbf{R}_1 \mathbf{x}_2 + \mathbf{x}_1, \mathbf{R}_1 \mathbf{R}_2)$, with $g_1, g_2 \in SE(d)$. Let $U : \mathbb{R}^3 \rtimes S^2 \to \mathbb{R}$ denote a function on the coupled space of positions and orientations. Then, its embedding $\tilde{U} : SE(3) \to \mathbb{R}$ is given by:

$$\tilde{U}(\mathbf{x}, \mathbf{R}) := U(\mathbf{x}, \mathbf{R}\mathbf{e}_z) \tag{1}$$

for all $\mathbf{x} \in \mathbb{R}^3$ and all rotations $\mathbf{R} \in SO(3)$. This embedding results in the axial symmetry in $\tilde{U}$ as a replacement $\mathbf{R} \mapsto \mathbf{R}\mathbf{R}_{\mathbf{e}_z, \alpha}$ does not affect $\tilde{U}$ in Eq. (1).

Throughout the document we will use the z-y-z Euler angles convention $\mathbf{R} = \mathbf{R}_{\mathbf{e}_z, \gamma} \mathbf{R}_{\mathbf{e}_y, \beta} \mathbf{R}_{\mathbf{e}_z, \alpha}$, with $\alpha \in [-\pi, \pi)$, $\beta \in [0, \pi]$ and $\gamma \in [-\pi, \pi)$. Just as in [6] we will use $\mathbf{R}_\mathbf{n}$ to denote any rotation such that $\mathbf{R}_\mathbf{n} \mathbf{e}_z = \mathbf{n}$. Due to the data symmetry induced by embedding according to Eq. (1), the choice of $\mathbf{R}_\mathbf{n}$ does not matter. Therefore, we can choose for each orientation a specific rotation. We set $\alpha = 0$ and define $\mathbf{R}_\mathbf{n}^0 = \mathbf{R}_{\mathbf{e}_z, \gamma} \mathbf{R}_{\mathbf{e}_y, \beta}$, where β and γ are standard spherical coordinates for the orientation: $\mathbf{n}(\beta, \gamma) = (\sin\beta \cos\gamma, \sin\beta \sin\gamma, \cos\beta)$.

2.2   The Hessian Matrix on SE(3)

By Eq. (1) we relate data U on positions and orientations to data $\tilde{U}$ on $SE(3)$. This is helpful to: (1) keep track of rotation and translation covariance as this boils down to left-invariance on the group. (2) work with moving frames of reference for each position and each orientation. Next, we explain the notion of left-invariance, followed by explicit formulas for the left-invariant vector fields on $SE(3)$ which are then used in the definition of the Hessian.

A vector field $g \mapsto \mathcal{A}|_g$ on $SE(3)$ is left-invariant if for all differentiable curves $\gamma : \mathbb{R} \mapsto SE(3)$ one has

$$\gamma'(0) = \mathcal{A}|_{\gamma(0)} \Rightarrow \forall_{g \in SE(3)} \ (g\gamma)'(0) = \mathcal{A}|_{g\gamma(0)}, \tag{2}$$

see Fig. 1(a) for a geometric explanation. The left-invariant vector fields are obtained via push-forward of the left multiplication $\mathcal{A}_i|_g = (L_g)_* \mathcal{A}_i|_e$ of the Lie algebra basis $\mathcal{A}_i|_e$. On $SE(3)$ the left-invariant vector fields are given by

$$\begin{pmatrix} \mathcal{A}_1 \\ \mathcal{A}_2 \\ \mathcal{A}_3 \end{pmatrix} = \mathbf{R}^T \begin{pmatrix} \partial_x \\ \partial_y \\ \partial_z \end{pmatrix}, \quad \begin{pmatrix} \mathcal{A}_4 \\ \mathcal{A}_5 \\ \mathcal{A}_6 \end{pmatrix} = \begin{pmatrix} \cos\alpha \cot\beta \, \partial_\alpha + \sin\alpha \, \partial_\beta - \frac{\cos\alpha}{\sin\beta} \partial_\gamma \\ -\sin\alpha \cot\beta \, \partial_\alpha + \cos\alpha \, \partial_\beta + \frac{\sin\alpha}{\sin\beta} \partial_\gamma \\ \partial_\alpha, \end{pmatrix}, \tag{3}$$

for $\beta \neq 0, \beta \neq \pi$, with $\mathbf{x} = (x, y, z)$ and recall that $\mathbf{R} = \mathbf{R}_{\mathbf{e}_z, \gamma} \mathbf{R}_{\mathbf{e}_y, \beta} \mathbf{R}_{\mathbf{e}_z, \alpha}$.

For defining the regularized Hessian matrix we use the following regularization kernel:

$$\tilde{G}_\mathbf{s}(g) := G_{s_p}^{\mathbb{R}^3}(\mathbf{x}) \, G_{s_o}^{S^2}(\mathbf{R}\mathbf{e}_z), \tag{4}$$

where $G_{s_p}^{\mathbb{R}^3}$ is the diffusion kernel on $\mathbb{R}^3$ and $G_{s_o}^{S^2}$ the diffusion kernel on the sphere S^2, and where $\mathbf{s} = (s_p, s_o)$, $s_p, s_o \geq 0$, are the spatial and angular scales of regularization respectively. Then, the 6×6 non-symmetric regularized Hessian[1] matrix at $g = (\mathbf{x}, \mathbf{R})$ is defined by

---

[1] In general the Hessian depends on the imposed connection on the tangent bundle $T(SE(3))$, where $\mathbf{H} = (\nabla_{\mathcal{A}_i}^* d\tilde{U})(\mathcal{A}_j)$. Here we follow [6, App. 4] and choose ∇ as the left Cartan connection, since it is the correct connection for left-invariant processing.

$$(\mathbf{H}^{\mathbf{s}}\tilde{U})(g) := (\mathbf{H}\tilde{V})(g) := [\mathcal{A}_j\mathcal{A}_i(\tilde{V})(g)]^6_{i,j=1}, \quad \text{with } \tilde{V} = \tilde{G}_{\mathbf{s}} * \tilde{U}, \qquad (5)$$

and where i, j denote the row and column index respectively. Here $*$ denotes convolution on the group $SE(3)$.

2.3   Exponential Curves on SE(3) and Spatial Projection

An exponential curve in $SE(3)$ is a curve obtained by the exponential mapping from Lie algebra to Lie group. For $g \in SE(3)$ and $t \in \mathbb{R}$ we write

$$\gamma^{\mathbf{c}}_g(t) = (\mathbf{x}(t), \mathbf{R}(t)) = g\, e^{t\sum\limits_{i=1}^{6} c^i A_i}, \qquad (6)$$

with $A_i = \mathcal{A}_i|_e$ denoting a basis of the Lie algebra $T_e(SE(d))$ and $\mathbf{c}^T = (\mathbf{c}^{(1)}, \mathbf{c}^{(2)})^T = (c^1, \ldots, c^6)^T \in \mathbb{R}^6$ be a given column vector, where $\mathbf{c}^{(1)} = (c^1, c^2, c^3) \in \mathbb{R}^3$ denotes the spatial velocity components and $\mathbf{c}^{(2)} = (c^4, c^5, c^6) \in \mathbb{R}^3$ denotes the rotational velocity components. The exponential curve has the crucial property that the components of the tangent vector expressed in the left-invariant basis are constant over the entire parametrization:

$$\dot{\gamma}^{\mathbf{c}}_g(t) = \sum_{i=1}^{6} c^i\, A_i|_{\gamma^{\mathbf{c}}_g(t)}, \qquad (7)$$

see Fig. 1(b). For formulae of the exponential curves in $SE(3)$ see [4]. Their spatial parts are circular spirals with constant curvature and torsion magnitude:

$$\|\kappa\| = \frac{\|\mathbf{c}^{(1)} \times \mathbf{c}^{(2)}\|}{\|\mathbf{c}^{(1)}\|^2} \text{ and } \|\tau\| = \frac{|\mathbf{c}^{(1)} \cdot \mathbf{c}^{(2)}| \cdot \|\kappa\|}{\|\mathbf{c}^{(1)}\|}. \qquad (8)$$

2.4   Exponential Curve Fits

The exponential curve fitting procedure minimizes

$$\mathbf{c}^*(g) = \underset{\mathbf{c}\in\mathbb{R}^6, \|\mathbf{c}\|_\mu=1}{\arg\min} \left\| \frac{d}{dt}\nabla\tilde{V}(\gamma^{\mathbf{c}}_g(t)) \right|_{t=0} \right\|^2_\mu,$$

$$\|\mathbf{c}\|_\mu := \|\mathbf{M}_\mu\mathbf{c}\|, \quad \mathbf{M}_\mu = \begin{pmatrix} \mu\mathbf{I}_3 & 0 \\ 0 & \mathbf{I}_3 \end{pmatrix} \in \mathbb{R}^{6\times6}, \qquad (9)$$

where $\mu > 0$ is a parameter used to balance spatial and angular distances. Its relation to the Hessian is that the normalized eigenvector $\mathbf{M}_\mu\mathbf{c}^*(g)$ with smallest eigenvalue of symmetric Hessian product matrix

$$\mathbf{M}^{-1}_\mu(\mathbf{H}\tilde{V}(g))^T\mathbf{M}^{-2}_\mu\mathbf{H}\tilde{V}(g)\mathbf{M}^{-1}_\mu \qquad (10)$$

provides the solution $\mathbf{c}^*(g)$ of optimization problem (9), see [6, Theorem 3] which shows the $SE(2)$ version of this problem. In contrast to [6], we do not use *external* regularization. In [6] this result for $SE(2)$ was not extended to $SE(3)$ because the optimization problem does not have a unique solution due to a non-trivial null-space of the matrix caused by the symmetry in our data. In practice however one needs to rely on a two-step method as explained in [6], where we first fit the optimal spatial tangent and then fit the curvature. The fact that the two-step method avoids the problems caused by the null-space was overlooked in [6]. Details follow in Sect. 4.

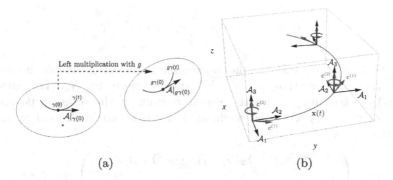

(a)   (b)

Fig. 1. (a) Schematic visualization of left-invariant vector fields, Eq. (2). A vector viewed as a tangent to a curve is used to construct a vector field by moving the curve to a different group element by group multiplication. (b) An exponential curve $\gamma_g^c(t)$, Eq. (6). The spatial part is a spiral (blue line). Its tangent $\dot{\gamma}_g^c(t)$, Eq. (7), has constant components w.r.t. the left-invariant vector fields $\mathcal{A}_i$ which act as a local frame of reference. Here $\mathbf{c}^{(1)}$ are components of the spatial tangent (red arrow) and $\mathbf{c}^{(2)}$ components of the angular tangent, shown here as the axis of rotation (green arrow). (Color figure online)

3   Implementation on Discrete Data

In practice we have discrete data on positions and orientations (e.g. a discrete orientation score) defined on a 3D rectangular grid parametrized by $\mathbf{x} = (x, y, z)$ with $x = 1, 2, \ldots, N_x$, $y = 1, 2, \ldots, N_y$ and $z = 1, 2, \ldots, N_z$, which is defined for a set of discrete orientations $\mathbf{n}_i = \mathbf{n}(\beta_i, \gamma_i)$ labeled by $i = 1, 2, \ldots, N_o$.

We will now focus on computing $\mathbf{H}\tilde{V}(g)$ for a group element $g = (\mathbf{x}, \mathbf{R}_\mathbf{n}^0)$. Note that $\mathbf{n} = \mathbf{R}\mathbf{e}_z$ may not be on the spherical grid requiring interpolation. Next we do this interpolation via spherical harmonics.

3.1   Signal Approximation with Spherical Harmonic

First we will approximate the signal by expressing it in a spherical harmonic basis. The spherical harmonics are given by

$$Y_l^m(\beta, \gamma) = \sqrt{\frac{2l+1}{4\pi}} \sqrt{\frac{(l-m)!}{(l+m)!}} e^{im\gamma} P_l^m(\cos\beta), \qquad (11)$$

where P_l^m is the associated Legendre function and with integer order $l \geq 0$ and integer phase factor $-l \leq m \leq l$. When doing computations it is more convenient to use an alternative indexing j for the basis functions, and we define:

$$Y_j = Y_m^l, \qquad \text{with } j := j(l,m) = (l^2 + l + 1) + m, \\ l_j = \lfloor \sqrt{j-1} \rfloor, \quad m_j = j - 1 - (l_j)^2 - l_j. \tag{12}$$

We approximate the data U at a discrete position $\mathbf{x}$ by

$$U(\mathbf{x}, \mathbf{n}(\beta, \gamma)) = \sum_{j=1}^{J} c_j(\mathbf{x}) \, Y_j(\beta, \gamma), \tag{13}$$

where $J = j(L, L)$, with L the maximum spherical harmonic order considered chosen such that $J < N_o$ and J close to N_o. Let $\mathbf{u}(\mathbf{x}) = (U(\mathbf{x}, \mathbf{n}_1), \ldots, U(\mathbf{x}, \mathbf{n}_{N_o}))^T$ be the vector containing the data at position $\mathbf{x}$, $\mathbf{c}(\mathbf{x}) = (c_1(\mathbf{x}), \ldots, c_J(\mathbf{x}))^T$ the coefficients of our approximation at $\mathbf{x}$, and $\mathbf{M}$ the matrix

$$\mathbf{M} = \begin{pmatrix} Y_1(\beta_1, \gamma_1) & Y_2(\beta_1, \gamma_1) & \cdots & Y_J(\beta_1, \gamma_1) \\ \vdots & \vdots & \ddots & \vdots \\ Y_1(\beta_{N_o}, \gamma_{N_o}) & Y_2(\beta_{N_o}, \gamma_{N_o}) & \cdots & Y_J(\beta_{N_o}, \gamma_{N_o}) \end{pmatrix} \in \mathbb{C}^{N_o \times J}, \tag{14}$$

then we have for each position $\mathbf{x}$ the overdetermined system $\mathbf{u} = \mathbf{Mc}$ and we can use a least square fitting procedure to find the coefficients $\mathbf{c}$, i.e. $\mathbf{c}(\mathbf{x}) = (\mathbf{M}^\dagger \mathbf{M})^{-1} \mathbf{M}^\dagger \mathbf{u}(\mathbf{x})$. We now have a description of the data for all (β, γ) but still for a discrete grid of positions.

3.2   Angular Regularization

Because of the choice of regularization kernel $\tilde{G}$ in Eq. (4) we can separately perform angular and isotropic spatial regularization and it does not matter which is performed first. First we apply angular regularization. Since spherical harmonics are eigenfunctions of the Laplace operator, i.e. $\Delta_{S^2} Y_m^l = -l(l+1)Y_m^l$, the regularized signal is given by

$$(G_{s_o}^{S^2} *_{S^2} U)(\mathbf{x}, \mathbf{n}(\beta, \gamma)) = \sum_{j=1}^{J} c_j^{s_o}(\mathbf{x}) \, Y_j(\beta, \gamma), \text{ with } c_j^{s_o} = c_j e^{-l_j(l_j+1)s_o}. \tag{15}$$

3.3   Spatial Regularization and Spatial Gaussian Derivatives

For all spatial derivatives we use Gaussian derivatives which are evaluated on the spherical harmonic coefficients, for example

$$(\partial_x G_{s_p}^{\mathbb{R}^3} *_{\mathbb{R}^3} U)(\mathbf{x}, \beta, \gamma) = \sum_{j=1}^{J} (\partial_x G_{s_p}^{\mathbb{R}^3} *_{\mathbb{R}^3} c_j)(\mathbf{x}) \, Y_j(\beta, \gamma). \tag{16}$$

Analogous procedures are used for all spatial derivatives on the coefficients $c_j^{s_o}$. For a group element $g = (\mathbf{x}, \mathbf{R}_{\mathbf{n}(\beta,\gamma)})$ we have the following spatial gradient and Hessian of regularized data $\tilde{V}$ in x-y-z coordinates

$$\nabla_{\mathbb{R}^3}\tilde{V}(g) = \sum_{j=1}^{J} \mathbf{c}_j^{\nabla_{\mathbb{R}^3}}(\mathbf{x})\, Y_j(\beta,\gamma), \ \text{ with } \mathbf{c}_j^{\nabla_{\mathbb{R}^3}} = \begin{pmatrix} \partial_x G_{s_p}^{\mathbb{R}^3} *_{\mathbb{R}^3} c_j^{s_o} \\ \partial_y G_{s_p}^{\mathbb{R}^3} *_{\mathbb{R}^3} c_j^{s_o} \\ \partial_z G_{s_p}^{\mathbb{R}^3} *_{\mathbb{R}^3} c_j^{s_o} \end{pmatrix}, \quad (17)$$

$$(\mathbf{H}_{\mathbb{R}^3}\tilde{V})(g) = \sum_{j=1}^{J} \mathbf{C}_j^{H_{\mathbb{R}^3}}(\mathbf{x})\, Y_j(\beta,\gamma), \ \text{ with } \mathbf{C}_j^{H_{\mathbb{R}^3}} = [\partial_{x_i}\partial_{x_j} G_{s_p}^{\mathbb{R}^3} *_{\mathbb{R}^3} c_j^{s_o}]_{i,j=1}^{3}, \ (18)$$

where $(x_1, x_2, x_3) = (x, y, z)$.

For computing the angular derivatives (e.g. $\mathcal{A}_4\mathcal{A}_4\tilde{V}$) we apply the same amount of spatial regularization:

$$\tilde{V}(g) = \sum_{j=1}^{J} c_j^{\tilde{V}}(\mathbf{x})\, Y_j(\beta,\gamma), \qquad \text{with } c_j^{\tilde{V}} = G_{s_p}^{\mathbb{R}^3} *_{\mathbb{R}^3} c_j^{s_o}. \quad (19)$$

3.4   Computation of the Hessian

For computation of the Hessian we use the commutator relations and the fact that by the invariance due to construction (1) we have $\mathcal{A}_6\tilde{V} = 0$ such that

$$\mathbf{H}\tilde{V} = \begin{pmatrix} \mathcal{A}_1^2 & \mathcal{A}_2\mathcal{A}_1 & \mathcal{A}_3\mathcal{A}_1 & \mathcal{A}_1\mathcal{A}_4 & \mathcal{A}_1\mathcal{A}_5 & \mathcal{A}_2 \\ \mathcal{A}_1\mathcal{A}_2 & \mathcal{A}_2^2 & \mathcal{A}_3\mathcal{A}_2 & \mathcal{A}_2\mathcal{A}_4 & \mathcal{A}_2\mathcal{A}_5 & -\mathcal{A}_1 \\ \mathcal{A}_1\mathcal{A}_3 & \mathcal{A}_2\mathcal{A}_3 & \mathcal{A}_3^2 & \mathcal{A}_3\mathcal{A}_4 - \mathcal{A}_2 & \mathcal{A}_3\mathcal{A}_5 + \mathcal{A}_1 & 0 \\ \mathcal{A}_1\mathcal{A}_4 & \mathcal{A}_2\mathcal{A}_4 & \mathcal{A}_3\mathcal{A}_4 & \mathcal{A}_4^2 & \mathcal{A}_5\mathcal{A}_4 & \mathcal{A}_5 \\ \mathcal{A}_1\mathcal{A}_5 & \mathcal{A}_2\mathcal{A}_5 & \mathcal{A}_3\mathcal{A}_5 & \mathcal{A}_4\mathcal{A}_5 & \mathcal{A}_5^2 & -\mathcal{A}_4 \\ 0 & 0 & 0 & 0 & 0 & 0 \end{pmatrix}\tilde{V} \quad (20)$$

recall Eq. (5). Due to the non-zero commutators we have for example $(\mathcal{A}_4\mathcal{A}_3)\tilde{V} = (\mathcal{A}_3\mathcal{A}_4 - \mathcal{A}_2)\tilde{V}$ which explains the $(3, 4)$ entry in the matrix. The derivatives can be split into three categories: spatial derivatives $(\mathcal{A}_3^2, \mathcal{A}_1, \mathcal{A}_2)$, angular derivatives $(\mathcal{A}_4\mathcal{A}_5 = \mathcal{A}_5\mathcal{A}_4, \mathcal{A}_4\mathcal{A}_4, \mathcal{A}_5\mathcal{A}_5)$ and mixed derivatives $(\mathcal{A}_3\mathcal{A}_4, \mathcal{A}_3\mathcal{A}_5)$.

Spatial Derivatives. For each $g = (\mathbf{x}, \mathbf{R}_{\mathbf{n}}^0)$ the spatial Hessian (rows and columns 1 to 3 of Eq. (20)) is given by

$$(\mathbf{H}^{spat}\tilde{V})(g) = (\mathbf{R}_{\mathbf{n}}^0)^T (\mathbf{H}_{\mathbb{R}^3}\tilde{V})(g)\mathbf{R}_{\mathbf{n}}^0, \quad (21)$$

where the spatial Hessian in x-y-z coordinates $\mathbf{H}_{\mathbb{R}^3}\tilde{V}$ at g is calculated from the coefficients $\mathbf{C}_j^{H_{\mathbb{R}^3}}(\mathbf{x}) \in \mathbb{R}^{3\times 3}$ according to Eq. (18). Likewise, we have

$$\begin{pmatrix} \mathcal{A}_1\tilde{V}(g) \\ \mathcal{A}_2\tilde{V}(g) \\ \mathcal{A}_3\tilde{V}(g) \end{pmatrix} = (\mathbf{R}_{\mathbf{n}}^0)^T \nabla_{\mathbb{R}^3}\tilde{V}(g), \quad (22)$$

for the first order spatial derivatives. More specifically we have $\mathcal{A}_3 = \mathbf{n} \cdot \nabla_{\mathbb{R}^3}$.

Angular Derivatives. For rotations of the form $\mathbf{R_n^0}$ the angular derivatives can be expressed in partial derivatives with respect to standard spherical coordinates (β, γ), recall Eq. (3) for $\alpha = 0$ and using Eq. (19):

$$
\begin{aligned}
\mathcal{A}_4 \tilde{V}(\mathbf{x}, \mathbf{R_n^0}) &= \frac{-1}{\sin\beta}\partial_\gamma \tilde{V}(\mathbf{x}, \mathbf{R_n^0}) = \sum\nolimits_{j=1}^{J} c_j^{\tilde{V}}(\mathbf{x})\frac{-1}{\sin\beta}\partial_\gamma Y_j(\beta, \gamma), \\
\mathcal{A}_5 \tilde{V}(\mathbf{x}, \mathbf{R_n^0}) &= \partial_\beta \tilde{V}(\mathbf{x}, \mathbf{R_n^0}) = \sum\nolimits_{j=1}^{J} c_j^{\tilde{V}}(\mathbf{x})\partial_\beta Y_j(\beta, \gamma),
\end{aligned}
\tag{23}
$$

$$
\begin{aligned}
\mathcal{A}_4\mathcal{A}_4 \tilde{V}(\mathbf{x}, \mathbf{R_n^0}) &= \sum\nolimits_{j=1}^{J} c_j^{\tilde{V}}(\mathbf{x})\left(\frac{1}{\sin^2\beta}\partial_\gamma\partial_\gamma + \frac{1}{\tan\beta}\partial_\beta\right)Y_j(\beta, \gamma), \\
\mathcal{A}_4\mathcal{A}_5 \tilde{V}(\mathbf{x}, \mathbf{R_n^0}) &= \sum\nolimits_{j=1}^{J} c_j^{\tilde{V}}(\mathbf{x})\left(\frac{-1}{\sin\beta}\partial_\gamma\partial_\beta + \frac{\cos\beta}{\sin^2\beta}\partial_\gamma\right)Y_j(\beta, \gamma), \\
\mathcal{A}_5\mathcal{A}_5 \tilde{V}(\mathbf{x}, \mathbf{R_n^0}) &= \sum\nolimits_{j=1}^{J} c_j^{\tilde{V}}(\mathbf{x})\partial_\beta\partial_\beta Y_j(\beta, \gamma),
\end{aligned}
\tag{24}
$$

recall that $\mathcal{A}_5\mathcal{A}_4 = \mathcal{A}_4\mathcal{A}_5$. Then, using Lemma 2 and Lemma 4 from [7] we eliminate the pole at $\beta = 0$ and obtain:

$$
\begin{aligned}
\mathcal{A}_4 Y_l^m &= a_l^m \tilde{Y}_{l-1}^{m,-1} + a_l^{-m}\tilde{Y}_{l-1}^{m,1}, \\
\mathcal{A}_5 Y_l^m &= b_l^m \tilde{Y}_l^{m,1} - b_l^{-m}\tilde{Y}_l^{m,-1}, \\
\mathcal{A}_4\mathcal{A}_4 Y_l^m &= -l(l+1)Y_l^m - \mathcal{A}_5\mathcal{A}_5 Y_l^m, \\
\mathcal{A}_4\mathcal{A}_5 Y_l^m &= h_l^m Y_{l-1}^m - g_l^{-m}\tilde{Y}_{l-1}^{m,-2} + g_l^m\tilde{Y}_{l-1}^{m,2}, \\
\mathcal{A}_5\mathcal{A}_5 Y_l^m &= k_l^m Y_l^m + j_l^{-m}\tilde{Y}_l^{m,-2} + j_l^m\tilde{Y}_l^{m,2},
\end{aligned}
\tag{25}
$$

with $\tilde{Y}_l^{m,p} = e^{-ip\gamma}Y_l^{m+p}$ and the following factors:

$$
\begin{aligned}
a_l^m &= \frac{i}{2}\sqrt{\frac{2l+1}{2l-1}}\sqrt{(l+m)(l+m-1)}, \qquad b_l^m = \frac{1}{2}\sqrt{(l-m)(l+m+1)}, \\
h_l^m &= a_l^m b_{l-1}^{m-1} - a_l^{-m}b_{l-1}^{-m-1}, \qquad\qquad\qquad g_l^m = a_l^{-m}b_{l-1}^{m+1}, \\
k_l^m &= -b_l^{-m}b_l^{m-1} - b_l^m b_l^{-m-1}, \qquad\qquad\qquad j_l^m = b_l^m b_l^{m+1}.
\end{aligned}
$$

Mixed Derivatives. Finally, the mixed derivatives are computed by

$$
\begin{pmatrix} \mathcal{A}_1\mathcal{A}_i\tilde{V}(g) \\ \mathcal{A}_2\mathcal{A}_i\tilde{V}(g) \\ \mathcal{A}_3\mathcal{A}_i\tilde{V}(g) \end{pmatrix} = (\mathbf{R_n^0}^T \nabla_{\mathbb{R}^3}\mathcal{A}_i\tilde{V})(g) = (\mathbf{R_n^0}^T \mathcal{A}_i\nabla_{\mathbb{R}^3}\tilde{V})(g), \quad i = 4,5,
\tag{26}
$$

with $\mathcal{A}_i\nabla_{\mathbb{R}^3} = (\mathcal{A}_i\partial_x, \mathcal{A}_i\partial_y, \mathcal{A}_i\partial_z)^T$. We combine Eq. (26) with Eqs. (17) and (23), and direct calculations yield:

$$
\begin{aligned}
\mathbf{R_n^0}^T \mathcal{A}_4\nabla_{\mathbb{R}^3}\tilde{V}(g) &= \mathbf{R_n^0}^T \sum_{j=1}^{J} \mathbf{c}_j^{\nabla_{\mathbb{R}^3}}(\mathbf{x})\frac{-1}{\sin\beta}\frac{\partial}{\partial\gamma}Y_j(\beta, \gamma), \\
\mathbf{R_n^0}^T \mathcal{A}_5\nabla_{\mathbb{R}^3}\tilde{V}(g) &= \mathbf{R_n^0}^T \sum_{j=1}^{J} \mathbf{c}_j^{\nabla_{\mathbb{R}^3}}(\mathbf{x})\frac{\partial}{\partial\beta}Y_j(\beta, \gamma).
\end{aligned}
\tag{27}
$$

Remark 1. In all implementations we use real valued spherical harmonics. The formulas for the derivatives are easily adapted for this using $\mathcal{A}_i \mathcal{A}_j \operatorname{Re}(Y_m^l) = \operatorname{Re}(\mathcal{A}_i \mathcal{A}_j Y_m^l)$.

4 Algorithm

We use the two-step method from [6] relying on a separate spatial and angular optimization using two submatrices of the symmetrized Hessian product. In the first step the spatial tangent is found and in the second step the curvature is estimated. In the second step we evaluate the Hessian at a different group element. Therefore we first apply some preparation steps such as approximating the signal using spherical harmonics, performing angular regularization and preparing spatial derivatives (Algorithm 1). Then we have the following two steps:

(1) **Determine spatial tangent.** First compute $\mathbf{H}\tilde{V}(g)$ using Algorithm 2, then compute rows and columns 1 to 3 of the symmetric Hessian product Eq. (10). Set $\mathbf{c}^{(1)}(g)$ equal to the eigenvector with smallest eigenvalue of this 3×3 matrix.

(2) **Determine curvature.** We determine the curvature at a different group element $g_{new} = (\mathbf{x}, \mathbf{R}_{\mathbf{n}_{new}})$, where $\mathbf{n}_{new} = \mathbf{R}_{\mathbf{n}} \mathbf{c}^{(1)}$, is the orientation given by the spatial tangent $\mathbf{c}^{(1)}(g)$ from step 1. Then compute $\mathbf{H}\tilde{V}(g_{new})$ using Algorithm 2, and compute rows and columns 3 to 5 of the symmetric Hessian product Eq. (10). Find the auxiliary coefficients $\mathbf{c}_{new}(g_{new}) = (0, 0, c^3(g_{new}), c^4(g_{new}), c^5(g_{new}), 0)^T$ where the components of the tangent vector $(\mu c^3, c^4, c^5)$ are set equal to the eigenvector with smallest eigenvalue of the 3×3 matrix.

We use the curvature determined at g_{new} for our curve fit at g (relying on neighboring exponential curves [6]). The coefficients of our fitted curve at g are given by

$$\mathbf{c}^*(g) = \begin{pmatrix} \mathbf{R}_\mathbf{n}^T \mathbf{R}_{\mathbf{n}_{new}} & \mathbf{0} \\ \mathbf{0} & \mathbf{R}_\mathbf{n}^T \mathbf{R}_{\mathbf{n}_{new}} \end{pmatrix} \mathbf{c}_{new}(g_{new}). \tag{28}$$

This gives the final, torsion-free, exponential curve fit $t \mapsto \gamma_g^{\mathbf{c}^*(g)}(t)$ in $SE(3)$. Implementations of the left-invariant derivatives are available in the *Mathematica* package *Lie Analysis*: Available at http://lieanalysis.nl/orientationscores.html.

5 Experiments

For the experiments 3 artificial datasets were constructed. The first is a spiral with increasing curvature which contains a wide range of curvature values. The second and third contain random tube patterns. First, data on positions and orientations was constructed from our 3D data via the orientation score transform using cake-wavelets [9] with $N_o = 42$. Then the curvature was estimated using the exponential curve fit algorithm from Sect. 4 with $(s_p, s_o) = (2, 0.08), \mu = 0.2$

---

input : $\mathbf{u} : N_x \times N_y \times N_z \times N_o$-array containing the input data.
    L : maximum order of spherical harmonics; initialize $J = j(L, L)$.
    s_o, s_p: scale of angular and spatial regularization.
output: $\mathbf{c}^{\nabla_{\mathbb{R}^3}} : N_x \times N_y \times N_z \times J \times 3$-array containing the spherical harmonic
    coefficients of the gradient.
    $\mathbf{c}^{\mathbf{H}_{\mathbb{R}^3}} : N_x \times N_y \times N_z \times J \times 3 \times 3$-array containing the spherical
    harmonic coefficients of the spatial Hessian.
    $\mathbf{c}^{\tilde{V}} : N_x \times N_y \times N_z \times J$-array containing the spherical harmonic
    coefficients of $\tilde{V}$.
Approximation by spherical harmonics;
$\mathbf{M} := $ Eq. (14); $\mathbf{M}^+ := \left(\mathbf{M}^\dagger \mathbf{M}\right)^{-1} \mathbf{M}^\dagger$;
for *all positions* $\mathbf{x}$ **do**
| $\mathbf{c}(\mathbf{x}, \cdot) = \mathbf{M}^+ \mathbf{U}(\mathbf{x}, \cdot)$;
end
Angular Regularization Eq. (15);
for *all positions* $\mathbf{x}$ *and all* j **do**
| $\mathbf{c}(\mathbf{x}, j) = \mathbf{c}(\mathbf{x}, j) e^{-l_j(l_j+1)s_o}$;
end
Spatial Derivatives and Spatial Regularization;
for *all* j **do**
| $\mathbf{c}^{\nabla_{\mathbb{R}^3}}(\cdot, j) := $ Eq. (17) (using Mathematica's GaussianFilter);
| $\mathbf{c}^{\mathbf{H}_{\mathbb{R}^3}}(\cdot, j) := $ Eq. (18) (using Mathematica's GaussianFilter);
| $\mathbf{c}^{\tilde{V}}(\cdot, j) := $ Eq. (19) (using Mathematica's GaussianFilter);
end

Algorithm 1. Preparation

---

input : $\mathbf{c}^{\nabla_{\mathbb{R}^3}}, \mathbf{c}^{\mathbf{H}_{\mathbb{R}^3}}, \mathbf{c}^{\tilde{V}}$: see output Algorithm 1.
    $\mathbf{n} : N_x \times N_y \times N_z \times N_o$-array containing the input orientations.
output: $\mathbf{H} : N_x \times N_y \times N_z \times N_o \times 6 \times 6$-array containing the Hessian.
Calculate Hessian;
for *all positions* $\mathbf{x}$ *and all orientations* i **do**
| Initialize Rotation;
| $\mathbf{R}(\mathbf{x}, i) := \mathbf{R}^0_{\mathbf{n}(\mathbf{x}, i)}$;
| Spatial Derivatives;
| $\mathbf{H}_{\mathbb{R}^3} := $ Eq. (18) with input $\mathbf{c}^{\mathbf{H}_{\mathbb{R}^3}}(\mathbf{x}, \cdot)$ and $\mathbf{n}(\mathbf{x}, i)$;
| $\mathbf{H}_{spat} := \mathbf{R}^T(\mathbf{x}, i) \mathbf{H}_{\mathbb{R}^3} \mathbf{R}(\mathbf{x}, i)$ (Eq. (21));
| $(\mathcal{A}_1, \mathcal{A}_2, \mathcal{A}_3) := $ Eq. (22) with input $\mathbf{c}^{\nabla_{\mathbb{R}^3}}(\mathbf{x}, \cdot)$ and $\mathbf{R}(\mathbf{x}, i)$;
| Angular Derivatives;
| $(\mathcal{A}_4, \mathcal{A}_5, \mathcal{A}_4\mathcal{A}_4, \mathcal{A}_4\mathcal{A}_5, \mathcal{A}_5\mathcal{A}_5) := $ Eqs. (23), (24) with input $\mathbf{c}^{\tilde{V}}(\mathbf{x}, \cdot)$ and
| $\mathbf{n}(\mathbf{x}, i)$;
| Mixed Derivatives;
| $\begin{pmatrix} \mathcal{A}_1\mathcal{A}_4 & \mathcal{A}_1\mathcal{A}_5 \\ \mathcal{A}_2\mathcal{A}_4 & \mathcal{A}_2\mathcal{A}_5 \\ \mathcal{A}_3\mathcal{A}_4 & \mathcal{A}_3\mathcal{A}_5 \end{pmatrix} := $ Eq. (27) with input $\mathbf{c}^{\nabla_{\mathbb{R}^3}}(\mathbf{x}, \cdot)$ and $\mathbf{n}(\mathbf{x}, i)$;
| Combine;
| $(\mathbf{H})(\mathbf{x}, i) := $ Eq. (20);
end

Algorithm 2. Hessian

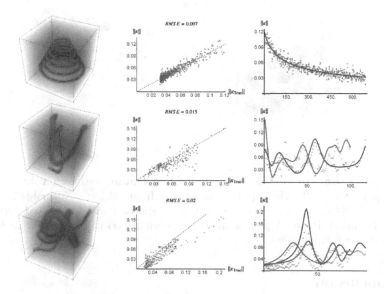

Fig. 2. Fit results on artificial datasets for $\sigma_{\text{Noise}} = 0.1$. Left: The data before adding noise. On a subset of points the spatial part of the fitted curves are shown (blue lines). Middle: Scatter plot of ground truth vs estimated curvatures. Right: Ground truth curvature at the selected points (lines) and estimated curvature (points) for the different structures represented by the different colors. RMSE: root-mean-square error. (Color figure online)

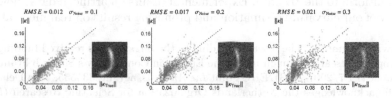

Fig. 3. Scatter plot of ground truth vs estimated curvatures for different amounts of noise. In these plots, the data from all four datasets is combined. Also a 2D slice through dataset 3 is shown for the different noise levels.

and $L = 5$, followed by Eq. (8). We compared estimated curvatures to the ground truth curvatures, see Fig. 2. A high correlation is observed between ground truth and estimated curvature. In the left column we also show in each figure the spatial projection of the fitted exponential curves.

To test the robustness to noise of our method, we added different levels of Gaussian noise to our data, see Fig. 3, with σ_{Noise} ranging from 0.1 to 0.3. The data has a Gaussian tube profile which has a maximum value of one.

Finally, we show some preliminary results of curvature estimation on magnetic resonance angiography data which can be valuable in 3D vessel biomarkers [3]. Visual inspection shows that the measured curvature is high at locations where the vessels are highly curved, see Fig. 4.

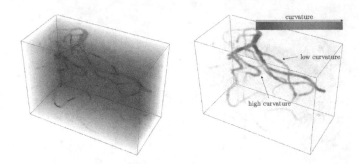

Fig. 4. Voxel-wise exponential curve fits for curvature estimation in 3D MR-anigography data. Left: The input patch (taken from subject "Normal-002" of the public database [3]). On a selection of points the spatial part of the fitted curves are shown (blue lines). Right: A plot of the corresponding curvature values at each voxel in color. (Color figure online)

6 Conclusion

We presented a method for calculating a Gaussian regularized Hessian of axially symmetric functions on the roto-translation group $SE(3)$ obtained from data on positions and orientations. After expressing our data in spherical harmonics, all computations are exact. Furthermore, we used this Hessian in curvature estimation of tubular structures in 3D data after first applying an orientation score transform to the 3D data. Experimental results on artificial data show high accuracy of our curvature estimation and promising results on real medical data.

Acknowledgements. The research leading to these results has received funding from the European Research Council under the European Community's Seventh Framework Programme (FP7/2007-2013)/ERC grant *Lie Analysis*, agr. nr. 335555. Tom Dela Haije gratefully acknowledges the Netherlands Organization for Scientific Research (NWO, No. 617.001.202) for financial support.

References

1. Bekkers, E.J., Zhang, J., Duits, R., ter Haar Romeny, B.M.: Curvature based biomarkers for diabetic retinopathy via exponential curve fits in SE(2). In: Proceedings of the Ophthalmic Medical Image Analysis Second International Workshop, pp. 113–120 (2015)
2. Boscain, U., Chertovskih, R.A., Gauthier, J.P., Remizov, A.O.: Hypoelliptic diffusion and human vision: a semidiscrete new twist. SIAM J. Imaging Sci. **7**(2), 669–695 (2014)
3. Bullitt, E., Zeng, D., Gerig, G., Aylward, S., Joshi, S., Smith, J.K., Lin, W., Ewend, M.G.: Vessel tortuosity and brain tumor malignancy: a blinded study. Acad. Radiol. **12**(10), 1232–1240 (2005)
4. Chirikjian, G.S., Kyatkin, A.B.: Engineering Applications of Noncommutative Harmonic Analysis: With Emphasis on Rotation and Motion Groups. CRC Press, Boca Raton (2000)

5. Creusen, E.J., Duits, R., Dela Haije, T.C.J.: Numerical schemes for linear and non-linear enhancement of DW-MRI. In: Bruckstein, A.M., Haar Romeny, B.M., Bronstein, A.M., Bronstein, M.M. (eds.) SSVM 2011. LNCS, vol. 6667, pp. 14–25. Springer, Heidelberg (2012). doi:10.1007/978-3-642-24785-9_2
6. Duits, R., Janssen, M.H.J., Hannink, J., Sanguinetti, G.R.: Locally adaptive frames in the roto-translation group and their applications in medical imaging. JMIV **56**(3), 367–402 (2016)
7. Eshagh, M.: Alternative expressions for gravity gradients in local north-oriented frame and tensor spherical harmonics. Acta Geophys. **58**(2), 215–243 (2009)
8. Frangi, A.F., Niessen, W.J., Vincken, K.L., Viergever, M.A.: Multiscale vessel enhancement filtering. In: Wells, W.M., Colchester, A., Delp, S. (eds.) MICCAI 1998. LNCS, vol. 1496, pp. 130–137. Springer, Heidelberg (1998). doi:10.1007/BFb0056195
9. Janssen, M., Duits, R., Breeuwer, M.: Invertible orientation scores of 3D images. In: Aujol, J.-F., Nikolova, M., Papadakis, N. (eds.) SSVM 2015. LNCS, vol. 9087, pp. 563–575. Springer, Cham (2015). doi:10.1007/978-3-319-18461-6_45
10. Savadjiev, P., Campbell, J.S.W., Pike, G.B., Siddiqi, K.: 3D curve inference for diffusion MRI regularization and fibre tractography. MIA **10**(5), 799–813 (2006)
11. Savadjiev, P., Strijkers, G.J., Bakermans, A.J., Piuze, E., Zucker, S.W., Siddiqi, K.: Heart wall myofibers are arranged in minimal surfaces to optimize organ function. PNAS **109**(24), 9248–9253 (2012)
12. Zweck, J., Williams, L.R.: Euclidean group invariant computation of stochastic completion fields using Shiftable-twistable functions. JMIV **21**(2), 135–154 (2004)

Semi-calibrated Near-Light Photometric Stereo

Yvain Quéau$^{(\boxtimes)}$, Tao Wu, and Daniel Cremers

Department of Informatics, Technical University of Munich, Munich, Germany
{yvain.queau,tao.wu,cremers}@tum.de

Abstract. We tackle the nonlinear problem of photometric stereo under close-range pointwise sources, when the intensities of the sources are unknown (so-called semi-calibrated setup). A variational approach aiming at robust joint recovery of depth, albedo and intensities is proposed. The resulting nonconvex model is numerically resolved by a provably convergent alternating minimization scheme, where the construction of each subproblem utilizes an iteratively reweighted least-squares approach. In particular, manifold optimization technique is used in solving the corresponding subproblems over the rank-1 matrix manifold. Experiments on real-world datasets demonstrate that the new approach provides not only theoretical guarantees on convergence, but also more accurate geometry.

1 Introduction

Photometric stereo [1] (PS) is a classic inverse problem arising from computer vision. It consists in estimating the shape and the reflectance of a surface, given $m \geq 2$ images $I^i : \mathbb{R}^2 \to \mathbb{R}$, $i \in [1, m]$, of this surface obtained from the same angle, but under varying lighting $\mathbf{s}^i$, $i \in [1, m]$. Figure 1 shows two PS images, and the 3D-reconstruction result obtained by the proposed approach.

Traditional PS methods assume that the lighting is induced by **infinitely distant point light sources**. Under this assumption, vector $\mathbf{s}^i \in \mathbb{R}^3$ represents a uniform light beam whose direction is that of the i-th source, and whose norm is related to its intensity $\phi^i > 0$. It is usually assumed that **the sources intensities are known**. From the user perspective, relaxing both these assumptions has two advantages: assuming close-range sources allows using low-cost lighting devices such as LEDs, and assuming unknown sources intensities (semi-calibrated PS) simplifies the calibration procedure.

Fully *uncalibrated* (*i.e.*, unknown intensities and locations of the sources) close-range photometric stereo has been studied in a few papers [2–4]. Nevertheless, calibration of the sources locations can easily be achieved using specular spheres [5], and assuming known sources locations considerably simplifies the numerical resolution. On the other hand, calibration of the sources intensities is not so easy, since they are relative to the radiometric parameters of the camera [6]. Hence, *semi-calibrated* close-range photometric stereo represents an interesting intermediate case: it retains the advantage of using known locations, but it is robust to uncontrolled radiometric variations, which allows for instance using the camera in "auto-exposure" mode.

This work was supported by the ERC Consolidator Grant "3D Reloaded".

© Springer International Publishing AG 2017
F. Lauze et al. (Eds.): SSVM 2017, LNCS 10302, pp. 656–668, 2017.
DOI: 10.1007/978-3-319-58771-4_52

Fig. 1. Left: 2 out of $m = 8$ images of a plaster statuette. Each image is acquired while turning on one different nearby LED with calibrated position and orientation, but uncalibrated intensity. Right: result of our semi-calibrated PS approach, which automatically estimates the shape, the reflectance (mapped on the 3D-reconstruction on the rightest figure) and the intensities.

However, existing methods for semi-calibrated PS [6,7] are restricted to distant sources. In addition, the semi-calibrated PS approach from [6] lacks robustness, as it is based on non-robust least-squares. The recent method in [7] solves this issue by resorting to a non-convex variational formulation: in the present paper we use the same numerical framework, but extend it to the case of nearby sources. Apart from fully uncalibrated ones [2–4], methods for PS with non-distant sources do not refine the intensities, and sometimes lack robustness. For instance, the near-light PS approach from [3] is based on least-squares, and it alternatively estimates the normals and integrates them into a depth map, which may be a source of drift. These issues are solved in [4] by using l^p-norm optimization, $p < 1$, to ensure robustness, and by treating the normals and the depth as two different entities. Still, the normals and the depth should correspond to the same geometry, hence approaches estimating directly the global geometry may be better suited. This is achieved in [8] by mesh deformation, yet again in a least-squares framework. PDE methods have also been suggested in [9]. The resulting Fast Marching-based numerical scheme is the only provably convergent strategy for near-light PS, yet it is restricted to the $m = 2$ images case, thus it has been recently replaced by variational methods in [10]. Still, this ratio-based procedure has several drawbacks: it results in a combinatorial number of equations to solve (limiting the approach to few and small images), it does not provide the albedo, and it biases the solution in shadowed areas.

Hence, there is still a need for a near-light PS method which is robust, provably convergent, and able to estimate the intensities. Our aim is to fill this gap. The proposed approach relies on a new variational formulation of PS under close-range sources, which is detailed in Sect. 2. Section 3 proposes an alternating minimization strategy to tackle the nonconvex variational model numerically. The construction of each subproblem utilizes the iteratively reweighted least-squares method. Convergence analysis on the generic version of the proposed algorithm is conducted in Sect. 4. Section 5 demonstrates an empirical evaluation of the new method, and Sect. 6 summarizes our achievements.

2   Variational Model for Semi-calibrated Near-Light PS

Photometric Model. Assuming $m \geq 3$ images of a Lambertian surface, the graylevel in a pixel $\mathbf{p} \in \mathbb{R}^2$ conjugate to a surface point $\mathbf{x} \in \mathbb{R}^3$ is given by:

$$I^i(\mathbf{p}) = \tilde{\rho}(\mathbf{x})\phi^i \left\{\mathbf{s}^i(\mathbf{x}) \cdot \mathbf{n}(\mathbf{x})\right\}_+, \ i \in [1, m], \tag{1}$$

where:

- $\tilde{\rho}(\mathbf{x}) > 0$ is the albedo in $\mathbf{x}$ (unknown);
- $\phi^i > 0$ represents the intensity of the i-th light source (unknown);
- $\mathbf{s}^i(\mathbf{x}) \in \mathbb{R}^3$ is a vector representing the i-th incident lighting (see Eq. (3));
- $\mathbf{n}(\mathbf{x}) \in \mathbb{S}^2 \subset \mathbb{R}^3$ is the outgoing normal vector to the surface in $\mathbf{x}$ (unknown);
- $\{\cdot\}_+$ encodes self-shadows (cf. Fig. 2-b), and it is defined as follows:

$$\{t\}_+ = \max\{t, 0\}. \tag{2}$$

We consider the imperfect Lambertian light source model, representing the i-th source by the parameters $\{\mathbf{n}_s^i, \mathbf{x}_s^i, \mu^i, \phi^i\}$, where $\mathbf{n}_s^i \in \mathbb{S}^2$ is the (unit-length) principal direction of the source, $\mathbf{x}_s^i \in \mathbb{R}^3$ is its location, $\mu^i > 0$ is its anisotropy parameter and $\phi^i > 0$ is its unknown intensity. Apart from ϕ^i, all the sources parameters are assumed to be known: anisotropy is provided by the manufacturer, the locations of the sources can be estimated by using reflective spheres [4,5], and their orientations can be deduced from images of a plane [5]. Vector $\mathbf{s}^i(\mathbf{x})$ in Eq. (1) is then written as follows:

$$\mathbf{s}^i(\mathbf{x}) = \left(\mathbf{n}_s^i \cdot \left[\frac{\mathbf{x} - \mathbf{x}_s^i}{\|\mathbf{x} - \mathbf{x}_s^i\|}\right]\right)^{\mu^i} \frac{1}{\|\mathbf{x} - \mathbf{x}_s^i\|^2} \frac{[\mathbf{x}_s^i - \mathbf{x}]}{\|\mathbf{x} - \mathbf{x}_s^i\|}, \ \forall i \in [1, m], \tag{3}$$

where the first factor represents attenuation due to anisotropy, the second factor stands for attenuation due to distance (inverse-of-square falloff), and the third one gives the unit-length lighting direction. This is illustrated in Fig. 2-a.

Geometric Setup. Under perspective projection, the conjugation relationship between $\mathbf{x}$ and $\mathbf{p} = [x, y]^\top$ reads as:

$$\mathbf{x}(x, y) = \tilde{z}(x, y)\mathbf{K}^{-1} [x, y, 1]^\top, \tag{4}$$

with $\tilde{z} : \Omega \subset \mathbb{R}^2 \to \mathbb{R}$ the depth map over the reconstruction domain Ω, and $\mathbf{K}$ the (calibrated) intrinsics matrix [11]:

$$\mathbf{K} = \begin{bmatrix} f_x & s & x_0 \\ 0 & f_y & y_0 \\ 0 & 0 & 1 \end{bmatrix}. \tag{5}$$

The normal vector $\mathbf{n}(\mathbf{x})$ in Eq. (1) is the unit-length vector proportional to $\partial_x \mathbf{x}(x, y) \times \partial_y \mathbf{x}(x, y)$. Using (4) and introducing the logarithmized depth $z = \log \tilde{z}$, we obtain after some algebra:

$$\mathbf{n}(\mathbf{x}) = \frac{1}{d(\mathbf{p}; z(\mathbf{p}))}\mathbf{J}(\mathbf{p})^\top \begin{bmatrix} \nabla z(\mathbf{p}) \\ -1 \end{bmatrix}, \tag{6}$$

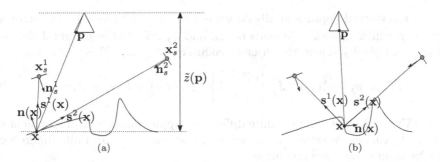

Fig. 2. (a) Near-light PS setup. Surface point $\mathbf{x}$ is conjugate to pixel $\mathbf{p}$ according to the pinhole camera model (4), where $\tilde{z}(\mathbf{p})$ is the unknown depth. According to Eq. (3), the lighting in $\mathbf{x}$ induced by the first source is strongly attenuated by anisotropy, while that induced by the second source is strongly attenuated by the distance to the source. (b) Pixel $\mathbf{p}$ appears shadowed in both images I^1 and I^2, because $\mathbf{x}$ is self-shadowed w.r.t. the first light source ($\mathbf{s}^1(\mathbf{x}) \cdot \mathbf{n}(\mathbf{x}) < 0$), and the second light source is occluded by the surface (cast-shadow). The first case is handled by our model (Eq. (2)), and the second one is treated as an outlier within a robust estimation framework (Eq. (12)).

where we denote:

$$z(\mathbf{p}) = \log \tilde{z}(\mathbf{p}), \ \mathbf{J}(\mathbf{p}) = \begin{bmatrix} f_x & -s & -(x - x_0) \\ 0 & f_y & -(y - y_0) \\ 0 & 0 & 1 \end{bmatrix}, \ d(\mathbf{p}; z(\mathbf{p})) = \left\| \mathbf{J}(\mathbf{p})^\top \begin{bmatrix} \nabla z(\mathbf{p}) \\ -1 \end{bmatrix} \right\|.$$
(7)

Discrete Variational Model. Instead of estimating the albedo $\tilde{\rho}(\mathbf{p})$ in each pixel $\mathbf{p}$, we follow [7] and rather estimate the following "pseudo"-albedo:

$$\rho(\mathbf{p}) := \frac{\tilde{\rho}(\mathbf{p})}{d(\mathbf{p}, z(\mathbf{p}))},$$
(8)

which eliminates the nonlinearity due to the denominator. Once the scaled albedo and the depth map are estimated, the "real" albedo is easily deduced.

Combining Eqs. (1), (6), (7) and (8), photometric model (1) is turned into the following system of nonlinear PDEs in $(\rho : \Omega \to \mathbb{R}, z : \Omega \to \mathbb{R}, \{\phi^i \in \mathbb{R}\}_i)$:

$$I^i(\mathbf{p}) = \phi^i \rho(\mathbf{p}) \left\{ [\mathbf{J}(\mathbf{p})\mathbf{s}^i(\mathbf{p}; z(\mathbf{p}))]^\top \begin{bmatrix} \nabla z(\mathbf{p}) \\ -1 \end{bmatrix} \right\}_+, \ \forall i \in [1, m], \ \forall \mathbf{p} \in \Omega, \quad (9)$$

where $\mathbf{s}^i(\mathbf{p}; z(\mathbf{p}))$ stands for $\mathbf{s}^i(\mathbf{x})$ as defined in Eq. (3), knowing that $\mathbf{x}$ depends on z and $\mathbf{p}$ according to Eq. (4), and where we denote from now on $\rho(\mathbf{p})$ instead of $\rho(\mathbf{x})$, knowing that there exists a bijection between $\mathbf{x}$ and $\mathbf{p}$ (Eq. (4)).

Instead of continuous images $I^i : \Omega \to \mathbb{R}$, we are given a finite list of graylevels over a discrete subset Ω of a 2D grid. Let us denote $j = 1 \ldots n$ the corresponding pixel indices, I^i_j the graylevel at pixel j in image I^i, $\mathbf{z} \in \mathbb{R}^n$ and

$\rho \in \mathbb{R}^n$ the stacked depth and albedo values, $\mathbf{s}_j^i(z_j) \in \mathbb{R}^3$ the lighting vector $\mathbf{s}^i$ at pixel j, which smoothly depends on z_j, and $\mathbf{J}_j \in \mathbb{R}^{3\times 3}$ the matrix $\mathbf{J}$ defined in Eq. (7) at pixel j. Then, the discrete counterpart of Eq. (9) is written as:

$$I_j^i = \phi^i \rho_j \left\{ (\mathbf{s}_j^i(z_j))^\top \mathbf{J}_j^\top \begin{bmatrix} (\nabla \mathbf{z})_j \\ -1 \end{bmatrix} \right\}_+ , \quad \forall i \in [1, m], \; \forall j \in [1, n], \qquad (10)$$

where $(\nabla \mathbf{z})_j \in \mathbb{R}^2$ represents a finite differences approximation of the gradient of z at pixel j (in our implementation, we used first-order forward finite differences with Neumann boundary conditions).

Our goal is to jointly estimate the albedo values $\rho \in \mathbb{R}^n$, the depth values $\mathbf{z} \in \mathbb{R}^n$ and the intensities $\phi \in \mathbb{R}^m$ from the set of nonlinear Eq. (10). Let $\mathcal{M}$ be the set of all rank-1 n-by-m matrices (known to be a smooth manifold [12]), $T_{\mathcal{M}}(\boldsymbol{\theta})$ the tangent space of $\mathcal{M}$ at $\boldsymbol{\theta}$, and $\mathcal{P}_{T_{\mathcal{M}}(\boldsymbol{\theta})}(\cdot)$ the (linear) projection onto $T_{\mathcal{M}}(\boldsymbol{\theta})$. By introducing the rank-1 matrix $\boldsymbol{\theta} \in \mathcal{M}$ such that $\theta_j^i \equiv \phi^i \rho_j$, we consider the following discrete optimization problem:

$$\min_{\mathbf{z}, \boldsymbol{\theta}: \boldsymbol{\theta} \in \mathcal{M}} F(\boldsymbol{\theta}, \mathbf{z}) = \sum_{j=1}^{n} \sum_{i=1}^{m} \Phi\left(r_j^i(\boldsymbol{\theta}, \mathbf{z})\right). \qquad (11)$$

Here, Φ is a robust estimator (possibly non-convex), *e.g.* Cauchy's estimator:

$$\Phi(x) = \lambda^2 \log(1 + x^2/\lambda^2) \qquad (12)$$

for some user-defined parameter $\lambda > 0$ (in our implementation $\lambda = 0.1$). We also define

$$r_j^i(\boldsymbol{\theta}, \mathbf{z}) = \theta_j^i \left\{ \Psi_j^i(\mathbf{z}) \right\}_{+,\delta} - I_j^i, \qquad \Psi_j^i(\mathbf{z}) = (\mathbf{s}_j^i(z_j))^\top \mathbf{J}_j^\top \begin{bmatrix} \nabla \mathbf{z})_j \\ -1 \end{bmatrix},$$

where it is convenient to avoid non-differentiability by smoothing $\{\cdot\}_+$ with

$$\{t\}_{+,\delta} = \begin{cases} t - \delta/2 & \text{if } t \geq \delta, \\ t^2/(2\delta) & \text{if } 0 \leq t < \delta, \\ 0 & \text{otherwise,} \end{cases}$$

for some $\delta > 0$. If $\delta = 0$, we regain $\{\cdot\}_{+,\delta} = \{\cdot\}_+$.

3   Optimization

Now we present a generic scheme which minimizes the nonconvex model (11) alternatively over variables $\boldsymbol{\theta}$ and $\mathbf{z}$. In each subproblem, we solve a local quadratic model of (11) with positive definite approximation of the Hessian. A backtracking line search is then performed to guarantee a sufficient descent in the objective. In particular, we note that in the $\boldsymbol{\theta}$-subproblem the rank-1 constraint is handled *implicitly*, and the resulting subproblem represents a weighted least-squares problem over the rank-1 matrix manifold. In the sequel, $\langle \cdot, \cdot \rangle$ denotes scalar product for either vectors or vectorized matrices.

Algorithm 1. (alternating minimization scheme)

Require: $\varepsilon, \delta > 0$.

1: Initialize $\mathbf{z}^{(0)} \in \mathbb{R}^n$, $\boldsymbol{\theta}^{(0)} \in \mathbb{R}^{n \times m}$ with $\boldsymbol{\theta}^{(0)} \in \mathcal{M}$.

2: **for** $k \in \{0, 1, 2, \dots\}$ **do**

3:    Choose a positive definite linear operator $H_\theta^{(k,k)} : \mathbb{R}^{n \times m} \to \mathbb{R}^{n \times m}$. Let $\widehat{\boldsymbol{\theta}}_{(k)}(\tau_\theta)$ be a local minimizer of the following problem:

$$\min_{\boldsymbol{\theta} \in \mathcal{M}} \; \tau_\theta \left\langle \frac{\partial F}{\partial \boldsymbol{\theta}}(\boldsymbol{\theta}^{(k)}, \mathbf{z}^{(k)}), \boldsymbol{\theta} - \boldsymbol{\theta}^{(k)} \right\rangle + \frac{1}{2} \left\langle \boldsymbol{\theta} - \boldsymbol{\theta}^{(k)}, H_\theta^{(k,k)}(\boldsymbol{\theta} - \boldsymbol{\theta}^{(k)}) \right\rangle. \quad (13)$$

4:    Set $\boldsymbol{\theta}^{(k+1)} := \widehat{\boldsymbol{\theta}}_{(k)}(\tau_\theta^{(k)})$, where $\tau_\theta^{(k)}$ is the largest element in $\{1, 1/2, 1/4, \dots\}$ satisfying the following descent condition:

$$F(\widehat{\boldsymbol{\theta}}_{(k)}(\tau_\theta^{(k)}), \mathbf{z}^{(k)}) \le F(\boldsymbol{\theta}^{(k)}, \mathbf{z}^{(k)}) - \varepsilon \|\widehat{\boldsymbol{\theta}}_{(k)}(\tau_\theta^{(k)}) - \boldsymbol{\theta}^{(k)}\|^2. \quad (14)$$

5:    Choose a positive definite linear operator $H_z^{(k+1,k)} : \mathbb{R}^n \to \mathbb{R}^n$. Let $\widehat{\mathbf{z}}_{(k)}(\tau_z)$ be the (global) minimizer of the following problem:

$$\min_{\mathbf{z}} \; \tau_z \left\langle \frac{\partial F}{\partial \mathbf{z}}(\boldsymbol{\theta}^{(k+1)}, \mathbf{z}^{(k)}), \mathbf{z} - \mathbf{z}^{(k)} \right\rangle + \frac{1}{2} \left\langle \mathbf{z} - \mathbf{z}^{(k)}, H_z^{(k+1,k)}(\mathbf{z} - \mathbf{z}^{(k)}) \right\rangle. \quad (15)$$

6:    Set $\mathbf{z}^{(k+1)} := \widehat{\mathbf{z}}_{(k)}(\tau_z^{(k)})$, where $\tau_z^{(k)}$ is the largest element in $\{1, 1/2, 1/4, \dots\}$ satisfying the following descent condition:

$$F(\boldsymbol{\theta}^{(k+1)}, \widehat{\mathbf{z}}_{(k)}(\tau_z^{(k)})) \le F(\boldsymbol{\theta}^{(k+1)}, \mathbf{z}^{(k)}) - \varepsilon \|\widehat{\mathbf{z}}_{(k)}(\tau_z^{(k)}) - \mathbf{z}^{(k)}\|^2. \quad (16)$$

7:    **if** the stopping criterion is satisfied **then**

8:       **return** $\boldsymbol{\theta}^{(k+1)}, \mathbf{z}^{(k+1)}$.

The iterates generated by the above algorithm are guaranteed to converge (subsequentially) to a critical point of the problem (11); see detailed analysis in Sect. 4.

Yet, the practical efficiency of the overall algorithm hinges on the choices of the scaling matrices $H_\theta^{(k,k)}$ and $H_z^{(k+1,k)}$ and the subroutines for solving (13) and (15). In this work, our choices for $H_\theta^{(k,k)}$ and $H_z^{(k+1,k)}$ (see formulas (18) and (21) below) will be structured Hessian approximations motivated from the iteratively reweighted least-squares (IRLS) method [13, 14]. The solution of the resulting sub-problem can be interpreted as a regularized Newton step; see [15–17].

For the ease of presentation, we introduce the following notations:

$$(r^{(\tilde{k},k)})_j^i = r_j^i(\boldsymbol{\theta}^{(\tilde{k})}, \mathbf{z}^{(k)}), \qquad (w^{(\tilde{k},k)})_j^i = \Phi'((r^{(\tilde{k},k)})_j^i)/(r^{(\tilde{k},k)})_j^i,$$

$$(\Psi^{(k)})_j^i = \Psi_j^i(\mathbf{z}^{(k)}), \qquad (\chi^{(k)})_j^i = \left\{\Psi_j^i(\mathbf{z}^{(k)})\right\}'_{+,\delta},$$

where $\tilde{k}$ is either k or $k+1$. Note that

$$\left(\frac{\partial F}{\partial \boldsymbol{\theta}}(\boldsymbol{\theta}^{(k)}, \mathbf{z}^{(k)})\right)_j^i = (w^{(k,k)})_j^i (r^{(k,k)})_j^i \left\{(\Psi^{(k)})_j^i\right\}_{+,\delta}. \tag{17}$$

By choosing $H_\theta^{k,k}$ such that

$$\left\langle \boldsymbol{\theta}, H_\theta^{(k,k)}\boldsymbol{\theta}\right\rangle = \sum_{j=1}^n \sum_{i=1}^m (w^{(k,k)})_j^i \left(\left\{(\Psi^{(k)})_j^i\right\}_{+,\delta} \theta_j^i\right)^2, \tag{18}$$

for all $\boldsymbol{\theta} \in \mathbb{R}^{n \times m}$, the $\boldsymbol{\theta}$-subproblem (13) with $\tau_\theta = 1$ is equivalent to the following weighted least-squares problem:

$$\min_{\boldsymbol{\theta} \in \mathcal{M}} \sum_{j=1}^n \sum_{i=1}^m (w^{(k,k)})_j^i \left|\left\{(\Psi^{(k)})_j^i\right\}_{+,\delta} \theta_j^i - I_j^i\right|^2. \tag{19}$$

Analogously for the $\mathbf{z}$-subproblem, we note that

$$\frac{\partial F}{\partial \mathbf{z}}(\boldsymbol{\theta}^{(k+1)}, \mathbf{z}^{(k)}) = \sum_{j=1}^n \sum_{i=1}^m (w^{(k+1,k)})_j^i (r^{(k+1,k)})_j^i (\boldsymbol{\theta}^{(k+1)})_j^i (\chi^{(k)})_j^i (\Psi_j^i)'(\mathbf{z}^{(k)}),$$

$$\tag{20}$$

and choose $H_z^{(k+1,k)}$ such that

$$\left\langle \mathbf{z}, H_z^{(k+1,k)}\mathbf{z}\right\rangle = \sum_{j=1}^n \sum_{i=1}^m (w^{(k+1,k)})_j^i \left((\boldsymbol{\theta}^{(k+1)})_j^i (\chi^{(k)})_j^i \mathbf{z}^\top (\Psi_j^i)'(\mathbf{z}^{(k)})\right)^2, \tag{21}$$

for all $\mathbf{z} \in \mathbb{R}^n$. As a result, the $\mathbf{z}$-subproblem (15) with $\tau_z = 1$ becomes

$$\min_{\mathbf{z}} \sum_{j=1}^n \sum_{i=1}^m (w^{(k+1,k)})_j^i \left|(r^{(k+1,k)})_j^i + (\boldsymbol{\theta}^{(k+1)})_j^i (\chi^{(k)})_j^i (\mathbf{z} - \mathbf{z}^{(k)})^\top (\Psi_j^i)'(\mathbf{z}^{(k)})\right|^2.$$

$$\tag{22}$$

We remark that $H_\theta^{(k,k)}$ and $H_z^{(k+1,k)}$ above are only sure to be positive semi-definite. To enforce their (uniform) positive definiteness along iterations (as being assumed in the convergence theory), one may always add cI (with arbitrarily small $c > 0$) to $H_\theta^{(k,k)}$ and $H_z^{(k+1,k)}$. This, however, seems unnecessary according to our numerical experiments.

In addition, it is empirically observed that $\tau_z^{(k)} = 1$ and $\tau_z^{(k)} = 1$ are always accepted by the backtracking line search, *i.e.* Steps 4 and 6 of Algorithm 1, for certain small ε even if δ is set zero. Thus, in practice, Algorithm 1 reduces to the following alternating reweighted least-squares (ARLS) scheme.

Algorithm 2. (alternating reweighted least-squares scheme)

Require: $\delta = 0$.
1: Initialize $\mathbf{z}^{(0)} \in \mathbb{R}^n$, $\boldsymbol{\theta}^{(0)} \in \mathbb{R}^{n \times m}$ with $\boldsymbol{\theta}^{(0)} \in \mathcal{M}$.
2: **for** $k \in \{0, 1, 2, \dots\}$ **do**
3:     Compute $\boldsymbol{\theta}^{(k+1)}$ as an approximate (local) solution of (19).
4:     Compute $\mathbf{z}^{(k+1)}$ as an approximate solution of (22).
5:     **if** the stopping criterion is satisfied **then**
6:         **return** $\boldsymbol{\theta}^{(k+1)}, \mathbf{z}^{(k+1)}$.

Concerning the subproblem solvers in Steps 3 and 4 of Algorithm 2, (22) can be solved by conjugate gradient iterations. Meanwhile, (19) represents the least-squares problem over the rank-1 matrix manifold, for which a local minimizer is pursued by a simple Riemannian gradient descent scheme in Algorithm 3. We refer to [18] for possibly more efficient numerical schemes for the same purpose.

Algorithm 3. (weighted rank-1 pursuit)

Require: $W_j^i := (w^{(k,k)})_j^i \left\{ (\Psi^{(k)})_j^i \right\}_{+,\delta}^2$, $Y_j^i := I_j^i / \max\left(\left\{ (\Psi^{(k)})_j^i \right\}_{+,\delta}, \epsilon \right)$, $\tau :=$
$1/\|W\|$, $\boldsymbol{\theta}^{(k)} \in \mathcal{M}$.
1: Initialize $s^{(0)} u^{(0)} (v^{(0)})^\top = \boldsymbol{\theta}^{(k)}$ for some $s^{(0)} > 0$ and unit vectors $u^{(0)} \in \mathbb{R}^n$, $v^{(0)} \in \mathbb{R}^m$,
2: **for** $l \in \{0, 1, 2, \dots\}$ **do**
3:     Set $(\bar{G}^{(l)})_j^i := W_j^i (s^{(l)} u_j^{(l)} v_i^{(l)} - Y_j^i)$.
4:     Set $G^{(l)} := u^{(l)} (u^{(l)})^\top \bar{G}^{(l)} + \bar{G}^{(l)} v^{(l)} (v^{(l)})^\top - u^{(l)} (u^{(l)})^\top \bar{G}^{(l)} v^{(l)} (v^{(l)})^\top$.
5:     Compute $\delta s^{(l)} := -(u^{(l)})^\top G^{(l)} v^{(l)}$, $\delta u^{(l)} := (-G^{(l)} v^{(l)} - u^{(l)} \delta s^{(l)})/s^{(l)}$, and $\delta v^{(l)} := (-(G^{(l)})^\top u^{(l)} - v^{(l)} \delta s^{(l)})/s^{(l)}$.
6:     Compute $s^{(l+1)} := s^{(l)} + \tau \delta s^{(l)}$, $u^{(l+1)} := u^{(l)} + \delta u^{(l)}/(1/\tau + \delta s^{(l)}/s^{(l)})$, $v^{(l+1)} := v^{(l)} + \delta v^{(l)}/(1/\tau + \delta s^{(l)}/s^{(l)})$.
7:     **if** the stopping criterion is satisfied **then**
8:         **return** $\boldsymbol{\theta}^{(k+1)} := s^{(l)} u^{(l)} (v^{(l)})^\top$.

4   Convergence Analysis

This section is devoted the convergence analysis of the Algorithm 1. We shall assume that the iterates $\{(\boldsymbol{\theta}^{(k)}, \mathbf{z}^{(k)})\}$ are contained in a bounded subset over which both $\frac{\partial F}{\partial \boldsymbol{\theta}}$ and $\frac{\partial F}{\partial \mathbf{z}}$ are Lipschitz continuous. We also assume that $\{\boldsymbol{\theta}^{(k)}\}$ are uniformly bounded away from 0, thus avoiding the pathological case of having 0 as a limit point. In addition, there exist constants $c, C > 0$ such that $cI \preceq H_{\boldsymbol{\theta}}^{(k,k)} \preceq CI$ and $cI \preceq H_z^{(k+1,k)} \preceq CI$ for all k. Without loss of generality, let $\frac{\partial F}{\partial \boldsymbol{\theta}}(\boldsymbol{\theta}^{(k)}, \mathbf{z}^{(k)})$ and $\frac{\partial F}{\partial \mathbf{z}}(\boldsymbol{\theta}^{(k+1)}, \mathbf{z}^{(k)})$ be nonzero throughout the iterations.

Lemma 1. *The admissible step sizes $\tau_{\boldsymbol{\theta}}^{(k)}$ and $\tau_z^{(k)}$ in Algorithm 1 can be found in finitely many trials.*

Proof. We only prove the case for $\tau_\theta^{(k)}$, since the other case is analogous (if not easier). Define

$$\kappa(\tau_\theta) = F(\widehat{\boldsymbol{\theta}}_{(k)}(\tau_\theta), \mathbf{z}^{(k)}) - F(\boldsymbol{\theta}^{(k)}, \mathbf{z}^{(k)}) + \varepsilon\|\widehat{\boldsymbol{\theta}}_{(k)}(\tau_\theta) - \boldsymbol{\theta}^{(k)}\|^2.$$

Note that $\widehat{\boldsymbol{\theta}}_{(k)}(0) = \boldsymbol{\theta}^{(k)}$, $\kappa(0) = 0$, and $\kappa'(0) = \left\langle \frac{\partial F}{\partial \boldsymbol{\theta}}(\boldsymbol{\theta}^{(k)}, \mathbf{z}^{(k)}), \widehat{\boldsymbol{\theta}}'_{(k)}(0) \right\rangle$. It suffices to show $\kappa'(0) < 0$.

Since $\widehat{\boldsymbol{\theta}}_{(k)}(\tau_\theta)$ is a local minimizer of (13), it must hold that

$$\tau_\theta \frac{\partial F}{\partial \boldsymbol{\theta}}(\boldsymbol{\theta}^{(k)}, \mathbf{z}^{(k)}) + H_\theta^{(k,k)}(\widehat{\boldsymbol{\theta}}_{(k)}(\tau_\theta) - \boldsymbol{\theta}^{(k)}) + \eta(\tau_\theta) = 0, \tag{23}$$

where $\eta(\tau_\theta)$ belongs to the normal space of $\mathcal{M}$ at $\widehat{\boldsymbol{\theta}}_{(k)}(\tau_\theta)$ for all $\tau_\theta \geq 0$ and $\eta(0) = 0$. By differentiating (23) at $\tau_\theta = 0$, and since $\eta'(0) = 0$, we obtain

$$\frac{\partial F}{\partial \boldsymbol{\theta}}(\boldsymbol{\theta}^{(k)}, \mathbf{z}^{(k)}) + H_\theta^{(k,k)}\widehat{\boldsymbol{\theta}}'_{(k)}(0) = 0. \tag{24}$$

It follows that $\kappa'(0) = -\left\langle \frac{\partial F}{\partial \boldsymbol{\theta}}(\boldsymbol{\theta}^{(k)}, \mathbf{z}^{(k)}), (H_\theta^{(k,k)})^{-1}\frac{\partial F}{\partial \boldsymbol{\theta}}(\boldsymbol{\theta}^{(k)}, \mathbf{z}^{(k)}) \right\rangle < 0$. $\square$

Theorem 1. *The iterates $\{(\boldsymbol{\theta}^{(k)}, \mathbf{z}^{(k)})\}$ generated by Algorithm 1 satisfy*

$$\liminf_{k\to\infty} \mathcal{P}_{T_\mathcal{M}(\boldsymbol{\theta}^{(k)})}\left(\frac{\partial F}{\partial \boldsymbol{\theta}}(\boldsymbol{\theta}^{(k)}, \mathbf{z}^{(k)})\right) = 0, \quad \liminf_{k\to\infty} \frac{\partial F}{\partial \mathbf{z}}(\boldsymbol{\theta}^{(k)}, \mathbf{z}^{(k)}) = 0.$$

Proof. Again, we only prove $\liminf_{k\to\infty} \mathcal{P}_{T_\mathcal{M}(\boldsymbol{\theta}^{(k)})}\left(\frac{\partial F}{\partial \boldsymbol{\theta}}(\boldsymbol{\theta}^{(k)}, \mathbf{z}^{(k)})\right) = 0$. Since $F(\boldsymbol{\theta}^{(k)}, \mathbf{z}^{(k)}) \leq F(\boldsymbol{\theta}^{(k+1)}, \mathbf{z}^{(k)}) \leq F(\boldsymbol{\theta}^{(k+1)}, \mathbf{z}^{(k+1)})$ for all k and $F(\cdot, \cdot)$ is bounded from below, we have $\lim_{k\to\infty}\|\boldsymbol{\theta}^{(k+1)} - \boldsymbol{\theta}^{(k)}\| = 0$. For brevity, we denote $g_\theta^{(k)} = \frac{\partial F}{\partial \boldsymbol{\theta}}(\boldsymbol{\theta}^{(k)}, \mathbf{z}^{(k)})$ in the remainder of the proof.

We first consider the case where $\liminf_{k\to\infty} \tau_\theta^{(k)} > 0$. In particular, the identity in (23) yields

$$\mathcal{P}_{T_\mathcal{M}(\boldsymbol{\theta}^{(k+1)})}\left(\tau_\theta^{(k)} g_\theta^{(k)} + H_\theta^{(k,k)}(\boldsymbol{\theta}^{(k+1)} - \boldsymbol{\theta}^{(k)})\right) = 0,$$

and ultimately $\lim_{k\to\infty} \mathcal{P}_{T_\mathcal{M}(\boldsymbol{\theta}^{(k)})}\left(g_\theta^{(k)}\right) = 0$.

Now consider the case $\tau_\theta^{(k)} \to 0$ along a subsequence indexed by $\tilde{k}$. Assume, for the sake of contradiction, that $\left\|\mathcal{P}_{T_\mathcal{M}(\boldsymbol{\theta}^{(k)})}\left(g_\theta^{(k)}\right)\right\|$ is uniformly bounded away from 0. Due to the nature of the backtracking line search, we have

$$F(\widehat{\boldsymbol{\theta}}_{(\tilde{k})}(2\tau_\theta^{(\tilde{k})}), \mathbf{z}^{(\tilde{k})}) - F(\boldsymbol{\theta}^{(\tilde{k})}, \mathbf{z}^{(\tilde{k})}) + \varepsilon\|\widehat{\boldsymbol{\theta}}_{(\tilde{k})}(2\tau_\theta^{(\tilde{k})}) - \boldsymbol{\theta}^{(\tilde{k})}\|^2 > 0,$$

which further implies $2\tau_\theta^{(\tilde{k})}\left\langle g_\theta^{(\tilde{k})}, \widehat{\boldsymbol{\theta}}'_{(\tilde{k})}(0)\right\rangle + o(2\tau_\theta^{(\tilde{k})}) > 0$. Thus, we must have $\liminf_{\tilde{k}\to\infty}\left\langle g_\theta^{(\tilde{k})}, \widehat{\boldsymbol{\theta}}'_{(\tilde{k})}(0)\right\rangle \geq 0$. Recalling (24), we obtain the contradiction:

$$0 \leq \liminf_{\tilde{k}\to\infty}\frac{\left\langle g_\theta^{(\tilde{k})}, \widehat{\boldsymbol{\theta}}'_{(\tilde{k})}(0)\right\rangle}{\left\|\mathcal{P}_{T_\mathcal{M}(\boldsymbol{\theta}^{(\tilde{k})})}\left(g_\theta^{(\tilde{k})}\right)\right\|^2} = \liminf_{\tilde{k}\to\infty} -\frac{\left\langle g_\theta^{(\tilde{k})}, (H_\theta^{(\tilde{k},\tilde{k})})^{-1}g_\theta^{(\tilde{k})}\right\rangle}{\left\|\mathcal{P}_{T_\mathcal{M}(\boldsymbol{\theta}^{(\tilde{k})})}\left(g_\theta^{(\tilde{k})}\right)\right\|^2}$$

$$\leq \limsup_{\tilde{k}\to\infty} -\frac{\left\langle g_\theta^{(\tilde{k})}, (H_\theta^{(\tilde{k},\tilde{k})})^{-1}g_\theta^{(\tilde{k})}\right\rangle}{\left\|\mathcal{P}_{T_\mathcal{M}(\boldsymbol{\theta}^{(\tilde{k})})}\left(g_\theta^{(\tilde{k})}\right)\right\|^2} \leq \limsup_{\tilde{k}\to\infty} -\frac{\left\|g_\theta^{(\tilde{k})}\right\|^2}{C\left\|\mathcal{P}_{T_\mathcal{M}(\boldsymbol{\theta}^{(\tilde{k})})}\left(g_\theta^{(\tilde{k})}\right)\right\|^2} \leq -\frac{1}{C}.$$

This completes the whole proof. □

5 Empirical Evaluation

We first consider the plaster statuette from Fig. 1, and compare existing calibrated near- and distant-light PS methods with the proposed near-light one. For competing methods, we used the calibrated intensities. For the proposed semi-calibrated one, intensities were initially set to the arbitrary (and wrong) values $\phi \equiv 1$. The result of distant-light PS was used as initial guess for the shape and

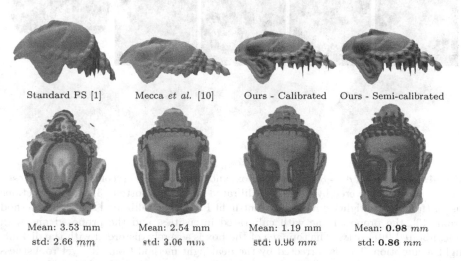

Standard PS [1]	Mecca *et al.* [10]	Ours - Calibrated	Ours - Semi-calibrated
Mean: 3.53 mm	Mean: 2.54 mm	Mean: 1.19 mm	Mean: **0.98** mm
std: 2.66 mm	std: 3.06 mm	std: 0.96 mm	std: **0.86** mm

Fig. 3. Comparison of several 3D-reconstructions obtained by PS. Top: 3D-reconstruction. Bottom: absolute error between the PS reconstruction and laser-scan ground truth (blue is zero, red is > 1 cm. State-of-the-art calibrated near-light PS [10] corrects the bias due to the distant-light assumption [1], yet it remains unsatisfactory in shadowed areas (*e.g.*, the ears), and it requires knowledge of the lighting intensities. Our approach is more robust, and it can be used without calibration of the intensities. (Color figure online)

the albedo, and then the proposed alternating scheme was run until the relative residual of the energy falls below 10^{-3}. Standard PS was used as initialization to accelerate the reconstruction, but we observed that this initalization had no impact on the final result. To evaluate our semi-calibrated method, this initial guess was obtained while assuming wrongly that $\phi \equiv 1$. The proposed method is thus entirely independent from the initial estimates of the intensities.

As shown in Fig. 3, the distant light assumption induces a bias, which is corrected by state-of-the-art calibrated near-light PS [10]. Yet, this result remains unsatisfactory in shadowed areas, because it treats self-shadows as outliers instead of modeling them. Our near-light approach provides more accurate results, because it explicitly accounts for self-shadows (cf. Eq. (1)) and it utilizes a more robust estimator (Cauchy's, instead of the L^1 norm one used in [10]). Interestingly, the semi-calibrated approach is more accurate than the calibrated one: this proves that calibration of intensities always induces a slight bias, which can be avoided by resorting to a semi-calibrated approach.

Figure 4 confirms on another dataset that the proposed method is more robust to shadows than state-of-the-art, because self-shadows are explicitly taken into account in the model and a robust M-estimator is used. Overall, the state-of-the-art is thus advanced both in terms of accuracy, simplicity of the calibration procedure, and convergence analysis.

Fig. 4. Top: 3 out of $m = 8$ images of a box, and 3D-model (3D-reconstruction and estimated albedo) recovered by our semi-calibrated approach. Bottom: 3D-reconstructions using (from left to right) standard distant-light PS [1], the calibrated near-light method from [10], the proposed one with calibrated intensities, and the proposed one with uncalibrated intensities. The top face of the box is severely distorted with the distant-light assumption. This is corrected by the near-light method from [10], yet robustness to shadows is not granted, which biases the 3D-reconstruction of both the other faces. Our approach is robust to shadows (self-shadows are handled in the model), and it removes the need for calibration of the intensities.

6   Conclusion

We have proposed a new variational approach for solving the near-light PS problem in a robust manner, considering unknown lighting intensities (semi-calibrated setup). Our numerical strategy relies on an alternating minimization scheme which builds upon manifold optimization. It is shown to overcome the state-of-the-art in terms of accuracy, while being the first approach to remove the need for intensity calibration and to be provably convergent.

As future work, the proposed approach could be extended to the fully uncalibrated case, by including inside the alternating scheme another step aiming at refining the positions and orientations of the sources.

References

1. Woodham, R.J.: Photometric method for determining surface orientation from multiple images. Opt. Eng. **19**, 139–144 (1980)
2. Koppal, S.J., Narasimhan, S.G.: Novel depth cues from uncalibrated near-field lighting. In: Proceedings of the ICCV (2007)
3. Papadhimitri, T., Favaro, P.: Uncalibrated near-light photometric stereo. In: Proceedings of the BMVC (2014)
4. Liao, J., Buchholz, B., Thiery, J.M., Bauszat, P., Eisemann, E.: Indoor scene reconstruction using near-light photometric stereo. IEEE Trans. Image Process. **26**, 1089–1101 (2017)
5. Nie, Y., Song, Z., Ji, M., Zhu, L.: A novel calibration method for the photometric stereo system with non-isotropic LED lamps. In: Proceedings of the RCAR (2016)
6. Cho, D., Matsushita, Y., Tai, Y.-W., Kweon, I.: Photometric stereo under non-uniform light intensities and exposures. In: Leibe, B., Matas, J., Sebe, N., Welling, M. (eds.) ECCV 2016. LNCS, vol. 9906, pp. 170–186. Springer, Cham (2016). doi:10.1007/978-3-319-46475-6_11
7. Quéau, Y., Wu, T., Lauze, F., Durou, J.D., Cremers, D.: A non-convex variational approach to photometric stereo under inaccurate lighting. In: Proceedings of the CVPR (2017)
8. Xie, W., Dai, C., Wang, C.C.L.: Photometric stereo with near point lighting: a solution by mesh deformation. In: Proceedings of the CVPR (2015)
9. Mecca, R., Wetzler, A., Bruckstein, A.M., Kimmel, R.: Near field photometric stereo with point light sources. SIAM J. Imaging Sci. **7**, 2732–2770 (2014)
10. Mecca, R., Quéau, Y., Logothetis, F., Cipolla, R.: A single-lobe photometric stereo approach for heterogeneous material. SIAM J. Imaging Sci. **9**, 1858–1888 (2016)
11. Hartley, R.I., Zisserman, A.: Multiple View Geometry in Computer Vision, 2nd edn. Cambridge University Press, Cambridge (2004)
12. Koch, O., Lubich, C.: Dynamical lowrank approximation. SIAM J. Matrix Anal. Appl. **29**, 434–454 (2007)
13. Vogel, C.R., Oman, M.E.: Iterative methods for total variation denoising. SIAM J. Sci. Comput. **17**, 227–238 (1996)
14. Chan, T.F., Mulet, P.: On the convergence of the lagged diffusivity fixed point method in total variation image restoration. SIAM J. Numer. Anal. **36**, 354–367 (1999)
15. Nikolova, M., Chan, R.H.: The equivalence of half-quadratic minimization and the gradient linearization iteration. IEEE Trans. Image Process. **16**, 1623–1627 (2007)

16. Hintermüller, M., Wu, T.: Nonconvex TV^q-models in image restoration: analysis and a trust-region regularization-based superlinearly convergent solver. SIAM J. Imaging Sci. **6**, 1385–1415 (2013)
17. Hintermüller, M., Wu, T.: A superlinearly convergent R-regularized Newton scheme for variational models with concave sparsity-promoting priors. Comput. Optim. Appl. **57**, 1–25 (2014)
18. Boumal, N., Mishra, B., Absil, P.A., Sepulchre, R.: Manopt, a Matlab toolbox for optimization on manifolds. J. Mach. Learn. Res. **15**, 1455–1459 (2014)

Shape Matching by Time Integration of Partial Differential Equations

Robert Dachsel$^{(\boxtimes)}$, Michael Breuß, and Laurent Hoeltgen

Institute for Mathematics, Brandenburg Technical University,
Platz der Deutschen Einheit 1, 03046, Cottbus, Germany
{dachsel,breuss,hoeltgen}@b-tu.de

Abstract. The main task in three dimensional shape matching is to retrieve correspondences between two similar three dimensional objects. To this end, a suitable point descriptor which is invariant under isometric transformations is required. A commonly used descriptor class relies on the spectral decomposition of the Laplace-Beltrami operator. Important examples are the heat kernel signature and the more recent wave kernel signature. In previous works, the evaluation of the descriptor is based on eigenfunction expansions. Thereby a significant practical aspect is that computing a complete expansion is very time and memory consuming. Thus additional strategies are usually introduced that enable to employ only part of the full expansion.

In this paper we explore an alternative solution strategy. We discretise the underlying partial differential equations (PDEs) not only in space as in the mentioned approaches, but we also tackle temporal parts by using time integration methods. Thus we do not perform eigenfunction expansions and avoid the use of additional strategies and corresponding parameters. We study here the PDEs behind the heat and wave kernel signature, respectively. Our shape matching experiments show that our approach may lead to quality improvements for finding correct correspondences in comparison to the eigenfunction expansion methods.

Keywords: Shape matching · Point descriptor · Shape analysis · Heat equation · Schrödinger equation

1 Introduction

The shape of a three dimensional geometric object can be described by its bounding surface $\mathcal{M}$. Two shapes may be considered similar if there exists an almost isometric transformation between them. In contrast to isometric transformations, an almost isometric transformation allows small elastic deformations such as stretching and contractions. For shape matching, the geometry of a given shape has to be analysed in order to explore relations between similar shapes. To this end, a point descriptor which captures the geometric information of its surrounding environment for each point on the shape is often employed. Ideally, a point descriptor should be invariant under almost isometric transformations.

© Springer International Publishing AG 2017
F. Lauze et al. (Eds.): SSVM 2017, LNCS 10302, pp. 669–680, 2017.
DOI: 10.1007/978-3-319-58771-4_53

Over the last decades a lot of point descriptors have been presented, however, classic point descriptors are invariant under rigid transformation only. Some examples are Shape Context [3], Spin Images [9], integral volume descriptors [8,14], or the multi-scale local features [10]. More recently, also approaches invariant under isometric transformations have been proposed. For example [11] extended the Shape Context descriptor making use of a geodesic framework, and in [12] the authors proposed a method based on the Möbius transform. Furthermore, spectral descriptors have been introduced which are based on the spectral decomposition of the Laplace-Beltrami operator. In the context of shape analysis these methods were first proposed in [13]. As an extension of that development, the Global Point Signature is constructed in [18] as a point descriptor by associating each point with a l^2 sequence based on the eigenfunctions and the eigenvalues of the Laplace-Beltrami operator. A major drawback of this descriptor is its dependence on the choice of a basis of eigenfunctions. This disadvantage was resolved in [20] by the introduction of the heat kernel signature (HKS). A main point in the construction is the use of fundamental solutions of the heat equation. This yields a series expansion of the heat kernel as an expression for the point descriptor. An important aspect for the geometric interpretation of this approach is that one can determine a connection between the heat kernel and intrinsic distances on a surface via Varadhan's formula [21]. Also a scale invariant version of the HKS was developed [5]. In [1] another point descriptor inspired by equations of theoretical physics was proposed. Based on the Schrödinger equation, the Wave Kernel Signature (WKS) represents the average probability of measuring a quantum mechanical particle at a specific location.

While the signature representation via the use of the eigenfunction expansions appears to be very elegant, in practice heuristics need to be introduced in order to avoid the computation of the full spectrum of corresponding operators, like e.g. a scaling of the time domain as employed in [20].

Our Contributions. In this paper we study to our best knowledge for the first time in the literature point descriptors based on the full numerical integration of the underlying partial differential equations (PDEs). While the eigenfunction expansion methods employ the spatial discretisation of the Laplace-Beltrami operator to account for the shape data, we perform in addition numerical time integration. We consider such integration-based point descriptors corresponding to the heat equation and the Schrödinger equation. In doing this we also study several possible time integrators. In experiments we demonstrate the benefits of our approach. Compared to the kernel based methods we especially observe a substantially higher accuracy in correct one-to-one correspondences at the first match.

2   PDEs and Spectral Point Descriptors

In this section we first recall briefly the PDEs used in this work. As indicated, these are the *heat equation* and the *Schrödinger equation*. The common property of both equations is that their spatial derivatives take the form of the Laplace operator when considering the Euclidean plane. In order to respect the curvature of a shape in 3D, techniques from differential geometry are employed [7]. The resulting Laplace-Beltrami operator is defined on smooth surfaces $\mathcal{M}$.

In this context, let us recall that for a given parameterisation of a surface, the Laplace-Beltrami operator can be expressed in local coordinates (ξ, η):

$$\Delta_{\mathcal{M}} u = \frac{1}{\sqrt{|g|}} \left(\partial_\xi \left(\frac{G \, \partial_\xi \tilde{u} - F \, \partial_\eta \tilde{u}}{\sqrt{|g|}} \right) + \partial_\eta \left(\frac{E \, \partial_\eta \tilde{u} - F \, \partial_\xi \tilde{u}}{\sqrt{|g|}} \right) \right) \tag{1}$$

where E, G and F are the coefficients of the metric tensor and $|g|$ represents its determinant. Further, $\tilde{u}$ is the function u expressed in local coordinates.

After presenting the PDEs, we also summarise the mechanism of the spectral eigenfunction expansion methods that are employed for comparison to our approach.

The Geometric Heat Equation. The heat equation

$$\partial_t u(x, t) = \Delta_{\mathcal{M}} \, u(x, t) \tag{2}$$

describes how a heat distribution $u(x, t)$ would propagate along a surface $\mathcal{M}$. In that regard, $x \in \mathcal{M}$ denotes the spacial component and $t \geq 0$ is the time. For $t = 0$, an initial heat distribution $u(x, 0)$ represents the initial condition.

The Geometric Schrödinger Equation. The free time-dependent Schrödinger equation

$$\partial_t u(x, t) = i \Delta_{\mathcal{M}} \, u(x, t) \tag{3}$$

allows to study how a free and massive quantum particle would move on the surface $\mathcal{M}$. In quantum mechanics, the dynamic of a particle is described by its complex wave function $u(x, t)$. This wave function is interpreted as the probability amplitude, and can be used to represent the probability density for finding the particle on the corresponding surface point at time t. The initial condition $u(x, 0)$ is a Gaussian wave packet. In contrast to the heat equation, the Schrödinger equation allows non-decaying oscillatory solutions.

The Spectral Methods. As an example for the spectral methods, the solution of the heat equation at time t can be expressed as convolution of the heat kernel $k_t(x, x')$ with the initial condition:

$$u(x, t) = \int_{\mathcal{M}} k_t(x, x') \, u(x', 0) \, dx' \tag{4}$$

According to the spectral decomposition of the Laplace-Beltrami operator, the heat kernel can be expressed as

$$k_t(x, x') = \sum_{i=1}^{\infty} e^{-\lambda_i t} \phi_i(x) \phi_i(x') \tag{5}$$

where λ_i are the (ordered) eigenvalues and ϕ_i the corresponding eigenfunctions. The quantity [20]

$$\mathrm{HKS}(x,t) = k_t(x,x) = \sum_{i=1}^{\infty} e^{-\lambda_i t} \phi_i^2(x) \tag{6}$$

describes the amount of heat present at point x at time t.

In [20], the authors proposed to associate each point x on the surface with a vector sampled at a finite set of times $t_1, \ldots, t_k$. This point descriptor is called the Heat Kernel Signature. The Wave Kernel Signature [1] can be written as:

$$\mathrm{WKS}(x,e) = C_e \sum_{i=1}^{\infty} \phi_i^2(x) e^{\frac{-(e-\log E_i)^2}{2\sigma^2}} \tag{7}$$

where a logarithmic energy scale e was introduced, the variance is denoted by σ and C_e represents a normalization factor.

As indicated, in contrast to this framework, we will construct a point descriptor by direct discretisation of the underlying PDEs.

3   Discretisation Aspects

In a first step, a discrete approximation of the underlying, continuous and closed surface has to be obtained. A suitable surface representation is given by a triangular mesh. In more detail, a triangulated surface is given by the tuple $\mathcal{M}_d = (P, E)$. The point cloud $P = \{p_1, \ldots, p_N\}$ contains the number of coordinate points a shape consist of. The edges E contain the neighborhood relations between the coordinate points. The entire mesh can be formed by connecting the coordinate points p_i so that one obtains two-dimensional triangular cells.

Many schemes have been proposed to estimate the Laplace-Beltrami operator for a triangular meshed surface [2,16,17]. A commonly used method is the cotangent weight scheme introduced in [15]. The authors present a formal derivation using the mixed Finite-Element/Finite-Volume paradigm. As a result, for a function $u(p_j)$ defined on a triangular mesh the discrete Laplace-Beltrami operator reduces to the following simple form:

$$\Delta_{\mathcal{M}} u(p_j) \approx \frac{1}{2A_j} \sum_{i \in N_j} (\cot \alpha_{ij} + \cot \beta_{ij})(u(p_i) - u(p_j)) \tag{8}$$

where N_j denotes the set of points adjacent to p_j, and A_j represents the barycentric area of the cell that corresponds to p_j. Furthermore, α_{ij} and β_{ij} denote the two angles opposite to the edge (i,j), for details we refer to the mentioned source. The arising formulae can be transfered into matrix notation:

$$L_{ij} = \begin{cases} -\frac{1}{2A_j} \sum\limits_{i \in N_j} (\cot \alpha_{ij} + \cot \beta_{ij}), & \text{if } i = j \\ \frac{1}{2A_j}(\cot \alpha_{ij} + \cot \beta_{ij}), & \text{if } i \neq j \text{ and } i \in N_j \\ 0, & \text{else} \end{cases} \tag{9}$$

where $L \in \mathbb{R}^{N \times N}$.

In the next step, the discrete representation of the time derivative $\partial_t u(p_j, t)$ has to be defined. In this paper we study the following, natural choices [19]:

$$\text{forward:} \qquad \frac{u(t + \tau, p_j) - u(t, p_j)}{\tau} =: \frac{u_j^{k+1} - u_j^k}{\tau} \qquad (10)$$

$$\text{backward:} \qquad \frac{u(t, p_j) - u(t - \tau, p_j)}{\tau} =: \frac{u_j^k - u_j^{k-1}}{\tau} \qquad (11)$$

$$\text{centered:} \qquad \frac{u(t + \tau, p_j) - u(t - \tau, p_j)}{2\tau} =: \frac{u_j^{k+1} - u_j^{k-1}}{2\tau} \qquad (12)$$

where τ denotes the time increment.

3.1 Some Details on Our Approach

For time integration, we replace the differential operators by its approximations as above. The vector $u^k = (u_1^k, \ldots, u_N^k)^T$ contains the spatial components from the kth time layer with $k = 1, \ldots, M$ and M being the number of time samples. For u^1, the initial heat point distribution and the initial wave packet are approximated by the discrete Dirac delta function $\delta_{p_j}(p)$, respectively. Thus we obtain three different time integration schemes.

Explicit Time Integration (FT Method). We approximate the time derivative by the forward difference, i.e. for the heat equation we obtain

$$\frac{u^{k+1} - u^k}{\tau} = L u^k \quad \Leftrightarrow \quad u^{k+1} = (I + \tau L) u^k \qquad (\text{FT+H})$$

and for the Schrödinger equation we have analogously

$$\frac{u^{k+1} - u^k}{\tau} = i L u^k \quad \Leftrightarrow \quad u^{k+1} = (I + i\tau L) u^k \qquad (\text{FT+S})$$

With these relations, and knowing the values of u^k at time k, we compute the corresponding values at time $k + 1$ by simple matrix-vector multiplication. This explicit scheme is known to be just conditionally stable. The stability requirement yields a limitation on the size of the time increment τ.

Implicit Time Integration (BT Method). Now the time derivative is approximated by the backward difference, i.e. for the heat equation this gives us

$$\frac{u^k - u^{k-1}}{\tau} = L u^k \quad \Leftrightarrow \quad (I - \tau L) u^{k+1} = u^k \qquad (\text{BT+H})$$

and for the Schrödinger equation one obtains analogously

$$\frac{u^k - u^{k-1}}{\tau} = i L u^k \quad \Leftrightarrow \quad (I - i\tau L) u^{k+1} = u^k \qquad (\text{BT+S})$$

Computing values at time $k+1$ requires here solving a system of linear equations at each time step. Therefore, for the same time step size, it is more numerically intensive than the explicit method. The considerable advantage is that the scheme is theoretically numerically stable independently of the time step size.

Centered in Time Integration (CT Method). We now approximate the time derivative by the central difference, so that we have for the heat equation

$$\frac{u^{k+1} - u^k}{2(\tau/2)} = Lu^{k+\frac{1}{2}} \quad \Leftrightarrow \quad \left(I - \frac{\tau}{2}L\right)u^{k+1} = \left(I + \frac{\tau}{2}L\right)u^k \qquad \text{(CT+H)}$$

and for the Schrödinger equation

$$\frac{u^{k+1} - u^k}{2(\tau/2)} = iLu^{k+\frac{1}{2}} \quad \Leftrightarrow \quad \left(I - \frac{i\tau}{2}L\right)u^{k+1} = \left(I + \frac{i\tau}{2}L\right)u^k \qquad \text{(CT+S)}$$

The centered in time scheme is, as the previous scheme, an implicit method. To obtain values at time $k+1$ it requires solving a system of linear equations as well as a matrix-vector multiplication in each time step. Therefore, it is numerically more intensive than the other investigated time integration methods, but it is the only one of these methods that has second-order accuracy in time.

Discrete Point Descriptor. From the solution $u(p,t)$ of the discretised PDEs the point descriptors at the location $p = p_i$ can be extracted as follows:

$$f_i(t) := u(p,t)|_{p=p_i} = (|u(p_i, t_1)|, \dots, |u(p_i, t_M)|)^\top \qquad (13)$$

The approximated solution is then considered at the point p_i, i.e. where the initial condition is triggered.

Let us note that there exists a physical interpretation of the point descriptors. The heat based point descriptor describes the rate of heat transfered away from the considered point p_i. Since the heat will always move from the hot initial spot to colder spots, the spectrum is monotonically decreasing. The Schrödinger based point descriptor gives the square root of the probability as a function of time to meet a quantum particle at the considered point p_i. As time progresses, the particle is more and more delocalised on the entire surface. Therefore, it becomes more improbable to meet the particle at the single point p_i. This is the reason why the spectrum is decreasing over time.

In comparison of the processes, the heat equation does not model interference effects as does the Schrödinger equation. However, the interference phenomenon may give the point descriptor a more unique signature, which leads us to conjecture that Schrödinger based methods may be superior to heat based methods in shape matching applications. For two selected points, the point descriptor for both equations and its application for point retrieval is illustrated in Fig. 1.

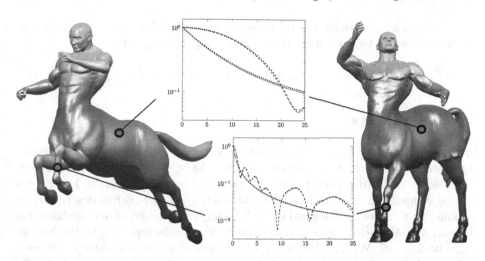

Fig. 1. The almost isometric centaur shapes and its point signature computed by backward time integration at the marked spots. The heat equation (solid) and Schrödinger equation (dashed) are resolved on the initial shape. Its counterpart descriptor on the deformed shapes is dotted.

4   The Shape Matching Process

Let us consider two isometric or almost isometric and triangular meshed surfaces $\mathcal{M}_d = (P, E)$ and $\tilde{\mathcal{M}}_d = (\tilde{P}, E)$ as given. We call $\mathcal{M}_d$ the initial shape because we are able to allocate a fixed labeling to its points $P = \{p_1, ..., p_N\}$. For a fixed labeling $p_i \subset P$ the assignment map

$$\text{match} : P \to \tilde{P}, i \mapsto j \tag{14}$$

gives $\tilde{p}_j \in \tilde{P}$ a label on the deformed shape, and the points with the same index belong together. Therefore we write

$$p_i \leftrightarrow \tilde{p}_j \Leftrightarrow \text{match}(i) = j \tag{15}$$

if p_i and $\tilde{p}_j$ describe the same point on $\mathcal{M}_d$ and $\tilde{\mathcal{M}}_d$.

This is the moment were the feature descriptors come into play. We employ the time evolution of the heat and Schrödinger equation to define an intrinsic descriptor, respectively.

The dynamics described by those equations is influenced by the intrinsic distance. For $f_i(t)$ and $\tilde{f}_j(t)$ the distance in feature space is measured by:

$$d(f_i, \tilde{f}_j)(t) := \frac{1}{M}\|f_i(t) - \tilde{f}_j(t)\|_1 = \frac{1}{M} \sum_{k=0}^{M} |f_i(t_k) - \tilde{f}_j(t_k)| \tag{16}$$

The points with the smallest feature distance should belong together. This condition can be written as a minimisation problem for all points:

$$p_i \leftrightarrow \tilde{p}_j \quad \Leftrightarrow \quad \text{match}(i) = \arg\min_j \left\{ d(f_i, \tilde{f}_j)(t) \right\} \tag{17}$$

5 Experiments

In the following we present a quantitative evaluation showing that the proposed time integration methods in combination with the heat and Schrödinger equation are in some interesting aspects superior to kernel based descriptors. For experimental comparison we considered the state-of-the-art wave kernel descriptor. Its parameters were set as described in [1]. The implementation of our methods was done in Matlab and the sparse linear system was prefactorised with the SuiteSparse package [6]. Without further run time optimisations our setup yields computational times in the order of up to a few minutes depending on the shape size on our hardware (Intel Core i7-3770 CPU with 4× 3.40 GHz and 7.7 GB RAM).

Evaluation Strategy. In our experimental setup the matching is known. As a quality criterion we define the *hit rate* by counting the percentage of correct matchings. In detail, the evaluation follows a procedure similar in logic to the one described in [1]:

- For both shapes $\mathcal{M}$ and $\tilde{\mathcal{M}}$ we compute the point descriptor for each point in a fixed time interval. After computation, a set of point descriptors $\{f_i(t)\}_{i=1}^N$ on initial shape and a set of point descriptors $\{\tilde{f}_i(t)\}_{i=1}^N$ on the matching deformed shape can be obtained.
- Starting with the first point descriptor $f_1(t)$ on the initial shape, the distances (16) are computed with respect to all point descriptors on the deformed shape. This leads to a set of distances $\{d(f_1, \tilde{f}_j)(t)\}_{j=1}^N$.
- The k smallest distances $\arg\min_j \left\{ d(f_1, \tilde{f}_j)(t) \right\}$ are taken and if the correct correspondence is among these k best matches, then the matching was successful.
- We proceed with the second point descriptor $f_2(t)$ on the initial shape and repeat the computation steps until $f_N(t)$.
- We visualise the hit rat showing the dependence on correspondences at the *first match*, $k = 1$, or the percentage of best matchings $100 \cdot k/N$.

For a point descriptor, let us note that it is a very challenging task to ensure correct correspondences at the first match $k = 1$.

Results of Quantitative Comparison. In the first experiment we will compare matching precision of the time integration methods and the WKS for an almost isometric shape matching scenario. For the experiment eight horse shapes are used, taken from the TOSCA data set [4], available in the public domain.

The time increment $\tau = 1$ was fixed for all experiments. In order to fulfill the stability condition for the explicit time integration scheme, the entire shapes were scaled by a factor of 10 for this method.

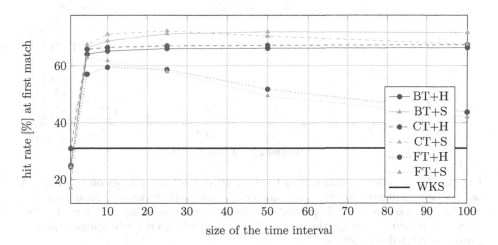

Fig. 2. Hit rate at the first best match as a function of the time interval size on the TOSCA horse shapes. Even for small time interval sizes of $T \geq 5$ the precision of the time integration methods is clearly superior to that of the WKS. The WKS descriptor with constant 100 evaluation steps is shown for reference

The evaluation in Fig. 2 shows that the matching precision of the time integration methods is superior to that of the WKS for already small time interval sizes $T \geq 5$ for the first match. This is a highly relevant aspect for computational efficiency. For small T the point descriptor contains geometric information of the local neighborhood. For larger time sizes the hit rate goes into saturation for the backward method and deteriorates for the forward/central method.

By comparing the several scheme combinations, the backward time integration with the Schrödinger equation gains best results by finding about 72% of correspondences. For medium times $5 \leq T \leq 25$ the centered in time integration of the Schrödinger equation is the best combination. The explicit time integration methods loose precision rapidly with increasing T.

In Fig. 3 the hit rate for increasing values of $100 \cdot k/N$ is shown. For values less then 0.1%, the backward time method with the Schrödinger equation clearly beats the WKS descriptor.

Evaluation of Robustness to Noise. In the second experiment two wolf shapes from the TOSCA data set are taken. On the deformed wolf shape an additional perturbation in form of an uniformly distributed number $rd \in (-a, a)$ to each coordinate point is added where the perturbation parameter is set to the range from $a = 0$ to $a = 0.3$. This simulates a given noisy data set which

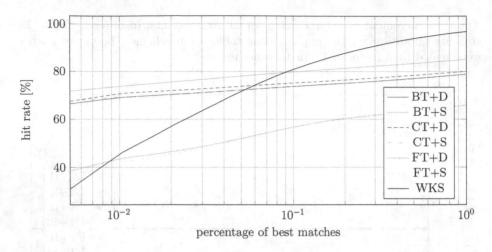

Fig. 3. The hit rate at points among the first 1% of the best matches on the TOSCA horse shapes is illustrated here. The time integration methods were evaluated for $T = 100$. In the total, the WKS descriptor benefits from this evaluation technique. For less then 0.1% of best matchings, the backward time method with the Schrödinger equation beats the WKS descriptor.

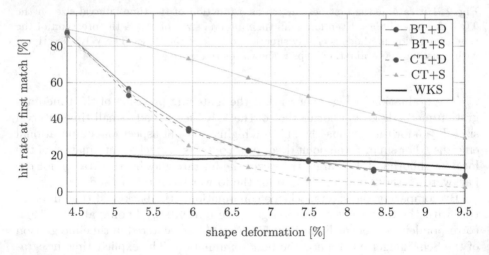

Fig. 4. Hit rate at the first best match as a function of the increasing the shape deformation on the TOSCA wolf shapes. The time integration methods were evaluated for $T = 100$.

could arise by measurement of point coordinates. The deformation strength of the two shapes can be expressed by the intrinsic area. We introduce the shape deformation $100 \cdot |A - \tilde{A}|/A$, where A and $\tilde{A}$ are the respective surface sizes of the shapes, normalised with respect to the initial shape.

As shown in Fig. 4 the precision of the hit rate deteriorates with increasing noise, as expected. The backward time integration in combination with the

Schrödinger equation gains the best results on the noisy dataset. In comparison, the WKS descriptor has a lower accuracy but performs somewhat more stable under noise as precision deteriorates more slowly when increasing the noise.

6   Summary and Conclusion

Based on the heat and Schrödinger equation we introduced a novel point descriptor class based on time integration methods. Experimental results confirm that our approach has a higher precision to find correct correspondences at the first match. This holds in particular for the implicit backward method integrating the Schrödinger equation. Therefore our approach is good for applications were a point descriptor with a high matching precision for the first matching is needed. Further, we demonstrated that the backward Schrödinger method gains a superior matching precision to that of the WKS for additional noise of strength up to 9.5% of the area of the initial shape which is a considerable noise level.

Let us point out here that for comparison we employed the WKS with all the heuristics proposed in [1], while in our approach a generic time step size was chosen and no further steps beyond the suitable discretisation of the model were taken. With a suitable fine tuning of numerical parameters we conjecture that we could obtain even better results.

References

1. Aubry, M., Schlickewei, U., Cremers, D.: The wave kernel signature: a quantum mechanical approach to shape analysis. In: IEEE Computer Vision Workshops (ICCV Workshops), pp. 1626–1633 (2011)
2. Belkin, M., Sun, J., Wang, Y.: Discrete laplace operator on meshed surfaces, pp. 278–287 (2008)
3. Belongie, S., Malik, J., Puzicha, J.: Shape context: a new descriptor for shape matching and object recognition. In: Advances in Neural Information Processing Systems, pp. 831–837 (2000)
4. Bronstein, A.M., Bronstein, M.M., Kimmel, R.: Numerical Geometry of Non-rigid Shapes. Springer, New York (2009)
5. Bronstein, M., Kokkinos, I.: Scale-invariant heat kernel signatures for non-rigid shape recognition. In: Proceedings of the International Conference on Computer Vision and Pattern Recognition, pp. 1704–1711 (2010)
6. Davis, T.A.: Algorithm 930: FACTORIZE: an object-oriented linear system solver for MATLAB. ACM Trans. Math. Softw. **39**(4), 1–18 (2013)
7. DoCarmo, M.P.: Differential Geometry of Curves and Surfaces: Revised and Updated Second Edition. Dover Puplications, New York (2016)
8. Gelfand, N., Mitra, N.J., Guibas, L.J., Pottmann, H.: Robust global registration. In: Proceedings of the Third Eurographics Symposium on Geometry Processing, pp. 197–206 (2005)
9. Johnson, A., Herbert, M.: Using spin images for efficient object recognition in cluttered 3D scenes. IEEE Trans. Pattern Anal. Mach. Intell. **21**(5), 433–449 (1999)

10. Li, X., Guskov, I.: Multi-scale features for approximate alignment of pointbased surfaces. In: Proceedings of the Third Eurographics Symposium on Geometry Processing, pp. 217–226 (2005)
11. Ling, H., Jacobs, D.: Shape classification using the inner-distance. IEEE Trans. Pattern Anal. Mach. Intell. **29**(2), 286–299 (2007)
12. Lipman, Y., Funkhouser, T.: Möbius voting for surface correspondence. ACM Trans. Graph. **28**(3), 1–12 (2009)
13. Lévy, B.: Laplace-beltrami eigenfunctions towards an algorithm that 'understands' geometry. In: International Conference on Shape Modeling and Applications (2006)
14. Manay, S., Hong, B.-W., Yezzi, A.J., Soatto, S.: Integral invariant signatures. In: Pajdla, T., Matas, J. (eds.) ECCV 2004. LNCS, vol. 3024, pp. 87–99. Springer, Heidelberg (2004). doi:10.1007/978-3-540-24673-2_8
15. Meyer, M., Desbrun, M., Schröder, P., Barr, A.H.: Discrete differential-geometry operators for triangulated 2-manifolds. In: Hege, H.C., Polthier, K. (eds.) Visualization and Mathematics III, pp. 35–57. Springer, Heidelberg (2002)
16. Pinkall, U., Polthier, K.: Computing discrete minimal surfaces and their conjugates. Exp. Math. **2**(1), 15–36 (1993)
17. Reuter, M., Wolter, F.E., Peinecke, N.: Laplace-beltrami spectra as shape-DNA of surfaces and solids. Comput.-Aided Des. **38**(4), 342–366 (2006)
18. Rustamov, R.: Laplace-beltrami eigenfunctions for deformation invariant shape representation. In: Symposium on Geometry Processing, pp. 225–233 (2007)
19. Strauss, W.A.: Partial Differential Equations: An Introduction, 2nd edn. Wiley, Hoboken (2007)
20. Sun, J., Ovsjanikov, M., Guibas, L.: A concise and provably informative multi-scale signature based on heat diffusion. Comput. Graph. Forum **28**(5), 1383–1392 (2009)
21. Varadhan, S.R.S.: On the behaviour of the fundamental solution of the heat equation with variable coefficients. Commun. Pure Appl. Math. **20**, 431–455 (1967)

Subspace Least Squares Multidimensional Scaling

Amit Boyarski[1]([✉]), Alex M. Bronstein[1,2,3], and Michael M. Bronstein[2,3,4]

[1] Technion, Haifa, Israel
{amitboy,bron}@cs.technion.ac.il
[2] Tel-Aviv University, Tel Aviv, Israel
michael.bronstein@usi.ch
[3] Intel Perceptual Computing, Haifa, Israel
[4] University of Lugano, Lugano, Switzerland

Abstract. Multidimensional Scaling (MDS) is one of the most popular methods for dimensionality reduction and visualization of high dimensional data. Apart from these tasks, it also found applications in the field of geometry processing for the analysis and reconstruction of non-rigid shapes. In this regard, MDS can be thought of as a *shape from metric* algorithm, consisting of finding a configuration of points in the Euclidean space that realize, as isometrically as possible, some given distance structure. In the present work we cast the least squares variant of MDS (LS-MDS) in the spectral domain. This uncovers a multiresolution property of distance scaling which speeds up the optimization by a significant amount, while producing comparable, and sometimes even better, embeddings.

Keywords: Multidimensional scaling · SMACOF · Majorization · Multi-resolution · Spectral regularization · Canonical forms

1 Introduction

Multidimensional Scaling (MDS) is one of the most popular techniques for dimensionality reduction, whose purpose is to represent dissimilarities between objects as distances between points in a low dimensional space. Since its invention in the 50's by Torgerson [31] within the field of psychometrics, it has been used in diverse fields including sociology, marketing, and colorimetry, to name a few [5, 22]. More recently, MDS has found applications in the field of geometry processing, in such tasks as analysis and synthesis of non-rigid shapes [6, 8]. In this regard, MDS can be thought of as a *shape from metric* algorithm, consisting of finding a configuration of points in the Euclidean space that realize, as isometrically as possible, some given distance structure. Least squares Multidimensional Scaling (LS-MDS) is a particular MDS model which seeks a low

© Springer International Publishing AG 2017
F. Lauze et al. (Eds.): SSVM 2017, LNCS 10302, pp. 681–693, 2017.
DOI: 10.1007/978-3-319-58771-4_54

dimensional Euclidean embedding by minimizing a geometrically meaningful criterion, namely the *Kruskal stress*

$$\sigma(\mathbf{X}) = \sum_{i<j} w_{ij} \left(\|\mathbf{x}_i - \mathbf{x}_j\| - d_{ij}\right)^2. \tag{1}$$

Here d_{ij} is a (symmetric) measure of dissimilarity between two sample points i and j; $w_{ij} > 0$ is a (symmetric) weight assigned to the pairwise term between those samples, and $\mathbf{X} \in \mathbb{R}^{N \times m}$ are the coordinates of the low-dimensional Euclidean embedding. Since (1) is a nonlinear non-convex function, a variety of nonlinear optimization techniques have been employed for its minimization, often resulting in local minima whose quality crucially depends on the initialization. Of these techniques, one of the most popular approaches is the SMACOF algorithm discovered by de-Leeuw [12], which stands for Scaling by Majorizing a Complicated Function. SMACOF is essentially a gradient based method, which suffers from the typical slow convergence associated with first order optimization methods. To supplement on this, a single iteration of SMACOF requires the computation of the Euclidean pairwise distances between all points participating in the optimization at their current configuration, a time consuming task on its own, which limits its application to small size data.

A related family of methods with the same goal in mind, confusingly called classical (multidimensional) scaling, aims at finding a low-dimensional Euclidean embedding $\mathbf{X} \in \mathbb{R}^{N \times m}$ by minimizing the following algebraic criterion called *strain*

$$s(\mathbf{X}) = \|\mathbf{X}\mathbf{X}^{\mathrm{T}} - \frac{1}{2}\mathbf{H}^{\mathrm{T}}\mathbf{D}\mathbf{H}\|_{\mathrm{F}}^2 \tag{2}$$

where $\mathbf{H} = \mathbf{I} - \frac{1}{n}\mathbf{1}\mathbf{1}^{\mathrm{T}}$ is a *double centering matrix* transforming a Euclidean squared-distance matrix $\mathbf{D}$ into a Gram matrix of inner products by fixing the origin, and $\mathbf{1}$ denotes the vector of ones. If $\mathbf{D}$ is a Euclidean squared-distance matrix between points in $\mathbb{R}^n$, $\frac{1}{2}\mathbf{H}^{\mathrm{T}}\mathbf{D}\mathbf{H}$ is a Gram matrix of rank n, and can be faithfully approximated by a Gram matrix of lower rank. However, if $\mathbf{D}$ is not a Euclidean squared-distance matrix, one can only hope that it is indeed well approximated by a low-rank Gram matrix after applying the double centering transformation.

Though (2) is not convex, it can be minimized globally by eigendecomposition techniques. On top of being expensive to apply, these techniques require the availability of the complete matrix $\mathbf{D}$, which may be time consuming in the best case, or impossible to obtain in the worst case. Iterative methods can also be used for strain minimization [10], which allows the incorporation of weights and missing distances, at the expense of losing the global convergence guarantees. Due to the lack of geometric intuition behind it, strain minimization results in inferior embeddings [15] and has some other drawbacks. For example, classical scaling exhibits large sensitivity to outliers since the double centering transformation spreads the effect of a single outlier to the rest of the points in the same row/column.

Contribution. Our work leverages the recent trend in geometry processing of using the truncated eigenbasis of the Laplace-Beltrami operator (LBO) to approximate smooth functions on manifolds. This favorable representation has been shown to improve classical scaling methods by orders of magnitude [2], as well as other key problems in geometry processing, e.g. non-rigid shape correspondence [23]. By constraining the embedding to an affine subspace spanned by the leading eigenvectors of the Laplace-Beltrami operator, we show that LS-MDS exhibits a multi-resolution property, and can be solved significantly faster, making it applicable to larger size problems and to new applications.

The rest of the article is arranged as follows: In Sect. 2 we review previous works and their relation to our work. In Sect. 3 we discuss the problem of stress minimization and describe in detail the SMACOF algorithm, a minimization-majorization type algorithm suited for this purpose. In Sect. 4 we give a short overview of the Laplace-Beltrami operator in the continuous and discrete settings, and the representation of band-limited signals on manifolds. In Sect. 5 we describe the core numerical scheme of our subspace LS-MDS approach, an algorithm we call *spectral SMACOF* and a multiresolution approach. Finally, in Sect. 6 we present our results, followed by a concluding discussion in Sect. 7.

2   Related Work

In this section we review previous work related to MDS, stress minimization techniques and subspace parametrization. The oldest version of MDS, called classical scaling, is due to Torgerson [31]. The formulation of MDS as a minimization over a loss function is due to Shepard [30] and Kruskal [20,21]. The SMACOF algorithm we describe in the next sections is due to de Leeuw [12], but in fact was previously developed by Guttman [17]. For a comprehensive overview of MDS problems and algorithms we refer the reader to [11]. A variety of methods have been proposed to accelerate classical scaling over the years, trying to reduce the size of the input pairwise distance matrix. [7,14] propose to embed only a subset of the points and find the rest by interpolation. [4] uses the Nyström method to perform out of sample extension to an existing embedding. However, it does not make use of the geometry of the data. [2] interpolate the distance matrix from a subset of pairwise distances by representing it in the Laplace-Beltrami eigenbasis and forcing it to be smooth on the manifold. [29] also uses the LBO and the Nyström method to interpolate the distance matrix from a set of known rows. This time the interpolation is formulated in the spatial domain so there is no need to compute a basis.

Regarding stress based scaling, [9] proposed a multi-grid approach. They rely heavily on the spatial representation of the shapes in switching between resolutions, which makes their scheme hard to generalize. [26] used vector extrapolation techniques to accelerate the convergence rate of the SMACOF algorithm. This acceleration technique is a meta-algorithm that can be put on top of our algorithm as well. [13] considers MDS problems with linear restrictions on the configurations, essentially constraining the embedding to belong to a subspace. [22] uses a subspace method for LS-MDS, but their subspace is an ad-hoc construction used for multi-channel image visualization.

Linear subspace methods are common in machine learning and pattern recognition applications where they are used to restrict a signal to some low-rank subspace, usually an eigenspace of some matrix, which preserves its important details. Examples include principle component analysis (PCA), locally linear embedding (LLE), linear discriminant analysis (LDA) and many more [27]. One of those methods which is related to our algorithm is the Laplacian eigenmaps method [3]. It is essentially an MDS problem using only local distances. Its outcome is an embedding of the distance matrix into the first m eigenvectors of the Laplace-Beltrami operator. In some sense, our proposed approach is a merge between Laplacian eigenmaps and LS-MDS. A related line of works uses Laplacian (spectral) regularization in the context of low-rank subspace constructions on graphs [18, 28].

Subspace methods are also common in numerical optimization to accelerate and stabilize optimization algorithms. A review can be found here [32]. It is also worth mentioning the work of [19] which uses the cotangent Laplacian as a proxy for the Hessian in various geometric optimization problems. Ours is a similar but different approach. We employ a subspace method which effectively projects the Hessian on the subspace of the leading eigenvectors of the Laplacian, thus solving a series of small dimensional problems, rather than approximate the Hessian using the Laplacian while retaining the dimension of the original problem.

3   LS-MDS and Stress Minimization

Given an $N \times N$ symmetric matrix $\mathbf{D}$ of dissimilarities, least squares MDS (LS-MDS) is an MDS model that looks for an Euclidean embedding $\mathbf{X} \in \mathbb{R}^{N \times m}$ by minimizing the stress function (1). The latter can be minimized by nonlinear optimization techniques, e.g. gradient descent[1]. One particularly elegant and popular algorithm is SMACOF [8, 12] – a majorization-minimization type algorithm which can be shown equivalent to gradient descent with a specific choice of the step size [8]. In light of that, we consider it as a representative for the class of first order methods for the minimization of (1). The idea is to use the Cauchy-Schwarz inequality to construct a *majorizing function* $h(\mathbf{X}, \mathbf{Z})$ for the stress, obeying $h(\mathbf{X}, \mathbf{Z}) \geq \sigma(\mathbf{X})$ for every $\mathbf{X}$ and $\mathbf{Z}$ and $h(\mathbf{X}, \mathbf{X}) = \sigma(\mathbf{X})$. To do so, one should first note that (1) can be written alternatively as

$$\sigma(\mathbf{X}) = \operatorname{tr}(\mathbf{X}^{\mathrm{T}}\mathbf{V}\mathbf{X}) - 2\operatorname{tr}(\mathbf{X}^{\mathrm{T}}\mathbf{B}(\mathbf{X})\mathbf{X}) + \sum_{i<j} w_{ij} d_{ij}^2 \tag{3}$$

where $\mathbf{V}$ and $\mathbf{B}(\mathbf{X})$ are symmetric row-and column-centered matrices given by

$$v_{ij} = \begin{cases} -w_{ij} & i \neq j \\ \sum_{k \neq i} w_{ik} & i = j \end{cases} \tag{4}$$

$$b_{ij} = \begin{cases} -w_{ij} d_{ij} \|\mathbf{x}_i - \mathbf{x}_j\|^{-1} & i \neq j, \mathbf{x}_i \neq \mathbf{x}_j \\ 0 & i \neq j, \mathbf{x}_i = \mathbf{x}_j \\ -\sum_{k \neq i} b_{ik} & i = j, \end{cases} \tag{5}$$

---

[1] Note also that (1) is not differentiable everywhere.

and define

$$h(\mathbf{X}, \mathbf{Z}) = \operatorname{tr}(\mathbf{X}^{\mathrm{T}}\mathbf{V}\mathbf{X}) - 2\operatorname{tr}(\mathbf{Z}^{\mathrm{T}}\mathbf{B}(\mathbf{Z})\mathbf{X}) + \sum_{i<j} w_{ij}d_{ij}^2, \tag{6}$$

which is a convex (quadratic) function in $\mathbf{X}$. Therefore, if we use the following iteration

$$\mathbf{X}_{k+1} = \operatorname*{argmin}_{\mathbf{X}} h(\mathbf{X}, \mathbf{X}_k) = \mathbf{V}^{\dagger}\mathbf{B}_k\mathbf{X}_k = \left(\mathbf{V} + \frac{1}{N}\mathbf{1}\mathbf{1}^{\mathrm{T}}\right)^{-1}\mathbf{B}_k\mathbf{X}_k, \tag{7}$$

where $\mathbf{B}_k \equiv \mathbf{B}(\mathbf{X}_k)$ and $\mathbf{V}^{\dagger}$ denotes the pseudo-inverse of the rank deficient matrix $\mathbf{V}$, we obtain a monotonically decreasing sequence of stress values

$$\sigma(\mathbf{X}_{k+1}) \le h(\mathbf{X}_{k+1}, \mathbf{X}_k) \le h(\mathbf{X}_k, \mathbf{X}_k) = \sigma(\mathbf{X}_k). \tag{8}$$

Equation (8) follows directly from (6) and (7); in the last passage, we used the fact that

$$\mathbf{V}^{\dagger} = \left(\mathbf{V} + \frac{1}{N}\mathbf{1}\mathbf{1}^{\mathrm{T}}\right)^{-1} - \frac{1}{N}\mathbf{1}\mathbf{1}^{\mathrm{T}} \tag{9}$$

and that $\mathbf{1}^{T}\mathbf{B}_k = \mathbf{0}^{T}$. The multiplicative update (7) suggests that at each iteration, each coordinate in the current embedding is a weighted mean of the coordinates of the previous embedding, starting with an initial embedding $\mathbf{X}_0$, where the weights are given by the ratio of the pairwise distances, $d_{ij}\|\mathbf{x}_i - \mathbf{x}_j\|^{-1}$. In what follows, we refer to (8) as the *majorization inequality*.

Each iteration of SMACOF requires the computation of the pairwise Euclidean distances between all points in the current embedding, a task of complexity $\mathcal{O}(N^2)$, and the solution of a linear system involving the pseudo-inverse of the matrix $\mathbf{V}$. Despite being rank deficient (in fact, $\mathbf{V}$ is the graph Laplacian of the graph encoded by the adjacency matrix $\mathbf{W}$, i.e., the pairwise weights), $\mathbf{V}$ is not necessarily sparse, and computing its pseudo-inverse is of order $\mathcal{O}(N^3)$, except when $\mathbf{V}$ has a special form. For example, in case all the weights w_{ij} are equal to 1, we get

$$\mathbf{V}^{\dagger} = \frac{1}{N}\left(\mathbf{I} - \frac{1}{N}\mathbf{1}\mathbf{1}^{\mathrm{T}}\right), \tag{10}$$

and the SMACOF iteration reduces to

$$\mathbf{X}_{k+1} = \frac{1}{N}\mathbf{B}_k\mathbf{X}_k. \tag{11}$$

To summarize, a single iteration of SMACOF consist of two steps: *Majorization* – the construction of $\mathbf{B}(\mathbf{X}_k)$ (5), which requires $\mathcal{O}(N^2)$ non-linear operations; and *Minimization* – the solution of (7), which in general requires $\mathcal{O}(N^3)$ for the factorization of $\mathbf{V} + \frac{1}{N}\mathbf{1}\mathbf{1}^{\mathrm{T}}$ in the first iteration, and $\mathcal{O}(N^2m)$ operations for solving the linear system using forward/backward substitution in the following iterations.

4   Laplace-Beltrami Operator and Band-Limited Signals

The Laplace-Beltrami operator is an analogue of the Euclidean Laplacian defined on a manifold, which has become a standard tool in the field of geometry processing. For a closed compact manifold surface S, let Δ denote its Laplace-Beltrami differential operator. Consider the equation $\Delta\phi = \lambda\phi$. The pair ϕ, λ are an eigenpair of Δ. Note that $\lambda = 0$ is always an eigenvalue, the corresponding eigenfunctions are constant functions. The eigenvalues of the Laplace-Beltrami operator are non-negative and constitute a discrete set. We will assume that the eigenvalues are distinct, so we can put them into ascending order, $0 = \lambda_0 < \lambda_1 < \lambda_2 < \cdots < \lambda_i < \dots$. The appropriately normalized eigenfunction corresponding to λ_i will be denoted by ϕ_i. The normalization is achieved using the L_2 inner product. Given two functions f and g on the surface, their inner product is denoted by $\langle f, g \rangle$, and is defined as the surface integral

$$\langle f, g \rangle = \int_S fg \, da. \tag{12}$$

Since the Laplace-Beltrami operator is Hermitian, the eigenfunctions corresponding to its different eigenvalues are orthogonal. Given a function f on the surface, one can expand it in terms of the eigenfunctions $f = \sum_{i=1}^{\infty} \alpha_i \phi_i$, where the coefficients are $\alpha_i = \langle f, \phi_i \rangle$. We refer to signals for which $\langle f, \phi_i \rangle = 0 \; \forall i > p$ as p-bandlimited. This intuitively suggests that to smooth a function one should simply discard the coefficients corresponding to the larger eigenvalues, i.e. truncate the infinite expansion above. A variety of discretizations exist for the Laplacian, each with its own pros and cons. We use the cotangent Laplacian of [24]. Instead of using the usual trigonometric construction, it can also be expressed in terms of the edge lengths and Heron's formula. See [6] for example. The result is a generalized eigenvalue problem $\mathbf{W}\phi = \lambda\mathbf{A}\phi$ where $\mathbf{W}$ is a symmetric positive definite matrix called *stiffness matrix* and $\mathbf{A}$ is a diagonal matrix called *the mass matrix*. Notice that in the discrete setting, this basis is orthonormal with respect to the inner product on the manifold $\langle \mathbf{f}, \mathbf{g} \rangle_{\mathbf{A}} = \mathbf{f}^{\mathsf{T}}\mathbf{A}\mathbf{g}$.

5   Subspace LS-MDS

The dependence of a single iteration of SMACOF on N^2 (or N^3) severely limits its applicability in embedding a large number of points. Deviating from the LS-stress model (1) makes things even worse. Different stress models like the L_1 stress, which could in theory be solved as a series of weighted MDS (WMDS) problems using an iteratively reweighted least squares technique, require very long time to converge if one uses the regular SMACOF iterations. Moreover, adding linear constraints on the configuration would require the solution of a large quadratic program in each iteration, making it practically impossible to use.

In order to reduce the dependence on N, we restrict the embedding to lie within a low-dimensional subspace of $\mathbb{R}^{N \times m}$. Low-rank representation of signals is a very popular approach in a variety of machine learning applications, and have also been applied previously to stress majorization [22]. Our goal is to show that for multidimensional scaling problems arising in geometry processing, a particular choice of subspace, namely the subspace of band-limited signals on a manifold, enables to accelerate stress majorization by a significant amount. Unlike the ad-hoc construction in [22], this subspace is a geometric construction. We also draw a connection between the number of samples, the band-limit, and the quality of the approximation. Although only an observational result at this stage, similar results have been obtained for the case of reconstruction of band-limited signals on graphs [25].

We assume that an initial manifold $\mathcal{M}_0$ embedded in $\mathbb{R}^m$ that encodes the local relationship between points is easily obtainable, and denote the discrete samples of this manifold by $\mathbf{X}_0$. The (discrete) embedding $\mathbf{X}$ can be written as $\mathbf{X} = \mathbf{X}_0 + \boldsymbol{\delta}$, and we can reformulate MDS in terms of the displacement field $\boldsymbol{\delta}$. Our observation is that since the embedding found by LS-MDS maintains the local relationship between samples, as encouraged by the stress term (1), $\boldsymbol{\delta}$ can be modeled as a band-limited signal (i.e. "smooth") on this manifold. We do that by explicitly representing the displacement field as a linear combination of the first p eigenvectors of the Laplace-Beltrami operator on the manifold $\mathcal{M}_0$. We denote the concatenation of the first p eigenvectors by $\boldsymbol{\Phi} \in \mathbb{R}^{N \times p}$, and the problem therefore becomes

$$\min_{\boldsymbol{\alpha} \in \mathbb{R}^{p \times m}} \sigma(\mathbf{X}_0 + \boldsymbol{\Phi}\boldsymbol{\alpha}) \tag{13}$$

The new update step in terms of $\boldsymbol{\alpha}$ is

$$\boldsymbol{\alpha}_{k+1} = \operatorname*{argmin}_{\boldsymbol{\alpha}} h(\mathbf{X}_0 + \boldsymbol{\Phi}\boldsymbol{\alpha}, \mathbf{X}_k) \tag{14}$$

$$= \left(\boldsymbol{\Phi}^{\mathsf{T}} \mathbf{V} \boldsymbol{\Phi}\right)^{\dagger} \boldsymbol{\Phi}^{\mathsf{T}} \left(\mathbf{B}_k \mathbf{X}_k - \mathbf{V} \mathbf{X}_0\right), \tag{15}$$

where $\mathbf{X}_{k+1} = \mathbf{X}_0 + \boldsymbol{\Phi}\boldsymbol{\alpha}_{k+1}$. Notice that the majorization inequality (8) still holds, since the requirement $\sigma(\mathbf{X}) \le h(\mathbf{X}, \mathbf{Z})$ is true for any $\mathbf{X}$ and $\mathbf{Z}$, so it must also be true for $\mathbf{X}$ restricted to an affine subspace

$$\sigma(\mathbf{X}_{k+1}) \le h(\mathbf{X}_0 + \boldsymbol{\Phi}\boldsymbol{\alpha}_{k+1}, \mathbf{X}_k) \le \sigma(\mathbf{X}_k). \tag{16}$$

Restricting the embedding to lie within a rank p subspace reduces the cost of solving the linear system (7) to $\mathcal{O}(p^2 m)$ (amortized $\mathcal{O}(p^3)$). This may have a profound effect on the *minimization* step of SMACOF for weighted MDS problems or when additional terms are added to the stress. However, the main bottleneck remains in the *majorization* step, which requires the computation of all pairwise Euclidean distances in the current embedding. Our main observation is that when the displacement field is p-bandlimited, i.e., can be written as a linear combination of the first p Laplace-Beltrami eigenvectors, it is enough to

---

Algorithm 1. SPECTRAL SMACOF

Input:
- $\mathcal{M}$ - A discretized manifold (e.g. triangular mesh, polygonal mesh, point cloud).
- **W** - A matrix of pairwise weights.
- p - Number of Laplace-Beltrami eigenfunctions.
- q - Number of samples (default: $q = 2p$).
- $\mathcal{M}_0$ - A discretized initial manifold on which we can define a Laplace-Beltrami operator.
- $\mathbf{X}_0 \in \mathbb{R}^{N \times m}$ - Initial embedding (discrete samples of $\mathcal{M}_0$).
- a_{tol} - Absolute tolerance.
- r_{tol} - Relative tolerance.
- maxiter - Maximum number of iterations.

Output: Euclidean embedding $\mathbf{X} \in \mathbb{R}^{N \times m}$.

1 $[\mathbf{D} , \mathbf{S}] = \text{FPS}(\mathcal{M})$ - Sample $\mathcal{M}$ with farthest point sampling and return sampling matrix **S** and matrix of geodesic distances between samples **D**.
2 $[\mathbf{\Phi} , \mathbf{\Lambda}] = \text{LBO\_basis}(\mathcal{M}_0, p)$ - Compute p leading eigenvectors $\mathbf{\Phi}$ and eigenvalues $\mathbf{\Lambda}$ of Laplace-Beltrami operator on $\mathcal{M}_0$.
3 Compute $\mathbf{V}^s$ according to (4).
4 Compute and store $(\mathbf{\Phi}^T \mathbf{S}^T \mathbf{V}^s \mathbf{S} \mathbf{\Phi})^\dagger$ and $\mathbf{V}^s \mathbf{S} \mathbf{X}_0$.
5 $k \leftarrow 1$
6 **while** $k \leq$ maxiter **and** $\sigma(\mathbf{SX}_k) > a_{\text{tol}}$ **and** $\left(1 - \frac{\sigma(\mathbf{SX}_k)}{\sigma(\mathbf{SX}_{k-1})}\right) > r_{\text{tol}}$ **do**
7 $\quad$ Compute $\mathbf{B}^s{}_k \equiv \mathbf{B}(\mathbf{SX}_k)$ according to (5).
8 $\quad$ $\alpha_{k+1} = \left(\mathbf{\Phi}^T \mathbf{S}^T \mathbf{V}^s \mathbf{S} \mathbf{\Phi}\right)^\dagger \mathbf{\Phi}^T \mathbf{S}^T \left(\mathbf{B}^s{}_k \mathbf{SX}_k - \mathbf{V}^s \mathbf{SX}_0\right)$
9 $\quad$ $\mathbf{X}_{k+1} = \mathbf{X}_0 + \mathbf{\Phi} \alpha_{k+1}$
10 $\quad$ $k \leftarrow k + 1$
11 **return** $\mathbf{X}_{k+1}$.

---

use $q = cp \ll N$ points to get an embedding which is almost as good, in terms of stress value, as the embedding achieved by using all the points. The quantity $1 < c = \frac{q}{p} \leq 2$ is a sampling ratio which can be found by experimentation. In practice, we set $c = 2$ in all our experiments. Denoting the set of sampled points by $\{s_1, \ldots, s_q\} \in \mathcal{S} \subset \{1, \ldots, N\}$, we define a sampling matrix $\mathbf{S}^{q \times N}$ with $\mathbf{S}_{ij} = 1$ if $j = s_i$ and 0 otherwise, and instead of minimizing the objective of (13), we minimize $\sigma(\mathbf{SX}_0 + \mathbf{S\Phi}\alpha)$. Each iteration of SMACOF now becomes

$$\alpha_{k+1} = \underset{\alpha}{\arg\min}\, h(\mathbf{SX}_0 + \mathbf{S\Phi}\alpha, \mathbf{X}_k) \tag{17}$$

$$= \left(\mathbf{\Phi}^T \mathbf{S}^T \mathbf{V}^s \mathbf{S} \mathbf{\Phi}\right)^\dagger \mathbf{\Phi}^T \mathbf{S}^T \left(\mathbf{B}^s{}_k \mathbf{SX}_k - \mathbf{V}^s \mathbf{SX}_0\right) \tag{18}$$

where $\mathbf{V}^s, \mathbf{B}^s$ are the matrices defined in (4), (5) constructed only from the q sampled points. We denote the solution and the final embedding by α_* and $\mathbf{X}_* = \mathbf{X}_0 + \mathbf{\Phi}\alpha_*$, respectively, referring to the latter as *spectral interpolation*. We summarize this algorithm, dubbed *spectral SMACOF*, in Algorithm 1.

Notice that the pairwise distances are only required between the sampled points. In order to sample the points, we employ the *farthest point sampling* strategy [16], computing the distances as part of the sampling process. Though the algorithm requires the computation of the truncated eigenbasis of the LBO, in order to apply (18) we do not need the full basis Φ, but only its sampled version $\mathbf{S}\Phi$. The full basis is only needed for the final interpolation of the displacement field δ, which can also be reformulated as an optimization problem

$$\min_{\delta} \|\mathbf{S}\delta - \mathbf{S}\Phi\alpha_*\|_F^2 + \lambda\langle\delta, \mathbf{L}\delta\rangle, \tag{19}$$

where $\mathbf{L}$ is the Laplacian matrix. This opens up the possibility of reducing the amount of time required to construct the basis, and is an issue we leave for future research.

To summarize, a single iteration of *spectral SMACOF* consist of two steps (excluding the interpolation which can be deferred to the final step): *Majorization* – the construction of $\mathbf{B}^s(\mathbf{X}_k)$, which requires $\mathcal{O}(q^2)$ operations; and *Minimization* – the solution of (18), which in general requires $\mathcal{O}(p^3)$ for the computation of $(\Phi^T\mathbf{S}^T\mathbf{V}^s\mathbf{S}\Phi)^\dagger$ in the first iteration, and $\mathcal{O}(p^2m)$ operations in the succeeding iterations.

5.1   Multi-resolution Scheme for Stress Minimization

To control the trade off between convergence speed and approximation quality, we employ a multi-resolution scheme. Multi-resolution and multi-grid methods have been previously employed for distance scaling with limited success [9]. Since those methods relied solely on the spatial representation of the embedding, the switch between resolution levels required cumbersome decimation and interpolation operators which were hard to generalize. The spectral formulation provides those operators practically "for free", where the decimation simply requires sampling the basis functions at the sampling points, and the interpolation is carried out using the full subspace basis.

The scheme consists of two distinct hierarchies, one for the spatial domain and one for the spectral domain. The two hierarchies are quantized and stored in the vectors $\mathbf{q} = [q_1, \cdots, q_{r_q}]^T$ and $\mathbf{p} = [p_1, \cdots, p_{r_p}]^T$, where the last level for both could possibly be N, i.e. using the full set of vertices, in which case we get a "pure" subspace MDS, or using the complete basis, in which case we get an equivalent of the landmark MDS method [14], or both, which reduces to applying a regular SMACOF iteration. It is important that each pair q_i, p_j complies with the "sampling criterion", $q_i \geq cp_j$.

We highlight two properties of this scheme: First, for a fixed q and varying p, it follows from the majorization inequality that if we intialize each resolution level with the embedding from the previous resolution, we get a monotonic decrease in stress values. i.e., in the "pure" subspace setting ($q = N$), spectral SMACOF produces a monotonically decreasing series of stress values, just like the regular SMACOF.

Second, for a fixed p with varying q, we observe that there is a jump in the stress value around $q \approx cp$, consistent with our observation in the derivation of the sampling criterion, and from there the approximation error and stress value decrease, though not monotonically.

6   Results

In this section we compare the spectral SMACOF algorithm to other LS-MDS algorithms in terms of running time and quality of the embedding. We implemented the algorithms in Matlab® using fast vector arithmetic. All the experiments were conducted on an Intel NUC6i7KYK equipped with Intel® Core™ i7-6770HQ CPU 2.6 GHz and 32 GB RAM. In all experiments we set $q = 2p$, and use three resolution levels $\mathbf{q} = [200, 600, N]$ and $\mathbf{p} = [100, 300, N]$. For the spectral SMACOF algorithm we use the following parameters: $a_{\text{tol}} = 0$, $r_{\text{tol}} = 10^{-4}$, maxiter $= 100$ (see Algorithm (1)), except for the full-resolution for which we set $r_{\text{tol}} = 10^{-5}$. For the SMACOF algorithm we use $r_{\text{tol}} = 10^{-5}$, maxiter $= 5000$. We run it until it reaches the same value of stress achieved by the spectral SMACOF algorithm or lower. We also compare to the algorithm proposed in [26] which uses vector extrapolation methods (RRE) to accelerate SMACOF. Every k iterations of regular SMACOF it tries to decrease the stress further by using a linear combination the previous descent directions. This acceleration technique is a meta-algorithm that can be put on top of the spectral SMACOF algorithm as well, and we only put it here for illustration purposes. In the following examples we set $k = 5$.

LS-MDS. We apply spectral SMACOF to compute *canonical forms* of several shapes from the low-res TOSCA dataset [1], which have 3400 vertices. The canonical form is an isometric embedding of a surface $\mathbf{X}$ equipped with a metric $\mathbf{d}_X$, e.g. the geodesic metric, into $(\mathbb{R}^3, d_{\mathbb{R}^3})$. This embedding allows us to reduce the problem of non-rigid shape correspondence into a much simpler problem of rigid shape correspondence. For more information see [8]. Figure (1a) shows running time for computing a canonical form using the unweighted stress. Figure (1b) shows running time for a canonical form obtained with $w_{ij} = {}^1/_{d_{ij}^2}$. This kind of stress is commonly known as *relative stress*. In both experiments we initialized with the original embedding. The convergence rate of spectral SMACOF, measured in CPU time, is faster by two orders of magnitudes than the convergence rate obtained by regular SMACOF, even though the iteration count is much higher. Since in the unweighted case the minimization step admits an especially simple form (see (11)), this effect is more pronounced in the weighted case. Additional results and applications will appear in a longer version of this article.

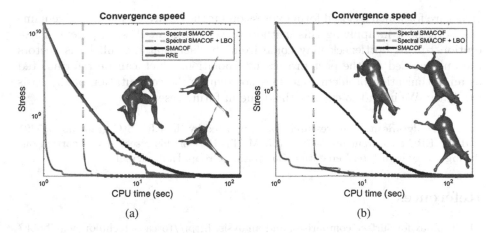

Fig. 1. Convergence rate of Spectral SMACOF compared to regular SMACOF and RRE SMACOF [26]. The dashed cyan plot is the accumulated time of spectral SMA-COF and the subspace computation. (a) shows an unweighted MDS embedding. (b) shows a weighted MDS embedding (relative stress). We can see a discontinuity when switching between resolution levels. The dark blue plot shows the convergence of the last resolution level, which is practically regular SMACOF iterations. The left shape on each plot is the original shape which was also used to initialize the algorithms. The right shapes are the embeddings generated by spectral SMACOF (top) and regular SMACOF (bottom). (Color figure online)

7   Conclusion

In this paper we showed that using a spectral representation for the embedding coordinates in LS-MDS problems arising in geometry processing uncovers a multi-resolution property of the numerical optimization scheme, which improves the convergence rate by orders of magnitude compared to other approaches, enabling its application to larger size problems and to more complex MDS models. The acceleration comes from two factors: First, we show experimentally that for various geometric optimization problems the displacement field between the final embedding and the initial embedding can be faithfully modeled as a bandlimited signal on the manifold, using only the first p eigenvectors of the Laplacian, reducing the number of variables by a factor of N/p. Second, we observed that for such signals we can sample the spatial data by a rate of $\approx ?p/N$ and still converge to a local minimum of the full stress as if all the data was used. The quality of the embedding depends on the number of eigenvectors used and the number of points sampled, and changes from shape to shape. The relationship between p, q and the approximation quality is only an observational result at this stage, and should be made more precise in future research.

In order to apply the method, the p leading eigenvectors of the discrete Laplace-Beltrami operator have to be computed in advance. Though this is possible for moderately sized meshes and for specific larger size meshes with special structure for which a closed form expression for the eigenvectors exist, it remains the bottleneck in applying this method to very large meshes. A potential resolution to this bottleneck may come from the fact that the full basis vectors are only needed for the post process interpolation, which can be reformulated as an optimization problem that does not require the computation of the basis explicitly. We intend to explore this issue in future research.

Acknowledgement. This research was supported by the ERC StG grant no. 335491 and the ERC StG grant no. 307048 (COMET). Part of this research was carried out during a stay with Intel Perceptual Computing Group, Haifa, Israel.

References

1. Toolbox for surface comparison and analysis. http://tosca.cs.technion.ac.il/book/resources_data.html
2. Aflalo, Y., Kimmel, R.: Spectral multidimensional scaling. Proc. Nat. Acad. Sci. **110**(45), 18052–18057 (2013)
3. Belkin, M., Niyogi, P.: Laplacian eigenmaps for dimensionality reduction and data representation. Neural Comput. **15**(6), 1373–1396 (2003)
4. Bengio, Y., Paiement, J.F., Vincent, P., Delalleau, O., Le Roux, N., Ouimet, M.: Out-of-sample extensions for LLE, Isomap, MDS, eigenmaps, and spectral clustering. In: Advances in Neural Information Processing Systems, pp. 177–184 (2004)
5. Borg, I., Groenen, P.J.: Modern Multidimensional Scaling: Theory and Applications. Springer Science & Business Media, Heidelberg (2005)
6. Boscaini, D., Eynard, D., Bronstein, M.M.: Shape-from-intrinsic operator. arXiv preprint arXiv:1406.1925 (2014)
7. Brandes, U., Pich, C.: Eigensolver methods for progressive multidimensional scaling of large data. In: Kaufmann, M., Wagner, D. (eds.) GD 2006. LNCS, vol. 4372, pp. 42–53. Springer, Heidelberg (2007). doi:10.1007/978-3-540-70904-6_6
8. Bronstein, A.M., Bronstein, M.M., Kimmel, R.: Numerical Geometry of Non-rigid Shapes. Springer Science & Business Media, Heidelberg (2008)
9. Bronstein, M.M., Bronstein, A.M., Kimmel, R., Yavneh, I.: Multigrid multidimensional scaling. Numer. Linear Algebra Appl. **13**(2–3), 149–171 (2006)
10. Buja, A., Swayne, D.F., Littman, M.L., Dean, N., Hofmann, H., Chen, L.: Data visualization with multidimensional scaling. J. Comput. Graph. Stat. **17**(2), 444–472 (2008)
11. Cox, T.F., Cox, M.A.: Multidimensional Scaling. CRC Press, Boca Raton (2000)
12. De Leeuw, J., Barra, I.J., Brodeau, F., Romier, G., Van Cutsem, B., et al.: Applications of convex analysis to multidimensional scaling. In: Recent Developments in Statistics. Citeseer (1977)
13. De Leeuw, J., Heiser, W.J.: Multidimensional scaling with restrictions on the configuration. Multivar. Anal. **5**, 501–522 (1980)
14. De Silva, V., Tenenbaum, J.B.: Global versus local methods in nonlinear dimensionality reduction. In: Advances in Neural Information Processing Systems, pp. 721–728 (2003)
15. Elad, A., Kimmel, R.: On bending invariant signatures for surfaces. IEEE Trans. Pattern Anal. Mach. Intell. **25**(10), 1285–1295 (2003)
16. Eldar, Y., Lindenbaum, M., Porat, M., Zeevi, Y.Y.: The farthest point strategy for progressive image sampling. IEEE Trans. Image Process. **6**(9), 1305–1315 (1997)

17. Guttman, L.: A general nonmetric technique for finding the smallest coordinate space for a configuration of points. Psychometrika **33**(4), 469–506 (1968)
18. Kalofolias, V., Bresson, X., Bronstein, M., Vandergheynst, P.: Matrix completion on graphs. arXiv preprint arXiv:1408.1717 (2014)
19. Kovalsky, S.Z., Galun, M., Lipman, Y.: Accelerated quadratic proxy for geometric optimization. ACM Trans. Graph. (TOG) **35**(4), 134 (2016)
20. Kruskal, J.B.: Multidimensional scaling by optimizing goodness of fit to a nonmetric hypothesis. Psychometrika **29**(1), 1–27 (1964)
21. Kruskal, J.B.: Nonmetric multidimensional scaling: a numerical method. Psychometrika **29**(2), 115–129 (1964)
22. Lawrence, J., Arietta, S., Kazhdan, M., Lepage, D., O'Hagan, C.: A user-assisted approach to visualizing multidimensional images. IEEE Trans. Vis. Comput. Graph. **17**(10), 1487–1498 (2011)
23. Ovsjanikov, M., Ben-Chen, M., Solomon, J., Butscher, A., Guibas, L.: Functional maps: a flexible representation of maps between shapes. ACM Trans. Graph. (TOG) **31**(4), 30 (2012)
24. Pinkall, U., Polthier, K.: Computing discrete minimal surfaces and their conjugates. Exp. Math. **2**(1), 15–36 (1993)
25. Puy, G., Tremblay, N., Gribonval, R., Vandergheynst, P.: Random sampling of bandlimited signals on graphs. Appl. Comput. Harmonic Anal. (2016, in press). http://doi.org/10.1016/j.acha.2016.05.005
26. Rosman, G., Bronstein, A.M., Bronstein, M.M., Sidi, A., Kimmel, R.: Fast multidimensional scaling using vector extrapolation. Technical report CIS-2008-01. Technnion, Israel Institute of Technology (2008)
27. Saul, L.K., Weinberger, K.Q., Ham, J.H., Sha, F., Lee, D.D.: Spectral methods for dimensionality reduction. In: Semisupervised Learning, pp. 293–308. MIT Press, Cambridge (2006)
28. Shahid, N., Kalofolias, V., Bresson, X., Bronstein, M., Vandergheynst, P.: Robust principal component analysis on graphs. In: Proceedings of the IEEE International Conference on Computer Vision, pp. 2812–2820 (2015)
29. Shamai, G., Aflalo, Y., Zibulevsky, M., Kimmel, R.: Classical scaling revisited. In: Proceedings of the IEEE International Conference on Computer Vision, pp. 2255–2263 (2015)
30. Shepard, R.N.: The analysis of proximities: multidimensional scaling with an unknown distance function. I. Psychometrika **27**(2), 125–140 (1962)
31. Torgerson, W.S.: Multidimensional scaling: I. Theory and method. Psychometrika **17**(4), 401–419 (1952)
32. Yuan, Y.: A review on subspace methods for nonlinear optimization. In: Proceedings of the International Congress of Mathematics, pp. 807–827 (2014)

Beyond Multi-view Stereo:
Shading-Reflectance Decomposition

Jean Mélou[1,3]([✉]), Yvain Quéau[2], Jean-Denis Durou[1], Fabien Castan[3],
and Daniel Cremers[2]

[1] IRIT, UMR CNRS 5505, Université de Toulouse, Toulouse, France
[2] Department of Informatics, Technical University Munich, Munich, Germany
[3] Mikros Image, Levallois-Perret, France
jeme@mikrosimage.eu

Abstract. We introduce a variational framework for separating shading
and reflectance from a series of images acquired under different angles,
when the geometry has already been estimated by multi-view stereo.
Our formulation uses an l^1-TV variational framework, where a robust
photometric-based data term enforces adequation to the images, total
variation ensures piecewise-smoothness of the reflectance, and an additional multi-view consistency term is introduced for resolving the arising
ambiguities. Optimisation is carried out using an alternating optimisation strategy building upon iteratively reweighted least-squares. Preliminary results on both a synthetic dataset, using various lighting and
reflectance scenarios, and a real dataset, confirm the potential of the
proposed approach.

Keywords: Reflectance · Multi-view · Shading · Variational methods

1 Introduction

Acquiring the shape and the reflectance of a scene is a key issue for the
movie industry, as it allows proper relighting. Well-established shape acquisition
techniques such as multi-view stereo can provide accurate 3D-reconstructions
in a robust manner. Nevertheless, they do not aim at recovering the surface
reflectance. Hence, the original input images are usually mapped onto the 3D-
reconstruction as texture. Since the images mix shading information (induced by
lighting and geometry) and reflectance (which characterises the surface), relighting based on this approach is usually unsatisfactory. To improve results, the
reflectance needs to be further extracted. As shown in Fig. 1, our aim is to
separate shading and reflectance using several images of a surface taken under
different angles, assuming known (but possibly gross) geometry.

We formulate this task as a variational problem, introducing the knowledge that the albedo (we assume Lambertian surface, hence albedo characterizes reflectance) is independent from the viewing angle as a prior within
the variational model. We further tackle the problem of robustness to specularities and imperfect alignment, using a robust l^1-norm-based photometric

© Springer International Publishing AG 2017
F. Lauze et al. (Eds.): SSVM 2017, LNCS 10302, pp. 694–705, 2017.
DOI: 10.1007/978-3-319-58771-4_55

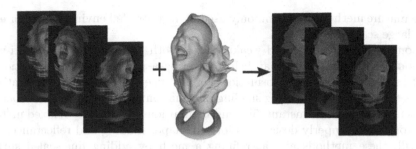

Fig. 1. Overview of our contribution. From a set of n images of a surface acquired under different angles, and a coarse geometry obtained for instance using multi-view stereo, we estimate a shading-free reflectance map per view. (Color figure online)

data term. Assuming that the albedo is piecewise-smooth, we further involve a TV-regularizer.

After reviewing related approaches in Sect. 2, we present our variational solution in Sect. 3. Our numerical strategy for solving this variational problem, which is presented in Sect. 4, is based on alternating optimisation of reflectance and lighting, and on an iteratively reweighted least-squares strategy for handling the l^1-terms. Preliminary experiments on both synthetic and real data are conducted in Sect. 5, which confirm the interest of multi-view shading-reflectance decomposition strategy. Our work is eventually summarised in Sect. 6.

2   Related Work

The problem of decomposing an image into a low-frequency component (representing reflectance) and a higher-frequency one has been tackled in various ways. One famous example is the so-called "cartoon-texture" image decomposition [2], which can be achieved efficiently using an l^1-TV approach [8]. Yet, such methods may fail in the presence of smooth brightness variations due to shading.

In this view, a photometric model would be helpful, as it would explicitly describe the interactions between the geometry, the potentially complex lighting and the reflectance. Yet, it is not possible to estimate all these parameters from a single image. In fact, estimating only the geometry, with known reflectance and lighting, is already an ill-posed problem, known as shape-from-shading [4]. It can be disambiguated by using several images obtained from the same angle, but under varying lighting, a variant known as photometric stereo [14] which can simultaneously recover shape, reflectance and lighting [3].

Still, photometric stereo requires very controlled acquisition environments, which limit potential applications. Multi-view stereo (MVS) methods [12], which focus on estimating the shape, are less restrictive. These techniques have seen significant growth over the last decade, an expansion which goes hand in hand with the development of structure-from-motion (SfM) solutions [10]. Indeed, MVS requires the cameras' parameters, outputs of the SfM algorithm. Nowadays, these mature methods are commonly used in uncontrolled environments, or even with large scale Internet data [1].

Considering strengths and weaknesses of both photometric and multi-view methods, a joint approach may help recovering a precise 3D-reconstruction as well as albedo and lighting information. For instance, the method in [5] iteratively refines the object surface using shading information, assuming that the albedo is constant or piecewise-constant [5]. This assumption was recently relaxed in [6,7], by resorting to properly designed priors on shape, shading and reflectance.

Still, these methods aim at refining a mesh by adding fine-scaled surface details, along with the associated reflectance information. As a result, the complexity of the mesh may be a source of concern when it comes to real-time manipulation by graphic artists. We argue that it may be more meaningful to keep the geometry simple, yet providing the artists with a series of 2D-maps representing reflectance and fine-scale geometry, under the form of albedo and depth maps. A first step in this direction has recently been achieved in [9], where a variational framework for the joint recovery of depth, reflectance and lighting maps is introduced. Yet, this approach relies on the choice of a single reference view, the other views being used only for the sake of stereo matching.

On the contrary, we target a symmetric approach, where all the reflectance maps corresponding to the different views are simultaneously recovered, thus avoiding the problem of selecting the main image. We focus in this exploratory work on separating shading and reflectance, using the MVS results, and not yet on refining fine-scale geometric surface details. Indeed, we will see that even with a smoothed geometry, reasonable reflectance estimation can be carried out. In this view, the next section introduces a simple and effective l^1-TV variational model for estimating a set of reflectance maps, assuming known geometry.

3   Joint Variational Estimation of the Albedo and of Spherical Harmonics Lighting

We consider a set of n pictures of an object, obtained under different angles (and, possibly, different lighting) $\{I^i : \Omega^i \subset \mathbb{R}^2 \to \mathbb{R}\}_{i=1\ldots n}$, where Ω^i represents the mask of the object of interest in image I^i. These masks are assumed to be known, as well as a (possibly inaccurate) representation of the geometry under the form of normal maps $\mathbf{n}^i : \Omega^i \to \mathbb{R}$ (which can be obtained by using SfM and MVS).

Our aim is to extract, from each image I^i, a representation of the surface reflectance through an albedo map $\rho^i : \Omega^i \to \mathbb{R}$, and an estimate of the lighting in this image. Assuming Lambertian reflectance and general lighting, a second-order spherical harmonics lighting model can be used [11], and thus the i-th lighting can be represented by a vector $\boldsymbol{\sigma}^i \in \mathbb{R}^9$. Our problem then comes down to solving the following set of equations[1]:

$$I^i(p) = \rho^i(p)\boldsymbol{\sigma}^i \cdot \boldsymbol{\nu}^i(p), \quad \forall p \in \Omega^i, \ \forall i = 1\ldots n, \tag{1}$$

where vectors $\boldsymbol{\nu}^i(p) \in \mathbb{R}^9$ can be deduced from the normals coordinates [3].

---

[1] This model is valid for greyscale images. To handle RGB images, our approach can be applied independently to each color channel.

Obviously, it is not possible to solve the set of Eq. (1) without introducing additional priors. Although a *global* (*i.e.*, same for each image and each pixel) scale ambiguity on the albedo is acceptable (because these values can always be normalized), the set of Eq. (1) exhibits such an ambiguity for each image. We tackle this issue by proposing a multi-view consistency prior on the albedo. Indeed, the albedo characterizes the surface, and is thus independent from the view. Besides, to ensure spatial consistency of the albedo estimate, a total variation prior is also introduced. Eventually, to ensure robustness to specularities, we solve the set of Eq. (1) in the l^1-norm sense. Overall, this leads us to estimate $\{\boldsymbol{\sigma}^i \in \mathbb{R}^9, \rho^i : \Omega^i \to \mathbb{R}\}_{i=1...n}$ as minimisers of the following energy:

$$\varepsilon(\{\boldsymbol{\sigma}^i, \rho^i\}_i) = \sum_{i=1}^{n} \varepsilon_{\text{Photo}}(\boldsymbol{\sigma}^i, \rho^i) + \lambda \sum_{i=1}^{n} \varepsilon_{\text{Smooth}}(\rho^i) + \mu \sum \sum_{i<j} \varepsilon_{\text{MV}}(\rho^i, \rho^j). \quad (2)$$

In Eq. (2), the first component ensures photometric consistency:

$$\varepsilon_{\text{Photo}}(\boldsymbol{\sigma}^i, \rho^i) = \sum_{p \in \Omega^i} |I^i(p) - \rho^i(p)\boldsymbol{\sigma}^i \cdot \boldsymbol{\nu}^i(p)|, \quad (3)$$

the second one ensures albedo smoothness:

$$\varepsilon_{\text{Smooth}}(\rho^i) = \sum_{p \in \Omega^i} |\partial_x \rho^i(p)| + |\partial_y \rho^i(p)|, \quad (4)$$

where $\nabla \rho^i(p) = [\partial_x \rho^i(p), \partial_y \rho^i(p)]^\top$ represents the gradient of ρ^i at pixel p (approximated, in practice, using first-order forward stencils), and the third component ensures multi-view consistency of the albedo estimate:

$$\varepsilon_{\text{MV}}(\rho^i, \rho^j) = \sum_{p^i \in \Omega^i} \sum_{p^j \in \Omega^j} C_{i,j}(p^i, p^j)|\rho^i(p^i) - \rho^j(p^j)|, \quad (5)$$

where $C_{i,j}$ is a "correspondence function" defined as follows:

$$C_{i,j}(p^i, p^j) = \begin{cases} 1 \text{ if pixels } p^i \text{ and } p^j \text{ correspond to the same surface point;} \\ 0 \text{ otherwise.} \end{cases} \quad (6)$$

At last, λ and μ are tunable hyper-parameters controlling the reflectance smoothness and the multi-view consistency, respectively.

The values of function $C_{i,j}$ are easily deduced from an initial geometry estimate, as proposed for instance by Langguth *et al.* in [7] for their evaluation of geometric error.

Applying an SfM algorithm to the images $\{I^i\}_{i=1...n}$, we obtain the cameras intrinsics $\mathbf{K}^i \in \mathbb{R}^{3 \times 3}$, and the poses of the cameras, represented by rotation matrices $\mathbf{R}^i \in \mathbb{R}^{3 \times 3}$ and translation vectors $\boldsymbol{t}^i \in \mathbb{R}^3$. Then, a point $X \in \mathbb{R}^3$ on the surface is projected to a pixel $p^i \in \mathbb{R}^2$ in the i-th image according to

$$[p^{i\top}, 1]^\top = \pi_i(X) = \mathbf{K}^i(\mathbf{R}^i X + \boldsymbol{t}^i), \quad (7)$$

where π_i stands for the projection from surface to image I^i.

Hence, the correspondence function $C_{i,j}$ defined in Eq. (6) can be redefined as follows, introducing some threshold $\epsilon > 0$ (we use $\epsilon = 3$, in the experiments) and using the known depth (obtained by MVS) to compute the inverse projections:

$$C_{i,j}(p^i, p^j) = \begin{cases} 1 \text{ if } \left\| \pi_i^{-1}([{p^i}^\top, 1]^\top) - \pi_j^{-1}([{p^j}^\top, 1]^\top) \right\| \leq \epsilon, \\ 0 \text{ otherwise.} \end{cases} \tag{8}$$

4   Resolution

Let us now introduce our numerical strategy for minimising the energy (2). This problem being bi-convex, we opt for an alternating estimation strategy: at iteration (k), we successively update the lighting and the albedo as:

$$\{\boldsymbol{\sigma}^{i,(k+1)}\}_i = \underset{\{\boldsymbol{\sigma}^i \in \mathbb{R}^9\}}{\operatorname{argmin}} \varepsilon(\{\boldsymbol{\sigma}^i, \rho^{i,(k)}\}_i), \tag{9}$$

$$\{\rho^{i,(k+1)}\}_i = \underset{\{\rho^i : \Omega^i \to \mathbb{R}\}_i}{\operatorname{argmin}} \varepsilon(\{\boldsymbol{\sigma}^{i,(k+1)}, \rho\}_i), \tag{10}$$

taking as initial guess $\rho^{i,(0)} \equiv I^i$ and $\boldsymbol{\sigma}^{i,(0)} = 1_{\mathbb{R}^9}$.

To handle the non-differentiable l^1-norm terms, we opt for an iteratively reweighted least-squares approach. Since the n lighting vectors $\boldsymbol{\sigma}^i$, $i = 1 \ldots n$, are independent, Eq. (9) is then replaced by the following n independent reweighted least-squares updates, which can be solved by resorting to the pseudo-inverse:

$$\boldsymbol{\sigma}^{i,(k+1)} = \underset{\boldsymbol{\sigma}^i \in \mathbb{R}^9}{\operatorname{argmin}} \sum_{p \in \Omega^i} w_i^{(k)}(p) |I^i(p) - \rho^{i,(k)}(p)\,\boldsymbol{\sigma}^i \cdot \boldsymbol{\nu}^i(p)|^2, \quad \forall i = 1 \ldots n, \tag{11}$$

with

$$w_i^{(k)}(p) = \frac{1}{|I^i(p) - \rho^{i,(k)}(p)\,\boldsymbol{\sigma}^{i,(k)} \cdot \boldsymbol{\nu}^i(p)|_\delta}, \tag{12}$$

where we denote $|\cdot|_\delta = \max\{\delta, |\cdot|\}$ (we use $\delta = 10^{-4}$, in the experiments).

Similarly, albedo update (10) is approximated as follows:

$$\{\rho^{i,(k+1)}\}_i = \underset{\{\rho^i : \Omega^i \to \mathbb{R}\}_i}{\operatorname{argmin}} \sum_{i=1}^n \sum_{p \in \Omega^i} w_i^{(k)}(p) |I^i(p) - \rho^i(p)\,\boldsymbol{\sigma}^{i,(k)} \cdot \boldsymbol{\nu}^i(p)|^2$$

$$+ \lambda \sum_{i=1}^n \sum_{p \in \Omega^i} w_{\partial_x \rho^i}^{(k)}(p) |\partial_x \rho^i(p)|^2 + w_{\partial_y \rho^i}^{(k)}(p) |\partial_y \rho^i(p)|^2$$

$$+ \mu \sum_{i<j} \sum_{p^i \in \Omega^i} \sum_{p^j \in \Omega^j} C_{i,j}(p^i, p^j) w_{i,j}^{(k)}(p^i, p^j) |\rho^i(p^i) - \rho^j(p^j)|^2, \tag{13}$$

with

$$w_{\partial_x \rho^i}^{(k)}(p) = \frac{1}{|\partial_x \rho^{i,(k)}(p)|_\delta}, \tag{14}$$

$$w_{\partial_y \rho^i}^{(k)}(p) = \frac{1}{|\partial_y \rho^{i,(k)}(p)|_\delta}, \tag{15}$$

$$w_{i,j}^{(k)}(p^i, p^j) = \frac{1}{|\rho^{i,(k)}(p^i) - \rho^{j,(k)}(p^j)|_\delta}. \tag{16}$$

This time, due to the multi-view consistency prior, the albedo estimates w.r.t. the different images are not independent: all estimations must be carried out simultaneously. Stacking all the albedo values in a large vector $\rho \in \mathbb{R}^N$, with $N = \sum_i |\Omega^i|$, the optimisation problem (13) can be turned into the following large, sparse, linear least-squares problem:

$$
\rho^{(k+1)} = \underset{\rho \in \mathbb{R}^N}{\mathrm{argmin}} \left\| \begin{bmatrix} \mathrm{Diag}(\{\sqrt{w_i^{(k)}(p)}\, \sigma^{i,(k+1)} \cdot \nu^i(p)\}_{i,p}) \\ \sqrt{\lambda}\, \mathrm{Diag}(\{\sqrt{w_{\partial_x \rho^i}^{(k)}(p)}\}_{i,p})\, \mathbf{D}_x \\ \sqrt{\lambda}\, \mathrm{Diag}(\{\sqrt{w_{\partial_y \rho^i}^{(k)}(p)}\}_{i,p})\, \mathbf{D}_y \\ \sqrt{\mu}\, \mathrm{Diag}(\{\sqrt{w_{i,j}^{(k)}(p^i, p^j)}\}_{i,j,p^i,p^j})\, \mathbf{C} \end{bmatrix} \rho \right.
$$

$$
\left. - \begin{bmatrix} \mathrm{Diag}(\{\sqrt{w_i^{(k)}(p)}\}_{i,p}) \boldsymbol{I} \\ \mathbf{0}_{N \times 1} \\ \mathbf{0}_{N \times 1} \\ \mathbf{0}_{\sum_{i=1}^{n-1}(n-i)|\Omega^i| \times 1} \end{bmatrix} \right\|_2^2. \tag{17}
$$

In the least-squares problem (17), the first matrix block stacks the weighted shading values, $\mathbf{D}_x$ and $\mathbf{D}_y$ are large sparse matrices obtained by concatenating the n finite differences matrices relative to each domain Ω^i, $i = 1 \dots n$, and the last one is a large $\sum_{i=1}^{n-1}(n-i)|\Omega^i| \times N$ matrix used to represent the correspondence functions defined in Eq. (6). As for the non-null vector in the second row of Eq. (17), it stacks all the intensity values in $\boldsymbol{I}$, and weights them. Each function $C_{i,j}$ is easily represented as an $|\Omega^i| \times |\Omega^j|$ matrix $\mathbf{C}_{i,j}$ with at most one nonzero element per row. By arranging these matrices by block in a matrix $\mathbf{C}$, all values $C_{i,j}(p^i, p^j)\left(\rho^i(p^i) - \rho^j(p^j)\right)$ can be compactly represented in matrix form as $\mathbf{C}\rho$. For instance, considering an $n = 4$ pictures set, we get the following matrix:

$$
\mathbf{C} = \begin{pmatrix} \mathbf{B}_{1,2} & \mathbf{C}_{1,2} & & \\ \mathbf{B}_{1,3} & & \mathbf{C}_{1,3} & \\ \mathbf{B}_{1,4} & & & \mathbf{C}_{1,4} \\ & \mathbf{B}_{2,3} & \mathbf{C}_{2,3} & \\ & \mathbf{B}_{2,4} & & \mathbf{C}_{2,4} \\ & & \mathbf{B}_{3,4} & \mathbf{C}_{3,4} \end{pmatrix}, \tag{18}
$$

where $\mathbf{B}_{i,j}$ is a diagonal $|\Omega^i| \times |\Omega^i|$ matrix with entries equal to -1 on the lines where $\mathbf{C}_{i,j}$ is non-null.

Problem (17) is a linear least-squares problem where the matrix is very sparse. For its resolution, we apply a conjugate gradient algorithm to the associated normal equations. We iterate optimisation steps (9) and (10) until convergence or a maximum iteration number is reached. In our experiments, we found 50 iterations were always sufficient to reach a stable solution (10^{-3} relative residual between two consecutive energy values). Proving convergence of our scheme is beyond the scope of this paper, but it was empirically observed in all experiments, although the convergence rate seems to be sublinear.

5   Results

We first test our shading-reflectance decomposition method in a very simple situation. Let us simulate $n = 13$ pictures of the object in Fig. 2-a, supposed purely-Lambertian, with a camera whose intrinsic and extrinsic parameters are known, under a "sky-dome" lighting. Since the object geometry is known, the problem unknowns are reflectance and lighting in each surface point.

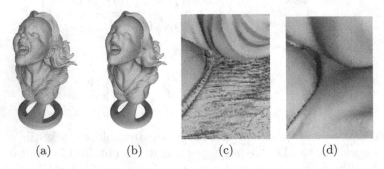

(a)   (b)   (c)   (d)

Fig. 2. (a) 3D-shape used in the tests (the well-known "Joyful Yell" 3D-model), which will be covered with two different albedos. (b) Same 3D-shape after smoothing, thus less accurate. (c)–(d) Zooms of (a) and (b), respectively, near the neck.

Figure 3 shows three of these pictures, of size 540×960, generated using a renderer, and the estimated colored albedo using our method.

As expected, since the lighting used in this simulation (sky-dome) is the most appropriate to a spherical harmonics modelisation, these first results are very satisfactory. As a comparison, the third row of Fig. 3 shows the results of the cartoon-texture decomposition method described in [8]. This method needs only one image. The "cartoon" part, which is more or less equivalent to an albedo, is far less uniform than the albedo estimated using shading-reflectance decomposition, in the four parts (hair, face, shirt and plinth) which have received a uniform albedo (compare the second and third lines of Fig. 3).

This comparison a posteriori confirms our basic idea i.e., that reflectance estimation benefits in two ways from the multi-view framework: indeed, this

Fig. 3. First line: Three (out of $n = 13$) synthetic views of the object of Fig. 2-a, computed with a purely-Lambertian reflectance divided into four parts (hair, face, shirt and plinth) which receive a uniform albedo, under "sky-dome" lighting. Second line: Colored estimated albedos, using the proposed approach. Geometry and camera parameters are supposed to be known, but the lighting is unknown. Third line: Empirical estimation of the albedo using the cartoon-texture decomposition described in [8]. (Color figure online)

allows us not only to estimate the 3D-shape, but also to constrain the albedo of each surface point to be the same in all the pictures where it is visible. In contrast, the cartoon-texture decomposition cannot correct the shading effects, which explains, for instance, why the cartoon is so dark inside the mouth.

As we dispose of the albedo ground truth, we can numerically evaluate these results by estimating the albedo variance in the $n = 13$ pictures, in each part of the object where the albedo is uniform[2]. The values presented in Table 1 confirm that our estimation is more accurate. As well, we observe that the albedo variance is higher for both zones which have concave parts, namely hair and face (in this last case, the albedo is largely under-estimated in the mouth). Indeed, such points only partly see the sky-dome, which causes a penumbra effect.

Since we also know the object geometry, it seems that we could compensate for penumbra. However, this would require that the lighting is known as well, which is not the case in the framework of the targeted usecase, since an outdoors lighting is uncontrolled. Moreover, we would have to consider not only the primary lighting, but also the successive bounces of light on the different parts of the scene (these were taken into account by the ray-tracing algorithm). Actually, one of the main difficulties of our problem is to consider unknown lighting.

---

[2] In order to compare comparable things, we scale the estimated albedos in each part, so that its median is equal to the associated ground truth value.

Table 1. Variances of the estimated albedos inside each of the four homogeneous parts of the colored 3D-model used for the tests of Fig. 3, computed after renormalization, in the three channels. In each box: the real value of the albedo is given on the left; on the right, the variances computed from our shading-reflectance decomposition, and from the cartoon-texture decomposition are given, respectively, above and below.

Channel	Hair		Face		Shirt		Plinth	
Red	1.0000	0.0135	1.0000	0.0015	0.0196	0.0002	0.1216	0.0004
		0.0274		0.0106		0.0006		0.0005
Green	0.0314	0.0007	0.5333	0.0016	0.0549	0.0000	0.1216	0.0003
		0.0007		0.0065		0.0001		0.0005
Blue	0.0000	0.0000	0.3608	0.0006	1.0000	0.0104	0.1216	0.0001
		0.0000		0.0031		0.0217		0.0003

Fig. 4. Same test as in Fig. 3, but the scene is illuminated by four extended light sources. Obviously, the results are not much affected by the light configuration, since the shading-reflectance decomposition is still effective. (Color figure online)

Another test, where the sky-dome lighting is replaced with four extended light sources, is thus appropriate. Figure 4 shows that, under the same assumptions as for Fig. 3, the results are really close. The proposed method seems little sensitive to the lighting configuration, which is a significant advantage.

As we use a TV-smoothing term, which favors piecewise-constant albedos, the satisfactory results of Figs. 3 and 4 were predictable. Let us now modify the shirt albedo in order to simulate thin stripes. Figure 5 shows that the proposed method still works well if the smoothing weight λ is well-tuned (λ is 12 times smaller for Fig. 5 than for Figs. 3 and 4).

The use of an l^1-term for photometric consistency offers a competitive advantage to our method: it is robust to outliers such as deviations from the Lambertian model (1), which are unavoidable in practice. We generated a new set of $n = 13$ pictures, considering now the hair and plinth reflectances as partly specular. Indeed, the results presented in Fig. 6 are similar to those of Fig. 5.

Fig. 5. Same tests as in Fig. 4, with a single extended light source, but the shirt has now a non-uniform albedo. Our method still works well, although the new configuration of the shirt albedo with fine stripes is a priori less adapted to a TV-smoothing term. (Color figure online)

Fig. 6. Same test as in Fig. 5, but the hair and plinth reflectances are now partly specular. Our method seems to be robust against outliers, due to the l^1-data term. (Color figure online)

For the next step, we suppose moreover that the scene geometry is inaccurately known. This will necessarily be the case with real data. The surface shown in Fig. 2-b (zoomed in Fig. 2-d) is obtained by smoothing the original 3D-shape of Fig. 2-a (zoomed in Fig. 2-c), using a tool from the meshlab software. The results provided in Fig. 7 show that our method is robust as well to small inaccuracies in the object geometry, and is thus relevant for the intended application.

As a digest of all these tests, Table 2 gives the variance of the albedo estimated inside the hair part in the red channel, which is the most significant.

Finally, we put this work in real context. The proposed algorithm is applied to the outputs of an SfM/MVS pipeline, which provides a rough geometry and camera parameters estimates. Figure 8 confirms that small inaccuracies in the geometry input do not degrade significantly the results of our method.

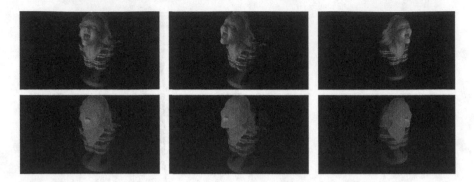

Fig. 7. Same test as in Fig. 6, using a coarse version of the 3D-shape (cf. Fig. 2-b and d). Our method is robust as well to small inaccuracies in the object geometry. (Color figure online)

Table 2. Variance of the estimated albedo inside the hair part in the red channel, for all tests on the synthetic dataset, except that of Fig. 5 (which would give the same value as that of Fig. 4).

Channel	Figure 3	Figure 4	Figure 6	Figure 7
Red	0.0135	0.0367	0.0475	0.0626

Fig. 8. Left: One real view of the object 'fountain-P11' [13]. Right: Colored estimated albedo, using the proposed approach. Geometry and camera parameters estimates are outputs of an SfM/MVS pipeline using 25 input images. Only 8 images have been used as inputs of our algorithm. (Color figure online)

6   Conclusion and Perspectives

We have proposed a variational framework for separating shading and reflectance from images based on an initial 3D-reconstruction obtained by SfM and MVS techniques. We have shown that the ambiguities can be raised by introducing a multi-view consistency prior on the reflectance. Robustness is further enforced by considering an l^1-norm-based photometric data term, and a piecewise-smoothness constraint on the albedo is introduced under the form of total variation regularization. Preliminary results on a synthetic dataset covered with two different albedos, and lit in various manners, as well as on a real dataset, demonstrate the potential of the approach.

We now plan to estimate not only the reflectance, but also fine-scale geometric details. In this view, our alternating scheme will be modified in order to include an additional step aiming at estimating the normals, in the spirit of the recent multi-view shape-from-shading approach presented in [9].

References

1. Agarwal, S., Snavely, N., Simon, I., Seitz, S.M., Szeliski, R.: Building Rome in a day. In: Proceedings of ICCV (2009)
2. Aujol, J.F., Gilboa, G., Chan, T., Osher, S.: Structure-texture image decomposition - modeling, algorithms, and parameter selection. Int. J. Comput. Vis. **67**(1), 111–136 (2006)
3. Basri, R., Jacobs, D., Kemelmacher, I.: Photometric stereo with general, unknown lighting. Int. J. Comput. Vis. **72**(3), 239–257 (2007)
4. Horn, B.K.P.: Shape from shading: a method for obtaining the shape of a smooth opaque object from one view. Ph.D. thesis, Department of Electrical Engineering and Computer Science, Massachusetts Institute of Technology (1970)
5. Jin, H., Cremers, D., Wang, D., Yezzi, A., Prados, E., Soatto, S.: 3-D reconstruction of shaded objects from multiple images under unknown illumination. Int. J. Comput. Vis. **76**(3), 245–256 (2008)
6. Kim, K., Torii, A., Okutomi, M.: Multi-view inverse rendering under arbitrary illumination and albedo. In: Leibe, B., Matas, J., Sebe, N., Welling, M. (eds.) ECCV 2016. LNCS, vol. 9907, pp. 750–767. Springer, Cham (2016). doi:10.1007/978-3-319-46487-9_46
7. Langguth, F., Sunkavalli, K., Hadap, S., Goesele, M.: Shading-aware multi-view stereo. In: Leibe, B., Matas, J., Sebe, N., Welling, M. (eds.) ECCV 2016. LNCS, vol. 9907, pp. 469–485. Springer, Cham (2016). doi:10.1007/978-3-319-46487-9_29
8. Le Guen, V.: Cartoon + Texture image decomposition by the TV-L1 model. Image Process. On Line **4**, 204–219 (2014). https://doi.org/10.5201/ipol.2014.103
9. Maurer, D., Ju, Y.C., Breuß, M., Bruhn, A.: Combining shape from shading and stereo: a variational approach for the joint estimation of depth, illumination and albedo. In: Proceedings of BMVC (2016)
10. Moulon, P., Monasse, P., Marlet, R.: openMVG: an open multiple view geometry library. https://github.com/openMVG/openMVG
11. Ramamoorthi, R., Hanrahan, P.: An efficient representation for irradiance environment maps. In: Proceedings of SIGGRAPH (2001)
12. Seitz, S.M., Curless, B., Diebel, J., Scharstein, D., Szeliski, R.: A comparison and evaluation of multi-view stereo reconstruction algorithms. In: Proceedings of CVPR (2006)
13. Strecha, C., Von Hansen, W., Van Gool, L.J., Fua, P., Thoennessen, U.: On benchmarking camera calibration and multi-view stereo for high resolution imagery. In: Proceedings of CVPR (2008)
14. Woodham, R.J.: Photometric method for determining surface orientation from multiple images. Opt. Eng. **19**(1), 139–144 (1980)

Author Index